Marketing

2014 Edition

William M. Pride | O.C. Ferrell

CENGAGE
Learning

Australia • Brazil • Japan • Korea • Mexico • Singapore • Spain • United Kingdom • United States

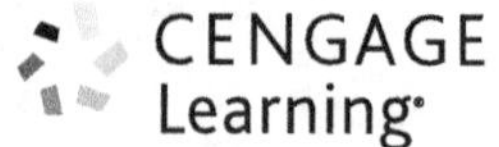

Marketing, 2014 Edition

Senior Project Development Manager:
Linda deStefano

Market Development Manager:
Heather Kramer

Senior Production/Manufacturing Manager:
Donna M. Brown

Production Editorial Manager:
Kim Fry

Sr. Rights Acquisition Account Manager:
Todd Osborne

Printed in the United States of America

Marketing 2014, 17th Edition
William M. Pride | O.C. Ferrell

For product information and technology assistance, contact us at
Cengage Learning Customer & Sales Support, 1-800-354-9706
For permission to use material from this text or product,
submit all requests online at **cengage.com/permissions**
Further permissions questions can be emailed to
permissionrequest@cengage.com

This book contains select works from existing Cengage Learning resources and was produced by Cengage Learning Custom Solutions for collegiate use. As such, those adopting and/or contributing to this work are responsible for editorial content accuracy, continuity and completeness.

ISBN-13: 978-1-285-90943-1

ISBN-10: 1-285-90943-7

Cengage Learning
5191 Natorp Boulevard
Mason, Ohio 45040
USA

Cengage Learning is a leading provider of customized learning solutions with office locations around the globe, including Singapore, the United Kingdom, Australia, Mexico, Brazil, and Japan. Locate your local office at:
international.cengage.com/region.
Cengage Learning products are represented in Canada by Nelson Education, Ltd.
For your lifelong learning solutions, visit **www.cengage.com/custom.**
Visit our corporate website at **www.cengage.com.**

To Nancy, Allen, Mike, Ashley, and Charlie Pride

To Linda Ferrell

brief contents

© Mike Stratton / © iStockphoto.com/hh5800 / © iStockphoto.com/sorendis

contents

© Mike Stratton / © iStockphoto.com/hh5800 / © iStockphoto.com/sorendis

Part 6: Distribution Decisions 479

Part 7: Promotion Decisions 563

Online Appendix: Careers in Marketing OA-1

preface

© Mike Stratton / © iStockphoto.com/hh5800 / © iStockphoto.com/sorendis

MARKETING IN A CHANGING ENVIRONMENT

The importance of marketing has continued to increase as dynamic changes in the environment evolve. As students prepare for careers in a globally competitive digital world, they will need to gain marketing knowledge that will prepare them to be successful. This new edition of Pride & Ferrell *Marketing* has been revised to engage students and provide the frameworks, concepts, and approaches to decision making that ensure comprehensive understanding of marketing. Our perspective goes beyond learning terminology and concepts to provide decision-making experiences for students through the use of cases, exercises, debate issues, and new themed role-play cases. As students prepare for the new digital world, they also need practice in developing communication skills, especially effective teamwork.

Pride & Ferrell *Marketing* has been developed to make sure that students receive the most comprehensive overview of marketing available. This means that students using this book should develop respect for the importance of marketing and understand that learning marketing requires in-depth knowledge and the mastering of essential concepts. Therefore, key concepts like digital marketing and social networking, services marketing, branding and packaging, and social responsibility and ethics in marketing all receive standalone chapters. We also provide numerous ancillary materials to aid in student comprehension of marketing concepts as well as for increasing instructor resources for teaching this important material. Online materials include quizzes, PowerPoint presentations, videos, and flashcards. Our marketing video case series enables students to learn about how real-world companies address marketing challenges. Our Interactive Marketing Plan Worksheets and video program provide students with practical knowledge of the challenges and the planning process of launching a new product. Together these revisions and additional materials will assist students in gaining a full understanding of pertinent marketing practices.

Online social networking has become an increasingly powerful tool for marketers. Most discussions about marketing today bring up issues like how digital media can lower costs, improve communications, provide better customer support, and achieve improved marketing research. All elements of the marketing mix should be considered when using digital media and social networking. We discuss how digital media and social networking tools can create effective digital marketing strategies that can enhance marketing efforts. In addition, the entire book integrates important digital marketing concepts and examples where appropriate.

We have paid careful attention to enhancing all key concepts in marketing and have built this revision to be current and to reflect important changes in marketing. Our book is a market leader because students find it readable and relevant. Our text reflects the real world of marketing and provides the most comprehensive coverage possible of important marketing topics.

Specific details of this extensive revision are available in the transition guide in the *Instructor's Resource Manual*. We have also made efforts to improve all teaching ancillaries and student learning tools. PowerPoint presentations continue to be a very popular teaching device, and a special effort has been made to upgrade the PowerPoint program to enhance classroom teaching. The *Instructor's Manual* continues to be a valuable tool updated with engaging in-class activities and projects. The authors and publisher have worked together to provide a comprehensive teaching package and ancillaries that are unsurpassed in the marketplace.

The authors have maintained a hands-on approach to teaching this material and revising the text and its ancillaries. This results in an integrated teaching package and approach that is accurate, sound, and successful in reaching students. The outcome of this involvement fosters trust and confidence in the teaching package and in student learning outcomes. Student feedback regarding this textbook is highly favorable.

WHAT'S NEW TO THIS EDITION?

Our goal is to provide the most up-to-date content, including concepts, examples, cases, exercises, and data, possible. Therefore, in this revision there are significant changes that make learning more engaging and interesting to the students. The following highlight the types of changes that were made in this revision.

- **Foundational content.** Each chapter has been updated with the latest knowledge available related to frameworks, concepts, and academic research. These additions have been seamlessly integrated into the text. Many examples are new and a review of footnotes at the end of chapters will reveal where new content has been added. Many of the new examples and content changes have been updated to 2012.
- **End-of-Part exercises.** At the end of each part, there is a new role-play case exercise. These eight new case exercises involve team participation where students engage in a discussion of the dilemma and provide a solution. The class breaks into teams and reaches decisions that relate to the short-term, intermediate-term, and long-term. Each team member is assigned a role and should take on that role in team decision making. The case dilemmas are disguised but are based on real-world marketing situations. All information, including the background section and the roles, are in the text. See the *Instructor's Manual* for more guidance on these exercises.

ROLE-PLAY TEAM CASE EXERCISE 1

This role-play team case exercise is designed to simulate actual marketing decision making in the real world. The entire team should read the overview and background. Each student will take on a role of a particular employee within the organization. Your instructor will provide additional information and instructions related to a team decision.

BIRMINGHAM HILL CHEESE COMPANY*

Background

In 1999, Ted and Delilah Yancey founded the Birmingham Hill Cheese company in Boulder, Colorado. The Yanceys wanted to capture a unique market niche by selling a product that was artisan, or handmade. Their first product, Raven Eye Goat Cheese, was an immediate hit and won first prize at a national cheese competition. The company was following the marketing concept of satisfying its target market of customers who wanted high-quality artisan cheese

MARKETING INSIGHTS

Walmart Returns to Its Roots

Walmart has long been admired for its skill in implementing a superior marketing strategy. Its everyday low prices (EDLP) and basic products strongly appeal to its target market, mainly households that make below $70,000 a year. However, trouble has come to Walmart due to changes in its marketing strategy. Walmart tried to broaden its customer base by selling more upscale products and compromising its position as a price leader. According to analysts, Walmart's attempt to be everything to everybody resulted in

some of its products, conflicting with Walmart's EDLP pricing strategy. Under normal economic conditions, this might not have been so problematic; however, during the most recent recession many of its customers were unhappy with Walmart's removal of basic items. They often switched to lower-priced rivals Dollar Tree and Family Dollar. Additionally, Walmart's upscale items failed to catch on with higher-income consumers.

After realizing its marketing mistakes, Walmart reintroduced many of

- **Opening vignettes: *Marketing Insights*.** All of the chapter-opening vignettes are new or updated. They are written to introduce the theme of each chapter by focusing on actual entrepreneurial companies and how they deal with real-world situations.
- **Boxed features.** Each chapter includes new or updated boxed features that highlight green marketing, marketing entrepreneurs, emerging trends in marketing, or controversial issues in marketing. The majority of the boxed features are new to this edition; a few have been significantly updated and revised to fit the themes of this edition.
- **New Snapshot features.** Many of the Snapshot features are new and engage students by highlighting interesting, up-to-date statistics that link marketing theory to the real world.
- **New research.** Throughout the text we have updated content with the most recent research that supports the frameworks and best practices for marketing.

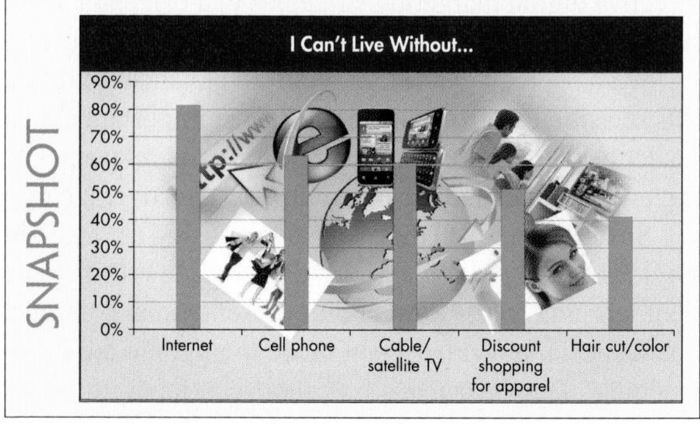

Source: BIGResearch-American Pulse Survey of 5,015 adult consumers, December 2010, www.stores.org/STORES%20 Magazine%20February%202011/adjusting-new-normal.

© iStockphoto.com/hocus-focus

Distribution
The growth in popularity of e-readers has lead to a greater direct distribution of magazines, newspapers, and books.

- **New illustrations and examples.** New advertisements from well-known firms are employed to illustrate chapter topics. Experiences of real-world companies are used to exemplify marketing concepts and strategies throughout the text. Most examples are new or updated to include digital marketing concepts as well as several new sustainable marketing illustrations.
- **End-of-chapter cases.** Each chapter contains two cases, including a video case, profiling firms to illustrate concrete application of marketing strategies and concepts. Many of our video cases are new to this edition and are supported by current and engaging videos.

FEATURES OF THE BOOK

As with previous editions, this edition of the text provides a comprehensive and practical introduction to marketing that is both easy to teach and to learn. Marketing continues to be one of the most widely adopted introductory textbooks in the world. We appreciate the confidence that adopters have placed in our textbook and continue to work hard to make sure that, as in previous editions, this edition keeps pace with changes. The entire text is structured to excite students about the subject and to help them learn completely and efficiently:

- An *organizational model* at the beginning of each part provides a "road map" of the text and a visual tool for understanding the connections among various components.
- *Objectives* at the start of each chapter present concrete expectations about what students are to learn as they read the chapter.
- Every chapter begins with an opening vignette. This feature provides an example of the real world of marketing that relates to the topic covered in the chapter. After reading the vignette, the student should be motivated to want to learn more about concepts and strategies that relate to the varying topics. Students will learn about topics, such as mystery shopping, the rise in gluten-free foods, the benefits of marketing ethics, and electronic book pricing. Students will also be introduced to such companies as The Melt, Legoland, Four Seasons, Bass Pro Shops, and Salesforce.com.
- Boxed features—*Emerging Trends in Marketing* and *Going Green*—capture dynamic changes in marketing. These changes are influencing marketing strategies and customer behavior. Strong feedback from adopters indicated the need for coverage in these areas.

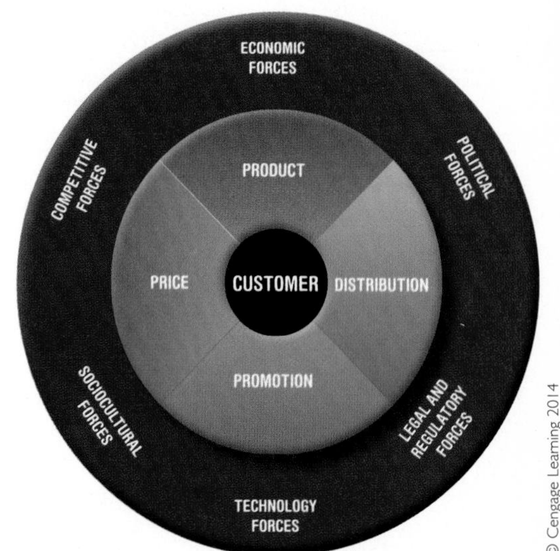

© Cengage Learning 2014

Emerging Trends

The Growing Trend of Eco-Friendly Funeral Services

The $12 billion funeral industry faces a dilemma: it is running out of burial space. In Europe cemeteries are reaching their maximum capacity. Cremations are being criticized due to the large amount of carbon emissions crematoriums release. These difficulties combined with a growing interest in environmentally friendly practices are inspiring more funeral companies to offer green burial services.

This emerging trend is reinventing the concept of funeral services. Green funerals not only help to solve the problem of decreasing land availability and pollution, but they also tend to cost less than traditional funerals. This is because many of the more costly services, such as embalming the body or buying a metal coffin, can be bypassed. Consumers can choose from many different "green" options, and companies are rushing to meet demand with their own solutions. For instance, Creative Coffins creates themed coffins that are biodegradable and Creative Reefs adds human ashes to an artificial reef ball placed on the ocean floor.

Not everyone is happy about green funerals, however. Some towns have blocked the creation of green cemeteries because residents fear that bodies buried without coffins could potentially contaminate groundwater. Other green funeral processes are thought to degrade human dignity. The topic of green burials has strained community relations in certain areas, a fact that funeral companies must keep in mind when marketing green funeral services.[b]

© iStockphoto.com/CTRd

- The *Emerging Trends* boxes cover such marketing phenomena as digital and interactive billboards, QR codes in marketing, weather-watching for inventory planning, mobile applications, virtual games, and branded stores. Featured companies include Netflix, Stage Stores, Clorox, Panera, and Zipcar.

Going Green

Italian Company Turns Sustainability into a Competitive Advantage

Italian company Sabox has come up with an innovative way to deal with overflowing trash in landfills: make furniture out of it. Sabox is a paper company that produces sustainable packaging from recycled paper. Its GreenProject initiative seeks to incorporate sustainability into all areas of the company, both with the products it sells and its operations. For instance, all of the company's products are certified by the Forest Stewardship Council, which signals that the materials are responsibly sourced. Even employees take the company's sustainability message seriously by carpooling to work.

Sabox is able to differentiate itself from competitors through its green message and its commitment to social responsibility. When Sabox founder Aldo Savarese saw the overflowing landfills in Naples, approximately 25 miles from company headquarters, he resolved to do something about it. For many years Naples has experienced problems with trash collection. The company believes it can help the area by turning discarded items into valuable products. Sabox has been able to create desks, tables, and chairs from discarded materials. And these items are not shoddily made either—some of the furniture has been designed by a famous Italian designer. Sabox also donates chairs to the Venice International Film Festival, a marketing tactic that increases goodwill for the company and spreads awareness of its products.[a]

- The *Going Green* boxes introduce students to such topics as green mobile applications, electric vehicles in China, LED light bulbs, reverse channels for recycling, greenwashing, and congestion pricing. Featured companies include General Electric, Samsung, Ikea, IBM, Chipotle, and Costco.
- In every chapter, there are two mini-features: *Marketing Debate and Entrepreneurship in Marketing.*
- The *Marketing Debate* marginal feature discusses controversial issues related to marketing, such as the relationship between marketing and value, the marketing of genetically modified seeds, the ability of consumers to opt out of online tracking, the practices of credit card companies, the marketing of brands on college campuses, and the pricing transparency of travel services.

Marketing Debate

The Payoffs for Being Ethical

ISSUE: Is Ethics a Cost or a Benefit to a Company?

As companies continue to struggle with "doing the right thing" for customers, employees, and communities, there is an ongoing debate around the costs/benefits of ethics programs. Critics argue that the cost to identify risks, create programs, train employees, implement hotlines and other reporting mechanisms, and establish checks and balances is tremendous for organizations and requires a significant investment. Those who support the cost of ethics programs recognize the benefits in providing employees with the guidance to navigate organizational risks and support the company's ethical culture, create trust in the marketplace that increases customer and employee loyalty, and prevent misconduct that can damage reputations and harm shareholder values. Those who support marketing ethics feel that any short-term costs are overshadowed by long-term gains, including financial performance.[e]

Entrepreneurship in Marketing

iModerate Takes a New Approach to Market Research

Entrepreneurs: Joel Benenson and Carl Rossow
Business: iModerate
Founded: 2004 | Denver, Colorado
Success: iModerate's clients have included 32 Fortune 100 companies, and 80 percent of initial clients return for additional projects.

Internet surveys are a popular marketing research method due to their ease and flexibility. However, entrepreneurs Joel Benenson and Carl Rossow saw something missing. They noticed that many Internet surveys do not provide enough information for each respondent. To solve this problem, they created the market research company iModerate. The company soon began making a name for itself in online market research, with clients including Kaiser Permanente, Business Roundtable, and Showtime.

Rather than simply surveying consumers, iModerate moderators also conduct one-on-one online discussions with consumers. Since its founding, the company has conducted more than 100,000 of these discussions. As a result, it has devised a unique framework called ThoughtPath™ to discover what consumers want. ThoughtPath™ combines the concepts of perception, identity, and experience to understand how consumers interpret a brand and view themselves in regard to the brand. This framework is used to provide meaningful consumer insights for iModerate clients. iModerate is an example of a company using evolving technologies to create more detailed methodologies for marketing research.[a]

- The *Entrepreneurship in Marketing* feature focuses on the role of entrepreneurship and the need for creativity in developing successful marketing strategies by featuring successful entrepreneurial companies like Skullcandy, Second City, Pixability, Quadlogic Controls, Tumblr, Kickstarter, Scentsy, and Warby Parker.
- *Key term definitions* appear in the margins to help students build their marketing vocabulary.
- Figures, tables, photographs, advertisements, and Snapshot features increase comprehension and stimulate interest.
- A complete *chapter summary* reviews the major topics discussed, and the list of important terms provides another end-of-chapter study aid to expand students' marketing vocabulary.
- *Discussion and review questions* at the end of each chapter encourage further study and exploration of chapter content, and *application questions* enhance students' comprehension of important topics.
- Additional application questions have been included to help students quantify and apply marketing strategies. These questions have been developed with higher-level Bloom's thinking in mind and for the sole purpose to guide students from basic knowledge of marketing concepts to application, analysis, and synthesis of marketing activities. Specific questions are intended to help students think through developing a marketing plan and are identified by the IMP icon.
- An *Internet exercise* at the end of each chapter asks students to examine a website and assess one or more strategic issues associated with the site. This section also points students toward the various learning tools that are available on the text's website.
- *Developing Your Marketing Plan* ties the chapter concepts into an overall marketing plan that can be created by completing the Interactive Marketing Plan activity found at www.cengagebrain.com. The *Developing Your Marketing Plan* feature allows students to explore each chapter topic in relation to developing and implementing a marketing campaign.

- Two *cases* at the end of each chapter help students understand the application of chapter concepts. One of the end-of-chapter cases is related to a video segment. Some examples of companies highlighted in the cases are Trek, Starbucks, Caterpillar, Dale Carnegie, Axe, Taza Chocolate, L.L.Bean, RogueSheep, New Belgium Brewery, Wyndham, and Standard Renewable Energy.
- A *strategic case* at the end of each part helps students integrate the diverse concepts that have been discussed within the related chapters. Examples include Apple Inc., Marriot, Chevrolet, GameStop, and Indy Racing League.
- A role-play case exercise at the end of each part encourages students to engage in a discussion of a marketing dilemma and provide a solution.
- *Appendixes* discuss marketing career opportunities, explore financial analysis in marketing, and present a sample marketing plan.
- A comprehensive *glossary* defines more than 625 important marketing terms.
- An online *Career Transitions* site will provide resources where students can search for marketing careers that meet their career goals, and search for suitable internships and full-time positions.

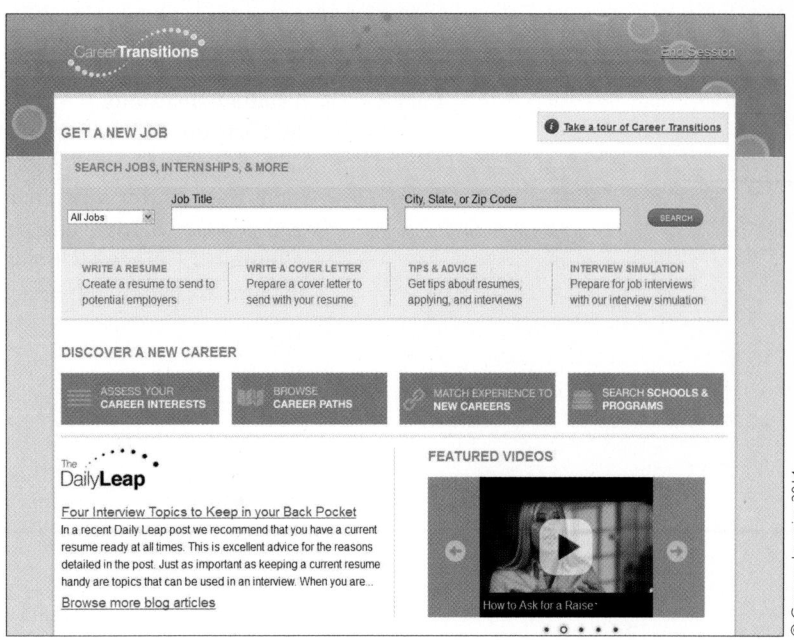

TEXT ORGANIZATION

We have organized the eight parts of *Marketing* to give students a theoretical and practical understanding of marketing decision making.

Part 1 **Marketing Strategy and Customer Relationships**

In **Chapter 1,** we define marketing and explore several key concepts: customers and target markets, the marketing mix, relationship marketing, the marketing concept, and value-driven marketing. In **Chapter 2,** we look at an overview of strategic marketing topics, such as the strategic planning process; corporate, business-unit, and marketing strategies; the implementation of marketing strategies; performance evaluation of marketing strategies; and the components of the marketing plan.

Part 2 **Environmental Forces and Social and Ethical Responsibilities**

We examine competitive, economic, political, legal and regulatory, technological, and sociocultural forces that can have profound effects on marketing strategies in **Chapter 3.** In **Chapter 4,** we explore social responsibility and ethical issues in marketing decisions.

Part 3 **Marketing Research and Target Market Analysis**

In **Chapter 5,** we provide a foundation for analyzing buyers with a look at marketing information systems and the basic steps in the marketing research process. We look at elements that affect buying decisions to better analyze customers' needs and evaluate how specific marketing strategies can satisfy those needs. In **Chapter 6,** we deal with how to select and analyze target markets—one of the major steps in marketing strategy development.

Part 4 **Buying Behavior, Global Marketing, and Digital Marketing**

We examine consumer buying decision processes and factors that influence buying decisions in **Chapter 7.** In **Chapter 8,** we explore business markets, business customers, the buying center, and the business buying decision process. **Chapter 9** focuses on the actions, involvement, and strategies of marketers that serve international customers. In **Chapter 10,** we discuss digital marketing, social media, and social networking.

Part 5 **Product Decisions**

In **Chapter 11,** we introduce basic concepts and relationships that must be understood to make effective product decisions. We analyze a variety of dimensions regarding product management in **Chapter 12,** including line extensions and product modification, new-product development, and product deletions. **Chapter 13** discusses branding, packaging, and labeling. In **Chapter 14,** we explore the nature, importance, and characteristics of services.

Part 6 **Distribution Decisions**

In **Chapter 15,** we look at supply-chain management, marketing channels, and the decisions and activities associated with the physical distribution of products, such as order processing, materials handling, warehousing, inventory management, and transportation. **Chapter 16** explores retailing and wholesaling, including types of retailers and wholesalers, direct marketing and selling, and strategic retailing issues.

Part 7 **Promotion Decisions**

We discuss integrated marketing communications in **Chapter 17.** The communication process and major promotional methods that can be included in promotion mixes are described. In **Chapter 18,** we analyze the major steps in developing an advertising campaign. We also define public relations and how it can be used. **Chapter 19** deals with personal selling and the role it can play in a firm's promotional efforts. We also explore the general characteristics of sales promotion and describe sales promotion techniques.

Part 8 **Pricing Decisions**

In **Chapter 20,** we discuss the importance of price and look at some characteristics of price and nonprice competition. We explore fundamental concepts like demand, elasticity, marginal analysis, and break-even analysis. We then examine the major factors that affect marketers' pricing decisions. In **Chapter 21,** we look at the six major stages of the process marketers use to establish prices.

A COMPREHENSIVE INSTRUCTIONAL RESOURCE PACKAGE

For instructors, this edition of *Marketing* includes an exceptionally comprehensive package of teaching materials.

Instructor's Manual

The instructor's manual has been revamped to meet the needs of an engaging classroom environment. It has been updated with diverse and dynamic discussion starters, classroom activities, and group exercises. It includes such tools as:

- Quick Reference Guide
- Purpose Statement

- Integrated Lecture Outline with features and multimedia (e.g., PowerPoint call-outs) incorporated
- Discussion Starter recommendations that encourage active exploration of the in-text examples
- Class Exercises, Semester Project Activities, and Chapter Quizzes
- Suggested Answers to end-of-chapter exercises, cases, and strategic cases
- Guide to teaching Role-Play Team Exercises.

Test Bank

The test bank provides more than 4,000 test items including true/false, multiple-choice, and essay questions. Each objective test item is accompanied by the correct answer, appropriate Learning Objective, level of difficulty, Bloom's level of thinking, main text page reference, and AACSB standard coding. Instructors are able to select, edit, and add questions, or generate randomly selected questions to produce a test master for easy duplication. This test bank has been updated by Dr. Phylis Mansfield, Pennsylvania State University–Erie.

American Marketing Association Professional Certified Marketer®

The American Marketing Association has recently started offering marketing graduates the opportunity of adding the AMA PCM® credentials to their undergraduate or MBA degree, which can serve as a symbol of professional excellence that affirms mastery of marketing knowledge and commitment to quality in the practice of marketing. Certification, which is voluntary, requires passing a rigorous and comprehensive exam and then maintaining your certification through continuing education. Earning your AMA PCM certification demonstrates to employers, peers and clients that you:

- Have mastered essential marketing knowledge and practices.
- Go the extra mile to stay current in the marketing field.
- Follow the highest professional standards.

The AMA recommends Pride and Ferrell *Marketing* as a suggested resource for AMA PCM students to utilize as they prepare for taking the AMA PCM Certification exam, and the text was used as a source to design the course and as a source for suitable examination questions. Now, more than ever, you need to stand out in the marketplace. AMA's Professional Certified Marketer (PCM®) program is the perfect way to showcase your expertise and set yourself apart.

To learn more about the American Marketing Association and the AMA PCM exam, visit www.marketingpower.com/Careers/Pages/ProfessionalCertifiedMarketer.aspx.

PowerPoint Slides

PowerPoint continues to be a very popular teaching device, and a special effort has been made to upgrade the PowerPoint program to enhance classroom teaching. Premium lecture slides, containing such content as advertisements, Web links, and unique graphs and data, have been created to provide instructors with up-to-date, unique content to increase student application and interest.

Discussion Point

Netflix alienates its target market

- Netflix revolutionized the video streaming and DVD rental business
- Netflix shocked customers when it announced price increases
- Over 82,000 angry comments were soon posted on the company's blog

? *Who is Netflix's target market?*

? *Have you ever provided feedback on a product through social media resources?*

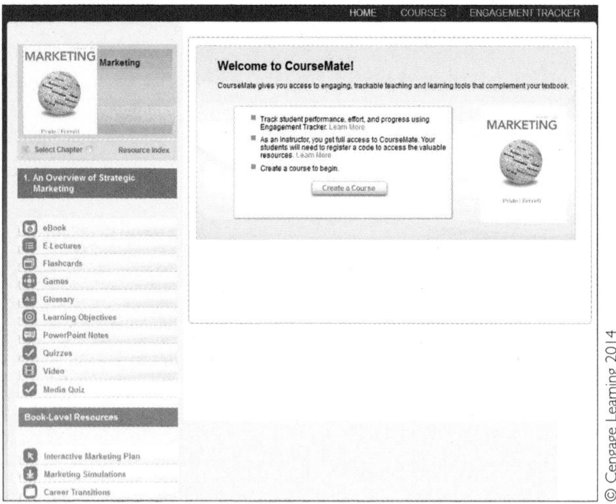

CourseMate

IMP Interested in a simple way to complement your text and course content with study and practice materials? Cengage Learning's Marketing CourseMate brings course concepts to life with interactive learning, study, and exam preparation tools that support the printed textbook. Watch student comprehension soar as your class works with the printed textbook and the textbook-specific website. Marketing CourseMate goes beyond the book to deliver what you need! Marketing CourseMate includes an interactive e-book as well as interactive teaching and learning tools including quizzes, flashcards, homework video cases, simulations, and more. Engagement Tracker monitors student engagement in the course.

Cengagenow (For WebCT® and Blackboard®)

IMP Ensure that your students have the understanding they need of marketing procedures and concepts they need to know with CengageNOW. This integrated, online course management and learning system combines the best of current technology to save time in planning and managing your course and assignments. You can reinforce comprehension with customized student learning paths and efficiently test and automatically grade assignments.

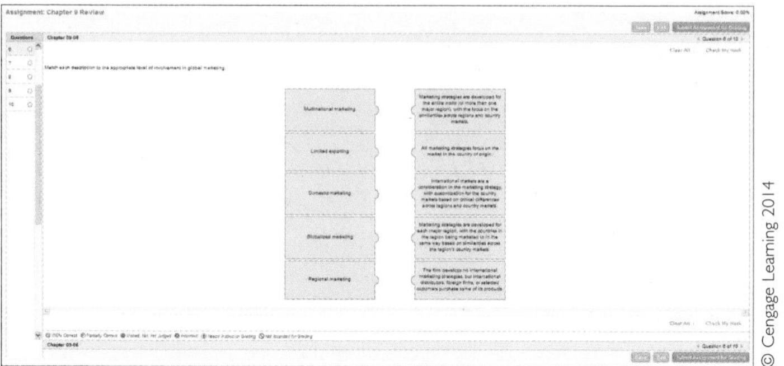

Marketing Video Case Series

IMP This series contains videos specifically tied to the video cases found at the end of the book. The videos include information about exciting companies, such as New Belgium Brewing, TOMS Shoes, Starbucks, Dale Carnegie, and Vans.

Author's Website

The authors also maintain a website at http://prideferrell.net to provide video resources that can be used as supplements and class exercises. The videos have been developed as marketing labs with worksheets for students to use on observing the videos. Some of the videos are accessible through links, and there is also information on where some of the videos can be obtained.

Interactive Marketing Plan

The Marketing Plan Worksheets have been revamped and reproduced within an interactive and multimedia environment. A video program has been developed around the worksheets, allowing students to follow a company through the trials and tribulations of launching a new product. This video helps place the conceptual marketing plan into an applicable light and is supported by a summary of the specific stages of the marketing plan as well as a sample plan based on the events of the video. These elements act as the 1-2-3 punch supporting the student while completing his or her own plan, the last step of the Interactive

Marketing Plan. The plan is broken up into three functional sections that can either be completed in one simple project or carried over throughout the semester.

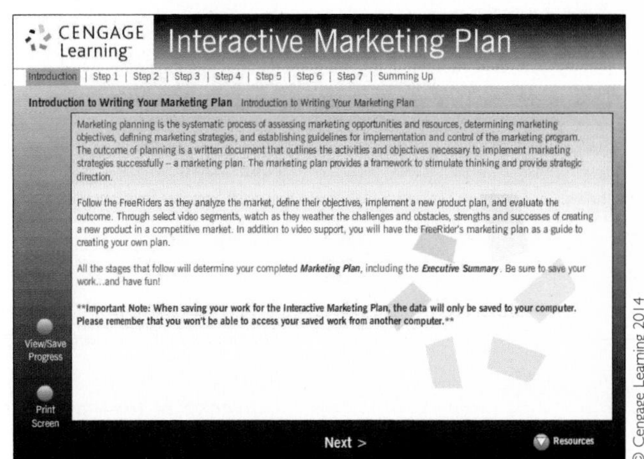

© Cengage Learning 2014

SUPPLEMENTS TO MEET STUDENT NEEDS

The complete package available with *Marketing* includes support materials that facilitate student learning. To access additional course materials, including Marketing CourseMate, please visit **www.cengagebrain.com**. At the CengageBrain.com home page, search for the ISBN of your textbook (from the back cover of your book) using the search box at the top of the page. This will take you to the product page, where the following resources can be found:

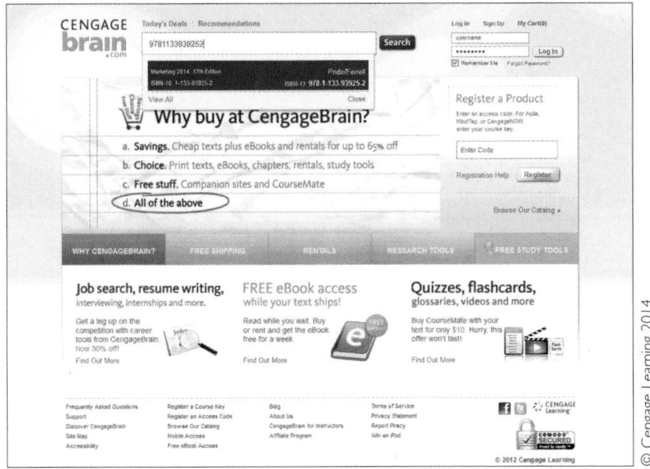

© Cengage Learning 2014

- Interactive teaching and learning tools, including:
    - Full-color e-book—Allows you to highlight and search for key terms.
    - Quizzes
    - Flashcards
    - Videos
    - An Interactive Marketing Plan
    - And more!

YOUR COMMENTS AND SUGGESTIONS ARE VALUED

As authors, our major focus has been on teaching and preparing learning materials for introductory marketing students. We have traveled extensively to work with students and to understand the needs of professors of introductory marketing courses. We both teach this marketing course on a regular basis and test the materials included in the book, test bank, and other ancillary materials to make sure they are effective in the classroom.

Through the years, professors and students have sent us many helpful suggestions for improving the text and ancillary components. We invite your comments, questions, and criticisms. We want to do our best to provide materials that enhance the teaching and learning of marketing concepts and strategies. Your suggestions will be sincerely appreciated. Please write us, or e-mail us at **w-pride@tamu.edu** or **OCFerrell@mgt.unm.edu**, or call 979-845-5857 (Bill Pride) or 505-277-3468 (O. C. Ferrell).

ACKNOWLEDGMENTS

Like most textbooks, this one reflects the ideas of many academicians and practitioners who have contributed to the development of the marketing discipline. We appreciate the opportunity to present their ideas in this book.

A number of individuals have made helpful comments and recommendations in their reviews of this or earlier editions. We appreciate the generous help of these reviewers:

Zafar U. Ahmed
Minot State University

Thomas Ainscough
University of Massachusetts–Dartmouth

Sana Akili
Iowa State University

Katrece Albert
Southern University

Joe F. Alexander
University of Northern Colorado

Mark I. Alpert
University of Texas at Austin

David M. Ambrose
University of Nebraska

David Andrus
Kansas State University

Linda K. Anglin
Minnesota State University

George Avellano
Central State University

Emin Babakus
University of Memphis

Julie Baker
Texas Christian University

Siva Balasubramanian
Southern Illinois University

Joseph Ballenger
Stephen F. Austin State University

Guy Banville
Creighton University

Frank Barber
Cuyahoga Community College

Joseph Barr
Framingham State College

Thomas E. Barry
Southern Methodist University

Charles A. Bearchell
California State University–Northridge

Richard C. Becherer
University of Tennessee–Chattanooga

Walter H. Beck, Sr.
Reinhardt College

Russell Belk
University of Utah

John Bennett
University of Missouri–Columbia

W. R. Berdine
California State Polytechnic Institute

Karen Berger
Pace University

Stewart W. Bither
Pennsylvania State University

Roger Blackwell
Ohio State University

Peter Bloch
University of Missouri–Columbia

Wanda Blockhus
San Jose State University

Nancy Bloom
Nassau Community College

Paul N. Bloom
University of North Carolina

James P. Boespflug
Arapahoe Community College

Joseph G. Bonnice
Manhattan College

John Boos
Ohio Wesleyan University

Peter Bortolotti
Johnson & Wales University

Jenell Bramlage
University of Northwestern Ohio

James Brock
Susquehanna College

John R. Brooks, Jr.
Houston Baptist University

William G. Browne
Oregon State University

John Buckley
Orange County Community College

Gul T. Butaney
Bentley College

James Cagley
University of Tulsa

Pat J. Calabros
University of Texas–Arlington

Linda Calderone
State University of New York College of Technology at Farmingdale

Joseph Cangelosi
University of Central Arkansas

William J. Carner
University of Texas–Austin

James C. Carroll
University of Central Arkansas

Terry M. Chambers
Westminster College

Lawrence Chase
Tompkins Cortland Community College

Larry Chonko
Baylor University

Barbara Coe
University of North Texas

Ernest F. Cooke
Loyola College–Baltimore

Robert Copley
University of Louisville

John I. Coppett
University of Houston–Clear Lake

Robert Corey
West Virginia University

Deborah L. Cowles
Virginia Commonwealth University

Sandra Coyne
Springfield College

Melvin R. Crask
University of Georgia

William L. Cron
Texas Christian University

Gary Cutler
Dyersburg State Community College

Bernice N. Dandridge
Diablo Valley College

Tamara Davis
Davenport University

Lloyd M. DeBoer
George Mason University

Sally Dibb
University of Warwick

Ralph DiPietro
Montclair State University

Paul Dishman
Idaho State University

Suresh Divakar
State University of New York–Buffalo

Casey L. Donoho
Northern Arizona University

Todd Donovan
Colorado State University

Peter T. Doukas
Westchester Community College

Kent Drummond
University of Wyoming

Tinus Van Drunen
University Twente (Netherlands)

Lee R. Duffus
Florida Gulf Coast University

Robert F. Dwyer
University of Cincinnati

Roland Eyears
Central Ohio Technical College

Thomas Falcone
Indiana University of Pennsylvania

James Finch
University of Wisconsin–La Crosse

Letty C. Fisher
SUNY/Westchester Community College

Renée Florsheim
Loyola Marymount University

Charles W. Ford
Arkansas State University

John Fraedrich
Southern Illinois University, Carbondale

David J. Fritzsche
University of Washington

Donald A. Fuller
University of Central Florida

Terry Gable
Truman State University

Ralph Gaedeke
California State University, Sacramento

Robert Garrity
University of Hawaii

Cathy Goodwin
University of Manitoba

Geoffrey L. Gordon
Northern Illinois University

Robert Grafton-Small
University of Strathclyde

Harrison Grathwohl
California State University–Chico

Alan A. Greco
North Carolina A&T State University

Blaine S. Greenfield
Bucks County Community College

Thomas V. Greer
University of Maryland

Sharon F. Gregg
Middle Tennessee University

Jim L. Grimm
Illinois State University

Charles Gross
University of New Hampshire

Joseph Guiltinan
University of Notre Dame

John Hafer
University of Nebraska at Omaha

David Hansen
Texas Southern University

Richard C. Hansen
Ferris State University

Nancy Hanson-Rasmussen
University of Wisconsin–Eau Claire

Robert R. Harmon
Portland State University

Mary C. Harrison
Amber University

Lorraine Hartley
Franklin University

Michael Hartline
Florida State University

Timothy Hartman
Ohio University

Salah S. Hassan
George Washington University

Manoj Hastak
American University

Del I. Hawkins
University of Oregon

Dean Headley
Wichita State University

Esther Headley
Wichita State University

Debbora Heflin-Bullock
California State Polytechnic University–Pomona

Merlin Henry
Rancho Santiago College

Tony Henthorne
University of Southern Mississippi

Lois Herr
Elizabethtown College

Charles L. Hilton
Eastern Kentucky University

Elizabeth C. Hirschman
Rutgers, State University of New Jersey

George C. Hozier
University of New Mexico

John R. Huser
Illinois Central College

Joan M. Inzinga
Bay Path College

Deloris James
University of Maryland

Ron Johnson
Colorado Mountain College

Theodore F. Jula
Stonehill College

Peter F. Kaminski
Northern Illinois University

Yvonne Karsten
Minnesota State University

Jerome Katrichis
Temple University

Garland Keesling
Towson University

James Kellaris
University of Cincinnati

Alvin Kelly
Florida A&M University

Philip Kemp
DePaul University

Sylvia Keyes
Bridgewater State College

William M. Kincaid, Jr.
Oklahoma State University

Roy Klages
State University of New York at Albany

Hal Koenig
Oregon State University

Douglas Kornemann
Milwaukee Area Technical College

Kathleen Krentler
San Diego State University

John Krupa, Jr.
Johnson & Wales University

Barbara Lafferty
University of South Florida

Patricia Laidler
Massasoit Community College

Bernard LaLond
Ohio State University

Richard A. Lancioni
Temple University

Irene Lange
California State University–Fullerton

Geoffrey P. Lantos
Stonehill College

Charles L. Lapp
University of Texas–Dallas

Virginia Larson
San Jose State University

John Lavin
Waukesha County Technical Institute

Marilyn Lavin
University of Wisconsin–Whitewater

Hugh E. Law
East Tennessee University

Monle Lee
Indiana University–South Bend

Ron Lennon
Barry University

Richard C. Leventhal
Metropolitan State College

Marilyn L. Liebrenz-Himes
George Washington University

Jay D. Lindquist
Western Michigan University

Terry Loe
Kennesaw State University

Mary Logan
Southwestern Assemblies of God College

Paul Londrigan
Mott Community College

Anthony Lucas
Community College of Allegheny County

George Lucas
U.S. Learning, Inc.

William Lundstrom
Cleveland State University

Rhonda Mack
College of Charleston

Stan Madden
Baylor University

Patricia M. Manninen
North Shore Community College

Gerald L. Manning
Des Moines Area Community College

Lalita A. Manrai
University of Delaware

Franklyn Manu
Morgan State University

Allen S. Marber
University of Bridgeport

Gayle J. Marco
Robert Morris College

Carolyn A. Massiah
University of Central Florida

James McAlexander
Oregon State University

Donald McCartney
University of Wisconsin–Green Bay

Anthony McGann
University of Wyoming

Jack McNiff
State University of New York College of Technology at Farmington

Lee Meadow
Eastern Illinois University

Carla Meeske
University of Oregon

Jeffrey A. Meier
Fox Valley Technical College

James Meszaros
County College of Morris

Brian Meyer
Minnesota State University

Martin Meyers
University of Wisconsin–Stevens Point

Stephen J. Miller
Oklahoma State University

William Moller
University of Michigan

Kent B. Monroe
University of Illinois

Carlos W. Moore
Baylor University

Carol Morris-Calder
Loyola Marymount University

David Murphy
Madisonville Community College

Keith Murray
Bryant College

Sue Ellen Neeley
University of Houston–Clear Lake

Carolyn Y. Nicholson
Stetson University

Francis L. Notturno, Sr.
Owens Community College

Terrence V. O'Brien
Northern Illinois University

James R. Ogden
Kutztown University of Pennsylvania

Lois Bitner Olson
San Diego State University

Mike O'Neill
California State University–Chico

Robert S. Owen
State University of New York–Oswego

Allan Palmer
University of North Carolina at Charlotte

David P. Paul III
Monmouth University

Terry Paul
Ohio State University

Teresa Pavia
University of Utah

John Perrachione
Truman State University

Michael Peters
Boston College

Linda Pettijohn
Missouri State University

Lana Podolak
Community College of Beaver County

Raymond E. Polchow
Muskingum Area Technical College

Thomas Ponzurick
West Virginia University

William Presutti
Duquesne University

Kathy Pullins
Columbus State Community College

Edna J. Ragins
North Carolina A&T State University

Daniel Rajaratnam
Baylor University

Mohammed Rawwas
University of Northern Iowa

James D. Reed
Louisiana State University–Shreveport

William Rhey
University of Tampa

Glen Riecken
East Tennessee State University

Winston Ring
University of Wisconsin–Milwaukee

Ed Riordan
Wayne State University

Bruce Robertson
San Francisco State University

Robert A. Robicheaux
University of Alabama–Birmingham

Linda Rose
Westwood College Online

Bert Rosenbloom
Drexel University

Robert H. Ross
Wichita State University

Tom Rossi
Broome Community College

Vicki Rostedt
The University of Akron

Catherine Roster
University of New Mexico

Michael L. Rothschild
University of Wisconsin–Madison

Kenneth L. Rowe
Arizona State University

Don Roy
Middle Tennessee State University

Catherine Ruggieri
St. John's University

Elise Sautter
New Mexico State University

Ronald Schill
Brigham Young University

Bodo Schlegelmilch
Vienna University of Economics and Business Administration

Edward Schmitt
Villanova University

Thomas Schori
Illinois State University

Donald Sciglimpaglia
San Diego State University

Stanley Scott
University of Alaska–Anchorage

Harold S. Sekiguchi
University of Nevada–Reno

Gilbert Seligman
Dutchess Community College

Richard J. Semenik
University of Utah

Beheruz N. Sethna
Lamar University

Morris A. Shapero
Schiller International University

Terence A. Shimp
University of South Carolina

Mark Siders
Southern Oregon University

Carolyn F. Siegel
Eastern Kentucky University

Dean C. Siewers
Rochester Institute of Technology

Lyndon Simkin
University of Warwick

Roberta Slater
Cedar Crest College

Paul J. Solomon
University of South Florida

Sheldon Somerstein
City University of New York

Eric R. Spangenberg
University of Mississippi

Rosann L. Spiro
Indiana University

William Staples
University of Houston–Clear Lake

Bruce Stern
Portland State University

Carmen Sunda
University of New Orleans

Claire F. Sullivan
Metropolitan State University

Robert Swerdlow
Lamar University

Crina Tarasi
Central Michigan University

Ruth Taylor
Texas State University

Steven A. Taylor
Illinois State University

Hal Teer
James Madison University

Ira Teich
Long Island University–C.W. Post

Debbie Thorne
Texas State University

Dillard Tinsley
Stephen F. Austin State University

Sharynn Tomlin
Angelo State University

Hale Tongren
George Mason University

James Underwood
University of Southwest Louisiana–Lafayette

Barbara Unger
Western Washington University

Dale Varble
Indiana State University

Bronis Verhage
Georgia State University

R. Vish Viswanathan
University of Northern Colorado

Charles Vitaska
Metropolitan State College

Kirk Wakefield
Baylor University

Harlan Wallingford
Pace University

Jacquelyn Warwick
Andrews University

James F. Wenthe
Georgia College

Sumner M. White
Massachusetts Bay Community College

Janice Williams
University of Central Oklahoma

Alan R. Wiman
Rider College

John Withey
Indiana University–South Bend

Ken Wright
West Australian College of Advanced Education

We would like to thank Charlie Hofacker and Michael Hartline, both of Florida State University, for many helpful suggestions and insights in developing the chapter on digital marketing and social networking. Michael Hartline also assisted in the development of the marketing plan outline and provided suggestions throughout the text. Catherine Roster, University of New Mexico, and Marty Meyers, University of Wisconsin–Stevens Point, provided important assistance in revising "Marketing Research and Information Systems," "Consumer Buying Behavior," and "Digital Marketing and Social Networking."

We thank Jennifer Sawayda and Courtney Bohannon for their research and editorial assistance in the revision of the chapters. We appreciate the efforts of Marian Wood for developing and revising a number of boxed features and cases. We are grateful to Harper Baird for editorial assistance and for her work on the *Instructor's Manual* and to Brett Nafziger for developing the PowerPoint program. We would like to acknowledge Jennifer Jackson, who helped provide updated examples for our text. In addition, we are grateful to Phylis Mansfield for her work on the test bank. We deeply appreciate the assistance of Courtney Monroe, Laurie Marshall, Clarissa Means, and Jamie Jahns for providing editorial technical assistance and support.

We express appreciation for the support and encouragement given to us by our colleagues at Texas A&M University and University of New Mexico. We are also grateful for the comments and suggestions we received from our own students, student focus groups, and student correspondents who provided feedback through the website.

A number of talented professionals at Cengage Learning and Integra have contributed to the development of this book. We are especially grateful to Mike Roche, Suzanna Bainbridge, Joanne Dauksewicz, Julie Klooster, Scott Dillon, Susan Nodine, Audrey Pettengill, Deanna Ettinger, Terri Miller, Stacy Shirley, Robin LeFevre, and Megan Fischer. Their inspiration, patience, support, and friendship are invaluable.

William M. Pride

O. C. Ferrell

ABOUT THE AUTHORS

William M. Pride is Professor of Marketing, Mays Business School, at Texas A&M University. He received his PhD from Louisiana State University. In addition to this text, he is the co-author of Cengage Learning's *Business* text, a market leader. Dr. Pride teaches principles of marketing at both undergraduate and graduate levels and constantly solicits student feedback important to revising a principles of marketing text.

Dr. Pride's research interests are in advertising, promotion, and distribution channels. His research articles have appeared in major journals in the fields of marketing, such as the *Journal of Marketing,* the *Journal of Marketing Research,* the *Journal of the Academy of Marketing Science,* and the *Journal of Advertising.*

Dr. Pride is a member of the American Marketing Association, Academy of Marketing Science, Society for Marketing Advances, and the Marketing Management Association. He has received the Marketing Fellow Award from the Society for Marketing Advances and the Marketing Innovation Award from the Marketing Management Association. Both of these are lifetime achievement awards.

O. C. Ferrell is University Distinguished Professor of Marketing and Bill Daniels Professor of Business Ethics, Anderson School of Management, University of New Mexico. He has also been on the faculties of the University of Wyoming, Colorado State University, University of Memphis, Texas A&M University, Illinois State University, and Southern Illinois University. He received his PhD in Marketing from Louisiana State University.

He is past president of the Academic Council of the American Marketing Association and chaired the American Marketing Association Ethics Committee. Under his leadership, the committee developed the AMA Code of Ethics and the AMA Code of Ethics for Marketing on the Internet. He is currently a member of the advisory committee for the AMA marketing certification program. In addition, he is a former member of the Academy of Marketing Science Board of Governors and is a Society of Marketing Advances and Southwestern Marketing Association Fellow and an Academy of Marketing Science Distinguished Fellow. He is the Academy of Marketing Science's vice president of publications. In 2010, he received a Lifetime Achievement Award from the Macromarketing Society and a special award for service to doctoral students from the Southeast Doctoral Consortium.

Dr. Ferrell is the co-author of 20 books and more than 100 published articles and papers. His articles have been published in the *Journal of Marketing Research*, the *Journal of Marketing,* the *Journal of Business Ethics*, the *Journal of Business Research,* the *Journal of the Academy of Marketing Science*, and the *Journal of Public Policy & Marketing,* as well as other journals.

part 1

Marketing Strategy and Customer Relationships

PART 1 introduces the field of marketing and offers a broad perspective from which to explore and analyze various components of the marketing discipline. CHAPTER 1 defines *marketing* and explores some key concepts, including customers and target markets, the marketing mix, relationship marketing, the marketing concept, and value. CHAPTER 2 provides an overview of strategic marketing issues, such as the effect of organizational resources and opportunities on the planning process; the role of the mission statement; corporate, business-unit, and marketing strategies; and the creation of the marketing plan.

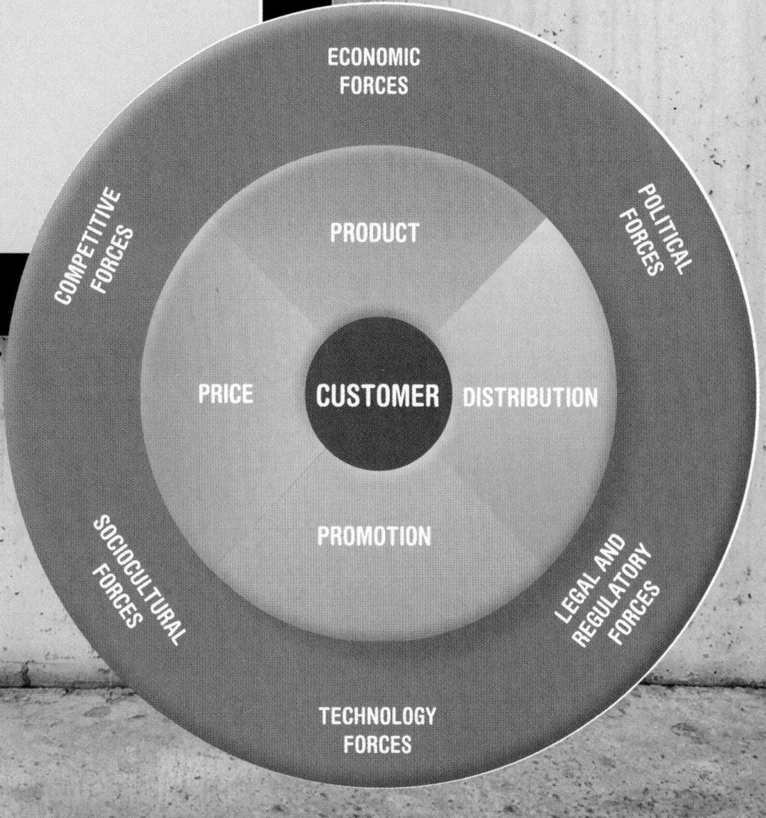

chapter 1

An Overview of Strategic Marketing

OBJECTIVES

1. To be able to define *marketing* as focused on customers
2. To identify some important marketing terms, including target market, marketing mix, marketing exchanges, and marketing environment
3. To understand the relationship between marketing and value
4. To become aware of the marketing concept and market orientation
5. To understand the importance of building customer relationships
6. To recognize the role of marketing in our society

MARKETING INSIGHTS

Walmart Returns to Its Roots

Walmart has long been admired for its skill in implementing a superior marketing strategy. Its everyday low prices (EDLP) and basic products strongly appeal to its target market, mainly households that make below $70,000 a year. However, trouble has come to Walmart due to changes in its marketing strategy. Walmart tried to broaden its customer base by selling more upscale products and compromising its position as a price leader. According to analysts, Walmart's attempt to be everything to everybody resulted in the alienation of its core market, which has likely contributed to its two years of declining U.S. sales.

To appeal to a higher-income market, Walmart began offering trendier items such as fashionable clothing and organic food. In the process, it removed items such as fishing tackle that were popular with its target market. The move resulted in higher prices for some of its products, conflicting with Walmart's EDLP pricing strategy. Under normal economic conditions, this might not have been so problematic; however, during the most recent recession many of its customers were unhappy with Walmart's removal of basic items. They often switched to lower-priced rivals Dollar Tree and Family Dollar. Additionally, Walmart's upscale items failed to catch on with higher-income consumers.

After realizing its marketing mistakes, Walmart reintroduced many of the basic products that it had removed and returned to its EDLP strategy. It even closed its fashion office in New York to return to its Bentonville, Arkansas, roots. However, many former Walmart shoppers have expressed their belief that Walmart no longer offers the best prices. It may take time for Walmart to regain domestic market share and get back to its roots.[1]

Like all organizations, Walmart attempts to provide products that customers want, communicate useful information about them to excite interest, price them appropriately, and make them available when and where customers want to buy them. Even if an organization does all these things well, however, competition from marketers of similar products, economic conditions, and other factors can impact the company's success. Such factors influence the decisions that all organizations must make in strategic marketing.

This chapter introduces the strategic marketing concepts and decisions covered throughout the text. First, we develop a definition of *marketing* and explore each element of the definition in detail. Next, we explore the importance of value-driven marketing. We also introduce the marketing concept and consider several issues associated with its implementation. Additionally, we take a look at the management of customer relationships and relationship marketing. Finally, we examine the importance of marketing in global society.

DEFINING *MARKETING*

If you ask several people what *marketing* is, you are likely to hear a variety of descriptions. Although many people think marketing is advertising or selling, marketing is much more complex than most people realize. In this book we define **marketing** as the process of creating, distributing, promoting, and pricing goods, services, and ideas to facilitate satisfying exchange relationships with customers and to develop and maintain favorable relationships with stakeholders in a dynamic environment. Our definition is consistent with that of the American Marketing Association (AMA), which defines *marketing* as "the activity, set of institutions, and processes for creating, communicating, delivering, and exchanging offerings that have value for customers, clients, partners, and society at large."[2]

marketing The process of creating, distributing, promoting, and pricing goods, services, and ideas to facilitate satisfying exchange relationships with customers and to develop and maintain favorable relationships with stakeholders in a dynamic environment

Marketing Focuses on Customers

As the purchasers of the products that organizations develop, price, distribute, and promote, **customers** are the focal point of all marketing activities (see Figure 1.1). Organizations have to define their products not as what the companies make or produce but as what they do to satisfy customers. The Walt Disney Company is not in the business of establishing theme parks;

customers The purchasers of organizations' products; the focal point of all marketing activities

© AP Images/PRNewsFoto/Gazillion Entertainment

Appealing to Target Markets Marvel provides online entertainment to satisfy its customers.

Figure 1.1 Components of Strategic Marketing

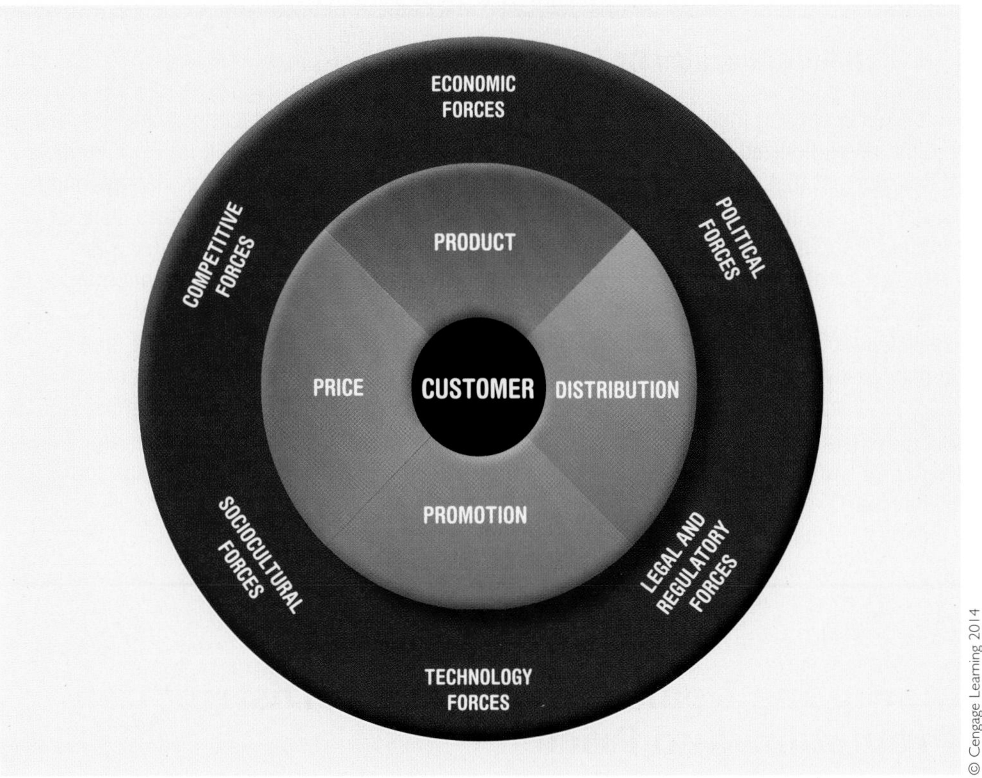

it is in the business of making people happy. At Disney World, customers are guests, the crowd is an audience, and employees are cast members. Customer satisfaction and enjoyment can come from anything received when buying and using a product.

The essence of marketing is to develop satisfying exchanges from which both customers and marketers benefit. The customer expects to gain a reward or benefit greater than the costs incurred in a marketing transaction. The marketer expects to gain something of value in return, generally the price charged for the product. Through buyer–seller interaction, a customer develops expectations about the seller's future behavior. To fulfill these expectations, the marketer must deliver on promises made. Over time, this interaction results in relationships between the two parties. Fast-food restaurants such as Taco Bell and Subway depend on repeat purchases from satisfied customers—many often live or work a few miles from these restaurants—whereas customer expectations revolve around tasty food, value, and dependable service.

Organizations generally focus their marketing efforts on a specific group of customers, called a **target market**. Marketing managers may define a target market as a vast number of people or a relatively small group. For instance, marketers are increasingly interested in Hispanic consumers. Within the last decade, Hispanics made up more than half of the population gains in the United States. The buying power of Hispanics is estimated to reach $1.5 trillion by 2015. Procter & Gamble is one of many companies trying to capitalize on this trend. Procter & Gamble is hoping to court more Hispanic shoppers with Spanish labeling and products customized toward Hispanic tastes, such as lavender-scented Downy detergent.[3] Other companies target multiple markets with different products, promotions, prices, and distribution systems for each one. Vans shoes targets a fairly narrow market segment, especially compared to more diverse athletic shoe companies such as Nike and Reebok. Vans targets skateboarders and snowboarders between the ages of 10 and 24, whereas Nike and Reebok target most sports, age ranges, genders, and price points.[4]

target market A specific group of customers on whom an organization focuses its marketing efforts

Emerging Trends

Netflix Alienates Its Target Market

Even popular companies make mistakes in serving their target market. Netflix, a company that revolutionized the video streaming and rental business, did just that. In 2011 Netflix shocked customers when it announced price increases for its rental and streaming plans. In the case of one popular streaming and DVD plan, Netflix raised the price from $9.99 to $15.98 per month.

Price is a flexible but sensitive element of the marketing mix. While it is easy for a company to lower prices, it is harder to raise prices without customer dissatisfaction. This is why many organizations choose to raise prices gradually. Netflix's large price increase was an unwelcome surprise for many loyal customers. Approximately 82,000 angry comments were soon posted on the company's blog.

In September 2011, CEO Reed Hastings's announcement that the company was going to split into two entities, one for the DVD rental services and one for the streaming services, upset customers even more. Investors disliked the idea, causing the price of Netflix stock to decrease. Pressure finally caused Netflix to scrap its intention of splitting services.

Customer satisfaction is difficult to achieve, and a company must coordinate the marketing mix of product, price, distribution, and promotion. Netflix, which became successful because of its marketing concept, experienced a serious reaction from customers. It is working hard to restore customer and investor confidence.[a]

Marketing Deals with Products, Distribution, Promotion, and Price

Marketing is more than simply advertising or selling a product; it involves developing and managing a product that will satisfy customer needs. It focuses on making the product available in the right place and at a price acceptable to buyers. It also requires communicating information that helps customers determine if the product will satisfy their needs. These activities are planned, organized, implemented, and controlled to meet the needs of customers within the target market. Marketers refer to these activities—product, pricing, distribution, and promotion—as the **marketing mix** because they decide what type of each element to use and in what amounts. Marketing creates value through the marketing mix. A primary goal of a marketing manager is to create and maintain the right mix of these elements to satisfy customers' needs for a general product type. Note in Figure 1.1 that the marketing mix is built around the customer.

Marketing managers strive to develop a marketing mix that matches the needs of customers in the target market. For example, REI targets consumers who are serious about the outdoors. Although they charge higher prices than discount stores, REI offers a broad range of quality products for a number of outdoor activities. REI stores also offer lifetime memberships for a $20 membership fee, which allows members to receive part of the company's profits based upon their purchases during the year.[5] Marketing managers must constantly monitor the competition and adapt their product, pricing, promotion, and distribution decisions to create long-term success.

Before marketers can develop a marketing mix, they must collect in-depth, up-to-date information about customer needs. Such information might include data about the age, income, ethnicity, gender, and educational level of people in the target market, their preferences for product features, their attitudes toward competitors' products, and the frequency with which they use the product. For instance, when Ursula Burns became CEO of Xerox, she knew that the company would have to change its focus. Consumers, particularly the younger generation, were choosing to use digital technology over photocopiers and traditional printers. On the other hand, research showed that offices still required services such as printing. By offering to manage these services for companies, Xerox has created a profitable business in which approximately half of its

marketing mix Four marketing activities—product, pricing, distribution, and promotion—that a firm can control to meet the needs of customers within its target market

revenue comes from its service business.[6] Armed with market information, marketing managers are better able to develop a marketing mix that satisfies a specific target market.

Let's look more closely at the decisions and activities related to each marketing mix variable.

The Product Variable

Successful marketing efforts result in products that become part of everyday life. Consider the satisfaction customers have had over the years from Coca-Cola, Levi's jeans, Visa credit cards, Tylenol pain relievers, and 3M Post-it Notes. The product variable of the marketing mix deals with researching customers' needs and wants and designing a product that satisfies them. A **product** can be a good, a service, or an idea. A good is a physical entity you can touch. Oakley sunglasses, Seven for All Mankind jeans, and Axe body spray are all examples of products. A service is the application of human and mechanical efforts to people or objects to provide intangible benefits to customers. Air travel, education, haircutting, banking, medical care, and day care are examples of services. Ideas include concepts, philosophies, images, and issues. For instance, a marriage counselor, for a fee, gives spouses ideas to help improve their relationship. Other marketers of ideas include political parties, churches, and schools.

The product variable also involves creating or modifying brand names and packaging and may include decisions regarding warranty and repair services. For example, the lawn care company TruGreen was originally branded as "Chemlawn." The company adapted its branding and products to provide a healthier and "greener" product offering.

Product variable decisions and related activities are important because they are directly involved with creating products that address customers' needs and wants. To maintain an assortment of products that helps an organization achieve its goals, marketers must develop new products, modify existing ones, and eliminate those that no longer satisfy enough buyers or that yield unacceptable profits.

The Distribution Variable

To satisfy customers, products must be available at the right time and in convenient locations. Subway, for example, locates not only in strip malls but also inside Walmarts, Home Depots, Laundromats, churches, and hospitals, as well as inside Goodwill stores, car dealerships, and appliance stores. There are more than 35,950 Subways in 98 different countries, surpassing McDonald's as the world's largest chain.[7]

In dealing with the distribution variable, a marketing manager makes products available in the quantities desired to as many target-market customers as possible, keeping total inventory,

product A good, a service, or an idea

© AP Images/ PRNewsFoto/VIZIO, Inc.

© NetPhotos/Alamy

Types of Products
Vizio produces 3D technology, a tangible good, to allow consumers a differentiated product experience, while Verizon provides an intangible product through its cellular services.

transportation, and storage costs as low as possible. A marketing manager also may select and motivate intermediaries (wholesalers and retailers), establish and maintain inventory control procedures, and develop and manage transportation and storage systems. The advent of the Internet and electronic commerce also has dramatically influenced the distribution variable. Companies now can make their products available throughout the world without maintaining facilities in each country. Apple has benefitted from the ability to download songs and apps over the Internet. Since the introduction of iTunes, 16 billion songs have been downloaded from its stores.[8] The company has supported growth and global success beyond the presence of physical Apple stores selling phones, computers, iPads, and accessories. We examine distribution issues in Chapters 15 and 16.

© Ruaridh Stewart/ZUMA Press/Newscom

Distribution
Starbucks increases its distribution channels by offering its coffee products through retail organizations, such as Barnes & Noble.

The Promotion Variable

The promotion variable relates to activities used to inform individuals or groups about the organization and its products. Promotion can aim to increase public awareness of the organization and of new or existing products. Adidas, for example, wanted to increase awareness of its brands among teenagers. The company released television and Internet commercials featuring famous athletes promoting its brands. Its online commercial contained links to Facebook and Twitter for more up-to-date information on its products.[9]

Promotional activities also can educate customers about product features or urge people to take a particular stance on a political or social issue, such as smoking or drug abuse. For example, the National Highway Safety Traffic Administration released an ad campaign to deter drunk driving during the holiday season. The campaign carried the message that cops "would see you before you see them." In the advertisement, a transparent cop watches drunk teenagers as they leave a party, only to have them arrested as they are driving home.[10]

Promotion can help to sustain interest in established products that have been available for decades, such as Arm & Hammer baking soda or Ivory soap. Many companies are using the Internet to communicate information about themselves and their products. Campbell's Kitchen provides a diverse array of recipes, coupons, and discussion boards online to support the sales of their soups.[11]

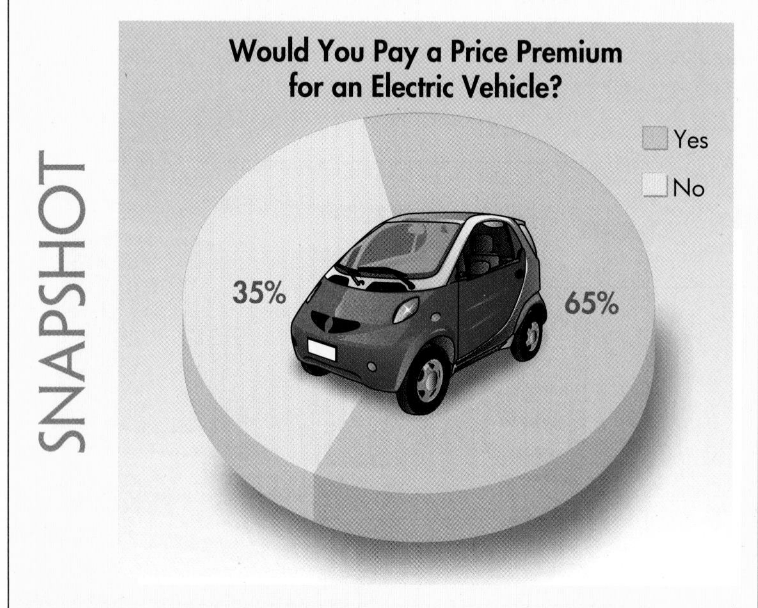

Source: "Global Consumers Not Plugging into Electric Vehicles: Deloitte Survey," October 4, 2011, www.deloitte.com/view/en_GX/global/86cc3bd8e9fc2310VgnVCM3000001c56f00aRCRD.htm (accessed May 16, 2012).

The Price Variable

The price variable relates to decisions and actions associated with establishing pricing objectives and policies and determining product prices. Price is a critical component of the marketing mix because customers are concerned about the value obtained in an exchange. Price is often used as a competitive tool, and intense price competition sometimes leads to price wars. High prices can be used competitively to establish a product's premium image. Waterman and Mont Blanc pens, for example, have an image of high quality and high price that has given them significant status. Other companies are skilled at providing products at prices lower than competitors. Amazon uses its vast network of partnerships and cost efficiencies to provide products at low prices. Brick-and-mortar retailers have not been able to offer comparable products with prices that low, providing Amazon with a considerable competitive advantage.

The marketing-mix variables are often viewed as controllable because they can be modified. However, there are limits to how much marketing managers can alter them. Economic conditions, competitive structure, and government regulations may prevent a manager from adjusting prices frequently or significantly. Making changes in the size, shape, and design of most tangible goods is expensive; therefore, such product features cannot be altered very often. In addition, promotional campaigns and methods used to distribute products ordinarily cannot be rewritten or revamped overnight.

Marketing Creates Value

Value is an important element of managing long-term customer relationships and implementing the marketing concept. We view **value** as a customer's subjective assessment of benefits relative to costs in determining the worth of a product (customer value = customer benefits – customer costs). Consumers develop a concept of value through the integration of their perceptions of product quality and financial sacrifice.[12] From a company's perspective, there is a trade-off between increasing the value offered to a customer and maximizing the profits from a transaction.[13]

Customer benefits include anything a buyer receives in an exchange. Hotels and motels, for example, basically provide a room with a bed and bathroom, but each firm provides a different level of service, amenities, and atmosphere to satisfy its guests. Hampton Inn offers the minimum services necessary to maintain a quality, efficient, low-price overnight accommodation. In contrast, the Ritz-Carlton provides every imaginable service a guest might desire. The hotel even allows its staff members to spend up to $2,000 to settle customer complaints.[14] Customers judge which type of accommodation offers the best value according to the benefits they desire and their willingness and ability to pay for the costs associated with the benefits.

Customer costs include anything a buyer must give up to obtain the benefits the product provides. The most obvious cost is the monetary price of the product, but nonmonetary costs can be equally important in a customer's determination of value. Two nonmonetary costs are the time and effort customers expend to find and purchase desired products. To reduce time and effort, a company can increase product availability, thereby making it more convenient for buyers to purchase the firm's products. Another nonmonetary cost is risk, which

value A customer's subjective assessment of benefits relative to costs in determining the worth of a product

Value-Driven Marketing
Cadbury provides a high-quality chocolate bar that satisfies customer desires at a premium price point.

Marketing Debate

The Relationship between Marketing and Value

ISSUE: Does marketing increase the value of products?

Value is a subjective assessment of benefits relative to costs. Marketing has the ability to increase consumers' perceptions of a product's quality and social approval. For instance, retailers like Neiman Marcus use marketing to create awareness and promote the quality of their products. Consumers may be willing to pay more for products when the image of the product is enhanced through advertising, personal selling, and publicity.

On the other hand, critics are concerned that consumers may pay more for products when benefits such as quality and functionality are not enhanced. For example, some name-brand pharmaceuticals have the exact same ingredients as generic brands. Additionally, certain products are advertised as natural and sustainable to justify higher prices. There is no evidence that consumers actually obtain more tangible benefits from these purchases.[b]

can be reduced by offering good basic warranties or extended warranties for an additional charge.[15] Another risk-reduction strategy is the offer of a 100 percent satisfaction guarantee. This strategy is increasingly popular in today's catalog/telephone/Internet shopping environment. L.L. Bean, for example, uses such a guarantee to reduce the risk involved in ordering merchandise from its catalogs.

The process people use to determine the value of a product is not highly scientific. All of us tend to get a feel for the worth of products based on our own expectations and previous experience. We can, for example, compare the value of tires, batteries, and computers directly with the value of competing products. We evaluate movies, sporting events, and performances by entertainers on the more subjective basis of personal preferences and emotions. For most purchases, we do not consciously try to calculate the associated benefits and costs. It becomes an instinctive feeling that Kellogg's Corn Flakes is a good value or that McDonald's is a good place to take children for a quick lunch. The purchase of an automobile or a mountain bike may have emotional components, but more conscious decision making also may figure in the process of determining value.

In developing marketing activities, it is important to recognize that customers receive benefits based on their experiences. For example, many computer buyers consider services such as fast delivery, ease of installation, technical advice, and training assistance to be important elements of the product. Customers also derive benefits from the act of shopping and selecting products. These benefits can be affected by the atmosphere or environment of a store, such as Red Lobster's nautical/seafood theme. Even the ease of navigating a website can have a tremendous impact on perceived value. For this reason, General Motors has developed a user-friendly way to navigate its website for researching and pricing vehicles. Using the Internet to compare a Chevrolet to a Mercedes could result in different users viewing each automobile as an excellent value. Owners have rated Chevrolet as providing reliable transportation and having dealers who provide acceptable service. A Mercedes may cost twice as much but has been rated as a better-engineered automobile that also has a higher social status than the Chevrolet. Different customers may view each car as being an exceptional value for their own personal satisfaction.

The marketing mix can be used to enhance perceptions of value. A product that demonstrates value usually has a feature or an enhancement that provides benefits. Promotional activities can also help to create image and prestige characteristics that customers consider in their assessment of a product's value. In some cases value may be perceived simply as the lowest price. Many customers may not care about the quality of the paper towels they buy; they simply want the cheapest ones for use in cleaning up spills because they plan to throw them in the trash anyway. On the other hand, more people are looking for the fastest, most convenient way to achieve a goal and therefore become insensitive to pricing. For example, many busy customers are buying more prepared meals in supermarkets to take home and serve quickly, even though these meals cost considerably more than meals prepared from scratch. In such cases the products with the greatest convenience may be perceived as having the greatest value. The availability or distribution of products also can enhance their value. Taco Bell wants to have its Mexican fast-food products available at any time and any place people are thinking about consuming food. It therefore has introduced Taco Bell products into supermarkets, vending machines, college campuses, and other convenient locations. Thus, the development of an effective marketing strategy requires understanding the needs and desires of customers and designing a marketing mix to satisfy them and provide the value they want.

Marketing Builds Relationships with Customers and Other Stakeholders

Marketing also creates value through the building of stakeholder relationships. Individuals and organizations engage in marketing to facilitate **exchanges**, the provision or transfer of goods, services, or ideas in return for something of value. Any product (good, service, or even idea) may be involved in a marketing exchange. We assume only that individuals and organizations expect to gain a reward in excess of the costs incurred.

For an exchange to take place, four conditions must exist. First, two or more individuals, groups, or organizations must participate, and each must possess something of value that the other party desires. Second, the exchange should provide a benefit or satisfaction to both parties involved in the transaction. Third, each party must have confidence in the promise of the "something of value" held by the other. If you go to a Coldplay concert, for example, you go with the expectation of a great performance. Finally, to build trust, the parties to the exchange must meet expectations.

Figure 1.2 depicts the exchange process. The arrows indicate that the parties communicate that each has something of value available to exchange. An exchange will not necessarily take place just because these conditions exist; marketing activities can occur even without an actual transaction or sale. You may see an ad for a Sub-Zero refrigerator, for instance, but you might never buy the luxury appliance. When an exchange occurs, products are traded for other products or for financial resources.

Marketing activities should attempt to create and maintain satisfying exchange relationships. To maintain an exchange relationship, buyers must be satisfied with the good, service, or idea obtained, and sellers must be satisfied with the financial reward or something else of

exchange The provision or transfer of goods, services, or ideas in return for something of value

© iStockphoto.com/Lya_Cattel

Satisfying Stakeholder Needs Apple continues to excel at creating products that satisfy customers, generate jobs, create shareholder wealth, and contribute to greater life enjoyment.

Figure 1.2 **Exchange between Buyer and Seller**

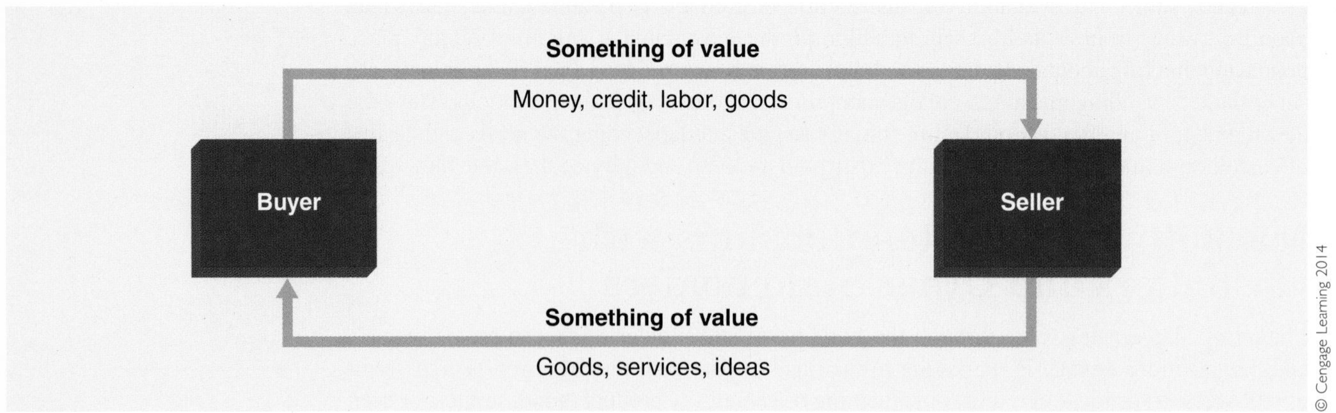

value received. A dissatisfied customer who lacks trust in the relationship often searches for alternative organizations or products.

Marketers are concerned with building and maintaining relationships not only with customers but also with relevant stakeholders. **Stakeholders** include those constituents who have a "stake," or claim, in some aspect of a company's products, operations, markets, industry, and outcomes; these include customers, employees, investors and shareholders, suppliers, governments, communities, and many others. Developing and maintaining favorable relations with stakeholders is crucial to the long-term growth of an organization and its products.

Marketing Occurs in a Dynamic Environment

Marketing activities do not take place in a vacuum. The **marketing environment**, which includes competitive, economic, political, legal and regulatory, technological, and sociocultural forces, surrounds the customer and affects the marketing mix (see Figure 1.1). The effects of these forces on buyers and sellers can be dramatic and difficult to predict. Their impact on value can be extensive as market changes can easily impact how stakeholders perceive certain products. They can create threats to marketers but also can generate opportunities for new products and new methods of reaching customers.

The forces of the marketing environment affect a marketer's ability to facilitate value-driven marketing exchanges in three general ways. First, they influence customers by affecting their lifestyles, standards of living, and preferences and needs for products. Because a marketing manager tries to develop and adjust the marketing mix to satisfy customers, effects of environmental forces on customers also have an indirect impact on marketing-mix components. For instance, high rates of obesity in America have created a demand for healthier food options. Responding to health concerns from consumers, Starbucks began offering Bistro Boxes at more than 5,000 locations. Bistro Boxes are small meals with fewer than 500 calories.[16] Second, marketing environment forces help to determine whether and how a marketing manager can perform certain marketing activities. Third, environmental forces may affect a marketing manager's decisions and actions by influencing buyers' reactions to the firm's marketing mix.

Marketing environment forces can fluctuate quickly and dramatically, which is one reason why marketing is so interesting and challenging. Because these forces are closely interrelated, changes in one may cause changes in others. For example, evidence linking children's consumption of soft drinks and fast foods to health issues has exposed marketers of such products to negative publicity and generated calls for legislation regulating the sale of soft drinks in public schools. Some companies have responded to these concerns by voluntarily reformulating products to make them healthier or even introducing new products.

stakeholders Constituents who have a "stake," or claim, in some aspect of a company's products, operations, markets, industry, and outcomes

marketing environment The competitive, economic, political, legal and regulatory, technological, and sociocultural forces that surround the customer and affect the marketing mix

McDonald's responded to accusations that its children's meals were unhealthy by decreasing the size of French fries and adding apple slices to its Happy Meals.[17]

Changes in the marketing environment produce uncertainty for marketers and at times hurt marketing efforts, but they also create opportunities. For example, when oil prices increase, consumers shift to potential alternative sources of transportation including bikes, buses, light rail, trains, carpooling, more energy-efficient vehicle purchases, or telecommuting when possible. Marketers who are alert to changes in environmental forces not only can adjust to and influence these changes but can also capitalize on the opportunities such changes provide. Marketing-mix variables—product, price, distribution, and promotion—are factors over which an organization has control; the forces of the environment, however, are subject to far less control. Even though marketers know that they cannot predict changes in the marketing environment with certainty, however, they must nevertheless plan for them. Because these environmental forces have such a profound effect on marketing activities, we explore each of them in considerable depth in Chapter 3.

UNDERSTANDING THE MARKETING CONCEPT

Some firms have sought success by buying land, building a factory, equipping it with people and machines, and then making a product they believe buyers need. However, these firms frequently fail to attract customers with what they have to offer because they define their business as "making a product" rather than as "helping potential customers satisfy their needs and wants." For example, when digital music became popular, businesses had opportunities to develop new products to satisfy customers' needs. Firms such as Apple developed the iTunes music store as well as new products like the iPod, iPhone, and iPad to satisfy consumers' desires for portable, customized music libraries. Other companies like Pandora and Spotify offered on-demand music streaming to computers and mobile devices. Companies that did not pursue such opportunities struggled to compete as digital music sales rose while physical album sales declined.

According to the **marketing concept**, an organization should try to provide products that satisfy customers' needs through a coordinated set of activities that also allows the organization to achieve its goals. Customer satisfaction is the major focus of the marketing concept. To implement the marketing concept, an organization strives to determine what buyers want and uses this information to develop satisfying products. It focuses on customer analysis, competitor analysis, and integration of the firm's resources to provide customer value and satisfaction, as well as to generate long-term profits.[18] The firm also must continue to alter, adapt, and develop products to keep pace with customers' changing desires and preferences. Howard Schultz, founder and CEO of Starbucks, demonstrates the company's grasp on the marketing concept by explaining that Starbucks is not a coffee business that serves people, but rather a "people business serving coffee." Starbucks' leadership sees the company as being "in the business of humanity," emphasizing the fact that Starbucks is not only concerned about customers but society as well.[19] Thus, the marketing concept emphasizes that marketing begins and ends with customers. Research has found a positive association between customer satisfaction and shareholder value,[20] and high levels of customer satisfaction also tend to attract and retain high-quality employees and managers.[21]

The marketing concept is not a second definition of marketing. It is a management philosophy guiding an organization's overall activities. This philosophy affects all organizational activities, not just marketing. Production, finance, accounting, human resources, and marketing departments must work together.

marketing concept A managerial philosophy that an organization should try to satisfy customers' needs through a coordinated set of activities that also allows the organization to achieve its goals

The marketing concept is also not a philanthropic philosophy aimed at helping customers at the expense of the organization. A firm that adopts the marketing concept must satisfy not only its customers' objectives but also its own, or it will not stay in business long. The overall

The Marketing Concept
Stew Leonard's corporate policy, etched in stone, reflects the essence of the marketing concept: customer satisfaction.

objectives of a business might relate to increasing profits, market share, sales, or a combination of all three. The marketing concept stresses that an organization can best achieve these objectives by being customer oriented. Thus, implementing the marketing concept should benefit the organization as well as its customers.

It is important for marketers to consider not only their current buyers' needs but also the long-term needs of society. Striving to satisfy customers' desires by sacrificing society's long-term welfare is unacceptable. For instance, there is significant demand for large SUVs and trucks. However, environmentalists and federal regulators are challenging automakers to produce more fuel-efficient vehicles with increased mpg standards. The question that remains is whether or not Americans are willing to give up their spacious SUVs for the good of the environment. Recent trends indicate that the popularity of SUVs is rebounding.[22]

Evolution of the Marketing Concept

The marketing concept may seem like an obvious approach to running a business. However, businesspeople have not always believed that the best way to make sales and profits is to satisfy customers.

The Production Orientation

During the second half of the nineteenth century, the Industrial Revolution was in full swing in the United States. Electricity, rail transportation, division of labor, assembly lines, and mass production made it possible to produce goods more efficiently. With new technology and new ways of using labor, products poured into the marketplace, where demand for manufactured goods was strong.

The Sales Orientation

While sales have always been needed to make a profit, during the first half of the twentieth century competition increased and businesses realized that they would have to focus more on selling products to buyers. Businesses viewed sales as the major means of increasing profits, and this period came to have a sales orientation. Businesspeople believed that the most important marketing activities were personal selling, advertising, and distribution. Today, some people incorrectly equate marketing with a sales orientation.

The Market Orientation

By the early 1950s, some businesspeople began to recognize that efficient production and extensive promotion did not guarantee that customers would buy products. These businesses, and many others since, found that they must first determine what customers want and then produce those products rather than making the products first and then trying to persuade customers that they need them. As more organizations realized the importance of satisfying customers' needs, U.S. businesses entered the marketing era, one of market orientation.

A **market orientation** requires the "organizationwide generation of market intelligence pertaining to current and future customer needs, dissemination of the intelligence across departments, and organizationwide responsiveness to it."[23] Market orientation is linked to new-product innovation by developing a strategic focus to explore and develop new products to serve target markets.[24] For example, with an increasing "green attitude" in this country, consumers like environmentally responsible products offered at fair prices. To meet this demand, Method laundry detergent is eight times more concentrated and can clean 50 loads of laundry from a container the size of a small soft-drink bottle. Top management, marketing managers, nonmarketing managers (those in production, finance, human resources, and so on), and customers are all important in developing and carrying out a market orientation. Trust, openness, honoring promises, respect, collaboration, and recognizing the market as the raison d'etre are six values required by organizations striving to become more market oriented.[25] Unless marketing managers provide continuous customer-focused leadership with minimal interdepartmental conflict, achieving a market orientation will be difficult. Nonmarketing managers must communicate with marketing managers to share information important to understanding the customer. Finally, a market orientation involves being responsive to ever-changing customer needs and wants. To accomplish this, eBay, the online auction and shopping site, acquired the online platform Hunch to help the ecommerce site create better product recommendations for its users. Hunch uses online data to make predictions based on users' likes and interests. It follows buyers' online purchases and recommends related topics.[26] Trying to assess what customers want, which is difficult to begin with, is further complicated by the speed with which fashions and tastes can change. Today, businesses want to satisfy customers and build meaningful long-term buyer–seller relationships. Doing so helps a firm boost its own financial value.[27]

Implementing the Marketing Concept

A philosophy may sound reasonable and look good on paper, but this does not mean that it can be put into practice easily. To implement the marketing concept, a market-oriented organization must accept some general conditions and recognize and deal with several problems. Consequently, the marketing concept has yet to be fully accepted by all businesses.

Management must first establish an information system to discover customers' real needs and then use the information to create satisfying products. For example, Rubbermaid is using a social commerce platform (customer/business interaction mechanism) that impacts product development and education as to how to use the product. In reviewing customer interaction, Rubbermaid noted that many consumers did not understand how to use its "Produce Saver" food storage container properly. When the company added use and care instructions to its website, the average star rating (a notation of satisfaction) increased significantly. Listening and responding to consumers' frustrations and appreciation is the key in implementing the marketing concept.[28] An information system is usually expensive; management must commit money and time for its development and maintenance. Without an adequate information system, however, an organization cannot be market oriented.

To satisfy customers' objectives as well as its own, a company also must coordinate all of its activities. This may require restructuring its internal operations, including production, marketing, and other business functions. This requires the firm to adapt to a changing external

market orientation An organizationwide commitment to researching and responding to customer needs

environment, including changing customer expectations. Companies who monitor the external environment can often predict major changes and adapt successfully. For instance, while the majority of Internet companies failed after the dot-com bubble burst in 2000, Amazon .com continued to thrive because it understood its customers and had created a website customized to their wants.[29] The company continues to expand its products and services and add new features to its website to better serve its customers. On the other hand, when Hewlett-Packard announced it intended to sell its personal computer business, company share prices plummeted. Investors felt HP's livelihood depended upon its PC sales. Additionally, because personal computers are such an integral part of HP, such a decision would require major changes in company operations and strategic direction. The plan was eventually scrapped.[30] If marketing is not included in the organization's top-level management, a company could fail to address actual customer needs and desires. Implementing the marketing concept demands the support not only of top management but also of managers and staff at all levels of the organization.

CUSTOMER RELATIONSHIP MANAGEMENT

Customer relationship management (CRM) focuses on using information about customers to create marketing strategies that develop and sustain desirable customer relationships. Achieving the full profit potential of each customer relationship should be the fundamental goal of every marketing strategy. Marketing relationships with customers are the lifeblood of all businesses. At the most basic level, profits can be obtained through relationships in the following ways: (1) by acquiring new customers, (2) by enhancing the profitability of existing customers, and (3) by extending the duration of customer relationships. In addition to retaining customers, companies also should focus on regaining and managing relationships with customers who have abandoned the firm.[31] Implementing the marketing concept means optimizing the exchange relationship, otherwise known as the relationship between a company's financial investment in customer relationships and the return generated by customers' loyalty and retention.

Relationship Marketing

Maintaining positive relationships with customers is an important goal for marketers. The term **relationship marketing** refers to "long-term, mutually beneficial arrangements in which both the buyer and seller focus on value enhancement through the creation of more satisfying exchanges."[32] Relationship marketing continually deepens the buyer's trust in the company, and as the customer's confidence grows, this, in turn, increases the firm's understanding of the customer's needs. Successful marketers respond to customer needs and strive to increase value to buyers over time. Eventually, this interaction becomes a solid relationship that allows for cooperation and mutual dependency. Whole Foods has implemented relationship marketing with the view that customers are its most important stakeholder. One of the company's core values involves "satisfying the customer first."[33]

Relationship marketing strives to build satisfying exchange relationships between buyers and sellers by gathering useful data at all customer contact points and analyzing that data to better understand customers' needs, desires, and habits. It focuses on building and using databases and leveraging technologies to identify strategies and methods that will maximize the lifetime value of each desirable customer to the company. It is imperative that marketers educate themselves about their customers' expectations if they are to satisfy their needs; customer dissatisfaction will only lead to defection.[34]

To build these long-term customer relationships, marketers are increasingly turning to marketing research and information technology. By increasing customer value over time,

customer relationship management (CRM) Using information about customers to create marketing strategies that develop and sustain desirable customer relationships

relationship marketing Establishing long-term, mutually satisfying buyer–seller relationships

organizations try to retain and increase long-term profitability through customer loyalty, which results from increasing customer value. The airline industry is a key player in CRM efforts with its frequent-flyer programs. Frequent-flyer programs enable airlines to track individual information about customers, using databases that can help airlines understand what different customers want and treat customers differently depending on their flying habits. Relationship-building efforts like frequent-flyer programs have been shown to increase customer value.[35]

Through the use of Internet-based marketing strategies (e-marketing), companies can personalize customer relationships on a nearly one-on-one basis. A wide range of products, such as computers, jeans, golf clubs, cosmetics, and greeting cards, can be tailored for specific customers. Customer relationship management provides a strategic bridge between information technology and marketing strategies aimed at long-term relationships. This involves finding and retaining customers by using information to improve customer value and satisfaction.

Customer Lifetime Value

Managing customer relationships requires identifying patterns of buying behavior and using that information to focus on the most promising and profitable customers.[36] Companies must be sensitive to customers' requirements and desires and establish communication to build their trust and loyalty. Pizza Hut, for example, is estimated to have a lifetime customer value of $8,000, whereas Cadillac estimates its lifetime customer's value at $332,000.[37] A customer's value over a lifetime represents an intangible asset to a marketer that can be augmented by addressing the customer's varying needs and preferences at different stages in his or her relationship with the firm.[38] In general, when marketers focus on customers chosen for their lifetime value, they earn higher profits in future periods than when they focus on customers selected for other reasons.[39]

The ability to identify individual customers allows marketers to shift their focus from targeting groups of similar customers to increasing their share of an individual customer's purchases. The emphasis changes from *share of market* to *share of customer.* Focusing on share of customer requires recognizing that all customers have different needs and that not all customers weigh the value of a company equally. The most basic application of this idea is the 80/20 rule: 80 percent of business profits come from 20 percent of customers. The goal is to assess the worth of individual customers and thus estimate their lifetime value to the company. The concept of *customer lifetime value* (CLV) may include not only an individual's tendency to engage in purchases but also his or her strong word-of-mouth communication about the company's products. Some customers—those who require considerable hand-holding or who return products frequently—may simply be too expensive to retain due to the low level of profits they generate. Companies can discourage these unprofitable customers by requiring them to pay higher fees for additional services.

CLV is a key measurement that forecasts a customer's lifetime economic contribution based on continued relationship marketing efforts. It can be calculated by taking the sum of the customer's present value contributions to profit margins over a specific time frame. For example, the lifetime value of a Lexus customer could be predicted by how many new automobiles Lexus could sell the customer over a period of years and a summation of the contribution to margins across the time period. Although this is not an exact science, knowing a customer's potential lifetime value can help marketers determine how best to allocate resources to marketing strategies to sustain that customer over a lifetime.

THE IMPORTANCE OF MARKETING IN OUR GLOBAL ECONOMY

Our definition of marketing and discussion of marketing activities reveal some of the obvious reasons the study of marketing is relevant in today's world. In this section we look at how marketing affects us as individuals and at its role in our increasingly global society.

Marketing Costs Consume a Sizable Portion of Buyers' Dollars

Studying marketing will make you aware that many marketing activities are necessary to provide satisfying goods and services. Obviously, these activities cost money. About one-half of a buyer's dollar goes toward marketing costs. If you spend $16 on a new CD, 50 to 60 percent goes toward marketing expenses, including promotion and distribution, as well as profit margins. The production (pressing) of the CD represents about $1, or 6 percent of its price. A family with a monthly income of $3,000 that allocates $600 to taxes and savings spends about $2,400 for goods and services. Of this amount, $1,200 goes toward marketing activities. If marketing expenses consume that much of your dollar, you should know how this money is being used.

Marketing Is Used in Nonprofit Organizations

Although the term *marketing* may bring to mind advertising for Burger King, Volkswagen, and Apple, marketing is also important in organizations working to achieve goals other than ordinary business objectives (such as profit). Government agencies at the federal, state, and local levels engage in marketing activities to fulfill their mission and goals. For instance, the Centers for Disease Control has promoted its new book about international health risks through its website for travelers' health.[40] Universities and colleges engage in marketing activities to recruit new students, as well as to obtain donations from alumni and businesses.

In the private sector, nonprofit organizations also employ marketing activities to create, price, distribute, and promote programs that benefit particular segments of society. The Red Cross provides disaster relief throughout the world and offers promotional messages to encourage donations to support their efforts. For example, the massive earthquakes in Haiti in 2010 and Japan in 2011 prompted the Red Cross to release many promotional messages encouraging people to donate money for those impacted by the disasters.

Nonprofit Organization
The National Highway Traffic Safety Administration creates awareness of the risks associated with drinking and driving during the holiday season.

Marketing Is Important to Businesses and the Economy

Businesses must engage in marketing to survive and grow, and marketing activities are needed to reach customers and provide products. Financial resources generated from sales are necessary for the operations of a firm and to provide financial returns to investors. Innovation in operations and products drive business success and customer loyalty. Even nonprofit businesses need to understand and utilize marketing to serve their audience.

Marketing activities help to produce the profits that are essential to the survival of individual businesses. Without profits, businesses would find it difficult, if not impossible, to buy more raw materials, hire more employees, attract more capital, and create additional products that, in turn, make more profits. Without profits, marketers cannot continue to provide jobs and contribute to social causes. Therefore, marketing helps create a successful economy and contributes to the well-being of society.

Marketing Fuels Our Global Economy

Marketing is necessary to advance a global economy. Advances in technology, along with falling political and economic barriers and the universal desire for a higher standard of living, have made marketing across national borders commonplace while stimulating global economic growth. As a result of worldwide communications and increased international travel, many U.S. brands have achieved widespread acceptance around the world. At the same time, customers in the United States have greater choices among the products they buy because foreign brands such as Toyota (Japan), Bayer (Germany), and Nestlé (Switzerland) sell alongside U.S. brands such as General Motors, Tylenol, and Chevron. People around the world watch CNN and MTV on Toshiba and Sony televisions they purchased at Walmart. Electronic commerce via the Internet now enables businesses of all sizes to reach buyers worldwide. We explore the international markets and opportunities for global marketing in Chapter 9.

Entrepreneurship in Marketing

Electronic Payments: From Beer Money to Multi-Million-Dollar Company

Entrepreneur: Michael Nardy
Business: Electronic Payments
Founded: 2001 | Long Island, New York
Success: Electronic Payments has annual sales of $42.7 million and has been featured on the Inc. 500 list of America's fastest growing companies for four consecutive years.

For entrepreneur Michael Nardy, the concept for his company Electronic Payments originated as a way to earn beer money. It has since come far from its humble origins; today Electronic Payments is an industry leader in payment processing. Electronic Payments processes business transactions, including credit, debit, and gift cards, for 25,000 organizations.

Nardy seems like an unusual founder of a successful payment processing business—his majors were in English and history. However, after recognizing a business need for efficient payment processing, this self-taught computer programmer launched Electronic Payments to meet this demand through technology. Customers receive superior customer service as part of the product. In fact, the company puts a great amount of emphasis on managing customer relationships and securing a greater share of a customer's business. For instance, it has invested significantly in an in-house network to meet various customer needs. In recognition for creating such a successful customer-centered business, Nardy was nominated as an Ernst & Young Entrepreneur of the Year 2011 New York Award finalist.[c]

Marketing Knowledge Enhances Consumer Awareness

Besides contributing to the well-being of our economy, marketing activities help to improve the quality of our lives. Studying marketing allows us to understand the importance of marketing to customers, organizations, and our economy. Thus, we can analyze marketing efforts that need improvement and how to attain that goal. Today the consumer has more power from information available through websites, social media, and required disclosure. As you become more knowledgeable, it is possible to improve purchasing decisions. In general, you have more accurate information about a product before you purchase it than at any other time in history. Understanding marketing enables us to evaluate corrective measures (such as laws, regulations, and industry guidelines) that could stop unfair, damaging, or unethical marketing practices. Thus, understanding how marketing activities work can help you to be a better consumer and increase your ability to maximize value from purchases.

Marketing Connects People through Technology

Technology, especially computers and telecommunications, helps marketers to understand and satisfy more customers than ever before. Over the phone and online, customers can provide feedback about their experiences with a company's products. Even products such as Dasani bottled water provide a customer service number and a website for questions or comments. This feedback helps marketers refine and improve their products to better satisfy customer needs. Today marketers must recognize the impact not only of websites but of instant messaging, blogs, online forums, online games, mailing lists, and wikis, as well as text messaging via cell phones and podcasts via MP3 players. Increasingly, these tools are facilitating marketing exchanges. For example, new apps are being released that allow consumers to pay for their purchases using their smartphones. These apps contain "virtual replicas" of the consumer's

Marketing Connects People through Technology
Social media sites, such as Facebook, allow consumers to share information on marketers' successes and failures through technology.

Table 1.1 Leading Mobile Internet Activities of U.S. Citizens

Activity	Percent of Time Spent on Activity
E-Mail	42
Search Engines and Portals	19
Social Networks	11
News, Sports, and Entertainment	10
Music and Videos	5
Weather	3
Other	10

Source: Nielson, reprinted in *Inc.*, December 2011/January 2012, p. 32.

credit or debit cards that can be used in lieu of plastic. Recognizing the convenience of this new method, more and more companies are adapting their operations to accept mobile payments.[41]

The Internet allows companies to provide tremendous amounts of information about their products to consumers and to interact with them through e-mail and websites. A consumer shopping for a new car, for example, can access automakers' webpages, configure an ideal vehicle, and get instant feedback on its cost. Consumers can visit Autobytel, Edmund's, and other websites to find professional reviews and obtain comparative pricing information on both new and used cars to help them find the best value. They can also visit a consumer opinion site, such as Epinions.com, to read other consumers' reviews of the products. They can then purchase a vehicle online or at a dealership. A number of companies employ social media to connect with their customers, utilizing blogs and social networking sites such as Facebook and Twitter. We consider social networking and other digital media in Chapter 10.

Marketers of everything from computers to travel reservations use the Internet for transactions. Southwest Airlines, for example, books most of its passenger revenue via its website.[42] The Internet also has become a vital tool for marketing to other businesses. Successful companies are using technology in their marketing strategies to develop profitable relationships with these customers. As more consumers adopt smartphones, mobile marketing is also becoming a major trend. Table 1.1 shows the most common mobile online activities. We will discuss mobile marketing in more detail in Chapter 10.

Socially Responsible Marketing: Promoting the Welfare of Customers and Stakeholders

The success of our economic system depends on marketers whose values promote trust and cooperative relationships in which customers and other stakeholders are treated with respect. The public is increasingly insisting that social responsibility and ethical concerns be considered in planning and implementing marketing activities. Although some marketers' irresponsible or unethical activities end up on the front pages of *USA Today* or *The Wall Street Journal,* more firms are working to develop a responsible approach to developing long-term relationships with customers and other stakeholders. In one such instance, OfficeMax partnered with Adopt-A-Classroom, a nonprofit organization, to create an event to end teacher-funded classrooms. Once a year, OfficeMax makes 1,000 teachers' days better all across the United States by surprising them at school with more than $1,000 in school supplies.[43]

In the area of the natural environment, companies are increasingly embracing the notion of **green marketing**, which is a strategic process involving stakeholder assessment to create

green marketing A strategic process involving stakeholder assessment to create meaningful long-term relationships with customers while maintaining, supporting, and enhancing the natural environment

Going Green

Legal Sea Foods Uses Edgy Ads to Hook Consumers

"Save the salmon...that our children can witness the beauty of this noble fish. Or just save it so that we can sauté it with our fabulous lemon chive butter sauce." This is one of three 15-second television advertisements the seafood restaurant chain Legal Sea Foods released. The ads show serene scenes of the fish in what initially look like environmental ads, with the narrator encouraging viewers to help these creatures. The narrator then concludes with why we should save the fish: so we can continue to eat them.

The ads have stirred up controversy. Greenpeace environmentalists believe that Legal Sea Foods' marketing campaign does not hit the heart of the issue. They feel that a cultural shift is needed in how consumers view the world, in which people will no longer place convenience and personal satisfaction over the planet's well-being. On the other hand, others believe that traditional environmental ads are ineffective because consumers do not feel connected enough to environmental issues to change their lifestyles. By making the issue into something to which consumers can relate—their love for good-tasting seafood—they feel that consumers will be more inclined to care. Whether Legal Sea Foods' ads were callous or not, they certainly attracted viewers' attention.[d]

meaningful long-term relationships with customers while maintaining, supporting, and enhancing the natural environment. Safeway, for example, was recognized by Greenpeace as the supermarket chain with the most sustainable seafood buying practices. Understanding that overfishing is a major concern, Safeway discontinued sales of several threatened fish populations and promoted the formation of a marine reserve in the southern Antarctic oceans to protect Chilean sea bass, a "red-list" fish.[44] Such initiatives not only reduce the negative impact that businesses have on the environment but also serve to enhance their reputations as sustainability concerns continue to grow.

By addressing concerns about the impact of marketing on society, a firm can contribute to society through socially responsible activities as well as increase its financial performance. For example, studies have revealed that market orientation combined with social responsibility improves overall business performance.[45] We examine these issues and many others as we develop a framework for understanding more about marketing in the remainder of this book.

Marketing Offers Many Exciting Career Prospects

From 25 to 33 percent of all civilian workers in the United States perform marketing activities. The marketing field offers a variety of interesting and challenging career opportunities throughout the world, such as personal selling, advertising, packaging, transportation, storage, marketing research, product development, wholesaling, and retailing. In the most recent recessionary period when unemployment was high, sales positions remained among the most attractive job opportunities. Marketing positions are among the most secure positions because of the need to manage customer relationships. In addition, many individuals working for nonbusiness organizations engage in marketing activities to promote political, educational, cultural, church, civic, and charitable activities. Whether a person earns a living through marketing activities or performs them voluntarily for a nonprofit group, marketing knowledge and skills are valuable personal and professional assets.

Summary

1. To be able to define *marketing* as focused on customers

Marketing is the process of creating, pricing, distributing, and promoting goods, services, and ideas to facilitate satisfying exchange relationships with customers and to develop and maintain favorable relationships with stakeholders in a dynamic environment. The essence of marketing is to develop satisfying exchanges from which both customers and marketers benefit. Organizations generally focus their marketing efforts on a specific group of customers called a target market.

2. To identify some important marketing terms, including target market, marketing mix, marketing exchanges, and marketing environment

A target market is the group of customers toward which a company directs a set of marketing efforts. Marketing involves developing and managing a product that will satisfy customer needs, making the product available at the right place and at a price acceptable to customers, and communicating information that helps customers determine if the product will satisfy their needs. These activities—product, price, distribution, and promotion—are known as the marketing mix because marketing managers decide what type of each element to use and in what amounts. Marketing managers strive to develop a marketing mix that matches the needs of customers in the target market. Before marketers can develop a marketing mix, they must collect in-depth, up-to-date information about customer needs. The product variable of the marketing mix deals with researching customers' needs and wants and designing a product that satisfies them. A product can be a good, a service, or an idea. In dealing with the distribution variable, a marketing manager tries to make products available in the quantities desired to as many customers as possible. The promotion variable relates to activities used to inform individuals or groups about the organization and its products. The price variable involves decisions and actions associated with establishing pricing policies and determining product prices. These marketing mix variables are often viewed as controllable because they can be changed, but there are limits to how much they can be altered.

Individuals and organizations engage in marketing to facilitate exchanges—the provision or transfer of goods, services, and ideas in return for something of value. Four conditions must exist for an exchange to occur. First, two or more individuals, groups, or organizations must participate, and each must possess something of value that the other party desires. Second, the exchange should provide a benefit or satisfaction to both parties involved in the transaction. Third, each party must have confidence in the promise of the "something of value" held by the other. Finally, to build trust, the parties to the exchange must meet expectations. Marketing activities should attempt to create and maintain satisfying exchange relationships.

The marketing environment, which includes competitive, economic, political, legal and regulatory, technological, and sociocultural forces, surrounds the customer and the marketing mix. These forces can create threats to marketers, but they also generate opportunities for new products and new methods of reaching customers. These forces can fluctuate quickly and dramatically.

3. To understand the relationship between marketing and value

Value is a customer's subjective assessment of benefits relative to costs in determining the worth of a product. Benefits include anything a buyer receives in an exchange, whereas costs include anything a buyer must give up to obtain the benefits the product provides. The marketing mix can be used to enhance perceptions of value. A product that demonstrates value usually has a feature or an enhancement that provides benefits. Promotional activities can also help to create image and prestige characteristics that customers consider in their assessment of a product's value. Marketing also creates value through the building of stakeholder relationships. Developing and maintaining favorable relations with stakeholders is crucial to the long-term growth of an organization and its products.

4. To become aware of the marketing concept and market orientation

According to the marketing concept, an organization should try to provide products that satisfy customers' needs through a coordinated set of activities that also allows the organization to achieve its goals. Customer satisfaction is the marketing concept's major objective. The philosophy of the marketing concept emerged in the United States during the 1950s after the production and sales eras. Organizations that develop activities consistent with the marketing concept become market-oriented organizations. To implement the marketing concept, a market-oriented organization must establish an information system to discover customers' needs and use the information to create satisfying products. It must also coordinate all its activities and develop marketing mixes that create value for customers in order to satisfy their needs.

5. To understand the importance of building customer relationships

Relationship marketing involves establishing long-term, mutually satisfying buyer–seller relationships. Customer relationship management (CRM) focuses on using information about customers to create marketing strategies that develop and sustain desirable customer relationships. Managing customer relationships requires identifying patterns of buying behavior and using that information to focus on the most promising and profitable customers. A customer's value over a lifetime represents an intangible asset to a marketer that can be augmented by addressing the customer's varying needs and preferences at different stages in his or her relationship with the firm. Customer lifetime value is a key measurement that forecasts a customer's lifetime economic contribution based on continued relationship marketing efforts. Knowing a customer's potential lifetime value can help marketers determine how to best allocate resources to marketing strategies to sustain that customer over a lifetime.

6. To recognize the role of marketing in our society

Marketing is important to society in many ways. Marketing costs absorb about half of each buyer's dollar. Marketing activities are performed in both business and nonprofit organizations. Marketing activities help business organizations to generate profits, and they help fuel the increasingly global economy. Knowledge of marketing enhances consumer awareness. New technology improves marketers' ability to connect with customers. Socially responsible marketing can promote the welfare of customers and society. Green marketing is a strategic process involving stakeholder assessment to create meaningful long-term relationships with customers while maintaining, supporting, and enhancing the natural environment. Finally, marketing offers many exciting career opportunities.

Go to www.cengagebrain.com for resources to help you master the content in this chapter as well as for materials that will expand your marketing knowledge!

Important Terms

marketing 4
customers 4
target market 5
marketing mix 6
product 7
value 9
exchange 11
stakeholders 12
marketing environment 12
marketing concept 13
market orientation 15
customer relationship management (CRM) 16
relationship marketing 16
green marketing 21

Discussion and Review Questions

1. What is *marketing*? How did you define the term before you read this chapter?
2. What is the focus of all marketing activities? Why?
3. What are the four variables of the marketing mix? Why are these elements known as variables?
4. What is value? How can marketers use the marketing mix to enhance the perception of value?
5. What conditions must exist before a marketing exchange can occur? Describe a recent exchange in which you participated.
6. What are the forces in the marketing environment? How much control does a marketing manager have over these forces?
7. Discuss the basic elements of the marketing concept. Which businesses in your area use this philosophy? Explain why.
8. How can an organization implement the marketing concept?
9. What is customer relationship management? Why is it so important to "manage" this relationship?
10. Why is marketing important in our society? Why should you study marketing?

Application Questions

1. Identify several businesses in your area that have *not* adopted the marketing concept. What characteristics of these organizations indicate nonacceptance of the marketing concept?
2. Identify possible target markets for the following products:
   a. Kellogg's Corn Flakes
   b. Wilson tennis rackets
   c. Disney World
   d. Diet Pepsi
3. Discuss the variables of the marketing mix (product, price, promotion, and distribution) as they might relate to each of the following:
   a. A trucking company
   b. A men's clothing store
   c. A skating rink
   d. A campus bookstore
4. IMP There are seemingly hundreds of different cell phones available on the market today. How do consumers choose? The answer is simple: consumer value. Compare the value of an Apple iPhone and a Samsung Galaxy smartphone. Begin by identifying the benefits and costs that you consider when evaluating cell phones—factors like ease of texting, overall look and feel, or purchasing price. Assign a weighting coefficient to each factor that reflects its importance to you. You could use 0–5, for example, with 0 meaning *no importance whatsoever* and 5 meaning *absolutely important*. Using the equation Value = Benefits/Costs, calculate the value for the iPhone and the Samsung Galaxy. Do these results match actual cell phone sales for the two products?

Internet Exercise

The American Marketing Association

The American Marketing Association (AMA) is the marketing discipline's primary professional organization. In addition to sponsoring academic research, publishing marketing literature, and organizing meetings of local businesspeople with student members, it helps individual members to find employment in member firms. Visit the AMA website at www.marketingpower.com.

a. What type of information is available on the AMA website to assist students in planning their careers and finding jobs?
b. If you joined a student chapter of the AMA, what benefits would you receive?
c. What marketing-mix variable does the AMA's Internet marketing effort exemplify?

developing your marketing plan

Successful companies develop strategies for marketing their products. The strategic plan guides the marketer in making many of the detailed decisions about the attributes of the product, its distribution, promotional activities, and pricing. A clear understanding of the foundations of marketing is essential in formulating a strategy and in the development of a specific marketing plan. To guide you in relating the information in this chapter to the development of your marketing plan, consider the following:

1. Discuss how the marketing concept contributes to a company's long-term success.
2. Describe the level of market orientation that currently exists in your company. How will a market orientation contribute to the success of your new product?
3. What benefits will your product provide to the customer? How will these benefits play a role in determining the customer value of your product?

The information obtained from these questions should assist you in developing various aspects of your marketing plan found in the "Interactive Marketing Plan" exercise at www.cengagebrain.com.

video case 1.1

Cruising to Success: The Tale of New Belgium Brewing

In 1991, electrical engineer Jeff Lebesch and Kim Jordan began making Belgian-style ales in their basement. The impetus for the brewery occurred after Lebesch had spent time in Belgium riding throughout the country on his mountain bike. He believed he could manufacture high-quality Belgian beers in America. After spending time in the Colorado Rockies deciding the values and directions of their new company, the two launched New Belgium Brewing (NBB), with Kim Jordan as marketing director. The company's first beer was named Fat Tire in honor of Lebesch's Belgian mountain biking trek. Fat Tire remains one of NBB's most popular ales.

NBB has come far from its humble basement origins. Today, the Fort Collins–based brewery is the third-largest craft brewer in the country with products available in 28 states. Kim Jordan helms the company as one of the few female CEOs of a large beer firm. "This entrepreneurial thing sneaks up on you," Jordan states. "And even after 20 years, I still have those pinch me moments where I think, wow, this is what we've created here together." While total beer sales are dropping in the United States, sales in the craft beer industry have increased to $8.7 billion. NBB has a sales growth rate of 15 percent.

© Tim Fleming/Alamy

Creating such success required a corporate culture that stressed creativity and an authentic approach to treating all stakeholders with respect. While the New Belgium product is a quality craft beer, just as important to the company is how it treats employees, the community, and the environment. Each element of the marketing mix was carefully considered. The company spends a significant amount of time researching and creating its beers, even collaborating with Seattle-based Elysian Brewing to co-create new products. This collaBEERation has led to products such as Ranger IPA and Kick. NBB's culture is focused on making a quality product and satisfying customers. It has even ventured into organic beer with its creation of Mothership Wit Organic Wheat Beer. The company has several product line varieties, including its more popular beers Fat Tire, 1554, and Sunshine Wheat; seasonal beers such as Dig and Snow Day; and its Lips of Faith line, a series of experimental beers including La Folie and Prickly Passion produced in smaller batches.

The distribution element of the product mix was complex at the outset. In her initial role as marketing director, Jordan needed to convince distributors to carry their products. Often, new companies must work hard to convince distributors to carry their brands as distributors are fearful of alienating more established rivals. However, Jordan tirelessly got NBB beer onto store shelves, even delivering beer in her Toyota station wagon. As a craft brewer, NBB uses a premium pricing strategy. Its products are priced higher than domestic brands such as Coors or Budweiser and have higher profit margins. The popularity of NBB beers has prompted rivals to develop competitive products such as MillerCoors' Blue Moon Belgian White.

Perhaps the most notable dimension of NBB's marketing mix is promotion. From the beginning the company based its brand on its core values, including practicing environmental stewardship and forming a participative environment in which all employees can exert their creativity. "For me brand is absolutely everything we are. It's the people here. It's how we interact with one another. And then there's the other piece of that creativity, obviously, which is designing beers," Kim Jordan said. NBB promotion has attempted to portray the company's creativity and its harmony with the natural environment. For instance, one NBB video features a tinkerer repairing a bicycle and riding down the road, while another features NBB "rangers" singing a hip-hop number to promote the company's Ranger IPA ale. The company has also heavily promoted its brand through Facebook and Twitter. This "indie" charm has served to position NBB as a company committed to having fun and being a socially responsible company.

NBB also markets itself as a company committed to sustainability. Sustainability has been a core value at NBB from day one. The company was the first fully wind-powered brewery in the United States. NBB recycles cardboard boxes, keg caps, office materials, and amber glass. The brewery stores spent barley and hop grains in an on-premise silo and invites local farmers to pick up the grains, free of charge, to feed their pigs. The company also provides employees with a cruiser bicycle after one year of employment so they can bike to work instead of drive.

NBB's popularity is allowing it to expand on the East Coast with plans to continue expanding throughout the United States. The combination of a unique brand image, strong marketing mix, and an orientation that considers all stakeholders has turned NBB into a multi-million dollar success.[46]

Questions for Discussion

1. How has New Belgium implemented the marketing concept?
2. What has Kim Jordan done to create success at New Belgium?
3. How does New Belgium's focus on sustainability as a core value contribute to its corporate culture and success?

case 1.2

Campbell's Wants to Show You the Value of Soup

The Campbell Soup Company is on a mission to create value in the minds of consumers. Value is the customer's subjective assessment of benefits relative to costs in determining the product's worth. Campbell's is very aware of the value equation and is concerned that some consumers may not appreciate the good value of Campbell's soups. To change this perception, Campbell's has intensified its marketing efforts to reposition its soup brands and differentiate them from the competition.

Campbell's Soup was founded in 1869 as a canned-food company. Its iconic red-and-white colors, first adopted in 1898 based upon the colors of the Cornell football team, have since become a core part of the company's brand identity. While most people associate Campbell's with soup, the company has adopted new product mixes through acquisitions and expansions. Campbell's is divided into three main divisions: Campbell North America, Pepperidge Farm, and International. The company owns such well-known brands as Campbell's, Pace, Pepperidge Farm, and V8.

Campbell's has been largely successful as a company, but in recent years its soup division in North America has diminished. Although product lines such as Pepperidge Farm have performed well globally, simple meal sales within the United States, which includes Campbell's soups, decreased 6 percent. With more than $1 billion in condensed soup sales, such a decrease is a serious threat to Campbell's Soup. In response the company is taking the bold marketing move of increasing its marketing by $100 million in order to reposition how consumers, particularly the younger generation, view condensed soup.

This is not Campbell's first endeavor to alter consumer perceptions of its flagship brand. In the last few years the company has performed extensive marketing research that culminated in changing its iconic labels and adopting a new advertising slogan. The bowls on the labels got bigger, the soup got steamier, the spoon was abandoned, and the logo was moved toward the bottom. To emphasize the quality and versatility of its soups, Campbell's adopted the tagline "It's Amazing What Soup Can Do" for all of its different soup lineups within the United States.

However, Campbell's newest marketing initiatives are set to push the limits of how its soups are perceived. For many years Campbell's has been emphasizing the healthy nature of its soups. As consumers have become more health-conscious, Campbell's responded by reducing the sodium in its soup products. Yet because the campaign was not successful in increasing purchases, Campbell's is taking the controversial step of de-emphasizing its health initiatives and pouring marketing dollars into re-portraying its brand as tasty and exciting.

Such a move comes with controversy because Campbell's has raised the amount of sodium in some of its soups. However, when companies try to address nutritional issues but consumers show little interest, the companies are faced with the dilemma of dropping their health campaigns in exchange for adopting attributes, such as taste, that customers value. Campbell's had also introduced discounts on its soups in the hopes of attracting price-conscious consumers. After the move failed to generate increased sales, Campbell's decided to stop discounting its soup products. Without these discounts, Campbell's will have to increase the perceived value of its products to convince consumers to pay more.

Yet Campbell's remains undeterred. The company aims to engage in what Campbell's' CEO calls "disruptive innovation" with the introduction of new product lines, new packaging, and new flavors. For instance, Campbell's released new exotic flavors in pouches to appeal to the younger generation. Campbell's has even tested marketing through new technology channels. The company has released iAds through Apple iPhones and iPads, a tactic which appears to aid brand recall. Initial studies found that consumers who viewed Campbell's iAds were five times more likely to recall them than those who had seen its TV ads. If Campbell's has its way, then a can of soup will become much more valuable to consumers.[47]

Questions for Discussion

1. Evaluate Campbell's success in implementing the marketing concept.
2. How would you define Campbell's target market for soup?
3. How is Campbell's trying to increase the customer's perceived value of its soup?

NOTES

[1]Miguel Bustillo, "Wal-Mart Merchandise Goes Back to Basics," *The Wall Street Journal,* April 11, 2011, B3; Miguel Bustillo, "Wal-Mart Tries to Recapture Mr. Sam's Winning Formula," *The Wall Street Journal,* February 22, 2011, A1, A11; Miguel Bustillo, "Wal-Mart Loses Edge," *The Wall Street Journal,* August 16, 2011, B1, B2; Reuters, "Wal-Mart Closing New York Fashion Office, Moving It Back to Arkansas," *The Chicago Tribune,* October 26, 2011, www.chicagotribune.com/business/breaking/chi-walmart-closing-new-york-fashion-office-moving-it-back-to-arkansas-20111026,0,6222767.story (accessed November 10, 2011).

[2]"Definition of Marketing," American Marketing Association, www.marketingpower.com/AboutAMA/Pages/DefinitionofMarketing.aspx (accessed July 7, 2010).

[3]Ellen Byron, "*Hola*: P&G Seeks Latino Shoppers," *The Wall Street Journal,* September 15, 2011, B1; Sam Fahmy, "Despite Recession, Hispanic and Asian Buying Power Expected to Surge in U.S., According to Annual UGA Selig Center Multicultural Economy Study," Terry College of Business, www.terry.uga.edu/news/releases/2010/minority-buying-power-report.html (accessed February 3, 2012).

[4]"Vans, Inc.," www.jiffynotes.com/a_study_guides/book_notes/cps_03/cps_03_00479.html (accessed December 27, 2010).

[5]"Recreational Equipment Incorporated (REI): A Responsible Retail Cooperative," in O. C. Ferrell, John Fraedrich, and Linda Ferrell, *Business Ethics: Ethical Decision Making and Cases*, 9th ed. (Mason, OH: South-Western Cengage Learning, 2013), 466–475.

[6]Dana Mattioli, "Xerox Chief Looks Beyond Photocopiers Toward Services," *The Wall Street Journal*, June 13, 2011, B9.

[7]Julie Jargon, "Subway Runs Past McDonald's Chain," *The Wall Street Journal*, March 9, 2011, B4; Subway, www.subway.com/subwayroot/default.aspx (accessed January 10, 2012).

[8]Donald Melanson, "Apple: 16 billion iTunes songs downloaded, 300 million iPods sold," engadget, October 4, 2011, www.engadget.com/2011/10/04/apple-16-billion-itunes-songs-downloaded-300-million-ipods-sol/ (accessed February 2, 2012).

[9]Allan Brettman, "Adidas Launching Biggest Marketing Campaign," Oregon*Live*.com, March 14, 2011, www.oregonlive.com/business/index.ssf/2011/03/adidas_launching_biggest_marke.html (accessed January 11, 2012).

[10]"Drive Sober or Get Pulled Over," National Highway Traffic Safety Administration, www.nhtsa.gov/drivesober/video/ (accessed June 29, 2012).

[11]Campbell's Kitchen, www.campbellskitchen.com/RecipeCategoryHome.aspx?fbid=DKtnA8n1vQ0 (accessed January 4, 2011).

[12]Rajneesh Suri, Chiranjeev Kohli, and Kent B. Monroe, "The Effects of Perceived Scarcity on Consumers' Processing of Price Information," *Journal of the Academy of Marketing Science* 35 (2007): 89–100.

[13]Natalie Mizik and Robert Jacobson, "Trading Off Between Value Creation and Value Appropriation: The Financial Implications and Shifts in Strategic Emphasis," *Journal of Marketing* (January 2003): 63–76.

[14]Kasey Wehrum, "How May We Help You?" *Inc.*, March 2011, 63–68.

[15]O. C. Ferrell and Michael Hartline, *Marketing Strategy.* (Mason, OH: South-Western, 2005), 108.

[16]Bruce Horovitz, "Marketers Go Huge with Lower-Calorie Offerings," *The Wall Street Journal*, July 12, 2011, 1B.

[17]Julie Jargon, "Kids Will Get Apple Slices, Fewer Fries in Happy Meals," *The Wall Street Journal*, July 27, 2011, B1.

[18]Ajay K. Kohli and Bernard J. Jaworski, "Market Orientation: The Construct, Research Propositions, and Managerial Implications," *Journal of Marketing* (April 1990): 1–18; O. C. Ferrell, "Business Ethics and Customer Stakeholders," *Academy of Management Executive* 18 (May 2004): 126–129.

[19]"Starbucks CEO Howard Schultz is all abuzz," *CBS News*, March 27, 2011, www.cbsnews.com/stories/2011/03/27/business/main20047618.shtml (accessed March 30, 2011).

[20]Eugene W. Anderson, Claes Fornell, and Sanal K. Mazvancheryl, "Customer Satisfaction and Shareholder Value," *Journal of Marketing* (October 2004): 172–185.

[21]Xeuming Luo and Christian Homburg, "Neglected Outcomes of Customer Satisfaction," *Journal of Marketing* 70, April 2007.

[22]Thomas Rice, "New Fuel-Efficiency Standards Would Choke U.S. Carmakers," *USA Today,* May 28, 2009; Mike Ramsey and Shirley Terlep, "Americans Embrace SUVs Again," *The Wall Street Journal*, December 22, 2011, http://online.wsj.com/article/SB10001424052970204012004577072132855087336.html (accessed January 10, 2012).

[23]Kohli and Jaworski, "Market Orientation: The Construct, Research Propositions, and Managerial Implications."

[24]Kwaku Atuahene-Gima, "Resolving the Capability-Rigidity Paradox in New Product Innovation," *Journal of Marketing* 69 (October 2005): 61–83.

[25]Gary F. Gebhardt, Gregory S. Carpenter, and John F. Sherry Jr., "Creating a Market Orientation," *Journal of Marketing* 70 (October 2006), www.marketingpower.com.

[26]"eBay Acquires Recommendation Engine Hunch.com," Business Wire, November 21, 2011, www.businesswire.com/news/home/20111121005831/en/eBay-Acquires-Recommendation-Engine-Hunch.com (accessed January 11, 2012).

[27]Sunil Gupta, Donald R. Lehmann, and Jennifer Ames Stuart, "Valuing Customers," *Journal of Marketing Research* (February 2004): 7–18.

[28]"Bazaarvoice Enables Rubbermaid to Listen, Learn, and Improve Products Based on Customer Conversations," Business Wire, January 21, 2010, www.businesswire.com/portal/site/home/permalink/?ndmViewId=news_view&newsId=20100121005613&newsLang=en (accessed January 12, 2012); "User-Generated R&D: Clay Shirky Explains How to Feed Innovation with Customer Insights," Bazaarvoice, May 3, 2011, www.bazaarvoice.com/blog/2011/05/03/user-generated-rd-clay-shirky-explains-how-to-feed-innovation-with-customer-insights/ (accessed January 12, 2012).

[29]Pradeep Korgaonkar and Bay O'Leary, "Management, Market, and Financial Factors Separating Winners and Losers in e-Business," *Journal of Computer-Mediated Communication* 11, no. 4 (2006): article 12.

[30]"Hewlett-Packard Replaces Leo Apotheker with Meg Whitman," BBC News, September 23, 2011, www.bbc.co.uk/news/business-15028509 (accessed February 3, 2012); James B. Stewart, "For Seamless Transitions, Don't Look to Hewlett," *The New York Times,* August 26, 2011,

www.nytimes.com/2011/08/27/business/for-seamless-transitions-at-the-top-dont-consult-hewlett-packard.html?pagewanted=all (accessed February 3, 2012).

[31]Jacquelyn S. Thomas, Robert C. Blattberg, and Edward J. Fox, "Recapturing Lost Customers," *Journal of Marketing Research* (February 2004): 31–45.

[32]Jagdish N. Sheth and Rajendras Sisodia, "More Than Ever Before, Marketing Is under Fire to Account for What It Spends," *Marketing Management* (Fall 1995): 13–14.

[33]"Whole Foods Market's Core Values," Whole Foods, www.wholefoodsmarket.com/values/corevalues.php (accessed January 10, 2012).

[34]Chezy Ofir and Itamar Simonson, "The Effect of Stating Expectations on Customer Satisfaction and Shopping Experience," *Journal of Marketing Research* XLIV (February 2007), 164-174.

[35]Robert W. Palmatier, Lisa K. Scheer, and Jan-Benedict E. M. Steenkamp, "Customer Loyalty to Whom? Managing the Benefits and Risks of Salesperson-Owned Loyalty," *Journal of Marketing Research* XLIV (May 2007), 185-199.

[36]Werner J. Reinartz and V. Kumar, "On the Profitability of Long-Life Customers in a Noncontractual Setting: An Empirical Investigation and Implications for Marketing," *Journal of Marketing* (October 2000): 17–35.

[37]Customer Insight Group, Inc., "Program Design: Loyalty and Retention," www.customerinsightgroup.com/loyalty_retention.php (accessed January 4, 2011).

[38]V. Kumar and Morris George, "Measuring and Maximizing Customer Equity: A Critical Analysis," *Journal of the Academy of Marketing Science* 35 (2007): 157–171.

[39]Rajkumar Venkatesan and V. Kumar, "A Customer Lifetime Value Framework for Customer Selection and Resource Allocation Strategy," *Journal of Marketing* (October 2004): 106–125.

[40]"Travelers' Health," Centers for Disease Control and Prevention, http://wwwnc.cdc.gov/travel/ (accessed January 11, 2012).

[41]Edward C. Baig, "Mobile Payments Gain Traction," *USA Today,* August 11, 2011, 1A–2A; Jefferson Graham, "Starbucks Expands Mobile Payments to 6,800 Sites," *USA Today,* January 19, 2011, 1B.

[42]"Southwest Airlines—Fact Sheet," Southwest Airlines, www.southwest.com/html/about-southwest/history/fact-sheet.html#fun_facts (accessed January 11, 2012).

[43]"OfficeMax and Store Customers Donate $1.7 Million in School Supplies Through 'A Day Made Better'," OfficeMax, October 4, 2011, www.adaymadebetter.com/newsroom (accessed January 11, 2012).

[44]Kim O'Donnel, "Safeway Scales the 'Seafood Scorecard' by Greenpeace," *USA Today*, April 18, 2011, 5D.

[45]Anis Ben Brik, Belaid Rettab, and Kemel Mallahi, "Market Orientation, Corporate Social Responsibility, and Business Performance," *Journal of Business Ethics*, 99 (2011): 307–324.

[46]New Belgium website, newbelgium.com (accessed March 27, 2012); "New Belgium Brewing: Ethical and Environmental Responsibility," in O. C. Ferrell, John Fraedrich, and Linda Ferrell, *Business Ethics: Ethical Decision Making and Cases,* 9th ed. (Mason, OH: South-Western Cengage Learning, 2013), 355–363; "New Belgium Brewery," Amalgamated, http://amalgamatednyc.com/project/tinkerer/ (accessed March 27, 2012); Norman Miller, "Craft Beer Industry Continues to Grow," *PJ Star,* March 26, 2012, www.pjstar.com/community/blogs/beer-nut/x140148153/Craft-Beer-industry-continues-to-grow (accessed March 27, 2012); "COLLABEERATIONS," Elysian Brewing Company, www.elysianbrewing.com/beer/collabeerations.html (accessed March 27, 2012); Devin Leonard, "New Belgium and the Battle of the Microbrews," *Bloomberg Businessweek,* December 1, 2011, www.businessweek.com/magazine/new-belgium-and-the-battle-of-the-microbrews-12012011.html (accessed March 27, 2012); "Our Joy Ride," www.newbelgium.com/Community/videos.aspx?id=1e15e412-9153-433d-9249-85134c24befa (accessed March 27, 2012).

[47]Campbell Soup Company website, www.campbellsoup.com/ (accessed March 2, 2012); Carly Weeks, "Campbell's Adding Salt Back to Its Soups," *The Globe and Mail*, July 15, 2011, www.theglobeandmail.com/life/health/new-health/health-news/campbells-adding-salt-back-to-its-soups/article2097659/ (accessed March 2, 2012); Ilan Brat, "The Emotional Quotient of Soup Shopping," *The Wall Street Journal,* February 17, 2010, http://online.wsj.com/article/SB10001424052748704804204575069562743700340.html (accessed March 2, 2012); "Campbell Launches *'It's Amazing What Soup Can Do'* Ad Campaign to Promote Campbell's U.S. Soup Brands," Business Wire, September 7, 2010, www.businesswire.com/news/home/20100907006087/en/Campbell-Launches-%E2%80%9CIt%E2%80%99s-Amazing-Soup-Do%E2%80%9D-Ad (accessed March 2, 2012); Lisa Terry, "How Campbell Soup Fixed Its Confusing Shelves," *Advertising Age,* July 25, 2011, http://adage.com/article/news/campbell-soup-fixed-confusing-shelves/228858/ (accessed March 2, 2012); Kunur Patel, "Apple, Campbell's Say iAds Twice as Effective as TV," *Advertising Age,* February 3, 2011, http://adage.com/article/digital/apple-campbell-s-iads-effective-tv/148630/ (accessed March 2, 2012); E. J. Schultz, "Campbell Soups Vows to Hold Line on Marketing," *Advertising Age*, September 2, 2011, http://adage.com/article/news/campbell-soup-vows-hold-line-marketing-economy/229611/ (accessed March 2, 2012); E. J. Schultz, "Campbell Counts on Soups in a Pouch to Spur Turnaround," *Advertising Age,* February 22, 2012, http://adage.com/article/cmo-strategy/campbell-counts-soups-a-pouch-spur-turnaround/232878/ (accessed March 2, 2012).

Feature Notes

[a]Reed Hastings, "An Explanation and Some Reflections," personal e-mail; Nick Wingfield, "Netflix Sidelines DVDs," *The Wall Street Journal*, July 13, 2011, B2; "Netflix Messes Up," *The Economist*, September 24, 2011, 79; Stu Woo and Shara Tibken, "Netflix Nixes Qwikster, Bowing to Complaints," *The Wall Street Journal,* October 10, 2011, http://online.wsj.com/article/SB10001424052970203499704576622674082410578.html?mod=WSJ_hp_mostpop_read (accessed October 10, 2011).

[b]Original material from O. C. Ferrell.

[c]Darren Dahl with Michael Nardy, "Leading the Charge," *Inc.*, September 2011, 28; "About Electronic Payments," www.electronicpayments.com/about.php (accessed December 1, 2011); Electronic Payments, "Electronic Payments Founder and CEO, Michael Nardy, Named Ernst & Young Entrepreneur of the Year 2011 New York Award Finalist," Retail Solutions Online, May 10, 2011, www.retailsolutionsonline.com/article.mvc/Electronic-Payments-Founder-And-CEO-Michael-0001 (accessed December 1, 2011).

[d]Bruce Horovitz, "Legal Sea Foods Ads Catch Some Flak," *USA Today*, September 13, 2011, 2B; Ariel Schwartz, "Legal Sea Foods Says Save Fish So We Can Eat Them," *Fast Company,* www.fastcoexist.com/1678637/legal-sea-foods-says-save-fish-so-we-can-eat-them (accessed November 3, 2011).

chapter 2

Planning, Implementing, and Evaluating Marketing Strategies

OBJECTIVES

1. To understand the strategic planning process
2. To examine what is necessary to effectively manage the implementation of marketing strategies
3. To describe the major elements of strategic performance evaluation
4. To understand the development of a marketing plan

MARKETING INSIGHTS

The Humble Grilled Cheese Sandwich Goes High Tech

What's the marketing potential of a grilled cheese sandwich? That's what Jonathan Kaplan wanted to know when planning his latest business after starting and selling two successful high-tech companies. As he thought about how to apply his background to a new challenge, he came up with the idea for The Melt, a high-tech restaurant featuring grilled cheese sandwiches.

Kaplan's research confirmed that grilled cheese sandwiches are a favorite comfort food for consumers of all ages. With help from celebrity chef Michael Mina, he sketched out a soup-and-sandwich menu for adult tastes, featuring sophisticated cheese fillings and savory soups.

Kaplan realized that technology was the key to faster service and better sandwiches. Because fast-food restaurants aren't always fast enough for consumers on the go, he planned to take advance orders via a smartphone app and website. For extra speed, customers can opt to have their smartphones alert the restaurant as they approach. Once customers arrive, they check in via smartphone and their sandwiches are immediately put onto a special grill that toasts everything to perfection in less than 60 seconds. One more minute to bag the order and process payment, and customers can be on their way.

Backed by a board of directors that includes a retail industry expert and businesspeople with financial and technical know-how, Kaplan has opened his first set of restaurants in California, with more in the works. Despite lots of fast-food competition, the entrepreneur sees The Melt's innovative technology as the way to turn grilled cheese sandwiches into profits.[1]

Whether it's The Melt or Microsoft, an organization must be able to create customer value and achieve its goals. This occurs through successful strategic marketing management. **Strategic marketing management** is the process of planning, implementing, and evaluating the performance of marketing activities and strategies, both effectively and efficiently. Effectiveness and efficiency are important dimensions of this definition. *Effectiveness* is the degree to which long-term customer relationships help achieve an organization's objectives. *Efficiency* refers to minimizing the resources an organization uses to achieve a specific level of desired customer relationships. Thus, the overall goal of strategic marketing management is to facilitate highly desirable customer relationships and to minimize the costs of doing so.

We begin this chapter with an overview of the strategic planning process and a discussion of the nature of marketing strategy. These elements provide a framework for the development, implementation, and evaluation of marketing strategies. Finally, we conclude this chapter by examining the development of a marketing plan.

THE STRATEGIC PLANNING PROCESS

strategic marketing management The process of planning, implementing, and evaluating the performance of marketing activities and strategies, both effectively and efficiently

strategic planning The process of establishing an organizational mission and formulating goals, corporate strategy, marketing objectives, and marketing strategy

Through the process of **strategic planning**, a company establishes an organizational mission and formulates goals, a corporate strategy, marketing objectives, and a marketing strategy.[2] A market orientation should guide the process of strategic planning to ensure that a concern for customer satisfaction is an integral part of the process and permeates the entire company. A market orientation is also important for the successful implementation of marketing strategies.[3]

Figure 2.1 shows the components of strategic planning. The process begins with the organization establishing or revising its mission and goals, and then developing corporate strategies to achieve those goals. Then, the company performs a detailed analysis of its own strengths and weaknesses and identifies opportunities and threats within the marketing environment

Figure 2.1 Components of the Strategic Planning Process

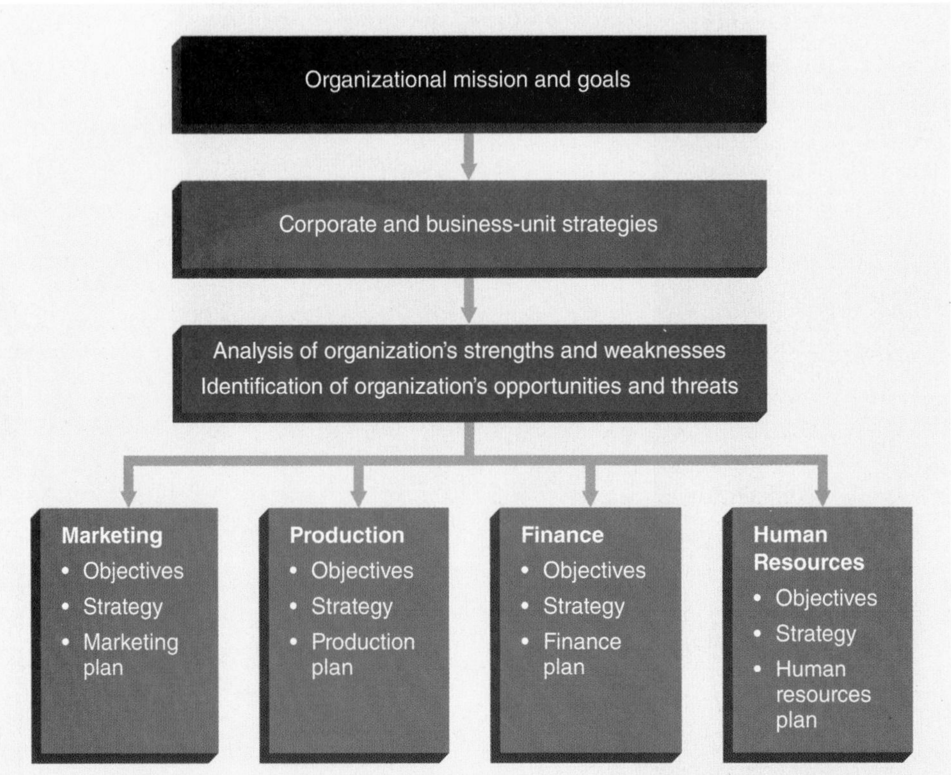

Source: Figure adopted from *Marketing Strategy*, Third Edition by OC Ferrell and Michael Hartline. Reprinted with permission of South-Western, a division of Cengage Learning www.cengage.com/permission/.

Strategic Marketing
Android executes strategic marketing by identifying and analyzing its target market and then developing a marketing mix to meet customers' needs.

and industry. Next, each functional area of the organization (marketing, production, finance, human resources, etc.) establishes its own objectives and develops strategies to achieve them that are in line with the company's corporate strategies. Thus, the objectives and strategies of each functional area must support the organization's overall goals and mission, and should also be coordinated with a focus on market orientation. Because our focus is marketing, we are, of course, most interested in the development of marketing objectives and strategies. We continue to examine the strategic planning process by taking a closer look at each component, beginning with organizational mission statements and goals.

Establishing Organizational Mission Statements and Goals

Once an organization has assessed its resources and opportunities, it can begin to establish goals and strategies to take advantage of those opportunities. The goals of any organization should derive from its **mission statement**, a long-term view, or vision, of what the organization wants to become. Ford Motor Company, for example, has a stated commitment to provide personal mobility for people around the world.[4]

mission statement A long-term view, or vision, of what the organization wants to become

Marketing Debate

Minding the Mission

ISSUE: Do organizations need a mission statement?

Too many mission statements contain buzz words and idealistic language that look good on paper but have no practical application. Some are so general that they don't mean much to employees or customers. And some are so wordy that they're not easy to understand or retain. "Our mission statement used to be a 200-word monster that nobody could remember," says the head of one Chamber of Commerce group.

Still, a mission statement can be valuable if it shows employees what the organization aims to achieve and guides their work activities in the right direction. High ideals can be both inspiring and motivating, encouraging employees to perform their very best. According to an Internet entrepreneur: "If you give people purpose, they will give you gold." However, when managers "talk the talk" but don't "walk the walk," they can turn the most carefully-crafted mission statement into a lot of empty words.[a]

When an organization decides on its mission, it really answers two questions. Who are our customers? What is our core competency? Although these questions appear very simple, they are two of the most important questions any company must answer. Defining customers' needs and wants gives direction to what the company must do to satisfy them.

Companies try to develop and manage their *corporate identity*—their unique symbols, personalities, and philosophies—to support all corporate activities, including marketing. Managing identity requires broadcasting a company's mission, goals, and values; sending a consistent image; and implementing a visual identity with stakeholders. Mission statements, goals, and objectives must be properly implemented to achieve the desired corporate identity. An organization's goals and objectives, derived from its mission statement, guide the remainder of its planning efforts. Goals focus on the end results the organization seeks. Ben & Jerry's ice cream is a brand well known for its commitment to social responsibility. It has a three-component mission statement to underscore this commitment. The social mission component focuses on improving the quality of life. The product mission, the second component, deals with maintaining high product quality through the use of natural ingredients. The third component is its economic mission. This component emphasizes growth, which includes expanding development and career opportunities for employees.[5]

Developing Corporate and Business-Unit Strategies

In most organizations, strategic planning typically begins at the corporate level and proceeds downward to the business-unit and marketing levels. However, more and more, organizations are developing strategies and conducting strategic planning both from the top-down and from the bottom-up. This means that companies often seek out the best expertise from multiple levels of the organization, not just from the corporate leadership, to do strategic planning. Corporate strategy is the broadest of the three levels of strategy (corporate, business unit, and marketing) and should be developed with the organization's overall mission in mind. Business-unit strategy should be consistent with the corporate strategy, and marketing strategy should be consistent with both the business-unit and corporate strategies. Figure 2.2 shows the relationships among these planning levels.

Figure 2.2 Levels of Strategic Planning

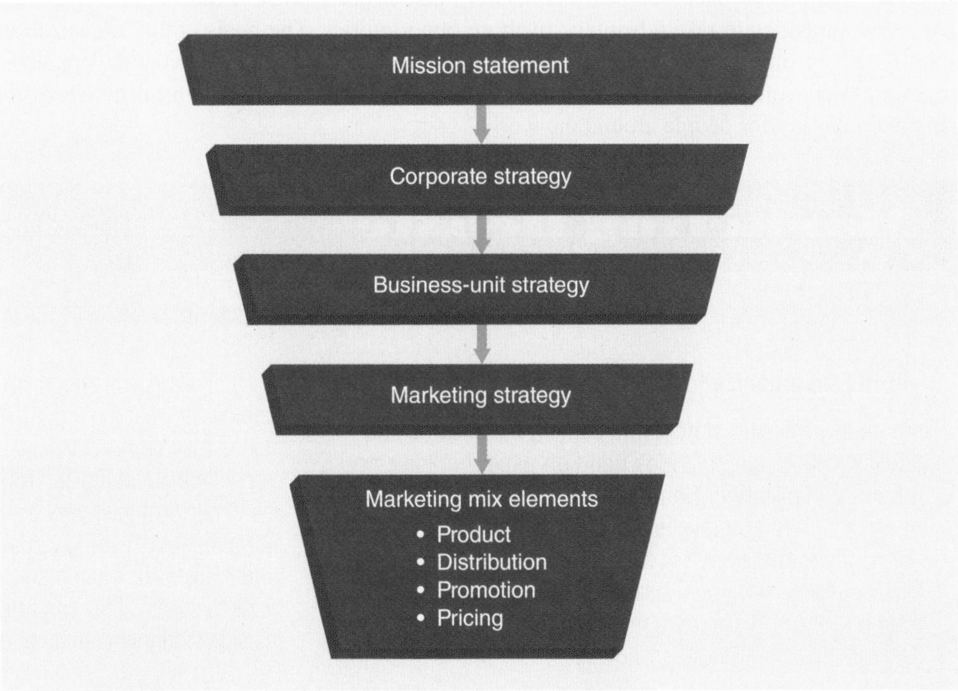

Corporate Strategies

Corporate strategy determines the means for utilizing resources in the functional areas of marketing, production, finance, research and development, and human resources to reach the organization's goals. A corporate strategy determines not only the scope of the business but also its resource deployment, competitive advantages, and overall coordination of functional areas. In particular, top management's level of marketing expertise and the effectiveness of their deployment of resources to address the company's markets affect sales growth and profitability. Corporate strategy addresses the two questions posed in the organization's mission statement. Who are our customers? What is our core competency? The term *corporate* in this context does not apply solely to corporations; corporate strategy is used by all organizations, from the smallest sole proprietorship to the largest multinational corporation. Corporate strategy simply refers to the top-level (i.e., highest) strategy developed within an organization.

Corporate Strategy
Samsung's corporate strategy includes frequent introductions of newly designed, technologically advanced products.

Corporate strategy planners are concerned with broad issues such as corporate culture, competition, differentiation, diversification, interrelationships among business units, and environmental and social issues. They attempt to match the resources of the organization with the opportunities and threats in the environment. Barnes & Noble, for example, took advantage of an opportunity to increase its market share when one of its competitors, Borders, declared bankruptcy. Barnes & Noble bought most of Borders' trademarks and intellectual property for $13.9 million, including Borders' online store and customer list, which included over 48 million people's information. The CEO of Barnes & Noble then sent out a letter to all Borders customers inviting them to shop at Barnes and Noble and join its reward program.[6] Corporate strategy planners are also concerned with defining the scope and role of the company's business units so the units are coordinated to reach the ends desired. How proactive or assertive a company's corporate strategy is can affect its capacity to be innovative.

Business-Unit Strategies

After analyzing corporate operations and performance, the next step in strategic planning is to determine future business directions and develop strategies for individual business units. A strategic business unit (SBU) is a division, product line, or other profit center within the parent company. Kraft's strategic business units, for example, consist of dairy products, snack foods, lunch meat, coffee, juice, and chocolate. Each of these units sells a distinct set of products to an identifiable group of customers, and each competes with a well-defined set of competitors. The revenues, costs, investments, and strategic plans of each SBU can be separated from those of the parent company and evaluated. SBUs operate in a variety of markets, all with differing growth rates, opportunities, degrees of competition, and profit-making potential. Business strategy is fundamentally focused on the measures required to create value for the company's target markets and achieve greater performance. Marketing research suggests that this requires implementing appropriate strategic actions and targeting appropriate market segments.[7]

Strategic planners should recognize the strategic performance capabilities of each SBU and carefully allocate scarce resources among those divisions. Several tools allow a company's portfolio of strategic business units, or even individual products, to be classified and visually displayed according to the attractiveness of various markets and the business's relative

corporate strategy A strategy that determines the means for utilizing resources in the various functional areas to reach the organization's goals

strategic business unit (SBU) A division, product line, or other profit center within the parent company

Going Green

GE's Ecomagination Saves and Earns Billions

General Electric launched Ecomagination as part of its corporate strategy to "imagine and build innovative solutions to today's environmental challenges while driving economic growth." Since embracing this green strategy in 2005, GE has saved billions of dollars through energy and water conservation, generated billions of dollars in new revenue, and polished its image as a socially-responsible firm.

Ecomagination combines GE's strengths in customer knowledge, design, and manufacturing to create and market dozens of green products for consumers and business customers. "This design signal we're getting from the marketplace is affordability, efficiency, and environmental sensitivity," says Mark Vachon, who heads Ecomagination. Given GE's global business presence, any green products it develops in one region can be distributed or adapted for distribution in other regions. For example, an energy-efficient portable ultrasound scanner designed for China was later introduced worldwide. Another product, the WattStation, is a user-friendly electric car charging station designed for use in suburban parking lots or on city streets.

Although Ecomagination products already account for 12 percent of GE's $150 billion annual revenue, the company is inviting new ideas from consumers and businesses. Watch for more green to flow to GE's bottom line as it continues its successful green strategy in the coming years.[b]

market share within those markets. A **market** is a group of individuals and/or organizations that have needs for products in a product class and have the ability, willingness, and authority to purchase those products. The percentage of a market that actually buys a specific product from a particular company is referred to as that product's (or business unit's) **market share**. Apple, for example, controls 78 percent of the market for digital music players in the United States with its iPod line, while Microsoft's Zune has only 1 percent.[8] Product quality, order of entry into the market, and market share have been associated with SBU success.[9]

One of the most helpful tools is the **market growth/market share matrix**, the Boston Consulting Group (BCG) approach, which is based on the philosophy that a product's market growth rate and its market share are important considerations in determining its marketing strategy. All the company's SBUs and products should be integrated into a single, overall matrix and evaluated to determine appropriate strategies for individual products and overall portfolio strategies. Managers can use this model to determine and classify each product's expected future cash contributions and future cash requirements. The BCG analytical approach is more of a diagnostic tool than a guide for making strategy prescriptions.

Figure 2.3, which is based on work by the BCG, enables the strategic planner to classify a company's products into four basic types: stars, cash cows, dogs, and question marks. *Stars* are products with a dominant share of the market and good prospects for growth. However, they use more cash than they generate to finance growth, add capacity, and increase market share. An example of a star might be Nintendo's Wii video game system. *Cash cows* have a dominant share of the market but low prospects for growth; typically they generate more cash than is required to maintain market share. Bounty, one of the best-selling paper towels in the United States, represents a cash cow for Procter & Gamble. *Dogs* have a subordinate share of the market and low prospects for growth; these products are often found in established markets. Portable compact disc (CD) players may be considered dogs at companies like Sony and Panasonic. The increasing popularity and affordability of iPods and other MP3 players has resulted in plummeting profits and market share for portable CD players. *Question marks,* sometimes called "problem children," have a small share of a growing market and generally require a large amount of cash to build market share. Mercedes carbon racing bikes, for example, are a question mark relative to Mercedes' automobile products.

market A group of individuals and/or organizations that have needs for products in a product class and have the ability, willingness, and authority to purchase those products

market share The percentage of a market that actually buys a specific product from a particular company

market growth/market share matrix A helpful business tool, based on the philosophy that a product's market growth rate and its market share are important considerations in determining its marketing strategy

Figure 2.3 Growth Share Matrix Developed by the Boston Consulting Group

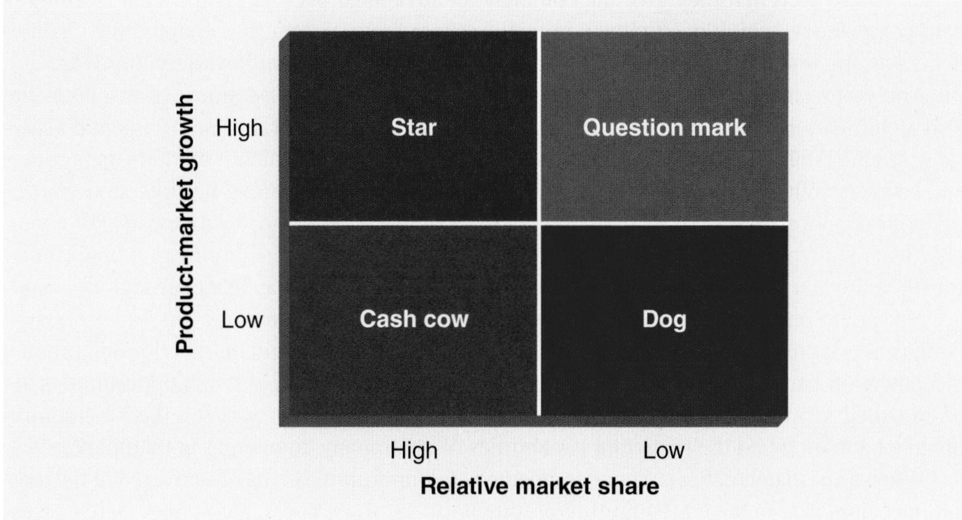

Source: *Perspectives*, No. 66, "The Product Portfolio." Reprinted by permission from The Boston Consulting Group, Inc., Boston, MA, Copyright © 1970.

The long-term health of an organization depends on having some products that generate cash (and provide acceptable profits) and others that use cash to support growth. Among the indicators of overall health are the size and vulnerability of the cash cows; the prospects for the stars, if any; and the number of question marks and dogs. Particular attention should be paid to those products with large cash appetites. Unless the company has an abundant cash flow, it cannot afford to sponsor many such products at one time. If resources, including debt capacity, are spread too thin, the company will end up with too many marginal products and will be unable to finance promising new-product entries or acquisitions in the future.

Assessing Organizational Resources and Opportunities

The strategic planning process begins with an analysis of the marketing environment, including a thorough analysis of the industry in which the company is operating or intends to sell its products. As we will see in Chapter 3, economic, competitive, political, legal and regulatory, sociocultural, and technological forces can threaten an organization and influence its overall goals; they also affect the amount and type of resources the company can acquire. However, these environmental forces can create favorable opportunities as well—opportunities that can be translated into overall organizational goals and marketing objectives. The organization's culture and the knowledge it has about the environment affect the extent to which managers perceive such opportunities as situations on which they can successfully capitalize in the marketplace.

Any strategic planning effort must assess the organization's available financial and human resources and capabilities as well as how the level of these factors is likely to change in the future, because additional resources may be needed to achieve the organization's goals and mission. Resources indirectly affect marketing and financial performance by helping to create customer satisfaction and loyalty. Resources can also include goodwill, reputation, and brand names. The reputation and well-known brand names of Rolex watches and BMW automobiles,

core competencies Things a company does extremely well, which sometimes give it an advantage over its competition

market opportunity A combination of circumstances and timing that permits an organization to take action to reach a particular target market

strategic windows Temporary periods of optimal fit between the key requirements of a market and the particular capabilities of a company competing in that market

competitive advantage The result of a company matching a core competency to opportunities it has discovered in the marketplace

for example, are resources that give these companies an advantage over their competitors. Such strengths also include **core competencies**, things a company does extremely well—sometimes so well that they give the company an advantage over its competition. Walmart's core competency, which is efficiency in supply chain management, has enabled the chain to build a strong reputation for low prices at high quality levels on a wide variety of goods.

Analysis of the marketing environment involves not only an assessment of resources but also identification of opportunities in the marketplace. An aspect of this environmental analysis is to understand the company's own industry or industries in which it markets its products and services. When the right combination of circumstances and timing permits an organization to take action to reach a particular target market, a **market opportunity** exists. For example, Brita, known for its water-filtering pitchers, has taken advantage of a market opportunity for filtered water without the bottled water waste. The company has branched out into product placement on television shows geared toward healthy living, such as *The Biggest Loser.* Brita is also taking advantage of the growing Spanish-language target market through product placement on Univision's weight-loss show, called *Dale Con Ganas.*[10] Such opportunities are often called **strategic windows**, temporary periods of optimal fit between the key requirements of a market and the particular capabilities of a company competing in that market.[11]

When a company matches a core competency to opportunities it has discovered in the marketplace, it is said to have a **competitive advantage**. In some cases, a company may possess manufacturing, technical, or marketing skills that it can match to market opportunities to create a competitive advantage. For instance, Tesco, a large-scale grocery chain from the United Kingdom, entered the western U.S. market with its Fresh & Easy Neighborhood Markets.

Competitive Advantage
Bulova has gained a competitive advantage through its use of an iPhone app.

The company seeks competitive advantage by offering cheap, healthy food options such as 98-cent produce packages and cheap cuts of meat. In addition to being a good value, the stores seek to source produce and meats locally as much as possible, offer organic and hormone-free foods, and use less energy than typical grocery stores.[12]

To help assess a firm's capabilities to achieve a competitive advantage, a marketer can employ SWOT analysis. To better understand the importance of timing to obtain a competitive advantage, a firm may gain insights by analyzing first-mover and late-mover advantages. We discuss SWOT analysis and first-mover and late-mover advantages next.

SWOT Analysis

One tool marketers use to assess an organization's strengths, weaknesses, opportunities, and threats is the **SWOT analysis**. Strengths and weaknesses are internal factors that can influence an organization's ability to satisfy its target markets. *Strengths* refer to competitive advantages or core competencies that give the company an advantage in meeting the needs of its target markets. John Deere, for example, promotes its service, experience, and reputation in the farm equipment business to emphasize the craftsmanship used in its lawn tractors and mowers for city dwellers. *Weaknesses* refer to any limitations a company faces in developing or implementing a marketing strategy. Consider Netflix, which once enjoyed a virtual monopoly on home-delivery movies, but has since encountered serious competition from brands like RedBox, Hulu, and others. One of Netflix's weaknesses has been a perceived lack of focus as the company tries to innovate ahead of the competition. As Netflix has struggled to address its internal weaknesses, the company's market value dwindled to around a quarter of its high value. Netflix has tried to address its weakness by expanding video streaming to Great Britain and Ireland to offset lackluster performance in the United States.[13] Both strengths and weaknesses should be examined from a customer perspective because they are meaningful only when they help or hinder the company in meeting customer needs. Only those strengths that relate to satisfying customers should be considered true competitive advantages. Likewise, weaknesses that directly affect customer satisfaction should be considered competitive disadvantages.

Opportunities and threats exist independently of the company and therefore represent issues to be considered by all organizations, even those that do not compete with the company. *Opportunities* refer to favorable conditions in the environment that could produce rewards for

SWOT analysis Assessment of an organization's strengths, weaknesses, opportunities, and threats

Emerging Trends

Watch That Weather Forecast!

Whether they might face a hurricane, blizzard, or tornado, some major marketers consult staff meteorologists as they work on marketing plans and implementation. For example, Walmart's meteorologists constantly monitor weather developments and update marketing planners and store personnel who must be ready to respond to bad weather systems. "It's great to have somebody in-house who can evaluate that information so that we can give real-time information to our associates, not only here at headquarters but out in the field," explains Walmart's head of emergency management. Planners analyze historical sales from each store in the affected area and then send out trucks filled with the specific goods each store will need during that type of storm (such as snow blowers for a blizzard or sump pumps for a hurricane).

Similarly, Home Depot's weather watchers keep the home improvement retailer ready for any type of storm, knowing that customers will need certain supplies before the bad weather and other supplies in its aftermath. When hurricane season opens, Home Depot has tractor-trailers preloaded with plywood, generators, and other products to restock stores in a storm's path. As a result, Home Depot is ready and able to remain open during a weather emergency.

Both FedEx and UPS have meteorologists on staff to help the delivery firms decide when their trucks should wait out a storm and how to reroute their cargo jets around severe weather systems. To maintain good customer relations, both firms alert customers as soon as they know pickups and deliveries will be delayed by bad weather.[c]

Figure 2.4 The Four-Cell SWOT Matrix

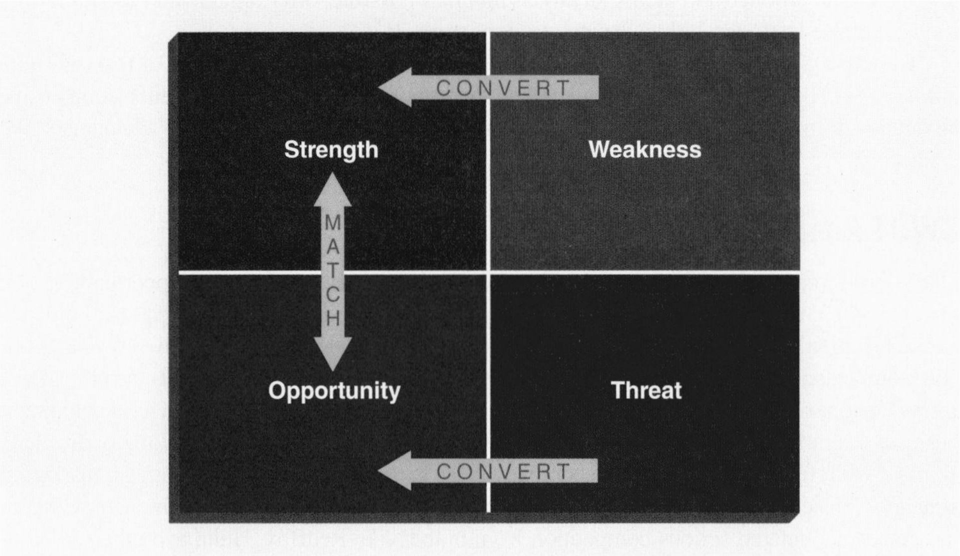

Source: Adapted from Nigel F. Piercy *Market-Led Strategic Change*. Copyright 1992 Butterworth-Heinemann Ltd. p. 371. Reprinted with permission.

the organization if acted on properly. That is, opportunities are situations that exist but must be exploited for the company to benefit from them. *Threats*, on the other hand, refer to conditions or barriers that may prevent the company from reaching its objectives. Threats must be acted upon to prevent them from limiting the organization's capabilities. Opportunities and threats can stem from many sources within the environment. When a competitor's introduction of a new product threatens a company, a defensive strategy may be required. If the company can develop and launch a new product that meets or exceeds the competition's offering, it can transform the threat into an opportunity.

Figure 2.4 depicts a four-cell SWOT matrix that can help managers in the planning process. When an organization matches internal strengths to external opportunities, it creates competitive advantages in meeting the needs of its customers. In addition, an organization should act to convert internal weaknesses into strengths and external threats into opportunities. Consider Apple's iPhone, which after a few years of being exclusively offered to only AT&T customers became widely available to Verizon customers as well. Although this development was a threat to AT&T's success, the company chose to convert it into a business opportunity. AT&T began running ads stating that iPhones worked faster and functioned better on its network. AT&T also worked to convert its own internal weaknesses into strengths by coming out with new devices, improving the quality of its network, cutting the prices of older iPhones, and giving current iPhone customers accelerated upgrades to the newest version of the iPhone when they signed a new long-term contract. These changes were part of an overall strategy by AT&T to minimize the number of customers lost to Verizon and possibly draw in some of Verizon's customers.[14]

SNAPSHOT

Source: Fall 2010 DLA Piper Technology Leaders Forecast Survey, www.dlapiper.com/files/upload/DLA_Piper_Tech_Survey_Report_2010.pdf (accessed May 16, 2012).

First-Mover and Late-Mover Advantage

An important factor that marketers must consider when identifying organizational resources and opportunities is if a company can have a first-mover advantage, or can choose to have a first-mover or late-mover advantage. A **first-mover advantage** is the ability of an innovative company to achieve long-term competitive advantages by being the first to offer a certain product in the marketplace. This creates benefits for marketers of that company in several ways. This initial entry into a market helps build a company's reputation as a pioneer and market leader. For a first mover, the market is, for at least a short period, free of competition as potential rival companies respond and work to create a substitute product. Consumers that want this product will have to buy that particular brand if it is the only one available. Therefore, a first-mover advantage also helps establish brand loyalty for the company due to its customers' costs to switch to competing products later on. Initial entry into a marketplace also gives the company an advantage by allowing it to protect its trade secrets or technology through patents. There are risks, however, of being the first to enter a market. There are usually high costs associated with creating a new product from scratch, including market research, product development, production, and marketing—or buyer education—costs. Also, early sales growth may not be as high as the company predicted if it makes mistakes with regard to the product or its marketing. The company runs the risk that the product will fail due to market uncertainty, or that the product might not completely meet consumers' expectations or needs.

A **late-mover advantage** is the ability of later market entrants to achieve long-term competitive advantages by not being the first to offer a certain product in a marketplace. Competitors that enter the market later can learn from the first mover's mistakes and thus create an updated and improved product design and marketing strategy that better responds to customers' needs. A late mover may have lower initial investment costs than the first mover to bring its product to the marketplace because the first mover has already developed an infrastructure and educated buyers about the product. By the time a late mover enters the market, there is more certainty about the success of the market for that product due to the previous company's sales data and other consumer response information. There are disadvantages of being a late mover, though. The company that entered the market first may have patents and other protections on its technology and trade secrets that prevent the late mover from reverse engineering

first-mover advantage The ability of an innovative company to achieve long-term competitive advantages by being the first to offer a certain product in the marketplace

late-mover advantage The ability of later market entrants to achieve long-term competitive advantages by not being the first to offer a certain product in a marketplace

First-Mover Advantage
The Kindle was the first reader to be introduced. What advantages did Amazon, the maker of the Kindle, experience by being first to market?

its product or producing a product that is too similar. Also, if customers who have already purchased the first mover's product believe that switching to the late mover's product will be too expensive or time-consuming for them, it will be difficult for the late mover to take market share away from the initial company's product. It is important to note that the timing of entry to the market is crucial and can determine the amount of late-mover advantage that is actually possible. Companies that are quick to enter the market after the first mover have a greater chance of building market share and brand loyalty. However, companies that enter the market later on, after many other companies have done so, face stronger competition and have more disadvantages.

Developing Marketing Objectives and Marketing Strategies

marketing objective A statement of what is to be accomplished through marketing activities

marketing strategy A plan of action for identifying and analyzing a target market and developing a marketing mix to meet the needs of that market

The next phase in strategic planning is the development of marketing objectives and marketing strategies. As we will soon discuss, marketing strategies are used to achieve marketing objectives. A **marketing objective** states what is to be accomplished through marketing activities. These objectives can be stated in terms of product introduction, product improvement or innovation, sales volume, profitability, market share, pricing, distribution, advertising, or employee training activities. A marketing objective of Ritz-Carlton hotels, for example, is to have more than 90 percent of its customers indicate that they had a memorable experience at the hotel. Marketing objectives should be based on a careful study of the SWOT analysis and should relate to matching strengths to opportunities and/or eliminating weaknesses or threats. With nearly one out of four consumer airline flights delayed, making significant improvements in on-time performance—such as having 90 percent on-time arrivals—would be a good marketing objective for an airline.

© AP/PRNewsFoto/Dominican Republic Ministry of Tourism

Marketing Objectives
What is the Dominican Republic Tourist Board hoping to achieve with this ad?

Marketing objectives should possess certain characteristics. First, a marketing objective should be expressed in clear, simple terms so all marketing and nonmarketing personnel in the company understand exactly what they are trying to achieve. Second, an objective should be written so it can be measured accurately. This allows the organization to determine if and when the objective has been achieved. For instance, if an objective is to increase market share by 10 percent in the U.S. marketplace, the company should be able to measure market share changes accurately in the United States. Third, a marketing objective should specify a time frame for its accomplishment. A company that sets an objective of introducing a new product should state the time period in which to do this. Finally, a marketing objective should be consistent with both business-unit and corporate strategy. This ensures that the company's mission is carried out at all levels of the organization and by both marketing and nonmarketing personnel.

Marketing objectives should be designed so their achievement will contribute to the corporate strategy and so they can be accomplished through efficient use of the company's marketing and nonmarketing resources. To achieve its marketing objectives, an organization must develop a marketing strategy.

A **marketing strategy** is the selection of a target market and the creation of a marketing mix that will satisfy the needs of target market members. A marketing strategy articulates the best use of the company's resources to achieve its marketing objectives. It should also match customers' desire for value with the organization's distinctive capabilities.

Selecting the Target Market

Selecting an appropriate target market may be the most important decision a company makes in the strategic planning process. The target market must be chosen before the organization can adapt its marketing mix to meet the customers' needs and preferences. Defining the target market and developing an appropriate marketing mix are the keys to strategic success. Toyota, for example, designed its Yaris sedan to appeal to 18- to 34-year-olds by giving the compact cars a "mischievous" personality to complement their quirky styling and then promoting them where Generation-Y consumers were likely to be. Toyota used Facebook, a user-generated-content website, and "mobisodes" (short mobile-phone episodes of popular television shows) to attract the attention of younger consumers. If a company selects the wrong target market, all other marketing decisions are likely to be made in vain.

Careful and accurate target market selection is crucial to productive marketing efforts. Products, and even whole companies, sometimes fail because marketers do not identify appropriate customer groups at whom to aim their efforts. Organizations that try to be all things to all people rarely satisfy the needs of any customer group very well. An organization's management therefore should designate which customer and stakeholder groups the company is trying to serve and gather adequate information about those groups. Identification and analysis of a target market provide a foundation on which the company can develop a marketing mix.

When exploring possible target markets, marketing managers try to evaluate how entering them would affect the company's sales, costs, and profits. Marketing information should be organized to facilitate a focus on the chosen target customers. Accounting and information systems, for example, can be used to track revenues and costs by customer (or group of customers). In addition, managers and employees need to be rewarded for focusing on profitable customers. Teamwork skills can be developed with organizational structures that promote a customer orientation that allows quick responses to changes in the marketing environment.

Marketers should also assess whether the company has the resources to develop the right mix of product, price, promotion, and distribution (i.e., marketing mix) to meet the needs of a particular target market. In addition, they should determine if satisfying those needs is consistent with the company's overall mission and objectives. The size and number of competitors already marketing products in potential target markets are concerns as well. Amazon.com was already the largest online bookseller when it made a strategic decision to start selling a variety of other products. The company believed that reaching a larger target audience through a wider range of products would broaden the company's appeal and result in larger sales. Clearly this was a wise decision, as Amazon.com is now the world's largest online retailer with revenues of over $48 billion annually. Customers can, and do, purchase virtually anything they want via Amazon.[15]

© AP Images/The Daily Nonpareil/Ben DeVrie

© AP Images/PRNewsFoto/hotels.com

Target Market Selection
Are Holiday Inn Express and the Four Seasons Hotel aiming at the same target market?

Creating Marketing Mixes

The selection of a target market serves as the basis for creating a marketing mix to satisfy the needs of that market. The decisions made in creating a marketing mix are only as good as the organization's understanding of its target market. This understanding typically comes from careful, in-depth research into the characteristics of the target market. Thus, although demographic information is important, the organization should also analyze customer needs, preferences, and behaviors with respect to product design, pricing, distribution, and promotion. Such is the case for Kimberly-Clark; its marketing researchers found that customers who buy Kleenex tissues have varied needs, so the company introduced a variety of packages, colors, and tissue types to meet the needs of its diverse target markets. These products ranged from tissues that are anti-viral; are for everyday use; come with lotion; have different expressions; and are ultra-soft. The box shapes come in square, rectangle, and oval.

Marketing mix decisions should have two additional characteristics: consistency and flexibility. All marketing mix decisions should be consistent with the business-unit and corporate strategies. Such consistency allows the organization to achieve its objectives on all three levels of planning. Flexibility, on the other hand, permits the organization to alter the marketing mix in response to changes in market conditions, competition, and customer needs. Marketing strategy flexibility has a positive influence on organizational performance.

The concept of the four marketing mix variables has stood the test of time, providing marketers with a rich set of questions for the four most important sets of decisions in strategic marketing. Consider the efforts of Harley-Davidson to improve its competitive position. The company worked to improve its product by eliminating oil leaks and other problems, and set prices that customers consider fair. The company used promotional tools to build a community of Harley riders renowned for their camaraderie. Harley-Davidson also fostered strong relationships with the dealers that distribute the company's motorcycles and related products and that reinforce the company's promotional messages.

At the marketing mix level, a company can detail how it will achieve a competitive advantage. To gain an advantage, the company must do something better than its competition. In other words, its products must be of higher quality, its prices must be consistent with its products' level of quality (value), its distribution methods must be efficient and cost as little as possible, and its promotion must be more effective than the competition's. It is also important that the company attempt to make these advantages sustainable. A **sustainable competitive advantage** is one that the competition cannot copy in the foreseeable future. Walmart, for example, maintains a sustainable competitive advantage in groceries over supermarkets because of its highly efficient and low-cost distribution system. This advantage allows Walmart to offer lower prices and helps it gain the largest share of the supermarket business. Maintaining a sustainable competitive advantage requires flexibility in the marketing mix when facing uncertain competitive environments.

MANAGING MARKETING IMPLEMENTATION

Marketing implementation is the process of putting marketing strategies into action. Through planning, marketing managers provide purpose and direction for an organization's marketing efforts. Likewise, understanding the problems and elements of marketing implementation sets the stage for implementing specific marketing strategies. As we have stated before, people are ultimately responsible for implementing marketing strategy. Therefore, the effective implementation of any and all marketing activities depends on the organization of the marketing department, motivating marketing personnel, effectively communicating within the marketing unit, coordinating all marketing activities, and establishing a timetable for the completion of each marketing activity.

sustainable competitive advantage An advantage that the competition cannot copy

marketing implementation The process of putting marketing strategies into action

Entrepreneurship in Marketing

At the Rogers Family Company, Coffee Is Not the Only Concern

Entrepreneur: Jon and Barbara Rogers
Business: Rogers Family Company
Founded: 1979 | Lincoln, California
Success: The company is the largest gourmet coffee roaster in the San Francisco Bay area.

In 1979, husband-and-wife entrepreneurs Jon and Barbara Rogers developed a high-quality coffee product that would stand out against the gourmet coffees marketed by larger rivals such as Starbucks. They didn't just want customers to "taste the difference" in flavor, they also wanted to "make a difference" in coffee-producing nations. First, they pay above-market prices for coffee beans, so small and mid-sized growers can make a decent living. Second, they support sustainability by sharing earth-friendly coffee growing methods. For example, thanks to successful experiments at the company's model farm in Panama, growers in Mexico and Nicaragua know they can use red earthworms to turn coffee waste into nutritious, organic fertilizer for coffee trees.

Much of the company's marketing efforts are aimed at building strong relationships with large wholesale customers such as Costco. In addition, it's introducing single-serve coffee products because this "is the fastest-growing segment of the coffee market right now," explains Jim Rogers, one of the family members in this two-generation company. The Rogers Family Company is brewing up more marketing activities to increase profits in the coming years.[d]

Organizing the Marketing Unit

The structure and relationships of a marketing unit, including lines of authority and responsibility that connect and coordinate individuals, strongly affect marketing activities. Companies that truly adopt the marketing concept develop a distinct organizational culture: a culture based on a shared set of beliefs that makes the customer's needs the pivotal point of the company's decisions about strategy and operations. Instead of developing products in a proverbial vacuum and then trying to persuade customers to purchase those products, companies that use the marketing concept begin with an orientation toward their customers' needs and desires. Recreational Equipment Inc. (REI), for example, gives customers a chance to try out sporting goods that approximate how the products will actually be used. Customers can try out hiking boots on a simulated hiking path with a variety of trail surfaces and inclines or test climbing gear on an indoor climbing wall. In addition, REI offers clinics to customers, such as "Rock Climbing Basics," "Basic Backpacking," and "REI's Outdoor School."

An important decision regarding structural authority is whether the marketing operation should be centralized or decentralized. In a **centralized organization**, top-level managers delegate little authority to lower levels. In a **decentralized organization**, decision-making authority is delegated as far down the chain of command as possible. The decision to centralize or decentralize the organization directly affects marketing. Most traditional organizations are highly centralized. In these organizations, most, if not all, marketing decisions are made at the top levels. However, as organizations become more marketing oriented, centralized decision making proves somewhat ineffective. In these organizations, decentralized authority allows the company to respond to customer needs more quickly.

How effectively a company's marketing management can implement marketing strategies also depends on how the marketing unit is organized. Organizing marketing activities in ways that mesh with a company's strategic marketing approach enhances performance. Effective organizational structure of a marketing department establishes the authority relationships among marketing personnel and specifies who is responsible for making certain decisions and performing particular activities. This internal structure helps direct marketing activities.

centralized organization A structure in which top-level managers delegate little authority to lower levels

decentralized organization A structure in which decision-making authority is delegated as far down the chain of command as possible

Recognition
Recognizing outstanding performance is one approach to motivating marketing personnel.

Motivating Marketing Personnel

People work to satisfy physical, psychological, and social needs. To motivate marketing personnel, managers must discover their employees' needs and then develop motivational methods that will help employees satisfy those needs. It is crucial that the plan to motivate employees be fair, ethical, and well understood by employees. In addition, rewards to employees should be tied to organizational goals. In general, to improve employee motivation, companies need to find out what workers think, how they feel, and what they want. Some of this information can be obtained from an employee attitude survey. A firm can motivate its workers by directly linking pay with performance, informing workers how their performance affects department and corporate results, following through with appropriate compensation, implementing a flexible benefits program, and adopting a participative management approach. Motivation is also facilitated by informing employees about how their performance affects their own compensation.

Besides tying rewards to organizational goals, managers should use a variety of other tools to motivate individuals. Selecting effective motivational tools has become more complex because of greater differences among workers in terms of race, ethnicity, gender, and age. Indeed, one of the most common forms of diversity in today's organizations is the diversity across generations of employees. Such differences broaden the range of individual value systems within an organization, which in turn calls for a more diverse set of motivational tools. For example, an employee might value autonomy or recognition more than a slight pay increase. Managers can reward employees not just with money and additional fringe benefits but also with such nonfinancial rewards as prestige or recognition, job autonomy, skill variety, task significance, increased feedback, or even a more relaxed dress code. It is crucial for management to show that it takes pride in its workforce and to motivate employees to take pride in their company.

Communicating within the Marketing Unit

With good communication, marketing managers can motivate personnel and coordinate their efforts. Poor communication can harm morale and reduce productivity. Poor communicating between managers and employees can be especially damaging in emotionally charged situations.

Marketing managers must be able to communicate with the firm's upper-level management to ensure marketing activities are consistent with the company's overall goals. Communication with top-level executives keeps marketing managers aware of the company's overall plans and achievements. It also guides the marketing unit's activities and indicates how they are to be integrated with those of other departments, such as finance, production, or human resources, with whose management the marketing manager must also communicate to coordinate marketing efforts. For example, marketing personnel should work with the production staff to help design products that customers want. To direct marketing activities, marketing managers must communicate with marketing personnel at the operations level, such as sales and advertising personnel, researchers, wholesalers, retailers, and package designers.

One of the most important types of communication in marketing is communication that flows upward from the frontline of the marketing unit to higher-level marketing managers. Customer-contact employees are in a unique position to understand customers' wants and needs. By taking steps to encourage upward communication, marketing managers can gain access to a rich source of information about what customers require, how well products are selling, whether marketing activities are working, and what problems are occurring in marketing implementation. Upward communication also allows marketing managers to understand the problems and needs of employees.

Training is a key part of communicating with marketing employees. Setting clear objectives and demonstrating that training adds value to the individual helps create a productive organizational climate. Through an effective training program, employees can learn, ask questions, and become accountable for marketing performance. Communication is also facilitated by an information system within the marketing unit. The marketing managers, sales managers, and sales personnel need to communicate with one another. Marketers need an information system to support a variety of activities, such as planning, budgeting, sales analyses, performance evaluations, and report preparation. An information system should also expedite communications with other departments in the organization and minimize destructive interdepartmental competition for organizational resources.

Coordinating Marketing Activities

Because of job specialization and differences among marketing activities, marketing managers must coordinate individuals' actions to achieve marketing objectives. They must work closely with managers in research and development, production, finance, accounting, and human resources to ensure that marketing activities mesh with other functions of the firm. They must coordinate the activities of marketing staff within the firm and integrate those activities with the marketing efforts of external organizations—advertising agencies, resellers (wholesalers and retailers), researchers, and shippers, among others. Marketing managers can improve coordination by making each employee aware of how his or her job relates to others and how his or her actions contribute to the achievement of marketing objectives.

Establishing a Timetable for Implementation

Successful marketing implementation requires that employees know the specific activities for which they are responsible and the timetable for completing each activity. One company that is very good at establishing implementation timetables is Domino's Pizza. Every activity involved in creating and delivering a pizza, from taking the phone order to handing the pizza to the customer, has an employee who is responsible for its implementation. In addition, all employees know the specified time frame for completion of their activities.

Establishing an implementation timetable involves several steps: (1) identifying the activities to be performed, (2) determining the time required to complete each activity, (3) separating the activities to be performed in sequence from those to be performed simultaneously, (4) organizing the activities in the proper order, and (5) assigning responsibility for completing each activity to

Courtesy of Angie's List

Evaluating Strategic Performance
An advertising campaign is frequently a part of a marketing strategy. Measuring the cost of an advertising campaign is not difficult. Evaluating the effectiveness of an advertising campaign is challenging.

one or more employees, teams, or managers. Some activities must be performed before others, whereas others can be performed at the same time or later in the implementation process. Completing all implementation activities on schedule requires tight coordination among departments—marketing, production, advertising, sales, and so on. Pinpointing those implementation activities that can be performed simultaneously will greatly reduce the total amount of time needed to put a given marketing strategy into practice. Since scheduling is a complicated task, most organizations use sophisticated computer programs to plan the timing of marketing activities.

EVALUATING MARKETING STRATEGIES

To achieve marketing objectives, marketing managers must effectively evaluate marketing strategies. **Strategic performance evaluation** consists of establishing performance standards, measuring actual performance, comparing actual performance with established standards, and modifying the marketing strategy, if needed.

Establishing Performance Standards

A **performance standard** is an expected level of performance against which actual performance can be compared. A performance standard might be a 20 percent reduction in customer complaints, a monthly sales quota of $150,000, or a 10 percent increase per month in new-customer accounts. Performance standards are derived from marketing objectives that are set while developing marketing strategies. By establishing marketing objectives, a marketer indicates what a marketing strategy is supposed to accomplish. Marketing objectives directly or indirectly set forth performance standards, usually in terms of sales, costs, or communication dimensions, such as brand awareness or product feature recall. Actual performance should be measured in similar terms to facilitate comparisons.

Analyzing Actual Performance

Analyzing actual performance is also driven by the marketing objective set by marketers. Analyzing actual performance associated with communication dimensions is usually achieved by conducting customer research. In this section, we focus on two bases—sales and cost—for evaluating the actual performance of marketing strategies.

Sales Analysis

Sales analysis uses sales figures to evaluate a firm's current performance. It is probably the most common method of evaluation because sales data partially reflect the target market's reactions to a marketing mix and often are readily available, at least in aggregate form. Marketers use current sales data to monitor the impact of current marketing efforts. However, that information alone is not enough. To provide useful analyses, current sales data must be compared with forecasted sales, industry sales, specific competitor's sales, or the costs incurred to achieve the sales volume. For example, knowing that a specialty store attained a $600,000 sales volume this year does not tell management whether its marketing strategy has succeeded. However, if managers

strategic performance evaluation Establishing performance standards, measuring actual performance, comparing actual performance with established standards, and modifying the marketing strategy, if needed

performance standard An expected level of performance against which actual performance can be compared

sales analysis Analysis of sales figures to evaluate a firm's performance

know expected sales were $550,000, they are in a better position to determine the effectiveness of the firm's marketing efforts. In addition, if they know the marketing costs needed to achieve the $600,000 volume were 12 percent less than budgeted, they are in an even better position to analyze their marketing strategy precisely. Although sales may be measured in several ways, the basic unit of measurement is the sales transaction. A sales transaction results in an order for a specified quantity of the organization's product sold under specified terms by a particular salesperson or sales team on a certain date. Many organizations record these bits of information about their transactions. With such a record, a company can analyze sales in terms of dollar volume or market share. Firms frequently use dollar volume in their sales analyses because the dollar is a common denominator of sales, costs, and profits. However, price increases and decreases affect total sales figures. This is especially true in the auto industry, where profit margins are being squeezed. Even though auto prices are increasing and its dollar sales volume is 10 percent greater than last year, the auto industry has not experienced any increase in unit sales. A marketing manager who uses dollar-volume analysis should factor out the effects of price changes.

A firm's market share is the firm's sales of a product stated as a percentage of industry sales of that product. Market share analysis lets a company compare its marketing strategy with competitors' strategies. The primary reason for using market share analysis is to estimate whether sales changes have resulted from the firm's marketing strategy or from uncontrollable environmental forces. When a company's sales volume declines but its share of the market stays the same, the marketer can assume industry sales declined (because of some uncontrollable factors) and this decline was reflected in the firm's sales. However, if a company experiences a decline in both sales and market share, it should consider the possibility that its marketing strategy is not effective or was improperly implemented.

Even though market share analysis can be helpful in evaluating the performance of a marketing strategy, the user must interpret results cautiously. When attributing a sales decline to uncontrollable factors, a marketer must keep in mind that such factors do not affect all firms in the industry equally. Not all firms in an industry have the same objectives and strategies, and some change strategies from one year to the next. Changes in the strategies of one company can affect the market shares of one or all companies in that industry. Ford Motor Company, for example, has a market share of just over 8 percent and is the second best-selling passenger car brand in Europe. Ford hopes to increase its own market share by releasing more than 10 new or redesigned models in Europe. If Ford's strategy works, competitors could experience declines in their market shares.[16] Within an industry, the entrance of new firms, the launch of new products by competing firms, or the demise of established products also affects a specific firm's market share, and market share analysts should attempt to account for these effects. Apple, for example, caused its competitors to reevaluate their marketing strategies when it introduced the iPad.

Marketing Cost Analysis

Although sales analysis is critical for evaluating the performance of a marketing strategy, it provides only a part of the picture. A marketing strategy that successfully generates sales may also be extremely costly. To get a complete picture, a firm must know the marketing costs associated with using a given strategy to achieve a certain sales level. **Marketing cost analysis** breaks down and classifies costs to determine which are associated with specific marketing efforts. By comparing costs of previous marketing activities with results generated, a marketer can better allocate the firm's marketing resources in the future. Marketing cost analysis lets a company evaluate the performance of marketing strategy by comparing sales achieved and costs incurred. By pinpointing exactly where a company is experiencing high costs, this form of analysis can help isolate profitable or unprofitable customers, products, and geographic areas.

A company that understands and manages its costs appropriately has a competitive advantage. By being a low-cost provider, an organization is then in a position to engage in aggressive price competition. Southwest Airlines, for example, uses a low-cost, no-frills approach to business that saves the company and its customers money. Southwest is able to market itself on the basis of a low price because it constantly analyzes its costs to look for new ways to reduce waste and make itself more competitive. After online booking became more popular, Southwest cut the

marketing cost analysis Analysis of costs to determine which are associated with specific marketing efforts

number of employees that handle reservations. Knowing that every minute that a plane spends sitting on the ground is a minute of lost profits, Southwest uses innovative technology to make its flight schedules and routes more efficient. Southwest has also reduced its fuel costs, which usually account for over 30 percent of an airline's costs, by improving the design of its planes to cut down on their fuel consumption and by hedging oil prices to avoid paying more when the cost of oil goes up. To measure costs against their competitors, many airlines calculate cost per available seat mile (CASM), which represents the average cost per mile to fly each seat on a plane. Southwest's CASM is currently about 9.6 cents per mile, whereas United, Continental, American, and Delta's CASMs are all over 12 cents per mile. Unlike its competitors, Southwest has reported a profit each year for over 35 straight years, due to its focus on marketing cost analysis.[17]

One way to analyze costs is by comparing a company's costs with industry averages. Many companies check the amount of money they spend on marketing efforts and other operations against average levels for the industry to look for areas of improvement. For example, a business could compare its advertising costs as a percentage of its sales with the industry average. A company might determine it spends 6 percent of its sales on advertising, while the industry average is 2 percent. When looking at industry averages, however, a company should take into account its own unique situation. The company's costs can differ from the industry average for several reasons, including its own marketing objectives, cost structure, geographic location, types of customers, and scale of operations. For example, the company mentioned above, when comparing its advertising costs with the industry average, might be spending 6 percent on advertising, even though the industry average is 2 percent, because it is a smaller company competing against industry giants. Perhaps this firm's advertising objectives are much more aggressive than those of other firms in the industry.

Costs can be categorized in different ways when performing marketing cost analysis. One way to categorize costs is to identify which ones are affected by sales or production volume, and which are not. Some costs are going to be a fixed amount of money for a certain period of time (such as a month) regardless of a company's production or sales volume. These costs could be rent, employees' salaries, office supplies, or utilities. Changes in the company's production or sales volumes won't affect the amount you pay for these costs. However, these costs often do not explain what marketing functions were performed using those funds. It does little good, for example, to know that $80,000 is spent for rent each year. The analyst has to do further research to find out what types of facilities are rented, and what function each of them serves in the business. For example, the analyst might determine that of the $80,000 spent on rent, only $32,000 was spent on facilities directly associated with marketing efforts. Some costs are directly attributable to production and sales volume. These costs are stated as a per quantity (or unit) cost, instead of as a cost per period of time. These costs could be the cost to produce or sell each unit of a specific product, such as the cost of the materials and labor that go into producing a product, or the amount of commissions that are paid to salespeople when products are sold.

Another way to categorize costs is based on whether or not they can be linked to a specific business function. Costs that can be linked are allocated, using one or several criteria, to the functions that they support. For example, if the firm spends $80,000 to rent space for production, storage, and sales facilities, the total rental cost can be allocated to each of the three functions if the analyst uses some sort of criteria, such as square footage of each, to do so. Some costs cannot be assigned according to any logical criteria; they are assignable only on an arbitrary basis. Interest paid on loans, taxes paid to the government, and the salaries of top management are examples of these difficult-to-assign costs.

Comparing Actual Performance with Performance Standards and Making Changes, if Needed

Comparing actual performance with established performance standards can result in actual performance exceeding performance standards or actual performance failing to meet performance standards. When actual performance exceeds performance standards, marketers view a marketing strategy as being effective, and they are usually satisfied with this outcome. It is important to try to gain an understanding of why the strategy is effective. This understanding can sometimes provide information that allows marketers to adjust a marketing strategy to make it even more successful. In some situations, it's possible that changes in the marketing environment resulted in conditions that helped this strategy be effective.

When actual performance does not meet performance standards, marketers usually will want to know why a marketing strategy was less effective. At times, decisions made regarding a specific marketing mix variable, such as price, were not the best. Such decisions can result in lower performance. The inadequate performance may occur due to conditions arising from environmental changes. Aggressive competitive behavior sometimes causes a marketing strategy to underperform.

When a marketing strategy is initially viewed as underperforming, a question sometimes arises as to whether the marketing objective, against which performance is measured, is realistic or not. Given the level of company resources available, it is possible that the marketing strategy is under-funded, resulting in lower performance. At times, the marketing objective may be unrealistic, independent of the level of company resources. To remedy this problem, marketers may have to alter the marketing objective to make it more realistic.

CREATING THE MARKETING PLAN

The strategic planning process ultimately yields a marketing strategy that is the framework for a **marketing plan**, a written document that specifies the marketing activities to be performed to implement and evaluate the organization's marketing strategies.

Developing a clear, well-written marketing plan, though time consuming, is important. The plan is the basis for internal communication among employees. It covers the assignment of responsibilities and tasks, as well as schedules for implementation. It presents objectives and specifies how resources are to be allocated to achieve those objectives. Finally, the marketing plan helps marketing managers monitor and evaluate the performance of a marketing strategy.

A single marketing plan can be developed and applied to the business as a whole, but it is more likely that a company will choose to develop multiple marketing plans, with each relating to a specific brand or product made by the company. If a company is using multiple marketing plans, these plans are part of a larger strategic business plan, and are used to implement specific parts of that overall strategy.

Marketing planning and implementation are closely linked in successful companies. The marketing plan provides a framework to stimulate thinking and provide strategic direction, whereas implementation occurs as an adaptive response to day-to-day issues, opportunities, and unanticipated situations—for example, increasing interest rates or an economic slowdown—that cannot be incorporated into marketing plans.

Organizations use many different formats when devising marketing plans. Plans may be written for strategic business units, product lines, individual products or brands, or specific markets. The key, however, is to make sure that the marketing plan is written in alignment with corporate and business-unit strategies and is accessible to and shared with all key employees. Marketing plans are critical parts of a company's overall strategy development, and they should go beyond the interests of marketing personnel to permeate the company's culture and all functional specialists in the company. Most plans share some common ground by including many of the same components.

Table 2.1 describes the major parts of a typical marketing plan. The first component of the marketing plan is the executive summary, which provides an overview of the entire marketing plan so that readers can quickly identify the key issues pertaining to their roles in the planning and implementation process. The executive summary includes an introduction, an explanation of the major aspects of the plan, and a statement about the costs of implementing the plan. The next component of the marketing plan is the environmental analysis, which supplies information about the company's current situation with respect to the marketing environment, the target market, and the firm's current objectives and performance. The first section of the environmental analysis includes an assessment of all the environmental factors—competitive, economic, political, legal, regulatory, technological, and sociocultural—that can affect marketing activities. In the

marketing plan A written document that specifies the activities to be performed to implement and control the organization's marketing strategies

Table 2.1 Components of the Marketing Plan

Plan Component	Component Summary	Highlights
Executive Summary	One- to two-page synopsis of the entire marketing plan	1. Stress key points 2. Include one to three key points that make the company unique
Environmental Analysis	Information about the company's current situation with respect to the marketing environment	1. Assessment of marketing environment factors 2. Assessment of target market(s) 3. Assessment of current marketing objectives and performance
SWOT Analysis	Assessment of the organization's strengths, weaknesses, opportunities, and threats	1. Strengths of the company 2. Weaknesses of the company 3. Opportunities in the environment and industry 4. Threats in the environment and industry
Marketing Objectives	Specification of the company's marketing objectives	1. Qualitative measures of what is to be accomplished 2. Quantitative measures of what is to be accomplished
Marketing Strategies	Outline of how the company will achieve its objectives	1. Target market(s) 2. Marketing mix
Marketing Implementation	Outline of how the company will implement its marketing strategies	1. Marketing organization 2. Activities and responsibilities 3. Implementation timetable
Performance Evaluation	Explanation of how the company will evaluate the performance of the implemented plan	1. Performance standards 2. Financial controls 3. Monitoring procedures (audits)

second section, the organization examines the current status of its target markets and assesses the current needs of each target market. In the final section of the environmental analysis, the company evaluates its current marketing objectives and performance to ensure that these objectives remain consistent with the changing environment. The next component of the marketing plan is the SWOT analysis, which assesses an organization's strengths, weaknesses, opportunities, and threats, using information gathered from the preceding component—the environmental analysis. Strengths and weaknesses of the company are a result of the firm's internal characteristics and conditions, whereas opportunities and threats are found by examining the firm's environment. The marketing objectives section of the marketing plan states what the company wants to accomplish through marketing activities, keeping the SWOT analysis results in mind. The marketing strategies component outlines how the firm plans to achieve its marketing objectives and discusses the company's target market selection(s) and marketing mix. The marketing implementation component of the plan outlines how marketing strategies will be implemented. The success of the marketing strategy depends on how feasible the marketing implementation is. Finally, the performance evaluation section of the marketing plan establishes the standards for how the results of the plan will be measured and evaluated, and what actions the company should take to reduce the differences between planned and actual performance.

It is important to note that most organizations have their own unique format and terminology to describe the marketing plan. Every marketing plan is and should be unique to the organization for which it was created.

The creation and implementation of a complete marketing plan will allow the organization to achieve not only its marketing objectives but its business-unit and corporate goals as well. However, a marketing plan is only as good as the information it contains and the effort and creativity that went into its development. Thus, the importance of having a good marketing information system cannot be overstated. Equally important is the role of managerial judgment throughout the strategic planning process. While the creation of a marketing plan is an important milestone in strategic planning, it is by no means the final step. To succeed, a company must have a plan that is closely followed yet flexible enough to allow for adjustments to reflect the changing marketing environment.

Summary

1. To understand the strategic planning process

Through the process of strategic planning, a company identifies or establishes an organizational mission and goals, corporate strategy, marketing goals and objectives, marketing strategy, and a marketing plan. To achieve its marketing objectives, an organization must develop a marketing strategy, which includes identifying a target market and developing a plan of action for developing, distributing, promoting, and pricing products that meet the needs of customers in that target market. The strategic planning process ultimately yields the framework for a marketing plan, a written document that specifies the activities to be performed for implementing and controlling an organization's marketing activities.

An organization's goals should be derived from its mission statement—a long-term view, or vision, of what the organization wants to become. A well-formulated mission statement helps give an organization a clear purpose and direction, distinguish it from competitors, provide direction for strategic planning, and foster a focus on customers. An organization's goals, which focus on the end results sought, guide the remainder of its planning efforts.

Corporate strategy determines the means for utilizing resources in the areas of production, finance, research and development, human resources, and marketing to reach the organization's goals. Business-unit strategy focuses on strategic business units (SBUs)—divisions, product lines, or other profit centers within the parent company used to define areas for consideration in a specific strategic marketing plan. The Boston Consulting Group's market growth/market share matrix integrates a company's products or SBUs into a single, overall matrix for evaluation to determine appropriate strategies for individual products and business units.

The marketing environment, including economic, competitive, political, legal and regulatory, sociocultural, and technological forces, can affect the resources a company can acquire and use to create favorable opportunities. Resources may include core competencies, which are things that a company does extremely well, sometimes so well that it gives the company an advantage over its competition. When the right combination of circumstances and timing permits an organization to take action toward reaching a particular target market, a market opportunity exists. Strategic windows are temporary periods of optimal fit between the key requirements of a market and the particular capabilities of a company competing in that market. When a company matches a core competency to opportunities it has discovered in the marketplace, it is said to have a competitive advantage. A marketer can use SWOT analysis to assess a firm's ability to achieve a competitive advantage. If marketers want to understand how the timing of entry into a marketplace can create competitive advantage, they can examine first-mover and late-mover advantages. The next phase of strategic planning involves the development of marketing objectives and strategies. Marketing objectives state what is to be accomplished through marketing activities, and should be consistent with both business-unit and corporate strategy. Marketing strategies, the most detailed and specific of the three levels of strategy, are composed of two elements: the selection of a target market and the creation of a marketing mix that will satisfy the needs of the target market members. The selection of a target market serves as the basis for the creation of the marketing mix to satisfy the needs of that market. Marketing mix decisions should also be consistent with business-unit and corporate strategies and be flexible enough to respond to changes in market conditions, competition, and customer needs. Different elements of the marketing mix can be changed to accommodate different marketing strategies.

2. To examine what is necessary to effectively manage the implementation of marketing strategies

Marketing implementation is the process of executing marketing strategies. Through planning, marketing managers provide purpose and direction for an organization's marketing efforts. Marketing managers must understand the problems and elements of marketing implementation before they can effectively implement specific marketing activities. Proper implementation requires creating efficient organizational structures, motivating marketing personnel, properly communicating within the marketing unit, coordinating the marketing activities, and establishing a timetable for implementation.

An internal structure for the marketing unit must be developed in order to organize the marketing department and help direct marketing efforts. In a centralized organization, top-level managers delegate very little authority to lower levels, whereas in decentralized organizations, decision-making authority is delegated as far down the chain of command as possible. Motivating marketing employees is crucial to effectively implementing marketing strategies. Marketing managers must discover marketing employees' needs and then develop different methods to motivate those employees to help the organization meet its goals. Proper communication within the marketing unit is a key element in successful marketing implementation. Communication should go both downward (from top management to the lower-level employees) and upward (from lower-level employees to top management). Marketing managers must also be able to effectively coordinate marketing activities. This entails both coordinating the activities of the marketing staff within the firms and integrating those activities with the marketing actions of external organizations that are also involved in implementing the marketing strategies. Finally, successful marketing implementation requires that a timetable for implementation be established. Establishment of an implementation timetable involves several steps, and ensures that employees know the specific activities for which they are responsible and the timeline for completing each activity. Completing all activities on schedule requires tight coordination among departments, and many organizations use sophisticated computer programs to plan the timing of marketing activities.

3. To describe the major elements of strategic performance evaluation

Strategic performance evaluation consists of establishing performance standards, analyzing actual performance, comparing actual performance with established standards, and modifying the marketing strategy, if needed. When actual performance is compared with performance standards, marketers must determine whether a discrepancy exists and, if so, whether it requires corrective action, such as changing the performance standard or improving actual performance. Two possible ways to evaluate the actual performance of marketing strategies are sales analysis and marketing cost analysis.

Sales analysis uses sales figures to evaluate a firm's current performance. It is probably the most common method of evaluation because sales data are a good indication of the target market's reaction to a marketing mix. Marketers analyze sales by comparing current sales to forecasted sales, industry sales, specific competitor's sales, or the costs incurred to achieve the sales volume. Companies can analyze sales in terms of the dollar volume or market share.

Marketing cost analysis breaks down and classifies costs to determine which are associated with specific marketing efforts. Marketing cost analysis helps marketers decide how to best allocate the firm's marketing resources for future years. Companies can use marketing cost analysis to identify profitable or unprofitable customers, products, and geographic areas. Marketers can compare current costs to previous years' costs, forecasted costs, industry averages, competitors' costs, or to the results generated by those costs. Companies should identify which of its costs are affected by sales and which are not related to sales volume. Companies should also categorize costs based on whether or not they can be linked to a specific business function, specifically marketing.

4. To understand the development of a marketing plan

A key component of marketing planning is the development of a marketing plan, which outlines all the activities necessary to implement marketing strategies. The plan fosters communication among employees, assigns responsibilities and schedules, specifies how resources are to be allocated to achieve objectives, and helps marketing managers monitor and evaluate the performance of a marketing strategy.

Go to www.cengagebrain.com for resources to help you master the content in this chapter as well as for materials that will expand your marketing knowledge!

Important Terms

strategic marketing management 32
strategic planning 32
mission statement 33
corporate strategy 35
strategic business unit (SBU) 35
market 36
market share 36
market growth/market share matrix 36
core competencies 38
market opportunity 38
strategic windows 38
competitive advantage 38
SWOT analysis 39
first-mover advantage 41
late-mover advantage 41
marketing objective 42
marketing strategy 42
sustainable competitive advantage 44
marketing implementation 44
centralized organization 45
decentralized organization 45
strategic performance evaluation 48
performance standard 48
sales analysis 48
marketing cost analysis 49
marketing plan 51

Discussion and Review Questions

1. Identify the major components of strategic planning, and explain how they are interrelated.
2. Explain how an organization can create a competitive advantage at the corporate strategy level and at the business unit strategy level.
3. What are some issues to consider in analyzing a company's resources and opportunities? How do these issues affect marketing objectives and marketing strategy?
4. What is SWOT analysis and why is it important?

5. How can an organization make its competitive advantages sustainable over time? How difficult is it to create sustainable competitive advantages?
6. How should organizations set marketing objectives?
7. What are the two major parts of a marketing strategy?
8. When considering the strategic planning process, what factors influence the development of a marketing strategy?
9. Identify and explain the major managerial actions that are a part of managing the implementation of marketing strategies.
10. Which element of the strategic planning process plays a major role in the establishment of performance standards? Explain.
11. When assessing actual performance of a marketing strategy, should a marketer perform marketing cost analysis? Why or why not?
12. Identify and explain the major components of a marketing plan.

Application Questions

1. Contact three companies that appear to be successful. Ask one of the company's managers if he or she would share with you the company's mission statement or organizational goals. For many companies, the mission statement and organizational goals can also be found on the company's webpage. Obtain as much information as possible about the mission statement and organizational goals. Discuss how the statement matches the criteria outlined in the text.
2. Assume you own a new, family-style restaurant that will open for business in the coming year. Formulate a long-term goal for the restaurant, and then develop short-term goals to help you achieve the long-term goal.
3. Amazon.com identified an opportunity to capitalize on a desire of many consumers to shop at home. This strategic window gave Amazon.com a very competitive position in a new market. Consider the opportunities that may be present in your city or your region. Identify a strategic window, and discuss how a company could take advantage of this opportunity. What types of core competencies are necessary?
4. Marketing units may be organized according to functions, products, regions, or types of customers. Describe how you would organize the marketing units for the following:
   a. A toothpaste with whitener; a toothpaste with sensitivity protection; a toothpaste with cinnamon flavor
   b. A national line offering all types of winter and summer sports clothing for men and women
   c. A life insurance company that provides life, health, and disability insurance
5. IMP After reading the case of Ford Motor Company, it should be apparent that the firm has major strengths and weaknesses in its operations. Additionally, as the external environment for the automobile industry continues to change, Ford is facing a number of new challenges and opportunities that it must address. Create a SWOT analysis based upon the case. Identify three strengths, three weaknesses, three opportunities, and three threats of Ford Motor Company. You should realize that not all strengths, weaknesses, opportunities, and threats have equal relevance. Some strengths might be stronger than weaknesses, while certain threats might be of more concern to a firm than others. Rank each of the strengths, weaknesses, opportunities, and threats from 1–10 depending upon how significant you feel each one is to the company. Do you feel that Ford has a high competitive position relative to other automobile companies?

Internet Exercise

Sony

Internet analysts have praised Sony's website as one of the best organized and most informative on the Internet. See why by accessing **www.sony.com**.

1. Based on the information provided on the website, describe Sony's SBUs. Does Sony have SBUs that are divisions, product lines, or some other profit-center structure within the parent company Sony?
2. Based on your existing knowledge of Sony as an innovative leader in the consumer electronics industry, describe the company's primary competitive advantage (i.e., what makes Sony strategically unique?). How does Sony's website support this competitive advantage?
3. Assess the quality and effectiveness of Sony's website. Specifically, perform a preliminary SWOT analysis comparing Sony's website with other high-quality websites you have visited.

developing your marketing plan

One of the foundations of a successful marketing strategy is a thorough analysis of your company. To make the best decisions about what products to offer, which markets to target, and how to reach those target market members, you must recognize your company's strengths and weaknesses. The information collected in this analysis should be referenced when making many of the decisions in your marketing plan. While writing the beginning of your plan, the information in this chapter can help you with the following issues:

1. Can you identify the core competencies of your company? Do they currently contribute to a competitive advantage? If not, what changes could your company make to establish a competitive advantage?
2. Conduct a SWOT analysis of your company to identify its strengths and weaknesses. Continue your analysis to include the business environment, discovering any opportunities that exist or threats that may impact your company.
3. Using the information from your SWOT analysis, have you identified any opportunities that are a good match with your company's core competencies? Likewise, have you discovered any weaknesses that could be converted to strengths through careful marketing planning?

The information obtained from these questions should assist you in developing various aspects of your marketing plan found in the "Interactive Marketing Plan" exercise at **www.cengagebrain.com**.

video case 2.1

White Rock's Sparkling Past Points the Way to Its Marketing Future

Larry Bodkin had a tough road ahead of him when he became president of White Rock Beverages. Founded in the late 1800s, White Rock's sparkling water reached its heyday in the early 20th century as the water of the upper class. However, by the end of the century, White Rock was struggling to survive in the face of intense competition from global brands with gigantic marketing budgets.

Now more than 140 years old, White Rock has used a combination of different marketing strategies to revitalize itself. For years it utilized a hybrid distribution system to sell to distributors in some markets and to retailers in other markets. In the process, White Rock uses customer service as a differentiator between its beverages and its competitors. Because customers find the company responsive to their needs, many stay loyal to the White Rock brand.

Another way in which White Rock differentiates itself from companies like Coca-Cola and Pepsi is by its branding strategy. The company recognizes that one of its key strengths is as a premium brand for a niche market segment. White Rock targets the health-food segment by marketing itself as a unique, healthy brand. It also capitalizes on its history as one of the oldest sparkling beverage companies in America. This brand appeal has become so important that White Rock challenged Coca-Cola after Coke claimed that it created today's modern image of Santa Claus. Bodkin demanded an apology from Coca-Cola when it was revealed that White Rock had been using the modern Santa Claus ad two decades prior to Coca-Cola's Santa ads. By developing a strong, authentic image for each of its brands, White Rock is building on recent trends toward "artisanal" foods that emphasize quality and distinctive traditions.

White Rock's marketing efforts have been successful in stimulating revenue growth. However, since the brand has matured (meaning that growth will likely be minimal), the company is adapting its strategy by introducing White Rock in new containers and sizes. For instance, it developed the White Rock Punch 'n' Fruity juice boxes, which are meant to appeal to on-the-go consumers and parents. Additionally, White Rock is breaking into the organic industry with its line of White Rock organics, made with cane sugar and natural fruit extracts.

White Rock is also pursuing an acquisition strategy of other brands. In addition to the White Rock brand, the company owns the Sioux City and Olde Brooklyn brands, brand names that seem connected to a bygone era. White Rock credits its nationally distributed Sioux City brand as one of the first brands of soft drinks to carry a Western theme. Olde Brooklyn's flavors are named after Brooklyn neighborhoods, a nostalgic appeal that connects with customers seeking brands with authenticity and history. Olde Brooklyn also lacks preservatives, which helps it appeal to the health-food market. By using brands such as Olde Brooklyn to gain entry into health-food stores like Trader Joe's, White Rock hopes to expand its market of distribution and secure more growth for the company.[18]

Questions for Discussion

1. How would you describe White Rock's strengths, weaknesses, opportunities, and threats?
2. What do you think White Rock should do to gain competitive advantage?
3. What elements of the marketing mix could White Rock change to improve its marketing strategy?

case 2.2

Ford's Hard-Driving Strategy for Competitive Advantage

Ford Motor Company's "One Ford" strategy has moved the company forward while the global economy pulls out of recession and competitors zig and zag. During the recent economic downturn, when car sales were in steep decline, both General Motors and Chrysler suffered such severe financial losses that they had to declare bankruptcy. Although Ford's sales also dropped, it gained status as the only major U.S. automaker to avoid bankruptcy. Meanwhile, Toyota was forced to recall millions of cars, and this also helped Ford's competitive situation.

"One Ford" reflects how the 110-year-old automotive company is using its engineering and manufacturing know-how, plus its in-depth market knowledge, to meet the needs of customers in markets worldwide. In the past, Ford (like its competitors) had a separate organization in each region to translate the needs of its local customers into vehicles that were suited to specific geographic areas. Now Ford is starting to steer away from that approach, choosing instead to apply its strengths to developing fuel-efficient, technology-packed vehicles with world-class design and engineering for a global marketplace. Simplifying the product line in this way will lead Ford to stronger, more profitable brands and products that appeal to broad market segments. Although advertising and other promotional efforts remain largely local, "One Ford" allows the company to spread development and production innovations through all markets much more quickly than when each region was in charge of its own design and engineering.

© AP Images/Reed Saxon

Ford's highly popular pickup trucks are still in the product line-up, but new models are being developed with multiple markets in mind. The Ford Focus, for instance, has styling flair that appeals to U.S. and European buyers as well as Chinese drivers. The basic body style remains the same in every market, with minor variations such as colors and interior materials tailored to local tastes. This affects the way Ford markets the brand in each market. Instead of a "one-size-fits-all effort," says Ford's head of product development, "the diversity of the marketing is created by the customers we want to reach, and not by the differences in the vehicles." The Ford Fiesta is another example. According to the CEO, this small, fuel-efficient car is to become "a world standard for car quality, design and comfort."

With models such as the Fusion, Ford targets particular customer segments and plans promotions that address those customers' interests and preferences. To market the Fusion to women, Ford sent the Fusion Studio on a road trip. This was a "pop-up store" that traveled to 10 malls across the United States where women could interact with the Fusion while they were being treated to beauty services, fitness training, and music. They were also given an opportunity to test-drive the car. The result: Fusion sales increased even as Ford's overall sales were struggling in the depth of the recession.

Ford is continually increasing its manufacturing capacities and refining its engineering as dealers in China and India are challenged to keep pace with higher demand from the growing middle class. For instance, the Ford Figo, a four-door subcompact hatchback sold in India, costs $7,700, and 10,000 orders were received in the first month of its launch. In one year, this tripled Ford's sales in India. "Indian customers want the best quality, high fuel efficiency, and safety at best value," explains

Ford's CEO. "These parameters have now become the pillars of design for the entire Ford family." In developing the Figo, Ford also learned how to handle the manufacturing demands of assembling vehicles with minor variations to fit specific customer orders. And many of Ford's India plants are highly automated, with the ability to produce any of six models at any one time, depending on demand.

As customers become more interested in environmentally-friendly vehicles, Ford has accelerated its marketing of innovative hybrid and electric cars such as the Fusion hybrid, Focus electric, and Explorer SUV hybrid. Nancy Gioia, Ford's Director of Sustainable Mobility, has been quoted as saying: "Electrification is not an option, it is the way forward." Japanese competitors have been very aggressive in this area, with Toyota's well-known Prius hybrid leading the way and Nissan's electric Leaf making inroads. General Motors is also moving into all-electric vehicles, with its Chevy Volt. All of this competition means Ford will have to carefully differentiate its green models from those made by U.S. and Japanese rivals, so that customers understand why they should drive a Ford.

Today, Ford continues to follow the "One Ford" strategy for higher market share in the global marketplace, with stronger brands that stretch across markets. Looking ahead, the Fiesta, Focus, Figo, and Fusion will be followed by newer models and new innovations, all bearing the familiar Ford logo in a blue oval, whether sold in India or Indiana. Just as important, Ford is on course for higher profitability in all regions, including recession-weary areas where sales are finally showing signs of turning around.[19]

Questions for Discussion

1. What is Ford's corporate strategy? Describe Ford's marketing strategies. How should Ford alter its corporate and marketing strategies?
2. What are Ford's core competencies, and how is the company using these in its "One Ford" program?
3. How can Ford use performance evaluation to stay on course toward the goals it seeks to achieve?

strategic case 1

Consumers Take a Shine to Apple Inc.

Few companies have fans who sleep outside their doors in order to be the first to snag their newest products. However, this is a common occurrence at Apple Inc. The new iPad (Apple's third generation of its iPad product) sold 3 million units four days after the launch. Headquartered in Cupertino, California, Apple went from near bankruptcy, with a 1997 share price of $3.30, to a brand valued at $153 billion and a share price of more than $600.

Apple first entered the public sphere in 1976 with the release of the computer Apple I, created by Apple co-founders Steve Jobs and Steve Wozniak. A few innovations later, the company had more than $1 million in sales. Yet Apple's luck did not last. Its downturn started during the 1980s with a series of product flops and resulted in near bankruptcy for the company. The return of Steve Jobs, who had been ousted in 1985 due to internal conflicts in the company, instituted major changes for Apple. The company successfully adopted a market orientation in which it was able to gather intelligence about customers' current and future needs—even before the customers themselves knew they needed it. For instance, the creation of the iPod and iTunes met customer needs for an efficient way to download a variety of music and listen to it on-the-go. While it was once unheard of to access the Internet from a cell phone, Apple's iPhone made it commonplace. Apple's investment in the iPad set off a massive surge in demand for tablet computers. Apple has become skilled at recognizing strategic windows of opportunity and acting upon them before the competition.

© Feng Li/Getty Images

Apple's Pricing and Promotion Strategies

In addition to its revolutionary products, Apple's success in pricing, promotion, and distribution have also contributed to its popularity. Apple products are traditionally priced high compared to competitors. For example, the new iPad retails for approximately $499 (although models with additional gigabytes are more expensive), while the Amazon Kindle Fire retails for $200. Apple's Mac computers are often more than $1,000. Yet rather than dissuading consumers from adopting the products, the high price point provides Apple with an image of prestige. Apple also stresses the convenience of its products as well as the revolutionary new capabilities they have to offer. Thus, it attempts to create value for customers, prompting them to pay more for Apple products than for those of its competitors.

Even with high-quality products, companies rarely achieve the success of Apple. Apple encourages demand for its products through several types of promotion, including word-of-mouth marketing. Early on, Apple supported "evangelism" of its products, even employing a chief evangelist to spread awareness about Apple and spur demand. Successful evangelists spread enthusiasm about a company among consumers, often through word-of-mouth marketing. These consumers in turn convince other people about the value of the product. Through product evangelism, Apple created a "Mac cult"—loyal customers eager to share their enthusiasm about the company with others.

Apple's Impact on Marketing

Apple's corporate culture of innovation and loyalty has created a company that massively impacts the marketing strategies of other industries. For some, this impact has been largely negative. Apple's iPhone increased competition in the cellular and smartphone industries, and its iPad competes with electronic readers like Amazon's Kindle. Apple has also taken market share away from competitors such as Research in Motion (RIM). Many RIM BlackBerry users are opting to exchange their BlackBerrys for iPads or Android devices. On the other hand, many companies are seizing upon the opportunity to learn from Apple. One industry in which Apple has made great changes is in retail.

Apple stores differentiate themselves significantly from other retailers; in fact, Apple took the concept of retail in an entirely new direction. Everything in the Apple store is carefully planned to align with the company's image, from the glass-and-steel design reminiscent of the company's technology to the stations where customers can try out Apple products. Apple stores are a place where customers can both shop and play. Customer service is also important to the Apple store image. Employees are expected to speak with customers within two minutes of them entering the store. Each employee has received extensive training and often receives greater compensation than those at other retail stores to encourage better customer service.

Apple executives constantly look for ways to improve stores, enhance customer service, and increase the time that customers spend in-store. In 2011 the company began to install iPad stations within its stores. The iPads feature a customer service app designed to answer customer questions. If the customer requires additional assistance, he or she can press a help button on the app. The app changes the customer service experience because rather than the customer seeking out the sales representative, the representative comes straight to the customer.

Due to the immense success of Apple stores, other companies are attempting to imitate its retail model. Microsoft and Sony opened some of their own stores, and others use Apple products to enhance their businesses. For instance, some pharmaceutical and car salespeople have adopted the iPad to aid in business transactions, and some restaurants even use the iPad to show menu items.

Apple Going Forward

The death of Steve Jobs concerned some people about the future of Apple. To many customers, Jobs appeared to be a savior who brought the company back from near bankruptcy and who was the driving force behind its innovative products. In the past, whenever rumors of Jobs's health reached the public, Apple's share prices dropped. However, the company remains optimistic. Although Apple must fill its leadership gap and continue innovating to deliver on its promises of quality, the loyalty that fans feel for Apple remains high.[20]

Questions for Discussion

1. How has Apple implemented the marketing concept?
2. Describe the role of Apple stores as an important part of its marketing strategy.
3. What will Apple need to do to maintain product innovation and customer loyalty?

ROLE-PLAY TEAM CASE EXERCISE 1

This role-play team case exercise is designed to simulate actual marketing decision making in the real world. The entire team should read the overview and background. Each student will take on a role of a particular employee within the organization. Your instructor will provide additional information and instructions related to a team decision.

BIRMINGHAM HILL CHEESE COMPANY*

Background

In 1999, Ted and Delilah Yancey founded the Birmingham Hill Cheese company in Boulder, Colorado. The Yanceys wanted to capture a unique market niche by selling a product that was artisan, or handmade. Their first product, Raven Eye Goat Cheese, was an immediate hit and won first prize at a national cheese competition. The company was following the marketing concept of satisfying its target market of customers who wanted high-quality artisan cheese products not available from larger companies.

An important part of the Birmingham Hill Cheese product is the process that Birmingham Hill employees take to ensure the product is of high quality. Birmingham Hill cheeses are mixed and sliced by hand and are inspected daily as a form of quality control. A new product is introduced every few months. This provides Birmingham Hill Cheese with a high-quality image and allows it to sell its products at a higher price than its rivals. The company's reputation and flavor for quality grew as it won award after award at national cheese festivals. Demand for its cheese products continued to rise, and soon Birmingham Hill cheeses were being sold in more than 150 Whole Foods stores. In order to meet this new demand, Birmingham Hill tripled the size of its facilities, hired more employees, and increased output. The company seemed to understand the marketing concept of satisfying customer desires for high-quality artisan cheese.

Despite the excitement the firm felt at its expansion, it was soon tempered by some disturbing news. A rival cheese maker in Wisconsin was coming out with a cheese identical to what Birmingham Hill was selling on the market. Birmingham Hill was certain that one of its former employees had divulged its top-secret recipe to its rival. Birmingham Hill knew it would have to vigorously defend its secrets and hired lawyer and business advisor John McDougall to provide advice on what to do next. This concerned Birmingham Hill because it was assumed that its recipe was unique and provided the firm with a distinct competitive advantage.

However, the theft of confidential information was not the only worry Birmingham Hill faced. Because the cheeses were handmade and required constant quality control, the Yanceys soon realized they could not meet the increase in demand at their current levels of production. The second part of the marketing concept of achieving company goals was not being met. With their funds strained from their rapid expansion, the Yanceys knew they would be unable to hire enough people to make up for the shortage. Delilah was constantly calling stores and telling them their shipments would be delayed. Distribution has to make the product available at the right time and in the right quantities.

Two weeks ago, Ted got a call from a Whole Foods representative. Despite the popularity of its cheeses, constant shortages kept the supermarket chain from making a sufficient return on investment. The representative informed Ted that, if the shortages continued, then Whole

---

 Jennifer Sawayda assisted with the development of this exercise under the direction of O.C. Ferrell and Linda Ferrell. This role-play case is not intended to represent the managerial decisions of an actual company.

Foods would eliminate the brand from their shelves. The main issue is availability. Ted and Delilah do not know how they can ramp up production with their current resources.

The two called an emergency meeting that includes Co-Owner Ted Yancey, responsible for distribution and pricing; Co-Owner Delilah Yancey, responsible for the product; Operations Manager Skylar Donaldson; Promotion Manager Ana Vigil; and John McDougall, the firm's lawyer and business advisor. The agenda for the meeting is to create a new marketing strategy and come up with a quick SWOT analysis to identify at least two strengths, opportunities, weaknesses, and threats. This will require the team to identify the firm's target market, marketing mix, core competencies, and ways to match its resources to market opportunities. They hope this course of action will help them discover solutions for how to deal with these problems.

Ted Yancey, Co-Owner

Although you are the co-owner of Birmingham Hill Cheese, the firm is so small that you have assumed the responsibilities of distribution and pricing. Under your and Delilah's leadership, Birmingham Hill Cheese has become nationally recognized for its high-quality, handmade cheese. Its reputation and specialty niche have allowed the company to successfully charge prices that are twice as high as cheeses from major corporations. You have enjoyed forming relationships with distributors and retailers, and your skills have gotten Birmingham Hill cheeses placed in some of the best locations on store shelves.

Until recently, you felt confident in your company's ability to overcome any challenge. For the first few years of the company's existence, you and Delilah had taken a conservative approach to your business operations. You both wanted to keep the business small and expand slowly. Yet, when Whole Foods took an interest in your product, both of you jumped at the chance to have it featured in an organization that you both admired.

The company had a solid marketing mix and a superior, unique product that appealed to the most avid cheese lovers. However, the past year has caused you many sleepless nights as you pondered how the two of you would be able to create enough product to meet demand. According to reports, the cheeses were barely placed on the shelf before they were snatched up by eager customers. While this was usually good news for a company, Birmingham Hill did not have the production capacity to fill all the new orders. Demand was going above and beyond the team's estimates. You and your team were working around the clock to fill orders and distribute them as quickly as possible, all while maintaining the high quality that had put its name on the map. You briefly considered outsourcing the product, but because Birmingham's cheeses are handmade, the idea was quickly discarded.

The recent call from a Whole Foods representative threatening to eliminate your brand if you could not meet demand worries you greatly. Losing this account could spell doom for the company, which is already in debt due to the recent expansion. You are also bothered by the fact that a former employee whom you had trusted sold one of your best secret recipes to a rival firm. You and Delilah are working with the company's legal and business advisor, John, to file a lawsuit. When filed, the lawsuit could take up to a year to resolve. You are hoping that this upcoming meeting will help shed some light on how to save the firm.

Delilah Yancey, Co-Owner

You have always been passionate about cheese. Before launching Birmingham Hill Cheese, you had traveled throughout Europe researching artisan cheeses to get ideas. You then got to work making your own cheeses and were rewarded for your efforts after your first cheese recipe, Raven's Eye Goat Cheese, won first prize at a national cheese competition. You are in charge of coming up with new product ideas. You also work very closely with Skylar to ensure that the cheeses are of the highest quality. You know the importance of making sure that your artisan cheeses live up to their reputation.

At first, you were skeptical about the Whole Foods account. You preferred selling your cheeses through smaller stores and specialty supermarkets. Even though Whole Foods was famous for its reputation as an ethical company, you thought that Birmingham Hill might lose its exclusive image. However, you also realized that the company would need to grab bigger accounts if it hoped to grow. You and Ted signed the contract with Whole Foods and approved the expansion of your facilities and production.

Almost from the beginning, however, the company encountered problems with meeting the increased production quotas. You constantly found yourself on the phone with Whole Foods stores telling them that their shipments would be delayed. Less of a people person than Ted, you would have much rather spent your time thinking up new cheese recipes and working with the operations manager to ensure the quality of the product. However, Ted's distribution responsibilities meant the hard task of negotiating with the stores fell to you.

Recently, Whole Foods threatened to drop the brand if the company continued to delay its shipments. However, you are more upset about the news that a previous employee divulged one of your top-secret recipes to a competitor in Wisconsin. The recipe, a type of organic blue cheese, had taken you months to perfect and is one of the company's best sellers. You are furious and want to sue the competing company and the former employee for all they're worth. You are less concerned with the threat by Whole Foods, since you believe that, even if the supermarket chain drops your brand, the popularity of your products will help you survive. On the other hand, Ted's anxiety has made you begin to question this assumption. Although you have little knowledge about the financial aspects of the company, you know that the latest expansion has put the company in debt. You wonder if your brand is strong enough to get the two of you through this crisis.

Skylar Donaldson, Operations Manager

You have been with Birmingham Hill Cheese almost since the beginning. A graduate from Colorado State University, you impressed the Yanceys with your hard work and dedication to the company. In turn, you loved the idea of creating a niche product that met the highest in quality standards. You are extremely devoted to the company and will go to great lengths to help it survive. In fact, you feel that this product has the potential to become a highly successful national brand.

You were also initially excited when you heard about the Whole Foods offer. You felt that Birmingham Hill had a major opportunity for market growth and that the national retailer could help the small firm grab market share from your prime competitors—particularly from a Wisconsin cheese maker that had been causing you trouble recently. However, the moment you looked at the Yanceys' expansion plans, your enthusiasm began to waver. Even with the hiring of more people, you had doubts about whether the company could maintain its high standards of quality. Birmingham Hill was known for inspecting its handmade cheeses daily. With Birmingham Hill's current output, the care that it took for its products was possible. But you recognized that, the greater the output, the more likely the possibility was that there would be slip-ups. The thought unnerved you, whose dedication to quality was almost an obsession. But you swallowed your anxiety and went along with the Yanceys' decision.

You now regret your decision not to speak up. The past few months have seen you working around the clock to produce more cheeses, inspecting more cheeses, and helping Ted ship more cheeses. Your lack of sleep has made you irritable, and you feel that it is only a matter of time before you make a mistake. You have heard about the recent theft of trade secrets by the rival firm in Wisconsin, but, at the moment, you think there are more pressing matters to pursue.

The recent news that Whole Foods might drop the brand has brought you to the limits of your patience. Although you want the company to succeed, you feel that it will be impossible if Birmingham Hill does not do something quickly.

Ana Vigil, Promotion Manager

You are Delilah's cousin and were hired by the Yanceys after they realized that the promotion variable of the marketing mix was too much for either to handle on their own. At the time, Birmingham Hill had only gained a very small following of fans. But through the years, Birmingham Hill cheeses gained in popularity, and you proved more and more valuable to the company. You appear to have a knack for identifying new market opportunities and coming up with promotional campaigns that attract cheese lovers to Birmingham's products.

As promotion manager, you are in charge of planning, organizing, implementing, and controlling the marketing of the Birmingham Hill brand to both retailers and consumers. You heavily promoted the fact that Birmingham Hill's artisan cheeses are handmade and inspected daily. It was your idea to label each package with the phrase "Ensuring the highest in quality and flavor," which was a hit among consumers as sales shot up afterward. You also recognized the opportunities of green marketing and heavily promoted Birmingham Hill's line of organic cheeses. As a result, its organic blue cheese has become a best seller.

You mainly focus on small retailers and large farmers' markets. Birmingham Hill Cheese is unique in that it does not use any media advertising but instead relies on word-of-mouth and digital marketing to promote the brand. You have become adept at reaching consumers through Twitter, Facebook, and the company's corporate blog. A good chunk of every day is spent communicating with small retailers and fans answering questions and providing updates about company activities. Because the company maintains a strong presence at local events and national contests, you love to use Twitter to inform fans about where they can find Birmingham Hill at particular events.

For years, you have been encouraging the Yanceys to look beyond their select line of specialty stores and pursue bigger accounts. You were happy when the Yanceys finally signed a deal with Whole Foods, and you prepared a large marketing campaign to announce the launch of the brand in Whole Foods stores. Although you knew that Birmingham Hill was having trouble keeping up with production, you were too busy trying to locate new accounts and promote the Birmingham Hill brand to worry too much about it. Then, a few months ago, you learned that a former employee had sold Birmingham's secret organic blue cheese recipe to your Wisconsin competitor. You knew the company had to protect its trade secrets and have offered to help the firm's lawyer and business advisor John McDougall by providing him with any marketing information he needs to make a case against them.

More trouble hit when it was announced that Whole Foods might eliminate the brand from their stores. You were shocked. You had no idea that production had fallen so far behind. You knew enough about the company's current situation to realize that, if Whole Foods pulled the brand, then the other larger accounts you were currently negotiating would fall through. Without an account with a large company, you know the company will be in trouble. As a single mother raising two children, you can ill afford to lose your job at this time.

John McDougall, Lawyer and Business Advisor

You graduated with a Bachelor's in Business Administration from Washington State and then went on to receive your law degree from Harvard. You have always loved the mountains and decided to move to Colorado to set up your own practice. Shortly after the move, you became friends with a young Ted Yancey. You were the first person Ted and Delilah came to with their idea to start an artisan cheese company. At first, you were skeptical about the idea, but after seeing their detailed business plan, you became convinced that such a firm could meet a market need. In fact, no one outside Birmingham Hill Cheese Company was more excited to see the firm succeed than you.

When you first heard about the deal with Whole Foods, and Birmingham Hill's subsequent expansion, you were uncertain about whether Birmingham Hill could handle the sudden increase in the firm's workload that would accompany such a deal. Now in your 50s, you have since moved away from Boulder and settled in Colorado Springs with your wife and two teenage sons, so you were unavailable to provide Ted with advice concerning the deal and did not know the preliminaries. You knew that a lot of good companies had overextended themselves by expanding too rapidly and hoped this would not happen to Birmingham Hill Cheese.

A few months ago, you received a call from Ted wanting to hire you to handle a dispute concerning the theft of confidential information by a rival firm. Semi-retired, you agreed to take the job on account of your long-standing friendship. After spending weeks looking at the evidence, you thought that Birmingham Hill Cheese had a compelling case. You warned Ted, however, that litigation might take as much as a year. If Birmingham Hill Cheese wins, they could receive a hefty settlement. On the other hand, if it loses, then Birmingham Hill would have the responsibility of paying all the legal fees itself, which would be hefty.

While working with Birmingham Hill to create a case, you were dismayed that your fears had proven true. It appeared that Birmingham Hill had overextended itself, first with the Whole Foods deal, and then with the wide-scale expansion. A few days ago, Ted called you in a panic. He told you that, because Birmingham Hill was not shipping products to Whole Foods stores quickly enough, the chain was threatening to eliminate the brand. You know the loss of this key account, coupled with the debt incurred from the recent expansion, could ruin the small company. You have agreed to attend a meeting with Delilah, Ted, and a small team of supervisors to provide advice on some of their options.

NOTES

[1]Linda Zavoral, "A La Carte: The Melt Oozes into Palo Alto," *San Jose Mercury News,* January 4, 2012, www.mercurynews.com; Sarah Duxbury, "Grilled Cheese Happiness for Melt Founder," *San Francisco Business Times,* November 3, 2011, www.bizjournals.com; Mark Milian, "Tech's Next Industry Trend: Grilled Cheese?" *CNN,* August 31, 2011, www.cnn.com; Brad Stone, "Comfort Food? There's an App for That," *Bloomberg BusinessWeek,* June 1, 2011, www.businessweek.com.

[2]O. C. Ferrell and Michael Hartline, *Marketing Strategy,* 5th ed. (Mason, OH: South-Western, 2011), 10.

[3]Christian Homburg, Karley Krohmer, and John P. Workman Jr., "A Strategy Implementation Perspective of Market Orientation," *Journal of Business Research* 57 (2004): 1331–1340.

[4]"Fortune 500 Mission Statements," www.missionstatements.com/fortune_500_mission_statements.html (accessed February 17, 2012).

[5]Ben & Jerry's Mission, www.benjerry.com/activism/mission-statement/ (accessed January 16, 2012).

[6]Tiffany Kary, "Borders to Sell Intellectual Property to Barnes & Noble," *BusinessWeek,* September 26, 2011, www.businessweek.com/news/2011-09-26/borders-to-sell-intellectual-property-to-barnes-noble.html.

[7]Stanley F. Slater, G. Tomas M. Hult, and Eric M. Olson, "On the Importance of Matching Strategic Behavior and Target Market Selection to Business Strategy in High-Tech Markets," *Journal of the Academy of Marketing Science* 35 (2007): 5–17.

[8]Sherilynn Macale, "Apple Has Sold 300M iPods, Currently Holds 78% of the Music Player Market," The Next Web, October 4, 2011, http://thenextweb.com/apple/2011/10/04/apple-has-sold-300m-ipods-currently-holds-78-of-the-music-player-market/.

[9]Robert D. Buzzell, "The PIMS Program of Strategy Research: A Retrospective Appraisal," *Journal of Business Research* 57 (2004): 478–483.

[10]Stuart Elliot, "Brita Puts its Brand in the Spotlight on a Univision Reality Show," *The New York Times,* January 9, 2012, www.time.com/time/specials/packages/article/0,28804,1877020_1877030_1990673,00.html.

[11]Derek F. Abell, "Strategic Windows," *Journal of Marketing* (July 1978): 21.

[12]"About Fresh and Easy Neighborhood Market," www.freshandeasy.com/Content/pdfs/FreshEasyFactSheet.pdf (accessed March 15, 2010).

[13]Nick Bilton, "Netflix Hops the Pond and Offers Video Streaming in Britain," *The New York Times,* January 9, 2012, http://bits.blogs.nytimes.com/2012/01/09/netflix-hops-the-pond-offers-video-streaming-in-u-k/?scp=3&sq=netflix&st=Search.

[14]Spencer E. Ante and Shayndi Raice, "AT&T Preps iPhone Plan," *The Wall Street Journal*, January 11, 2011, http://online.wsj.com/article/SB10001424052748704458204576074301611973530.html.

[15]Amazon.com 2011 Annual Report, page 37, accessed via http://phx.corporate-ir.net/phoenix.zhtml?c=97664&p=irol-reportsannual (accessed March 20, 2012).

[16]"Ford's Total Sales Rise in Europe in 2011 Despite Economic Headwinds," Ford Motor Company, Press Release, January 13, 2012, http://media.ford.com/article_display.cfm?article_id=35848&utm_source=dlvr.it&utm_medium=twitter.

[17]"Southwest Airlines Co.," www.hoovers.com/company/Southwest_Airlines_Co/rrykki-1.html (accessed January 4, 2012); Scott McCartney, "The Gap Between Airlines is Shrinking," *The Wall Street Journal*, February 17, 2011, http://blogs.wsj.com/middleseat/2011/02/17/the-gap-between-airlines-is-shrinking/.

[18]Joel Rose, "White Rock Beverages Still Thirsty After 140 Years," NPR, December 5, 2011, www.npr.org; "After 140 Years, White Rock Still Solid," BevNet, July 6, 2011, BevNET.com; White Rock, www.whiterockbeverages.com; "Creative Beverage Merchandising," Creative Beverage, April/May 2005, www.creativemag.com; PR Newswire, "Coca-Cola's Santa Claus: Not the Real Thing!" PR News Online, December 15, 2006, www.prnewsonline.com.

[19]N. Madhavan, "In Driver's Seat," Business Today (India), March 18, 2012, http:// http://businesstoday.intoday.in/story/ford-india-transformation/1/22688.html; Bill Vlasic, "Ford's Bet: It's a Small World After All," *The New York Times,* January 10, 2010, www.nytimes.com; D. Goldman, "Battered Auto Sales Show Improvement," CNN Money, June 2, 2009, http://money.cnn.com; S. Arvizu, "Electric Cars for the Masses," Triple Pundit, April 2009, www.triplepundit.com; David Kiley, "One World, One Car, One Name," *BusinessWeek,* March 13, 2008, www.businessweek.com; Mike Thomas, "Fiesta Is New Ford Small Car," Ford, February 15, 2008, www.ford.com/about-ford/news-announcements/featured-stories/featured-

stories-detail/ford-fiesta-geneva; Keith Bradsher and Vikas Baja, "Ford Shifts and Gains Ground in Asia," *The New York Times,* March 31, 2010, www.nytimes.com.

[20]"Apple Chronology," CNN Money, January 6, 1998, http://money.cnn.com/1998/01/06/technology/apple_chrono/ (accessed June 6, 2011); Amanda Cantrell, "Apple's Remarkable Comeback Story," CNN Money, March 29, 2006, http://money.cnn.com/2006/03/29/technology/apple_anniversary/?cnn=ye (accessed June 6, 2011); Scott Martin, "How Apple Rewrote the Rules of Retailing," *USA Today*, May 19, 2011, 1B; Millward Brown Optimor, *BrandZ Top 100 2011*, www.millwardbrown.com/libraries/optimor_brandz_files/2011_brandz_top100_chart.sflb.ashx (accessed June 6, 2011); "World's Most Admired Companies: Apple," CNN Money, http://money.cnn.com/magazines/fortune/mostadmired/2011/snapshots/670.html (accessed June 6, 2011); Alan Deutschman, "The Once and Future Steve Jobs," *Salon,* October 11, 2000, www.salon.com/technology/books/2000/10/11/jobs_excerpt/ (accessed June 6, 2011); Martyn Williams, "Timeline: iTunes Store at 10 Billion," *ComputerWorld,* February 24, 2010, www.computerworld.com/s/article/9162018/Timeline_iTunes_Store_at_10_billion (accessed June 6, 2011); "Former Apple Evangelist on Company's History," CNET News, March 29, 2006, http://news.cnet.com/1606-2_3-6055676.html (accessed June 6, 2011); Nilofer Merchant, "Apple's Startup Culture," *Bloomberg BusinessWeek,* June 24, 2010, www.businessweek.com/innovate/content/jun2010/id20100610_525759.htm (accessed June 6, 2011); "The Evangelist's Evangelist," Creating Customer Evangelists, www.creatingcustomerevangelists.com/resources/evangelists/guy_kawasaki.asp (accessed June 6, 2011); Jefferson Graham, "At Apple Stores, iPads at Your Service," *USA Today*, May 23, 2011, 1B; "Apple Boss Steve Jobs Takes 'Medical Leave'," BBC News, January 17, 2011, www.bbc.co.uk/news/technology-12205173 (accessed June 6, 2011); Jefferson Graham, "At Apple Stores, iPads at Your Service," *USA Today*, May 23, 2011, 1B; Rob Waugh, "Hit New iPad Sells Three Million in Just Four Days Since Launch—Apple's First Tablet Took 80 Days to Hit Same Figure," *Daily Mail,* March 20, 2012, www.dailymail.co.uk/sciencetech/article-2117581/New-iPad-sells-million-days-launch--figure-iPad-took-80-days-reach.html (accessed March 21, 2012); "Apple, Inc. (APPL)," *YAHOO! Finance,* http://finance.yahoo.com/q?s=AAPL (accessed March 21, 2012); Peter Svensson, "Review: New iPad Screen Is Eye-Opening Upgrade," *Denver Post,* March 21, 2012, www.denverpost.com/technology/ci_20223806/review-new-ipad-screen-is-eye-opening-upgrade (accessed March 21, 2012); "BlackBerry Market Share Slides Again Amid Takeover Talk," *The Telegraph,* January 1, 2012, www.telegraph.co.uk/technology/blackberry/8985101/BlackBerry-market-share-slides-again-amid-takeover-talk.html (accessed March 21, 2012).

Feature Notes

[a]Based on information in Michelle Ertel, "Forecast Sunny for Seminole," *Seminole Voice* (Florida), January 4, 2012, www.seminolevoice.com; Leanne Hoagland-Smith, "Why Most Mission Statements Fail to Deliver the Desired Results," Sun-Times Media (Chicago), December 19, 2011, http://posttrib.suntimes.com; Marla Tabaka, "Crucial Keys to Business Success in 2012, *Inc.,* December 29, 2011, www.inc.com; Mitchell Harper, "Eight Rules for a Kick-Ass Company Culture," Sydney Morning Herald, December 29, 2011, www.smh.com.au.

[b]Based on information in Todd Woody, "GE's New Ecomagination Chief: Green Tech Innovation Goes Global," *Forbes,* May 3, 2011, www.forbes.com; Kate Maddox, "'B to B' Names GE's Boff Digital Marketer of the Year," BtoB, October 3, 2011, 3; "GE's Ecomagination Challenge Phase Two to Focus on Eco-Home Technology," TechCrunch, January 7, 2011, www.techcrunch.com; Kerry A. Dolan, "Yves Behar's Latest Design: GE's WattStation," *Forbes,* July 13, 2010, www.forbes.com; www.ecomagination.com.

[c]Based on information in Dhanya Skariachan and Phil Wahba, "Home Depot, Walmart, Grocers Get Boost from Irene," Reuters, August 26, 2011, www.reuters.com; John Hamilton, "Big-Box Stores' Hurricane Prep Starts Early," NPR, August 26, 2011, www.npr.org; J. Cashman, "Generators, Batteries Big Sellers Ahead of Irene," *New England Post,* August 27, 2011, www.newenglandpost.com; "Snow Disrupts Package Pickup, Delivery in Oklahoma," *Oklahoman,* February 2, 2011, http://newsok.com; Arielle Kass, "George Companies Prepared for Hurricane Well in Advance," *Atlanta Journal Constitution,* August 26, 2011, www.ajc.com/business.

[d]Based on information in Brian Hickey, "Lincoln Coffee Company Unveils Single-Serve Coffee," KCRA (Sacramento), October 25, 2011, www.kcra.com; Kathie Canning, "Consider the Source," Progressive Grocer's Store Brands, January 1, 2011, www.progressivegrocer.com; "Rogers Family Company Rolls Out Single Serve Coffee Product," Food & Beverage Close-Up, October 27, 2011, n.p.

Environmental Forces and Social and Ethical Responsibilities

part 2

PART 2 deals with the marketing environment, social responsibility, and marketing ethics. CHAPTER 3 examines competitive, economic, political, legal and regulatory, technological, and sociocultural forces in the marketing environment, which can have profound effects on marketing strategies. CHAPTER 4 explores the role of social responsibility and ethical issues in marketing decisions.

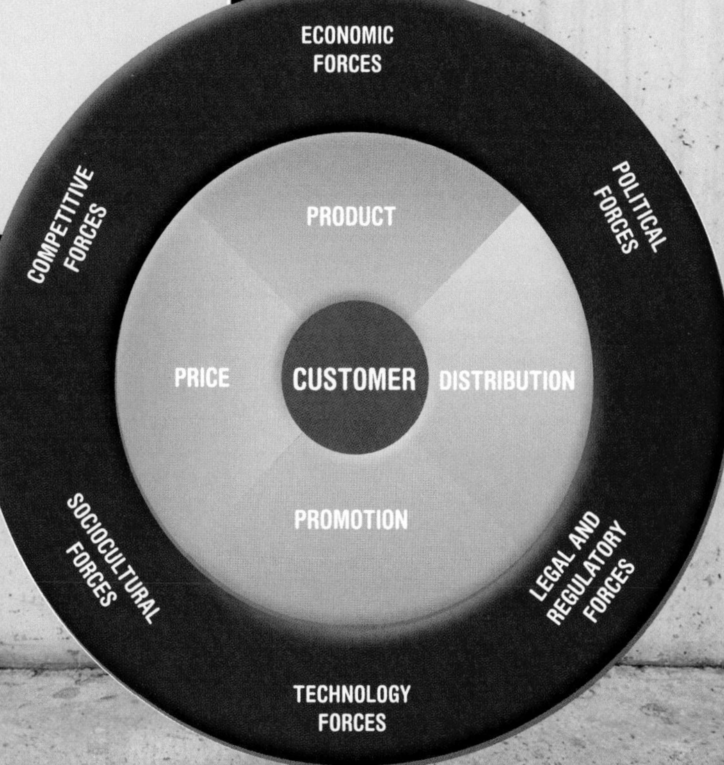

chapter 3

The Marketing Environment

OBJECTIVES

1. To recognize the importance of environmental scanning and analysis
2. To understand how competitive and economic factors affect an organization's ability to compete and a customer's ability and willingness to buy products
3. To identify the types of political forces in the marketing environment
4. To understand how laws, government regulations, and self-regulatory agencies affect marketing activities
5. To explore the effects of new technology on society and on marketing activities
6. To analyze sociocultural issues marketers must deal with as they make decisions

MARKETING INSIGHTS

Lululemon Takes Advantage of the Yoga Craze

Lululemon has turned fashionable yoga gear into a lifestyle. The retailer has revolutionized women's athletic apparel by combining its unique philosophy with its premium products and customer service. Lululemon's clothes are designed to make women feel and look good. The company's stretching and wicking fabrics keep athletes warm and dry while allowing for better movement, and unlike many athletic brands, Lululemon offers specific numbered sizes instead of small, medium, and large. Other Lululemon products include bags, yoga mats, and athletic equipment.

The company's products appeal to women who want yoga to be a social experience. Lululemon locations offer free yoga classes, workshops, and community events in their showrooms. In addition, Lululemon's grassroots marketing strategy features "ambassadors" who embody the company's lifestyle. The stores and ambassadors work hard to emphasize Lululemon's values of quality, product, integrity, balance, entrepreneurship, and fun.

This combination of workout clothing and lifestyle is powerful. Lululemon grew 52 percent over just four years and has annual sales of over $712 million. However, the company's sales are starting to slow as competition increases. Other retailers have noticed the company's success, and Nike, Gap, and Nordstrom each have their own lines of high-end athletic gear that are priced slightly lower. Because the last recession negatively impacted discretionary income, consumers may no longer be willing to pay $98 for a pair of yoga pants. Despite these challenges, Lululemon remains committed to promoting a fun and healthy lifestyle among its customers.[1]

Companies like Lululemon are modifying marketing strategies in response to changes in the marketing environment. Because recognizing and addressing such changes in the marketing environment are crucial to marketing success, we will focus in detail on the forces that contribute to these changes.

This chapter explores the competitive, economic, political, legal and regulatory, technological, and sociocultural forces that constitute the marketing environment. First, we define the marketing environment and consider why it is critical to scan and analyze it. Next, we discuss the effects of competitive forces and explore the influence of general economic conditions: prosperity, recession, depression, and recovery. We also examine buying power and look at the forces that influence consumers' willingness to spend. We then discuss the political forces that generate government actions that affect marketing activities and examine the effects of laws and regulatory agencies on these activities. After analyzing the major dimensions of the technological forces in the environment, we consider the impact of sociocultural forces on marketing efforts.

EXAMINING AND RESPONDING TO THE MARKETING ENVIRONMENT

The marketing environment consists of external forces that directly or indirectly influence an organization's acquisition of inputs (human, financial, natural resources and raw materials, and information) and creation of outputs (goods, services, or ideas). As we saw in Chapter 1, the marketing environment includes six such forces: competitive, economic, political, legal and regulatory, technological, and sociocultural.

Whether fluctuating rapidly or slowly, environmental forces are always dynamic. Changes in the marketing environment create uncertainty, threats, and opportunities for marketers. Firms providing digital products such as software, music, and movies face many environmental threats as well as opportunities. Advancing technology provides digital delivery of these products, which is an efficient and effective way to reach global markets. On the other hand, sites such as Pirate Bay allow peer-to-peer transfers and are referred to as file-sharing sites or cyberlockers. These sites can operate in countries such as Russia, where intellectual property rights are weak. The movie and music industries want more effective legislation in place to crack down on the theft of their products. Most of these developments involve trying to influence controls to stop this threat.[2] The marketing environment constantly fluctuates, requiring marketers to monitor it regularly.

Although the future is sometimes hard to predict, marketers try to forecast what may happen. We can say with certainty that marketers continue to modify their marketing strategies and plans in response to dynamic environmental forces. Consider how technological changes have affected the products offered by the mobile phone industry and how the public's growing concern with health and fitness has influenced the products of clothing, food, exercise equipment, and health-care companies. Marketing managers who fail to recognize changes in environmental forces leave their firms unprepared to capitalize on marketing opportunities or to cope with threats created by those changes. Consider Kodak's failure to make the switch from film development to digital photos. The firm filed for bankruptcy in 2012. Monitoring the environment is crucial to an organization's survival and to the long-term achievement of its goals.

Environmental Scanning and Analysis

environmental scanning The process of collecting information about forces in the marketing environment

To monitor changes in the marketing environment effectively, marketers engage in environmental scanning and analysis. **Environmental scanning** is the process of collecting information about forces in the marketing environment. Scanning involves observation;

secondary sources such as business, trade, government, and general-interest publications; and marketing research. The Internet has become a popular scanning tool because it makes data more accessible and allows companies to gather needed information quickly. Environmental scanning gives companies an edge over competitors in allowing them to take advantage of current trends. However, simply gathering information about competitors and customers is not enough; companies must know *how* to use that information in the strategic planning process. Managers must be careful not to gather so much information that sheer volume makes analysis impossible.

Environmental analysis is the process of assessing and interpreting the information gathered through environmental scanning. A manager evaluates the information for accuracy, tries to resolve inconsistencies in the data, and, if warranted, assigns significance to the findings. Evaluating this information should enable the manager to identify potential threats and opportunities linked to environmental changes. Understanding the current state of the marketing environment and recognizing threats and opportunities that might arise from changes within it help companies in their strategic planning. A threat could be rising interest rates or commodity prices. An opportunity could be increases in consumer income, decreases in the unemployment rate, or adoption of new technology. In particular, environmental analysis can help marketing managers assess the performance of current marketing efforts and develop future marketing strategies.

Responding to Environmental Forces

Marketing managers take two general approaches to environmental forces: accepting them as uncontrollable or attempting to influence and shape them. An organization that views environmental forces as uncontrollable remains passive and reactive toward the environment. Instead of trying to influence forces in the environment, its marketing managers adjust current marketing strategies to environmental changes. They approach with caution market opportunities discovered through environmental scanning and analysis. On the other hand, marketing managers who believe environmental forces can be shaped adopt a more proactive approach. For example, if a market is blocked by traditional environmental constraints, proactive marketing managers may apply economic, psychological, political, and promotional skills to gain access to and operate within it. Once they identify what is constraining a market opportunity, they assess the power of the various parties involved and develop strategies to overcome the obstructing environmental forces. Microsoft, Intel, and Google, for example, have responded to political, legal, and regulatory concerns about their power in the computer industry by communicating the value of their competitive approaches to various publics. The computer giants contend that their competitive success results in superior products for their customers.

environmental analysis The process of assessing and interpreting the information gathered through environmental scanning

Responding to the Marketing Environment
The sponsors of this ad are trying to educate drivers about the dangers associated with texting and driving.

A proactive approach can be constructive and bring desired results. To influence environmental forces, marketing managers seek to identify market opportunities or to extract greater benefits relative to costs from existing market opportunities. Consider a firm that is losing sales to competitors with lower-priced products. If this firm develops a technology that makes its production processes more efficient, it will be able to lower the prices of its own products. Political action is another way to affect environmental forces. The pharmaceutical industry, for example, has lobbied very effectively for fewer restrictions on prescription drug marketing. However, managers must recognize that there are limits to the degree that environmental forces can be shaped. Although an organization may be able to influence legislation through lobbying—as the movie and music industries are doing to try and stop the piracy of their products—it is unlikely that a single organization can significantly change major economic factors such as recessions, interest rates, or commodity prices.

Whether to take a reactive or a proactive approach to environmental forces is a decision for a firm to make based on its strengths or weaknesses. For some organizations the passive, reactive approach is more appropriate, but for others the aggressive approach leads to better performance. Selection of a particular approach depends on an organization's managerial philosophies, objectives, financial resources, customers, and human resources skills, as well as on the environment within which the organization operates. Both organizational factors and managers' personal characteristics affect the variety of responses to changing environmental conditions. Microsoft, for example, can take a proactive approach because of its financial resources and the highly visible image of its founder, Bill Gates. However, Microsoft has also been the target of various lawsuits regarding anticompetitive practices, demonstrating that even Microsoft is limited in how far it can influence the business environment.

In the remainder of this chapter, we explore in greater detail the six environmental forces—competitive, economic, political, legal and regulatory, technological, and sociocultural—that interact to create opportunities and threats that must be considered in strategic planning.

COMPETITIVE FORCES

Few firms, if any, operate free of competition. In fact, for most goods and services, customers have many alternatives from which to choose. For example, although the five best-selling soft drinks in the United States are Coke, Diet Coke, Pepsi-Cola, Mountain Dew, and Dr Pepper, soft-drink sales in general have flattened as consumers have turned to alternatives such as bottled water, flavored water, fruit juice, and iced tea products.[3] Thus, when marketing managers define the target market(s) their firm will serve, they simultaneously establish a set of competitors.[4] In addition, marketing managers must consider the type of competitive structure in which the firm operates. In this section, we examine types of competition and competitive structures, as well as the importance of monitoring competitors' actions.

competition Other organizations that market products that are similar to or can be substituted for a marketer's products in the same geographic area

brand competitors Firms that market products with similar features and benefits to the same customers at similar prices

product competitors Firms that compete in the same product class but market products with different features, benefits, and prices

generic competitors Firms that provide very different products that solve the same problem or satisfy the same basic customer need

Types of Competitors

Broadly speaking, all firms compete with one another for customers' dollars. More practically, however, a marketer generally defines **competition** as other firms that market products that are similar to or can be substituted for its products in the same geographic area. These competitors can be classified into one of four types. **Brand competitors** market products with similar features and benefits to the same customers at similar prices. For instance, a thirsty, calorie-conscious customer may choose a diet soda such as Diet Coke or Diet Pepsi from the soda machine. However, these sodas face competition from other types of beverages. **Product competitors** compete in the same product class but market products with different features, benefits, and prices. The thirsty dieter, for instance, might purchase iced tea, juice, a sports beverage, or bottled water instead of a soda.

Generic competitors provide very different products that solve the same problem or satisfy the same basic customer need. Our dieter, for example, might simply have a glass of

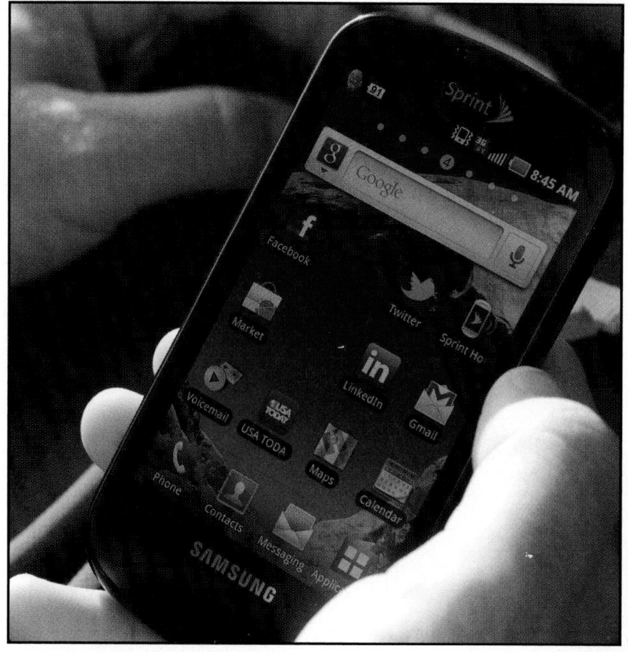

Product Competition
Apple and Samsung compete directly with one another and closely monitor new product developments.

water from the kitchen tap to satisfy her thirst. **Total budget competitors** compete for the limited financial resources of the same customers.[5] Total budget competitors for Diet Coke, for example, might include gum, a newspaper, and bananas. Although all four types of competition can affect a firm's marketing performance, brand competitors are the most significant because buyers typically see the different products of these firms as direct substitutes for one another. Consequently, marketers tend to concentrate environmental analyses on brand competitors.

total budget competitors Firms that compete for the limited financial resources of the same customers

Entrepreneurship in Marketing

Crepes in the Fast Lane

Entrepreneur: Matt Chatham
Business: SkyCrepers
Founded: 2011 | North Attleboro, Massachusetts
Success: Chatham's business concept for SkyCrepers won the 2011 business-plan competition at Babson College and provided him with $60,000 in funding and services to launch his restaurant.

What do crepes and linebackers have in common? For former Patriots football linebacker Matt Chatham, crepes are his new business. Chatham entered the MBA program at Babson College, where he launched his concept for a fast-food crepe shop as part of the school's business plan competition. Chatham's mission is to eliminate the fancy French perception of crepes and create bigger, bolder, more Americanized versions. Chatham won the competition and received funding to launch SkyCrepers, a fast-food shop offering crepes and 25 types of gourmet coffee, along with other food choices.

In addition to challenging his brand competitors, Chatham also wants to take on his product competitors by placing his crepe shops in mall food courts. In August 2011 he opened his first shop in the Emerald Square Mall in North Attleboro, Massachusetts, with several of his former Patriot team members in attendance. Although still a start-up, Chatham has big plans for SkyCrepers. He plans to see several shops throughout New England and plans to eventually become "the #1 mall snack provider in the U.S."[a]

Types of Competitive Structures
The cruise ship industry is an example of an oligopoly.

Types of Competitive Structures

The number of firms that supply a product may affect the strength of competitors. When just one or a few firms control supply, competitive factors exert a different form of influence on marketing activities than when many competitors exist. Table 3.1 presents four general types of competitive structures: monopoly, oligopoly, monopolistic competition, and pure competition.

A **monopoly** exists when an organization offers a product that has no close substitutes, making that organization the sole source of supply. Because the organization has no competitors, it controls the supply of the product completely and, as a single seller, can erect barriers to potential competitors. In reality, most monopolies surviving today are local utilities, which are heavily regulated by local, state, or federal agencies. These monopolies are tolerated because of the tremendous financial resources needed to develop and operate them. For example, few organizations can obtain the financial or political resources to mount any competition against a local water supplier. On the other hand, competition is increasing in the electric and cable television industries.

An **oligopoly** exists when a few sellers control the supply of a large proportion of a product. In this case, each seller considers the reactions of other sellers to changes in marketing activities. Products facing oligopolistic competition may be homogeneous, such as aluminum, or differentiated, such as packaged delivery services. Usually barriers of some sort make it difficult to enter the market and compete with oligopolies. For example, because of the enormous financial outlay required, few companies or individuals could afford to enter the oil-refining or steel-producing industry. Moreover, some industries demand special technical or marketing skills, a qualification that deters the entry of many potential competitors.

Monopolistic competition exists when a firm with many potential competitors attempts to develop a marketing strategy to differentiate its product. For example, Wrangler and Seven 4 All Mankind have established an advantage for their blue jeans through well-known trademarks, designs, advertising, and a reputation for quality. Wrangler is associated with a cowboy image, while Seven 4 All Mankind tries to maintain a premium designer image. Although many competing brands of blue jeans are available, this firm has carved out a market niche by emphasizing differences in its products.

Pure competition, if it existed at all, would entail an extremely large number of sellers, none of which could significantly influence price or supply. Products would be homogeneous,

monopoly A competitive structure in which an organization offers a product that has no close substitutes, making that organization the sole source of supply

oligopoly A competitive structure in which a few sellers control the supply of a large proportion of a product

monopolistic competition A competitive structure in which a firm has many potential competitors and tries to develop a marketing strategy to differentiate its product

pure competition A market structure characterized by an extremely large number of sellers, none strong enough to significantly influence price or supply

Table 3.1 Selected Characteristics of Competitive Structures

Type of Structure	Number of Competitors	Ease of Entry into Market	Product	Examples
Monopoly	One	Many barriers	Almost no substitutes	Water utilities
Oligopoly	Few	Some barriers	Homogeneous or differentiated (with real or perceived differences)	UPS, FedEx, Postal Service (package delivery)
Monopolistic competition	Many	Few barriers	Product differentiation, with many substitutes	Wrangler, Levi Strauss (jeans)
Pure competition	Unlimited	No barriers	Homogeneous products	Agricultural corn market

and entry into the market would be easy. The closest thing to an example of pure competition is an unregulated farmers' market, where local growers gather to sell their produce. Commodities such as soybeans, corn, and wheat have their markets subsidized or regulated by the government.

Pure competition is an ideal at one end of the continuum, and a monopoly is at the other end. Most marketers function in a competitive environment somewhere between these two extremes.

Monitoring Competition

Marketers need to monitor the actions of major competitors to determine what specific strategies competitors are using and how those strategies affect their own. Competitive intensity influences a firm's strategic approach to markets.[6] Price is one marketing strategy variable that most competitors monitor. When Delta or Southwest Airlines lowers its fare on a route, most major airlines attempt to match the price. Monitoring guides marketers in developing competitive advantages and in adjusting current marketing strategies and planning new ones. When an airline such as Southwest acquires a competitor such as AirTran, then there is the potential for less competition.

In monitoring competition, it is not enough to analyze available information; the firm must develop a system for gathering ongoing information about competitors and potential competitors. Information about competitors allows marketing managers to assess the performance of their own marketing efforts and to recognize the strengths and weaknesses in their own marketing strategies. In addition, organizations are rewarded for taking risks and dealing with the uncertainty created by inadequate information.[7] Data about market shares, product movement, sales volume, and expenditure levels can be useful. However, accurate information on these matters is often difficult to obtain.

ECONOMIC FORCES

Economic forces in the marketing environment influence both marketers' and customers' decisions and activities. In this section, we examine the effects of general economic conditions as well as buying power and the factors that affect people's willingness to spend.

Economic Conditions

The overall state of the economy fluctuates in all countries. Changes in general economic conditions affect (and are affected by) supply and demand, buying power, willingness to spend, consumer expenditure levels, and intensity of competitive behavior. Therefore, current economic conditions and changes in the economy have a broad impact on the success of organizations' marketing strategies.

Fluctuations in the economy follow a general pattern, often referred to as the **business cycle**. In the traditional view, the business cycle consists of four stages: prosperity, recession, depression, and recovery. From a global perspective, different regions of the world may be in different stages of the business cycle during the same period. Throughout much of the 1990s, for example, the United States experienced booming growth (prosperity). The U.S. economy began to slow in 2000, with a brief recession, especially in high-technology industries, in 2001. Japan, however, endured a recession during most of the 1990s and into the early 2000s. Economic variation in the global marketplace creates a planning challenge for firms that sell products in multiple markets around the world. In 2008, the United States experienced an economic downturn due to higher energy prices, falling home values, increasing unemployment, the financial crisis in the banking industry, and fluctuating currency values. That recession was the longest since the Great Depression of the 1930s.

During **prosperity**, unemployment is low and total income is relatively high. Assuming a low inflation rate, this combination ensures high buying power. If the economic outlook

business cycle A pattern of economic fluctuations that has four stages: prosperity, recession, depression, and recovery

prosperity A stage of the business cycle characterized by low unemployment and relatively high total income, which together ensure high buying power (provided the inflation rate stays low)

remains prosperous, consumers generally are willing to buy. In the prosperity stage, marketers often expand their product offerings to take advantage of increased buying power. They can sometimes capture a larger market share by intensifying distribution and promotion efforts.

Because unemployment rises during a **recession**, total buying power declines. These factors, usually accompanied by consumer pessimism, often stifle both consumer and business spending. As buying power decreases, many customers may become more price and value conscious, and look for basic, functional products. For example, when buying power decreased during the recession, department store sales dropped. Consumers began shopping at off-price retailers such as T.J. Maxx and Ross. These stores attracted middle-income consumers because they sell brand-name goods at a discount. Even during the recovery cycle, many consumers opted to continue shopping at off-price retailers to take advantage of the lower prices.[8]

During a recession, some firms make the mistake of drastically reducing their marketing efforts, thus damaging their ability to survive. Obviously, however, marketers should consider some revision of their marketing activities during a recessionary period. Because consumers are more concerned about the functional value of products, a company should focus its marketing research on determining precisely what functions buyers want and make sure those functions become part of its products. Promotional efforts should emphasize value and utility. Marketers must also carefully monitor the needs and expectations of their companies' target markets. Walmart tried to upgrade its products to appeal to a higher-income demographic, but the campaign backfired. A significant number of customers switched to lower-priced retailers such as Dollar General and Dollar Tree.[9]

A prolonged recession may become a **depression**, a period in which unemployment is extremely high, wages are very low, total disposable income is at a minimum, and consumers lack confidence in the economy. A depression usually lasts for an extended period, often years, and has been experienced by Russia, Mexico, and Brazil in the 2000s. Although evidence supports maintaining or even increasing spending during economic slowdowns, marketing budgets are more likely to be cut in the face of an economic downturn.

During **recovery**, the economy moves from recession or depression toward prosperity. During this period, high unemployment begins to decline, total disposable income increases, and the economic gloom that reduced consumers' willingness to buy subsides. Both the ability and the willingness to buy rise. Marketers face some problems during recovery; for example, it is difficult to ascertain how quickly and to what level prosperity will return. Large firms such as Procter & Gamble must try to assess how quickly consumers will increase their purchase of higher-priced brands versus economy brands. In this stage, marketers should maintain as much flexibility in their marketing strategies as possible so they can make the needed adjustments.

recession A stage of the business cycle during which unemployment rises and total buying power declines, stifling both consumer and business spending

depression A stage of the business cycle when unemployment is extremely high, wages are very low, total disposable income is at a minimum, and consumers lack confidence in the economy

recovery A stage of the business cycle in which the economy moves from recession or depression toward prosperity

buying power Resources, such as money, goods, and services, that can be traded in an exchange

income For an individual, the amount of money received through wages, rents, investments, pensions, and subsidy payments for a given period

disposable income After-tax income

Buying Power

The strength of a person's **buying power** depends on economic conditions and the size of the resources—money, goods, and services that can be traded in an exchange—that enable the individual to make purchases. The major financial sources of buying power are income, credit, and wealth. For an individual, **income** is the amount of money received through wages, rents, investments, pensions, and subsidy payments for a given period, such as a month or a year. Normally this money is allocated among taxes, spending for goods and services, and savings. The median annual household income in the United States is approximately $49,445.[10] However, because of differences in people's educational levels, abilities, occupations, and wealth, income is not equally distributed in this country.

Marketers are most interested in the amount of money left after payment of taxes because this **disposable income** is used for spending or saving. Because disposable income is a ready source of buying power, the total amount available in a nation is important to marketers. Several factors determine the size of total disposable income. One is the total amount of income, which is affected by wage levels, the rate of unemployment, interest rates, and dividend rates. Because disposable income is income left after taxes are paid, the number and amount of taxes directly affect the size of total disposable income. When taxes rise, disposable income declines; when taxes fall, disposable income increases.

Disposable income that is available for spending and saving after an individual has purchased the basic necessities of food, clothing, and shelter is called **discretionary income**. People use discretionary income to purchase entertainment, vacations, automobiles, education, pets, furniture, appliances, and so on. Changes in total discretionary income affect sales of these products, especially automobiles, furniture, large appliances, and other costly durable goods.

Credit enables people to spend future income now or in the near future. However, credit increases current buying power at the expense of future buying power. Several factors determine whether people use, acquire, or forgo credit. First, credit must be available. Interest rates also affect buyers' decisions to use credit, especially for expensive purchases such as homes, appliances, and automobiles. When interest rates are low, the total cost of automobiles and houses becomes more affordable. In the United States, low interest rates in the 2000s induced many buyers to take on the high level of debt necessary to own a home, fueling a tremendous boom in the construction of new homes and the sale of older homes. In contrast, when interest rates are high, consumers are more likely to delay buying such expensive items. Use of credit is also affected by credit terms, such as size of the down payment and amount and number of monthly payments.

Discretionary Income
Consumers may use their discretionary income to purchase tickets to Broadway shows.

Wealth is the accumulation of past income, natural resources, and financial resources. It exists in many forms, including cash, securities, savings accounts, jewelry, and real estate. Global wealth is increasing, with 12.5 million millionaires worldwide, double the number 10 years ago.[11] This growth in millionaires has been spearheaded by Asia, which surpassed Europe for the first time in 2011.[12] Like income, wealth is unevenly distributed. A person can have a high income and very little wealth. It is also possible, but not likely, for a person to have great wealth but little income. The significance of wealth to marketers is that as people become wealthier, they gain buying power in three ways: they can use their wealth to make current purchases, to generate income, and to acquire large amounts of credit.

Income, credit, and wealth equip consumers with buying power to purchase goods and services. Marketing managers must be aware of current levels and expected changes in buying power in their own markets because buying power directly affects the types and quantities of goods and services customers purchase. Information about buying power is available from government sources, trade associations, and research agencies. One of the most current and comprehensive sources of buying power data is the Sales & Marketing Management Survey of Buying Power, published annually by *Sales & Marketing Management* magazine. Having buying power, however, does not mean consumers will buy. They must also be willing to use their buying power.

discretionary income Disposable income available for spending and saving after an individual has purchased the basic necessities of food, clothing, and shelter

wealth The accumulation of past income, natural resources, and financial resources

willingness to spend An inclination to buy because of expected satisfaction from a product, influenced by the ability to buy and numerous psychological and social forces

Willingness to Spend

People's **willingness to spend**—their inclination to buy because of expected satisfaction from a product—is, to some degree, related to their ability to buy. That is, people are sometimes more

Figure 3.1 American Customer Satisfaction Index

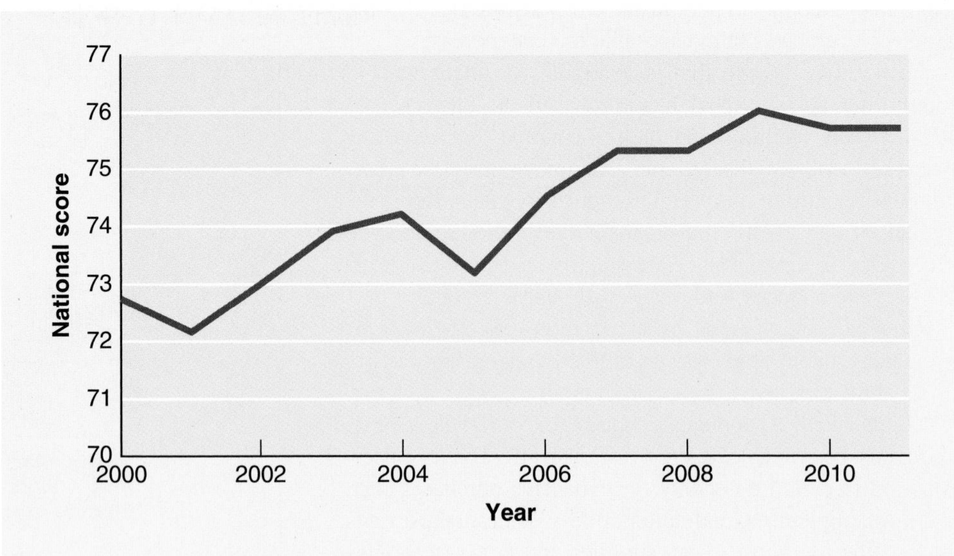

Source: "National Quarterly Scores," American Customer Satisfaction Index, 2012, www.theacsi.org/index.php?option=com_content&view=article&id=31&Itemid=117 (accessed May 16, 2012).

willing to buy if they have the buying power. However, a number of other elements also influence willingness to spend. Some elements affect specific products; others influence spending in general. A product's price and value influence almost all of us. Cross pens, for example, appeal to customers who are willing to spend more for fine writing instruments even when lower-priced pens are readily available. The amount of satisfaction received from a product already owned may also influence customers' desire to buy other products. Satisfaction depends not only on the quality of the currently owned product but also on numerous psychological and social forces. The American Customer Satisfaction Index, computed by the National Quality Research Center at the University of Michigan (see Figure 3.1), offers an indicator of customer satisfaction with a wide variety of businesses. The American Customer Satisfaction Index helps marketers to understand how consumers perceive their industries and businesses. By understanding how satisfied (or dissatisfied) customers are with their business or industry, marketers can take this information and adapt their marketing strategies accordingly.

Factors that affect consumers' general willingness to spend are expectations about future employment, income levels, prices, family size, and general economic conditions. Willingness to spend ordinarily declines if people are unsure whether or how long they will be employed, and it usually increases if people are reasonably certain of higher incomes in the future. Expectations of rising prices in the near future may also increase willingness to spend in the present. For a given level of buying power, the larger the family, the greater the willingness to spend. One reason for this relationship is that as the size of a family increases, more dollars must be spent to provide the basic necessities to sustain family members.

POLITICAL FORCES

Political, legal, and regulatory forces of the marketing environment are closely interrelated. Legislation is enacted, legal decisions are interpreted by courts, and regulatory agencies are created and operated, for the most part, by elected or appointed officials. Legislation and regulations (or the lack thereof) reflect the current political outlook. For instance, after the financial crisis caused a worldwide recession, the government passed the Dodd-Frank Wall

Marketing Debate

The Product Safety of Genetically Modified Seeds

ISSUE: Should countries ban genetically modified products?

Monsanto, the world's top producer of genetically modified (GM) seeds, has a problem. Many stakeholders believe that because GM seeds produce greater yields and hardier crops, they could decrease starvation rates. GM seeds have revolutionized farming, with 10 percent of the world's croplands consisting of GM crops. However, opponents contend that GM products could have unforeseen negative health implications on those that consume them. A blow to Monsanto came when India banned a type of GM eggplant for this reason. Because India is the second-largest producer of eggplant worldwide, this could have massive consequences not only for Monsanto but also for the 1.4 million farmers in India. Is it fair to ban GM food when it cannot be proven that it negatively impacts health?[b]

Street Reform and Consumer Protection Act of 2010. This agency was created to increase accountability and transparency in the financial industry.[13] The legislation established a new Consumer Financial Protection Bureau to protect consumers from deceptive financial practices.[14] On the other hand, many political leaders blamed this legislation for slowing down the economic recovery and adding extra costs and uncertainty to business decision making. Consequently, the political forces of the marketing environment have the potential to influence marketing decisions and strategies.

Marketing organizations strive to maintain good relations with elected and appointed political officials for several reasons. Political officials well disposed toward particular firms or industries are less likely to create or enforce laws and regulations unfavorable to those companies. For example, political officials who believe oil companies are making honest efforts to control pollution are unlikely to create and enforce highly restrictive pollution-control laws. Government contracts can be very profitable, so understanding the competitive bidding process for obtaining contracts is important. Finally, political officials can play key roles in helping organizations secure foreign markets. For example, government officials will sometimes organize trade missions in which business executives go to foreign countries to meet with potential clients or buyers.[15] Massachusetts governor Duval Patrick organized a trade mission to Brazil and Chile to promote business and trade opportunities between Massachusetts and the two countries.[16]

Many marketers view political forces as beyond their control and simply adjust to conditions that arise from those forces. Some firms, however, seek to influence the political process. In some cases, organizations publicly protest the actions of legislative bodies. More often, organizations help elect individuals to political offices who regard them positively. Much of this help is in the form of campaign contributions. AT&T is an example of a company that has attempted to influence legislation and regulation over a long period of time. Since 1990, AT&T has made more than $47 million in corporate donations for use in supporting the campaign funds of political candidates.[17] Some companies choose to donate to the campaign funds of opponents when it is believed to be a close race. Until recently, laws have limited corporate contributions to political campaign funds for specific candidates, and company-sponsored political advertisements could primarily focus only on topics (e.g., health care) and not on candidates. In the 2010 ruling for *Citizens United v. Federal Election Commission*, the Supreme Court ruled that the government is not authorized to ban corporate spending in candidate elections.[18] This means that future elections can be affected by large corporate donations to candidates. Marketers also can influence the political process through political action committees (PACs) that solicit donations from individuals and then contribute those funds to candidates running for political office.

Companies can also participate in the political process through lobbying to persuade public and/or government officials to favor a particular position in decision making. Many organizations

© AP Images/John Minchillo

Political Forces
Protestors attempt to influence the legal and regulatory environment.

concerned about the threat of legislation or regulation that may negatively affect their operations employ lobbyists to communicate their concerns to elected officials. For instance, when the United States was debating the Health Care and Education Reconciliation Act of 2010, several organizations, including medical associations, private insurance providers, and pharmaceutical companies, sent lobbyists to give their respective viewpoints regarding the health-care bill.

LEGAL AND REGULATORY FORCES

A number of federal laws influence marketing decisions and activities. Table 3.2 lists some of the most important laws. In addition to discussing these laws, which deal with competition and consumer protection, this section examines the effects of regulatory agencies and self-regulatory forces on marketing efforts.

Procompetitive Legislation

Procompetitive laws are designed to preserve competition. Most of these laws were enacted to end various antitrade practices deemed unacceptable by society. The Sherman Antitrust Act, for example, was passed in 1890 to prevent businesses from restraining trade and monopolizing markets. Examples of illegal anticompetitive practices include stealing trade secrets or obtaining other confidential information from a competitor's employees, trademark and copyright infringement, price fixing, false advertising, and deceptive selling methods such as "bait and switch" and false representation of products. For example, the Lanham Act (1946) and the Federal Trademark Dilution Act (1995) help companies protect their trademarks (brand names, logos, and other registered symbols) against infringement. The latter also requires users of names that match or parallel existing trademarks to relinquish them to prevent confusion among consumers. Antitrust laws also authorize the government to punish companies that engage in such anticompetitive practices. For instance, the Justice Department filed a lawsuit against Wachovia, now a part of Wells Fargo, alleging that bank employees had engaged in anticompetitive behavior by manipulating the bidding process on certain contracts. The company was fined $148 million.[19]

Table 3.2 Major Federal Laws That Affect Marketing Decisions

Name and Date Enacted	Purpose
Sherman Antitrust Act (1890)	Prohibits contracts, combinations, or conspiracies to restrain trade; establishes as a misdemeanor monopolizing or attempting to monopolize
Clayton Act (1914)	Prohibits specific practices such as price discrimination, exclusive-dealer arrangements, and stock acquisitions whose effect may noticeably lessen competition or tend to create a monopoly
Federal Trade Commission Act (1914)	Created the Federal Trade Commission; also gives the FTC investigatory powers to be used in preventing unfair methods of competition
Robinson-Patman Act (1936)	Prohibits price discrimination that lessens competition among wholesalers or retailers; prohibits producers from giving disproportionate services or facilities to large buyers
Wheeler-Lea Act (1938)	Prohibits unfair and deceptive acts and practices regardless of whether competition is injured; places advertising of foods and drugs under the jurisdiction of the FTC
Lanham Act (1946)	Provides protections for and regulation of brand names, brand marks, trade names, and trademarks
Celler-Kefauver Act (1950)	Prohibits any corporation engaged in commerce from acquiring the whole or any part of the stock or other share of the capital assets of another corporation when the effect would substantially lessen competition or tend to create a monopoly
Fair Packaging and Labeling Act (1966)	Prohibits unfair or deceptive packaging or labeling of consumer products
Magnuson-Moss Warranty (FTC) Act (1975)	Provides for minimum disclosure standards for written consumer product warranties; defines minimum consent standards for written warranties; allows the FTC to prescribe interpretive rules in policy statements regarding unfair or deceptive practices
Consumer Goods Pricing Act (1975)	Prohibits the use of price maintenance agreements among manufacturers and resellers in interstate commerce
Trademark Counterfeiting Act (1980)	Imposes civil and criminal penalties against those who deal in counterfeit consumer goods or any counterfeit goods that can threaten health or safety
Trademark Law Revision Act (1988)	Amends the Lanham Act to allow brands not yet introduced to be protected through registration with the Patent and Trademark Office
Nutrition Labeling and Education Act (1990)	Prohibits exaggerated health claims; requires all processed foods to contain labels with nutritional information
Telephone Consumer Protection Act (1991)	Establishes procedures to avoid unwanted telephone solicitations; prohibits marketers from using an automated telephone dialing system or an artificial or prerecorded voice to certain telephone lines
Federal Trademark Dilution Act (1995)	Grants trademark owners the right to protect trademarks and requires relinquishment of names that match or parallel existing trademarks
Digital Millennium Copyright Act (1996)	Refined copyright laws to protect digital versions of copyrighted materials, including music and movies
Children's Online Privacy Protection Act (2000)	Regulates the collection of personally identifiable information (name, address, e-mail address, hobbies, interests, or information collected through cookies) online from children under age 13
Do Not Call Implementation Act (2003)	Directs the FCC and FTC to coordinate so their rules are consistent regarding telemarketing call practices including the Do Not Call Registry and other lists, as well as call abandonment; in 2008, the FTC amended its rules and banned prerecorded sales pitches for all but a few cases
Credit Card Act (2009)	Implements strict rules on credit card companies regarding topics such as issuing credit to youths, terms disclosure, interest rates, and fees
Dodd–Frank Wall Street Reform and Consumer Protection Act (2010)	Promotes financial reform to increase accountability and transparency in the financial industry, protects consumers from deceptive financial practices, and establishes the Bureau of Consumer Financial Protection

Laws have also been created to prevent businesses from gaining an unfair advantage through bribery. The U.S. Foreign Corrupt Practices Act (FCPA) prohibits American companies from making illicit payments to foreign officials in order to obtain or keep business. For instance, Siemens AG paid $1.6 billion to the United States and Germany to settle allegations that it had bribed government officials in different countries to win contracts.[20] The FCPA does allow for small facilitation ("grease") payments to expedite routine government transactions. However, the passage of the U.K. Bribery Act does not allow for facilitation payments.[21] The U.K. Bribery Act is more encompassing than the FCPA and has significant implications for global business. Under this law companies can be found guilty of bribery even if the bribery did not take place within the U.K., and company officials without explicit knowledge about the misconduct can still be held accountable. The law applies to any business with operations in the U.K.[22] It also can hold companies liable if its joint-venture partners or subsidiaries are found guilty of bribery. However, the U.K. Bribery Law does allow for leniency if the company has an effective compliance program and undergoes periodic ethical assessments.[23] In response to the law, companies have begun to strengthen their compliance programs related to bribery. For instance, Kimberly-Clark now requires some of its business partners to consent to audits and keep thorough documentation of their payments.[24]

Consumer Protection Legislation

Consumer protection legislation is not a recent development. During the mid-1800s, lawmakers in many states passed laws to prohibit adulteration of food and drugs. However, consumer protection laws at the federal level mushroomed in the mid-1960s and early 1970s. A number of them deal with consumer safety, such as the food and drug acts, and are designed to protect people from actual and potential physical harm caused by adulteration or mislabeling. Other laws prohibit the sale of various hazardous products, such as flammable fabrics and toys that may injure children. Others concern automobile safety.

Congress has also passed several laws concerning information disclosure. Some require that information about specific products, such as textiles, furs, cigarettes, and automobiles, be provided on labels. Other laws focus on particular marketing activities: product development and testing, packaging, labeling, advertising, and consumer financing. For example, concerns about companies' online collection and use of personal information, especially about children, resulted in the passage of the Children's Online Privacy Protection Act (COPPA), which prohibits websites and Internet providers from seeking personal information from children under age 13 without parental consent. Fines for violating the COPPA can be severe. Playdom

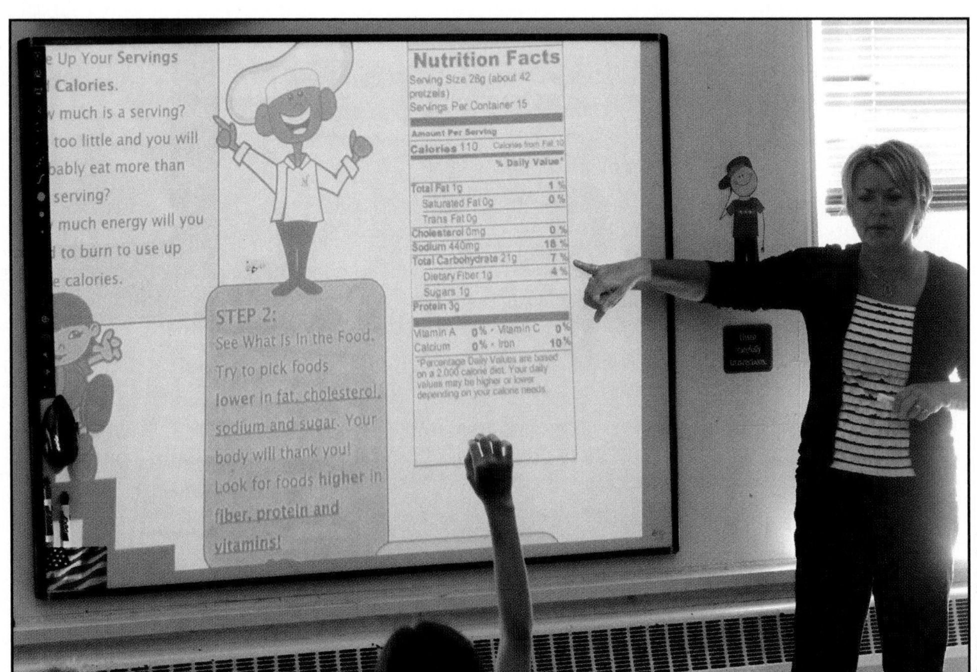

© AP Images/Seth Perlman

Consumer Protection Legislation
The Nutrition Labeling and Education Act requires that processed foods be labeled with specific nutrition information.

Inc., which operates online social games, was forced to pay $3 million in penalties for allegedly collecting and disclosing children's personal information without parental consent.[25]

An example of more recent consumer protection legislation is the Credit Card Accountability, Responsibility and Disclosure (or Credit CARD) Act of 2009, which restricts credit card companies' ability to change interest rates, charge unfair late fees, use complicated or unclear wording in their terms, and issue credit to individuals under 21.[26]

Encouraging Compliance with Laws and Regulations

Marketing activities are sometimes at the forefront of organizational misconduct, with fraud and antitrust violations the most frequently sentenced organizational crimes. Legal violations usually begin when marketers develop programs that unwittingly overstep legal bounds. Many marketers lack experience in dealing with complex legal actions and decisions. Some test the limits of certain laws by operating in a legally questionable way to see how far they can get with certain practices before being prosecuted. Other marketers interpret regulations and statutes very strictly to avoid violating a vague law. When marketers interpret laws in relation to specific marketing practices, they often analyze recent court decisions both to better understand what the law is intended to do and to predict future court interpretations.

The current trend is moving away from legally based organizational compliance programs. Instead, many companies are choosing to provide incentives that foster a culture of ethics and responsibility that encourages compliance with laws and regulations. Developing best practices and voluntary compliance creates rules and principles that guide decision making. Many companies are encouraging their employees to take responsibility for avoiding legal misconduct themselves. The New York Stock Exchange, for example, requires all member companies to have a code of ethics, and some firms try to go beyond what is required by the law. Many firms are trying to develop ethical cultures based on values and proactive assessments of risks to prevent misconduct.

Regulatory Agencies

Federal regulatory agencies influence many marketing activities, including product development, pricing, packaging, advertising, personal selling, and distribution. Usually these bodies have the power to enforce specific laws, as well as some discretion in establishing operating rules and regulations to guide certain types of industry practices. Because of this discretion and overlapping areas of responsibility, confusion or conflict regarding which agencies have jurisdiction over which marketing activities is common.

Of all the federal regulatory units, the **Federal Trade Commission (FTC)** most heavily influences marketing activities. Although the FTC regulates a variety of business practices, it allocates a large portion of resources to curbing false advertising, misleading pricing, and deceptive packaging and labeling. For instance, the FTC filed charges against Reebok for making false claims regarding its Reebok's EasyTone walking shoes, flip flops, and RunTone running shoes. Reebok claimed that these shoes would help tone the legs and buttocks, but the FTC found no evidence to support these claims. Reebok agreed to pay $25 million to resolve these claims.[27] When it has reason to believe a firm is violating a law, the commission typically issues a complaint stating that the business is in violation and takes appropriate action. If, after it is issued a complaint, a company continues the questionable practice, the FTC can issue a cease-and-desist order demanding that the business stop doing whatever caused the complaint. The firm can appeal to the federal courts to have the order rescinded. However, the FTC can seek civil penalties in court, up to a maximum penalty of $10,000 a day for each infraction if a cease-and-desist order is violated. The commission can require companies to run corrective advertising in response to previous ads deemed misleading (see Figure 3.2).

Federal Trade Commission (FTC) An agency that regulates a variety of business practices and curbs false advertising, misleading pricing, and deceptive packaging and labeling

Figure 3.2 Federal Trade Commission Enforcement Tools

Cease-and-desist order	Consent decree	Redress	Corrective advertising	Civil penalties
A court order to a business to stop engaging in an illegal practice	An order for a business to stop engaging in questionable activities to avoid prosecution	Money paid to customer to settle or resolve a complaint	A requirement that a business make new advertisement to correct misinformation	Court-ordered civil fines for up to $10,000 per day for violating a cease-and-desist order

Source: www.ftc.gov.

The FTC also assists businesses in complying with laws and evaluates new marketing methods every year. For example, the agency has held hearings to help firms establish guidelines for avoiding charges of price fixing, deceptive advertising, and questionable telemarketing practices. It has also held conferences and hearings on electronic (Internet) commerce, identity theft, and childhood obesity. When general sets of guidelines are needed to improve business practices in a particular industry, the FTC sometimes encourages firms within that industry to establish a set of trade practices voluntarily. The FTC may even sponsor a conference that brings together industry leaders and consumers for this purpose.

Unlike the FTC, other regulatory units are limited to dealing with specific products, services, or business activities. Consider the Food and Drug Administration (FDA), which enforces regulations that prohibit the sale and distribution of adulterated, misbranded, or hazardous food and drug products. For instance, the FDA ordered the diabetes pill Avandia to be pulled from retail shelves after it was discovered that the pill significantly increases the risks of heart trouble.[28] Table 3.3 outlines the areas of responsibility of seven federal regulatory agencies.

Table 3.3 Major Federal Regulatory Agencies

Agency	Major Areas of Responsibility
Federal Trade Commission (FTC)	Enforces laws and guidelines regarding business practices; takes action to stop false and deceptive advertising, pricing, packaging, and labeling
Food and Drug Administration (FDA)	Enforces laws and regulations to prevent distribution of adulterated or misbranded foods, drugs, medical devices, cosmetics, veterinary products, and potentially hazardous consumer products
Consumer Product Safety Commission (CPSC)	Ensures compliance with the Consumer Product Safety Act; protects the public from unreasonable risk of injury from any consumer product not covered by other regulatory agencies
Federal Communications Commission (FCC)	Regulates communication by wire, radio, and television in interstate and foreign commerce
Environmental Protection Agency (EPA)	Develops and enforces environmental protection standards and conducts research into the adverse effects of pollution
Federal Power Commission (FPC)	Regulates rates and sales of natural gas producers, thereby affecting the supply and price of gas available to consumers; also regulates wholesale rates for electricity and gas, pipeline construction, and U.S. imports and exports of natural gas and electricity
Consumer Financial Protection Bureau (CFPB)	Regulates the offering and provision of consumer financial products and serves to protect consumers from deceptive financial practices

Source: "Subtitle A—Bureau of Consumer Financial Protection," *One Hundred Eleventh Congress of the United States of America*, 589.

In addition, all states, as well as many cities and towns, have regulatory agencies that enforce laws and regulations regarding marketing practices within their states or municipalities. State and local regulatory agencies try not to establish regulations that conflict with those of federal regulatory agencies. They generally enforce laws dealing with the production and sale of particular goods and services. The utility, insurance, financial, and liquor industries are commonly regulated by state agencies. Among these agencies' targets are misleading advertising and pricing. Recent legal actions suggest that states are taking a firmer stance against perceived deceptive pricing practices and are using basic consumer research to define deceptive pricing.

State consumer protection laws offer an opportunity for state attorneys general to deal with marketing issues related to fraud and deception. Most states have consumer protection laws that are very general in nature and provide enforcement when new schemes evolve that injure consumers. For example, the New York Consumer Protection Board is very proactive in monitoring consumer protection and providing consumer education. New York became the first state to implement an airline passenger rights law. More recently, the New York Consumer Protection Board has taken measures to protect consumers from scams or data breaches. For example, it provided contact information on its website to assist those who were victims of data breaches at New York State Electric and Gas and Rochester Gas and Electric.[29]

Self-Regulatory Forces

In an attempt to be good corporate citizens and prevent government intervention, some businesses try to regulate themselves. Similarly, a number of trade associations have developed self-regulatory programs. Though these programs are not a direct outgrowth of laws, many were established to stop or stall the development of laws and governmental regulatory groups that would regulate the associations' marketing practices. Sometimes trade associations establish ethics codes by which their members must abide or risk censure or exclusion from the association. For instance, the Pharmaceutical Research and Manufacturers of America released its "Guiding Principles" to function as a set of voluntary industry rules for drug companies to follow when advertising directly to consumers.[30]

Self-Regulatory Forces
The Better Business Bureau is one of the best known self-regulatory organizations.

Table 3.4 Self-Regulatory Issues in Marketing

1	Truthful Advertising Messages
2	Health and Childhood Obesity
3	Internet Tracking/User Privacy
4	Concern for Vulnerable Populations
5	Failure to Deliver on Expectations and Promises
6	Sustainable Marketing Practices and Greenwashing
7	Transparent Pricing
8	Understandable Labeling and Packaging
9	Supply Chain Relationships/Ethical Sourcing
10	Marketing of Dangerous Products
11	Product Quality Failures
12	Nonresponse to Customer Complaints

Perhaps the best-known self-regulatory group is the **Better Business Bureau (BBB)**, which is a system of nongovernmental, independent, local regulatory agencies that are supported by local businesses. More than 150 bureaus help settle problems between consumers and specific business firms. Each bureau also acts to preserve good business practices in a locality, although it usually lacks strong enforcement tools for dealing with firms that employ questionable practices. When a firm continues to violate what the Better Business Bureau believes to be good business practices, the bureau warns consumers through local newspapers or broadcast media. If the offending organization is a BBB member, it may be expelled from the local bureau. For example, the Better Business Bureau expelled four contractors in New York for failing to respond to customer complaints.[31] Table 3.4 describes some of the major self-regulatory issues that often occur in the marketing industry.

The Council of Better Business Bureaus is a national organization composed of all local Better Business Bureaus. The National Advertising Division (NAD) of the council operates a self-regulatory program that investigates claims regarding alleged deceptive advertising. For instance, in an investigation of Johnson & Johnson's (J&J) advertising for its REACH Total Care + Whitening Toothbrush, NAD determined that the product did whiten teeth. However, it recommended that J&J modify its product claims slightly to indicate that its whitening properties come from the toothbrush's bristles. NAD believes consumers might interpret the claims to mean that the toothbrush bleaches teeth, which is inaccurate.[32]

Another self-regulatory entity, the **National Advertising Review Board (NARB)**, considers cases in which an advertiser challenges issues raised by the NAD about an advertisement. Cases are reviewed by panels drawn from NARB members that represent advertisers, agencies, and the public. For example, the NARB concurred with the NAD regarding claims about Time Warner's fiber optic network. The NARB believed that Time Warner's advertising led consumers to believe that fiber-optic technology was used throughout its entire network, while in reality it was not used throughout the whole system. Although Time Warner disagreed with the NARB's conclusion, it agreed to modify its advertising.[33] The NARB, sponsored by the Council of Better Business Bureaus and three advertising trade organizations, has no official enforcement powers. However, if a firm refuses to comply with its decision, the NARB may publicize the questionable practice and file a complaint with the FTC.

Self-regulatory programs have several advantages over governmental laws and regulatory agencies. Establishment and implementation are usually less expensive, and guidelines are generally more realistic and operational. In addition, effective self-regulatory programs reduce the need to expand government bureaucracy. However, these programs have several limitations. When a trade association creates a set of industry guidelines for its members, nonmember firms do not have to abide by them. Furthermore, many self-regulatory programs lack the tools or authority to enforce guidelines. Finally, guidelines in self-regulatory programs are often less strict than those established by government agencies.

Better Business Bureau (BBB) A system of nongovernmental, independent, local regulatory agencies supported by local businesses that helps settle problems between customers and specific business firms

National Advertising Review Board (NARB) A self-regulatory unit that considers challenges to issues raised by the National Advertising Division (an arm of the Council of Better Business Bureaus) about an advertisement

TECHNOLOGICAL FORCES

The word *technology* brings to mind scientific advances such as information technology and biotechnology, which have resulted in the Internet, cell phones, cloning, stem-cell research, electric vehicles, iPads, and more. Technology has revolutionized the products created and offered by marketers and the channels by which they communicate about those products.

© AP Images/PRNewsFoto/Bang & Olufsen, Peter Krasilnikoff

Impact of Technology
Changes in technology create opportunities for marketers to stimulate consumer interest.

However, even though these innovations are outgrowths of technology, none of them *are* technology. **Technology** is the application of knowledge and tools to solve problems and perform tasks more efficiently. Technology grows out of research performed by businesses, universities, government agencies, and nonprofit organizations. More than half of this research is paid for by the federal government, which supports research in such diverse areas as health, defense, agriculture, energy, and pollution.

The rapid technological growth of the last several decades is expected to accelerate. It has transformed the U.S. economy into the most productive in the world and provided Americans with an ever-higher standard of living and tremendous opportunities for sustained business expansion. Technology and technological advancements clearly influence buyers' and marketers' decisions, so let's take a closer look at the impact of technology and its use in the marketplace.

Impact of Technology

Technology determines how we, as members of society, satisfy our physiological needs. In various ways and to varying degrees, eating and drinking habits, sleeping patterns, sexual activities, health care, and work performance are all influenced by both existing technology and changes in technology. Because of the technological revolution in communications, for example, marketers can now reach vast numbers of people more efficiently through a variety of media. Social networks, smartphones, and tablet computers help marketers stay in touch with clients, make appointments, and handle last-minute orders or cancellations. A growing number of U.S. households, as well as many businesses, have given up their land-lines in favor of using cell phones as their primary phones. Currently, about one-fourth of Americans have exchanged their land-lines for cell phones.[34] An estimated 35 percent of American adults own the more advanced smartphones.[35]

The proliferation of mobile devices has led marketers to employ text and multimedia messaging on cell phones to reach their target markets. Restaurants, for example, can send their lunch specials to subscribers' cell phones. Because many mobile devices are able to access the Internet, marketers have an increasing number of opportunities for mobile advertising. In 2011, mobile advertising in the United States hit $1.2 billion, a 41.2 percent increase from

technology The application of knowledge and tools to solve problems and perform tasks more efficiently

Going Green

Samsung Uses Green Strategy for New Market Opportunities

If Samsung has its way, it will not only be known for its information technology but also for green technologies and health-care products. Samsung has decided to expand into the green energy and health-care sectors to take advantage of growing market opportunities. It plans to invest $21 billion into these business sectors by 2020. In terms of green technology, Samsung will create three new businesses: solar panels, LED lighting, and electronic vehicle batteries. Samsung hopes to go from being what it calls an "infortainment" company to a "lifecare" company, creating products that can benefit consumers and the environment.

Although Samsung desires to improve people's lives, its motives are not totally philanthropic; rather, it embraces the marketing concept of satisfying customer needs while at the same time achieving its own financial goals. Samsung believes the green sector will grow by leaps and bounds. The company is so confident that it announced that it will invest $7 billion into a green energy industrial park. The park will specialize in such areas as wind power generators and solar batteries. Investing in a completely new market area is risky, but if Samsung's predictions come true, then the company will get a head start in a profitable industry.[c]

the year before. As consumers become more tech-savvy, marketers must adapt their strategies to take advantage of these new opportunities.[36] Mobile marketing will be discussed in more detail in Chapter 10.

Computers have become a staple in American homes, but the type of computer has been changing drastically in this past decade. Traditional desktop computers appear to be on the decline. Laptops became immensely popular due to their mobility, but analysts estimate that laptops might be entering the maturity stage of the product life cycle. Conversely, tablet computers such as the iPad are experiencing immense growth and may soon supersede laptops in sales.[37] In response many companies are creating apps specifically made for the iPad and similar devices. The rapidly evolving state of technology requires marketers to familiarize themselves with the latest technological changes.

The Internet has become a major tool in most households for communicating, researching, shopping, and entertaining. The use of video online, especially through websites such as YouTube, has exploded from 7 percent of Internet traffic in 2005 to more than 25 percent in 2010.[38] Cisco estimated that online videos comprised more than 50 percent of consumer Internet traffic in 2012.[39] Time spent on social networks also makes up a significant portion of a consumer's online activities. One study estimates that users worldwide spend 19 percent of their time online on social networking sites.[40]

Although technology has had many positive impacts on our lives, there are also many negative impacts to consider. We enjoy the benefits of communicating through the Internet; however, we are increasingly concerned about protecting our privacy and intellectual property. Hackers and those who steal digital property are also using advanced technology to harm others. Likewise, technological advances in the areas of health and medicine have led to the creation of new drugs that save lives; however, such advances have also led to cloning and genetically modified foods that have become controversial issues in many segments of society. Consider the impact of cell phones. The ability to call from almost any location has many benefits, but it also has negative side effects, including increases in traffic accidents, increased noise pollution, and fears about potential health risks.[41]

The effects of technology relate to such characteristics as dynamics, reach, and the self-sustaining nature of technological progress. The *dynamics* of technology involve the constant change that often challenges the structures of social institutions, including social relationships, the legal system, religion, education, business, and leisure. *Reach* refers to the broad nature of technology as it moves through society.

The *self-sustaining* nature of technology relates to the fact that technology acts as a catalyst to spur even faster development. As new innovations are introduced, they stimulate the need for more advancement to facilitate further development. For example, Apple advances the capabilities of each new model of its iPhone and iPad. Companies such as Research in Motion failed to update technology for its BlackBerry as fast as Apple did for its products, losing market share as a result. Technology initiates a change process that creates new opportunities for new technologies in every industry segment or personal life experience that it touches. At some point, there is a multiplier effect that causes still greater demand for more change to improve performance.[42]

The expanding opportunities for e-commerce, the sharing of business information, the ability to maintain business relationships, and the ability to conduct business transactions via digital networks are changing the relationship between businesses and consumers.[43] Many people use the Internet to purchase consumer electronics, clothing, software, books, furniture, and music. More people now opt to purchase music online or simply listen for free on social networking sites. As a result, CD sales have decreased over the years. In addition, consumers go online to acquire travel-related services, financial services, and information. The forces unleashed by the Internet are particularly important in business-to-business relationships, where uncertainties are being reduced by improving the quantity, reliability, and timeliness of information.

Adoption and Use of Technology

Many companies lose their status as market leaders because they fail to keep up with technological changes. It is important for firms to determine when a technology is changing the industry and to define the strategic influence of the new technology. For example, the Internet has created the need for ever-faster transmission of signals through 4G, cable broadband, satellite, Wi-Fi, or fiber optic technology. To remain competitive, companies today must keep up with and adapt to technological advances.

The extent to which a firm can protect inventions that stem from research also influences its use of technology. How secure a product is from imitation depends on how easily others can copy it without violating its patent. If groundbreaking products and processes cannot be protected through patents, a company is less likely to market them and make the benefits of its research available to competitors.

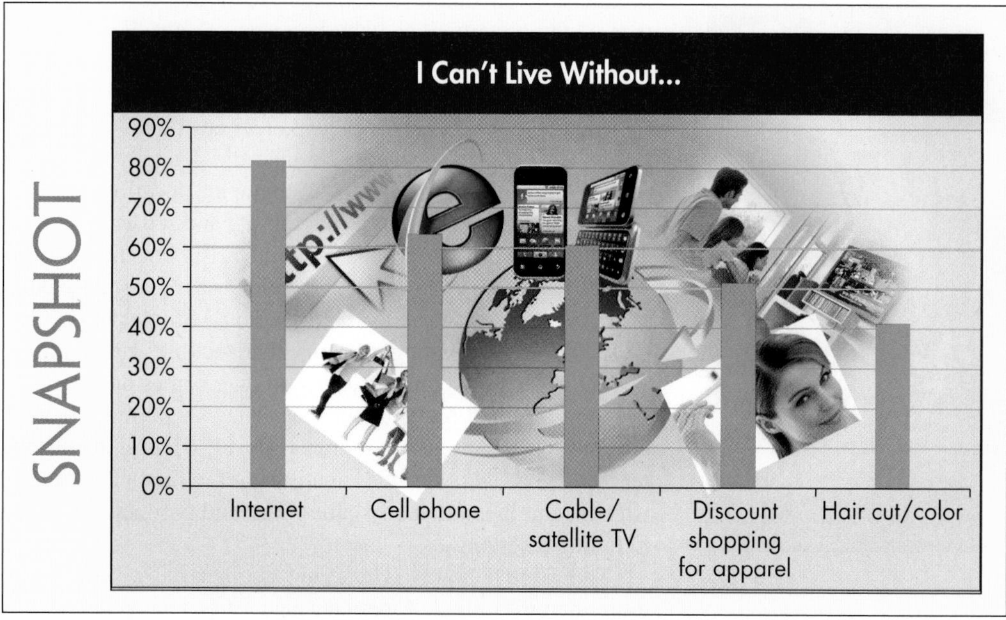

Source: BIGResearch-American Pulse Survey of 5,015 adult consumers, December 2010, www.stores.org/STORES%20 Magazine%20February%202011/adjusting-new-normal.

Through a procedure known as *technology assessment,* managers try to foresee the effects of new products and processes on their firm's operations, on other business organizations, and on society in general. With information obtained through a technology assessment, management tries to estimate whether benefits of adopting a specific technology outweigh costs to the firm and to society at large. The degree to which a business is technologically based also influences its managers' response to technology.

SOCIOCULTURAL FORCES

Sociocultural forces are the influences in a society and its culture(s) that bring about changes in people's attitudes, beliefs, norms, customs, and lifestyles. Profoundly affecting how people live, these forces help determine what, where, how, and when people buy products. Like the other environmental forces, sociocultural forces present marketers with both challenges and opportunities. For a closer look at sociocultural forces, we examine three major issues: demographic and diversity characteristics, cultural values, and consumerism.

Demographic and Diversity Characteristics

Changes in a population's demographic characteristics—age, gender, race, ethnicity, marital and parental status, income, and education—have a significant bearing on relationships and individual behavior. These shifts lead to changes in how people live and ultimately in their consumption of such products as food, clothing, housing, transportation, communication, recreation, education, and health services. We'll look at a few of the changes in demographics and diversity that are affecting marketing activities.

sociocultural forces The influences in a society and its culture(s) that change people's attitudes, beliefs, norms, customs, and lifestyles

Demographic Changes
Changing demographics motivated the U.S. government to implement a more diverse marketing campaign during the 2010 Census.

One demographic change that is affecting the marketplace is the increasing proportion of older consumers. According to the U.S. Bureau of the Census, the number of people age 65 and older is expected to more than double by the year 2050, reaching 88.5 million.[44] Consequently, marketers can expect significant increases in the demand for health-care services, recreation, tourism, retirement housing, and selected skin-care products. Even online companies are trying to take advantage of the opportunities baby boomers present. For example, several online dating sites directed toward boomers were recently launched, such as BabyBoomerPeopleMeet.com and SeniorPeopleMeet.com.[45] To reach older customers effectively, of course, marketers must understand the diversity within the mature market with respect to geographic location, income, marital status, and limitations in mobility and self-care.

The number of singles is also on the rise. For the first time singles have surpassed married couples, which currently comprise 48 percent of American households.[46] Single people have quite different spending patterns than couples and families with children. They are less likely to own homes and thus buy less furniture and fewer appliances. They spend more heavily on convenience foods, restaurants, travel, entertainment, and recreation. In addition, they tend to prefer smaller packages, whereas families often buy bulk goods and products packaged in multiple servings.

The United States is entering another baby boom, with more than 84 million Americans age 19 or younger. The new baby boom represents 27.1 percent of the total population; the original baby boomers, born between 1946 and 1964, account for about 27 percent.[47] The children of the original baby boomers differ from one another radically in terms of race, living arrangements, and socioeconomic status. Thus, the newest baby boom is much more diverse than in previous generations.

Despite this trend, the birthrate has begun to decline. The U.S. population experienced the slowest rate of growth in the last decade since the Great Depression. The population grew 9.7 percent to more than 310 million. While the birth rate is declining, new immigrants help with population gains.[48]

Another noteworthy population trend is the increasingly multicultural nature of U.S. society. Because of this, the federal government decided to produce the advertisements for the 2010 Census in 28 different languages rather than only in English.[49] The number of immigrants into the United States has steadily risen during the last 40 years. In the 1960s, 3.3 million people immigrated to the United States; in the 1970s, 4.4 million immigrated; in the 1980s, 7.3 million arrived; in the 1990s, the United States received 9.1 million immigrants; and in the 2000s, more than 8.3 million people have immigrated to the United States.[50] In contrast to earlier immigrants, very few recent ones are of European origin. Another reason for the increasing cultural diversification of the United States is that most recent immigrants are relatively young, whereas U.S. citizens of European origin are growing older. These younger immigrants tend to have more children than their older counterparts, further shifting the population balance. By the turn of the 20th century, the U.S. population had shifted from one dominated by whites to one consisting largely of three racial and ethnic groups: whites, blacks, and Hispanics. The U.S. government projects that by the year 2050, more than 133 million Hispanics, 66 million blacks, and 41 million Asians will call the United States home.[51] Table 3.5 provides a glimpse into the multicultural nature of the U.S. population. Although the majority of

Sociocultural Forces
Whole Foods broadens its appeal to health-conscious consumers by offering in-store dining options.

Emerging Trends

Stage Stores Target Small Towns

While many retailers locate in large cities to take advantage of a larger customer base, some target smaller towns. Walmart grew by initially focusing on small to mid-sized areas. Another company that has widespread success in small towns is apparel retailer Stage Stores. Stage Stores is the parent company of Palais Royale, Bealls, Steele's, Goody's, Peebles, and Stage retailers. The firm has 800 stores, usually located in towns with fewer than 50,000 people. Rather than being limited by the smaller environment, Stage is adept at seizing the competitive, economic, and sociocultural opportunities these towns offer.

Because many national retailers do not focus on small towns, competition for Stage Stores tends to be low. Eighty percent of its sales come from branded apparel such as Levi's and Nike. This emphasis on branded apparel differentiates it from Walmart, allowing Stage Stores to succeed in towns with a Walmart presence. It also takes advantage of the lower rents found in smaller areas. Finally, Stage recognizes the value that consumers in small towns place on relationships. Each year Stage rewards loyal customers with Hallmark gift cards for their birthdays, making them feel appreciated. Its ability to recognize the marketing environment has helped the company and its shareholders prosper. In fact, Stage Stores was able to increase 2010 dividends 50 percent from the previous year despite the difficult economic climate.[d]

Table 3.5 The Multicultural Nature of the U.S. Population

Race	% Population	% Change (2000–2010)
White	72	6
Hispanic	16	43
Black or African American	13	12
Asian	5	29
American Indian or Alaska Native	0.9	18
Native Hawaiian or Pacific Islander	0.2	35

Source: United States Census 2010, http://2010.census.gov/2010census/ (accessed May 17, 2012); "2010 Census Shows America's Diversity," U.S. Census Bureau, March 24, 2011, www.census.gov/newsroom/releases/archives/2010_census/cb11-cn125.html (accessed May 17, 2012).

the population still identify themselves as white, Hispanic and Asian ethnicities made major population gains between 2000 and 2010.

Marketers recognize that these profound changes in the U.S. population bring unique problems and opportunities. But a diverse population means a more diverse customer base, and marketing practices must be modified—and diversified—to meet its changing needs. For example, Hispanics wield about $1 trillion in annual buying power, and experts project that figure will grow to $1.5 trillion by 2015.[52] In an effort to target this expanding demographic, MillerCoors is sponsoring a Mexican soccer league and placing more Spanish language on its cartons and labels. Not to be outdone, competitor Anheuser-Busch InBev is creating more Spanish advertisements and sponsored Cuban-American rapper Pitbull. The companies hope to create a rapport with Hispanic consumers in order to gain their loyalty.[53]

Cultural Values

Changes in cultural values have dramatically influenced people's needs and desires for products. Although cultural values do not shift overnight, they do change at varying speeds. Marketers try to monitor these changes, knowing this information can equip them to predict changes in consumers' needs for products, at least in the near future.

Starting in the late 1980s, issues of health, nutrition, and exercise grew in importance. People today are more concerned about the foods they eat and thus are choosing healthier products. Compared to those in the previous two decades, Americans today are more likely to favor smoke-free environments and to consume less alcohol. They have also altered their sexual behavior to reduce the risk of contracting sexually transmitted diseases. Marketers have responded with a proliferation of foods, beverages, and exercise products that fit this new lifestyle, as well as with programs to help people quit smoking and contraceptives that are safer and more effective. Americans are also becoming increasingly open to alternative medicines and nutritionally improved foods. As a result, sales of organic foods, herbs and herbal remedies, vitamins, and dietary supplements have escalated. In addition to the proliferation of new organic brands, such as Earthbound Farm, Horizon Dairy, and Whole Foods' 365, many conventional marketers have introduced organic versions of their products, including Orville Redenbacher, Heinz, and even Walmart.

The major source of cultural values is the family. For years, when asked about the most important aspects of their lives, adults specified family issues and a happy marriage. Today, however, only one out of two marriages is predicted to last. Values regarding the permanence of marriage are changing. Because a happy marriage is prized so highly, more people are willing to give up an unhappy one and seek a different marriage partner or opt to stay single.

Children continue to be very important. Marketers have responded with safer, upscale baby gear and supplies, children's electronics, and family entertainment products. Marketers are also aiming more marketing efforts directly at children because children often play pivotal roles in purchasing decisions. A recent study in Austria reported that children influence twice as many purchase decisions in the supermarket than parents are aware of, and the majority of items children requested are products positioned at their eye level.[54]

Children and family values are also factors in the trend toward more eat-out and take-out meals. Busy families in which both parents work generally want to spend less time in the kitchen and more time together enjoying themselves. Beneficiaries of this trend have primarily been fast-food and casual restaurants like McDonald's, Taco Bell, and Applebee's, but most supermarkets have added more ready-to-cook and ready-to-serve meal components to meet the needs of busy customers. Some also offer dine-in cafés.

Green marketing helps establish long-term consumer relationships by maintaining, supporting, and enhancing the natural environment. One of society's environmental hurdles is proper disposal of waste, especially of nondegradable materials such as disposable diapers and polystyrene packaging. Companies have responded by developing more environmentally sensitive products and packaging. Procter & Gamble, for example, uses recycled materials in some of its packaging and sells environment-friendly refills. Companies like Seventh Generation, which sells products like paper towels and bathroom tissue made from recycled paper as well as eco-friendly cleaning products, have entered the mainstream. Everything the company produces is as environmentally friendly as it can be, in hopes of having as little impact on the next seven generations as possible.[55] A number of marketers sponsor recycling programs and encourage their customers to take part in them.

Consumerism

Consumerism involves organized efforts by individuals, groups, and organizations to protect consumers' rights. The movement's major forces are individual consumer advocates, consumer organizations and other interest groups, consumer education, and consumer laws.

To achieve their objectives, consumers and their advocates write letters or send e-mails to companies, lobby government agencies, broadcast public service announcements, and boycott companies whose activities they deem irresponsible. Consider that a number of consumers would like to eliminate telemarketing and e-mail spam, and some of them have joined organizations and groups attempting to stop these activities. Businesses that engage in questionable practices invite additional regulation. For example, several organizations evaluate children's products for safety, often announcing dangerous products before Christmas so parents can avoid them. Other actions by the consumer movement have resulted in seat belts and air bags in automobiles, dolphin-friendly tuna, the banning of unsafe three-wheel motorized vehicles, and numerous laws regulating product safety and information. We take a closer look at consumerism in the next chapter.

consumerism Organized efforts by individuals, groups, and organizations to protect consumers' rights

Summary

1. To recognize the importance of environmental scanning and analysis

The marketing environment consists of external forces that directly or indirectly influence an organization's acquisition of inputs (personnel, financial resources, raw materials, and information) and generation of outputs (goods, services, and ideas). The marketing environment includes competitive, economic, political, legal and regulatory, technological, and sociocultural forces.

Environmental scanning is the process of collecting information about forces in the marketing environment; environmental analysis is the process of assessing and interpreting information obtained in scanning. This information helps marketing managers predict opportunities and threats associated with environmental fluctuation. Marketing managers may assume either a passive, reactive approach or a proactive, aggressive approach in responding to these environmental fluctuations. The choice depends on the organization's structures and needs and on the composition of environmental forces that affect it.

2. To understand how competitive and economic factors affect an organization's ability to compete and a customer's ability and willingness to buy products

All businesses compete for customers' dollars. A marketer, however, generally defines *competition* as other firms that market products that are similar to or can be substituted for its products in the same geographic area. These competitors can be classified into one of four types: brand competitors, product competitors, generic competitors, and total budget competitors. The number of firms controlling the supply of a product may affect the strength of competitors. The four general types of competitive structures are monopoly, oligopoly, monopolistic competition, and pure competition. Marketers monitor what competitors are currently doing and assess changes occurring in the competitive environment.

General economic conditions, buying power, and willingness to spend can strongly influence marketing decisions and activities. The overall state of the economy fluctuates in a general pattern known as the business cycle, which consists of four stages: prosperity, recession, depression, and recovery. Consumers' goods, services, and financial holdings make up their buying power, or ability to purchase. Financial sources of buying power are income, credit, and wealth. After-tax income used for spending or saving is disposable income. Disposable income left after an individual has purchased the basic necessities of food, clothes, and shelter is discretionary income. Factors affecting buyers' willingness to spend include product price; level of satisfaction obtained from currently used products; family size; and expectations about future employment, income, prices, and general economic conditions.

3. To identify the types of political forces in the marketing environment

The political, legal, and regulatory forces of the marketing environment are closely interrelated. Political forces may determine what laws and regulations affecting specific marketers are enacted, how much the government purchases, and from which suppliers. They can also be important in helping organizations secure foreign markets. Companies influence political forces in several ways, including maintaining good relationships with political officials, protesting the actions of legislative bodies, helping elect individuals who regard them positively to public office through campaign contributions, and employing lobbyists to communicate their concerns to elected officials.

4. To understand how laws, government regulations, and self-regulatory agencies affect marketing activities

Federal legislation affecting marketing activities can be divided into procompetitive legislation—laws designed to preserve and encourage competition—and consumer protection laws, which generally relate to product safety and information disclosure. Actual effects of legislation are determined by how marketers and courts interpret the laws. Federal guidelines for sentencing concerning violations of these laws represent an attempt to force marketers to comply with the laws.

Federal, state, and local regulatory agencies usually have power to enforce specific laws. They also have some discretion in establishing operating rules and drawing up regulations to guide certain types of industry practices. Industry self-regulation represents another regulatory force; marketers view this type of regulation more favorably than government action because they have more opportunity to take part in creating guidelines. Self-regulation may be less expensive than government regulation, and its guidelines are generally more realistic. However, such regulation generally cannot ensure compliance as effectively as government agencies.

5. To explore the effects of new technology on society and on marketing activities

Technology is the application of knowledge and tools to solve problems and perform tasks more efficiently. Consumer demand, buyer behavior, product development, packaging, promotion, prices, and distribution systems are all influenced directly by technology. The rapid technological growth of the last few decades is expected to accelerate. Revolutionary changes in communication technology have allowed marketers to reach vast numbers of people; however, with this expansion of communication has come concern about privacy and intellectual property. And while science and medical research have brought many great advances, cloning and genetically modified foods are controversial issues in many segments of society. Home, health, leisure, and work are all influenced to varying degrees by technology and technological advances. The *dynamics* of technology involves the constant change that challenges every aspect of our society. *Reach* refers to the broad nature of technology as it moves through and affects society.

Many companies lose their status as market leaders because they fail to keep up with technological changes. The ability to protect inventions from competitor imitation is also an important consideration when making marketing decisions.

6. To analyze sociocultural issues marketers must deal with as they make decisions

Sociocultural forces are the influences in a society and its culture that result in changes in attitudes, beliefs, norms, customs, and lifestyles. Major sociocultural issues directly affecting marketers include demographic and diversity characteristics, cultural values, and consumerism.

Changes in a population's demographic characteristics, such as age, income, race, and ethnicity, can lead to changes in that population's consumption of products. Changes in cultural values, such as those relating to health, nutrition, family, and the natural environment, have had striking effects on people's needs for products and therefore are closely monitored by marketers. Consumerism involves the efforts of individuals, groups, and organizations to protect consumers' rights. Consumer rights organizations inform and organize other consumers, raise issues, help businesses develop consumer-oriented programs, and pressure lawmakers to enact consumer protection laws.

Go to www.cengagebrain.com for resources to help you master the content in this chapter as well as materials that will expand your marketing knowledge!

Important Terms

environmental scanning 70
environmental analysis 71
competition 72
brand competitors 72
product competitors 72
generic competitors 72
total budget competitors 73
monopoly 74
oligopoly 74
monopolistic competition 74
pure competition 74
business cycle 75
prosperity 75
recession 76
depression 76
recovery 76
buying power 76
income 76
disposable income 76
discretionary income 77
wealth 77
willingness to spend 77
Federal Trade Commission (FTC) 83
Better Business Bureau (BBB) 86
National Advertising Review Board (NARB) 86
technology 87
sociocultural forces 90
consumerism 93

Discussion and Review Questions

1. Why are environmental scanning and analysis important to marketers?
2. What are the four types of competition? Which is most important to marketers?
3. In what ways can each of the business cycle stages affect consumers' reactions to marketing strategies?
4. What business cycle stage are we experiencing currently? How is this stage affecting business firms in your area?
5. Define *income, disposable income,* and *discretionary income.* How does each type of income affect consumer buying power?
6. How do wealth and consumer credit affect consumer buying power?
7. What factors influence a buyer's willingness to spend?
8. Describe marketers' attempts to influence political forces.
9. What types of problems do marketers experience as they interpret legislation?
10. What are the goals of the Federal Trade Commission? List the ways in which the FTC affects marketing activities. Do you think a single regulatory agency should have such broad jurisdiction over so many marketing practices? Why or why not?
11. Name several nongovernmental regulatory forces. Do you believe self-regulation is more or less effective than governmental regulatory agencies? Why?
12. What does the term *technology* mean to you? Do the benefits of technology outweigh its costs and potential dangers? Defend your answer.
13. Discuss the impact of technology on marketing activities.
14. What factors determine whether a business organization adopts and uses technology?
15. What evidence exists that cultural diversity is increasing in the United States?
16. In what ways are cultural values changing? How are marketers responding to these changes?
17. Describe consumerism. Analyze some active consumer forces in your area.

Application Questions

1. Assume you are opening one of the following retail stores. Identify publications at the library or online that provide information about the environmental forces likely to affect the store. Briefly summarize the information each source provides.
   a. Convenience store
   b. Women's clothing store
   c. Grocery store
   d. Fast-food restaurant
   e. Furniture store
2. For each of the following products, identify brand competitors, product competitors, generic competitors, and total budget competitors.
   a. Chevrolet Tahoe
   b. Levi's jeans
   c. Travelocity
3. Technological advances and sociocultural forces have a great impact on marketers. Identify at least one technological advance and one sociocultural change that has affected you as a consumer. Explain the impact of each change on your needs as a customer.
4. IMP Competitive forces are very important to companies, particularly those that operate in many different countries. However, the importance of each competitive force might vary depending upon the industry. For instance, legal and regulatory forces limit many of the activities of cigarette firms. While rising prices might affect the purchase of luxury goods, necessities like diapers and antibiotics will not experience as much of an impact, because people require them whether the prices are high or not. With this in mind, examine the impact that economic forces, political forces, legal and regulatory forces, technological forces, and sociocultural forces have upon ExxonMobil, General Motors, and Procter & Gamble. Rate each of these factors on a scale of 1–5, from 5 meaning *most important* to 1 meaning *least important*. Based on these companies, which environmental variable do you think would be the highest priority for each company, and why? Based on these three companies, which environmental variable do you feel would be most important for marketers?

Internet Exercise

The Federal Trade Commission

To learn more about the Federal Trade Commission and its functions, visit the FTC's website at **www.ftc.gov**.

1. Based on information on the website, describe the FTC's impact on marketing.
2. Examine the sections entitled Newsroom and Formal Actions. Describe three recent incidents of illegal or inappropriate marketing activities and the FTC's response to those actions.
3. How could the FTC's website assist a company in avoiding misconduct?

developing your marketing plan

A marketing strategy is dynamic. Companies must constantly monitor the marketing environment not only to create their marketing strategy but to revise it if necessary. Information about various forces in the marketplace is collected, analyzed, and used as a foundation for several marketing plan decisions. The following questions will help you to understand how the information in this chapter contributes to the development of your marketing plan.

1. Describe the current competitive market for your product. Can you identify the number of brands or market share they hold? Expand your analysis to include other products that are similar or could be substituted for yours.
2. Using the business cycle pattern, in which of the four stages is the current state of the economy? Can you identify any changes in consumer buying power that would affect the sale and use of your product?
3. Referring to Tables 3.2 and 3.3, do you recognize any laws or regulatory agencies that would have jurisdiction over your type of product?
4. Conduct a brief technology assessment, determining the impact that technology has on your product, its sale, or its use.
5. Discuss how your product could be affected by changes in social attitudes, demographic characteristics, or lifestyles.

The information obtained from these questions should assist you in developing various aspects of your marketing plan found in the "Interactive Marketing Plan" exercise at **www.cengagebrain.com**.

video case 3.1

Preserve Products Challenge Traditional Brands with Green Alternatives

When entrepreneur Eric Hudson started Preserve® Products in 1996, people thought he was crazy. "When we first started the company, a lot of people looked at us like we had three heads, saying, 'Recycled materials are for ashtrays. Recycled materials are for pen holders,' " Hudson said. However, Hudson recognized that cultural values were beginning to shift toward green products. He founded Preserve Products, with the mission "to deliver consumer products that offer great looking design, high performance and are better for the environment than alternative products." The first Preserve product was its recyclable toothbrush. The toothbrush has become one of the organization's more popular products and even had an appearance as Will Ferrell's toothbrush in the movie *Stranger than Fiction*.

More than 15 years later, the green revolution is in full swing and Preserve has become a multi-million dollar company with products available in over a dozen countries. Preserve takes plastics from products at the end of their life cycle and recycles them to create consumer goods such as toothbrushes, razors, kitchenware, mixing bowls, and storage containers. As green products become more mainstream, Preserve has seen an increase in demand from both retailers and consumers. Preserve products can now be found in Wegman's, Whole Foods, Trader Joe's, and Target.

In addition to being recyclable, Preserve products are dishwasher safe and are manufactured in the United States. The company also guarantees that no products have been tested on animals and that it never uses ingredients that could potentially harm consumers. Preserve works to ensure that its products are well-designed and will last for a long time. In 2010 the company won the Spark International Design Silver Award for responsible packaging.

Being a green company is not easy, particularly because many consumers believe that green products are costlier than traditional products. Economic forces like the latest recession have made the cost of goods an even greater concern for consumers. Additionally, greenwashing, or marketing products as being more environmentally-friendly than they really are, is also a problem for Preserve because then consumers become more cautious of trusting green marketing claims. As a result, Preserve works hard to deliver price-competitive, trustworthy products through legitimate retailers.

In order to make its business work, Preserve forms partnerships with both organizations and consumers to get the materials it needs. It has strong relationships with companies like Brita and Seventh Generation, which send their waste to Preserve to be recycled into new products. For instance, Preserve uses the plastic from Stonyfield Farm yogurt cups to create the handles of its recycled toothbrush. Support from these companies is crucial for Preserve to maintain its competitive advantage as a company that offers quality green products.

Additionally, Preserve has been able to use consumers as suppliers. The company encourages their customers to send them used products when they reach the end of their life cycles rather than throwing them into landfills. In 2010 Preserve introduced the Mail-Back package at Whole Foods and Target for its recycled toothbrushes. The package not only protects the toothbrush but also allows consumers to use the package as a mailer to send it back to the company when they are finished with the product. Preserve can therefore reduce costs and widen its distribution range by incorporating consumers into the process. "They can facilitate being part of our supply chain," Hudson said.

Despite its advantages, Preserve must constantly engage in environmental scanning and analysis to effectively respond to changing environmental forces. For instance, Preserve must try to understand consumer perceptions toward green products. One way Preserve achieves this is by remaining in constant dialogue with its customers. "We've sought to have a very innovative approach of really reaching out to our advocates," Hudson said. Preserve uses personal e-mails and electronic newsletters to answer concerns and update consumers on recent events.

Preserve also must constantly analyze the competition. Brand competitors include not only other green consumer product firms but also big brand companies that sell more traditional products. Because the company operates in an environment of monopolistic competition, Preserve strives to differentiate its products and communicate their benefits to relevant stakeholders. Its recent initiative is to work with partners to recycle #5 plastic, which makes up 25 percent of plastic waste but is one of the least-recycled types of plastic.

Preserve has come far in its short history, witnessing a sociocultural shift from little stakeholder concern for green products to strong stakeholder support. As the company continues to research innovative approaches toward reusing products and researching consumers, Preserve appears well poised to compete in the green marketplace.[56]

Questions for Discussion

1. Describe the target market for Preserve products.
2. What environmental forces will be most important to understand for Preserve to be successful?
3. Which elements of the marketing mix are key to Preserve in dealing with competition?

case 3.2

Whole Foods Capitalizes on Consumer Desires for Organic Food

Whole Foods Market's emphasis on organic food and sustainable fishing practices is not just socially responsible business but also good marketing. Whole Foods has adopted the value of putting the customer first. It keeps this value in mind when conducting environmental scanning to understand the different forces in the marketing environment. By paying careful attention to changing trends, Whole Foods has been able to identify major concerns and tailor its business practices accordingly. For instance, Whole Foods banned the use of the chemical compound Bisphenol-A from its baby bottles and cups even before the Food and Drug Administration recognized that it could be potentially harmful for children.

Whole Foods was started as a natural foods market in 1980. Through a series of acquisitions the company expanded from a small Austin-based market into a national organic food chain. However, as organic food became more popular, competition increased. Its rival Trader Joe's, for instance, guarantees that products sold under its private-label brand are free from preservatives, genetically-modified ingredients, and trans fats. Whole Foods products are often more expensive than the competition, requiring consumers to spend more disposable income at its stores. These factors require Whole Foods to constantly examine its environment and modify its marketing strategies to increase consumers' willingness to spend in its stores.

One way that Whole Foods has successfully grabbed market share in the organic food industry is by offering a superior product. Whole Foods Market created its own system of quality standards for its food products to assure consumers that it is purchasing superior products, including promoting organically grown foods, selling food that is free from preservatives and sweeteners, and carefully choosing each product in the mix. Whole Foods also tries to create an exciting customer experience in its stores with its free in-store samples, quality customer service, and environmentally-friendly practices.

In 2009, Whole Foods decided to embark upon a healthy living marketing initiative. CEO and co-founder John Mackey believed Whole Foods was deviating from its core principles by selling certain products that were unhealthy. That year Whole Foods adopted a new core value: "Promoting the health of our stakeholders through healthy eating education." Whole Foods partnered with healthy-eating partners to help it educate its stakeholders about healthy food choices. Whole Foods stores began to post healthy eating information and recipes throughout its stores and began selling healthy eating cookbooks. For its employee stakeholders, Whole Foods began offering programs to help employees live more healthy lives and provided additional employee discounts to those who achieved health objectives.

Whole Foods also recognizes the importance of environment, particularly regarding the precarious nature of the world's fisheries. Whole Foods became the first supermarket to offer Marine Stewardship Council (MSC)-certified seafood. Whole Foods has a rating system that color codes the wild-caught seafood it sells into three ratings: green (sustainable seafood), yellow (medium danger of being overfished), and red (in serious danger of being overfished). Whole Foods has committed to phasing out all red-rated seafood species by 2013.

Whole Foods' products and sustainability initiatives have factors on its side. The company has been able to benefit from sociocultural perspectives supporting natural and organic food. Whole Foods can also profit, albeit indirectly, from political forces. With the government's fight against childhood obesity and its push for healthier eating, companies like Whole Foods that market healthy food options are likely to prosper. However, Whole Foods does have one major disadvantage: its higher price points, while signaling the fact that it sells premium products, can also harm the company during a recession. When the recession hit, Whole Foods had to make quick changes to its pricing strategies to retain customers. It lowered prices on some of its brands and began to sell "extreme value items" at very low prices. Its adaptions to economic conditions have allowed the company to survive and even prosper. Whole Foods is a good example of a company that offers premium products consumers desire. Whole Foods customers like the company so much that the company has made *Fortune*'s list for "World's Most Admired Companies."[57]

Questions for Discussion

1. How has Whole Foods been successful in the highly competitive supermarket industry?
2. How does the company adjust to changes in economic conditions?
3. How will changes in sociocultural forces provide opportunities for Whole Foods in the future?

NOTES

[1]Ashley Lutz, "Rivals Rush to Copy Lululemon's Yoga Pose," *Bloomberg Businessweek,* September 8, 2011, www.businessweek.com/magazine/rivals-rush-to-copy-lululemons-yoga-pose-09082011.html (accessed October 6, 2011); "Lululemon Athletica: Our Company History," Lululemon, www.lululemon.com/about/history (accessed October 6, 2011); Solarina Ho, "Lululemon Seen Growing in Lucrative Niche Market," Reuters, November 2, 2010, www.reuters.com/article/2010/11/02/idUSN0116446120101102 (accessed October 6, 2011); Matt Townsend and Cotton Timberlake, "Shoppers Buy Quality at Lululemon, Victoria's Secret," *Bloomberg Businessweek*, January 26, 2011, www.sddt.com/News/article.cfm?SourceCode=20110126fai (accessed July 12, 2012).

[2]"Dotcom Bust," *Economist*, January 28, 2012, 66.

[3]Jon Sicher, "Top 10 CSD Results for 2008," *Beverage Digest*, March 30, 2009; Natalie Zmuda, "Major Changes at PepsiCo as Marketing Department Reorganizes," *Ad Age,* June 16, 2011, http://adage.com/article/cmo-strategy/pepsico-reorganizes-marketing-department-beverages/228259/ (accessed January 12, 2012).

[4]O. C. Ferrell and Michael Hartline, *Marketing Strategy* (Mason, OH: South-Western, 2011).

[5]Ferrell and Hartline, *Marketing Strategy.*

[6]Aron O'Cass and Liem Viet Ngo, "Balancing External Adaptation and Internal Effectiveness: Achieving Better Brand Performance," *Journal of Business Research* 60 (January 2007): 11–20.

[7]Eberhard Stickel, "Uncertainty Reduction in a Competitive Environment," *Journal of Business Research* 51 (2001): 169–177.

[8]John Jannarone, "Discounters Are Still in Fashion" *The Wall Street Journal,* February 25, 2011, C8.

[9]Miguel Bustillo, "Wal-Mart Loses Edge," *The Wall Street Journal,* August 16, 2011, B1, B; Miguel Bustillo, "Wal-Mart Merchandise Goes Back to Basics," *The Wall Street Journal,* April 11, 2011, B3.

[10]Dennis Cauchon and Barbara Hansen, "Typical U.S. Family Got Poorer During the Past 10 Years," *USA Today,* September 14, 2011, www.usatoday.com/news/nation/story/2011-09-13/census-household-income/50383882/1 (accessed January 12, 2011).

[11]Alexis Leondis, "World's Millionaires Increased by 12% on Market, Study Says," *Bloomberg Businessweek,* May 31, 2011, www.businessweek.com/news/2011-05-31/world-s-millionaires-increased-by-12-on-market-study-says.html (accessed January 13, 2012).

[12]Joseph A. Giannone, "Asia Surpasses Europe in Millionaires and Wealth," June 22, 2011, www.reuters.com/article/2011/06/22/us-wealthreport-merrill-idUSTRE75L3O420110622 (accessed January 13, 2012).

[13]Joshua Gallu, "Dodd–Frank May Cost $6.5 Billion and 5,000 Workers," *Bloomberg,* February 14, 2011, www.bloomberg.com/news/2011-02-14/dodd-frank-s-implementation-calls-for-6-5-billion-5-000-staff-in-budget.html (accessed February 22, 2011); Binyamin Appelbaum and Brady Dennis, "Dodd's Overhaul Goes Well Beyond Other Plans," *The Washington Post,* November 11, 2009, www.washingtonpost.com/wp-dyn/content/article/2009/11/09/AR2009110901935.html?hpid=topnews&sid=ST2009111003729 (accessed February 22, 2011).

[14]"Wall Street Reform: Bureau of Consumer Financial Protection (CFPB)," U.S. Treasury, www.treasury.gov/initiatives/Pages/cfpb.aspx (accessed February 22, 2011).

[15]"Trade Mission," BusinessDictionary.com, www.businessdictionary.com/definition/trade-mission.html (accessed February 7, 2012).

[16]"Governor Patrick Announces Trade Mission To Brazil, Chile," Mass.gov, November 16, 2011, www.mass.gov/governor/pressoffice/pressreleases/2011/20111116braziltrademission.html (accessed February 7, 2012).

[17]"Top All-Time Donors, 1989-2012," OpenSecrets.org, www.opensecrets.org/orgs/list.php (accessed January 13, 2012).

[18]"Campaign Finance," *The New York Times,* October 8, 2010, http://topics.nytimes.com/top/reference/timestopics/subjects/c/campaign_finance/index.html (accessed January 24, 2011).

[19]"Wachovia Bank N.A. Admits to Anticompetitive Conduct by Former Employees in the Municipal Bond Investments Market and Agrees to Pay $148 Million to Federal and State Agencies," Department of Justice, December 8, 2011, www.justice.gov/atr/public/press_releases/2011/278076.htm (accessed January 13, 2012).

[20]Chad Bray, "U.S. Charges Ex-Siemens Executives in Alleged Bribery Scheme," *The Wall Street Journal,* December 14, 2011, http://online.wsj.com/article/SB10001424052970203430404577096283680373586.html?KEYWORDS=Siemens+bribery (accessed February 7, 2012).

[21]Dionne Searcey, "U.K. Law on Bribes Has Firms in a Sweat," *The Wall Street Journal*, December 28, 2010, B1; Julius Melnitzer, "U.K. Enacts 'Far-Reaching' Anti-Bribery Act," *Law Times,* February 13, 2011, www.lawtimesnews.com/201102148245/Headline-News/UK-enacts-far-reaching-anti-bribery-act (accessed March 28, 2011).

[22]Julius Melnitzer, "U.K. Enacts 'Far-Reaching' Anti-Bribery Act," *Law Times,* February 13, 2011, www.lawtimesnews.com/201102148245/Headline-News/UK-enacts-far-reaching-anti-bribery-act (accessed March 28, 2011).

[23]Ibid.

[24]Sarah Johnson, "Don't Trust, Verify," *CFO,* February 1, 2012, www.cfo.com/article.cfm/14615752?f=singlepage (accessed February 7, 2012).

[25]Matt Jerzemsky, "Playdom Settles with FTC," *The Wall Street Journal,* May 13, 2011, B6.

[26]David Stout, "Senate Passes Bill to Restrict Credit Card Practices," *The New York Times*, May 19, 2009.

[27]Sara Forden, Peggy Fisk, and Matt Townsend, "Reebok Settles FTC False Sneaker-Claims Case for $25 Million," *Bloomberg Businessweek,* September 28, 2011, www.businessweek.com/news/2011-09-28/reebok-settles-ftc-false-sneaker-claims-case-for-25-million.html (accessed January 13, 2012).

[28]Steve Sternburg, "Avandia to Be Pulled from Retail Shelves," *USA Today*, May 19, 2011, 3A.

[29]"Welcome to the Division of Consumer Protection," Department of State, Division of Consumer Protection, www.dos.ny.gov/consumerprotection/ (accessed February 7, 2012).

[30]"PhRMA Guiding Principles: Direct to Consumer Advertisements," Pharmaceutical Research and Manufacturers of America, December 2008, www.phrma.org.

[31]"BBB expels four contractors," Better Business Bureau, August 31, 2011, www.buffalo.bbb.org/article/bbb-expels-four-contractors-29242 (accessed January 13, 2012).

[32]"NAD Recommends J&J Healthcare Products Modify Claims," *RDH,* www.rdhmag.com/index/display/article-display/7340140924/articles/dentisryiq/industry/2011/09/nad-recommends_j_j.html (accessed January 13, 2012).

[33]Jorgen Wouters, "Verizon Forces Time Warner to Drop Fiber Optic Claims," *Daily Finance,* February 9, 2011, www.dailyfinance.com/2011/02/09/verizon-forces-time-warner-to-drop-fiber-optic-claims/ (accessed January 13, 2012).

[34]Mike Snider, "A Quarter of American Homes Have Hung up on Land Lines," *USA Today*, April 21, 2011, 1A.

[35]Aaron Smith, "Cellphone Adoption and Usage," Pew Internet, June 11, 2011, http://pewinternet.org/Reports/2011/Smartphones.aspx (accessed January 13, 2012).

[36]Melissa Hoffman, "Mobile Marketing to 'Explode' in 2012," *Direct Marketing News,* January 12, 2012, www.dmnews.com/mobile-marketing-to-explode-in-2012/article/222991/ (accessed January 13, 2012).

[37]David Sarno, "The Rise of Tablet Computers," *Los Angeles Times,* May 6, 2011, http://articles.latimes.com/2011/may/06/business/la-fi-tablet-era-20110506 (accessed January 13, 2012).

[38]Cisco, reproduced in *Bloomberg Businessweek Year in Review*, 2010, 24.

[39]"Cisco Visual Networking Index: Forecast and Methodology, 2010-2015," Cisco, June 1, 2011, www.cisco.com/en/US/solutions/collateral/ns341/ns525/ns537/ns705/ns827/white_paper_c11-481360_ns827_Networking_Solutions_White_Paper.html (accessed January 13, 2012).

[40]Nick Clayton, "Social Networks Account for 20% of Time Spent Online," *The Wall Street Journal*, December 22, 2011, http://blogs.wsj.com/tech-europe/2011/12/22/social-networks-account-for-20-of-time-spent-online/ (accessed January 13, 2012).

[41]Debbie McAlister, Linda Ferrell, and O. C. Ferrell, *Business and Society* (Mason, OH: South-Western Cengage Learning, 2011), 352–353.

[42]Ibid.

[43]Vladmir Zwass, "Electronic Commerce: Structures and Issues," *International Journal of Electronic Commerce* (Fall 2000): 3–23.

[44]"Grayson K. Vincent and Victoria A. Velkoff, "The Next Four Decades: The Older Population in the United States: 2010 to 2050," May 2010, www.census.gov/prod/2010pubs/p25-1138.pdf (accessed January 13, 2012).

[45]www.seniorpeoplemeet.com, babyboomerpeoplemeet.com (accessed March 8, 2010).

[46]Sabrina Tavernise, "Married Couples Are No Longer a Majority, Census Finds," *The New York Times,* May 26, 2011, www.nytimes.com/2011/05/26/us/26marry.html (accessed January 13, 2012).

[47]U.S. Bureau of the Census, *Statistical Abstract of the United States, 2011* (Washington, DC: Government Printing Office, 2009), 12.

[48]Haya El Nasser, Gregory Korte, and Paul Overberg, "308.7 Million," *USA Today*, December 22, 2010, 1A; "U.S. and World Population Clocks," U.S. Census Bureau, www.census.gov/main/www/popclock.html (accessed February 7, 2012).

[49]U.S. Bureau of the Census, "Census Bureau Launches 2010 Census Advertising Campaign," January 14, 2010, http://2010.census.gov/news/releases/operations/ad-campaign-release.html.

[50]U.S. Bureau of the Census, *Statistical Abstract of the United States, 2010*, 58.

[51]U.S. Bureau of the Census, "Projections of the Population by Sex, Race, and Hispanic Origin for the United States: 2010 to 2050," August 14, 2008, www.census.gov/population/www/projections/summarytables.html.

[52]Sam Fahmy, "Despite Recession, Hispanic and Asian Buying Power Expected to Surge in U.S., According to Annual UGA Selig Center Multicultural Economy Study," Terry College of Business, November 4, 2010, www.terry.uga.edu/news/releases/2010/minority-buying-power-report.html (accessed January 13, 2012).

[53]David Kesmodel, "Brewers Go Courting Hispanics," *The Wall Street Journal*, July 12, 2011, B8.

[54]"Parents Grossly Underestimate the Influence Their Children Wield Over In-Store Purchases," *Science News*, March 17, 2009, www.sciencedaily.com.

[55]"About Seventh Generation," www.seventhgeneration.com/about (accessed March 10, 2010).

[56]*Recycline* [DVD], Cengage Learning; Preserve Products website, www.preserveproducts.com/ (accessed March 13, 2012); *Preserve Press Kit*, www.preserveproducts.com/media/presskits/Preserve_MediaKit_2012.pdf (accessed March 13, 2012); Nick Leiber, "America's Most Promising Social Entrepreneurs 2011: Preserve Products," *Bloomberg Businessweek*, http://images.businessweek.com/slideshows/20110621/america-s-most-promising-social-entrepreneurs-2011/slides/19 (accessed March 13, 2012); "Eric Hudson, Recycline," [Interview], YouTube, August 13, 2010, www.youtube.com/watch?v=6hhFPUSMtMg (accessed March 13, 2012); *Recyclables Newsletter: Recycline,* Fall 2006, www.preserveproducts.com/newsletter/newsletter-fall-06.html (accessed March 14, 2012).

[57]"Bisphenol-A," Whole Foods Market, www.wholefoodsmarket.com/products/bisphenol-a.php (accessed March 2, 2012); Joe Dickson, "The FDA Changes Its Tune on Bisphenol-A," Whole Foods Market, http://blog.wholefoodsmarket.com/2010/01/the-fda-changes-its-tune-on-bisphenol-a/ (accessed March 2, 2012); "About Whole Foods Market," Whole Foods Market, www.wholefoodsmarket.com/company/ (accessed March 2, 2012); "Trader Joe's Product FAQs," Trader Joe's, www.traderjoes.com/about/product-faq.asp (accessed March 2, 2012); "Seafood Sustainability," Whole Foods Market, www.wholefoodsmarket.com/values/seafood.php (accessed March 2, 2012); "Our Quality Standards," Whole Foods Market, www.wholefoodsmarket.com/products/quality-standards.php (accessed March 2, 2012); "Health Starts Here™ Launches at Whole Foods Market®," Whole Foods Market Press Room, January 20, 2010, http://wholefoodsmarket.com/pressroom/blog/2010/01/20/health-starts-here%E2%84%A2-launches-at-whole-foods-market%C2%AE/ (accessed March 2, 2012); Lisa Baertlein, "Whole Foods Boosts 2011 View, Shares Up," Reuters, July 27, 2011, www.reuters.com/article/2011/07/27/us-wholefoods-idUSTRE76Q6EU20110727 (accessed March 2, 2012); Katy McLaughlin and Timothy W. Martin, "As Sales Slip, Whole Foods Tries Health Push," *The Wall Street Journal,* August 5, 2009, http://online.wsj.com/article/SB124941849645105559.html (accessed March 2, 2012); "World's Most Admired Companies: Whole Foods Market," CNNMoney, http://money.cnn.com/magazines/fortune/most-admired/2012/snapshots/10572.html (accessed March 2, 2012).

Feature Notes

[a]Nadine Heintz, "Close-up: Matt Chatham," *Inc.*, September 2011, 32; "SkyCrepers," Facebook, www.facebook.com/#!/group.php?gid=303410209155&v=wall (accessed December 1, 2011); "Former Patriots Player Matt Chatham Is Opening SkyCrepers in North Attleboro," Boston Restaurant Talk, http://bostonrestaurants.blogspot.com/2011/07/former-patriots-player-matt-chatham-is.html (accessed December 1, 2011); Michael Chmura, "2011 MBA Business Plan Competition Winner SkyCrepers, LLC Announces Grand Opening At Emerald Square Mall," Babson, August 1, 2011, www.babson.edu/News-Events/babson-news/Pages/SkyCrepersOpening8-11.aspx (accessed December 1, 2011).

[b]Rina Chadran, "Debate over GM Eggplant Consumes India," Reuters, February 16, 2010, www.reuters.com/article/2010/02/16/us-india-food-idUSTRE61F0RS20100216 (accessed November 15, 2011); "India Bans GM Eggplant," *ABC Rural,* November 2, 2010, www.abc.net.au/rural/news/content/201002/s2816662.htm (accessed November 15, 2011); Elizabeth Weise, "More of World's Crops Are Genetically Engineered," *USA Today,* February 22, 2011, www.usatoday.com/tech/news/biotech/2011-02-22-biotech-crops_N.htm (accessed November 15, 2011).

[c]"The Next Big Bet," *The Economist,* October 1, 2011, 75–77; Reuters, "Samsung CEO Urges M&As in New Areas," *The Times of India,* October 31, 2011, http://articles.timesofindia.indiatimes.com/2011-10-31/strategy/ 30341477_1_samsung-electronics-chip-business-new-growth-areas (accessed November 3, 2011); "RPT-Update 1—S. Korea's Samsung to Spend $7 Bln on Green Energy Complex," Reuters Africa, April 27, 2011, http://af.reuters.com/article/energyOilNews/idAFL3E7FR11X20110427 (accessed November 3, 2011).

[d]David Kaplan, "Winning Small," *Houston Chronicle,* July 31, 2011, D1, D3; "Stage Stores Board Declares Quarterly Cash Dividend," *Business Wire,* August 27, 2010, www.businesswire.com/news/home/20100827005117/en/Stage-Stores-Board-Declares-Quarterly-Cash-Dividend (accessed November 4, 2011); "Stage Stores Launches New Steele's Concept," *Houston Business Journal,* October 12, 2011, www.bizjournals.com/houston/morning_call/2011/10/stage-stores-launches-new-steeles.html (accessed November 4, 2011).

chapter 4

Social Responsibility and Ethics in Marketing

OBJECTIVES

1. To understand the concept and dimensions of social responsibility
2. To define and describe the importance of marketing ethics
3. To become familiar with ways to improve ethical decisions in marketing
4. To understand the role of social responsibility and ethics in improving marketing performance

MARKETING INSIGHTS

Marketers Win by Being Ethical

The traditional view of marketing is that ethics and social responsibility are good supplements to business activities but may not be essential. Some marketers believe that ethics and social responsibility initiatives drain resources that could be better used for other marketing activities. Yet research has shown that ethical behavior can not only enhance a company's reputation but also contribute significantly to the bottom line.

According to the Ethisphere Institute, the stock prices of the world's most ethical companies have outperformed the stock prices of companies on the Standard & Poor's 500 and Financial Times and Stock Exchange 100 indexes. This is no accident. Consumers worldwide are embracing fair treatment of employees, green practices, and high-integrity products. Consumers want to build trust and develop relationships with ethical companies. According to one study, 41 percent of respondents indicated that they purchased products from companies because those companies supported social, ethical, or environmental causes.

So how can marketers profit from this information? Marketers can promote their companies' social responsibility initiatives to attract more business. Whole Foods, for instance, scores high on customer service and for its organic and natural products. Social responsibility initiatives can also help a company distinguish itself from competitors. The hotel chain Wyndham Worldwide is known for its strong customer service and dedication toward energy conservation. The company has a team of 100 leaders committed toward improving the hotel chain's sustainability practices. Finally, companies whose ethical conduct earns them endorsements from institutions such as *Fortune* magazine or the Ethisphere Institute appear more trustworthy. Consumers can feel more confident that their ethical claims are true.[1]

© Helen Sessions/Alamy

Most businesses operate responsibly and within the limits of the law, but organizations often walk a fine line between acting ethically and engaging in questionable behavior. Research shows that ethical companies often have better stock performance, but too often companies are distracted by the short-term costs of implementing ethics programs and the fleeting benefits of cutting ethical corners. Another common mistake companies make is a tendency to believe that because an activity is legal, it is also ethical. In fact, ethics often goes above and beyond the law and should therefore be a critical concern of marketers.

Some of the most common types of unethical practices among companies include deceptive sales practices, bribery, price discrimination, deceptive advertising, misleading packaging, and marketing defective products. Deceptive advertising in particular causes consumers to become defensive toward all promotional messages and distrustful of all advertising, so it hurts not only consumers but marketers as well.[2] Practices of this kind raise questions about marketers' obligations to society. Inherent in these questions are the issues of social responsibility and marketing ethics.

Because social responsibility and ethics often have profound impacts on the success of marketing strategies, we devote this chapter to their role in marketing decision making. We begin by defining social responsibility and exploring its dimensions. We then discuss social responsibility issues, such as sustainability and the marketer's role as a member of the community. Next, we define and examine the role of ethics in marketing decisions. We consider ethical issues in marketing, the ethical decision-making process, and ways to improve ethical conduct in marketing. Finally, we incorporate social responsibility and ethics into strategic market planning.

THE NATURE OF SOCIAL RESPONSIBILITY

In marketing, **social responsibility** refers to an organization's obligation to maximize its positive impact and minimize its negative impact on society. Social responsibility thus deals with the total effect of all marketing decisions on society. In marketing, social responsibility includes the managerial processes needed to monitor, satisfy, and even exceed stakeholder expectations and needs.[3] Remember from Chapter 1 that stakeholders are groups that have a "stake," or claim, in some aspect of a company's products, operations, markets, industry, and outcomes. CEOs such as Indra Nooyi, chairperson and CEO of PepsiCo, are increasingly recognizing that in the future companies will have to "do better by doing better." She goes on to say that "performance without purpose is not a long-term sustainable formula."[4]

Ample evidence demonstrates that ignoring stakeholders' demands for responsible marketing can destroy customers' trust and even prompt government regulations. Irresponsible actions that anger customers, employees, or competitors may not only jeopardize a marketer's financial standing but have legal repercussions as well. For instance, GlaxoSmithKline settled with the U.S. Justice Department for $3 billion after the Justice Department accused it of defrauding Medicaid and marketing certain drugs illegally. One of the accusations levied against GlaxoSmithKline was that it marketed its drug Wellbutrin for uses not approved by the Food and Drug Administration. Such off-label marketing is illegal.[5]

In contrast, socially responsible activities can generate positive publicity and boost sales. IBM, for example, has established a corporate volunteer program that sends employees to developing countries to create opportunities for their citizens. Through this program, IBM has helped Kenya reform its postal system and has aided Tanzania in developing eco-tourism opportunities. Although the program is costly, IBM's efforts have created positive relationships with stakeholders in these countries and have generated approximately $5 million in new business.[6]

social responsibility An organization's obligation to maximize its positive impact and minimize its negative impact on society

Socially responsible efforts have a positive impact on local communities; at the same time, they indirectly help the sponsoring organization by attracting goodwill, publicity, and potential customers and employees. Thus, although social responsibility is certainly a positive concept in itself, most organizations embrace it in the expectation of indirect long-term benefits. Our own research suggests that an organizational culture that supports social responsibility generates greater employee commitment and improved business performance.[7] Table 4.1 provides a sampling of companies that have chosen to make social responsibility a strategic long-term objective.

Table 4.1 Best Corporate Citizens

1	Johnson Controls, Inc.
2	Campbell Soup Co.
3	IBM Corp.
4	Bristol Myers Squibb Co.
5	Mattel, Inc.
6	3M Corp.
7	Accenture plc
8	Kimberly Clark Corp.
9	Hewlett-Packard Co.
10	Nike, Inc.

Source: "CR's 100 Best Corporate Citizens 2011," *CR*, http://thecro.com/files/100Best2011_List_revised.pdf (accessed May 17, 2012).

The Dimensions of Social Responsibility

Socially responsible organizations strive for **marketing citizenship** by adopting a strategic focus for fulfilling the economic, legal, ethical, and philanthropic social responsibilities that their stakeholders expect of them. Companies that consider the diverse perspectives of stakeholders in their daily operations and strategic planning are said to have a *stakeholder orientation,* an important element of social responsibility.[8] A stakeholder orientation in marketing goes beyond customers, competitors, and regulators to include understanding and addressing the needs of all stakeholders, including communities and special-interest groups. As a result, organizations are now under pressure to undertake initiatives that demonstrate a balanced perspective on stakeholder interests.[9] Pfizer, for example, has secured stakeholder input on a number of issues including rising health-care costs and health-care reform.[10] As Figure 4.1 shows, the economic, legal, ethical, and philanthropic dimensions of social responsibility can be viewed as a pyramid.[11]

marketing citizenship The adoption of a strategic focus for fulfilling the economic, legal, ethical, and philanthropic social responsibilities expected by stakeholders

The Nature of Social Responsibility
Many car companies are embracing the electric car as a long-term, socially responsible benefit to their product offerings.

At the most basic level, all companies have an economic responsibility to be profitable so that they can provide a return on investment to their owners and investors, create jobs for the community, and contribute goods and services to the economy. How organizations relate to stakeholders affects the economy. When economic downturns or poor decisions lead companies to lay off employees, communities often suffer as they attempt to absorb the displaced employees. Customers may experience diminished levels of service as a result of fewer experienced employees. Stock prices often decline when layoffs are announced, reducing the value of shareholders' investment portfolios. An organization's sense of economic responsibility is especially significant for employees, raising such issues as equal job opportunities, workplace diversity, job safety, health, and employee privacy. Economic responsibilities require finding a balance in stakeholder interests while recognizing that a firm must make a profit to be sustainable in the long run.

Marketers also have an economic responsibility to engage in fair competition and build ethical customer relationships. Government regulatory agencies often define the activities that constitute fair competition along with unethical issues such as price fixing, deceptive sales practices, false advertising, bribery, and questionable distribution practices. This misconduct can be considered unfair competition that is also damaging to consumers. Companies that engage in questionable conduct damage their reputation and can destroy customer trust. On the other hand, the "World's Most Ethical Companies"—a designation given by the Ethisphere Institute—have a track record of avoiding these types of issues. For example, Starbucks, Cummins, Johnson Controls, Adobe, and Juniper Networks are profitable and have excellent reputations with their customers. Marketers are also expected, of course, to obey laws and regulations. Laws and regulations are designed to keep U.S. companies' actions within the

Figure 4.1 The Pyramid of Corporate Social Responsibility

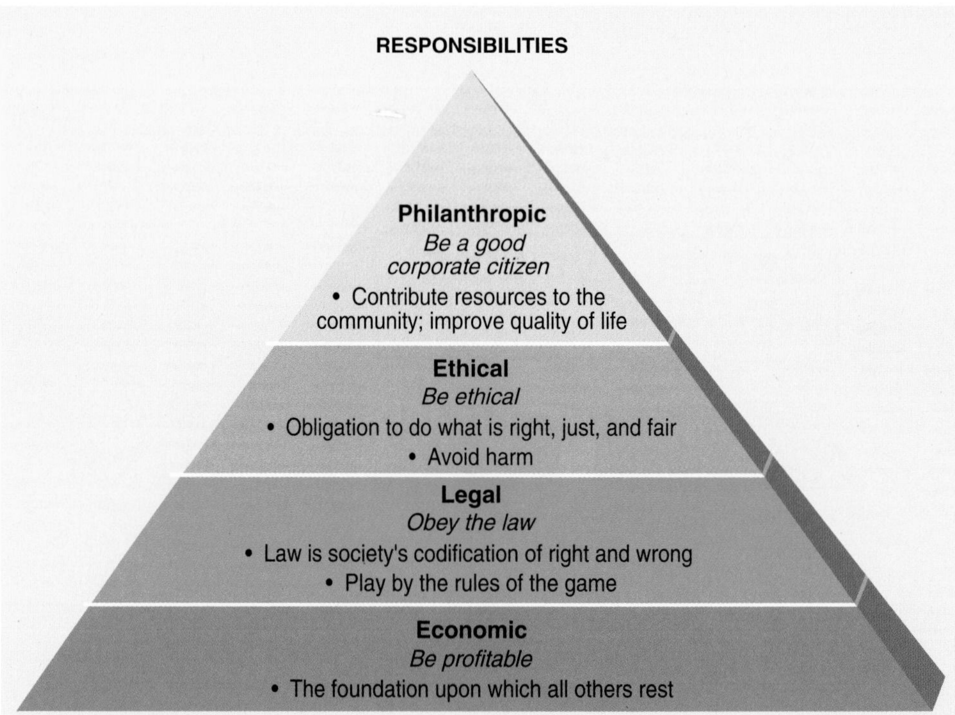

Source: From Archie B. Carroll, "The Pyramid of Corporate Social Responsibility: Toward the Moral Management of Organizational Stakeholders," adaptation of Figure 3, p. 42. Reprinted from *Business Horizons,* July/August 1991, by the Foundation for the School of Business at Indiana University. Reprinted with permission.

range of acceptable conduct and fair competition. When customers, interest groups, or businesses become outraged over what they perceive as misconduct on the part of a marketing organization, they may urge their legislators to draft new legislation to regulate the behavior or engage in litigation to force the organization to "play by the rules." For example, complaints from merchants about high debit card fees prompted new legislation that capped how much banks could charge for processing debit card transactions.[12]

Economic and legal responsibilities are the most basic levels of social responsibility for a good reason: failure to consider them may mean that a marketer is not around long enough to engage in ethical or philanthropic activities. Beyond these dimensions is **marketing ethics**, principles and standards that define acceptable conduct in marketing as determined by various stakeholders, including the public, government regulators, private-interest groups, consumers, industry, and the organization itself. The most basic of these principles have been codified as laws and regulations to encourage marketers to conform to society's expectations for conduct. However, marketing ethics goes beyond legal issues. Ethical marketing decisions foster trust, which helps build long-term marketing relationships. We take a more detailed look at the ethical dimension of social responsibility later in this chapter.

At the top of the pyramid of corporate responsibility (see Figure 4.1) are philanthropic responsibilities. These responsibilities, which go beyond marketing ethics, are not required of a company, but they promote human welfare or goodwill, as do the economic, legal, and ethical dimensions of social responsibility. That many companies have demonstrated philanthropic responsibility is evidenced by the more than $15 billion in annual corporate donations and contributions to environmental and social causes.[13] Even small companies participate in philanthropy through donations and volunteer support of local causes and national charities, such as the Red Cross and the United Way. For example, Charlotte Street Computers in Asheville, North Carolina, has developed a refurbishing center that refurbishes computers and then donates them to those in need. The small business also sponsors several community events and fundraising for charities.[14]

More companies than ever are adopting a strategic approach to corporate philanthropy. Many firms link their products to a particular social cause on an ongoing or short-term basis, a practice known as **cause-related marketing**. General Mills, for example, has implemented its Box Tops for Education program to raise money for schools. Consumers can raise money for their children's schools by cutting Box Top coupons found on participating products. These coupons can then be redeemed for cash. The program has generated approximately $400 million for schools since it was implemented in 1996.[15] Such cause-related programs tend to appeal to consumers because they provide an additional reason to "feel good" about a particular purchase. Marketers like the programs because well-designed ones increase sales and create feelings of respect and admiration for the companies involved. Indeed, research suggests that 85 percent of American consumers have a more positive opinion of an organization when it supports causes that they care about.[16]

On the other hand, some companies are beginning to extend the concept of corporate philanthropy beyond financial contributions by adopting a **strategic philanthropy** approach, the synergistic use of organizational core competencies and resources to address key stakeholders' interests and achieve both organizational and social benefits. Strategic philanthropy involves employees, organizational resources and expertise, and the ability to link those assets to the concerns of key stakeholders, including employees, customers, suppliers, and social needs. Strategic philanthropy involves both financial and nonfinancial contributions to stakeholders (employee time, goods and services, company technology and equipment, etc.), while also benefiting the company.[17] Salesforce.com, for example, believes in the benefits of strategic philanthropy so strongly that it incorporates community service into its corporate culture. Salesforce.com allows employees 1 percent of their time to volunteer in their communities, sets aside 1 percent of the company's capital for the Salesforce.com Foundation, and donates or discounts licenses of its Customer Relationship Management software to over 8,000 nonprofits worldwide.[18]

marketing ethics Principles and standards that define acceptable marketing conduct as determined by various stakeholders

cause-related marketing The practice of linking products to a particular social cause on an ongoing or short-term basis

strategic philanthropy The synergistic use of organizational core competencies and resources to address key stakeholders' interests and achieve both organizational and social benefits

Strategic Philanthropy
Home Depot pairs with Peter Facinelli, of Twilight fame, and MasterCard to raise money for Habitat for Humanity.

Social Responsibility Issues

Although social responsibility may seem to be an abstract ideal, managers make decisions related to social responsibility every day. To be successful, a business must determine what customers, government regulators, competitors, and society want or expect in terms of social responsibility. Table 4.2 summarizes three major categories of social responsibility issues: sustainability, consumerism, and community relations.

sustainability The potential for the long-term well-being of the natural environment, including all biological entities, as well as the interaction among nature and individuals, organizations, and business strategies

Sustainability

One of the more common ways marketers demonstrate social responsibility is through programs designed to protect and preserve the natural environment. **Sustainability** is the potential for the long-term well-being of the natural environment, including all biological

Table 4.2 Social Responsibility Issues

Issue	Description	Major Social Concerns
Sustainability	Consumers insisting not only on a good quality of life but on a healthful environment so they can maintain a high standard of living during their lifetimes	Conservation Water pollution Air pollution Land pollution
Consumerism	Activities undertaken by independent individuals, groups, and organizations to protect their rights as consumers	The right to safety The right to be informed The right to choose The right to be heard
Community relations	Society eager to have marketers contribute to its well-being, wishing to know what marketers do to help solve social problems	Equality issues Disadvantaged members of society Safety and health Education and general welfare

Sustainability
Timberland reports its "Green Index" on all of its footwear.

entities, as well as the interaction among nature and individuals, organizations, and business strategies. Sustainability includes the assessment and improvement of business strategies, economic sectors, work practices, technologies, and lifestyles—all while maintaining the natural environment. Many companies are making contributions to sustainability by adopting more eco-friendly business practices and/or supporting environmental initiatives. For instance, Walmart has taken steps to reduce waste and decrease greenhouse gas emissions in its supply chain. Walmart's example is convincing other large retailers to take similar actions.[19] Such efforts generate positive publicity and often increase sales for the companies involved.

Many products have been certified as "green" by environmental organizations such as Green Seal and carry a special logo identifying their organization as green marketers. Lumber products at Home Depot, for example, may carry a seal from the Forest Stewardship Council to indicate that they were harvested from sustainable forests using environmentally friendly methods.[20]

Going Green

Italian Company Turns Sustainability into a Competitive Advantage

Italian company Sabox has come up with an innovative way to deal with overflowing trash in landfills: make furniture out of it. Sabox is a paper company that produces sustainable packaging from recycled paper. Its GreenProject initiative seeks to incorporate sustainability into all areas of the company, both with the products it sells and its operations. For instance, all of the company's products are certified by the Forest Stewardship Council, which signals that the materials are responsibly sourced. Even employees take the company's sustainability message seriously by carpooling to work.

Sabox is able to differentiate itself from competitors through its green message and its commitment to social responsibility. When Sabox founder Aldo Savarese saw the overflowing landfills in Naples, approximately 25 miles from company headquarters, he resolved to do something about it. For many years Naples has experienced problems with trash collection. The company believes it can help the area by turning discarded items into valuable products. Sabox has been able to create desks, tables, and chairs from discarded materials. And these items are not shoddily made either—some of the furniture has been designed by a famous Italian designer. Sabox also donates chairs to the Venice International Film Festival, a marketing tactic that increases goodwill for the company and spreads awareness of its products.[a]

Figure 4.2 **The EU Ecolabel**

Likewise, most Chiquita bananas are certified through the Rainforest Alliance's Better Banana Project as having been grown with more environmentally and labor-friendly practices.[21] In Europe, companies can voluntarily apply for the EU Ecolabel to indicate that their products are less harmful to the environment than competing products, based on scientifically determined criteria (see Figure 4.2).

Although demand for economic, legal, and ethical solutions to environmental problems is widespread, the environmental movement in marketing includes many different groups whose values and goals often conflict. Some environmentalists and marketers believe companies should work to protect and preserve the natural environment by implementing the following goals:

1. *Eliminate the concept of waste.* Recognizing that pollution and waste usually stem from inefficiency, the question is not what to do with waste but how to make things without waste.
2. *Reinvent the concept of a product.* Products should be reduced to only three types and eventually just two. The first type is consumables, which are eaten or, when placed in the ground, turn into soil with few harmful side effects. The second type is durable goods—such as cars, televisions, computers, and refrigerators—that should be made, used, and returned to the manufacturer within a closed-loop system. Such products should be designed for disassembly and recycling. The third category is unsalables and includes such products as radioactive materials, heavy metals, and toxins. These products should always belong to the original makers, who should be responsible for the products and their full life-cycle effects. Reclassifying products in this way encourages manufacturers to design products more efficiently.
3. *Make prices reflect the cost.* Every product should reflect or at least approximate its actual cost—not only the direct cost of production but also the cost of air, water, and soil. For example, the cost of a gallon of gasoline is higher when pollution, waste disposal, health effects, and defense expenditures are factored in. Major disasters like the BP oil leak in the Gulf of Mexico also impact the price of gas.

4. *Make environmentalism profitable.* Consumers are beginning to recognize that competition in the marketplace should not occur between companies that are harming the environment and those that are trying to save it.[22]

Courtesy of Aubrey Organics, Inc.

Green Marketing
Companies, such as Aubrey Organics, make consumers aware of its energy saving programs and technology through a marketing communications campaign.

Consumerism

Another significant issue in socially responsible marketing is consumerism, which we defined in Chapter 3 as the efforts of independent individuals, groups, and organizations to protect the rights of consumers. A number of interest groups and individuals have taken action against companies they consider irresponsible by lobbying government officials and agencies, engaging in letter-writing campaigns and boycotts, and making public-service announcements. Some consumers choose to boycott firms and products out of a desire to support a cause and make a difference.[23] How a firm handles customer complaints affects consumer evaluations and in turn customer satisfaction and loyalty.[24] Consumer reaction had a significant impact on Verizon when it announced plans to charge customers a $2 fee for paying their bills online or over the phone. The resulting consumer backlash caused Verizon to drop the idea for the extra charge.[25]

The consumer movement has been helped by news-format television programs, such as *Dateline, 60 Minutes,* and *Prime Time Live,* as well as by 24-hour news coverage from CNN, MSNBC, and Fox News. The Internet too has changed the way consumers obtain information about companies' goods, services, and activities. Consumers can share their opinions about goods and services and about companies they see as irresponsible at consumer-oriented websites, such as epinions.com and ConsumerReview.com, and through blogs and social networking sites.

Ralph Nader, one of the best-known consumer activists, continues to crusade for consumer rights. Consumer activism by Nader and others has resulted in legislation requiring many features that make cars safer: seat belts, air bags, padded dashboards, stronger door latches, head restraints, shatterproof windshields, and collapsible steering columns. Activists' efforts have also facilitated the passage of several consumer protection laws, including the Wholesome Meat Act of 1967, the Radiation Control for Health and Safety Act of 1968, the Clean Water Act of 1972, and the Toxic Substance Act of 1976.

Also of great importance to the consumer movement are four basic rights spelled out in a consumer "bill of rights" that was drafted by President John F. Kennedy. These rights include the right to safety, the right to be informed, the right to choose, and the right to be heard.

Ensuring consumers' *right to safety* means marketers are obligated not to market a product that they know could harm consumers. This right can be extended to imply that all products must be safe for their intended use, include thorough and explicit instructions for proper and safe use, and have been tested to ensure reliability and quality.

Consumers' *right to be informed* means consumers should have access to and the opportunity to review all relevant information about a product before buying it. Many laws require specific labeling on product packaging to satisfy this right. In addition, labels on alcoholic and tobacco products must inform consumers that these products may cause illness and other problems.

The *right to choose* means consumers should have access to a variety of products and services at competitive prices. They should also be assured of satisfactory quality and service at a fair price. Activities that reduce competition among businesses in an industry might jeopardize this right.

The *right to be heard* ensures that consumers' interests will receive full and sympathetic consideration in the formulation of government policy. The right to be heard also promises

Emerging Trends

The Growing Trend of Eco-Friendly Funeral Services

The $12 billion funeral industry faces a dilemma: it is running out of burial space. In Europe cemeteries are reaching their maximum capacity. Cremations are being criticized due to the large amount of carbon emissions crematoriums release. These difficulties combined with a growing interest in environmentally friendly practices are inspiring more funeral companies to offer green burial services.

This emerging trend is reinventing the concept of funeral services. Green funerals not only help to solve the problem of decreasing land availability and pollution, but they also tend to cost less than traditional funerals. This is because many of the more costly services, such as embalming the body or buying a metal coffin, can be bypassed. Consumers can choose from many different "green" options, and companies are rushing to meet demand with their own solutions. For instance, Creative Coffins creates themed coffins that are biodegradable and Creative Reefs adds human ashes to an artificial reef ball placed on the ocean floor.

Not everyone is happy about green funerals, however. Some towns have blocked the creation of green cemeteries because residents fear that bodies buried without coffins could potentially contaminate groundwater. Other green funeral processes are thought to degrade human dignity. The topic of green burials has strained community relations in certain areas, a fact that funeral companies must keep in mind when marketing green funeral services.[b]

consumers fair treatment when they complain to marketers about products. This right benefits marketers too because when consumers complain about a product, the manufacturer can use this information to modify the product and make it more satisfying.

The Federal Trade Commission provides a wealth of consumer information at its website (**www.ftc.gov/bcp/consumer.shtm**) on a variety of topics ranging from automobiles and the Internet to diet, health, fitness, and identity theft.

Community Relations

On the other hand, being a good community citizen also means avoiding harmful actions that could damage the community. Examples include pollution, urban sprawl, and exploitation of the work force. A firm that participates in the economic viability of the community improves community relations. For example, Cutco Corp. in Olean, New York, gives its employees gift certificates to local stores at Christmas. This supports local businesses and helps build good relationships with the community.

Although most charitable donations come from individuals, corporate philanthropy is on the rise. Target, for example, committed $1 billion in its ongoing efforts to improve education. Through the retailer's Take Charge of Education program, customers who use a Target REDcard can designate a specific school to which Target donates 1 percent of their total purchase. The company also provides funds for building new school libraries.[26]

Smaller firms can also make positive contributions to their communities. For example, California-based clothing company Patagonia donates 1 percent of its sales toward preserving and restoring the environment.[27] From a positive perspective, a marketer can significantly improve its community's quality of life through employment opportunities, economic development, and financial contributions to educational, health, cultural, and recreational causes.

MARKETING ETHICS

As noted earlier, marketing ethics is a dimension of social responsibility that involves principles and standards that define acceptable conduct in marketing. Acceptable standards of conduct in making individual and group decisions in marketing are determined by various

Figure 4.3 American Trust in Different Institutions

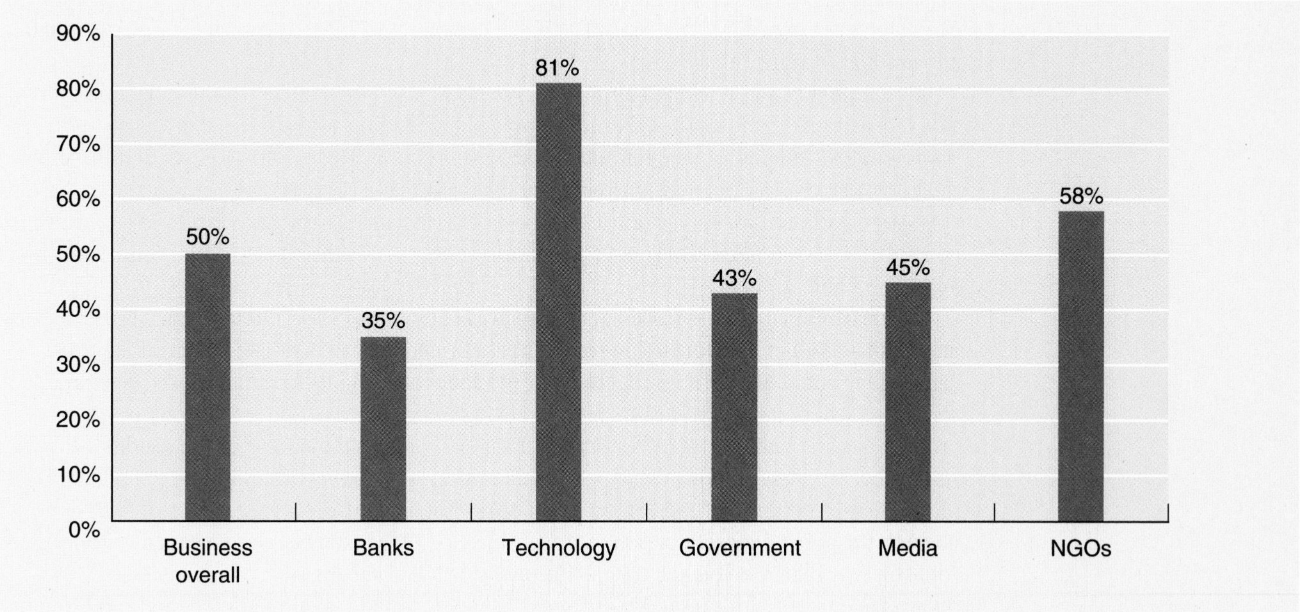

Source: Edelman, *2012 Edelman Trust Barometer Global Results*, p. 7, http://trust.edelman.com/trust-download/global-results/ (accessed January 25, 2012).

stakeholders and by an organization's ethical climate. Marketers must also use their own values and knowledge of ethics to act responsibly and provide ethical leadership for others.

Marketers should be aware of stakeholders including customers, employees, regulators, suppliers, and the community. When marketing activities deviate from accepted standards, the exchange process can break down, resulting in customer dissatisfaction, lack of trust, and lawsuits. In recent years, a number of ethical scandals have resulted in a massive loss of confidence in the integrity of U.S. businesses. A recent study shows that about 50 percent of U.S. consumers trust businesses today.[28] Trust is an important concern for marketers since it is the foundation for long-term relationships. Consumer lack of trust has increased in recent years due to the financial crisis and deep recession. The questionable conduct of high-profile financial institutions and banks has caused many consumers to critically examine the conduct of all companies. Trust must be built or restored to gain the confidence of customers. Figure 4.3 describes the trust Americans have for different institutions. Once trust is lost, it can take a lifetime to rebuild. The way to deal with ethical issues is proactively during the strategic planning process, not after major problems materialize.

Our focus here is on the ethical conduct of marketers. It is not our purpose to examine the conduct of consumers, although some do behave unethically (engaging, for instance, in coupon fraud, shoplifting, intellectual property piracy, and other abuses). We discuss consumer misbehavior and ethical issues associated with this misconduct in Chapter 7. Our goal in this chapter is to underscore the importance of resolving ethical issues in marketing and to help you learn about marketing ethics.

Ethical Issues in Marketing

An **ethical issue** is an identifiable problem, situation, or opportunity that requires an individual or organization to choose from among several actions that must be evaluated as right or wrong, ethical or unethical. Any time an activity causes marketing managers or customers in their target market to feel manipulated or cheated, a marketing ethical issue exists, regardless of the legality of that activity. For instance, the Girl Scouts have been criticized because their three most popular cookies—Samoas, Tagalongs, and Thin Mints—contain partially

ethical issue An identifiable problem, situation, or opportunity requiring a choice among several actions that must be evaluated as right or wrong, ethical or unethical

hydrogenated oils (trans fat). Yet the organization has carried a "0 percent trans fat" label on its cookie boxes since 2007. By law companies are allowed to label their food products as containing 0 percent trans fat as long as the product contains less than 0.5 grams of trans fat per serving. However, critics feel that the label is misleading as long as the cookies contain any amount of trans fat.[29]

Regardless of the reasons behind specific ethical issues, marketers must be able to identify those issues and decide how to resolve them. Doing so requires familiarity with the many kinds of ethical issues that may arise in marketing. Research suggests that the greater the consequences associated with an issue, the more likely it will be recognized as an ethics issue and the more important it will be in making an ethical decision.[30] Some examples of ethical issues related to product, promotion, price, and distribution (the marketing mix) appear in Table 4.3.

Product-related ethical issues generally arise when marketers fail to disclose risks associated with a product or information regarding the function, value, or use of a product. Pressures can build to substitute inferior materials or product components to reduce costs. Ethical issues also arise when marketers fail to inform customers about existing conditions or changes in product quality; such failure is a form of dishonesty about the nature of the product. *Product recalls* occur when companies ask customers to return products found to be defective. Companies that issue product recalls are often criticized for not having adequate quality controls to catch the defective product before it was released. For instance, a few years ago Johnson & Johnson was highly criticized for instituting 50 product recalls of its medicines in 15 months due to bad smelling odors, flakes of metal or wood found in the medicine, and other quality issues.[31] The failure to maintain product quality and integrity in production is a significant ethical issue.

Promotion can create ethical issues in a variety of ways, among them false or misleading advertising and manipulative or deceptive sales promotions, tactics, and publicity. One controversial issue in the area of promotion is *greenwashing*, which occurs when products are promoted as being more environmentally friendly than they really are. As green products gain in popularity, companies are increasingly selling products that they claim to be "green." However, there are no formal criteria for what constitutes a green product, so it is hard to determine whether a company's product is truly green. Another major ethical issue is promoting products to children that might be construed as harmful, such as violent video games or fatty foods. Many other ethical issues are linked to promotion, including the use of bribery in personal selling situations. *Bribery* occurs when an incentive (usually money or expensive gifts) is offered in exchange for an illicit advantage. Even a bribe that is offered to benefit the organization is usually considered unethical. Because it jeopardizes trust and fairness, it hurts the organization in the long run. For this reason, sales promotion activities such as games, contests, and other sales attempts must be communicated accurately and transparently.

Table 4.3 Sample Ethical Issues Related to the Marketing Mix

Product Issue *Product information*	Covering up defects that could cause harm to a consumer; withholding critical performance information that could affect a purchase decision.
Distribution Issue *Counterfeiting*	Counterfeit products are widespread, especially in the areas of computer software, clothing, and audio and video products. The Internet has facilitated the distribution of counterfeit products.
Promotion Issue *Advertising*	Deceptive advertising or withholding important product information in a personal selling situation.
Pricing Issue *Pricing*	Indicating that an advertised sale price is a reduction below the regular price when in fact that is not the case.

In pricing, common ethical issues are price fixing, predatory pricing, and failure to disclose the full price of a purchase. The emotional and subjective nature of price creates many situations in which misunderstandings between the seller and buyer cause ethical problems. Marketers have the right to price their products to earn a reasonable profit, but ethical issues may crop up when a company seeks to earn high profits at the expense of its customers. Some pharmaceutical companies, for example, have been accused of *price gouging,* or pricing products at exorbitant levels, and taking advantage of customers who must purchase the medicine to survive or to maintain their quality of life. Various forms of *bait and switch* pricing schemes attempt to gain consumer interest with a low-priced product, then switch the buyer to a more expensive product or add-on service. One way companies do this is by telling customers that the lower-priced product they wanted is unavailable. Another issue relates to quantity surcharges that occur when consumers are effectively overcharged for buying a larger package size of the same grocery product.[32]

Ethical issues in distribution involve relationships among producers and marketing intermediaries. Marketing intermediaries, or middlemen (wholesalers and retailers), facilitate the flow of products from the producer to the ultimate customer. Each intermediary performs a different role and agrees to certain rights, responsibilities, and rewards associated with that role. For example, producers expect wholesalers and retailers to honor agreements and keep them informed of inventory needs. Serious ethical issues with regard to distribution include manipulating a product's availability for purposes of exploitation and using coercion to force intermediaries to behave in a specific manner. Several companies have been accused of *channel stuffing*, which involves shipping surplus inventory to wholesalers and retailers at an excessive rate, typically before the end of a quarter. The practice may conceal declining demand for a product or inflate financial statement earnings, which misleads investors.[33] Another ethical issue that has become a worldwide problem is *counterfeiting*. The market for fake or pirated goods is enormous, with an estimated global value of $600 billion. Counterfeit products on the Internet are becoming a major concern due to the ease of distribution and the greater difficulty in detecting whether a product is authentic. To prevent counterfeiting some companies have begun to invest in technology that can identify the authenticity of a product.[34] As this section has shown, the nature of marketing ethics involves the ethics of all marketing channel members. However, the member managing the product is often held accountable for ethical conduct throughout the total supply chain. Hershey found this out when it was criticized by the International Labor Rights Forum for purchasing chocolate from suppliers using child labor. Hershey agreed to improve its labor practices and invested $10 million into its West African suppliers.[35]

Ethical Dimensions of Managing Supply Chain Relationships

Managing supply chains responsibly is one of the greatest difficulties of marketing ethics and therefore needs some additional explanation. Supply chains require constant vigilance on the part of marketers as well as the need to anticipate unforeseen circumstances. For instance, sending free goldfish to media companies might seem like a unique idea for a marketing promotion, but not if the goldfish die in transit. This is exactly what happened to an Australian firm that sent media companies 50 goldfish that perished on the way. The firm issued an apology and donated money to animal protection organizations.[36] Such examples might seem extreme, but the supply chain is a difficult area to conquer in regard to ethics.[37] Consider Apple Inc., which has a stellar reputation for its high-quality products and technological innovation. Human rights issues have emerged at Chinese suppliers that Apple uses to build and clean its products. Instances of forced overtime, underage workers, explosions, and improper disposal of waste have been recorded at Apple's supplier factories. In 2010 more than 100 workers became ill after using harmful chemicals to clean iPod screens. Although Apple has a Supplier Code of Conduct, problems at its supplier factories have continued.[38]

The issues that Apple has faced highlight the numerous risks that occur in global supply chains. Although companies often create a Supplier Code of Conduct, it requires regular audits to ensure that factories are following compliance standards—which in turn can incur significant costs to companies in both time and finances. Countries with lax labor laws, such as China and Russia, require even more diligent monitoring. Often suppliers hire sub-contractors to do some of the work, which increases a company's network of suppliers and the costs of trying to monitor all of them. Finally, company compliance requirements may conflict with the mission of the procurement office. Because it is the procurement division's job to procure resources at the lowest price possible, the division may very well opt to source from less expensive suppliers with questionable ethical practices rather than from more expensive ethical suppliers. Nike faced this problem during the 1990s when it was highly criticized for worker abuses in its supplier factories.[39]

Managing supply chain ethical decision making is important because many stakeholders hold the firm responsible for all ethical conduct related to product availability. This requires the company to exercise oversight over all of the supplies used in producing a product. Developing good supply chain ethics is important because it ensures the integrity of the product and the firm's operations in serving customers. For instance, leading health care supply company Novation has been recognized for its strong corporate governance and reporting mechanisms in its supply chain. To encourage its suppliers to report misconduct, the company has instituted a vendor grievance and feedback system. This allows vendors to report potential problems before they reach the next level of the supply chain, which reduces the damage such problems will cause if the products continue down the supply chain unchecked.[40]

Fortunately, organizations have been coming up with solutions to promote ethical sourcing practices. First, it is essential for all companies that work with global suppliers to adopt a Global Supplier Code of Conduct and ensure that it is effectively communicated to suppliers. Additionally, companies should encourage compliance and procurement employees to work together to find ethical suppliers at reasonable costs. Marketers must also work to make certain that their company's supply chains are diverse. This can be difficult because sometimes the best product manufacturers are located in a single country. Yet although it is expensive to diversify a company's supply chain, disasters can incapacitate a country.[41] Companies like Jabil Circuit and Goodyear Tire & Rubber found their supply chains at risk due to the Japanese tsunami of 2011 and severe flooding in Thailand.[42] Finally, and perhaps most importantly, companies must perform regular audits on its suppliers and, if necessary, discipline those found to be in violation of company standards.[43] More on supply chain management will be discussed in Chapter 15.

The Nature of Marketing Ethics

To grasp the significance of ethics in marketing decision making, it is helpful to examine the factors that influence the ethical decision-making process. As Figure 4.4 shows, individual

Figure 4.4 Factors That Influence the Ethical Decision-Making Process in Marketing

factors, organizational relationships, and opportunity interact to determine ethical decisions in marketing.

Source: Wi-Fi Alliance/Wakefield survey of 1,054 adults, www.wakefieldresearch.com/blog/2011/05/16/wi-fi-alliancewakefield-research-snapshot.

Individual Factors

When people need to resolve ethical conflicts in their daily lives, they often base their decisions on their own values and principles of right or wrong. For example, a study by the Josephson Institute of Ethics reported that 59 percent of students admitted to cheating on an exam at least once in the past year, and over 40 percent admitted to lying to save money.[44] People learn values and principles through socialization by family members, social groups, religion, and formal education. Because of different levels of personal ethics in any organization, there will be significant ethical diversity among employees. Therefore, shared ethical values and compliance standards are required to prevent deviation from desired ethical conduct. In the workplace, however, research has established that an organization's culture often has more influence on marketing decisions than an individual's own values.[45]

Organizational Relationships

Although people can and do make ethical choices pertaining to marketing decisions, no one operates in a vacuum.[46] Ethical choices in marketing are most often made jointly, in work groups and committees, or in conversations and discussions with coworkers. Marketing employees resolve ethical issues based not only on what they learned from their own backgrounds but also on what they learn from others in the organization. The outcome of this learning process depends on the strength of each individual's personal values, opportunity for unethical behavior, and exposure to others who behave ethically or unethically. Superiors, peers, and subordinates in the organization influence the ethical decision-making process. Although people outside the organization, such as family members and friends, also influence decision makers, organizational culture and structure operate through organizational relationships to influence ethical decisions.

Organizational, or **corporate**, **culture** is a set of values, beliefs, goals, norms, and rituals that members of an organization share. These values also help shape employees' satisfaction with their employer, which may affect the quality of the service they provide to customers. A firm's culture may be expressed formally through codes of conduct, memos, manuals, dress codes, and ceremonies, but it is also conveyed informally through work habits, extracurricular activities, and stories. An organization's culture gives its members meaning and suggests rules for how to behave and deal with problems within the organization.

With regard to organizational structure, most experts agree that the chief executive officer or vice president of marketing sets the ethical tone for the entire marketing organization. Lower-level managers obtain their cues from top managers, but they too impose some of their personal values on the company. Top-performing sales representatives may influence the conduct of other salespersons as they serve as role models for success. This interaction between corporate culture and executive leadership helps determine the firm's ethical value system.

Coworkers' influence on an individual's ethical choices depends on the person's exposure to unethical behavior. Especially in gray areas, the more a person is exposed to unethical activity by others in the organizational environment, the more likely he or she is to behave unethically. Most marketing employees take their cues from coworkers in learning

organizational (corporate) culture A set of values, beliefs, goals, norms, and rituals that members of an organization share

Organizational Culture
Bill Gates, founder of Microsoft, reflects the company's organizational culture through his and his wife's personal convictions. Microsoft has been elected as one of the World's Most Ethical Companies.

how to solve problems, including ethical problems.[47] For instance, the most recent National Business Ethics Survey (NBES) found that 45 percent of employees had observed at least one type of misconduct in the past year; about 35 percent of them chose not to report the misconduct to management.[48] Table 4.4 compares the percentage of observed misconduct in the United States between 2009 and 2011. Moreover, research suggests that marketing employees who perceive their work environment as ethical experience less role conflict and ambiguity, are more satisfied with their jobs, and are more committed to their employer.[49]

Organizational pressure plays a key role in creating ethical issues. For example, because of pressure to meet a schedule, a superior may ask a salesperson to lie to a customer over the phone about a late product shipment. Similarly, pressure to meet a sales quota may result in overly aggressive sales tactics. Research in this area indicates that superiors and coworkers can generate organizational pressure, which plays a key role in creating ethical issues. Nearly all marketers face difficult issues whose solutions are not obvious or that present conflicts between organizational objectives and personal ethics.

Opportunity

Another factor that may shape ethical decisions in marketing is opportunity—that is, conditions that limit barriers or provide rewards. A marketing employee who takes advantage of an opportunity to act unethically and is rewarded or suffers no penalty may repeat such acts as other opportunities arise. For instance, a salesperson who receives a raise after using a deceptive sales presentation to increase sales is being rewarded and thus will probably continue the behavior. Indeed, opportunity to engage in unethical conduct is often a better predictor of unethical activities than are personal values.[50] Beyond rewards and the absence of punishment, other elements in the business environment may create opportunities. Professional codes of conduct and ethics-related corporate policy also influence opportunity by prescribing what behaviors are acceptable. The larger the rewards and the milder the punishment for unethical conduct, the greater is the likelihood that unethical behavior will occur.

However, just as the majority of people who go into retail stores do not try to shoplift at each opportunity, most marketing managers do not try to take advantage of every opportunity for unethical behavior in their organizations. Although marketing managers often perceive

Table 4.4 Percentage of U.S. Workforce Observing Specific Forms of Misconduct

Behavior	2009 (%)	2011 (%)
Misuse of company time	n/a	33
Abusive behavior	22	21
Lying to employees	19	20
Company resource abuse	23	20
Violating company Internet use policies	n/a	16
Discrimination	14	15
Conflicts of interest	16	15
Inappropriate social networking	n/a	14
Health or safety violations	11	13
Lying to outside stakeholders	12	12
Stealing	9	12
Falsifying time reports or hours worked	n/a	12
Employee benefits violations	11	12
Sexual harassment	7	11
Employee privacy breach	10	11

Source: Ethics Resource Center, *2011 National Business Ethics Survey®: Ethics in Transition* (Arlington, VA: Ethics Resource Center, 2012), 39–40.

many opportunities to engage in unethical conduct in their companies and industries, research suggests that most refrain from taking advantage of such opportunities. Moreover, most marketing managers do not believe that unethical conduct in general results in success.[51] Individual factors as well as organizational culture may influence whether an individual becomes opportunistic and tries to take advantage of situations unethically.

Codes of Conduct

Without compliance programs and uniform standards and policies regarding conduct, it is hard for employees to determine what conduct is acceptable within the company. In the absence of such programs and standards, employees will generally make decisions based on their observations of how coworkers and superiors behave. To improve ethics, many organizations have developed **codes of conduct** (also called *codes of ethics*) that consist of formalized rules and standards that describe what the company expects of its employees. Most large corporations have formal codes of conduct, but not all codes are effective if implemented improperly. Codes must be periodically revised to identify and eliminate weaknesses in the company's ethical standards and policies. Most codes address specific ethical risk areas in marketing. For instance, IBM's code of conduct has a bribery policy that prohibits accepting gifts of nominal value if the gift in any way influences IBM's business relationship with the giver. However, employees are allowed to accept promotional premiums or gifts of nominal value if based upon bonus programs (such as with hotels and airlines) or if the gift is routinely offered to all other parties with similar relationships to the gift giver.[52] Codes of conduct promote ethical behavior by reducing opportunities for unethical behavior; employees know both what is expected of them and what kind of punishment they face if they violate the rules. Codes help

codes of conduct Formalized rules and standards that describe what the company expects of its employees

Entrepreneurship in Marketing

Second City Brings Ethics Training to Life

Entrepreneur: Paul Sills, Howard Alk, and Bernie Sahlins
Business: The Second City
Founded: 1959 | Chicago, Illinois
Success: Over 80 companies have expressed an interest in licensing Second City Communication's RealBiz shorts, which it created with the help of companies like Dow Jones, Best Buy, and MasterCard.

Second City Communications (SCC), a division of the Second City comedy theater company, seeks to bring comedy to ethics training. The Second City was founded as a cabaret theater, and although the company never lost its theater roots, it has expanded into many different areas. SCC, for instance, focuses on the power of comedy to tackle important business issues.

In response to employee perceptions that business ethics training is dull, SCC has released 40 videos called RealBiz shorts showing humorous scenarios of what *not* to do in business. For instance, in one video, the boss unveils the number of the company ethics hotline as 1-800-RAT-FINK. The videos introduce issues such as reporting misconduct, and it is assumed that the firm will address how reporting works within its own organization.

The purpose is to engage workers and encourage them to listen to what their businesses have to say. There may be a downside, however. Some businesses are wary of poking fun at issues that could have legal consequences. Despite this issue, SCC believes its shorts will change the dynamics of ethics training by making employees eager to learn.[c]

marketers deal with ethical issues or dilemmas that develop in daily operations by prescribing or limiting specific activities.

Codes of conduct do not have to be so detailed that they take every situation into account, but they should provide guidelines that enable employees to achieve organizational objectives in an ethical manner. The American Marketing Association Code of Ethics, reprinted in Table 4.5, does not cover every possible ethical issue, but it provides a useful overview of what marketers believe are sound principles for guiding marketing activities. This code serves as a helpful model for structuring an organization's code of conduct.

Improving Marketing Ethics

It is possible to improve ethical conduct in an organization by hiring ethical employees and eliminating unethical ones, and by improving the organization's ethical standards. One way to approach improvement of an organization's ethical standards is to use a "bad apple–bad barrel" analogy. Some people always do things in their own self-interest, regardless of organizational goals or accepted moral standards; they are sometimes called "bad apples." To eliminate unethical conduct, an organization must rid itself of bad apples through screening techniques and enforcement of the firm's ethical standards. However, organizations sometimes become "bad barrels" themselves, not because the individuals within them are unethical but because the pressures to survive and succeed create conditions (opportunities) that reward unethical behavior. One way to resolve the problem of the bad barrel is to redesign the organization's image and culture so that it conforms to industry and societal norms of ethical conduct.[53]

If top management develops and enforces ethical and legal compliance programs to encourage ethical decision making, it becomes a force to help individuals make better decisions. According to a National Business Ethics Survey (NBES), a company's ethical culture is the greatest determinant of future misconduct. Thus, a well-implemented ethics program

Table 4.5 Code of Ethics of the American Marketing Association

Ethical Norms and Values for Marketers
PREAMBLE
The American Marketing Association commits itself to promoting the highest standard of professional ethical norms and values for its members. Norms are established standards of conduct expected and maintained by society and/or professional organizations. Values represent the collective conception of what people find desirable, important, and morally proper. Values serve as the criteria for evaluating the actions of others. Marketing practitioners must recognize that they serve not only their enterprises but also act as stewards of society in creating, facilitating, and executing the efficient and effective transactions that are part of the greater economy. In this role, marketers should embrace the highest ethical norms of practicing professionals as well as the ethical values implied by their responsibility toward stakeholders (e.g., customers, employees, investors, channel members, regulators, and the host community).
GENERAL NORMS
1. Marketers must first do no harm. This means doing work for which they are appropriately trained or experienced so they can actively add value to their organizations and customers. It also means adhering to all applicable laws and regulations, as well as embodying high ethical standards in the choices they make.
2. Marketers must foster trust in the marketing system. This means that products are appropriate for their intended and promoted uses. It requires that marketing communications about goods and services are not intentionally deceptive or misleading. It suggests building relationships that provide for the equitable adjustment and/or redress of customer grievances. It implies striving for good faith and fair dealing so as to contribute toward the efficacy of the exchange process.
3. Marketers should embrace, communicate, and practice the fundamental ethical values that will improve consumer confidence in the integrity of the marketing exchange system. These basic values are intentionally aspirational and include: Honesty, Responsibility, Fairness, Respect, Openness, and Citizenship.
Ethical Values
Honesty—this means being truthful and forthright in our dealings with customers and stakeholders.
We will tell the truth in all situations and at all times.
We will offer products of value that do what we claim in our communications.
We will stand behind our products if they fail to deliver their claimed benefits.
We will honor our explicit and implicit commitments and promises.
Responsibility—this involves accepting the consequences of our marketing decisions and strategies.
We will make strenuous efforts to serve the needs of our customers.
We will avoid using coercion with all stakeholders.
We will acknowledge the social obligations to stakeholders that come with increased marketing and economic power.
We will recognize our special commitments to economically vulnerable segments of the market such as children, the elderly, and others who may be substantially disadvantaged.
Fairness—this has to do with justly trying to balance the needs of the buyer with the interests of the seller.
We will clearly represent our products in selling, advertising, and other forms of communication; this includes the avoidance of false, misleading, and deceptive promotion.
We will reject manipulations and sales tactics that harm customer trust.
We will not engage in price fixing, predatory pricing, price gouging, or "bait and switch" tactics.
We will not knowingly participate in material conflicts of interest.
Respect—this addresses the basic human dignity of all stakeholders.
We will value individual differences even as we avoid customer stereotyping or depicting demographic groups (e.g., gender, race, sexual) in a negative or dehumanizing way in our promotions.
We will listen to the needs of our customers and make all reasonable efforts to monitor and improve their satisfaction on an ongoing basis.
We will make a special effort to understand suppliers, intermediaries, and distributors from other cultures.

(continued)

Table 4.5 Code of Ethics of the American Marketing Association (*continued*)

We will appropriately acknowledge the contributions of others, such as consultants, employees, and coworkers, to our marketing endeavors.
Openness—this focuses on creating transparency in our marketing operations.
We will strive to communicate clearly with all our constituencies.
We will accept constructive criticism from our customers and other stakeholders.
We will explain significant product or service risks, component substitutions, or other foreseeable eventualities affecting the customer or their perception of the purchase decision.
We will fully disclose list prices and terms of financing as well as available price deals and adjustments.
Citizenship—this involves a strategic focus on fulfilling the economic, legal, philanthropic, and societal responsibilities that serve stakeholders.
We will strive to protect the natural environment in the execution of marketing campaigns.
We will give back to the community through volunteerism and charitable donations.
We will work to contribute to the overall betterment of marketing and its reputation.
We will encourage supply-chain members to ensure that trade is fair for all participants, including producers in developing countries.
Implementation
Finally, we recognize that every industry sector and marketing subdiscipline (e.g., marketing research, e-commerce, direct selling, direct marketing, advertising, etc.) has its own specific ethical issues that require policies and commentary. An array of such codes can be accessed via links on the AMA website. We encourage all such groups to develop and/or refine their industry and discipline-specific codes of ethics in order to supplement these general norms and values.

Source: Copyright © 2010 by the American Marketing Association, www.marketingpower.com/AboutAMA/Pages/Statement%20of%20Ethics.aspx (accessed May 17, 2012).

© AP Images/PRNewsFoto/ESCS Ethics & Safety Compliance Standards, Inc.

Implementing Ethical Compliance
Firms like Global Compliance have been established to help companies integrate ethical and compliance solutions into their organizations.

and a strong corporate culture result in the greatest decrease in ethical risks for an organization. Companies that wish to improve their ethics, then, should implement a strong ethics and compliance program and encourage organization-wide commitment to an ethical culture.[54] Ethics programs that include written standards of conduct, ethics training, and hotlines increase the likelihood that employees will report misconduct observed in the workplace. When top managers talk about the importance of ethics and model ethical behavior themselves, employees observe significantly fewer instances of unethical conduct. When marketers understand the policies and requirements for ethical conduct, they can more easily resolve ethical conflicts. However, marketers can never fully abdicate their personal ethical responsibility in making decisions. Claiming to be an agent of the business ("the company told me to do it") is unacceptable as a legal excuse and is even less defensible from an ethical perspective.[55] It is also unacceptable for managers to punish those who do report ethical misconduct, although retaliation is still fairly prevalent. The NBES study stated that 22 percent of respondents who reported misconduct said they experienced retaliation, from getting the cold shoulder from other employees to being demoted.[56] Figure 4.5 shows the most common types of retaliation whistle blowers have said they have experienced.

Figure 4.5 Forms of Retaliation Experienced as a Result of Reported Misconduct

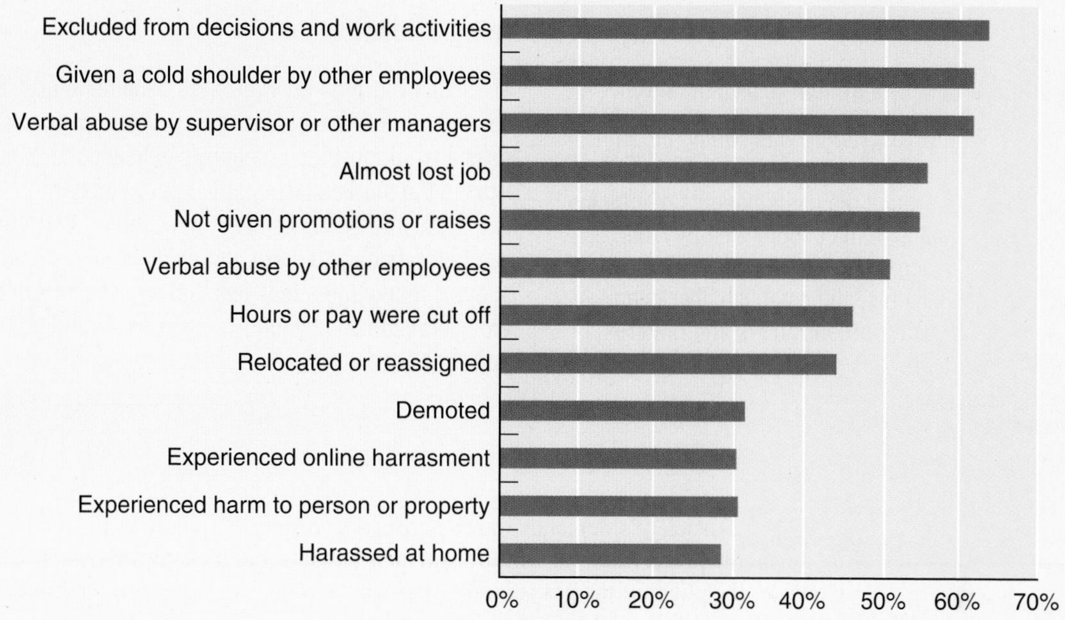

Source: Ethics Resource Center, *2011 National Business Ethics Survey®: Ethics in Transition* (Arlington, VA: Ethics Resource Center, 2012), 16.

INCORPORATING SOCIAL RESPONSIBILITY AND ETHICS INTO STRATEGIC PLANNING

Although the concepts of marketing ethics and social responsibility are often used interchangeably, it is important to distinguish between them. *Ethics* relates to individual and group decisions—judgments about what is right or wrong in a particular decision-making situation—whereas *social responsibility* deals with the total effect of marketing decisions on society. The two concepts are interrelated because a company that supports socially responsible decisions and adheres to a code of conduct is likely to have a positive effect on society. Because ethics and social responsibility programs can be profitable as well, an increasing number of companies are incorporating them into their overall strategic market planning.

As we have emphasized throughout this chapter, ethics is one dimension of social responsibility. Being socially responsible relates to doing what is economically sound, legal, ethical, and socially conscious. One way to evaluate whether a specific activity is ethical and socially responsible is to ask other members of the organization if they approve of it. Contact with concerned consumer groups and industry or government regulatory groups may be helpful. A check to see whether there is a specific company policy about an activity may help resolve ethical questions. If other organizational members approve of the activity and it is legal and customary within the industry, chances are that the activity is acceptable from both an ethical and a social responsibility perspective.

A rule of thumb for resolving ethical and social responsibility issues is that if an issue can withstand open discussion that results in agreement or limited debate, an acceptable solution may exist. Nevertheless, even after a final decision is reached, different viewpoints on the issue may remain. Openness is not the end-all solution to the ethics problem. However, it creates trust and facilitates learning relationships.[57]

Marketing Debate

The Payoffs for Being Ethical

ISSUE: Is Ethics a Cost or a Benefit to a Company?

As companies continue to struggle with "doing the right thing" for customers, employees, and communities, there is an ongoing debate around the costs/benefits of ethics programs. Critics argue that the cost to identify risks, create programs, train employees, implement hotlines and other reporting mechanisms, and establish checks and balances is tremendous for organizations and requires a significant investment. Those who support the cost of ethics programs recognize the benefits in providing employees with the guidance to navigate organizational risks and support the company's ethical culture, create trust in the marketplace that increases customer and employee loyalty, and prevent misconduct that can damage reputations and harm shareholder values. Those who support marketing ethics feel that any short-term costs are overshadowed by long-term gains, including financial performance.[d]

Many of society's demands impose costs. For example, society wants a cleaner environment and the preservation of wildlife and their habitats, but it also wants low-priced products. Consider the plight of the gas station owner who asked his customers if they would be willing to spend an additional 1 cent per gallon if he instituted an air filtration system to eliminate harmful fumes. The majority indicated they supported his plan. However, when the system was installed and the price increased, many customers switched to a lower-cost competitor across the street. Thus, companies must carefully balance the costs of providing low-priced products against the costs of manufacturing, packaging, and distributing their products in an environmentally responsible manner.

In trying to satisfy the desires of one group, marketers may dissatisfy others. Regarding the smoking debate, for example, marketers must balance nonsmokers' desire for a smoke-free environment against smokers' desires, or needs, to continue to smoke. Some anti-tobacco crusaders call for the complete elimination of tobacco products to ensure a smoke-free world. However, this attitude fails to consider the difficulty smokers have in quitting (now that tobacco marketers have admitted their product is addictive) and the impact on U.S. communities and states that depend on tobacco crops for their economic survival. Thus, this issue, like most ethical and social responsibility issues, cannot be viewed in black and white.

Balancing society's demands to satisfy all members of society is difficult, if not impossible. Marketers must evaluate the extent to which members of society are willing to pay for what they want. For instance, customers may want more information about a product but be unwilling to pay the costs the firm incurs in providing the data. Marketers who want to make socially responsible decisions may find the task a challenge because, ultimately, they must ensure their economic survival.

SOCIAL RESPONSIBILITY AND ETHICS IMPROVE MARKETING PERFORMANCE

The challenges of ethical conduct are an important part of marketing success. Increasing evidence indicates that being socially responsible and ethical results in increased profits. Research suggests that a relationship exists between a stakeholder orientation and an organizational climate that supports marketing ethics and social responsibility. Marketing is often the most visible interaction that consumers have with a firm. Also, stakeholders observe marketing activities such as promotion and learn about their activities through the mass media.

© AP Images/Tom Uhlman

Social Responsibility Improves Marketing
Walmart deals with consumer environmental concerns through reducing waste in the supply chain and using alternative fuel in some fleet trucks.

Anytime there is a product recall or potential unethical act, reputational damage can occur. On the other hand, firms that are highly ethical and build trust with customers are usually not headline stories in the mass media. The evidence is strong that a broad stakeholder view of the firm can help improve marketing practices that contribute to improved financial, social, and ethical performance.[58] This relationship implies that being ethically and socially concerned is consistent with meeting the demands of customers and other stakeholders. By encouraging employees to understand their markets, companies can help them respond to stakeholders' demands.[59] A stakeholder orientation helps to broaden and redefine marketing beyond a market orientation that focuses on customers and competitors by considering primary stakeholders such as employees, suppliers, regulators, shareholders, customers, and the community. Marketers need to analyze stakeholder relationships to maximize value for specific target markets.

This creates a need to prioritize stakeholders, deal with conflicting demands, and respond with a marketing strategy to provide balance. For instance, car auction company Barrett-Jackson incorporates customer satisfaction into its business model. The company provides its buyers with access to insurance, undergoes extensive background checks to vouch for the authenticity of the classic and custom cars that it auctions, and has hired independent auditors to ensure the fairness and transparency of its business operations.[60] By incorporating ethics into its marketing strategy, Barrett-Jackson has balanced the needs of its stakeholders and developed a solid reputation of trust. All of these actions should be grounded in social responsibility and marketing ethics. The results should be positive relationships with customers and increased financial performance.[61]

A direct association exists between corporate social responsibility and customer satisfaction, profits, and market value.[62] In a survey of consumers, 80 percent indicated that when quality and price are similar among competitors, they would be more likely to buy from the company associated with a particular cause. In addition, young adults aged 18 to 25 are especially likely to take a company's citizenship efforts into account when making not only purchasing but also employment and investment decisions.[63]

Thus, recognition is growing that the long-term value of conducting business in an ethical and socially responsible manner far outweighs short-term costs.[64] To demonstrate the

Figure 4.6 ***Ethisphere's* 2011 World's Most Ethical Companies versus S&P 500**

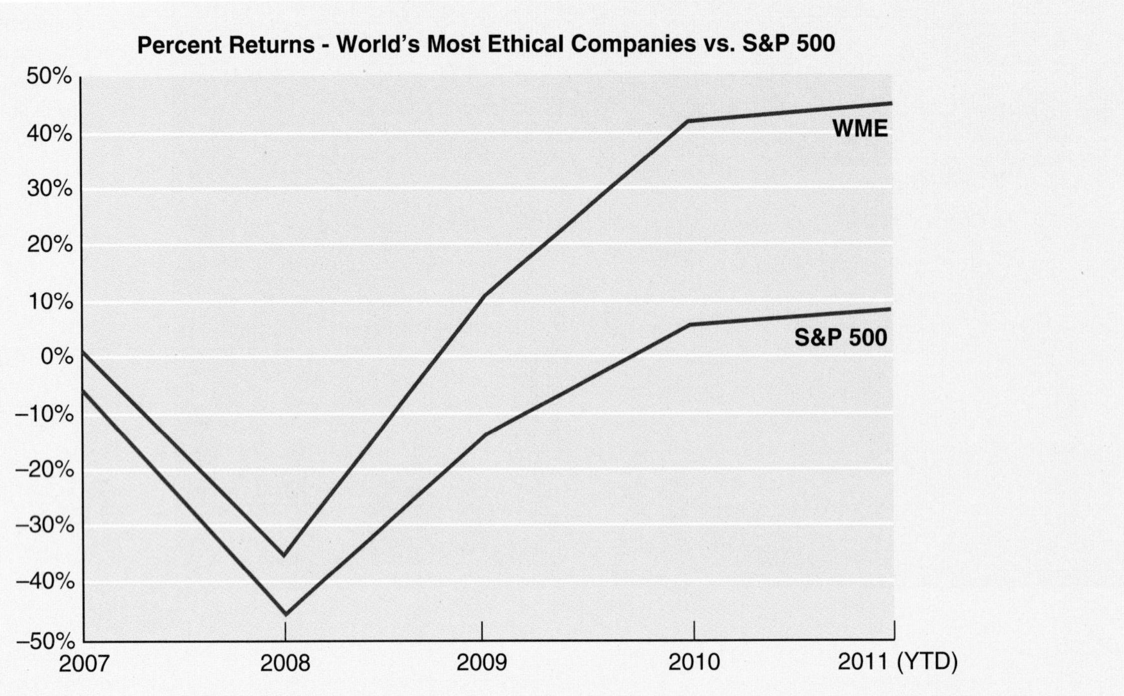

Source: "2011 World's Most Ethical Companies," *Ethisphere,* http://ethisphere.com/past-wme-honorees/wme2011/ (accessed May 17, 2012).

financial benefits of ethical companies, the Ethisphere Institute compared the stock prices of the winners of the World's Most Ethical (WME) companies award with companies listed on Standard & Poor's (S&P) 500 index. As Figure 4.6 reveals, the percent returns of WME companies surpasses those on the S&P 500. Companies that fail to develop strategies and programs to incorporate ethics and social responsibility into their organizational culture may pay the price with poor marketing performance and the potential costs of legal violations, civil litigation, and damaging publicity when questionable activities are made public. Because marketing ethics and social responsibility are not always viewed as organizational performance issues, many managers do not believe they need to consider them in the strategic planning process. Individuals also have different ideas as to what is ethical or unethical, leading them to confuse the need for workplace ethics and the right to maintain their own personal values and ethics. Although the concepts are undoubtedly controversial, it is possible—and desirable—to incorporate ethics and social responsibility into the planning process.

Summary

1. To understand the concept and dimensions of social responsibility

Social responsibility refers to an organization's obligation to maximize its positive impact and minimize its negative impact on society. It deals with the total effect of all marketing decisions on society. Although social responsibility is a positive concept, most organizations embrace it in the expectation of indirect long-term benefits. Marketing citizenship involves adopting a strategic focus for fulfilling the economic, legal, ethical, and philanthropic social responsibilities expected of organizations by their stakeholders, those constituents who have a stake, or claim, in some aspect of the company's products, operations, markets, industry, and outcomes. At the most basic level, companies have an economic responsibility to be profitable so that they can provide a return on investment to their stockholders, create jobs for the community, and contribute goods and services to the economy. Marketers are also expected to obey laws and regulations. Marketing ethics refers to principles and standards that define acceptable conduct in marketing as determined by various stakeholders, including the public, government regulators, private-interest groups, industry, and the organization itself. Philanthropic responsibilities go beyond marketing ethics; they are not required of a company, but they promote human welfare or goodwill. Many firms use cause-related marketing, the practice of linking products to a social cause on an ongoing or short-term basis. Strategic philanthropy is the synergistic use of organizational core competencies and resources to address key stakeholders' interests and achieve both organizational and social benefits.

Three major categories of social responsibility issues are sustainability, consumerism, and community relations. One of the more common ways marketers demonstrate social responsibility is through programs designed to protect and preserve the natural environment. Sustainability is the potential for the long-term well-being of the natural environment, including all biological entities, as well as the interaction among nature and individuals, organizations, and business strategies. Consumerism consists of the efforts of independent individuals, groups, and organizations to protect the rights of consumers. Consumers expect to have the right to safety, the right to be informed, the right to choose, and the right to be heard. Many marketers view social responsibility as including contributions of resources (money, products, and time) to community causes such as the natural environment, arts and recreation, disadvantaged members of the community, and education.

2. To define and describe the importance of marketing ethics

Whereas social responsibility is achieved by balancing the interests of all stakeholders in the organization, ethics relates to acceptable standards of conduct in making individual and group decisions. Marketing ethics goes beyond legal issues. Ethical marketing decisions foster mutual trust in marketing relationships.

An ethical issue is an identifiable problem, situation, or opportunity requiring an individual or organization to choose from among several actions that must be evaluated as right or wrong, ethical or unethical. A number of ethical issues relate to the marketing mix (product, promotion, price, and distribution).

Individual factors, organizational relationships, and opportunity interact to determine ethical decisions in marketing. Individuals often base their decisions on their own values and principles of right or wrong. However, ethical choices in marketing are most often made jointly, in work groups and committees, or in conversations and discussions with coworkers. Organizational culture and structure operate through organizational relationships (with superiors, peers, and subordinates) to influence ethical decisions. Organizational, or corporate, culture is a set of values, beliefs, goals, norms, and rituals that members of an organization share. The more a person is exposed to unethical activity by others in the organizational environment, the more likely he or she is to behave unethically. Organizational pressure plays a key role in creating ethical issues, as do opportunity and conditions that limit barriers or provide rewards.

3. To become familiar with ways to improve ethical decisions in marketing

It is possible to improve ethical behavior in an organization by hiring ethical employees and eliminating unethical ones, and by improving the organization's ethical standards. If top management develops and enforces ethics and legal compliance programs to encourage ethical decision making, it becomes a force to help individuals make better decisions. To improve company ethics, many organizations have developed codes of conduct—formalized rules and standards that describe what the company expects of its employees. To nurture ethical conduct in marketing, open communication is essential. Firms should also periodically monitor and audit their operations, including their supply chain, to ensure the integrity of the product and the firm's activities. Companies must consistently enforce standards and impose penalties or punishment on those who violate codes of conduct.

4. To understand the role of social responsibility and ethics in improving market performance

An increasing number of companies are incorporating ethics and social responsibility programs into their overall strategic market planning. To promote socially responsible and ethical behavior while achieving organizational goals, marketers must monitor changes and trends in society's values.

They must determine what society wants and attempt to predict the long-term effects of their decisions. Costs are associated with many of society's demands, and balancing those demands to satisfy all of society is difficult. However, increasing evidence indicates that being socially responsible and ethical results in valuable benefits: an enhanced public reputation (which can increase market share), costs savings, and profits.

Go to www.cengagebrain.com for resources to help you master the content in this chapter as well as for materials that will expand your marketing knowledge!

Important Terms

social responsibility 104
marketing citizenship 105
marketing ethics 107
cause-related marketing 107
strategic philanthropy 107
sustainability 108
ethical issue 113
organizational (corporate) culture 117
codes of conduct 119

Discussion and Review Questions

1. What is social responsibility? Why is it important?
2. What are stakeholders? What role do they play in strategic marketing decisions?
3. What are four dimensions of social responsibility? What impact do they have on marketing decisions?
4. What is strategic philanthropy? How does it differ from more traditional philanthropic efforts?
5. What are some major social responsibility issues? Give an example of each.
6. What is the difference between ethics and social responsibility?
7. Why is ethics an important consideration in marketing decisions?
8. How do the factors that influence ethical or unethical decisions interact?
9. What ethical conflicts may exist if business employees fly on certain airlines just to receive benefits for their personal frequent-flyer programs?
10. Give an example of how ethical issues can affect each component of the marketing mix.
11. How can the ethical decisions involved in marketing be improved?
12. How can people with different personal values work together to make ethical decisions in organizations?
13. What trade-offs might a company have to make to be socially responsible and responsive to society's demands?
14. What evidence exists that being socially responsible and ethical is worthwhile?

Application Questions

1. Some organizations promote their social responsibility. These companies often claim that being ethical is good business and that it pays to be a "good corporate citizen." Identify an organization in your community that has a reputation for being ethical and socially responsible. What activities account for this image? Is the company successful? Why or why not?
2. If you had to conduct a social audit of your organization's ethics and social responsibility, what information would most interest you? What key stakeholders would you want to communicate with? How could such an audit assist the company in improving its ethics and social responsibility?
3. Suppose that in your job you face situations that require you to make decisions about what is right or wrong and then act on these decisions. Describe such a situation. Without disclosing your actual decision, explain what you based it on. What and whom did you think of when you were considering what to do? Why did you consider them?
4. Consumers interact with many businesses daily and weekly. Not only do companies in an industry acquire a reputation for being ethical or unethical, entire industries also become known as ethical or unethical. Identify two types of businesses with which you or others you know have had the most conflict involving ethical issues. Describe those ethical issues.

5. IMP Socially responsible organizations strive for marketing citizenship by adopting a strategic focus for fulfilling the economic, legal, ethical, and philanthropic social responsibilities that their stakeholders expect of them. So how would you rate real-world companies on social responsibility? Compare Google and Microsoft in the areas of economic, legal, ethical, and philanthropic responsibilities. Assign a weighting coefficient to each factor. You could use 0–5, for example, with 0 meaning *not socially responsible at all* and 5 meaning *very socially responsible.* How do the two companies compare as socially responsible citizens? What are some ways that each company might improve their scores?

Internet Exercise

Business for Social Responsibility

Business for Social Responsibility (BSR) is a nonprofit organization for companies who want to operate responsibly and demonstrate respect for ethical values, people, communities, and the natural environment. Founded in 1992, BSR offers members practical information, research, educational programs, and technical assistance, as well as the opportunity to network with peers on current social responsibility issues. To learn more about this organization and access its many resources, visit **www.bsr.org**.

1. What types of businesses join BSR, and why?
2. Describe the services available to member companies. How can these services help companies improve their performances?
3. Peruse the "BSR Conference" link, located at the top of the home page. What are some advantages to attending the BSR conference and listening to industry leaders and experts in corporate social responsibility?

developing your marketing plan

When developing a marketing strategy, companies must consider that their decisions affect not only their own company but also society in general. Many socially responsible and ethical companies identify their intentions as part of their mission statement, which serves as a guide for making all decisions about the company, including those in the marketing plan. To assist you in relating the information in this chapter to the development of your marketing plan, consider the following:

1. Determine the level of importance that marketing citizenship holds in your company. Identify the various stakeholders who would be affected by your strategic decisions.
2. Referring to Table 4.2 as a guide, discuss how the negative impact of your product's production and use could be minimized.
3. Using Table 4.3, identify additional issues related to your product for each of the 4Ps.

The information obtained from these questions should assist you in developing various aspects of your marketing plan found in the "Interactive Marketing Plan" exercise at **www.cengagebrain.com**.

video case 4.1

TOMS Shoes Expands One-to-One Model to Eyewear

While many organizations try to incorporate cause-related marketing into their business operations, TOMS Shoes takes the concept of philanthropy one step further. TOMS blends a for-profit business with a philanthropic component in what it terms the one-to-one model. For every pair of shoes sold, another pair is provided to a child in need. Recently, TOMS has also expanded into eyewear. For every pair of sunglasses sold, a person with vision problems in developing countries receives surgery, prescription glasses, or medical treatment to help restore his or her sight. Unlike many nonprofits,

TOMS' for-profit business enables the company to support its philanthropic component, which keeps the company from having to solicit donations.

The idea for TOMS Shoes occurred after founder Blake Mycoskie witnessed the immense poverty in Argentinean villages—poverty so bad that many families could not afford to purchase shoes for their children. Recognizing the importance of shoes to health and education, Mycoskie decided to create a new business that would consist of two parts: TOMS Shoes, a for-profit business that would sell the shoes, and Friends of TOMS, the company's nonprofit subsidiary that would distribute shoes to those in need.

For his original product, Mycoskie decided to adopt the *alpargata* shoe worn in Argentina. The *alpargata* is a slip-on shoe made from canvas or fabric with rubber soles. After a *Los Angeles Times* article featured Mycoskie's new business, demand for the shoes exploded. Unfortunately for Mycoskie, he did not have enough shoes to fill the orders. Mycoskie was able to work out the product shortage, and today TOMS is a thriving business.

After distributing its one-millionth pair of shoes in 2010, TOMS began to consider other products that could be used in the one-to-one model. "When I thought about launching another product with the TOMS model, vision seemed the most obvious choice," Blake Myscoskie explained. Because 80 percent of vision impairment in developing countries is preventable or curable, TOMS decided that for every pair of sunglasses it sold, the company would provide treatment or prescription glasses for those in need. TOMS chose Nepal as the first country to apply its one-to-one model.

TOMS takes its obligations for social responsibility seriously. The company builds the cost of the extra pair of shoes and eye care into the price of the products it sells. TOMS also works closely with local humanitarian organizations. "With TOMS we always work with local nonprofits or NGOs to understand what the need is in a community before we just go in and start giving," said Liza De La Torre, VP of sales and marketing at TOMS.

Customers who do business with TOMS feel committed to the company because they know that their purchases are going toward a good cause, even if they might pay a bit more in the process. TOMS goes to great lengths to educate the public about the importance of its mission. Although it does not have a marketing budget, the company provides internship opportunities and engages brand ambassadors at universities to spread the TOMS message. Every year the company promotes the One Day Without Shoes campaign, in which participants spend one day without shoes to understand what children in developing countries must undergo daily. These events have been supported by celebrities such as Charlize Theron, Kris Ryan, and the Dallas Cowboys Cheerleaders.

Despite TOMS' clear philanthropic component, risks for misconduct still exist. The company uses factories in China, Argentina, and Ethiopia for manufacturing, which creates complex supply chain relationships that must be carefully managed. TOMS created a set of manufacturing standards based upon International Labor Organization compliance standards for its manufacturers. The company regularly performs audits to check that the factories are complying with company standards. TOMS also seeks to create strong organizational relationships with its employees and volunteers. The company often allows employees to participate in Shoe Drops (distributing the shoes to children) so they can see firsthand how their efforts are helping others.

Despite its success, TOMS' mission is far from complete. As its expansion into eyewear demonstrates, the company is looking for new opportunities for applying its one-to-one model. TOMS demonstrates how an innovative concept and the ability to incorporate philanthropy into business operations can create a successful company that can make a difference.[65]

Questions for Discussion

1. Do you think TOMS is successful because of its unique products, or is it the firm's approach to social responsibility?
2. How does TOMS manage its supply chain in order to ensure ethical and socially responsible conduct?
3. How does TOMS' business model relate to the understanding of stakeholders and strategic philanthropy?

case 4.2

Ethics Drives Barrett-Jackson Auto Auction Company to Success

Monitoring the ethical behavior of auction companies can be tricky. Consumers might not know the value of the product until after they purchase it, and not all items purchased at auction companies come with sufficient documentation to prove the product's authenticity. It has not been unheard of for sellers to falsify documentation to secure better deals. To avoid these ethical issues, classic and vintage car auction company Barrett-Jackson LLC has created an ethical culture that considers the needs of buyers, sellers, and the community. The company has been recognized as one of the world's most ethical companies by *Ethisphere* magazine.

Barrett-Jackson was founded in 1971 in Scottsdale, Arizona, by classic car lovers Russ Jackson and Tom Barrett. The two men had met a decade earlier when Jackson was considering buying a 1933 Cadillac V16 Town Car from Barrett. The two became lifelong friends and began organizing their own auctions. From the beginning the men recognized the special nature of the products they were auctioning. Buyers place great value on the cars they purchase, with some having searched for years to locate their classic "dream" car. The company would have to exert great delicacy to ensure a fair auction process and authentic products.

© Todd Oren/Getty Images for Barrett-Jackson

After Russ Jackson passed away, his son Craig Jackson began running the company. Like his predecessors, Craig recognized the importance of adopting values to ensure an ethical auction process. "We will separate ourselves and do things in an ethical manner to make sure we set the right standards for our customers. These are the things that have been entrenched in our corporate culture since the beginning," Craig stated.

The company has instituted a number of programs to make certain that the auction process between buyer and seller remains fair. These programs recognize the inherent rights of the stakeholders involved in the transaction. For instance, Barrett-Jackson protects buyers' rights to choose by working to prevent false bids meant to raise the price of the cars. Sometimes car owners will try to bid on their own cars to boost the price. Barrett-Jackson acts to make certain that prices remain fair so that consumers can choose their dream car at a competitive price. Barrett-Jackson also protects the right to safety of both buyers and sellers by using security cameras to monitor stakeholders during the auction and making sure that buyers have the ability to pay. The company also offers access to Barrett-Jackson–endorsed insurance coverage, which reduces the risk of purchase by assuring buyers that their cars can be restored in case of an accident. Barrett-Jackson protects consumers' rights to be informed by making sure to the best of their ability that documentation is truthful and rejects sellers who do not meet their stringent requirements.

Barrett-Jackson also tries to ensure that their stakeholders are provided with a forum to make their voices heard. This includes thoroughly investigating stakeholder concerns even if it might interfere with the sale of a product. For instance, one of the collector vehicles sold by Barrett-Jackson was allegedly the ambulance that carried President John F. Kennedy to the hospital after he was shot. Shortly after the auction of the ambulance was announced, questions concerning the authenticity of these claims arose. Barrett-Jackson responded by undertaking a thorough investigation of the documentation provided on the ambulance. The company responded that it could not offer a 100 percent guarantee that the ambulance was authentic but that the claims were true to the best of its knowledge. By acting to investigate the available documentation and releasing a disclaimer, Barrett-Jackson not only took these claims seriously but told potential buyers about the possible risks involved so they could make an informed decision.

Additionally, Barrett-Jackson practices social responsibility by giving back to the communities in which it does business. Barrett-Jackson has helped raise $5.8 million for charities nationwide. The company also engages in strategic philanthropy and created the Barrett-Jackson Cancer Research Fund at the Translational Genomics Research Institute (TGen) in 2010. In honor of Russ Jackson and his son Brian, both victims of cancer, the company raises money to fund research to fight colon and prostate cancer and search for a cure. For example, in 2012 the company raised $125,000 for TGen by auctioning a 1993 Chevrolet Corvette 40th Anniversary coupe.

Barrett-Jackson's emphasis on community relations and customer satisfaction has helped secure its reputation as an ethical company. Buyers and sellers alike can feel confident that they will be treated fairly when doing business with the firm. Barrett-Jackson is a good example of how ethical conduct can increase company success.[66]

Questions for Discussion

1. Why is ethical behavior so important for an auction company such as Barrett-Jackson?
2. In what ways does Barrett-Jackson protect the rights of its buyers and sellers?
3. How do solid community relations help Barrett-Jackson succeed?

strategic case 2

At Timberland, Doing Well and Doing Good Are Laced Together

Timberland's well-known name and tree logo are good clues as to how much this multinational firm cares about sustainability. The company, headquartered in Stratham, New Hampshire, started out manufacturing shoes and boots and later expanded into apparel and accessories. Today, Timberland sells through its own network of stores as well as through thousands of department and specialty stores worldwide. It also operates e-business websites in the United States, the United Kingdom, Japan, and France. The firm was so profitable that it was acquired by VF Corporation, owner of brands North Face and Wrangler, for $2.3 billion. The acquisition was the largest in the corporation's history.

© xymmus/Shutterstock.com

Timberland's $1.5 billion in revenue comes from sales in North America, Europe, and Asia. To stay on top of fast-changing trends in the world of fashion, Timberland maintains an international design center in London. It seeks to develop high-quality outdoor products to improve the lives of its customers and communities, as well as to inspire them to make a difference in the world. As a result, the company's long-term strategy for success combines a comprehensive social responsibility agenda with careful planning for the ever-changing marketing environment.

Four Pillars of Social Responsibility

Timberland's social responsibility agenda rests on the four "pillars" of energy, products, workplaces, and service. Each pillar is associated with specific short- and long-term targets that Timberland has established with the input of its stakeholders. Under the first pillar—energy—the company has reduced energy consumption, slashed harmful greenhouse gas emissions, and increased its use of power from renewable sources. It is also increasing the use of virtual meetings to cut down on employee travel, which saves energy as well as time and money.

The second pillar, earth-friendly products, is a key element in Timberland's social responsibility agenda. More than one-third of its shoes contain some recycled material. Its Earthkeepers shoes have been specially designed to incorporate a combination of organic, renewable, and recyclable materials. Some Earthkeepers are not only made from old plastic bottles and other recycled content, they can be completely disassembled and the components can be reworked into new Timberland shoes. Soon, all Timberland products will be labeled to show their impact on the planet.

The third pillar relates to the workplace. Timberland sets tough standards for fair and safe working conditions at all the factories and facilities that make its shoes and clothing products. Although it owns and operates a factory in the Dominican Republic, the company buys most of its products from a global network of suppliers that employs 175,000 workers in approximately 300 factories spread across 35 countries. Timberland works with the VF Corporation's audit team to ensure that suppliers are complying with their detailed code of conduct, which forbids discrimination, child labor, and unsafe practices. Factories are audited regularly and when violations are found, Timberland follows up to be sure that the necessary workplace improvements are made. Timberland employees are encouraged to call the Integrity Line, a 24-hour hotline answered by a third party, whenever they want to report workplace concerns, submit ideas, or ask questions.

The fourth pillar, service, has long been part of Timberland's cultural fabric. Every full-time Timberland employee can take up to 40 hours, with pay, to volunteer in his or her community. In addition, Timberland's former CEO began the tradition of Serv-a-palooza in 1998 when he set aside one work day for global volunteerism. Today, employees are encouraged (but not required) to devote this annual day of service to volunteering in their communities.

Some employees use the day to clear nature trails, some pick up trash from riverbanks, and others grab their tool belts to build arts facilities or repair neighborhood schools. In more than a decade with Timberland, the former vice president of corporate culture enthusiastically laced up his Timberland boots and volunteered on three continents, doing everything from protecting the rainforest to improving the gardens around a senior center.

The Changing Marketing Environment

Because Timberland has a diverse product portfolio and is active in retailing and wholesaling as well as manufacturing, it has to keep an eye on competitors in several industries. One strong U.S.-based rival is Wolverine World Wide, which manufactures Hush Puppies, Sebago, Merrell, Patagonia Footwear, and other brands of casual and work shoes. Like Timberland, Wolverine operates company stores in the United States and the United Kingdom. The U.K.-based R. Griggs Group, maker of Doc Martens boots, shoes, and sandals, is a key competitor. Finally, particular Timberland shoe styles compete directly with footwear marketed by the world's largest athletic shoe companies.

Economic conditions can also affect Timberland's marketing situation. During the recent recession, when many consumers held back on discretionary purchases, the company's overall revenue fell. However, sales of its work boots remained flat, even as some competitors saw their sales drop. Timberland's marketing executives realized that the brand was holding its own among construction workers and other buyers who need tough, reliable footwear to use day in and day out.

Timberland's marketers have also noticed that the challenging global economic situation is influencing the way consumers think and feel about buying products such as shoes and clothing. When unemployment was low and buying power was high, consumers often used such purchases as a way to display their wealth. As the economy moved into recession, however, many cash-strapped consumers cut back on purchases of showy, expensive items, in favor of products that conveyed a more subtle message about cultural values such as concern for the environment. Today, "self worth is tied to thoughtful purchases as a way to impress your peers, instead of conspicuous consumption," states Timberland's senior director of merchandising.

In addition to its international marketing initiatives in China and Europe, Timberland sees promising opportunities for growth in India. It signed a strategic alliance with Reliance Industries, a local company known for marketing international brands. Reliance distributes shoes, boots, and clothing through Timberland-branded stores and through selected department stores in major Indian cities. Timberland's CEO says that Reliance has "a clear understanding of the Timberland brand and consumer" and, just as important, it's "as committed as we are to our ideology and passion for the outdoors."

High-Tech Shoes and Communications

Timberland is applying technological advances to improve its footwear products and to reach out to customers through digital media. For example, to satisfy customers' needs for comfort, the company has introduced patented "Smart Comfort" footbeds in its shoes. As part of its commitment to sustainability, Timberland makes Green Rubber soles from recycled rubber and is designing its new footwear products for easy disassembly and recycling at the end of their useful lives.

Moving into digital media is helping Timberland bring its marketing messages to the attention of consumers who use the Web. Through brand-specific sites, Facebook fan pages, blog entries, a Twitter feed, YouTube videos, and online games, Timberland supplements its traditional marketing activities and engages consumers who seek a deeper level of involvement with their favorite brands.[67]

Questions for Discussion

1. What forces in the marketing environment appear to pose the greatest challenges to Timberland's marketing performance? Explain.
2. What kinds of ethical issues does Timberland face in its marketing? What is the company doing to address these issues?
3. How does Timberland's reputation for social responsibility serve as a strength when consumers are turning away from showy, expensive products?
4. Over time, Timberland plans to add labels to show how eco-friendly each of its products really is. What are the marketing advantages and disadvantages of this move?

ROLE-PLAY TEAM CASE EXERCISE 2

This role-play team case exercise is designed to simulate actual marketing decision making in the real world. The entire team should read the overview and background. Each student will take on a role of a particular employee within the organization. Your instructor will provide additional information and instructions related to a team decision.

NATIONAL FARM AND GARDEN INC.*

Background

National Farm and Garden Inc. (NFG) was founded in Nebraska in 1935 and has been a leading supplier of farming equipment for more than 60 years. Over the last five years, however, demand for NFG's flagship product, the Ultra Tiller, has been declining. To make matters worse, NFG's market lead was overtaken by the competition for the first time two years ago.

Last year, NFG expanded its product line with the "Turbo Tiller," a highly advertised and much anticipated upgrade to the Ultra Tiller. The product launch was timed to coincide with last year's fall tilling season. Due to the timing of the release, the research and development process was shortened, and the manufacturing department was pressed to produce high numbers to meet anticipated demand. All responsible divisions approved the product launch and schedule. In order to release the product as scheduled, however, the manufacturing department was forced to employ the safety shield design from the Ultra Tiller. When attached, the shield protects the user from the tilling blades; however, it is necessary to remove the shield in order to clean the product. Because of differences between the Ultra and Turbo models, the Turbo's shield is very difficult to reattach after cleaning, and the process requires specialized tools. Owners can have the supplier make modifications on site or at the sales location, or leave the shielding off and continue operation. All product documentation warns against operating the tiller without the shielding, and the product itself has three distinct warning labels on it. Modifications are now available that allow for the shield to be removed and replaced quite easily, and these modifications are covered by the factory warranty. However, most owners have elected to operate the Turbo Tiller without the safety shielding after its first cleaning.

Over the last year, a number of farm animals (chickens, cats, a dog, and two goats) have been killed by Turbo Tillers being operated without the guard. Two weeks ago, a 7-year-old Nebraska boy riding on the back of an unshielded tiller fell off. When the tiller caught the sleeve of his shirt, his arm was permanently mangled, requiring amputation. One of the child's parents owns the local newspaper, which ran a story about the accident on the front page of the local paper the next day. NFG's chief executive officer (CEO) has called an emergency meeting with the company's divisional vice president, director of product development, director of manufacturing, director of sales, and vice president of public relations to discuss the situation and develop a plan of action.

 The research and conceptual assistance of Larry Gonzales, Pat Hansen, Heidi Hollenbeck, Marilynn Hill, Michael Mitchell, Craig Hurst, Bill Haskins, and Dana Schubert is gratefully acknowledged. This role-play case is not intended to represent the managerial decisions of an actual company.

Divisional Vice President

You are the divisional vice president and have been with the company for many years. Historically, you have not been a pushy individual and generally prefer to stay in the background. When there are major decisions to be made or crises to address, you are frequently not available. The CEO recently put you on a 60-day "action plan" to improve your division's output; failure to achieve this plan will result in your termination, even though you are just a few years shy of retirement. Therefore, you now find it necessary to satisfy not only your own objectives but the CEO's very high expectations as well. This has caused great turmoil within all divisions as you place increasing pressure on your subordinates.

As the divisional vice president, you are focused on coordinating all departments. You are responsible for output from the sales, manufacturing, and field service engineering departments. The research and development (R&D) department, which must sign off on all new products before they are approved for production, is not under your supervision.

Recently, you received a memorandum from the director of product development outlining some potential problems with the development and testing of the Turbo Tiller. The memo was copied to you, the director of manufacturing, and the director of sales. You agreed with the director of manufacturing not to share the contents of the memo with your CEO, because you felt that bringing this small concern to his attention would cause unnecessary problems for each division. Moreover, the CEO is known for his abrasive personality and has a history of yelling at bearers of bad news.

The CEO has called an all-hands emergency meeting. You are expected to bring all knowledge of this situation with you for discussion and creation of a comprehensive action plan.

Director of Product Development

You are the director of product development in the R&D department. Although you have a master's degree in mechanical engineering from Stanford University, you are originally from the inner city of Chicago, where you grew up in the school of "hard knocks." From previous experience, you tend to be rather uncompromising about products that are engineered within your organization. Your engineering team has been very successful in the past, and you are quite proud of the many new successful products your department has developed.

You originally fast-tracked the Turbo Tiller product due to constant pressure, particularly from the director of sales. However, upon further investigation, you became concerned about the implementation of the product's safety shield. Consequently, you recently sent a memorandum to the director of manufacturing, director of sales, and the divisional vice president outlining the fact that consumers could sue National Farm and Garden under the state's *strict liability doctrine*, which holds manufacturers, distributors, wholesalers, retailers, and others in the chain of distribution of a defective product liable for the damages caused by the defect regardless of fault. Moreover, plaintiffs could cite the state's *concept of defect of manufacture* when the manufacturer fails to (1) properly assemble a product, (2) properly test a product, and (3) adequately check the quality of the product's component parts or materials used in manufacturing. You now believe that NFG has violated all of these "defects of manufacture."

Having received no response to this memo, you are contemplating whether to escalate the issue by going to the CEO. The only reason you have not already done so is the CEO's historic temper when confronted with negative situations.

The CEO has called an all-hands emergency meeting. You are expected to bring all knowledge of this situation with you for discussion and creation of a comprehensive action plan.

Director of Manufacturing

You are the director of manufacturing. A graduate from the University of Alabama with a bachelor's degree in industrial manufacturing, you have worked for NFG for 20 years. You are required to provide reports to top management on a weekly, monthly, and quarterly basis. Top management creates the exact measures of performance that you provide; although you have a say in what these reports focus on, you often disagree with their exact focus. Your overall performance is evaluated based more on numbers of units produced than on quality. Despite this, you enjoy working for the company. You consider the group like family and especially appreciate the effort the CEO has made to make you feel valued and supported.

You are aware of the difficulties the Ultra Tiller guard poses when used on the Turbo Tiller. Due to the Turbo Tiller's larger size, the guard is nearly impossible to replace after removal. Reattachment of the shield requires a professional machine shop and additional assistance. However, with your knowledge of statistics, you know that, even without the shield in place, the chances of an animal or a person being injured by the Turbo Tiller are small. Thus, you agreed with the divisional vice president to bury a memo sent by the director of product development stating related concerns. You both felt that the risks were small enough and that raising these concerns to your superiors would only cause headaches and paperwork. Furthermore, you needed to stay on schedule in order to reach your volume goals if you were to earn your bonus.

You also received several e-mails from the manager of the field service engineering department about reports of farmers operating the Turbo Tiller without the guard. When you requested statistical data regarding the number and location of occurrences and any related accidents, the field service engineering manager replied with field data indicating that more than 85 percent of all Turbo Tillers are eventually operated without the guard.

The CEO has called an all-hands emergency meeting. You are expected to bring all knowledge of this situation with you for discussion and creation of a comprehensive action plan.

Director of Sales

You are the director of sales and have been with NFG for more than 10 years. You were recruited from a competing firm and have more than 25 years of sales experience in the industry. Because of sagging sales, you face extreme pressure from above to meet your numbers. However, you feel that sales forecasts have been set unrealistically high. Furthermore, these aggressive forecasts create churning within your department as your sales staff consistently complain that their quotas are unrealistic. Although you are adamant that declining sales are industry and product offering issues, you are reluctant to raise these concerns to the CEO because of his history of ripping the heads off messengers bearing bad news. You have witnessed this phenomenon firsthand as the CEO literally screamed at a coworker who brought a problem to his attention. On the other hand, the CEO has promised you a new Dodge Ram if your department reaches its numbers this year. Of course, you enthusiastically promised to achieve these results and quickly ran from the room.

The Turbo Tiller has been a much-anticipated addition to your stagnant product portfolio, but you were concerned that it would be delayed due to red tape and wrote daily e-mails to the director of product development about getting it to market on a timely basis. You have received a memo from the director of product development about some legal concerns over the Turbo Tiller. However, you feel that these concerns are manufacturing's problem, not your department's. Furthermore, because the director of manufacturing received a carbon copy of the memo, you are sure that the concerns will be addressed appropriately.

You have organized training on this product for your sales staff that included proper operating procedures and the dangers of standing within 5 feet of the tilling blades. Independent of these training sessions, you arranged a separate class on how to address and downplay these concerns with customers.

The CEO has called an all-hands emergency meeting. You are expected to bring all knowledge of this situation with you for discussion and creation of a comprehensive action plan.

Vice President of Public Relations

You are the most recent addition to the management staff at NFG, having been with the company for just three years. You obtained a bachelor's degree in human resources from Ohio State University, and a master's degree in communications from Florida State University.

Prior to working with NFG, you handled public relations at a nonprofit organization for five years. You took this job because you thought it would be a personal challenge to represent a larger for-profit business. Besides, you were raised in Nebraska, and you are a farmer at heart.

Nearly six months ago, you learned that the company had developed and released a product that has some safety concerns. Most department heads were not concerned about the problem because of a lack of solid evidence that a danger existed. You have been monitoring the situation, although it has not been your highest priority due to recent union negotiations. Recently, the CEO informed you that a corporate meeting is eminent. As the vice president of public relations, it is your responsibility to gain information about public opinion to present to the CEO. As you begin to collect this information, you find disturbing news. Many consumers don't trust NFG because of its handling of a chemical spill five years ago. Additionally, many rumors are circulating about NFG's hiring practices.

You know that a single negative event can wipe out a company's reputation and destroy favorable customer attitudes established through years of expensive advertising campaigns and other promotional efforts. In this situation, you need to minimize the negative publicity, yet still address the media. You suddenly wish the company had developed a crisis plan before this happened.

The CEO has called an all-hands emergency meeting. You are expected to bring all knowledge of this situation with you for discussion and creation of a comprehensive action plan.

NOTES

[1]"Ethisphere's 2010 World's Most Ethical Companies," *Ethisphere,* Q1, 26–28; "Even as Cause Marketing Grows, 83 Percent of Consumers Still Want to See More," Cone Communications, September 15, 2010, www.coneinc.com/cause-grows-consumers-want-more (accessed November 14, 2011); "'Best Companies to Work For' Rankings," www.wholefoodsmarket.com/careers/fortune100.php (accessed November 9, 2011); "Wyndham Worldwide Excels at Stakeholder Management," Case developed for the Daniels Fund Ethics Initiative, University of New Mexico, http://danielsethics.mgt.unm.edu/pdf/Wyndham%20Case.pdf (accessed February 10, 2012).

[2]Peter R. Darke and Robin J. B. Ritchie, "The Defensive Consumer: Advertising Deception, Defensive Processing, and Distrust," *Journal of Marketing Research*, 4, no. 1 (February 2007): 114–127.

[3]Isabelle Maignan and O. C. Ferrell, "Corporate Social Responsibility and Marketing: An Integrative Framework," *Journal of the Academy of Marketing Science* 32 (January 2004): 3–19.

[4]Indra Nooyi, "The Responsible Company," *The Economist,* March 31, 2008, 132.

[5]Jeanne Whalen, "Glaxo to Pay U.S. $3 Billion to Settle," November 4, 2011, http://online.wsj.com/article/SB10001424052970203804204577015234100584756.html (accessed January 13, 2012).

[6]Anne Tergesen, "Doing Good to Do Well," *The Wall Street Journal*, January 9, 2012, B7.

[7]Isabelle Maignan and O. C. Ferrell, "Antecedents and Benefits of Corporate Citizenship: An Investigation of French Businesses," *Journal of Business Research* 51 (2001): 37–51.

[8]Debbie Thorne, Linda Ferrell, and O. C. Ferrell, *Business and Society: A Strategic Approach to Social Responsibility*, 4th ed. (Boston: Houghton Mifflin, 2011), 38–40.

[9]O. C. Ferrell, "Business Ethics and Customer Stakeholders," *Academy of Management Executive* 18 (May 2004): 126–129.

[10]"2007 Corporate Citizenship Report," Pfizer, www.pfizer.com/files/corporate_citizenship/cr_report_2007.pdf (accessed February 10, 2010).

[11]Archie Carroll, "The Pyramid of Corporate Social Responsibility: Toward the Moral Management of Organizational Stakeholders," *Business Horizons* (July/August 1991): 42.

[12]Hadley Malcolm, "Retailers Sue Fed, Say Debit Card Fees Are Still Too High," *USA Today*, November 23, 2011, 3B; Richard A. Epstein, "The Dangerous Experiment of the Durbin Amendment," *Regulation*, Spring 2011, 24–29.

[13]"Giving and Volunteering in America," *USA Today*, November 29, 2011, 8D.

[14]Lindsay Blakely, "Erasing the Line Between Marketing and Philanthropy," *CBS News,* April 21, 2011, www.cbsnews.com/8301-505143_162-40244368/erasing-the-line-between-marketing-and-philanthropy/ (accessed January 17, 2012); "The Best of 2011," Charlotte Street Computers, http://charlottestreetcomputers.com/the-best-of-2011/ (accessed January 17, 2012).

[15]Box Tops for Education, www.boxtops4education.com/Default.aspx (accessed January 17, 2012); Mike Eiman, "Boosters Compete, Kids Come Out on 'Top'," *Hanford Sentinel,* January 14, 2012, www.hanfordsentinel.com/news/local/boosters-compete-kids-come-out-on-top/article_36a3ad60-3e51-11e1-b225-001871e3ce6c.html (accessed January 17, 2012).

[16]"Cone LLC Releases the 2010 Cone Cause Evolution Study," Cone, www.coneinc.com/cause-grows-consumers-want-more (accessed January 17, 2012).

[17]Thorne, Ferrell, and Ferrell, *Business and Society*, 335.

[18]"2010 World's Most Ethical Companies—Company Profile: Salesforce .com," *Ethisphere*, Q1, 32.

[19]Christine Birkner, "Green Global Brands," *Marketing News*, September 30, 2011, 12–16.

[20]"Welcome to Eco Options: Sustainable Forestry," Home Depot, www .homedepot.com/ecooptions/index.html? (accessed February 5, 2010).

[21]"Better Banana Project," Chiquita, www.chiquita.com/chiquita/discover/ owbetter.asp (accessed February 5, 2010).

[22]Paul Hawken and William McDonough, "Seven Steps to Doing Good Business," *Inc.* (November 1993): 79–90.

[23]Jill Gabrielle Klein, N. Craig Smith, and Andrew John, "Why We Boycott: Consumer Motivations for Boycott Participation," *Journal of Marketing* 68 (July 2004): 92–109.

[24]Christian Homburg and Andreas Fürst, "How Organizational Complaint Handling Drives Customer Loyalty: An Analysis of the Mechanistic and the Organic Approach," *Journal of Marketing* 69 (July 2005): 95–114.

[25]Greg Bensinger, "Verizon Drops Plan for New $2 Fee," *The Wall Street Journal,* December 31, 2011, http://online.wsj.com/article/SB10001424052970204720204577130802272138184.html (accessed January 17, 2012).

[26]Christie Garton, "Corporations Add Their Know-How to Charitable Efforts," *USA Today,* July 25, 2011, www.usatoday.com/money/companies/management/2011-07-22-corporate-giving-chronicle-of-philanthropy_n.htm (accessed June 29, 2012); REDcard, https://redcard.target.com/redcard/rc_main.jsp (accessed January 17, 2012).

[27]"Environmentalism: What We Do," Patagonia, www.patagonia.com/us/patagonia.go?assetid=1960 (accessed January 17, 2012).

[28]Edelman, *2012 Edelman Trust Barometer Global Results*, http://trust .edelman.com/trust-download/global-results/ (accessed January 25, 2012).

[29]Monica Eng, "Girl Scout Cookies and Other Sweets Offer Confusing Labeling on Trans Fats," *Los Angeles Times,* January 25, 2011, www.latimes .com/health/ct-met-girl-scout-cookies-trans-fat-20110125,0,1426933.story (accessed January 26, 2011).

[30]Tim Barnett and Sean Valentine, "Issue Contingencies and Marketers' Recognition of Ethical Issues, Ethical Judgments and Behavioral Intentions," *Journal of Business Research* 57 (2004): 338–346.

[31]David Voreacos, Alex Nussbaum, and Greg Farrell, "Johnson and Johnson Fights to Clear its Once-Trusted Name," *Bloomberg Businessweek*, April 4, 2011, 69.

[32]David E. Sprott, Kenneth C. Manning, and Anthony D. Miyazaki, "Grocery Price Setting and Quantity Surcharges," *Journal of Marketing* (July 2003): 34–46.

[33]Stephen Taub, "SEC Probing Harley Statements," *CFO.com*, July 14, 2005, www.cfo.com/article.cfm/4173321/c_4173841?f=archives&origin=archive.

[34]Elizabeth Holmes, "The Finer Art of Faking It," *The Wall Street Journal*, June 30, 2011, D1, D4.

[35]Ari Lavaux, "Chocolate's Dark Side," *The Weekly Alibi*, February 9–15, 2012, 22.

[36]"Mouthing Off By the Numbers," *Ethisphere*, 2011, Q3, 9.

[37]"Monitoring and Auditing Global Supply Chains Is a Must," *Ethisphere,* 2011, Q3, 38–45.

[38]Charles Duhigg and David Barboza, "Apple's iPad and the Human Costs for Workers in China," *The New York Times,* January 25, 2012, www .nytimes.com/2012/01/26/business/ieconomy-apples-ipad-and-the-human-costs-for-workers-in-china.html?pagewanted=all (accessed February 8, 2012).

[39]Ibid.

[40]"Health Care Supply Company Novation Earns Ethics Inside Certification," *Ethisphere,* November 8, 2011, http://ethisphere.com/leading-health-care-supply-contracting-company-novation-earns-ethics-inside-certification/ (accessed February 8, 2012).

[41]Maxwell Murphy, "Reinforcing the Supply Chain," *The Wall Street Journal*, January 11, 2012, B6; "Monitoring and Auditing Global Supply Chains Is a Must," 38–45.

[42]Murphy, B6.

[43]"Monitoring and Auditing Global Supply Chains Is a Must," 38–45.

[44]Josephson Institute Center for Youth Ethics, "The Ethics of American Youth: 2010," February 10, 2011, http://charactercounts.org/programs/reportcard/2010/installment02_report-card_honesty-integrity.html (accessed January 17, 2012).

[45]Peggy H. Cunningham and O. C. Ferrell, "The Influence of Role Stress on Unethical Behavior by Personnel Involved in the Marketing Research Process" (working paper, Queens University, Ontario, 2004), 35.

[46]Joseph W. Weiss, *Business Ethics: A Managerial, Stakeholder Approach* (Belmont, CA: Wadsworth, 1994), 13.

[47]O. C. Ferrell, Larry G. Gresham, and John Fraedrich, "A Synthesis of Ethical Decision Models for Marketing," *Journal of Macromarketing* (Fall 1989): 58–59.

[48]Ethics Resource Center, *2011 National Business Ethics Survey®: Ethics in Transition* (Arlington, VA: Ethics Resource Center, 2012).

[49]Barry J. Babin, James S. Boles, and Donald P. Robin, "Representing the Perceived Ethical Work Climate Among Marketing Employees," *Journal of the Academy of Marketing Science* 28 (2000): 345–358.

[50]Ferrell, Gresham, and Fraedrich, "A Synthesis of Ethical Decision Models for Marketing."

[51]Lawrence B. Chonko and Shelby D. Hunt, "Ethics and Marketing Management: A Retrospective and Prospective Commentary," *Journal of Business Research* 50 (2000): 235–244.

[52]IBM, *Business Conduct Guidelines* (Armonk, New York: International Business Machines Corp., 2011).

[53]Linda K. Trevino and Stuart Youngblood, "Bad Apples in Bad Barrels: A Causal Analysis of Ethical Decision Making Behavior," *Journal of Applied Psychology* 75 (1990): 378–385.

[54]Ethics Resource Center, "The Ethics Resource Center's 2009 National Business Ethics Survey," 41.

[55]Ethics Resource Center, "The Ethics Resource Center's 2007 National Business Ethics Survey," ix.

[56]Ethics Resource Center, *2011 National Business Ethics Survey®: Ethics in Transition* (Arlington, VA: Ethics Resource Center, 2012).

[57]Sir Adrian Cadbury, "Ethical Managers Make Their Own Rules," *Harvard Business Review* (September/October 1987): 33.

[58]Isabelle Maignan, Tracy L. Gonzalez-Padron, G. Tomas M. Hult, and O. C. Ferrell, "Stakeholder Orientation: Development and Testing of a Framework for Socially Responsible Marketing," 90, no. 4, (July 2011): 313–338.

[59]Ferrell, Fraedrich, and Ferrell, *Business Ethics*, 27–30.

[60]"Barrett-Jackson Auction Company: Family, Fairness, and Philanthropy," http://danielsethics.mgt.unm.edu/pdf/Barrett-Jackson%20Case.pdf (accessed February 10, 2012).

[61]G. Thomas Hult, Jeannette Mena, O. C. Ferrell, and Linda Ferrell, "Stakeholder Marketing: A Definition and Conceptual Framework," *AMS Review* 1, no. 1 (2011): 44–65.

[62]Marjorie Kelly, "Holy Grail Found: Absolute, Definitive Proof That Responsible Companies Perform Better Financially," *Business Ethics,* Winter 2005, www.business-ethics.com/current_issue/winter_2005_holy_grail_article.html; Xueming Luo and C. B. Bhattacharya, "Corporate Social Responsibility, Customer Satisfaction, and Market Value," *Journal of Marketing* 70 (October 2006), www.marketingpower.com; Isabelle Maignan, O. C. Ferrell, and Linda Ferrell, "A Stakeholder Model for Implementing Social Responsibility in Marketing," *European Journal of Marketing* 39 (September/October 2005): 956–977.

[63]"Cone LLC Releases the 2010 Cone Cause Evolution Study," Cone, www.coneinc.com/cause-grows-consumers-want-more (accessed January 17, 2012).

[64]Maignan, Ferrell, and Ferrell, "A Stakeholder Model for Implementing Social Responsibility in Marketing."

[65]Athima Chansanchai, "Happy Feet: Buy a Pair of TOMS Shoes and a Pair Will Be Donated to a Poor Child Abroad," *Seattle Pi,* June 11, 2007, www.seattlepi.com/default/article/Happy-feet-Buy-a-pair-of-TOMS-shoes-and-a-pair-1240201.php (accessed June 3, 2011); Patrick Cole, "Toms Free Shoe Plan, Boosted by Clinton, Reaches Million Mark," *Bloomberg,* September 15, 2010, www.bloomberg.com/news/2010-09-16/toms-shoe-giveaway-for-kids-boosted-by-bill-clinton-reaches-million-mark.html (accessed June 2, 2011); "Don't Be An Intern At TOMS," TOMS, www.toms.com/our-movement/intern (accessed June 9, 2011); "How We Give," TOMS, www.toms.com/how-we-give (accessed June 3, 2011); "How We Wear Them," TOMS, www.toms.com/how-we-wear-them/ (accessed June 3, 2011); Booth Moore, "Toms Shoes' Model Is Sell a Pair, Give a Pair Away," *Los Angeles Times,* April 19, 2009, www.latimes.com/features/image/la-ig-greentoms19-2009apr19,0,3694310.story (accessed June 9, 2011); "One Day Without Shoes," TOMS, www.onedaywithoutshoes.com/ (accessed June 3, 2011); "One for One," TOMS, www.toms.com/our-movement/movement-one-for-one (accessed June 3, 2011); "Our Movement," TOMS, www.toms.com/our-movement/ (accessed March 5, 2012); Stacy Perman, "Making a Do-Gooder's Business Model Work," *Bloomberg Businessweek,* January 23, 2009, www.businessweek.com/smallbiz/content/jan2009/sb20090123_264702.htm (accessed June 3, 2011); Michelle Prasad, "TOMS Shoes Always Feels Good," *KENTON Magazine*, March 19, 2011, http://kentonmagazine.com/toms-shoes-always-feel-good/ (accessed June 3, 2011); Craig Sharkton, "Toms Shoes—Philanthropy as a Business Model," sufac.com, August 23, 2008, http://sufac.com/2008/08/toms-shoes-philanthropy-as-a-business-model/ (accessed June 3, 2011); *TOMS Campus Club Program*, http://images.toms.com/media/content/images/campus-clubs-assets/TOMSCampushandbook_082510_International_final.pdf (accessed June 2, 2011); "TOMS Company Overview," TOMS, www.toms.com/corporate-info/ (accessed June 3, 2011); "TOMS Manufacturing Practices," TOMS, www.toms.com/manufacturing-practices (accessed June 3, 2011); *TOMS One for One Giving Report,* http://images.toms.com/media/content/images/giving-report/TOMS-Giving-Report-2010.pdf (accessed June 3, 2011); TOMS Shoes, www.toms.com/ (accessed June 3, 2011); Mike Zimmerman, "The Business of Giving: TOMS Shoes," *Success Magazine,* September 30, 2009, www.successmagazine.com/the-business-of-giving/PARAMS/article/852 (accessed June 3, 2011); "TOMS Eyewear," www.toms.com/eyewear/ (accessed March 5, 2012); "TOMS Founder Shares Sole-ful Tale," *North Texas Daily,* April 14, 2011, www.ntdaily.com/?p=53882 (accessed March 5, 2012).

[66]"2010 Most Ethical Companies in the World," Barrett-Jackson website, www.barrett-jackson.com/articles/most-ethical-auction-company.asp (accessed June 9, 2011). "2010 World's Most Ethical Companies," *Ethisphere*, http://ethisphere.com/wme2010 (accessed June 8, 2011); "Barrett-Jackson Cancer Research Fund and TGen," TGen website, https://www.tgenfoundation.org/NetCommunity/Page.aspx?pid=828 (accessed June 9, 2011). "The Barrett-Jackson Legacy," Barrett-Jackson website, www.barrett-jackson.com/about (accessed June 8, 2011); Barrett-Jackson News, "Barrett-Jackson Celebrates Four Decades Of Charitable Work At 40th Annual Scottsdale Auction," Barrett-Jackson website, January 18, 2011, http://news.barrett-jackson.com/barrett-jackson-celebrates-four-decades-of-charitable-work-at-40th-annual-scottsdale-auction (accessed June 9, 2011). Paul M. Barrett, "Barrett-Jackson Auction: Dude, There's My Car!" *Bloomberg Businessweek*, January 28, 2011, www.businessweek.com/magazine/content/11_06/b4214071705361.htm (accessed June 7, 2011); Larry Edsall, "Real Buyers. Real Sellers. Real Auctions," Barrett-Jackson website, www.barrett-jackson.com/articles/real-auctions.asp (accessed June 9, 2011). "Reserve Consignments at Barrett-Jackson Palm Beach Auction," *Sports Car Digest*, February 16, 2011, www.sportscardigest.com/reserve-consignments-at-barrett-jackson-palm-beach-auction (accessed June 9, 2011); Beth Schwartz, "Dream Chasers," *Luxury Las Vegas*, November 2009, http://luxurylv.com/2009/11/features/3495 (accessed June 9, 2011); Barrett-Jackson, "Barrett-Jackson Calls Upon Collector Car Specialist Gordon McCall to Run Salon Collection Offering Division," January 22, 2012, http://news.barrett-jackson.com/barrett-jackson-calls-upon-collector-car-specialist-gordon-mccall-to-run-salon-collection-offering-division/ (accessed March 20, 2012); Bob Golfen, "Dream Cars for Sale at Barrett-Jackson Auction," *Fox News,* January 13, 2012, www.foxnews.com/leisure/2012/01/13/dream-cars-for-sale-at-barrett-jackson-auction/ (accessed March 20, 2012); Hannah Elliot, "Update: Barrett-Jackson Stands Behind JFK Ambulance," *Forbes*, January 21, 2011, www.forbes.com/sites/hannahelliott/2011/01/21/update-barrett-jackson-stands-behind-jfk-ambulance/2/ (accessed March 20, 2012); Barrett-Jackson, "Corvette Coupe Raises $125,000 for Cancer Investigations at TGen," January 24, 2012, http://news.barrett-jackson.com/corvette-coupe-raises-125000-for-cancer-investigations-at-tgen/ (accessed March 20, 2012).

[67]Francine Kopun, "Earth-friendly Shoes," *Toronto Star*, April 12, 2010, www.thestar.com; "Timberland to Increase Use of Digital through New European Manager Role," *New Media Age*, March 4, 2010, p. 7; "Consumer Spending Shifts Down as Mindset Changes," *Food Institute Report*, January 11, 2010, p. 8; Desda Moss, "The Value of Giving," *HR Magazine,* December 2009, 22ff; "Timberland Partners with Reliance Brands," *Professional Services Close-up*, December 9, 2009; "Timberland Reduces GHG Emissions 36%," *Environmental Leader*, April 8, 2010, www.environmentalleader.com; Timberland website, www.Timberland.com; "Timberland Responsibility," http://responsibility.timberland.com/ (accessed October 15, 2012); Barney Jopson, "Timberland Boosts VF Revenue," *Financial Times*, February 16, 2012, www.ft.com/cms/s/0/c29013ea-58c3-11e1-b118-00144feabdc0.html#axzz1zD4HzKBc (accessed June 29, 2012).

Feature Notes

[a]Alessandra Migliaccio and Flavia Rotondi, "Turning Trash Into Tables in Naples," *Bloomberg Businessweek,* October 24–30, 2011, 59–60; "Big Green Effort by Italian Sabox," *Packaging Today,* January 2010, www.packagingtoday.co.uk/story.asp?storycode=61406 (accessed November 4, 2011); Sabox website, www.saboxgreen.it/sito%20in%20inglese/index.html (accessed November 4, 2011).

[b]Eric Spitznagel, "The Greening of Death," *Bloomberg Businessweek,* November 7–13, 2011, 101–103; Cheryl Corley, "Burials and Cemeteries Go Green," NPR, December 16, 2007, www.npr.org/templates/story/story.php?storyId=17232879 (accessed November 11, 2011); Bill Briggs, "When You're Dying for a Lower Carbon Footprint," MSNBC, January 18, 2011, http://today.msnbc.msn.com/id/41003238/ns/business-oil_and_energy/ (November 11, 2011); Frank Thadeusz, "A Rotten Way to Go," Der Spiegel, January 7, 2008, www.spiegel.de/international/germany/0,1518,527134,00.html (accessed November 11, 2011); John McDonnell, "No Room for the Dead: Cemeteries to Be Full by the End of the Decade," Daily Mail Online, www.dailymail.co.uk/news/article-1387932/Cemeteries-end-decade.html (accessed November 11, 2011); Philip Shishkin, "Green Revolution Hits Dead End in Georgia Cemetery Proposal," *The Wall Street Journal,* January 2, 2009, http://online.wsj.com/article/SB123085771149647839.html (accessed November 11, 2011); "Exit Strategies," *The Economist,* September 16, 2010, www.economist.com/node/17043348 (accessed November 11, 2011); "What Is Green Burial?" Green Burial Council, www.greenburialcouncil.org/faqs-fiction (accessed November 15, 2011).

[c]Bill Briggs, "Business Ethics, with a Chuckle," MSNBC, June 11, 2010, www.msnbc.msn.com/id/37595722/ns/business-small_business// (accessed December 1, 2011); "RealBiz Shorts," Second City Communications, www.realbizshorts.com/ (accessed December 1, 2011); Lauren Bloom, "Watch Second City's Ethics Shorts, Laugh, and Learn," Lauren Bloom's Blog, June 14, 2010, www.thebusinessethicsblog.com/watch-second-citys-ethics-shorts-laugh-and-learn (accessed December 1, 2011); "History of The Second City," The Second City, www.secondcity.com/history/ (accessed December 1, 2011).

[d]Stefan Ambec and Paul Lanoie, "Does It Pay to Be Green? A Systematic Overview," *Academy of Management Perspective* 22, no. 4 (November 2008): 47; Mary K. Pratt, "The High Cost of Ethics Compliance," *ComputerWorld,* August 24, 2009, www.computerworld.com/s/article/341268/Ethics_Harder_in_a_Recession_ (accessed November 21, 2011).

part 3

Marketing Research and Target Market Analysis

PART 3 examines how marketers use information and technology to better understand and reach customers. CHAPTER 5 provides a foundation for analyzing buyers through a discussion of marketing information systems and the basic steps in the marketing research process. Understanding elements that affect buying decisions enables marketers to better analyze customers' needs and to evaluate how specific marketing strategies can satisfy those needs. CHAPTER 6 deals with selecting and analyzing target markets, which is one of the major steps in marketing strategy development.

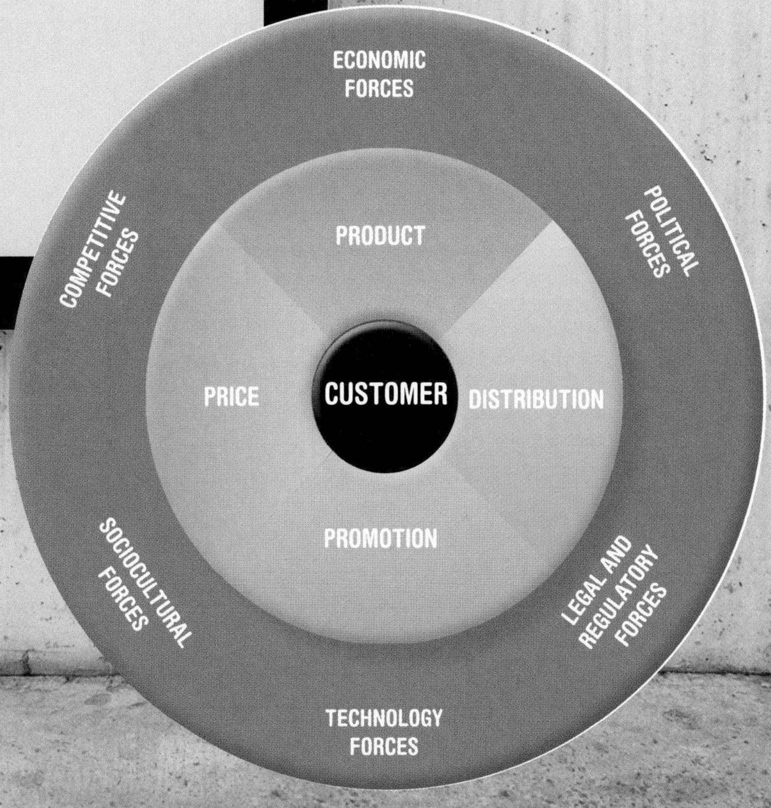

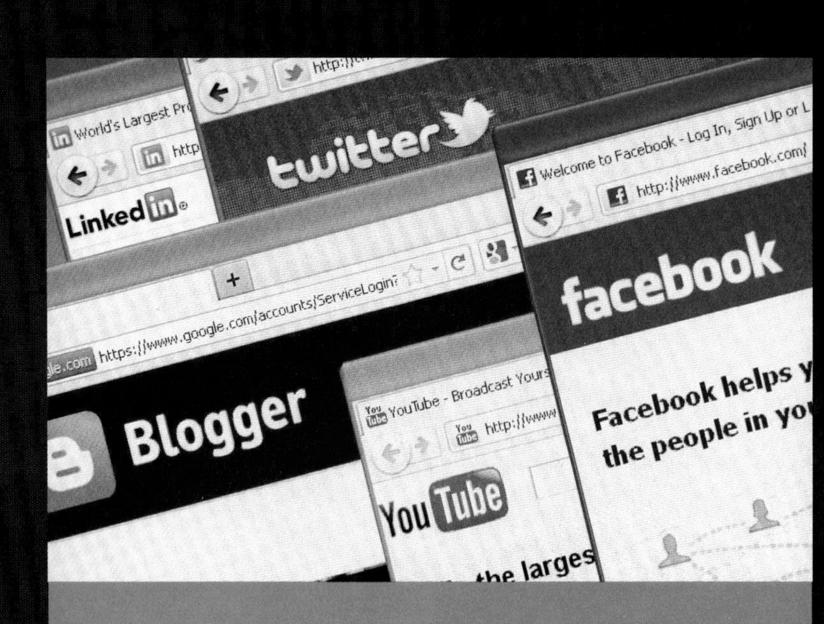

chapter 5

Marketing Research and Information Systems

OBJECTIVES

1. To describe the basic steps in conducting marketing research
2. To explore the fundamental methods of gathering data for marketing research
3. To describe the nature and roles of tools, such as databases, decision support systems, and the Internet, in marketing decision making
4. To identify key ethical and international considerations in marketing research

MARKETING INSIGHTS

Mystery Shoppers Provide Insights

In the 1940s, companies began using volunteer "mystery shoppers" to visit their stores and report back on whether employees were adhering to the companies' standards of service. These volunteer shoppers were unrecognizable to employees and often willing to work for small fees or free items. Today, mystery shopping has become a $1.5 billion industry, and mystery shoppers are valuable information-gatherers who help companies improve their marketing strategies. For example, mystery shopping helped the president of Office Depot recognize serious weaknesses in customer service at its retail establishments. By going undercover, the president learned that company metrics used by employees and mystery shoppers were flawed. He changed the metrics to better evaluate service components.

Mystery shoppers enter establishments pretending to be regular customers. They scrutinize not only how they are treated but also how the stores appear. Some may use digital cameras and computer equipment in their observations. Many mystery shoppers work on a part-time basis and earn free merchandise, meals, movies, and other goods. Mystery shoppers engage in meaningful observations to improve the implementation of marketing strategies.

Companies rely on the information provided by mystery shoppers to ensure that employees are following company guidelines. Some companies base bonuses on employee performance during mystery inspections. A survey by American Express supports the importance of customer service. In the study, 70 percent of respondents replied that they would be willing to spend an additional 13 percent with companies that demonstrate quality customer service. Mystery shoppers are therefore an asset to companies who want to identify strengths and weaknesses in their operations and adapt their marketing tactics to improve company performance.[1]

Marketing research enables marketers to implement the marketing concept by helping them acquire information about whether and how their goods and services satisfy the desires of target market customers. When used effectively, such information facilitates relationship marketing by helping marketers focus their efforts on meeting and even anticipating the needs of their customers. Marketing research and information systems that can provide practical and objective information to help firms develop and implement marketing strategies are therefore essential to effective marketing.

In this chapter, we focus on how marketers gather information needed to make marketing decisions. First, we define marketing research and examine the individual steps of the marketing research process, including various methods of collecting data. Next, we look at how technology aids in collecting, organizing, and interpreting marketing research data. Finally, we consider ethical and international issues in marketing research.

THE IMPORTANCE OF MARKETING RESEARCH

Marketing research is the systematic design, collection, interpretation, and reporting of information to help marketers solve specific marketing problems or take advantage of marketing opportunities. As the word *research* implies, it is a process for gathering information that is not currently available to decision makers. The purpose of marketing research is to inform an organization about customers' needs and desires, marketing opportunities for particular goods and services, and changing attitudes and purchase patterns of customers. Market information increases the marketer's ability to respond to customer needs, which leads to improved organizational performance. Detecting shifts in buyers' behaviors and attitudes helps companies stay in touch with the ever-changing marketplace. Organic food marketers, for example, would be interested to know that demand for high-end organic food brands is declining, while demand for private-label organic brands, such as those sold by Albertsons, Trader Joe's, and Whole Foods, is growing. In fact, consumer confidence in private-label organic brands has boosted

marketing research The systematic design, collection, interpretation, and reporting of information to help marketers solve specific marketing problems or take advantage of marketing opportunities

Courtesy of Irwin Research

Importance of Marketing Research
Irwin provides services to help companies better understand their customers' needs.

confidence in private-label brands overall.[2] Strategic planning requires marketing research to facilitate the process of assessing such opportunities or threats.

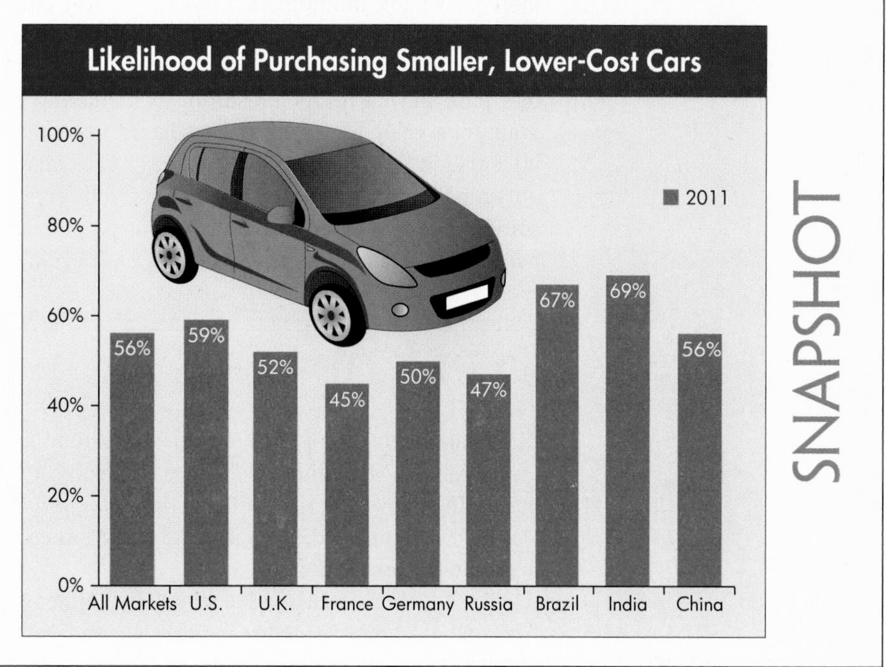

Source: Capgemini Cars, *Cars Online 11/12: Changing Dynamics Drive New Developments in Technology and Business Models*, www.capgemini.com/m/en/tl/Cars_Online_11_12.pdf (accessed May 24, 2012).

Marketing research can help a firm better understand market opportunities, ascertain the potential for success for new products, and determine the feasibility of a particular marketing strategy. It can also reveal some surprising trends. For instance, a recent survey of 15,000 fast-food customers showed that while Starbucks remained the most popular coffee franchise, coffee drinkers tend to exhibit more loyalty to McDonald's coffee beverages. The study revealed that 53 percent of frequent customers at Starbucks and Dunkin' Donuts were likely to patronize rival coffee outlets during the month, versus 29 percent of frequent McDonald's customers. This higher rate of loyalty for its coffee beverages is a significant victory for McDonald's. As the fast-food market for coffee becomes saturated, loyal customers are becoming more and more crucial to a company's success.[3]

Many types of organizations use marketing research to help them develop marketing mixes to match the needs of customers. Supermarkets, for example, have learned from marketing research that roughly half of all Americans prefer to have their dinners ready in 15 to 30 minutes. Such information highlights a tremendous opportunity for supermarkets to offer high-quality "heat-and-eat" meals to satisfy this growing segment of the food market. Political candidates also depend on marketing research to understand the scope of issues their constituents view as important. National political candidates may spend millions surveying voters to better understand issues and craft their images accordingly.

Changes in the economy, especially the most recent recession, have dramatically changed marketers' decision-making strategies. Increasingly, businesses need speed and agility to survive and to react quickly to changing consumer behaviors. The snapshot indicates the percentage of consumers that plan to purchase a smaller, lower-cost car. On the other hand, premium brands like BMW, Mercedes Benz, Audi, and Lexus are seeing an increase in demand in the United States, Europe, and even in developing countries such as China. As premium carmakers open new production lines, companies making cheaper brands of cars are starting to struggle.[4] Marketing research has shifted its focus toward smaller studies like test marketing, small-scale surveys, and short-range forecasting in order to learn about changing dynamics in the marketplace. However, large, high-value research projects remain necessary for long-term success. While it is acceptable to conduct studies that take six months or more, many companies need real-time information to help them make good decisions. Firms may benefit from historical or secondary data, but due to changes in the economy and buyer behavior, such data are not as useful in today's decision-making environment. As we discuss in this chapter, online research services are helping to supplement and integrate findings in order to help companies make tactical and strategic decisions. In the future, the marketing researcher will need to be able to identify the most efficient and effective ways of gathering information.[5]

The real value of marketing research is measured by improvements in a marketer's ability to make decisions. For example, the television channel Nickelodeon decided to target more shows toward mothers. Mothers in the United States spend approximately $2.1 trillion annually, making this a lucrative market for companies. After conducting marketing research on this demographic, Nickelodeon found that mothers tend to "unwind" between the hours of 9 p.m. and 1 a.m. As a result of its marketing research, Nickelodeon plans to launch programming geared toward mothers based upon their viewing habits.[6] Marketers should treat information the same way as other resources, and they must weigh the costs and benefits of obtaining information. Information should be considered worthwhile if it results in marketing activities that better satisfy the firm's target customers, lead to increased sales and profits, or help the firm achieve some other goal.

TYPES OF RESEARCH

The nature and type of research vary based on the research design and the hypotheses under investigation. Marketing research can involve two forms of data. *Qualitative data* yields descriptive non-numerical information. *Quantitative data* yields empirical information that can be communicated through numbers. Marketers may choose to collect either depending upon the research required.

To collect this data, marketers conduct either exploratory research or conclusive research. Although each has a distinct purpose, the major differences between them are formalization and flexibility rather than the specific research methods used. Table 5.1 summarizes the differences.

Exploratory Research

exploratory research Research conducted to gather more information about a problem or to make a tentative hypothesis more specific

When marketers need more information about a problem or want to make a tentative hypothesis more specific, they may conduct **exploratory research**. The main purpose of exploratory research is to better understand a problem or situation and/or to help identify additional data needs or decision alternatives.[7] Consider that until recently, there was no research available to help marketers understand how consumers perceive the terms *clearance* versus *sale* in describing a discounted price event. An exploratory study asked one group of 80 consumers to write down their thoughts about a store window sign that said "sale" and another group of

Table 5.1 Differences between Exploratory and Conclusive Research

Research Project Components	Exploratory Research	Conclusive Research
Research purpose	General: to generate insights about a situation	Specific: to verify insights and aid in selecting a course of action
Data needs	Vague	Clear
Data sources	Ill-defined	Well-defined
Data collection form	Open-ended, rough	Usually structured
Sample	Relatively small; subjectively selected to maximize generalization of insights	Relatively large; objectively selected to permit generalization of findings
Data collection	Flexible; no set procedure	Rigid; well-laid-out procedure
Data analysis	Informal; typically nonquantitative	Formal; typically quantitative
Inferences/ recommendations	More tentative than final	More final than tentative

Source: A. Parasuraman, *Marketing Research*, Second Edition. © 2007 South-Western, a part of Cengage Learning, Inc. Reproduced by permission, www.cengage.com/permissions.

80 consumers to write about a store window sign that read "clearance." The results revealed that consumers expected deeper discounts when the term *clearance* was used, and they expected the quality of the clearance products to be lower than that of products on sale.[8] This exploratory research helped marketers better understand how consumers view these terms and opened up the opportunity for additional research hypotheses about options for retail pricing.

More organizations are starting **customer advisory boards**, which are small groups of actual customers who serve as sounding boards for new-product ideas and offer insights into their feelings and attitudes toward a firm's products, promotion, pricing, and other elements of marketing strategy. While these advisory boards help companies maintain strong relationships with valuable customers, they can also provide great insight into marketing research questions. Dallas-based supply chain technology company Transplace maintains a customer advisory board of 15 rotating members. Members of the board brainstorm and provide recommendations on how to improve company services and resources to meet the needs of its global customers.[9]

customer advisory boards Small groups of actual customers who serve as sounding boards for new-product ideas and offer insights into their feelings and attitudes toward a firm's products and other elements of its marketing strategy

focus group A study in which a small group of 8 to 12 people are interviewed often informally, without a structured questionnaire, to observe interaction when members are exposed to an idea or a concept

One common method for conducting exploratory research is through a focus group. A **focus group** brings together multiple people to discuss a certain topic in a group setting led by a moderator. Focus groups are often conducted informally, without a structured questionnaire. They allow customer attitudes, behaviors, lifestyles, needs, and desires to be explored in a flexible and creative manner. Questions are open-ended and stimulate respondents to answer in their own words. A traditional focus group session consists of approximately 8 to 12 individuals and is led by a moderator, an independent individual hired by the research firm or the company. The moderator encourages group discussion among all of the participants and can direct the discussion by occasionally asking questions.

Focus groups can provide companies with ideas for new products or be used for initial testing of different marketing strategies for existing products. For example, Ford may use focus groups to determine whether to change its advertising to emphasize a vehicle's safety features rather than its style and performance. Netflix has used focus groups extensively in the past to test new product ideas or changes. Interestingly, the company deviated from its use of focus groups with its disastrous decision to split the company into two separate entities, Netflix and Qwikster. It instead relied upon data about customer preferences, which did not allow Netflix to gather feedback as to how consumers felt about the move.[10] The less-structured format of focus groups, where participants can interact with one another and build on each other's comments, is beneficial to marketers because it can yield more detailed information to researchers, including information that they might not have necessarily thought to ask participants about beforehand.

A current trend for researchers is online focus groups. In this method, participants sign in to a website and type their comments and responses there. Online focus groups can gather data from large and geographically diverse groups in a less intensive manner than focus-group interviews. California-based watch company Modify has used online focus groups to understand its target market and improve its marketing strategy.[11] Online focus groups are also more convenient for the participants than traditional focus groups. However, this method makes it more difficult to ask participants about a product's smell or taste, if that is relevant to the product being tested. Researchers also cannot observe the participants' nonverbal cues and body language in this setting, which can often reveal "gut" reactions to questions asked or topics discussed. Ford Motor Company prefers traditional live focus groups because of these advantages.[12]

Focus Groups
Companies like FocusVision help administer video-enabled online focus groups with the use of platforms, such as InterVu.

Focus groups do have a few disadvantages for marketers. Sometimes, the focus group's discussion can be hindered by overly talkative, confrontational, or shy individuals. Some participants may be less than honest in an effort to be sociable or to receive money and/or food in exchange for their participation.[13] For these reasons, focus groups provide only qualitative, not quantitative, data and are thus best used to uncover issues that can then be explored using quantifiable marketing research techniques.

Conclusive Research

Conclusive research is designed to verify insights through an objective procedure to help marketers make decisions. It is used when the marketer has one or more alternatives in mind and needs assistance in the final stages of decision making. Consider exploratory research that has revealed that the terms *clearance* and *sale* send different signals to consumers. To make a decision about how to use this information, marketers would benefit from a well-defined and structured research project that will help them decide which approach is best for a specific set of products and target consumers. The typically quantitative study should be specific in selecting a course of action and using methods that can be verified. Two such types of conclusive research are descriptive research and experimental research.

If marketers need to understand the characteristics of certain phenomena to solve a particular problem, **descriptive research** can aid them. Descriptive studies may range from general surveys of customers' educations, occupations, or ages to specifics on how often teenagers consume sports drinks or how often customers buy new pairs of athletic shoes. For example, if Nike and Reebok want to target more young women, they might ask 15- to 35-year-old females how often they work out, how frequently they wear athletic shoes for casual use, and how many pairs of athletic shoes they buy in a year. Such descriptive research can be used to develop specific marketing strategies for the athletic-shoe market. Descriptive studies generally demand much prior knowledge and assume that the problem or issue is clearly defined. Some descriptive studies require statistical analysis and predictive tools. The marketer's major task is to choose adequate methods for collecting and measuring data.

Descriptive research is limited in providing evidence necessary to make causal inferences (i.e., that variable X causes a variable Y). **Experimental research** allows marketers to make causal deductions about relationships. Such experimentation requires that an independent variable (one not influenced by or dependent on other variables) be manipulated and the resulting changes in a dependent variable (one contingent on, or restricted to, one value or set of values assumed by the independent variable) be measured. For instance, when Coca-Cola introduced Dasani flavored waters, managers needed to estimate sales at various potential price points. In some markets, Dasani was introduced at $6.99 per six-pack. By holding variables such as advertising and shelf position constant, Coca-Cola could manipulate the price variable to study its effect on sales. If sales increased 40 percent when the price was reduced by $2, then managers could make an informed decision about the effect of price on sales. Coca-Cola could also use experimental research to manipulate other variables such as advertising or in-store shelf position to determine their effect on sales. Manipulation of the causal variable and control of other variables are what make experimental research unique. As a result, they can provide much stronger evidence of cause and effect than data collected through descriptive research.

conclusive research Research designed to verify insights through objective procedures and to help marketers in making decisions

descriptive research Research conducted to clarify the characteristics of certain phenomena to solve a particular problem

experimental research Research that allows marketers to make causal inferences about relationships

THE MARKETING RESEARCH PROCESS

To maintain the control needed to obtain accurate information, marketers approach marketing research as a process with logical steps: (1) locating and defining problems or issues, (2) designing the research project, (3) collecting data, (4) interpreting research findings, and (5) reporting research findings (see Figure 5.1). These steps should be viewed as an overall approach to conducting research rather than as a rigid set of rules to be followed in each

Figure 5.1 **The Five Steps of the Marketing Research Process**

project. In planning research projects, marketers must consider each step carefully and determine how they can best adapt the steps to resolve the particular issues at hand.

Locating and Defining Problems or Research Issues

The first step in launching a research study is problem or issue definition, which focuses on uncovering the nature and boundaries of a situation or question related to marketing strategy or implementation. The first sign of a problem is typically a departure from some normal function, such as the failure to attain objectives. If a corporation's objective is a 12 percent sales increase and the current marketing strategy resulted in a 6 percent increase, this discrepancy should be analyzed to help guide future marketing strategies. Declining sales, increasing expenses, and decreasing profits also signal problems. Customer relationship management (CRM) is frequently based on analysis of existing customers. Armed with this knowledge, a firm could define a problem as finding a way to adjust for biases stemming from existing customers when gathering data or to develop methods for gathering information to help find new customers. Conversely, when an organization experiences a dramatic rise in sales or some other positive event, it may conduct marketing research to discover the reasons and maximize the opportunities stemming from them.

Marketing research often focuses on identifying and defining market opportunities or changes in the environment. When a firm discovers a market opportunity, it may need to conduct research to understand the situation more precisely so it can craft an appropriate marketing strategy. Such market research is quite common in the film industry. Hollywood studios often use pre-screenings or hire market research firms such as Nielsen National Research Group to determine how the audience might respond. These market research firms will also warn studios if their movie release dates are set to "collide" with similar movies with the same target market demographic.[14] Market research has yet to catch on for the Indian film industry Bollywood, however. Indian filmmakers depend less upon market research and more on their individual experiences when creating movies for the public.[15]

To pin down the specific boundaries of a problem or an issue through research, marketers must define the nature and scope of the situation in a way that requires probing beneath the superficial symptoms. The interaction between the marketing manager and the marketing researcher should yield a clear definition of the research needed. Researchers and decision makers should remain in the problem or issue definition stage until they have determined precisely what they want from marketing research and how they will use it. Deciding how to refine a broad, indefinite problem or issue into a precise, researchable statement is a prerequisite for the next step in the research process.

Designing the Research Project

Once the problem or issue has been defined, the next step is to create a **research design**, an overall plan for obtaining the information needed to address it. This step requires formulating a hypothesis and determining what type of research is most appropriate for testing the hypothesis to ensure the results are reliable and valid.

research design An overall plan for obtaining the information needed to address a research problem or issue

Courtesy of Booshaka.com

Locating and Defining Research Issues and Problems Companies like Booshaka assist in identifying market opportunities or changes in the competitive environment.

Developing a Hypothesis

The objective statement of a marketing research project should include a hypothesis based on both previous research and expected research findings. A **hypothesis** is an informed guess or assumption about a certain problem or set of circumstances. It is based on all the insight and knowledge available about the problem or circumstances from previous research studies and other sources. As information is gathered, the researcher can test the hypothesis. For example, a food marketer such as H.J. Heinz might propose the hypothesis that children today have considerable influence on their families' buying decisions regarding ketchup and other grocery products. A marketing researcher would then gather data, perhaps through surveys of children and their parents, and draw conclusions as to whether the hypothesis is correct. Movie theater, sports arena, and concert venue owners who may be wondering why sales are down have hypothesized that consumers are staying home more because of rising event prices, widespread availability of home theater systems and broadband Internet access, and families' increasingly busy schedules. Marketers could test this hypothesis by manipulating prices or offering strong incentives for consumers to return. Sometimes, several hypotheses are developed during an actual research project; the hypotheses that are accepted or rejected become the study's chief conclusions.

Research Reliability and Validity

In designing research, marketing researchers must ensure that research techniques are both reliable and valid. A research technique has **reliability** if it produces almost identical results in repeated trials. However, a reliable technique is not necessarily valid. To have **validity**, the research method must measure what it is supposed to measure, not something else. For example, although a group of customers may express the same level of satisfaction based on a rating scale, as individuals they may not exhibit the same repurchase behavior because of different personal characteristics. If the purpose of rating satisfaction was to estimate potential repurchase behavior, this result may cause the researcher to question the validity of the satisfaction scale.[16] A study to measure the effect of advertising on sales would be valid if advertising could be isolated from other factors or from variables that affect sales. The study would be reliable if replications of it produced the same results.

hypothesis An informed guess or assumption about a certain problem or set of circumstances

reliability A condition that exists when a research technique produces almost identical results in repeated trials

validity A condition that exists when a research method measures what it is supposed to measure

Collecting Data

The next step in the marketing research process is collecting data to help prove (or disprove) the research hypothesis. The research design must specify what types of data to collect and how they will be collected.

Types of Data

Marketing researchers have two types of data at their disposal. **Primary data** are observed and recorded or collected directly from respondents. This type of data must be gathered by observing phenomena or surveying people of interest. **Secondary data** are compiled both inside and outside the organization for some purpose other than the current investigation. Secondary data include general reports supplied to an enterprise by various data services and internal and online databases. Such reports might concern market share, retail inventory levels, and customers' buying behavior. Commonly, secondary data are already available in private or public reports or have been collected and stored by the organization itself. Due to the opportunity to obtain data via the Internet, more than half of all marketing research now comes from secondary sources.

primary data Data observed and recorded or collected directly from respondents

secondary data Data compiled both inside and outside the organization for some purpose other than the current investigation

Sources of Secondary Data

Marketers often begin the data-collection phase of the marketing research process by gathering secondary data. They may use available reports and other information from both internal and external sources to study a marketing problem.

Internal sources of secondary data can contribute tremendously to research. An organization's own database may contain information about past marketing activities, such as sales records and research reports, which can be used to test hypotheses and pinpoint problems. From sales reports, for example, a firm may be able to determine not only which product sold best at certain times of the year but also which colors and sizes customers preferred. Such information may have been gathered using customer relationship management tools for marketing, management, or financial purposes.

Accounting records are also an excellent source of data but, surprisingly, are often overlooked. The large volume of data an accounting department collects does not automatically flow to other departments. As a result, detailed information about costs, sales, customer accounts, or profits by product category may not be easily accessible to the marketing area. This condition develops particularly in organizations that do not store marketing information on a systematic basis. A third source of internal secondary data is competitive information gathered by the sales force.

External sources of secondary data include trade associations, periodicals, government publications, unpublished sources, and online databases. Trade associations such as the American Marketing Association offer guides and directories that are full of information. Periodicals such as *Bloomberg Businessweek, The Wall Street Journal, Sales & Marketing Management, Advertising Age, Marketing Research,* and *Industrial Marketing* publish general information that can help marketers define problems and develop hypotheses. *Survey of Buying Power,* an annual supplement to *Sales & Marketing Management,* contains sales data for major industries on a

Collecting Data
Tobii Technology assists clients in providing technology to study eye movements on screen to collect primary data and gain insight into customers' responses to marketing communications.

Table 5.2 Popular Internet Activities

Activity	Percent of Internet Users That Use Each Activity
Send or read e-mail	92%
Use a search engine	92
Get news online	76
Buy a product online	71
Visit social network sites	65

Source: The Pew Research Center's Internet & American Life Project tracking surveys, 2002–2011, pewinternet.org.

county-by-county basis. Many marketers also consult federal government publications such as the *Statistical Abstract of the United States,* the *Census of Business,* the *Census of Agriculture,* and the *Census of Population;* most of these government publications are available online. Although the government still conducts its primary census every 10 years, it also conducts the American Community Survey, an ongoing survey sent to population samples on a regular basis.[17] This provides marketers with a more up-to-date demographic picture of the nation's population every year. A company might use survey census data to determine, for example, whether or not to construct a shopping mall in a specific area.[18]

In addition, companies may subscribe to services, such as ACNielsen or Information Resources Inc. (IRI), that track retail sales and other information. For example, IRI tracks consumer purchases using in-store, scanner-based technology. Marketing firms can purchase information from IRI about a product category, such as frozen orange juice, as secondary data.[19] Small businesses may be unable to afford such services, but they can still find a wealth of information through industry publications and trade associations.

Companies such as TiVo are challenging services like ACNielson by offering year-round second-by-second information about the show and advertising viewing habits of consumers who own the company's DVRs. The data are anonymous and are recorded by the TV viewers' boxes. ACNielson only measures local program viewing for four months a year. However, TiVo's data gathering is limited. Its privacy-protection policies prevent the company from collecting information that Nielson can provide, such as demographic breakdowns and the number of people watching each TV set. On the other hand, TiVo information can aid local TV news programs in their programming decisions by helping them choose when to air sports and weather and how much time to devote to each segment.[20]

The Internet can be especially useful to marketing researchers. Search engines such as Google can help marketers locate many types of secondary data or to research topics of interest. Of course, companies can mine their own websites for useful information by using CRM tools. Amazon.com, for example, has built a relationship with its customers by tracking the types of books, music, and other products they purchase. Each time a customer logs on to the website, the company can offer recommendations based on the customer's previous purchases. Such a marketing system helps the company track the changing desires and buying habits of its most valued customers. Furthermore, marketing researchers are increasingly monitoring blogs to discover what consumers are saying about their products—both positive and negative. Some, including yogurt maker Stonyfield Farms, have even established their own blogs as a way to monitor consumer dialogue on issues of their choice. There are many reasons people go online, which can make the job of using the Internet complicated for marketers. Table 5.2 lists the main reasons people go online, and Table 5.3 summarizes the external sources of secondary data, excluding syndicated services.

Methods of Collecting Primary Data

Collecting primary data is a lengthier, more expensive, and more complex process than collecting secondary data. To gather primary data, researchers use sampling procedures, survey methods, and observation. These efforts can be handled in-house by the firm's own research department or contracted to a private research firm such as ACNielsen, Information Resources Inc., or IMS International.

population All the elements, units, or individuals of interest to researchers for a specific study

Sampling Because the time and resources available for research are limited, it is almost impossible to investigate all the members of a target market or other population. A **population**, or "universe," includes all the elements, units, or individuals of interest to researchers for a

Table 5.3 Sources of Secondary Information

Government Sources	
Economic census	www.census.gov/econ/census07
Export.gov—country and industry market research	www.export.gov/mrktresearch/index.asp
National Technical Information Services	www.ntis.gov
Strategis—Canadian trade	www.strategis.ic.gc.ca/engdoc/main.html
Trade Associations and Shows	
American Society of Association Executives	www.asaecenter.org
Directory of Associations	www.marketingsource.com/associations
Trade Show News Network	www.tsnn.com
Magazines, Newspapers, Video, and Audio News Programming	
Blinkx	www.blinkx.com
Resource Library	http://findarticles.com
Google Video Search	www.video.google.com
Google News Directory	www.google.com/news/directory
Yahoo! Video Search	www.video.search.yahoo.com
Corporate Information	
Annual Report Service	www.annualreportservice.com
Bitpipe	www.bitpipe.com
Business Wire—press releases	www.businesswire.com
Hoover's Online	www.hoovers.com
Open Directory Project	www.dmoz.org
PR Newswire—press releases	www.prnewswire.com

Source: Adapted from "Data Collection: Low-Cost Secondary Research," *KnowThis.com*, www.knowthis.com/principles-of-marketing-tutorials/data-collection-low-cost-secondary-research/ (accessed May 24, 2012).

specific study. Consider a Gallup poll designed to predict the results of a presidential election. All registered voters in the United States would constitute the population. By systematically choosing a limited number of units—a **sample**—to represent the characteristics of a total population, researchers can project the reactions of a total market or market segment. (In the case of the presidential poll, a representative national sample of several thousand registered voters would be selected and surveyed to project the probable voting outcome.) **Sampling** in marketing research, therefore, is the process of selecting representative units from a total population. Sampling techniques allow marketers to predict buying behavior fairly accurately on the basis of the responses from a representative portion of the population of interest. Most types of marketing research employ sampling techniques.

There are two basic types of sampling: probability sampling and nonprobability sampling. With **probability sampling**, every element in the population being studied has a known chance of being selected for study. Random sampling is a form of probability sampling. When marketers employ **random sampling**, all the units in a population have an equal chance of appearing in the sample. The various events that can occur have an equal or known chance of taking place. For example, a specific card in a regulation deck should have a 1 in 52 probability of being drawn at any one time. Sample units are ordinarily chosen by selecting from a table of random numbers statistically generated so that each digit, 0 through 9, will have an equal probability of occurring in each position in the sequence. The sequentially numbered elements of a population are sampled randomly by selecting the units whose numbers appear in the table of random numbers.

sample A limited number of units chosen to represent the characteristics of a total population

sampling The process of selecting representative units from a total population

probability sampling A type of sampling in which every element in the population being studied has a known chance of being selected for study

random sampling A form of probability sampling in which all units in a population have an equal chance of appearing in the sample, and the various events that can occur have an equal or known chance of taking place

Sampling
Companies like uSamp assist customers in creating samples and consumer panels.

Another type of probability sampling is **stratified sampling**, in which the population of interest is divided into groups according to a common attribute, and a random sample is then chosen within each group. The stratified sample may reduce some of the error that could occur in a simple random sample. By ensuring that each major group or segment of the population receives its proportionate share of sample units, investigators avoid including too many or too few sample units from each group. Samples are usually stratified when researchers believe there may be variations among different types of respondents. For instance, many political opinion surveys are stratified by gender, race, age, and/or geographic location.

The second type of sampling, **nonprobability sampling**, is more subjective than probability sampling because there is no way to calculate the likelihood that a specific element of the population being studied will be chosen. Quota sampling, for example, is highly judgmental because the final choice of participants is left to the researchers. In **quota sampling**, researchers divide the population into groups and then arbitrarily choose participants from each group. In quota sampling, there are some controls—usually limited to two or three variables, such as age, gender, or race—over the selection of participants. The controls attempt to ensure that representative categories of respondents are interviewed. A study of people who wear eyeglasses, for example, may be conducted by interviewing equal numbers of men and women who wear eyeglasses. Because quota samples are not probability samples, not everyone has an equal chance of being selected, and sampling error therefore cannot be measured statistically. Quota samples are used most often in exploratory studies, when hypotheses are being developed. Often a small quota sample will not be projected to the total population, although the findings may provide valuable insights into a problem. Quota samples are useful when people with some common characteristic are found and questioned about the topic of interest. A probability sample used to study people who are allergic to cats, for example, would be highly inefficient.

stratified sampling A type of probability sampling in which the population is divided into groups with a common attribute and a random sample is chosen within each group

nonprobability sampling A sampling technique in which there is no way to calculate the likelihood that a specific element of the population being studied will be chosen

quota sampling A nonprobability sampling technique in which researchers divide the population into groups and then arbitrarily choose participants from each group

mail survey A research method in which respondents answer a questionnaire sent through the mail

Survey Methods Marketing researchers often employ sampling to collect primary data through mail, telephone, personal interview, online, or social networking surveys. The results of such surveys are used to describe and analyze buying behavior. The survey method chosen depends on the nature of the problem or issue; the data needed to test the hypothesis; and the resources, such as funding and personnel, available to the researcher. Marketers may employ more than one survey method depending on the goals of the research. Surveys can be quite expensive (Procter & Gamble spends about $350 million on consumer research and conducts more than 15,000 research studies annually), but small businesses can turn to sites such as SurveyMonkey.com[21] and zoomerang.com for inexpensive or even free online surveys. Table 5.4 summarizes and compares the advantages of the various survey methods.

Gathering information through surveys is becoming increasingly difficult because fewer people are willing to participate. Many people believe responding to surveys requires too much scarce personal time, especially as surveys become longer and more detailed. Others have concerns about how much information marketers are gathering and whether their privacy is being invaded. The unethical use of selling techniques disguised as marketing surveys has also led to decreased cooperation. These factors contribute to nonresponse rates for any type of survey.

In a **mail survey**, questionnaires are sent to respondents, who are encouraged to complete and return them. Mail surveys are used most often when the individuals in the sample are spread over a wide area and funds for the survey are limited. A mail survey is less expensive than a telephone or personal interview survey as long as the response rate is high enough to

Table 5.4 Comparison of the Four Basic Survey Methods

	Mail Surveys	Telephone Surveys	Online Surveys	Personal Interview Surveys
Economy	Potentially lower in cost per interview than telephone or personal surveys if there is an adequate response rate.	Avoids interviewers' travel expenses; less expensive than in-home interviews.	The least expensive method if there is an adequate response rate.	The most expensive survey method; shopping mall and focus-group interviews have lower costs than in-home interviews.
Flexibility	Inflexible; questionnaire must be short and easy for respondents to complete.	Flexible because interviewers can ask probing questions, but observations are impossible.	Less flexible; survey must be easy for online users to receive and return; short, dichotomous, or multiple-choice questions work best.	Most flexible method; respondents can react to visual materials; demographic data are more accurate; in-depth probes are possible.
Interviewer bias	Interviewer bias is eliminated; questionnaires can be returned anonymously.	Some anonymity; may be hard to develop trust in respondents.	Interviewer bias is often eliminated with e-mail, but e-mail address on the return eliminates anonymity.	Interviewers' personal characteristics or inability to maintain objectivity may result in bias.
Sampling and respondents' cooperation	Obtaining a complete mailing list is difficult; nonresponse is a major disadvantage.	Sample limited to respondents with telephones; devices that screen calls, busy signals, and refusals are a problem.	The available e-mail address list may not be a representative sample for some purposes. Social media surveys might be skewed as fans may be more likely to take the survey.	Not-at-homes are a problem, which may be overcome by focus-group and shopping mall interviewing.

produce reliable results. The main disadvantages of this method are the possibility of a low response rate and of misleading results if respondents differ significantly from the population being sampled. One method of improving response rates involves attaching a brief personal message on a Post-it® Note to the survey packet. Response rates to these surveys are higher, and the quality and timeliness of the responses are also improved.[22] As a result of these issues, companies are increasingly moving to Internet surveys and automated telephone surveys.

Premiums or incentives that encourage respondents to return questionnaires have been effective in developing panels of respondents who are interviewed regularly by mail. Such mail panels, selected to represent a target market or market segment, are especially useful in evaluating new products and providing general information about customers, as well as records of their purchases (in the form of purchase diaries). Mail panels and purchase diaries are much more widely used than custom mail surveys, but both panels and purchase diaries have shortcomings. People who take the time to fill out a diary may differ from the general population based on income, education, or behavior, such as the time available for shopping activities. Internet and social networking surveys have also greatly gained in popularity, although they are similarly limited as well—given that not all demographics utilize these media equally.

In a **telephone survey**, an interviewer records respondents' answers to a questionnaire over a phone line. A telephone survey has some advantages over a mail survey. The rate of response is higher because it takes less effort to answer the telephone and talk than to fill out and return a questionnaire. If enough interviewers are available, a telephone survey can be conducted very quickly. Thus, political candidates or organizations that want an immediate reaction to an event may choose this method. In addition, a telephone survey permits interviewers to gain rapport with respondents and ask probing questions. Automated telephone surveys, also known as interactive voice response or "robosurveys," rely on a recorded voice to ask the questions while a computer program records respondents' answers. The primary benefit of automated surveys is the elimination of any bias that might be introduced by a live researcher.

telephone survey A research method in which respondents' answers to a questionnaire are recorded by an interviewer on the phone

Entrepreneurship in Marketing

iModerate Takes a New Approach to Market Research

Entrepreneurs: Joel Benenson and Carl Rossow
Business: iModerate
Founded: 2004 | Denver, Colorado
Success: iModerate's clients have included 32 Fortune 100 companies, and 80 percent of initial clients return for additional projects.

Internet surveys are a popular marketing research method due to their ease and flexibility. However, entrepreneurs Joel Benenson and Carl Rossow saw something missing. They noticed that many Internet surveys do not provide enough information for each respondent. To solve this problem, they created the market research company iModerate. The company soon began making a name for itself in online market research, with clients including Kaiser Permanente, Business Roundtable, and Showtime.

Rather than simply surveying consumers, iModerate moderators also conduct one-on-one online discussions with consumers. Since its founding, the company has conducted more than 100,000 of these discussions. As a result, it has devised a unique framework called ThoughtPath™ to discover what consumers want. ThoughtPath™ combines the concepts of perception, identity, and experience to understand how consumers interpret a brand and view themselves in regard to the brand. This framework is used to provide meaningful consumer insights for iModerate clients. iModerate is an example of a company using evolving technologies to create more detailed methodologies for marketing research.[a]

Another option is the **telephone depth interview**, which combines the traditional focus group's ability to probe with the confidentiality provided by a telephone survey. This type of interview is most appropriate for qualitative research projects among a small targeted group that is difficult to bring together for a traditional focus group because of members' professions, locations, or lifestyles. Respondents can choose the time and day for the interview. Although this method is difficult to implement, it can yield revealing information from respondents who otherwise would be unwilling to participate in marketing research.

However, only a small proportion of the population likes to participate in telephone surveys or interviews. This can significantly limit participation and distort representation. Moreover, surveys and interviews conducted over the telephone are limited to oral communication; visual aids or observation cannot be included. Interpreters of results must make adjustments for individuals who are not at home or do not have telephones. Many households are excluded from telephone directories by choice (unlisted numbers) or because the residents moved after the directory was published. Potential respondents often use telephone answering machines, voice mail, or caller ID to screen or block calls; additionally, millions have signed up for "Do Not Call Lists." Moreover, an increasing number of younger Americans are giving up their fixed telephone lines in favor of cellular or wireless phones. These issues have serious implications for the use of telephone samples in conducting surveys or interviews.

In a **personal interview survey**, participants respond to questions face-to-face. Various audiovisual aids—pictures, products, diagrams, or prerecorded advertising copy—can be incorporated into a personal interview. Rapport gained through direct interaction usually permits more in-depth interviewing, including probes, follow-up questions, or psychological tests. In addition, because personal interviews can be longer, they may yield more information. Respondents can be selected more carefully, and reasons for nonresponse can be explored. One such research technique is the **in-home (door-to-door) interview**. The in-home interview offers a clear advantage when thoroughness of self-disclosure and elimination of group influence are important. In an in-depth interview of 45 to 90 minutes, respondents can be probed to reveal their true motivations, feelings, behaviors, and aspirations.

telephone depth interview An interview that combines the traditional focus group's ability to probe with the confidentiality provided by telephone surveys

personal interview survey A research method in which participants respond to survey questions face-to-face

in-home (door-to-door) interview A personal interview that takes place in the respondent's home

The nature of personal interviews has changed. In the past, most personal interviews, which were based on random sampling or prearranged appointments, were conducted in the respondent's home. Today, many personal interviews are conducted in shopping malls.

Shopping mall intercept interviews involve interviewing a percentage of individuals who pass by an "intercept" point in a mall. Like any face-to-face interviewing method, mall intercept interviewing has many advantages. The interviewer is in a position to recognize and react to respondents' nonverbal indications of confusion. Respondents can view product prototypes, videotapes of commercials, and the like, and provide their opinions. The mall environment lets the researcher deal with complex situations. For instance, in taste tests, researchers know that all the respondents are reacting to the same product, which can be prepared and monitored from the mall test kitchen. In addition to the ability to conduct tests requiring bulky equipment, lower cost and greater control make shopping mall intercept interviews popular.

An **on-site computer interview** is a variation of the shopping mall intercept interview in which respondents complete a self-administered questionnaire displayed on a computer monitor. A computer software package can be used to conduct such interviews in shopping malls. After a brief lesson on how to operate the software, respondents proceed through the survey at their own pace. Questionnaires can be adapted so that respondents see only those items (usually a subset of an entire scale) that may provide useful information about their attitudes.

Online and Social Media Surveys We give online surveys and Internet research its own section because as more and more consumers gain Internet access, Internet surveys are likely to become the predominate tool for general population sampling. The amount that marketers spend on Internet surveys has increased 33 percent since 2005.[23] In an **online survey**, questionnaires can be transmitted to respondents either through e-mail or through a website. Marketing researchers often send these surveys to online panel samples purchased from professional brokers or put together by the company. Because e-mail is semi-interactive, recipients can ask for clarification of specific questions or pose questions of their own. The potential advantages of online surveys are quick response and lower cost than traditional mail, telephone, and personal interview surveys if the response rate is adequate. In addition, more firms use their websites to conduct surveys.

Social networking sites can also be used to conduct surveys. Marketers can use digital media forums such as chat rooms, blogs, newsgroups, social networks, and research communities to identify trends in interests and consumption patterns. However, using these forums for conducting surveys has some limitations. Often consumers choose to go to a particular social media site or blog and then take the survey; this eliminates randomness and makes it more difficult to obtain

shopping mall intercept interview A research method that involves interviewing a percentage of individuals passing by "intercept" points in a mall

on-site computer interview A variation of the shopping mall intercept interview in which respondents complete a self-administered questionnaire displayed on a computer monitor

online survey A research method in which respondents answer a questionnaire via e-mail or on a website

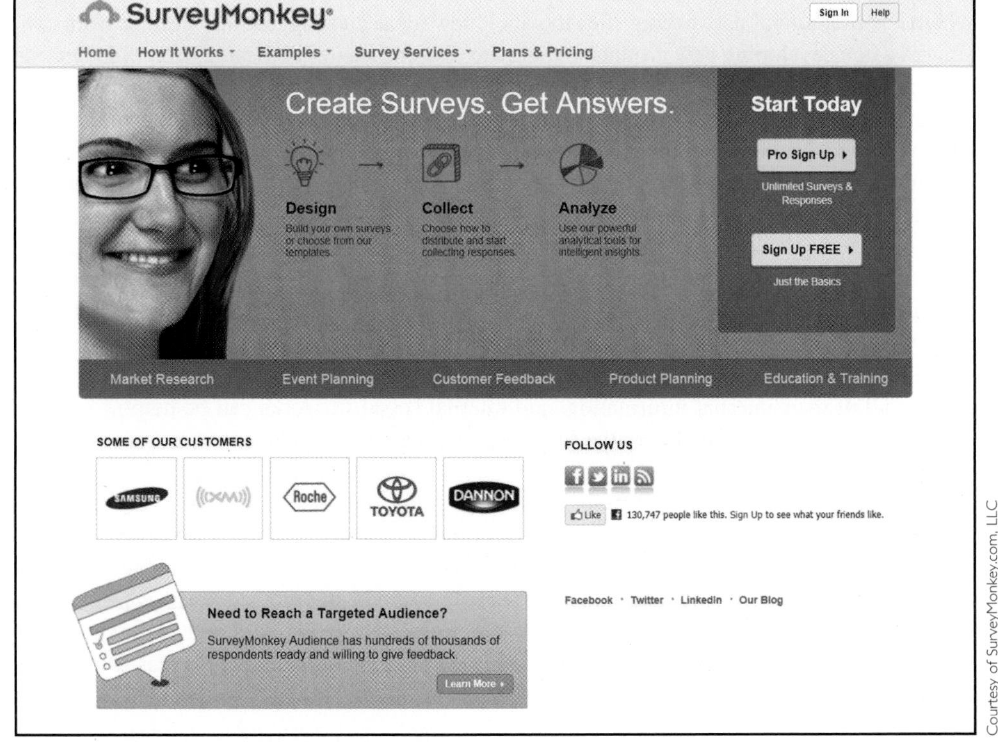

Online Surveys
SurveyMonkey provides its customers with research delivered by a readily available online survey panel.

Going Green

Stakeholder Feedback Helps Companies Be Greener

Businesses are often wary of creating open stakeholder dialogue. Many believe that public discussions in which stakeholders can publically express their opinions, such as Web forums, could open them up to criticism. However, businesses that engage in a dialogue with stakeholders usually find that the benefits outweigh the risks.

This is especially true when stakeholder feedback can help companies become greener. For instance, Dell created an online platform called IdeaStorm to solicit customer recommendations. Although customers are free to discuss any topic, several respondents have posted suggestions on environmental initiatives they believe the company should take. Green dialogue can also incorporate suggestions from suppliers, employees, and business partners. Eaton participates in symposiums to stimulate discussions between the company, business partners, and public leaders. Kimball International holds a Green Supplier conference to talk with suppliers about green expectations.

Finally, dialogue can help stakeholders to learn more about a company's sustainable products. Bardo Furniture engages its consumers in conversations about its green product lines. And unlike one-way forms of communication, discussing these topics with stakeholders enables companies to understand what stakeholders need and provide them with sustainable options. Engaging in dialogue seems to be an effective means of conducting green market research.[b]

a representative sample size. On the other hand, they can provide a very general idea of consumer trends and preferences. Movies, consumer electronics, food, and computers are popular topics in many online communities. Indeed, by "listening in" on these ongoing conversations, marketers may be able to identify new-product opportunities and consumer needs. Moreover, this type of online data can be gathered at little incremental cost compared to alternative data sources.

Crowdsourcing combines the words *crowd* and *outsourcing* and calls for taking tasks usually performed by a marketer or researcher and outsourcing them to a crowd, or potential market, through an open call. In the case of digital marketing, crowdsourcing is often used to obtain the opinions or needs of the crowd (or potential markets). Consider Procter & Gamble, which has used social networking sites to solicit new ideas and suggestions straight from consumers when developing new products. There are also entire sites dedicated to crowdsourcing. On threadless.com participants can submit and score T-shirt designs. Designs with the highest votes are printed and then sold. Crowdsourcing is a way for marketers to gather input straight from willing consumers and to actively listen to people's ideas and evaluations on products.

Nutritional-supplement firm GNC views social networking as an important marketing research tool that allows it to venture into consumers' lives and test product ideas. For example, GNC launched a social media campaign to promote its coconut-water beverage through Google AdWords, Twitter, and a microsite. Initial feedback was negative regarding the product's taste, prompting GNC to begin revamping the beverage. Although the initial product was unsuccessful, social media enabled the company to receive instant feedback and provided it with the information it needed to understand the issue.[24] It is also important for organizations to harness all of their internal information, and internal social networks can be helpful for that. California-based Blue Shield uses the internal social networking platform Chatter to connect its employees.[25]

Marketing research will likely rely heavily on online surveys in the future. Furthermore, as negative attitudes toward telephone surveys render that technique less representative and more expensive, the integration of e-mail and voice mail functions into one computer-based system provides a promising alternative for survey research. Internet surveys have especially strong potential within organizations whose employees are networked and for associations that publish members' e-mail addresses. However, there are some ethical issues to consider when using e-mail for marketing research, such as unsolicited e-mail, which could be viewed

crowdsourcing Combines the words *crowd* and *outsourcing* and calls for taking tasks usually performed by a marketer or researcher and outsourcing them to a crowd, or potential market, through an open call

as "spam," and privacy, as some potential survey respondents fear their personal information will be given or sold to third parties without their knowledge or permission.

Another challenge for researchers is obtaining a sample that is representative of the desired population. While Internet surveys allow respondents to retain their anonymity and flexibility, it can also enable survey takers to abuse the system. For instance, some survey takers take multiple surveys or pose as other people to make more money. To get around this problem, companies are developing screening mechanisms and instituting limits on how many surveys one person can take.[26] Survey programs such as Qualtrics can also delete surveys that appear suspicious.

Questionnaire Construction A carefully constructed questionnaire is essential to the success of any survey. Questions must be clear, easy to understand, and directed toward a specific objective; that is, they must be designed to elicit information that meets the study's data requirements. Researchers need to define the objective before trying to develop a questionnaire because the objective determines the substance of the questions and the amount of detail. A common mistake in constructing questionnaires is to ask questions that interest the researchers but do not yield information useful in deciding whether to accept or reject a hypothesis. Finally, the most important rule in composing questions is to maintain impartiality. The questions are usually of three kinds: open-ended, dichotomous, and multiple-choice. Problems may develop in the analysis of dichotomous or multiple-choice questions when responses for one outcome outnumber others. For example, a dichotomous question that asks respondents to choose between "buy" or "not buy" might require additional sampling from the disproportionately smaller group if there were not enough responses to analyze.[27]

Researchers must also be very careful about questions that a respondent might consider too personal or that might require an admission of activities that other people are likely to condemn. Questions of this type should be worded to make them less offensive.

Observation Methods In using observation methods, researchers record individuals' overt behavior, taking note of physical conditions and events. Direct contact with them is avoided; instead, their actions are examined and noted systematically. For instance, researchers might use observation methods to answer the question, "How long does the average McDonald's restaurant customer have to wait in line before being served?" Observation may include the use of ethnographic techniques, such as watching customers interact with a product in a real-world environment. To increase its ability to observe consumer behavior, Time Warner opened a media lab in New York equipped with eye-tracking stations, a home theater, a mock retail store with a checkout, and gaming stations. The lab tries to simulate a real-world environment to test how consumers would react naturally to different forms of media. Researchers can watch the proceedings from observation rooms in the lab.[28] Observation may also be combined with interviews. For instance, during a personal interview, the condition of a respondent's home or other possessions may be observed and recorded. The interviewer can also directly observe and confirm such demographic information as race, approximate age, and gender. In addition to observation rooms, the Time Warner lab also has areas for focus group interviews.[29]

Data gathered through observation can sometimes be biased if the subject is aware of the observation process. However, an observer can be placed in a natural market environment, such as a grocery store, without influencing shoppers' actions. If the presence of a human observer is likely to bias the outcome or if human sensory abilities are inadequate, mechanical means may be used to record behavior. Mechanical observation devices include cameras, recorders, counting machines, scanners, and equipment that records physiological changes. A special camera can be used to record the eye movements of people as they look at an advertisement; the camera detects the sequence of reading and the parts of the advertisement that receive the greatest attention. The electronic scanners used in supermarkets are very useful in marketing research: they provide accurate data on sales and customers' purchase patterns, and marketing researchers may buy such data from the supermarkets.

Observation is straightforward and avoids a central problem of survey methods: motivating respondents to state their true feelings or opinions. However, observation tends to be descriptive. When it is the only method of data collection, it may not provide insights into causal relationships. Another drawback is that analyses based on observation are subject to the observer's biases or the limitations of the mechanical device.

Interpreting Research Findings

After collecting data to test their hypotheses, marketers need to interpret the research findings. Interpretation of the data is easier if marketers carefully plan their data analysis methods early in the research process. They should also allow for continual evaluation of the data during the entire collection period. Marketers can then gain valuable insights into areas that should be probed during the formal analysis.

The first step in drawing conclusions from most research is to display the data in table format. If marketers intend to apply the results to individual categories of the things or people being studied, cross-tabulation may be useful, especially in tabulating joint occurrences. For example, using the two variables of gender and purchase rates of automobile tires, a cross-tabulation could show how men and women differ in purchasing automobile tires.

After the data are tabulated, they must be analyzed. **Statistical interpretation** focuses on what is typical and what deviates from the average. It indicates how widely responses vary and how they are distributed in relation to the variable being measured. When marketers interpret statistics, they must take into account estimates of expected error or deviation from the true values of the population. The analysis of data may lead researchers to accept or reject the hypothesis being studied. Data require careful interpretation by the marketer. If the results of a study are valid, the decision maker should take action; if a question has been incorrectly or poorly worded, however, the results may produce poor decisions. Consider the research conducted for a food marketer that asked respondents to rate a product on criteria such as "hearty flavor," as well as how important each criterion was to the respondent. Although such results may have had utility for advertising purposes, they are less helpful in product development because it is not possible to discern each respondent's meaning of the phrase "hearty flavor." Managers must understand the research results and relate them to a context that permits effective decision making.

statistical interpretation Analysis of what is typical and what deviates from the average

Statistical Interpretation
Qualtrics assists customers with data collection and analysis.

Reporting Research Findings

The final step in the marketing research process is to report the research findings. Before preparing the report, the marketer must take a clear, objective look at the findings to see how well the gathered facts answer the research question or support or negate the initial hypotheses. In most cases, it is extremely doubtful that the study can provide everything needed to answer the research question. Thus, the researcher must point out the deficiencies in the research and their causes in the report. Research should be meaningful to all participants, especially top managers who develop strategy. Therefore, researchers must try to make certain that their findings are relevant and not just interesting. Research is not useful unless it supports the organization's overall strategy objectives. The more knowledge researchers have about the opportunities and challenges facing an organization, the more meaningful their research report will be. If an outside research agency conducts research, it is even more important to understand the client's business. After conducting research, a research report is the next step. Those responsible for preparing the report must facilitate adjusting the findings to the environment, as elements change over time. Most importantly, the report should be helpful to marketers and managers on an ongoing basis.[30]

The report of research results is usually a formal, written document. Researchers must allow time for the writing task when they plan and schedule the project. Because the report is a means of communicating with the decision makers who will use the research findings, researchers need to determine beforehand how much detail and supporting data to include. They should keep in mind that corporate executives prefer reports that are short, clear, and simply expressed. Researchers often give their summary and recommendations first, especially if decision makers do not have time to study how the results were obtained. A technical report allows its users to analyze data and interpret recommendations because it describes the research methods and procedures and the most important data gathered. Thus, researchers must recognize the needs and expectations of the report user and adapt to them.

Marketing researchers want to know about behavior and opinions, and they want accurate data to help them in making decisions. Careful wording of questions is very important because a biased or emotional word can dramatically change the results. Marketing research and marketing information systems can provide an organization with accurate and reliable customer feedback, which a marketer must have to understand the dynamics of the marketplace. As managers recognize the benefits of marketing research, they assign it a much larger role in decision making.

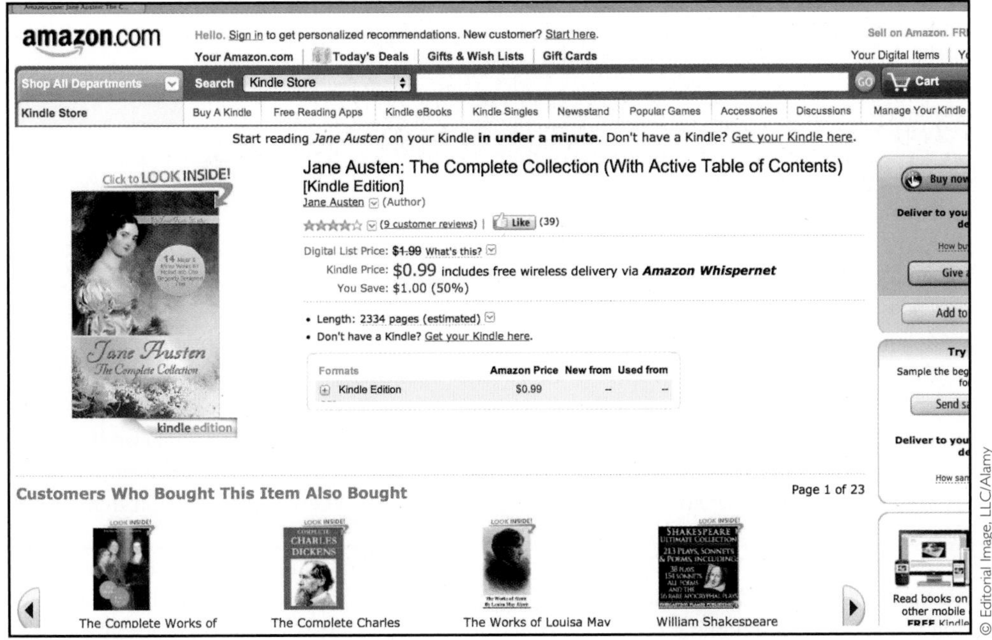

Using Technology
Amazon and other online retailers have developed technology that makes recommendations to a customer for music or movies that he or she might like based on prior purchases.

USING TECHNOLOGY TO IMPROVE MARKETING INFORMATION GATHERING AND ANALYSIS

Technology makes information for marketing decisions increasingly accessible. The ability of marketers to track customer buying behavior and to better discern what buyers want is changing the nature of marketing. Customer relationship management is being enhanced by integrating data from all customer contacts and combining that information to improve customer retention. Information technology permits internal research and quick information gathering to help marketers better understand and satisfy customers. For instance, company responses to e-mail complaints—as well as to communications through mail, telephone, and personal contact—can be used to improve customer satisfaction, retention, and value. Armed with such information, marketers can fine-tune marketing mixes to satisfy their customers' needs.

Consumer feedback is an important aspect of marketing research, and new technology such as digital media is enhancing this process. Ratings and reviews on Internet forums are becoming increasingly popular, with 25 percent of the U.S. online population reading these types of consumer-generated feedback.[31] Online retailers such as Amazon, Netflix, and Priceline are capitalizing on these ratings and reviews by allowing consumers to post comments on their sites concerning books, movies, hotels, and more. Marketers can use these social media forums to closely monitor what their customers are saying. In the case of negative feedback, marketers can communicate with consumers to address problems or complaints more easily than with traditional marketing channels. In one survey, 40 percent of respondents replied that they would be likely to consider a local business that takes the time to respond to negative reviews.[32] By researching what consumers are saying about their products, companies can understand what features of their product mixes should be promoted or modified.

Finally, the integration of telecommunications and computer technologies allows marketers to access a growing array of valuable information sources related to industry forecasts, business trends, and customer buying behavior. Electronic communication tools can be effectively used to gain accurate information with minimal customer interaction. Most marketing researchers have e-mail, voice mail, teleconferencing, and fax machines at their disposal. In fact, many firms use marketing information systems and CRM technologies to network all these technologies and organize all the marketing data available to them. In this section, we look at marketing information systems and specific technologies that are helping marketing researchers obtain and manage marketing research data.

Marketing Information Systems

A **marketing information system (MIS)** is a framework for the day-to-day management and structuring of information gathered regularly from sources both inside and outside the organization. As such, an MIS provides a continuous flow of information about prices, advertising expenditures, sales, competition, and distribution expenses. Marketing information systems can be an important asset for developing effective marketing strategies. Procter & Gamble managers, for instance, search through P&G's proprietary MIS for data to help the company predict which products will work best in different countries.[33] The main focus of the MIS is on data storage and retrieval, as well as on computer capabilities and management's information requirements. Regular reports of sales by product or market categories, data on inventory levels, and records of salespeople's activities are examples of information that is useful in making decisions. In the MIS, the means of gathering data receive less attention than do the procedures for expediting the flow of information.

marketing information system (MIS) A framework for managing and structuring information gathered regularly from sources inside and outside the organization

An effective MIS starts by determining the objective of the information—that is, by identifying decision needs that require certain information. The firm can then specify an information system for continuous monitoring to provide regular, pertinent information on both the

Emerging Trends

The Billboard of the Future

Traditionally, when a person looks at a billboard, information goes one way: from billboard to consumer. However, new marketing research technology now allows information to go two ways. The consumer collects information from the billboard's message, and the billboard in turn collects information about the consumer.

In Japan, digital billboards have been invented that estimate a consumer's age and gender. Based on the estimated age and gender, the display then creates advertising tailored to the appropriate demographic. An East Japan Railway subsidiary introduced vending machines with this technology that use information gleaned from consumers to suggest drinks.

Similar billboards are appearing across the world. In the United States, marketers are creating displays that recognize gestures and facial expressions of consumers. This data can determine whether the consumer is actually looking at the display. For marketers, the technology can help them understand who is attracted to their messages and perhaps create customized messages for each consumer based upon this data collection. However, privacy advocates are wary of this technology. They fear that it can be misused to identify people, a violation of individual privacy. So far there is little regulation to limit how marketers will use information collected from billboards. As this technology becomes more popular, clearer laws will be needed to allow marketers to gather information without abusing consumer privacy.[c]

external and internal environment. FedEx, for example, has interactive marketing systems that provide instantaneous communication between the company and customers. Customers can track their packages and receive immediate feedback concerning delivery via the Internet. The company's website provides information about customer usage and allows customers to convey what they think about company services. The evolving telecommunications and computer technologies allow marketers to use information systems to cultivate one-to-one relationships with customers.

Databases

Most marketing information systems include internal databases. A **database** is a collection of information arranged for easy access and retrieval. Databases allow marketers to tap into an abundance of information useful in making marketing decisions: internal sales reports, newspaper articles, company news releases, government economic reports, bibliographies, and more, often accessed through a computer system. Information technology has made it possible to develop databases to guide strategic planning and help improve customer services. Customer relationship management (CRM) employs database marketing techniques to identify different types of customers and develop specific strategies for interacting with each customer. CRM incorporates these three elements:

1. Identifying and building a database of current and potential consumers, including a wide range of demographic, lifestyle, and purchase information.
2. Delivering differential messages according to each consumer's preferences and characteristics through established and new media channels.
3. Tracking customer relationships to monitor the costs of retaining individual customers and the lifetime value of their purchases.[34]

Many commercial websites require consumers to register and provide personal information to access the site or to make a purchase. Frequent-flyer programs permit airlines to ask loyal customers to participate in surveys about their needs and desires and to track their best customers' flight patterns by time of day, week, month, and year. Also, supermarkets gain a significant amount of data through checkout scanners tied to store discount cards.

database A collection of information arranged for easy access and retrieval

Marketing Debate

The Privacy of Purchase Data

ISSUE: Do the proposals of MasterCard and Visa infringe on users' privacy?

MasterCard and Visa announced plans to compile information about consumers' purchases and sell it to marketers for online advertising purposes. Rather than targeting a particular individual, the companies would use aggregate data to create market segments that marketers could use to target ads toward specific areas or predict buying behavior. One of Visa's proposals is to create user profiles based on credit card transactions in stores as well as data from social networks, insurance claims, or even DNA databanks. These profiles can then be used to target ads to specific market segments. According to one senator, these plans have "unprecedented and alarming" implications. The companies respond that the information will be kept anonymous and that current laws limit how customer data is used.[d]

Marketing researchers can also use databases, such as LexisNexis, to obtain useful information for marketing decisions. Many commercial databases are accessible online for a fee. Sometimes, they can be obtained in printed form or digitally. With most commercial databases, the user typically conducts a computer search by keyword, topic, or company, and the database service generates abstracts, articles, or reports that can then be printed out.

Information provided by a single firm on household demographics, purchases, television viewing behavior, and responses to promotions such as coupons and free samples is called **single-source data**. For example, BehaviorScan, offered by Information Resources Inc., screens markets with populations between 75,000 and 215,000.[35] This single-source information service monitors consumer household televisions and records the programs and commercials watched. When buyers from these households shop in stores equipped with scanning registers, they present Hotline cards (similar to credit cards) to cashiers. This enables each customer's identification to be electronically coded so the firm can track each product purchased and store the information in a database. The firm also offers new product testing. It is important to gather longitudinal (long-term) information on customers to maximize the usefulness of single-source data.

Marketing Decision Support Systems

A **marketing decision support system (MDSS)** is customized computer software that aids marketing managers in decision making by helping them anticipate the effects of certain decisions. Some decision support systems have a broader range and offer greater computational and modeling capabilities than spreadsheets; they let managers explore a greater number of alternatives. For instance, an MDSS can determine how sales and profits might be affected by higher or lower interest rates or how sales forecasts, advertising expenditures, production levels, and the like might affect overall profits. For this reason, MDSS software is often a major component of a company's marketing information system. Some decision support systems incorporate artificial intelligence and other advanced computer technologies.

single-source data Information provided by a single marketing research firm

marketing decision support system (MDSS) Customized computer software that aids marketing managers in decision making

ISSUES IN MARKETING RESEARCH

Marketers should identify concerns that influence the integrity of research. Ethical issues are a constant risk in gathering and maintaining the quality of information. International issues relate to environmental differences, such as culture, legal requirements, level of technology, and economic development.

The Importance of Ethical Marketing Research

Marketing managers and other professionals are relying more and more on marketing research, marketing information systems, and new technologies to make better decisions. Therefore, it is essential that professional standards be established by which to judge the reliability of marketing research. Such standards are necessary because of the ethical and legal issues that develop in gathering marketing research data. In the area of online interaction, for example, consumers remain wary of how the personal information collected by marketers will be used, especially whether it will be sold to third parties. In addition, the relationships between research suppliers, such as marketing research agencies, and the marketing managers who make strategy decisions require ethical behavior. Organizations such as the Marketing Research Association have developed codes of conduct and guidelines to promote ethical marketing research. To be effective, such guidelines must instruct marketing researchers on how to avoid misconduct. Table 5.5 recommends explicit steps interviewers should follow when introducing a questionnaire.

Consumer privacy has also become a significant issue. Firms now have the ability to purchase data on customer demographics, interests, and more personal matters such as bankruptcy filings and past marriages. This information has allowed companies to predict customer behavior or current life changes more accurately but may also infringe upon consumer privacy.[36] The popularity of the Internet has also enabled marketers to collect data on Internet users who visit their websites. Many companies have been able to use this to their advantage. For instance, Amazon, Netflix, and eBay use data to make customized recommendations based on their customers' interests, ratings, or past purchases. Companies such as Capital One Financial have used data collected by firms who specialize in tracking consumers' online behavior. While such data enable companies to offer more personalized services, policy makers fear that it could also allow them to discriminate among consumers who do not appear to make "valuable" customers.[37] Many consumers also believe that their online behavior could be used to identify them personally. Google, for instance, collects and stores data from its users' searches. These search queries are kept indefinitely, although Google claims that the data is "anonymized" after 18 months.[38] Internet privacy concerns have become so great that policy makers have begun proposing a "Do Not Track" bill for the Internet. More on the "Do Not Track" bill will be discussed in Chapter 10.

Table 5.5 Guidelines for Questionnaire Introduction

• Allow interviewers to introduce themselves by name.
• State the name of the research company.
• Indicate that this questionnaire is a marketing research project.
• Explain that no sales will be involved.
• Note the general topic of discussion (if this is a problem in a "blind" study, a statement such as "consumer opinion" is acceptable).
• State the likely duration of the interview.
• Assure the anonymity of the respondent and the confidentiality of all answers.
• State the honorarium, if applicable (for many business-to-business and medical studies, this is done up-front for both qualitative and quantitative studies).
• Reassure the respondent with a statement such as, "There are no right or wrong answers, so please give thoughtful and honest answers to each question" (recommended by many clients).

Source: Reprinted with the permission of The Marketing Research Association.

International Issues
Companies like Asia Insight assist other businesses to understand the environmental forces, such as sociocultural differences, that might introduce challenges when attempting to research foreign customers.

International Issues in Marketing Research

As we shall see in Chapter 9, sociocultural, economic, political, legal, and technological forces vary in different regions of the world. These variations create challenges for the organizations that are attempting to understand foreign customers through marketing research. The marketing research process we describe in this chapter is used globally, but to ensure the research is valid and reliable, data-gathering methods may have to be modified to allow for regional differences. To make certain that global and regional differences are satisfactorily addressed, many companies retain a research firm with experience in the country of interest. Most of the largest marketing research firms derive a significant share of their revenues from research conducted outside the United States. As Table 5.6 indicates, the Nielsen Company, the largest marketing research firm in the world, received more than half of its revenues from outside the United States.[39]

Experts recommend a two-pronged approach to international marketing research. The first phase involves a detailed search for and analysis of secondary data to gain a greater understanding of a particular marketing environment and to pinpoint issues that must be taken into account in gathering primary research data. Secondary data can be particularly helpful in building a general understanding of the market, including economic, legal, cultural, and demographic issues, as well as in assessing the risks of doing business in that market and in forecasting demand. Marketing researchers often begin by studying country trade reports from the U.S. Department of Commerce, as well as country-specific information from local sources, such as a country's website, and trade and general business publications such as *The Wall Street Journal*. These sources can offer insights into the marketing environment in a particular country and can even indicate untapped market opportunities abroad.

The second phase involves field research using many of the methods described earlier, including focus groups and telephone surveys, to refine a firm's understanding of specific customer needs and preferences. Specific differences among countries can have a profound influence on data gathering. For instance, in-home (door-to-door) interviews are illegal in some countries. In developing countries, few people have land-line telephones, as many opt for cell phones, making telephone surveys less practical and less representative of the total population. Primary data gathering may have a greater chance of

Table 5.6 Top U.S. Marketing Research Firms

Rank	Company	Global Revenues (in Millions of U.S. Dollars)	Percent of Revenues from Outside the United States
1	The Nielsen Co.	$5,353.00	53.0%
2	The Kantar Group	3,331.8	72.1
3	Ipsos	2,754.7	77.3
4	Westat Inc.	506.5	TB
5	SymphonyIRI Group	764.1	39.1

Source: "Top 50 U.S. Market Research Organizations," *Marketing News*, June 30, 2012, p. 25.

success if the firm employs local researchers who better understand how to approach potential respondents and can do so in their own languages.[40] Regardless of the specific methods used to gather primary data, whether in the United States or abroad, the goal is to recognize the needs of specific target markets to craft the best marketing strategy to satisfy the needs of customers in each market, as we will see in the next chapter.

Summary

1. To describe the basic steps in conducting marketing research

Marketing research is the systematic design, collection, interpretation, and reporting of information to help marketers solve specific marketing problems or take advantage of marketing opportunities. It is a process for gathering information not currently available to decision makers. Marketing research can help a firm better understand market opportunities, ascertain the potential for success for new products, and determine the feasibility of a particular marketing strategy. The value of marketing research is measured by improvements in a marketer's ability to make decisions.

To maintain the control needed to obtain accurate information, marketers approach marketing research as a process with logical steps: (1) locating and defining problems or issues, (2) designing the research project, (3) collecting data, (4) interpreting research findings, and (5) reporting research findings.

2. To explore the fundamental methods of gathering data for marketing research

The first step in launching a research study, the problem or issue definition, focuses on uncovering the nature and boundaries of a situation or question related to marketing strategy or implementation. When a firm discovers a market opportunity, it may need to conduct research to understand the situation more precisely so it can craft an appropriate marketing strategy. In the second step, marketing researchers design a research project to obtain the information needed to address it. This step requires formulating a hypothesis and determining what type of research to employ to test the hypothesis so the results are reliable and valid. A hypothesis is an informed guess or assumption about a problem or set of circumstances. Marketers conduct exploratory research when they need more information about a problem or want to make a tentative hypothesis more specific; they use conclusive research to verify insights through an objective procedure. Research is considered reliable if it produces almost identical results in repeated trials; it is valid if it measures what it is supposed to measure.

For the third step of the research process, collecting data, two types of data are available. Primary data are observed and recorded or collected directly from respondents; secondary data are compiled inside or outside the organization for some purpose other than the current investigation. Sources of secondary data include an organization's own database and other internal sources, periodicals, government publications, unpublished sources, and online databases. Methods of collecting primary data include sampling, surveys, observation, and experimentation. Sampling involves selecting representative units from a total population. In probability sampling, every element in the population being studied has a known chance of being selected for study. Nonprobability sampling is more subjective than probability sampling because there is no way to calculate the likelihood that a specific element of the population being studied will be chosen. Marketing researchers employ sampling to collect primary data through mail, telephone, online, or personal interview surveys. A carefully constructed questionnaire is essential to the success of any survey. In using observation methods, researchers record respondents' overt behavior and take note of physical conditions and events. In an experiment, marketing researchers attempt to maintain certain variables while measuring the effects of experimental variables.

To apply research data to decision making, marketers must interpret and report their findings properly—the final two steps in the marketing research process. Statistical interpretation focuses on what is typical or what deviates from the average. After interpreting the research findings, the researchers must prepare a report on the findings that the decision makers can understand and use. Researchers must also take care to avoid bias and distortion.

3. To describe the nature and role of tools, such as databases, decision support systems, and the Internet, in marketing decision making

Many firms use computer technology to create a marketing information system (MIS), a framework for managing and structuring information gathered regularly from sources both inside and outside the organization. A database is a collection of information arranged for easy access and retrieval. A marketing decision support system (MDSS) is customized computer software that aids marketing managers in decision making by helping them anticipate the effects of certain decisions. Online information services and the Internet also enable marketers to communicate with customers and obtain information.

Go to www.cengagebrain.com for resources to help you master the content in this chapter as well as materials that will expand your marketing knowledge!

4. To identify key ethical and international considerations in marketing research

Eliminating unethical marketing research practices and establishing generally acceptable procedures for conducting research are important goals of marketing research. Both domestic and international marketing use the same marketing research process, but international marketing may require modifying data-gathering methods to address regional differences.

Important Terms

marketing research 144
exploratory research 146
customer advisory boards 147
focus group 147
conclusive research 148
descriptive research 148
experimental research 148
research design 149
hypothesis 150
reliability 150
validity 150
primary data 151
secondary data 151
population 152
sample 153
sampling 153
probability sampling 153
random sampling 153
stratified sampling 154
nonprobability sampling 154
quota sampling 154
mail survey 154
telephone survey 155
telephone depth interview 156
personal interview survey 156
in-home (door-to-door) interview 156
shopping mall intercept interview 157
on-site computer interview 157
online survey 157
crowdsourcing 158
statistical interpretation 160
marketing information system (MIS) 162
database 163
single-source data 164
marketing decision support system (MDSS) 164

Discussion and Review Questions

1. What is marketing research? Why is it important?
2. Describe the five steps in the marketing research process.
3. What is the difference between defining a research problem and developing a hypothesis?
4. Describe the different types of approaches to marketing research, and indicate when each should be used.
5. Where are data for marketing research obtained? Give examples of internal and external data.
6. What is the difference between probability sampling and nonprobability sampling? In what situation would random sampling be best? Stratified sampling? Quota sampling?
7. Suggest some ways to encourage respondents to cooperate in mail surveys.
8. If a survey of all homes with listed telephone numbers is to be conducted, what sampling design should be used?
9. Describe some marketing problems that could be solved through information gained from observation.
10. What is a marketing information system, and what should it provide?
11. Define a database. What is its purpose, and what does it include?
12. How can marketers use online services and the Internet to obtain information for decision making?
13. What role do ethics play in marketing research? Why is it important that marketing researchers be ethical?
14. How does marketing research in other countries differ from marketing research in the United States?

Application Questions

1. After observing customers' traffic patterns, Bashas' Markets repositioned the greeting card section in its stores, and card sales increased substantially. To increase sales for the following types of companies, what information might marketing researchers want to gather from customers?
   a. Furniture stores
   b. Gasoline outlets service stations
   c. Investment companies
   d. Medical clinics
2. When a company wants to conduct research, it must first identify a problem or possible opportunity to market its goods or services. Choose a company in your city that you think might benefit from a research project. Develop a research question and outline a method to approach this question. Explain why you think the research question is relevant to the organization and why the particular methodology is suited to the question and the company.
3. Input for marketing information systems can come from internal or external sources. ACNielsen Corporation is the largest provider of single-source marketing research in the world. Identify two firms in your city that might benefit from internal sources and two that might benefit from external sources. Explain why these sources would be useful to these companies. Suggest the type of information each company should gather.

4. IMP Suppose you are opening a health insurance brokerage firm and want to market your services to small businesses with fewer than 50 employees. Determine which database for marketing information you will use in your marketing efforts, and explain why you will use it.
5. You work as a marketing researcher for a manufacturer of energy drinks. Your company is designing a new product that will be targeted at college and university students. In order to learn more about their energy drink habits, the company plans to conduct a survey. After conducting some research, you determine that the best survey method that fits your firm's budget is a mail survey. You know from past experience that the response rate for mail surveys is approximately 10 percent. Your manager tells you that he wants at least 550 completed surveys in order to make an informed decision. You also know that approximately 14 percent of respondents who mail surveys back to you fail to answer certain questions. Given the low response rate and the rate of unfinished surveys, how large will the sample size need to be to comply with your manager's request? With this estimated response rate and the number of surveys that the company plans to distribute, do you feel that this sample will be representative of the entire population of college and university students?

Internet Exercise

European Society for Opinion and Marketing Research
ESOMAR, the European Society for Opinion and Marketing Research, was founded in 1948. It is a nonprofit association for marketing research professionals. ESOMAR promotes the use of opinion and marketing research to improve marketing decisions in companies worldwide and works to protect personal privacy in the research process. Visit the association's website at www.esomar.org.

1. How can ESOMAR help marketing professionals conduct research to guide marketing strategy?
2. How can ESOMAR help marketers to protect the privacy of research subjects when conducting marketing research in other countries?
3. ESOMAR introduced the first professional code of conduct for marketing research professionals in 1948. The association continues to update the document to address new technology and other changes in the marketing environment. According to ESOMAR's code, what are the specific professional responsibilities of marketing researchers?

developing your marketing plan

Decisions about which market opportunities to pursue, what customer needs to satisfy, and how to reach potential customers are not made in a vacuum. The information provided by marketing research activities is essential in developing both the strategic plan and the specific marketing mix. Focus on the following issues as you relate the concepts in this chapter to the development of your marketing plan.

1. Define the nature and scope of the questions you must answer with regard to your market. Identify the types of information you will need about the market to answer those questions. For example, do you need to know about the buying habits, household income levels, or attitudes of potential customers?
2. Determine whether or not this information can be obtained from secondary sources. Visit the websites provided in Table 5.3 as possible resources for the secondary data.
3. Using Table 5.4, choose the appropriate survey method(s) you would use to collect primary data for one of your information needs. What sampling method would you use?

The information obtained from these questions should assist you in developing various aspects of your marketing plan found in the "Interactive Marketing Plan" exercise at www.caaengagebrain.com.

video case 5.1

Marketing Research Reveals Marketing Opportunities in the Baby Boomer Generation

For many years, marketers have focused upon consumers between the ages of 18 and 34 to promote products. Marketers feel that wooing consumers early in life will ensure that they become lifetime loyal customers. While this seems logical, research is revealing that Baby Boomers might be a more profitable demographic. Statistics show that while spending for Millennials is actually shrinking, Baby Boomer spending has been increasing. Baby Boomers are estimated to have \$3.4 trillion in annual buying power.

The Baby Boomer generation is vastly different from the generations preceding it. Baby Boomers desire to have a variety of products available to them. Many of the products traditionally thought to belong to the younger generation are actually bought the most by older generations, such as cars and technological products. With approximately 20 percent of the U.S. population estimated to be 65 years or older by 2030, marketers are beginning to research better ways for marketing to Baby Boomers.

In one study researchers attempted to understand how older consumers shop and interact in stores. Because store marketers often target younger generations of consumers, little thought has been given to how accessible these stores are for older generations. The research design involved equipping a person with gloves, neck braces, helmets, blurry goggles, and other equipment to simulate how a person in his or her 70s with arthritis is feeling. Researchers would then observe how the person takes items off of shelves, gets into his or her car, and gets up from chairs.

This research has been shared with many businesses, who have interpreted the findings to create a retail environment better suited to this demographic. CVS, for instance, has lowered its shelves, made its store lighting softer, and installed magnifying glasses for hard-to-read labels. Other businesses are using this information to redesign their products. Diamond Foods Inc., for example, has designed the packaging of its Emerald snack nuts to be easier to open, a great help for older consumers whose hands become less mobile as they age. The company also studied consumers with arthritis and decreased the time it takes to rotate the caps to open its products.

Additionally, Baby Boomers have created an opportunity for businesses to market entirely new products. Baby Boomers tend to embrace fitness and exercise regimens as a way to stay fit and prolong their lives. Technology firms are seeing an opportunity to develop products to be installed in the homes of older consumers. These products monitor the movements of the inhabitants and alert family or experts if there are any changes in the inhabitants' movements. A decrease in mobility could signal a change in the person's physical and mental state, which may require medical attention. Although these devices might otherwise seem intrusive, Baby Boomers' desires to stay healthy and prolong life are increasing their demand. Many Baby Boomers are also concerned with preserving their more youthful appearance. Lingerie maker Maidenform has created shapewear, or clothes that help to "tone" the body, targeted toward those ages 35 to 54.

There is one description that marketers must avoid when marketing to Baby Boomers: any words or phrases that make them feel old. Marketing research has revealed that Baby Boomers do not like to be reminded that they are aging. Therefore, many marketing initiatives aimed at older consumers must be subtle. For this reason, Diamond Foods does not market the fact that its packages are easier to open because it does not want to make Baby Boomers feel aged. Even marketers of products that are for older people have overhauled their promotional campaigns to focus less on the concept of aging. Kimberly-Clark's Depend brand for incontinence was widely regarded as "adult diapers." This negative connotation led many to avoid them. To try to counteract this view, Kimberly-Clark released commercials that discussed the benefits of the product but also tried to "de-myth" the brand by discussing its similarity in look and feel to underwear. Many other businesses that sell similar products are following suit.

Although marketers have long focused on Millennials, the demand for products by Baby Boomers is changing the ways that businesses market to consumers. Marketing research is key to understanding the Baby Boomer demographic and creating the goods and services that best meet their needs.[41]

Questions for Discussion

1. Why are Baby Boomers such a lucrative market?
2. How has the marketing research process been used to understand how Baby Boomers shop and interact in stores?
3. How have stores used marketing research findings to tailor their stores and products to appeal to Baby Boomers?

case 5.2

At Threadless, Customers Design the Product

Loyal customers are also loyal designers at Threadless, a fast-growing T-shirt company based in Chicago. The idea for Threadless grew out of Jake Nickell's hobby of creating digital designs for T-shirts. In 2000, after one of his designs won a contest, 20-year-old Nickell teamed up with his friend Jacob DeHart to start a new business. Their unique marketing twist was that the T-shirts they sold would feature digital designs submitted and selected by customers through online voting. Threadless became a crowdsourcing company, in which tasks usually performed by a marketer or researcher—in this case, product design—are outsourced to the market.

© iStockphoto.com/GoodMood Photo

The first contest, which offered a grand prize of two free T-shirts, drew dozens of entries. The designs were placed on the Threadless website, and participants voted on the ones they preferred. Threadless printed and sold 24 copies each of the five top vote-getters. Soon the company began paying $100 for each winning design, an amount it gradually raised above $2,000. By 2002, Threadless had 10,000 customers voting on designs and was selling $100,000 worth of T-shirts.

A decade after its founding, the company's annual sales have skyrocketed beyond $30 million, and customers submit 300 designs per day. Threadless has 1.8 million members registered with its site, creating a large sample size from which to solicit feedback and votes. By marketing only designs that customers approve with their votes, Threadless keeps costs down and profit margins high. Sooner or later, all of its T-shirts sell out, and customers can click to vote for reprinting sold-out designs. Winners receive $2,000 along with a $500 Threadless gift card and $500 for every time the design is printed.

Threadless not only allows aspiring artists and designers to submit and potentially sell their work, but it also acts as a forum for market research. Blogging and critiquing on the Threadless website give designers the ability to interact with one another and receive recommendations on their ideas. This interaction often follows the five-step process of marketing research. For instance, a designer defines a problem she has with her design. She then thinks about what she wants to ask and posts the problem, as well as a picture of the design, on the Threadless blog. Other members post their recommendations, enabling the designer to collect relevant data for solving the problem. She can then interpret the findings to find the best solution and redesign the T-shirt before submitting it. Such interactions are common among the Threadless online community.

After the designers submit their ideas, Threadless creates the equivalent of an online focus group consisting of members from across the world. The T-shirt submissions are posted for members to vote upon, and voters can choose from a score of 0 to 5 on whether this shirt should be printed. They also have the chance to submit their own comments. For those who fall in love with the shirt, Threadless provides a button that the voter can click on to receive an alert. If the shirt gets chosen, the voter will receive a notification that the shirt is available for purchase. Threadless T-shirts and other company apparel can be purchased through the website. By using online customer reviews to create the final product, Threadless is able to eliminate the costs of test marketing.

Threadless has been so successful that it has opened its own retail store in Chicago to feature and sell its newest collections. Other companies are also getting involved. In 2012 Threadless partnered with Gap to sell T-shirt collections through Gap's website and retail outlets. The company also partnered with the Whole Planet Foundation to create the Whole Planet Foundation T-shirt Design Challenge. Designers submitted their designs for a chance to win a trip abroad, and part of the proceeds for their designs went toward funding entrepreneurs in developing countries.

As cofounder of Threadless, Nickell cannot imagine doing business any other way. "Why wouldn't you want to make the products that people want you to make?" he asks. By paying close attention to its customers' preferences, Threadless now sells 100,000 T-shirts every month. Customers are loyal because they know that their design ideas and votes really count.[42]

Questions for Discussion

1. How has Threadless used crowdsourcing as the foundation of its marketing research?
2. How does Threadless create the equivalent of an online focus group to provide feedback on designs?
3. How has Threadless eliminated the cost of test marketing?

NOTES

[1]Kevin Peters, "Office Depot's President on How 'Mystery Shopping' Helped Spark a Turnaround," *Harvard Business Review*, November 2011, http://hbr.org/2011/11/office-depots-president-mystery-shopping-turnaround/ar/1 (accessed November 10, 2011); MSPA Staff, "American Express Survey Reinforces Value of Mystery Shopping," Mystery Shopping Providers Association, May 9, 2011, www.mysteryshop.org/news/article_pr.php?art_ID=116 (accessed November 10, 2011); Paula Andruss, "Missing Research Insights," *Marketing News*, May 20, 2010, 23–25; "MSPA North America," MysteryShopping Providers Association, www.mysteryshop.org/index-na.php (accessed April 1, 2010).

[2]"J.D. Power and Associates Reports: For Private Label Grocery Brands, Organic Products Drive Gain in Prestige Among Customers," March 25, 2009, http://businesscenter.jdpower.com/news/pressrelease.aspx?ID=2009047 (accessed January 20, 2011).

[3]Julie Jargon, "Tracking the Loyalty of Coffee Drinkers," *The Wall Street Journal*, April 14, 2011, D5.

[4]"Too Many Cars, Too Few Buyers," *The Economist*, February 18, 2012, 65.

[5]Allison Enright, "Surviving 2010," *Marketing News,* February 28, 2010, 30–33.

[6]Lauren A. E. Shucker, "What Busy Moms Sneak In...TV Time," *The Wall Street Journal*, November 9, 2011, http://online.wsj.com/article/SB10001424052970204554204577025941886057630.html (accessed February 5, 2012).

[7]Dhruv Grewal Parasuraman and R. Krishnan, *Marketing Research* (Boston: Houghton Mifflin, 2007).

[8]Ken Manning, O. C. Ferrell, and Linda Ferrell, "Consumer Expectations of Clearance vs. Sale Prices," University of New Mexico, working paper, 2010.

[9]Amy Roach Partridge, "Managing a Customer-Driven Supply Chain," *Logistics,* December 2010, www.inboundlogistics.com/cms/article/managing-a-customer-driven-supply-chain/ (accessed July 9, 2012); Lisa Nirell, "The Secret Life of Customer Advisory Boards," *Fast Company,* March 7, 2011, www.fastcompany.com/1736109/the-secret-life-of-customer-advisory-boards-part-2 (accessed February 7, 2012).

[10]Cliff Edwards and Ronald Grover, "Can Netflix Regain Lost Ground?," *Bloomberg Businessweek*, October 19, 2011, www.businessweek.com/magazine/can-netflix-regain-lost-ground-10192011.html (accessed February 6, 2012).

[11]David H. Freedman, "Turning Facebook Followers Into Online Focus Groups," *The New York Times*, January 5, 2012, http://boss.blogs.nytimes.com/2012/01/05/turning-facebook-followers-into-online-focus-groups/ (accessed February 8, 2012).

[12]Piet Levy, "In With the Old, in Spite of the New," *Marketing News*, May 30, 2009, 19.

[13]Daniel Gross, "Lies, Damn Lies, and Focus Groups," *Slate*, October 10, 2003, www.slate.com/articles/business/moneybox/2003/10/lies_damn_lies_and_focus_groups.html (accessed July 9, 2012).

[14]Stephen Miller, "Researcher's Data Rewrote Hollywood Endings," *The Wall Street Journal*, December 9, 2011, http://online.wsj.com/article/SB10001424052970204319004577086782750362996.html?KEYWORDS=market+research+hollywood (accessed February 7, 2012); Edward Jay Epstein, "Hidden Persuaders," *Slate*, July 18, 2005, www.slate.com/articles/arts/the_hollywood_economist/2005/07/hidden_persuaders.html (accessed February 7, 2012).

[15]Diksha Sahni, "Does Bollywood Need Market Research?" *The Wall Street Journal*, March 24, 2011, http://blogs.wsj.com/indiarealtime/2011/03/24/does-bollywood-need-market-research/ (accessed February 7, 2012).

[16]Vikas Mittal and Wagner A. Kamakura, "Satisfaction, Repurchase Intent, and Repurchase Behavior: Investigating the Moderating Effects of Customer Characteristics," *Journal of Marketing Research* (February 2001): 131–142.

[17]U.S. Census Bureau, *American Community Survey,* www.census.gov/acs/www/ (accessed January 20, 2011).

[18]Aaron Gilchrist, "Census Forms Confusion: 'American Community Survey' Is Legit," *nbc12.com*, January 27, 2010, www.nbc12.com/Global/story.asp?S= 11890921 (accessed January 21, 2011).

[19]Symphony IRI Group, "About Us," http://symphony iri.com/About/History/tabid/60/Default.aspy (accessed January 21, 2011).

[20]David Lieberman, "TiVo to Sell Data on What People Watch, Fast-Forward," *USA Today*, April 20, 2010, www.usatoday.com/tech/news/2009-04-20-tivo-data-new-plan_N.htm (accessed March 19, 2010).

[21]Proctor & Gamble 2009 Annual Report, February 24, 2010, 3, http://annualreport.pg.com/annualreport2009/index.shtml (accessed March 20, 2010).

[22]Warren Davies, "How to Increase Survey Response Rates Using Post-it Notes," *GenerallyThinking.com*, August 3, 2009, http://generallythinking.com/blog/how-to-increase-survey-response-rates-using-post-it-notes/ (accessed March 9, 2010); Randy Garner, "Post-It Note Persuasion: A Sticky Influence," *Journal of Consumer Psychology* 15 (2005): 230–237.

[23]Sue Shellenbarger, "A Few Bucks for Your Thoughts?" *The Wall Street Journal*, May 18, 2011, http://online.wsj.com/article/SB10001424052748703509104576329110724411724.html (accessed February 7, 2012).

[24]David Rosenbaum, "Who's Out There?" *CFO*, January/February 2012, 44–49.

[25]Ibid.

[26]Shellenbarger, "A Few Bucks for Your Thoughts?"

[27]Bas Donkers, Philip Hans Franses, and Peter C. Verhoef, "Selective Sampling for Binary Choice Models," *Journal of Marketing Research* (November 2003): 492–497.

[28]James Verrinder, "Time Warner Unveils Hi-Tech Media Lab," *Research*, January 25, 2012, www.research-live.com/news/news-headlines/time-warner-unveils-hi-tech-media-lab/4006765.article (accessed February 7, 2012).

[29]Ibid.

[30]Piet Levy, "10 Minutes with…Gregory A. Reid," *Marketing News*, February 28, 2010, 34.

[31]Charlene Li and Josh Bernoff, *Groundswell* (Boston: Harvard Business Press, 2008), 26–27.

[32]"RatePoint Survey Reveals 70 Percent of Consumers Appreciate Being Asked to Write an Online Review," *PR Newswire*, www.prnewswire.com/

news-releases/ratepoint-survey-reveals-70-percent-of-consumers-appreciate-being-asked-to-write-an-online-review-130353633.html (accessed February 10, 2012).

[33]Lauren Coleman-Lochner, "Why Procter & Gamble Needs to Shave More Indians," *Bloomberg Buinessweek*, June 9, 2011, www.businessweek.com/magazine/content/11_25/b4233021703857.htm (accessed February 7, 2012).

[34]David Aaker, V. Kumar, George Day, and Robert Lane, *Marketing Research,* 10th ed. (New York: Wiley & Sons, 2010).

[35]*BehaviorScan® Testing*, 2011, www.symphonyiri.com/LinkClick.aspx?fileticket=da0Vpb7a728%3D&tabid=348 (accessed February 8, 2012).

[36]Chares Duhigg, "How Companies Learn Your Secrets," *The New York Times*, February 15, 2012, www.nytimes.com/2012/02/19/magazine/shopping-habits.html?_r=1&pagewanted=all (accessed February 28, 2012).

[37]Emily Steel and Julia Angwin, "The Web's Cutting Edge, Anonymity in Name Only," *The Wall Street Journal*, August 4, 2010, http://online.wsj.com/article/SB10001424052748703294904575385532109190198.html (accessed February 7, 2012).

[38]Morgan Downs (Producer), *Inside the Mind of Google* [DVD], United States: CNBC Originals, 2010.

[39]"Top 50 U.S. Market Research Organizations," *Marketing News*, June 30, 2011, 17.

[40]Reprinted with permission of The Marketing Research Association, P.O. Box 230, Rocky Hill, CT 06067-0230, 860-257-4008.

[41]Ellen Byron, "From Diapers to 'Depends': Marketers Discreetly Retool for Aging Boomers," *The Wall Street Journal*, February 5, 2011, http://online.wsj.com/article/SB10001424052748704013604576104394209062996.html (accessed March 30, 2012); Bruce Horovitz, "Big-Spending Baby Boomers Bend the Rules of Marketing," *USA Today*, November 16, 2010, www.usatoday.com/money/advertising/2010-11-16-1Aboomerbuyers16_CV_N.htm (accessed March 30, 2012).

[42]Threadless website, www.threadless.com/ (accessed March 6, 2012); Katie Schuppler, "GAP + Threadless," Chicago NOW, March 5, 2012, www.chicagonow.com/fashion-speak/2012/03/gap-threadless/ (accessed March 6, 2012); Tina Baine, "'Threadless' Hints at Art's Crowdsourced Future," *Santa Cruz (CA) Sentinel,* December 11, 2010, www.santacruzsentinel.com/localnews/ci_16832324 (accessed March 6, 2012); Micha Maidenberg, "Threadless Eyes West Loop," *Chicago Journal,* May 5, 2010, www.chicagojournal.com/news/05-05-2010/Threadless_eyes_West_Loop (accessed March 6, 2012); Julie Shaffer, "Social Climbing," *American Printer,* January 1, 2010, http://americanprinter.com (accessed March 6, 2012); Laurie Burkitt, "Need to Build a Community? Learn from Threadless," *Forbes,* January 7, 2010, www.forbes.com (accessed March 6, 2012); Alicia Wallace, "5 Questions for Jake Nickell, Founder and Chief Strategy Officer of Threadless," *Daily Camera* (Boulder, CO), May 18, 2009, www.dailycamera.com; Max Chafkin, "The Customer Is the Company," *Inc.,* June 1, 2008, www.inc.com/magazine/20080601/the-customer-is-the-company.html (accessed March 6, 2012).

Feature Notes

[a]iModerate website, www.imoderate.com/company/our-company; Eric Peterson, "Tech Startup of the Month," *Colorado-Biz*, August 2007, 20.

[b]Holly Barbo, "Start a 'Green' Dialogue in Your Store," Western Home Furnishings Association, www.whfa.org/articles/sustainablebiz/start-a-green-dialogue-in-your-store/ (accessed December 6, 2011); "Corporations Foster Dialogue On the Environment," Marketing Green, January 14, 2008, http://marketinggreen.wordpress.com/category/green-consumer-research/ (accessed December 6, 2011); "Suppliers & Vendors," Kimball International, www.kimball.com/suppliersenvironment.aspx (accessed December 6, 2011); Eaton Corporation, "Eaton Leads Dialogue on Green Transportation and Sustainable Urbanization at Energy Evolution Symposium," June 9, 2011, www.eaton.com/Eaton/OurCompany/NewsEvents/NewsReleases/PCT_277951 (accessed December 6, 2011); Adrian, "Could Dell Own Green," IdeaStorm, February 1, 2007, www.ideastorm.com/ideaView?id=087700000000006iDAAQ (accessed December 6, 2011).

[c]Daisuke Wakabayashi and Juro Osawa, "Billboard That Can See You," *The Wall Street Journal*, September 3, 2010, B5; Emily Steel, "The Billboard That Knows," *The Wall Street Journal*, February 29, 2011, B5.

[d]Emily Steel, "Using Credit Cards To Target Web Ads," *The Wall Street Journal*, October 25, 2011, A1, A16; "U.S. Senator Wants Details on How MasterCard, Visa Use Customer Data," *The Wall Street Journal,* October 27, 2011, http://blogs.wsj.com/digits/2011/10/27/u-s-senator-wants-details-on-how-mastercard-visa-use-customer-data/ (accessed November 10, 2011).

chapter 6

Target Markets: Segmentation and Evaluation

OBJECTIVES

1. To learn about *markets*
2. To understand the differences among general targeting strategies
3. To become familiar with the major segmentation variables
4. To know what segment profiles are and how they are used
5. To understand how to evaluate market segments
6. To identify the factors that influence the selection of specific market segments for use as target markets
7. To become familiar with sales forecasting methods

MARKETING INSIGHTS

Block Party at LEGOLAND Florida

LEGOLAND Florida, located less than an hour's drive from Disney World in Orlando, is a theme park with 50 million plastic bricks and a name based on one of the world's best-known brands. Its parent company, Merlin Entertainments Group, is using the worldwide appeal of Lego bricks to attract families with young children. Merlin has invested more than $125 million to build LEGOLAND on the renovated site of Cypress Gardens, a failed theme park. Nearly everything is made of Lego blocks, from a roller coaster to a mini-Golden Gate Bridge, and soon young visitors will be able to build rafts from oversized Lego blocks to ride the child-sized rapids in the adjacent water park.

Whereas Disney and many other theme parks reach out to visitors of all ages, LEGOLAND is aiming at families with children in the 2-to-12 age group. In fact, some attractions are for tots only, part of LEGOLAND's plan to provide fun for children too young for the rides in most theme parks. Children can also build Lego race cars and robots in supervised play areas, an interactive experience that sets the park apart from competitors.

Merlin saved millions of dollars by renovating an existing theme park instead of building a new one, which means it can turn a profit with fewer than 1 million visitors per year. By contrast, Disney World's yearly attendance exceeds 15 million visitors. LEGOLAND's admission prices are lower than at Disney World, and it offers discount tickets to nearby schools and church groups. Can LEGOLAND Florida build a loyal following among local families and families that come to Florida on vacation?[1]

Like most organizations that are trying to compete effectively, LEGOLAND Florida has identified specific customer groups toward which it will direct its marketing efforts. Any organization that wants to succeed must identify its customers and develop and maintain marketing mixes that satisfy the needs of those customers.

In this chapter, we explore markets and market segmentation. Initially, we define the term *market* and discuss the major requirements of a market. Then we examine the steps in the target market selection process, including identifying the appropriate targeting strategy, determining which variables to use for segmenting consumer and business markets, developing market segment profiles, evaluating relevant market segments, and selecting target markets. Finally, we discuss various methods for developing sales forecasts.

WHAT ARE MARKETS?

In Chapter 2, we defined a *market* as a group of people who, as individuals or as organizations, have needs for products in a product class and have the ability, willingness, and authority to purchase such products. Students, for example, are part of the market for textbooks, as well as for computers, clothes, food, music, and other products. Individuals can have the desire, the buying power, and the willingness to purchase certain products, but may not have the authority to do so. For example, teenagers may have the desire, the money, and the willingness to buy liquor, but a liquor producer does not consider them a market because teenagers are prohibited by law from buying alcoholic beverages. Thus, a group of people that lacks any one of the four requirements does not constitute a market.

Markets fall into one of two categories: consumer markets and business markets. These categories are based on the characteristics of the individuals and groups that make up a specific market and the purposes for which they buy products. A **consumer market** consists of purchasers and household members who intend to consume or benefit from the purchased products and do not buy products for the main purpose of making a profit. Consumer markets are sometimes also referred to as *business-to-consumer (B2C) markets.* Each of us belongs to numerous consumer markets. The millions of individuals with the ability, willingness, and authority to buy make up a multitude of consumer markets for products such as housing, food, clothing, vehicles, personal services, appliances, furniture, recreational equipment, and so on, as we shall see in Chapter 7.

consumer market Purchasers and household members who intend to consume or benefit from the purchased products and do not buy products to make profits

© AP Images/PRNewsFoto/Dockers

Courtesy of The Advertising Archives

Types of Markets
Dockers advertises to consumers, whereas Xerox advertises to businesses.

A **business market** consists of individuals or groups that purchase a specific kind of product for one of three purposes: resale, direct use in producing other products, or use in general daily operations. For instance, a lamp producer that buys electrical wire to use in the production of lamps is part of a business market for electrical wire. This same firm purchases dust mops to clean its office areas. Although the mops are not used in the direct production of lamps, they are used in the operations of the firm; thus, this manufacturer is part of a business market for dust mops. Business markets also may be called *business-to-business (B2B), industrial,* or *organizational markets.* They also can be classified into producer, reseller, government, and institutional markets, as we shall see in Chapter 8.

TARGET MARKET SELECTION PROCESS

As indicated earlier, the first of two major components of developing a marketing strategy is to select a target market. Although marketers may employ several methods for target market selection, generally they use a five-step process. This process is shown in Figure 6.1, and we discuss it in the following sections.

Step 1: Identify the Appropriate Targeting Strategy

A target market is a group of people or organizations for which a business creates and maintains a marketing mix specifically designed to satisfy the needs of group members. The strategy used to select a target market is affected by target market characteristics, product attributes, and the organization's objectives and resources. Figure 6.2 illustrates the three basic targeting strategies: undifferentiated, concentrated, and differentiated.

Undifferentiated Targeting Strategy

An organization sometimes defines an entire market for a particular product as its target market. When a company designs a single marketing mix and directs it at the entire market for a particular product, it is using an **undifferentiated targeting strategy**. As Figure 6.2 shows, the strategy assumes that all customers in the target market for a specific kind of product have similar needs, and thus the organization can satisfy most customers with a single marketing mix. This mix consists of one type of product with little or no variation, one price, one promotional program aimed at everybody, and one distribution system to reach most customers in the total market. Products marketed successfully through the undifferentiated strategy include commodities and staple food items, such as sugar and salt, and certain kinds of farm produce.

The undifferentiated targeting strategy is effective under two conditions. First, a large proportion of customers in a total market must have similar needs for the product, a situation termed a **homogeneous market**. A marketer using a single marketing mix for a total market of customers with a variety of needs would find that the marketing mix satisfies very few people. A "universal car" meant to suit everyone would fulfill very few customers' needs for

business market Individuals, organizations, or groups that purchase a specific kind of product for resale, direct use in producing other products, or use in general daily operations

undifferentiated targeting strategy A strategy in which an organization designs a single marketing mix and directs it at the entire market for a particular product

homogeneous market A market in which a large proportion of customers have similar needs for a product

Figure 6.1 Target Market Selection Process

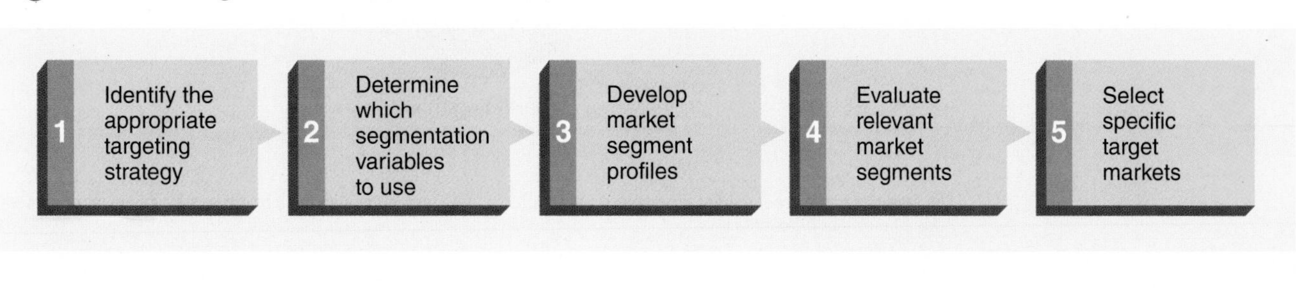

Figure 6.2 Targeting Strategies

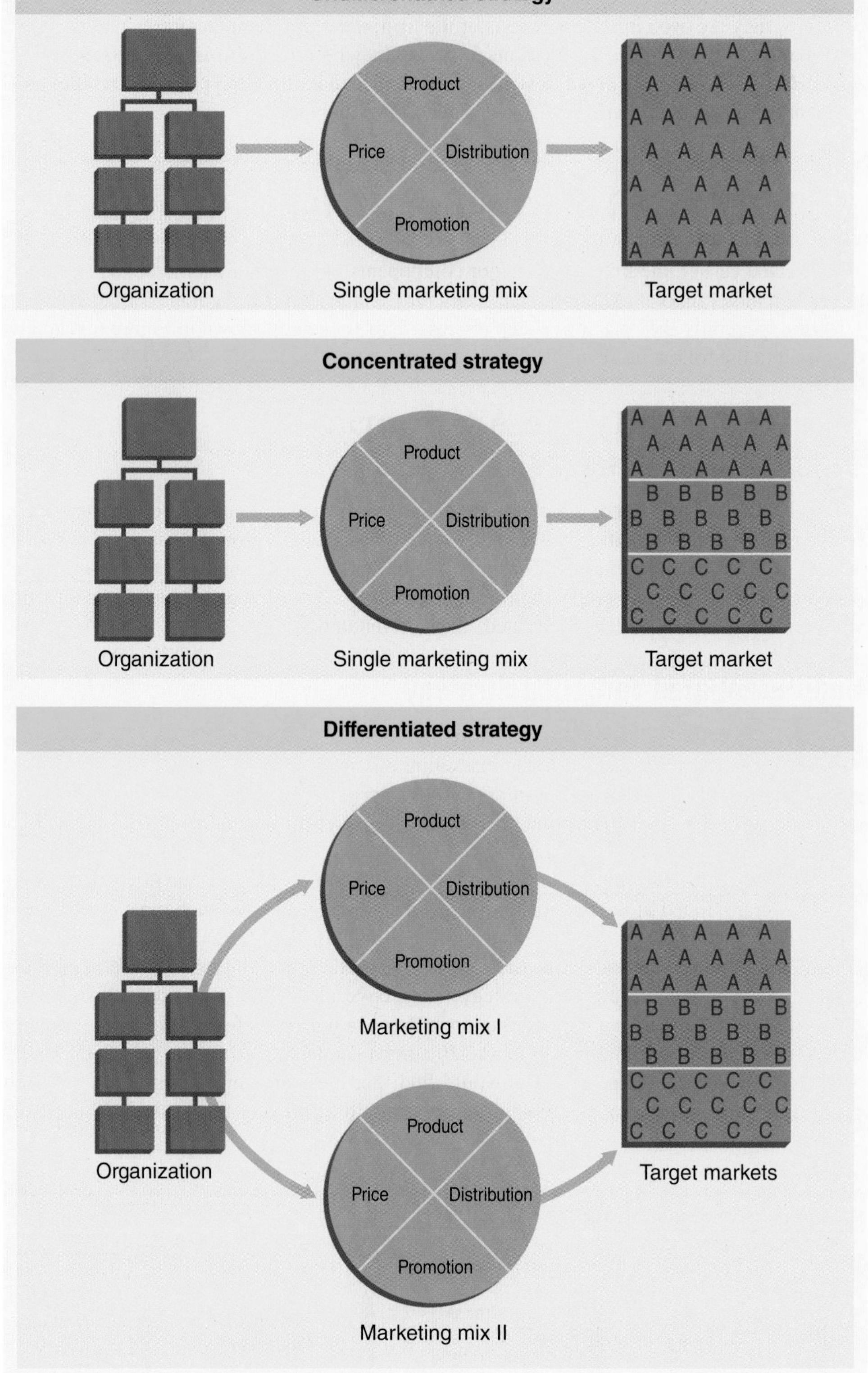

The letters in each target market represent potential customers. Customers with the same letters have similar characteristics and similar product needs.

cars because it would not provide the specific combination of attributes sought by a particular person. Second, the organization must be able to develop and maintain a single marketing mix that satisfies customers' needs. The company must be able to identify a set of needs common to most customers in a total market and have the resources and managerial skills to reach a sizable portion of that market.

The reality is that although customers may have similar needs for a few products, for most products their needs decidedly differ. In such instances, a company should use a concentrated or a differentiated strategy.

Concentrated Targeting Strategy through Market Segmentation

A market made up of individuals or organizations with diverse product needs is called a **heterogeneous market**. Not everyone wants the same type of car, furniture, or clothes. For example, some individuals want an economical car, whereas others desire a status symbol, and still others seek a roomy and comfortable or fuel-efficient vehicle. The automobile market thus is heterogeneous.

For heterogeneous markets, market segmentation is appropriate. **Market segmentation** is the process of dividing a total market into groups, or segments, that consist of people or organizations with relatively similar product needs. The purpose is to enable a marketer to design a marketing mix that more precisely matches the needs of customers in the selected market segment. A **market segment** consists of individuals, groups, or organizations that share one or more similar characteristics that cause them to have relatively similar product needs. The automobile market is divided into many different market segments. Consider the Lexus LS Hybrid, a luxury hybrid sedan with a base price of about $112,750. This car targets high-income individuals who are environmentally conscious. This is not a vehicle that is purchased by the masses.[2]

The main rationale for segmenting heterogeneous markets is that a company is better able to develop a satisfying marketing mix for a relatively small portion of a total market than to develop a mix that meets the needs of all people. Market segmentation is widely used. Fast-food

heterogeneous market A market made up of individuals or organizations with diverse needs for products in a specific product class

market segmentation The process of dividing a total market into groups with relatively similar product needs to design a marketing mix that matches those needs

market segment Individuals, groups, or organizations sharing one or more similar characteristics that cause them to have similar product needs

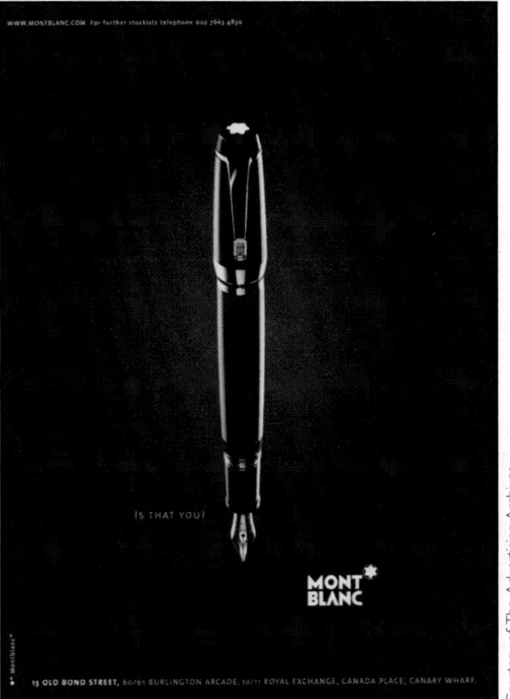

Courtesy of The Advertising Archives

© AP Images/PRNewsFoto/BIC

Concentrated Targeting Strategy
Both Mont Blanc and Bic use a concentrated targeting strategy to aim at a different, single market segment. They are not competing for the same customers.

Marketing Debate

Targeting by Religion or Sexual Orientation

ISSUE: Should marketers be allowed to target consumers on the basis of religion or sexual orientation?

U.S. companies are generally not allowed to discriminate on the basis of religion or sexual orientation when hiring. For marketing purposes, should they be allowed to target consumer segments using these same two variables?

Absolut vodka targets gay and lesbian consumers with ads in specialized publications, part of its positioning as an "open-minded brand," according to an executive. Philadelphia recently ran a successful tourism advertising campaign focusing on gay and lesbian consumers. "It's a way to help people understand that they're accepted," explains a Philadelphia tourism expert.

Whole Foods carries halal-certified foods for Muslim consumers. "If we have a customer base where there's a big Muslim population," says a manager, "it makes sense for us to service that population."

However, targeting by religion or sexual orientation raises the possibility that consumers may be stereotyped or depicted in a negative way. It also calls attention to religious and sexual differences that may be offensive to some and embarrassing to others. When Best Buy began referring to Muslim holidays in some of their ads, some consumers complained—and others cheered.[a]

chains, soft-drink companies, magazine publishers, hospitals, and banks are just a few types of organizations that employ market segmentation.

For market segmentation to succeed, five conditions must exist. First, customers' needs for the product must be heterogeneous; otherwise, there is little reason to segment the market. Second, segments must be identifiable and divisible. The company must find a characteristic or variable for effectively separating individuals in a total market into groups containing people with relatively uniform needs for the product. Third, the total market should be divided so segments can be compared with respect to estimated sales potential, costs, and profits. Fourth, at least one segment must have enough profit potential to justify developing and maintaining a special marketing mix for that segment. Finally, the company must be able to reach the chosen segment with a particular marketing mix. Some market segments may be difficult or impossible to reach because of legal, social, or distribution constraints. For instance, marketers of Cuban rum and cigars cannot market to U.S. consumers because of political and trade restrictions.

When an organization directs its marketing efforts toward a single market segment using one marketing mix, it is employing a **concentrated targeting strategy**. Porsche focuses on the luxury sports car segment and directs almost all of its marketing efforts toward high-income individuals who want to own high-performance sports cars. Notice in Figure 6.2 that the organization that is using the concentrated strategy is aiming its marketing mix only at "B" customers.

The chief advantage of the concentrated strategy is that it allows a firm to specialize. The firm analyzes the characteristics and needs of a distinct customer group and then focuses all its energies on satisfying that group's needs. A firm may generate a large sales volume by reaching a single segment. Also, concentrating on a single segment permits a firm with limited resources to compete with larger organizations that may have overlooked smaller segments.

concentrated targeting strategy A market segmentation strategy in which an organization targets a single market segment using one marketing mix

Specialization, however, means that a company puts all its eggs in one basket, which can be hazardous. If a company's sales depend on a single segment and the segment's demand for the product declines, the company's financial strength also deteriorates. Moreover, when a firm penetrates one segment and becomes well entrenched, its popularity may keep it from moving into other segments. For example, it is very unlikely that Mont Blanc could or would want to compete with Bic in the low-end, disposable-pen market segment.

Differentiated Targeting Strategy through Market Segmentation

With a **differentiated targeting strategy**, an organization directs its marketing efforts at two or more segments by developing a marketing mix for each segment (refer to Figure 6.2). After a firm uses a concentrated strategy successfully in one market segment, it sometimes expands its efforts to include additional segments. For instance, Dove has traditionally been aimed at one segment: women. However, the company now also markets care and cleansing products to men, including face washes, soap, and a dual-sided shower tool.[3]

Marketing mixes for a differentiated strategy may vary as to product features, distribution methods, promotion methods, and prices. A firm may increase sales in the aggregate market through a differentiated strategy because its marketing mixes are aimed at more people. For example, the Kate Spade brand, which includes women's clothing, handbags, and other accessories, once only targeted suburban mothers in their 40s. Recently though, the company began creating new products that target a new market—urban, professional women between 26 and 36—in addition to its previous target market. The brand adopted this differentiated strategy by marketing new younger and hip-looking products along with its other products in an effort to revitalize the brand and increase sales. Since its products now appeal to more people than they did before, sales for the Kate Spade brand have doubled.[4] A company with excess production capacity may find a differentiated strategy advantageous because the sale of products to additional segments may absorb excess capacity. On the other hand, a differentiated strategy often demands more production processes, materials, and people. Thus, production costs may be higher than with a concentrated strategy.

differentiated targeting strategy A strategy in which an organization targets two or more segments by developing a marketing mix for each segment

Step 2: Determine Which Segmentation Variables to Use

Segmentation variables are the characteristics of individuals, groups, or organizations used to divide a market into segments. For instance, location, age, gender, and rate of product usage can all be bases for segmenting markets. Most marketers use several variables in combination. Faced with declining attendance and aging audiences, the new CEO of the Metropolitan Opera

segmentation variables Characteristics of individuals, groups, or organizations used to divide a market into segments

Gender Segmentation
Harley-Davidson segments based on gender, aiming some of its products at women and most of its merchandise at men.

House, Peter Gelb, decided to attract new market segments by using different segmentation variables. He targets younger audiences by offering edgier works. He attracts audiences from wider geographic areas and lower income segments by beaming MET productions to movie houses around the world. Gelb has managed to turn around the MET's dire financial situation. Revenue was up 50 percent in 2011 over 2010, while the average age of attendees was down by about 3 years. Broadcasting MET operas in HD in theaters now generates over $11 million annually.[5] To select a segmentation variable, several factors are considered. The segmentation variable should relate to customers' needs for, uses of, or behavior toward the product. Television marketers might segment the television market based on income and age but not on religion because people's television needs do not differ due to religion. Furthermore, if individuals or organizations in a total market are to be classified accurately, the segmentation variable must be measurable. Age, location, and gender are measurable because such information can be obtained through observation or questioning. In contrast, segmenting a market on the basis of, say, intelligence is extremely difficult because this attribute is harder to measure accurately.

A company's resources and capabilities affect the number and size of segment variables used. The type of product and degree of variation in customers' needs also dictate the number and size of segments targeted. In short, there is no best way to segment markets.

Choosing one or more segmentation variables is a critical step in targeting a market. Selecting an inappropriate variable limits the chances of developing a successful marketing strategy. To help you better understand potential segmentation variables, we next examine the major types of variables used to segment consumer markets and the types used to segment business markets.

Variables for Segmenting Consumer Markets

A marketer that is using segmentation to reach a consumer market can choose one or several variables from an assortment of possibilities. As Figure 6.3 shows, segmentation variables can be grouped into four categories: demographic, geographic, psychographic, and behavioristic.

Demographic Variables Demographers study aggregate population characteristics such as the distribution of age and gender, fertility rates, migration patterns, and mortality rates. Demographic characteristics that marketers commonly use in segmenting markets include age, gender, race, ethnicity, income, education, occupation, family size, family life cycle,

Figure 6.3 Segmentation Variables for Consumer Markets

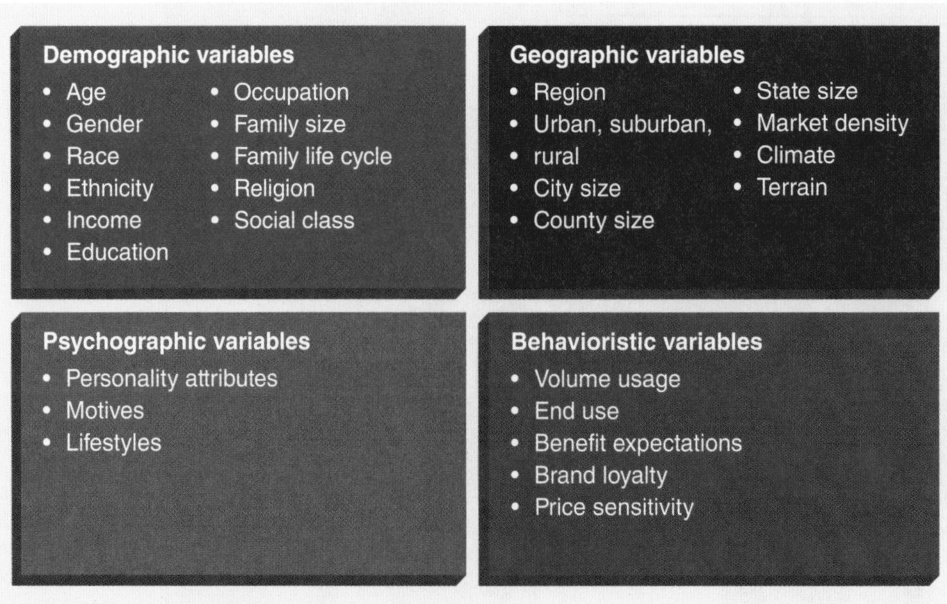

religion, and social class. Marketers rely on these demographic characteristics because they are often closely linked to customers' needs and purchasing behaviors and can be readily measured. Like demographers, a few marketers even use mortality rates. Service Corporation International (SCI), the largest U.S. funeral services company, attempts to locate its facilities in higher-income suburban areas with high mortality rates. SCI operates more than 1,800 funeral service locations, cemeteries, and crematoriums.[6]

Age is a commonly used variable for segmentation purposes. A trip to the shopping mall highlights the fact that many retailers, including Abercrombie & Fitch, Aeropostale, and American Eagle Outfitters, target teens and very young adults. Some of these retailers are now looking to create new marketing mixes for their customers as they age by opening new concept stores with new brand names. Several clothing companies, for example, created new brands for their own stores to provide more mature clothing options to aging Generation Y customers (born between 1980 and 1996). Marketers need to be aware of age distribution and how that distribution is changing. All age groups under 55 are expected to decrease by the year 2025, whereas all age categories 55 and older are expected to increase. In 1970, the average age of a U.S. citizen was 27.9; currently it is about 37.2.[7] As Figure 6.4 shows, Americans 65 and older spend as much or more on housing and health care compared to Americans in the two younger age groups.

Figure 6.4 **Spending Levels of Three Age Groups for Selected Product Categories**

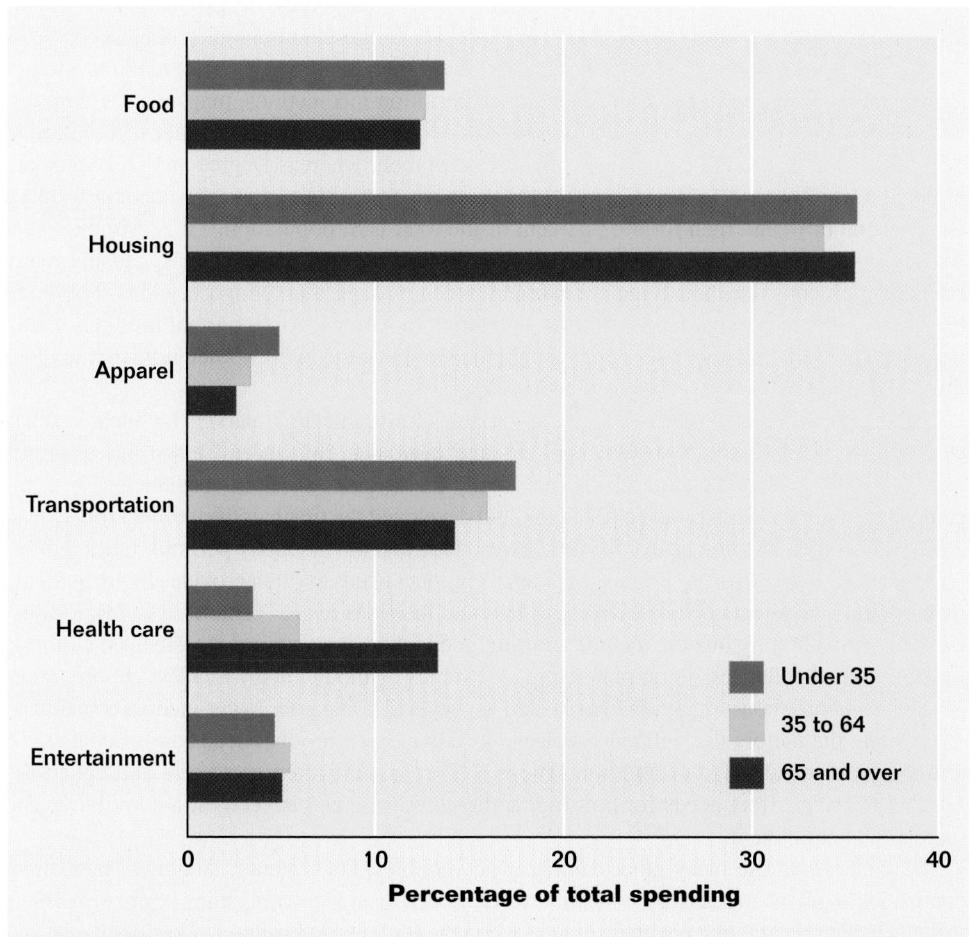

Source: U.S. Department of Labor, Bureau of Labor Statistics, "Age of Reference Person: Average Annual Expenditures and Characteristics," *Consumer Expenditure Survey*, 2010, Table 3, www.bls.gov/cex/2010/Standard/age.pdf (accessed May 24, 2012).

Source: T. Rowe Price survey of 1,008 parents.

Many marketers recognize the purchase influence of children and are targeting more marketing efforts at them. VTech, for example, recently created the InnoTab, a durable tablet computer for children ages 4 to 9 that provides interactive reading, educational games, and other creative activities on a five-inch color touchscreen.[8] Numerous products are aimed specifically at children—toys, clothing, food and beverages, and entertainment such as movies and TV cable channels. In addition, children ages 16 and under influence over $1.1 trillion of overall family spending every year.[9] In households with only one parent or those in which both parents work, children often take on additional responsibilities such as cooking, cleaning, and grocery shopping, and thus influence the types of products and brands these households purchase.

Gender is another demographic variable that is commonly used to segment markets, including the markets for clothing, soft drinks, nonprescription medications, magazines, cigarettes, and personal care products. For example, some deodorant marketers use gender segmentation: Secret and Soft & Dri are targeted specifically at women, whereas Degree and Old Spice are directed toward men. The U.S. Census Bureau reports that girls and women account for 50.8 percent, and boys and men for 49.2 percent of the total U.S. population.[10] It is estimated that women influence more than 80 percent of all consumer purchasing decisions, causing many companies to consider their female customers when making marketing decisions. Food and beverage companies in particular pay close attention to women. All important food marketing trends are partially the result of women's influence in the home, with women influencing more than 90 percent of food purchasing decisions.[11]

Marketers also use race and ethnicity as variables for segmenting markets for such products as food, music, clothing, cosmetics, banking, and insurance. SoftSheen-Carson, for example, makes hair care and skin care products specifically for African American consumers. The company has been in business for over 100 years, and developed the first hair dye product for African American women, the first no-lye hair relaxer product, and the first body perm for black hair.[12]

Because income strongly influences people's product needs, it often provides a way to divide markets. Income affects people's ability to buy and their desires for certain lifestyles. Product markets segmented by income include sporting goods, housing, furniture, cosmetics, clothing, jewelry, home appliances, automobiles, and electronics. Although many retailers choose to target higher-income consumers, some marketers are instead going after lower-income consumers.

Among the factors that influence household income and product needs are marital status and the presence and age of children. These characteristics, often combined and called the *family life cycle,* affect needs for housing, appliances, food and beverages, automobiles, and recreational equipment.

Marketers also use many other demographic variables. For instance, dictionary publishing companies segment markets by education level. Some insurance companies segment markets using occupation, targeting health insurance at college students and young workers with employers that do not provide health coverage. Family life cycles can be broken down in various ways. Figure 6.5 shows a breakdown into nine categories. The composition of the U.S. household in relation to the family life cycle has changed considerably over the last several decades.

Single-parent families are on the rise, meaning that the "typical" family no longer consists of a married couple with children. Since 1970, the number of households headed by a single mother increased from 12 to 19 percent of total family households, and that number grew from 1 to 7 percent for families headed by a single father. Another factor that influences the family life cycle is that the increase in median marrying age for women has increased from 20.8 to 26.5 years old since 1970, while for men it increased from 23.2 to 28.7 years old. Additionally, the proportion of women ages 20 to 24 who have never been married has more than doubled over this time, and for women ages 30 to 34 this number has nearly tripled. Other important changes in the family life cycle include the rise in the number of people living alone and the number of unmarried couples living together.[13] Tracking these changes helps marketers satisfy the needs of particular target markets through new marketing mixes.

Figure 6.5 Family Life Cycle Stages as a Percentage of All Households

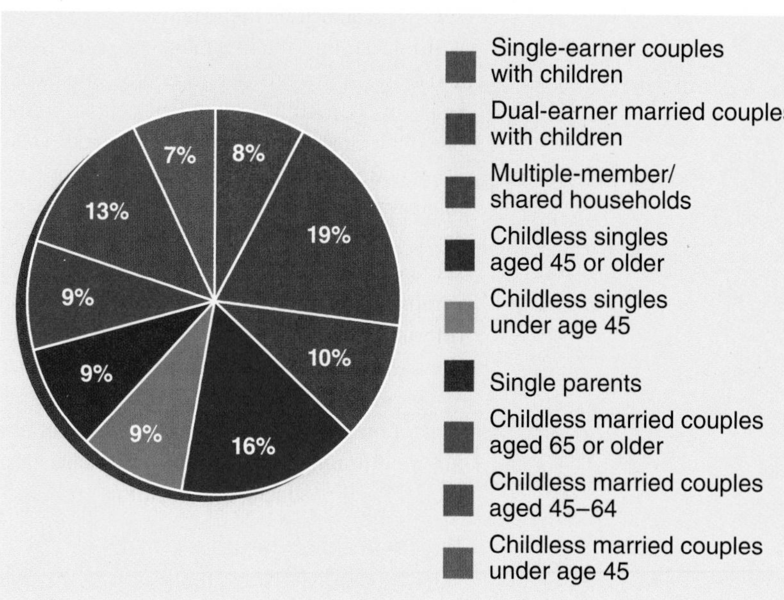

Geographic Variables Geographic variables—climate, terrain, city size, population density, and urban/rural areas—also influence consumer product needs. Markets may be divided into regions because one or more geographic variables can cause customers to differ from one region to another. Consumers in the South, for instance, rarely have need for snow tires. A company that sells products to a national market might divide the United States into the following regions: Pacific, Southwest, Central, Midwest, Southeast, Middle Atlantic, and New England. A firm that is operating in one or several states might regionalize its market by counties, cities, zip code areas, or other units.

City size can be an important segmentation variable. Some marketers focus efforts on cities of a certain size. Consider one franchised restaurant organization that will not locate in cities of fewer than 200,000 people. It concluded that a smaller population base would result in inadequate profits. Other firms actively seek opportunities in smaller towns. A classic example is Walmart, which initially was located only in small towns.

Because cities often cut across political boundaries, the U.S. Census Bureau developed a system to classify metropolitan areas (any area with a city or urbanized area with a population of at least 50,000 and a total metropolitan population of at least 100,000). Metropolitan areas are categorized as one of the following: a metropolitan statistical area (MSA), a primary metropolitan statistical area (PMSA), or a consolidated metropolitan statistical area (CMSA). An MSA is an urbanized area encircled by nonmetropolitan counties and is neither socially nor economically dependent on any other metropolitan area. A metropolitan area within a complex of at least 1 million inhabitants can elect to be named a PMSA. A CMSA is a metropolitan area of at least 1 million that has two or more PMSAs. Of the 20 CMSAs, the five largest—New York, Los Angeles, Chicago, San Francisco, and Philadelphia—account for 20 percent of the U.S. population. The federal government provides a considerable amount of socioeconomic information about MSAs, PMSAs, and CMSAs that can aid in market analysis and segmentation.

Market density refers to the number of potential customers within a unit of land area, such as a square mile. Although market density relates generally to population density, the correlation is not exact. For example, in two different geographic markets of approximately equal size and population, market density for office supplies would be much higher in one area if it contained a much greater proportion of business customers than the other area. Market density may be a useful segmentation variable because low-density markets often require different sales, advertising, and distribution activities than do high-density markets.

market density The number of potential customers within a unit of land area

A number of marketers are using geodemographic segmentation. **Geodemographic segmentation** clusters people in zip code areas and even smaller neighborhood units based on lifestyle and demographic information. These small, precisely described population clusters help marketers isolate demographic units as small as neighborhoods where the demand for specific products is strongest. Information companies such as Donnelley Marketing Information Services, Claritas, and C.A.C.I. Inc. provide geodemographic data services called Prospect Zone, PRIZM, and Acorn, respectively. PRIZM is based on a classification of the more than 500,000 U.S. neighborhoods into one of 66 cluster types, such as "shotguns and pickups," "money and brains," and "gray power."

Geodemographic segmentation allows marketers to engage in micromarketing. **Micromarketing** is the focusing of precise marketing efforts on very small geographic markets, such as community and even neighborhood markets. Providers of financial and health-care services, retailers, and consumer products companies use micromarketing. Special advertising campaigns, promotions, retail site location analyses, special pricing, and unique retail product offerings are a few examples of micromarketing facilitated through geodemographic segmentation. Many retailers use micromarketing to determine the merchandise mix for individual stores.

Climate is commonly used as a geographic segmentation variable because of its broad impact on people's behavior and product needs. Product markets affected by climate include air-conditioning and heating equipment, fireplace accessories, clothing, gardening equipment, recreational products, and building materials.

Psychographic Variables Marketers sometimes use psychographic variables, such as personality characteristics, motives, and lifestyles, to segment markets. A psychographic dimension can be used by itself to segment a market or it can be combined with other types of segmentation variables.

geodemographic segmentation A method of market segmentation that clusters people in zip code areas and smaller neighborhood units based on lifestyle and demographic information

micromarketing An approach to market segmentation in which organizations focus precise marketing efforts on very small geographic markets

Personality characteristics can be useful for segmentation when a product resembles many competing products and consumers' needs are not significantly related to other segmentation variables. However, segmenting a market according to personality traits can be risky. Although marketing practitioners have long believed consumer choice and product use vary with personality, until recently marketing research had indicated only weak relationships. It is hard to measure personality traits accurately, especially because most personality tests were developed for clinical use, not for segmentation purposes.

When appealing to a personality characteristic, a marketer almost always selects one that many people view positively. Individuals with this characteristic, as well as those who

Geographic Segmentation Climate affects numerous markets. Customers' needs for automotive accessories, such as tires, vary based on climate.

would like to have it, may be influenced to buy that marketer's brand. Marketers taking this approach do not worry about measuring how many people have the positively valued characteristic; they assume a sizable proportion of people in the target market either have it or want to have it.

When motives are used to segment a market, the market is divided according to consumers' reasons for making a purchase. Personal appearance, affiliation, status, safety, and health are examples of motives affecting the types of products purchased and the choice of stores in which they are bought. Marketing efforts based on health and fitness motives can be a point of competitive advantage. For instance, Taco Bell, a fast-food chain known more for its low prices than its healthfulness, is now offering healthier, fresh options. The chain is rolling out breakfast items and a "Cantina Bell" menu, which feature burritos and salads containing black beans, marinated meats, cilantro rice, fresh guacamole, grilled corn salsa, and fresh vegetables. The chain hopes to compete with other healthy fast-food establishments like Chipotle by offering healthier options that are cheaper than the competition.[14]

Courtesy of The Advertising Archives

Lifestyle Segmentation
Lifestyle segmentation is based on people's activities, interests, and opinions.

Lifestyle segmentation groups individuals according to how they spend their time, the importance of things in their surroundings (homes or jobs, for example), beliefs about themselves and broad issues, and some demographic characteristics, such as income and education.[15] Lifestyle analysis provides a broad view of buyers because it encompasses numerous characteristics related to people's activities (work, hobbies, entertainment, sports), interests (family, home, fashion, food, technology), and opinions (politics, social issues, education, the future).

One of the most popular lifestyle frameworks is VALS™ from Strategic Business Insights (SBI), a spin-out of SRI International. VALS classifies consumers based on psychological characteristics (personality characteristics) that are correlated with purchase behavior and key demographics. The VALS classification questionnaire, which is used to determine a consumers' VALS type, can be integrated into larger questionnaires to find out about consumers' lifestyle choices. Figure 6.6 is an example of VALS data that shows the proportion of each VALS group that purchased a mountain bike, purchased golf clubs, owns a fishing rod, or goes hunting. VALS research is also used to create new products as well as to segment existing markets. VALS systems have been developed for the United States, Japan, the United Kingdom, Venezuela, and the Dominican Republic.[16]

Behavioristic Variables Firms can divide a market according to some feature of consumer behavior toward a product, commonly involving some aspect of product use. For example, a market may be separated into users—classified as heavy, moderate, or light—and nonusers. To satisfy a specific group, such as heavy users, marketers may create a distinctive product, set special prices, or initiate special promotion and distribution activities. Per capita consumption data help identify different levels of usage.

How customers use or apply products may also determine the method of segmentation. To satisfy customers who use a product in a certain way, some feature—say, packaging, size, texture, or color—may be designed precisely to make the product easier to use, safer, or more convenient.

Benefit segmentation is the division of a market according to benefits that consumers want from the product. Although most types of market segmentation assume a relationship between the variable and customers' needs, benefit segmentation differs in that the benefits customers seek *are* their product needs. Consider that a customer who purchases over-the-counter cold relief medication may be specifically interested in two benefits: stopping a runny nose and relieving chest congestion. Thus, individuals are segmented directly according to their needs. By determining the desired benefits, marketers may be able to divide people into

benefit segmentation The division of a market according to benefits that consumers want from the product

groups seeking certain sets of benefits. The effectiveness of such segmentation depends on three conditions: (1) the benefits sought must be identifiable; (2) using these benefits, marketers must be able to divide people into recognizable segments; and (3) one or more of the resulting segments must be accessible to the firm's marketing efforts. Both Timberland and Avia, for example, segment the foot apparel market based on benefits sought.

As this discussion shows, consumer markets can be divided according to numerous characteristics. Business markets are segmented using different variables, as we will see in the following section.

Variables for Segmenting Business Markets

Like consumer markets, business markets are frequently segmented, often by multiple variables in combination. Marketers segment business markets according to geographic location, type of organization, customer size, and product use.

Geographic Location Earlier, we noted that the demand for some consumer products can vary considerably among geographic areas because of differences in climate, terrain, customer preferences, and similar factors. Demand for business products also varies according to geographic location. For instance, producers of certain types of lumber divide their markets geographically because their customers' needs vary from region to region. Geographic

Figure 6.6 **VALS Types and Sports Preferences**

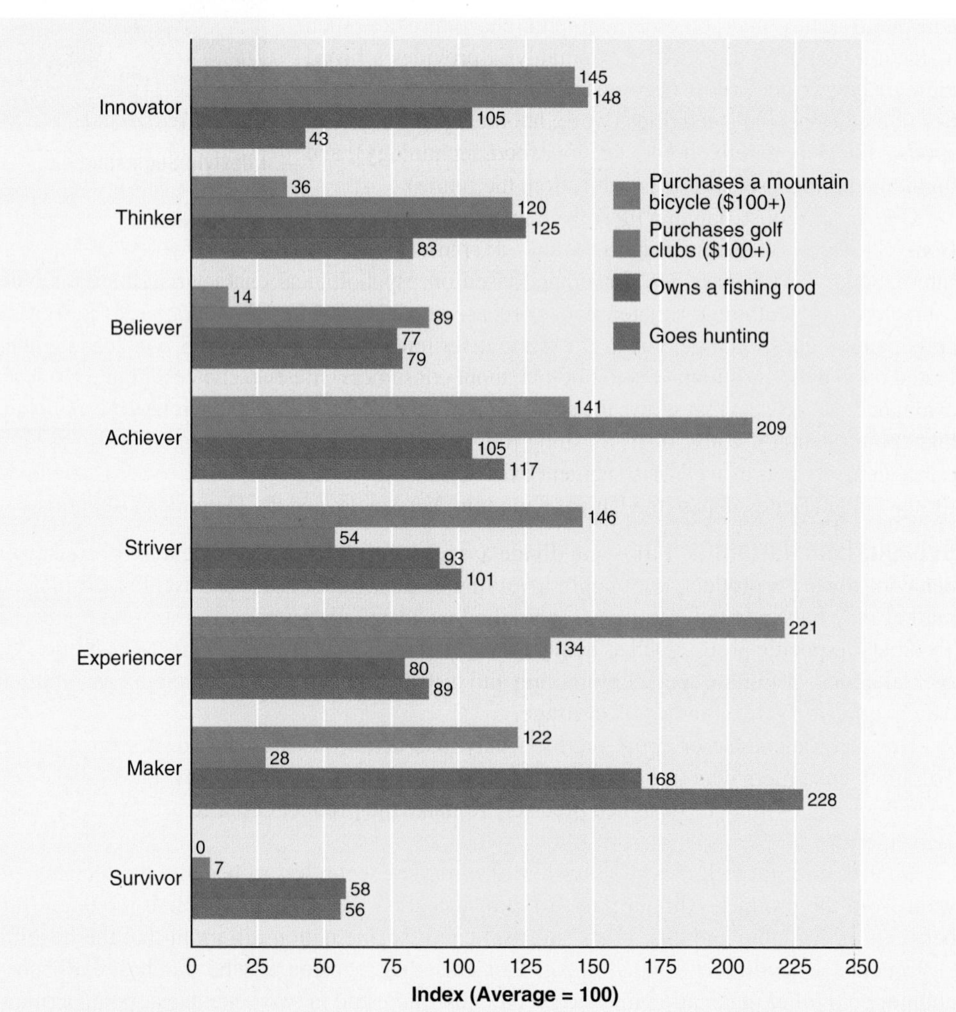

Source: VALS/GfK MRI Survey of the American Consumer, Strategic Business Insights (SBI), www.strategicbusinessinsights.com/VALS.

Going Green

IKEA Adds to the Green Lifestyle

IKEA, the global retailer known for its stylish, affordable, assemble-it-yourself furniture, has added interest in sustainability as a key element in its segmentation strategy. Spotlighting environmental efforts gives IKEA an edge with the growing segment of eco-minded customers and helps the company's bottom line, as well. "What is good for our customers is also good for us in the long run," says CEO Mikael Ohlsson.

Consumers who want to live a greener lifestyle appreciate the way IKEA puts its environmental values into practice, making its stores, its products, and even its shipping materials more eco-friendly every year. More than three-quarters of IKEA's U.S. stores and distribution centers are equipped with solar panels to generate clean energy. Instead of the wooden pallets traditionally used for shipping merchandise, IKEA now uses single-use pallets made from recyclable cardboard. The new pallets are more compact and much lighter than wooden pallets, which means less fuel is consumed when they're transported—and IKEA pays less for transportation.

IKEA recently began rating its products using an 11-point sustainability scorecard, tracking attributes such as the product's percentage of recycled content and the amount of clean energy used in production. Such detailed information appeals to customers seeking a greener lifestyle, who are interested in each product's environmental impact.[b]

segmentation may be especially appropriate for reaching industries concentrated in certain locations. Furniture and textile producers, for example, are concentrated in the Southeast.

Type of Organization A company sometimes segments a market by types of organizations within that market. Different types of organizations often require different product features, distribution systems, price structures, and selling strategies. Given these variations, a firm may either concentrate on a single segment with one marketing mix (a concentration targeting strategy) or focus on several groups with multiple mixes (a differentiated targeting strategy). A carpet producer, for example, could segment potential customers into several groups, such as automobile makers, commercial carpet contractors (firms that carpet large commercial buildings), apartment complex developers, carpet wholesalers, and large retail carpet outlets.

Customer Size An organization's size may affect its purchasing procedures and the types and quantities of products it wants. Size can thus be an effective variable for segmenting a business market. To reach a segment of a particular size, marketers may have to adjust one or more marketing mix components. For example, customers who buy in extremely large quantities are sometimes offered discounts. In addition, marketers often must expand personal selling efforts to serve large organizational buyers properly. Because the needs of large and small buyers tend to be quite distinct, marketers frequently use different marketing practices to reach various customer groups.

Product Use Certain products, especially basic raw materials like steel, petroleum, plastics, and lumber, are used in numerous ways. How a company uses products affects the types and amounts of products purchased, as well as the purchasing method. Consider computers, which are used for engineering purposes, basic scientific research, and business operations such as word processing, accounting, and telecommunications. A computer maker, therefore, may segment the computer market by types of use because organizations' needs for computer hardware and software depend on the purpose for which products are purchased.

Step 3: Develop Market Segment Profiles

A market segment profile describes the similarities among potential customers within a segment and explains the differences among people and organizations in different segments. A profile may cover such aspects as demographic characteristics, geographic factors, product benefits sought, lifestyles, brand preferences, and usage rates. Individuals and organizations within segments should be relatively similar with respect to several characteristics and product needs and differ considerably from those within other market segments. Marketers use market segment profiles to assess the degree to which their possible products can match or fit potential customers' product needs. Market segment profiles help marketers understand how a business can use its capabilities to serve potential customer groups.

The use of market segment profiles benefits marketers in several ways. Such profiles help a marketer determine which segment or segments are most attractive to the organization relative to the firm's strengths, weaknesses, objectives, and resources. Although marketers may initially believe certain segments are quite attractive, development of market segment profiles may yield information that indicates the opposite. For the market segment or segments chosen by the organization, the information included in market segment profiles can be highly useful in making marketing decisions.

Step 4: Evaluate Relevant Market Segments

After analyzing the market segment profiles, a marketer is likely to identify several relevant market segments that require further analysis and eliminate certain segments from consideration. To further assess relevant market segments, several important factors, including sales estimates, competition, and estimated costs associated with each segment, should be analyzed.

Sales Estimates

Potential sales for a market segment can be measured along several dimensions, including product level, geographic area, time, and level of competition.[17] With respect to product level, potential sales can be estimated for a specific product item (e.g., Diet Coke) or an entire product line (Coca-Cola Classic, Caffeine-Free Coke, Diet Coke, Caffeine-Free Diet Coke, Vanilla Coke, Diet Vanilla Coke, Cherry Coke, and Diet Cherry Coke comprise one product line). A manager must also determine the geographic area to include in the estimate. In relation to time, sales estimates can be short range (one year or less), medium range (one to five years), or long range (longer than five years). The competitive level specifies whether sales are being estimated for a single firm or for an entire industry.

Market potential is the total amount of a product that customers will purchase within a specified period at a specific level of industrywide marketing activity. Market potential can be stated in terms of dollars or units. A segment's market potential is affected by economic, sociocultural, and other environmental forces. Marketers must assume a certain general level of marketing effort in the industry when they estimate market potential. The specific level of marketing effort varies from one firm to another, but the sum of all firms' marketing activities equals industrywide marketing efforts. A marketing manager must also consider whether and to what extent industry marketing efforts will change.

Company sales potential is the maximum percentage of market potential that an individual firm within an industry can expect to obtain for a specific product. Several factors influence company sales potential for a market segment. First, the market potential places absolute limits on the size of the company's sales potential. Second, the magnitude of industrywide marketing activities has an indirect but definite impact on the company's sales potential. Those activities have a direct bearing on the size of the market potential. When Domino's Pizza advertises home-delivered pizza, for example, it indirectly promotes pizza in general; its commercials may indirectly help sell Pizza Hut's and other competitors' home-delivered pizza. Third, the intensity and effectiveness of a company's marketing activities relative to competitors' activities affect the size of the company's sales potential. If a company spends twice as much as any of its competitors on marketing efforts and if each dollar spent is more effective in generating sales, the firm's sales potential will be quite high compared to competitors'.

Two general approaches that measure company sales potential are breakdown and buildup. In the **breakdown approach**, the marketing manager first develops a general economic forecast for a specific time period. Next, the manager estimates market potential based on this economic forecast. Then the manager derives the company's sales potential from the general economic forecast and estimate of market potential. In the **buildup approach**, the marketing manager begins by estimating how much of a product a potential buyer in a specific geographic

market potential The total amount of a product that customers will purchase within a specified period at a specific level of industrywide marketing activity

company sales potential The maximum percentage of market potential that an individual firm within an industry can expect to obtain for a specific product

breakdown approach Measuring company sales potential based on a general economic forecast for a specific period and the market potential derived from it

buildup approach Measuring company sales potential by estimating how much of a product a potential buyer in a specific geographic area will purchase in a given period, multiplying the estimate by the number of potential buyers, and adding the totals of all the geographic areas considered

Emerging Trends

Remember That Toy?

Parents and grandparents with fond memories of toys from their childhood are now the target market for Colorforms, the Smurfs, and other long-lived toy brands. Demographics clearly play a role: children who enjoy the toys grow up, start a family, and choose the toys they liked when they buy for their children (and, later, their grandchildren). Psychographics are also a factor: Nostalgia motivates these adults to buy toy brands they remember from when they were young.

When Colorforms celebrated its 60th anniversary, parent company University Games launched a multimedia campaign targeting grownups who, as children, played with these sets of colorful vinyl shapes. "We're trying to say to the American public, 'Colorforms is still here,'" explained the president of University Games. "Everything you loved about it as a child will be appealing to your children."

Sony Pictures used nostalgia marketing to encourage purchasing of Smurfs merchandise when it released *The Smurfs* movie. The Smurf characters, introduced in comic strips more than 50 years ago, were familiar because of the 1980s-era Smurfs cartoon series. Sony arranged various promotions, including a float in the Macy's Thanksgiving Day parade, to remind parents of their positive associations with the Smurfs. Thanks to nostalgia, both the movie and the merchandise did well worldwide.[c]

area, such as a sales territory, will purchase in a given period. The manager then multiplies that amount by the total number of potential buyers in that area. The manager performs the same calculation for each geographic area in which the firm sells products and then adds the totals for each area to calculate market potential. To determine company sales potential, the manager must estimate, based on planned levels of company marketing activities, the proportion of the total market potential the company can obtain.

Competitive Assessment

Besides obtaining sales estimates, it is crucial to assess competitors that are already operating in the segments being considered. Without competitive information, sales estimates may be misleading. A market segment that initially seems attractive based on sales estimates may turn out to be much less so after a competitive assessment. Such an assessment should ask several questions about competitors: How many exist? What are their strengths and weaknesses? Do several competitors have major market shares and together dominate the segment? Can our company create a marketing mix to compete effectively against competitors' marketing mixes? Is it likely that new competitors will enter this segment? If so, how will they affect our firm's ability to compete successfully? Answers to such questions are important for proper assessment of the competition in potential market segments.

The actions of a national food company that considered entering the dog food market illustrate the importance of competitive assessment. Through a segmentation study, the company determined that dog owners could be divided into three segments according to how they viewed their dogs and dog foods. One group treated their dogs as companions and family members. These individuals were willing to pay relatively high prices for dog foods and wanted a variety of types and flavors so their dogs would not get bored. The second group saw their dogs as performing a definite utilitarian function, such as protecting family members, playing with children, guarding the property, or herding farm animals. These people wanted a low-priced, nutritious dog food and were not interested in a wide variety of flavors. Dog owners in the third segment were found to actually hate their dogs. These people wanted the cheapest dog food they could buy and were not concerned with nutrition, flavor, or variety. The food company examined the extent to which competitive brands were serving all these dog owners and found that each segment contained at least three well-entrenched competing brands, which together dominated the segment. The company's management decided not to enter the dog food market because of the strength of the competing brands.

Cost Estimates

To fulfill the needs of a target segment, an organization must develop and maintain a marketing mix that precisely meets the wants and needs of individuals and organizations in that segment. Developing and maintaining such a mix can be expensive. Distinctive product features, attractive package design, generous product warranties, extensive advertising, attractive promotional offers, competitive prices, and high-quality personal service consume considerable organizational resources. Indeed, to reach certain segments, the costs may be so high that a marketer concludes the segment is inaccessible. Another cost consideration is whether the organization can effectively reach a segment at costs equal to or below competitors' costs. If the firm's costs are likely to be higher, it will be unable to compete in that segment in the long run. When Apple decided to enter the digital textbook market, the company had to consider its strengths and weaknesses compared to existing competitors in a rapidly growing industry. Apple hoped to leverage the strength of the brand and brand loyalty among consumers to convince students to trade in their books for an iPad. Apple contracted with textbook publishers McGraw Hill, Pearson, and Houghton Mifflin to offer a range of titles digitally for less money than the print versions. Its iBooks Author feature should make books more interactive and easier for authors to update—in order to give students the most cutting-edge information. The digital textbook industry is small, but it is growing fast and competition is fierce. Before introducing its own titles, Apple had to weigh the costs of entering the market, the competition, and the potential benefits of doing so. A major barrier for widespread adoption of the Apple digital books is the cost of an iPad, which many schools and students cannot yet afford. An impediment to future growth is that other digital book titles are available on multiple devices, making adoption easier for consumers. Apple is, nevertheless, optimistic about its future in the digital textbook industry.[18]

Step 5: Select Specific Target Markets

An important initial consideration in selecting a target market is whether customers' needs differ enough to warrant the use of market segmentation. If segmentation analysis shows customer needs to be fairly homogeneous, the firm's management may decide to use the undifferentiated approach, discussed earlier. However, if customer needs are heterogeneous, which is much more likely, one or more target markets must be selected. On the other hand, marketers may decide not to enter and compete in any of the segments.

Assuming one or more segments offer significant opportunities to achieve organizational objectives, marketers must decide in which segments to participate. Ordinarily information gathered in the previous step—about sales estimates, competitors, and cost estimates—requires careful consideration in this final step to determine long-term profit opportunities. Also, the firm's management must investigate whether the organization has the financial resources, managerial skills, employee expertise, and facilities to enter and compete effectively in selected segments. Furthermore, the requirements of some market segments may be at odds with the firm's overall objectives, and the possibility of legal problems, conflicts with interest groups, and technological advancements could make certain segments unattractive. In addition, when prospects for long-term growth are taken into account, some segments may appear very attractive and others less desirable.

Selecting appropriate target markets is important to an organization's adoption and use of the marketing concept philosophy. Identifying the right target market is the key to implementing a successful marketing strategy, whereas failure to do so can lead to low sales, high costs, and severe financial losses. A careful target market analysis places an organization in a better position to both serve customers' needs and achieve its objectives.

DEVELOPING SALES FORECASTS

sales forecast The amount of a product a company expects to sell during a specific period at a specified level of marketing activities

After a company targets its market, it needs a **sales forecast**—the amount of a product the company expects to sell during a specific period at a specified level of marketing activities. The sales forecast differs from the company sales potential. It concentrates on what actual sales will

Entrepreneurship in Marketing

How Skullcandy Segments Its Market

Entrepreneur: Rick Alden
Business: Skullcandy
Founded: 2003 | Park City, Utah
Success: Skullcandy now sells its products in 70 countries and has more than $200 million in annual revenues.

Rick Alden, an avid snowboarder, founded Skullcandy in 2003 with the idea of making trendy, functional headphones for music lovers who enjoy active sports and want to look stylish. The iPod era was in full swing, and consumers could now take their digital music collections anywhere and everywhere—even on snow-capped mountains. "I wanted to integrate headphones into backpacks, beanies, helmets—to make an easier music delivery device," he remembers.

Although age was a consideration—many of the consumers in his target market were in their teens or twenties—lifestyle and attitude turned out to be more important variables for segmenting the overall market. Skullcandy's headphones and earbuds are specially made for snowboarders and others who listen to music while engaging in snow or sun sports. Instead of the usual black or white earbuds, Skullcandy's earbuds are brightly colored to appeal to sports-minded consumers with fashion flair.

With more than $200 million in annual revenue and distribution in 70 countries, Skullcandy now competes against global giants such as Sony. To continue growing, the company has adjusted its segmentation to reach consumers involved in a wider variety of active-sports lifestyles, including skateboarders, surfers, inline skaters, and motocrossers.[d]

be at a certain level of company marketing effort, whereas the company sales potential assesses what sales are possible at various levels of marketing activities, assuming certain environmental conditions will exist. Businesses use the sales forecast for planning, organizing, implementing, and controlling their activities. The success of numerous activities depends on this forecast's accuracy. Common problems in failing companies are improper planning and lack of realistic sales forecasts. Overly ambitious sales forecasts can lead to overbuying, overinvestment, and higher costs.

To forecast sales, a marketer can choose from a number of forecasting methods, some arbitrary and others more scientific, complex, and time consuming. A firm's choice of method or methods depends on the costs involved, type of product, market characteristics, time span of the forecast, purposes of the forecast, stability of the historical sales data, availability of required information, managerial preferences, and forecasters' expertise and experience.[19] Common forecasting techniques fall into five categories: executive judgment, surveys, time series analysis, regression analysis, and market tests.

Executive Judgment

At times, a company forecasts sales chiefly on the basis of **executive judgment**: the intuition of one or more executives. This approach is unscientific but expedient and inexpensive. Executive judgment may work reasonably well when product demand is relatively stable and the forecaster has years of market-related experience. However, because intuition is swayed most heavily by recent experience, the forecast may be overly optimistic or overly pessimistic. Another drawback to intuition is that the forecaster has only past experience as a guide for deciding where to go in the future.

executive judgment A sales forecasting method based on the intuition of one or more executives

Surveys

Another way to forecast sales is to question customers, sales personnel, or experts regarding their expectations about future purchases. In a **customer forecasting survey**, marketers ask customers what types and quantities of products they intend to buy during a specific period. This approach may be useful to a business with relatively few customers. Consider Intel,

customer forecasting survey A survey of customers regarding the types and quantities of products they intend to buy during a specific period

which markets to a limited number of companies (primarily computer manufacturers). Intel could conduct customer forecasting surveys effectively. PepsiCo, in contrast, has millions of customers and could not feasibly use a customer survey to forecast future sales.

In a **sales force forecasting survey**, the firm's salespeople estimate anticipated sales in their territories for a specified period. The forecaster combines these territorial estimates to arrive at a tentative forecast. A marketer may survey the sales staff for several reasons. The most important is that the sales staff is closer to customers on a daily basis than other company personnel and therefore should know more about customers' future product needs. Moreover, when sales representatives assist in developing the forecast, they are more likely to work toward its achievement. In addition, forecasts can be prepared for single territories, divisions consisting of several territories, regions made up of multiple divisions, and the total geographic market. Thus, the method provides sales forecasts from the smallest geographic sales unit to the largest.

sales force forecasting survey A survey of a firm's sales force regarding anticipated sales in their territories for a specified period

expert forecasting survey Sales forecasts prepared by experts outside the firm, such as economists, management consultants, advertising executives, or college professors

When a company wants an **expert forecasting survey**, it hires professionals to help prepare the sales forecast. These experts are usually economists, management consultants, advertising executives, college professors, or other individuals outside the firm with solid experience in a specific market. Drawing on this experience and their analyses of available information about the company and the market, experts prepare and present forecasts or answer questions regarding a forecast. Using experts is expedient and relatively inexpensive. However, because they work outside the firm, these forecasters may be less motivated than company personnel to do an effective job.

A more complex form of the expert forecasting survey incorporates the Delphi technique. In the **Delphi technique**, experts create initial forecasts, submit them to the company for averaging, and have the results returned to them so they can make individual refined forecasts. The premise is that the experts will use the averaged results when making refined forecasts and these forecasts will be in a narrower range. The procedure may be repeated several times until the experts, each working separately, reach a consensus on the forecasts. The ultimate goal in using the Delphi technique is to develop a highly accurate sales forecast.

Delphi technique A procedure in which experts create initial forecasts, submit them to the company for averaging, and then refine the forecasts

time series analysis A forecasting method that uses historical sales data to discover patterns in the firm's sales over time and generally involves trend, cycle, seasonal, and random factor analyses

Time Series Analysis

With **time series analysis**, the forecaster uses the firm's historical sales data to discover a pattern or patterns in the firm's sales over time. If a pattern is found, it can be used to forecast

Sales Forecasting
A business organization can obtain the services of other organizations, like salesforce.com, to help with sales forecasting efforts.

sales. This forecasting method assumes that past sales patterns will continue in the future. The accuracy, and thus usefulness, of time series analysis hinges on the validity of this assumption.

In a time series analysis, a forecaster usually performs four types of analyses: trend, cycle, seasonal, and random factor. **Trend analysis** focuses on aggregate sales data, such as the company's annual sales figures, covering a period of many years to determine whether annual sales are generally rising, falling, or staying about the same. Through **cycle analysis**, a forecaster analyzes sales figures (often monthly sales data) for a three- to five-year period to ascertain whether sales fluctuate in a consistent, periodic manner. When performing a **seasonal analysis**, the analyst studies daily, weekly, or monthly sales figures to evaluate the degree to which seasonal factors, such as climate and holiday activities, influence sales. In a **random factor analysis**, the forecaster attempts to attribute erratic sales variations to random, nonrecurrent events, such as a regional power failure, a natural disaster, or political unrest in a foreign market. After performing each of these analyses, the forecaster combines the results to develop the sales forecast. Time series analysis is an effective forecasting method for products with reasonably stable demand, but not for products with highly erratic demand.

Regression Analysis

Like time series analysis, regression analysis requires the use of historical sales data. In **regression analysis**, the forecaster seeks to find a relationship between past sales (the dependent variable) and one or more independent variables, such as population, per capita income, or gross domestic product. Simple regression analysis uses one independent variable, whereas multiple regression analysis includes two or more independent variables. The objective of regression analysis is to develop a mathematical formula that accurately describes a relationship between the firm's sales and one or more variables; however, the formula indicates only an association, not a causal relationship. Once an accurate formula is established, the analyst plugs the necessary information into the formula to derive the sales forecast.

Regression analysis is useful when a precise association can be established. However, a forecaster seldom finds a perfect correlation. Furthermore, this method can be used only when available historical sales data are extensive. Thus, regression analysis is futile for forecasting sales of new products.

Market Tests

A **market test** involves making a product available to buyers in one or more test areas and measuring purchases and consumer responses to distribution, promotion, and price. Test areas are often cities with populations of 200,000 to 500,000, but they can be larger metropolitan areas or towns with populations of 50,000 to 200,000.

A market test provides information about consumers' actual rather than intended purchases. In addition, purchase volume can be evaluated in relation to the intensity of other marketing activities such as advertising, in-store promotions, pricing, packaging, and distribution. Forecasters base their sales estimates for larger geographic units on customer response in test areas. Taco Bell utilized the city of Bakersfield, California, as a test market for three of its recent ideas: the Doritos Locos tacos, with a cheesy Dorito shell, its First Meal breakfast items, and its healthier Cantina Bell menu options. Releasing items in a limited number of cities generates nationwide buzz and desire in those cities that do not have the items yet. Test marketing menu items in a limited number of cities before a full roll out allows businesses to gauge consumer response and how the products will perform nationally.[20]

Because it does not require historical sales data, a market test is effective for forecasting sales of new products or sales of existing products in new geographic areas. A market test also gives a marketer an opportunity to test various elements of the marketing mix. However, these tests are often time consuming and expensive. In addition, a marketer cannot be certain that consumer response during a market test represents the total market response or that such a response will continue in the future.

trend analysis An analysis that focuses on aggregate sales data over a period of many years to determine general trends in annual sales

cycle analysis An analysis of sales figures for a three- to five-year period to ascertain whether sales fluctuate in a consistent, periodic manner

seasonal analysis An analysis of daily, weekly, or monthly sales figures to evaluate the degree to which seasonal factors influence sales

random factor analysis An analysis attempting to attribute erratic sales variations to random, nonrecurrent events

regression analysis A method of predicting sales based on finding a relationship between past sales and one or more independent variables, such as population or income

market test Making a product available to buyers in one or more test areas and measuring purchases and consumer responses to marketing efforts

Using Multiple Forecasting Methods

Although some businesses depend on a single sales forecasting method, most firms use several techniques. Sometimes a company is forced to use multiple methods when marketing diverse product lines, but even a single product line may require several forecasts, especially when the product is sold to different market segments. Thus, a producer of automobile tires may rely on one technique to forecast tire sales for new cars and on another to forecast sales of replacement tires. Variation in the length of needed forecasts may call for several forecasting methods. A firm that employs one method for a short-range forecast may find it inappropriate for long-range forecasting. Sometimes a marketer verifies results of one method by using one or more other methods and comparing outcomes.

Summary

1. To learn about *markets*

A market is a group of people who, as individuals or as organizations, have needs for products in a product class and have the ability, willingness, and authority to purchase such products. Markets can be categorized as consumer markets or business markets based on the characteristics of the individuals and groups that make up a specific market and the purposes for which they buy products. A consumer market, also known as a *business-to-consumer (B2C) market,* consists of purchasers and household members who intend to consume or benefit from the purchased products and do not buy products for the main purpose of making a profit. A business market, also known as *business-to-business (B2B), industrial,* or *organizational market,* consists of individuals or groups that purchase a specific kind of product for one of three purposes: resale, direct use in producing other products, or use in general daily operations.

2. To understand the differences among general targeting strategies

In general, marketers employ a five-step process when selecting a target market. Step 1 is to identify the appropriate targeting strategy. When a company designs a single marketing mix and directs it at the entire market for a particular product, it is using an undifferentiated targeting strategy. The undifferentiated strategy is effective in a homogeneous market, whereas a heterogeneous market needs to be segmented through a concentrated targeting strategy or a differentiated targeting strategy. Both of these strategies divide markets into segments consisting of individuals, groups, or organizations that have one or more similar characteristics and thus can be linked to similar product needs. When using a concentrated strategy, an organization directs marketing efforts toward a single market segment through one marketing mix. With a differentiated targeting strategy, an organization directs customized marketing efforts at two or more segments.

Certain conditions must exist for effective market segmentation. First, customers' needs for the product should be heterogeneous. Second, the segments of the market should be identifiable and divisible. Third, the total market should be divided so segments can be compared with respect to estimated sales, costs, and profits. Fourth, at least one segment must have enough profit potential to justify developing and maintaining a special marketing mix for that segment. Fifth, the firm must be able to reach the chosen segment with a particular marketing mix.

3. To become familiar with the major segmentation variables

Step 2 is determining which segmentation variables to use. Segmentation variables are the characteristics of individuals, groups, or organizations used to divide a total market into segments. The segmentation variable should relate to customers' needs for, uses of, or behavior toward the product. Segmentation variables for consumer markets can be grouped into four categories: demographic (e.g., age, gender, income, ethnicity, family life cycle), geographic (population, market density, climate), psychographic (personality traits, motives, lifestyles), and behavioristic (volume usage, end use, expected benefits, brand loyalty, price sensitivity). Variables for segmenting business markets include geographic location, type of organization, customer size, and product use.

4. To know what segment profiles are and how they are used

Step 3 in the target market selection process is to develop market segment profiles. Such profiles describe the similarities among potential customers within a segment and explain the differences among people and organizations in different market segments. They are used to assess the degree to which the firm's products can match potential customers' product needs. Segments, which may seem at first quite attractive, may be shown to be quite the opposite after a market segment profile is completed.

5. To understand how to evaluate market segments

Step 4 is evaluating relevant market segments. Marketers analyze several important factors, such as sales estimates, competition, and estimated costs associated with each segment. Potential sales for a market segment can be measured along several dimensions, including product level, geographic area, time, and level of competition. Besides obtaining sales estimates, it is crucial to assess competitors that are already operating in the segments being considered. Without competitive information, sales estimates may be misleading. The cost of developing a marketing mix that meets the wants and needs of individuals in that segment must also be considered. If the firm's costs to compete in that market are very high, it may be unable to compete in that segment in the long run.

6. To identify the factors that influence the selection of specific market segments for use as target markets

Step 5 involves the actual selection of specific target markets. In this final step, the company considers whether customers' needs differ enough to warrant segmentation and which segments to target. If customers' needs are heterogeneous, the decision must be made which segment to target, or whether to enter the market at all. Considerations such as resources, managerial skills, employee expertise, facilities, the firm's overall objectives, possible legal problems, conflicts with interest groups, and technological advancements must be considered when deciding which segments to target.

7. To become familiar with sales forecasting methods

A sales forecast is the amount of a product the company actually expects to sell during a specific period at a specified level of marketing activities. To forecast sales, marketers can choose from a number of methods. The choice depends on various factors, including the costs involved, type of product, market characteristics, and time span and purposes of the forecast. There are five categories of forecasting techniques: executive judgment, surveys, time series analysis, regression analysis, and market tests. Executive judgment is based on the intuition of one or more executives. Surveys include customer, sales force, and expert forecasting surveys. Time series analysis uses the firm's historical sales data to discover patterns in the firm's sales over time and employs four major types of analyses: trend, cycle, seasonal, and random factor. With regression analysis, forecasters attempt to find a relationship between past sales and one or more independent variables. Market testing involves making a product available to buyers in one or more test areas and measuring purchases and consumer responses to distribution, promotion, and price. Many companies employ multiple forecasting methods.

Go to www.cengagebrain.com for resources to help you master the content in this chapter as well as for materials that will expand your marketing knowledge!

Important Terms

consumer market 176
business market 177
undifferentiated targeting strategy 177
homogeneous market 177
heterogeneous market 179
market segmentation 179
market segment 179
concentrated targeting strategy 180
differentiated targeting strategy 181
segmentation variables 181
market density 185
geodemographic segmentation 186
micromarketing 186
benefit segmentation 187
market potential 190
company sales potential 190
breakdown approach 190
buildup approach 190
sales forecast 192
executive judgment 193
customer forecasting survey 193
sales force forecasting survey 194
expert forecasting survey 194
Delphi technique 194
time series analysis 194
trend analysis 195
cycle analysis 195
seasonal analysis 195
random factor analysis 195
regression analysis 195
market test 195

Discussion and Review Questions

1. What is a market? What are the requirements for a market?
2. In your local area, identify a group of people with unsatisfied product needs who represent a market. Could this market be reached by a business organization? Why or why not?
3. Outline the five major steps in the target market selection process.
4. What is an undifferentiated strategy? Under what conditions is it most useful? Describe a present market situation in which a company is using an undifferentiated strategy. Is the business successful? Why or why not?
5. What is market segmentation? Describe the basic conditions required for effective segmentation. Identify several firms that use market segmentation.

6. List the differences between concentrated and differentiated strategies, and describe the advantages and disadvantages of each.
7. Identify and describe four major categories of variables that can be used to segment consumer markets. Give examples of product markets that are segmented by variables in each category.
8. What dimensions are used to segment business markets?
9. Define *geodemographic segmentation.* Identify several types of firms that might employ this type of market segmentation, and explain why.
10. What is a market segment profile? Why is it an important step in the target market selection process?
11. Describe the important factors that marketers should analyze to evaluate market segments.
12. Why is a marketer concerned about sales potential when trying to select a target market?
13. Why is selecting appropriate target markets important for an organization that wants to adopt the marketing concept philosophy?
14. What is a sales forecast? Why is it important?
15. What are the two primary types of surveys a company might use to forecast sales? Why would a company use an outside expert forecasting survey?
16. Under what conditions are market tests useful for sales forecasting? What are the advantages and disadvantages of market tests?
17. Under what conditions might a firm use multiple forecasting methods?

Application Questions

1. Cable channels, such as Lifetime and Spike TV, each target a specific market segment. Identify another product marketed to a distinct target market. Describe the target market, and explain how the marketing mix appeals specifically to that group.
2. Generally, marketers use one of three basic targeting strategies to focus on a target market: undifferentiated, concentrated, or differentiated. Locate an article that discusses the target market for a specific product. Describe the target market, and explain the targeting strategy used to reach that target market.
3. The car market may be segmented according to income and age. Discuss two ways the market for each of the following products might be segmented.
   a. Candy bars
   b. Travel services
   c. Bicycles
   d. Cell phones
4. If you were using a time series analysis to forecast sales for your company for the next year, how would you use the following sets of sales figures?

a.

2003	$145,000	2008	$149,000
2004	$144,000	2009	$148,000
2005	$147,000	2010	$180,000
2006	$145,000	2011	$191,000
2007	$148,000	2012	$227,000

b.

	2010	2011	2012
Jan.	$12,000	$14,000	$16,000
Feb.	$13,000	$14,000	$15,500
Mar.	$12,000	$14,000	$17,000
Apr.	$13,000	$15,000	$17,000
May	$15,000	$17,000	$20,000
June	$18,000	$18,000	$21,000
July	$18,500	$18,000	$21,500
Aug.	$18,500	$19,000	$22,000
Sep.	$17,000	$18,000	$21,000
Oct.	$16,000	$15,000	$19,000
Nov.	$13,000	$14,000	$19,000
Dec.	$14,000	$15,000	$18,000

c. In 2010, sales increased 21.2 percent. In 2011, sales increased 18.8 percent. New stores were opened in 2010 and 2011.

5. IMP Despite the use of cell phones to tell the time these days, the U.S. watch market is still worth about $10 billion. A new watch company that manufactures classic American watches in the style of the Elgin and Hamilton brands has been segmenting the U.S watch market. It has identified the following five main segments, using a combination of demographic, psychographic, and behavioristic variables.

Carrie is a 25- to 40-year-old woman. She might be single or married, with or without children, but she values her independence. She is a professional, living an urban lifestyle. She is brand conscious and makes well-informed purchasing decisions. She is often a fashion leader. Her annual household income exceeds $100,000. She enjoys jazz, opera, ballet, and “intellectual” popular music. She dines out often, usually trying the most fashionable restaurants. She watches television, especially PBS, Discovery Channel, and HGTV. She has three watches, each of which is priced around $500: a stylish daytime watch for the office, a glamorous watch for evening events, and a sporty watch for weekends and recreational pursuits.

Brittney is a 12- to 18-year-old female. She is all about fashion. She has about $50 to spend per week, either from a part-time job or as an allowance from her parents. She enjoys spending time with her friends and can often be seen at malls or cafés, chatting or texting. She is very aware of different brands and tries to imitate the latest fashions from her favorite celebrities. Her musical tastes are mainstream, and she is addicted to reality programs and MTV. She has six watches, each of which costs less than $100. Watches to her are an accessory, and she replaces them frequently when fashion changes.

Skater Boy is a 12- to 23-year-old male. He is a self-described "individual." He thinks of himself as being different, and his style and activities are beyond the mainstream. He often buys clothing at "underground" shops, and his favorite brands are often not branded at all or defined as anti-establishment. He has a part-time job or receives an allowance but spends the majority of this money on music, games, and other lifestyle pursuits. He watches some television, mostly extreme sports, cartoons, and comedy programs. He has one watch, which he wears as a statement of his personality. It is rugged and even clunky and costs less than $200.

Executives are men and women, aged 45 and above. They are married with children and consider themselves elite, with annual household incomes of more than $400,000. They belong to exclusive clubs and sit on boards of not-for-profit organizations. They have a high regard for quality and often buy products that are somewhat exotic. They watch little television, preferring evenings out at the opera, ballet, or symphony, of which they are members. Like **Carrie**, they have three watches (daytime, evening, and weekend), but each is worth more than $1,000.

Joe Lunchbox is a 25- to 65-year-old man. He is married with two children, and earns about $40,000 per year. He is very family-oriented and spends his spare time camping, attending sporting events, and working on do-it-yourself projects. He often buys American and prefers the basic casual style of jeans, T-shirts, and running shoes. His music tastes range from country to classic rock. He loves television, especially sports. He has one watch, which was received as a gift. It serves only one function: telling time.

Develop a rating scale of 1–5, with 1 as the most desirable market segment and 5 as the least desirable. If you decided to market a watch that was under $100 and would compete against lower-priced Swatch or Timex watches, rate the attractiveness of each market based on these criteria. What will be the unique features that will give your watch a competitive advantage?

What if you wanted to develop a higher-priced watch that targets those individuals with an active lifestyle? Which market segment would you choose, and why?

Internet Exercise

iExplore

iExplore is an Internet company that offers a variety of travel and adventure products. Learn more about its goods, services, and travel advice through its website at www.iexplore.com.

a. Based on the information provided at the website, what are some of iExplore's basic products?
b. What market segments does iExplore appear to be targeting with its website? What segmentation variables is the company using to segment these markets?
c. How does iExplore appeal to comparison shoppers?

developing your marketing plan

Identifying and analyzing a target market is a major component of formulating a marketing strategy. A clear understanding and explanation of a product's target market is crucial to developing a useful marketing plan. References to various dimensions of a target market are likely to appear in several locations in a marketing plan. To assist you in understanding how information in this chapter relates to the creation of your marketing plan, focus on the following considerations:

1. What type of targeting strategy is being used for your product? Should a different targeting strategy be employed?
2. Select and justify the segmentation variables that are most appropriate for segmenting the market for your product. If your product is a consumer product, use Figure 5.3 for ideas regarding the most appropriate segmentation variables. If your marketing plan focuses on a business product, review the information in the section entitled "Variables for Segmenting Business Markets."
3. Discuss how your product should be positioned in the minds of customers in the target market relative to the product positions of competitors.

The information obtained from these questions should assist you in developing various aspects of your marketing plan found in the "Interactive Marketing Plan" exercise at www.cengagebrain.com.

video case 6.1

Raleigh Wheels Out Steel Bicycle Marketing

From its 19th-century roots as a British bicycle company, Raleigh has developed a worldwide reputation for marketing sturdy, comfortable, steel-frame bicycles. The firm, named for the street in Nottingham, England, where it was originally located, was a trendsetter in designing and manufacturing bicycles. When Raleigh introduced steel-frame bicycles equipped with three-speed gear hubs in 1903, it revolutionized the industry and set off a never-ending race to improve the product's technology. In the pre-auto era, its bicycles became a two-wheeled status symbol for British consumers, and the brand maintained its cachet for decades. Although Raleigh's chopper-style bicycles were hugely popular in the 1970s, international competition and changing consumer tastes have taken a toll during the past few decades.

Now Raleigh markets a wide variety of bicycles to consumers in Europe, Canada, and the United States, focusing not just on performance but also styling. Its U.S. division, based in Kent, Washington, has been researching new bicycles for contemporary consumers and developing models that are lighter, faster, and better. Inspired by the European lifestyle and tradition of getting around on bicycles, and its long history in the business, Raleigh is looking to reinvigorate sales and capture a larger share of the $6 billion U.S. bicycle market.

Raleigh's U.S. marketers have been observing the "messenger market," customers who ride bicycles through downtown streets to deliver documents and small packages to businesses and individuals. They have also noted that many everyday bicycle riders dress casually, in T-shirts and jeans, rather than in special racing outfits designed for speed. Targeting consumers who enjoy riding bicycles as a lifestyle, Raleigh's marketers are focusing on this segment's specific needs and preferences as they develop, price, promote, and distribute new models.

In recent years, Raleigh's marketers have stepped up the practice of bringing demonstration fleets to public places where potential buyers can hop on one of the company's bicycles and pedal for a few minutes. The idea is to allow consumers who enjoy bicycling to actually experience the fun feeling of riding a Raleigh. The marketers are also fanning out to visit bicycle races and meet bicyclists in cities and towns across America, encouraging discussions about Raleigh and about bicycling in general and seeking feedback about particular Raleigh products.

Listening to consumers, Raleigh's marketers recognized that many had misperceptions about the weight of steel-frame bicycles. Although steel can be quite heavy, Raleigh's bicycles are solid yet light, nimble, and easy to steer. Those who have been on bicycles with steel frames praise the quality of the ride, saying that steel "has a soul," according to market research.

To stay in touch with its target market, Raleigh is increasingly active in social media. Ten thousand fans visit its Facebook page to see the latest product concepts and post their own photos and comments about Raleigh bicycles. It also uses Twitter to keep customers informed and answer questions about its bicycles and upcoming demonstration events. The company's main blog communicates the latest news about everything from frame design and new bike colors under consideration to product awards and racing activities. It has a separate blog about both the fun and the challenges of commuting on bicycle, a topic in which its customers are intensely interested because so many do exactly that. By listening to customers and showing that it understands the daily life of its target market, Raleigh is wheeling toward higher sales in a highly competitive marketplace.[21]

Questions for Discussion

1. Of the four categories of variables, which is most important to Raleigh's segmentation strategy, and why?
2. How would you describe Raleigh's positioning for its steel-frame bicycles?
3. Raleigh sells exclusively through retail dealers, not directly to consumers. How does this affect its ability to segment the bicycle market using geographic variables?

case 6.2

Is There a Trek Bicycle for Everybody?

Trek Bicycle, founded in 1976, gets a marketing boost whenever high-profile professional racers speed off on their Trek bikes or world-class cyclists power through dirt-bike races. Based in Waterloo, Wisconsin, Trek is North America's largest bicycle manufacturer, with more than $800 million in annual sales and a worldwide network of 1,000 dealers. Knowing it can't be all things to all cyclists, Trek focuses its marketing efforts on satisfying the needs of serious cyclists seeking top-quality, high-performance bicycles for athletic training and competition, recreation, or commuting.

© iStockphoto.com/Brigitte Smith

For example, Trek has found that the lifestyles and behavior of consumers who like mountain biking are distinctly different from those of consumers who ride in city streets. Even among mountain bikers, some consumers prefer to feel the rough terrain under their wheels, while others want a smoother ride. Similarly, some urban riders are interested in style, while others care about a bike's environmental impact. Professional athletes want the very best performance, whether they're competing in a fast-paced triathlon or the grueling Tour de France.

Targeting the segments it can satisfy most effectively, Trek now offers two separate lines of mountain bikes, "hardtails" for feeling the ride and "full-suspension" for comfort. For urban riders, it markets seven models of pedal-power bikes and five bikes equipped with electric motors. For consumers who wheel around on bike paths or take a spin on city streets, Trek offers a wide variety of options, including one tandem model. The company's triathlon bicycles are designed with aerodynamics in mind, to help speed cyclists on their way to victory or through a high-powered workout.

Because one size does not fit all cyclists, Trek also designs bikes specifically for women. In addition, customers can design and equip their own bikes online using Trek's Project One configuration tool. To ensure proper fit, customers must visit a local dealer to be measured before their bikes are manufactured and delivered.

Trek's choices of product names reflect the interests of each targeted segment. For example, the Madone product line, for dedicated athletes, is named for Col de la Madone, a French mountain where Lance Armstrong has famously tested his cycling strength. Some of the commuter models are named after cities where cyclists can be seen pedaling along downtown, such as the Portland (Oregon) and the Soho (New York).

Prices for Trek's high-end Madone models can top $8,000, depending on exact specifications and customizing touches. The urban bikes range in price from $500 to more than $1,000. Many of its children's bicycles are priced above $200. These are well-made bicycles for people who want advanced engineering, stylish looks, and a great riding experience—and are willing to pay for it.

Just as Trek tailors its bikes to the needs of each customer group, it also tailors its promotional efforts. These include targeted advertising, training programs to help cyclists build their skills, and product demonstrations at parks and sporting events. Trek uses Facebook, blogs, Twitter, online videos, and e-mail newsletters to stay in touch with customers, answer questions, and gather feedback.

Supporting charitable groups such as the Lance Armstrong Foundation and the Breast Cancer Research Foundation helps the company show its commitment to social responsibility. Trek also funds DreamBikes, a nonprofit organization that recycles used bikes and trains teenagers in repair and retail sales techniques. DreamBikes asks for donations of bicycles that are unwanted or in disrepair and hires high school students to refurbish and resell the bikes, which are priced for affordability. Currently, DreamBikes has two stores in Wisconsin, with more in the planning stage.

Trek started with the mission of building the world's best bicycle. Today, it markets the bicycle as a way to be fit, reduce traffic, and make the world a greener place. Its Eco Design bicycles incorporate environmentally friendly materials and can be disassembled to recycle the parts at the end of their useful lives. The company practices what it preaches about environmental issues, using renewable power to run its manufacturing plant and providing convenient parking for employees who bicycle to work. Green targeting helps Trek attract like-minded customers as well as employees. Employees—cycling enthusiasts, like their customers—often come up with new product ideas and enjoy testing new products along the way. Where will targeting take Trek next?[22]

Questions for Discussion

1. Is Trek using an undifferentiated, concentrated, or differentiated strategy for targeting? How do you know?
2. Identify the segmentation variables that Trek is applying to consumer markets. What additional variables would you suggest that it apply, and why?
3. If marketers at Trek were trying to determine anticipated sales for a specific period, what method of forecasting would they be using?

strategic case 3

Marriott: Getting Down to Business with Business Travelers

Imagine marketing more than 3,600 hotels and resorts under 18 brands in 71 countries. That's the challenge facing Marriott, a multinational marketer that provides lodging services to millions of customers every day. The company, founded by J. Willard Marriott in 1927, started with a single root-beer stand and the "spirit to serve." Today it rings up $12 billion in global sales from guest room revenue, meals, meeting and special-event revenue, and other services.

© AP Images/Paul Sakuma

Each of Marriott's brands has its own positioning. The flagship Marriott brand, for example, stands for full service. Its properties have restaurants, meeting rooms, fitness centers, and other facilities. The JW Marriott brand is more upscale, and the Ritz-Carlton brand is known for top-quality service. Marriott's newest hotel brand is Edition, a chain of stylish, luxury hotels. TownePlace Suites are mid-priced suite hotels for customers who plan an extended stay away from home. Fairfield Inn & Suites are for businesspeople and vacationers seeking value-priced accommodations.

Sluggish economic conditions have only intensified rivalry within the hyper-competitive hotel industry. Major hotel companies such as Hilton, Hyatt, InterContinental, and Starwood all offer a wide range of hotel and resort brands for different customers' needs and tastes. In addition, local hotels and regional chains compete on the basis of location, ambience, price, amenities, and other elements. To compete effectively in this pressured environment, Marriott is relying on extensive marketing research, expert segmentation, and careful targeting.

Focus on the Customer

What exactly do hotel customers want? Marriott uses a variety of research techniques to find out about customer needs and behavior, including focus groups, online surveys, and in-room questionnaires. For example, when it conducted focus groups with customers who had stayed at its Marriott and Renaissance properties, it discovered some interesting differences. Renaissance customers said they like to open the curtains and look out the window when they first enter their rooms. In contrast, Marriott guests said they get unpacked quickly and get right to work in their rooms. "That's when we started making connections about the individual personalities that gravitate toward the Marriott brand," says the vice president of marketing strategy.

With this research in hand, marketers for the Marriott hotel brand targeted a segment they call "achievers," business travelers who feel driven to get a lot done in a short time. They created an advertising campaign to communicate that "Marriott is about productivity and performance," according to one marketing executive. The print and online ads featured interviews with six real customers, who discussed their drive to accomplish personal and professional goals.

When Marriott looked at visitors who prefer SpringHill Suites, one of its suite hotel brands, it found a slightly different profile. These are businesspeople who travel often and see a suite hotel as a place to spread out, feel refreshed, and take a break from the stress of being on the road. These customers are also heavy users of technology, especially mobile communication devices such as smartphones. In reaching out to this target market, Marriott uses mobile marketing as well as traditional media to get its message across. It invites business travelers to download its iPhone app, for example, and runs ads designed especially for viewing on smartphone screens. Customers can click on the mobile ad to check availability online or to speak with the reservations department.

One of the newer brands, Marriott Executive Apartments, combines the spacious comfort of an upscale apartment with the elegance of a luxury hotel. This brand targets affluent business and professional travelers, and their families, who plan to be in a city for several weeks or even longer. Ranging in size from a studio to three bedrooms, these accommodations have an upscale, residential ambiance and offer extras such as room service and an on-site café.

More Business from Business Customers

Marriott also targets companies that need hotel space to hold meetings and seminars. In most cases, these companies bring in attendees from outside the immediate area, which means Marriott can fill more guest rooms during meetings. Meetings usually involve additional purchases, such as snacks or meals, another profitable reason to target businesses. Sales reps at major Marriott properties are ready to help companies plan employee workshops, supplier and distributor events, and other meetings for a handful to a ballroom full of people.

Studying the needs and buying patterns of companies that hold business meetings, Marriott's marketers have found that a growing number are interested in videoconferencing and other high-tech extras. To appeal to this segment, Marriott has equipped many of its meeting rooms with the latest in recording and communications technology. Because planning and managing a business meeting of any size can be a complicated process, Marriott offers online special tools for one-stop assistance. Meeting planners can log on to view photos and floor plans of different meeting rooms, reserve space, and book hotel rooms for individual attendees. They can also use Marriott's web-based calculators to determine how large a meeting space they'll need and estimate costs. Downloadable checklists guide companies through every step, from selecting a site to promoting their meetings to attendees. Marriott understands that when a business meeting goes smoothly, the company is more likely to pick a Marriott meeting place next time around.

Targeting Green Travelers

The segment of consumers and business travelers who care about the environment is sizable these days, and Marriott wants its share of this growing market. The company has developed prototype green hotels for several of its brands, designing the public space and guest rooms with an eye toward conserving both water and energy. Marriott will build hundreds of these green hotels during the next decade. Thanks to the company's emphasis on saving power, 275 of its hotels already qualify for the U.S. Environmental Protection Agency's Energy Star designation.

Marriott is also going green by working with suppliers that operate in environmentally friendly ways. It provides pads made from recycled paper for attendees of business meetings held at its properties, for example, and buys key cards made from recycled plastic. Even the pillows in guest rooms are made from recycled plastic bottles.

Getting the Database Details Right

Marriott set up a central database to capture details such as how long customers stay and what they purchase when they stay at any of its hotels or resorts. It also stores demographic data and tracks individual preferences so it can better serve customers. By analyzing the information in this huge database, Marriott discovered that many of its customers visit more than one of its brands.

Therefore, the company created sophisticated statistical models to target customers for future marketing offers based on their history with Marriott. In one campaign, for instance, Marriott sent out 3 million e-mail messages customized according to each recipient's unique history with the hotel chain. Because of its database capabilities, Marriott was able to track whether recipients returned to one of its properties after this campaign—and actual sales results exceeded corporate expectations. This database technology has paid for itself many times over with improved targeting efficiency and higher response rates.

Watch for Marriott to continue its expansion into new markets and new brands with marketing initiatives targeting vacationers, business travelers, and meeting planners.[23]

Questions for Discussion

1. How is Marriott segmenting the market for hotel services?
2. Which of the three targeting strategies is Marriott using? Explain your answer.
3. As Marriott builds more green hotels, should it reposition its hotel brands as being environmentally friendly? Why or why not?
4. What specific types of data should Marriott have in its customer database for segmentation purposes?

ROLE-PLAY TEAM CASE EXERCISE 3

This role-play team case exercise is designed to simulate actual marketing decision making in the real world. The entire team should read the overview and background. Each student will take on a role of a particular employee within the organization. Your instructor will provide additional information and instructions related to a team decision.

SEASCAPE COMMUNICATIONS*

Background

Seascape Communications was founded in 1991 in Chicago, Illinois, by Theodore Sullivan. Sullivan had worked six years at the Apex Corporation, a company whose core product was pagers. Sullivan left the company determined to create a more sophisticated product that would meet customers' changing communication needs. Seascape Communications initially struggled against more established rivals but finally made a breakthrough in 1996 with the release of the Seascape 1, a handheld pager that operated using a wireless network.

Building upon its success, Seascape Communications continued to perform extensive market research to identify changing environmental trends. Seascape explored its core competencies and conducted a SWOT analysis that included environmental scanning and analysis to discover opportunities and threats. The company discovered that there was a significant market desire for the benefits that could be provided through smartphones. This constant monitoring enabled Seascape Communications to gain first mover advantages in an emerging industry that would soon take the world by storm: the smartphone industry.

In 2002, Seascape Communications released its first smartphone product, the Wave phone. The Wave was a combination of a pager, phone, personal calendar, and mini-computer all rolled into one. Later versions perfected the Wave so that it had advanced Internet capabilities, data storage capacity, and the ability to send e-mail, faxes, or text messages. The Wave was particularly popular in the business industry due to its portability and strong communication capabilities. Seascape quickly gained 35 percent of the smartphone market.

Recent years, however, have seen a significant increase in competition from other smartphone companies. While the Wave was a first mover in the smartphone industry, Apple's iPhone and iPad as well as the Google Android's operating system posed significant competitive threats. The Wave began to lose its edge. Although Seascape released new generations of the Wave, its features could not compare with the advanced features of its rivals. Still, the Wave managed to barely hang on due to its popularity among some of its largest business customers.

With shares lower than they have ever been, a takeover of Seascape Communications is a possibility. Seascape management knows they must act quickly to implement changes that will maintain and attract customers. With its market share decreasing, Seascape launched a major marketing research study to better understand its customer base and determine how to maintain its current market share. Because of the need to obtain feedback quickly, the company launched social media surveys to get feedback. A marketing research firm was also hired to conduct two focus groups with business customers and two focus groups with consumer customers in the United States, along with two focus groups of business customers in Europe.

---

*© O.C. Ferrell and Linda Ferrell, 2012. Jennifer Sawayda assisted with the development of this exercise under the direction of O.C. Ferrell and Linda Ferrell. This role-play case is not intended to represent the managerial decisions of an actual company.

CEO Morgan Stanton realizes that the company must act quickly if it hopes to survive. Stanton has scheduled a meeting that will consist of himself, Marketing Research Director Lyle Patrecco, and Chief Marketing Officer Stacy McDougall, who helped conduct the study. He also invited Dylan Wilder, public relations director, to provide insight from a public relations perspective and give an update on the corporate blog that she manages. Randy Cho, operations manager, will also be joining to discuss the feasibility of certain options from an operational standpoint. Stanton hopes that, by the end of the meeting, they will have constructed a list of recommendations the company can take to save Seascape from extinction. He hopes to use early findings from exploratory research to determine how to improve marketing strategies. A key concern is to recommend the appropriate target market for Seascape.

Morgan Stanton, Chief Executive Officer

You arrived at Seascape Communications in 1999 after a 10-year stint at cell phone company Sunset Inc., where you gained an in-depth knowledge of handheld devices. Your knowledge made you invaluable to then-CEO Theodore Sullivan, and you were largely influential in perfecting the initial Wave product. Seascape Communications became your life, so much so that your spouse left after claiming that you spent more time worrying about work instead of your marriage.

After taking over the reins from Sullivan in 2005, you spearheaded initiatives to grab more of the business market. Soon, Seascape was releasing upgraded Wave products with features that would appeal to business executives. At first, the initiative was largely successful. When rivals began introducing similar products to the consumer market, you didn't feel threatened, because you believed the consumer market for handheld devices and the business market were vastly different. At first, research and development seemed to keep Seascape ahead of competitors. It soon became evident, however, that this wasn't the case in the long-term. The iPad, for instance, was quickly adopted by businesses as well as consumers, becoming quite popular in the sales industry. For some time, you have been concerned about the market share that your competitors have been gaining. Your company has begun to place features on the newest Wave, such as mobile applications and games, to appeal to the consumer market, but sales in this market have been lackluster so far.

With Seascape stock hitting an all-time low, investors are getting anxious. You know Seascape will have to do something quick if it wants to save the product. To accomplish this objective, you strongly support a marketing research study to examine options. Although you are eager to take action, you know it is important to correctly assess the findings. You are especially interested in knowing how both businesses and consumers perceive your brand, whether they see it as more of a consumer product, a business product, or both. This information might help the company determine which features to add and whether it needs to be repositioned in the minds of your target market.

You are aware that the firm has tried to develop a database to improve customer services, and you are hopeful that some of this data can help provide answers. On the other hand, you are concerned about the research and development needed to develop a competitive edge in the market. One thing is for certain: you have worked too hard and sacrificed too much to see this brand go down without a fight. You know that if the company is forced to eliminate the Wave from its line, then Seascape will likely not survive. The two have become almost synonymous throughout the years.

Dylan Wilder, Public Relations Director

You joined Seascape Communications in 2009 from a small public relations company. You felt that working for such a large company was a step up and were particularly proud that you had achieved such a high managerial position before you turned 30. At first, you found the work exhilarating. You love talking to reporters and being in front of the camera.

Lately, however, the questions asked about your company have all been negative. In a recent television interview, you were bombarded with questions about why the company feels it is losing market share, how it plans on competing against competitors, and whether the rumors about selling the company were true. Fans on the Wave's Facebook page have dropped, and you know from postings that the public views the Wave as inferior to the competition. Otherwise, you know very little about why the Wave is failing except for the little information that corporate gives you. Although you have sent several press releases to major news outlets, many of them are no longer running your releases. Rather, criticism about the company seems to be increasing in volume. All these factors make it much harder to do your job.

Part of your job is to manage the company's corporate blog on the Wave, while other members of your department manage the company's Twitter and Facebook accounts. You have never been very adept at computers, so this is not your favorite part of the job. Still, it gives you the chance to post updates and respond to blog comments. Most of the people who respond are fans. Even in the midst of trouble, you are happy to see that there are still people who are committed to the company. However, fewer people are responding compared to a year ago, and some of the comments on the blog have been negative.

You heard something about a marketing research study being conducted and know very little about how this will get the company back on track, but you are anxious to learn more. As part of the study, you were told to create a blog post asking users "How do you like your Wave?" and "How do you use your Wave?", along with a series of 10 survey questions. You are excited to see that many people have commented. From your observations, a large number of fans seem to like the Wave, but it is obvious that some feel competing products are easier to use and have many more applications. Although it is the job of the chief marketing officer and the marketing research director to analyze the results, what you have learned so far may provide you with more information for your media interviews.

You are not sure what actions management will pursue, but you will try to portray their actions in the most positive light possible. You have been called to attend a meeting tomorrow to provide input on the best way to handle the situation from a public relations perspective.

Stacy McDougall, Chief Marketing Officer

You have been with the company since it was first founded and are a close friend of Theodore Sullivan. In the beginning, you felt that Seascape did a wonderful job of identifying market opportunities and creating a quality product that the market desired. You even began opening a chain of Wave stores, starting with the company's first trial store outside of Chicago. In the past few years, however, you have felt that the company was not reacting quickly enough to market changes. The most recent Wave model was a flop, and you feel it is because it tried too hard to appeal to both business and consumer markets and ended up doing neither. Without a clear brand identity and target market, you don't know how the Wave is going to make it. Wave's troubles have halted any thought of opening additional Wave stores in the near future.

As chief marketing officer, you are so busy with your responsibilities that you were able to give little thought to marketing research. A few months ago, Seascape decided to hire a marketing research firm. You were excited that Seascape finally seemed to take the job of marketing research so seriously but wonder if it is too late. The Wave has lost so much market share in the smartphone market that you have heard rumors of selling the brand. You sincerely hope this does not happen as you do not know how Seascape Communications will survive otherwise.

Seascape asked the marketing research firm it hired to conduct studies identifying why the Wave was losing market share to its competitors. As a result, you were asked to help the marketing research director, Lyle Patrecco, create the study and analyze the data by constructing questions to place on Wave's Facebook page and blog and arranging focus groups in America and Europe. You felt that it was important to learn more about business customers that were the most loyal target market in the past. You also helped interpret the results when they came in. You knew that the marketing research you were helping to conduct would be difficult to interpret in making a decision about improving the marketing strategy. The firm needed to also identify the existing databases, such as industry trade articles, internal sales reports, and data from the customer relationship management (CRM) system, which recognized different types of customers as they were asked to register their Wave purchases.

Although it took you and Lyle several weeks to come up with quantitative results from all the data, the two of you have finally put together a report to share with the CEO. Some of the results are very interesting. For instance, only about 5 percent of respondents that do not currently own a Wave indicated that they would purchase a Wave over a rival product. However, another 25 percent stated that they might consider purchasing the Wave if it was easier to use and had more features. The majority of respondents that currently use the Wave product, about 85 percent, indicated that they primarily use it for work purposes. One of the biggest questions is whether the Wave should be modified even further to appeal to both the consumer and business markets to compete more head-to-head with Apple's products and Google's Android, or whether it should stick to its original target market of corporate buyers. The CEO expects you to use what you learned from the marketing research study to make recommendations on how Seascape can improve market share.

Lyle Patrecco, Marketing Research Director

You graduated at the top of your class from Brown University with an MBA in marketing and immediately left to found your own marketing research firm. A few months ago, your firm was hired by Seascape Communications to conduct a marketing research study. The study's main purpose was to determine why businesses and consumers were choosing rival products over the Wave as well as to provide some insight into what Seascape could do to regain market share.

You decided to use two different methods to collect information. To get consumers' initial reactions as well as recommendations on how to make the Wave a better product, you used social media surveys. You worked with Seascape's chief marketing officer, Stacy McDougall, to create a Facebook page along with a short list of survey questions, such as "What are features you would like to see on the Wave?" You asked the public relations director to post similar questions on Wave's corporate blog, and comments immediately started to roll in.

To get more detailed information about how people feel about the Wave, you decided to conduct focus group interviews. While the key concern was retaining business customers, two of the focus groups were done with U.S. consumers that didn't use the phone for their businesses. You arranged to have four focus groups total in the United States and two in Europe, with members of your firm observing. By asking questions similar to "How do you like your Wave?", "How do you use your Wave?", and "Would you purchase the Wave over a competitor's product?", your firm hoped it could understand why the Wave was losing market share so rapidly.

From the studies, you realize now that the public sees the Wave as failing to keep up with new technological features. In general, it's perceived as a device that's harder to use than competitor products and cannot run some of the software and applications that consumers desire the most. One focus group participant stated, "I can use the iPhone both at work and home. So why would I need the Wave? It's a business product." On the other hand, another business focus group participant responded, "But the Wave should purely be a business product. That's what I use it for. Why have the last few products been tailored toward the consumer market? It doesn't make sense."

While the Wave has the largest share of the business market (firms purchase the phone for employees), the iPhone is making advances into the market segment. The business focus groups indicated that employees started bringing their iPhones and iPads to work and created buzz about how much easier these devices were to use. There were also indications that the iPhone was considered a higher quality product, and the applications available on the iPhone kept coming up in all of the focus groups. The consumer focus groups and Facebook postings confirmed that consumers saw the iPhone and Android operating systems as superior to the Wave's operating system. It was obvious that the consumer market needed better technology to keep up with the competition. Many Facebook users indicated a desire to see a better designed, easier-to-use product that could play the most popular games and applications. You have great faith in social media as a marketing research tool and are thinking about suggesting to Seascape's CEO the idea of using crowdsourcing to try to solicit more detailed product suggestions. Perhaps the company could offer a prize for the best consumer idea.

Randy Cho, Operations Manager

You have been with the company for more than eight years and love the Wave brand. It seems strange to you that other consumers do not share your enthusiasm for the product. You prefer simpler products and don't understand how consumers could possibly prefer the more complicated rival products. In your view, all those extra gadgets simply take away from the main purpose of the core product.

As operations manager, you are responsible for overseeing and controlling the production process. The latest version of the Wave has been more complicated than previous generations and has caused your team some problems. With management hoping to appeal more to the consumer market, the newest Wave came equipped with more applications and features to create a more integrated experience for consumers. Unfortunately, you failed to realize the extra amount of time it would take to build in these features. With only a small amount of time before the launch date, you were forced to redesign the production process at the last minute to make sure the products would be produced in time. As you half-expected, consumers did not warm up to the new features, and sales were lackluster. There have also been reports that the newer versions of the Wave have not performed as well as previous generations. You strongly believe that the Wave is a business product; hence, all the extra features put into the latest version to appeal to the consumer market were a waste of time. It is clear that research and development has not been linked to an understanding of market segments. Now, all of the Wave products seem to be falling behind the iPhone and Android products.

You know that Seascape's stock has dropped quite a bit and have begun to hear rumors that Seascape might have to sell the Wave brand. Although you doubt CEO Morgan Stanton would agree to this, if changes are not made to begin regaining market share, there may be few options left. You hope the new marketing research study you heard about will identify opportunities to salvage the Wave brand. You have been invited to the meeting to discuss the feasibility of options from an operational standpoint. The CEO is counting on your expertise to help him understand whether the company's manufacturing facilities have enough capacity to handle the alternatives that will be discussed, as well as how long it might take to implement certain changes in the production process. You know that any wide-scale changes in the product will take a long time to implement at the company's current level of quality.

NOTES

[1]Based on information in Mark Albright, "LEGOLAND Rolls Out a Park Plan," *St. Petersburg Times (Florida),* November 30, 2011, 5B; William Harvey, "Block Party!" *St. Petersburg Times (Florida)*, October 27, 2011, 8; Mark Albright, "Hope Building that LEGOLAND Will Prosper," *St. Petersburg Times (Florida),* October 15, 2011, 1B; Brooks Barnes, "From Britain, It's LEGOLAND," *The New York Times,* October 16, 2011, www.nytimes.com.

[2]"LS Hybrid," Lexus, www.lexus.com/models/LSh/features/pricing.html (accessed February 21, 2012).

[3]Jack Neff and Rupal Parekh, "Dove Takes Its New Men's Line to the Super Bowl," *Ad Age*, January 5, 2010.

[4]Cotton Timberlake, "Kate Spade's Got a Brand New Bag," *Bloomberg Businessweek*, February 24, 2011, www.businessweek.com/magazine/content/11_10/b4218023895330.htm?chan=innovation_branding_top+stories.

[5]Shelly DuBois, "The Metropolitan Opera's New Act," CNN, January 11, 2012, http://management.fortune.cnn.com/2012/01/11/metropolitan-opera-peter-gelb/?iid=HP_River.

[6]Service Corporation International, www.sci-corp.com/SCICORP/home.aspx (accessed February 21, 2012).

[7]Lindsay M. Howden and Julie A. Meyer, "Age and Sex Composition: 2010," U.S. Census Bureau, May 2011, www.census.gov/prod/cen2010/briefs/c2010br-03.pdf.

[8]"VTech Debuts Tablet for Kids—InnoTab," Press Release, February 10, 2011, www.vtech.com/en/press/press-release/2011/292-vtech-debuts-tablet-for-kids-innopad.

[9]Bruce Horovitz, "Marketing to Kids Gets More Savvy with New Technologies," *USA Today*, August 15, 2011, www.usatoday.com/money/industries/retail/2011-07-27-new-technolgies-for-marketing-to-kids_n.htm.

[10]U.S. Census Bureau, *Statistical Abstract of the United States, 2012*, Table 7, www.census.gov/compendia/statab/cats/population.html (accessed March 22, 2012).

[11]"Marketing to Women—Quick Facts," She-Conomy, http://she-conomy.com/report/marketing-to-women-quick-facts/ (accessed February 21, 2012).

[12]"About Us," SoftSheen-Carson, www.softsheen-carson.com/_us/_en/about-us/index.aspx (accessed February 21, 2012).

[13]"Families and Living Arrangements," U.S. Census Bureau, www.census.gov/population/www/socdemo/hh-fam.html (accessed February 21, 2012), Tables F1 and MS-2.

[14]Tiffany Hsu, "Taco Bell Trying 'First Meal' Break and Fresh 'Cantina' Options," *Los Angeles Times,* January 21, 2012, www.latimes.com/business/money/la-fi-mo-taco-bell-breakfast-20120120,0,1543035.story.

[15]Joseph T. Plummer, "The Concept and Application of Life Style Segmentation," *Journal of Marketing* (January 1974): 33.

[16]SRI Consulting Business Intelligence, "About VALS™," www.strategicbusinessinsights.com/vals/international.shtml (accessed February 21, 2012).

[17]Philip Kotler and Kevin Keller, *Marketing Management*, 14th ed. (Englewood Cliffs, NJ: Prentice Hall, 2012).

[18]Jessica E. Vascellaro, Shara Tibken, and Jeffrey A. Trachtenberg, "Apple Jumps into Textbooks," *The Wall Street Journal,* January 20, 2012, http://online.wsj.com/article/SB10001424052970204555904577169523446883172.html?mod=WSJ_Tech_RightMostPopular.

[19]Charles W. Chase Jr., "Selecting the Appropriate Forecasting Method," *Journal of Business Forecasting* (Fall 1997): 2, 23, 28–29.

[20]"Fresher Taco Bell? Bakersfield Becoming Go-To Test Market," *Bakersfield Now*, January 20, 2012, www.bakersfieldnow.com/news/business/A-fresher-Taco-Bell-Bakersfield-becoming-go-to-test-market-137782233.html.

[21]Mark Sutton, "Raleigh Trade Show: Teaching an Old Bike New Tricks," Bike Biz, March 16, 2012, www.bikebiz.com; "BRAINy Awards Honor Individuals," Bicycle Retailer and Industry News, April 15, 2010, www.bicycleretailer.com; Francis Lawell, "Raleigh: Cycling to Success?" Business Review (UK), February 2009, 16ff; "Industry Overview 2008," National Bicycle Dealers Association, http://nbda.com; www.raleighusa.com.

[22]"Tim's Travels: Building a Better Bike," NBC 15 (Madison, WI), February 29, 2012, www.nbc15.com; "Trek's John Burke Testifies in Congress," Bicycle Retailer, March 31, 2011, www.bicycleretailer.com; Tom Held, "DreamBikes Opens a Store and Opportunities in Milwaukee," *Journal Sentinel,* April 7, 2010, www.jsonline.com; "Trek Announces Title Sponsorship of 2010 Dirt Series," Mountain Bike Review, February 3, 2010, http://reviews.mtbr.com/; Joe Vanden Plas, "CIO Leadership: Trek's Brent Leland Cycles through Business-IT Alignment," Wisconsin Technology Network FusionCIO, February 24, 2009, http://wistechnology.com; www.trekbikes.com.

[23]Scott Mayerowitz, "CEO Bill Marriott Reflects on 40 Years Leading Hotel Giant," Associated Press, March 18, 2012, www.seattletimes.com; Ghazanfar Ali Khan, "World-Class Marriott Project in Riyadh Targets Booming Business Travel Trade," Arab News, March 12, 2012, http://arabnews.com; Rick Swanborg, "How Marriott Broke Down Customer Data Siloes," CIO, November 11, 2009, www.cio.com; "Marriott Partners with AT&T and Cisco for Virtual Meetings," Hotel Marketing, January 28, 2010, www.hotelmarketing.com; Dan Butcher, "Marriott Exec Reveals Multichannel Mobile Strategy for SpringHill Suites," Mobile Marketer, November 25, 2009, www.mobilemarketer.com; Helen Coster and Laurie Burkitt, "In These Ads, Customers Are the Celebrities," Forbes, September 2, 2009, www.forbes.com; www.marriott.com.

Feature Notes

[a]Based on information in Stuart Elliott, "Absolut Celebrates Its 30 Years of Marketing to Gay Consumers," *The New York Times,* October 26, 2011, www.nytimes.com; Melissa Dribben, "How Philadelphia Welcomed Gay and Lesbian Tourism," *Philadelphia Inquirer,* July 14, 2011, www.philly.com; "USA—The Halal Meat Trade," *Meat Trade Daily* (UK), January 15, 2011, www.meattradedaily.uk.com.

[b]Based on information in "Ikea Adding Solar Power in Canton, Other Midwest Stores," CBS Detroit, January 12, 2012, http://Detroit.cbslocal.com; "Ikea: Stock Market Pressures Hinder Sustainability," Environmental Leader, September 20, 2011, www.environmentalleader.com; Ola Kinnander, "Ikea's Challenge to the Wooden Shipping Pallet," *Bloomberg Businessweek,* November 23, 2011, www.businessweek.com; "Ikea Installs Electric Car Charging Stations in Costa Mesa," Los Angeles Business, December 7, 2011, www.bizjournals.com; Jonathan Bardelline, "IKEA Boosting Stock of Sustainable Goods with Eco Scoreboard," Green Biz, March 30, 2011, www.greenbiz.com.

[c]Based on information in Gregory Schmidt, "Toy Companies Turn to Nostalgia to Celebrate Anniversaries," *The New York Times,* July 11, 2011, www.nytimes.com; Michelle Kung, "Sony Whips Up 'Smurfs' Marketing Frenzy," *The Wall Street Journal,* July 28, 2011, www.wsj.com; Fu Yu, "Smurfs Head Back to China's Screens," *China Daily,* April 8, 2011, http://usa.chinadaily.com.cn; Alex Ben Block, "'Smurfs' vs. 'Cars 2,'" *Hollywood Reporter,* August 16, 2011, www.hollywoodreporter.com.

[d]Based on information in Richard Nieva, "Skullcandy's Delicious Ride," *Fortune,* November 22, 2011, www.fortune.com; Margaret Heffernan, "Skullcandy: How a Small Company Reaches a Big Market," *CBS Marketwatch,* January 11, 2011, www.cbsnews.com; Steven Oberbeck, "Utah's Skullcandy Continues Turnaround in Q2," *Salt Lake City Tribune,* August 16, 2011, www.sltrib.com; "The Service Dude," *Fortune,* December 26, 2011, 21.

Buying Behavior, Global Marketing, and Digital Marketing

PART 4 continues the focus on the customer. Understanding elements that affect buying decisions enables marketers to analyze customers' needs and evaluate how specific marketing strategies can satisfy those needs. CHAPTER 7 examines consumer buying decision processes and factors that influence buying decisions. CHAPTER 8 stresses business markets, organizational buyers, the buying center, and the organizational buying decision process. In CHAPTER 9, the actions, involvement, and strategies of marketers that serve international customers are considered. CHAPTER 10 examines digital marketing strategies, new communication channels, such as social networking, and customer behavior related to these emerging technologies and trends.

part 4

chapter 7

Consumer Buying Behavior

OBJECTIVES

1. To recognize the stages of the consumer buying decision process
2. To understand the types of consumer decision making and the level of involvement
3. To explore how situational influences may affect the consumer buying decision process
4. To understand the psychological influences that may affect the consumer buying decision process
5. To examine the social influences that may affect the consumer buying decision process
6. To examine consumer misbehavior

MARKETING INSIGHTS

General Mills Gobbles Up Gluten-Free Sales

Betty Crocker's smiling face has new meaning these days for the millions of U.S. consumers who are unable to tolerate foods with gluten, a protein commonly found in wheat, barley, and rye. Until recently, these consumers had very limited choices when shopping for gluten-free cereals, cakes, and other packaged foods in local grocery stores. Now General Mills, which owns Betty Crocker, Chex, and many other well-known food brands, has begun a major initiative to put hundreds of gluten-free foods onto supermarket shelves.

Consumers with celiac disease must stick to a gluten-free diet. In addition, many other consumers are sensitive to gluten or choose to eliminate it from their diets for health reasons. As a result, demand for gluten-free foods is growing quickly, and annual purchases are currently estimated at $6 billion. General Mills recognized this as an opportunity in 2007, when its food scientists first cooked up gluten-free Rice Chex. Next, the company began reformulating cakes and cookies, a difficult task because gluten helps give baked goods both height and texture. After hundreds of experiments, however, General Mills succeeded. Now the company markets more than 300 foods prominently marked as gluten-free, and every year it introduces dozens more.

To educate consumers about the benefits of a gluten-free diet, offer suitable recipes, and sell gluten-free foods, General Mills became the driving force behind GlutenFreely.com. Despite increased competition from Kellogg's and other mainstream food marketers that now offer gluten-free products, General Mills is building a loyal and lucrative following among consumers who need or want to avoid gluten.[1]

© ZUMA Press/Newscom

General Mills and many other traditional and online marketers go to great lengths to understand their customers' needs and gain a better grasp of customers' **buying behavior**: the decision processes and actions of people involved in buying and using products. **Consumer buying behavior** refers to the buying behavior of ultimate consumers—those who purchase products for personal or household use and not for business purposes. Marketers attempt to understand buying behavior for several reasons. First, customers' overall opinions and attitudes toward a firm's products have a great impact on the firm's success. Second, as we saw in Chapter 1, the marketing concept stresses that a firm should create a marketing mix that satisfies customers. To find out what satisfies buyers, marketers must examine the main influences on what, where, when, and how consumers buy. Third, by gaining a deeper understanding of the factors that affect buying behavior, marketers are in a better position to predict how consumers will respond to marketing strategies.

In this chapter, we first examine the major stages of the consumer buying decision process, beginning with problem recognition, information search, and evaluation of alternatives and proceeding through purchase and postpurchase evaluation. We follow this with an examination of how the customer's level of involvement affects the type of decision making employed and discuss the types of consumer decision-making processes. Next, we examine situational influences—surroundings, time, purchase reason, and buyer's mood and condition—that affect purchasing decisions. We go on to consider psychological influences on purchasing decisions: perception, motives, learning, attitudes, personality and self-concept, and lifestyles. Next, we discuss social influences that affect buying behavior, including roles, family, reference groups and opinion leaders, social classes, and culture and subcultures. We conclude with a discussion of consumer misbehavior.

buying behavior The decision processes and actions of people involved in buying and using products

consumer buying behavior The decision processes and purchasing activities of people who purchase products for personal or household use and not for business purposes

consumer buying decision process A five-stage purchase decision process that includes problem recognition, information search, evaluation of alternatives, purchase, and postpurchase evaluation

CONSUMER BUYING DECISION PROCESS

The **consumer buying decision process**, shown in Figure 7.1, includes five stages: problem recognition, information search, evaluation of alternatives, purchase, and postpurchase evaluation. Before we examine each stage, consider these important points. First, as shown in

Figure 7.1 Consumer Buying Decision Process and Possible Influences on the Process

Possible influences on the decision process

Situational influences
- Physical surroundings
- Social surroundings
- Time
- Purchase reason
- Buyer's mood and condition

Psychological influences
- Perception
- Motives
- Learning
- Attitudes
- Personality and self-concept
- Lifestyles

Social influences
- Roles
- Family
- Reference groups
- Opinion leaders
- Social classes
- Culture and subcultures

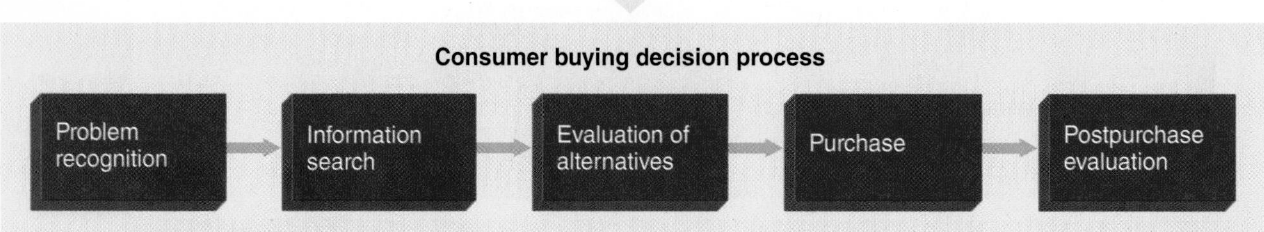

Figure 7.1, this process can be affected by situational, psychological, and social influences. Second, the actual act of purchasing is just one stage in the process and usually not the first stage. Third, even though we indicate that a purchase occurs, not all decision processes lead to a purchase; individuals may end the process at any stage. Finally, not all consumer decisions include all five stages.

Problem Recognition

Problem recognition occurs when a buyer becomes aware of a difference between a desired state and an actual condition. Consider a female student who owns an older, out-of-date calculator, and she learns that a newer calculator is going to be necessary to run software required for class. She recognizes that a difference exists between the desired state—having a programmable calculator—and her actual condition. She therefore decides to buy a new calculator.

The speed of consumer problem recognition can be quite rapid or rather slow. Sometimes a person has a problem or need but is unaware of it. Marketers use sales personnel, advertising, and packaging to help trigger recognition of such needs or problems. For example, a university bookstore may advertise programmable calculators in the school newspaper at the beginning of the term. Students who see the advertisement may recognize that they need these calculators for their course work.

Problem Recognition
This advertisement is attempting to stimulate problem recognition regarding the protection of one's computer.

Information Search

After recognizing the problem or need, a buyer (if continuing the decision process) searches for product information that will help resolve the problem or satisfy the need. To reference the example given earlier, after recognizing her need for a new calculator, the student may search for information about different types and brands of calculators. She acquires information over time from her surroundings. However, the information's impact depends on how she interprets it.

An information search has two aspects. In an **internal search**, buyers search their memories for information about products that might solve their problem. If they cannot retrieve enough information from memory to make a decision, they seek additional information from outside sources in an **external search**. The external search may focus on communication with friends or relatives, comparison of available brands and prices, marketer-dominated sources, and/or public sources. An individual's personal contacts—friends, relatives, and coworkers—often are influential sources of information because the person trusts and respects them. However, research suggests that consumers may overestimate friends' knowledge about products and their ability to evaluate them. Using marketer-dominated sources of information, such as salespeople, advertising, websites, package labeling, and in-store demonstrations and displays, typically requires little effort on the consumer's part. Indeed, the Internet has become a major information source during the consumer buying decision process, especially for product and pricing information. Buyers also obtain information from independent sources—for instance, government reports, news presentations, publications such as *Consumer Reports,* and reports from product-testing organizations. Consumers frequently view information from these sources as highly credible because of their factual and unbiased nature.

Repetition, a technique well-known to advertisers, increases consumers' learning of information. When they see or hear an advertising message for the first time, recipients may not grasp all its important details, but they learn more details as the message is repeated. Nevertheless, even when commercials are initially effective, repetition eventually may cause wear-out, meaning consumers pay less attention to the commercial and respond to it less favorably than they did at first. Information can be presented verbally, numerically, or visually. Marketers pay great attention to the visual components of their advertising materials.

internal search An information search in which buyers search their memories for information about products that might solve their problem

external search An information search in which buyers seek information from sources other than their memories

Evaluation of Alternatives

A successful information search within a product category yields a group of brands that a buyer views as possible alternatives. This group of brands is sometimes called a **consideration set** (also called an *evoked set*). For example, a consideration set of computers might include desktop, laptop, and notebook computers from Dell, Toshiba, and HP. Research suggests that consumers assign a greater value to a brand they have heard of than to one they have not—even when they do not know anything else about the brand. Thus, when attempting to choose between two airlines for an emergency trip, most consumers will choose the one they have heard of over an unfamiliar name.

To assess the products in a consideration set, the buyer uses **evaluative criteria**: objective characteristics (such as the size) and subjective characteristics (such as style) that are important to him or her. Consider that one buyer may want a large display, whereas another may want a computer with a large amount of memory. The buyer also assigns a certain level of importance to each criterion: some features and characteristics carry more weight than others. The buyer rates and eventually ranks brands in the consideration set using the preceding criteria. The evaluation stage may yield no brand the buyer is willing to purchase. In that case, a further information search may be necessary.

Marketers may influence consumers' evaluations by *framing* the alternatives—that is, describing the alternatives and their attributes in a certain manner. Framing can make a characteristic seem more important to a consumer and facilitate its recall from memory. For example, by stressing a car's superior comfort and safety features over those of a competitor's, a carmaker can direct consumers' attention toward these points of superiority. Framing probably influences the decision processes of inexperienced buyers more than those of experienced ones. If the evaluation of alternatives yields one or more brands that the consumer is willing to buy, he or she is ready to move on to the next stage of the decision process: the purchase.

consideration set A group of brands within a product category that a buyer views as alternatives for possible purchase

evaluative criteria Objective and subjective product characteristics that are important to a buyer

Purchase

In the purchase stage, the consumer chooses the product or brand to be bought. Selection is based on the outcome of the evaluation stage and on other dimensions. Product availability may influence which brand is purchased. For instance, if the brand that ranked highest in evaluation is unavailable, the buyer may purchase the brand that ranked second. If a consumer

Going Green

How Green Is That Product? Check the App!

In a world filled with alternatives, how do you evaluate products or brands that offer similar benefits? The answer, for many consumers, is to check a product's environmental record before making a buying decision. There's an app for that—actually, any number of mobile apps are available to help consumers determine which goods or services are the greenest alternatives.

Consumers who download the GoodGuide app, for example, first select the criteria they want to apply to a product, such as how energy efficient it is and whether it contains natural ingredients. Next, they scan the product's bar code with a cell phone. The app instantly checks GoodGuide's database of 140,000 products and displays a numerical score, from 0 to 10. The higher the score, the greener the product.

The Green Fuel app helps consumers find the nearest gas station offering alternative fuels such as compressed natural gas. The Light Bulb Finder app suggests energy-efficient alternatives to traditional incandescent light bulbs, personalized for each user's zip code and power situation. The Find Green app directs users toward local businesses that offer green goods and services. And the eLabel app reveals a product's carbon and water footprint.[a]

wants a pair of black Nikes and cannot find them in his size, he may buy a pair of black Reeboks.

During this stage, buyers also pick the seller from which they will buy the product. The choice of seller may affect final product selection and therefore the terms of sale, which, if negotiable, are determined at this stage. Other issues, such as price, delivery, warranties, maintenance agreements, installation, and credit arrangements, are also settled. Finally, the actual purchase takes place during this stage, unless the consumer decides to terminate the buying decision process.

Postpurchase Evaluation

After the purchase, the buyer begins evaluating the product to ascertain if its actual performance meets expected levels. Many criteria used in evaluating alternatives are applied again during postpurchase evaluation. The outcome of this stage is either satisfaction or dissatisfaction, which influences whether the consumer complains, communicates with other possible buyers, and repurchases the brand or product.

Shortly after the purchase of an expensive product, evaluation may result in **cognitive dissonance**, doubts in the buyer's mind about whether purchasing the product was the right decision. For instance, a customer who spends extra to purchase a hybrid car because of its high gas mileage might have second thoughts upon finding out that the vehicle's actual mileage is not nearly as good as promised. Cognitive dissonance is most likely to arise when a person has recently bought an expensive, high-involvement product that lacks some of the desirable features of competing brands. A buyer who is experiencing cognitive dissonance may attempt to return the product or seek positive information about it to justify choosing it. Marketers sometimes attempt to reduce cognitive dissonance by having salespeople telephone or e-mail recent purchasers to make sure they are satisfied with their new purchases. At times, recent buyers are sent results of studies showing that other consumers are very satisfied with the brand.

As Figure 7.1 shows, three major categories of influences are believed to affect the consumer buying decision process: situational, psychological, and social. In the remainder of this chapter, we focus on these influences. Although we discuss each major influence separately, their effects on the consumer decision process are interrelated.

TYPES OF CONSUMER DECISION MAKING AND LEVEL OF INVOLVEMENT

To acquire products that satisfy their current and future needs, consumers must engage in decision making. People engage in different types of decision-making processes depending on the nature of the products involved. The amount of effort, both mental and physical, that buyers expend in solving problems also varies considerably. A major determinant of the type of decision-making process employed depends on the customer's **level of involvement**: the degree of interest in a product and the importance the individual places on that product. High-involvement products tend to be those that are visible to others (such as clothing, furniture, or automobiles) and are expensive. High-importance issues, such as health care, are also associated with high levels of involvement. Low-involvement products tend to be less expensive and have less associated social risk, such as many grocery items. A person's interest in a product or product category that is ongoing and long term is referred to as *enduring involvement.* For instance, a consumer who is interested in technology might always have the most advanced electronic devices, read electronics magazines, and work in a related field. However, most consumers have an enduring involvement with only a very few activities or items. In contrast, *situational involvement* is temporary and dynamic, and it results from a particular set of circumstances, such as the need to buy a new car after being involved in an accident. For a short

cognitive dissonance A buyer's doubts shortly after a purchase about whether the decision was the right one

level of involvement An individual's degree of interest in a product and the importance of the product for that person

Table 7.1 Consumer Decision Making

	Routinized Response	Limited	Extended
Product cost	Low	Low to moderate	High
Search effort	Little	Little to moderate	Extensive
Time spent	Short	Short to medium	Lengthy
Brand preference	More than one is acceptable, although one may be preferred	Several	Varies; usually many

time period, the consumer will visit car dealerships, visit a car company's website, or even purchase automotive-related magazines or books. However, once the car purchase is made, the consumer's interest and involvement taper off. Consumer involvement may be attached to product categories (such as sports), loyalty to a specific brand, interest in a specific advertisement (e.g., a funny commercial) or a medium (such as a particular television show), or to certain decisions and behaviors (e.g., a love of shopping). On the other hand, a consumer may find a particular advertisement entertaining but still not get involved with the brand advertised because of loyalty to another brand. Involvement level, as well as other factors, affects a person's selection of one of three types of consumer decision making: routinized response behavior, limited decision making, or extended decision making (Table 7.1).

routinized response behavior A consumer decision-making process used when buying frequently purchased, low-cost items that require very little search-and-decision effort

limited decision making A consumer decision-making process used when purchasing products occasionally or needing information about an unfamiliar brand in a familiar product category

A consumer uses **routinized response behavior** when buying frequently purchased, low-cost items that require very little search-and-decision effort. When buying such items, a consumer may prefer a particular brand but is familiar with several brands in the product class and views more than one as acceptable. Typically, low-involvement products are bought through routinized response behavior—that is, almost automatically. For example, most buyers spend little time or effort selecting soft drinks or cereals.

Buyers engage in **limited decision making** when they buy products occasionally or when they need to obtain information about an unfamiliar brand in a familiar product category. This type of decision making requires a moderate amount of time for information gathering and deliberation. For instance, if Procter & Gamble introduces an improved Tide laundry

Low-Involvement Products
Soft drinks are low-involvement products, because they are inexpensive and purchased frequently. When buying soft drinks, consumers usually employ routinized response behavior.

detergent, interested buyers will seek additional information about the new product, perhaps by asking a friend who has used it, watching a commercial about it, or visiting the company's website, before making a trial purchase.

The most complex type of decision making, **extended decision making**, occurs when purchasing unfamiliar, expensive, or infrequently bought products—for instance, a car, home, or college education. The buyer uses many criteria to evaluate alternative brands or choices and spends much time seeking information and deciding on the purchase. Extended decision making is frequently used for purchasing high-involvement products.

Purchase of a particular product does not always elicit the same type of decision-making process. In some instances, we engage in extended decision making the first time we buy a certain product but find that limited decision making suffices when we buy it again. If a routinely purchased, formerly satisfying brand no longer satisfies us, we may use limited or extended decision making to switch to a new brand. Thus, if we notice that the brand of pain reliever we normally buy is no longer working well, we may seek out a different brand through limited decision making. Most consumers occasionally make purchases solely on impulse and not on the basis of any of these three decision-making processes. **Impulse buying** involves no conscious planning but results from a powerful urge to buy something immediately.

SITUATIONAL INFLUENCES ON THE BUYING DECISION PROCESS

Situational influences result from circumstances, time, and location that affect the consumer buying decision process. Imagine buying an automobile tire after noticing, while washing your car, that the current tire is badly worn; this is a different experience from buying a tire right after a blowout on the highway spoils your vacation. Situational factors can influence the buyer during any stage of the consumer buying decision process and may cause the individual to shorten, lengthen, or terminate the process. Situational factors can be classified into five categories: physical surroundings, social surroundings, time perspective, reason for purchase, and the buyer's momentary mood and condition.[2]

Physical surroundings include location, store atmosphere, aromas, sounds, lighting, weather, and other factors in the physical environment in which the decision process occurs. Retail chains should try to design their store environment and layout in a way that makes shopping as enjoyable

extended decision making A consumer decision-making process employed when purchasing unfamiliar, expensive, or infrequently bought products

impulse buying An unplanned buying behavior resulting from a powerful urge to buy something immediately

situational influences Influences that result from circumstances, time, and location that affect the consumer buying decision process

Situational Influences
Because physical surroundings are situational influences, retailers spend considerable resources on store interiors, and sometimes exteriors, to make the customer's experience more favorable.

and easy as possible, so consumers are more willing to buy items from that store. In order to keep up with changing consumer buying habits and to maintain high productivity, major grocery chain, Kroger, has been working to remodel many of its stores around the nation.[3] Marketers at banks, department stores, and specialty stores go to considerable effort and expense to create physical settings that are conducive to making purchase decisions. Most restaurant chains, such as Olive Garden and Chili's, invest heavily in facilities, often building from the ground up, to provide special surroundings that enhance customers' dining experiences. In some settings, dimensions such as weather, traffic sounds, and odors are clearly beyond the marketers' control; instead, marketers must try to make customers more comfortable. General climatic conditions, for example, may influence a customer's decision to buy a specific type of vehicle (such as an SUV) and certain accessories (such as four-wheel drive). Current weather conditions, depending on whether they are favorable or unfavorable, may be either encouraging or discouraging to consumers when they are deciding whether to go shopping to seek out specific products.

Social surroundings include characteristics and interactions of others who are present during a purchase decision, such as friends, relatives, salespeople, and other customers. Buyers may feel pressured to behave in a certain way because they are in a public place such as a restaurant, store, or sports arena. Thoughts about who will be around when the product is used or consumed are another dimension of the social setting. An overcrowded store or an argument between a customer and a salesperson may cause consumers to leave the store.

The time dimension, too, influences the buying decision process in several ways, such as the amount of time required to become knowledgeable about a product, to search for it, and to buy and use it. For instance, more men are buying diamond engagement rings online, partly to make an informed decision at their own convenience. An online jeweler like Blue Nile features a comfortable, anonymous, easy-to-use website to help men educate themselves about diamonds and then select a unique combination from its large inventory of diamonds and settings.[4] Time plays a major role in that the buyer considers the possible frequency of product use, the length of time required to use the product, and the length of the overall product life. Other time dimensions that influence purchases include time of day, day of the week or month, seasons, and holidays. The amount of time pressure a consumer is under affects how much time is devoted to purchase decisions. A customer under severe time constraints is likely to either make a quick purchase decision or delay a decision.

The purchase reason raises the questions of what exactly the product purchase should accomplish and for whom. Generally, consumers purchase an item for their own use, for household use, or as a gift. For example, people who are buying a gift may buy a different product from one they would buy for themselves. If you own a Mont Blanc pen, for example, it is unlikely that you bought it for yourself.

The buyer's momentary moods (such as anger, anxiety, or contentment) or momentary conditions (fatigue, illness, or the possession of cash) may have a bearing on the consumer buying decision process. These moods or conditions immediately precede the current situation and are not chronic. Any of these moods or conditions can affect a person's ability and desire to search for information, receive information, or seek and evaluate alternatives. Research suggests that sad buyers are more inclined to take risks, whereas happy buyers are more likely to be risk averse when making buying decisions. Moods can also significantly influence a consumer's postpurchase evaluation.

PSYCHOLOGICAL INFLUENCES ON THE BUYING DECISION PROCESS

psychological influences Factors that in part determine people's general behavior, thus influencing their behavior as consumers

Psychological influences partly determine people's general behavior and thus influence their behavior as consumers. Primary psychological influences on consumer behavior are perception, motives, learning, attitudes, personality and self-concept, and lifestyles. Even though these psychological factors operate internally, they are very much affected by social forces outside the individual.

Perception

Different people perceive the same thing at the same time in different ways. When you first look at the illustration at the bottom of the page, do you see fish or birds? Similarly, an individual may perceive the same item in a number of ways at different times. **Perception** is the process of selecting, organizing, and interpreting information inputs to produce meaning. **Information inputs** are sensations received through sight, taste, hearing, smell, and touch. When we hear an advertisement, see a friend, smell food cooking at a nearby restaurant, or touch a product, we receive information inputs. Perception is a complicated thing. For instance, research has shown that advertisements for food items that appeal to multiple senses at once are more effective than ones that focus on taste alone.[5] Marketers are increasingly taking a multisensory approach. They sometimes even use scent to help attract consumers who may be in the problem recognition or information search stages of the buying decision process. Sony uses a scent that includes mandarin, vanilla, bourbon, and other special ingredients in its electronics stores. The company's marketers say every ingredient in this scent has a purpose: mandarin is supposed to denote class, vanilla relaxes female customers, and bourbon entices male customers to enter the store. Hotels, retailers, and even car makers use scents to create a certain atmosphere, which affects the consumers' behavior and spending.[6]

perception The process of selecting, organizing, and interpreting information inputs to produce meaning

information inputs Sensations received through sight, taste, hearing, smell, and touch

selective exposure The process by which some inputs are selected to reach awareness and others are not

selective distortion An individual's changing or twisting of information that is inconsistent with personal feelings or beliefs

selective retention Remembering information inputs that support personal feelings and beliefs and forgetting inputs that do not

As the definition indicates, perception is a three-step process. Although we receive numerous pieces of information at once, only a few reach our awareness. We select some inputs and ignore others because we cannot be conscious of all inputs at one time. This process is called **selective exposure** because an individual selects which inputs will reach awareness. If you are concentrating on this paragraph, you probably are not aware that cars outside are making noise, that the room light is on, that a song is playing on your MP3 player, or that you are touching this page. Even though you receive these inputs, they do not reach your awareness until they are pointed out.

An individual's current set of needs affects selective exposure. Information inputs that relate to one's strongest needs at a given time are more likely to be selected to reach awareness. It is not by random chance that many fast-food commercials are aired near mealtimes. Customers are more likely to tune in to these advertisements at these times.

The selective nature of perception may result not only in selective exposure but also in two other conditions: selective distortion and selective retention. **Selective distortion** is changing or twisting received information; it occurs when a person receives information inconsistent with personal feelings or beliefs, and he or she selectively interprets the information. Selective distortion describes the tendency for people to reject information that is inconsistent with their beliefs, even when presented with information to the contrary. Selective distortion can both help and hurt marketers. For example, a consumer may become loyal to a brand and remain loyal even when confronted with evidence that another brand performs better. Selective distortion can also lessen the effect of the advertisement on the individual substantially. In **selective retention**, a person remembers information inputs that support personal feelings and beliefs and forgets inputs that do not. After hearing a sales presentation

Fish or Fowl?
Do you see fish or birds?

Marketing Debate

Digital Stalking: Your Choice?

ISSUE: Should consumers have to take the initiative to opt out of online tracking, or should they be excluded unless they opt in?

Since the dawn of the Internet age, marketers have studied online behavior to better understand what consumers do and why. The goal is to deliver relevant online marketing messages when and where a consumer is likely to be interested.

Privacy advocates worry that consumers don't know how much data marketers actually collect online. Few people dig deeply into privacy policies or learn about the tracking techniques being used to follow their activities online. That's why critics say consumers should be tracked only if they consent by opting in. Legal or regulatory action may result in a "Do Not Track" list similar to the "Do Not Call" list that currently prevents consumers from receiving unwanted telemarketing calls.

Marketers point out that tracking adds convenience, allowing them to personalize pages and offers according to consumers' preferences. Still, the online advertising industry has set up a program to more prominently disclose tracking and make it easier to opt out. In addition, most Internet browsers can be configured to detect tracking and let consumers opt out. Finally, by offering special privileges or other incentives, marketers have found many consumers very willing to provide personal data and allow tracking.[b]

and leaving a store, for example, a customer may forget many selling points if they contradict personal beliefs or preconceived notions.

The second step in the process of perception is perceptual organization. Information inputs that reach awareness are not received in an organized form. To produce meaning, an individual must mentally organize and integrate new information with what is already stored in memory. People use several methods to organize. One method, called *closure,* occurs when a person mentally fills in missing elements in a pattern or statement. In an attempt to draw attention to its brand, an advertiser will capitalize on closure by using incomplete images, sounds, or statements in its advertisements.

Interpretation, the third step in the perceptual process, is the assignment of meaning to what has been organized. A person bases interpretation on what he or she expects or what is familiar. For this reason, a manufacturer who changes a product or its package faces a major problem: when people are looking for the old, familiar product or package, they may not recognize the new one. Consider Coca-Cola, who pulled the plug on its seasonal package redesign for its regular Coca-Cola cans. The company often changes the design of its regular Coca-Cola cans for the holidays or a special event, but it had always kept the can the traditional red color. However, when Coca-Cola introduced a white can for the winter holidays to highlight global warming's effect on polar bears' Arctic habitat, many consumers complained about the new design, and Coca-Cola had to change the seasonal design back to one with a red can. Many customers complained that they bought the white cans thinking they were Diet Coke, which is sold in a silver can. Others thought that the regular Coca-Cola tasted different in the white cans, and some were simply outraged over the change to a color other than red.[7] Unless a product or package change is accompanied by a promotional program that makes people aware of the change, an organization may suffer a sales decline.

Although marketers cannot control buyers' perceptions, they often try to influence them through information. Several problems may arise from such attempts, however. First, a consumer's perceptual process may operate so that a seller's information never reaches that person. For example, a buyer may block out a salesperson's presentation. Second, a buyer may receive a seller's information but perceive it differently than was intended, as occurs in selective distortion. For instance, when a toothpaste producer advertises that "35 percent of the people who use this toothpaste have fewer cavities," a customer might infer that

65 percent of users have more cavities. Third, a buyer who perceives information inputs to be inconsistent with prior beliefs is likely to forget the information quickly, as is the case with selective retention.

Motives

A **motive** is an internal energizing force that directs a person's activities toward satisfying needs or achieving goals. Buyers' actions are affected by a set of motives rather than by just one motive. At a single point in time, some of a person's motives are stronger than others. For example, a person's motives for having a cup of coffee are much stronger right after waking up than just before going to bed. Some motives may help an individual achieve his or her goals, whereas others create barriers to goal achievement. Motives also affect the direction and intensity of behavior. For example, with e-commerce on the rise, researchers feel an increasing need to understand the motives of online shoppers and how it affects their buying behavior. Recent research into this area divided online shoppers by two basic motivations: utilitarian (or functional) shoppers and hedonic (or nonfunctional) shoppers. Utilitarian consumers shop online because it is a useful and fast way to purchase certain items, whereas hedonic consumers shop online because it is a fun and enjoyable way to find bargains. The research found that hedonic consumers spent more time on the Internet for each purchase and shopped online more often than utilitarian consumers. Hedonic consumers were also more likely to make impulse buys online and engage in bidding wars on sites like eBay.[8]

Abraham Maslow, an American psychologist, conceived a theory of motivation based on a hierarchy of needs. According to Maslow, humans seek to satisfy five levels of needs, from most important to least important, as shown in Figure 7.2. This sequence is known as **Maslow's hierarchy of needs**. Once needs at one level are met, humans seek to fulfill needs at the next level up in the hierarchy.

At the most basic level are *physiological needs,* requirements for survival such as food, water, sex, clothing, and shelter, which people try to satisfy first. Food and beverage marketers often appeal to physiological needs. Marketers of whitening toothpastes such as Rembrant sometimes promote their brands based on sex appeal.

At the next level are *safety needs,* which include security and freedom from physical and emotional pain and suffering. Life insurance, automobile air bags, carbon monoxide detectors, vitamins, and decay-fighting toothpastes are products that consumers purchase to meet safety needs.

Next are *social needs:* the human requirements for love and affection and a sense of belonging. Advertisements frequently appeal to social needs. Ads for cosmetics and other

motive An internal energizing force that directs a person's behavior toward satisfying needs or achieving goals

Maslow's hierarchy of needs The five levels of needs that humans seek to satisfy, from most to least important

Figure 7.2 Maslow's Hierarchy of Needs

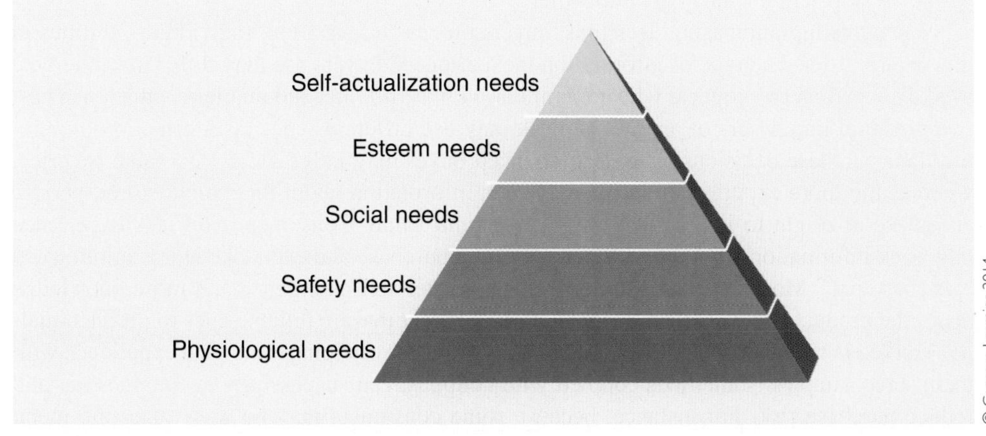

Safety Needs
Breathe Right nasal strips help an individual sleep better by facilitating improved breathing. This product contributes to achieving safety needs.

beauty products, jewelry, and even cars often suggest that purchasing these products will bring love. Certain types of trendy clothing, such as Abercrombie jeans, Nike athletic shoes, or T-shirts imprinted with logos or slogans, appeal to the customer's need to belong.

At the level of *esteem needs,* people require respect and recognition from others as well as self-esteem, a sense of one's own worth. Owning a Lexus automobile, having a beauty makeover, or flying first class can satisfy esteem needs. Many consumers are more willing to purchase products, even if they cost more, from firms that have a reputation for making charitable contributions. Part of this may be motivated by a desire by consumers to be perceived as caring about socially responsible causes.

At the top of the hierarchy are *self-actualization needs.* These refer to people's needs to grow and develop and to become all they are capable of becoming. Some products that satisfy these needs include fitness center memberships, education, self-improvement workshops, and skiing lessons. In its recruiting advertisements, the U.S. Army told potential enlistees to "be all that you can be in the Army," a message that implies that people can reach their full potential by enlisting in the U.S. Army.

Motives that influence where a person purchases products on a regular basis are called **patronage motives**. A buyer may shop at a specific store because of such patronage motives as price, service, location, product variety, or friendliness of salespeople. To capitalize on patronage motives, marketers try to determine why regular customers patronize a particular store and to emphasize these characteristics in the store's marketing mix.

Learning

Learning refers to changes in a person's thought processes and behavior caused by information and experience. Consequences of behavior strongly influence the learning process. Behaviors that result in satisfying consequences tend to be repeated. For example, a consumer who buys a Snickers candy bar and enjoys the taste is more likely to buy a Snickers again. In fact, the individual will probably continue to purchase that brand until it no longer provides satisfaction. When outcomes of the behavior are no longer satisfying, the person may switch brands or stop eating candy bars altogether.

When making purchasing decisions, buyers process information. Individuals' abilities in this regard differ. The type of information inexperienced buyers use may differ from the type used by experienced shoppers who are familiar with the product and purchase situation. Thus, two potential purchasers of an antique desk may use different types of information in making their purchase decisions. The inexperienced buyer may judge the desk's value by price, whereas the more experienced buyer may seek information about the manufacturer, period, and place of origin to judge the desk's quality and value. Consumers who lack experience may seek information from others when making a purchase and even take along an informed "purchase pal." More experienced buyers have greater self-confidence and more knowledge about the product and can recognize which product features are reliable cues to product quality. Marketers help customers learn about their products by helping them gain experience with them. Free samples, sometimes coupled with coupons, can successfully encourage trial and reduce purchase risk. For instance, because some consumers may be wary of exotic menu

patronage motives Motives that influence where a person purchases products on a regular basis

learning Changes in an individual's thought processes and behavior caused by information and experience

items, restaurants sometimes offer free samples. In-store demonstrations foster knowledge of product uses. A software producer may use point-of-sale product demonstrations to introduce a new product. Test drives give potential new-car purchasers some experience with the automobile's features.

Consumers also learn by experiencing products indirectly through information from salespeople, advertisements, websites, friends, and relatives. Through sales personnel and advertisements, marketers offer information before (and sometimes after) purchases to influence what consumers learn and to create more favorable attitudes toward the product. However, their efforts are seldom fully successful. Marketers encounter problems in attracting and holding consumers' attention, providing consumers with important information for making purchase decisions, and convincing them to try the product.

Attitudes

An **attitude** is an individual's enduring evaluation of feelings about and behavioral tendencies toward an object or idea. The objects toward which we have attitudes may be tangible or intangible, living or nonliving. For example, we have attitudes toward sex, religion, politics, and music, just as we do toward cars, football, and breakfast cereals. Although attitudes can change over time, they generally tend to remain stable and do not vary much in the short term. However, all of a person's attitudes do not have equal impact at any one time; some are stronger than others. Individuals acquire attitudes through experience and interaction with other people.

An attitude consists of three major components: cognitive, affective, and behavioral. The cognitive component is the person's knowledge and information about the object or idea. The affective component comprises the individual's feelings and emotions toward the object or idea. Emotions involve both psychological and biological elements. They relate to feelings and can create visceral responses related to behavior. Love, hate, and anger are emotions that can influence behavior. For some people, certain brands, such as Apple Inc., Starbucks, or their favorite sports franchise, elicit an emotional response. Firms that create an emotional experience or connection establish a positive brand image and will contribute to customer affinity and loyalty. This means it is important for marketers to generate authentic, genuine messages that consumers can relate to emotionally. The behavioral component manifests itself in the person's actions regarding the object or idea. Changes in one of these components may

attitude An individual's enduring evaluation of feelings about and behavioral tendencies toward an object or idea

Emerging Trends

Smartphone + QR = Unlimited Marketing Opportunity

From store windows to magazine ads, the boxy patterns known as QR codes are popping up in many marketing situations to guide consumers toward additional information, on demand. As long as the consumer has a smartphone equipped with a QR-reading app, he or she can "crack the code" and learn more about the product, its manufacturer, and its availability, at any time and from anywhere.

Macy's has been using QR codes to give consumers special "behind the scenes" fashion insights. The department store inserts QR codes into advertising and displays promoting fashion apparel so consumers can watch video interviews with the designers. It also puts QR codes on beauty products for easy access to videos offering makeup tips. Home Depot prints QR codes on potted plants so consumers can determine the best planting time and plan for grouping plants that grow well together.

Some marketers reward consumers for scanning QR codes with special pricing and exclusive product promotions. For example, scanning QR codes from the Pottery Barn Teen retail chain leads consumers to discount coupons, as well as news of new furniture and bedding products. Others, such as real estate agents, see QR codes as a way to give consumers convenient, 24/7 access to multiple details, such as price and special features.[c]

or may not alter the other components. Thus, a consumer may become more knowledgeable about a specific brand without changing the affective or behavioral components of his or her attitude toward that brand.

Consumer attitudes toward a company and its products greatly influence success or failure of the firm's marketing strategy. When consumers have strong negative attitudes toward one or more aspects of a firm's marketing practices, they may not only stop using its products but also urge relatives and friends to do likewise.

Because attitudes play an important part in determining consumer behavior, marketers should measure consumer attitudes toward prices, package designs, brand names, advertisements, salespeople, repair services, store locations, features of existing or proposed products, and social responsibility efforts. Seeking to understand attitudes has resulted in two major academic models: the attitude toward the object (the Fishbein model) and the behavioral intentions model (also known as the Theory of Reasoned Action). These models provide an understanding of the role of attitudes in decision making.

The attitude toward the object model can be used to understand, and possibly predict, a consumer's attitude. The three elements of this model include beliefs about product attributes, the strength of the belief, and the evaluation of the belief. These elements combine to form what is called the overall attitude toward the object.[9] The behavioral intentions model, rather than focusing on attributes, focuses on intentions to act or purchase. This model considers consumer perceptions of what other people, such as peers, believe is the best choice among a set of alternatives. This model also focuses on attitudes toward the buying behavior, not toward the object. The subjective norm component is important in recognizing that individuals live in an inherently social environment and are influenced by what others think and believe. Consider attitudes toward personal appearance (such as what clothes people wear, hairstyles, or body modifications such as piercings or tattoos). Consumers will take into account what others will think of their decisions. Many people are motivated to comply with what others hold to be an acceptable norm and stay in close communication through traditional word-of-mouth communications, media, and online social networking.

Several methods help marketers gauge consumer attitudes. One of the simplest ways is to question people directly. The Internet and social networking sites have become valuable tools for marketers seeking information on consumer attitudes. Using sites like Facebook, companies can ask consumers directly for feedback and reviews of their products. Marketers also evaluate attitudes through attitude scales. An **attitude scale** usually consists of a series of adjectives, phrases, or sentences about an object. Respondents indicate the intensity of their feelings toward the object by reacting to the adjectives, phrases, or sentences in a certain way. For example, a marketer who is measuring people's attitudes toward shopping might ask respondents to indicate the extent to which they agree or disagree with a number of statements, such as "shopping is more fun than watching television." By using an attitude scale, a marketing research company was able to identify and classify six major types of clothing purchasers. The scale was based on such attributes as demographics, media use, and purchase behavior.

When marketers determine that a significant number of consumers have negative attitudes toward an aspect of a marketing mix, they may try to change those attitudes to make them more favorable. This task is generally lengthy, expensive, and difficult and may require extensive promotional efforts. After being touted as the low-cost car of the future, Tata's Nano did not perform nearly as well as expected. After suffering from lower-than-expected interest and safety problems, the brand was suffering from a poor international reputation. Tata is now working to reposition itself as a low-cost family-friendly car, not a "poor man's vehicle," in anticipation of Nano launches in Europe and the United States. After years of negative publicity over safety issues and production problems, Nano marketers at Tata will have to work hard to win over skeptical customers in new markets.[10] To alter consumers' responses so that more of them buy a given brand, a firm might launch an information-focused campaign to change the cognitive component of a consumer's attitude or a persuasive

attitude scale A means of measuring consumer attitudes by gauging the intensity of individuals' reactions to adjectives, phrases, or sentences about an object

© Paul Souders/Corbis

Communication to Influence Attitudes
Hartford's Farms is trying to influence resident's attitudes about purchasing from local businesses, rather than buying from sellers not in the community.

(emotional) campaign to influence the affective component. Distributing free samples might help change the behavioral component. Both business and nonbusiness organizations try to change people's attitudes about many things, from health and safety to prices and product features.

Personality and Self-Concept

Personality is a set of internal traits and distinct behavioral tendencies that result in consistent patterns of behavior in certain situations. An individual's personality arises from hereditary characteristics and personal experiences that make the person unique. Personalities typically are described as having one or more characteristics, such as compulsiveness, ambition, gregariousness, dogmatism, authoritarianism, introversion, extroversion, and competitiveness. Marketing researchers look for relationships between such characteristics and buying behavior. Even though a few links between several personality traits and buyer behavior have been determined, results of many studies have been inconclusive. The weak association between personality and buying behavior may be the result of unreliable measures rather than a lack of a relationship. A number of marketers are convinced that consumers' personalities do influence types and brands of products purchased. For example, the type of clothing, jewelry, or automobile a person buys may reflect one or more personality characteristics. The VALS™ program is one consumer framework, based on individual personality differences, that is successful. (See the following "Lifestyles" section.)

At times, marketers aim advertising at certain types of personalities. For instance, ads for certain cigarette brands are directed toward specific personality types. Marketers focus on positively valued personality characteristics, such as security consciousness, sociability, independence, or competitiveness, rather than on negatively valued ones, such as insensitivity or timidity.

A person's self-concept is closely linked to personality. **Self-concept** (sometimes called *self-image*) is a perception or view of oneself. Individuals develop and alter their self-concepts based on an interaction between psychological and social dimensions. Research shows that buyers purchase products that reflect and enhance their self-concepts and that

personality A set of internal traits and distinct behavioral tendencies that result in consistent patterns of behavior in certain situations

self-concept A perception or view of oneself

Entrepreneurship in Marketing

Gelato Fiasco: Marketing Frozen Food in a Sub-Freezing Community

Entrepreneurs: Josh Davis and Bruno Tropeano
Business: Gelato Fiasco
Founded: 2007 | Brunswick, Maine
Success: The company has grown to over $1 million in annual sales from its two retail locations and wholesale operations.

The motto of the Gelato Fiasco, a fast-growing small business owned by Josh Davis and Bruno Tropeano, is "inspired by Italy, perfected in Maine." Based in Brunswick, Maine, the Gelato Fiasco rings up more than $1 million in annual sales from two retail locations and a thriving wholesale business.

The co-owners started from scratch, mixing small batches of fresh ingredients to create a unique gelato taste. They also found that creating a wide variety of seasonal flavors gave them a competitive edge in appealing to consumers who enjoy trying new things. As a result, the Gelato Fiasco offers an ever-changing menu of at least 24 flavors, priced at a premium to reflect the all-natural ingredients and special production process that sets this gelato apart from competing brands.

Because Brunswick had few late-night food places, "we realized that late hours might be a big draw," Davis says. Now the Gelato Fiasco remains open until 11 p.m. every night, even in snow storms. In fact, by offering a discount when the outside temperature drops below freezing, the stores draw crowds even on the chilliest winter evenings.[d]

purchase decisions are important to the development and maintenance of a stable self-concept. For example, consumers who feel insecure about their self-concept may purchase products that help them bolster the image of themselves that they would like to project.[11] Consumers' self-concepts may influence whether they buy a product in a specific product category and may affect brand selection as well as where they buy. Founded by environmentalist Yvon Chouinard, the outfitting company Patagonia appeals to consumers with a self-concept as being outdoor enthusiasts. Many consumers are loyal to the brand because its products and values represent their lifestyle. Patagonia is highly committed to its mission of sustainability so that people can continue to enjoy nature. It reincorporated under a new organizational structure, a benefit corporation, meaning that it values doing good as much as making profits.[12]

Lifestyles

As we saw in Chapter 5, many marketers attempt to segment markets by lifestyle. A **lifestyle** is an individual's pattern of living expressed through activities, interests, and opinions. Lifestyle patterns include the ways people spend time, the extent of their interaction with others, and their general outlook on life and living. People partially determine their own lifestyles, but the pattern is also affected by personality and by demographic factors such as age, education, income, and social class. Lifestyles are measured through a lengthy series of questions.

Lifestyles have a strong impact on many aspects of the consumer buying decision process, from problem recognition to postpurchase evaluation. Lifestyles influence consumers' product needs, brand preferences, types of media used, and how and where they shop.

lifestyle An individual's pattern of living expressed through activities, interests, and opinions

One of the most popular frameworks for exploring consumer lifestyles is a survey from Strategic Business Insights (SBI), a spin-out of SRI International. The company's VALS Program uses a short questionnaire to help classify consumers into eight basic groups: Innovators, Thinkers, Achievers, Experiencers, Believers, Strivers, Makers, and Survivors (see Figure 7.3). The segmentation is based on psychological characteristics that are cor-

Figure 7.3 VALS™ Types

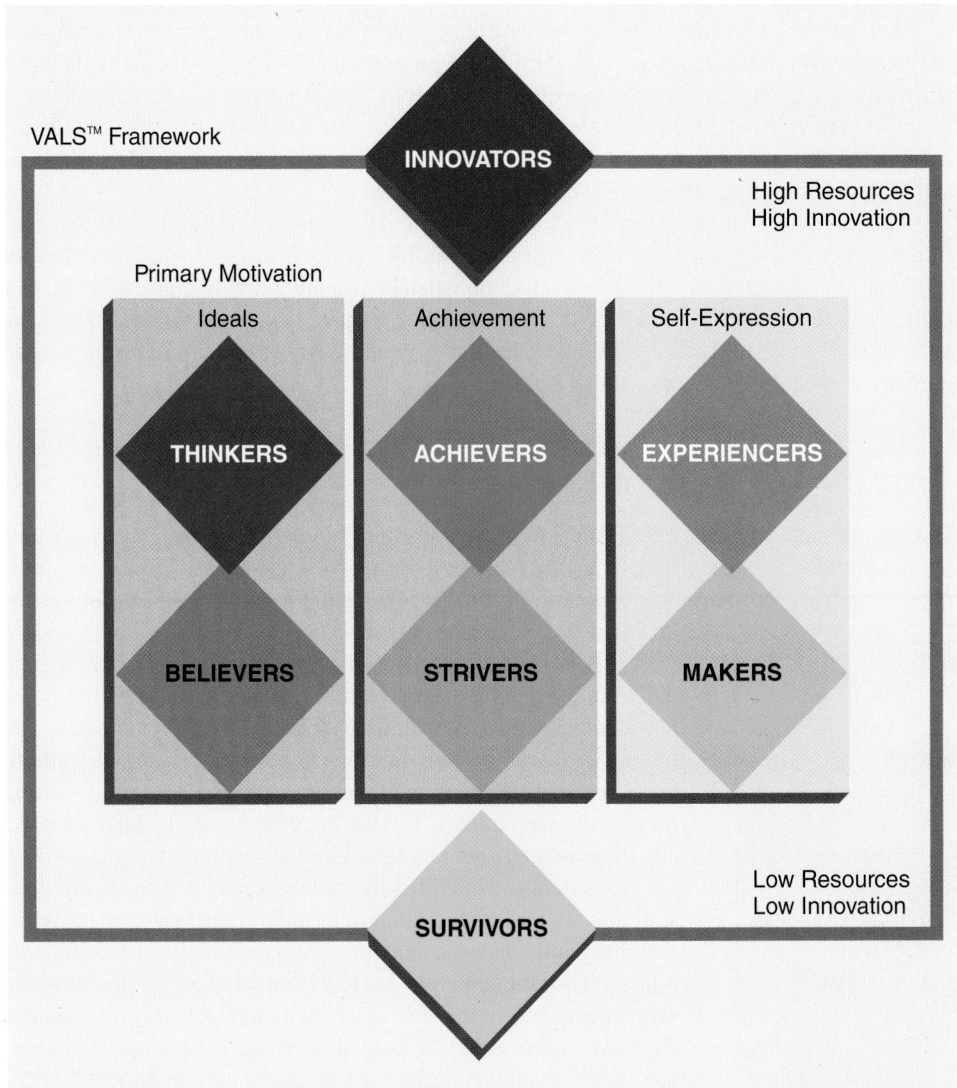

Source: VALS™ Program, Strategic Business Insights (SBI), www.strategicbusinessinsights.com/VALS.

related with purchase behavior and four key demographics. This VALS questionnaire is then attached to larger surveys, such as GfK MRI's Survey of the American Consumer, that focus on particular products, services, leisure activities, or media preferences to learn about the lifestyles of the eight groups.[13] VALS is a framework that links personality with consumers' lifestyles.

SOCIAL INFLUENCES ON THE BUYING DECISION PROCESS

Forces that other people exert on buying behavior are called **social influences**. As Figure 7.1 shows, they are grouped into five major areas: roles, family, reference groups and opinion leaders, social classes, and culture and subcultures.

social influences The forces other people exert on one's buying behavior

Roles

All of us occupy positions within groups, organizations, and institutions. As part of each position, we all play one or more **roles**, which are sets of actions and activities a person in a particular position is supposed to perform based on expectations of both the individual and surrounding persons. Because people occupy numerous positions, they have many roles. For example, a man may perform the roles of son, husband, father, employee or employer, church member, civic organization member, and student in an evening college class. Thus, multiple sets of expectations are placed on each person's behavior.

An individual's roles influence both general behavior and buying behavior. The demands of a person's many roles may be diverse and even inconsistent. Consider the various types of clothes that you buy and wear depending on whether you are going to class, to work, to a party, or to the gym. You and others involved in these settings have expectations about what is acceptable clothing for these events. Thus, the expectations of those around us affect our purchases of clothing and many other products.

roles Actions and activities that a person in a particular position is supposed to perform based on expectations of the individual and surrounding persons

consumer socialization The process through which a person acquires the knowledge and skills to function as a consumer

Family Influences

Family influences have a direct impact on the consumer buying decision process. Parents teach children how to cope with a variety of problems, including those dealing with purchase decisions. **Consumer socialization** is the process through which a person acquires the knowledge and skills to function as a consumer. Often, children gain this knowledge and set of skills by observing parents and older siblings in purchase situations, as well as through their own purchase experiences. Children observe brand preferences and buying practices in their families and, as adults, retain some of these brand preferences and buying practices as they establish and raise their own families. Buying decisions made by a family are a combination of group and individual decision making.

The extent to which family members take part in family decision making varies among families and product categories. Traditionally, family decision-making processes have been grouped into four categories: autonomic, husband dominant, wife dominant, and syncratic, as shown in Table 7.2. Although female roles continue to change, women still make buying decisions related to most household items, including health-care products, laundry supplies, paper products, and foods. Indeed, research indicates that women are the primary decision makers for 85 percent of all consumer buying decisions.[14] Spouses participate jointly in the purchase of a variety of products, especially durable goods.

The family life-cycle stage affects individual and joint needs of family members. For example, consider how the car needs of recently married "twenty-somethings" differ from those of the same couple when they are "forty-somethings" with a 13-year-old daughter and a 17-year-old son. Family life-cycle changes can affect which family members are involved in purchase decisions and the types of products purchased. Children make many purchase decisions and influence numerous household purchase decisions.

When two or more family members participate in a purchase, their roles may dictate that each is responsible for performing certain purchase-related tasks, such as initiating the idea, gathering information, determining if the product is affordable, deciding whether to buy the product, or selecting the specific brand. The

Family Influences
The decision process related to purchasing a home is influenced by parents and children. In addition, children learn about buying housing, which they will apply when making similar decisions when they are adults.

Table 7.2 Types of Family Decision Making

Decision-Making Type	Decision Maker	Types of Products
Husband dominant	Male head of household	Lawn mowers, hardware and tools, stereos, automobile parts
Wife dominant	Female head of household	Children's clothing, women's clothing, groceries, household furnishings
Autonomic	Equally likely to be made by the husband or wife, but not by both	Men's clothing, luggage, toys and games, sporting equipment, cameras
Syncratic	Made jointly by husband and wife	Vacations, TVs, living room furniture, carpets, financial planning services, family cars

specific purchase tasks performed depend on the types of products being considered, the kind of family purchase decision process typically employed, and the amount of influence children have in the decision process. Thus, different family members may play different roles in the family buying process.

Within a household, an individual may perform one or more roles related to making buying decisions. The gatekeeper is the household member who collects and controls information. This may include price and quality comparisons, locations of sellers, and assessment of which brand best suits the family's needs. For example, if a family is planning a summer vacation, the gatekeeper might compare prices for hotels and airfare. The influencer is a family member who expresses his or her opinions and tries to influence buying decisions. In the vacation example, an influencer might be a child who wants to go to Disney World or a teenager who only wants to go snowboarding. The decider is a member who makes the buying choice. This role switches based on the type and expense of the product being purchased. In the case of a vacation, the decider will more likely be the adults, who use a combination of information, influences, and their own preferences. The buyer is a member who actually makes the purchase. After the family has decided to go to Disney World, the buyer will make all of the actual travel purchases. The user is a household member who consumes or uses the product. In this Disney World example, all members of the family would be users.

reference group A group that a person identifies with so strongly that he or she adopts the values, attitudes, and behavior of group members

Source: American Express Spending & Saving Tracker.

Reference Groups

A **reference group** is a group that a person identifies with so strongly that he or she adopts the values, attitudes, and behavior of group members. Reference groups can be large or small.

Most people have several reference groups, such as families, work-related groups, fraternities or sororities, civic clubs, professional organizations, or church-related groups.

In general, there are three major types of reference groups: membership, aspirational, and disassociative. A membership reference group is one to which an individual actually belongs; the individual identifies with group members strongly enough to take on the values, attitudes, and behaviors of people in that group. An aspirational reference group is a group to which a person aspires to belong; the individual desires to be like those group members. A group that a person does not wish to be associated with is a disassociative or negative reference group; the individual does not want to take on the values, attitudes, and behavior of group members.

A reference group may serve as an individual's point of comparison and source of information. A customer's behavior may change to be more in line with actions and beliefs of group members. For instance, a person may stop buying one brand of shirts and switch to another based on reference group members' advice. An individual may also seek information from the reference group about other factors regarding a prospective purchase, such as where to buy a certain product.

The extent to which a reference group affects a purchase decision depends on the product's conspicuousness and on the individual's susceptibility to reference group influence. Generally, the more conspicuous a product, the more likely that reference groups will influence the purchase decision. A product's conspicuousness is determined by whether others can see it and whether it can attract attention. Reference groups can affect whether a person does or does not buy a product at all, buys a type of product within a product category, or buys a specific brand.

A marketer sometimes tries to use reference group influence in advertisements by suggesting that people in a specific group buy a product and are highly satisfied with it. In this type of appeal, the advertiser hopes that many people will accept the suggested group as a reference group and buy (or react more favorably to) the product. Whether this kind of advertising succeeds depends on three factors: how effectively the advertisement communicates the message, the type of product, and the individual's susceptibility to reference group influence.

Opinion Leaders

An **opinion leader** is a member of an informal group who provides information about a specific topic, like software, to other group members who seek that information. He or she is in a position or has knowledge or expertise that makes him or her a credible source of information about a few topics. Opinion leaders are easily accessible, and they are viewed by other group members as being well informed about a particular topic. Opinion leaders are not the foremost authority on all topics, but because such individuals know they are opinion leaders, they feel a responsibility to remain informed about a topic and thus seek out advertisements, manufacturers' brochures, salespeople, and other sources of information. Opinion leaders have a strong influence on the behavior of others in their group, particularly relating to product adoption and purchases.

An opinion leader is likely to be most influential when consumers have high product involvement but low product knowledge, when they share the opinion leader's values and attitudes, and when the product details are numerous or complicated. Possible opinion leaders and topics are shown in Table 7.3.

opinion leader A member of an informal group who provides information about a specific topic to other group members

social class An open group of individuals with similar social rank

Social Classes

In all societies, people rank others into higher or lower positions of respect. This ranking process, called social stratification, results in social classes. A **social class** is an open aggregate of people with similar social rank. A class is referred to as *open* because people can move into and out of it. Criteria for grouping people into classes vary from one society to another. In the

Table 7.3 Examples of Opinion Leaders and Topics

Opinion Leader	Possible Topics
Local religious leader	Charities to support, political ideas, lifestyle choices
Sorority president	Clothing and shoe purchases, hair styles, nail and hair salons
"Movie buff" friend	Movies to see in theaters, rent, or buy, television programs to watch
Family doctor	Prescription drugs, vitamins, health products
"Techie" acquaintance	Computer and other electronics purchases, software purchases, Internet service choices, video game purchases

United States, we take into account many factors, including occupation, education, income, wealth, race, ethnic group, and possessions. A person who is ranking someone does not necessarily apply all of a society's criteria. Sometimes, too, the role of income tends to be overemphasized in social class determination. Although income does help determine social class, the other factors also play a role. Within social classes, both incomes and spending habits differ significantly among members.

Analyses of social class in the United States commonly divide people into three to seven categories. Social scientist Richard P. Coleman suggests that, for purposes of consumer analysis, the population is divided into the three major status groups shown in Table 7.4. However, he cautions marketers that considerable diversity exists in people's life situations within each status group.

To some degree, individuals within social classes develop and assume common behavioral patterns. They may have similar attitudes, values, language patterns, and possessions. Social class influences many aspects of people's lives. Because people have the most frequent interaction with people from within their own social class, most people are more likely to be influenced by others within their own class than by those in other classes. For example, it affects their chances of having children and their children's chances of surviving infancy. It influences their childhood training, choice of religion, financial planning decisions, access to higher education, selection of occupation, and leisure time activities. Because social class has a bearing on so many aspects of a person's life, it also affects buying decisions.

Social class influences people's spending, saving, and credit practices. It determines to some extent the type, quality, and quantity of products a person buys and uses. For instance, it affects purchases of clothing, foods, financial and health-care services, travel, recreation, entertainment, and home furnishings. The behaviors of people in one class can influence consumers in others. Most common is the "trickle-down" effect, in which members of lower classes attempt to emulate members of higher social classes, such as purchasing expensive automobiles, homes, appliances, and other status symbols. For example, couture fashions designed for the upper class influence the clothing sold in department stores frequented by the middle class, which eventually influences the working class who shop at discount clothing stores. Less often, status float will occur, when a product that is traditionally associated with a lower class gains status and usage among upper classes. Blue jeans, for example, were originally worn exclusively by the working class. Youth of the 1950s began wearing them as a symbol of rebellion against their parents. By the 1970s and 1980s, jeans had also been adopted by upper-class youth when they began to acquire designer labels. Today, blue jeans are acceptable attire for all social classes and cost anywhere from a few dollars to thousands of dollars, depending on the brand.

Social class also affects an individual's shopping patterns and types of stores patronized. In some instances, marketers attempt to focus on certain social classes through store location

Table 7.4 Social Class Behavioral Traits and Purchasing Characteristics

Class (Percent of Population)	Behavioral Traits	Buying Characteristics
Upper Americans		
Upper-upper (0.5)	Social elite Of aristocratic, prominent families Inherited their position in society	Children attend private preparatory schools and best colleges Do not consume ostentatiously Spend money on private clubs, various causes, and the arts
Lower-upper (3.8)	Newer social elite Successful professionals earning very high incomes Earned their position in society	Purchase material symbols of their status, such as large, suburban houses and expensive automobiles Provide a substantial market for luxury product offerings Visit museums and attend live theater Spend money on skiing, golf, swimming, and tennis
Upper-middle (13.8)	Career-oriented, professional degree holders Demand educational attainment of their children	Provide a substantial market for quality product offerings Family lifestyle characterized as gracious yet careful Spend money on movies, gardening, and photography
Middle Americans		
Middle class (32.8)	"Typical" Americans Work conscientiously and adhere to culturally defined standards Average-pay white-collar workers Attend church and obey the law Often very involved in children's school and sports activities	Greatly value living in a respected neighborhood and keep their homes well furnished Generally price sensitive Adopt conventional consumption tastes and consult category experts Spend on family-oriented, physical activities, such as fishing, camping, boating, and hunting
Working class (32.3)	Average-pay blue-collar workers Live a routine life with unchanging day-to-day activities Hold jobs that entail manual labor and moderate skills Some are union members Socially not involved in civic or church activities; limit social interaction to close neighbors and relatives	Reside in small houses or apartments in depressed areas Impulsive as consumers yet display high loyalty to national brands Seek best bargains Enjoy leisure activities like local travel and recreational parks
Lower Americans		
Upper-lower (9.5)	Low-income individuals who generally fail to rise above this class Reject middle-class morality	Living standard is just above poverty Seek pleasure whenever possible, especially through impulse purchases Frequently purchase on credit
Lower-lower (7.3)	Some are on welfare and may be homeless Poverty stricken Some have strong religious beliefs Some are unemployed In spite of their problems, often good-hearted toward others May be forced to live in less desirable neighborhoods	Spend on products needed for survival Able to convert discarded goods into usable items

Sources: Roger D. Blackwell, Paul W. Miniard, and James F. Engel, *Consumer Behavior,* 10th ed. (Mason, OH: South-Western, 2005); "The Continuing Significance of Social Class Marketing," *Journal of Consumer Research* 10 (Dec. 1983): 265–280; Eugene Sivadas, George Mathew, and David J. Curry, "A Preliminary Examination of the Continued Significance of Social Class in Marketing," *Journal of Consumer Marketing* 14, no. 6 (1997): 463–469.

and interior design, product design and features, pricing strategies, personal sales efforts, and advertising. Many companies focus on the middle and working classes because they account for such a large portion of the population. Outside the United States, the middle class is growing in India, China, Mexico, and other countries, making these consumers increasingly desirable to marketers as well. Some firms target different classes with different products. For example, luxury brands BMW and Mercedes-Benz have both released more moderately priced vehicles ($30,000 to $45,000) to target middle-class consumers, although it usually targets upper-class customers with more expensive vehicles ($70,000 plus).[15]

Courtesy of The Advertising Archives

Subcultures
Cosmetic companies create products for customers who are a part of a specific subculture.

Culture and Subcultures

Culture is the accumulation of values, knowledge, beliefs, customs, objects, and concepts that a society uses to cope with its environment and passes on to future generations. Examples of objects are foods, furniture, buildings, clothing, and tools. Concepts include education, welfare, and laws. Culture also includes core values and the degree of acceptability of a wide range of behaviors in a specific society. For example, in U.S. culture, customers as well as businesspeople are expected to behave ethically.

Culture influences buying behavior because it permeates our daily lives. Our culture determines what we wear and eat and where we reside and travel. Society's interest in the healthfulness of food affects food companies' approaches to developing and promoting their products. Culture also influences how we buy and use products and our satisfaction from them. In U.S. culture, makers of furniture, cars, and clothing strive to understand how people's color preferences are changing.

Because culture determines product purchases and uses to some degree, cultural changes affect product development, promotion, distribution, and pricing. Food marketers, for example, have made a multitude of changes in their marketing efforts. Thirty years ago, most U.S. families ate at least two meals a day together, and the mother spent four to six hours a day preparing those meals. Today, the majority of women work outside the home before they reach retirement age, and average family incomes have risen considerably. These shifts, along with scarcity of time, have resulted in dramatic changes in the national per capita consumption of certain food products, such as take-out foods, frozen dinners, and shelf-stable foods.

When U.S. marketers sell products in other countries, they realize the tremendous impact those cultures have on product purchases and use. Global marketers find that people in other regions of the world have different attitudes, values, and needs, which call for different methods of doing business as well as different types of marketing mixes. Some international marketers fail because they do not or cannot adjust to cultural differences.

A culture consists of various subcultures. A **subculture** is a group of individuals whose characteristics, values, and behavioral patterns are similar within the group and different from those of people in the surrounding culture. Subcultural boundaries are usually based on geographic designations and demographic characteristics, such as age, religion, race, and ethnicity. U.S. culture is marked by many different subcultures. Among them are West Coast, teenage, Asian American, and college students. Within subcultures, greater similarities exist in people's attitudes, values, and actions than within the broader culture. Relative to other subcultures, individuals in one subculture may have stronger preferences for specific types

culture The accumulation of values, knowledge, beliefs, customs, objects, and concepts that a society uses to cope with its environment and passes on to future generations

subculture A group of individuals whose characteristics, values, and behavioral patterns are similar within the group and different from those of people in the surrounding culture

of clothing, furniture, food, or consumer electronics. Consider that usage of different types of cell phones can be explained based on the different subcultures that exist and their needs for phones. Out of all of the adults in the United States, 35 percent have a smartphone. However, 59 percent of adults with higher household incomes ($75,000 and up) are smartphone owners. Nearly half of all adults with a college degree own a smartphone. Also, urban and suburban residents are twice as likely to own a smartphone as those living in a rural area.[16] Research has shown that subcultures can play a significant role in how people respond to advertisements, particularly when pressured to make a snap judgment. It is important to understand that a person can be a member of more than one subculture and that the behavioral patterns and values attributed to specific subcultures do not necessarily apply to all group members.

The percentage of the U.S. population consisting of ethnic and racial subcultures is expected to grow. By 2050, about one-half of the U.S. population will be members of racial and ethnic minorities. The U.S. Census Bureau reports that the three largest and fastest-growing ethnic U.S. subcultures are African Americans, Hispanics, and Asians.[17] Approximately 46 percent of children in the United States are minorities.[18] The population growth of these subcultures interests marketers. Businesses recognize that, to succeed, their marketing strategies will have to take into account the values, needs, interests, shopping patterns, and buying habits of various subcultures.

African American Subculture

In the United States, the African American subculture represents 12.6 percent of the population.[19] Like all subcultures, African American consumers possess distinct buying patterns. For example, African American consumers spend much of their money on depreciable products such as phone services, children's clothing, and shoes. The combined buying power of African American consumers is projected to reach $1.2 trillion by 2015.[20]

Many companies are renewing their focus on the African American community. A recent marketing initiative by Ford Motor Company included two advertising campaigns targeted specifically at African American consumers. The first program, called "Inspired by Color," highlighted how the various colors and features available for Ford's Fiesta fit different consumers' personalities. The second campaign, called "All In," featured African American executives from Ford that were an important part of revitalizing the company during the recent economic recession.[21]

Hispanic Subculture

Hispanics represent 16.3 percent of the U.S. population.[22] Hispanic buying power is expected to reach $1.5 trillion by 2015, an increase of 50 percent.[23] This development makes this subculture a powerful and attractive consumer group for marketers. When considering the buying behavior of Hispanics, marketers must keep in mind that this subculture is really composed of many diverse cultures coming from a huge geographic region that encompasses nearly two dozen nationalities, including Cuban, Mexican, Puerto Rican, Caribbean, Spanish, and Dominican. Each has its own history and unique culture that affect consumer preferences and buying behavior. Marketers should also recognize that the terms *Hispanic* and *Latino* refer to an ethnic category rather than a racial distinction. Because of the group's growth and purchasing power, understanding the Hispanic subculture is critical to marketers. Like African American consumers, Hispanics spend more of their income on groceries, phone services, clothing, and shoes, while they spend less than average on health care, entertainment, and education.[24]

To attract this powerful subculture, marketers are developing products and creating advertising and promotions with Hispanic values and preferences in mind. Clorox launched an advertising campaign directed exclusively at Hispanics with "Hogar + Sanito en Tres Pasitos." The campaign encourages families to get a flu shot, wash hands, and disinfect surfaces in their home with Clorox products in order to stay healthy.[25] Insurance company Allstate partnered with Spanish-language network Telemundo to create a digital award show based upon viewers' favorite "novela moments." (Novelas are Spanish-language soap operas.) Viewers watched novelas on http://msnlatino.telemundo.com and voted for their favorite moments using 20 different categories. Before the shows began, viewers saw an Allstate advertisement that promoted the company's insurance services. The campaign was meant to educate the Hispanic market about insurance and create brand awareness for the company.[26]

Asian American Subculture

The term *Asian American* includes people from more than 15 ethnic groups, encompassing Filipinos, Chinese, Japanese, Asian Indians, Koreans, and Vietnamese, and this group represents 4.8 percent of the U.S. population.[27] The individual language, religion, and value system of each group influences its members' purchasing decisions. Some traits of this subculture, however, carry across ethnic divisions, including an emphasis on hard work, strong family ties, and a high value placed on education. The combined buying power of Asian American consumers is projected to reach $775 billion by 2015, a growth rate of 43 percent. Asian Americans spend more of their income on housing, clothing, education, and personal insurance, while they spend less than average on vehicles, entertainment, alcohol, and tobacco.[28]

Marketers are targeting the diverse Asian American market in many ways. Subaru, for example, recently targeted the Chinese group of Asian American consumers with its "Sweet Tomorrow" advertising campaign for its Legacy sedan. Elements of this campaign included a billboard in San Francisco's Chinatown district, TV ads featured on Subaru's Chinese language site and its YouTube channel, and print ads in both Mandarin and Cantonese in publications in Los Angeles and San Francisco.[29]

CONSUMER MISBEHAVIOR

Approaching the topic of inappropriate consumer behavior requires some caution because of varying attitudes and cultural definitions of what comprises misbehavior. However, there is general agreement that some conduct, such as shoplifting or purchasing illegal drugs, falls under the category of activities that are not accepted by established norms. Therefore, we will define **consumer misbehavior** as simply behavior that violates generally accepted norms of a particular society. Shoplifting is one of the most obvious misconduct areas, with organized retail crime (where people are paid to shoplift certain goods from retail stores) on the rise. Experts estimate that organized retail crime alone costs businesses nearly $30 billion annually.[30] Consumer motivation for shoplifting includes the low risk of being caught, a desire to be accepted by a group of peers (particularly among young people), and the excitement associated with the activity.

Consumer fraud includes purposeful actions to take advantage of and/or damage others. Fraudulently obtaining credit cards, checks, bank accounts, or false insurance claims fall into this category. Even large companies with sophisticated security systems can be vulnerable to consumer fraud. Zappos shoes, a subsidiary of Amazon.com, was the victim of a cyber-attack that revealed names, information, and partial credit card numbers for 24 million customers. Sony's Playstation network fell under a similar attack that exposed information on an estimated 77 million customers.[31] Some consumers engage in identity theft, which is a serious and growing legal problem. Another example of consumer fraud would be purchasing a dress for a special event, wearing it once, and then returning it.

Copying computer software, video games, movies, or music (also known as piracy) is illegal and costs the electronics and entertainment industries an estimated $59 billion annually.[32] The recording industry broadcasts messages explaining why sharing music may not be acceptable. Understanding motivations for piracy can be helpful in developing a plan to combat the issue. (See Table 7.5.)

consumer misbehavior
Behavior that violates generally accepted norms of a particular society.

Table 7.5 Motivations for Unethical or Illegal Misbehavior

• Justification/rationalization	• The thrill of getting away with it
• Economic reasons	• There is little risk of getting caught
• It is accepted by peers	• People think they are smarter than others

Source: Kevin J. Shanahan and Michael J. Hyman, "Motivators and Enablers of SCOURing: A Study of Online Piracy in the US and UK," *Journal of Business Research* 63 (September–October 2010): 1095–1102.

Yet another area of concern with consumer misbehavior is abusive consumers. Rude customers engage in verbal or physical abuse, can be uncooperative, and may even break policies. Airlines remove abusive customers because they represent a threat to employees and other passengers. Belligerently drunk customers, especially in environments like bars and restaurants, have to be removed in order to protect others. Understanding the psychological and social reasons for consumer misconduct can be helpful in preventing or responding to the problem.

Summary

1. To recognize the stages of the consumer buying decision process

The consumer buying decision process includes five stages: problem recognition, information search, evaluation of alternatives, purchase, and postpurchase evaluation. Not all decision processes culminate in a purchase, nor do all consumer decisions include all five stages. Problem recognition occurs when buyers become aware of a difference between a desired state and an actual condition. After recognizing the problem or need, buyers search for information about products to help resolve the problem or satisfy the need. In the internal search, buyers search their memories for information about products that might solve the problem. If they cannot retrieve from memory enough information for a decision, they seek additional information through an external search. A successful search yields a group of brands, called a consideration set, which a buyer views as possible alternatives. To evaluate the products in the consideration set, the buyer establishes certain criteria by which to compare, rate, and rank different products. Marketers can influence consumers' evaluations by framing alternatives. In the purchase stage, consumers select products or brands on the basis of results from the evaluation stage and on other dimensions. Buyers also choose the seller from whom they will buy the product. After the purchase, buyers evaluate the product to determine if its actual performance meets expected levels.

2. To understand the types of consumer decision making and the level of involvement

Buying behavior consists of the decision processes and acts of people involved in buying and using products. Consumer buying behavior is the buying behavior of ultimate consumers. An individual's level of involvement—the importance and intensity of interest in a product in a particular situation—affects the type of decision-making process used. Enduring involvement is an ongoing interest in a product class because of personal relevance, whereas situational involvement is a temporary interest that stems from the particular circumstance or environment in which buyers find themselves. There are three kinds of consumer decision making: routinized response behavior, limited decision making, and extended decision making. Consumers rely on routinized response behavior when buying frequently purchased, low-cost items requiring little search-and-decision effort. Limited decision making is used for products purchased occasionally or when buyers need to acquire information about an unfamiliar brand in a familiar product category. Consumers engage in extended decision making when purchasing an unfamiliar, expensive, or infrequently bought product. Purchase of a certain product does not always elicit the same type of decision making. Impulse buying is not a consciously planned buying behavior but involves a powerful urge to buy something immediately.

3. To explore how situational influences may affect the consumer buying decision process

Three major categories of influences affect the consumer buying decision process: situational, psychological, and social. Situational influences are external circumstances or conditions existing when a consumer makes a purchase decision. Situational influences include surroundings, time, reason for purchase, and the buyer's mood and condition.

4. To understand the psychological influences that may affect the consumer buying decision process

Psychological influences partly determine people's general behavior, thus influencing their behavior as consumers. The primary psychological influences on consumer behavior are perception, motives, learning, attitudes, personality and self-concept, and lifestyles. Perception is the process of selecting, organizing, and interpreting information inputs (sensations received through sight, taste, hearing, smell, and touch) to produce meaning. The three steps in the perceptual process are selection, organization, and interpretation. Individuals have numerous perceptions of packages, products, brands, and organizations that affect their buying decision processes. A motive is an internal energizing force that orients a person's activities toward satisfying needs or achieving goals. Learning refers to changes in a person's thought processes and behavior caused by information and experience. Marketers try to shape what consumers learn in order to influence what they buy. An attitude is an individual's enduring evaluation, feelings, and behavioral tendencies toward an object or idea and consists of three major components: cognitive, affective, and behavioral. Personality is the set of traits and behaviors that make a person unique. Self-concept, closely linked to personality, is one's perception or view of oneself. Researchers have found that buyers purchase products that reflect and enhance their self-concepts. Lifestyle is an individual's pattern of living expressed through activities, interests, and opinions. Lifestyles influence consumers' needs, brand preferences, and how and where they shop.

5. To examine the social influences that may affect the consumer buying decision process

Social influences are forces that other people exert on buying behavior. They include roles, family, reference groups and opinion leaders, electronic networks, social class, and culture and subcultures. Everyone occupies positions within groups, organizations, and institutions, and each position has a role—a set of actions and activities that a person in a particular position is supposed to perform based on expectations of both the individual and surrounding persons. In a family, children learn from parents and older siblings how to make decisions, such as purchase decisions. Consumer socialization is the process through which a person acquires the knowledge and skills to function as a consumer. The consumer socialization process is partially accomplished through family influences. A reference group is a group that a person identifies with so strongly that he or she adopts the values, attitudes, and behavior of group members. The three major types of reference groups are membership, aspirational, and disassociative. An opinion leader is a member of an informal group who provides information about a specific topic to other group members. A social class is an open group of individuals with similar social rank. Social class influences people's spending, saving, and credit practices. Culture is the accumulation of values, knowledge, beliefs, customs, objects, and concepts that a society uses to cope with its environment and passes on to future generations. A culture is made up of subcultures, groups of individuals whose characteristic values and behavior patterns are similar but different from those of the surrounding culture. U.S. marketers focus on three major ethnic subcultures: African American, Hispanic, and Asian American.

6. To examine consumer misbehavior

Consumer misbehavior is defined as behavior that violates generally accepted norms of a particular society. One form of consumer misbehavior involves shoplifting, or stealing goods from retail stores. Organized retail crime is on the rise and involves people paying others to shoplift certain goods from retail stores, which are then usually sold on the black market. Another form of consumer misbehavior is consumer fraud, which involves purposeful actions to take advantage of and/or damage others. Common examples of consumer fraud are false insurance claims, identity theft, returning an item of clothing after wearing it, and fraudulently obtaining credit cards, checks, and bank accounts. Another form of consumer misbehavior is the copying or sharing of music, movies, video games, and computer software. One final area of concern with regards to consumer misbehavior is abusive consumers, which include customers who are rude, verbally or physically abusive, and/or uncooperative, which may violate some companies' policies. In order to respond to or even prevent these growing problems, organizations need to understand the psychological and social reasons for consumer misbehavior.

Go to www.cengagebrain.com for resources to help you master the content in this chapter as well as for materials that will expand your marketing knowledge!

Important Terms

buying behavior 214
consumer buying behavior 214
consumer buying decision process 214
internal search 215
external search 215
consideration set 216
evaluative criteria 216
cognitive dissonance 217
level of involvement 217
routinized response behavior 218
limited decision making 218
extended decision making 219
impulse buying 219
situational influences 219
psychological influences 220
perception 221
information inputs 221
selective exposure 221
selective distortion 221
selective retention 221
motive 223
Maslow's hierarchy of needs 223
patronage motives 224
learning 224
attitude 225
attitude scale 226
personality 227
self-concept 227
lifestyle 228
social influences 229
roles 230
consumer socialization 230
reference group 231
opinion leader 232
social class 232
culture 235
subculture 235
consumer misbehavior 237

Discussion and Review Questions

1. What are the major stages in the consumer buying decision process? Are all these stages used in all consumer purchase decisions? Why or why not?
2. How does a consumer's level of involvement affect his or her choice of decision-making process?
3. Name the types of consumer decision-making processes. List some products you have bought using each type. Have you ever bought a product on impulse? If so, describe the circumstances.
4. What are the categories of situational factors that influence consumer buying behavior? Explain how each of these factors influences buyers' decisions.
5. What is selective exposure? Why do people engage in it?
6. How do marketers attempt to shape consumers' learning?
7. Why are marketers concerned about consumer attitudes?
8. In what ways do lifestyles affect the consumer buying decision process?
9. How do roles affect a person's buying behavior? Provide examples.
10. What are family influences, and how do they affect buying behavior?
11. What are reference groups? How do they influence buying behavior? Name some of your own reference groups.
12. How does an opinion leader influence the buying decision process of reference group members?
13. How might consumer behavior be influenced by digital networks?
14. In what ways does social class affect a person's purchase decisions?
15. What is culture? How does it affect a person's buying behavior?
16. Describe the subcultures to which you belong. Identify buying behavior that is unique to one of your subcultures.
17. What is consumer misbehavior? Describe the various forms of consumer misbehavior.

Application Questions

1. Consumers use one of three decision-making processes when purchasing goods or services: routinized response behavior, limited decision making, or extended decision making. Describe three buying experiences you have had (one for each type of decision making), and identify which decision-making type you used. Discuss why that particular process was appropriate.
2. The consumer buying process consists of five stages: problem recognition, information search, evaluation of alternatives, purchase, and postpurchase evaluation. Not every buying decision goes through all five stages, and the process does not necessarily conclude in a purchase. Interview a classmate about the last purchase he or she made. Report the stages used and those skipped, if any.
3. Attitudes toward products or companies often affect consumer behavior. The three components of an attitude are cognitive, affective, and behavioral. Briefly describe how a beer company might alter the cognitive and affective components of consumer attitudes toward beer products and toward the company.

4. An individual's roles influence that person's buying behavior. Identify two of your roles, and give an example of how they have influenced your buying decisions.
5. Select five brands of toothpaste and explain how the appeals used in advertising these brands relate to Maslow's hierarchy of needs.
6. IMP Assume that Reebok has developed two new types of athletic shoes. One is designed for distance runners, and the other has been developed for teenage skateboarders. As a marketer, you need to evaluate the potential psychological influences for each of these distinct target markets.

   Rank each of the following on a scale of 1 to 5 in order of importance for distance runners versus teenage skateboarders. Consider 1 as the most important variable and 5 as the least important.

   Roles
   Family Influences
   Reference Groups
   Opinion Leaders
   Social Classes
   Culture and Subcultures

   Are your top two ranks for the distance runner and skateboarder markets the same or different? If they're dissimilar, explain why various social influences affect contrasting target markets.

Internet Exercise

Amazon

Some mass-market e-commerce sites, such as Amazon, have extended the concept of customization to their customer base. The company has created an affinity group by drawing on certain users' likes and dislikes to make product recommendations to other users. Check out this pioneering online retailer at www.amazon.com.

1. What might motivate some consumers to read a "Top Selling" list?
2. Is the consumer's level of involvement with an online book purchase likely to be high or low?
3. Discuss the consumer buying decision process as it relates to a decision to purchase from Amazon.

developing your marketing plan

Understanding the process that an individual consumer goes through when purchasing a product is essential for developing marketing strategy. Knowledge about the potential customer's buying behavior will become the basis for many of the decisions in the specific marketing plan. Using the information from this chapter, you should be able to determine the following:

1. See Table 7.1.What type of decision making are your customers likely to use when purchasing your product?
2. Determine the evaluative criteria that your target market(s) would use when choosing between alternative brands.
3. Using Table 7.2, what types of family decision making, if any, would your target market(s) use?
4. Identify the reference groups or subcultures that may influence your target market's product selection.

The information obtained from these questions should assist you in developing various aspects of your marketing plan found in the "Interactive Marketing Plan" exercise at www.cengagebrain.com.

video case 7.1

Starbucks Refines the Customer Experience

Starbucks—the Seattle-based company that popularized the "coffee culture"—is brewing up higher sales through new beverages and new cafés in global markets. A stop at Starbucks has become part of many consumers' daily routines. Some are attracted by the high-quality, brewed-to-order coffees, while others look forward to relaxing and socializing in the "third place" between home and work.

Starbucks has researched and refined every aspect of the customer experience, from the size of its coffees ("tall" is actually "small") to the number of minutes that customers spend waiting in line. To speed up purchases, it offers a pay-by-cell phone option called "mobile pay." Consumers with iPhone or Android cell phones simply download the app and let cashiers scan the Starbucks code on the screen during checkout. The app links to the customer's Starbucks Card, which combines the rewards of a loyalty program with the convenience of a prepaid card for making purchases. Mobile pay is a big hit: in its first 15 months, customers used their cell phones to make more than 42 million payments to Starbucks.

© ITAR-TASS Photo Agency/Alamy

Well established in the intensely competitive U.S. market, Starbucks is growing much more quickly in Asian markets. The company will soon have 1,500 cafés and 30,000 employees in China, where consumers drink, on average, just three cups of coffee every year. By opening in more locations and encouraging consumers to bring their friends for coffee and conversation, Starbucks aims to increase demand and boost sales throughout China. In Japan, where Starbucks now has more than 1,000 cafés, consumers have long enjoyed the tradition of meeting in neighborhood coffee shops.

Through market research, Starbucks stays in touch with what its customers like and what their lifestyles are like. Coffee lovers are still buying their espressos or lattes, but they're also "looking for a healthier lifestyle," says a Starbucks executive. In response to this trend, the company bought Evolution Fresh, which makes premium juices, and opened its first Evolution Fresh store in Bellevue, Washington. On the menu: all-natural, freshly-blended drinks from nutritious fruits and vegetables, plus salads and wraps. Over time, Starbucks is adding Evolution Fresh drinks to the menu in all of its cafés and opening additional Evolution Fresh stores on the East and West Coasts. Although expanding into fresh juices means competing with Jamba Juice and other rivals, Starbucks is relying on its brand-building expertise to juice up this part of its business.

Taking note of consumer interest in energy drinks, which has blossomed into an $8 billion market, Starbucks has also launched Starbucks Refreshers, a line of carbonated drinks with more than half the caffeine content of an espresso shot. Available in supermarkets and in Starbucks cafés, these all-natural drinks combine green, unroasted coffee with fruit juices for a fruity, non-coffee flavor. To gain significant market share, Starbucks must battle Red Bull, Rockstar, and other well-known marketers of energy drinks.

Starbucks also believes in social responsibility. It offers health-insurance benefits to both part-time and full-time employees and donates generously to community projects. It also protects the environment by recycling in every café and constructing buildings designed to save energy and water. Finally, the company follows ethical purchasing practices to ensure that coffee growers get a fair price for their premium beans.[33]

Questions for Discussion

1. In terms of situational influences and level of involvement, what are the benefits of mobile pay?
2. With Evolution Fresh, which psychological influences on consumer buying decisions does Starbucks seem to be addressing?
3. Why would Starbucks want customers to know that it believes in social responsibility?

case 7.2

Iams and Eukanuba Understand People Who Love Pets

Many people treat their pets like family members and want to buy them the best, creating opportunities for marketing pet foods, treats, and even insurance. Marketers at Iams and Eukanuba, both owned by Procter & Gamble, are using their knowledge of consumer behavior to market these goods and services to pet "parents." "The humanization trend continues in pet care, as pet parents continue to increase in willingness to invest in their pets," observes the Iams brand manager at parent company Procter & Gamble.

Food for cats and dogs has become a $19 billion business. As in the overall market for people food, pet foods with all-natural or special ingredients are increasingly attractive choices for consumers who are focused on pet health. For example, Iams ProActive Health pet foods include PreBiotics, good bacteria that promote healthy digestion. The company also has a Healthy Naturals line containing no artificial colors, flavors, or preservatives. New lines of Iams and Eukanuba pet foods meet the nutritional needs of "senior" dogs and cats (older than nine). The popularity of such products indicates that consumers are highly involved in buying decisions about pet food, seeing pets as family members entitled to the same quality food and nutrition as everyone else in the family.

Iams and Eukanuba use research to uncover the specific needs and preferences of consumers with pets. For example, customers with more than one cat were concerned about how to feed them when one cat is overweight but others are not. As a result, Iams created a Multi-Cat formula with ingredients aimed at reducing fat in heavy cats while still providing protein for lean cats. The company's Savory Sauce formulas for dogs are bottled just like barbecue sauces or marinades for people. The sauces are fortified with vitamins, minerals, and antioxidants, are low in calories and fat, and come in flavors such as Pot Roast or Country Style Chicken.

Eukanuba also markets special foods for dogs with sensitive skin or a sensitive stomach, as well as breed-specific foods (for boxers, Labradors, and other dog breeds). More than 100,000 people have clicked to "like" Eukanuba's Facebook page, which features pet-care tips and videos, new-product information, and links to sponsorships of events such as the American Kennel Club/Eukanuba National Championships. Through Facebook and Twitter, Eukanuba invites pet owners to submit questions for expert answers, showcasing the brand's connection with pet well-being. Eukanuba's YouTube channel offers tutorials on puppy training, highlights of dog-show winners, and videos about individual dog breeds.

To help consumers learn more about training pets, feeding them properly, and what to expect as pets age, Iams partners with *Dog Fancy* and *Cat Fancy* magazines to provide free online classes at Dog College and Cat College. The curriculum includes courses on physiology, natural nutrition, communication, genetics, environmental science, health science, and art history. Participants can also enter to win pet food and, when they finish a course, print a Dog College "bark-alaureate" diploma. In addition, Iams and Eukanuba partner with the Veterinary Pet Insurance Co. to provide health insurance for cats, dogs, birds, and more exotic pets. By offering a wide variety of goods and services for pet health and well-being, Iams and Eukanuba are clearly paying attention to the needs of pet owners and making it possible for them to create healthy lifestyles for their pets.[34]

Questions for Discussion

1. Which of the psychological influences on pet owners should marketers at Iams and Eukanuba pay particular attention to, and why?
2. During which stages of the buying decision process would you expect the educational resources of Dog College and Cat College to have the most influence on consumers' behavior?
3. Why would consumers continue spending on their pets even during an economic downturn? Explain your answer in terms of consumer buying behavior concepts.

NOTES

[1]Based on information in Keith O'Brien, "Should We All Go Gluten-Free?" *The New York Times,* November 25, 2011, www.nytimes.com; Mike Hughlett, "Demonized Gluten Means Major Dough," *Minneapolis Star Tribune,* May 8, 2011, 1A; Jenni Spinner, "General Mills Cereal Packaging Spotlights Whole Grains," *Packaging Digest,* January 13, 2012, www.packagingdigest.com; www.glutenfreely.com.

[2]Russell W. Belk, "Situational Variables and Consumer Behavior," *Journal of Consumer Research* (December 1975): 157–164.

[3]"Kroger Stays Neutral," Zacks Investment Research, January 19, 2012, www.zacks.com/stock/news/68142/Kroger+Stays+Neutral.

[4]Blue Nile, *Diamond Education,* www.bluenile.com/diamonds/diamond-education (accessed February 22, 2012).

[5]Ryan S. Elder and Ariadna Krishna, "The Effects of Advertising Copy on Sensory Thoughts and Perceived Taste," *Journal of Consumer Research* 36, no. 5 (February 2010): 748–756.

[6]Dalia Fahmy, "Smells Like Profit: Scents in Stores, on Products, Makes Shoppers Buy More," ABC News, July 1, 2010, http://abcnews.go.com/Business/smells-profit-scents-stores-products-makes-shoppers-buy/story?id=11053555.

[7]Mark McNeilly, "Coke Discovers the Hard Way that People Can Taste Color," *Fast Company*, January 3, 2012, www.fastcompany.com/1804825/coke-discovers-people-can-taste-color.

[8]Sojung Kim and Matthew S. Eastin, "Hedonic Tendencies and the Online Consumer: An Investigation of the Online Shopping Process," *Journal of Internet Commerce* 10, no. 1 (2011): 68–90.

[9]Barry J. Babin and Eric G. Harris, *CB3* (Mason, OH: South-Western Cengage Learning, 2012), 130.

[10]Paul Beckett and Santanu Choudhury, "Tata Chairman Assails Early Nano Sales Efforts," *The Wall Street Journal,* January 5, 2012, http://online.wsj.com/article/SB10001424052970203513604577142072569802382.html?KEYWORDS=nano.

[11]Aric Rindfleisch, James E. Burroughs, and Nancy Wong, "The Safety of Objects: Materialism, Existential Insecurity, and Brand Connection," *Journal of Consumer Research* 36, no. 1 (June 2009): 1–16.

[12]"Common Threads Initiative," Patagonia, www.patagonia.com/us/common-threads/ (accessed February 22, 2012); Angus Loten, "With New Law, Profits Take a Back Seat," *The Wall Street Journal,* January 19, 2012, http://online.wsj.com/article/SB10001424052970203735304577168591470161630.html?KEYWORDS=Patagonia.

[13]Strategic Business Insights, www.strategicbusinessinsights.com/vals/ (accessed March 31, 2011).

[14]"Fast Facts," Marketing to Women Conference, www.m2w.biz/fast_facts.php (accessed February 22, 2012).

[15]Mercedes-Benz USA, *Vehicles Menu,* www.mbusa.com/mercedes/vehicles (accessed February 22, 2012); BMW North America, *All BMWs,* www.bmwusa.com/standard/content/allbmws/default.aspx (accessed February 22, 2012).

[16]"35% of American Adults Own a Smartphone," Pew Research Center, July 11, 2011, http://pewresearch.org/pubs/2054/smartphone-ownership-demographics-iphone-blackberry-android.

[17]Jeffrey M. Humphreys, "The Multicultural Economy 2010," Selig Center for Economic Growth, www.terry.uga.edu/selig/buying_power.html (accessed February 22, 2012).

[18]William H. Frey, "America's Diverse Future: Initial Glimpses at the U.S. Child Population from the 2010 Census," Metropolitan Policy Program at Brookings, April 2011, www.brookings.edu/~/media/Files/rc/papers/2011/0406_census_ diversity_frey/0406_census_diversity_frey.pdf.

[19]U.S. Census Bureau, *2010 Census Data*, http://2010.census.gov/2010census/data/index.php (accessed February 22, 2012).

[20]Humphreys, "The Multicultural Economy 2010."

[21]Brittany Hutson, "7 Companies Effectively Marketing to African American Consumers," *Atlanta Post*, November 2, 2010, http://atlantapost.com/2010/11/02/7-companies-effectively-marketing-to-african-american-consumers/.

[22]U.S. Census Bureau, *2010 Census Data.*

[23]Humphreys, "The Multicultural Economy 2010."

[24]Ibid.

[25]"Clorox Launches Hogar + Sanitos en Tres Pasitos Campaign Encouraging Hispanic Families to Have a Healthier Home," PR Newswire, January 23, 2012, www.prnewswire.com/news-releases/clorox-launches-hogar--sanito-en-tres-pasitos-campaign-encouraging-hispanic-families-to-have-a-healthier-home-137895548.html.

[26]Laurel Wentz, "Allstate, Telemundo Start Online Awards for Telenovela Fans," *Ad Age,* June 20, 2011, http://adage.com/article/hispanic-marketing/allstate-telemundo-start-online-awards-telenovela-fans/228293/.

[27]U.S. Census Bureau, *2010 Census Data.*

[28]Humphreys, "The Multicultural Economy 2010."

[29]Tim Peterson, "Subaru Campaign Targets Asian-American Consumers," *Direct Marketing News*, May 20, 2011, www.dmnews.com/subaru-campaign-targets-asian-american-consumers/article/203383/.

[30]"Organized Retail Theft: A $30 Billion-a-Year Industry," Federal Bureau of Investigation, January 3, 2011, www.fbi.gov/news/stories/2011/january/retail_010311.

[31]Stu Woo and Ben Worthen, "Lessons from Zappos Attack," *The Wall Street Journal*, January 17, 2012, http://online.wsj.com/article/SB10001424052970203735304577167282373793846.html?KEYWORDS=retail+crime.

[32]"Emerging Markets Drive Software Piracy to a Record $59 Billion in 2010, BSA Reports," Business Software Alliance, May 12, 2011, www.bsa.org/country/News%20and%20Events/News%20Archives/global/05062011-idc-globalpiracystudy.aspx.

[33]Rose Yu, "Starbucks to Brew a Bigger China Pot," *The Wall Street Journal,* April 1, 2012, www.wsj.com; Bruce Horovitz, "Starbucks to Jolt

Consumers with Refreshers Energy Drink," *USA Today,* March 22, 2012, www.usatoday.com; Bruce Horovitz, "Starbucks to Open First Evolution Fresh Juice Store," *USA Today,* March 18, 2012, www.usatoday.com; Jennifer Van Grove, "Starbucks Apps Account for 42M Payments," *VentureBeat,* April 9, 2012, www.venturebeat.com.

[34]Allison Cerra, "Iams Boosts Pet Care Offerings for Older Four-Legged Friends," Drug Store News, March 9, 2012, www.drugstorenews.com; "Ongoing 'Humanization' of Pets Good for Business," MMR, January 23, 2012, 18; Teddy Wayne, "Gourmet Dog Food," *Bloomberg Businessweek,* March 15, 2012, www.businessweek.com; www.iams.com; www.eukanuba.com.

Feature Notes

[a.] Based on information in "Values for Money," *Economist,* November 19, 2011, 66; "New Devices for an 'Appy' Environment," *Environmental Technology Online,* December 23, 2011, www.envirotech-online.com; Jefferson Graham, "Mobile Apps Make It Easier to Go Green," *USA Today,* May 12, 2011, www.usatoday.com; Jefferson Graham, "GoodGuide App Helps Navigate Green Products," *USA Today,* May 13, 2011, www.usatoday.com.

[b.] Based on information in Byron Acohido, "Consumers Turn to Do-Not-Track Software to Maintain Privacy," *USA Today,* December 29, 2011, www.usatoday.com; Byron Acohido, "Internet Advertisers Begin Offering New Do Not Track Icon," *USA Today,* August 29, 2011, www.usatoday.com; Ryan LaSalle and Rafae Bhatti, "A Privacy-Centered Economy," *TechWorld,* January 13, 2012, www.techworld.com.

[c.] Based on information in Blythe Lawrence, "Real-Estate Pros Hopeful about Apps, Social Media in New Year," *Seattle Times,* January 6, 2012, http://seattletimes.nwsource.com; Kunur Patel, "Why Marketers Love for QR Codes Is Not Shared by Consumers," *Advertising Age,* January 2, 2012, www.adage.com; Kevin Woodward, "Retailers Stuff Their Stores with QR Codes," *Internet Retailer,* January 4, 2012, www.internetretailer.com.

[d.] Based on information in Meredith Goad, "Fiasco Stirs the Gelato Pot on Sweet Stretch of Fore Street," *Press Herald* (Portland, OR), October 19, 2011, www.pressherald.com; Josh Davis, "Five Lessons from Gelato Fiasco Co-Founder Josh Davis," *Bowdoin Orient Express* (Maine), September 11, 2010, http://bowdoinorientexpress.com; Elaine Pofeldt, "David vs. Goliath: The Gelato Fiasco vs. Haagen Dazs," *Fortune,* November 7, 2011, 50.

chapter 8

Business Markets and Buying Behavior

OBJECTIVES

1. To distinguish among the various types of business markets
2. To identify the major characteristics of business customers and transactions
3. To understand several attributes of demand for business products
4. To become familiar with the major components of a buying center
5. To understand the stages of the business buying decision process and the factors that affect this process
6. To describe industrial classification systems, and explain how they can be used to identify and analyze business markets

MARKETING INSIGHTS

Staying Ahead of Technology

Cisco Systems, founded five years before the World Wide Web was born, has grown into a $43 billion company by helping corporations, government agencies, utility companies, and small businesses prepare for an increasingly networked future. Its earliest products were software and equipment for moving data between computer networks. Over the years, Cisco has evolved into a full-service provider of cutting-edge equipment and services that enable business organizations to do more with the information that moves through their networks.

Cisco's personnel visit customers regularly to discuss their networking needs, with an eye toward introducing new products. Nearly a decade ago, Cisco began asking the different departments within its customer businesses about how they move data, voice (such as phone calls), and video (such as sales presentations) through their networks. Cisco realized that its customers would soon need a more powerful, flexible networking system to handle everything. It decided to develop its own line of blade servers, versatile networking products that save both space and energy. By helping businesses solve three networking problems with one product, Cisco quickly became the number-two U.S. marketer of blade servers.

Looking ahead, Cisco has created special "smart grid" technology for utilities that are starting to upgrade their power systems for more efficiency and security. It has also won market share in the competitive world of data centers by partnering with multiple vendors to deliver its Unified Computing System, meeting customers' exacting standards for reliability and performance. Finally, Cisco offers services like WebEx that allow businesses of all sizes to hold virtual meetings and presentations as they move into the networked future.[1]

Serving business markets effectively requires understanding those markets. Marketers at Cisco go to considerable lengths to understand their customers so they can provide better products and develop and maintain long-term customer relationships. Like consumer marketers, business marketers are concerned about satisfying their customers.

In this chapter, we look at business markets and business buying decision processes. We first discuss various kinds of business markets and the types of buyers that comprise those markets. Next, we explore several dimensions of business buying, such as characteristics of transactions, attributes and concerns of buyers, methods of buying, and distinctive features of demand for products sold to business purchasers. We then examine how business buying decisions are made and who makes the purchases. Finally, we consider how business markets are analyzed.

BUSINESS MARKETS

As defined in Chapter 6, a business market (also called a *business-to-business market* or *B2B market*) consists of individuals, organizations, or groups that purchase a specific kind of product for one of three purposes: resale, direct use in producing other products, or use in general daily operations. Marketing to businesses employs the same concepts as marketing to ultimate consumers—such as defining target markets, understanding buying behavior, and developing effective marketing mixes—but we devote a complete chapter to business marketing because there are structural and behavioral differences in business markets. A company that markets to another company must understand how its product will affect other firms in the marketing channel, such as resellers and other manufacturers. Business products can also be technically complex, and the market often consists of sophisticated buyers.

Because the business market consists of relatively smaller customer populations, a segment of the market could be as small as a few customers.[2] The market for railway equipment in the United States, for example, is limited to a few major carriers. On the other hand, a business product can be a commodity, such as corn or a bolt or screw, but the quantity purchased and the buying methods differ significantly from the consumer market. Business marketing is often based on long-term mutually profitable relationships across members of the marketing channel. Networks of suppliers and customers recognize the importance of building strong alliances based on cooperation, trust, and collaboration.[3] Manufacturers may even co-develop new products, with business customers sharing marketing research, production, scheduling, inventory management, and information systems. Although business marketing can be based on collaborative long-term buyer–seller relationships, there are also transactions based on timely exchanges of basic products at highly competitive market prices. For most business marketers, the goal is understanding customer needs and providing a value-added exchange that shifts from attracting customers to keeping customers and developing relationships.

The four categories of business markets are producer, reseller, government, and institutional. In the remainder of this section, we discuss each of these types of markets.

Producer Markets
Fellowes manufactures shredders. The companies that sell raw materials, equipment, and component parts to Fellowes and other manufacturers are serving producer markets.

Producer Markets

Individuals and business organizations that purchase products for the purpose of making a profit by using them to produce other products or using them in their operations are classified

Table 8.1 Number of Establishments in Industry Groups

Industry	Number of Establishments
Forestry, fishing, hunting, and agriculture	231,000
Mining, quarrying, and oil/gas extraction	109,000
Construction	2,528,000
Manufacturing	314,000
Transportation, warehousing, and utilities	1,057,000
Finance, insurance, and real estate	2,864,000

Source: U.S. Bureau of the Census, *Statistical Abstract of the United States, 2012*, Table 757, www.census.gov/compendia/statab/2012/tables/12s0757.pdf.

as **producer markets**. Producer markets include buyers of raw materials, as well as purchasers of semifinished and finished items, used to produce other products. For instance, manufacturers buy raw materials and component parts for direct use in product creation. Grocery stores and supermarkets are part of producer markets for numerous support products, such as paper and plastic bags, shelves, counters, and scanners. Farmers are part of producer markets for farm machinery, fertilizer, seed, and livestock. Producer markets include a broad array of industries ranging from agriculture, forestry, fisheries, and mining to construction, transportation, communications, and utilities. As Table 8.1 indicates, the number of business establishments in national producer markets is enormous.

Manufacturers are geographically concentrated. More than half are located in just seven states: New York, California, Pennsylvania, Illinois, Ohio, New Jersey, and Michigan. This concentration sometimes enables businesses that sell to producer markets to serve them more efficiently. Within certain states, production in a specific industry may account for a sizable proportion of that industry's total production. However, the United States is not the manufacturing powerhouse that it once was. In fact, the country has lost 28 percent of its high-tech manufacturing jobs since 2000. Most of this loss is attributable to outsourcing, cutbacks on funding for research and development, and increasingly competitive workforces in other countries, primarily in Asia.[4]

Reseller Markets

Reseller markets consist of intermediaries, such as wholesalers and retailers, which buy finished goods and resell them for a profit. Aside from making minor alterations, resellers do not change the physical characteristics of the products they handle. Except for items producers sell directly to consumers, all products sold to consumer markets are first sold to reseller markets.

Wholesalers purchase products for resale to retailers, other wholesalers, producers, governments, and institutions. Of the nearly 430,000 wholesalers in the United States, a large number are located in New York, California, Illinois, Texas, Ohio, Pennsylvania, New Jersey, and Florida.[5] Although some products are sold directly to end users, many manufacturers sell their products to wholesalers, which in turn sell the products to other firms in the distribution system. Thus, wholesalers are very important in helping producers get products to customers.

Retailers purchase products and resell them to final consumers. There are approximately 1.1 million retailers in the United States, employing almost 16 million people and generating approximately $3.9 trillion in annual sales.[6] Half of the top 10 largest retail companies in the world are based in the United States. These retailers include Walmart, The Kroger Co., Home Depot, Costco, and Target.[7] Some retailers—Home Depot, PetSmart, and Staples, for

producer markets Individuals and business organizations that purchase products to make profits by using them to produce other products or using them in their operations

reseller markets Intermediaries that buy finished goods and resell them for a profit

example—carry a large number of items. Supermarkets may handle as many as 50,000 different products. In small, individually owned retail stores, owners or managers make purchasing decisions. In chain stores, a central office buyer or buying committee frequently decides whether a product will be made available for selection by store managers. For many products, however, local managers make the actual buying decisions for a particular store.

When making purchase decisions, resellers consider several factors. They evaluate the level of demand for a product to determine in what quantity and at what prices the product can be resold. Retailers assess the amount of space required to handle a product relative to its potential profit, sometimes on the basis of sales per square foot of selling area. Because customers often depend on resellers to have products available when needed, resellers typically appraise a supplier's ability to provide adequate quantities when and where wanted. Resellers also take into account the ease of placing orders and the availability of technical assistance and training programs from producers. When resellers consider buying a product not previously carried, they try to determine whether the product competes with or complements products they currently handle. These types of concerns distinguish reseller markets from other markets.

Government Markets

Federal, state, county, and local governments make up **government markets**. These markets spend billions of dollars annually for a variety of goods and services, ranging from office supplies and health-care services to vehicles, heavy equipment, and weapons, to support their internal operations and provide citizens with such products as highways, education, water, energy, and national defense. Total government spending accounts for around 39 percent of the United States' total gross domestic product. A significant portion of this goes to national defense. As the national debt grows, there has been mounting pressure to reduce government spending. The president has proposed cuts to government spending, including 10 percent of the Pentagon's budget, which concerns businesses and contractors who rely on government work.[8] Besides the federal government, there are 50 state governments, 3,033 county governments, and 89,476 local governments.[9] The amount spent by federal, state, and local units during the past 30 years has increased rapidly because the total number of government units, and the services they provide, have both increased. Costs of providing these services have also risen.

government markets
Federal, state, county, or local governments that buy goods and services to support their internal operations and provide products to their constituencies

Going Green

IBM: Big Blue Is Really Green

IBM (aka: Big Blue), known worldwide for business-to-business technology products and services, has made eco-friendly operations a priority since 1971. Early on, the company sought to reduce production waste and prevent pollution. Decades later, the ongoing effort to spread these and other practices throughout its global supply chain has won the $100 billion company high marks for green leadership.

Today, IBM's 28,000 suppliers in nearly 100 countries are required to measure and report on their environmental impact, including energy use, greenhouse gas emissions, and recycling results. Year by year, IBM suppliers must also make progress toward green goals such as conserving natural resources and reducing waste. Just as important, IBM suppliers are expected to push *their* suppliers toward greener practices. Being green adds to IBM's bottom line, says the company's chief procurement officer, because conserving scarce resources will keep costs under control—an important consideration for its suppliers and business customers, as well.

Finally, IBM's green leadership is also attracting attention in government markets, because many of those buyers are responsible for environmental initiatives on the national, state, and local levels. It has already been honored by the U.S. Environmental Protection Agency, by New York State, and by other government groups for its earth-friendly programs. Watch for Big Blue to go even greener in the future.[a]

Government contracts are awarded to firms of all sizes and across a wide variety of industries. One example is New Jersey-based VaxInnate, a biotechnology company that specializes in developing vaccines. The U.S. Department of Health and Human Services (HHS) recently awarded VaxInnate a contract worth up to $196 million to develop flu vaccines for the public.[10] Although it is common to hear of large corporations being awarded government contracts, in fact, businesses of all sizes market to government agencies.

Because government agencies spend public funds to buy the products needed to provide services, they are accountable to the public. This accountability explains their relatively complex set of buying procedures. Some firms do not even try to sell to government buyers because they want to avoid the tangle of red tape. However, many marketers have learned to deal efficiently with government procedures and do not find them to be a stumbling block. For certain products, such as defense-related items, the government may be the only customer. The U.S. Government Printing Office publishes and distributes several documents that explain buying procedures and describe the types of products various federal agencies purchase.

Governments make purchases through bids or negotiated contracts. Although companies may be reluctant to approach government markets because of the complicated bidding process, once they understand the rules of this process, some firms routinely penetrate government markets. To make a sale under the bid system, firms must apply and be approved for placement on a list of qualified bidders. When a government unit wants to buy, it sends out a detailed description of the products to qualified bidders. Businesses that want to sell such products submit bids. The government unit is usually required to accept the lowest bid.

institutional markets Organizations with charitable, educational, community, or other nonbusiness goals

When buying nonstandard or highly complex products, a government unit often uses a negotiated contract. Under this procedure, the government unit selects only a few firms and then negotiates specifications and terms; it eventually awards the contract to one of the negotiating firms. Most large defense-related contracts, once held by such companies as Lockheed Martin and Northrop Grumman, traditionally were negotiated in this fashion. However, as the number and size of such contracts have declined, these companies have had to strengthen their marketing efforts and look to other markets. Although government markets can impose intimidating requirements, they can also be very lucrative.

Institutional Markets

Organizations with charitable, educational, community, or other nonbusiness goals constitute **institutional markets**. Members of institutional markets include churches, some hospitals, fraternities and sororities, charitable organizations, and private colleges. Institutions purchase millions of dollars' worth of products annually to provide goods, services, and ideas to congregations, students, patients, and others. Because institutions often have different goals and fewer resources than other types of organizations, marketers may use special marketing efforts to serve them. Aramark provides a variety of services and products to institutional markets, from schools to hospitals, to senior living centers. It is one of *Fortune* magazine's most admired companies and has demonstrated a commitment to reducing waste and increasing sustainability. The positive publicity related to its social responsibility efforts helps Aramark gain new clients. For areas like its university food service, Aramark aims its marketing efforts directly at students.[11]

Institutional Markets
This pipe organ producer supplies products mainly to churches, which are a part of institutional markets.

DIMENSIONS OF MARKETING TO BUSINESS CUSTOMERS

Now that we have considered different types of business customers, we look at several dimensions of marketing to them, including transaction characteristics, attributes of business customers and some of their primary concerns, buying methods, major types of purchases, and the characteristics of demand for business products (see Figure 8.1).

Characteristics of Transactions with Business Customers

Transactions between businesses differ from consumer sales in several ways. Orders by business customers tend to be much larger than individual consumer sales. Consider that Turkish Airlines recently placed an order for 15 of Boeing's 737 aircraft. In total, the order was worth more than $1.2 billion.[12] Suppliers often must sell products in large quantities to make profits; consequently, they prefer not to sell to customers who place small orders.

Some business purchases involve expensive items, such as computer systems. Other products, such as raw materials and component items, are used continuously in production, and their supply may need frequent replenishing. The contract regarding terms of sale of these items is likely to be a long-term agreement.

Discussions and negotiations associated with business purchases can require considerable marketing time and selling effort. Purchasing decisions are often made by committee, orders are frequently large and expensive, and products may be custom built. Several people or departments in the purchasing organization are often involved. For example, one department expresses a need for a product, a second department develops the specifications, a third stipulates maximum expenditures, and a fourth places the order.

reciprocity An arrangement unique to business marketing in which two organizations agree to buy from each other

One practice unique to business markets is **reciprocity**, an arrangement in which two organizations agree to buy from each other. Reciprocal agreements that threaten competition are

Figure 8.1 Dimensions of Marketing to Business Customers

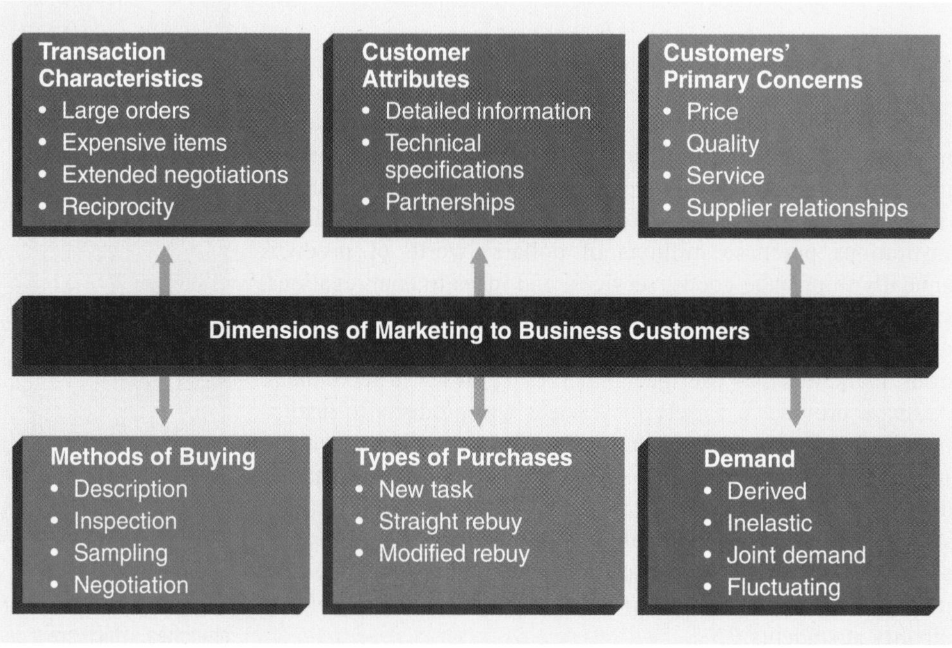

illegal. The Federal Trade Commission and the Justice Department take actions to stop anticompetitive reciprocal practices. Nonetheless, a certain amount of reciprocal activity occurs among small businesses and, to a lesser extent, among larger companies. Because reciprocity influences purchasing agents to deal only with certain suppliers, it can lower morale among agents and lead to less than optimal purchases.

Attributes of Business Customers

Business customers differ from consumers in their purchasing behavior because they are better informed about the products they purchase. They typically demand detailed information about a product's functional features and technical specifications to ensure that it meets their needs. Personal goals, however, may also influence business buying behavior. Most purchasing agents seek the psychological satisfaction that comes with organizational advancement and financial rewards. Agents who consistently exhibit rational business buying behavior are likely to attain these personal goals because they help their firms achieve organizational objectives. Today, many suppliers and their customers build and maintain mutually beneficial relationships, sometimes called *partnerships.* Researchers find that even in a partnership between a small vendor and a large corporate buyer, a strong partnership exists because high levels of interpersonal trust can lead to higher levels of commitment to the partnership by both organizations.[13]

Primary Concerns of Business Customers

When making purchasing decisions, business customers take into account a variety of factors. Among their chief considerations are price, product quality, service, and supplier relationships. Obviously, price matters greatly to business customers because it influences operating costs and costs of goods sold, which in turn affect selling price, profit margin, and ultimately the ability to compete. When purchasing major equipment, a business customer views price as the amount of investment necessary to obtain a certain level of return or savings. A business customer is likely to compare the price of a product with the benefits the product will yield to the organization, often over a period of years.

Most business customers try to achieve and maintain a specific level of quality in the products they buy. To achieve this goal, most firms establish standards (usually stated as a percentage of defects allowed) for these products and buy them on the basis of a set of expressed characteristics, commonly called *specifications.* A customer evaluates the quality of the products being considered to determine whether they meet specifications. If a product fails to meet specifications or malfunctions for the ultimate consumer, the customer may drop that product's supplier and switch to a different one. On the other hand, customers are ordinarily cautious about buying products that exceed specifications because such products often cost more, thus increasing the organization's overall costs. Specifications are designed to meet a customer's wants, and anything that does not contribute to meeting those wants may be considered wasteful.

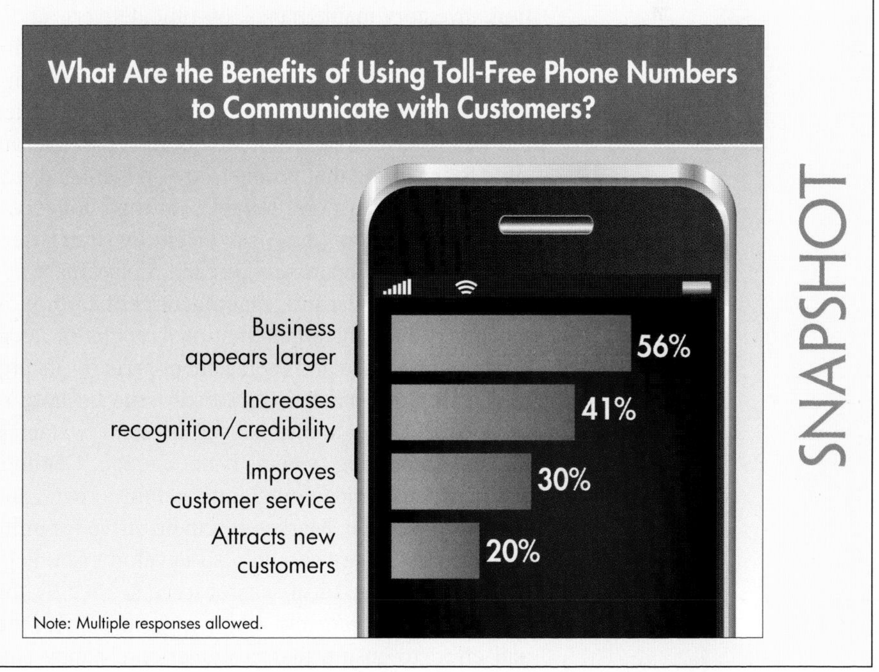

Source: eVoice survey of 308 small-business owners.

Concerns of Business Customers
Business customers are concerned about several major factors, including costs, acquiring the right product that works effectively, and customer service.

© AP Images/PRNewsFoto/Cloud Cruiser

Business buyers value service. Services offered by suppliers directly and indirectly influence customers' costs, sales, and profits. In some instances, the mix of customer services is the major means by which marketers gain a competitive advantage. WaterFurnace, a manufacturer of geothermal energy equipment for residential and commercial markets, recently launched a web-based platform just for businesses. WeDoGeo.com provides business customers with information on equipment selection and pricing, ordering, and answers to construction questions. The platform improves communication and ease of ordering, and attracts customers looking for strong customer service.[14] Typical services customers desire are market information, inventory maintenance, on-time delivery, and repair services. Business buyers are likely to need technical product information, data regarding demand, information about general economic conditions, or supply and delivery information. Maintaining adequate inventory is critical because it helps make products accessible when a customer needs them and reduces the customer's inventory requirements and costs. Because business customers are usually responsible for ensuring that products are on hand and ready for use when needed, on-time delivery is crucial. Furthermore, reliable, on-time delivery saves business customers money because it enables them to carry less inventory. Purchasers of machinery are especially concerned about obtaining repair services and replacement parts quickly because inoperable equipment is costly. Caterpillar Inc., manufacturer of earth-moving, construction, and materials-handling machinery, has built an international reputation, as well as a competitive advantage, by providing prompt service and replacement parts for its products around the world.[15]

Quality of service is a critical issue because customer expectations about service have broadened. Using traditional service quality standards based only on traditional manufacturing and accounting systems is not enough. Communication channels that allow customers to ask questions, voice complaints, submit orders, and trace shipments are indispensable components of service. Marketers should strive for uniformity of service, simplicity, truthfulness, and accuracy. They should also develop customer service objectives and monitor customer service programs. Firms can observe service by formally surveying customers or informally calling on customers and asking questions about the service they receive. Expending the time and effort to ensure that customers are happy can greatly benefit marketers by increasing customer retention.

Emerging Trends

Apps Help Business Marketers Go Mobile

Now that many business customers carry mobile devices, such as smartphones and tablet computers, business marketers are stepping up their use of mobile marketing to reach buyers, sellers, and users. For example, Emerson Climate Technologies, which makes thermostats and other climate-control equipment, offers a variety of mobile apps (applications) to help customers make buying decisions and use its products more effectively. Another ECT app allows sellers to show homeowners how much energy and money will be saved by installing new, high-efficiency systems. A third app helps technicians diagnose malfunctioning climate-control systems and identify the appropriate replacement parts needed to make repairs.

CBS Outdoor, which markets advertising space on billboards, offers a map app that allows advertising agencies and media buyers to pinpoint its North American billboard locations. The app also shows nearby transportation facilities and offers access to a gallery of billboard ads, to help agencies evaluate traffic patterns and plan creative strategies.

The office supply retailer Office Max reaches out to small businesses with apps that promote weekly product specials, help customers find the closest store and check loyalty rewards, show customers' purchase history for quick and easy reordering, and enable customers to order copies of printed documents on the go. As an added convenience, Office Max will send a text alert when a customer's print order is ready to be picked up.[b]

Finally, business customers are concerned about the costs of developing and maintaining relationships with their suppliers. By developing relationships and building trust with a particular supplier, buyers can reduce their search efforts and uncertainty about monetary prices. Research also demonstrates that satisfaction and perceived product quality in B2B relationships foster loyalty and future purchase intentions. Business customers have to keep in mind the overall fit of a purchase, including its potential to reduce inventory and carrying costs, and increase inventory turnover and ability to move the right products to the right place at the right time.

Methods of Business Buying

Although no two business buyers do their jobs the same way, most use one or more of the following purchase methods: *description, inspection, sampling,* and *negotiation.* When products are standardized according to certain characteristics (such as size, shape, weight, and color) and graded using such standards, a business buyer may be able to purchase simply by describing or specifying quantity, grade, and other attributes. Agricultural products often fall into this category. Sometimes buyers specify a particular brand or its equivalent when describing the desired product. Purchases on the basis of description are especially common between a buyer and seller with an ongoing relationship built on trust.

Certain products, such as industrial equipment, used vehicles, and buildings, have unique characteristics and may vary with regard to condition. For example, a particular used truck may have a bad transmission. Consequently, business buyers of such products must base purchase decisions on inspection.

Sampling entails taking a specimen of the product from the lot and evaluating it on the assumption that its characteristics represent the entire lot. This method is appropriate when the product is homogeneous—for instance, grain—and examining the entire lot is not physically or economically feasible.

Some purchases by businesses are based on negotiated contracts. In certain instances, buyers describe exactly what they need and ask sellers to submit bids. They then negotiate with the suppliers that submit the most attractive bids. This approach may be used when acquiring commercial vehicles, for example. In other cases, the buyer may be unable to identify specifically what is to be purchased and can provide only a general description, as might be the case for a piece of custom-made equipment. A buyer and seller might negotiate a contract that specifies a base price and provides for the payment of additional costs and fees. These contracts are most commonly used for onetime projects such as buildings, capital equipment, and special projects.

new-task purchase An organization's initial purchase of an item to be used to perform a new job or solve a new problem

straight rebuy purchase A routine purchase of the same products under approximately the same terms of sale by a business buyer

modified rebuy purchase A new-task purchase that is changed on subsequent orders or when the requirements of a straight rebuy purchase are modified

derived demand Demand for business products that stems from demand for consumer products

Types of Business Purchases

Most business purchases are one of three types: new-task, straight rebuy, or modified rebuy purchase. Each type is subject to different influences and thus requires business marketers to modify their selling approaches appropriately. For a **new-task purchase**, an organization makes an initial purchase of an item to be used to perform a new job or solve a new problem. A new-task purchase may require development of product specifications, vendor specifications, and procedures for future purchases of that product. To make the initial purchase, the business buyer usually needs much information. New-task purchases are important to suppliers, because if business buyers are satisfied with the products, suppliers may be able to sell buyers large quantities of them for many years.

A **straight rebuy purchase** occurs when buyers purchase the same products routinely under approximately the same terms of sale. Buyers require little information for these routine purchase decisions and tend to use familiar suppliers that have provided satisfactory service and products in the past. These marketers try to set up automatic reordering systems to make reordering easy and convenient for business buyers. A supplier may even monitor the business buyer's inventories and indicate to the buyer what should be ordered and when.

For a **modified rebuy purchase**, a new-task purchase is changed the second or third time it is ordered, or requirements associated with a straight rebuy purchase are modified. A business buyer might seek faster delivery, lower prices, or a different quality level of product specifications. A modified rebuy situation may cause regular suppliers to become more competitive to keep the account because other suppliers could obtain the business. When a firm changes the terms of a service contract, such as for telecommunication services, it has made a modified purchase.

Courtesy of Hewlett-Packard

Types of Business Purchases
When purchasing this type of equipment, business customers are prone to use a modified rebuy.

Demand for Business Products

Unlike consumer demand, demand for business products (also called *industrial demand*) can be characterized as (1) derived, (2) inelastic, (3) joint, or (4) fluctuating.

Derived Demand

Because business customers, especially producers, buy products for direct or indirect use in the production of goods and services to satisfy consumers' needs, the demand for business products derives from the demand for consumer products; it is therefore called **derived demand**. In the long run, no demand for business products is totally unrelated to the demand for consumer products. The derived nature of demand is usually multilevel. Business marketers at different levels are affected by a change in consumer demand for a particular product. For instance, consumers have become concerned with health and good nutrition and, as a result, are purchasing more products with less fat, cholesterol, and sodium. When consumers reduced their purchases of high-fat foods, a change occurred in the demand for products marketed by food processors, equipment manufacturers, and suppliers of raw materials associated with these products. Change in consumer demand for a product affects demand for all firms involved in the production of that product.

© iStockphoto.com/4kodiak

Derived Demand
Intel attempts to generate derived demand by promoting that its products are inside many brands of computers. Thus, the sale of computers generates demand for Intel products.

Inelastic Demand

With **inelastic demand**, a price increase or decrease will not significantly alter demand for a business product. Because some business products contain a number of parts, price increases that affect only one or two parts may yield only a slightly higher per-unit production cost. When a sizable price increase for a component represents a large proportion of the product's cost, demand may become more elastic because the price increase in the component causes the price at the consumer level to rise sharply. For example, if aircraft engine manufacturers substantially increase the price of engines, forcing Boeing to raise the prices of the aircraft it manufactures, the demand for airliners may become more elastic as airlines reconsider whether they can afford to buy new aircraft. An increase in the price of windshields, however, is unlikely to greatly affect either the price of or the demand for airliners.

Inelasticity applies only to industry demand for business products, not to the demand an individual firm faces. Suppose a spark plug producer increases the price of spark plugs sold to small-engine manufacturers, but its competitors continue to maintain lower prices. The spark plug company will probably experience reduced unit sales because most small-engine producers will switch to lower-priced brands. A specific firm is vulnerable to elastic demand, even if industry demand for a specific business product is inelastic.

Joint Demand

Demand for certain business products, especially raw materials and components, is subject to joint demand. **Joint demand** occurs when two or more items are used in combination to produce a product. Consider a firm that manufactures axes. The firm will need the same number of ax handles as it does ax blades; these two products thus are demanded jointly. If a shortage of ax handles exists, the producer buys fewer ax blades. Understanding the effects of joint demand is particularly important for a marketer that sells multiple jointly demanded items. Such a marketer realizes that when a customer begins purchasing one of the jointly demanded items, a good opportunity exists to sell related products.

inelastic demand Demand that is not significantly altered by a price increase or decrease

joint demand Demand involving the use of two or more items in combination to produce a product

Fluctuating Demand

Because the demand for business products is derived from consumer demand, it may fluctuate enormously. In general, when particular consumer products are in high demand, their producers buy large quantities of raw materials and components to ensure meeting long-run production requirements. In addition, these producers may expand production capacity, which entails acquiring new equipment and machinery, more workers, and more raw materials and component parts. Conversely, a decline in demand for certain consumer goods significantly reduces demand for business products used to produce those goods.

Marketers of business products may notice changes in demand when customers alter inventory policies, perhaps because of expectations about future demand. For example, if several dishwasher manufacturers that buy timers from one producer increase their inventory of timers from a two-week to a one-month supply, the timer producer will have a significant, immediate increase in demand.

Sometimes, price changes lead to surprising temporary changes in demand. A price increase for a business product may initially cause business customers to buy more of the item because they expect the price to rise further. Similarly, demand for a business product may decrease significantly following a price cut because buyers are waiting for further price reductions. Fluctuations in demand can be substantial in industries in which prices change frequently.

BUSINESS BUYING DECISIONS

Business (organizational) buying behavior refers to the purchase behavior of producers, government units, institutions, and resellers. Although several factors that affect consumer buying behavior (discussed in the previous chapter) also influence business buying behavior, a number of factors are unique to the latter. In this section, we first analyze the buying center to learn who participates in business purchase decisions. Then we focus on the stages of the buying decision process and the factors that affect it.

The Buying Center

Relatively few business purchase decisions are made by just one person; often they are made through a buying center. The **buying center** is the group of people within the organization who make business purchase decisions. They include users, influencers, buyers, deciders, and gatekeepers.[16] One person may perform several roles. These participants share some goals and risks associated with their decisions.

Users are the organizational members who actually use the product being acquired. They frequently initiate the purchase process and/or generate purchase specifications. After the purchase, they evaluate product performance relative to the specifications.

Influencers are often technical personnel, such as engineers, who help develop the specifications and evaluate alternative products. Technical personnel are especially important influencers when the products being considered involve new, advanced technology.

Buyers select suppliers and negotiate terms of purchase. They may also become involved in developing specifications. Buyers are sometimes called purchasing agents or purchasing managers. Their choices of vendors and products, especially for new-task purchases, are heavily influenced by people occupying other roles in the buying center. For straight rebuy purchases, the buyer plays a major role in vendor selection and negotiations.

Deciders actually choose the products. Although buyers may be deciders, it is not unusual for different people to occupy these roles. For routinely purchased items, buyers are commonly deciders. However, a buyer may not be authorized to make purchases that exceed a certain dollar limit, in which case higher-level management personnel are deciders.

Finally, *gatekeepers,* such as secretaries and technical personnel, control the flow of information to and among people who occupy other roles in the buying center. Buyers who deal directly with vendors also may be gatekeepers because they can control information flows. The flow of information from a supplier's sales representatives to users and influencers is often controlled by personnel in the purchasing department.

business (organizational) buying behavior The purchase behavior of producers, government units, institutions, and resellers

buying center The people within an organization who make business purchase decisions

The number and structure of an organization's buying centers are affected by the organization's size and market position, the volume and types of products being purchased, and the firm's overall managerial philosophy regarding exactly who should be involved in purchase decisions. The size of a buying center is influenced by the stage of the buying decision process and by the type of purchase (new task, straight rebuy, or modified rebuy). The size of the buying center likely would be larger for a new-task purchase than for a straight rebuy. Varying goals among members of a buying center can have both positive and negative effects on the purchasing process.

A marketer attempting to sell to a business customer should determine who is in the buying center, the types of decisions each individual makes, and which individuals are most influential in the decision process. Because in some instances many people make up the buying center, marketers cannot feasibly contact all participants. Instead, they must be certain to contact a few of the most influential.

Stages of the Business Buying Decision Process

Like consumers, businesses follow a buying decision process. This process is summarized in the lower portion of Figure 8.2. In the first stage, one or more individuals recognize that a problem or need exists. Problem recognition may arise under a variety of circumstances—for instance, when machines malfunction or a firm modifies an existing product or introduces a new one. Individuals in the buying center, such as users, influencers, or buyers, may be involved in problem recognition, but it may be stimulated by external sources, such as sales representatives or advertisements.

The second stage of the process, development of product specifications, requires that buying center participants assess the problem or need and determine what is necessary to resolve or satisfy it. During this stage, users and influencers, such as engineers, often provide information and advice for developing product specifications. By assessing and describing needs, the organization should be able to establish product specifications.

Searching for and evaluating potential products and suppliers is the third stage in the decision process. Search activities may involve looking in company files and trade directories; contacting suppliers for information; soliciting proposals from known vendors; and examining websites,

Figure 8.2 **Business (Organizational) Buying Decision Process and Factors That May Influence It**

Possible influences on the decision process

Environmental
- Competitive factors
- Economic factors
- Political forces
- Legal and regulatory forces
- Technological changes
- Sociocultural issues

Organizational
- Objectives
- Purchasing policies
- Resources
- Buying center structure

Interpersonal
- Cooperation
- Conflict
- Power relationships

Individual
- Age
- Education level
- Personality
- Tenure
- Position in organization

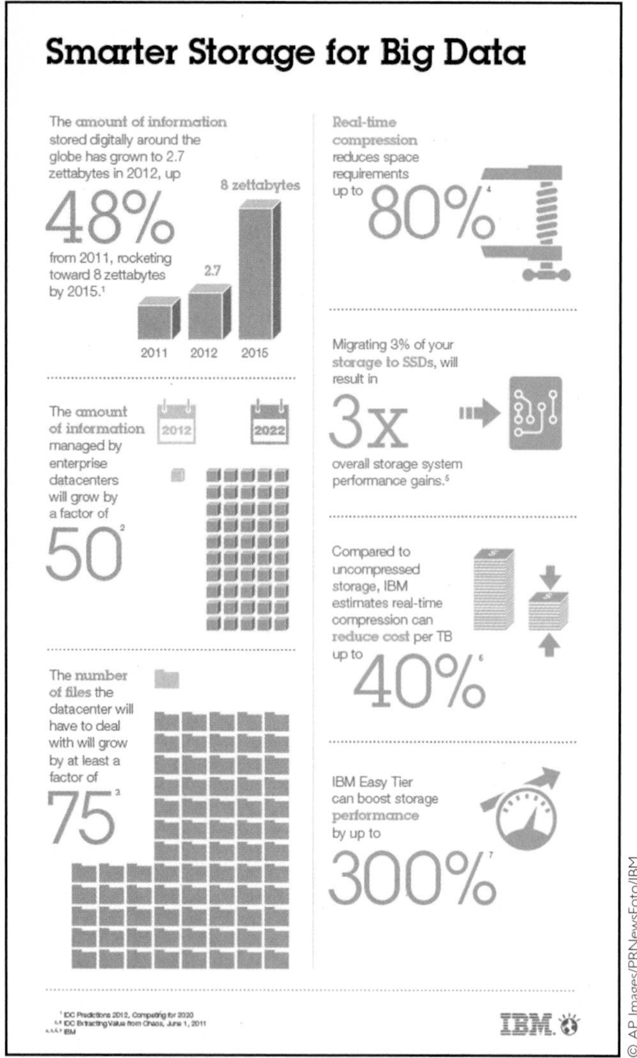

© AP Images/PRNewsFoto/IBM

Problem Recognition
This advertisement is attempting to stimulate problem recognition among business customers.

catalogs, and trade publications. To facilitate a vendor search, some organizations, such as Walmart, advertise their desire to build partnerships with specific types of vendors, such as those owned by women or by minorities. During this stage, some organizations engage in value analysis, an evaluation of each component of a potential purchase. **Value analysis** examines quality, design, materials, and possibly item reduction or deletion to acquire the product in the most cost-effective way. Some vendors may be deemed unacceptable because they are not large enough to supply needed quantities; others may be excluded because of poor delivery and service records. Sometimes the product is not available from any existing vendor and the buyer must find a company known for its innovation, such as 3M, to design and make it. Products are evaluated to make sure they meet or exceed product specifications developed in the second stage. Usually suppliers are judged according to multiple criteria. A number of firms employ **vendor analysis**, a formal, systematic evaluation of current and potential vendors, focusing on such characteristics as price, product quality, delivery service, product availability, and overall reliability.

Results of deliberations and assessments in the third stage are used during the fourth stage to select the product to be purchased and the supplier from which to buy it. In some cases, the buyer selects and uses several suppliers, a process known as **multiple sourcing**. At times, only one supplier is selected, a situation called **sole sourcing**. Firms with federal government contracts are required to have several sources for an item. Sole sourcing has traditionally been discouraged except when a product is available from only one company. Sole sourcing is much more common today, however, partly because such an arrangement means better communications between buyer and supplier, stability and higher profits for suppliers, and often lower prices for buyers. However, many organizations still prefer multiple sourcing because this approach lessens the possibility of disruption caused by strikes, shortages, or bankruptcies. The actual product is ordered in this fourth stage, and specific details regarding terms, credit arrangements, delivery dates and methods, and technical assistance are finalized. During the fifth stage, the product's performance is evaluated by comparing it with specifications. Sometimes the product meets the specifications, but its performance fails to adequately solve the problem or satisfy the need recognized in the first stage. In that case, product specifications must be adjusted. The supplier's performance is also evaluated during this stage. If supplier performance is inadequate, the business purchaser seeks corrective action from the supplier or searches for a new one. Results of the evaluation become feedback for the other stages in future business purchase decisions.

This business buying decision process is used in its entirety primarily for new-task purchases. Several stages, but not necessarily all, are used for modified rebuy and straight rebuy situations.

value analysis An evaluation of each component of a potential purchase

vendor analysis A formal, systematic evaluation of current and potential vendors

multiple sourcing An organization's decision to use several suppliers

sole sourcing An organization's decision to use only one supplier

Influences on the Business Buying Decision Process

Figure 8.2 also lists four major categories of factors that influence business buying decisions: environmental, organizational, interpersonal, and individual.

Environmental factors include competitive and economic factors, political forces, legal and regulatory forces, technological changes, and sociocultural issues. These factors generate

Marketing Debate

Self-Regulation Helps to Manage Supplier Diversity

ISSUE: When corporations and institutions make a special effort to encourage supplier diversity, how should "diversity" be defined?

Many large corporations encourage supplier diversity by reaching out to businesses that are small or owned by veterans, women, or members of minority groups. Although small businesses that meet "supplier diversity" qualifications don't automatically receive orders—they must compete, just like every other supplier—such programs help them get a foot in the door.

Can "diversity" cover too many or too few suppliers? At Kroger, the supermarket company, diversity suppliers must be at least 51 percent owned by a U.S. citizen who is Hispanic, African American, Asian-Indian, Asian-Pacific, Native American, female, gay or lesbian, bisexual, transgender, a military veteran, or a disabled military veteran. Suppliers must also be certified by a recognized group such as the National Minority Supplier Development Council or the U.S. Department of Veteran Affairs. For Dell, the computer company, diversity extends to small businesses owned by socially or economically disadvantaged people and to small businesses located in underutilized business zones, as designated by the U.S. Small Business Association.

Are these programs going too far or not far enough in providing potential opportunities for suppliers? Should diversity extend to businesses owned by teens, seniors, families, and first-time entrepreneurs? What do you think?[c]

considerable uncertainty for an organization, which can make individuals in the buying center apprehensive about certain types of purchases. Changes in one or more environmental forces can create new purchasing opportunities and threats. For example, changes in competition and technology can make buying decisions difficult for products such as software, computers, and telecommunications equipment. On the other hand, technological innovations and the Internet can help streamline business market decisions, reduce customer service costs, and improve communications and relationships with business customers.

Organizational factors that influence the buying decision process include the company's objectives, purchasing policies, and resources, as well as the size and composition of its buying center. An organization may have certain buying policies to which buying center participants must conform. For instance, a firm's policies may mandate unusually long- or short-term contracts, perhaps longer or shorter than most sellers desire. An organization's financial resources may require special credit arrangements. Any of these conditions could affect purchase decisions.

Interpersonal factors are the relationships among people in the buying center. Trust is crucial in collaborative partnerships. This is especially true when customized products are involved, as the buyer may not see the product until it is finished. Trust and clear communication will ensure that all parties are satisfied with the outcome. The use of power and the level of conflict among buying center participants influence business buying decisions. Certain individuals in the buying center may be better communicators and more persuasive than others. Often, these interpersonal dynamics are hidden, making them difficult for marketers to assess.

Individual factors are personal characteristics of participants in the buying center, such as age, education level, personality, and tenure and position in the organization. Consider a 55-year-old manager who has been in the organization for 25 years. This manager may affect decisions made by the buying center differently than a 30-year-old person employed only two years. How influential these factors are depends on the buying situation; the type of product being purchased; and whether the purchase is new-task, modified rebuy, or straight rebuy. Negotiating styles of people vary within an organization and from one organization to another. To be effective, marketers must know customers well enough to be aware of these individual factors and their potential effects on purchase decisions.

Entrepreneurship in Marketing

Pixability Helps Small Businesses Compete through Videos

Founder: Bettina Hein
Business: Pixability
Founded: 2008 | Cambridge, Massachusetts
Success: This company is growing fast, with about 85 percent of its customers located outside of the Boston area.

Bettina Hein, the founder and CEO of Pixability, says that she is in the business of "trying to democratize video." In today's wired world, YouTube and other sites are now the go-to place for how-to videos, customer testimonials, and product demonstrations. Yet small businesses rarely have the expertise and equipment to make, edit, and post professional-looking videos online. And that's where Pixability comes in.

Based in Cambridge, Massachusetts, Pixability helps small businesses turn their ideas into completed, uploaded videos in about two weeks, at an affordable price. First, Pixability talks with each customer about the purpose of the video. Then it sends out a handheld video camera and a list of suggested video shots for the customer to film. Once the customer has uploaded about 30 minutes of raw footage, Pixability's specialists edit everything down to two minutes, add music and captions, and insert the customer's logo and contact information. The result is a video that conveys the customer's message for as long as it's available on the Web.

Knowing how effective online videos can be, Pixability practices what it preaches. The fast-growing small business now has dozens of instructional videos on its website to help customers make the most of their video marketing.[d]

INDUSTRIAL CLASSIFICATION SYSTEMS

Marketers have access to a considerable amount of information about potential business customers, since much of this information is available through government and industry publications and websites. Marketers use this information to identify potential business customers and to estimate their purchase potential.

Much information about business customers is based on industrial classification systems. In the United States, marketers traditionally have relied on the *Standard Industrial Classification (SIC) system,* which the federal government developed to classify selected economic characteristics of industrial, commercial, financial, and service organizations. However, the SIC system has been replaced by a new industry classification system called the **North American Industry Classification System (NAICS)**. NAICS is a single industry classification system used by the United States, Canada, and Mexico to generate comparable statistics among the three partners of the North American Free Trade Agreement (NAFTA). The NAICS classification is based on the types of production activities performed. NAICS is similar to the International Standard Industrial Classification (ISIC) system used in Europe and many other parts of the world. Whereas the SIC system divided industrial activity into 10 divisions, NAICS divides it into 20 sectors. NAICS contains 1,170 industry classifications, compared with 1,004 in the SIC system. NAICS is more comprehensive and up-to-date, and it provides considerably more information about service industries and high-tech products.[17] Table 8.2 shows some NAICS codes for Apple Inc. and AT&T Inc. Over the next few years, all three NAFTA countries will convert from previously used industrial classification systems to NAICS.

North American Industry Classification System (NAICS) An industry classification system that generates comparable statistics among the United States, Canada, and Mexico

Industrial classification systems are ready-made tools that enable marketers to categorize organizations into groups based mainly on the types of goods and services provided. Although an industrial classification system is a vehicle for segmentation, it is most appropriately used

Table 8.2 Examples of NAICS Classification

NAICS Hierarchy for AT&T Inc.		NAICS Hierarchy for Apple Inc.	
Sector 51	Information	Sector 31–33	Manufacturing
Subsector 517	Telecommunications	Subsector 334	Computer and Electronic Manufacturing
Industry Group 5171	Wired Telecommunication Carriers	Industry Group 3341	Computer and Peripheral Equipment Manufacturing
Industry Group 5172	Wireless Telecommunications Carriers		
Industry 51711	Wired Telecommunication Carriers	Industry 33411	Computer and Peripheral Equipment Manufacturing
Industry 51721	Wireless Telecommunications Carriers		
Industry 517110	Wired Telecommunication Carriers	U.S. Industry 334111	Electronic Computer Manufacturing
Industry 517210	Wireless Telecommunications Carriers		

Source: NAICS Association, www.census.gov/eos/www/naics/ (accessed February 23, 2012).

in conjunction with other types of data to determine exactly how many and which customers a marketer can reach.

A marketer can take several approaches to determine the identities and locations of organizations in specific groups. One approach is to use state directories or commercial industrial directories, such as *Standard & Poor's Register* and Dun & Bradstreet's *Million Dollar Database.* These sources contain information about a firm, including its name, industrial classification, address, phone number, and annual sales. By referring to one or more of these sources, marketers isolate business customers with industrial classification numbers, determine their locations, and develop lists of potential customers by desired geographic area. A more expedient, although more expensive, approach is to use a commercial data service. Dun & Bradstreet, for example, can provide a list of organizations that fall into a particular industrial classification group. For each company on the list, Dun & Bradstreet gives the name, location, sales volume, number of employees, type of products handled, names of chief executives, and other pertinent information. Either method can effectively identify and locate a group of potential customers. However, a marketer probably cannot pursue all organizations on the list. Because some companies have greater purchasing potential than others, marketers must determine which customer or customer group to pursue.

To estimate the purchase potential of business customers or groups of customers, a marketer must find a relationship between the size of potential customers' purchases and a variable available in industrial classification data, such as the number of employees. For example, a paint manufacturer might attempt to determine the average number of gallons purchased by a specific type of potential customer relative to the number of employees. A marketer with no previous experience in this market segment will probably have to survey a random sample of potential customers to establish a relationship between purchase sizes and numbers of employees. Once this relationship is established, it can be applied to customer groups to estimate their potential purchases. After deriving these estimates, the marketer is in a position to select the customer groups with the most sales and profit potential.

Despite their usefulness, industrial classification data pose several problems. First, a few industries do not have specific designations. Second, because a transfer of products from one establishment to another is counted as a part of total shipments, double counting may occur when products are shipped between two establishments within the same firm. Third, because the Census Bureau is prohibited from providing data that identify specific business organizations, some data, such as value of total shipments, may be understated. Finally, because government agencies provide industrial classification data, a significant lag usually exists between data-collection time and the time the information is released.

Summary

1. To distinguish among the various types of business markets

Business (B2B) markets consist of individuals, organizations, and groups that purchase a specific kind of product for resale, direct use in producing other products, or use in day-to-day operations. Producer markets include those individuals and business organizations that purchase products for the purpose of making a profit by using them to produce other products or as part of their operations. Intermediaries that buy finished products and resell them to make a profit are classified as reseller markets. Government markets consist of federal, state, county, and local governments, which spend billions of dollars annually for goods and services to support internal operations and to provide citizens with needed services. Organizations with charitable, educational, community, or other nonprofit goals constitute institutional markets.

2. To identify the major characteristics of business customers and transactions

Transactions that involve business customers differ from consumer transactions in several ways. Such transactions tend to be larger, and negotiations occur less frequently, though they are often lengthy. They frequently involve more than one person or department in the purchasing organization. They may also involve reciprocity, an arrangement in which two organizations agree to buy from each other. Business customers are usually better informed than ultimate consumers and are more likely to seek information about a product's features and technical specifications.

When purchasing products, business customers are particularly concerned about quality, service, price, and supplier relationships. Quality is important because it directly affects the quality of products the buyer's firm produces. To achieve an exact level of quality, organizations often buy products on the basis of a set of expressed characteristics, called specifications. Because services have such a direct influence on a firm's costs, sales, and profits, factors such as market information, on-time delivery, and availability of parts are crucial to a business buyer. Although business customers do not depend solely on price to decide which products to buy, price is of primary concern because it directly influences profitability.

Business buyers use several purchasing methods, including description, inspection, sampling, and negotiation. Most organizational purchases are new-task, straight rebuy, or modified rebuy. In a new-task purchase, an organization makes an initial purchase of items to be used to perform new jobs or solve new problems. A straight rebuy purchase occurs when a buyer purchases the same products routinely under approximately the same terms of sale. In a modified rebuy purchase, a new-task purchase is changed the second or third time it is ordered or requirements associated with a straight rebuy purchase are modified.

3. To understand several attributes of demand for business products

Industrial demand differs from consumer demand along several dimensions. Industrial demand derives from demand for consumer products. At the industry level, industrial demand is inelastic. If an industrial item's price changes, product demand will not change as much proportionally. Some industrial products are subject to joint demand, which occurs when two or more items are used in combination to make a product. Finally, because organizational demand derives from consumer demand, the demand for business products can fluctuate widely.

4. To become familiar with the major components of a buying center

Business (or organizational) buying behavior refers to the purchase behavior of producers, resellers, government units, and institutions. Business purchase decisions are made through a buying center, the group of people involved in making such purchase decisions. Users are those in the organization who actually use the product. Influencers help develop specifications and evaluate alternative products for possible use. Buyers select suppliers and negotiate purchase terms. Deciders choose the products. Gatekeepers control the flow of information to and among individuals occupying other roles in the buying center.

5. To understand the stages of the business buying decision process and the factors that affect this process

The stages of the business buying decision process are problem recognition, development of product specifications to solve problems, search for and evaluation of products and suppliers, selection and ordering of the most appropriate product, and evaluation of the product's and supplier's performance.

Four categories of factors influence business buying decisions: environmental, organizational, interpersonal, and individual. Environmental factors include competitive forces, economic conditions, political forces, laws and regulations, technological changes, and sociocultural factors. Business factors include the company's objectives, purchasing policies, and resources, as well as the size and composition of its buying center. Interpersonal factors are the relationships among people in the buying center. Individual factors are personal characteristics of members of the buying center, such as age, education level, personality, and tenure and position in the organization.

6. To describe industrial classification systems, and explain how they can be used to identify and analyze business markets

Business marketers have a considerable amount of information available for use in planning marketing strategies. Much of this information is based on an industrial classification system, which categorizes businesses into major industry groups, industry subgroups, and detailed industry categories. An industrial classification system—like the North American Industry Classification System (NAICS) used by the United States, Canada, and Mexico—provides marketers with information needed to identify business customer groups. It can best be used for this purpose in conjunction with other information. After identifying target industries, a marketer can obtain the names and locations of potential customers by using government and commercial data sources. Marketers then must estimate potential purchases of business customers by finding a relationship between a potential customer's purchases and a variable available in industrial classification data.

Go to www.cengagebrain.com for resources to help you master the content in this chapter as well as for materials that will expand your marketing knowledge!

Important Terms

producer markets 249
reseller markets 249
government markets 250
institutional markets 251
reciprocity 252
new-task purchase 256
straight rebuy purchase 256
modified rebuy purchase 256
derived demand 256
inelastic demand 257
joint demand 257
business (organizational) buying behavior 258
buying center 258
value analysis 260
vendor analysis 260
multiple sourcing 260
sole sourcing 260
North American Industry Classification System (NAICS) 262

Discussion and Review Questions

1. Identify, describe, and give examples of the four major types of business markets.
2. Why might business customers generally be considered more rational in their purchasing behavior than ultimate consumers?
3. What are the primary concerns of business customers?
4. List several characteristics that differentiate transactions involving business customers from consumer transactions.
5. What are the commonly used methods of business buying?
6. Why do buyers involved in straight rebuy purchases require less information than those making new-task purchases?
7. How does demand for business products differ from consumer demand?
8. What are the major components of a firm's buying center?
9. Identify the stages of the business buying decision process. How is this decision process used when making straight rebuys?
10. How do environmental, business, interpersonal, and individual factors affect business purchases?
11. What function does an industrial classification system help marketers perform?

Application Questions

1. Identify organizations in your area that fit each business market category: producer, reseller, government, and institutional. Explain your classifications.
2. Indicate the method of buying (description, inspection, sampling, or negotiation) an organization would be most likely to use when purchasing each of the following items. Defend your selections.

   a. A building for the home office of a light bulb manufacturer
   b. Wool for a clothing manufacturer

c. An Alaskan cruise for a company retreat, assuming a regular travel agency is used
d. One-inch nails for a building contractor

3. Purchases by businesses may be described as new-task, modified rebuy, or straight rebuy. Categorize the following purchase decisions and explain your choices.

   a. Bob has purchased toothpicks from Smith Restaurant Supply for 25 years and recently placed an order for yellow toothpicks rather than the usual white ones.
   b. Jill's investment company has been purchasing envelopes from AAA Office Supply for a year and now needs to purchase boxes to mail year-end portfolio summaries to clients. Jill calls AAA to purchase these boxes.
   c. Reliance Insurance has been supplying its salespeople with small personal computers to assist in their sales efforts. The company recently agreed to begin supplying them with faster, more sophisticated computers.

4. Identifying qualified customers is important to the survival of any organization. NAICS provides helpful information about many different businesses. Find the NAICS manual at the library or online at www.naics.com and identify the NAICS code for the following items.

   a. Chocolate candy bars
   b. Automobile tires
   c. Men's running shoes

5. IMP The United States is the largest producer of corn in the world. Each year, a corn farmer must decide what the end market for the corn crop will be and what type of seed to use. In approximately a decade, corn production for livestock, poultry, and fish has fallen from 80 percent of production to 40 percent. At the same time, corn produced for ethanol production has soared to 40 percent of corn production. In addition, the shift to ethanol has taken corn out of the supply chain for the agricultural feed market, causing an impact on food costs. About 12 percent of corn is used for direct human consumption, in the form of cereal and corn chips, for example. It is much less costly for farmers to produce corn for ethanol, because it can be produced using more efficient genetically modified seeds. To plant genetically modified corn for ethanol, the seed costs around $200/bushel, and the yields are significantly higher than other corn crops because insecticides and herbicides are built into the seed. Non-genetically modified seed produces more revenue at market per bushel but will have a lower overall crop yield and is more costly to produce. If you assume that the non-genetically modified crop sells for $10.00/bushel and that the genetically modified seed crop sells for $7.00/bushel, rank each of the following variables from 1–5. Think of 1 as the most important variable and 5 as the least important. Based on health, environment, and dependency on foreign energy sources, what would you do as a farmer purchasing seed for next year's crop?

   Rate the decision of whether to use genetically modified or non-genetically modified seed based on the following considerations:

   Safety to the Environment
   Ability to Control Production Costs
   Impact on Food Prices
   Overall Health Concerns
   Contribution to Reducing Dependence on Foreign Energy Sources

Internet Exercise

Boeing

Boeing is the world's leading aerospace corporation and largest manufacturer of commercial and military aircraft. Visit the company's website at www.boeing.com.

1. At what types of business markets are Boeing's products targeted?
2. How does Boeing address some of the concerns of business customers?
3. What environmental factors do you think affect demand for Boeing products?

developing your marketing plan

When developing a marketing strategy for business customers, it is essential to understand the process the business goes through when making a buying decision. Knowledge of business buying behavior is important when developing several aspects of the marketing plan. To assist you in relating the information in this chapter to the creation of a marketing plan for business customers, consider the following issues:

1. What are the primary concerns of business customers? Could any of these concerns be addressed with the strengths of your company?
2. Determine the type of business purchase your customer will likely be using when purchasing your product. How would this impact the level of information required by the business when moving through the buying decision process?
3. Discuss the different types of demand that the business customer will experience when purchasing your product.

The information obtained from these questions should assist you in developing various aspects of your marketing plan found in the "Interactive Marketing Plan" exercise at **www.cengagebrain.com**.

video case 8.1

Dale Carnegie Focuses on Business Customers

Dale Carnegie was a highly successful entrepreneur and one of the most legendary speakers of the 20th century. His simple but effective two-step formula for connecting with customers and colleagues in business situations was (1) win friends and (2) influence people. He began teaching his methods as part of the Dale Carnegie Course in 1912. In 1936, he published his ground-breaking book, *How to Win Friends and Influence People,* which went on to become an international best seller and is still available in print, as an audio book, and as an e-book. The original manuscript of this famous book remains on view in the Hauppauge, New York, headquarters of the company that Dale Carnegie founded, inspiring the new leaders who have brought the firm into the 21st century.

Today, Dale Carnegie operates in 85 countries, from China to Cameroon, with 2,700 trainers teaching his methods in 25 languages. In all, more than 8 million people have taken a Dale Carnegie course. The company has trained managers, employees, and teams in multinational corporations, such as Ford, Honda, Adidas, John Deere, 3M, Verizon, American Express, and Apple. It also provides training to people in government agencies, such as the U.S. Department of Veteran Affairs, as well as to small business owners and individuals who want to learn the Carnegie way.

Carnegie's methods can help marketers build a relationship with people at all levels, from the mail room to the board room. Whether the conversation involves a sales call or a factory visit to see a particular piece of equipment, "you can change people's behavior by changing your attitude towards them," says Peter Handal, CEO of Dale Carnegie. Listening carefully, wearing a smile, and being courteous is common sense, yet "it's not common practice," Handal explains, which is where the Dale Carnegie course comes in.

Dale Carnegie's principles still apply in this era of digital communications. For example, choosing positive words in a business e-mail can give recipients a good feeling about the message and the sender. Businesspeople are busy, so many value the efficiency of brief messages sent via text or Twitter. At the same time, adding a personal touch with a quick Skype conversation or recording a relevant video message can be a very effective way to engage business customers. And there's nothing like a face-to-face meeting where the customer can sit with a supplier or technical expert, ask questions, watch a live demonstration or handle a product, and build trust.

As CEO, Peter Handal travels the world to hear what customers and trainers have to say about Dale Carnegie's operations and about their own business situations. He emphasizes the need for managers to listen to what others have to say, even if the news is bad. "That's a very dangerous situation," Handal says. "You can't have everyone on the team in charge, but you have to have everyone be able to speak openly and honestly." In other words, it's important to be nice, but it's also important to speak up so decision makers have all the information they need to proceed.[18]

Questions for Discussion

1. How would you apply Dale Carnegie's methods if you were trying to make a sale to a company with a large buying center?
2. From a marketing perspective, why would people who work for the U.S. Department of Veteran Affairs be as interested in taking a Dale Carnegie course as people who work for American Express?
3. Which concerns of business customers should Dale Carnegie's marketers pay close attention to when selling training services to a company like American Express?

case 8.2

Bombardier Serves Multiple Business Markets

Bombardier is all about trains and planes. Founded by Joseph-Armand Bombardier in 1942, the company originally marketed snowmobiles for transportation through the wintry terrain of Canada's Quebec province. Among its earliest products were snowmobiles for delivering mail, shuttling students to and from schools, and moving commercial freight shipments. The company also served consumer markets through its Ski-Doo, a pioneer of the personal snowmobile industry, and its Sea-Doo, a pioneer of the personal watercraft industry.

Today, however, Bombardier's primary markets are governments and businesses that purchase aerospace and railroad-related products. For example, Bombardier markets its narrow-body jetliners to commercial airlines. To seal such sales, Bombardier emphasizes fuel efficiency, low operating costs, and other bottom-line benefits that airlines seek when buying new planes. Competition for orders is especially intense as the global economy recovers from recession and airlines plan ahead to replace the oldest models in their aging fleets. Depending on their needs, airlines may look at aircraft made by Airbus, Boeing, Embraer, Mitsubishi, or other competitors, not just at Bombardier's products. The exact configuration of each jet is customized airline by airline, which means every order represents a major investment of time, energy, and negotiation for buyer and seller alike.

© John MacDougall/AFP/Getty Images

Bombardier also markets corporate jets, under the brand names of Learjet, Challenger, and Global, to big businesses that fly executives from state to state, across the country, or halfway around the world. Because different businesses have different needs, Bombardier listens carefully to learn where and when the aircraft will be used. Business customers that don't need a jet standing by every day may be good prospects for other Bombardier offerings. If they anticipate using a jet for 50 or more flight hours per year, they can become part-owners of a plane through Bombardier's Flexjet program. If they occasionally need a private plane for specific trips, they may prefer Bombardier's Skyjet charter program.

Both commercial airlines and corporate buyers expect a high level of customer service when they purchase a new jet. To meet their needs, Bombardier operates round-the-clock customer response centers staffed by specialists who understand each product inside and out, from engineering and technical systems to parts and supplies. When customers call, the company is ready to help get their planes back in the air as quickly as possible.

Government markets are the focus of Bombardier's rail transportation division. During the 1970s, with a global oil crisis hurting sales of gasoline-powered vehicles, such as snowmobiles, Bombardier diversified by winning a large and lucrative contract to make subway trains for its headquarters city of Montreal. This paved the way for marketing to other municipalities who were expanding or modernizing their mass-transit systems. Now the company markets all manner of train and railway equipment, including passenger cars, high-speed locomotives, mass-transit systems, signal and control mechanisms, and railway-related maintenance and services.

Rail transportation is booming these days as countries and urban centers upgrade their infrastructures. Although no two government buyers have exactly the same requirements, Bombardier knows that quality, reliability, safety, and price are always major concerns in such purchases. Therefore, to compete with General Electric, Siemens, and other rivals, the company showcases its manufacturing expertise and points with pride to its many satisfied customers worldwide. Sustainability is an increasingly important factor for government buyers as well. "Everybody accepts that rail transportation is an eco-friendly way to move people in large cities," says Bombardier's CEO. As a result, Bombardier's marketing communicates that the firm's new energy-efficient, low-emission rail products have been designed with the environment in mind.

Knowing that business and government customers care about the reputation of their vendors, Bombardier requires all employees, managers, suppliers, and agents to follow its strict code of ethics and business conduct. Its social-responsibility initiatives include programs to reduce waste, conserve water and energy, and obtain electricity from renewable power sources. From its current level of $19 billion in annual sales and a workforce of 70,000 employees on five continents, Bombardier is poised for even better performance as its business marketing takes off.[19]

Questions for Discussion

1. How does derived demand apply to the demand for commercial jets purchased by airlines? What are the implications for Bombardier's marketing efforts?
2. When an airline wants to order new jets to replace older jets in its fleet, do you think it would approach the decision as a new-task purchase, a straight rebuy, or a modified rebuy purchase? Explain. Also, which methods of business buying are Bombardier's customers most likely to use? Why?
3. In which stage of the business buying decision process is Bombardier's reputation likely to have the most influence on a government that is considering the purchase of new subway cars?

NOTES

[1]Based on information in David Chernicoff, "Cisco Takes a Bite Out of the Datacenter Server Market," *ZDNet,* January 26, 2012, www.zdnet.com; Rich Karlgaard, "Cisco's Chambers: Driving Change," *Forbes,* January 25, 2012, www.forbes.com; Heather Clancy, "Cisco Seeks to Lock Up Smart Grid Influence," *ZDNet,* January 17, 2012, www.zdnet.com; Art Wittmann, "Cisco Leads Tight Pack in Data Center Networking," *Information Week,* January 5, 2012, www.informationweek.com.

[2]"STP: Segmentation, Targeting, Positioning," American Marketing Association, www.marketingpower.com (accessed March 22, 2012).

[3]Ibid.

[4]Manufacturing Employment Concentrations, http://geocommons.com/maps/1534; Corilyn Shropshire, "U.S. Lost Quarter of Its High-Tech Jobs in Past Decade," *Chicago Tribune,* January 18, 2012, http://articles.chicagotribune.com/2012-01-18/business/ct-biz-0118-tech-jobs-20120118_1_high-tech-manufacturing-jobs-job-losses-research.

[5]U.S. Bureau of the Census, *Statistical Abstract of the United States, 2012,* Table 1044, www.census.gov/compendia/statab/cats/wholesale_retail_trade.html.

[6]Ibid. (Tables 1048, 1051).

[7]"Global Powers of Retailing 2011," Deloitte, www.deloitte.com/view/en_GX/global/industries/consumer-business-transportation/retail/272d8abc8fa5d210VgnVCM3000001c56f00aRCRD.htm (accessed February 23, 2012).

[8]"Total Government Spending, Fiscal Year 2012," www.usgovernmentspending.com/percent_gdp; Binyamin Applebaum, "A Shrinking Military Budget May Take Neighbors With It," *The New York Times,* January 6, 2012, www.nytimes.com/2012/01/07/us/a-hidden-cost-of-military-cuts-could-be-invention-and-its-industries.html?scp=4&sq=military%20spending&st=cse.

[9]U.S. Bureau of the Census, *Statistical Abstract of the United States, 2012,* Table 428, www.census.gov/compendia/statab/2012/tables/12s0428.pdf.

[10]"VaxInnate Awarded Contract by the U.S. Government to Develop Recombinant Seasonal and Pandemic Flu Vaccines," *Business Wire*, March 1, 2011, www.businesswire.com/news/home/20110301006065/en/VaxInnate-Awarded-Contract-U.S.-Government-Develop-Recombinant.

[11]"About Aramark," Aramark, www.aramark.com/AboutARAMARK/; Christina Holloway, "Advertise in Disguise," *Daily Helmsman,* January 11, 2012, www.dailyhelmsman.com/news/advertise-in-disguise-1.2740791.

[12]"Boeing, Turkish Airlines Sign Order for 15 Planes," *Reuters,* April 1, 2011, www.reuters.com/article/2011/04/01/us-boeing-turkishairlines-idUSTRE7300ZV20110401.

[13]Das Narayandas and V. Kasturi Rangan, "Building and Sustaining Buyer-Seller Relationships in Mature Industrial Markets," *Journal of Marketing* (July 2004): 63.

[14]Press release, "WaterFurnace Introduces WeDeGeo.com, a Comprehensive B2B Selection Software for Applied Commercial Representatives," MarketWatch, January 25, 2012, www.marketwatch.com/story/waterfurnace-introduces-wedogeocom-a-comprehensive-b2b-selection-software-for-applied-commercial-representatives-2012-01-25?reflink=MW_news_stmp.

[15]Caterpillar Inc., "Code of Conduct," www.caterpillar.com/company/strategy/code-of-conduct (accessed April 6, 2011).

[16]Frederick E. Webster Jr. and Yoram Wind, "A General Model for Understanding Organizational Buyer Behavior," *Marketing Management* (Winter/Spring 1996): 52–57.

[17]"Development of NAICS," U.S. Census Bureau, www.census.gov/epcd/www/naicsdev.htm (accessed March 22, 2012).

[18]Sunny Thao, "Social Media as a Strategy," *Star Tribune* (Minneapolis), April 7, 2012, www.startribune.com; "Dale Carnegie Wins Friends in a Digital Age," *CBS News,* January 15, 2012, www.cbsnews.com; Paul Harris, "Digital Makeover for the Self-Help Bible that Helped Millions to Make Friends," *Observer* (London), October 9, 2011, 25; www.dalecarnegie.com.

[19]Susan Taylor, "Bombardier Sees 2012 Dip in Plane Deliveries, Margins," Reuters, March 1, 2012, www.reuters.com; Caroline van Hasselt, "Bombardier's Profit Dips," *The Wall Street Journal,* April 1, 2010, www.wsj.com; Scott Deveau, "Bombardier in Finance Deal with China," *Financial Post,* March 31, 2010, www.montrealgazette.com; Andrea Rothman, "Airbus, Boeing Confront Bombardier on Financing Rules," *Bloomberg Businessweek,* March 26, 2010, www.businessweek.com; "Start Your Engines," *The Economist,* March 20, 2010, 59; Stephen Gandel, "Trains, Planes, and Bombardier," *Time,* March 8, 2010, GB8; www.bombardier.com.

Feature Notes

[a]Based on information in Melissa Hincha-Ownby, "Newsweek Names IBM Greenest Company in America," *Forbes,* October 18, 2011, www.forbes.com; Susan Campriello, "IBM Is Environmental Leader," *Poughkeepsie Journal* (New York), June 11, 2011, www.poughkeepsiejournal.com; Todd Woody, "IBM Suppliers Must Track Environmental Data," *The New York Times,* April 14, 2010, www.nytimes.com; "IBM, Accenture Lead Responsible Government Suppliers," *Environmental Leader,* July 21, 2011, www.environmentalleader.com.

[b]Based on information in Chantal Tode, "OfficeMax Puts Customer Benefits Before ROI in Mobile," *Mobile Commerce Daily,* January 20, 2012, www.mobilecommercedaily.com; Kate Maddox, "Mobile Apps, Social Integration, Content Are Key Trends," *BtoB Online,* January 16, 2012, www.btobonline.com; Heather Taylor, "CBS Outdoor B2B site Goes Mobile in Canada," *Econsultancy,* January 16, 2012, http://econsultancy.com; www.emersonclimate.com.

[c]Based on information in "Kroger Ranks High for Multicultural Opportunities," *Progressive Grocer,* January 16, 2012, www.progressivegrocer.com; Victoria Fraza Kickham, "Supplier Diversity a Boon to Small Business," *Electronic Design,* August 11, 2011, 60; www.dell.com; www.kroger.com.

[d]Based on information in Scott Kirsner, "Pixability Pulls in $1 Million, to Help Small Businesses Add Video to Their Marketing Toolkit," *Boston Globe,* February 18, 2011, www.boston.com; Joel Brown, "Claim to Frame: Helping Businesses Polish Images," *Boston Globe,* May 25, 2010, www.boston.com; Verne Harnish, "5 Business Myths to Ditch Now," *Fortune,* January 19, 2011, www.fortune.com.

chapter 9

Reaching Global Markets

OBJECTIVES

1. To understand the nature of global marketing strategy
2. To analyze the environmental forces that affect international marketing efforts
3. To understand several important international trade agreements
4. To identify methods of international market entry
5. To examine various forms of global organizational structures
6. To examine the use of the marketing mix internationally

MARKETING INSIGHTS

KFC Experiences Explosive Growth in China

Although KFC is struggling in its home market, it is rapidly growing in China. KFC parent company Yum! Brands makes a greater profit in China than it does in the United States and has even surpassed McDonald's in popularity. How did a foreign firm with dwindling domestic sales manage to out-compete both local and global restaurants in the Chinese market? While most multinational fast-food chains, including McDonald's, tend to take a standardized approach to their operations, KFC restaurants customize to meet the tastes of Chinese consumers.

KFC entered the Chinese market in 1987. From the start, the company faced a number of economic and government obstacles. There was a lack of sufficient infrastructure to ensure quality distribution and logistics operations, and the Chinese government did not view foreign firms favorably. To overcome these challenges, KFC hired a local team of Chinese managers who spoke the language, understood Chinese consumers, and had a knowledge of Western business practices. This team was able to help KFC create a mix of American menu items, such as its trademark chicken recipes, and local Chinese dishes. To overcome the infrastructure barriers, KFC began to build its own distribution and logistics system from the ground up, which enabled it to ensure quality products and have more control over its operations. Finally, KFC entered into joint ventures with local government-owned entities that helped it form connections with the Chinese government.

Thanks to its clear understanding of the market, KFC currently has more than 3,000 restaurants in 650 Chinese cities. Its adaptation to local tastes and values has made it a favorite among Chinese consumers across the nation.[1]

Technological advances and rapidly changing political and economic conditions are making it easier than ever for companies to market their products overseas as well as at home. With most of the world's population and two-thirds of total purchasing power outside the United States, international markets represent tremendous opportunities for growth. Accessing these markets can promote innovation, while intensifying competition can spur companies to develop global strategies. For instance, Coca-Cola has adopted a strategy to expand into Africa. With sales falling flat in many developed markets, Coca-Cola views Africa as a new frontier for growth.[2]

In deference to the increasingly global nature of marketing, we devote this chapter to the unique features of global markets and international marketing. We begin by considering the nature of global marketing strategy and the environmental forces that create opportunities and threats for international marketers. Next, we consider several regional trade alliances, markets, and agreements. Then we examine the modes of entry into international marketing and companies' degree of involvement in it, as well as some of the structures that can be used to organize multinational enterprises. Finally, we examine how firms may alter their marketing mixes when engaging in international marketing efforts. All of these factors must be considered in any marketing plan that includes an international component.

THE NATURE OF GLOBAL MARKETING STRATEGY

international marketing Developing and performing marketing activities across national boundaries

International marketing involves developing and performing marketing activities across national boundaries. For instance, Walmart has approximately 740,000 employees and operates 5,366 stores in 27 countries outside the United States; Starbucks serves tens of millions of customers a week at more than 5,500 shops in over 50 countries.[3] General Motors sells more cars in China than in the United States.

© Honey Salvadori/Alamy

International Marketing
As a part of an extensive international marketing program, Pepsi uses global celebrities to promote its product.

Firms are finding that international markets provide tremendous opportunities for growth. To encourage international growth, many countries offer significant practical assistance and valuable benchmarking research that will help their domestic firms become more competitive globally. One example is Export.gov, a website managed by the U.S. Department of Commerce's International Trade Administration. Export.gov collects a variety of resources to help businesses who want to export to other countries.[4] A major element of the assistance that governmental organizations can provide for firms (especially small and medium-sized firms) is knowledge of the internationalization process of firms.

Traditionally, most companies—such as McDonald's and KFC—have entered the global marketplace incrementally as they gained knowledge about various markets and opportunities. Beginning in the 1990s, however, some firms—such as eBay, Google, and Logitech—were founded with the knowledge and resources to expedite their commitment and investment in the global marketplace. These "born globals"—typically small technology-based firms earning as much as 70 percent of their sales outside the domestic home market—export their products almost immediately after being established in market niches in which they compete with larger, more established firms.[5] Whether a firm adopts the traditional approach, the born global approach, or an approach that merges attributes of both approaches to market products and services, international marketing strategy is a critical element of a firm's global operations. Today, global competition in most industries is intense and becoming increasingly fierce with the addition of newly emerging markets and firms.

ENVIRONMENTAL FORCES IN GLOBAL MARKETS

Firms that enter international markets often find that they must make significant adjustments in their marketing strategies. The environmental forces that affect foreign markets may differ dramatically from those that affect domestic markets. It took McDonald's 14 years of intense negotiations before it was able to open its restaurants in Russia, but the past 20 years of operating restaurants in 60 Russian cities has been an enormous success. The first location in Russia was the Pushkin Square location, which remains the single busiest McDonald's in the world.[6] Thus, a successful international marketing strategy requires a careful environmental analysis. Conducting research to understand the needs and desires of international customers is crucial to global marketing success. Many firms have demonstrated that such efforts can generate tremendous financial rewards, increase market share, and heighten customer awareness of their products around the world. In this section, we explore how differences in the sociocultural; economic; political, legal, and regulatory; social and ethical; competitive; and technological forces in other countries can profoundly affect marketing activities.

Sociocultural Forces

Cultural and social differences among nations can have significant effects on marketing activities. Because marketing activities are primarily social in purpose, they are influenced by beliefs and values regarding family, religion, education, health, and recreation. In terms of families, the world population is over the 7 billion mark, with half residing in countries where fertility is at or below 2.1. Because of these lower fertility rates, the next wave of major population growth will likely take longer and be driven by developing countries.[7] By identifying such major sociocultural deviations among countries, marketers lay groundwork for an effective adaptation of marketing strategy. In India, for instance, half of Taco Bell's menu is vegetarian to appeal to Indian tastes. Chicken is used instead of beef, and many of the options are spicier than their American counterparts. Meal options include potato crunchy tacos and fajita and paneer stuffed burritos.[8]

Local preferences, tastes, and idioms can all prove complicated for international marketers. Although football is a popular sport in the United States and a major opportunity for many television advertisers, soccer is the most popular televised sport in Europe and Latin America. And, of course, marketing communications often must be translated into other languages. Sometimes, the true meaning of translated messages can be misinterpreted or lost. Consider some translations that went awry in foreign markets: KFC's long-running slogan "Finger lickin' good" was translated into Spanish as "Eat your fingers off," and Coors' "Turn it loose" campaign was translated into Spanish as "Drink Coors and get diarrhea."[9]

It can be difficult to transfer marketing symbols, trademarks, logos, and even products to international markets, especially if these are associated with objects that have profound religious or cultural significance in a particular culture. Gerber began marketing their baby food products in Africa and made minimal changes to the traditional packaging, showing the Gerber baby on the label. When baby food sales fell way below expectations, the company did some investigation and learned that, because the literacy rate is low in many parts of Africa, it is customary to put a picture of what is in the container on the package. Many consumers were not buying the product because they thought Gerber was selling baby meat. Cultural differences may also affect marketing negotiations and decision-making behavior. Although U.S. and Taiwanese sales agents are equally sensitive to customer interests, research suggests that the Taiwanese are more sensitive to the interests of their companies and competitors and less attuned to the interests of colleagues. Identifying such differences in work-related values of employees across different nationalities helps companies design more effective sales management practices. Cultural differences in the emphasis placed on personal relationships, status, and decision-making styles have been known to complicate dealings between Americans and businesspeople from other countries. In many parts of Asia, a gift may be considered a necessary introduction before negotiation, whereas in the United States or Canada, a gift may be misconstrued as an illegal bribe.

Buyers' perceptions of other countries can influence product adoption and use. Multiple research studies have found that consumer preferences for products depend on both the country of origin and the product category of competing products.[10] When people are unfamiliar with products from another country, their perceptions of the country as a whole may affect their attitude toward the product and influence whether they will buy it. If a country has a reputation for producing quality products and therefore has a positive image in consumers'

Cultural Differences
L'Oréal uses dramatic advertising to promote its products in public venues in China.

minds, marketers of products from that country will want to make the country of origin well known. For example, a generally favorable image of Western computer technology has fueled sales of U.S.-made Dell, Apple, and Microsoft computers and software in Japan. On the other hand, marketers may want to dissociate themselves from a particular country in order to build a brand's reputation as truly global or because a country does not have a good reputation for quality. Because China has had issues with product quality in the past, a Chinese company that purchased Volvo is keeping Volvo positioned as a Swedish brand. The extent to which a product's brand image and country of origin influence purchases is subject to considerable variation based on national culture characteristics.

When products are introduced from one nation into another, acceptance is far more likely if similarities exist between the two cultures. In fact, many similar cultural characteristics exist across countries. For international marketers, cultural differences have implications for product development, advertising, packaging, and pricing. When the original Mini automobile was introduced in England in 1959, its dimensions were 10 feet in length, 4 feet in width, and 4 feet in height. Although BMW was reluctant to export the car to the United States, the company gave it a try in 2002 and was surprised that Americans who drove SUVs, trucks, and minivans were very interested in the Mini. In light of its surprising success and its desire to grow market share for the Mini in the United States, BMW introduced the Countryman, a larger version of the Mini, to appeal to a potentially broader American audience.[11]

Economic Forces

Global marketers need to understand the international trade system, particularly the economic stability of individual nations, as well as trade barriers that may stifle marketing efforts. Economic differences among nations—differences in standards of living, credit, buying power, income distribution, national resources, exchange rates, and the like—dictate many of the adjustments firms must make in marketing internationally.

Instability is one of the guaranteed constants in the global business environment. The United States and the European Union are more stable economically than many other regions of the world. However, even these economies have downturns in regular cycles, and the most recent recession significantly slowed business growth. A number of other countries, including Korea, Russia, Singapore, and Thailand, have all experienced economic problems, such as depressions, high unemployment, corporate bankruptcies, instability in currency markets,

Emerging Trends

Demand for Luxury Goods Grows in the East

The demand for luxury goods is switching from the West to the East. While the luxury goods market is decreasing in Europe, it is quickly increasing in Asia. China now ranks number two among luxury goods markets, and analysts estimate that it might become number one by 2015.

Demand is so high that some individuals in Asian countries will make significant sacrifices, including skipping meals, to afford luxury goods. As a result, the Asian market is increasingly making up a significant percentage of the fashion industry's revenue. Sales in Asia generated $9.7 billion in revenues for luxury group LVMH Moët Hennessy Louis Vuitton, versus $6.3 billion in the United States. Italian menswear company Zegna owes much of its success to China, which makes up one-quarter of the company's annual sales.

However, China isn't the only avenue for growth in Asia. South Korea, Japan, and Saudi Arabia also offer opportunities for luxury goods makers. Louis Vuitton is even selling its luxury bags in Mongolia. As demand grows, some luxury goods makers are creating brands specifically for Asia, such as Burberry's Blue Label brand in Japan. The Asian market may eventually become the new face of the luxury goods industry.[a]

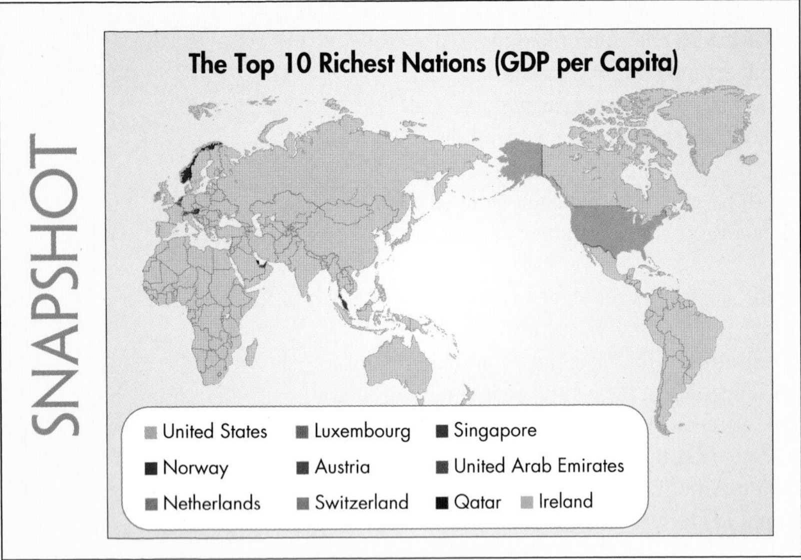

Source: Abby Rogers and Robert Johnson, "The 10 Richest Countries In The World," *Business Insider*, September 25, 2011, www.businessinsider.com/worlds-richest-countries-2011-9# (accessed July 4, 2012).

trade imbalances, and financial systems that need major reforms. For instance, the rising power of raw materials could increase inflation in developing countries where demand is growing.[12] The constantly fluctuating conditions in different economies require global marketers to carefully monitor the global environment and make changes quickly. Even more stable developing countries, such as Mexico and Brazil, tend to have greater fluctuations in their business cycles than the United States does. Despite this fact, the United States had its debt rating downgraded in 2011 due to continual deficit spending. Economic instability can also disrupt the markets for U.S. products in places that otherwise might be excellent marketing opportunities. On the other hand, competition from the sustained economic growth of countries like China and India can disrupt markets for U.S. products.

The value of the dollar, euro, and yen has a major impact on the prices of products in many countries. An important economic factor in the global business environment is currency valuation. Many countries have adopted a floating exchange rate, which allows the currencies of those countries to fluctuate, or float, according to the foreign exchange market. China is constantly being criticized for undervaluing its currency, or valuing its currency below the market value. This gives it an advantage in selling exports, since the Chinese yuan has a lower value than other nations' currencies. It also decreases demand for manufacturers and exporters from other countries.[13] In 2010, China allowed for the yuan to rise against the U.S. dollar, but most economists believe the change had a negligible impact.[14] Latin American countries, Brazil, China, and several economists have also accused the United States government of purposely devaluing its currency by issuing more money (which subsequently weakens the dollar). Although the United States defended its practices as legitimate, the rapid influx of U.S. dollars into the economy could spark a disruption in international currencies. Because many countries float their exchange rates around the dollar, too much or too little U.S. currency in the economy could create inflationary effects or harm exports.[15]

In terms of the value of all products produced by a nation, the United States has the largest gross domestic product in the world with more than $15 trillion.[16] **Gross domestic product (GDP)** is an overall measure of a nation's economic standing; it is the market value of a nation's total output of goods and services for a given period. However, it does not take into account the concept of GDP in relation to population (GDP per capita). The United States has a GDP per capita of $48,100. Switzerland is roughly 230 times smaller than the United States—a little larger than the state of Maryland—but its population density is six times greater than that of the United States. Although Switzerland's GDP is about one-forty-fifth the size of the United States' GDP, its GDP per capita is not that much lower. Even Canada, which is comparable in size to the United States, has a lower GDP and GDP per capita.[17] Table 9.1 provides a comparative economic analysis of 15 countries, including the United States. Knowledge about per capita income, credit, and the distribution of income provides general insights into market potential.

gross domestic product (GDP) The market value of a nation's total output of goods and services for a given period; an overall measure of economic standing

Opportunities for international trade are not limited to countries with the highest incomes. The countries of Brazil, Russia, India, China, and South Africa (BRICS) have attracted attention as their economies appear to be rapidly advancing. Other nations are progressing at a much faster rate than they were a few years ago, and these countries—especially in Latin America, Africa, eastern Europe, and the Middle East—have great market potential. Many

Table 9.1 Comparative Analysis of Selected Countries

Country	Population (in Millions)	GDP (U.S.$ in Billions)	Exports (U.S.$ in Billions)	Imports (U.S.$ in Billions)	Internet Users (in Millions)	Cell Phones (in Millions)
Brazil	206	2,282	250.8	219.6	75.98	202.94
Canada	34	1,389	450.6	459.6	26.96	24.04
China	1,343	11,290	1,898	1,743	389	859
Honduras	8.3	35.6	6.8	10.04	.73	9.5
India	1,205	4,463	298.2	357.7	61.34	752
Japan	127	4,389	800.8	794.7	99.18	121
Jordan	6.5	36.8	8.07	14	1.64	6.62
Kenya	43	66.03	5.44	11.9	4	24.97
Mexico	115	1,657	336.3	341.9	31.02	91.36
Russia	138	2,380	498.6	310.1	40.85	238
South Africa	49	554.6	94.2	92.9	4.42	50.37
Switzerland	7.7	340.5	308.3	299.6	6.15	9.48
Turkey	80	1,026	133	212.2	27.23	61.77
Thailand	67	601.4	244.4	214.6	17.48	69.68
U.S.	313	15,087.7	1,511	2,314	245	279

Source: The CIA, *The World Fact Book,* www.cia.gov/library/publications/the-world-factbook/rankorder/rankorderguide.html (accessed April 2, 2012); U.S. Department of Commerce Bureau of Economic Analysis, www.bea.gov/national/index.htm#gdp (accessed February 1, 2012); U.S. Census Bureau, Foreign Trade Division, *U.S. Trade in Goods and Services—Balance of Payments (BOP)* ***Basis,*** February 10, 2012, www.census.gov/foreign-trade/statistics/historical/gands.pdf (accessed February 27, 2012).

of these countries are now being classified into two new categories. "Overlooked" countries, including Saudi Arabia and Morocco, are nations whose economic advancements are beginning to rival the BRICS. "Frontier" countries, such as Sri Lanka, Kenya, and Nigeria, are riskier but nonetheless have potential for growth.[18] Consider the market potential for health-care services, which are growing rapidly in developing countries. In India, for example, demand for dialysis to treat diseases like diabetes has exploded. Within a five-year period, the market is expected to grow from $97 million to $152 million. Unfortunately, although dialysis services in India are only a fraction of what they cost in the United States, most Indians still cannot afford treatment.[19] This demonstrates the complex situation that marketers of goods and services in developing countries face: how to price products high enough to earn a profit and yet make them affordable for lower income consumers. Marketers must also understand the political and legal environments before they can convert buying power of customers in these countries into actual demand for specific products.

Political, Legal, and Regulatory Forces

The political, legal, and regulatory forces of the environment are closely intertwined in the United States. To a large degree, the same is true in many countries internationally. Typically, legislation is enacted, legal decisions are interpreted, and regulatory agencies are operated by elected or appointed officials. A country's legal and regulatory infrastructure is a direct reflection of the political climate in the country. In some countries, this political climate is determined by the people via elections, whereas in other countries leaders are appointed or have assumed leadership based on certain powers. Although laws and regulations have direct effects on a firm's operations in a country, political forces are indirect and often not clearly known in all countries. For example, although China has opened to international investment in recent years, government censorship prevents Facebook, the world's largest online social media network, from interacting

Table 9.2 The Best Countries for Entrepreneurs

Rank*	Country
1	Singapore
2	Hong Kong SAR, China
3	New Zealand
4	United States
5	Denmark
6	Norway
7	United Kingdom
8	Republic of Korea
9	Iceland
10	Ireland

*Rankings created by the Small Business Administration on which nations provide the most favorable environment for entrepreneurs.

Source: Alicia Ciccone, "10 Best Countries For Starting A Business," *Huffington Post,* January 10, 2012, www.huffingtonpost.com/2012/01/10/10-easiest-countries-to-s_n_1194511.html (accessed January 20, 2012).

with consumers.[20] Working to establish operations in China has been a highly political process since the advent of Communist rule. China is an example of state-directed capitalism. The government owns a majority of or has a partial stake in many businesses. State-backed firms accounted for one-third of the emerging world's foreign direct investment in the last decade. In fact, the world's largest oil and gas companies are backed by the state. The problem with state-owned enterprises versus private ones is the nature of competition. State-backed companies do not have as many competitors because the government is supporting them. Unless state-owned firms work hard to remain competitive, costs for these companies will most likely increase.[21]

On the other hand, some countries have political climates that make it easier for international entrepreneurs to start their own businesses. Table 9.2 lists some of the best countries in which to start a business, according to the Small Business Administration.

The political climate in a country or region, political officials in a country, and political officials in charge of trade agreements directly affect the legislation and regulations (or lack thereof). Within industries, elected or appointed officials of influential industry associations also set the tone for the regulatory environment that guides operations in a particular industry. Consider the American Marketing Association, which has one of the largest professional associations for marketers with 30,000 members worldwide in every area of marketing. It has established a statement of ethics, called "Ethical Norms and Values for Marketers," that guides the marketing profession in the United States.[22]

import tariff A duty levied by a nation on goods bought outside its borders and brought into the country

A nation's political system, laws, regulatory bodies, special-interest groups, and courts all have a great impact on international marketing. A government's policies toward public and private enterprise, consumers, and foreign firms influence marketing across national boundaries. Some countries have established import barriers, such as tariffs. An **import tariff** is any duty levied by a nation on goods bought outside its borders and brought into the country.

Political Forces
Activists protest against the Indian government's increasingly restrictive regulation of the Internet in New Delhi.

Because they raise the prices of foreign goods, tariffs impede free trade between nations. Tariffs are usually designed either to raise revenue for a country or to protect domestic products. In the United States, tariff revenues account for less than 2 percent of total federal revenues, down from about 50 percent of total federal revenues in the early 1900s.[23]

Nontariff trade restrictions include quotas and embargoes. A **quota** is a limit on the amount of goods an importing country will accept for certain product categories in a specific period of time. The United States maintains tariff-rate quotas on imported raw cane sugar, refined and specialty sugar, and sugar-containing products. The goal is to allow countries to export specific products to the United States at a relatively low tariff but acknowledges higher tariffs above predetermined quantities.[24] An **embargo** is a government's suspension of trade in a particular product or with a given country. Embargoes are generally directed at specific goods or countries and are established for political, health, or religious reasons. An embargo may be used to suspend the purchase of a commodity like oil from a country that is involved in questionable conduct, such as human rights violations or terrorism. Products that were created in the United States or by U.S. companies or those containing more than 20 percent of U.S.-manufactured parts cannot be sold to Cuba. Until recently, most Americans were banned from visiting Cuba because of the embargo. However, the administration has begun to allow more Americans to visit Cuba with certain restrictions, suggesting that the tension between the two countries might be diminishing.[25] Laws regarding competition may also serve as trade barriers. For example, the European Union has stronger antitrust laws than the United States. Being found guilty of anticompetitive behavior has cost companies like Intel billions of dollars. Because some companies do not have the resources to comply with more stringent laws, this can act as a barrier to trade.

Exchange controls, government restrictions on the amount of a particular currency that can be bought or sold, may also limit international trade. They can force businesspeople to buy and sell foreign products through a central agency, such as a central bank. On the other hand, to promote international trade, some countries have joined to form free trade zones, multinational economic communities that eliminate tariffs and other trade barriers. Such regional trade alliances are discussed later in the chapter. As mentioned earlier, foreign currency exchange rates also affect the prices marketers can charge in foreign markets. Fluctuations in the international monetary market can change the prices charged across national boundaries on a daily basis. Thus, these fluctuations must be considered in any international marketing strategy.

Countries may limit imports to maintain a favorable balance of trade. The **balance of trade** is the difference in value between a nation's exports and its imports. When a nation exports more products than it imports, a favorable balance of trade exists because money is flowing into the country. The United States has a negative balance of trade for goods and services of more than $600 billion.[26] A negative balance of trade is considered harmful, because it means U.S. dollars are supporting foreign economies at the expense of U.S. companies and workers. At the same time, U.S. citizens benefit from the assortment of imported products and their typically lower prices.

Many nontariff barriers, such as quotas and minimum price levels set on imports, port-of-entry taxes, and stringent health and safety requirements, still make it difficult for U.S. companies to export their products. For instance, the collectivistic nature of Japanese culture and the high-context nature of Japanese communication make some types of direct marketing messages less effective and may predispose many Japanese to support greater regulation of direct marketing practices.[27] A government's attitude toward importers has a direct impact on the economic feasibility of exporting to that country.

quota A limit on the amount of goods an importing country will accept for certain product categories in a specific period of time

embargo A government's suspension of trade in a particular product or with a given country

exchange controls Government restrictions on the amount of a particular currency that can be bought or sold

balance of trade The difference in value between a nation's exports and its imports

Ethical and Social Responsibility Forces

Differences in national standards are illustrated by what the Mexicans call *la mordida*: "the bite." The use of payoffs and bribes is deeply entrenched in many governments. Because U.S. trade and corporate policy, as well as U.S. law, prohibits direct involvement in payoffs and bribes, U.S. companies may have a hard time competing with foreign firms that engage in these practices. Some U.S. businesses that refuse to make payoffs are forced to hire local consultants, public relations firms, or advertising agencies, which results in indirect payoffs. The ultimate

Ethical and Social Responsibility
Protestors gather in the Philippines, opposing genetically modified foods that raise health concerns.

© AP Images/Aaron Favila

decision about whether to give small tips or gifts where they are customary must be based on a company's code of ethics. However, under the Foreign Corrupt Practices Act of 1977, it is illegal for U.S. firms to attempt to make large payments or bribes to influence policy decisions of foreign governments. Nevertheless, facilitating payments, or small payments to support the performance of standard tasks, are often acceptable. The Foreign Corrupt Practices Act also subjects all publicly held U.S. corporations to rigorous internal controls and record-keeping requirements for their overseas operations.

Many other countries have also outlawed bribery. As we discussed in Chapter 3, the U.K. Bribery Act does not permit facilitating payments in many circumstances. It has also redefined what many companies consider to be bribery versus gift-giving, causing multinational firms to update their codes of ethics. Companies with operations in the United Kingdom could still face penalties for bribery, even if the bribery occurred outside the country and managers were not aware of the misconduct.[28] In this case, the U.K. Bribery Law might be considered stricter than the Foreign Corrupt Practices Act. It is thus essential for global marketers to understand the major laws in the countries in which their companies operate.

Differences in ethical standards can also affect marketing efforts. In China and Vietnam, for example, standards regarding intellectual property differ dramatically from those in the United States, creating potential conflicts for marketers of computer software, music, and books. Pirated consumer goods, according to the International Anti-Counterfeiting Coalition, cost $600 billion annually.[29] See Table 9.3 for the top 10 counterfeited consumer goods. Even the widely admired company Apple is not immune. As Apple expands into China, it has had to contend with knock-offs of its Apple stores. Some of these knock-offs are so close to official stores in their design and product mix that consumers mistake them as being authentic.[30] The enormous amount of counterfeit products available worldwide, the time it takes to track them down, and legal barriers in certain countries make the pursuit of counterfeiters challenging for many companies.

Table 9.3 Top 10 Seized Counterfeit Goods

Rank	Product
1	Brand Name Clothing
2	Electronics
3	Handbags/Luxury Accessories
4	Medicine
5	CDs/DVDs/Video Games
6	Automotive Parts
7	Toys
8	Cosmetics/Personal Hygiene Products
9	Cigarettes
10	Food/Beverages

Source: "Counterfeit Culture," *CBC News*, www.cbc.ca/news/interactives/map-counterfeit-goods (accessed July 4, 2012).

When marketers do business abroad, they sometimes perceive that other business cultures have different modes of operation. This uneasiness is especially pronounced for marketers who have not traveled extensively or interacted much with foreigners in business or social settings. For example, a perception exists among many in the United States that U.S. firms are different from those in other countries. This implied perspective of "us" versus "them" is also common in other countries. In business, the idea that "we" differ from "them" is called the self-reference criterion (SRC). The SRC is the unconscious reference to one's own cultural values, experiences, and knowledge. When confronted with a situation, we react on the basis of knowledge we have accumulated over a lifetime, which is usually grounded in our culture of origin. Our reactions are based on meanings, values, and symbols that relate to our culture but may not have the same relevance to people of other cultures.

However, many businesspeople adopt the principle of "When in Rome, do as the Romans do." These businesspeople adapt to the cultural practices of the country they are in and use the host country's cultural practices as the rationalization for sometimes straying from their own ethical values when doing business internationally. For instance, by defending the payment of bribes or "greasing the wheels of business" and other questionable practices in this fashion, some businesspeople are resorting to **cultural relativism**—the concept that morality varies from one culture to another and that business practices are therefore differentially defined as right or wrong by particular cultures. Table 9.4 indicates the countries that businesspeople, risk analysts, and the general public perceive as having the most and least corrupt public sectors.

Because of differences in cultural and ethical standards, many companies work both individually and collectively to establish ethics programs and standards for international business conduct. Levi Strauss' code of ethics, for example, bars the firm from manufacturing in countries where workers are known to be abused. Many firms, including Texas Instruments, Coca-Cola, Du Pont, Hewlett-Packard, Levi Strauss & Company, Texaco, and Walmart, endorse following international business practices responsibly. These companies support a globally based resource system called Business for Social Responsibility (BSR). BSR tracks emerging issues and trends, provides information on corporate leadership and best practices, conducts educational workshops and training, and assists organizations in developing practical

cultural relativism The concept that morality varies from one culture to another and that business practices are therefore differentially defined as right or wrong by particular cultures

Table 9.4 Ranking of Countries Based Upon Corruption of Public Sector

Country Rank	CPI Score*	Least Corrupt	Country Rank	CPI Score*	Most Corrupt
1	9.5	New Zealand	182	1.0	Somalia
2	9.4	Denmark	182	1.0	North Korea
2	9.4	Finland	180	1.5	Myanmar
4	9.3	Sweden	180	1.5	Afghanistan
5	9.2	Singapore	177	1.6	Uzbekistan
6	9.0	Norway	177	1.6	Turkmenistan
7	8.9	Netherlands	177	1.6	Sudan
8	8.8	Australia	175	1.8	Iraq
8	8.8	Switzerland	175	1.8	Haiti
10	8.7	Canada	172	1.9	Venezuela
11	8.5	Luxembourg	172	1.9	Equatorial Guinea
12	8.4	Hong Kong	172	1.9	Burundi

* CPI score relates to perceptions of the degree of public sector corruption as seen by businesspeople and country analysts and ranges between 10 (highly clear) and 0 (highly corrupt). The United States is perceived as the 24th least-corrupt nation.

Source: © Transparency International, *Corruption Perceptions Index 2011* (Berlin, Germany, 2011). All rights reserved.

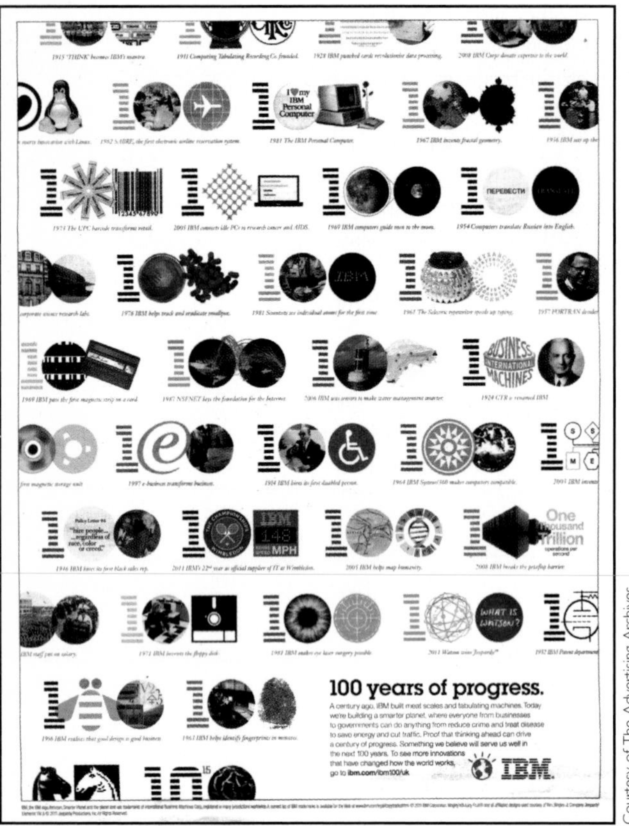

Courtesy of The Advertising Archives

Competitive Forces
IBM maintains a global competitive advantage by focusing on innovation, product quality, and customer satisfaction.

business ethics tools. It addresses such issues as community investment, corporate social responsibility, the environment, governance, and accountability.[31]

Competitive Forces

Competition is often viewed as a staple of the global marketplace. Customers thrive on the choices offered by competition, and firms constantly seek opportunities to outmaneuver their competition to gain customers' loyalty. Firms typically identify their competition when they establish target markets worldwide. Customers who are seeking alternative solutions to their product needs find the firms that can solve those needs. However, the increasingly interconnected international marketplace and advances in technology have resulted in competitive forces that are unique to the international marketplace.

Beyond the types of competition (i.e., brand, product, generic, and total budget competition) and types of competitive structures (i.e., monopoly, oligopoly, monopolistic competition, and pure competition), which are discussed in Chapter 3, firms that operate internationally must do the following:

- Be aware of the competitive forces in the countries they target.
- Identify the interdependence of countries and the global competitors in those markets.
- Be mindful of a new breed of customers: the global customer.

Each country has unique competitive aspects—often founded in the other environmental forces (i.e., sociocultural, technological, political, legal, regulatory, and economic forces)—that are often independent of the competitors in that market. The most globally competitive countries are listed in Table 9.5. Although competitors drive competition, nations establish the infrastructure and the rules for the types of competition that can take place. For example, the laws against antitrust in the European Union are often perceived as being stricter than those in the United States.

Table 9.5 Ranking of the Most Competitive Countries in the World

Rank	Country	Rank	Country
1	Switzerland	11	Hong Kong SAR
2	Singapore	12	Canada
3	Sweden	13	Taiwan, China
4	Finland	14	Qatar
5	United States	15	Belgium
6	Germany	16	Norway
7	Netherlands	17	Saudi Arabia
8	Denmark	18	France
9	Japan	19	Austria
10	United Kingdom	20	Australia

Source: Xavier Sala-i-Martin and Klaus Schwab (ed.), *The Global Competitiveness Report 2011–2012,* www3.weforum.org/docs/WEF_GCR_Report_2011-12.pdf (accessed July 4, 2012).

© Andia/Alamy

Staying Ahead of the Competition
DHL supports its competitive advantage by providing efficient and effective global shipping services.

The New York Stock Exchange found this out firsthand after European antitrust regulators argued against its merger with Germany's marketplace organizer Deutsche Börse. The regulators felt that the merger would give the company too much power in the marketplace.[32] Like the United States, other countries allow some monopoly structures to exist. Consider Sweden; their alcohol sales are made through the governmental store Systembolaget, which is legally supported by the Swedish Alcohol Retail Monopoly. According to Systembolaget, the Swedish Alcohol Retail Monopoly exists for one reason: "to minimize alcohol-related problems by selling alcohol in a responsible way."[33]

A new breed of customer—the global customer—has changed the landscape of international competition drastically. In the past, firms simply produced goods or services and provided local markets with information about the features and uses of their goods and services. Customers seldom had opportunities to compare products from competitors, know details about the competing products' features, and compare other options beyond the local (country or regional) markets. Now, however, not only do customers who travel the globe expect to be able to buy the same product in most of the world's more than 200 countries, but they also expect that the product they buy in their local store in Miami will have the same features as similar products sold in London or even in Beijing. If either the quality of the product or the product's features are more advanced in an international market, customers will soon demand that their local markets offer the same product at the same or lower prices.

Technological Forces

Advances in technology have made international marketing much easier. Interactive Web systems, instant messaging, and podcast downloads (along with the traditional vehicles of voice mail, e-mail, and cell phones) make international marketing activities more affordable and convenient. Internet use and social networking activities have accelerated dramatically within the United States and abroad. In Japan, 99 million have Internet access, and more than 41 million Russians, 61 million Indians, and 389 million Chinese are logging on to the Internet (refer back to Table 9.1).[34]

Going Green

Electric Cars Penetrate Chinese Vehicle Industry

China is considered to be the next big market for electric vehicles (EVs). The Chinese government plans to have half a million EVs on its roadways by 2015 and 5 million by 2020. The government is offering 60,000 yuan in subsidies to Chinese consumers who purchase EVs. If current trends continue, it is estimated that EVs will make up 7 percent of Chinese vehicle sales by 2020.

Despite wide-scale government support, EVs face many challenges in the Chinese market. Firstly, China's car manufacturers are having trouble competing with global automakers. One way to solve this problem is for Chinese EV manufacturers to increase their brand awareness by entering into joint ventures with global companies. These joint ventures allow for the sharing of EV technology and branding. In fact, the Chinese government has created barriers to limit the expansion of foreign EV makers in China without entering into joint ventures.

In response, foreign automakers are releasing EVs into China with caution. While many are entering into joint ventures with domestic companies, some are limiting which intellectual property to share. For instance, although General Motors announced it would enter into a joint venture to create an EV with a Chinese firm, it has decided to import its Chevy Volt and forgo government subsidies to avoid sharing the Volt's EV technologies.[b]

In many developing countries that lack the level of technological infrastructure found in the United States and Japan, marketers are beginning to capitalize on opportunities to leapfrog existing technology. For example, cellular and wireless phone technology is reaching many countries at a more affordable rate than traditional hard-wired telephone systems. Consequently, opportunities for growth in the cell phone market remain strong in Southeast Asia, Africa, and the Middle East. One opportunity created by the rapid growth in mobile devices in Kenya is mobile payment services. Approximately 8.5 million Kenyans use their mobile phones to transfer money. London-based Vodafone has taken advantage of this market opportunity with its M-PESA money transfer service, the most popular money transfer service in Kenya. Because banks tend to avoid catering to lower income populations, such services are likely to grow.[35]

REGIONAL TRADE ALLIANCES, MARKETS, AND AGREEMENTS

Although many more firms are beginning to view the world as one huge marketplace, various regional trade alliances and specific markets affect companies engaging in international marketing; some create opportunities, and others impose constraints. In fact, while trade agreements in various forms have been around for centuries, the last century can be classified as the trade agreement period in the world's international development. Today, there are nearly 200 trade agreements around the world compared with only a select handful in the early 1960s. In this section, we examine several of the more critical regional trade alliances, markets, and changing conditions affecting markets. These include the North American Free Trade Agreement, European Union, Southern Common Market, Asia-Pacific Economic Cooperation, Association of Southeast Asian Nations, and World Trade Organization.

The North American Free Trade Agreement (NAFTA)

North American Free Trade Agreement (NAFTA) An alliance that merges Canada, Mexico, and the United States into a single market

The **North American Free Trade Agreement (NAFTA)**, implemented in 1994, effectively merged Canada, Mexico, and the United States into one market of nearly 444 million consumers. NAFTA eliminated virtually all tariffs on goods produced and traded among Canada, Mexico, and the United States to create a free trade area. The estimated annual output for this trade alliance is more than $17 trillion.[36]

NAFTA makes it easier for U.S. businesses to invest in Mexico and Canada; provides protection for intellectual property (of special interest to high-technology and entertainment industries); expands trade by requiring equal treatment of U.S. firms in both countries; and simplifies country-of-origin rules, hindering Japan's use of Mexico as a staging ground for further penetration into U.S. markets. Although most tariffs on products coming to the United States were lifted, duties on more sensitive products, such as household glassware, footwear, and some fruits and vegetables, were phased out over a 15-year period.

Canada's more than 34 million consumers are relatively affluent, with a per capita GDP of $39,400.[37] Trade between the United States and Canada totals approximately $545 billion.[38] Canada is the single largest trading partner of the United States, which in turn supports millions of U.S. jobs. The United States purchases 73 percent of Canada's exports and supplies 63 percent of Canada's imports.[39] NAFTA has also enabled additional trade between Canada and Mexico. Mexico is Canada's fifth largest export market and third largest import market.[40]

With a per capita GDP of $13,900, Mexico's more than 113 million consumers are less affluent than Canadian consumers.[41] However, they bought more than $181 billion worth of U.S. products last year.[42] Many U.S. companies, including Hewlett-Packard, IBM, and General Motors, have taken advantage of Mexico's low labor costs and close proximity to the United States to set up production facilities, sometimes called *maquiladoras*. Production at the *maquiladoras*, especially in the automotive, electronics, and apparel industries, has grown rapidly as companies as diverse as Ford, John Deere, Motorola, Kimberly-Clark, and VF Corporation set up facilities in north-central Mexican states. Although Mexico experienced financial instability throughout the 1990s and is experiencing another bout of instability because of drug cartel violence, privatization of some government-owned firms as well as other measures instituted by the Mexican government and businesses have helped Mexico's economy. Moreover, increasing trade between the United States and Canada constitutes a strong base of support for the ultimate success of NAFTA.

Mexico's membership in NAFTA links the United States and Canada with other Latin American countries, providing additional opportunities to integrate trade among all the nations in the Western Hemisphere. Indeed, efforts to create a free trade agreement among the 34 nations of North and South America are under way. A related trade agreement—the Dominican Republic–Central American Free Trade Agreement (CAFTA-DR)—among Costa Rica, the Dominican Republic, El Salvador, Guatemala, Honduras, Nicaragua, and the United States has also been ratified in all those countries except Costa Rica. The United States exports $20 billion to the CAFTA-DR countries annually.[43]

Despite its benefits, NAFTA has been controversial, and disputes continue to arise over its implementation. The three countries have found it difficult to agree on the best way for enforcing the trade agreement. For instance, the Mexican president has called for a union among the three economies that would allow the trade bloc to compete against Asia. However, his vision has not been accepted by the other leaders. Leaders in the trading bloc are meeting less often, and many of the goals that were first set for the years following NAFTA have not been met. One reason was the September 11th attacks that prompted the United States to increase border controls. It has been estimated that less than 1 percent of the border between the United States and Canada is secure, and the drug wars near the Mexican border make it unlikely that the United States will loosen its border controls anytime soon. Another problem with the trilateral agreement is the fact that Mexico and Canada seem more intent on their relationships with the United States than with each other.[44] Firms have also faced difficulties under NAFTA. ExxonMobil filed a lawsuit against the Canadian government for damages resulting from Canada's imposition of new costs on offshore petroleum projects, which the company believes violates the provisions of the trade agreement.[45]

Although many Americans feared the agreement would erase jobs in the United States, Mexicans have been disappointed that it failed to create more jobs. Although NAFTA has been controversial, it has become a positive factor for U.S. firms that want to engage in international marketing. Because licensing requirements have been relaxed under the pact, smaller businesses that previously could not afford to invest in Mexico and Canada are able to do business in those markets without having to locate there. NAFTA's long phase-in period provided ample time for adjustment for those firms affected by reduced tariffs on imports. Furthermore, increased competition should lead to a more efficient market, and the long-term prospects of including most Western Hemisphere countries in the alliance promise additional opportunities for U.S. marketers.

The European Union (EU)

The **European Union (EU)**, sometimes also referred to as the *European Community* or *Common Market*, was established in 1958 to promote trade among its members, which initially included Belgium, France, Italy, West Germany, Luxembourg, and the Netherlands. In 1991, East and West Germany united, and by 2013, the EU included the United Kingdom, Spain, Denmark, Greece, Portugal, Ireland, Austria, Finland, Sweden, Cyprus, Poland, Hungary, the Czech Republic, Slovenia, Estonia, Latvia, Lithuania, Slovakia, Malta, Romania, Bulgaria, and Croatia. The Former Yugoslav Republic of Macedonia and Turkey are candidate countries that hope to join the European Union in the near future.[46]

The European Union consists of nearly half a billion consumers and has a combined GDP of more than $14 trillion.[47] Although it only makes up 7 percent of the population, the EU generates nearly 22 percent of the world's GDP.[48] The EU is a relatively diverse set of democratic European countries. It is not a state that is intended to replace existing country states, nor is it an organization for international cooperation. Instead, its member states have common institutions to which they delegate some of their sovereignty to allow specific matters of joint interest to be decided at the European level. The primary goals of the EU are to establish European citizenship; ensure freedom, security, and justice; promote economic and social progress; and assert Europe's role in world trade.[49] To facilitate free trade among members, the EU is working toward standardizing business regulations and requirements, import duties, and value-added taxes; eliminating customs checks; and creating a standardized currency for use by all members. Many European nations (Austria, Belgium, Finland, France, Germany, Ireland, Italy, Luxembourg, the Netherlands, Portugal, Greece, and Spain) are linked to a common currency, the *euro*, but several EU members have rejected the euro in their countries (e.g., Denmark, Sweden, and the United Kingdom). Although the common currency may necessitate that marketers modify their pricing strategies and subjects them to increased competition, it also frees companies that sell products among European countries from the complexities of exchange rates. The long-term goals are to eliminate all trade barriers within the EU, improve the economic efficiency of the EU nations, and stimulate economic growth, thus making the union's economy more competitive in global markets, particularly against Japan and other Pacific Rim nations and North America.

European Union (EU) An alliance that promotes trade among its member countries in Europe

Marketing Debate

Productivity vs. Vacation Time

ISSUE: Does less vacation time make the United States more or less competitive?

The United States is the most productive country in the world. Some argue that this is because Americans work harder. On average, Americans take about 13 days of vacation annually, versus 15 in Japan, 19 in Australia, and 38 days in France. It might be easy to assume that the United States' higher productivity is therefore a result of more days worked, but others are not so sure. Although total productivity might be high in the United States, studies show that gross domestic product per hours worked is higher in some European countries, including Belgium and Luxembourg. Research also reveals that breaks from work actually increase productivity.[c]

As the EU nations attempt to function as one large market, consumers in the EU may become more homogeneous in their needs and wants. Marketers should be aware, however, that cultural differences among the nations may require modifications in the marketing mix for customers in each nation. Differences in tastes and preferences in these diverse markets are significant for international marketers. But there is evidence that such differences may be diminishing, especially within the younger population that includes teenagers and young professionals. Gathering information about these distinct tastes and preferences is likely to remain a very important factor in developing marketing mixes that satisfy the needs of European customers.

The latest worldwide recession has slowed Europe's economic growth and created a debt crisis. Several members have budget deficits and are struggling to recover. Ireland, Greece, and Portugal required significant bailouts from the European Union, followed by bailout requests from Spain and Cyprus.[50] Greece experienced the worst trouble. It did not have the funds needed to pay back its bondholders, even after the bailout. A default by one nation negatively impacts all EU members as it lowers investor confidence and potentially leads to credit downgrades.[51] In early 2012, Standard & Poor's dealt a blow to the EU by downgrading the sovereign debt ratings of nine of its member countries, including France, Portugal, Italy, and Austria.[52] Germany, on the other hand, is seeing its impact on the euro-zone increase. Germany is home to many exporting companies, its exports are in high demand in fast-growing economies, and it has a smaller budget deficit and household debt. As a result, Germany is doing better economically than its European counterparts.[53] It continues to maintain its AAA+ rating, signaling to investors that the country is a safe investment.[54]

The Southern Common Market (MERCOSUR)

The **Southern Common Market (MERCOSUR)** was established in 1991 under the Treaty of Asunción to unite Argentina, Brazil, Paraguay, and Uruguay as a free trade alliance. Venezuela joined in 2006. Currently, Bolivia, Chile, Colombia, Ecuador, and Peru are associate members. The alliance represents two-thirds of South America's population and has a combined GDP of more than $2.4 trillion, making it the fourth-largest trading bloc behind NAFTA and the EU. Like NAFTA, MERCOSUR promotes "the free circulation of goods, services, and production factors among the countries" and establishes a common external tariff and commercial policy.[55]

South America and Latin America are catching the attention of many international businesses. The region is advancing economically with an estimated growth rate of four to five percent. Another trend is that several of the countries, including some of the MERCOSUR alliance, are starting to experience more stable democracies. Even Cuba, one of the traditionally harshest critics of capitalism in Latin America, is accepting more privatization. After up to 1 million state workers were laid off in 2011, many Cubans had to try to earn their living in the county's expanding private sector.[56]

The Asia-Pacific Economic Cooperation (APEC)

The **Asia-Pacific Economic Cooperation (APEC)**, established in 1989, promotes open trade and economic and technical cooperation among member nations, which initially included Australia, Brunei Darussalam, Canada, Indonesia, Japan, Korea, Malaysia, New Zealand, the Philippines, Singapore, Thailand, and the United States. Since then, the alliance has grown to include China, Hong Kong, Taiwan, Mexico, Papua New Guinea, Chile, Peru, Russia, and Vietnam. The 21-member alliance represents approximately 41 percent of the world's population, 54 percent of world GDP, and nearly 44 percent of global trade. APEC differs from other international trade alliances in its commitment to facilitating business and its practice of allowing the business/private sector to participate in a wide range of APEC activities.[57]

Companies of the APEC have become increasingly competitive and sophisticated in global business in the last few decades. Moreover, the markets of the APEC offer tremendous opportunities to marketers who understand them. In fact, the APEC region has consistently

Southern Common Market (MERCOSUR) An alliance that promotes the free circulation of goods, services, and production factors, and has a common external tariff and commercial policy among member nations in South America

Asia-Pacific Economic Cooperation (APEC) An alliance that promotes open trade and economic and technical cooperation among member nations throughout the world

Going Green
Electric cars have been very successful in China.

been one of the most economically dynamic parts of the world. In its first decade, the APEC countries generated almost 70 percent of worldwide economic growth, and the APEC region consistently outperformed the rest of the world.[58]

Japanese firms in particular have made tremendous inroads on world markets for automobiles, motorcycles, watches, cameras, and audio and video equipment. Products from Sony, Sanyo, Toyota, Mitsubishi, Canon, Suzuki, and Toshiba are sold all over the world and have set standards of quality by which other products are often judged. Despite the high volume of trade between the United States and Japan, the two economies are less integrated than the U.S. economy is with Canada and the European Union. If Japan imported goods at the same rate as other major nations, the United States would sell billions of dollars more each year to Japan.

The most important emerging economic power is China, which has become one of the most productive manufacturing nations. China, which is now the United States' second-largest trading partner, has initiated economic reforms to stimulate its economy by privatizing many industries, restructuring its banking system, and increasing public spending on infrastructure. China is a manufacturing powerhouse with an economy growing at a rate of about 8.9 percent.[59] Many foreign companies, including Nike and Adidas, have factories in China to take advantage of its low labor costs, and China has become a major global producer in virtually every product category.

For international businesses, the potential of China's consumer market is so vast that it is almost impossible to measure. However, doing business in China entails many risks. China's state capitalism has yielded many economic benefits, including a high average annual growth rate. Yet, at the same time, economists believe that such high growth will not last unless the country focuses less upon exports and more upon the spending power and domestic consumption of its consumers.[60] Political and economic instability—especially inflation, corruption, and erratic policy shifts—have undercut marketers' efforts to stake a claim in what could become the world's largest market. Moreover, piracy is a major issue, and protecting a brand name in China is difficult. Because copying is a tradition in China, and laws that protect copyrights and intellectual property are weak and minimally enforced, the country is flooded with counterfeit media, computer software, furniture, and clothing.

Global Alliances
Presidents and leaders from South American countries come together for a meeting of the Union of the South American Nations in Argentina.

Pacific Rim regions like South Korea, Thailand, Singapore, Taiwan, and Hong Kong are also major manufacturing and financial centers. Even before Korean brand names, such as Samsung, Daewoo, and Hyundai, became household words, these products prospered under U.S. company labels, including GE, GTE, RCA, and JCPenney. Singapore boasts huge global markets for rubber goods and pharmaceuticals. Hong Kong is still a strong commercial center after being transferred to Chinese control. Vietnam is one of Asia's fastest-growing markets for U.S. businesses, but Taiwan, given its stability and high educational attainment, has the most promising future of all the Pacific Rim nations as a strong local economy and low import barriers draw increasing imports. The markets of APEC offer tremendous opportunities to marketers who understand them. For instance, YUM! Brands gets 60 percent of its profits from overseas.[61]

Another important trade agreement is the Trans-Pacific Partnership. The Trans-Pacific Strategic Economic Partnership is a trade agreement between Singapore, Brunei, Chile, and New Zealand, with the United States, Vietnam, Malaysia, Japan, Peru, and Australia seeking to join.[62] Signed in 2005, the partnership seeks to encourage free trade by phasing out import tariffs between member countries.[63] If the partnership succeeds, the trade bloc will become the fifth largest trading partner for the United States.[64] The agreement would create standards for state-owned enterprises, labor, international property, and the environment.[65]

Although the agreement has gained praise from many stakeholders, some countries are wary about eliminating tariffs on certain items. Japanese farmers, for instance, have criticized the agreement, as they believe that eliminating import tariffs on agricultural products will put them out of business.[66] China also has high import duties, making the country more likely to be placed in the lower qualified category of the partnership.[67] Supporters of the partnership, however, believe it will increase the overall global competitiveness of member countries and could act as a standard for future trade agreements.[68]

Association of Southeast Asian Nations (ASEAN)

Association of Southeast Asian Nations (ASEAN) An alliance that promotes trade and economic integration among member nations in Southeast Asia

The **Association of Southeast Asian Nations (ASEAN)**, established in 1967, promotes trade and economic integration among member nations in Southeast Asia. The trade pact includes

Malaysia, the Philippines, Singapore, Thailand, Brunei Darussalam, Vietnam, Laos, Myanmar, and Cambodia.[69] The region is home to 600 million people with a combined GDP of $2 trillion.[70] With its motto "One Vision, One Identity, One Community," member nations have expressed the goal of encouraging free trade, peace, and collaboration between member countries.[71] In 1993, the trade bloc passed the Common Effective Preferential Tariff to reduce or phase out tariffs between countries over a 10-year period as well as eliminate non-tariff trade barriers.[72]

The economies of ASEAN countries are expanding at an average of 5 percent, with Singapore listed among the top richest nations in the world.[73] Yet, despite these positive growth rates, ASEAN is facing many obstacles in becoming a unified trade bloc. Unlike members of the European Union, the countries in ASEAN are vastly different, with political systems including a military dictatorship (Myanmar), democracies (Philippines, Indonesia, and Malaysia), constitutional monarchies (Thailand and Cambodia), and communism (Vietnam).[74] Other countries outside of ASEAN have placed pressure on the trade bloc for its inclusion of Myanmar, which has been criticized for human rights abuses. There have also been conflicts between members themselves. For instance, in 2011, Thailand and Cambodia clashed militarily over disputed territory between the two countries.[75]

On the other hand, while many choose to compare ASEAN with the European Union, ASEAN members are careful to point out their differences. Although members hope to increase economic integration by 2015, they expressed that there will be no common currency or fully free labor flows between members. In this way, ASEAN plans to avoid some of the pitfalls that occurred among nations in the EU during the latest worldwide recession.[76]

The World Trade Organization (WTO)

The **World Trade Organization (WTO)** is a global trade association that promotes free trade among 153 member nations. The WTO is the successor to the **General Agreement on Tariffs and Trade (GATT)**, which was originally signed by 23 nations in 1947 to provide a forum for tariff negotiations and a place where international trade problems could be discussed and resolved. Rounds of GATT negotiations reduced trade barriers for most products and established rules to guide international commerce, such as rules to prevent **dumping**, the selling of products at unfairly low prices.

The WTO came into being in 1995 as a result of the Uruguay Round (1988–1994) of GATT negotiations. Broadly, WTO is the main worldwide organization that deals with the rules of trade between nations; its main function is to ensure that trade flows as smoothly, predictably, and freely as possible between nations. In 2011, 153 nations were members of the WTO.[77]

Fulfilling the purpose of the WTO requires eliminating trade barriers; educating individuals, companies, and governments about trade rules around the world; and assuring global markets that no sudden changes of policy will occur. At the heart of the WTO are agreements that provide legal ground rules for international commerce and trade policy. Based in Geneva, Switzerland, the WTO also serves as a forum for dispute resolution.[78] For example, Mexico, the United States, and the EU complained to the WTO that China was unfairly placing restrictions on the export of nine raw materials. The WTO determined that China's export restrictions violated international trade rules.[79]

World Trade Organization (WTO) An entity that promotes free trade among member nations by eliminating trade barriers and educating individuals, companies, and governments about trade rules around the world

General Agreement on Tariffs and Trade (GATT) An agreement among nations to reduce worldwide tariffs and increase international trade

dumping Selling products at unfairly low prices

MODES OF ENTRY INTO INTERNATIONAL MARKETS

Marketers enter international markets and continue to engage in marketing activities at several levels of international involvement. Traditionally, firms have adopted one of four different modes of entering an international market; each successive "stage" represents different degrees of international involvement.

Figure 9.1 Levels of Involvement in Global Marketing

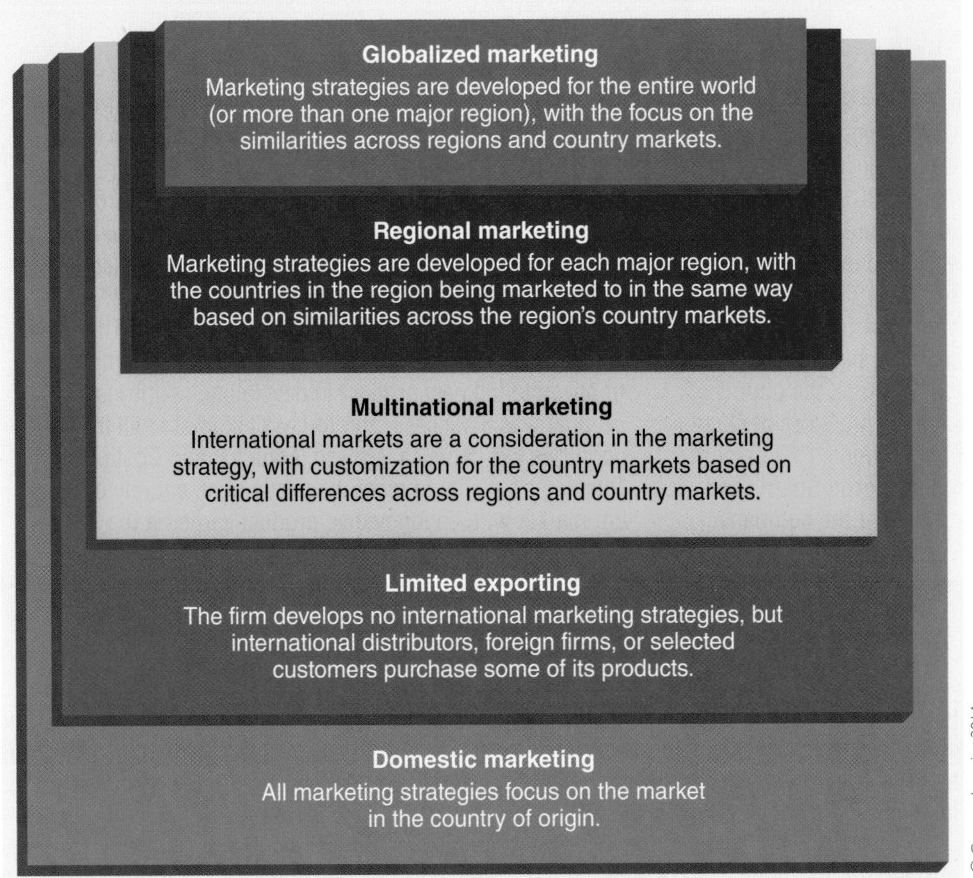

- Stage 1: No regular export activities
- Stage 2: Export via independent representatives (agents)
- Stage 3: Establishment of one or more sales subsidiaries internationally
- Stage 4: Establishment of international production/manufacturing facilities[80]

As Figure 9.1 shows, companies' international involvement today covers a wide spectrum, from purely domestic marketing to global marketing. Domestic marketing involves marketing strategies aimed at markets within the home country; at the other extreme, global marketing entails developing marketing strategies for the entire world (or at least more than one major region of the world). Many firms with an international presence start out as small companies serving local and regional domestic markets and expand to national markets before considering opportunities in foreign markets (the born global firm, described earlier, is one exception to this internationalization process). Limited exporting may occur even if a firm makes little or no effort to obtain foreign sales. Foreign buyers may seek out the company and/or its products, or a distributor may discover the firm's products and export them. The level of commitment to international marketing is a major variable in global marketing strategies. In this section, we examine importing and exporting, trading companies, licensing and franchising, contract manufacturing, joint ventures, direct ownership, and some of the other approaches to international involvement.

Importing and Exporting

importing The purchase of products from a foreign source

exporting The sale of products to foreign markets

Importing and exporting require the least amount of effort and commitment of resources. **Importing** is the purchase of products from a foreign source. **Exporting**, the sale of products

Entrepreneurship in Marketing

Quadlogic Profits during Recession with Help from Developing Countries

Entrepreneurs: Doron Shafrir and Sayre Swarztrauber
Business: Quadlogic Controls Corporation
Founded: 1982 | Long Island, New York
Success: Quadlogic Controls won the 2011 Wall Street Journal Small-Business Innovation Award for adapting its products to create innovative, environmentally friendly solutions for international markets.

While most companies tightened their belts during the recent recession, Quadlogic Controls took the opportunity to go global. When the recession hit, sales of Quadlogic's energy-tracking products plummeted 70 percent. But rather than panicking, founders Doron Shafrir and Sayre Swarztrauber decided to reinvent the company and focus on a new market: developing countries. As a result, sales have increased 170 percent from before the recession.

In developing countries, energy theft is a severe problem. Quadlogic had already started developing a product to address this need, but it was still in the experimental stages when the recession hit. The founders decided to speed up production of the product Energy Guard™, which was designed to detect and prevent energy theft. The company then went on an extensive marketing campaign to promote the new product in developing countries. The product was a success, and today, customers hail from countries like Jamaica, Mexico, Ecuador, and Costa Rica. Quadlogic's ability to meet the needs of an entirely different market with an innovative product earned it the 2011 Wall Street Journal Small-Business Innovation Award.[d]

to foreign markets, enables firms of all sizes to participate in global business. A firm may find an exporting intermediary to take over most marketing functions associated with marketing to other countries. This approach entails minimal effort and cost. Modifications in packaging, labeling, style, or color may be the major expenses in adapting a product for the foreign market.

Export agents bring together buyers and sellers from different countries and collect a commission for arranging sales. Export houses and export merchants purchase products from different companies and then sell them abroad. They are specialists at understanding customers' needs in global markets. Using exporting intermediaries involves limited risk because no foreign direct investment is required.

Buyers from foreign companies and governments provide a direct method of exporting and eliminate the need for an intermediary. These buyers encourage international exchange by contacting overseas firms about their needs and the opportunities available in exporting to them. Indeed, research suggests that many small firms tend to rely heavily on such native contacts, especially in developed markets, and remain production oriented rather than market oriented in their approach to international marketing.[81] Domestic firms that want to export with minimal effort and investment should seek out export intermediaries. Once a company becomes involved in exporting, it usually develops more knowledge of the country and becomes more confident in its competitiveness.[82]

Trading Companies

Marketers sometimes employ a **trading company**, which links buyers and sellers in different countries but is not involved in manufacturing and does not own assets related to manufacturing. Trading companies buy products in one country at the lowest price consistent with quality and sell them to buyers in another country. For instance, SCiNet World Trade System offers a 24-hour-per-day online world trade system that connects 20 million companies in 245 countries, offering more than 60 million products and services.[83] A trading company acts like a wholesaler, taking on much of the responsibility of finding markets while facilitating all marketing aspects of a transaction. An important function of trading companies is taking title to products and performing all the activities necessary to move the products to the targeted

trading company A company that links buyers and sellers in different countries foreign country. For instance, large grain-trading companies that operate out-of-home offices in both the United States and overseas control a major portion of world trade of basic food commodities. These trading companies sell homogeneous agricultural commodities that can be stored and moved rapidly in response to market conditions.

Trading companies reduce risk for firms that want to get involved in international marketing. A trading company provides producers with information about products that meet quality and price expectations in domestic and international markets. Additional services a trading company may provide include consulting, marketing research, advertising, insurance, product research and design, legal assistance, warehousing, and foreign exchange.

Licensing and Franchising

When potential markets are found across national boundaries, and when production, technical assistance, or marketing know-how is required, **licensing** is an alternative to direct investment. The licensee (the owner of the foreign operation) pays commissions or royalties on sales or supplies used in manufacturing. The licensee may also pay an initial down payment or fee when the licensing agreement is signed. Exchanges of management techniques or technical assistance are primary reasons for licensing agreements. Yoplait, for example, is a French yogurt that is licensed for production in the United States; the Yoplait brand tries to maintain a French image. Similarly, sports organizations like the International Olympic Committee (IOC), which is responsible for the Olympic Games, typically concentrate on organizing their sporting events while licensing the merchandise and other products that are sold.

Licensing is an attractive alternative when resources are unavailable for direct investment or when the core competencies of the firm or organization are not related to the product being sold (such as in the case of Olympics merchandise). Licensing can also be a viable alternative when the political stability of a foreign country is in doubt. In addition, licensing is especially advantageous for small manufacturers wanting to launch a well-known brand internationally. For example, Questor Corporation owns the Spalding name but does not produce a single golf club or tennis ball itself; all Spalding sporting products are licensed worldwide.

licensing An alternative to direct investment that requires a licensee to pay commissions or royalties on sales or supplies used in manufacturing

Global Franchises
KFC offers an extensive global franchise network.

Franchising is a form of licensing in which a company (the franchiser) grants a franchisee the right to market its product, using its name, logo, methods of operation, advertising, products, and other elements associated with the franchiser's business, in return for a financial commitment and an agreement to conduct business in accordance with the franchiser's standard of operations. This arrangement allows franchisers to minimize the risks of international marketing in four ways: (1) the franchiser does not have to put up a large capital investment; (2) the franchiser's revenue stream is fairly consistent because franchisees pay a fixed fee and royalties; (3) the franchiser retains control of its name and increases global penetration of its product; and (4) franchise agreements ensure a certain standard of behavior from franchisees, which protects the franchise name.[84]

Contract Manufacturing

Contract manufacturing occurs when a company hires a foreign firm to produce a designated volume of the firm's product (or a component of a product) to specification and the final product carries the domestic firm's name. The Gap, for example, relies on contract manufacturing for some of its apparel; Reebok uses Korean contract manufacturers to produce many of its athletic shoes. Marketing may be handled by the contract manufacturer or by the contracting company.

Three specific forms of contract manufacturing have become popular in the last decade: outsourcing, offshoring, and offshore outsourcing. **Outsourcing** is defined as the contracting of noncore operations or jobs from internal production within a business to an external entity that specializes in that operation. For example, outsourcing certain elements of a firm's operations to China and Mexico has become popular. The majority of all footwear is now produced in China, regardless of the brand name on the shoe you wear. Over the last 20 years, U.S. domestic apparel manufacturing fell from 41 percent to 3 percent due to outsourcing.[85] Services can also be outsourced. The Food and Drug Administration (FDA) announced that it plans to outsource more overseas safety inspections to third parties.[86]

Offshoring is defined as moving a business process that was done domestically at the local factory to a foreign country, regardless of whether the production accomplished in the foreign country is performed by the local company (e.g., in a wholly owned subsidiary) or a third party (e.g., subcontractor). Typically, the production is moved to reap the advantages of lower cost of operations in the foreign location. **Offshore outsourcing** is the practice of contracting with an organization to perform some or all business functions in a country other than the country in which the product or service will be sold. Today, some clothing manufacturers that previously engaged in offshore outsourcing are moving production back to the United States to maintain quality and tighter inventory control.[87]

contract manufacturing The practice of hiring a foreign firm to produce a designated volume of the domestic firm's product or a component of it to specification; the final product carries the domestic firm's name

outsourcing The practice of contracting noncore operations with an organization that specializes in that operation

offshoring The practice of moving a business process that was done domestically at the local factory to a foreign country, regardless of whether the production accomplished in the foreign country is performed by the local company (e.g., in a wholly owned subsidiary) or a third party (e.g., subcontractor)

offshore outsourcing The practice of contracting with an organization to perform some or all business functions in a country other than the country in which the product or service will be sold

joint venture A partnership between a domestic firm and a foreign firm or government

Joint Ventures

In international marketing, a **joint venture** is a partnership between a domestic firm and a foreign firm or government. Joint ventures are especially popular in industries that require large investments, such as natural resources extraction or automobile manufacturing. Control of the joint venture may be split equally, or one party may control decision making. Joint ventures are often a political necessity because of nationalism and government restrictions on foreign ownership. In spite of an unpredictable political environment under democratically elected socialist president Hugo Chávez, many nations are eager to form joint ventures with Venezuelan national oil companies in order to gain access to Venezuela's petroleum resources. Brazilian conglomerate Odebrecht paid $50 million to state-owned oil company Petroleos de Venezuela for a 40 percent stake in the venture. The joint venture will search for oil in the Venezuelan state of Zulia.[88] However, the Chávez regime has been hostile to some direct foreign investment from capitalist countries, particularly that of U.S. companies. Joint ventures may also occur when acquisition or internal development is not feasible or when the risks and constraints leave no other alternative.

© Harry Page/Bloomberg via Getty Images

Strategic Alliances
American Airlines, British Airlines, and Iberia formed an alliance in serving transatlantic routes called One World.

Joint ventures also provide legitimacy in the eyes of the host country's citizens. Local partners have firsthand knowledge of the economic and sociopolitical environment and the workings of available distribution networks, and they may have privileged access to local resources (raw materials, labor management, and so on). However, joint venture relationships require trust throughout the relationship to provide a foreign partner with a ready means of implementing its own marketing strategy. Joint ventures are assuming greater global importance because of cost advantages and the number of inexperienced firms that are entering foreign markets. They may be the result of a trade-off between a firm's desire for completely unambiguous control of an enterprise and its quest for additional resources.

Strategic alliances are partnerships formed to create a competitive advantage on a worldwide basis. They are very similar to joint ventures, but while joint ventures are defined in scope, strategic alliances are typically represented by an agreement to work together (which can ultimately mean more involvement than a joint venture). In an international strategic alliance, the firms in the alliance may have been traditional rivals competing for the same market. They may also be competing in certain markets while working together in other markets where it is beneficial for both parties. One such collaboration is the Sky Team Alliance—involving KLM, Aeromexico, Air France, Alitalia, CSA Czech Airlines, Delta, Korean Air, Kenya Airways, Aeroflot, AirEuropa, Vietnam Airlines, China Airlines, MEA, Saudia, Tarom Romanian Air Transport, China Eastern, and China Southern—which is designed to improve customer service among the firms.[89] Whereas joint ventures are formed to create a new identity, partners in strategic alliances often retain their distinct identities, with each partner bringing a core competency to the union.

The success rate of international alliances could be higher if a better fit between the companies existed. A strategic alliance should focus on a joint market opportunity from which all partners can benefit. In the automobile, computer, and airline industries, strategic alliances are becoming the predominant means of competing internationally. Competition in these industries is so fierce and the costs of competing on a global basis are so high that few firms have all the resources needed to do it alone. Firms that lack the internal resources essential for international success may seek to collaborate with other companies. A shared mode of leadership among partner corporations combines joint abilities and allows collaboration from a distance. Focusing on customer value and implementing innovative ways to compete create a winning strategy.

strategic alliance A partnership that is formed to create a competitive advantage on a worldwide basis

Direct Ownership

Once a company makes a long-term commitment to marketing in a foreign country that has a promising market as well as a suitable political and economic environment, **direct ownership** of a foreign subsidiary or division is a possibility. Most foreign investment covers only manufacturing equipment or personnel because the expenses of developing a separate foreign distribution system can be tremendous. The opening of retail stores in Europe, Canada, or Mexico can require a staggering financial investment in facilities, research, and management.

The term **multinational enterprise**, sometimes called *multinational corporation*, refers to a firm that has operations or subsidiaries in many countries. Often, the parent company is based in one country and carries on production, management, and marketing activities in other countries. The firm's subsidiaries may be autonomous so they can respond to the needs of individual international markets, or they may be part of a global network that is led by the headquarters' operations.

At the same time, a wholly owned foreign subsidiary may be allowed to operate independently of the parent company to give its management more freedom to adjust to the local environment. Cooperative arrangements are developed to assist in marketing efforts, production, and management. A wholly owned foreign subsidiary may export products to the home country, its market may serve as a test market for the firm's global products, or it may be a component of the firm's globalization efforts. Some U.S. automobile manufacturers, for example, import cars built by their foreign subsidiaries. A foreign subsidiary offers important tax, tariff, and other operating advantages. Table 9.6 lists the 10 largest global corporations, most of which have operations in several different countries.

One of the greatest advantages of a multinational enterprise is the cross-cultural approach. A subsidiary usually operates under foreign management so it can develop a local identity. In particular, the firm (i.e., seller) is often expected to adapt, if needed, to the buyer's culture. Interestingly, the cultural values of customers in the younger age group (30 years and younger) are becoming increasingly similar around the world. Today, a 20-year-old in Russia is increasingly similar in mindset to a 20-year-old in China and a 20-year-old in the United States, especially with regard to their tastes in music, clothes, and cosmetics. This makes marketing goods and services to the younger population easier today than it was only a generation ago. Nevertheless, there is still great danger involved in having a wholly owned subsidiary in some parts of the world due to political uncertainty, terrorism threats, and economic instability.

direct ownership A situation in which a company owns subsidiaries or other facilities overseas

multinational enterprise A firm that has operations or subsidiaries in many countries

Whereas the most well-known multinational corporations (MNCs) come from developed countries, the world is seeing a rise in MNCs from emerging economies as well. Brazil's Embraer (an aircraft company) and South Africa's MTN (a mobile phone company) are two

Table 9.6 The 10 Largest Global Corporations

Rank	Company	Revenue (U.S.$ in Millions)	Country
1	Royal Dutch Shell	$484,489	Netherlands
2	ExxonMobil	452,926	United States
3	Wal-Mart Stores	446,950	United States
4	BP	386,463	United Kingdom
5	Sinopec Group	375,214	China
6	China National Petroleum	352,338	China
7	State Grid	259,141.8	China
8	Chevron	245,621	United States
9	ConocoPhillips	237,272	United States
10	Toyota Motor	235,364	Japan

Source: "Global 500: Fortune's Annual Ranking of the World's Largest Corporations," *Fortune*, July 23, 2012, F1–F2.

examples. India's Tata group is even beginning to rival more established MNCs. Tata owns several firms that qualify as MNCs, specializing in such diverse products as cars, hotels, steel, and chemicals. These conglomerates—in which one major entity owns several companies—are becoming an organizational trend among multinationals from developing nations.[90]

GLOBAL ORGANIZATIONAL STRUCTURES

Firms develop their international marketing strategies and manage their marketing mixes (i.e., product, distribution, promotion, and price) by developing and maintaining an organizational structure that best leverages their resources and core competencies. This organizational structure is defined as the way a firm divides its operations into separate functions and/or value-adding units and coordinates its activities. Most firms undergo a step-by-step development in their internationalization efforts of the firm's people, processes, functions, culture, and structure. The pyramid in Figure 9.2 symbolizes how deeply rooted the international operations and values are in the firm, with the base of the pyramid—structure—being the most difficult to change (especially in the short term). Three basic structures of international organizations exist: export departments, international divisions, and internationally integrated structures (e.g., product division structures, geographic area structures, and matrix structures). The existing structure of the firm, or the structure that the firm chooses to adopt, has implications for international marketing strategy.

Export Departments

For most firms, the early stages of international development are often informal and not fully planned. During this early stage, sales opportunities in the global marketplace motivate a

Figure 9.2 Organizational Architecture

company to engage internationally. For instance, born global firms make exporting a primary objective from their inceptions. For most firms, however, very minimal, if any, organizational adjustments take place to accommodate international sales. Foreign sales are typically so small that many firms cannot justify allocating structural or other resources to the internationalization effort in the infancy of internationalization. Exporting, licensing, and using trading companies are preferred modes of international market entry for firms with an export department structure.

Some firms develop an export department as a subunit of the marketing department, whereas others organize it as a department that structurally coexists at an equal level with the other functional units. Additionally, some companies choose to hire outside export departments to handle their international operations. Lone Star Distribution, a distributor for sports and nutritional supplements, has an export department that helps its clients transport their goods internationally.[91] Another unique case of developing a successful export operation early after its inception is the born global firm of Logitech International. Founded in 1981, Logitech is a Swiss company that designs personal computer peripherals that enable people to effectively work, play, and communicate in the digital world.

As demand for a firm's goods and services grows or its commitments increase due to its internationalization efforts, it develops an international structure. Many firms evolve from using their export department structure to forming an international division.

International Divisions

A company's international division centralizes all of the responsibility for international operations (and in many cases, all international activities also become centralized in the international division). The typical international division concentrates human resources (i.e., international expertise) into one unit and serves as the central point for all information flow related to international operations (e.g., international market opportunities, international research and development). At the same time, firms with an international division structure take advantage of economies of scale by keeping manufacturing and related functions within the domestic divisions. Firms may develop international divisions at a relatively early stage, as well as a mature stage, of their international development. However, an increasing number of firms are recognizing the importance of going global early on. As such, these firms use exporting, licensing and franchising, trading companies, contract manufacturing, and joint ventures as possible modes of international market entry.

This international division structure illustrates the importance of coordination and cooperation among domestic and international operations. Frequent interaction and strategic planning meetings are required to make this structure work effectively. In particular, firms that use an international division structure are often organized domestically on the basis of functions or product divisions, whereas the international division is organized on the basis of geography. This means that coordination and strategic alignment across domestic divisions and the international division are critical to success. At the same time, lack of coordination between domestic and international operations is commonly the most significant flaw in the international division structure.

An example of a firm that has used the international division structure to achieve worldwide success is Abbott Laboratories, a $30 billion diversified health-care company that develops products and services that span prevention and diagnosis to treatment and cures. As international sales grew in the late 1960s, the firm added an international division to its structure. This international division structure has benefits and drawbacks for Abbott, as it does for other firms that use it.[92]

Some argue that to offset the natural "isolation" that may result between domestic and international operations in this structure, the international division structure should be used only when a company (1) intends to market only a small assortment of goods or services internationally and (2) when foreign sales account for only a small portion of total sales. When the product assortment increases or the percentage of foreign sales becomes significant, an internationally integrated structure may be more appropriate.

Internationally Integrated Structures

A number of different internationally integrated structures have been developed and implemented by firms in their quest to achieve global success. The three most common structures are the product division structure, the geographic area structure, and the global matrix structure. Firms with these varied structures have multiple choices for international market entry similar to international divisions (e.g., exporting, licensing and franchising, trading companies, contract manufacturing, and joint ventures). However, firms that have internationally integrated structures are the most likely to engage in direct ownership activities internationally.

The product division structure is the form used by the majority of multinational enterprises. This structure lends itself well to firms that are diversified, often driven by their current domestic operations. Each division is a self-contained entity with responsibility for its own operations, whether it is based on a country or regional structure. However, the worldwide headquarters maintains the overall responsibility for the strategic direction of the firm, whereas the product division is in charge of implementation. Procter & Gamble has a long-standing tradition of operating in a product division structure, with leading brands like Pampers, Tide, Pantene, Bounty, Folgers, Pringles, Charmin, Downy, Crest, and Olay.

The geographic area structure lends itself well to firms with a low degree of diversification. Under this domestically influenced functional structure, the world is divided into logical geographical areas based on the firms' operations and the customers' characteristics. Accenture, a global management consulting firm, operates worldwide largely based on a geographic area structure. Each area tends to be relatively self-contained, and integration across areas is typically via the worldwide or the regional headquarters. This structure facilitates local responsiveness, but it is not ideal for reducing global costs and transferring core knowledge across the firm's geographic units. A key issue in geographic area structures, as in almost all multinational corporations, is the need to become more regionally and globally integrated.

The global matrix structure was designed to achieve both global integration and local responsiveness. Asea Brown Boveri (ABB), a Swedish-Swiss engineering multinational, is the best-known firm to implement a global matrix structure. ABB is an international leader in power and automation technologies that enable customers to improve their performance while lowering environmental impact. Global matrix structures theoretically facilitate a simultaneous focus on realizing local responsiveness, cost efficiencies, and knowledge transfers. However, few firms can operate a global matrix well, since the structure is based on, for example, product and geographic divisions simultaneously (or a combination of any two traditional structures). This means that employees belong to two divisions and often report to two managers throughout the hierarchies of the firm. An effectively implemented global matrix structure has the benefit of being global in scope while also being nimble and responsive locally. However, a poorly implemented global matrix structure results in added bureaucracy and indecisiveness in leadership and implementation.

CUSTOMIZATION VERSUS GLOBALIZATION OF INTERNATIONAL MARKETING MIXES

Like domestic marketers, international marketers develop marketing strategies to serve specific target markets. Traditionally, international marketing strategies have customized marketing mixes according to cultural, regional, and national differences. Table 9.7 provides a sample of international issues related to product, distribution, promotion, and price. For example, many developing countries lack the infrastructure needed for expansive distribution networks, which can make it harder to get the product to consumers. Nestlé is finding ways to get past these obstacles in Africa by employing local sales agents to promote and deliver its products. These agents often travel by taxi, bicycle, or on foot. Although such distribution

Table 9.7 Marketing Mix Issues Internationally

	Sample International Issues
Product Element	
Core Product	Is there a commonality of the customer's needs across countries? What will the product be used for and in what context?
Product Adoption	How is awareness created for the product in the various country markets? How and where is the product typically bought?
Managing Products	How are truly new products managed in the country markets vis-à-vis existing products or products that have been modified slightly?
Branding	Is the brand accepted widely around the world? Does the home country help or hurt the brand perception of the consumer?
Distribution Element	
Marketing Channels	What is the role of the channel intermediaries internationally? Where is value created beyond the domestic borders of the firm?
Physical Distribution	Is the movement of products the most efficient from the home country to the foreign market or to a regional warehouse?
Retail Stores	What is the availability of different types of retail stores in the various country markets?
Retailing Strategy	Where do customers typically shop in the targeted countries—downtown, in suburbs, or in malls?
Promotion Element	
Advertising	Some countries' customers prefer firm-specific advertising instead of product-specific advertising. How does this affect advertising?
Public Relations	How is public relations used to manage the stakeholders' interests internationally? Are the stakeholders' interests different worldwide?
Personal Selling	What product types require personal selling internationally? Does it differ from how those products are sold domestically?
Sales Promotion	Is coupon usage a widespread activity in the targeted international markets? What other forms of sales promotion should be used?
Pricing Element	
Core Price	Is price a critical component of the value equation of the product in the targeted country markets?
Analysis of Demand	Is the demand curve similar internationally and domestically? Will a change in price drastically change demand?
Demand, Cost, and Profit Relationships	What are the fixed and variable costs when marketing the product internationally? Are they similar to the domestic setting?
Determination of Price	How do the pricing strategy, environmental forces, business practices, and cultural values affect price?

methods might seem unconventional, Nestlé has already seen an increase in sales in the area.[93] Realizing that both similarities and differences exist across countries is a critical first step to developing the appropriate marketing strategy effort targeted to particular international markets. Today, many firms strive to build their marketing strategies around similarities that exist instead of customizing around differences.

For many firms, **globalization** of marketing is the goal; it involves developing marketing strategies as though the entire world (or its major regions) were a single entity: a globalized firm markets standardized products in the same way everywhere. Nike and Adidas shoes, for example, are standardized worldwide. Other examples of globalized products include electronic communications equipment, Western-style clothing, movies, soft drinks, rock and alternative music, cosmetics, and toothpaste. Sony televisions, Starbucks coffee, and many products sold at Walmart all post year-to-year gains in the world market.

globalization The development of marketing strategies that treat the entire world (or its major regions) as a single entity

© AP Images//Mary Altaffer

Globalization
Lay's customizes their products in many countries throughout the world.

For many years, organizations have attempted to globalize their marketing mixes as much as possible by employing standardized products, promotion campaigns, prices, and distribution channels for all markets. The economic and competitive payoffs for globalized marketing strategies are certainly great. Brand name, product characteristics, packaging, and labeling are among the easiest marketing mix variables to standardize; media allocation, retail outlets, and price may be more difficult. In the end, the degree of similarity among the various environmental and market conditions determines the feasibility and degree of globalization. A successful globalization strategy often depends on the extent to which a firm is able to implement the idea of "think globally, act locally."[94] Even take-out food lends itself to globalization: McDonald's, KFC, and Taco Bell restaurants satisfy hungry customers in both hemispheres, although menus may be altered slightly to satisfy local tastes. When Dunkin' Donuts entered the Chinese market, it served coffee, tea, donuts, and bagels, just as it does in the United States, but in China, the donut case also includes items like green tea and honeydew melon donuts and mochi rings, which are similar to donuts but are made with rice flour. The company has experienced success in China and plans to expand into Vietnam.[95]

International marketing demands some strategic planning if a firm is to incorporate foreign sales into its overall marketing strategy. International marketing activities often require customized marketing mixes to achieve the firm's goals. Globalization requires a total commitment to the world, regions, or multinational areas as an integral part of the firm's markets; world or regional markets become as important as domestic ones. Regardless of the extent to which a firm chooses to globalize its marketing strategy, extensive environmental analysis and marketing research are necessary to understand the needs and desires of the target market(s) and successfully implement the chosen marketing strategy.

A global presence does not automatically result in a global competitive advantage. However, a global presence generates five opportunities for creating value: (1) to adapt to local market differences, (2) to exploit economies of global scale, (3) to exploit economies of global scope, (4) to mine optimal locations for activities and resources, and (5) to maximize the transfer of knowledge across locations.[96] To exploit these opportunities, marketers need to conduct marketing research and work within the constraints of the international environment and regional trade alliances, markets, and agreements.

Summary

1. To understand the nature of global marketing strategy

International marketing involves developing and performing marketing activities across national boundaries. International markets can provide tremendous opportunities for growth and renewed opportunity for the firm.

2. To analyze the environmental forces that affect international marketing efforts

A detailed analysis of the environment is essential before a company enters an international market. Environmental aspects of special importance include sociocultural; economic, political, legal, and regulatory; social and ethical; competitive; and technological forces. Because marketing activities are primarily social in purpose, they are influenced by beliefs and values regarding family, religion, education, health, and recreation. Cultural differences may affect marketing negotiations, decision-making behavior, and product adoption and use. A nation's economic stability and trade barriers can affect marketing efforts. Significant trade barriers include import tariffs, quotas, embargoes, and exchange controls. Gross domestic product (GDP) and GDP per capita are common measures of a nation's economic standing. Political and legal forces include a nation's political system, laws, regulatory bodies, special-interest groups, and courts. In the area of ethics, cultural relativism is the concept that morality varies from one culture to another and that business practices are therefore differentially defined as right or wrong by particular cultures. In addition to considering the types of competition and the types of competitive structures that exist in other countries, marketers also need to consider the competitive forces at work and recognize the importance of the global customer who is well informed about product choices from around the world. Advances in technology have greatly facilitated international marketing.

3. To understand several important international trade agreements

Various regional trade alliances and specific markets create both opportunities and constraints for companies engaged in international marketing. Important trade agreements include the North American Free Trade Agreement, European Union, Southern Common Market, Asia-Pacific Economic Cooperation, Association of Southeast Asian Nations, and World Trade Organization.

4. To identify methods of international market entry

There are several ways to enter international marketing. Importing (the purchase of products from a foreign source) and exporting (the sale of products to foreign markets) are the easiest and most flexible methods. Marketers may employ a trading company, which links buyers and sellers in different countries but is not involved in manufacturing and does not own assets related to manufacturing. Licensing and franchising are arrangements whereby one firm pays fees to another for the use of its name, expertise, and supplies. Contract manufacturing occurs when a company hires a foreign firm to produce a designated volume of the domestic firm's product to specification, and the final product carries the domestic firm's name. Joint ventures are partnerships between a domestic firm and a foreign firm or government. Strategic alliances are partnerships formed to create competitive advantage on a worldwide basis. Finally, a firm can build its own marketing or production facilities overseas. When companies have direct ownership of facilities in many countries, they may be considered multinational enterprises.

5. To examine various forms of global organizational structures

Firms develop their international marketing strategies and manage their marketing mixes by developing and maintaining an organizational structure that best leverages their resources and core competencies. Three basic structures of international organizations include export departments, international divisions, and internationally integrated structures (e.g., product division structures, geographic area structures, and matrix structures).

6. To examine the use of the marketing mix internationally

Although most firms adjust their marketing mixes for differences in target markets, some firms standardize their marketing efforts worldwide. Traditional full-scale international marketing involvement is based on products customized according to cultural, regional, and national differences. Globalization, however, involves developing marketing strategies as if the entire world (or regions of it) were a single entity; a globalized firm markets standardized products in the same way everywhere. International marketing demands some strategic planning if a firm is to incorporate foreign sales into its overall marketing strategy.

Go to www.cengagebrain.com for resources to help you master the content in this chapter as well as for materials that will expand your marketing knowledge!

Important Terms

international marketing 274
gross domestic product (GDP) 278
import tariff 280
quota 281
embargo 281
exchange controls 281
balance of trade 281
cultural relativism 283
North American Free Trade Agreement (NAFTA) 286
European Union (EU) 288
Southern Common Market (MERCOSUR) 289
Asia-Pacific Economic Cooperation (APEC) 289
Association of Southeast Asian Nations (ASEAN) 291
World Trade Organization (WTO) 292
General Agreement on Tariffs and Trade (GATT) 292
dumping 292
importing 293
exporting 293
trading company 294
licensing 295
contract manufacturing 296
outsourcing 296
offshoring 296
offshore outsourcing 296
joint venture 296
strategic alliance 297
direct ownership 298
multinational enterprise 298
globalization 302

Discussion and Review Questions

1. How does international marketing differ from domestic marketing?
2. What factors must marketers consider as they decide whether to engage in international marketing?
3. Why are the largest industrial corporations in the United States so committed to international marketing?
4. Why do you think this chapter focuses on an analysis of the international marketing environment?
5. If you were asked to provide a small tip (or bribe) to have a document approved in a foreign nation where this practice is customary, what would you do?
6. How will NAFTA affect marketing opportunities for U.S. products in North America (the United States, Mexico, and Canada)?
7. What should marketers consider as they decide whether to license or enter into a joint venture in a foreign nation?
8. Discuss the impact of strategic alliances on international marketing strategies.
9. Contrast globalization with customization of marketing strategies. Is one practice better than the other?
10. What are some of the product issues that you need to consider when marketing luxury automobiles in Australia, Brazil, Singapore, South Africa, and Sweden?

Application Questions

1. To successfully implement marketing strategies in the international marketplace, a marketer must understand the complexities of the global marketing environment. Which environmental forces (sociocultural, economic, political/legal/regulatory, ethical, competitive, or technological) might a marketer need to consider when marketing the following products in the international marketplace, and why?
   a. Barbie dolls
   b. Beer
   c. Financial services
   d. Television sets
2. Many firms, including Procter & Gamble, FedEx, and Occidental Petroleum, wish to do business in eastern Europe and in the countries that were once part of the former Soviet Union. What events could occur that would make marketing in these countries more difficult? What events might make it easier?

3. This chapter discusses various organizational approaches to international marketing. Which would be the best arrangements for international marketing of the following products, and why?
   a. Construction equipment
   b. Cosmetics
   c. Automobiles
4. Procter & Gamble has made a substantial commitment to foreign markets, especially in Latin America. Its actions may be described as a "globalization of marketing." Describe how a shoe manufacturer (e.g., Wolverine World Wide) would go from domestic marketing to limited exporting, to international marketing, and finally to a globalization of marketing. Give examples of some activities that might be involved in this process.
5. IMP Windshield wipers were invented by Mary Anderson in 1903, when she observed that streetcar drivers in New York City had to open the window when it rained in order to see. Her invention consisted of a long arm with a rubber blade that was operated by hand from inside the cab. By 1916, all passenger vehicles were fitted with these manual windshield wipers; starting in the early 1920s, a variety of automatic systems began to appear. In 1936, the first windshield washer unit became available as an option, adding another technological breakthrough in automotive technology.

   Flash forward to the present. Now, every vehicle utilizes windshield-washing fluids—usually consisting of a mixture of ethylene glycol, isoproponal, and water—that are reasonably effective at removing dirt, bugs, and other debris. The efficacy of windshield washing fluids decreases, however, in cold weather. Indeed, in winter months, these fluids do not spray properly and can sometimes even freeze.

   Recently, a few companies have begun to manufacture windshield-washing fluid heaters, which instantly heat the windshield-washing fluid to approximately 50°C (132°F) at the driver's touch. The system comes in a kit, which takes only 15 minutes to install. The first benefit, of course, is that the heated windshield-washer fluid reduces the amount of scraping of ice and snow needed by the driver beforehand. Heated windshield-washing fluid also sprays more consistently, helping to reach all parts of the windshield and is more effective at dissolving dirt and bugs. The manufacturing companies also claim that the fluid will help windshield wipers last longer.

   Many countries have long and cold winters, but Russia instantly comes to mind as a potential global market. Evaluate Russia in terms of its environmental forces for these manufacturers of windshield-washer fluid heaters. Based on approximately 275 motor vehicles per 1,000 people in the Russian population, what percentage of the market do you think that companies selling this product can capture (industry sales)? Which mode of entry seems best for one of these manufacturers? They are usually mid-sized companies with limited capital, international experience, and knowledge. How much customization would a product like this require for Russia?

Internet Exercise

FTD

Founded in 1910 as Florists' Telegraph Delivery, FTD was the first company to offer a "flowers-by-wire" service. FTD does not deliver flowers itself, but it depends on local florists to do it. In 1994, FTD expanded its toll-free telephone-ordering service by establishing a website. Visit the site at www.ftd.com.

a. Click on "International" near the bottom of the Web page. Select a country to which you would like to send flowers. Summarize the delivery and pricing information that would apply to that country.
b. Determine the cost of sending fresh-cut seasonal flowers to Germany.
c. What are the benefits of this global distribution system for sending flowers worldwide? What other consumer products could be distributed globally through the Internet?

developing your marketing plan

When formulating marketing strategy, one of the issues a company must consider is whether or not to pursue international markets. Although international markets present increased marketing opportunities, they also require more complex decisions when formulating marketing plans. To assist you in relating the information in this chapter to the development of your marketing plan, focus on the following:

1. Review the environmental analysis that was completed in Chapter 3. Extend the analysis for each of the seven factors to include global markets.
2. Using Figure 9.1 as a guide, determine the degree of international involvement that is appropriate for your product and your company.
3. Discuss the concepts of customization and globalization for your product when moving to international markets. Refer to Table 9.7 for guidance in your discussion.

The information obtained from these questions should assist you in developing various aspects of your marketing plan found in the "Interactive Marketing Plan" exercise at www.cengagebrain.com.

video case 9.1

Evo: The Challenge of Going Global

While Bryce Phillips, founder of active sports retailer evo, was skiing in Japan, he was surprised to learn that several skiers at the lodge owned evo products. Although it is evo's intention to become a more global company, the organization does not regularly export to other countries. Yet, even with little export activities, customers from other countries are seeking out evo sports gear.

© Ilja Mašík/Shutterstock.com

Evo, short for "evolution," was founded as an online retailer in 2001 and opened its Seattle-based retail store four years later. While the retail store provides customers with a physical location to look for products, the online store allows evo to carry a greater selection and extend its global reach. The company caters to active sports enthusiasts with products like ski gear, wakeboards, snowboards, skateboard gear, and street wear. From the beginning, Phillips wanted to use the Web to spread the word about evo worldwide. "When we think about the future, we think about being a global brand in the context that, for the kind of customers that we'd like to attract, we'd like to attract them all over the world," Phillips said. "And being on the Web, the word travels, and your brand can travel very, very quickly."

Approximately 5 percent of evo's business comes from outside the United States, and the Web's global reach has increased demand for evo's products. Yet, despite these favorable global prospects, evo has been constrained somewhat in its ability to ship internationally. "We are confined in some ways by a lot of our dealer agreements," said Nathan Decker, senior director of e-commerce at evo. He provides two reasons for why vendors create exclusive dealer arrangements with evo: (1) to avoid saturating markets overseas; and (2) to maintain control over their products in order to compete fairly in the global marketplace. By limiting distribution, manufacturers are able to exert some control over other elements of the marketing mix, such as price. The evo website contains a list of brands that the company cannot ship overseas due to contractual agreements. If consumers from foreign countries try to order these brands, they will receive notification that their order has been canceled.

Because retailers often do not own many of the brands they sell, manufacturers can maintain the right to determine where their products are sold and how much to distribute to the company. This represents a major challenge for retailers that want to go global. On the other hand, large retail companies that have a lot of power, such as Walmart, have a better ability to negotiate with manufacturers on global distribution. As evo grows as a brand, the company may gain the power to negotiate more favorable distribution terms with its vendors.

Additionally, dealer contracts cannot prevent consumers themselves from sending the products overseas. As Phillips found out firsthand, the company's popularity has spilled over into other countries. Technology has enabled the company to engage in viral marketing, which aids in increasing the company's global brand exposure. For instance, when mountain gear manufacturer Rossignol decided to launch its skis globally through the evo website, the news was posted on ski websites throughout the world. Evo has also been featured in magazines that have international circulations.

Evo hopes to work with its vendors to make global selling more feasible. "Once we kind of work through that and get the green light from some of our bigger vendors, I think that it'll become more of a strategic focus," Decker said. In the meantime, evo is finding additional ways to increase its global presence. For instance, the company launched evoTrip as a service for adventurous sports enthusiasts who want to travel. EvoTrip arranges the trips with the goal to connect people to local cultures, communities, and sports. In addition to increasing its customer base, evoTrip allows the organization to form relationships with consumers overseas.

Global opportunities are likely to increase as evo continues to grow. In 2011, the company released its first customer catalogue, and Phillips has expressed a desire to open more stores across the nation. The organization is also exploring the possibility of expanding its own line of evo-branded products. In doing so, the organization would not be constrained by contractual obligations from its vendors. Creating a global brand remains an important part of evo's endeavors. According to Phillips, "Everything we do, whether it be something we buy or something we sell [or] something we invest in, is connected globally."[97]

Questions for Discussion

1. What are both the positive and negative outcomes from using exclusive dealer agreements that restrict global distribution?
2. What are the unique product features that could make evo a global brand?
3. What should evo's marketing strategy be to go global?

case 9.2

Starbucks Faces Global Opportunities and Barriers

Although Starbucks has become an important part of America's coffee culture heritage, the idea for the company came from outside its country of origin. While on a business trip in Milan, Italy, in 1983, Starbucks founder and CEO Howard Schultz noticed the popularity of coffee shops as a community gathering place. He realized that, for Italians, coffee was not so much a beverage as it was a social experience. Schultz decided to replicate this coffee culture in the United States, turning Starbucks into the "third place" consumers would frequent after home and work.

Starbucks opened up its first international store in Vancouver, British Columbia, in 1987. Today, the company is a multinational powerhouse with more than 15,000 stores in 50 countries. Globalization offers many advantages to Starbucks. As the coffee industry becomes increasingly saturated in the United States, international expansion allows Starbucks to take advantage of untapped opportunities in other countries.

However, global expansion has not always been so easy. Starbucks has learned that while it must ensure consistency of quality, it must also customize to adapt to local tastes. For example, in the United Kingdom, Starbucks was not initially popular with British consumers. In response, Starbucks began to renovate its stores to create a unique look so that each store fit into the local neighborhood environment. The company rebounded, and today it has approximately 700 stores in the UK with plans to begin opening franchises in the country.

Starbucks also faces sociocultural barriers in China. The company entered China in 1999 and has since grown to about 550 stores, but what has been particularly challenging for Starbucks is to find a way to get past cultural barriers. In 2007, the company closed its store in the Forbidden City after criticism from the Chinese media.

Due to the backlash from Chinese citizens, Starbucks once again customized its offerings, with more Chinese-inspired food products and coffee-free beverages (Chinese consumers drink an average of three cups of coffee annually). To show support for Chinese business operations, the company opened a coffee farm and processing facilities within the country and reorganized to form a new China and Asia Pacific division.

Starbucks must work to ensure that its Western roots and expansion plans do not clash with Chinese values, since the country offers a highly lucrative market. Sales in the coffee market grew 20 percent in 2011 from the year before. However, while the coffee market is booming, Starbucks has also come across economic barriers. Because operating costs are higher in China, and labor costs are increasing, the price of Starbucks drinks in China is 50 to 75 percent higher than in the United States. This makes it harder for Starbucks to attract China's large population of lower-income consumers, and plans to increase prices to keep up with rising costs have angered middle-income customers. Starbucks must additionally find a way to overcome these barriers to increase its reach among the Chinese population.

Perhaps one of Starbucks' most celebrated successes is its entry into the Indian market. This success is particularly significant due to political barriers for foreign multinationals in India. Until recently, the Indian government mandated that foreign firms could only operate in the country if they created 50-50 joint ventures with domestic firms. The Indian government changed the law to allow companies that only sell one brand of products to develop wholly owned subsidiaries in the country. However, Starbucks opted to create a 50-50 joint venture with Indian firm Tata Global Beverages. Such a joint venture has many advantages, including an easier transition into the Indian market (Tata Global Beverages is part of the largest business group in the country). On the other hand, Starbucks must still contend with socioeconomic and economic barriers. Not only is India more of a tea-driven society, but most domestic coffee companies sell their beverages at a fraction of Starbucks' prices in the United States. Becoming affordable enough to attract the average Indian consumer will require changes in Starbucks' marketing strategies.

Interestingly, there is one notable country in which Starbucks is absent: Italy. While Starbucks modeled itself after Italian-style coffee shops, major differences between the two coffee cultures might hinder Starbucks' acceptance. For instance, the amount of espresso and the proper times to offer certain drinks like cappuccinos (never for breakfast or after heavy meals in Italy) are very different from American coffee-drinking habits. To succeed in Italy may require Starbucks to significantly customize its shops and beverages to appeal to Italian tastes.[98]

Questions for Discussion

1. Describe Starbucks' global strategy. Is it engaging in more of a globalization or customization approach?
2. What appear to be some of the most significant barriers Starbucks is facing when expanding into foreign countries?
3. What are some of the most significant obstacles to expansion in Italy, and how can Starbucks overcome them?

NOTES

[1]William Mellor, "McDonald's No Match for KFC in China as Colonel Rules Fast Food," *Bloomberg Businessweek*, January 26, 2011, www.bloomberg.com/news/2011-01-26/mcdonald-s-no-match-for-kfc-in-china-where-colonel-sanders-rules-fast-food.html (accessed December 8, 2011); Maggie Starvish, "KFC's Explosive Growth in China," *Harvard Business School*, June 17, 2011, http://hbswk.hbs.edu/item/6704.html (accessed December 8, 2011); Warren Liu and Young Entrepreneur Foundation, "The World Is Flat #3: How KFC Went Global," Young Entrepreneur Foundation, October 1, 2009, http://youngentrepreneurfoundation.wordpress.com/2009/10/01/the-world-is-flat-3-how-kfc-went-global/ (accessed December 8, 2011).

[2]Duane Stanford, "Africa: Coke's Last Frontier," *Bloomberg Businessweek*, October 28, 2010, www.businessweek.com/magazine/content/10_45/b4202054144294.htm (accessed December 20, 2010); Trefis Team, "Coca-Cola Stock Fizzing Up To $75 Through Middle East, Africa,"*Forbes*, December 21, 2011, www.forbes.com/sites/greatspeculations/2011/12/21/coca-cola-stock-fizzing-up-to-75-through-middle-east-africa/ (accessed February 21, 2012).

[3]Walmart Corporate International, http://walmartstores.com/aboutus/246.aspx (accessed January 20, 2012); Starbucks Coffee International, http://walmartstores.com/aboutus/246.aspx (accessed January 20, 2012).

[4]"Export Assistance," Office of the United States Trade Representative, www.ustr.gov/trade-topics/trade-toolbox/export-assistance (accessed February 21, 2012).

[5]Gary A. Knight and S. Tamer Cavusgil, "Innovation, Organizational Capabilities, and the Born-Global Firm," *Journal of International Business Studies* (March 2004): 124–141.

[6]Jessica Golloher, "McDonald's Still Thriving in Russia After 20 Years," February 2, 2010, www1.voanews.com/english/news/europe/McDonalds-Still-Thriving-in-Russia-After-20-Years-83327327.html (accessed January 20, 2012).

[7]John Parker, "Another Year, Another Billion," *The Economist: The World in 2011 Special Edition*, 28.

[8]Taco Bell Indian website, http://tacobell.co.in/tacomenu.aspx# (accessed January 23, 2012); Associated Press, "Taco Bell Comes to India," *Huffington Post*, June 22, 2010, www.huffingtonpost.com/2010/04/22/taco-bell-to-india_n_548427.html (accessed January 23, 2012).

[9]Anton Piësch, "Speaking in Tongues," *Inc.* (June 2003): 50.

[10]Sadrudin A. Ahmed and Alain D'Astous, "Moderating Effects of Nationality on Country-of-Origin Perceptions: English-Speaking Thailand Versus French-Speaking Canada," *Journal of Business Research* 60 (March 2007): 240–248; George Balabanis and Adamantios Diamantopoulos, "Domestic Country Bias, Country-of-Origin Effects, and Consumer Ethnocentrism: A Multidimensional Unfolding Approach," *Journal of the Academy of Marketing Science* (January 2004): 80–95; Harri T. Luomala, "Exploring the Role of Food Origin as a Source of Meanings for Consumers and as a Determinant of Consumers' Actual Food Choices," *Journal of Business Research* 60 (February 2007): 122–129; Durdana Ozretic-Dosen, Vatroslav Skare, and Zoran Krupka, "Assessments of Country of Origin and Brand Cues in Evaluating a Croatian, Western and Eastern European Food Product," *Journal of Business Research* 60 (February 2007): 130–136.

[11]William R. Snyder, "Mini's Small Victory," *The Wall Street Journal*, March 11, 2010, http://magazine.wsj.com/gatherer/behind-the-brand/small-victory (accessed March 15, 2010).

[12]Philip Coggan, "Markets in a Muddle," *The Economist: The World in 2011 Special Edition,* 145.

[13]Adam Davidson, "How China's Currency Policy Affects You," NPR, April 20, 2006, www.npr.org/templates/story/story.php?storyId=5353313 (accessed January 20, 2012).

[14]Coggan, "Markets in a Muddle," 146.

[15]Parmy Olson, "Greenspan Accuses U.S. of Dollar Weakening," *Forbes,* November 11, 2010, www.forbes.com/2010/11/11/greenspan-dollar-weakening-markets-currencies-g20-us-china-fed.html (accessed January 20, 2012); Inti Landauro, "Colombia, Mexico Criticize Rich Countries On Monetary, Fiscal Policies," *The Wall Street Journal,* January 24, 2011, http://online.wsj.com/article/BT-CO-20110124-710562.html (accessed January 20, 2012).

[16]U.S. Department of Commerce Bureau of Economic Analysis, www.bea.gov/national/index.htm#gdp (accessed February 1, 2012).

[17]The CIA, *The World Fact Book*, www.cia.gov/library/publications/the-world-factbook/rankorder/rankorderguide.html (accessed April 11, 2012); Abby Rogers and Robert Johnson,"The 10 Richest Countries In The World," *Business Insider*, September 25, 2011, www.businessinsider.com/worlds-richest-countries-2011-9# (accessed January 20, 2012).

[18]Adrian Wooldridge, "The Emerging Emerging Markets," *The Economist: The World in 2011 Special Edition*, 131–132.

[19]Adi Narayan, "The Big Market for Dialysis in India," *Bloomberg Businessweek*, January 9–January 15, 2012, 26.

[20]"Censorship: The Trade Barrier That Dare Not Speak Its Name," *Bloomberg Businessweek*, March 14, 2011, 29–30.

[21]"The Rise of Capitalism," *The Economist*, January 21, 2012, 11.

[22]Code of Ethics, American Marketing Association, www.marketingpower.com/content435.php (accessed March 8, 2010).

[23]Mark Djarem, "Polyester Shirts to $3 Shoes Face Highest U.S. Tariffs," *Bloomberg,* June 14, 2011, www.bloomberg.com/news/2011-06-14/polyester-shirts-to-3-shoes-face-top-u-s-duties-study-finds.html (accessed January 23, 2012);"Will the New Congress Shift Gears on Free Trade?" *The Wall Street Journal,* November 18–19, 2006, A7.

[24]"U.S. Trade Representative Announces Fiscal 2010 Tariff-Rate Quota Allocations for Raw Cane Sugar, Refined Specialty Sugar, Sugar Containing Products," October 1, 2009, www.highbeam.com/doc/1P3-1870093731.html (accessed March 15, 2010).

[25]"USA: President Obama Should Take the Lead on Lifting Embargo against Cuba," Amnesty International, September 2, 2009, www.amnesty.org/en/for-media/press-releases/usa-president-obama-should-take-lead-lifting-embargo-against-cuba-200909 (accessed March 15, 2010); Kitty

Bean Yancey, "Back to Cuba: 'People-to-people trips' get the green light," *USA Today*, August 4, 2011, 4A.

[26]U.S. Census Bureau, Foreign Trade Division, "U.S. Trade in Goods and Services—Balance of Payments (BOP) Basis," March 9, 2012, www.census.gov/foreign-trade/statistics/historical/gands.pdf (accessed April 2, 2012).

[27]Charles R. Taylor, George R. Franke, and Michael L. Maynard, "Attitudes Toward Direct Marketing and Its Regulation: A Comparison of the United States and Japan," *Journal of Public Policy & Marketing* (Fall 2000): 228–237.

[28]Julius Melnitzer, "U.K. Enacts 'Far-Reaching' Anti-Bribery Act," *Law Times*, February 13, 2011, www.lawtimesnews.com/201102148245/Headline-News/UK-enacts-far-reaching-anti-bribery-act (accessed March 28, 2011).

[29]"About Counterfeiting," IACC, https://iacc.org/about-counterfeiting/ (accessed January 23, 2012).

[30]Loretta Chao, "The Ultimate Knock-Off: A Fake Apple Store," *The Wall Street Journal,* July 20, 2011, http://blogs.wsj.com/digits/2011/07/20/the-ultimate-knock-off-a-fake-apple-store/ (accessed January 24, 2012).

[31]Business for Social Responsibility, www.bsr.org (accessed March 8, 2010).

[32]Stephen Fidler and Jacob Bunge, "NYSE Deal Nears Collapse," *The Wall Street Journal*, January 11, 2012, A1, A9.

[33]"This Is Systembolaget," www.systembolaget.se/Applikationer/Knappar/InEnglish/Swedish_alcohol_re.htm (accessed March 23, 2010).

[34]The CIA, *The World Fact Book*, www.cia.gov/library/publications/the-world-factbook/rankorder/rankorderguide.html (accessed January 20, 2012).

[35]Pete Guest, "Switching On: Africa's Vast New Tech Opportunity," July 12, 2011, Wired.co,uk, www.wired.co.uk/magazine/archive/2011/08/features/switching-on?page=all (accessed January 24, 2012); "Africa's Mobile Phone Industry 'Booming'," *BBC*, November 9, 2011, www.bbc.co.uk/news/world-africa-15659983 (accessed January 24, 2012).

[36]"The North American Free Trade Agreement (NAFTA)," export.gov, http://export.gov/FTA/nafta/index.asp (accessed January 23, 2012).

[37]The CIA, *The World Fact Book*, www.cia.gov/library/publications/the-world-factbook/rankorder/rankorderguide.html (accessed January 20, 2012).

[38]"Trade in Goods with Canada," U.S. Census Bureau: Foreign Trade, www.census.gov/foreign-trade/balance/c1220.html#2011 (accessed January 23, 2012).

[39]"The Border Two-Step," *The Economist*, December 10, 2011, 41.

[40]"Canada's Major Trading Partners—2010," Ontario Canada website, www.sse.gov.on.ca/medt/investinontario/en/Pages/coca_401.aspx (accessed January 24, 2012).

[41]The CIA, *The World Fact Book*, www.cia.gov/library/publications/the-world-factbook/rankorder/rankorderguide.html (accessed January 20, 2012).

[42]"Trade in Goods with Mexico," U.S. Census Bureau: Foreign Trade, www.census.gov/foreign-trade/balance/c2010.html (accessed January 23, 2012).

[43]"CAFTA-DR (Dominican Republic-Central America FTA)," Office of the United States Trade Representative, www.ustr.gov/trade-agreements/free-trade-agreements/cafta-dr-dominican-republic-central-america-fta (accessed January 23, 2012).

[44]"To Each His Own," *The Economist*, February 26, 2011, 44.

[45]"Exxon Mobil Expected to File 40 mln USD NAFTA Suit Against Canada in November," *CNNMoney*, October 16, 2007, www.abcmoney.co.uk/news/162007146139.htm (accessed March 23, 2010).

[46]"The History of the European Union," Europa, http://europa.eu/abc/history/index_en.htm (accessed March 10, 2010); "Europe in 12 Lessons," Europa, http://europa.eu/abc/12lessons/lesson_2/index_en.htm (accessed March 3, 2010).

[47]The CIA, "European Union," *The World Fact Book*, www.cia.gov/library/publications/the-world-factbook/geos/ee.html (accessed January 23, 2012).

[48]Herman Van Rompuy, "Europe in the New Global Game," *The Economist: The World in 2011 Special Edition*, 97.

[49]"About the European Union," Europa, http://europa.eu/about-eu/index_en.htm (accessed March 10, 2010).

[50]Bruno Waterfield, "Ireland Forced to Take EU and IMF Bail-Out Package," *The Telegraph*, November 22, 2010, www.telegraph.co.uk/finance/financetopics/financialcrisis/8150137/Ireland-forced-to-take-EU-and-IMF-bail-out-package.html (accessed January 10, 2011); Jonathon House and Alkman Granitsas, "Spain, Cyprus Request Bailout Aid," *The Wall Street Journal*, June 25, 2012, http://online.wsj.com/article/SB100014240527023044586045774888913242104 70.html (accessed July 16, 2012).

[51]Charles Forelle and Marcus Walker, "Dithering at the Top Turned EU Crisis to Global Threat," *The Wall Street Journal*, December 29, 2011; Jeff Cox, "US, Europe Face More Ratings Cuts in Coming Years," *CNBC*, January 20, 2012, www.cnbc.com/id/46072354?__source=google%7Ceditorspicks%7C&par=google (accessed January 20, 2012).

[52]David Gauthier-Villars, "Europe Hit by Downgrades," *The Wall Street Journal*, January 14, 2012, http://online.wsj.com/article/SB10001424052970204542404577158561838264378.html (accessed February 1, 2012).

[53]"Powerhouse Deutschland," *Bloomberg Businessweek*, January 3, 2011, 93; Alan S. Blinder, "The Euro Zone's German Crisis," *The Wall Street Journal*, http://online.wsj.com/article/SB100014240529702034304045777094313707190708.html (accessed January 20, 2012).

[54]David Gauthier-Villars, "Europe Hit by Downgrades."

[55]"Common Market of the South (MERCOSUR): Agri-Food Regional Profile Statistical Overview," Agriculture and Agrifood Canada, March 2009, www.ats.agr.gc.ca/lat/3947-eng.htm (accessed March 10, 2010); Joanna Klonsky and Stephanie Hanson, "Mercosur: South America's Fractious Trade Bloc," Council on Foreign Relations, August 20, 2009, www.cfr.org/publication/12762/mercosur.html (accessed March 18, 2010).

[56]Michael Reid, "Latin America Changes Its Guard," *The Economist: The World in 2011 Special Edition*, 55–56.

[57]"About APEC," Asia-Pacific Economic Cooperation, www.apec.org/apec/about_apec.html (accessed February 25, 2010).

[58]Asian Pacific Economic Cooperation, www.apec.org/apec/about_apec/achievements_and_benefits.html (accessed March 10, 2010).

[59]Charles Sizemore, "China Won't Blow Up in 2012," *Forbes*, January 23, 2012, www.forbes.com/sites/moneybuilder/2012/01/23/china-wont-blow-up-in-2012/ (accessed January 23, 2012).

[60]"China and the Paradox of Prosperity," *The Economist*, January 28, 2012, 9.

[61]Karen Cho, "KFC China's Recipe for Success," *INSEAD Knowledge*, July 1, 2009, http://knowledge.insead.edu/KFCinChina090323.cfm?vid=195; "Yum! China," Yum! Brands www.yum.com/company/china.asp (accessed March 18, 2010); Ben Rooney, "China: The New Fast Food Nation," *CNNMoney*, July 14, 2010, http://money.cnn.com/2010/07/13/news/companies/Yum_Brands/index.htm (accessed January 20, 2012); Kathy Chu, "For Some U.S. Companies, China Sales Rule," *USA Today*, February 3, 2011, 1B.

[62]David Pilling, "Trans-Pacific Partnership: Far-Reaching Agreement Could Form Powerful New Trade Bloc," *Financial Times*, November 8, 2011, www.ft.com/cms/s/0/47dd4d14-06cc-11e1-90de-00144feabdc0.html#axzz1kIownbPm (accessed January 23, 2012).

[63]Hiroko Tabuchi, "Premier Says Japan Will Join Pacific Free Trade Talks," *The New York Times*, November 11, 2011, www.nytimes.com/2011/11/12/world/asia/japan-to-join-talks-on-pacific-trade-pact.html (accessed January 23, 2012).

[64]Tom Barkley,"Framework Is Set For New Trade Bloc," *The Wall Street Journal*, November 14, 2011, http://online.wsj.com/article/SB10001424052970203503204577036553639815214.html (accessed January 23, 2012).

[65]Pilling, "Trans-Pacific Partnership: Far-Reaching Agreement Could Form Powerful New Trade Bloc."

[66]Tabuchi, "Premier Says Japan Will Join Pacific Free Trade Talks."

[67]Li Jiabao and Lan Lan, "Trade Pact Complicates Prospects for Asia," *China Daily*, November 11-13, 2011, 3.

[68]Tabuchi, "Premier Says Japan Will Join Pacific Free Trade Talks"; Tom Barkley, "Framework Is Set For New Trade Bloc."

[69]"Overview," Association of Southeast Asian Nations, www.aseansec.org/64.htm (accessed January 23, 2012).

[70]Wang Yan, "ASEAN Works to 'Act as Unison' on Global Stage," *China Daily*, November 19, 2011, www.chinadaily.com.cn/cndy/2011-11/19/content_14122972.htm (accessed January 27, 2012).

[71]ASEAN website, www.aseansec.org/ (accessed January 23, 2012).

[72]"Common Effective Preferential Tariff (CEPT)," The Malaysia Government's Official Portal, www.malaysia.gov.my/EN/Relevant%20Topics/IndustryInMalaysia/Business/BusinessAndEBusiness/BusinessAndAgreement/CEPT/Pages/CEPT.aspx (accessed January 23, 2012).

[73]Eric Bellman, "Najib Says Asean To Avoid EU Errors," *The Wall Street Journal*, November 17, 2011, http://online.wsj.com/article/SB1000142405297020451720457704411302023870\8.html (accessed January 27, 2012); Abby Rogers and Robert Johnson,"The 10 Richest Countries In The World," *Business Insider*, September 25, 2011, www.businessinsider.com/worlds-richest-countries-2011-9# (accessed January 20, 2012).

[74]R.C., "No Brussels Sprouts in Bali," *The Economist*, November 18, 2011, www.economist.com/blogs/banyan/2011/11/asean-summits (accessed January 23, 2012).

[75]Kathy Quiano, "ASEAN Summit Starts amid Cloud of Thai-Cambodia Border Row," CNN, May 7, 2011, http://articles.cnn.com/2011-05-07/world/asia.asean.summit_1_asean-leaders-asean-summit-southeast-asian-nations?_s=PM:WORLD (accessed January 23, 2012).

[76]Eric Bellman, "Asia Seeks Integration Despite EU's Woes," *The Wall Street Journal*, July 22, 2011, A9.

[77]"Members and Observers," World Trade Organization, www.wto.org/english/thewto_e/whatis_e/tif_e/org6_e.htm (accessed January 23, 2012.

[78]"What Is the WTO?" World Trade Organization, www.wto.org/english/thewto_e/whatis_e/whatis_e.htm (accessed January 20, 2012).

[79]Matthew Dalton, "Beijing Sparks Ire of WTO Over Curbs," *The Wall Street Journal*, July 6, 2011, A9.

[80]Jan Johanson and Finn Wiedersheim-Paul, "The Internationalization of the Firm," *Journal of Management Studies* (October 1975): 305–322; Jan Johanson and Jan-Erik Vahlne, "The Internationalization Process of the Firm—A Model of Knowledge Development and Increasing Foreign Commitments," *Journal of International Business Studies* (Spring/Summer 1977): 23–32; S. Tamer Cavusgil and John R. Nevin, "Internal Determinants of Export Marketing Behavior: An Empirical Investigation," *Journal of Marketing Research* (February 1981): 114–119.

[81]Pradeep Tyagi, "Export Behavior of Small Business Firms in Developing Economies: Evidence from the Indian Market," *Marketing Management Journal* (Fall/Winter 2000): 12–20.

[82]Berrin Dosoglu-Guner, "How Do Exporters and Non-Exporters View Their 'Country of Origin' Image Abroad?" *Marketing Management Journal* (Fall/Winter 2000): 21–27.

[83]SciNet World Trade System, www.scinet-corp.com/associates/index.htm, (accessed January 23, 2012).

[84]Farok J. Contractor and Sumit K. Kundu, "Franchising Versus Company-Run Operations: Model Choice in the Global Hotel Sector," *Journal of International Marketing* (November 1997): 28–53.

[85]"Suddenly, Made in USA Looks Like a Strategy," *Bloomberg Businessweek*, March 28, 2011, 57–58.

[86]Catherine Larkin and Anna Edney, "More Outsourcing Planned for FDA Overseas Factory Inspections," *Bloomberg Businessweek*, February 10, 2011, www.businessweek.com/news/2011-02-10/more-outsourcing-planned-for-fda-overseas-factory-inspections.html (accessed January 24, 2012).

[87]"Suddenly, Made in USA Looks Like a Strategy."

[88]Kejal Vyas, "Venezuela's PdVSA Forms Joint Venture With Brazil's Odebrecht," *The Wall Street Journal*, September 29, 2011, http://online.wsj.com/article/BT-CO-20110929-710025.html (accessed January 24, 2012).

[89]Sky Team website, www.skyteam.com/ (accessed January 20, 2012).

[90]"The 2011 Oil Shock," *The Economist*, March 5, 2011, 14–16.

[91]"Export Department," Lone Star Distribution, www.lonestardistribution.com/index.php/our-companies/export-department (accessed January 20, 2012).

[92]Abbott, www.abbott.com/global/url/content/en_US/10.17:17/general_content/General_Content_00054.htm (accessed March 23, 2010).

[93]Devon Maylie, "By Foot, by Bike, by Taxi, Nestlé Expands in Africa," *The Wall Street Journal*, December 1, 2011, B1, B16.

[94]Deborah Owens, Timothy Wilkinson, and Bruce Keillor, "A Comparison of Product Attributes in a Cross-Cultural/Cross-National Context," *Marketing Management Journal* (Fall/Winter 2000): 1–11.

[95]Patrick Barta, "Dunkin' Brands to Expand in Asia," *The Wall Street Journal*, March 8, 2011, http://online.wsj.com/article/SB10001424052748703386704576185910821716404.html (accessed January 24, 2012); "Dunkin' Donuts Coming to Mainland China," *USA Today,* January 25, 2008, www.usatoday.com/money/world/2008-01-25-dunkin-shanghai_N.htm (accessed January 24, 2012).

[96]Anil K. Gupta and Vijay Govindarajan, "Converting Global Presence into Global Competitive Advantage," *Academy of Management Executive* (May 2001): 45–58.

[97]*Evo* [DVD], Cengage Learning, 2012; evo website, www.evo.com/ (accessed March 13, 2012); Jessica Naziri, "Retailer Grows Up, Along with His Business," *CNBC*, February 15, 2012, www.cnbc.com/id/46386774 (accessed March 13, 2012); "Evo Goes Against The Grain With First Winter Sports," New Schoolers, October 15, 2011, www.newschoolers.com/readnews/4209.0/Evo-Goes-Against-The-Grain-With-First-Winter-Sports-Consumer-Catalog?c=2 (accessed March 13, 2012); "Evo Shares its Retail Secrets," *Skiing Business*, February 7, 2012, http://skiingbusiness.com/11874/profiles/evo-shares-its-retail-secrets/ (accessed March 14, 2012); "About evoTrip," evo, www.evo.com/about-evotrip.aspx (accessed March 14, 2012).

[98]"Our Heritage," Starbucks, www.starbucks.com/about-us/our-heritage (accessed March 12, 2012); "Timeline," http://news.starbucks.com/images/10041/Timeline-TheAmericas_Q3FY09.pdf (accessed March 12, 2012); David Teather, "Starbucks Legend Delivers Recovery by Thinking Smaller," *The Guardian*, January 21, 2010, www.guardian.co.uk/business/2010/jan/21/starbucks-howard-schultz (accessed July 19, 2011); "How Starbucks Colonised the World," *The Sunday Times,* February 17, 2008, http://business.timesonline.co.uk/tol/business/industry_sectors/leisure/article3381092.ece (accessed July 19, 2011); Rosie Baker, "Starbucks Launches Mobile Payments," *MarketingWeek*, November 24, 2011, www.marketingweek.co.uk/starbucks-launches-mobile-payments/3032181.article (accessed March 14, 2012); "Starbucks to Open UK Franchises as Profits Jump," *The Telegraph*, March 14, 2012, www.telegraph.co.uk/finance/newsbysector/retailandconsumer/9043202/Starbucks-to-open-UK-franchises-as-profits-jump.html (accessed March 14, 2012); Lauren Pollock, "Starbucks Adds Division Focused on Asia," *The Wall Street Journal,* July 11, 2011, http://online.wsj.com/article/SB10001424052702303678704576440292712481616.html (accessed July 15, 2011); Matt Hodges, "Schultz Brews Up Major Push in China," *China Daily,* June 10-11, 2011, 5; "Starbucks Company Profile," http://assets.starbucks.com/assets/aboutuscompanyprofileq12011final13111.pdf (accessed July 15, 2011); Mariko Sanchanta, "Starbucks Plans Big Expansion in China," *The Wall Street Journal,* April 14, 2010, B10; "Asia Pacific," Starbucks Newsroom, http://news.starbucks.com/about+starbucks/starbucks+coffee+international/asia+pacific/ (accessed July 19, 2011); David Teather, "Starbucks Legend Delivers Recovery by Thinking Smaller," *The Guardian*, January 21, 2010, www.guardian.co.uk/business/2010/jan/21/starbucks-howard-schultz (accessed July 19, 2011); "How Starbucks Colonised the World," *The Sunday Times,* February 17, 2008, http://business.timesonline.co.uk/tol/business/industry_sectors/leisure/article3381092.ece (accessed July 19, 2011); "Greater China," http://news.starbucks.com/about+starbucks/starbucks+coffee+international/greater+china (accessed July 19, 2011); Laurie Burkitt, "Starbucks Price Increase Stirs China's Netizens," *The Wall Street Journal,* February 1, 2012, http://blogs.wsj.com/chinarealtime/2012/02/01/starbucks-price-increase-stirs-chinas-netizens/ (accessed March 14, 2012); Vikas Bajaj, "After a Year of Delays, the First Starbucks Is to Open in Tea-Loving India This Fall," *The New York Times,* January 30, 2012, www.nytimes.com/2012/01/31/business/global/starbucks-to-open-first-indian-store-this-autumn.html (accessed March 14, 2012); Stephan Faris, "Grounds Zero: A Starbucks-Free Italy," *Bloomberg Businessweek,* February 9, 2012, http://mobile.businessweek.com/magazine/grounds-zero-a-starbucksfree-italy-02092012.html (accessed March 14, 2012).

Feature Notes

[a]"The Glossy Posse," *The Economist*, October 1, 2011, 67; Kathy Chu, "Marketers Create Brands Just for Asia," *USA Today*, September 11, 2011, 1B; Sherry Lee, "E-commerce Rewrites the Rules of Retail," *CommonWealth Magazine,* May 19, 2011, http://english.cw.com.tw/print.do?action=print&id=12842 (accessed November 7, 2011); Joel Backaler, "What Are China's Luxury Consumers Buying?," *Forbes,* May 16, 2010, http://blogs.forbes.com/china/2010/05/16/what-are-chinas-luxury-consumers-buying (accessed November 7, 2011); Carol Matlack, "High-End Tailor Zegna's Marco Polo Moment," *Bloomberg Businessweek*, June 10, 2010, www.businessweek.com/magazine/content/10_25/b4183018327399.htm (accessed November 7, 2011).

[b]"Highly Charged," *The Economist*, July 2, 2011, 58; Won-Joon Lee, "Green Road Is Being Laid: Now, for the Cars," *China Daily,* November 18–November 24, 2011, 8; Keith Bradsher, "G.M. Plans to Develop Electric Cars with China," *The New York Times,* September 20, 2011, www.nytimes.com/2011/09/21/business/global/gm-plans-to-develop-electric-cars-with-chinese-automaker.html (accessed December 2, 2011); Norihiko Shirouzu, "China Spooks Auto Makers," *The Wall Street Journal,* September 16, 2010, http://online.wsj.com/article/SB10001424052748704394704575495480368918268.html (accessed December 2, 2011).

[c]"Crunching the Numbers," *Inc.,* September 2011, 34; Mark Scott, "Do Longer Holidays Translate to Greater Productivity," *Der Spiegel,* August 20, 2009, www.spiegel.de/international/business/0,1518,643900,00.html (accessed November 21, 2011); Reuters, "Why Summer Vacations (and the Internet) Make You More Productive," *The Atlantic,* August 29, 2011, www.theatlantic.com/business/archive/2011/08/why-summer-vacations-and-the-internet-make-you-more-productive/244289/ (accessed November 21, 2011).

[d]Sarah E. Needleman, Vanessa O'Connell, Emily Maltby, and Angus Loten, "Small Business Big Innovation," *The Wall Street Journal*, November 14, 2011, R1, R4; "Quadlogic Controls is Named Winner of Wall Street Journal Small-Business Innovation Award," PR Newswire, November 14, 2011, www.prnewswire.com/news-releases/quadlogic-controls-is-named-winner-of-wall-street-journal-small-business-innovation-award-133849928.html (accessed December 9, 2011); "Products," Quadlogic, www.quadlogic.com/productsEG.html (accessed December 9, 2011).

chapter 10

Digital Marketing and Social Networking

OBJECTIVES

1. To define *digital media* and *electronic marketing* and recognize their increasing importance in strategic planning
2. To identify and understand the role of digital media in a marketing strategy and how each type of social media can be used as an effective marketing tool
3. To understand digital marketing consumer behavior
4. To understand and identify how digital media affects the marketing mix
5. To identify legal and ethical considerations in digital media and electronic marketing

MARKETING INSIGHTS

Facebook Befriends Small Businesses

Although more than 9 million small businesses have "free" Facebook pages to promote their organizations, not as many choose to pay for advertising. Facebook Chief Operations Officer Sheryl Sandberg wants to change this. Sandberg, formerly vice president of global online sales and operations at Google, began offering incentives to small businesses to advertise on Facebook. In 2012, Facebook began offering $50 of advertising credits to as many as 200,000 small businesses.

Normally, Facebook charges the advertising business a set rate for each time a user clicks on the ad. With this new campaign, Facebook will forgo charging until the number of clicks surpasses $50. Because rates are often 25 cents or less per click, the business has an opportunity to target a wide range of consumers with its $50 credit.

Sandberg hopes that businesses that take advantage of this incentive will soon realize the valuable word-of-mouth marketing opportunities that Facebook offers. Indeed, many small businesses have already succeeded in their marketing campaigns due to Facebook's ability to help businesses attract specific target markets. For instance, one wedding photographer used Facebook advertising to successfully target women who just changed their Facebook status to "engaged." Another advantage of Facebook is the ease of creating a marketing platform and interacting directly with consumers through free pages. Sandberg believes Facebook is the key to helping small companies achieve growth. According to Sandberg, she will not "stop until all of them are using it to grow their business."[1]

© bloomua/Shutterstock.com

Since the 1990s, the Internet and information technology have dramatically changed the marketing environment and the strategies that are necessary for marketing success. Digital media have created exciting opportunities for companies to target specific markets more effectively, develop new marketing strategies, and gather more information about customers. Using digital media channels, marketers are better able to analyze and address consumer needs.

One of the defining characteristics of information technology in the 21st century is accelerating change. New systems and applications advance so rapidly that a chapter on this topic has to strain to incorporate the possibilities of the future. For example, when Google first arrived on the scene in 1998, a number of search engines were fighting for dominance. Google, with its fast, easy-to-use format, soon became the number-one search engine. Today, Google provides additional competition to many industries, including advertising, newspaper, mobile phone services, book publishing, and social networking. However, even Google must constantly innovate to keep its competitive advantage. For instance, the Chinese search engine Baidu is gaining ground with 75 percent of the Chinese search engine market. Baidu has also announced it will create its own mobile technology to challenge Google's more than 40 percent market share in mobile operating systems in China.[2] As you can see, the environment for marketing is changing rapidly based on these factors, as well as unknown future developments within information technology.

In this chapter, we focus on digital marketing strategies, particularly new communication channels such as social networks, and discuss how consumers are changing their information searches and consumption behaviors to fit with these emerging technologies and trends. Most importantly, we analyze how marketers can use new media to their advantage to better connect with consumers, gather more information about their target markets, and convert this information into successful marketing strategies.

GROWTH AND BENEFITS OF DIGITAL MARKETING

digital media Electronic media that function using digital codes; when we refer to digital media, we are referring to media available via computers, cellular phones, smartphones, and other digital devices that have been released in recent years

Before we move on, we must first provide a definition of digital media. **Digital media** are electronic media that function using digital codes—when we refer to digital media, we are referring to media available via computers, cellular phones, smartphones, and other digital devices

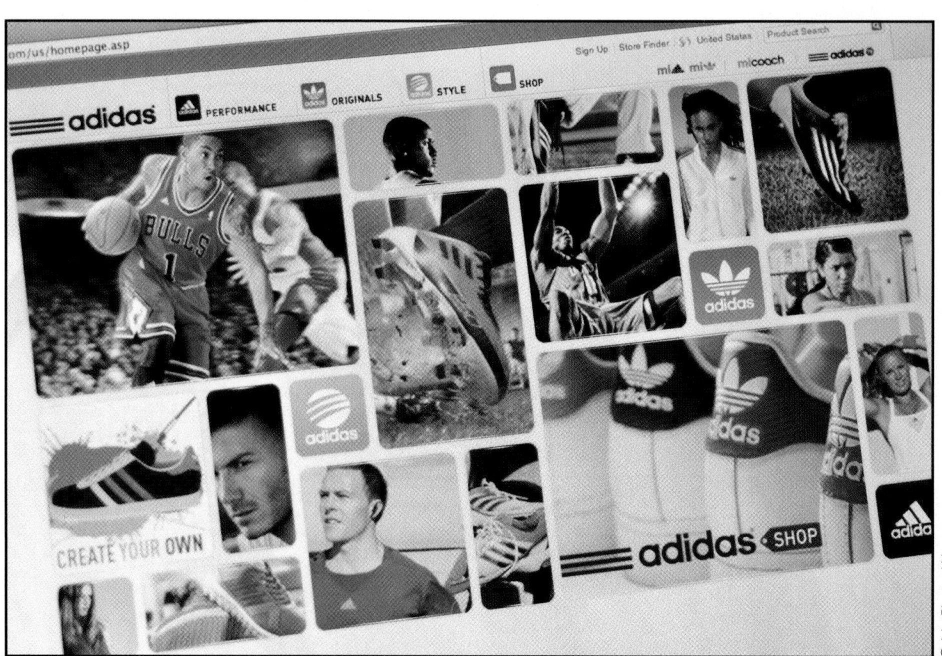

Digital Marketing
Companies like Adidas build their brand equity and gain market share with their digital marketing strategies.

that have been released in recent years. A number of terms have been coined to describe marketing activities on the Internet. **Digital marketing** uses all digital media, including the Internet and mobile and interactive channels, to develop communication and exchanges with customers. In this chapter, we focus on how the Internet relates to all aspects of marketing, including strategic planning. Thus, we use the term **electronic marketing**, or **e-marketing**, to refer to the strategic process of distributing, promoting, and pricing products, and discovering the desires of customers using digital media and digital marketing. Our definition of e-marketing goes beyond the Internet and also includes mobile phones, banner ads, digital outdoor marketing, and social networks.

The phenomenal growth of the Internet has provided unprecedented opportunities for marketers to forge interactive relationships with consumers. As the Internet and digital communication technologies have advanced, they have made it possible to target markets more precisely and reach markets that were previously inaccessible. Because of its ability to enhance the exchange of information between the marketer and the customer, the Internet has become an important component of firms' marketing strategies. As the world of digital media continues to develop, Internet marketing has been integrated into strategies that include all digital media, including television advertising and other mobile and interactive media that do not use the Internet (advertising media are discussed in detail in Chapter 18). In fact, marketers are using the term *digital marketing* as a catch-all for capturing all digital channels for reaching customers. This area is evolving quickly, and the digital world is still in an early stage of integration into marketing strategy.[3]

One of the most important benefits of e-marketing is the ability of marketers and customers to share information. Through websites, social networks, and other digital media, consumers can learn about everything they consume and use in life. Since 274 million Americans now have Internet access, the Internet is changing the way marketers communicate and develop relationships.[4] Today's marketers can use the Internet to form relationships with a variety of stakeholders, including customers, employees, and suppliers. Many companies use not just e-mail and mobile phones, but also social networking, wikis, media sharing sites, podcasts, blogs, videoconferencing, and other technologies to coordinate activities and communicate with employees. Modes of communication are changing as well. For instance, many consumers prefer to text rather than call on their cell phones. Among those who text on their cell phones, men send an average of 555 text messages monthly, while women send 716 text

digital marketing Uses all digital media, including the Internet and mobile and interactive channels, to develop communication and exchanges with customers

electronic marketing (e-marketing) The strategic process of distributing, promoting, and pricing products, and discovering the desires of customers using digital media and digital marketing

© Newsies Media/Alamy

Characteristics of E-Marketing
Wendy's encourages customers to go to their website to get a free order of their new French fries.

messages.[5] Women also lead the way in social networking, with 53 percent of women and 47 percent of men using blogs or social networks.[6]

Some digital forms of communication merge two or more technologies. Twitter, considered both a social network and micro blog, illustrates how these digital technologies are combined to create new communication opportunities. Social networking in particular is changing the dynamics of marketing and business communication. Because of the way they facilitate communications while significantly reducing costs, these new information technologies represent a tremendous opportunity for any industry or activity that depends on the flow of information.

For many businesses, engaging in digital and online marketing activities is essential to maintaining competitive advantages. Increasingly, small businesses can use digital media to develop strategies to reach new markets and access inexpensive communication channels. In addition, large companies like Target use online catalogs and company websites to supplement their brick-and-mortar stores. At the other end of the spectrum, companies like Amazon .com, which lack physical stores and sell products solely online, are emerging to challenge traditional brick-and-mortar businesses. Social networking sites are advancing e-marketing by providing features, such as Facebook developing its own currency to purchase products, send gifts, and engage in the entire shopping experience.[7] Finally, some corporate websites and social media sites provide feedback mechanisms through which customers can ask questions, voice complaints, indicate preferences, and otherwise communicate about their needs and desires.

One of the biggest mistakes a marketer can make when engaging in digital marketing is to treat it like a traditional marketing channel. Digital media offer a whole new dimension to marketing that marketers must consider when concocting their companies' marketing strategies. Some of the characteristics that distinguish online media from traditional marketing include addressability, interactivity, accessibility, connectivity, and control, as defined in Table 10.1.

Table 10.1 Characteristics of Online Media

Characteristic	Definition	Example
Addressability	The ability of the marketer to identify customers before they make a purchase	Amazon installs cookies on a user's computer that allow the company to identify the user when he or she returns to the website
Interactivity	The ability of customers to express their needs and wants directly to the firm in response to its marketing communications	Texas Instruments interacts with its customers on its Facebook page by answering concerns and posting updates
Accessibility	The ability for marketers to obtain digital information	Google can use Web searches done through its search engine to learn about customer interests
Connectivity	The ability for consumers to be connected with marketers along with other consumers	The Avon Voices website encourages singers to upload their singing videos, which can then be voted on by other users for the chance to be "discovered"
Control	The customer's ability to regulate the information they view as well as the rate and exposure to that information	Consumers use Kayak.com to discover the best travel deals

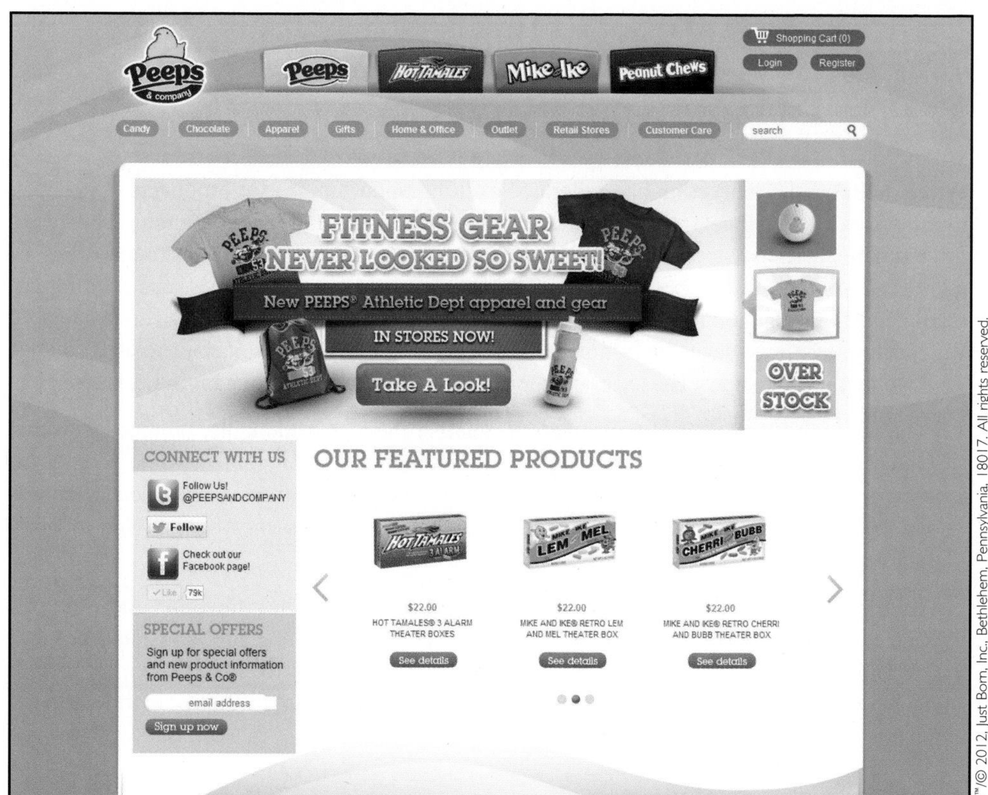

Connectivity
Companies can bring networks of individuals together to share their love of a product, as illustrated by the classic PEEPS® marshmallow chick.

THE INTERACTIVITY OF SOCIAL MEDIA

The main distinguishing characteristic of digital media is their interactivity. From a business perspective, the interactivity of digital media enables the firm to engage with its stakeholders. Conversely, traditional marketing usually involves one-way forms of communication. The marketer contacts the customer through an advertising message, and if the customer has questions or concerns, he or she contacts company representatives by phone or other feedback mechanisms. This sometimes lengthy process requires companies to employ service representatives and/or call centers to interact with customers. Customers often experience a waiting period of some duration from between the time they issue the request to when they receive an answer. Too much waiting can result in customer dissatisfaction.

Interactivity helps to solve this problem by focusing on the kinds of digital media that can make interpersonal connections possible. By utilizing appropriate digital media, companies can facilitate interactivity and enable a conversation with the customer. Features like interactive links on websites, for example, allow Internet users to view marketing messages at their own pace, which is different from the more "intrusive" advertisements like television commercials or sales calls. Digital media like blogs and some social networks allow marketers to interact with prospective customers in real time (or a close approximation of it). The one-sided communication common to traditional marketing channels is being replaced with interactive conversations between customer and marketer. Thus, digital communication can move marketing away from being an intrusion into developing relationships through greater interaction between business and consumer.

Interactivity helps marketers maintain high-quality relationships with existing customers by shaping customer expectations and perceptions. Additionally, digital media has created a myriad of relationships. Where traditionally a relationship existed between a company and a consumer, the Internet now allows consumers to form relationships with one another as well—through online chats, blogs, and electronic word of mouth.[8] By providing information, ideas, and a context for interacting with other customers, interactive marketers can enhance customers' interest in and involvement with their products.

TYPES OF CONSUMER-GENERATED MARKETING AND DIGITAL MEDIA

While digital and e-marketing has generated exciting opportunities for producers of products to interact with consumers, it is essential to recognize that social media are more consumer-driven than traditional media. Consumer-generated material is having a profound effect on marketing. As the Internet becomes more accessible worldwide, consumers are creating and reading consumer-generated content like never before. Social networks and advances in software technology provide an environment for marketers to utilize consumer-generated content.

Two major trends have caused consumer-generated information to gain importance:

1. The increased tendency of consumers to publish their own thoughts, opinions, reviews, and product discussions through blogs or digital media.
2. Consumers' tendencies to trust other consumers over corporations. Consumers often rely on the recommendations of friends, family, and fellow consumers when making purchasing decisions.

By understanding where online users are likely to express their thoughts and opinions, marketers can use these forums to interact with consumers, address problems, and promote their companies. Types of digital media in which Internet users are likely to participate include social networking sites, blogs, wikis, media-sharing sites, virtual reality sites, mobile devices, applications and widgets, and more.

Social Networks

Social networks have evolved quickly in a short period of time. A **social network** is defined as "a web-based meeting place for friends, family, coworkers, and peers that allows users to create a profile and connect with other users for the purposes that range from getting acquainted, to keeping in touch, to building a work related network."[9] They are widely used by marketers, and marketing strategies are using social networking sites to develop relationships with customers. Each wave of social network has become increasingly sophisticated. Today's social networks offer a multitude of consumer benefits, including music downloads, apps, forums, and games. Marketers are thereby using these sites and their popularity with consumers to promote products, handle questions and complaints, and provide information to assist customers in buying decisions.

As the number of social network users increases, interactive marketers are finding opportunities to reach out to consumers in new target markets. CafeMom is a social networking site that offers mothers a forum in which to connect and write about parenting and other topics important to them. At 12.5 million unique monthly visitors, this particular site is an opportunity to reach out to mothers, a demographic that has a significant influence on family purchasing behavior. Walmart, Playskool, General Mills, and Johnson & Johnson have all advertised through this site.[10] Many countries have their own much smaller social networking sites as well. Orkut is a Google-owned service that has gained popularity in India and Brazil. In China, QQ is a major social networking site; some of its counterparts are VKONTAKTE in Russia and CyWorld in South Korea. Social networking sites also offer ways for marketers to promote their companies. More information on how marketers use social networks is provided in later sections of this chapter.

social network Web-based meeting place for friends, family, coworkers, and peers that allow users to create a profile and connect with other users for purposes that range from getting acquainted, keeping in touch, and building a work-related network

Internet users join social networks for many reasons, from chatting with friends to professional networking. Social networks have become very popular in a number of countries, as mentioned earlier in this chapter. As Figure 10.1 demonstrates, Israel has the highest percentage of adults who use social networking sites, followed by the United States.[11] One in five Kenyans and one in four Japanese adults participate in social networks.[12] As social networks evolve, both marketers and the owners of social networking sites are realizing the incredible

Figure 10.1 Social Networking Usage by Adult Population

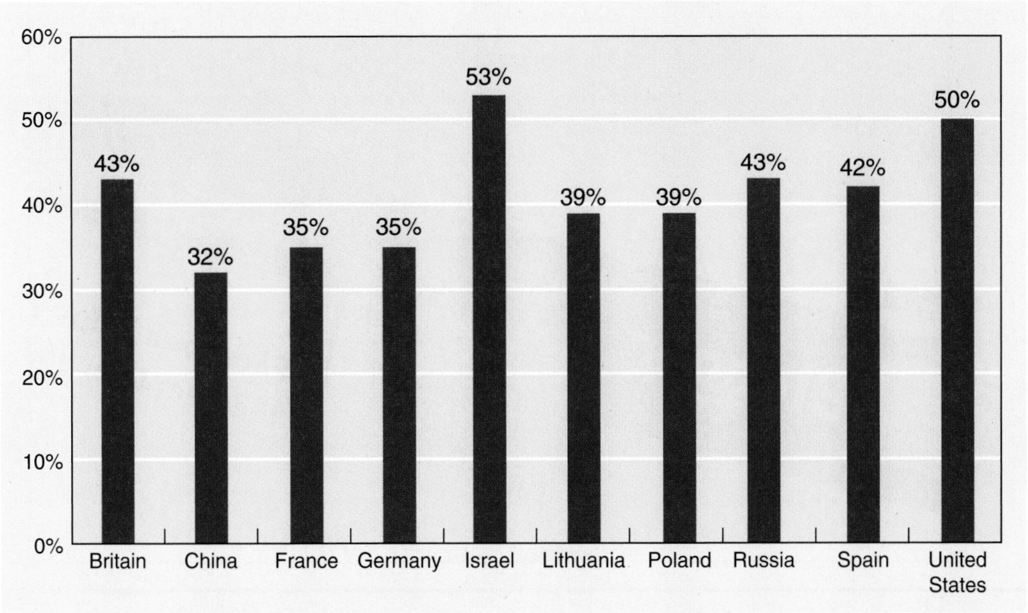

Source: Pew Research Center, "53%—Social Networking Popular Worldwide, with Israel in the Lead," February 10, 2012, http://pewresearch.org/databank/dailynumber/?NumberID=1408 (accessed July 8, 2012).

opportunities such networks offer—an influx of advertising dollars for social networking owners and a large reach for the advertiser. As a result, marketers have begun investigating and experimenting with promotion on social networks.

Although social networks are often used to refer to consumer relationships, businesses can also use digital media as internal mechanisms. *Enterprise 2.0* in the business environment is a term coined to describe firms' efforts to use cutting-edge technology associated with social networks and blogs to assist in workplace connections. It involves software modifications to contribute to traditional software platforms used by large companies. Companies like the telecom firm Alcatel Lucent have designed their own internal social networks for in-house networking. By using the company's own social network, employees can find data faster. Internal social networks are a great way to capture knowledge and identify experts on different subjects within an organization.[13]

An important question relates to how social media sites are adding value to the economy. Marketers at companies like Ford and Zappos, for instance, are using social media to promote products and build consumer relationships. Many corporations are supporting Facebook pages and Yammer accounts for employees to communicate across departments and divisions. Professionals like doctors, professors, and engineers also share ideas on a regular basis. Even staffing organizations use social media, bypassing the traditional e-mail and telephone channels. While billions of dollars in investments are being funneled into social media, it may be too early to assess the exact economic contribution of social media to the entire economy.[14]

Facebook

When Facebook surpassed Myspace in its number of members, it became the most popular social networking site in the world.[15] Internet users create Facebook profiles and then search the network for people with whom to connect. Facebook markets to parents and grandparents as well as to teenagers. In fact, the fastest-growing group on Facebook is consumers 55 and over.[16]

For this reason, many marketers are turning to Facebook to market products, interact with consumers, and take advantage of free publicity. It is possible for consumers to become

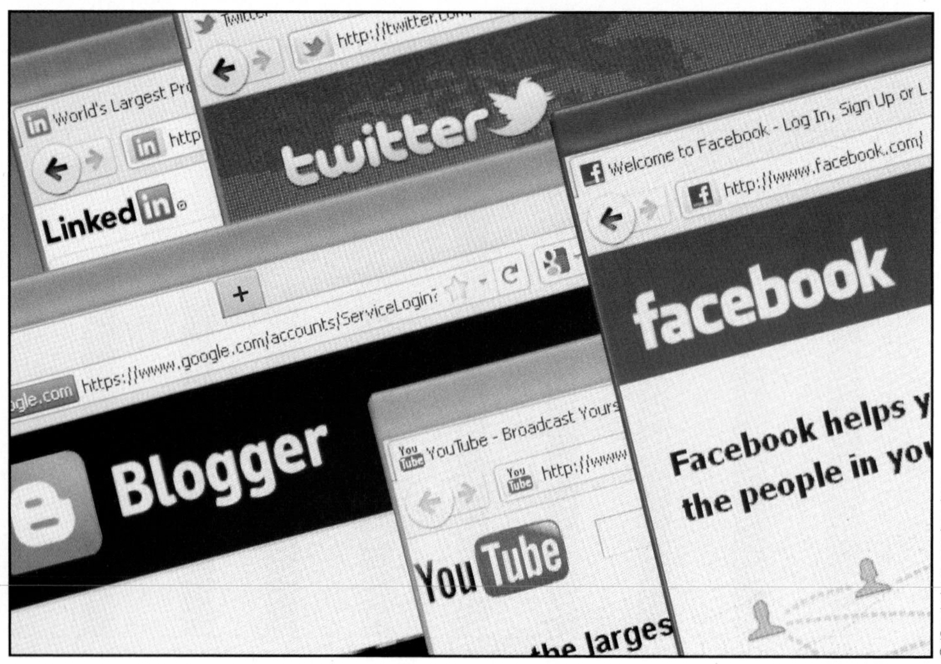

Social Networks
The wide variety of social networks allows consumers to connect for both personal and business purposes.

"fans" of major companies like Avon by clicking on the "like" icon on their Facebook pages. Facebook is also partnering with businesses to offer unique incentives to businesses. American Express allows participants in its Members Rewards program to redeem reward points for Facebook ads.[17]

Additionally, social networking sites are useful for relationship marketing, or the creation of relationships that mutually benefit the marketing business and the customer. Companies are using relationship marketing through Facebook to help consumers feel more connected to their products. For instance, New Belgium Brewing has 38 local Facebook pages and uses the website to target advertisements toward its fan base. After conducting a study on its Facebook fans, the company determined that its fans generate half of the company's annual sales.[18] Thanks to Facebook, companies like New Belgium are able to understand who their customers are and how they can meet their needs.

Myspace

Myspace is a social networking site that offers users the chance to create profiles and connect with other Myspace members across the world. Like Facebook, Myspace allows users to watch videos, listen to and promote music, instant message friends, write on various topics (called forums), network with friends/colleagues, play games, and more. Due to what some analysts say was a failure to innovate, Myspace now trails behind Facebook in popularity. Myspace hopes that redesign and content changes will help to reinvigorate the site. In 2011, News Corporation sold Myspace to Specific Media for $35 million. Pop star Justin Timberlake became co-owner of the site.[19]

Despite its decrease in popularity, Myspace retains a loyal following who prefer its layout and interface to other online social networking sites. Myspace also offers aspiring artists a chance to demonstrate their talent, becoming the largest artist community on the Web. Emerging musicians are using Myspace to record and share their music, and users can create social playlists of music from famous artists.[20] Justin Timberlake is determined to use Myspace's library of songs and music videos to turn the site around. He announced the company would launch Myspace TV, a way to integrate television with instant communication among Myspace members.[21] For businesses, Myspace can be a creative means of marketing through the use of profiles, advertising, music, videos, and other forms of online media.

Twitter

Twitter is a hybrid mix of a social networking site and a micro-blogging site that asks viewers one simple question: "What's happening?" Users can post answers of up to 140 characters, which are then available for their "followers" to read. A limitation of 140 characters may not seem like enough for companies to send an effective message, but some have become experts at using Twitter in their marketing strategies. For instance, Southwest Airlines has an entire team monitor its Twitter account during its business operations to answer questions ranging from refunds to lost baggage.[22] These efforts are having an impact; approximately 23 percent of users report that they follow businesses on Twitter.[23]

Like other social networking sites, Twitter is also being used to enhance customer service and create publicity about company products. For example, Zappos posts on Twitter to update followers on company activities and address customer complaints.[24] Other companies are paying influencers to use Twitter to create "buzz" around their products. To avoid deceiving consumers about the nature of these messages, the Federal Trade Commission (FTC) created guidelines requiring influencers who are receiving pay for company tweets to disclose this fact to viewers.[25] Finally, companies are using Twitter to gain a competitive advantage. Marketers can pay Twitter to highlight advertisements or company brands to a wider range of users when they search for specific terms or topics.[26] The race is on for companies who want to use Twitter to get an edge over the competition.

Blogs and Wikis

Today's marketers must recognize the impact of consumer-generated material like blogs and wikis, as their significance to online consumers has increased a great deal. **Blogs** (short for "weblogs") are web-based journals in which writers can editorialize and interact with other Internet users. More than three-fourths of Internet users read blogs.[27]

Blogs give consumers control, sometimes more than companies would like. Whether or not the blog's content is factually accurate, bloggers can post whatever opinions they like about a company or its products. Although companies have filed lawsuits against bloggers for defamation, they usually cannot prevent the blog from going viral. Responding to a negative review is a delicate matter. When a Korean Dunkin' Donuts worker created a blog alleging that a company factory had unsanitary conditions, the company forced him to remove

blogs Web-based journals (short for "weblogs") in which writers editorialize and interact with other Internet users

© Rob Wilkinson/Alamy

Wikis
Wikipedia is an online encyclopedia that allows users to add or edit information in more than 250 languages.

the blog. However, readers had already created copies of the blog, and they spread it across the Internet after the original's removal.[28] Similarly, one author made the mistake of angrily responding to a negative blog post about her book. The comments quickly went viral and were used as an example of how *not* to treat criticism on the Internet.[29] In other cases, a positive review of a product or service posted on a popular blog can result in large increases in sales. Thus, blogs can represent a potent threat to corporations as well as an opportunity.

Blogs have major advantages as well. Rather than trying to eliminate blogs that cast their companies in a negative light, some businesses are using such blogs to answer consumer concerns or defend their corporate reputations. Many major corporations have created their own blogs or encourage employees to blog about the company. Boeing operates a corporate blog to highlight company news and to post correspondence from Boeing enthusiasts from all over the world.[30] As blogging changes the face of media, companies like Boeing are using blogs to build enthusiasm for their products and create relationships with consumers.

A **wiki** is a type of software that creates an interface that enables users to add or edit the content of some types of websites. One of the best known is Wikipedia, an online encyclopedia with more than 17 million entries in more than 250 languages on nearly every subject imaginable (*Encyclopedia Britannica* only has 120,000 entries).[31] Wikipedia is consistently one of the top 10 most popular sites on the Web. Because Wikipedia can be edited and read by anyone, it is easy for online consumers to correct inaccuracies in content.[32] This site is expanded, updated, and edited by a large team of volunteer contributors. For the most part, only information that is verifiable through another source is considered appropriate. Access to some entries, however, is restricted because of increased risk for vandalism. Because of its open format, Wikipedia has suffered from some high-profile instances of vandalism in which incorrect information was disseminated. Such problems have usually been detected and corrected quickly. Like all social media, wikis have advantages and disadvantages for companies. Wikis on controversial companies like Walmart and Nike often contain negative publicity about the companies, such as worker rights violations. However, some companies have begun to use wikis as internal tools for teams working on a project requiring lots of documentation.[33] Additionally, monitoring wikis provides companies with a better idea of how consumers feel about the company brand.

wiki Type of software that creates an interface that enables users to add or edit the content of some types of websites

There is too much at stake financially for marketers to ignore blogs and wikis. Despite this fact, statistics show that less than one-fourth of Fortune 500 companies have a corporate blog.[34] Marketers who want to form better customer relationships and promote their company's products must not underestimate the power of these two tools as new media outlets.

Entrepreneurship in Marketing

High School Dropout Founds Fastest-Growing Blogging Service

Entrepreneur: David Karp
Business: Tumblr
Founded: 2007 | New York
Success: Tumblr is the fastest-growing blogging service online and has a value of $800 million.

David Karp did not finish high school, but he knew his computer coding. At 16, he became chief technology officer of the parenting site UrbanBaby. Four years later, Karp went on to found the blogging service Tumblr, which has grown so quickly that, even though the company has yet to generate much revenue, many investors are eager to get involved.

Karp created Tumblr to make the blogging process simpler. This simplicity extends to the look and feel of the site: for every new feature placed on Tumblr, an older feature is removed to keep the site from becoming too cluttered. Joining Tumblr is free, and users can share posts, hyperlinks, and pictures. They also have the ability to customize their pages. The freedom Tumblr provides resonates with consumers. In one year, the number of blog posts went from 8 million to 30 million. With 13 billion monthly views, Tumblr seems poised to revolutionize the blogging industry.[a]

Media-Sharing Sites

Businesses can also share their corporate messages in more visual ways through media sharing sites. Media-sharing sites allow marketers to share photos, videos, and podcasts but are more limited in scope in how companies interact with consumers. They tend to be more promotional rather than reactive. This means that while firms can promote their products through videos or photos, they usually do not interact with consumers through personal messages or responses. At the same time, the popularity of these sites provides the potential to reach a global audience of consumers.

Photo-sharing sites allow users to upload and share their photos with the world. Well-known photo sharing sites include Flickr, SmugMug, Picasa Web Albums, and Photobucket. Flickr is owned by Yahoo! and is the most popular photo-sharing site on the Internet. A Flickr user can upload images, edit them, classify the images, create photo albums, and share photos or videos with friends without having to e-mail bulky image files or send photos through the mail. Photo sharing represents an opportunity for companies to market themselves visually by displaying snapshots of company events, company staff, and/or company products. Keller Williams, for example, has used Flickr to show photographs of employees performing philanthropic services in their communities, a type of cause-related marketing.[35] Companies can direct viewers to their photostreams (sets of photographs) by marking their pictures with the appropriate keywords or tags.[36] Many businesses with pictures on Flickr have a link connecting their Flickr photostreams to their corporate websites.[37]

Video-sharing sites allow virtually anybody to upload videos, from professional marketers at Fortune 500 corporations to the average Internet user. Some of the most popular video-sharing sites include YouTube, Metacafe.com, and Hulu. Video-sharing sites give companies the opportunity to upload ads and informational videos about their products. A few videos become viral at any given time, and although many of these gain popularity because they embarrass the subject in some way, others reach viral status because people find them entertaining (viral marketing will be discussed in more detail in Chapter 17). Marketers are seizing upon opportunities to utilize this viral nature to promote awareness of their companies. McDonald's, for instance, has partnered with YouTube to have advertisements posted during videos by YouTube's partners. With YouTube's biggest partner generating more than 5 million subscribers, such exposure guarantees that McDonald's will reach a large audience.[38]

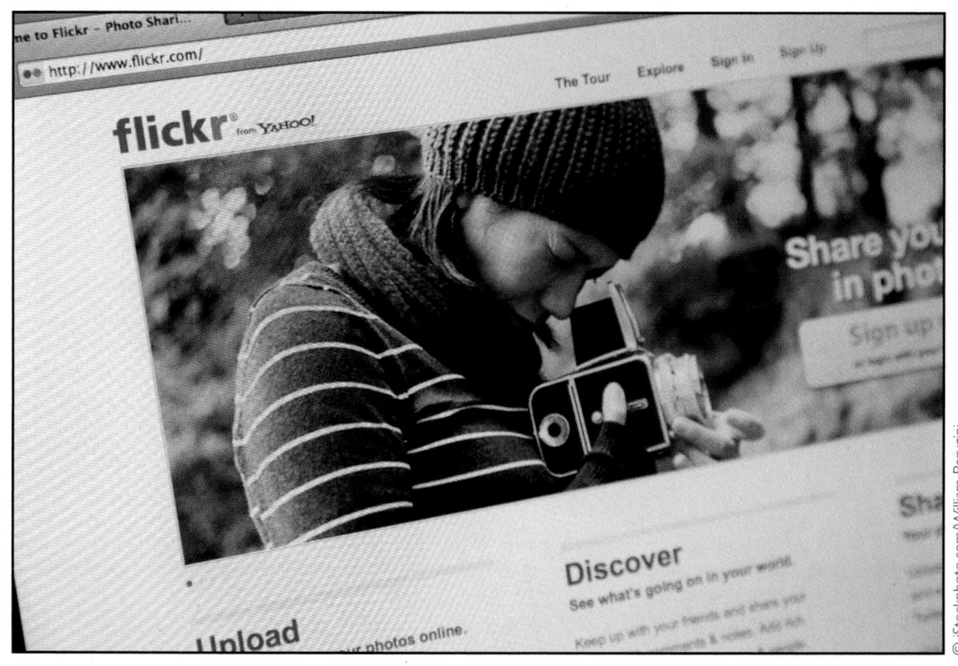

Photo-Sharing
Flickr is a very popular site that allows photo and video sharing.

A new trend in video marketing is the use of amateur filmmakers. Businesses have begun to realize that they can use consumer-generated content, which saves companies a lot of money because they do not have to hire advertising firms to develop professional advertising campaigns. GoPro was transformed from a small camera firm into a $250 million company due to the videos consumers took of themselves using GoPro cameras. The company is partnering with YouTube to create its own network for consumer-generated GoPro videos.[39] Marketers believe consumer videos appear more authentic and create enthusiasm for the product among consumer participants.

Podcasting, traditionally used for music and radio broadcasts, is also an important digital marketing tool. **Podcasts** are audio or video files that can be downloaded from the Internet with a subscription that automatically delivers new content to listening devices or personal computers. Podcasts offer the benefit of convenience, giving users the ability to listen to or view content when and where they choose. The fact that the majority of current podcast users are between 18 and 29 years of age makes podcasts a key tool for businesses marketing to this demographic.[40] For instance, the podcast *Mad Money*, hosted by Jim Cramer, gives investment advice and teaches listeners how to analyze stocks and other financial instruments.[41] Companies can use podcasts to demonstrate how to use their products or understand certain features. As podcasting continues to catch on, radio and television networks like CBC Radio, NPR, MSNBC, and PBS are creating podcasts of their shows to profit from this growing trend. Through podcasting, many companies hope to create brand awareness, promote their products, and encourage customer loyalty.

Virtual Sites

podcast Audio or video file that can be downloaded from the Internet with a subscription that automatically delivers new content to listening devices or personal computers; podcasts offer the benefit of convenience, giving users the ability to listen to or view content when and where they choose

Virtual sites are offering significant opportunities for marketers to connect with consumers in unique ways. Virtual sites include Second Life, Everquest, Sim City, and the role-playing game World of Warcraft. Such virtual worlds can be classified as social networks with a twist. Virtual realities are user-created, three-dimensional worlds that have their own economies and currencies, lands, and residents who come in every shape and size. Internet users who participate in virtual realities like Second Life choose a fictional persona called an *avatar.* Residents of Second Life connect with other users, communicate with one another, purchase goods with virtual Linden dollars (which are convertible to real dollars on a floating exchange rate of around 250 Linden dollars per $1), and even own virtual businesses. For entertainment

Virtual Realities
World of Warcraft is an example of a virtual reality game that allows consumers to completely immerse themselves in a fictional environment.

Emerging Trends

Selling Products with Virtual Games

Would you pay $5 for a chicken or $3 for a skyscraper? What if they didn't physically exist? Zynga, a virtual gaming company, is one of several organizations selling virtual products. Less than 5 percent of Zynga's users purchase virtual goods, but with 150 million unique monthly players, selling virtual goods has become highly profitable. Virtual goods were estimated to be a $6.1 billion global market in 2011.

Perhaps the greatest advantage virtual companies have is their ability to use social networking to gather information about their users. When a Facebook user accepts a Zynga game's application, the company receives information about that person's interests and friends, which increases Zynga's accessibility to other users.

Some companies also use virtual games to promote their products. Wrigley created buzz marketing around its Wrigley 5 gum through an alternate-reality game called "The Human Preservation Project." To acquire the codes needed to advance to higher levels of the game, users had to buy packs of Wrigley 5 gum. Rather than dissuading consumers, those who were eager to continue playing were willing to purchase the products. With the popularity of virtual games increasing, more products will likely be sold or promoted through this new form of social media.[b]

purposes, residents can shop, attend concerts, or travel to virtual environments—all while spending real money.

Real-world marketers and organizations have been eager to capitalize on the popularity of virtual realities. Second Life allows businesses to reach consumers in a way that is creative and fun. For instance, in an effort to connect with consumers and build brand loyalty, Domino's Pizza created a shop in Second Life that allows users to order pizza online.[42] Other businesses are looking toward virtual worlds to familiarize consumers with their products and services. For instance, McDonald's has partnered with the virtual gaming site Zynga to bring its virtual store and brand to Zynga's popular virtual gaming site Cityville.[43]

Firms are also using virtual technology for recruiting purposes. Major companies like Boeing, Procter & Gamble, Citigroup, and Progressive Corp. have held virtual career fairs to recruit candidates from across the world. The companies promoted the fairs on Facebook and Twitter. By interacting with the public virtually, businesses hope to connect with younger generations of consumers.[44]

Mobile Devices

Mobile devices, such as smartphones, mobile computing devices, and tablet computers, allow customers to leave their desktops and access digital networks from anywhere. More than 80 percent of Americans have a mobile device.[45] Many of these mobile devices are smartphones, which have the ability to access the Internet, download apps, listen to music, take photographs, and more. Figure 10.2 breaks down smartphone usage by age. Mobile marketing is exploding—marketers spent $1.2 billion on mobile marketing in 2011, and this number is expected to dramatically increase.[46]

Mobile marketing has proven effective in grabbing consumers' attention. In one study, 88 percent of smartphone users replied that they have noticed mobile advertisements. This rate is unusually high in a world where consumers are often inundated with ads. Despite these promising trends, many brands have yet to take advantage of mobile marketing opportunities. Although most major businesses have websites, not all of these websites are easily viewable on mobile devices.[47] Additionally, while most brands engage in e-mail marketing, these e-mail messages are often not mobile friendly.[48]

To avoid being left behind, brands must recognize the importance of mobile marketing. E-commerce sales on smartphones totaled $5 billion in 2011, but marketers expect this number to rise in upcoming years.[49] This makes it essential for companies to understand how to use mobile

Figure 10.2 Smartphone Usage by Age

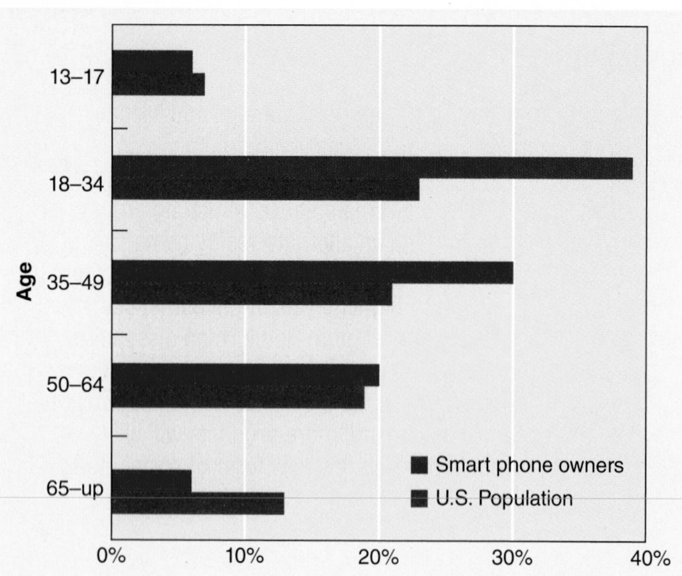

Source: Nielsen/NM Incite and U.S. Census Bureau. Reprinted in *USA Today*, February 24, 2012, 4A.

tools to create effective campaigns. Some of the more common mobile marketing tools include the following:

- SMS Messages: SMS messages are text messages of 160 words or less. SMS messages have been an effective way to send coupons to prospective customers.[50]
- Multimedia Messages: Multimedia messaging takes SMS messaging a step further by allowing companies to send video, audio, photos, and other types of media over mobile devices. For instance, Motorola's House of Blues multimedia campaign allowed users to receive access to discounts, tickets, music, and other digital content on their mobile phones.[51]
- Mobile advertisements: Mobile advertisements are visual advertisements that appear on mobile devices. Companies might choose to advertise through search engines, websites, or even games accessed on mobile devices. Orville Redenbacher has used mobile advertisements to promote its healthy snacks.[52]
- Mobile websites: Mobile websites are websites designed for mobile devices. Mobile devices constitute 7 percent of Web traffic.[53]
- Location-based networks: Location-based networks are built for mobile devices. One of the most popular location-based networks is Foursquare, which lets users check in and share their location with others. Businesses like Walgreens and Chili's Grill & Bar have partnered with Foursquare to offer incentives to consumers who check in at their venues.[54]
- Mobile applications: Mobile applications are software programs that run on mobile devices and give users access to certain content.[55] Businesses release apps to help consumers access more information about their company or to provide incentives. These are discussed in further detail in the next section.

Applications and Widgets

Applications, or apps, are adding an entirely new layer to the marketing environment, as approximately half of all American adult cell phone users have applications on their mobile devices.[56] The most important feature of apps is the convenience and cost savings they offer to the consumer. Certain apps allow consumers to scan a product's barcode and then compare it with the prices of identical products in other stores. Mobile apps also enable customers to download in-store discounts. Shoppers using the Shopkick application can download rewards at Best Buy, Macy's, Target, and other retailers.[57] As the "Snapshot" feature demonstrates, more than 30 percent of cell phone owners use mobile devices to download applications.

To remain competitive, companies are beginning to use mobile marketing to offer additional incentives to consumers. International Hotel Group, for instance, has both a mobile website and a Priority Club Reward app. As a result of its mobile marketing strategy, the company experienced a 20 percent boost in mobile site jumps per month.[58] Another application that marketers are finding useful is the QR scanning app. QR codes are black-and-white squares that sometimes appear in magazines, posters, and storefront displays. Smartphone users that have downloaded the QR scanning application can open their smartphones and scan the code, which contains a hidden message accessible with the app. The QR scanning app recognizes the code and opens the link, video, or image on the phone's screen. Marketers are using QR codes to promote their companies and offer consumer discounts.[59]

Mobile technology is also making inroads in transforming the shopping experience. Not only can shoppers use mobile applications to compare prices or download electronic discounts, they can also use mobile applications to tally up purchases and pay through their smartphones. For instance, a system called Scan It has been implemented in half of the Stop

& Shop and Giant supermarkets throughout the Northeast. The Scan It device, located on shopping carts, allows shoppers to scan their purchases, add them up, and upload their bill to the self-checkout kiosks. Initial studies show that shoppers using the system spend approximately 10 percent more on purchases in the store.[60]

Mobile payments are also gaining traction, and companies like Google are working to capitalize on this opportunity.[61] Google Wallet is a mobile app that stores credit card information on the smartphone. When the shopper is ready to check out, he or she can tap the phone at the point of sale for the transaction to be registered.[62] The success of mobile payments in revolutionizing the shopping experience will largely depend upon retailers to adopt this payment system, but companies like Starbucks are already jumping at the opportunity. Since an estimated 70 percent of U.S. consumers will own smartphones by 2014, businesses cannot afford to miss out on the chance to profit from these new trends.[63]

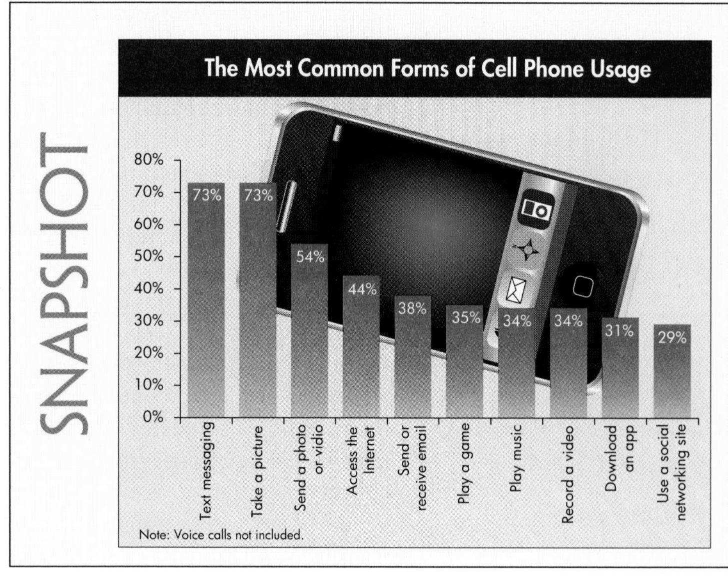

Source: The Pew Research Center's Internet & American Life Project, April 26–May 22, 2011 Spring Tracking Survey.

Widgets are small bits of software on a website, desktop, or mobile device that enables users "to interface with the application and operating system." Marketers might use widgets to display news headlines, clocks, or games on their webpages.[64] Widgets have been used by companies like A&E Television Network as a form of viral marketing—users can download the widget and send it to their friends with a click of a button.[65] Widgets downloaded to a user's desktop can update the user on the latest company or product information, enhancing relationship marketing between companies and their fans. For instance, Krispy Kreme® Doughnuts developed a widget that will alert users when their Original Glazed® doughnuts are hot off the oven at their favorite Krispy Kreme shop.[66] Widgets are an innovative digital marketing tool to personalize webpages, alert users to the latest company information, and spread awareness of the company's products.

CHANGING DIGITAL MEDIA BEHAVIORS OF CONSUMERS

Since the beginning of e-marketing, businesses have witnessed a range of changes in consumer behavior. Today, with a click of a button, consumers expect to be able to gain access to a vast amount of information on companies, products, and issues that can aid them in their purchasing decisions. Deal websites have emerged that now allow online shoppers to find the best deals, giving retailers a run for their money. E-marketers like Amazon.com, eBay, and Netflix have taken market share away from brick-and-mortar bookstores and movie rental stores. Companies are working to provide creative incentives to consumers and market to them in new ways.

With the onset of social networking sites and digital media like blogs, consumers are able to connect with each other in ways unheard of a decade ago. Through these connections, consumers can share information and experiences without company interference, allowing consumers to get more of the "real story" on a product or company. In many ways, some of the power of the professional marketer to control and dispense information has been placed in the hands of the consumer. Consumers now have a greater ability to regulate the information that they view as well as the rate and sequence of their exposure to that information. The Internet is sometimes referred to as a *pull* medium because users determine which websites they are going to view; the marketer has only limited ability to control the content to which users are exposed, and in what sequence. Today, blogs, wikis, podcasts, and ratings are used to publicize, praise, or challenge companies. Digital media certainly require marketers to approach their jobs differently compared with traditional marketing.[67] However, most companies in the United States do not routinely monitor consumers' postings to online social networking sites. In many cases, this represents a missed opportunity to gather information.

However, the changing social behavior of consumers does not have to be a sign of doom to marketers who choose to harness the power of the consumer and Internet technology. Some companies are using the power of the consumer to their advantage. While negative ratings and reviews are damaging to a company, positive customer feedback is free publicity that often helps the company more than corporate messages do. Because consumer-generated content appears more authentic than corporate messages, it can go far in increasing a company's credibility. Additionally, while consumers can use digital media to access more information, marketers can also use the same sites to get information on the consumer—often more information than could be garnered through traditional marketing venues. They can examine how consumers are using the Internet to better target marketing messages to their audience. Marketers increasingly use consumer-generated content to aid in their own marketing efforts, even going so far as to incorporate Internet bloggers in their publicity campaigns. Finally, marketers are also using the Internet to track the success of their online marketing campaigns, creating an entirely new way of gathering marketing research.

Online Consumer Behavior

As Internet technology evolves, digital media marketers must constantly adapt to new technologies and changing consumer patterns. Unfortunately, with so many new technologies emerging, the attrition rate for digital media channels is very high, with some dying off each year

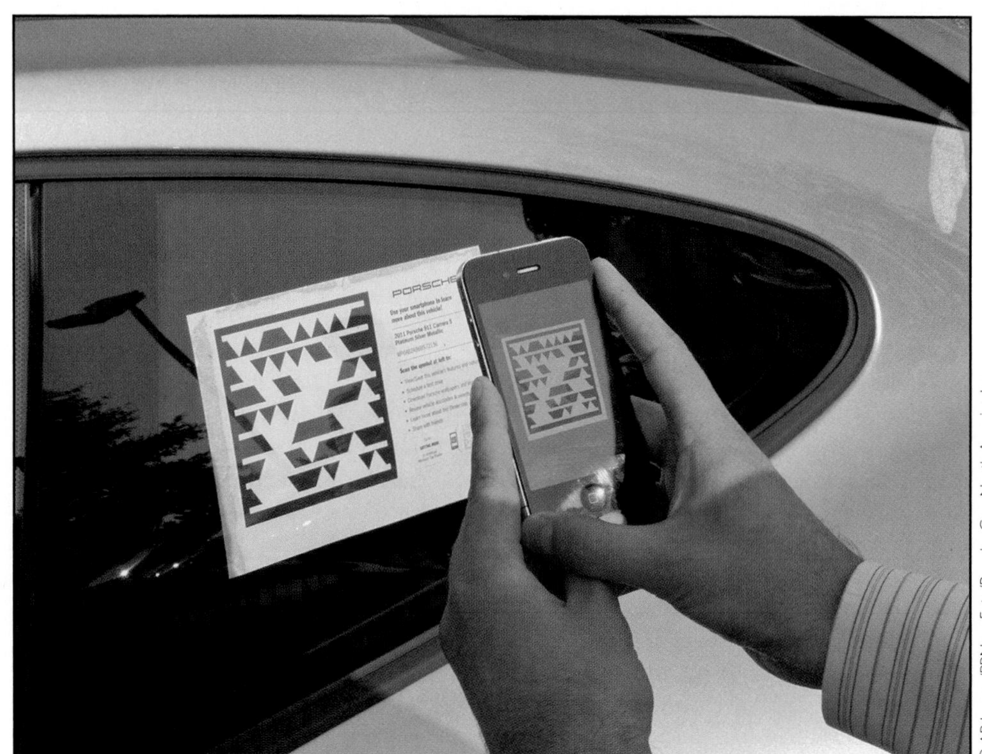

Online Consumer Behavior
QR Code scanning offers consumers the option of comparing prices between retailers, assuring the opportunity to get the best value.

as new ones emerge. Social networks are no exception: the earliest social networks like Six Degrees were dropped when they failed to catch on with the general public. As time passes, digital media are becoming more sophisticated so as to reach consumers in more effective ways. Those that are not able to adapt and change eventually fail.

Mastering digital media presents a daunting task for marketers, particularly those used to more traditional means of marketing. For this reason, it is essential that marketers focus on the changing social behaviors of consumers and how they interact with digital media. Social networking and new digital technologies, as their adoption becomes more widespread, are changing how consumers gather and use information. Consumers have access to more information than ever before, and the Internet is enabling the average consumer to get involved in the marketing process.

Forrester Research, a technology and market research company, emphasizes the importance of understanding these changing relationships in the online media world. By grouping online consumers into different segments based on how they utilize digital online media, marketers can gain a better understanding of the online market and how best to proceed.[68]

The Social Technographics Profile developed by Forrester Research groups the online community into seven segments according to how they interact with new digital media. It is important to note that these segments overlap; many online consumers may belong to multiple segments simultaneously. Table 10.2 provides a description of these seven different groups. *Creators* are those consumers who create their own media outlets, such as blogs, podcasts, consumer-generated videos, and wikis.[69] Creators are becoming increasingly important to online marketers as a conduit for addressing consumers directly. These types of consumer-generated media are becoming a major part of companies' public relations strategies. For instance, many marketers are pitching new products or stories to professional reporters and bloggers. Bloggers who post this information can reach online consumers as well as reporters in the mainstream media, who often read blogs for story ideas.[70]

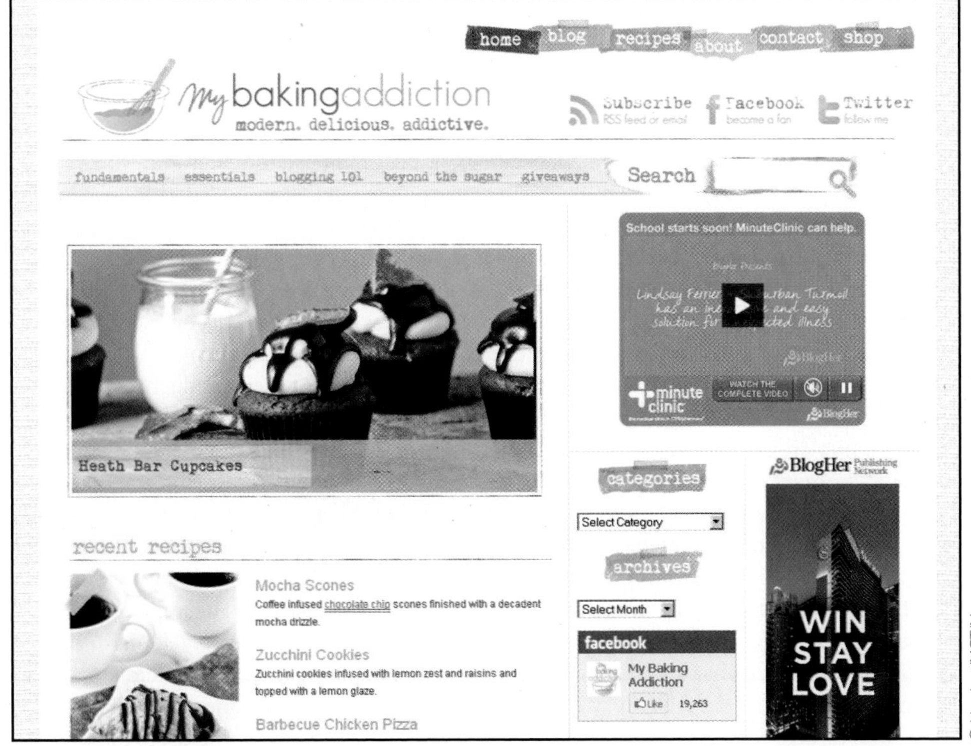

Creators
Marketers work hard to reach consumers who review products and post blogs that are widely read by other consumers or journalists.

Table 10.2 Social Technographics

Creators	Publish a blog Publish personal webpages Upload original video Upload original audio/music Write articles or stories and post them
Conversationalists	Update status on social networking sites Post updates on Twitter
Critics	Post ratings/reviews of products or services Comment on someone else's blog Contribute to online forums Contribute to/edit articles in a wiki
Collectors	Use RSS feeds Add tags to webpages or photos "Vote" for websites online
Joiners	Maintain profile on a social networking site Visit social networking sites
Spectators	Read blogs Watch video from other users Listen to podcasts Read online forums Read customer ratings/reviews
Inactives	None of the activities

Source: Charlene Li and Josh Bernoff, *Groundswell* (Boston: Harvard Business Press, 2008), 43; "Forrester Unveils New Segment of Social Technographics—The Conversationalists," 360 Digital Connections, January 21, 2010, http://blog.360i.com/social-media/forrester-new-segment-social-technographics-conversationalists (accessed July 8, 2012).

The Technographics profile calls its second group of Internet users *conversationalists.* Conversationalists regularly update their Twitter feeds or status updates on social networking sites. Although they are less involved than creators, conversationalists spend time at least once a week (and often more) on digital media sites posting updates.[71] The third category is *critics.* Critics are people who comment on blogs or post ratings and reviews. If you've ever posted a product review or rated a movie, you have engaged in this activity. Critics need to be an important component in a company's digital marketing strategy, because the majority of online shoppers read ratings and reviews to aid in their purchasing decisions. As mentioned before, consumer-generated content like ratings and reviews are viewed as more credible than corporate messages. Consumers often visit review websites like Yelp for recommendations on businesses. Yelp is one of the most comprehensive review sites on businesses. Hence, marketers should carefully monitor what consumers are saying about their products and address consumer concerns that may affect their corporate reputation.

Collectors are perhaps the least recognized group of the seven. Collectors gather information and organize content generated by critics and creators. The growing popularity of this segment is leading to the creation of social networking sites like Digg, del.icio.us, reddit, and RSS feeds. Want to know the top 10 stories according to online consumers? Collectors gather this type of information and post their findings to social networking sites like reddit, where users vote on the sites they like the best. Collectors usually constitute a smaller part of the online population than the other groups; however, they can still have a significant impact on marketing activities.[72] Because collectors are active members in the online community, a company story or site that catches the eye of a collector is likely to be posted and discussed on collector sites and made available to other online users looking for information.

Another Technographic segment, known as *joiners*, is growing dramatically. Anyone who becomes a member of Myspace, Twitter, Facebook, or other social networking sites is a joiner.[73] It is not unusual for consumers to be members of several social networking sites at once. Joiners participate in these sites to connect and network with other users, but, as previously discussed, marketers can take significant advantage of these sites to connect with consumers and form customer relationships.

The last two segments are classified as *spectators* and *inactives*. Inactives are online users who do not participate in any digital online media, but as more and more people begin to use computers as a resource, this number is dwindling. Spectators are the largest group in most countries, and it is not hard to see why. Spectators are those consumers who read what other consumers produce but do not create any content themselves.

Marketers who want to capitalize on social and digital media marketing will need to consider what portion of online consumers are creating, conversing, rating, collecting, joining, or simply reading online materials. As with traditional marketing efforts, marketers need to know the best ways to reach their target market. In markets where spectators make up the majority of the online population, companies should post their own corporate messages through blogs and websites promoting their organizations. In a population of joiners, companies could try to connect with their target audience by creating profile pages and inviting consumers to post their thoughts. In areas where a significant portion of the online community consists of creators, marketers should continually monitor what other consumers are saying and incorporate bloggers into their public relations strategies. Companies must exercise care, however. The firms that try to use their influence to stifle online criticism can get hit with consumer backlash. The power of the consumer in the online world should not be underestimated by the online marketer. By knowing how to segment the online population, marketers can better tailor their messages to their target markets.

E-MARKETING STRATEGY

Although the Internet has yet to take off in many countries due to a lack of infrastructure, basic Internet literacy is increasingly common. More than one-fourth of the world's population uses the Internet, and this number is growing at a high rate. In North America, more than three-fourths of the population has Internet access.[74] These trends display a growing need for businesses to use the Internet to reach an increasingly Web-savvy population. As more and more shoppers go online for purchases, the power of traditional brick-and-mortar businesses is lessening. Online retailers like Amazon.com are challenging more traditional retailers like Barnes & Noble or Walmart, and even small businesses are finding ways to reach customers and grab share away from established competitors.

This makes it essential for businesses, small and large alike, to learn how to effectively use new social media. Most businesses are finding it necessary to use digital marketing to grab or maintain market share. When Amazon.com first became popular as an online bookstore in the 1990s, the brick-and-mortar bookseller chain Barnes & Noble quickly made online shopping possible through its website, but did not abandon its physical stores. This "brick-and-clicks" model is now standard for businesses from neighborhood family-owned restaurants to national chain retailers. In the process, companies that use digital marketing well can receive the added benefit of streamlining their organizations and offering entirely new benefits and convenience to consumers. The following sections will examine how businesses are effectively using these social media forums to create effective marketing strategies on the Web.

Product Considerations

In traditional marketing, marketers must anticipate consumer needs and preferences and then tailor their products to meet these needs. The same is true with marketing products using digital media. Digital media provide an opportunity to add a service dimension to traditional products and create new products that could only be accessible on the Internet. The applications available on the iPad, for instance, provide examples of products that are only available in the digital world. The ability to access product information for any product can have a major impact on buyer decision making. However, with larger companies now launching their own extensive marketing campaigns, and with the constant sophistication of digital technology, many businesses are finding it necessary to continually upgrade their product offerings to meet consumer needs. As has been discussed throughout this chapter, the Internet represents a large resource to marketers for learning more about consumer wants and needs.

Some companies now use online advertising campaigns and contests to help develop better products. Netflix, the online movie rental-by-mail service, offers a much wider array of movies and games than what is available at the average movie rental store, plus a number of convenience features: no late fees, a one-month free trial service, quick delivery times, and online video streaming of some movies. Netflix also prides itself on its recommendation engine that suggests movies for users based on their previous rental history and ratings. Other companies have also begun selling their products through social networking sites. With social media e-commerce applications, shoppers can add a company's products into a cart through Facebook and then transfer back to the company website to complete the transaction. Some newer applications, such as Off the Wall and Payvment, are now allowing shoppers to purchase a company's products directly from Facebook.[75]

Distribution Considerations

The role of distribution is to make products available at the right time, at the right place, and in the right quantities. Digital marketing can be viewed as a new distribution channel that helps businesses increase efficiency. The ability to process orders electronically and increase the speed of communications via the Internet reduces inefficiencies, costs, and redundancies while increasing speed throughout the marketing channel. Shipping times and costs have become an important consideration in attracting consumers, prompting many companies to offer consumers low shipping costs or next-day delivery. Walmart, for example, has a "site-to-store" system, whereby consumers get free shipping if they pick up their purchases at a Walmart store of their choice. The company has even tested the concept of delivering groceries to individual

Going Green

Are Electronic Textbooks Really Better for the Environment?

College textbooks are going digital. E-textbooks are growing 50 percent per year and are expected to constitute over 11 percent of the industry by 2013. With the help of an application created by technology company Inkling, students can even read e-textbooks on their iPads. However, despite the benefits of e-textbooks, they also have a number of challenges to overcome. One of these lies in the realm of sustainability.

E-books require e-readers, which, in turn, require resources that are not always sustainable. On average, manufacturing an e-reader requires 33 pounds of minerals, 300 liters of water, and emits about 66 pounds of carbon dioxide. The iPad also requires what is known as "conflict minerals"—minerals that are either hard to extract or that come from parts of the world undergoing severe conflict.

On the other hand, traditional books use approximately 1.5 million metric tons of paper annually, and the average book emits about 8.85 pounds of carbon dioxide. Thus, much of the debate comes down to how many books a consumer reads during the year. One study indicates that, for those who read fewer than 10 books a year, traditional books are the greener option. Those who read many books a year would be better off using digital books. Of course, there is one option that trumps both of these in sustainability: the library.[c]

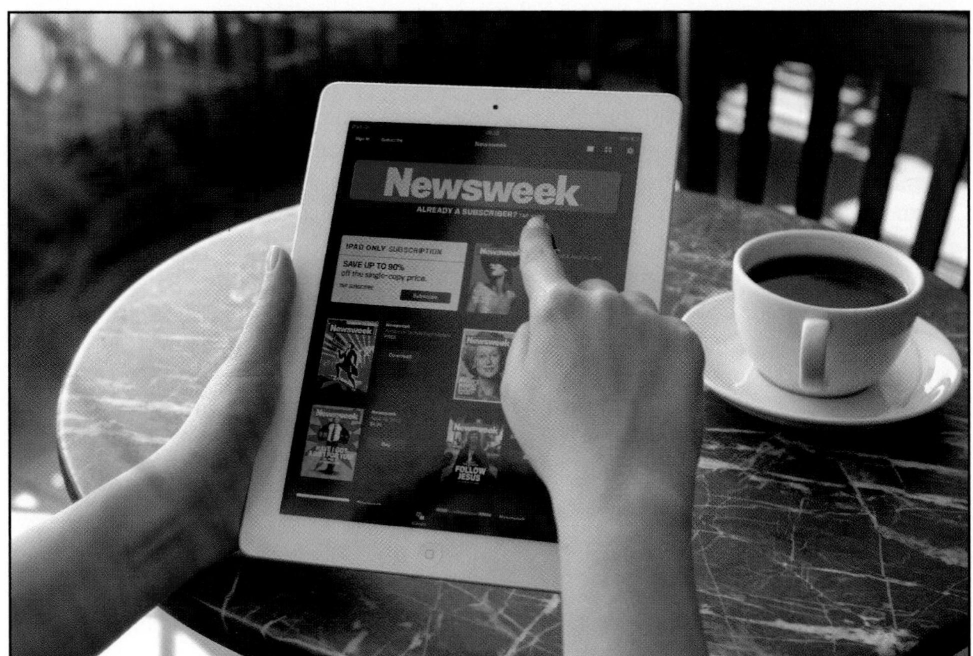

© iStockphoto.com/hocus-focus

Distribution
The growth in popularity of e-readers has lead to a greater direct distribution of magazines, newspapers, and books.

homes. Walmart hopes to become an online success and eventually take market share away from competitors like Amazon.[76]

Distribution involves a push–pull dynamic: the firm that provides a product will push to get that product in front of the consumer, while at the same time connectivity aids those channel members that desire to find each other—the pull side of the dynamic. For example, an iPhone application can help consumers find the closest Starbucks, McDonald's, or KFC. On the other hand, a blog or Twitter feed can help a marketer communicate the availability of products and how and when they can be purchased. This process can help push products through the marketing channel to consumers or enable customers to pull products through the marketing channel.

These changing distribution patterns are not just limited to the Western world. Businesses around the world are choosing to sell products over the Internet. This represents a revolutionary shift in countries like China, where online shopping had not been widely adopted by consumers. One of the first Chinese companies to adopt Internet selling was Taobao, an auction site for consumers that also features sections for Chinese brands and retailers. Taobao has been successful, with the majority of online sales in China going through its site.[77] The changing consumer trends in China demonstrate that the shift to digital media is well underway.

Promotion Considerations

The majority of this chapter has discussed ways that marketers use digital media and social networking sites to promote products, from creating profiles on social networking sites to connecting with consumers (New Belgium) to using Twitter to build customer relationships (Southwest Airlines) to taking advantage of virtual worlds like Second Life to increase consumer interest (Domino's). Social networking sites also allow marketers to approach promotion in entirely new, creative ways. For instance, Facebook's launch of "Sponsored Stories" lets advertisers pay to have Facebook highlight users' status updates or "likes" so their friends can see them. Burberry's and Ben & Jerry's have used the "Sponsored Stories" feature to capitalize on this opportunity for word-of-mouth marketing. Facebook's "Sponsored Stories" has been moved into its "News Feed," since that is the place where most users look first.[78] Marketers who choose to capitalize on these opportunities have the chance to boost their firms' brand exposure.

These digital promotions all attempt to increase brand awareness and market to consumers. As a result of online promotion, consumers are more informed, reading consumer-generated content before making purchasing decisions and increasingly shopping at Internet stores. Consumer consumption patterns are changing radically, and marketers must adapt their promotional efforts to meet these new patterns.

Almost any traditional promotional event can be enhanced or replaced by digital media. To prepare for the 2012 Super Bowl game, General Motors released a mobile application that enabled users to play trivia, interact with other users, and have the chance to win a new car.[79] Banks are using blogs, podcasts, and Twitter to post rates and financial products and to answer financial questions. Even direct selling representatives from firms like Avon or Amway are gathering their consumers on Facebook to discuss products, much like socializing around the kitchen table or engaging in a focus group.

Pricing Considerations

Pricing relates to perceptions of value and is the most flexible element of the marketing mix. Digital online media marketing facilitates both price and nonprice competition, because Internet marketing gives consumers access to more information about costs and prices. As consumers become more informed about their options, the demand for low-priced products has grown, leading to the creation of daily deal sites like Groupon, CrowdCut, and Living Social. These companies partner with local businesses to offer major discounts to subscribers in order to generate new business. Groupon and LivingSocial have been so successful that they are looking to expand their partnerships to larger firms like Fandango and Whole Foods.[80] Several marketers are also offering buying incentives like online coupons or free samples to generate consumer demand for their product offerings.

Digital connections can help the customer find the price of the product available from various competitors in an instant. Websites provide price information, and mobile applications can help the customer find the lowest price. Consumers can even bargain with retailers in the store by using a smartphone to show the lowest price available during a transaction. While this new access to price information benefits the consumer, it also places new pressures on the seller to be competitive and to differentiate products so that customers focus on attributes and benefits other than price.

Until recently, social networks like Facebook and Twitter were mainly used for promotional purposes and customer service. Those who wanted to purchase items were often redirected to the company's website. However, retailers and other organizations are developing e-commerce stores on Facebook so that consumers will not have to leave the site to purchase items. Delta sells airline tickets through Facebook, while the apparel retailer Express has begun to sell its product line on its Facebook page.[81] For the business that wants to compete on price, digital marketing provides unlimited opportunities.

ETHICAL AND LEGAL ISSUES

How marketers use technology to gather information—both online and offline—raises numerous legal and ethical issues. The popularity and widespread use of the Internet grew so quickly in the 1990s that global regulatory systems were unable to keep pace, although today there are a number of laws in place to protect businesses and consumers. Among the issues of concern are personal privacy, fraud, and misappropriation of copyrighted intellectual property.

Privacy

One of the most significant privacy issues involves the use of personal information that companies collect from website visitors in their efforts to foster long-term relationships with customers. Some people fear that the collection of personal information from website users may violate users' privacy, especially when it is done without their knowledge. Hackers may break into websites and steal users' personal information, enabling them to commit identity theft. Mobile phone payments are another source of concern. Consumers worry that their information could be hacked, or their phones could be targeted with malware.[82] Many of these breaches occur at banks, universities, and other businesses that contain sensitive consumer information.[83] This requires organizations to implement increased security measures to prevent database theft.

Facebook and other social networking sites have also come under fire for privacy issues. Facebook and Google both agreed to undergo independent privacy audits for 20 years due to alleged privacy transgressions. The FTC determined that Facebook's 2009 changes to its privacy policies were done without warning users. The commission also charged Google with using the personal information from its Gmail users for its Google Buzz service, despite telling users otherwise. Such changes were deemed to have violated users' rights to know how their information was being utilized.[84] Another Internet privacy issue occurring more frequently is "scraping," an activity where companies offer to collect personal information from social networking sites and other forums. Such events have prompted both consumers and the federal government alike to consider an online privacy "Bill of Rights" to protect consumers from having their information tracked without permission. Such a bill might also require more companies to submit to privacy audits.[85]

Due to consumer concerns over privacy, the FTC is considering developing regulations that would better protect consumer privacy by limiting the amount of consumer information that businesses can gather online. Other countries are pursuing similar actions. The European Union passed a law requiring companies to get users' consent before using cookies to track their information. In the United States, one proposed solution for consumer Internet privacy is a "do not track" bill, similar to the "do not call" bill for telephones, to

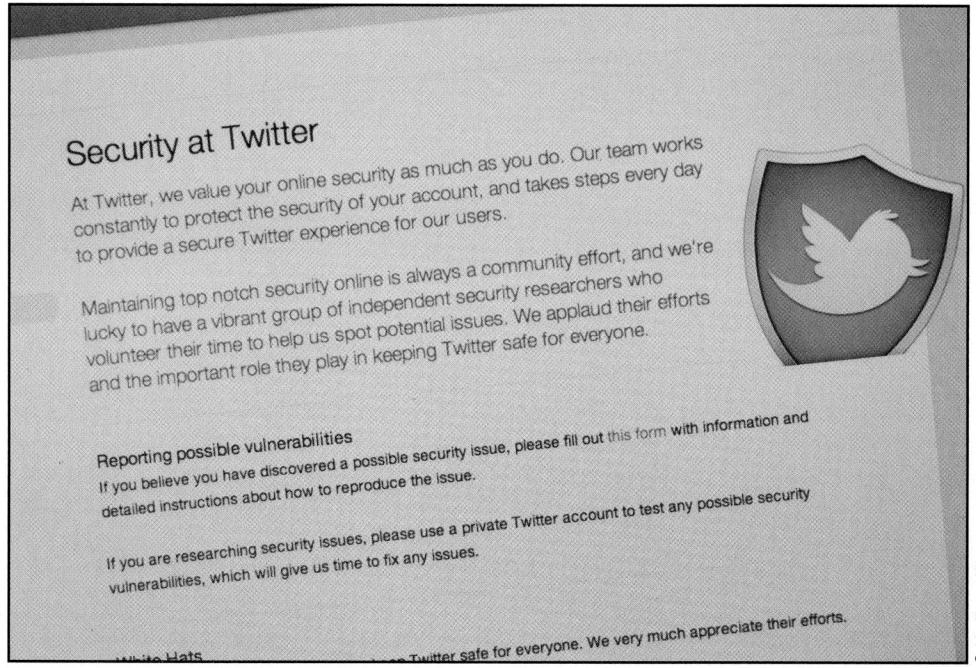

Ethical and Legal Issues in Digital Media
Twitter freely shares its online security measures with consumers.

allow users to opt out of having their information tracked.[86] While consumers may welcome such added protections, Web advertisers, who use consumer information to better target advertisements to online consumers, see it as a threat. In response to impending legislation, many Web advertisers are attempting self-regulation in order to stay ahead of the game. For instance, the Interactive Advertising Board is encouraging its members to adopt a do-not-track icon that users can click on to avoid having their online activity monitored. However, it is debatable whether members will choose to participate or honor users' do-not-track requests.[87]

Online Fraud

Online fraud includes any attempt to conduct dishonest activities online. Online fraud includes, among other things, attempts to deceive consumers into releasing personal information. It is becoming a major source of frustration with social networking sites. Cybercriminals are discovering ways to use sites like Facebook and Twitter to carry out fraudulent activities. For instance, it has become common for cybercriminals to create profiles under a company's name. These fraudulent profiles are often created to either damage the company's reputation (this is particularly common with larger, more controversial companies) or as a way to lure that company's customers into releasing personal information that the cybercriminal can then use for monetary gain. Another tactic some fraudsters have used is to create typosquatting sites based on common misspellings of search engines or social networks (e.g. Faecbook vs. Facebook). Fraudsters then trick visitors into releasing their information.[88] Perhaps the most disturbing is the practice of using social networking sites to pose as charitable institutions. For instance, fake charities were established on Facebook after the 2011 earthquake and tsunami disaster in Japan. The Better Business Bureau worked with the FBI to compile and release a list of suspected scams seeking to benefit from natural disasters though social networking.

Organizations and social networking sites alike are developing ways to combat fraudulent activity on new digital media sites. For instance, organizations known as brand-protection firms monitor social networks for fraudulent accounts. Whenever these sites are found, the organizations notify their clients about the fraud and help them to remove the fraudulent account.[89] However, the best protection for consumers is to be careful when divulging information online. Privacy advocates advise that the best way to stay out of trouble is to avoid giving out personal information, such as social security numbers or credit card information, unless the site is definitely legitimate.

online fraud Any attempt to conduct fraudulent activities online, including deceiving consumers into releasing personal information

Marketing Debate

Social Networking in the Workplace

ISSUE: Should employees be allowed to use social networking sites at work?

While employers agree that social media isn't going away, they disagree on what to do about its use in the workplace. It is estimated that the average employee spends one hour a day on social media sites during work time and that distractions from social media and other devices can cost a large company over $10 million annually. As a result, some companies block social media sites. However, employees indicate that blocking social media might actually decrease their productivity and lower their morale, because these restrictions indicate distrust in the employee. Additionally, younger generations often want to work at companies where social media is permitted and might forgo working at places that block these sites.[d]

Intellectual Property

The Internet has also created issues associated with intellectual property, the copyrighted or trademarked ideas and creative materials developed to solve problems, carry out applications, and educate and entertain others. Each year, intellectual property losses in the United States total billions of dollars stemming from the illegal copying of computer programs, movies, compact discs, and books. YouTube has often faced lawsuits on intellectual property infringement. With millions of users uploading content to YouTube, it can be hard for Google to monitor and remove all the videos that may contain copyrighted materials. Additionally, the file hosting service Megaupload was shut down, and owner Kim Dotcom arrested after prosecutors accused the site of being a front for massive Internet piracy. Unfortunately, legitimate users of the site were cut off from their files as well.[90]

Online piracy has become such an issue that the U.S. government proposed two bills, the Stop Online Piracy Act and Protect Intellectual Property Act, that would enable the government to shut down sites that appeared to violate another stakeholder's intellectual property. Although studios and record labels supported the bills, online Internet companies and many consumers were against them. They feared that giving Congress more authority to regulate the Internet would infringe on freedom of speech. To protest the proposed bill, Wikipedia went offline for a day, and Google blacked out its "Google" lettering on its main page. The pressure caused the government to drop the bills.[91] The fine line between protecting intellectual property and maintaining freedom of speech makes this a continual controversy.

The software industry is particularly hard-hit when it comes to the pirating of materials and illegal file sharing. The Business Software Alliance estimates that the global computer software industry loses more than $50 billion a year to illegal theft.[92] Consumers view illegal downloading in different ways, depending on the motivation for the behavior. If the motivation is primarily utilitarian, or for personal gain, then the act is viewed as less ethically acceptable than if it is for a hedonistic reason, or just for fun.[93]

Consumers rationalize pirating software, video games, and music for a number of reasons. First, many consumers feel that they just do not have the money to pay for what they want. Second, because their friends engage in piracy and swap digital content, they feel influenced to engage in this activity. Third, for some, the attraction is the thrill of getting away with it and the slim risk of consequences. Fourth, to some extent, there are people who think they are smarter than others; engaging in piracy allows them to show how tech savvy they are.[94]

As digital media continues to evolve, more legal and ethical issues will certainly arise. As a result, marketers and all other users of digital media should make an effort to learn and abide by ethical practices to ensure that they get the most out of the resources available in this growing medium. Doing so will allow marketers to maximize the tremendous opportunities digital media has to offer.

Summary

1. To define *digital media* and *electronic marketing* and recognize their increasing importance in strategic planning

Digital media are electronic media that function using digital codes—when we refer to digital media, we are referring to media available via computers, cellular phones, smartphones, and other digital devices that have been released in recent years. Digital marketing uses all digital media, including the Internet and mobile and interactive channels, to develop communication and exchanges with customers. Electronic marketing refers to the strategic process of distributing, promoting, and pricing products, and discovering the desires of customers using digital media and digital marketing. Our definition of e-marketing goes beyond the Internet and also includes mobile phones, banner ads, digital outdoor marketing, and social networks.

2. To identify and understand the role of digital media in a marketing strategy and how each type of digital media can be used as an effective marketing tool

Digital media in marketing is advancing at a rapid rate. The self-sustaining nature of digital technology means that current advances act as a catalyst to spur even faster development. As faster digital transmissions evolve, marketing applications are emerging that offer an opportunity for companies to reach consumers in entirely new ways.

As a result, digital marketing is moving from a niche strategy to becoming a core consideration in the marketing mix. At the same time, digital technologies are largely changing the dynamic between marketer and consumer. Consumers use social networking sites and mobile applications to do everything from playing games to booking airline and hotel reservations. The menu of digital media alternatives continues to grow, requiring marketers to make informed decisions about strategic approaches.

3. To understand digital marketing consumer behavior

It is essential that marketers focus on the changing social behaviors of consumers and how they interact with digital media. Consumers now have a greater ability to regulate the information that they view as well as the rate and sequence of their exposure to that information. This is why the Internet is sometimes referred to as a *pull* medium because users determine which websites they are going to view; the marketer has only limited ability to control the content to which users are exposed, and in what sequence. Marketers must modify their marketing strategies to adapt to the changing behaviors of online consumers.

Forrester Research groups online consumers into seven categories depending upon how they use digital media. Creators are those consumers who create their own media outlets. Conversationalists regularly update their Twitter feeds or status updates on social networking sites. Critics are people who comment on blogs or post ratings and reviews. Collectors gather information and organize content generated by critics and creators. Joiners are those who become members of social networking sites. Spectators are those consumers who read what other consumers produce but do not produce any content themselves. Finally, inactives are online users who do not participate in any digital online media, but this number is decreasing as the popularity of digital media grows. Marketers who want to capitalize on social and digital media marketing will need to consider what portion of online consumers are creating, conversing, rating, collecting, joining, or simply reading online materials.

4. To understand and identify how digital media affects the marketing mix

The reasons for a digital marketing strategy are many. The low costs of many digital media channels can provide major savings in promotional budgets. Laptops, smartphones, mobile broadband, webcams, and other digital technologies can provide low-cost internal communication as well as external connections with customers. Digital marketing is allowing companies to connect with market segments that are harder to reach with traditional media. Despite the challenges involved in such a strategy, digital marketing is opening up new avenues in the relationship between businesses and consumers.

Because digital tools, strategies, tactics, and channels are not static, marketers must prepare to learn new ways to reach customers. There is still a need to balance traditional media with new digital media. Developing skills to manage the appropriate mix of traditional and digital media is important for success. Assuming that everything has changed to digital can be a mistake in reaching some market segments. Collaboration across the organization is necessary to make digital decisions that break down the walls between products and customers. Customers should be engaged to help this bond evolve. Finally, marketers must find ways to address the challenges that come with digital marketing, such as formulating ways to evaluate the effectiveness of a digital marketing campaign. The implementation of an effective digital marketing strategy will help businesses reap the rewards that digital technologies have to offer.

5. To identify legal and ethical considerations in digital media and electronic marketing

How marketers use technology to gather information—both online and offline—has raised numerous legal and ethical issues.

Privacy is one of the most significant issues, involving the use of personal information that companies collect from website visitors in their efforts to foster long-term relationships with customers. Some people fear that the collection of personal information from website users may violate users' privacy, especially when it is done without their knowledge. Another concern is that hackers may break into websites and steal users' personal information, enabling them to commit identity theft.

Online fraud includes any attempt to conduct dishonest activities online. Online fraud includes, among other things, attempts to deceive consumers into releasing personal information. It is becoming a major source of frustration with social networking sites. Cybercriminals are discovering entirely new ways to use sites like Facebook and Twitter to carry out fraudulent activities. Organizations and social networking sites alike are developing ways to combat fraudulent activity on new digital media sites.

The Internet has also created issues associated with intellectual property, the copyrighted or trademarked ideas and creative materials developed to solve problems, carry out applications, and educate and entertain others. Each year, intellectual property losses in the United States total billions of dollars stemming from the illegal copying of computer programs, movies, compact discs, and books. The software industry is particularly hard-hit when it comes to pirating material and illegal file sharing.

Go to www.cengagebrain.com for resources to help you master the content in this chapter as well as for materials that will expand your marketing knowledge!

Important Terms

digital media 316
digital marketing 317
electronic marketing (e-marketing) 317
social network 320
blogs 323
wiki 324
podcast 326
online fraud 338

Discussion and Review Questions

1. How does e-marketing differ from traditional marketing?
2. Define interactivity and explain its significance. How can marketers exploit this characteristic to improve relations with customers?
3. Explain the distinction between push and pull media. What is the significance of control in terms of using websites to market products?
4. Why are social networks becoming an increasingly important marketing tool? Find an example online in which a company has improved the effectiveness of its marketing strategy by using social networks.
5. How has new media changed consumer behavior? What are the opportunities and challenges that face marketers with this in mind?
6. Describe the different technographic segments. How can marketers use this segmentation in their strategies?
7. How can marketers exploit the characteristics of the Internet to improve the product element of their marketing mixes?
8. How do the characteristics of e-marketing affect the promotion element of the marketing mix?
9. How has digital media affected the pricing of products? Give examples of the opportunities and challenges presented to marketers in light of these changes.
10. Name and describe the major ethical and legal issues that have developed in response to the Internet. How should policymakers address these issues?

Application Questions

1. Amazon.com is one of the Web's most recognizable marketers. Visit the company's website at www.amazon.com and describe how the company adds value to its customers' buying experiences.
2. Social networking has become a popular method of communication not only for individuals but for businesses as well. Visit the various social networking sites, such as Facebook and Twitter, and identify how companies are utilizing each of these sites in their marketing strategies.
3. Some products are better suited than others to electronic marketing activities. For example, Art.com specializes in selling art prints via its online store. The ability to display a variety of prints in many different categories gives customers a convenient and efficient way to search for art. On the other hand, General Electric has a website displaying its appliances, but customers must visit a retailer to purchase them. Visit www.art.com and www.geappliances.com and compare how each firm uses the electronic environment of the Internet to enhance its marketing efforts.
4. Visit the information technology company website www.covisint.com and evaluate the nature of the business customers attracted. Who is the target audience for this business marketing site? Describe the types of firms currently doing business through this exchange. What other types of organizations might be attracted? Is it appropriate to sell any banner advertising on a site such as this? What other industries might benefit from developing similar digital media exchange hubs?
5. IMP Marketers have a keen interest in social media because of the notion of influence. The assumption is that you have certain friends on Facebook, or specific authors whom you follow on Twitter, who affect the kinds of products that you buy. A recent start-up called Klout attempts to quantify this online influence by assigning people a Klout score, which ranges from 0 to 100 and which, according to the company, reflects a person's influence across the social network. Marketers can then try to use people with high Klout scores as influencers of consumption behaviors. Critiques of Klout suggest that the algorithm that it uses to calculate the Klout score is too reliant on Facebook and Twitter, does not account for the quality of the online interactions, and neglects other important social media. But its rise as an Internet darling (and the growth of other similar services like Kred and PeerIndex) suggests that it has some influence over social media marketing.

   Identify and map your social habits on social networking sites for the past week. Did you create content through blogs? Did you rate or recommend products or companies? Did you post photos of yourself at particular events or places on Facebook? Rate each of your online social activities according to how much influence you think they have had upon your friends or followers. Use 0 if you believe a particular activity had zero influence, 1 for slight influence, 2 for moderate influence, and 3 for significant influence. After you are finished ranking how much of an impact each of your online activities has had upon your friends and followers, determine whether you are an influencer of consumption behaviors. Do you think your friends would agree with you?

Internet Exercise

Victors & Spoils

To learn more about the world's first creative ad agency built on crowdsourcing principles, including an opportunity to engage the world's most talented creatives, look at the Victors & Spoils site at http://victorsandspoils.com.

1. How can Victors & Spoils be used to outsource advertising campaigns through co-creation and mass collaboration?
2. Victors & Spoils and crowdsourcing is built on the foundation that good ideas should come from anywhere. Is it possible that this new approach will eliminate traditional ad agencies and creative departments?
3. If you want to engage in activities related to what would be found in the creative department of an advertising agency, how can Victors & Spoils help you launch your career?

developing your marketing plan

When developing a marketing strategy using new digital media, a marketer must be aware of the strengths and weaknesses of these new media. Digital media are relatively new to the field of marketing and have different pros and cons relative to traditional media sources. Different products and target markets may be more or less suited for different digital media outlets.

1. Review the key concepts of addressability, interactivity, accessibility, connectivity, and control in Table 10.1, and explain how they relate to social media. Think about how a marketing strategy focused on social media differs from a marketing campaign reliant on traditional media sources.
2. No matter what marketing media are used, determining the correct marketing mix for your company is always important. Think about how social media might affect the marketing mix.
3. Discuss different digital media and the pros and cons of using each as part of your marketing plan.

The information obtained from these questions should assist you in developing various aspects of your marketing plan found in the "Interactive Marketing Plan" exercise at **www.cengagebrain.com**.

video case 10.1

RogueSheep's Postage App: The Postcard of the Future

That 25-cent postcard in the gift shop may soon become a thing of the past. RogueSheep's postage application is giving the traditional postcard a run for its money, as it allows users to send a digital postcard to their family members quickly and efficiently. RogueSheep is a software development and consulting company based in Seattle. Co-founders Christopher Parrish, Daniel Guenther, Matt Joss, and Jeff Argast founded RogueSheep as an Adobe Development shop.

The company specializes in graphics and publishing software while acting as a consultant to clients with their software development projects. One of the company's most popular products is its mobile app "Postage," iPhone's first postcard application. The idea for Postage came from a business conference when Parrish's business partner wanted to send a postcard back to his wife. The founders of RogueSheep thought this would make a great iPhone app, and development of this app began.

For $4.99, iPhone users can purchase the app, choose from more than 90 postcard designs, customize the design by inserting their own photos, and send the postcard to their friends or relatives. Customers can personalize their postcards by adding effects, rotating or zooming in on the picture, and changing the font or style of the message. What takes a few days by regular mail can now take only seconds. Connectivity based on digital communication keeps people connected in an instant. Social networking sites provide a way that consumers can connect and express their feelings, emotions, and opinions.

In the case of the RogueSheep Postage app, it provides better and more personalized connections than a traditional postcard. Each pixel of the app's screens has been designed by RogueSheep designers. RogueSheep has become a major success in the software design world, winning Apple's 2009 Design Award. Much of its success likely comes from the great care that RogueSheep puts into its Postage designs. Each postcard in the app is created by the application designer, and designs are continually added to give customers a range of options to choose from. Additionally, RogueSheep has broken into the social networking world by creating ways that users can share their customized postcards with friends and followers on Facebook and Twitter. Now that social networking is more popular for personal communication than e-mail, RogueSheep's app is perfect for social networks. Social networking also allows RogueSheep to spread the word about its Postage app and create buzz around the product.

To create awareness of the product, RogueSheep uses a combination of digital and traditional media, utilizing Web advertising and traditional magazines like *Macworld* as promotional tools. RogueSheep has also encouraged trials of its Postage app by giving out promotional codes through Twitter to enable free trials of its product. In the business realm, RogueSheep's Postage app could be used to send postcards to remind customers about their products or special events. This application could potentially be customized to be a less expensive, more impactful business-to-consumer promotional postcard.

As more and more people become familiar with iPhone apps, RogueSheep must constantly adapt its products to anticipate and meet customer needs. Recently, RogueSheep expanded its product offerings with apps like RoseGlobe—which allows users to place pictures of their sweethearts in a globe with swirling hearts that move as the iPhone moves—and an Instaview app that allows users of the mobile photo sharing application Instagram to show and share these photos on a Mac computer. RogueSheep also offers holiday- and romance-themed Postage apps for special occasions. The company regularly investigates new designs for its digital postcards. By creating a new, efficient way to meet a consumer need, RogueSheep's Postage app may supplant printed materials to become the future of postcards. The business applications of sending RogueSheep postcards are unlimited and can be another form of digital marketing. RogueSheep's postage application, like all digital marketing activities, should be integrated into a marketing strategy that relates to the target market's ability and interest in digital communication.[95]

Questions for Discussion:

1. How do you think businesses could effectively use RogueSheep postcards in their communications program?
2. Is it possible for RogueSheep to advance its digital postcards to those who do not have access to iPhone apps?
3. What are the advantages of the RogueSheep digital postcard over traditional postcards?

case 10.2

Twitter Emerges as a Digital Marketing Tool

Businesses big and small are tweeting to inform the world about their companies. By asking the question "What's happening?," Twitter allows users to tell their followers about moments in their daily lives. Twitter users post messages of up to 140 characters through SMS, instant messaging, or the Twitter website. Based out of a San Francisco warehouse, Twitter was founded by Biz Stone, Noah Glass, Jack Dorsey, and Evan Williams. It started as a podcasting company but quickly morphed into its current social networking form. People use Twitter for everything from "I'm catching some zzz's in class," to organizing protests, to fielding questions during presidential town hall meetings. On Facebook, users are able to communicate directly only if the users have agreed to be "friends." On Twitter, anyone can sign up to follow any public tweets available. For instance, actor Ashton Kutcher has more than 9 million followers.

© iStockphoto.com/Simone Becchetti

Many marketers have been quick to jump on the Twitter bandwagon, finding it to be an effective communications tool for attracting consumers. For example, direct selling jewelry company Stella & Dot uses Twitter to post updates about the company and its products. Many of its product postings are accompanied by a link that displays product photos; thus, the posting calls attention to the product, while the photo enables interested users to see what it looks like without having to leave the site.

Additionally, Twitter has been helpful for entrepreneurs to share their expertise. Gary Vaynerchuck, who co-owns a wine retailer, shares his wine expertise with more than 900,000 followers. The bottom line is that a Twitter post can tell others what you are up to in your business. These posts can then be forwarded to others to create a buzz.

"Follow us on Twitter" signs are appearing on the doors and windows of businesses around the globe. A survey conducted by Social Media Examiner indicates that more than 90 percent of marketers use Facebook, more than 80 percent use Twitter, and about 70 percent use LinkedIn. Kogi BBQ in Los Angeles, which uses vans to cater Korean food, has incorporated Twitter as part of its core promotional strategy. The company has more than 97,000 followers on Twitter and uses the service to tell customers where its mobile Korean food vans can be found each day. The most important benefit marketers claim that social media sites like Twitter offer is increasing the exposure of their businesses.

For its first years of existence, revenue generation was not a strong priority for Twitter. Rather, its mission statement is "to constantly connect people everywhere to what is most meaningful to them." However, because no business can survive without revenue, Twitter decided to investigate unique advertising opportunities that would benefit businesses while maintaining its core values. Although businesses can still post tweets for free, they can pay to have their posts made more prominent on the Twitter site. Twitter adopted three major promotional methods to help businesses call attention to their messages among non-followers. "Promoted tweets" are tweets that businesses pay to have placed at the top of relevant search results. "Promoted trends" are placed at the top of Twitter's popular topics page for a day at a cost of approximately $120,000. "Promoted accounts" are when businesses pay to have Twitter recommend their businesses for users to follow based upon their interests.

These promotional techniques have generated revenue from marketers at Budweiser, Starbucks, and Walt Disney. General Motors used Twitter promotions to supplement its television commercials during the 2012 Super Bowl, including one that took a combative approach to competitor Ford Motor (Ford responded with its own tweets). General Motors estimates these ads doubled its amount of Twitter followers. Twitter has also made promoted tweets available over mobile devices.

Of course, with the success of Twitter comes criticism as well. Some feel that many Twitter users post mundane details of their lives just to kill time. Security issues have also been a problem. Security breaches have sometimes released users' personal information, causing Twitter to invest in security measures to guard against such problems. But these challenges have not dulled Twitter's success. With more than 100 million active Twitter users, the craze is continuing at full force.[96]

Questions for Discussion

1. Why is Twitter appealing to companies?
2. How could Twitter be used as a tool to strengthen customer relationships and to gather consumer feedback?
3. What are some of the drawbacks of using Twitter as a marketing tool?

strategic case 4

McDonald's Continues to Be a Global Marketing Success

Serving 68 million people in 33,000 locations worldwide is all in a day's work for McDonald's—an ordinary day for a company that rings up $27 billion in annual sales in 119 nations. Through smart marketing and an understanding of what, when, where, why, and how customers want to eat, McDonald's has been able to withstand competition from traditional fast-food rivals like Burger King and KFC, as well as from casual dining chains like Panera. Growth-minded McDonald's never stops looking for new ways to reinforce customer loyalty and build profits.

© Asia Photopress/Alamy

What's in Store?

One key to McDonald's success is its menu of core items that are inextricably linked to the McDonald's brand and other items that are adapted to regional tastes. In Moscow, consumers have made Fresh McMuffin sausage sandwiches a top-selling morning item. In Argentina, the Ranchero hamburger sandwich, with a special salsa sauce, is a particular customer favorite. In France, the Croque McDo is McDonald's version of the popular croque monsieur hot ham-and-cheese sandwich. In India, the McVeggie sandwich satisfies local needs for vegetarian dishes. Taking advantage of seasonal tastes, McDonald's adds some menu items for limited periods, which encourages customers to enjoy these special foods while they can.

Although McDonald's built its reputation on burgers and fries, its marketers recognize that many consumers have become more health conscious. That's why McDonald's has developed lighter fast-food fare for adults and children alike, including fresh salads, wrap sandwiches, and apple slices. It reduced the amount of sodium in

McNuggets and lowered the calorie count in Happy Meals. In fact, McDonald's now sells more chicken in the United States than beef. Consumers can access the company's website for detailed nutrition and ingredient information about every menu item.

Ready for Customers Early, Late, and on the Go

Another way McDonald's has increased sales and profits is by opening stores early to serve the breakfast crowd and keeping select stores open until midnight or later. Some units operate drive-through service 24 hours a day. In China, where McDonald's has more than 1,500 outlets, late-night hours are popular and have helped significantly increase revenues. Breakfast is a big draw as well, accounting for up to 10 percent of McDonald's China sales. Knowing that car ownership is on the rise in China, and few competitors have drive-through locations, McDonald's is equipping new stores with drive-through capabilities, and most are open around the clock. At the same time, its stores in China offer to deliver meals to the home or office because local restaurants have traditionally provided this service.

To fuel faster growth in China, McDonald's wants to pick up the pace of franchising. Currently, fewer than 10 percent of its units in China are owned by franchisees, in contrast to the 80 percent of McDonald's units worldwide that are owned by franchisees. Meanwhile, the company is opening 200 new restaurants each year across China and diversifying its menu to appeal to customers' tastes.

Dealing with the Dollar Menu

To appeal to cash-strapped customers on a budget, McDonald's highlights its Dollar Menu of breakfast entrees and sandwiches. It has also developed an Extra Value Menu, bundling foods and beverages at a special price. Because of rising costs, however, some foods that had previously been on the Dollar Menu are now priced above a dollar and, in their place, the company has added beverages and snacks.

Rising costs are a problem for McDonald's international stores as well. In countries like Russia, for example, McDonald's boosts menu prices more than once a year to cope with inflation that drives up the cost of ingredients. The company increases the price of less-expensive menu items by about half the inflation rate but increases the price of premium menu items by more than the inflation rate because, as one executive explains, "We still have a huge amount of people who are price sensitive."

Despite the price hikes, Moscow's Pushkin Square is usually the busiest McDonald's on the planet, with 26 cash registers and seating for 900. For a few weeks during the 2012 Olympic Games in London, the McDonald's restaurant built expressly for this event exceeded the records set by the Pushkin Square unit by serving 1,200 customers per hour. Constructed as the official restaurant of the Olympic Games, this unit had a dining area built for 1,500 customers and served some 50,000 Big Mac burgers and 180,000 packs of fries during its six weeks of operation. At the end of the Olympics, McDonald's dismantled the restaurant and reused or recycled nearly all of the materials, equipment, and fixtures as part of its sustainability agenda.

Social Responsibility on the Menu

Ronald McDonald House Charities, a nonprofit group started by McDonald's, provides accommodations for families while their critically ill children are treated in hospitals far from home. Now more than three decades old, the group runs houses in 52 nations. This isn't the company's only philanthropic activity. Local McDonald's outlets support their communities by contributing to neighborhood charities and causes.

Prodded in part by animal activists, the company has established animal-handling standards for its meat suppliers. It's also going green by using paper and cardboard packaging made from recycled materials. In addition, McDonald's is involving its employees in suggesting and implementing a wide range of changes to make its restaurants and operations more eco-friendly. Its U.K. division has 600 employees volunteering as Planet Champions to investigate and recommend such changes. Thanks to their efforts, McDonald's U.K. has been able to cut its energy and water consumption even as its 1,200 restaurants are serving thousands more customers each year. The corporation showcases its environmental and charitable accomplishments in a yearly corporate responsibility report posted on its website.

Not all of McDonald's community activities are well received. For instance, McDonald's restaurants in Seminole County, Florida, arranged to give Happy Meals to local elementary school students as rewards for good grades and attendance. But some parents and child advocates raised concerns when students brought home report card jackets with a picture of Ronald McDonald. "It's a terribly troubling trend because it really, clearly links doing well in school with getting a Happy Meal," the head of the Campaign for a Commercial-Free Childhood told *The New York Times.*

Viral Videos and Blogging about Beef

McDonald's has a strong presence on the Internet and in social media, with country-specific Facebook pages and Twitter accounts. Its U.S. Facebook page has 20 million "likes," and its U.S. Twitter account has more than 500,000 followers. The company also posts videos online. A YouTube video by McDonald's Canada, intended to "open the virtual doors" and reveal what happens behind the scenes, received more than 3 million views within days of being posted. This video demonstrated why Quarter Pounders with cheese look better in McDonald's ads than they do in person. In the video, the director of marketing for McDonald's Canada showed how food stylists and photographers fuss over every tiny detail of preparing a burger for an ad, from the exact placement of mustard to the angle of the top bun. Then she bought a Quarter Pounder with cheese from a local McDonald's and brought it to the studio to be photographed. By comparison, the store-bought burger lacked the perfect shape and careful construction of the mouthwatering version in the ads. Not only did this video go viral, it also attracted considerable media attention worldwide.

To generate grassroots word-of-mouth communications about food and service quality, the company has enlisted a handful of Mom's Quality Correspondents to visit headquarters, suppliers' facilities, and individual McDonald's stores. The moms are free to look around, ask questions, videotape what they see, and then blog about their reactions, including video snippets. A McDonald's marketing official says these bloggers can say whatever they like because "if moms were out there speaking to their communities and online communities unedited, it would get us far more credibility than just posting an article or doing website copy." After the moms traveled to a McDonald's beef supplier in Oklahoma City, one wrote on the blog, "Hey, moms across America—it is really 100% beef!" McDonald's marketing and nutrition executives are continuing the outreach to keep the conversation going. Some have attended the annual BlogHer conference and hosted lunches where bloggers can ask about nutrition, Happy Meals, and anything else on their minds.

McDonald's social media initiatives don't always go the way its marketers would like. Not long ago, the company created commercials featuring some of the local farmers and ranchers who supply its restaurants with fresh potatoes, beef, and other ingredients. It paid Twitter for the privilege of being at the top of the trending list and created two hashtags, #MeetTheFarmers and #McDStories, to highlight related tweets. The objectives of this campaign were to build buzz, encourage interactivity, and lead consumers to the online commercials. Twitter users generally reacted positively to #MeetTheFarmers and the videos. However, conversations tagged as #McDStories took a negative turn, with many users posting complaints and sarcastic comments about the company. McDonald's social media director quickly decided to remove #McDStories from Twitter's home page but left #MeetTheFarmers in place because "we got lots of great engagement on that, lots of uptick from it."

Selling the Arch Card

Although McDonald's has sold gift certificates for many years, it now has a corporate sales division that targets businesses interested in giving small incentives to employees or customers. The incentive that McDonald's offers is its Arch Card, a prepaid gift card issued in the amount of $5, $10, $25, or $50. Businesses can buy up to 25 Arch Cards through local McDonald's outlets. The corporate sales division handles bulk purchases and gives business customers a discount if they buy $10,000 worth of Arch Cards. After recipients spend the initial gift amount, they can reload up to $110 on each card. The next time they visit a McDonald's restaurant, they'll be ready to grab and go with just a swipe of plastic.[97]

Questions for Discussion

1. In what ways is McDonald's generating positive attitudes toward its brand and offerings?
2. Why would McDonald's select businesses as a target market for its Arch Cards?
3. What are the advantages and disadvantages of McDonald's using franchising to grow more quickly in China?
4. Do you agree with how McDonald's handled the situation with Twitter messages marked #McDStories? Explain, in terms of addressability, accessibility, interactivity, connectivity, and control, why you think this part of McDonald's Twitter campaign didn't go as planned.

ROLE-PLAY TEAM CASE EXERCISE 4

This role-play team case exercise is designed to simulate actual marketing decision making in the real world. The entire team should read the overview and background. Each student will take on a role of a particular employee within the organization. Your instructor will provide additional information and instructions related to a team decision.

PARCEL INTERNATIONAL EXPRESS*

Background

Parcel International Express (PIE), located in Europe, provides international shipping of documents and freight as well as contract logistics. PIE's global headquarters are located in Paris and Brussels in Europe, Atlanta in North America, and Hong Kong in Asia. Major competitors include FedEx, DHL, UPS, TNT, and national post carriers like the United States Postal Service and Royal Mail. The goal of PIE is to practice customer orientation by developing loyalty through efficiency and quality of all services offered. While PIE must conform with all regulatory agencies in the areas that it operates, it functions in a highly competitive environment that requires employees to meet specific performance requirements. Therefore, PIE faces many risks related to organizational decisions, especially in its attempts to understand its customers' behavior, operate in an international environment, and adapt to changes in technology.

In the past, PIE was the shipping service of choice for many businesses and consumers. However, it has fallen behind its competitors lately, particularly in the United States. American consumers are increasingly turning to PIE rivals FedEx and UPS for shipping services. Although PIE still maintains a significant market share among business customers, its market share in the industry also appears to be decreasing. An initial investigation revealed a surprising finding. Although PIE has high rankings for speed of delivery, it is ranked one of the worst in customer service. Customers complain that customer service representatives are abrasive and have little knowledge about how to address their problems when they call the company's customer service hotline. Postpurchase evaluations are terrible, and even loyal PIE customers say that they are considering alternative shipping companies if this problem is not addressed.

PIE is also having trouble with its international operations. The company currently has operations in more than 100 countries. However, not all of these countries are profitable. Consumers from developing countries are often choosing low cost domestic postal carriers rather than PIE. The company is struggling to comply with the many different regulations in these different markets. There has been news of potential misconduct among PIE's joint venture partners. Recently, the company received news that was even more distressing. One of their top sales managers, Peter Hult, is suspected of bribing government officials in China, Russia, and Mexico. If true, this could subject the company to serious penalties. Because the company has operations in both the United States and the United Kingdom, these bribes could be seen as violations of the Foreign Corrupt Practices Act and the U.K. Bribery Act. Both these laws can impose serious penalties on businesses found guilty of bribery.

 Jennifer Sawayda assisted with the development of this exercise under the direction of O.C. Ferrell and Linda Ferrell. This role-play case is not intended to represent the managerial decisions of an actual company.

One suggestion that the vice president of marketing has for restoring relationships with customers is by increasing the company's presence on social media sites. Although the company has a Facebook account, the account is outdated and has minimal information. The company has otherwise invested little in digital media marketing. In the past, top managers did not seem concerned with digital media, but the VP of marketing is convinced that PIE is missing an opportunity for using these evolving channels to reach customers. As more people use social media, PIE managers are carefully considering ways to use this new marketing channel to their advantage. However, because social media changes so quickly, the company is unsure how to implement a digital marketing strategy.

An executive marketing committee has been formed to address issues related to declining sales. In general, customer relationships, including concerns about the effective use of social media in an international environment, are at the heart of the discussion. As with most discussions relating to operations, there are some concerns about the challenges of the legal and ethical issues across national boundaries. PIE hopes that this executive marketing committee can help prioritize issues and take appropriate steps. The committee includes Manager of Customer Relationship Management Casey Evans; Vice President of Marketing Robin Maignan; Vice President of Operations Loren Chanchey; Vice President of International Marketing Sidney Dolce; and Customer Service Manager Terry Nely. Their charge is to develop a plan for improving customer relationships, dealing with employee issues related to the payment of bribes, and developing ideas for a digital marketing strategy. The goal is to make recommendations for immediate action and a longer-term strategic approach toward improving marketing related to these areas of concern.

Casey Evans, Manager of Customer Relationship Management

You have been with PIE for the past 20 years. You started working in a customer contact center while you finished a college degree in management. After finishing your degree, you became a front-line manager and supervised operations in a transportation center. Next, you moved to two corporate headquarters working in human resources. After finishing your master of business administration on a part-time basis, you developed an interest in customer relationship management (CRM). You were invited to join this newly formed customer relationship management department. Last year, you were offered the newly established position of manager of customer relationship management.

Your department's job is to use information about customers to create marketing strategies to develop long-term customer relationships. You helped to spearhead a customer loyalty rewards program for businesses. The rewards program provides frequent business customers with discounts on the shipping of certain items. This was an extremely popular program among your business buyers. Your department works very closely with PIE's sales force and has become skilled at identifying the buying centers at businesses. Once the sales force has identified the group of people within a particular business that makes the buying decision, your department works hard to form relationships with them to ensure that their business needs are being met. For consumer customers, your company offers competitive rates for overseas packaging and shipping guarantees of one week for domestic shipping and two weeks for international. As a result, PIE has earned a name for itself for its speed of delivery.

You are shocked to hear about the customer service problems at your company. You are even more shocked at how quickly the news has spread. Apparently, dissatisfied customers posted about their experiences on blogs, Facebook, and Twitter. Someone even made a video blasting the company on YouTube. A few of these postings went viral, and now your company's reputation has been tarnished. You are set to meet with the executive committee tomorrow to discuss plans for managing and restoring relationships with customers.

Robin Maignan, Vice President of Marketing

You have been vice president of marketing for the past five years. During this time, you have noticed that sales have been increasing at a slower rate. You are faced with managing the numbers and driving revenue for PIE. Before joining PIE, you were the marketing manager for the European division of FedEx. In this position, you faced severe competition and had to work hard to make the numbers. As you have moved from positions as a middle manager and local manager, you have excelled at operational and tactical plans to achieve goals set by the CEO. You develop marketing strategies for PIE to become an industry benchmark for innovation and performance. Without new ideas, the company will become stagnant and lose market share. By being innovative, the marketing department can continue to put forth the best possible performance. You don't believe that it is possible to maintain performance without being entrepreneurial and allowing employees to be creative.

You are particularly concerned about the bribery allegations against the sales manager Peter Hult. While paying off government officials is clearly unethical in the United States and many nations in the Western world, in other cultures it is an expected business practice. You know that giving payments to officials in countries like China, Mexico, and Russia are expected in order to do business there. You feel that salespeople must be aggressive and persuasive or they will lose out to the competition. You also believe that businesses must adhere to a cultural relativist approach to remain competitive and accept the fact that morality differs from culture to culture.

You are concerned about changes in digital marketing and customer relationships. You would like to create a company blog to increase PIE's global presence. You also feel that a blog will enhance the company's customer service so it can be used to answer simple questions and free up the customer service representatives at the call center to spend more time on difficult issues. However, you also know that managing such a blog requires a serious time commitment that you don't have. You feel that investing in CRM technologies might help PIE to better identify specific customers, establish dialogues with them, and use this information to increase PIE's level of customer service. It is something you wish to discuss with the manager of customer relationship management and the customer service manager in the upcoming meeting.

Loren Chanchey, Vice President of Operations

As the vice president of operations, you're responsible for coordinating the efforts of PIE's global operations and focusing on the importance of staying competitive. This past year, when profits began to slow, the CEO expressed concern that operations needed to improve its performance, because the cost of basic commodities and supplies are increasing at a rapid rate. There is no room in your operations to slow down or fail to push employees to perform.

Last year, your spouse filed for divorce and called you a workaholic. Now, your career and loyalty to PIE is your main focus in life. Each month, you travel to different operational facilities to witness firsthand the efficiencies that are being achieved with new technology. You have all the processes in place and do not want to disrupt the system. You feel that employee misconduct and customer relationship issues are not your responsibilities. You are not happy at being at this meeting, because it is a threat to operational efficiency. In your position, you can't afford to compromise competitive advantages and performance objectives. You will be out of a job if you don't deliver operational excellence.

You are, however, interested in discussing digital technologies that can improve efficiency. Since more than one-fourth of the world's population has Internet access, you feel that this would be a great technology to use to reach customers in far off places and coordinate shipping and distribution. You are particularly interested in using social media as a way to help customers or businesses track their shipments. While you currently have such technology available through your website, you feel that using the popularity of social media for these purposes will provide PIE with an edge. You also hope that investing more in digital technologies and e-marketing will increase operational efficiencies and affordability.

You have been asked to voice both opportunities and risk areas related to operations. In your area, good employees are encouraged to be creative, and everyone seems to be willing to forgive stellar performers for minor issues of misconduct. You agree to try to identify some opportunities and risk areas in your department.

Sidney Dolce, Vice President of International Marketing

You joined PIE 10 years ago after leaving a position as vice president of international marketing with a trucking company. You enjoy evaluating projects to see if they will be profitable and deciding how to best develop favorable relationships with businesses and consumers in different countries. The industry is expanding but faces many challenges, such as how to reach customers in countries with less infrastructure and development.

You have found your career educational and rewarding but very stressful. Every night, you take long walks and mentally review the international issues that constantly arise, whether they be economic, regulatory, political, or sociocultural. For instance, you have been trying to reduce the costs for shipping packages in developing countries to compete with low-cost local competitors. You also work closely with the legal department to understand the relevant laws for each of the 100 countries in which PIE does business. You are used to a regulatory environment that provides rules for exact procedures to maintain compliance. In addition, you believe that, if you obey the law and follow the regulations, there should be no misconduct issues. You do not want to question the ethics of employees because you view that as their concern. Although you are very supportive of following the rules, you feel that some issues, such as bribery, are nearly impossible to get around in certain countries. Trying to maintain compliance while also following the provisions of the Foreign Corrupt Practices Act, the U.K. Bribery Act, and other regulations is a continual challenge.

Figuring out how to enter a country is a major challenge as well. In China and India, PIE has formed joint ventures, or partnerships with domestic firms, to enter the country. While these partnerships have been extremely beneficial, there has been talk about misconduct in the partners' firms. You worry that, if this is true, PIE could be held liable. As if these issues weren't enough, you are learning how to navigate different trade alliances, such as NAFTA and ASEAN, as these alliances affect operations in different countries with different regulations. For instance, member countries of these trade alliances are often able to forgo certain taxes, whereas PIE, as a foreign company, is not provided with these benefits.

You understand that it is your responsibility to contribute to this meeting by identifying international marketing risks in your area. You have created a list of international issues that you feel must be addressed immediately for PIE to maintain its global competitiveness.

Terry Nely, Customer Service Manager

You are a member of the seasoned management team. You started working at PIE in 2002, three weeks after finishing your undergraduate studies in customer service. Being a customer service manager at PIE has posed several challenges, including not having an equally weighted voice in important decisions. Although it is negligible to outsiders, several employees have noticed your lack of clout. You worked diligently to move up through the ranks to obtain your current position and have a mild resentment for those who consider you and your department as trivial. Nobody better understands the pool of employees than you.

Corporate culture is an important aspect at PIE, and the company's leaders have strived to make the job enjoyable. Creativity and risk-taking are both encouraged. PIE's mission statement even emphasizes the importance of "intrapreneurship" (an entrepreneurship-like attitude within the company's framework) and innovation to the company's success. PIE has been a leader in providing employee compensation and benefits. At the same time, you feel that your employees are overworked and undertrained. Essentially, your job in the consumer buying process is to ensure that the customer has a positive postpurchase evaluation. This means that your department must provide the highest in quality and service, including coordinating reimbursements for lost or damaged items and answering questions or complaints.

As a customer service manager, you tend to emphasize business market customer services more than consumer customer services. You know that businesses use PIE's shipping services much more frequently on a daily basis than individual consumers. Hence, you spend more time communicating with business customers than consumer customers when they call or e-mail. PIE has several contracts with large businesses that involve straight rebuy purchases, which occur when the business customer uses PIE's products routinely under approximately the same terms of sales. It is interesting to note that most complaints about the quality of PIE's customer services come from consumers, not businesses.

Rarely do consumer complaints deal with the service quality of the actual delivery, as PIE has become known for its speed. Most of the complaints that the customer service department receives involve damaged goods or missing packages. The number of complaints received does not appear to be any greater than any other shipping company, so you are disheartened to hear so many complaints about customer service. You feel that your representatives, many with only a high school diploma, get easily frustrated with customers. You recognize this job is not easy. For instance, despite a clear policy stating that PIE is not liable for any damages not reported within 30 days after delivery (or, in the case of lost packages, 30 days after the expected arrival), customer service representatives are constantly receiving calls from irate customers expecting to be reimbursed after the 30-day time period. You feel that perhaps if PIE had clearer policies in place alerting customers to the rules, as well as investing in better customer service training for representatives, then this situation could be avoided.

You have been asked to identify potential risk areas in the customer service area. Specifically, you are supposed to address the nature of customer complaints as well as how customer sales representatives respond to them.

NOTES

[1]Sarah E. Needleman, "Facebook 'Likes' Small Business," *The Wall Street Journal*, September 26, 2011, B11; Jefferson Graham, "Facebook wants to be big among small businesses," *USA Today*, September 16, 2011, 3B; Edward Lovett and Melinda Arons, "Facebook Is Friend to Jobless and Small Business, Says Company COO," *ABC News*, September 15, 2011, http://abcnews.go.com/Business/facebook-friend-jobless-small-business-creates-jobs-coo/story?id=14521237 (accessed November 8, 2011).

[2]Trefis Team, "Baidu Girds For Google Battle In China," *Forbes*, www.forbes.com/sites/greatspeculations/2011/12/07/baidu-girds-for-google-battle-in-china/ (accessed February 10, 2012).

[3]Piet Levy, "The State of Digital Marketing," *Marketing News*, March 15, 2010, 20–21.

[4]Mike Snider, "Study Details Digital Lives by Age, Sex and Race," *USA Today*, February 24, 2012, 4A.

[5]"Crunching the Numbers," *Inc.*, April 2011, 24.

[6]Ibid.

[7]Don Fletcher, "Gift Giving on Facebook Gets Real," *Time*, February 15, 2010, www.time.com/time/magazine/article/0,9171,1960260,00.html (accessed April 12, 2011).

[8]"17 Key Differences Between Social Media and Traditional Marketing," *Microgeist*, April 20, 2009, http://microgeist.com (accessed February 18, 2010).

[9]"2009 Digital Handbook," *Marketing News*, April 30, 2009, 13.

[10]"CafeMom," Highland Capital Partners, www.hcp.com/cafemom (accessed February 10, 2012); "Top 15 Most Popular Social Networking Sites," *eBiz*, February 2012, www.ebizmba.com/articles/social-networking-websites (accessed February 10, 2012).

[11]Pew Research Center, "53%—Social Networking Popular Worldwide, with Israel in the Lead," February 10, 2012, http://pewresearch.org/databank/dailynumber/?NumberID=1408 (accessed February 10, 2012).

[12]Pew Research Center, "53%—Social Networking Popular Worldwide, with Israel in the Lead," February 10, 2012, http://pewresearch.org/databank/dailynumber/?NumberID=1408 (accessed February 10, 2012).

[13]Sharon Gaudin, "Alcatel-Lucent Gets Social with Company Communication," *Computerworld*, July 15, 2010, www.computerworld.com/s/article/9179169/Alcatel_Lucent_gets_social_with_company_communication (accessed July 5, 2011); Alison Diana, "Yammer Beefs Up Executive Suite," *InformationWeek*, February 10, 2011, www.informationweek.com/news/software/productivity_ apps/229215134 (accessed July 5, 2011).

[14]Zachary Karabell, "To Tweet or Not to Tweet," *Time*, April 12, 2011, 24.

[15]"Facebook: Largest, Fastest Growing Social Network," *Tech Tree*, August 13, 2008, www.techtree.com/India/News/Facebook_Largest_Fastest_Growing_Social_Network/551-92134-643.html (accessed April 12, 2011).

[16]Courtney Rubin, "Internet Users Over Age 50 Flocking to Social Media," *Inc.*, August 30, 2010, www.inc.com/news/articles/2010/08/users-over-50-are-fastest-growing-social-media-demographic.html (accessed February 13, 2012).

[17]Bruce Horovitz, "AmEx Rewards Points Now Buy You Facebook Ads," *USA Today*, June 29, 2011, 1B.

[18]Cotton Delo, "New Belgium Toasts to Its Facebook Fans," *Advertising Age*, February 13, 2012, http://adage.com/article/news/belgium-toasts-facebook-fans/232681/ (accessed February 27, 2012).

[19]Jon Swartz, "Timberlake Could Revive Popularity of Myspace," *USA Today*, July 5, 2011, 5B.

[20]Myspace website, www.myspace.com/ (accessed April 11, 2011).

[21]"Justin Timberlake Debuts Myspace TV," *Rolling Stone*, January 10, 2012, www.rollingstone.com/music/news/justin-timberlake-debuts-myspace-tv-20120110 (accessed February 10, 2012).

[22]Elizabeth Holmes, "Tweeting Without Fear," *The Wall Street Journal*, December 9, 2011, B1.

[23]Bruce Horowitz, "Marketers Step Up Their Rewards for Twitter Buzz," *USA Today*, November 17, 2010, 2B.

[24]Zachary Karabell, "To Tweet or Not to Tweet," *TIME*, April 11, 2011, 24.

[25]Suzanne Vranica, "Tweeting to Sell Cars," *The Wall Street Journal*, November 15, 2010, B12.

[26]"As Twitter Grows and Evolves, More Manpower Is Needed," *Marketing News*, March 15, 2011, 13.

[27]"Social Media Summit," Harrisburg University, 2012, www.harrisburgu.edu/academics/professional/socialmedia/index-2012.php (accessed February 16, 2012).

[28]"Couldn't Stop the Spread of the Conversation in Reactions from Other Bloggers," from Hyejin Kim's May 4, 2007, blog post, "Korea: Bloggers and Donuts" on the blog *Global Voices*, http://groundswell.forrester.com/site1-16 (accessed April 12, 2011).

[29]"How Not to Handle Bad Reviews," *The Guardian*, www.guardian.co.uk/books/booksblog/2011/mar/30/jacqueline-howett-bad-review (accessed February 16, 2012).

[30]Randy Tinseth, "Randy's Journal," *Boeing*, http://boeingblogs.com/randy (accessed April 12, 2011).

[31]Drake Bennett, "Ten Years of Inaccuracy and Remarkable Detail: Wikipedia," *Bloomberg Businessweek*, January 10, 2011, 57–61.

[32]Charlene Li and Josh Bernoff, *Groundswell* (Boston: Harvard Business Press, 2008), 24.

[33]Ibid., 25–26.

[34]Nora Ganim Barnes and Justina Andonian, "The 2011 Fortune 500 and Social Media Adoption: Have America's Largest Companies Reached a Social Media Plateau?" University of Massachusetts, 2011, www.umassd.edu/cmr/studiesandresearch/2011fortune500/ (accessed February 16, 2012).

[35]"Keller Williams Reality Photostream," www.flickr.com/photos/kellerwilliamsrealty/ (accessed February 16, 2012).

[36]Bianca Male, "How to Promote Your Business on Flickr," *The Business Insider*, December 1, 2009, www.businessinsider.com/how-to-promote-your-business-on-flickr-2009-12?utm_source=feedburner&utm_medium=feed&utm_campaign=Feed%3A+businessinsider+(The+Business+Insider) (accessed April 12, 2011).

[37]"How to Market on Flickr," Small Business Search Marketing, www.smallbusinesssem.com/articles (accessed April 12, 2011).

[38]Emily Glazer, "Who Is Ray WJ? YouTube's Top Star," *The Wall Street Journal*, February 2, 2012, B1.

[39]Tom Foster, "The GoPro Army," *Inc.*, February 2012, 52–59.

[40]"2009 Digital Handbook," *Marketing News,* April 30, 2009, 14.

[41]"About Made Money," *CNBC,* www.cnbc.com/id/17283246/ (accessed February 28, 2012).

[42]"Dominos Pizza," Second Places, www.secondplaces.net/opencms/opencms/portfolio/caseStudies/caseStudy_dominospizza.html (accessed February 16, 2012).

[43]Brandy Shaul, "CityVille Celebrates the Golden Arches with Branded McDonald's Restaurant," Games.com, October 19, 2011, http://blog.games.com/2011/10/19/cityville-mcdonalds-restaurant.

[44]Emily Glazer, "Virtual Fairs Offer Real Jobs," *The Wall Street Journal*, October 31, 2011, B9.

[45]Aaron Smith, "Americans and Their Cell Phones," Pew Internet & American Life Project, August 15, 2011, http://pewinternet.org/Reports/2011/Cell-Phones.aspx (accessed February 28, 2012).

[46]Melissa Hoffman, "Mobile Marketing to Explode in 2012," *Direct Marketing News*, January 12, 2012, www.dmnews.com/mobile-marketing-to-explode-in-2012/article/222991/ (accessed February 28, 2012).

[47]Thomas Claburn, "Google Tells Businesses 'Fall In Love With Mobile'," *Information Week,* February 28, 2012, www.informationweek.com/news/mobility/business/232601587 (accessed February 28, 2012).

[48]"Brands Continue Limited Mobile Site Offerings," eMarketer, January 30, 2012, www.emarketer.com/Article.aspx?id=1008803&R=1008803 (accessed February 28, 2012).

[49]"Mobile Marketing Advertising Budgets Will Increase in 2012 Due to Smartphone Sales," PR Web, January 11, 2012, www.prweb.com/releases/2012/1/prweb9095950.htm (accessed February 28, 2012).

[50]Mark Milian, "Why Text Messages Are Limited to 160 Characters," *Los Angeles Times*, May 3, 2009, http://latimesblogs.latimes.com/technology/2009/05/invented-text-messaging.html (accessed February 28, 2012); "Eight Reasons Why Your Business Should Use SMS Marketing," Mobile Marketing Ratings, www.mobilemarketingratings.com/eight-reasons-sms-marketing.html (accessed February 28, 2012).

[51]Lauren Folino and Michelle V. Rafter, "How to Use Multimedia for Business Marketing," *Inc.,* January 25, 2010, www.inc.com/guides/multimedia-for-business-marketing.html (accessed February 28, 2012); "Motorola Powers House of Blues®," *PR Newswire,* www.prnewswire.com/news-releases/motorola-powers-house-of-bluesr-54990822.html (accessed February 28, 2012).

[52]Lauren Johnson, "Orville Redenbacher Promotes Healthy Snacks with Mobile Banner Ads," Mobile Marketer, October 26, 2011, www.mobilemarketer.com/cms/news/advertising/11321.html (accessed February 28, 2012).

[53]Nick Bilton, "Mobile Devices Account for a Growing Portion of Web Traffic," *The New York Times,* October 12, 2011, http://bits.blogs.nytimes.com/2011/10/12/mobile-accounts-for-7-percent-of-web-traffic-report-says/ (accessed February 28, 2012).

[54]Foursquare website, https://foursquare.com/ (accessed February 16, 2012).

[55]Anita Campbell, "What the Heck Is an App?" Small Business Trends, March 7, 2011, http://smallbiztrends.com/2011/03/what-is-an-app.html (accessed February 28, 2012).

[56]"Half of All Adult Cell Phone Owners Have Apps on Their Phones," Pew Internet and American Life Project, November 2, 2011, http://pewinternet.org/~/media/Files/Reports/2011/PIP_Apps-Update-2011.pdf (accessed February 28, 2012).

[57]Jefferson Graham, "Shopkick App Knocking on Doors of Local Retailers to Offer Deals," *USA Today*, June 22, 2011, 3B.

[58]Todd Wasserman, "5 Innovative Mobile Marketing Campaigns," Mashable, March 8, 2011, http://mashable.com/2011/03/08/mobile-marketing-campaigns/ (accessed February 13, 2012).

[59]Umika Pidaparthy, "Marketers Embracing QR Codes, for Better or Worse," *CNN Tech,* March 28, 2011, http://articles.cnn.com/2011-03-28/tech/qr.codes.marketing_1_qr-smartphone-users-symbian?_s=PM:TECH (accessed April 11, 2011).

[60]Ann Zimmerman, "Check Out the Future of Shopping," *The Wall Street Journal*, May 18, 2011, D1.

[61]Brad Stone and Olga Kharif, "Pay As You Go," *Bloomberg Businessweek,* July 18–July 24, 2011, 66–71.

[62]"Google Wallet," www.google.com/wallet/what-is-google-wallet.html (accessed February 16, 2012).

[63]Miriam Gottfried, "Mobile Banking Gets Riskier," *The Wall Street Journal*, July 10, 2011, B7.

[64]Vangie Beal, "All About Widgets," Webopedia™, August 31, 2010, www.webopedia.com/DidYouKnow/Internet/2007/widgets.asp (accessed February 28, 2012).

[65]Rachael King, "Building a Brand with Widgets," *Bloomberg Businessweek,* March 3, 2008, www.businessweek.com/technology/content/feb2008/tc20080303_000743.htm (accessed February 28, 2012).

[66]PR Newswire, "Barkley Develops Krispy Kreme® 'Hot Light' App and Widget," *The Wall Street Journal,* December 23, 2011, http://online.wsj.com/article/PR-CO-20111223-904499.html (accessed February 28, 2012).

[67]"17 Key Differences Between Social Media and Traditional Marketing."

[68]Li and Bernoff, *Groundswell,* 41.

[69]Ibid., 41–42.

[70]Scott, *The New Rules of Marketing and PR*, 195–196.

[71]"Forrester Unveils New Segment of Social Technographics - The Conversationalists," 360 Digital Connections, January 21, 2010, http://blog.360i.com/social-media/forrester-new-segment-social-technographics-conversationalists (accessed April 17, 2012).

[72]Li and Bernoff, *Groundswell,* 44.

[73]Ibid, 44–45.

[74]"Internet Usage Statistics," Internet World Stats, www.internetworldstats.com/stats.htm (accessed February 16, 2012).

[75]Paula Andruss, "Social Shopping," *Marketing News*, January 30, 2011, 22–23.

[76]Matthew Boyle and Douglas MacMillan, "Wal-Mart's Rocky Path From Bricks to Clicks," *Bloomberg Businessweek,* July 25–July 31, 2011, 31–33; "Free Shipping With Site to Store®," Walmart, www.walmart.com/cp/Site-to-Store/538452 (accessed February 10, 2012).

[77]Aaron Back, "China's Big Brands Tackle Web Sales," *The Wall Street Journal*, December 1, 2009, B2; "The Taobao Affair from China Largest Auction Website," PR Log, February 7, 2010, www.prlog.org/10552554-the-taobao-affair-from-china-largest-auction-website.html (accessed February 16, 2012).

[78]Shayndi Raice, "The Man Behind Facebook's Marketing," *The Wall Street Journal*, February 3, 2012, B7; "About Sponsored Stories," Facebook, www.facebook.com/help/?page=154500071282557 (accessed February 13, 2012).

[79]Larry D. Woddard, "Super Bowl Advertisers Heavy Up on the Social Media," *ABC News,* February 5, 2012, http://abcnews.go.com/Business/chevy-super-bowl-advertisers-big-social-media/story?id=15482527 (accessed February 16, 2012).

[80]"Who You Calling Copycat," *Bloomberg Businessweek,* September 26–October 2, 2011, 45–46.

[81]Bruce Horovitz, "Retailers Set up Shop on Facebook," *USA Today*, May 11, 2011, 1A.

[82]Stone and Kharif, 69.

[83]Larry Barrett, "Data Breach Costs Surge in 2009: Study," *eSecurity Planet,* January 26, 2010, www.esecurityplanet.com/features/article.php/3860811/article.htm (accessed April 12, 2011).

[84]Julia Angwin, Shayndi Raice, and Spencer E. Ante, "Facebook Retreats on Privacy," *The Wall Street Journal*, November 11, 2011, http://online.wsj.com/article/SB10001424052970204224604577030383745515166.html (accessed February 16, 2012).

[85]Julia Angwin, "U.S. Seeks Web Privacy 'Bill of Rights,'" *The Wall Street Journal*, December 17, 2010, A1–A2; Julia Angwin and Steve Stecklow, "'Scrapers' Dig Deep for Data on Web," *The Wall Street Journal*, October 12, 2010, A1, A18.

[86]Jon Swartz, "Facebook Changes Its Status in Washington," *USA Today*, January 13, 2011, 1B–2B; John W. Miller, "Yahoo Cookie Plan in Place," *The Wall Street Journal*, March 19, 2011, http://online.wsj.com/article/ SB10001424052748703512404576208700813815570.html (accessed July 5, 2011).

[87]Byron Acohido, "Net Do-Not-Track Option Kicks Off to Criticism," *USA Today*, August 30, 2011, 2B.

[88]"Friend Me On Faecbook," *Bloomberg Businessweek*, November 7–November 13, 2011, 36–37.

[89]Sarah Needleman, "Social-Media Con Game," *The Wall Street Journal*, October 12, 2009, http://online.wsj.com/article/SB10001424052748704471504574445502831219412.html (accessed April 12, 2011).

[90]Brett Molina, "Legit Megaupload Users Cut Off from Their Files," *The Wall Street Journal*, February 1, 2012, 3B.

[91]Derek Broes, "Why Should You Fear SOPA and PIPA?" *Forbes*, January 20, 2012, www.forbes.com/sites/derekbroes/2012/01/20/why-should-you-fear-sopa-and-pipa/ (accessed February 16, 2012); "SOPA And PIPA Bills: Online Companies Win Piracy Fight," *Huffington Post,* www.huffingtonpost.com/2012/01/21/sopa-and-pipa-bills-anti-piracy-legislation_n_1220817.html (accessed February 16, 2012).

[92]"2010 Global PC Software Theft Reaches Record 59 Billion," *BSA,* http://portal.bsa.org/globalpiracy2010/ (accessed February 16, 2012).

[93]Aubry R. Fowler III, Barry J. Babin, and May K. Este, "Burning for Fun or Money: Illicit Consumer Behavior in a Contemporary Context," presented at the Academy of Marketing Science Annual Conference, May 27, 2005, Tampa, FL.

[94]Kevin Shanahan and Mike Hyman, "Motivators and Enablers of SCOURing: A Study of Online Piracy in the US and UK," *Journal of Business Research,* 63 (2010): 1095–1102.

[95]"Postage - Postcards," iTunes Preview, http://itunes.apple.com/app/postage-postcards/id312231322?mt=8# (accessed March 14, 2012); "Welcome to Rogue Sheep," RogueSheep website, www.roguesheep.com/ (accessed March 14, 2012); Philip Michaels, "Macworld's 2009 App Gems Awards," *Macworld*, December 15, 2009, www.macworld.com/article/145088/2009/12/appgems_2009.html?lsrc=top_1 (accessed March 14, 2012); "Company," RogueSheep website, www.roguesheep.com/company (accessed April 22, 2010); Brier Dudley, "Rogue Sheep Wins Apple's Stamp of Approval," *The Seattle Times*, June 11, 2009, seattletimes.nwsource.com/html/brierdudley/2009325474_brier11.html (accessed March 14, 2012); "RogueSheep," Marketing Video Series, Cengage Learning.

[96]Michael S. Malone, "The Twitter Revolution," *The Wall Street Journal*, April 18, 2009, A11; "A Peach of an Opportunity," *The Economist,* January 30, 2010, 13–15; Stella & Dot Twitter page, http://twitter.com/#!/stelladot (accessed March 15, 2012); Ashton Kutcher Twitter page, http://twitter.com/#!/aplusk (accessed March 15, 2012); Kogi BBQ Twitter page, http://twitter.com/#!/kogibbq (accessed March 15, 2012); Jeff Mason and Steve Holland, "Obama Tweets for the First Time, Tweaks Republicans," *Reuters,* July 6, 2011, www.reuters.com/article/2011/07/06/us-obama-twitter-idUSTRE7652VO20110706 (accessed March 15, 2012); Michael A. Stelzner, *2011 Social Media Marketing Industry Report,* April 2011, www.socialmediaexaminer.com/SocialMediaMarketingReport2011.pdf (accessed March 15, 2012); "Promoted Promotions," Twitter Blog, October 4, 2010, http://blog.twitter.com/2010/10/promoted-promotions.html (accessed March 15, 2012); Brad Stone, "Twitter, the Startup That Wouldn't Die," *Bloomberg Businessweek,* March 1, 2012, www.businessweek.com/articles/2012-03-01/twitter-the-startup-that-wouldnt-die#p1 (accessed March 15, 2012); Sarah E. Needleman, "Twitter's Small-Business Big Shots," *The Wall Street Journal,* June 28, 2011, http://online.wsj.com/article/SB10001424052702304314404576414182020501492.html (accessed March 15, 2012); "Twitter Settles Charges that It Failed to Protect Consumers' Personal Information; Company Will Establish Independently Audited Information Security Program," Federal Trade Commission, June 24, 2010, www.ftc.gov/opa/2010/06/twitter.shtm (accessed March 15, 2012).

[97]Based on information in Wenguang Huang, "McDonald's China CEO on Bringing McMuffins to the Masses," *Fortune,* May 10, 2012, http://management.fortune.cnn.com; Rebecca Smithers, "McDonald's Pops-Up Its Biggest Ever Restaurant for Olympics," *Guardian* (U.K.), June 25, 2012, www.guardian.co.uk; Tiffany Hsu, "The Secret to a Camera-Ready Burger? McDonald's Tells All," *Los Angeles Times,* June 23, 2012, www.latimes.com; Brad Tuttle, "McDonald's Dollar Menu Shakeup," *Time,* March 8, 2012, www.time.com; Nicolette Fox, "McDonald's: Flush with Success,"

Guardian (UK), May 30, 2012, www.guardian.co.uk; Keith O'Brien, "How McDonald's Came Back Bigger than Ever," *The New York Times,* May 4, 2012, www.nytimes.com; Esther Fung, "McDonald's to Double Restaurants in China," *The Wall Street Journal,* March 29, 2010, www.wsj.com; Meg Marco, "McDonald's Rolls Out Breakfast Dollar Menu," *The Consumerist,* August 28, 2099, http://consumerist.com; Janet Adamy, "Steady Diet: As Burgers Boom in Russia, McDonald's Touts Discipline," *The Wall Street Journal,* October 16, 2007, A1; www.mcdonalds.com.

Feature Notes

[a]Liz Welch and David Karp, "The Way I Work: David Karp, Tumblr," *Inc.*, June 2011, 115–118; Spencer E. Ante, "Tumblr Valued At $800 Million," *The Wall Street Journal*, September 7, 2011, B3; "About Us," Tumblr, www.tumblr.com/about (accessed November 10, 2011).

[b]Nick Wingfield, "Virtual Products, Real Profits," *The Wall Street Journal*, September 9, 2011, A1, A11; Julie Jargon, "Wrigley Targets Web Gamers," *The Wall Street Journal*, August 23, 2011, B6; Douglas MacMillan, "Getting Social Media Games to Play Overseas," *Bloomberg Businessweek,* February 21, 2011, www.businessweek.com/magazine/content/11_10/b4218036715963.htm (accessed December 12, 2011).

[c]"Hitting the e-books," *Inc.*, September 2011, 36; Leon Kaye, "Will iPads Kindle a Massive Carbon Footprint," April 13, 2011, *The Guardian,* www.guardian.co.uk/sustainable-business/carbon-footprint-ipad-kindle (accessed December 8, 2011); Nancy Davis Kho, "E-readers or Print Books—which Is Greener?" *San Francisco Chronicle,* December 4, 2011, www.sfgate.com/cgi-bin/article.cgi?f=/c/a/2011/12/01/HOCR1M0J6B.DTL (accessed December 8, 2011); Nick Bilton, "Replacing a Pile of Textbooks With an iPad," *The New York Times,* August 23, 2010, http://bits.blogs.nytimes.com/2010/08/23/replacing-a-pile-of-textbook-with-an-ipad/ (accessed December 8, 2011).

[d]Tim Mullaney, "Distractions for Workers Add Up," *USA Today*, May 18, 2011, 1B; Anthony Balderrama, "Social Media at Work—Bane or Boon?" *CNN,* March 8, 2010, www.cnn.com/2010/LIVING/worklife/03/08/cb.social.media.banned/index.html (accessed November 22, 2011); Carlos Dominguez, "A Case for Social Media at Work," Cisco blog, November 16, 2011, http://blogs.cisco.com/news/a-case-for-social-media-at-work/ (accessed November 22, 2011).

part 5

Product Decisions

We are now prepared to analyze the decisions and activities associated with developing and maintaining effective marketing mixes. In Parts 5 through 8, we focus on the major components of the marketing mix: product, distribution, promotion, and price. PART 5 explores the product component of the marketing mix. CHAPTER 11 introduces basic concepts and relationships that must be understood to make effective product decisions. CHAPTER 12 analyzes a variety of dimensions regarding product management, including line extensions and product modification, new-product development, and product deletions. CHAPTER 13 explores the nature, importance, and characteristics of services. CHAPTER 14 discusses branding, packaging, and labeling.

chapter 11

Product Concepts

OBJECTIVES

1. To understand the concept of a product
2. To explain how to classify products
3. To examine the concepts of product item, product line, and product mix, and understand how they are connected
4. To understand the product life cycle and its impact on marketing strategies
5. To describe the product adoption process
6. To understand why some products fail and some succeed

MARKETING INSIGHTS

The Future Is Denim for Gap Inc.

Domestically, Gap Inc. clothing has reached the maturity level of the product life cycle, characterized by little or no growth. But Gap is not about to remain at this level without a fight. It intends to jump back into the growth stage. One way it will try and accomplish this is through international expansion. While Gap will close 189 underperforming American stores by 2013, it plans to open stores in Hong Kong to capture China's growing demand for quality clothing lines. It has also opened stores in South Africa and Australia. The company is working to create awareness and encourage product trial and adoption among global consumers.

However, Gap is also repositioning its clothing lines in the United States. Under the leadership of Chief Marketing Officer Seth Farbman, Gap is going back to its roots by focusing on denim as its core product. One of its most recent clothing lines, 1969 jeans, emphasizes its strong heritage in the American fashion industry (1969 was the year Gap was founded). Gap views the line as a premium product that it makes accessible with reasonable prices. Gap has also taken steps to make its jeans an experiential product. During one fashion launch, Gap partnered with taco trucks in Los Angeles to provide $1.69 tacos, along with a Gap coupon. According to Farbman, Gap clothing lines are not just functional but also emotional. Thus, while the core product might be jeans, consumers who purchase from Gap are also buying an experience.[1]

The product is a key variable in the marketing mix. Products, such as the 1969 jeans sold by Gap, are typically a firm's most important asset. If a company's products do not meet customers' desires and needs, the firm will fail, unless it is willing to make adjustments. Developing successful products and carrying out strategic moves requires highly sophisticated knowledge of fundamental marketing and product concepts.

In this chapter, we first define *product* and discuss how buyers view products. Next, we examine the concepts of product line and product mix. We then explore the stages of the product life cycle and the effect of each life cycle stage on marketing strategies. Then we outline the product adoption process. Finally, we discuss the factors that contribute to a product's failure or success.

WHAT IS A PRODUCT?

As defined in Chapter 1, a *product* is a good, a service, or an idea received in an exchange. It can be either tangible or intangible and includes functional, social, and psychological utilities or benefits. It also includes supporting services, such as installation, guarantees, product information, and promises of repair or maintenance. Thus, the four-year/50,000-mile warranty that covers most new automobiles is part of the product itself. A **good** is a tangible physical entity, such as an iPad or a Quiznos sandwich. A **service**, in contrast, is intangible; it is the result of the application of human and mechanical efforts to people or objects. Examples of services include a performance by Lady Gaga, an online travel agency booking, a medical examination, child day care, real estate services, and martial arts lessons (Chapter 13 provides a detailed discussion of services). An **idea** is a concept, philosophy, image, or issue. Ideas provide the psychological stimulation that aids in solving problems or adjusting to the environment. For example, MADD (Mothers Against Drunk Driving) promotes safe consumption of alcoholic beverages and stricter enforcement of laws against drunk driving.

good A tangible physical entity

service An intangible result of the application of human and mechanical efforts to people or objects

idea A concept, philosophy, image, or issue

It is helpful to think of a total product offering as having a combination of three interdependent elements: the core product itself, its supplemental features, and its symbolic or experiential value (Figure 11.1). Consider that some people buy new tires for their basic utility

What Is a Product?
A product can be an idea, a good, or service, such as this concert by One Direction in New York.

(e.g., Goodyear), whereas some look for safety (e.g., Michelin), and others buy on the basis of brand name or exemplary performance (e.g., Pirelli).

The core product consists of a product's fundamental utility or main benefit. For example, Chipotle's core product uses the finest sustainable ingredients. Its core product is therefore high-quality fast food.[2] The core product usually addresses a fundamental need of the consumer. When you buy bottled water, you can buy name brands like Dasani and Aquafina or more exclusive brands, such as Fiji, Voss, or Evian. Regardless of price, each alternative will quench your thirst. Retailers like Target and Walmart specialize in offering core products (store brands and generics) of a generally acceptable quality level at competitive prices. Hotels, such as Clarion and the Hampton Inn, specialize in providing quality services at affordable prices.

A product's supplemental features provide added value or attributes in addition to its core utility or benefit. Supplemental products can also provide installation, delivery, training, and financing. These supplemental attributes are not required to make the core product function effectively, but they help differentiate one product brand from another. For example, the Mercedes-Benz dealership in Manhattan is trying to set a model for its national dealerships by reinventing the showroom experience. Its showroom includes a coffee bar, designer furniture, flat-screen televisions, and a service bay that can be viewed from the sales floor. The picture and name of the technician working on the customer's car is displayed on the TV. The goal of Mercedes-Benz is to have the atmosphere of its dealerships reflect the luxury of its products.[3] These supplemental features add real value to the core product of car shopping and car repair.

Figure 11.1 The Total Product

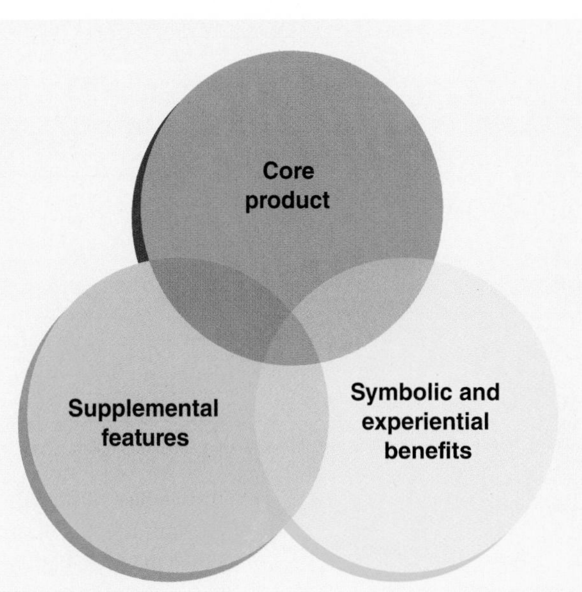

Luxury Products
When individuals buy Patek Philippe watches, they are buying the specialty status and symbols of success more than they're purchasing mere timepieces.

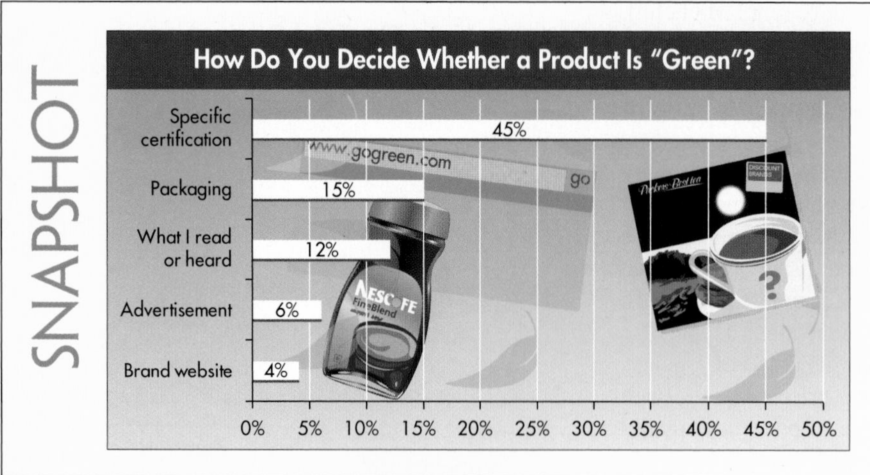

Source: 2011 ImagePower Green Brands survey of 1,200 people.

Finally, customers also receive benefits based on their experiences with the product. For some consumers, the simple act of shopping gives symbolic value and improves their attitudes. Some stores capitalize on this value by striving to create a special experience for customers. For instance, co-creation encourages the customer to participate in creating the purchase, service, or consumption event. This personalized experience can not only serve to increase customer satisfaction but can also make the development of the product more cost-effective.[4] Build-A-Bear creates such an experience for its customers. You can buy stuffed toys at many retailers, but at Build-A-Bear, you can choose the type of animal, stuff it yourself, give it a heart, and create a name complete with a birth certificate, as well as give the toy a bath and clothe and accessorize it. The atmosphere and décor of a retail store, the variety and depth of product choices, the customer support, and even the sounds and smells all contribute to the experiential element. When you check into a Hotel Monaco, not only do you get a great room with down comforters, bed toppers, and pillows, but you can also "check out" a fish as your companion during your stay. Many customers credit the Hotel Monaco with providing a differentiated, enjoyable stay and become loyal customers. In addition, Hotel Monacos offer complementary wine happy hours to allow guests to socialize in their lobby. These symbolic and experiential features are all part of the Hotel Monaco total product.

Thus, when buyers purchase a product, they are really buying the benefits and satisfaction they think the product will provide. A Rolex or Patek Philippe watch is purchased to make a statement of success, not just for telling time. Services in particular are purchased on the basis of expectations. Expectations, suggested by images, promises, and symbols, as well as processes and delivery, help consumers make judgments about tangible and intangible products. For example, some restaurants offer 10-15 minute lunch guarantees to assure customers that they are an efficient and quick place to dine. Products are formed by the activities and processes that help satisfy expectations. Starbucks did not invent the coffee shop, but it did make high-quality coffee beverages readily available around the world with standardized service and in stylish, comfortable stores. Starbucks has conducted extensive consumer research to develop a "consumer sensory preference map." The sensory map helps Starbucks understand the preferences of coffee-drinkers across the world.[5] Often, symbols and cues are used to make intangible products more tangible, or real, to the consumer. Allstate Insurance Company, for example, uses giant hands to symbolize security, strength, and friendliness, whereas Travelers Insurance uses an umbrella to signify protection.

CLASSIFYING PRODUCTS

Products fall into one of two general categories. Products that are purchased to satisfy personal and family needs are **consumer products**. Products bought to use in a firm's operations, to resell, or to make other products are **business products**. Consumers buy products to satisfy their personal wants, whereas business buyers seek to satisfy the goals of their organizations.

consumer products Products purchased to satisfy personal and family needs

business products Products bought to use in a firm's operations, to resell, or to make other products

The same item can be classified as both a consumer product and a business product. When a person buys a 100-watt light bulb for lighting a home closet, it is classified as a consumer product. However, when an organization purchases a 100-watt light bulb for lighting a reception area, it is considered a business product, because it is used in daily operations. Thus, the buyer's intent—or the ultimate use of the product—determines whether an item is classified as a consumer or business product. In addition, the sizes of business product purchases are often very large, as they are used to accommodate an office, manufacturing facility, or warehouse.

Product classifications are important, because classes of products are aimed at particular target markets; this targeting, in turn, affects distribution, promotion, and pricing decisions. Furthermore, appropriate marketing strategies vary among the classes of consumer and business products. In short, how a product is classified can affect the entire marketing mix. In this section, we examine the characteristics of consumer and business products and explore the marketing activities associated with some of these products.

Consumer Products

The most widely accepted approach to classifying consumer products is based on characteristics of consumer buying behavior. It divides products into four categories: convenience, shopping, specialty, and unsought products. However, not all buyers behave in the same way when purchasing a specific type of product. Thus, a single product can fit into several categories. To minimize this problem, marketers think in terms of how buyers *generally* behave when purchasing a specific item. In addition, they recognize that the "correct" classification can be determined only by considering a particular firm's intended target market. Examining the four traditional categories of consumer products can provide further insight.

Convenience Products

Convenience products are relatively inexpensive, frequently purchased items for which buyers exert only minimal purchasing effort. They range from bread, soft drinks, and chewing gum to gasoline and newspapers. The buyer spends little time planning the purchase or comparing available brands or sellers. Today, time has become one of our most precious assets, and many consumers therefore buy products at the closest location to preserve time for other activities. Even a buyer who prefers a specific brand will often willingly choose a substitute if the preferred brand is not readily available.

Classifying a product as a convenience product has several implications for a firm's marketing strategy. A convenience product is normally marketed through many retail outlets. Examples of typical outlets include 7-Eleven, Conoco gas stations, and Starbucks. Starbucks coffee is available in airports, hotels, and grocery stores, and many of the Starbucks company-owned stores now have drive-thru lanes to ensure that customers can get coffee whenever or wherever the desire strikes.[6] Because sellers experience high inventory turnover, per-unit gross margins can be relatively low. Producers of convenience products, such as Altoid mints, expect little promotional effort at the retail level and thus must provide it themselves with

convenience products Relatively inexpensive, frequently purchased items for which buyers exert minimal purchasing effort

Marketing Debate

The Authenticity of Stress-Relief Drinks

ISSUE: Do stress-relief drinks really work?

In a stressful world, demand for relaxation products is at an all-time high. Marketers of "stress-busting" drinks, such as Mini Chill, GEM, and Be Happy, are seizing upon this opportunity by touting the "anti-stress" qualities of their products. Stress-relief drinks consist of herbs or natural growth hormones that appear to help with sleep deprivation or anxiety. However, while some of the ingredients seem to have relaxation properties, nutritionists caution against trusting the products' marketing claims too much. Some ingredients found in certain drinks might be harmful if consumed excessively, such as the hormone melatonin found in stress-relief drinks like Dream Water. Because these drinks have not gone through extensive clinical trials, many nutritionists are also questioning whether they even work.[a]

advertising and sales promotion. Packaging is also an important element of the marketing mix for convenience products. The package may have to sell the product because many convenience items are available only on a self-service basis at the retail level.

Shopping Products

shopping products Items for which buyers are willing to expend considerable effort in planning and making purchases

Shopping products are items for which buyers are willing to expend considerable effort in planning and making the purchase. Buyers spend a lot of time comparing stores and brands with respect to prices, product features, qualities, services, and even warranties. Shoppers may compare products at a number of outlets, such as Best Buy, Amazon.com, Lowe's, or Home Depot. Appliances, bicycles, furniture, stereos, cameras, and shoes exemplify shopping products. These products are expected to last a fairly long time and, thus, are purchased less frequently than convenience items. Although shopping products are more expensive than convenience products, few buyers of shopping products are particularly brand loyal. As an example, most consumers are not brand loyal for home appliances and decorations. If they were, they would be unwilling to shop and compare among brands. Even when they are brand loyal, they may still spend considerable time comparing the features of different models of a brand. A consumer who is looking for a new LG washing machine may explore the company's website to compare the features of different washers before visiting a store and talking to a salesperson. Regardless of the number of brands of interest, buyers may also consult buying guides, such as *Consumer Reports*, or visit consumer information websites like www.epinions.com or the consumer review website www.yelp.com to view others' opinions or ratings of brands before they are ready to make an actual purchase.

To market a shopping product effectively, a marketer considers several key issues. Shopping products require fewer retail outlets than convenience products. Because shopping products are

Convenience Products vs. Shopping Products
M&M candies are an example of a convenience product, whereas people spend considerable time buying cameras, such as the Canon EOS, which are usually considered shopping products.

© AP Images

Comsumer Reports* and *ShopSmart
Consumers who spend considerable time researching product attributes and comparisons find *Consumer Reports* and *ShopSmart* very appealing.

purchased less frequently, inventory turnover is lower, and marketing channel members expect to receive higher gross margins. Although large sums of money may be required to advertise shopping products, an even larger percentage of resources are likely to be used for personal selling. The producer and the marketing channel members usually expect some cooperation from one another with respect to providing parts and repair services and performing promotional activities. In certain situations, both shopping products and convenience products may be marketed in the same location. Both Target and Walmart carry shopping products, such as televisions, computers, and cameras, as well as groceries and other convenience products.

specialty products Items with unique characteristics that buyers are willing to expend considerable effort to obtain

Specialty Products

Specialty products possess one or more unique characteristics, and generally buyers are willing to expend considerable effort to obtain them. Buyers actually plan the purchase of a specialty product; they know exactly what they want and will not accept a substitute. Examples of specialty products include a Mont Blanc pen and a one-of-a-kind piece of baseball memorabilia, such as a ball signed by Babe Ruth. When searching for specialty products, buyers do not compare alternatives; they are concerned primarily with finding an outlet that has the preselected product available. Racing fans interested in a high-status way to commemorate attending the Indy 500 doubtless found the specially designed Tag Heuer Indy 500 wristwatch very attractive.

The fact that an item is a specialty product can affect a firm's marketing efforts in several ways. Specialty products are often distributed through a limited number of retail outlets. Like shopping products, they are purchased infrequently, causing lower inventory turnover and thus requiring relatively high gross margins. However, just because specialty products are purchased less frequently does not necessarily make them less profitable. For example, the Swatch Group, the maker of a European line of wrist watches, sells significantly more limited edition "swatches" than traditional ones.

Courtesy of The Advertising Archives

Specialty Products
DeBeers has specialized in diamond jewelry for over 100 years.

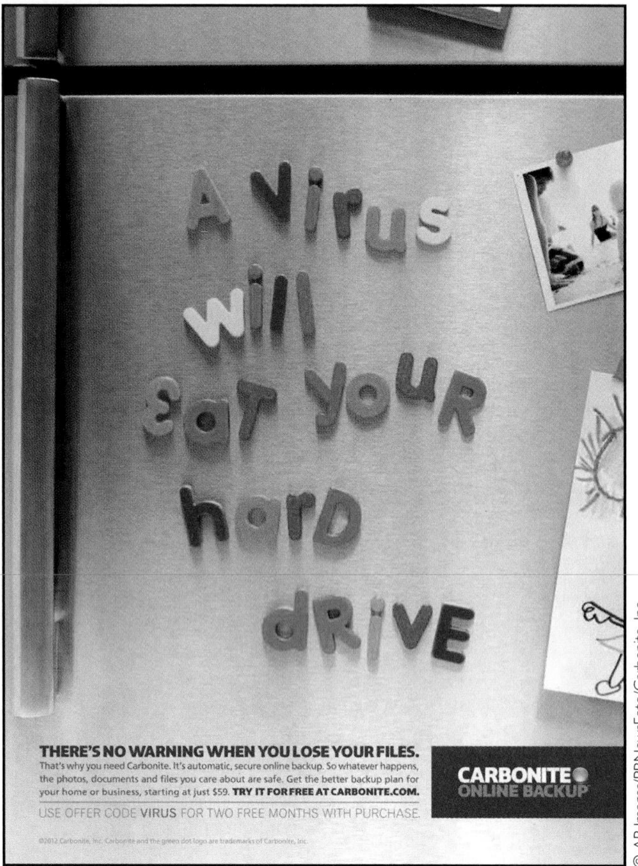

© AP Images/PRNewsFoto/Carbonite, Inc.

Unsought Products
Carbonite provides online security to prevent file and data loss. Unfamiliar information technology is sometimes not purchased, because there may be limited consciousness of the need until a breach of the system's security occurs.

Unsought Products

Unsought products are products purchased when a sudden problem must be solved, products of which customers are unaware, and products that people do not necessarily think of purchasing. Emergency medical services and automobile repairs are examples of products needed quickly to solve a problem. A consumer who is sick or injured has little time to plan to go to an emergency medical center or a hospital. Likewise, in the event of a broken fan belt on the highway, a consumer will likely seek out the nearest auto repair facility or call AAA to get back on the road as quickly as possible. Computer users must purchase antivirus and spyware detection software to protect their computers even though they may not want to make such purchases. In these cases, speed and problem resolution are far more important than price, in addition to other features buyers might consider if they had more time for decision making. Companies like ServiceMaster, which markets emergency services like disaster recovery and plumbing repair, are making the purchases of these unsought products more bearable by building trust with consumers through recognizable brands (ServiceMaster Clean and Rescue Rooter) and superior functional performance.

Business Products

Business products are usually purchased on the basis of an organization's goals and objectives. Generally, the functional aspects of the product are more important than the psychological rewards sometimes associated with consumer products. Business products can be classified into seven categories according to their characteristics and intended uses: installations, accessory equipment, raw materials, component parts, process materials, MRO supplies, and business services.

Installations

Installations include facilities, such as office buildings, factories, and warehouses, as well as major pieces of equipment that are nonportable, such as production lines and very large machines. Major equipment is normally used for production purposes. Some major equipment is custom made to perform specific functions for a particular organization; other items are standardized and perform similar tasks for many types of firms. Normally, installations are expensive and intended to be used for a considerable length of time. Because they are so expensive and typically involve a long-term investment of capital, purchase decisions are often made by high-level management. Marketers of installations frequently must provide a variety of services, including training, repairs, maintenance assistance, and even financial assistance.

unsought products Products purchased to solve a sudden problem, products of which customers are unaware, and products that people do not necessarily think of buying

installations Facilities and nonportable major equipment

accessory equipment Equipment that does not become part of the final physical product but is used in production or office activities

Accessory Equipment

Accessory equipment does not become a part of the final physical product but is used in production or office activities. Examples include file cabinets, fractional-horsepower motors, calculators, and tools. Compared with major equipment, accessory items are usually much cheaper, purchased routinely with less negotiation, and treated as expense items rather than capital items, because they are not expected to last as long. Accessory products are standardized

Going Green

What Makes a Green Product?

Is a chainsaw "green" when it runs on electricity instead of gasoline? What about cigarettes that use organic tobacco? This is a red-hot issue as sales of green products rise, and both marketers and consumers try to determine what makes a product green.

Consider what happened when Home Depot invited suppliers to nominate green products for its Eco Options promotional campaign. Of the 176,000 items carried in its stores, suppliers believed more than 60,000 to be worthy of the "green" designation. After screening the products using the Environmental Protection Agency's Energy Star designation, Home Depot allowed only 2,500 of them into the Eco Option program. Obviously, different stakeholders have differing opinions on what makes a product green.

Companies must also make tradeoffs when creating green products. Some of these tradeoffs are problematic. For instance, when SunChips introduced its bioplastic bag, the bag was so noisy that the company discontinued it. Compact fluorescent light bulbs save energy, but they also contain mercury that could harm consumers if they break. The truth of the matter is that all products have some effect on the environment. Rather than making a 100 percent green product, marketers could instead look for ways to increase sustainability throughout its operations to decrease its negative environmental impact.[b]

items that can be used in several aspects of a firm's operations. More outlets are required for distributing accessory equipment than for installations, but sellers do not have to provide the numerous services expected of installations marketers.

Raw Materials

Raw materials are the basic natural materials that are used in marketing a physical product. They include minerals, chemicals, agricultural products, and materials from forests and oceans. They are usually bought and sold according to grades and specifications, and in relatively large quantities. Corn, for example, is a raw material that is found in many different products, including food, beverages (as corn syrup), and even fuel (ethanol). Consider an unusual raw material—killer wasps. Bug Agentes Biológicos produces wasps to combat larvae and stink bugs that threaten sugarcane and soybean plants. The wasps are sprayed onto the fields via airplane just like a pesticide.[7]

Component Parts

Component parts become part of the physical product and are either finished items ready for assembly or products that need little processing before assembly. Although they become part of a larger product, component parts often can be easily identified and distinguished. Spark plugs, tires, clocks, brakes, and headlights are all component parts of an automobile. India-based Dynamatic Technologies is a company that specializes in component parts for a variety of companies. Its clients include Airbus, Ford, Honeywell, and Cummins.[8] These companies purchase such items according to their own specifications or industry standards. They expect the parts to be of specified quality and delivered on time so that production is not slowed or stopped. Producers that are primarily assemblers, such as most lawn mower and computer manufacturers, depend heavily on suppliers of component parts.

Process Materials

Process materials are used directly in the production of other products. Unlike component parts, however, process materials are not readily identifiable. A salad dressing manufacturer may include vinegar in its salad dressing; the vinegar is a process material, because it is

raw materials Basic natural materials that become part of a physical product

component parts Items that become part of the physical product and are either finished items ready for assembly or items that need little processing before assembly

process materials Materials that are used directly in the production of other products but are not readily identifiable

included in the salad dressing but is not identifiable. As with component parts, process materials are purchased according to industry standards or the purchaser's specifications.

Business Products
Accenture provides global management consulting, technology services, and outsourcing to businesses.

MRO Supplies

MRO supplies are maintenance, repair, and operating items that facilitate production and operations but do not become part of the finished product. Paper, pencils, oils, cleaning agents, and paints are in this category. Although you might be familiar with Tide, Downy, and Febreze as consumer products, to restaurants and hotels, they are MRO supplies required to wash dishes and launder sheets and towels. Selling MRO supplies can be a profitable business. Procter & Gamble is increasingly targeting business customers in the $3.6 billion market for janitorial and housekeeping products.[9] MRO supplies are commonly sold through numerous outlets and are purchased routinely. To ensure supplies are available when needed, buyers often deal with more than one seller.

Business Services

Business services are the intangible products that many organizations use in their operations. They include financial, legal, market research, information technology, and janitorial services. Firms must decide whether to provide their own services internally or obtain them from outside the organization. For example, E-Verify quickly confirms an employee's eligibility to work in the United States. Most firms cannot provide this service. This decision to purchase services depends on the costs associated with each alternative and how frequently the services are needed. As an example, IBM focuses on services that help companies with business processes and management systems and with integrating advanced technology into their operations.

PRODUCT LINE AND PRODUCT MIX

Marketers must understand the relationships among all the products of their organization to coordinate the marketing of the total group of products. The following concepts help describe the relationships among an organization's products.

A **product item** is a specific version of a product that can be designated as a distinct offering among an organization's products. An Abercrombie and Fitch polo shirt represents a product item. A **product line** is a group of closely related product items that are considered to be a unit because of marketing, technical, or end-use considerations. For example, Purina's Fancy Feast includes five different varieties of wet, dry, or kitten gourmet cat food in the same product line.[10]

The exact boundaries of a product line (although sometimes blurred) are usually indicated by the use of descriptive terms, such as "frozen dessert product line" or "shampoo product line." Specific product items in a product line, such as different dessert flavors or shampoos for oily and dry hair, usually reflect the desires of different target markets or the different needs of consumers. Thus, to develop the optimal product line, marketers must understand buyers' goals. Firms with high market share are likely to expand their product lines aggressively, as are marketers with relatively high prices or limited product lines.[11] This pattern can be seen in the personal computer industry, where companies are likely to expand their product lines when industry barriers are low or perceived market opportunities exist.

A **product mix** is the composite, or total, group of products that an organization makes available to customers. Procter & Gamble's product mix comprises all the health-care, beauty-care,

MRO supplies Maintenance, repair, and operating items that facilitate production and operations but do not become part of the finished product

business services Intangible products that many organizations use in their operations

product item A specific version of a product that can be designated as a distinct offering among a firm's products

product line A group of closely related product items viewed as a unit because of marketing, technical, or end-use considerations

product mix The composite, or total, group of products that an organization makes available to customers

Product Line vs. Product Mix
Burberry produces a line of coats and also maintains a diverse product mix, including watches, handbags, shoes, sunglasses, and other clothing items.

laundry and cleaning, food and beverage, paper, cosmetic, and fragrance products that the firm manufactures. The **width of product mix** is measured by the number of product lines a company offers. General Electric offers multiple product lines, including consumer products like housewares, health-care products like molecular imaging, and commercial engines for the military.[12] The **depth of product mix** is the average number of different products offered in each product line. Figure 11.2 shows the width and depth of a part of Procter & Gamble's product mix. Procter & Gamble is known for using distinctive branding, packaging, segmentation, and consumer advertising to promote individual items in its detergent product line. Tide,

width of product mix The number of product lines a company offers

depth of product mix The average number of different products offered in each product line

Figure 11.2 The Concepts of Product Mix Width and Depth Applied to U.S. Procter & Gamble Products

Laundry detergents	Toothpastes	Bar soaps	Deodorants	Shampoos	Tissue/Towel
Ivory Snow 1930	Gleem 1952	Ivory 1879	Old Spice 1948	Pantene 1947	Charmin 1928
Dreft 1933	Crest 1955	Camay 1926	Secret 1956	Head & Shoulders 1961	Puffs 1960
Tide 1946		Zest 1952	Sure 1972	Vidal Sassoon 1974	Bounty 1965
Cheer 1950		Safeguard 1963		Pert Plus 1979	
Bold 1965		Oil of Olay 1993		Ivory 1983	
Gain 1966				Infusium 23 1986	
Era 1972				Physique 2000	
Febreze Clean Wash 2000				Herbal Essence 2001	

Depth (vertical axis) — Width (horizontal axis)

Bold, Gain, Cheer, and Era—all Procter & Gamble detergents—share the same distribution channels and similar manufacturing facilities, but each is promoted as a distinctive product, adding depth to the product line.

PRODUCT LIFE CYCLES AND MARKETING STRATEGIES

Just as biological cycles progress from birth through growth and decline, so do product life cycles. As Figure 11.3 shows, a **product life cycle** has four major stages: introduction, growth, maturity, and decline. As a product moves through its life cycle, the strategies that relate to competition, promotion, distribution, pricing, and market information must be periodically evaluated and possibly changed. Astute marketing managers use the life-cycle concept to make sure the introduction, alteration, and termination of a product are timed and executed properly. By understanding the typical life-cycle pattern, marketers are better able to maintain profitable products and drop unprofitable ones.

Introduction

The **introduction stage** of the product life cycle begins at a product's first appearance in the market, when sales start at zero and profits are negative. Profits are below zero because initial revenues are low, and the company generally must cover large expenses for promotion and distribution. Notice in Figure 11.3 how sales should move upward from zero, and profits should also move upward from a position in which they are negative because of high expenses in developing new products.

product life cycle The progression of a product through four stages: introduction, growth, maturity, and decline

introduction stage The initial stage of a product's life cycle; its first appearance in the marketplace when sales start at zero and profits are negative

Developing and introducing a new product can mean an outlay of millions. Consider that the battery pack for the recently introduced Nissan Leaf cost the company $18,000 per pack. The Leaf is not expected to be profitable until its third year.[13] And although the importance of new products is significant, the risk of new-product failure is quite high, depending on the industry. For instance, many television manufacturers were disappointed to see the initially slow adoption rate of 3D televisions in North America. But a combination of forces, including an uncertain economy, the expense of 3D televisions and glasses, and consumers' reluctance

Figure 11.3 **The Four Stages of the Product Life Cycle**

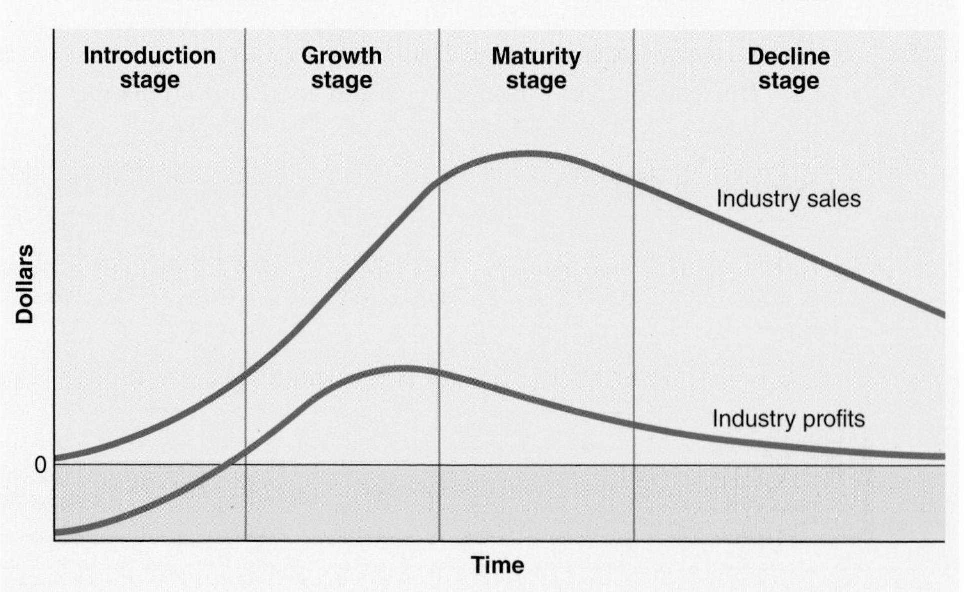

to change their television viewing habits, have made 3D television a risky investment for many consumers.[14]

Because of high risks and costs, few product introductions represent revolutionary inventions. More typically, product introductions involve a new variety of packaged convenience food, a new model of automobile, or a new fashion in clothing rather than a major product innovation. For instance, Kraft released its Philadelphia Cooking Cremes in 10-oz containers after discovering that consumers liked to use its cream cheese varieties in cooking. Its new product line comes in four different flavors of cream cheese.[15] The more market-oriented the firm, the more likely it will be to launch innovative, new-to-the-market products.[16]

Potential buyers must be made aware of the new product's features, uses, and advantages. Efforts to highlight a new product's value can create a foundation for building brand loyalty and customer relationships.[17] Two difficulties may arise at this point. First, sellers may lack the resources, technological knowledge, and marketing know-how to launch the product successfully. Firms without large budgets can still attract attention by giving away free samples, as Essence of Vali did with its aromatherapy products. Another small-budget tactic is to gain visibility through media appearances. Dave Dettman, a.k.a. Dr. Gadget, specializes in promoting new products on television news and talk programs. Companies like Sony, Disney, Warner Brothers, and others have hired Dr. Gadget to help with the introduction of new products.[18] Second, the initial product price may have to be high to recoup expensive marketing research or development costs. Given these difficulties, it is not surprising that many products never get beyond the introduction stage.

Most new products start off slowly and seldom generate enough sales to bring immediate profits. Less than 10 percent of new products succeed in the marketplace, and 90 percent of successes come from a handful of companies.[19] As buyers learn about the new product, marketers should be alert for product weaknesses and make corrections quickly to prevent the product's early demise. Marketing strategy should be designed to attract the segment that is most interested in the product and has the fewest objections. As the sales curve moves upward and the break-even point is reached, the growth stage begins.

Growth

During the **growth stage**, sales rise rapidly, profits reach a peak, and then they start to decline (see Figure 11.3). The growth stage is critical to a product's survival, because competitive reactions to the product's success during this period will affect the product's life expectancy. When Truvia, a natural sugar substitute, was introduced, demand rose quickly. Although Truvia is more expensive than other sugar substitutes, its popularity has prompted Coca-Cola, Pepsi, and Kraft to begin using Truvia in certain products.[20]

Profits begin to decline late in the growth stage as more competitors enter the market, driving prices down and creating the need for heavy promotional expenses. At this point, a typical marketing strategy encourages strong brand loyalty and competes with aggressive emulators of the product. During the growth stage, the organization tries to strengthen its market share and develop a competitive niche by emphasizing the product's benefits. As coconut water grows as a sports drink, marketers for the beverage are attempting to promote its benefits, such as its natural electrolytes, over those of traditional sports drinks.[21] Marketers should also analyze competing brands' product positions relative to their own brands and take corrective actions. Aggressive pricing, including price cuts, is also typical during this stage.

As sales increase, management must support the momentum by adjusting the marketing strategy. The goal is to establish and fortify the product's market position by encouraging brand loyalty. To achieve greater market penetration, segmentation may have to be used more intensely. This would require developing product variations—a deeper product mix—to satisfy the needs of people in several different market segments. Apple, for example, introduced more variations on its wildly popular iPod MP3 player, including the affordable iPod shuffle, the smaller iPod nano, and the iPod touch, all of which helped expand Apple's market penetration in the competitive MP3 player industry. On the other hand, Netflix adjusted its strategy and not only lost money and customers but also saw its profits and stock price sink.

growth stage The product life-cycle stage when sales rise rapidly, profits reach a peak, and then they start to decline

Cargill, Inc.

Growth
Truvia is a natural sweetener that is in the growth stage of the product life cycle.

When Netflix announced plans to separate its DVD-by-mail service into a separate company named Qwikster, consumers were outraged. They felt that having to navigate between two websites—the Internet-streaming Netflix site and the DVD-by-mail Qwikster—would be too complicated.[22]

Gaps in geographic market coverage should be filled during the growth period. As a product gains market acceptance, new distribution outlets usually become easier to obtain. Marketers sometimes move from an exclusive or a selective exposure to a more intensive network of dealers to achieve greater market penetration. Marketers must also make sure the physical distribution system is running efficiently so that customers' orders are processed accurately and delivered on time.

Promotion expenditures may be slightly lower than during the introductory stage but are still quite substantial. As sales increase, promotion costs should drop as a percentage of total sales. A falling ratio between promotion expenditures and sales should contribute significantly to increased profits. The advertising messages should stress brand benefits. Coupons and samples may be used to increase market share.

After recovering development costs, a business may be able to lower prices. As sales volume increases, efficiencies in production can result in lower costs. These savings may be passed on to buyers, as in the case of flat-screen televisions; when they were initially introduced, the price was $5,000 or more. As demand soared, manufacturers of both LCD and plasma technologies were able to take advantage of economies of scale to reduce production costs and lower prices to less than $1,000 within several years. If demand remains strong and there are few competitive threats, prices tend to remain stable. If price cuts are feasible, they can help a brand gain market share and discourage new competitors from entering the market.

Entrepreneurship in Marketing

Kickstarter Allows Entrepreneurs to Unleash Products

Entrepreneurs: Perry Chen, Yancey Strickler, and Charles Adler
Business: Kickstarter
Founded: 2009 | New York City, New York
Success: Since its launch, Kickstarter has raised over $75 million for creative projects and has a 44 percent success rate.

Got a project idea, but you can't find funding? Kickstarter might be the answer. Kickstarter is a Web platform that engages in "crowd-sourced financing." Entrepreneurs post their ideas on the site, and funders can choose whether to fund them. In return, funders either get a free item or a finished product at a steep discount. Since its launch, the site has featured 26,000 creative projects in fields like technology, design, music, and art. Kickstarter takes an all-or-nothing approach, so entrepreneurs must reach a certain financing goal on the website in order to receive any funding.

In an uncertain economic climate where funding is scarce, Kickstarter enables funders to find and choose projects and share in the financial risks. Entrepreneurs benefit not only from funding but also from feedback provided by consumers and investors. This feedback enables entrepreneurs to understand market needs and tailor their products accordingly, a significant component to product success. Thanks to Kickstarter, many of the products featured on its site have the chance to move quickly from the introduction to the growth stage.[c]

Maturity

During the **maturity stage**, the sales curve peaks and starts to decline and profits continue to fall (see Figure 11.3). This stage is characterized by intense competition, because many brands are now in the market. Competitors emphasize improvements and differences in their versions of the product. As a result, during the maturity stage, stronger companies tend to squeeze out their weaker competitors or consumers begin to lose interest in the product.

During the maturity phase, the producers who remain in the market are likely to change their promotional and distribution efforts. Advertising and dealer-oriented promotions are typical during this stage of the product life cycle. Marketers must also take into account that, as the product matures, buyers' knowledge of it reaches a high level. Consumers of the product are no longer inexperienced generalists; instead they are experienced specialists. Marketers of mature products sometimes expand distribution into global markets.

Often, the products have to be adapted to more precisely fit the differing needs of customers. For instance, after 40 years of the traditional single serve ketchup packet, Heinz determined that the packets were too frustrating to open, particularly for drivers eating in their cars. This was problematic as the company receives two-thirds of its fast-food revenue from drive-thru lanes. To solve this problem, Heinz introduced the larger "Dip and Squeeze" ketchup packet. These packets allow the consumer to either peel off a corner of the packet or squeeze out the ketchup.[23]

Because many products are in the maturity stage of their life cycles, marketers must know how to deal with these products and be prepared to adjust their marketing strategies. As Table 11.1 shows, there are many approaches to altering marketing strategies during the maturity stage. As noted in the table, to increase the sales of mature products, marketers may suggest new uses for them. Arm & Hammer, through refrigerator freshening and partnerships with toothpaste manufacturers, has boosted demand for its baking soda with this method, providing multiple uses for this product.

As customers become more experienced and knowledgeable about products during the maturity stage (particularly about business products), the benefits they seek may change as well, necessitating product modifications. Consider that traditional truck-based sport utility

maturity stage The stage of a product's life cycle when the sales curve peaks and starts to decline, and profits continue to fall

Table 11.1 Selected Approaches for Managing Products in the Maturity Stage

Approach	Examples
Develop new-product uses	Knox gelatin used as a plant food Arm & Hammer baking soda marketed as a refrigerator and cat litter deodorant as well as co-branded in toothpastes Frankincense oil used to eliminate skin age spots
Increase product usage among current users	Multiple packaging used for products in which a larger supply at the point of consumption actually increases consumption (such as for soft drinks with "The Cube" 24-pack package design)
Increase number of users	Global markets or small niches in domestic markets pursued
Add product features	Traditional SUVs slowly replaced by crossover vehicles Satellite radio and park-assist systems in automobiles
Change package sizes	Single-serving sizes introduced Travel-size packages of personal-care products introduced Concentrated versions of cleaning products in smaller packages
Increase product quality	Life of light bulbs increased Reliability and durability of U.S.-made automobiles increased
Change nonproduct marketing mix variables—promotion, price, distribution	Focus of Dr Pepper advertisements shifted from teenagers to people ages 18 to 54 A package of dishwasher detergent containing one-third more product offered for the same price Computer hardware marketed through mail-order outlets

vehicles, such as the Ford Explorer and GMC Tahoe, have reached maturity. Consumers seem more interested in "crossovers": car-based utility vehicles like the Chevrolet Equinox, Honda CR-V, Audi Q5, and Volvo XC60. Hybrid SUVs are also an option for consumers who like the horsepower of traditional SUVs. Automakers are responding to this interest with more models and features. With their improved ride, handling, and fuel economy, crossovers and hybrids are in a rapid sales growth stage at the expense of traditional SUVs.[24]

Three general objectives can be pursued during the maturity stage:

1. *Generate cash flow.* This is essential for recouping the initial investment and generating excess cash to support new products.
2. *Maintain share of market.* Companies with marginal market share must decide whether they have a reasonable chance to improve their position or whether they should drop out.
3. *Increase share of customer.* Whereas *market share* refers to the percentage of total customers a firm holds, *share of customer* relates to the percentage of each customer's needs that the firm is meeting. For example, many banks have added new services (brokerage, financial planning, auto leasing, etc.) to gain more of each customer's financial services business. Likewise, many supermarkets are seeking to increase share of customer by adding services, such as restaurants, movie rentals, banking, and dry cleaning, to provide one-stop shopping for their customers' household needs.[25]

During the maturity stage, marketers actively encourage dealers to support the product. Resellers may be offered promotional assistance in lowering their inventory costs. In general, marketers go to great lengths to serve resellers and provide incentives for selling their brands.

Maintaining market share during the maturity stage requires moderate, and sometimes large, promotion expenditures. Advertising messages focus on differentiating a brand from the field of competitors, and sales promotion efforts are aimed at both consumers and resellers.

A greater mixture of pricing strategies is used during the maturity stage. Strong price competition is likely and may ignite price wars. Firms also compete in ways other than price, such as through product quality or service. In addition, marketers develop price flexibility to differentiate offerings in product lines. Markdowns and price incentives are common. Prices may have to be increased, however, if distribution and production costs rise.

Even something as simple as packaging can be used to revitalize a product. For instance, Procter & Gamble, PepsiCo, and General Mills have begun resurrecting their old packaging designs for their products in the hopes that older, less cluttered designs will appeal to consumers' perceptions of "better times."[26]

Decline

During the **decline stage**, sales fall rapidly (refer to Figure 11.3). When this happens, the marketer considers pruning items from the product line to eliminate those that are no longer earning a profit. The marketer may also cut promotion efforts, eliminate marginal distributors, and finally plan to phase out the product. This can be seen in the decline in demand for most carbonated beverages, which has been continuing for several years as consumers turn away from higher-calorie soft drinks. Experts predict that soft-drink sales will continue to fall at least 1.5 percent each year for the next 5 to 10 years. This shift in consumer preferences is already changing the way companies produce and market bottled beverages, with companies expanding their offerings of juices, waters, and more healthful drink options.[27]

An organization can justify maintaining a product only as long as the product contributes to profits or enhances the overall effectiveness of a product mix. For instance, HP discontinued its TouchPad after a failed attempt to compete against the Apple iPad.[28]

In the decline stage, marketers must determine whether to eliminate the product or try to reposition it to extend its life. Usually, a declining product has lost its distinctiveness because similar competing or superior products have been introduced. Competition engenders increased substitution and brand switching as buyers become insensitive to minor product differences. For these reasons, marketers do little to change a product's style, design, or other attributes during its decline. New technology or social trends, product substitutes, or environmental

decline stage The stage of a product's life cycle when sales fall rapidly

Figure 11.4 Products at Different Stages of Life Cycle

Introduction	Growth	Maturity	Decline
• 3D televisions • Internet-streamed movies • Google Wallet	• DVRs • E-book readers • Tablet computers	• Flat-panel televisions • Internet movie rentals • Laptop computers	• Retail-store movie rentals • Gas SUVs • DVD players

considerations may also indicate that the time has come to delete the product. Consider the incandescent light bulb. As consumers switch to "greener" compact fluorescent bulbs and LED lighting—increasingly prompted by government bans on incandescent bulbs—manufacturers had to implement plans to phase the old bulbs out of their product mixes.

During a product's decline, outlets with strong sales volumes are maintained and unprofitable outlets are eliminated. An entire marketing channel may be eliminated if it does not contribute adequately to profits. An outlet that was not previously used, such as a factory outlet or Internet retailer, is sometimes used to liquidate remaining inventory of an obsolete product. As sales decline, the product becomes more inaccessible, but loyal buyers seek out resellers who still carry it.

Spending on promotion efforts is usually reduced considerably. Advertising of special offers may slow the rate of decline. Sales promotions, such as coupons and premiums, may temporarily recapture buyers' attention. As the product continues to decline, the marketing manager has two options during the decline stage: attempt to postpone the decline or accept its inevitability. Many firms lack the resources to renew a product's demand and are forced to consider harvesting or divesting the product or the strategic business unit (SBU). The *harvesting* approach employs a gradual reduction in marketing expenditures and a less resource-intensive marketing mix. A company adopting the *divesting* approach withdraws all marketing support from the declining product or SBU. It may continue to sell the product until losses are sustained, or it may arrange for another firm to acquire the product. For instance, GlaxoSmithKline divested its noncore over-the-counter medications to Prestige Brands Holdings Inc. so that it could focus on more profitable brands.[29]

Because most businesses have a product mix that consists of multiple products, a firm's destiny is rarely tied to one product. A composite of life-cycle patterns forms when various products in the mix are at different cycle stages: as one product is declining, other products are in the introduction, growth, or maturity stages. Marketers must deal with the dual problem of prolonging the lives of existing products and introducing new products to meet organizational sales goals. Figure 11.4 shows products at different stages of the product life cycle.

THE PRODUCT ADOPTION PROCESS

Acceptance of new products—especially new-to-the-world products—usually doesn't happen overnight. In fact, it can take a very long time. People are sometimes cautious or even skeptical about adopting new products, as indicated by some of the remarks quoted in Table 11.2. Consumers sometimes wait until the "second generation" of a new product to assure a more reliable product experience.

Customers who eventually accept a new product do so through an adoption process. Figure 11.5 details the product adoption process. The stages of the **product adoption process** are as follows:

product adoption process The five-stage process of buyer acceptance of a product: awareness, interest, evaluation, trial, and adoption

1. *Awareness.* The buyer becomes aware of the product.
2. *Interest.* The buyer seeks information and is receptive to learning about the product.

Table 11.2 Most New Ideas Have Their Skeptics

"I think there is a world market for maybe five computers." —Thomas Watson, chairman of IBM, 1943
"This 'telephone' has too many shortcomings to be seriously considered as a means of communication. The device is inherently of no value to us." —Western Union internal memo, 1876
"The wireless music box has no imaginable commercial value. Who would pay for a message sent to nobody in particular?" —David Sarnoff's associates in response to his urgings for investment in the radio in the 1920s
"The concept is interesting and well-formed, but in order to earn better than a 'C', the idea must be feasible." —A Yale University Management professor in response to Fred Smith's paper proposing reliable overnight delivery service (Smith went on to found Federal Express Corporation)
"Who the hell wants to hear actors talk?" —H. M. Warner, Warner Brothers, on the movie industry's future after silent films, 1927
"A cookie store is a bad idea. Besides, the market research reports say America likes crispy cookies, not soft and chewy cookies like you make." —Banker's response to Debbie Fields's idea of starting Mrs. Fields' Cookies
"We don't like their sound, and guitar music is on the way out." —Decca Recording Company rejecting the Beatles, 1962

3. *Evaluation*. The buyer considers the product's benefits and decides whether to try it, considering its value versus the competition.
4. *Trial*. The buyer examines, tests, or tries the product to determine if it meets his or her needs.
5. *Adoption*. The buyer purchases the product and can be expected to use it again whenever the need for this product arises.[30]

In the first stage, when individuals become aware that the product exists, they have little information about it and are not concerned about obtaining more. Consumers enter the interest stage when they are motivated to get information about the product's features, uses, advantages, disadvantages, price, or location. During the evaluation stage, individuals consider whether the product will satisfy certain criteria that are crucial to meeting their particular needs. In the trial stage, they use or experience the product for the first time, possibly by purchasing a small quantity, taking advantage of free samples, or borrowing the product from someone. Supermarkets, for instance, frequently offer special promotions to encourage consumers to taste new food products. During this stage, potential adopters determine the usefulness of the product under the specific conditions for which they need it.

Individuals move into the adoption stage by choosing a specific product when they need a product of that general type. However, entering the adoption process does not mean the person will eventually adopt the new product. Rejection may occur at any stage, including the adoption stage. Both product adoption and product rejection can be temporary or permanent. This

Figure 11.5 Product Adoption Process

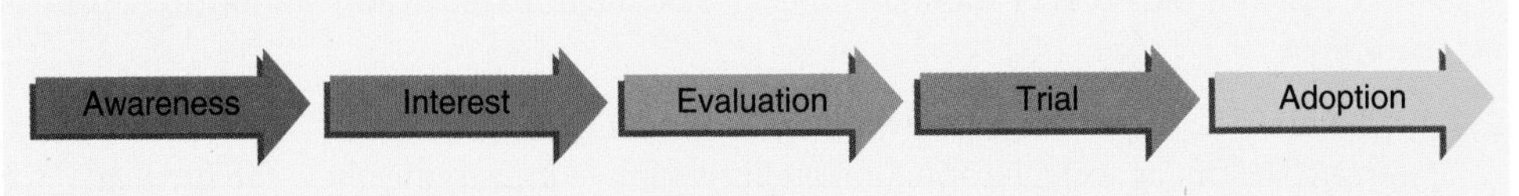

adoption model has several implications when launching a new product. First, the company must promote the product to create widespread awareness of its existence and its benefits. Samples or simulated trials should be arranged to help buyers make initial purchase decisions. At the same time, marketers should emphasize quality control and provide solid guarantees to reinforce buyer opinion during the evaluation stage. Finally, production and physical distribution must be linked to patterns of adoption and repeat purchases.

When an organization introduces a new product, people do not begin the adoption process at the same time, nor do they move through the process at the same speed. Of those who eventually adopt the product, some enter the adoption process rather quickly, whereas others start considerably later. For most products, there is also a group of nonadopters who never begin the process. For business marketers, success in managing production innovation, diffusion, and adoption requires great adaptability and significant effort in understanding customers.[31]

Depending on the length of time it takes them to adopt a new product, consumers fall into one of five major adopter categories: innovators, early adopters, early majority, late majority, and laggards.[32] **Innovators** are the first to adopt a new product; they enjoy trying new products and tend to be venturesome. **Early adopters** choose new products carefully and are viewed as "the people to check with" by those in the remaining adopter categories. People in the **early majority** adopt a new product just prior to the average person; they are deliberate and cautious in trying new products. Individuals in the **late majority** are quite skeptical of new products but eventually adopt them because of economic necessity or social pressure. **Laggards**, the last to adopt a new product, are oriented toward the past. They are suspicious of new products, and when they finally adopt the innovation, it may already have been replaced by a new product.

innovators First adopters of new products

early adopters People who adopt new products early, choose new products carefully, and are viewed as "the people to check with" by later adopters

early majority Individuals who adopt a new product just prior to the average person

late majority Skeptics who adopt new products when they feel it is necessary

laggards The last adopters, who distrust new products

WHY SOME PRODUCTS FAIL AND OTHERS SUCCEED

Thousands of new products are introduced annually, and many fail. Statistical bureaus, consulting firms, and trade publications estimate that one out of every three new products fails each year; others report an annual new-product failure rate as high as 80 to 90 percent. The annual cost of product failures to U.S. firms can reach $100 billion. Failure and success rates vary from organization to organization, but consumer products fail more often than business products in general.

Emerging Trends

Companies Reward Product Failures

At ad agency Grey New York, the "Heroic Failure" award isn't an insult but an honor. The agency is one of several companies who are changing their views toward failure after recognizing that high risks can lead to failures—or greater payouts. Indeed, with as many as 95 percent of new products failing annually, the best products are often accompanied by high failure rates. Unfortunately, many employees are taught to fear the consequences of failure. Although this may help companies avoid losses from failed products, it also stifles creativity. According to Segway inventor Dean Kamen, such fear creates a risk-averse culture with little innovation.

To avoid this outcome, companies have begun to reward employees for taking risks and trying new and innovative ideas. Some organizations even like failure because it allows employees to learn from mistakes. Research shows that businesses tend to learn more from failure then they do from success. The trick for encouraging a culture of innovation is for top management to openly acknowledge failure and stress its importance to the innovation process. For instance, the Consumer Electronics Association requires employees to openly admit their mistakes so the organization can learn from them. This trend of innovative risk-taking may be what businesses need to jumpstart new innovations.[d]

Many believe that the first business to release a revolutionary new product into the market will have the best chance of succeeding. The Apple iPad is a good example of such success. Launched in 2010, the iPad was a milestone in the tablet computer industry. When the iPad 2 was launched a year later, 70 percent of customers were first-time iPad buyers. The product quickly sold out. The third iteration of the iPad (the "new iPad") sold 3 million units a few days after its launch. The iPad may even be moving traditional PCs toward the decline stage; traditional computer makers have been seeing their PC sales decline in recent years.[33] However, being one of the first brands launched in a product category is no guarantee of success. Google was not the first search engine in the market, but it quickly assumed dominance after it was launched. Researchers now believe companies can profit just as much, and sometimes even more, by being fast followers and learning from the mistakes of first movers.[34]

Products fail for many reasons. One of the most common reasons is the company's failure to match product offerings to customer needs. When products do not offer value and lack the features customers want, they fail in the marketplace. At one time, Kodak held 90 percent of the camera film industry. In 2012, it declared bankruptcy after more than 100 years of business. Analysts believe Kodak's prime mistake was focusing on its core product (film) without being receptive to customers' changing needs. Kodak largely avoided digital technology because the technology would cannibalize its film business. This missed opportunity cost Kodak dearly once digital technology supplanted film.[35] Ineffective or inconsistent branding has also been blamed for product failures. Examples of products that failed because they didn't convey the right message or image include Gerber Singles (gourmet food for adults packaged in baby food jars), Microsoft's Bob (a "social interface" cartoon character that many users perceived as juvenile), and Gillette's For Oily Hair Only shampoo (whose name gave an unappealing mental image, because even though many people have oily hair, few are proud of it).[36] Other reasons cited for new-product failure include technical or design problems, poor timing, overestimation of market size, ineffective promotion, and insufficient distribution. Table 11.3 shows examples of recent product successes and failures.

When examining the problem of product failure, it is important to distinguish the degree of failure. Absolute failure occurs when an organization loses money on a new product because it is unable to recover development, production, and marketing costs. This product is usually deleted from the product mix. Relative product failure occurs when a product returns a profit but does not meet a company's profit or market share objectives. If a company repositions or improves a relative product failure, that product may become a successful member of the product line. On the other hand, some products experience relative product failure after years of success. Gramophone records, for example, were the main medium for music for most of the 20th century. However, they experienced relative product failure in the 1980s, when the

Table 11.3 Product Successes and Failures

Successes	Failures
Apple iPhone	R. J. Reynolds Premier smokeless cigarettes
Vita Coco	Ben-Gay Aspirin
Chevy Cruze	Heinz Salsa Ketchup
Red Bull	Qwikster–Netflix
Facebook	Arch Deluxe McDonald's hamburger
Tequila Avión	Dryel home dry cleaning kits by Procter & Gamble
Procter & Gamble Swiffer mop and dusting cloths	S. C. Johnson Allercare aerosol spray, carpet powder, and dust mite powder
Bluetooth earpieces by Jawbone	New Coke

Why Some Products Fail and Others Succeed
Cocaine energy drink is an example of a product that was poorly branded and poorly positioned relative to the target market.

record was supplanted by cassettes and compact discs. Despite its past popularity, the gramophone record is little more than an antique today.

In contrast to this gloomy picture of product failures, some new products are very successful. In order to compete against smoothie chains like Jamba Juice, McDonald's introduced its McCafe Real Fruit smoothies in 2010. Although many criticized the idea of a burger chain entering the smoothie market, McDonald's has experienced success in the beverage market. Beverages are estimated to account for approximately 25 percent of McDonalds' revenue.[37]

Perhaps the most important ingredient for success is the product's ability to provide a significant and perceivable benefit to a sizable number of customers. New products with an observable advantage over similar available products, such as more features, ease of operation, or improved technology, have a greater chance to succeed. Sometimes a product is simply in touch with consumers' feelings and taste. Consider the Whoopie Pie, a Maine product similar to the Moon Pie sold in the South. Critical to launching a product that will achieve market success is effective planning and management. Companies that follow a systematic, customer-focused plan for new-product development, such as Procter & Gamble and 3M, are well-positioned to launch successful products.

Summary

1. To understand the concept of a product

A product is a good, a service, or an idea received in an exchange. It can be either tangible or intangible; either way, it includes functional, social, and psychological utilities or benefits. When consumers purchase a product, they are buying the benefits and satisfaction they think the product will provide.

2. To explain how to classify products

Products can be classified on the basis of the buyer's intentions. Consumer products are those purchased to satisfy personal and family needs. Business products are purchased for use in a firm's operations, to resell, or to make other products. Consumer products can be subdivided into convenience, shopping, specialty, and unsought products. Business products can be classified as installations, accessory equipment, raw materials, component parts, process materials, MRO supplies, or business services.

3. To examine the concepts of product item, product line, and product mix, and understand how they are connected

A product item is a specific version of a product that can be designated as a distinct offering among an organization's products. A product line is a group of closely related product items that are viewed as a unit because of marketing, technical, or end-use considerations. The product mix is the composite, or total, group of products that an organization makes available to customers. The width of the product mix is measured by the number of product lines the company offers. The depth of the product mix is the average number of different products offered in each product line.

4. To understand the product life cycle and its impact on marketing strategies

The product life cycle describes how product items in an industry move through four stages: introduction, growth, maturity, and decline. The life-cycle concept is used to ensure that the introduction, alteration, and termination of a product are timed and executed properly. The sales curve is at zero at introduction, rises at an increasing rate during growth, peaks at maturity, and then declines. Profits peak toward the end of the growth stage of the product life cycle. The life expectancy of a product is based on buyers' wants, the availability of competing products, and other environmental conditions. Most businesses have a composite of life-cycle patterns for various products. It is important to manage existing products and develop new ones to keep the overall sales performance at a desired level.

5. To describe the product adoption process

When customers accept a new product, they usually do so through a five-stage adoption process. The first stage is awareness, when buyers become aware that a product exists. Interest, the second stage, occurs when buyers seek information about the product. In the third stage, evaluation, buyers consider the product's benefits and decide whether to try it. The fourth stage is trial, when buyers examine, test, or try the product to determine if it meets their needs. The last stage is adoption, when buyers actually purchase the product and use it whenever a need for this general type of product arises.

6. To understand why some products fail and some succeed

Of the thousands of new products introduced every year, many fail. Absolute failure occurs when an organization loses money on a new product. Absolute failures are usually removed from the product mix. Relative failure occurs when a product returns a profit but fails to meet a company's objectives. Reasons for product failure include failure to match product offerings to customer needs, poor timing, and ineffective or inconsistent branding. New products that succeed provide significant and observable benefits to customers. Products that have perceivable advantages over similar products also have a better chance to succeed. Effective marketing planning and product management are important factors in a new product's chances of success.

Go to www.cengagebrain.com for resources to help you master the content in this chapter as well as for materials that will expand your marketing knowledge!

Important Terms

good 360
service 360
idea 360
consumer products 362
business products 362
convenience products 363
shopping products 364
specialty products 365
unsought products 366
installations 366
accessory equipment 366
raw materials 367
component parts 367
process materials 367
MRO supplies 368
business services 368

product item 368
product line 368
product mix 368
width of product mix 369
depth of product mix 369
product life cycle 370
introduction stage 370
growth stage 371
maturity stage 373
decline stage 374
product adoption process 375
innovators 377
early adopters 377
early majority 377
late majority 377
laggards 377

Discussion and Review Questions

1. List the tangible and intangible attributes of a pair of Nike athletic shoes. Compare its benefits with those of an intangible product, such as hairstyling in a salon.
2. A product has been referred to as a "psychological bundle of satisfaction." Is this a good definition of a product? Why or why not?
3. Is a personal computer sold at a retail store a consumer product or a business product? Defend your answer.
4. How do convenience products and shopping products differ? What are the distinguishing characteristics of each type of product?
5. In the category of business products, how do component parts differ from process materials?
6. How does an organization's product mix relate to its development of a product line? When should an enterprise add depth to its product lines rather than width to its product mix?
7. How do industry profits change as a product moves through the four stages of its life cycle?
8. What is the relationship between the concepts of product mix and product life cycle?
9. What are the stages in the product adoption process, and how do they affect the commercialization phase?
10. What are the five major adopter categories describing the length of time required for a consumer to adopt a new product, and what are the characteristics of each?
11. In what ways does the marketing strategy for a mature product differ from the marketing strategy for a growth product?
12. What are the major reasons for new-product failure?

Application Questions

1. Choose a familiar clothing store. Describe its product mix, including its depth and width. Evaluate the mix and make suggestions to the owner.
2. Tabasco pepper sauce is a product that has entered the maturity stage of the product life cycle. Name products that would fit into each of the four stages: introduction, growth, maturity, and decline. Describe each product and explain why it fits into that stage.
3. Generally, buyers go through a product adoption process before becoming loyal customers. Describe your experience in adopting a product you now use consistently. Did you go through all the stages of the process?
4. Identify and describe a friend or family member who fits into each of the following adopter categories. How would you use this information if you were product manager for a fashion-oriented, medium-priced clothing retailer such as J.Crew or JCPenney?
   a. Innovator
   b. Early adopter
   c. Early majority
   d. Late majority
   e. Laggard
5. IMP It is helpful to think of a total product offering as having a combination of three interdependent elements: the core product itself, its supplemental features, and its symbolic or experiential value. For example, Southwest Airlines does not just offer safe passage to your destination (core product). It also offers two free checked bags (supplemental product offerings) and tries to create a fun environment to emphasize its culture of "luv" (experiential product offerings). Use the following matrix to list the core products, supplemental benefits, and experiential benefits for the four different companies listed.

	Core Products	Supplemental Benefits	Experiential Benefits
BMW			
Starbucks			
McDonald's			
Whole Foods			

Internet Exercise

Goodyear Tire & Rubber Company

In addition to providing information about the company's products, Goodyear's website helps consumers find the exact products they want and will even direct them to the nearest Goodyear retailer. Visit the Goodyear site at www.goodyear.com.

1. How does Goodyear use its website to communicate information about the quality of its tires?
2. How does Goodyear's website demonstrate product design and features?
3. Based on what you learned at the website, describe what Goodyear has done to position its tires.

developing your marketing plan

Identifying the needs of consumer groups and developing products that satisfy those needs are essential when creating a marketing strategy. Successful product development begins with a clear understanding of fundamental product concepts. The product concept is the basis on which many of the marketing plan decisions are made. When relating the information in this chapter to the development of your marketing plan, consider the following:

1. Using Figure 11.2 as a guide, create a matrix of the current product mix for your company.
2. Discuss how the profitability of your product will change as it moves through each of the phases of the product life cycle.
3. Create a brief profile of the type of consumer who is likely to represent each of the product adopter categories for your product.
4. Discuss the factors that could contribute to the failure of your product. How will you define product failure?

The information obtained from these questions should assist you in developing various aspects of your marketing plan found in the "Interactive Marketing Plan" exercise at www.cengagebrain.com.

video case 11.1

Artistry Meets Affordability with Blu Dot Furniture

The phrase "not cheap, but affordable," summarizes the pricing strategy of Blu Dot, a Minneapolis-based furniture maker. Blu Dot prides itself on selling artistically modern, high-quality furniture at prices that it feels are more affordable for consumers. Blu Dot's pricing decisions stem from the personal experiences of co-founders John Christakos, Maurice Blanks, and Charles Lazor. When furnishing their first apartments, the three men quickly realized that the furniture they wanted was beyond their price range. They saw a market need for quality furniture that was affordable. With a background in architecture and art, the men felt they could use innovation, simple manufacturing processes, and off-the-shelf materials to fill this need. In 1997, Blu Dot was started using $50,000 of the founders' savings.

Today, Blu Dot's products can be found in boutiques and independent retailers nationwide, with products available to order online as well. The founders of Blu Dot have designed their furniture using inspiration from the modernism art movement, which includes artists like Marcel Duchamp and Donald Judd. For consumer products, Blu Dot can be considered more of a shopping product than a specialty product. Blu Dot differentiates its products as quality and affordable furniture with more of a modern design appeal. In terms of its target market, Blu Dot sees consumers' desires for furniture as operating on a scale. On the one end of the scale are consumers who are looking for very basic, inexpensive furniture. On the other end are consumers who are looking for custom designed furniture and will spend great amounts to obtain it. Blu Dot targets those who are more in the middle: customers who do not want to spend large amounts on furniture but would like to have well-designed, artistic products.

Blu Dot also offers trade discounts to store buyers, interior designers, architects, exporters, and corporate gift buyers. This market represents the business products that are usually purchased due to the functional aspects of the product more than fashion or psychological involvement. Business products are considered accessory equipment that does not become a part of the final product and assists with office activities. By having different product lines, Blu Dot is able to market a closely related group of product items because of marketing, end-use considerations. The company sells several product lines—tables, storage, accessories, desks, beds, seating, and shelving. Blu Dot has been highly successful, with sales doubling in recent years and a sustained growth rate of 40 to 60 percent since 1996. By having both consumer products and business products, Blu Dot has managed to serve two distinct markets.

© bludot.com

However, the challenges Blu Dot encounters have not diminished with its success. Blu Dot still struggles with keeping affordability at the lower end of the spectrum and craftsmanship at the high end. When pricing products, the designers add up their fixed and variable costs plus the markup needed to allow the business to function. Creative pricing strategies are often employed to make the appropriate margins. For example, when selling a set of coffee tables, one table may have a higher markup while another one has a slightly lower markup in order to appeal to the price-conscious consumer and create profit.

Blu Dot recognizes that it has to think of the total product offering as having a combination of three interdependent elements: the core product itself, its supplemental features, and its symbolic or experiential value. While some customers focus on the artistic aspects of the product, other consumers are more concerned with value. Therefore, Blu Dot must synchronize its marketing mix to make product and price consistent.

The designers have also found ways to keep costs lower through innovative and efficient uses of materials, processes, and distribution methods. For instance, Blu Dot contracts with suppliers that make industrial products due to the more efficient technologies and processes used. Blu Dot furniture is designed to be able to ship easily, cutting down on distribution costs. Additionally, the designers use simple manufacturing processes and straightforward materials to create what they term "a by-product of the process." Blu Dot also ensures that its products can ship efficiently and are easy for its customers to put together. Add aesthetics into the equation, and the designers have significant challenges indeed.

Despite these difficulties, the designers thrive on their ability to blend manufacturing and art to create high-end furniture at more affordable prices than their competitors. For those with a flair for modern, affordable furnishings, Blu Dot offers a range of products to suit your artistic palate.[38]

Questions for Discussion

1. What are the different challenges for Blu Dot in selling consumer products versus business products?
2. Do you think that the product life cycle would be an important marketing concept in developing and managing Blu Dot products?
3. Describe the product mix and the importance of different product lines in Blu Dot's marketing strategy.

case 11.2

Wyndham Hotels Portfolio of Brands Satisfies Diverse Customer Needs

Wyndham Worldwide is a global provider of hotels and travel-related services. Its more than 7,200 franchised hotels include Wyndham Grand Collection, Days Inn, Howard Johnson, Wingate at Wyndham, Super 8, Ramada, and Planet Hollywood. While the core product, a place to stay, is virtually the same no matter the hotel, the supplemental and experiential benefits of its hotel chains differ. Wyndham has worked to ensure that each hotel chain maintains its own unique feel to appeal to the appropriate target market.

In many ways, Wyndham's wide range of hotels benefits the company by allowing it to target both budget-conscious consumers and vacationers willing to spend extra money for the resort experience. However, the company must always be careful to market these hotels consistently. For some time, people viewed Wyndham hotels as inconsistent in the quality of services and benefits. The Wyndham CEO believed that past marketing initiatives conflicted with one another to muddle the company's brand identity.

To rectify the problem, Wyndham redesigned some of its hotels and sought to create a solid identity for each hotel chain that would capture the feel of the chain's history and purpose. For instance, the Howard Johnson hotel chain's longer history prompted Wyndham to create an "iconic" atmosphere for these hotels that target leisure travelers and families. The experiential benefits of the Howard Johnson chain therefore include a family-friendly environment and the ability to stay in a classic hotel at a reasonable price.

On the other hand, Wyndham's more upscale hotel chains offer a completely different experience. Its Night Hotel in New York City claims to be "for the traveler who revels in all things after dark." The hotel tries to imbue a "sexy" feel with a chic eatery and bar as well as dark-colored furnishings. Wyndham's TRYP hotels are located in some of the world's biggest cities in Europe, South America, and North America. The hotels are designed to fit in with the local environment and, thus, range from modernistic to historical designs. The hotels are meant to be an extension of the city in which they are located, enabling visitors to experience the excitement of the city even before leaving the hotel's doors.

The hotel product is far from complete without the numerous supplemental benefits that accompany the core product. Travelers have their own expectations of supplemental items that hotels should offer, ranging from intangible items like friendly service to tangible products, such as ample towels and toiletries, pillows, and television. Hotels that do not meet these expectations tend to receive bad reviews and are often shunned by even budget-conscious families. Hotels that go above and beyond these expectations, however, manage to obtain an advantage over their competitors.

Wyndham offers a range of supplemental goods and services to its guests, from discounted hotel packages to large meeting rooms for company conferences. Many Wyndham hotel chains offer their own unique supplemental benefits as well. Wyndham Gardens offers library lounges for customer comfort, while the more economical Knight's Inn provides a free continental breakfast. Wyndham also provides a reward program for customers that frequently stay at Wyndham hotels. Customers who receive enough points for staying at Wyndham hotels can receive extra days for free. Another program, Wyndham's ByRequest, awards members with free Internet access, expedited check-in, and—after three nights—a snack and drink, extra items like pillows, and the option to have the room personalized to the customer's preferences. Wyndham also rewards female business travelers with its Women on Their Way program. The program's website offers advice and special packages for businesswomen planning their trips.

Wyndham's hotel chains are at different levels of the life cycle. Its Night and TRYP hotel chains, for example, are in the introductory and growth stages, while its Howard Johnson hotel chains are likely in the maturity phase. As a result, Wyndham is more likely to engage in heavy marketing to spread awareness of its newer brands. However, the company is not neglecting its more mature brands. It has worked hard to portray Howard Johnson as an iconic brand and continues to offer benefits packages to encourage families to stay at the chain. The company makes sure to adjust its marketing strategies to suit both the product's benefits and its stage in the product life cycle.

Wyndham has achieved great success in creating a successful product mix to meet the needs of different customers. The company's ability to adapt its marketing strategies to suit its various chains has provided it with unique advantages that make it a formidable competitor to rival hotel companies.[39]

Questions for Discussion

1. How is Wyndham using symbolic and experiential benefits to target its hotels to certain groups of travelers?
2. How is Wyndham using supplemental features at its hotels to create a competitive advantage?
3. How should Wyndham market its hotels according to their stages in the product life cycle?

NOTES

[1]Christine Birkner with Seth Farbman, "Back to Basics," *Marketing News,* November 30, 2011, 14–20; Kathy Chu, "Clothing Retailers in U.S. Open in China," *USA Today,* November 16, 2011, 7B; Shirley Brady, "Gap's New Global Brand Story: Denim, Design, Food Trucks and a Dog Named Louie," *BrandChannel,* August 1, 2011, www.brandchannel.com/home/post/Gap-Global-Branding-Campaign-Fall-2011.aspx (November 18, 2011).

[2]Danielle Sacks, "50 Most Innovative Companies: Chipotle," *Fast Company*, March 2012, 125–126.

[3]Chris Woodyard, "Showrooms Get More Showy," *USA Today,* September 8, 2011, 1B–2B.

[4]Anne L. Roggeveen, Michael Tsiros, and Dhruv Grewal, "Understanding the Co-Creation Effect: When Does Collaborating with Customers Provide a Lift to Service Recovery?" *Journal of the Academy of Marketing Science*, July 14, 2011, www.springerlink.com/content/u467183wx3550700/ (accessed April 23, 2012).

[5]Jon Gertner, "50 Most Innovative Companies," *Fast Company,* March 2012, 112–115, 148.

[6]"Company Profile," *Starbucks,* February 2010, www.starbucks.com/about-us/company-information (accessed April 14, 2011).

[7]David Lidsky, "50 Most Innovative Companies: Bug Agentes Biológicos," *Fast Company,* March 2012, 122.

[8]Peerzada Abrar and Radhika P. Nair, "Airbus Parts-Maker Dynamatic Acquires German Automotive Component Maker Eisenwerke Erla," *The Economic Times,* June 2, 2011, http://articles.economictimes.indiatimes.com/2011-06-02/news/29613018_1_automotive-business-new-acquisition-manufacturing (accessed January 18, 2012).

[9]"Janitorial and Housekeeping Cleaning Products: USA 2010: Market Analysis and Opportunities," The Kline Group, www.klinegroup.com/reports/brochures/x30i/factsheet.pdf (accessed January 18, 2012).

[10]Purina Fancy Feast, www.fancyfeast.com/all-products/ (accessed January 18, 2012).

[11]William P. Putsis Jr and Barry L. Bayus, "An Empirical Analysis of Firms' Product Line Decisions," *Journal of Marketing Research* (February 2001): 110–118.

[12]General Electric website, Products & Services, www.ge.com/products_services/index.html (accessed April 7, 2010).

[13]Eric Loveday, "WSJ: Nissan Leaf Profitable by Year Three; Battery Cost Closer to $18,000," *Auto Blog Green,* May 15, 2010, http://green.autoblog.com/2010/05/15/nissan-leaf-profitable-by-year-three-battery-cost-closer-to-18/ (accessed January 18, 2012).

[14]David Kender, "3D TV Not Ready for Prime Time," *USA Today,* September 7, 2011, www.usatoday.com/tech/products/story/2011-09-07/3D-TV-not-ready-for-prime-time/50296416/1 (accessed January 18, 2012); "The Difference Engine: Beyond HDTV," *The Economist,* July 28, 2011, www.economist.com/node/21524524 (accessed January 18, 2012).

[15]"Product Trends for 2011," *USA Today*, http://mediagallery.usatoday.com/Product-trends-for-2011/G1992 (accessed March 5, 2012).

[16]Brian A. Lukas and O. C. Ferrell, "The Effect of Market Orientation on Product Innovation," *Journal of the Academy of Marketing Science* (February 2000): 239–247.

[17]Michael D. Johnson, Andreas Herrmann, and Frank Huber, "Evolution of Loyalty Intentions," *Journal of Marketing* 70 (April 2006), via www.marketingpower.com.

[18]The Dettman Group, www.doctorgadget.com (accessed January 18, 2012).

[19]Narendra Rao, "The Keys to New Product Success (Part-1)—Collecting Unarticulated & Invisible Customer-Needs," *Product Management & Strategy,* June 19, 2007, http://productstrategy.wordpress.com/ (accessed April 1, 2010).

[20]Anne Marie Chaker, "Bracing for the Fake Sugar Rush," *The Wall Street Journal,* January 4, 2012, http://online.wsj.com/article/SB10001424052970203462304577138521022594412.html (accessed January 18, 2012).

[21]Dr. Mercola, "Help Your Heart: 71% of Those Who Drank This Lowered Their Blood Pressure," Mercola.com, November 27, 2011, http://articles.mercola.com/sites/articles/archive/2011/11/27/coconut-water-ultimate-rehydrator.aspx (accessed February 24, 2012).

[22]Stu Woo, "Under Fire, Netflix Rewinds DVD Plan," *The Wall Street Journal,* October 11, 2011, http://online.wsj.com/article/SB10001424052970203499704576622674082410578.html (accessed January 18, 2012).

[23]Sarah Nassauer, "Old Ketchup Packet Heads for Trash," *The Wall Street Journal*, September 9, 2011, B1–B2.

[24]Jonathan Welsh, "Two Crossovers Ahead of the Class," *The Wall Street Journal*, August 28, 2009, http://online.wsj.com/article/SB10001424052970203706604574378532004773694.html?KEYWORDS=crossovers (accessed April 14, 2011); "KBB Sees Strong Hybrid Growth in Used Market," Auto Remarketing, September 20, 2010, www.autoremarketing.com/content/trends/kbb-sees-strong-hybrid-growth-used-market (accessed January 19, 2012).

[25]O. C. Ferrell and Michael Hartline, *Marketing Strategy* (Mason, OH: South-Western, 2011), 221.

[26]Sarah Nassauer, "New! Improved! (and Very Old)," *The Wall Street Journal*, May 25, 2011, D1.

[27]Valerie Bauerlein, "U.S. Soda Sales Fell at Slower Rate Last Year," *The Wall Street Journal*, March 25, 2010, http://online.wsj.com/article/SB10001424052748704266504575141710213338560.html (accessed April 14, 2011); Jeremiah McWilliams, "Diet Coke Passes Pepsi as Soft Drinks Decline," *Atlanta-Constitution Journal*, March 17, 2011, www.ajc.com/business/diet-coke-passes-pepsi-875437.html (accessed January 19, 2012).

[28]Scott Martin, "HP's $99 Fire Sale on Discontinued TouchPad Sells Out," *USA Today,* August 22, 2011, www.usatoday.com/tech/products/story/2011-08-22/HPs-99-fire-sale-on-discontinued-TouchPad-sells-out/50097032/1 (accessed January 18, 2012).

[29]Jana Weigand, "GlaxoSmithKline Sells OTC Brands In US, Canada To Prestige Brands For GBP426M," *The Wall Street Journal,* http://online.wsj.com/article/BT-CO-20111220-705736.html (accessed January 18, 2012); "GlaxoSmithKline Announces Non-Core OTC Products to Be Divested," GlaxoSmithKline, April 14, 2011, www.gsk.com/media/pressreleases/2011/2011-pressrelease-402902.htm (accessed January 18, 2012).

[30]Adapted from Everett M. Rogers, *Diffusion of Innovations* (New York: Macmillan, 1962), 81–86.

[31]Arch G. Woodside and Wim Biemans, "Managing Relationships, Networks, and Complexity in Innovation, Diffusion, and Adoption Processes," *Business & Industrial Marketing* 20 (July 2005): 335–338.

[32]Ibid., 247–250.

[33]Aaron Ricadela and Dina Bass, "Apple iPad's 'Buzz Saw' Success Cuts PC Sales at HP, Dell," *Bloomberg,* May 18, 2011, www.bloomberg.com/news/2011-05-18/apple-ipad-s-buzz-saw-success-cuts-into-pc-sales-at-hp-dell.html (accessed January 18, 2012); Philip Elmer-DeWitt, "Piper Jaffray: iPad 2 Totally Sold Out, 70% to New Buyers," *CNNMoney,* March 13, 2011, http://tech.fortune.cnn.com/2011/03/13/piper-jaffray-ipad-2-totally-sold-out-70-to-new-buyers/ (accessed January 18, 2012); Brett Molina, "Apple Sells 3 Million New iPads," *USA Today,* March 19, 2012, http://content.usatoday.com/communities/technologylive/post/2012/03/apple-confirms-record-weekend-for-ipad/1 (accessed March 30, 2012).

[34]"Steve Blank: Here's Why The First-Mover Advantage Is Extremely Overrated," *Business Insider,* October 19, 2010, http://articles.businessinsider.com/2010-10-19/tech/30027432_1_market-bad-idea-failure-rate (accessed January 19, 2012).

[35]Avi Dan, "Kodak Failed By Asking The Wrong Marketing Question," *Forbes,* January 23, 2012, www.forbes.com/sites/avidan/2012/01/23/kodak-failed-by-asking-the-wrong-marketing-question/ (accessed February 24, 2012).

[36]Susan Casey, "Object-Oriented: Everything I Ever Needed to Know About Business I Learned in the Frozen Food Aisle," *Business 2.0,* October 2000.

[37]Dan Macsai, "Jamba Juice to McDonald's: You Selling Smoothies is Just as Crazy as Us Blending Cheeseburgers," *Fast Company,* July 30, 2010, www.fastcompany.com/1676088/jamba-juice-to-mcdonalds-you-selling-smoothies-is-just-as-crazy-as-us-blending-cheeseburgers (accessed January 18, 2012); Associated Press, "McDonald's Adds New Smoothie to Roster," Boston.com, June 27, 2011, http://articles.boston.com/2011-06-27/business/29709429_1_smoothie-banana-mango-pineapple (accessed January 18, 2012).

[38]John Christakos, "American Furniture." Blu Dot website, www.bludot.com/blu_dot_info/in_print/american_furniture (accessed April 21, 2010); "The Blu Dot Story," Blu Dot website, www.bludot.com/blu_dot_info/the_blu_dot_story (accessed April 21, 2010); "Trade," Blu Dot website, www.bludot.com/blu_dot_info/trade (accessed April 21, 2010); "[Stuff]," Blu Dot website, originally published in *Minnesota Monthly*, www.bludot.com/blu_dot_info/in_print/minnesota_monthly (accessed April 21, 2010); Carl Alviani, "Taking the Middle Ground: Massive Design for the Masses?" *Core77*, www.core77.com/reactor/07.05_mIddleground.asp (accessed April 21, 2010); "Blu Dot," Marketing Video Series, Cengage Learning.

[39]"At a Glance," Wyndham Worldwide, www.wyndhamworldwide.com/about/at_a_glance.cfm (accessed May 18, 2011); "Wyndham Hotels and Resorts," Wyndham Hotel Group, http://hotelfranchise.wyndhamworldwide.com/international/wyndham_hotels_resorts/ (accessed May 18, 2011); Roger Yu, "New Spinoff Wyndham Hopes to Re-Establish Hotels with Fresh Look," *USA Today*, August 2, 2006, www.usatoday.com/money/biztravel/2006-08-01-wyndham-usat_x.htm (accessed May 19, 2011); Roger Yu, "Travel Q&A: Wyndham CEO Eric Danziger," *USA Today,* January 29, 2009, www.usatoday.com/travel/hotels/2009-01-29-qa-eric-danzinger_N.htm (accessed May 19, 2011); "Corporate Information," Wyndham, www.wyndham.com/corporate/franchise/main.wnt (accessed May 26, 2011); "Wyndham Rewards® With ByRequest®," Wyndham, www.wyndham.com/servlet/rewards_benefits.wnt? (accessed June 14, 2011); "Finally, A Program That Rewards You," Wyndham Rewards, www.wyndhamrewards.com/trec/consumer/aboutWR.action?variant (accessed June 14, 2011); "About Women on Their Way," Women On Their Way by Wyndham Worldwide, www.womenontheirway.com/about/ (accessed June 14, 2011); "Howard Johnson," Wyndham Hotel Group, http://hotelfranchise.wyndhamworldwide.com/portfolio/howard_johnson/ (accessed March 20, 2012); Night Hotel New York main page, www.nighthotelny.com/index.html (accessed March 20, 2012); TYRP by Wyndham main page, www.tryphotels.com/en/index.html (accessed March 20, 2012); "Wyndham Garden," Wyndham Worldwide, http://wynres.wyndham.com/Wyndham/control/wyndhamgarden?variant (accessed March 20, 2012).

Feature Notes

[a]Bruce Horovitz, "Stress-Busting Drinks Taking Off," *USA Today*, May 16, 2011, 1A; Laura Johannes, "Drinks Intended to Calm You," *The Wall Street Journal*, March 30, 2010, http://online.wsj.com/article/SB10001424052702304370304575151990923047492.html (accessed November 22, 2011).

[b]Paul Keegan, "The Trouble with Green Ratings," *CNNMoney*, July 13, 2011, http://money.cnn.com/2011/07/12/technology/problem_green_ratings.fortune/index.htm (accessed November 15, 2011); Matthew McDermott, "Is Noise Really Why SunChips Should Ditch Bioplastic Packaging," *Treehugger*, October 5, 2010, www.treehugger.com/corporate-responsibility/is-noise-really-why-sunchips-should-ditch-bioplastic-packaging.html (accessed November 15, 2011); Bruce Geiselman, "Aisle 7 for Eco Options," *Waste News*, April 30, 2007, 35; Home Depot, www.homedepot.com; "Home Depot Hammers Out Eco Options ID Program," *Brandweek*, April 23, 2007, 5; Clifford Krauss, "Can They Really Call the Chainsaw Eco-Friendly?" *The New York Times*, June 25, 2007, A1.

[c]Steven Kurutz, "On Kickstarter, Designers' Dreams Materialize," *The New York Times*, September 21, 2011, www.nytimes.com/2011/09/22/garden/on-kickstarter-designers-dreams-materialize.html?pagewanted=all (accessed December 7, 2011); Jenna Wortham, "A Few Dollars at a Time, Patrons Support Artists on the Web," *The New York Times*, August 24, 2009, www.nytimes.com/2009/08/25/technology/start-ups/25kick.html?_r=1&em (accessed December 7, 2011); Brittany Shammas, "Funding Sites Match Entrepreneurs, Contributors," Indy.com, August 6, 2011, www.indy.com/posts/funding-sites-match-entrepreneurs-contributors-2 (accessed December 7, 2011); "What Is Kickstarter?!" Kickstarter, www.kickstarter.com/ (accessed December 7, 2011).

[d]Sue Shellenbarger, "Better Ideas Through Failure," *The Wall Street Journal*, September 27, 2011, D1, D4; Laurie Burkitt and Ken Bruno, "New, Improved…and Failed," *Forbes*, March 24, 2010, www.msnbc.msn.com/id/36005036/ns/business-forbes_com/t/new-improved-failed/ (accessed November 10, 2011); Jason Koebler, "Segway Inventor: Fear of Failure Kills U.S. Innovation," *U.S. News*, November 2, 2011, www.usnews.com/news/blogs/stem-education/2011/11/02/segway-inventor-fear-of-failure-kills-us-innovation (accessed November 10, 2011); "Organizations Learn More from Failure Than Success, Study Finds; Knowledge Gained from Failure Lasts Longer," *ScienceDaily*, August 23, 2010, www.sciencedaily.com/releases/2010/08/100823162322.htm (accessed November 10, 2011).

chapter 12

Developing and Managing Products

OBJECTIVES

1. To understand how companies manage existing products through line extensions and product modifications
2. To describe how businesses develop a product idea into a commercial product
3. To understand the importance of product differentiation and the elements that differentiate one product from another
4. To understand how businesses position their products
5. To examine how product deletion is used to improve product mixes
6. To describe organizational structures used for managing products

MARKETING INSIGHTS

GM Modifies Products to Rebound

General Motors is becoming a rebound success story. After declaring bankruptcy in 2008 and receiving a $50 billion government bailout, GM has reduced its debt and has created more profitable and efficient operations. Despite its comeback, however, GM faces a number of challenges from competitors, changing customer tastes, and government regulations. For GM to continue to prosper, it must innovate and adapt its products regularly. The company also must do so in a shorter time frame—GM's CEO announced plans to reduce the time period for new-product development while decreasing costs.

GM has already made significant changes to its product line. It eliminated half its brands, including Pontiac, Saturn, Saab, and Hummer. It also deleted several of its "gas-guzzler" SUVs that lost the company money before the recession. These product changes have allowed GM to focus more on improving its existing brands. GM brands are undergoing quality, functional, and aesthetic modifications to meet government regulations and create a positive consumer perception.

Perhaps the company's biggest challenge is creating vehicles that will meet new government mileage requirements. By 2025, all vehicles must be able to reach 54.5 miles per gallon. As a result, GM is making functional and quality modifications by using lighter materials, new energy-conserving technology, and a "global core architecture" in which products have a universal design but are adapted slightly for different markets. GM is also attempting to reposition its Buick brand as a luxury car with an aesthetically-pleasing design. GM's ability to successfully adapt its products will determine whether it will maintain its status as the world's largest automaker.[1]

To compete effectively and achieve their goals, organizations must be able to adjust their products' features in response to changes in customers' needs. To provide products that satisfy target markets and achieve the firm's objectives, a marketer must develop, alter, and maintain an effective product mix. An organization's product mix may require adjustment for a variety of reasons. Because customers' attitudes and product preferences change over time, their desire for certain products may wane. Coca-Cola, for example, has seen sales of its traditional carbonated beverages decline as consumers become more health-conscious. As a result, the company has released 12.5-ounce and 16-ounce bottles as well as "mini" 7.5-ounce cans. Consumers can choose these smaller options over the traditional 20-ounce or 2-liter bottles and the 12-ounce cans.[2] Coke also introduced healthier beverages like NESTEA Red Tea Pomegranate Passion Fruit (red tea is a touted source of antioxidants) and Odwalla Reduced Calorie Quenchers (sweetened with TRUVIA and organic evaporated cane juice).

In some cases, a company needs to alter its product mix for competitive reasons. A marketer may have to delete a product from the mix because a competitor dominates the market for that product. Similarly, a firm may have to introduce a new product or modify an existing one to compete more effectively. A marketer may expand the firm's product mix to take advantage of excess marketing and production capacity.

In this chapter, we examine several ways to improve an organization's product mix. First, we discuss managing existing products through effective line extension and product modification. Next, we examine the stages of new-product development, including idea generation, screening, concept testing, business analysis, product development, test marketing, and commercialization. Then we look at how companies differentiate their products in the marketplace through quality, design, and support services. Next, we examine the importance of deleting weak products and the methods companies use to eliminate them. Finally, we look at the organizational structures used to manage products.

MANAGING EXISTING PRODUCTS

A company can benefit by capitalizing on its existing products. By assessing the composition of the current product mix, a marketer can identify weaknesses and gaps. This analysis can then lead to improvement of the product mix through line extension and product modification.

Line Extensions

A **line extension** is the development of a product that is closely related to one or more products in the existing product line but designed specifically to meet somewhat different customer needs. For example, the Porsche Cayenne S Hybrid V-1 can drive short distances using electric power but at high speeds can switch to gas and match the power of a V-8 engine. This product extension of the Cayenne model provides an added benefit of fuel economy without compromising the performance that is a hallmark of the brand.

Many of the so-called new products introduced each year are in fact line extensions. Line extensions are more common than new products because they are a less-expensive, lower-risk alternative for increasing sales. A line extension may focus on a different market segment or attempt to increase sales within the same market segment by more precisely satisfying the needs of people in that segment. Researchers have found that the success of a line extension is enhanced if the parent brand has a high-quality brand image and if there is a good fit between the line extension and its parent.[3] San Francisco–based meat processor and distributor Niman Ranch, for example, extended its successful line of natural meats by launching a line of cage-free liquid eggs.[4] On the other hand, Burger King boxer shorts were an unsuccessful line extension because fast food seems to have little in common with underwear.[5]

line extension Development of a product that is closely related to existing products in the line but is designed specifically to meet different customer needs

© AP Images/Procter & Gamble Co.

Line Extensions
Tide Pods represent a line extension of the successful Tide laundry product line.

Line extensions are also used to take market share from competitors. For instance, the Ford Fusion Hybrid is a product line extension that was designed to compete directly with the Toyota Prius. However, one side effect of employing a line extension is that it may result in a more negative evaluation of the core product. To avoid this concern, Procter & Gamble introduced Tide Pods for consumers who dislike pouring laundry detergent. The pods come in shells that dissolve in the wash. P&G hopes Tide Pods will reinvigorate its stagnating Tide brand.[6]

Product Modifications

Product modification means changing one or more characteristics of a product. A product modification differs from a line extension in that the original product does not remain in the line. For example, Ford is abandoning the "retro trend" for its Ford Mustangs and is choosing to adopt a more modern design to appeal to the younger market.[7] Once the new models are introduced, the manufacturers stop producing the previous model. Like line extensions, product modifications entail less risk than developing new products.

Product modification can indeed improve a firm's product mix, but only under certain conditions. First, the product must be modifiable. Second, customers must be able to perceive that a modification has been made. Third, the modification should make the product more consistent with customers' desires so it provides greater satisfaction. One drawback to modifying a successful product is that the consumer who had experience with the original version of the product may view a modified version as a riskier purchase. There are three major types of modifications that can be made to products: quality, functional, and aesthetic modifications.

Quality Modifications

Quality modifications are changes relating to a product's dependability and durability. The changes usually are executed by altering the materials or the production process. For instance, for a service, quality modifications may involve American Airlines increasing the leg room for passengers or improving its performance regarding on-time departures.

Reducing a product's quality may allow an organization to lower its price and direct the item at a different target market. In contrast, increasing the quality of a product may give a firm

product modifications Changes in one or more characteristics of a product

quality modifications Changes relating to a product's dependability and durability

an advantage over competing brands. Higher quality may enable a company to charge a higher price by creating customer loyalty and lowering customer sensitivity to price. For example, organic milk is higher quality because it has fewer hormones and antibiotics. However, higher quality may require the use of more expensive components and processes, thus forcing the organization to cut costs in other areas. Some firms, such as Caterpillar, are finding ways to increase quality while reducing costs.

Functional Modifications

Changes that affect a product's versatility, effectiveness, convenience, or safety are called **functional modifications**; they usually require redesign of the product. Product categories that have undergone considerable functional modification include office and farm equipment, appliances, cleaning products, and telecommunications services. For example, Sub-Zero modified its refrigerators with dual compressors. This feature allows for independent climate control of different compartments in the unit. The functional benefit is fresher food.

Functional modifications can make a product useful to more people and thus enlarge its market. One example is the new features on the iPhone 5. Powered by Apple's iOS 6 mobile operating system, the iPhone 5 comes with expanded voice recognition capabilities and is the world's thinnest smartphone made entirely of glass and aluminum.[8] This technology, along with other modifications, makes the iPhone 5 significantly different from previous models. Companies like Apple can place a product in a favorable competitive position by providing benefits that competing brands do not offer. They can also help an organization achieve and maintain a progressive image. Finally, functional modifications are sometimes made in response to product shortcomings and assist in reducing the possibility of product liability lawsuits.

functional modifications Changes affecting a product's versatility, effectiveness, convenience, or safety

aesthetic modifications Changes relating to the sensory appeal of a product

Aesthetic Modifications

Aesthetic modifications change the sensory appeal of a product by altering its taste, texture, sound, smell, or appearance. A buyer making a purchase decision is swayed by how a product looks, smells, tastes, feels, or sounds. Thus, an aesthetic modification may strongly affect purchases. The fashion industry relies heavily on aesthetic modifications from season to season. For example, Louis Vuitton clothing, handbags, and leather goods are leaders in the haute couture industry. In order to maintain its reputation for the utmost level of quality and style, the company performs aesthetic modifications on its products regularly. This ensures that Louis Vuitton maintains its reputation for cutting-edge design and quality. In addition, aesthetic modifications attempt to minimize the amount of illegal product counterfeiting that occurs through constant change in design and quality.

Aesthetic modifications can help a firm differentiate its product from competing brands and thus gain a sizable market share. The major drawback in using aesthetic modifications is that consumers determine their value subjectively. Although a firm

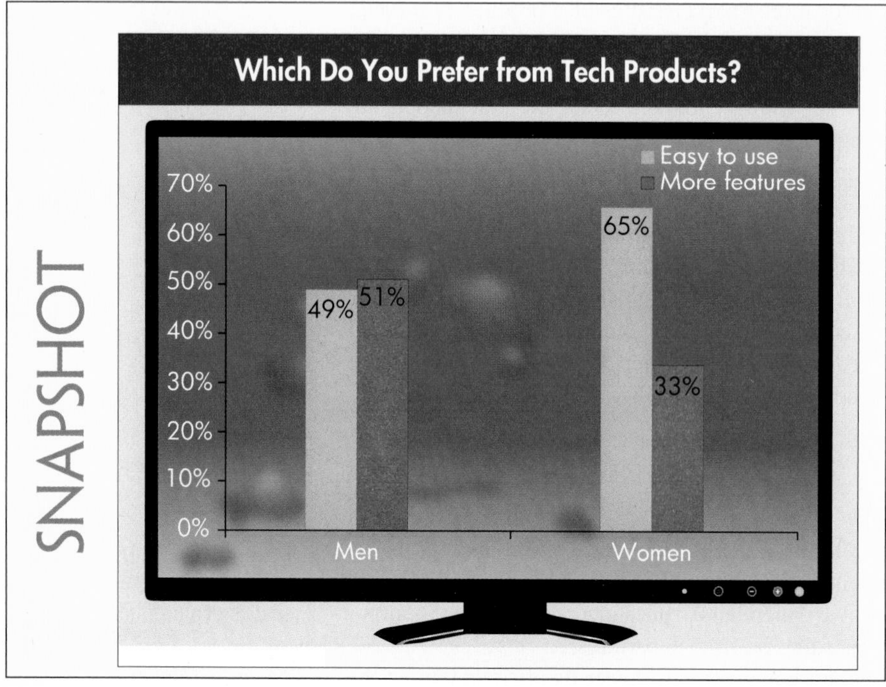

Source: NBCUniversal's Women at NBCU survey of 1,650 adults 18-54 years old.

may strive to improve the product's sensory appeal, some customers may actually find the modified product less attractive.

DEVELOPING NEW PRODUCTS

A firm develops new products as a means of enhancing its product mix and adding depth to a product line. However, developing and introducing new products is frequently expensive and risky. For instance, Microsoft's Vista operating system launched to lackluster reviews and abundant problems, causing many PC users to refuse to upgrade from Microsoft's XP. Microsoft responded to the negative reviews by creating Windows 7, which was formulated as a replacement to Vista. Windows 7 was in turn replaced by Windows 8 when it came out in 2012. As we discussed in the previous chapter, new-product failures occur frequently and can create major financial problems for organizations, sometimes even causing them to go out of business. Failure to introduce new products is also risky. Eastman Kodak lost market share and entered bankruptcy due, in part, to its failure to innovate and keep up with competitive products.[9]

New Products
Through licensing to Heinz, T.G.I. Friday's restaurants have launched new products, including ready-to-heat, frozen snacks in grocery stores.

The term *new product* can have more than one meaning. A genuinely new product offers innovative benefits. For example, Twitter co-founder Jack Dorsey developed a device called the Square reader, a small credit card reader that plugs into the audio jack of mobile phones. Dorsey hopes that this new device will eliminate the need for plastic credit cards.[10] However, products that are different and distinctly better are often viewed as new. For instance, Crest 3D 2-Hour Express Whitestrips are perceived as a new product, even though whitening strips have been on the market for years. The core difference between the new product and earlier products is that Crest 3D 2-Hour Express Whitestrips will whiten teeth in two hours versus three weeks.[11] Some product innovations of the past 30 years include Post-it Notes, cell phones, laptops, PDAs, MP3 players, satellite radio, and digital video recorders. Thus, a new product can be an innovative product that has never been sold by any organization, like the digital camera was when introduced for the first time, or a modified product that existed previously. A radically new product involves a complex developmental process, including an extensive business analysis to determine the potential for success.

Entrepreneurship in Marketing

Entrepreneur Creates Invention to Meet French Demand for Baguettes

Entrepreneur: Jean-Louis Hecht
Business: The Baguette Vending Machine
Founded: 2011 | France
Success: During its first month of operation, Jean-Louise Hecht's two machines sold 1,600 baguettes.

Two years ago, baker Jean-Louis Hecht got an idea for a new product. Hecht, who lived above his bakery, kept getting interrupted after closing hours by consumers who wanted freshly-baked baguettes, the long, crisp loaves of bread that are popular among French consumers. To meet this demand, Hecht began to develop a baguette vending machine. His initial designs failed due to technical difficulties, but after working out the kinks, Hecht now has two automated baguette machines to satisfy his customers' late-night cravings. The machines are simple. As many as 120 partially precooked baguettes are inserted into the machines. When the customer makes a selection, the machine bakes the bread and distributes it to the consumer. Each baguette costs 1 euro ($1.35). Realizing the risks involved with this new product concept, Hecht initially tested it by only operating two machines. However, early demand appears promising: shortly after opening, the company sold thousands of baguettes, with sales continuing to rise.[a]

© AP Images/PRNewsFoto/Red Mango

New Products as Line Extensions
Many new products are line extensions related to existing products. Red Mango low-fat frozen yogurt introduced dark chocolate as a new product item to satisfy consumers.

A new product can also be a product that a given firm has not marketed previously, although similar products have been available from other companies. When Denver-based Russian coffee company DAZBOG introduced tea, it was a new product line with 25 varieties of full-leaf teas and herbal infusions.[12] Finally, a product can be viewed as new when it is brought to one or more markets from another market. When Daimler brought its Smart Car to the United States, it was viewed as a new product, although the Smart had been out in Europe for years.[13]

Before a product is introduced, it goes through the seven phases of the **new-product development process** shown in Figure 12.1: (1) idea generation, (2) screening, (3) concept testing, (4) business analysis, (5) product development, (6) test marketing, and (7) commercialization. A product may be dropped (and many are) at any stage of development. In this section, we look at the process through which products are developed, from idea inception to fully commercialized product.

Idea Generation

Businesses and other organizations seek product ideas that will help them achieve their objectives. This activity is **idea generation**. The fact that only a few ideas are good enough to be commercially successful underscores the challenge of the task.

Although some organizations get their ideas almost by chance, firms that try to manage their product mixes effectively usually develop systematic approaches for generating new product ideas. Indeed, in organizations there is a relationship between the amount of market information gathered and the number of ideas generated by work groups. At the heart of innovation is a purposeful, focused effort to identify new ways to serve a market. One trend that has been emerging in new product idea development is the incorporation of consumers into the process. As more global consumers become interconnected through the Internet, marketers have the chance to tap into consumer ideas by building online communities with them. These communities provide consumers with a sense of empowerment and allow them to provide insight for new product ideas that can prove invaluable to the firm.[14]

New product ideas can come from several sources. They may stem from internal sources: marketing managers, researchers, sales personnel, engineers, or other organizational personnel. Brainstorming and incentives or rewards for good ideas are typical intra-firm devices for stimulating development of ideas. For example, the idea for 3M Post-it adhesive-backed notes came from an employee. As a church choir member, he used slips of paper to mark songs in his hymnal. Because the pieces of paper kept falling out, he suggested developing an adhesive-backed note.

In the restaurant industry, ideas may come from franchisees. At McDonald's, for example, franchise owners invented the Big Mac, Filet-O-Fish, and Egg McMuffin.[15] New product ideas may also arise from sources outside the firm, such as customers, competitors, advertising agencies, management consultants, and private research organizations. The interactivity of the Internet allows stakeholders to not only suggest and analyze new product ideas but also interact with one another on evaluating and filtering these ideas. Employees are becoming more empowered to express their own product ideas to their supervisors. This collaborative process can be particularly useful to help marketers iron out the details of a new product concept.[16]

new-product development process A seven-phase process for introducing products: idea generation, screening, concept testing, business analysis, product development, test-marketing, and commercialization

idea generation Seeking product ideas to achieve organizational objectives

Procter & Gamble is one company that gets nearly half of its ideas from inventors and outside consultants.[17] Such consultants are often used as sources for stimulating new product ideas. For example, Fahrenheit 212 serves as an "idea factory" that provides ready-to-go product ideas, together with market potential analysis for major Fortune 500 firms including

Campbell's, Best Buy, Citibank, Starbucks, Samsung, and Clorox, to name a few.[18] When outsourcing new-product development activities to outside organizations, the best results are achieved by spelling out the specific tasks with detailed contractual specifications. Asking customers what they want from products and organizations has helped many firms become successful and remain competitive. Today, marketers are using online social networking sites, such as quirky.com and crowdspring.com, to communicate with customers and gather new product ideas.

Figure 12.1 Phases of New-Product Development

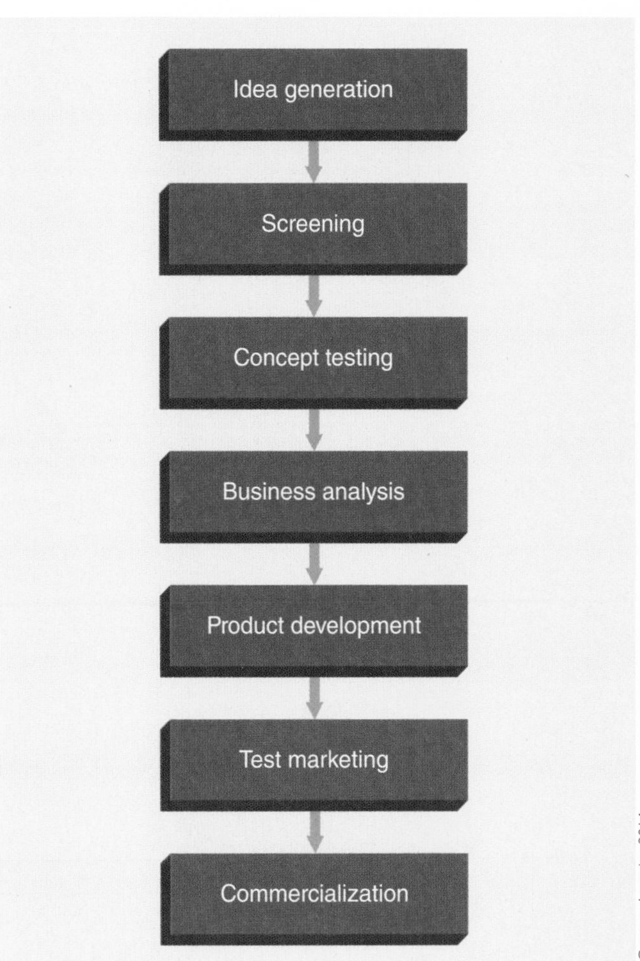

Screening

In the process of **screening**, the ideas with the greatest potential are selected for further review. During screening, product ideas are analyzed to determine whether they match the organization's objectives and resources. Consider that Howard Schultz, the founder of Starbucks, got the idea for a coffee café while visiting Italy. While Starbucks has 730 stores in the United Kingdom, the company has not opened a single store in Italy. As Starbucks screened opportunities for global expansion, the coffee drinking habits and types of coffee Italians drink did not match the Starbucks product.[19] The company's overall abilities to produce and market the product are also analyzed. Keeping the product idea in focus and on track by understanding consumer needs and wants is the key to success. Other aspects of an idea to be weighed are the nature and wants of buyers and possible environmental changes. At times, a checklist of new-product requirements is used when making screening decisions. This practice encourages evaluators to be systematic and thus reduces the chances of overlooking some pertinent fact. Most new product ideas are rejected during the screening phase.

Concept Testing

To evaluate ideas properly, it may be necessary to test product concepts. In **concept testing**, a small sample of potential buyers is presented with a product idea through a written or oral description (and perhaps a few drawings) to determine their attitudes and initial buying intentions regarding the product. For a single product idea, an organization can test one or several concepts of the same product. Concept testing is a low-cost procedure that allows a company to determine customers' initial reactions to a product idea before it invests considerable resources in research and development. Input from online communities may also be beneficial in the product development process. The results of concept testing can help product development personnel better understand which product attributes and benefits are most important to potential customers.

Figure 12.2 shows a concept test for a proposed tick and flea control product. Notice that the concept is briefly described and then a series of questions is presented. The questions vary considerably depending on the type of product being tested. Typical questions include the following: In general, do you find this proposed product attractive? Which benefits are especially attractive to you? Which features are of little or no interest to you? Do you feel that this proposed product would work better for you than the product you currently use? Compared with your current product, what are the primary advantages of the proposed product? If this product were available at an appropriate price, would you buy it? How often would you buy this product? How could this proposed product be improved?

screening Selecting the ideas with the greatest potential for further review

concept testing Seeking a sample of potential buyers' responses to a product idea

Figure 12.2 Concept Test for a Tick and Flea Control Product

Product description

An insecticide company is considering the development and introduction of a new tick and flea control product for pets. This product would consist of insecticide and a liquid-dispensing brush for applying the insecticide to dogs and cats. The insecticide is in a cartridge that is installed in the handle of the brush. The insecticide is dispensed through the tips of the bristles when they touch the pet's skin (which is where most ticks and fleas are found). The actual dispensing works very much like a felt-tip pen. Only a small amount of insecticide actually is dispensed on the pet because of this unique dispensing feature. Thus, the amount of insecticide that is placed on your pet is minimal compared to conventional methods of applying a tick and flea control product. One application of insecticide will keep your pet free from ticks and fleas for 14 days.

Please answer the following questions:

1. In general, how do you feel about using this type of product on your pet?
2. What are the major advantages of this product compared with the existing product that you are currently using to control ticks and fleas on your pet?
3. What characteristics of this product do you especially like?
4. What suggestions do you have for improving this product?
5. If it is available at an appropriate price, how likely are you to buy this product?

   Very likely   Semi-likely   Not likely
6. Assuming that a single purchase would provide 30 applications for an average-size dog or 48 applications for an average-size cat, approximately how much would you pay for this product?

Business Analysis

During the **business analysis** stage, the product idea is evaluated to determine its potential contribution to the firm's sales, costs, and profits. In the course of a business analysis, evaluators ask a variety of questions: Does the product fit in with the organization's existing product mix? Is demand strong enough to justify entering the market, and will this demand endure? What types of environmental and competitive changes can be expected, and how will these changes affect the product's future sales, costs, and profits?

When HP launched its TouchPad tablet computer, the business analysis did not signal to the company that the competitive environment and profit margins would cause the firm to withdraw this product shortly after its launch. Are the organization's research, development, engineering, and production capabilities adequate to develop the product? If new facilities must be constructed, how quickly can they be built, and how much will they cost? Is the necessary financing for development and commercialization on hand or obtainable at terms consistent with a favorable return on investment?

business analysis Evaluating the potential impact of a product idea on the firm's sales, costs, and profits

In the business analysis stage, firms seek market information. The results of customer surveys, along with secondary data, supply the specifics needed to estimate potential sales, costs, and profits.

For many products in this stage (when they are still just product ideas), forecasting sales accurately is difficult. This is especially true for innovative and completely new products. Organizations sometimes employ break-even analysis to determine how many units they would have to sell to begin making a profit. At times, an organization also uses payback analysis, in which marketers compute the time period required to recover the funds that would be invested in developing the new product. Because break-even and payback analyses are based on estimates, they are usually viewed as useful but not particularly precise during this stage.

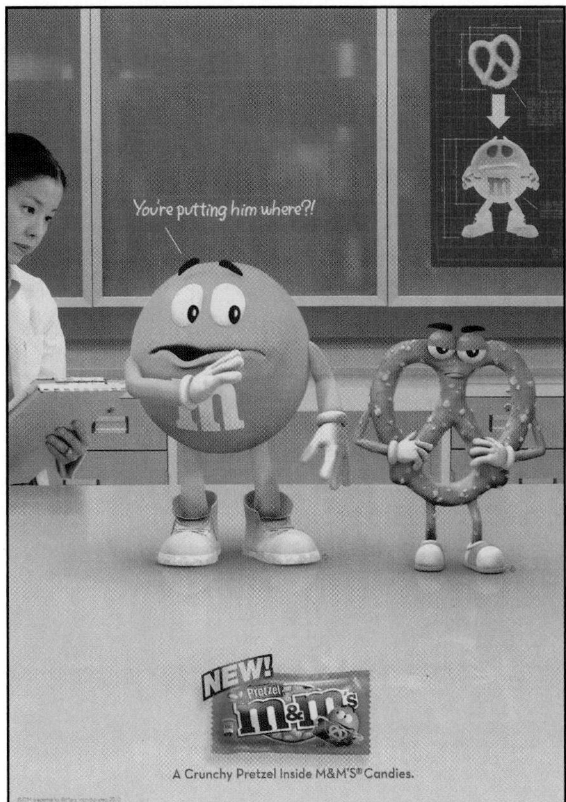

Concept Testing
Before the M&M'S® Brand introduced a crunchy, chocolate-covered pretzel candy, they had to determine consumer interest in the new product.

Product Development

Product development is the phase in which the organization determines if it is technically feasible to produce the product and if it can be produced at costs low enough to make the final price reasonable. To test its acceptability, the idea or concept is converted into a prototype, or working model. The prototype should reveal tangible and intangible attributes associated with the product in consumers' minds. The product's design, mechanical features, and intangible aspects must be linked to wants in the marketplace. Through marketing research and concept testing, product attributes important to buyers are identified. These characteristics must be communicated to customers through the design of the product. GreenTech Automotive, for example, has developed a series of hybrid prototypes meant to appeal to consumers looking for efficient hybrid vehicles.

After a prototype is developed, its overall functioning must be tested. Its performance, safety, convenience, and other functional qualities are tested both in a laboratory and in the field. Functional testing should be rigorous and lengthy enough to test the product thoroughly. Studies have revealed that the form or design of a product can actually influence how consumers view the product's functional performance.[20] For instance, the design and style of an automobile often influences how the consumer perceives its performance. However, companies should take care to ensure that their products live up to expectations, as a well-designed product that does not work well will not survive on the market for very long. Manufacturing issues that come to light at the prototype stage may require adjustments. When Nintendo and Opera Software partnered on the Wii, Nintendo engineers had to come up with many prototypes before the two companies could agree on a final version.

A crucial question that arises during product development is how much quality to build into the product. For example, a major dimension of quality is durability. Higher quality often calls for better materials and more expensive processing, which increase production costs and, ultimately, the product's price. In determining the specific level of quality, a marketer must ascertain approximately what price the target market views as acceptable. In addition, a marketer usually tries to set a quality level consistent with that of the firm's other products. Obviously the quality of competing brands is also a consideration.

The development phase of a new product is frequently lengthy and expensive; thus, a relatively small number of product ideas are put into development. If the product appears sufficiently successful during this stage to merit test marketing, marketers begin to make decisions regarding branding, packaging, labeling, pricing, and promotion for use in the test marketing stage.

Test Marketing

Test marketing is a limited introduction of a product in geographic areas chosen to represent the intended market. Altria Group, for example, conducted market tests of its new smokeless

product development Determining if producing a product is technically feasible and cost effective

test marketing A limited introduction of a product in geographic areas chosen to represent the intended market

Going Green

Will LEDs Become the New Light Bulb?

Thomas Edison's light bulb may soon be a thing of the past. In 2007, the U.S. Congress passed a bill to completely phase out the incandescent light bulb by 2014. Because incandescent bulbs convert just 10 percent of the energy they use into light, substituting them with more efficient alternatives will reduce energy loss and carbon emissions.

At first, compact fluorescent light bulbs (CFLs) were considered to be the best replacement for incandescent light bulbs. CFLs are more energy efficient and last longer. However, consumers soon began to question the product quality of these bulbs. Turning a CFL on and off rapidly can burn out the light bulb and reduce its product life. CFLs also contain mercury, and consumers fear that if the bulbs break, they could be exposed to this toxic substance.

These considerations are paving the way for another type of bulb: light-emitting diodes (LEDs), semiconductors that don't use filaments to give off light. Switching to LEDs could reduce CO_2 emissions from electric power lighting sources by as much as 50 percent within two decades. Although the initial cost for LED bulbs is high, experts believe they will become less expensive over time. LED light bulbs might still be in the introduction stage of the product life cycle, but continued product development could soon make them ready for wide-scale commercialization.[b]

tobacco sticks at select Kansas retailers.[21] The aim of test marketing is to determine the extent to which potential customers will buy the product. It is not an extension of the development stage but a sample launching of the entire marketing mix. Test marketing should be conducted only after the product has gone through development and initial plans have been made regarding the other marketing mix variables. Companies use test marketing to lessen the risk of product failure. The dangers of introducing an untested product include undercutting already profitable products and, should the new product fail, loss of credibility with distributors and customers.

Test marketing provides several benefits. It lets marketers expose a product in a natural marketing environment to measure its sales performance. The company can strive to identify weaknesses in the product or in other parts of the marketing mix. A product weakness discovered after a nationwide introduction can be expensive to correct. Moreover, if consumers' early reactions are negative, marketers may be unable to persuade consumers to try the product again. Thus, making adjustments after test marketing can be crucial to the success of a new product. On the other hand, test marketing results may be positive enough to warrant accelerating the product's introduction. Test marketing also allows marketers to experiment with variations in advertising, pricing, and packaging in different test areas and to measure the extent of brand awareness, brand switching, and repeat purchases resulting from these alterations in the marketing mix.

Selection of appropriate test areas is very important because the validity of test marketing results depends heavily on selecting test sites that provide accurate representation of the intended target market. Table 12.1 lists some of the most popular test market cities. The criteria used for choosing test market cities depend on the product's attributes, the target market's characteristics, and the firm's objectives and resources.

Test marketing is not without risks. It is expensive, and competitors may try to interfere. A competitor may attempt to "jam" the test program by increasing its own advertising or promotions, lowering prices, and offering special incentives, all to combat recognition and purchase of the new brand or product. Such competitor-thwarting tactics can invalidate test results. Sometimes, too, competitors copy the product in the testing stage and rush to introduce a similar product. This is the time to conduct research to identify issues that might drive potential customers to market-leading competitors instead. It is therefore

Table 12.1 **Popular Test Markets in the United States**

Rank	City
1	Albany, NY
2	Rochester, NY
3	Greensboro, NC
4	Birmingham, AL
5	Syracuse, NY
6	Charlotte, NC
7	Nashville, TN
8	Eugene, OR
9	Wichita, KS
10	Richmond, VA

Source: "Which American City Provides the Best Consumer Test Market?" *Business Wire*, May 24, 2004.

desirable to move to the commercialization phase as soon as possible after successful testing. On the other hand, some firms have been known to heavily promote new products long before they are ready for the market to discourage competitors from developing similar new products.

Because of these risks, many companies use alternative methods to measure customer preferences. One such method is simulated test marketing. Typically, consumers at shopping centers are asked to view an advertisement for a new product and are given a free sample to take home. These consumers are subsequently interviewed over the phone or through online panels and asked to rate the product. The major advantages of simulated test marketing are greater speed, lower costs, and tighter security, which reduce the flow of information to competitors and reduce jamming. Gillette's Personal Care Division, for example, spends less than $200,000 for a simulated test that lasts three to five months. A live test market costs Gillette $2 million, counting promotion and distribution, and takes one to two years to complete. Several marketing research firms, such as ACNielsen Company, offer test marketing services to provide independent assessment of proposed products.

Clearly not all products that are test-marketed are launched. At times, problems discovered during test marketing cannot be resolved. Procter & Gamble, for example, test-marketed a new plastic wrap product called Impress in Grand Junction, Colorado, but decided not to launch the brand nationally based on the results of test marketing.

Commercialization

During the **commercialization** phase, plans for full-scale manufacturing and marketing must be refined and finalized and budgets for the project prepared. Early in the commercialization phase, marketing management analyzes the results of test marketing to find out what changes in the marketing mix are needed before introducing the product. The results of test marketing may tell marketers to change one or more of the product's physical attributes, modify the distribution plans to include more retail outlets, alter promotional efforts, or change the product's price. However, as more and more changes are made based on test marketing findings, the test marketing projections may become less valid.

commercialization Refining and finalizing plans and budgets for full-scale manufacturing and marketing of a product

© AP Images/PRNewsFoto/Peapod

Test Marketing
Peapod, the nation's leading online grocer, has placed a virtual store in Chicago to test market the virtual store concept versus maintaining a strictly online presence before finalizing commercialization.

During the early part of this stage, marketers must not only gear up for larger-scale production but also make decisions about warranties, repairs, and replacement parts. The type of warranty a firm provides can be a critical issue for buyers, especially for expensive, technically complex goods such as appliances or frequently used items such as mattresses. Tempur-Pedic offers a 90-day, no-risk, in-home trial of its innovative mattresses. If, after 90 days, the customer is not satisfied, the retailer will pick up the mattress for a modest return fee. Maytag also provides a money-back guarantee on its refrigerators. Establishing an effective system for providing repair services and replacement parts is necessary to maintain favorable customer relationships. Although the producer may furnish these services directly to buyers, it is more common for the producer to provide such services through regional service centers. Regardless of how services are provided, it is important to customers that they be performed quickly and correctly.

The product enters the market during the commercialization phase. When introducing a product, a firm may spend enormous sums for advertising, personal selling, and other types of promotion, as well as more manufacturing facilities and equipment. Such expenditures may not be recovered for several years. Smaller firms may find this process difficult, but even so they may use press releases, blogs, podcasts, and other tools to capture quick feedback as well as to promote the new product. Another low-cost promotional tool is product reviews in newspapers and magazines, which can be especially helpful when they are positive and target the same customers.

Usually, products are not launched nationwide overnight but are introduced through a process called a *roll-out.* With a roll-out, a product is introduced in stages, starting in one set of geographic areas and gradually expanding into adjacent areas. It may take several years to market the product nationally. Sometimes, the test cities are used as initial marketing areas, and the introduction of the product becomes a natural extension of test marketing. A product test-marketed in Sacramento, California; Fort Collins, Colorado; Abilene, Texas; Springfield, Illinois; and Jacksonville, Florida could be introduced first in those cities. After the stage 1 introduction is complete, stage 2 could include market coverage of the states where the test cities are located. In stage 3, marketing efforts might be extended into adjacent states. All remaining states would then be covered in stage 4. Figure 12.3 shows these four stages of commercialization.

Gradual product introductions do not always occur state by state; other geographic combinations, such as groups of counties that overlap across state borders, are sometimes

Figure 12.3 **Stages of Expansion into a National Market During Commercialization**

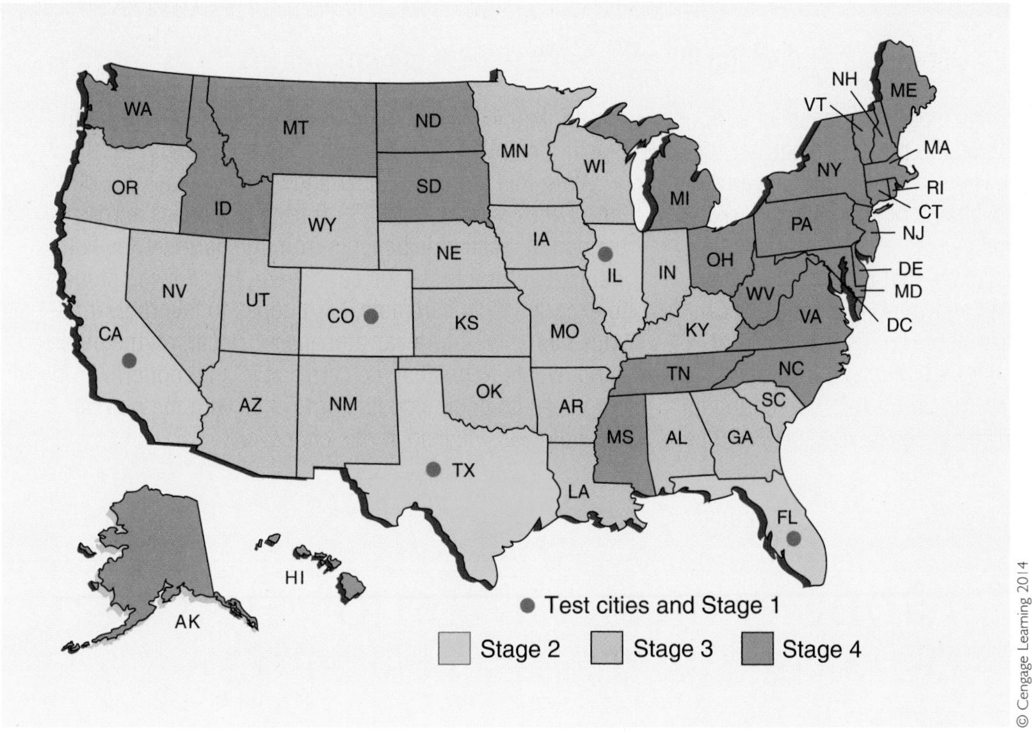

used. Products destined for multinational markets may also be rolled out one country or region at a time. For instance, Sky Zone (a company marketing locations filled with giant trampolines on which people can pay to play dodge ball, take fitness classes, or simply jump around for $9 per hour) first opened in Las Vegas, Nevada. After realizing success there, the company tested in St. Louis and Sacramento. It now has arenas scattered across the United States and one in Ontario, Canada.[22] Gradual product introduction is desirable for several reasons. First, it reduces the risks of introducing a new product. If the product fails, the firm will experience smaller losses if it introduced the item in only a few geographic areas than if it marketed the product nationally. Second, a company cannot introduce a product nationwide overnight because a system of wholesalers and retailers to distribute the product cannot be established so quickly; developing a distribution network may take considerable time. Third, if the product is successful, the number of units needed to satisfy nationwide demand for it may be too large for the firm to produce in a short time. Finally, it allows for fine-tuning of the marketing mix to better satisfy target customers. Procter & Gamble, for example, originally conceived of Febreze deodorizer as a fabric-care product, but over time, the company's view of the highly successful brand evolved into an air-freshening line because that is how consumers indicated they were using it.[23]

Despite the good reasons for introducing a product gradually, marketers realize this approach creates some competitive problems. A gradual introduction allows competitors to observe what the firm is doing and monitor results just as the firm's own marketers are doing. If competitors see that the newly introduced product is successful, they may quickly enter the same target market with similar products. In addition, as a product is introduced region by region, competitors may expand their marketing efforts to offset promotion of the new product. Marketers should realize that too much delay in launching a product can cause the firm to miss out on seizing market opportunities, creating competitive offerings, and forming cooperative relationships with channel members.[24]

Emerging Trends

Ford and Zipcar Partnership Mutually Beneficial

It doesn't seem like a company that encourages its customers not to purchase cars would be a good partner for a major auto manufacturer. However, Ford and Zipcar are working together to take advantage of a lucrative market opportunity: college students.

Zipcar is a car-sharing service that promotes itself as an alternative to the "hassle" of owning an expensive car. The company's 605,000 members can reserve and rent cars by the hour or by the day, with gas and insurance included for up to 180 miles. Zipcar claims that renting its cars versus driving one's own car can save $300–$600 per month. Many college students do not own cars, making Zipcar a popular choice on college campuses.

With this in mind, Zipcar and Ford are placing 1,000 Ford Focus sedans onto 250 college campuses across the nation. Each side benefits from the partnership. Ford wants to attract first-time car buyers. By allowing students to experience its cars now, Ford hopes to favorably influence students' future car purchases. Zipcar, on the other hand, wants to position its cars as hip and modern. Ford's emphasis on equipping its Ford Focus with the newest technologies will help in this endeavor.[c]

PRODUCT DIFFERENTIATION THROUGH QUALITY, DESIGN, AND SUPPORT SERVICES

Some of the most important characteristics of products are the elements that distinguish them from one another. **Product differentiation** is the process of creating and designing products so customers perceive them as different from competing products. Customer perception is critical in differentiating products. Perceived differences might include quality, features, styling, price, or image. A crucial element used to differentiate one product from another is the brand, discussed in Chapter 14. In this section, we examine three aspects of product differentiation that companies must consider when creating and offering products for sale: product quality, product design and features, and product support services. These aspects involve the company's attempt to create real differences among products.

Product Quality

Quality refers to the overall characteristics of a product that allow it to perform as expected in satisfying customer needs. The words *as expected* are very important to this definition because quality usually means different things to different customers. For some, durability signifies quality. Among the most durable products on the market today is the Craftsman line of tools at Sears; indeed, Sears provides a lifetime guarantee on the durability of its tools. Similarly, in the household market, Cutco provides a lifetime warranty on its high-quality line of knives and cutlery. For other consumers, a product's ease of use may indicate quality.

The concept of quality also varies between consumer and business markets. Consumers consider high-quality products to be reliable, durable, and easy to maintain. For business markets, technical suitability, ease of repair, and company reputation are important characteristics. Unlike consumers, most organizations place far less emphasis on price than on product quality.

One important dimension of quality is **level of quality**: the amount of quality a product possesses. The concept is a relative one; that is, the quality level of one product is difficult to describe unless it is compared with that of other products. The American Customer

product differentiation Creating and designing products so that customers perceive them as different from competing products

quality The overall characteristics of a product that allow it to perform as expected in satisfying customer needs

level of quality The amount of quality a product possesses

Satisfaction Index, compiled by the National Quality Research Center at the University of Michigan, ranks customer satisfaction among a wide variety of businesses. Dissatisfied customers may curtail their overall spending, which could stifle economic growth. In the full-service restaurant category, Olive Garden tied with Red Lobster in receiving the highest satisfaction score.[25]

A second important dimension is consistency. **Consistency of quality** refers to the degree to which a product has the same level of quality over time. Consistency means giving consumers the quality they expect every time they purchase the product. Like level of quality, consistency is a relative concept; however, it implies a quality comparison within the same brand over time. For example, if FedEx delivers more than 99 percent of overnight packages on time, its service has a consistent quality.

The consistency of product quality can also be compared across competing products. It is at this stage that consistency becomes critical to a company's success. Companies that can provide quality on a consistent basis have a major competitive advantage over rivals. UPS, for example, is viewed as more consistent in delivery schedules than the U.S. Postal Service, which has earned UPS a higher consumer satisfaction rating for express deliveries.[26] In simple terms, no company has ever succeeded by creating and marketing low-quality products. Many companies have taken major steps, such as implementing total quality management (TQM), to improve the quality of their products.

By and large, higher product quality means marketers will charge a higher price for the product. This fact forces marketers to consider quality carefully in their product planning efforts. Not all customers want or can afford the highest-quality products available. Thus, some companies offer products with moderate quality.

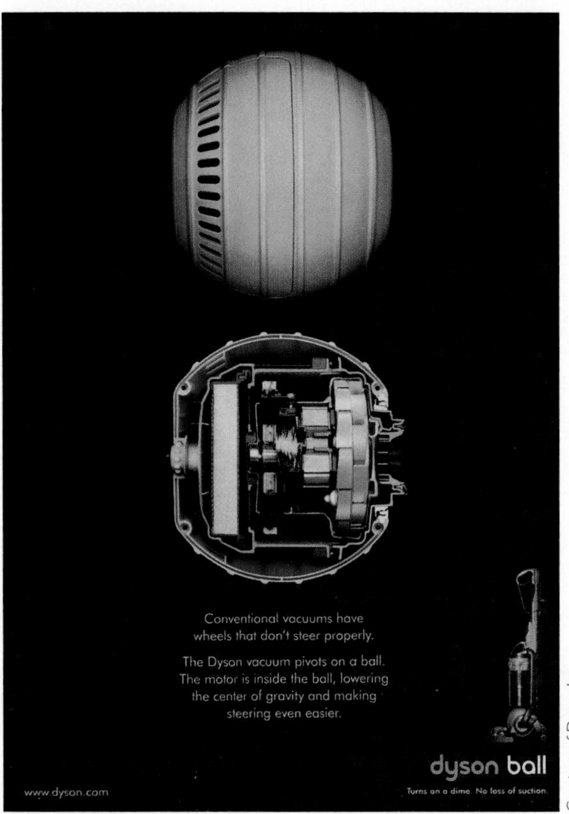

Courtesy of Dyson Inc.

Product Quality
Dyson provides high-quality products known for exceptional design and performance.

Product Design and Features

Product design refers to how a product is conceived, planned, and produced. Design is a very complex topic because it involves the total sum of all the product's physical characteristics. Many companies are known for the outstanding designs of their products: Sony for personal electronics, Hewlett-Packard for printers, and JanSport for backpacks. Good design is one of the best competitive advantages any brand can possess.

One component of design is **styling**, or the physical appearance of the product. The style of a product is one design feature that can allow certain products to sell very rapidly. Good design, however, means more than just appearance; it also involves a product's functioning and usefulness. For instance, a pair of jeans may look great, but if they fall apart after three washes, clearly the design was poor. Most consumers seek out products that both look good and function well.

Product features are specific design characteristics that allow a product to perform certain tasks. By adding or subtracting features, a company can differentiate its products from those of the competition. With the tagline "Get Used to More," GM promotes its Chevrolet Cruze as having more of everything that consumers desire, including safety features, technology, and space.[27] Product features can also be used to differentiate products within the same company. For example, Nike offers both a walking shoe and a run-walk shoe for specific consumer needs as well as technology that can link to your iPod to track your distance traveled and calories burned. In these cases, the company's products are sold with a wide range of features, from low-priced "base" or "stripped-down" versions to high-priced, prestigious "feature-packed" ones. The automotive industry regularly sells products with a wide range of features. In general, the more features a product has, the higher its price and, often, the higher its perceived quality.

consistency of quality The degree to which a product has the same level of quality over time

product design How a product is conceived, planned, and produced

styling The physical appearance of a product

product features Specific design characteristics that allow a product to perform certain tasks

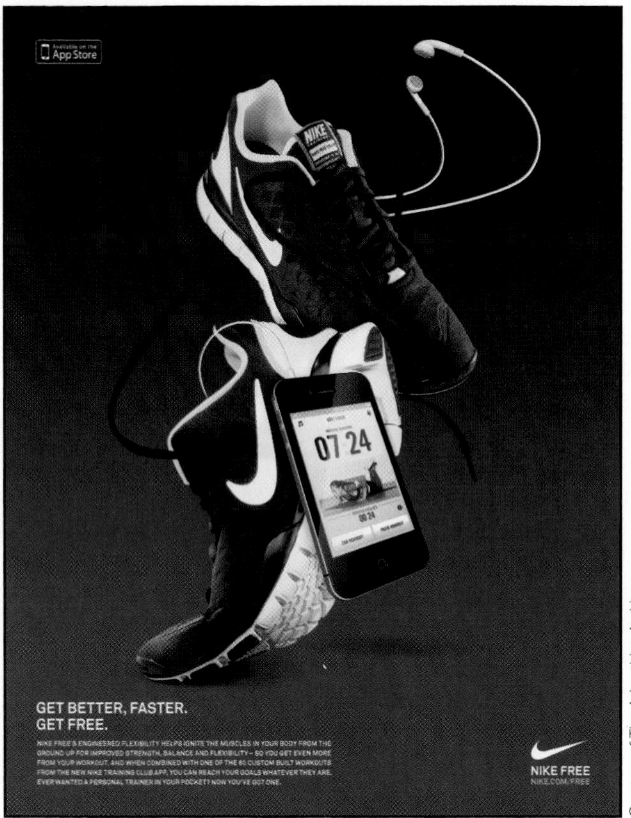

Courtesy of The Advertising Archives

Product Design
Nike carefully designed the Nike Free shoes to be stylish and integrated with Apple performance-monitoring apps.

For a brand to have a sustainable competitive advantage, marketers must determine the product designs and features that customers desire. Information from marketing research efforts and databases can help in assessing customers' product design and feature preferences. Being able to meet customers' desires for product design and features at prices they can afford is crucial to a product's long-term success. Marketers must be careful not to misrepresent or overpromise regarding product features or product performance.

Product Support Services

Many companies differentiate their product offerings by providing support services. Usually referred to as **customer services**, these services include any human or mechanical efforts or activities a company provides that add value to a product. Examples of customer services include delivery and installation, financing arrangements, customer training, warranties and guarantees, repairs, layaway plans, convenient hours of operation, adequate parking, and information through toll-free numbers and websites. The department store Nordstrom has earned a reputation for excellent customer service, in part due to its return policy and considerate employees.[28]

Whether as a major or minor part of the total product offering, all marketers of goods sell customer services. Providing good customer service may be the only way a company can differentiate its products when all products in a market have essentially the same quality, design, and features. This is especially true in the computer industry. When buying a laptop computer, for example, consumers shop more for fast delivery, technical support, warranties, and price than for product quality and design, as witnessed by the high volume of "off-the-shelf," noncustomized, sometimes lagging-in-technology, discount laptops sold at Best Buy, Costco, Walmart, Target, etc. Through research, a company can discover the types of services customers want and need. For example, some customers are more interested in financing, whereas others are more concerned with installation and training. The level of customer service a company provides can profoundly affect customer satisfaction. Add-on features can enhance a product in the eyes of the consumer. Consumers often infer a higher level of quality from the mere availability of add-on services.[29]

customer services Human or mechanical efforts or activities that add value to a product

Marketing Debate

The Authenticity of the Artisan Food Label

ISSUE: Are artisan food labels authentic?

Artisan food has traditionally been used to describe handcrafted food. However, as artisan food becomes more popular, marketers are taking notice. Tostitos, Wendy's, and Subway have all used the term artisan on some of their product labels. The latest is Domino's pizza, which sells artisan pizzas in boxes signed by the employee who made them. But is this term misleading? In the past, artisan food was created in small batches, which is obviously not the case with these items. Domino's uses unique quality toppings for its artisan pizzas. Is this enough to classify these products as artisan?[d]

PRODUCT POSITIONING AND REPOSITIONING

Once a target market is selected, a firm must consider how to position its product. Product positioning refers to the decisions and activities intended to create and maintain a certain concept of the firm's product (relative to competitive brands) in customers' minds. When marketers introduce a product, they try to position it so that it appears to have the characteristics that the target market most desires. This projected image is crucial. Crest is positioned as a fluoride toothpaste that fights cavities, whereas Rembrandt is positioned to fight intense stains.

Perceptual Mapping

A product's position is the result of customers' perceptions of the product's attributes relative to those of competitive brands. Buyers make numerous purchase decisions on a regular basis. To avoid a continuous reevaluation of numerous products, buyers tend to group, or "position," products in their minds to simplify buying decisions. Rather than allowing customers to position products independently, marketers often try to influence and shape consumers' concepts or perceptions of products through advertising. Marketers sometimes analyze product positions by developing perceptual maps, as shown in Figure 12.4. Perceptual maps are created by questioning a sample of consumers about their perceptions of products, brands, and organizations with respect to two or more dimensions. To develop a perceptual map like the one in Figure 12.4, respondents would be asked how they perceive selected pain relievers in regard to price and type of pain for which the products are used. Also, respondents would be asked about their preferences for product features to establish "ideal points" or "ideal clusters," which represent a consensus about what a specific group of customers desires in terms of product features. Then marketers can compare how their brand is perceived compared with the ideal points.

Figure 12.4 Hypothetical Perceptual Map for Pain Relievers

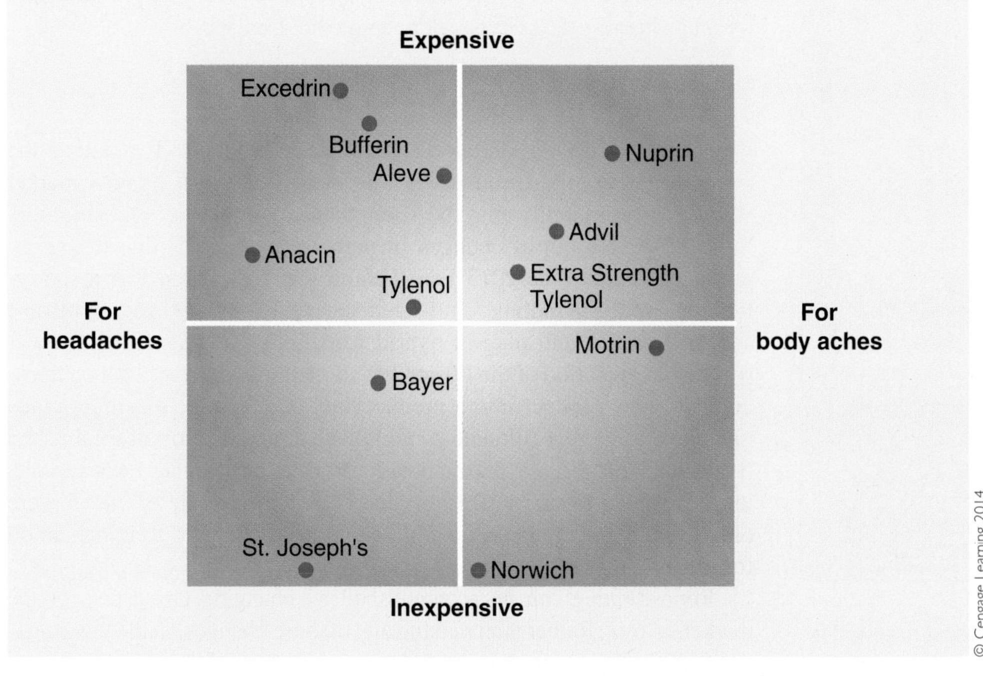

Bases for Positioning

Marketers can use several bases for product positioning. A common basis for positioning products is to use competitors. A firm can position a product to compete head-on with another brand, as PepsiCo has done against Coca-Cola, or to avoid competition, as 7UP has done relative to other soft-drink producers. Head-to-head competition may be a marketer's positioning objective if the product's performance characteristics are at least equal to those of competitive brands and if the product is priced lower. Head-to-head positioning may be appropriate even when the price is higher if the product's performance characteristics are superior. General Motors used a head-to-head positioning strategy in its "Dear Corolla" Chevrolet Cruze commercials. The commercials addressed the Toyota Corolla's lack of Bluetooth technology and the superiority of the Chevy Cruze.[30]

Conversely, positioning to avoid competition may be best when the product's performance characteristics do not differ significantly from competing brands. Moreover, positioning a brand to avoid competition may be appropriate when that brand has unique characteristics that are important to some buyers. Volvo, for example, has for years positioned itself away from competitors by focusing on the safety characteristics of its cars. Whereas some auto companies mention safety issues in their advertisements, many are more likely to focus on style, fuel efficiency, performance, or terms of sale. Avoiding competition is critical when a firm introduces a brand into a market in which the company already has one or more brands. Marketers usually want to avoid cannibalizing sales of their existing brands, unless the new brand generates substantially larger profits.

A product's position can be based on specific product attributes or features. For instance, Apple's iPhone is positioned based on product attributes such as its unique shape, easy-to-use touchscreen, and its access to iTunes' music store. If a product has been planned properly, its features will give it the distinct appeal needed. Style, shape, construction, and color help create the image and the appeal. If buyers can easily identify the benefits, they are, of course, more likely to purchase the product. When the new product does not offer certain preferred attributes, there is room for another new product.

© Terri Miller/E-Visual Communications, Inc.

Positioning
Tide to Go is positioned as a portable spot remover for use when away from home.

Other bases for product positioning include price, quality level, and benefits provided by the product. For example, Era detergent provides stain treatment and stain removal. Also, a positioning basis employed by some marketers is the target market. This type of positioning relies heavily on promoting to the types of people who use the product.

Repositioning

Positioning decisions are not just for new products. Evaluating the positions of existing products is important because a brand's market share and profitability may be strengthened by product repositioning. Repositioning requires changes in perception and usually changes in product features. The 2013 Ford Fusion was repositioned as a sporty-looking, sporty-handling, mid-sized car with gas savings, EcoBoost standard power, and plug-in hybrid capabilities. Ford claimed the car was not an evolution of the Fusion but something different.[31] When introducing a new product into a product line, one or more existing brands may have to be repositioned to minimize cannibalization of established brands and ensure a favorable position for the new brand. For example, the 2013 Ford Fusion has a long list of features, some of which were only available on Lincoln models. There is a danger of cannibalization for this brand.[32]

Repositioning can be accomplished by changing any aspect of the marketing mix. Rather than making any of these changes, marketers sometimes reposition a product by changing its image through promotional efforts. Finally, a marketer may reposition a product by aiming it at a completely different target market. For instance, Dr Pepper Snapple Group repositioned Dr Pepper Ten as "not for women" with a macho advertising campaign, because the company found that men consume a much smaller amount of diet drinks. Unfortunately for Dr Pepper, some men do not like being made self-conscious about their purchases, and women did not like being excluded. This demonstrates how hard it is to reposition target markets through promotion.[33]

PRODUCT DELETION

Generally, a product cannot satisfy target market customers and contribute to the achievement of the organization's overall goals indefinitely. **Product deletion** is the process of eliminating a product from the product mix, usually because it no longer satisfies a sufficient number of customers. Honda, for example, discontinued its Honda Element due to lackluster sales.[34] A declining product reduces an organization's profitability and drains resources that could be used to modify other products or develop new ones. A marginal product may require shorter production runs, which can increase per-unit production costs. Finally, when a dying product completely loses favor with customers, the negative feelings may transfer to some of the company's other products.

Most organizations find it difficult to delete a product. A decision to drop a product may be opposed by managers and other employees who believe the product is necessary to the product mix. Salespeople who still have some loyal customers are especially upset when a product is dropped. In such cases, companies may spend considerable resources and effort to change a slipping product's marketing mix to improve its sales and thus avoid having to eliminate it. Products constantly undergo reformulation and redesign to fortify their fit in the product line and avoid deletion.

Some organizations delete products only after the products have become heavy financial burdens. A better approach is some form of systematic review in which each product is evaluated periodically to determine its impact on the overall effectiveness of the firm's product mix. Such a review should analyze the product's contribution to the firm's sales for a given period, as well as estimate future sales, costs, and profits associated with the product. It should also gauge the value of making changes in the marketing strategy to improve the product's performance. A systematic review allows an organization to improve product performance and ascertain when to delete products. General Motors decided to delete the Hummer, Saturn, Saab, and Pontiac brands in order to lower costs, improve reputation, and become more profitable.

Basically, a product can be deleted in three ways: phase it out, run it out, or drop it immediately (see Figure 12.5). A *phase-out* allows the product to decline without a change in the marketing

product deletion Eliminating a product from the product mix when it no longer satisfies a sufficient number of customers

Figure 12.5 Product Deletion Process

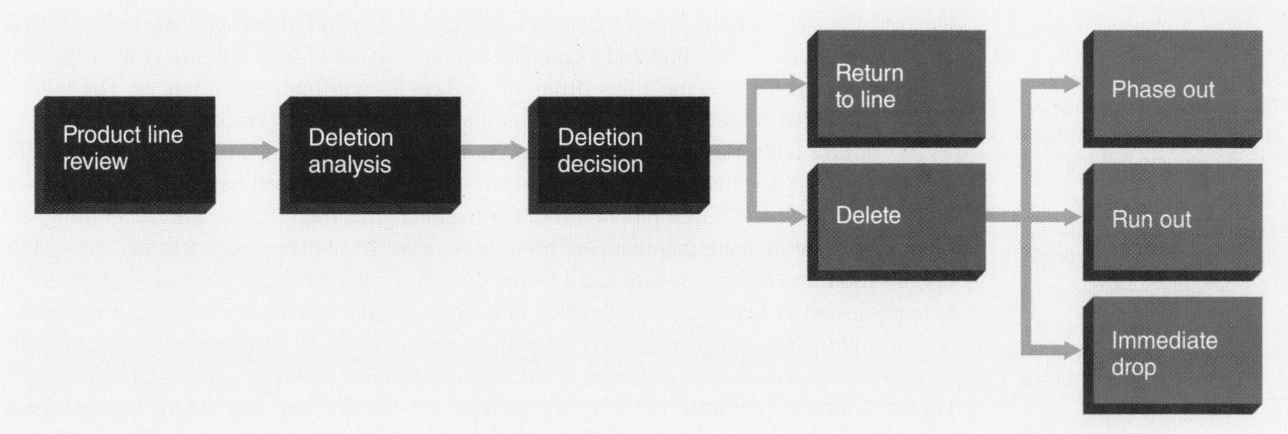

Source: Martin L. Bell. *Marketing: Concepts and Strategy*, 3rd ed., p. 267; Copyright © 1979, Houghton Miffl in Company. Reprinted by permission of Mrs. Martin L. Bell.

strategy; no attempt is made to give the product new life. A *run-out* exploits any strengths left in the product. Intensifying marketing efforts in core markets or eliminating some marketing expenditures, such as advertising, may cause a sudden jump in profits. This approach is commonly taken for technologically obsolete products, such as older models of computers and CD players. Often, the price is reduced to generate a sales spurt. The third alternative, an *immediate drop* of an unprofitable product, is the best strategy when losses are too great to prolong the product's life.

ORGANIZING TO DEVELOP AND MANAGE PRODUCTS

After reviewing the concepts of product line, mix, and life cycles, it should be obvious that managing products is a complex task. Often, the traditional functional form of an organization, in which managers specialize in such business functions as advertising, sales, and distribution, does not fit a company's needs. In this case, management must find an organizational approach that accomplishes the tasks necessary to develop and manage products. Alternatives to functional organization include the product or brand manager approach, the market manager approach, and the venture team approach.

A **product manager** is responsible for a product, a product line, or several distinct products that make up an interrelated group within a multiproduct organization. A **brand manager** is responsible for a single brand. Kraft, for example, has one brand manager for Nabisco Oreos, its number-one-selling cookie, and one for Oscar Mayer Lunchables. Both product and brand managers operate cross-functionally to coordinate the activities, information, and strategies involved in marketing an assigned product. Product managers and brand managers plan marketing activities to achieve objectives by coordinating a mix of distribution, promotion (especially sales promotion and advertising), and price. They must consider packaging and branding decisions and work closely with personnel in research and development, engineering, and production. Marketing research helps product managers understand consumers and find target markets. Because luxury brands like BMW and Porsche can have their brand image reduced by association with their producers' other mass-market brands, brand managers must balance their brands' independent image with associated brands of the firm. The product or brand manager approach to organization is used by many large, multiple-product companies.

A **market manager** is responsible for managing the marketing activities that serve a particular group of customers. This organizational approach is particularly effective when a firm engages in different types of marketing activities to provide products to diverse customer groups. A company might have one market manager for business markets and another for consumer markets. Markets also could be divided by geographic region. For example, the Jack-in-the-Box fast-food chain offers different menu items in New Mexico than it does in Oregon. Because Hindus believe cows are sacred, and India has a large vegetarian population, McDonald's offers lamb and vegetarian options in lieu of beef burgers at its restaurants in India. The chains recognize that different markets have different preferences. These broad market categories might be broken down into more limited market responsibilities.

A **venture team** creates entirely new products that may be aimed at new markets. Unlike a product or market manager, a venture team is responsible for all aspects of developing a product: research and development, production and engineering, finance and accounting, and marketing. Venture team members are brought together from different functional areas of the organization. In working outside established divisions, venture teams have greater flexibility to apply inventive approaches to develop new products that can take advantage of opportunities in highly segmented markets. Companies are increasingly using such cross-functional teams for product development in an effort to boost product quality. Quality may be positively related to information integration within the team, customers' influence on the product development process, and a quality orientation within the firm. When a new product has demonstrated commercial potential, team members may return to their functional areas, or they may join a new or existing division to manage the product.

product manager The person within an organization who is responsible for a product, a product line, or several distinct products that make up a group

brand manager The person responsible for a single brand

market manager The person responsible for managing the marketing activities that serve a particular group of customers

venture team A cross-functional group that creates entirely new products that may be aimed at new markets

Summary

1. To understand how companies manage existing products through line extensions and product modifications

Organizations must be able to adjust their product mixes to compete effectively and achieve their goals. A product mix can be improved through line extension and product modification. A line extension is the development of a product closely related to one or more products in the existing line but designed specifically to meet different customer needs. Product modification is the changing of one or more characteristics of a product. This approach can be effective when the product is modifiable, when customers can perceive the change, and when customers want the modification. Quality modifications relate to a product's dependability and durability. Functional modifications affect a product's versatility, effectiveness, convenience, or safety. Aesthetic modifications change the sensory appeal of a product.

2. To describe how businesses develop a product idea into a commercial product

Before a product is introduced, it goes through a seven-phase new-product development process. In the idea-generation phase, new product ideas may come from internal or external sources. In the process of screening, ideas are evaluated to determine whether they are consistent with the firm's overall objectives and resources. Concept testing, the third phase, involves having a small sample of potential customers review a brief description of the product idea to determine their initial perceptions of the proposed product and their early buying intentions. During the business analysis stage, the product idea is evaluated to determine its potential contribution to the firm's sales, costs, and profits. In the product development stage, the organization determines if it is technically feasible to produce the product and if it can be produced at a cost low enough to make the final price reasonable. Test marketing is a limited introduction of a product in areas chosen to represent the intended market. Finally, in the commercialization phase, full-scale production of the product begins and a complete marketing strategy is developed.

3. To understand the importance of product differentiation and the elements that differentiate one product from another

Product differentiation is the process of creating and designing products so that customers perceive them as different from competing products. Product quality, product design and features, and product support services are three aspects of product differentiation that companies consider when creating and marketing products. Product quality includes the overall characteristics of a product that allow it to perform as expected in satisfying customer needs. The level of quality is the amount of quality a product possesses. Consistency of quality is the degree to which a product has the same level of quality over time. Product design refers to how a product is conceived, planned, and produced. Components of product design include styling (the physical appearance of the product) and product features (the specific design characteristics that allow a product to perform certain tasks). Companies often differentiate their products by providing support services, usually called customer services. Customer services are human or mechanical efforts or activities that add value to a product.

4. To understand how businesses position their products

Product positioning relates to the decisions and activities that create and maintain a certain concept of the firm's product in customers' minds. Buyers tend to group, or "position," products in their minds to simplify buying decisions. Marketers try to position a new product so that it appears to have all the characteristics that the target market most desires. Positioning plays a role in market segmentation. Organizations can position a product to compete head-to-head with another brand or to avoid competition. Positioning a product away from competitors by focusing on a specific attribute not emphasized by competitors is one strategy. Other bases for positioning include price, quality level, and benefits provided by the product. Repositioning by making physical changes in the product, changing its price or distribution, or changing its image can boost a brand's market share and profitability.

5. To examine how product deletion is used to improve product mixes

Product deletion is the process of eliminating a product that no longer satisfies a sufficient number of customers. Although a firm's personnel may oppose product deletion, weak products are unprofitable, consume too much time and effort, may require shorter production runs, and can create an unfavorable impression of the firm's other products. A product mix should be systematically reviewed to determine when to delete products. Products to be deleted can be phased out, run out, or dropped immediately.

6. To describe organizational structures used for managing products

Often, the traditional functional form of organization does not lend itself to the complex task of developing and managing products. Alternative organizational forms include the product or brand manager approach, the market manager approach, and the venture team approach. A product manager is responsible for a product, a product line, or several distinct products that make up an interrelated group within a multiproduct organization. A brand manager is responsible for a single brand. A market manager is responsible for managing the marketing activities that serve a particular group or class of customers. A venture team is sometimes used to create entirely new products that may be aimed at new markets.

Go to www.cengagebrain.com for resources to help you master the content in this chapter as well as materials that will expand your marketing knowledge!

Important Terms

line extension 390
product modifications 391
quality modifications 391
functional modifications 392
aesthetic modifications 392
new-product development process 394
idea generation 394
screening 395
concept testing 395
business analysis 396
product development 397
test marketing 397
commercialization 399
product differentiation 402
quality 402
level of quality 402
consistency of quality 403
product design 403
styling 403
product features 403
customer services 404
product deletion 407
product manager 408
brand manager 408
market manager 408
venture team 408

Discussion and Review Questions

1. What is a line extension, and how does it differ from a product modification?
2. Compare and contrast the three major approaches to modifying a product.
3. Identify and briefly explain the seven major phases of the new-product development process.
4. Do small companies that manufacture just a few products need to be concerned about developing and managing products? Why or why not?
5. Why is product development a cross-functional activity—involving finance, engineering, manufacturing, and other functional areas—within an organization?
6. What is the major purpose of concept testing, and how is it accomplished?
7. What are the benefits and disadvantages of test marketing?
8. Why can the process of commercialization take a considerable amount of time?
9. What is product differentiation, and how can it be achieved?
10. Explain how the term *quality* has been used to differentiate products in the automobile industry in recent years. What are some makes and models of automobiles that come to mind when you hear the terms *high quality* and *poor quality?*
11. What is product positioning? Under what conditions would head-to-head product positioning be appropriate? When should head-to-head positioning be avoided?
12. What types of problems does a weak product cause in a product mix? Describe the most effective approach for avoiding such problems.
13. What type of organization might use a venture team to develop new products? What are the advantages and disadvantages of such a team?

Application Questions

1. When developing a new product, a company often test-markets the proposed product in a specific area or location. Suppose you wish to test-market your new, revolutionary SuperWax car wax, which requires only one application for a lifetime finish. Where and how would you test-market your new product?
2. A product manager may make quality, functional, or aesthetic modifications when modifying a product. Identify a familiar product that recently was modified, categorize the modification (quality, functional, or aesthetic), and describe how you would have modified it differently.
3. Phasing out a product from the product mix often is difficult for an organization. Visit a retail store in your area, and ask the manager what products he or she has had to discontinue in the recent past. Find out what factors influenced the decision to delete the product and who was

involved in the decision. Ask the manager to identify any products that should be but have not been deleted, and try to ascertain the reason.

4. IMP Marketers use different approaches in new-product development in order to identify the relative importance of different product attributes. These approaches help marketers optimize product design, predict purchasing likelihood, and estimate market share in a competitive situation. As an example, different restaurants have varying attributes, including ambience, breadth of menu, service level, location, and price. Consumers place different value on each of these attributes and are consequently willing to make "trade-offs." Higher service levels often mean a higher price, for example. A broader menu often accompanies a restaurant with a nicer ambience, but it comes at a higher price. Marketers can assign weights to the different values that consumers place on the product attributes, and thereby understand the trade-offs that are made.

   You are designing a new tablet computer. Begin by identifying the set of all product attributes. Rate these attributes on a scale of 1 to 10, with 1 being the most important and 10 being the least important. For instance, would you rate ease of use higher than the aesthetic design of the product? How important is it for the tablet to have the newest technological features? Remember, the more sophisticated and tech-savvy the product, the more expensive it is likely to be. Finally, make a recommendation for the new tablet computer design.

Internet Exercise

Merck & Company

Merck, a leading global pharmaceutical company, develops, manufactures, and markets a broad range of health-care products. In addition, the firm's Merck-Medco Managed Care Division manages pharmacy benefits for more than 40 million Americans. The company has established a website to serve as an educational and informational resource for Internet users around the world. To learn more about the company and its research, visit its award-winning site at www.merck.com.

1. What products has Merck developed and introduced recently?
2. What role does research play in Merck's success? How does research facilitate new-product development at Merck?
3. Find Merck's mission statement. Is Merck's focus on research consistent with the firm's mission and values?

developing your marketing plan

A company's marketing strategy may be revised to include new products as it considers its SWOT analysis and the impact of environmental factors on its product mix. When developing a marketing plan, the company must decide whether new products are to be added to the product mix or if existing ones should be modified. The information in this chapter will assist you in the creation of your marketing plan as you consider the following:

1. Identify whether your product will be a modification of an existing one in your product mix or a completely new product.
2. If the product is an extension of one in your current product mix, determine the type(s) of modifications that will be performed.
3. Using Figure 12.1 as a guide, discuss how your product idea would move through the stages of new-product development. Examine the idea, using the tests and analyses included in the new-product development process.
4. Discuss how the management of this product will fit into your current organizational structure.

The information obtained from these questions should assist you in developing various aspects of your marketing plan found in the "Interactive Marketing Plan" exercise at www.cengagebrain.com.

video case 12.1

Do AXE Products Make Men More Desirable?

Whether you love them or hate them, the AXE commercials leave an indelible impression. The AXE brand, owned by Unilever, is meant to exude masculinity. First released under the Lynx brand name in France in 1983, AXE products did not hit American shelves until 2002. However, in a short time period, AXE products have revolutionized the male grooming market. AXE is the number-one male grooming brand in both the United States and Canada.

The company features provocative advertisements of women falling over men who wear the AXE body spray. AXE body sprays are its most popular product, but when it first entered the U.S. market, the company was taking a risk. Until that time, body sprays were not marketed to men, as they were considered to be more of a girl's item. Yet AXE quickly gained popularity by honing in on what many young men care about.

"Our target is really 18 to 24," said AXE brand manager Mike Dwyer. "Our ads are exactly what an 18-to-24-year-old guy is thinking about. It's gears and gadgets, it's sports, or it's girls. We focus very much on girls."

AXE's product features are both tangible and psychological. On the tangible side, the smell of the product needs to be pleasing to both men and women. The psychological features of the product include desirability, masculinity, and seductiveness.

To effectively manage the AXE brand, Unilever has to regularly develop new products and manage existing lines. Over the years, it has introduced several line extensions, including hairstyling, aftershave, skin care, and shower gel products. The company has also released an AXE fragrance called Anarchy for Her in Canada, so that girls can experience the "AXE Effect." Anarchy for Her is meant to complement the Anarchy for Him male fragrance and has more fruity and flowery scents.

Each year, the company introduces a new fragrance. For example, one of its more recent fragrances includes a chocolate ice cream scent. In order to create scents that resonate with its young male demographic, AXE hires professional perfumers to develop the fragrance and even employs expert "smellers." Such efforts not only made AXE a market leader but also helped the male grooming industry as a whole. It is estimated that, by 2015, male grooming products will be a $33.2 billion industry.

AXE's sexualized marketing and its appeal to young men have become what Dwyer has called the "AXE Lifestyle." The styling of the product's package is meant to convey seductiveness (the traditional package is black, but the color changes depending on the product). AXE advertisements try to connect the action of attracting a woman to the product itself. For instance, the chocolate ice cream fragrance featured a commercial where women were licking the man after he used that particular scented body spray. Although AXE promotes itself through Twitter and events, its commercials tend to be its most notable promotion.

Young men have gravitated toward the idea that AXE body spray can make them more desirable. However, what AXE perhaps did not anticipate was its popularity among younger generations: male teenagers and tweens (those between the ages of 10 and 12). Although these younger generations do not have jobs, they have significant influence in the family. Mothers often purchase these products for their children after they request them.

Many of the promotions that appeal to young men seem to appeal to preadolescents—namely, the desire to be accepted and feel "sexy." Because preadolescence is the age when many young men become more conscientiousness of their looks, AXE provides a way for them to feel more confident about their body image. Unfortunately, preadolescents tend to over-spray, and some schools have even banned the body spray because it is distracting in class.

Although the AXE brand can profit from its popularity among the tween generation, this trend can also backfire. Young men traditionally have shied away from products that are popular with those young enough to be their "kid brothers." Therefore, AXE makes it clear that its target market is for those between the ages of 18 and 24. To respond to these changing trends, AXE will need to continue developing and adapting products to meet the needs of its target market and take advantage of new market opportunities.[35]

Questions for Discussion

1. How has AXE managed its product mix?
2. How has AXE used line extensions to increase its reach among consumers?
3. Why are younger generations attracted to AXE products?

case 12.2

Caterpillar Inc. Crawls Over the Competition with Product Development

Caterpillar Inc. is a global manufacturer of construction and mining equipment, machinery, and engines. The company is best known for its more than 300 machines, including tractors, forest machines, off-highway trucks, wheel dozers, and underground mining machines. Many of these machines are sold under the Cat brand, which consists of a Cat logo with the yellow pyramid over part of the "A." Since Caterpillar's machines and equipment are by far their most popular products, the organization must continually develop new products, modify existing ones, and spread awareness of its offerings to maintain its global competitive edge.

The development of new products at Caterpillar involves a series of stages. Overseeing the product development process are product managers. Under their direction, the Caterpillar division will brainstorm ideas for new products or discuss ways to modify existing ones. The company screens relevant product ideas and then undergoes concept testing and business analysis to determine the likely demand and feasibility of the proposed ideas. When it comes to actually developing the product, quality is everything for Caterpillar. Creating high-quality products is embedded in Caterpillar's Code of Conduct as one of its highest values. Therefore, the company has adopted the quality control process of Six Sigma to detect, correct, and reduce problems before the product is released.

© Jim R. Bounds/Bloomberg via Getty Images

After a working product is developed, Caterpillar releases the product on a limited scale and, should these test markets prove favorable, commercializes it on a national or global scale. This allows Caterpillar to gauge not only customer reaction to the product but also work out any manufacturing issues or problems that occur before launching it on a massive scale. When Caterpillar released its Cat CT660 Vocational Truck, it first released the truck into limited markets to make certain that it met quality standards and avoided major glitches. Once it passed these inspection processes, the Cat CT660 Vocational Truck was made available for large-scale shipment.

Not all of Caterpillar's products are new. Many of the company's machines and much of its equipment are modified to meet changing customer needs or adhere to new governmental requirements. For instance, after being criticized for violating the Clean Air Act in 2000, Caterpillar began modifying its engines to be more eco-friendly. Previously, the company's engines were releasing too much pollution into the air, so Caterpillar created Advanced Combustion Emissions Reduction Technology (ACERT) engines to reduce the amount of gases released. Caterpillar's ACERT technology surpassed federal regulation requirements. However, tighter gas emission laws are requiring Caterpillar to modify its products once more. To meet new requirements, Caterpillar has partnered with Tenneco Inc. to create the Clean Emissions Module (CME) to reduce emissions even further. These modules are being placed in Caterpillar's ACERT engines. Caterpillar also refurbishes old machines to increase their life spans, a type of functional modification.

Caterpillar has extended its product line into several different areas, including apparel, watches, toys, and jackets. Line extensions have both benefits and potential downsides. If the line extension has little to do with the core product, then the extension could fail or, even worse, contaminate the brand. On the other hand, line extensions can allow companies to branch out into other areas and increase brand awareness. For instance, Caterpillar-branded toy trucks and tractors allow consumers to become familiar with the Caterpillar name at a young age.

Caterpillar has begun taking its line extensions a step further by licensing the Cat brand name to create Cat-branded lifestyle stores across the world. When first considering Cat-branded stores, Caterpillar was uncertain whether consumers would accept items like apparel and footwear in a retail environment. The company test-marketed the stores over a two-year period with outlets in the United Arab Emirates and China. Caterpillar has since decided to open stores on a wider global scale. The company has licensed its brand to Wolverine World Wide Inc. for Cat footwear and Summit Resource Imports/SRI Apparel for Cat-branded apparel. Although it is riskier to create a product extension that is vastly different from Caterpillar's core products of machinery and equipment, Caterpillar expects to profit from these licensing arrangements with increased revenue and global brand awareness.

Caterpillar is a company that must continually develop and manage its products to maintain its leadership in the construction industry. Its success at product management will likely lead the company to take advantage of future opportunities in the global market.[36]

Questions for Discussion

1. Why is it so important for Caterpillar to develop new products on a regular basis?
2. Why is Caterpillar so careful to test-market its products prior to commercialization?
3. What are some of the benefits and risks of Caterpillar's line extensions?

NOTES

[1]Jon Gertner, "How Do You Solve a Problem Like GM, Mary?" *Fast Company*, October 2011, 104–108, 148; Sharon Terlep, "The Secrets of the GM Diet," *The Wall Street Journal*, August 5, 2011, B1, B4; John D. Stoll, "GM Deeply Discounts Pontiacs and Saturns," MSN Money Central, December 29, 2009, http://articles.moneycentral.msn.com/SavingandDebt/SaveonaCar/gm-deeply-discounts-saturns-and-pontiacs.aspx (accessed December 12, 2011).

[2]Mike Esterl, "Coke Tailors Its Soda Sizes," *The Wall Street Journal*, September 19, 2011, B4.

[3]Robert E. Carter and David J. Curry, "Perceptions versus Performance When Managing Extensions: New Evidence about the Role of Fit between a Parent Brand and an Extension," *Journal of the Academy of Marketing Science*, www.springerlink.com/content/8030v6q35851821t (accessed April 20, 2012).

[4]"Niman Ranch Cage-Free Eggs Are the Perfect Protein for Earth Day," Niman Ranch, April 18, 2011, http://admin.specialtyfood.com/fileManager/65930NimanRanchEarth_Day_Eggs_Final_4-14.pdf (accessed January 19, 2012).

[5]Kenneth Hein, "BK Boxers Leads Pack of Worst Line Extensions," *Ad Week*, www.adweek.com/news/advertising-branding/bk-boxers-leads-pack-worst-line-extensions-104927 (accessed April 20, 2012).

[6]Bruce Horovitz, "Trend Alert: 10 New Products to Watch for in 2012," *USA Today*, January 9, 2012, www.usatoday.com/money/industries/retail/story/2012-01-09/product-trends/52472380/1 (accessed March 5, 2012).

[7]Mike Ramsey, "Old Mustang Is Put Out to Pasture," *The Wall Street Journal*, April 16, 2012, B1.

[8]Sam Grobart and Brad Stone, "With iPhone 5, Apple Again Raises the Smartphone Bar," *Bloomberg Businessweek*, September 12, 2012, www.businessweek.com/articles/2012-09-12/with-iphone-5-apple-again-raises-the-smartphone-bar (accessed September 13, 2012).

[9]Panos Mourdoukoutas, "The Entrepreneurial Failure of Eastman Kodak," *Forbes*, October 2, 2011, www.forbes.com/sites/panosmourdoukoutas/2011/10/02/the-entrepreneurial-failure-of-eastman-kodak (accessed January 19, 2012).

[10]Michael Lev-Ram, "A Twitter Guy Takes on Banks," *Fortune*, February 7, 2011, 37–42.

[11]"Product Trends for 2011," *USA Today*, http://mediagallery.usatoday.com/Product-trends-for-2011/G1992 (accessed January 19, 2012).

[12]"Introducing DAZBOG Tea," *Marketing News*, March 30, 2011, 16.

[13]"About Us," *Smart USA*, www.smartusa.com (accessed March 15, 2010).

[14]Christoph Fuchs and Martin Schreier, "Customer Empowerment in New Product Development," *Journal of Product Innovation Management* 28, no. 1 (January 2011): 17–31.

[15]"The Ray Kroc Story," McDonald's, www.mcdonalds.com/us/en/our_story/our_history/the_ray_kroc_story.html (accessed January 19, 2012).

[16]Arina Soukhoroukova, Martin Spann, and Bernd Skiera, "Sourcing, Filtering, and Evaluating New Product Ideas: An Empirical Exploration of the Performance of Idea Markets," *Journal of Product Innovation Management* 29, no. 1 (January 2012): 100–112.

[17]"P&G Open to New Ideas, But Not to Embalming Kits," *Taipei Times*, January 3, 2010, www.taipeitimes.com/News/biz/archives/2010/01/03/2003462552 (accessed January 19, 2012).

[18]"Our Clients," Fahrenheit 212, www.fahrenheit-212.com/#/innovation/our-work/our-clients (accessed January 19, 2012); Nadira A. Hira, "Fahrenheit 212—The Innovator's Paradise," *Fortune*, December 16, 2009, http://money.cnn.com/2009/12/15/news/companies/fahrenheit_212.fortune/index.htm (accessed March 19, 2010).

[19]Stephan Faris, "Ground Zero," *Bloomberg Businessweek*, February 13–19, 2012, 68–69.

[20]JoAndrea Hoegg and Joseph W. Alba, "Seeing Is Believing (Too Much): The Influence of Product Form on Perceptions of Functional Performance," *Journal of Product Innovation Management* 28, no. 3 (May 2011): 346–359.

[21]"Altria Plans to Test-Market Smokeless 'Tobacco Sticks'," *The Wall Street Journal*, February 23, 2011, http://online.wsj.com/article/SB10001424052748703842004576162920066342358.html (accessed January 19, 2012).

[22]Sky Zone website, http://skyzonesports.com/ (accessed January 19, 2012); Jason Daley, "The Big Bounce," *Entrepreneur*, April 2010, 108.

[23]Jack Neff, "Swiffer by Another Name," *Advertising Age*, April 11, 2005, 11.

[24]Roger J. Calantone and C. Anthony Di Benedetto, "The Role of Lean Launch Execution and Launch Timing on New Product Performance," *Journal of the Academy of Marketing Science*, June 2011, http://rd.springer.com/article/10.1007/s11747-011-0258-1 (accessed April 20, 2012).

[25]"Scores by Industry: Full Service Restaurants," The American Consumer Satisfaction Index, www.theacsi.org/index.php?option=com_content&view=article&id=149&catid=&Itemid=214&c=All+Others&i=Full+Service+Restaurants (accessed January 19, 2012).

[26]"Scores by Industry: Express Delivery," ACSI, www.theacsi.org/index.php?option=com_content&view=article&id=147&catid=&Itemid=212&i=Express+Delivery+%28Consumer+Shipping%29 (accessed January 19, 2012).

[27]"The All-New Chevrolet Cruze. Get Used to 'More'." Chevrolet, www.chevrolet.com/assets/pdf/en/overview/11_Spec_Sheet_Cruze.pdf (accessed January 19, 2011).

[28]Karen Aho, "The 2011 Customer Service Hall of Fame," MSN Money, http://money.msn.com/investing/the-2011-customer-service-hall-of-fame.aspx?cp-documentid=6820771 (accessed January 19, 2012).

[29]Marco Bertini, Elie Ofek, and Dan Ariely, "The Impact of Add-On Features on Consumer Product Evaluations," *Journal of Consumer Research* 36, no. 1 (June 2009): 17–28.

[30]"The Chevrolet Cruze—Dear Corolla," YouTube, www.youtube.com/watch?v=nnVkXh4f-Tw (accessed January 30, 2012).

[31]"2013 Ford Fusion," *Motor Trend*, March 2012, 51–52.

[32]Ibid., 54.

[33]Mae Anderson, "Dr Pepper Ten 'Not for Women'," *USA Today*, October 10, 2011, www.usatoday.com/money/industries/food/story/2011-10-10/dr-pepper-for-men/50717788/1 (accessed March 5, 2012).

[34]Christian Seabaugh, "Rest in Pieces—Cars That Bit the Dust in 2011," *Motor Trend*, December 28, 2011, http://wot.motortrend.com/rest-in-pieces-cars-that-bit-the-dust-in-2011-150683.html (accessed January 19, 2012).

[35]John Berman and Lauren Effron, "The World of AXE Is 'Lick-able, Addictive'," *ABC News,* March 25, 2011, http://abcnews.go.com/Entertainment/lick-inside-axe-popular-male-grooming-products-brand/story?id=13224549 (accessed March 30, 2012); "AXE Unleashes Anarchy in Canada with First-Ever Female Fragrance," Canadian Newswire, February 7, 2012, www.newswire.ca/en/story/917149/axe-unleashes-anarchy-in-canada-with-first-ever-female-fragrance (accessed March 30, 2012); Jan Hoffman, "Masculinity in a Spray Can," *The New York Times*, January 29, 2010, www.nytimes.com/2010/01/31/fashion/31smell.html?pagewanted=1&_r=1 (accessed March 30, 2012); "Axe," Unilever, www.unilever.ca/brands/personal carebrands/Axe.aspx (accessed March 30, 2012).

[36]Caterpillar, *2010 Sustainability Report*, www.caterpillar.com/cda/files/2646184/7/2010SustainabilityReport.pdf (accessed April 30, 2011); "Certified Rebuild," *2010 Sustainability Report*, www.caterpillar.com/cda/layout?m=389975&x=7&ids=2646281 (accessed April 23, 2011); "Clean Air Villain of the Month," Clean Air Trust, www.cleanairtrust.org/villain.0800.html (accessed April 23, 2011); "Vision, Mission, Strategy," Caterpillar, www.caterpillar.com/sustainability/vision-mission-strategy (accessed April 23, 2011); "Caterpillar Inc. (CAT)," Yahoo! Finance, http://finance.yahoo.com/q/pr?s=CAT+Profile (accessed May 24, 2011); "Equipment," CAT, www.cat.com/equipment (accessed May 24, 2011); "CATERPILLAR INC (CAT: New York)," *Bloomberg Businessweek,* http://investing.businessweek.com/research/stocks/snapshot/snapshot.asp?ticker=CAT:US (accessed May 24, 2011); "Caterpillar," Business Insider, www.businessinsider.com/blackboard/caterpillar (accessed May 24, 2011); "CAT," Caterpillar, www.caterpillar.com/brands/cat (accessed May 25, 2011); "Products," CAT, www.cat.com/products/ (accessed May 25, 2011); Marc Gunther, "Caterpillar Jumps on the Green Bandwagon," CNNMoney, May 3, 2007, http://money.cnn.com/ 2007/05/02/magazines/fortune/pluggedin_Gunther.fortune/index.htm (accessed May 27, 2011); David Paper and Steve Dickinson, "A Comprehensive Process Improvement Methodology: Experiences at Caterpillar's Mossville Engine Center (MEC)," in Jay Liebowitz and Mehdi Khosrowpour (eds.), *Cases on Information Technology Management in Modern Organizations,* (Hershey, PA: Idea Group Publishing, 1997), 100; "CAT® Branded Lifestyle Stores Expand Worldwide," Caterpillar, www.caterpillar.com/cda/components/fullArticle?m=393446&x=7&id=2994324 (accessed March 20, 2012); Heather McBroom, "6 Sigma: Foundation for Quality at Caterpillar," *Peoria Magazines,* July 2009, www.peoriamagazines.com/ibi/2009/jul/6-sigma (accessed March 20, 2012); "Caterpillar Product Manager Gary Blood Speaks about the CT660," YouTube, February 9, 2011, www.youtube.com/watch?v=poqQMOk3pIQ (accessed March 20, 2012); "Cat® CT660 Vocational Trucks Ready for Work," Caterpillar Press Release, September 2011.

Feature Notes

[a]"The Baguette Vending Machine," *TIME*, August 2011, 80; Jamey Keaten, "French Baker Builds Vending Machine for Baguettes," August 8, 2011, www.msnbc.msn.com/id/44061368/ns/business-small_business/t/french-baker-builds-vending-machine-baguettes (accessed November 21, 2011); Douglas Stanglin, "Daring French Baker Unveils Baguette Vending Machine," *USA Today,* August 9, 2011, http://content.usatoday.com/communities/ondeadline/post/2011/08/daring-french-baker-unveils-baguette-vending-machine/1 (accessed November 21, 2011); "Baguette Vending Machine Filling Gap," *The Australian,* August 9, 2011, www.theaustralian.com.au/news/world/baguette-vending-machine-filling-gap/story-e6frg6so-1226111450643 (accessed November 21, 2011).

[b]Terri Bennett, "The Good, Bad & Ugly about CFLs," *The Chicago Tribune,* April 26, 2010, www.chicagotribune.com/health/sc-home-0426-clfs-20100426,0,2225600.story (accessed November 17, 2011); Elisabeth Rosenthal and Felicity Barringer, "Green Promise Seen in Switch to LED Lighting," *The New York Times,* May 29, 2009, www.nytimes.com/2009/05/30/science/earth/30degrees.html?ref=lightemitting_diodes (accessed November 17, 2011); Wendy Koch, "American Hazy on U.S. Phaseout of Incandescent Lights," *USA Today,* December 21, 2010, http://content.usatoday.com/communities/greenhouse/post/2010/12/americans-hazy-us-energy-efficiency-rules/1 (accessed November 17, 2011); Dan Koeppel, "The Future of Lights Is the LED," *Wired*, August 19, 2011, www.wired.com/magazine/2011/08/ff_lightbulbs (accessed November 17, 2011).

[c]James R. Healey, "Ford, Zipcar Send Focus to College," *USA Today,* August 31, 2011, 1B; Zipcar, www.zipcar.com (accessed March 15, 2010); Joseph Pisani, "Car Sharing Takes Off," CNBC, December 4, 2009, www.cnbc.com/id/34257797 (accessed March 15, 2010); Paul Keegan, "The Best in Business," *Fortune*, September 14, 2009, 42–52; Kunur Patel, "Zipcar: An America's Hottest Brands Study Case," *Advertising Age*, November 16, 2009, http://adage.com/article?article_id=140495 (accessed March 15, 2010); "Zipcar, San Francisco Launch Plug-in Hybrid Pilot Program," SustainableBusiness.com, February 19, 2009, www.sustainablebusiness.com/index.cfm/go/news.display/id/17703 (accessed March 15, 2010).

[d]Tiffany Hsu, "Food Products Described as Artisan Go Mainstream," *The Los Angeles Times*, September 28, 2011, http://articles.latimes.com/2011/sep/28/business/la-fi-artisan-food-20110928 (accessed November 2, 2011); Bruce Horovitz, "But Is It Art(isan)? Food Labels Say Yes," *USA Today*, October 25, 2011, 3B.

chapter 13

Services Marketing

OBJECTIVES

1. To understand the growth and importance of services
2. To identify the characteristics of services that differentiate them from goods
3. To describe how the characteristics of services influence the development of marketing mixes for services
4. To understand the importance of service quality and explain how to deliver exceptional service quality
5. To explore the nature of nonprofit marketing

MARKETING INSIGHTS

Four-Season Personal Service at the Four Seasons

Whether they're checking into the glittering Four Seasons high-rise hotel in Manhattan or the Four Seasons tropical resort in Bali, guests expect more than top-quality facilities—they expect top-notch service. Toronto-based Four Seasons, which operates 86 hotels in 35 countries, has made its name by delivering services geared to each guest's individual preferences. As the hotel company's vice president of marketing explains: "We create personal experiences."

Four Seasons personnel go out of their way to be accommodating. For example, the company offers a 15-minute room service menu for hotel guests in a hurry. Customers can have their orders brought to the front desk at checkout, to their guest rooms before checkout, or directly to their cars. For those who are headed for flights, the Four Seasons also prepares meals and snacks that can be taken through airport security checkpoints.

In addition, the Four Seasons uses digital marketing to engage and serve its customers. One of its blogs offers suggestions for family activities in Four Seasons cities. Another posts special recipes and profiles the chefs at different Four Seasons properties. The company hosts virtual wine tastings, in which participants and experts post comments on the Four Seasons Twitter account while sipping the wines at a Four Seasons hotel or on their own. Finally, the Four Seasons' website links to visitors' reviews of its service because, says the marketing vice president, "what we're offering to our guest is something that stands up to that level of scrutiny."[1]

The products offered by the Four Seasons are service products rather than tangible goods. This chapter explores concepts that apply specifically to products that are services. The organizations that market services include for-profit firms, such as those offering financial, personal, and professional services, and nonprofit organizations, such as educational institutions, churches, charities, and governments.

We begin this chapter with a focus on the growing importance of service industries in our economy. We then address the unique characteristics of services. Next, we deal with the challenges these characteristics pose in developing and managing marketing mixes for services. We then discuss customers' judgment of service quality and the importance of delivering high-quality services. Finally, we define nonprofit marketing and examine the development of nonprofit marketing strategies.

THE GROWTH AND IMPORTANCE OF SERVICES

All products, whether goods, services, or ideas, are intangible to some extent. We previously defined a service as an intangible product that involves a deed, a performance, or an effort that cannot be physically possessed.[2] Services are usually provided through the application of human and/or mechanical efforts that are directed at people or objects. For example, a service such as education involves the efforts of service providers (teachers) that are directed at people (students), whereas janitorial and interior decorating services direct their efforts at objects. Services can also involve the use of mechanical efforts directed at people (air transportation) or objects (freight transportation). A wide variety of services, such as health care and landscaping, involve both human and mechanical efforts. Although many services entail the use of tangibles such as tools and machinery, the primary difference between a service and a good is that a service is dominated by the intangible portion of the total product.

Services as products should not be confused with the related topic of customer service. Customer service involves any human, mechanical, or electronic activity that adds value to the product. Although the core product may be a good or electronic, complementary services help create the total product, and although customer service is a part of the marketing of goods,

© NetPhotos/Alamy

The Importance of Services
The marketing of services can be challenging, because services are intangible products, as opposed to goods, which are physical and tangible products.

service marketers also provide customer services. For instance, many service companies offer guarantees to their customers in an effort to increase value. Hampton Inn, a national chain of mid-price hotels, gives its guests a free night if they are not 100 percent satisfied with their stay (less than one-half of 1 percent of Hampton customers ask for a refund). In some cases, a 100 percent satisfaction guarantee or similar service commitment may motivate employees to provide high-quality service, not because failure to do so leads to personal penalties but because they are proud to be part of an organization that is so committed to good service.

The increasing importance of services in the U.S. economy has led many people to call the United States the world's first service economy. In most developed countries, including Germany, Japan, Australia, and Canada, services account for about 70 percent of the gross domestic product (GDP). More than one-half of new businesses are service businesses, and service employment is expected to continue to grow. These industries have absorbed much of the influx of women and minorities into the workforce. A practice that has gained popularity among a number of U.S. businesses is **homesourcing**, in which customer-contact jobs, especially at call centers, are outsourced into the homes of workers. Staffing agencies like Rhema Business Solutions are dedicated to providing homesourcing employees to organizations in a variety of industries, including nursing, marketing and sales, advertising, Web development, and writing. Companies as diverse as 1-800-FLOWERS, J.Crew, and Office Depot all utilize homesourcing for some tasks.[3]

One major catalyst in the growth of consumer services has been long-term economic growth (slowed only by a few recessions) in the United States, which has led to increased interest in financial services, travel, entertainment, and personal care. Lifestyle changes have similarly encouraged expansion of the service sector. The need for child care, domestic services, online dating services, and other time-saving services has increased, and many consumers want to avoid such tasks as meal preparation, house cleaning, yard maintenance, and tax preparation. Hampton Inn Hotels, Subway, 7-Eleven, and Days Inn are all franchises that are experiencing rapid growth.[4] Also, because Americans have become more health, fitness, and recreation oriented, the demand for exercise and recreational facilities has escalated. In terms of demographics, the U.S. population is growing older, a fact that has spurred tremendous expansion of health-care services. Finally, the increasing number and complexity of high-tech goods have spurred demand for support services. Indeed, the services sector has been enhanced by dramatic changes in information technology. Consider service companies like Google, eBay, and Amazon.com, which use technology to provide services to challenge and change traditional ways of conducting business.

Business services have prospered as well. Business services include support and maintenance, consulting, installation, equipment leasing, marketing research, advertising, temporary office personnel, and janitorial services. Expenditures for business services have risen even faster than expenditures for consumer services. The growth in business services has been attributed to the increasingly complex, specialized, and competitive business environment. IBM, for example, has shifted from a focus on computer hardware to consulting services and software applications.

One way to view services is from a theater framework with production elements, such as actors, audience, a setting, and a performance. The actors (service workers) create a performance (service) for the audience (customers) in a setting (service environment) where the performance unfolds. Costumes (uniforms), props (devices, music, machines), and the setting (face-to-face or indirect through telephone or Internet) help complete the theatrical metaphor.[5] At Disney World, for example, all employees wear costumes, there is an entertainment setting, and most service contact with employees involves playing roles and engaging in planned skits. But you can also see theatrical components of services in many organizations, from the uniforms employees wear to the style of delivery, such as the joking tone of Southwest Airlines flight attendants or the upbeat and reliable service of a Starbucks barista. In addition, a performance involves a "script," a chronologically ordered representation of the steps that comprise the service performance from the customer's perspective.[6] Even sports events like football, basketball, and hockey have sequences of events and rules that standardize the performance, even if the outcome depends on the performance itself.

homesourcing A practice whereby customer contact jobs are outsourced into workers' homes

CHARACTERISTICS OF SERVICES

The issues associated with marketing service products differ somewhat from those associated with marketing goods. To understand these differences, we need to look at the distinguishing characteristics of services. Services have six basic characteristics: intangibility, inseparability of production and consumption, perishability, heterogeneity, client-based relationships, and customer contact.[7]

Intangibility

As already noted, the major characteristic that distinguishes a service from a good is intangibility. **Intangibility** means a service is not physical and therefore cannot be perceived by the senses. For example, it is impossible to touch the education that students derive from attending classes; the intangible benefit is becoming more knowledgeable. In addition, services cannot be physically possessed. Students obviously cannot physically touch knowledge as they can an iPod or a car. The level of intangibility of a product or service has an effect on the overall importance of the brand when a customer is deciding which brand to purchase. When there is an intangible product involved, there are fewer factors for the customer to use when deciding on which brand to select, so a customer trying to select an intangible product usually relies more heavily on the brand to act as a cue to the nature and quality of the service.

Figure 13.1 depicts a tangibility continuum from pure goods (tangible) to pure services (intangible). Pure goods, if they exist at all, are rare because practically all marketers of goods also provide customer services. Even a tangible product like sugar must be delivered to the store, priced, and placed on a shelf before a customer can purchase it. Intangible, service-dominant products, such as education or health care, are clearly service products. But what about products near the center of the continuum? Is a restaurant like Chili's a goods marketer or a service marketer? Services like airline flights have something tangible to offer, such as seats and drinks. An Internet search engine like Google or a news site, such as CNN or MSNBC, is service-dominant. Knowing where the product lies on the continuum is important in creating marketing strategies for service-dominant products.

intangibility The characteristic that a service is not physical and cannot be perceived by the senses

Figure 13.1 The Tangibility Continuum

Inseparability of Production and Consumption

Another important characteristic of services that creates challenges for marketers is **inseparability**, which refers to the fact that the production of a service cannot be separated from its consumption by customers. For instance, an airline flight is produced and consumed simultaneously—that is, services are often produced, sold, and consumed at the same time. In goods marketing, a customer can purchase a good, take it home, and store it until ready for use. The manufacturer of the good may never see an actual customer. Customers, however, often must be present at the production of a service (such as investment consulting or surgery) and cannot take the service home. Indeed, both the service provider and the customer must work together to provide and receive the service's full value. Because of inseparability, customers not only want a specific type of service but expect it to be provided in a specific way by a specific individual. For example, the production and consumption of a medical exam occur simultaneously, and the patient knows in advance who the physician is and generally understands how the exam will be conducted. Inseparability implies a shared responsibility between the customer and service provider. Training programs for employees in the service sector should stress the importance of the customer in the service experience so that employees understand that the shared responsibility exists.

Perishability

Services are characterized by **perishability** in that the unused service capacity of one time period cannot be stored for future use. For instance, empty seats on an airline flight today cannot be stored and sold to passengers at a later date. Other examples of service perishability include unsold basketball tickets, unscheduled dentists' appointment times, and empty hotel rooms. Although some goods, such as meat, milk, and produce, are perishable, goods generally are less perishable than services. If a pair of jeans has been sitting on a department store shelf for a week, someone can still buy them the next day. Goods marketers can handle the supply-demand problem through production scheduling and inventory techniques. Service marketers do not have the same advantage and face several hurdles in trying to balance supply and demand. They can, however, plan for demand that fluctuates according to day of the week, time of day, or season.

inseparability The quality of being produced and consumed at the same time

perishability The inability of unused service capacity to be stored for future use

Inseparability of Production and Consumption
An airline flight is characterized by inseparability. Production and consumption occur simultaneously.

Heterogeneity

Services delivered by people are susceptible to **heterogeneity**, or variation in quality. Quality of manufactured goods is easier to control with standardized procedures, and mistakes are easier to isolate and correct. Because of the nature of human behavior, however, it is very difficult for service providers to maintain a consistent quality of service delivery. This variation in quality can occur from one organization to another, one service person to another within the same service facility, and one service facility to another within the same organization. For example, one bank may provide more convenient hours and charge fewer fees than the one next door, or the retail clerks in one bookstore may be more knowledgeable and therefore more helpful than those in another bookstore owned by the same chain. In addition, the service a single employee provides can vary from customer to customer, day to day, or even hour to hour. Although many service problems are one-time events that cannot be predicted or controlled ahead of time, training and establishment of standard procedures can help increase consistency and reliability. Employee training should educate employees in ways that will help them provide quality service consistently to customers, thus mitigating the issue of heterogeneity. For example, a business that provides services in a cross-cultural environment may want to train its employees to be more sensitive toward people of different countries and cultures.

Heterogeneity usually increases as the degree of labor intensiveness increases. Many services, such as auto repair, education, and hairstyling, rely heavily on human labor. Other services, such as telecommunications, health clubs, grocery delivery, and public transportation, are more equipment intensive. People-based services are often prone to fluctuations in quality from one time period to the next. For instance, the fact that a hairstylist gives a customer a good haircut today does not guarantee that customer a haircut of equal quality from the same hairstylist at a later date or even a later hour. A morning customer may receive a better haircut than an end-of-the-day customer from the same stylist. Equipment-based services suffer from this problem to a lesser degree than people-based services. For instance, automated teller machines have reduced inconsistency in the quality of teller services at banks, and bar-code scanning has improved the accuracy of service at checkout counters in grocery stores.

heterogeneity Variation in quality

Heterogeneity
Do you like to go to the same hair care professional most of the time? If so, it is probably because you want the same quality of hair care, such as a haircut that you have received from this individual in the past.

Client-Based Relationships

The success of many services depends on creating and maintaining **client-based relationships**: interactions that result in satisfied customers who use a service repeatedly over time.[8] In fact, some service providers, such as lawyers, accountants, and financial advisers, call their customers *clients* and often develop and maintain close, long-term relationships with them. For such service providers, it is not enough to attract customers. They are successful only to the degree to which they can maintain a group of clients who use their services on an ongoing basis. For example, an accountant may serve a family in his or her area for decades. If the members of this family like the quality of the accountant's services, they are likely to recommend the accountant to other families. If several families repeat this positive word-of-mouth communication, the accountant will likely acquire a long list of satisfied clients before long. Social media have made it easier for customers to share information about service companies. Pinterest is one of these sites that help increase traffic to company websites. It is a social media site that resembles notice boards to which users can pin information about services and products that they like or plan to use. Users create separate pinboards for different categories, such as a wedding or party they are planning, and other users can utilize these boards for ideas and inspiration. Pinterest is growing by leaps and bounds and is most popular among young and middle-aged women—the market segment in charge of most household purchasing decisions.[9] Word-of-mouth is a key factor in creating and maintaining client-based relationships. To ensure that it actually occurs, the service provider must take steps to build trust, demonstrate customer commitment, and satisfy customers so well that they become very loyal to the provider and unlikely to switch to competitors.

client-based relationships Interactions that result in satisfied customers who use a service repeatedly over time

customer contact The level of interaction between provider and customer needed to deliver the service

Customer Contact

Not all services require a high degree of customer contact, but many do. **Customer contact** refers to the level of interaction between the service provider and the customer necessary to deliver the service. High-contact services include health care, real estate, legal, and spa services. Examples of low-contact services are tax preparation, auto repair, travel reservations, and dry cleaning. Some service-oriented businesses are reducing their level of customer

Entrepreneurship in Marketing

Via: Best Small Ad Agency Attracts National Clients

Entrepreneur: John Coleman
Business: Via
Founded: 1993 | Portland, Maine
Success: Via was named the best small agency of the year by *Advertising Age.*

Headquartered in a 19th-century building that once served as the public library of Portland, Maine, Via is a small advertising agency with big ideas for the 21st century. The award-winning agency is known as much for its responsive, results-oriented service as for its creativity. Founded by John Coleman in 1993, Via develops advertising campaigns for all media, including social media, helping its business clients market more effectively to their customers.

The chief marketing officer of Samsung Electronics observes that Via's creative experts are good listeners, work collaboratively with clients, and understand the need for measurable results. When Samsung introduced its Galaxy Tab tablet computer, which competes with Apple's iPad, Via was able to crank up a multimedia launch program in only five weeks. Thanks in part to Via's high-performing campaign, Samsung sold more than 1 million Galaxy Tabs in the first three months.

Via's top-notch service has attracted a growing roster of clients from different industries, including Unilever ice creams, Macaroni Grill, Perdue chicken products, and People's United Bank. No wonder *Advertising Age* named Via the best small agency of the year in 2011.[a]

Level of Customer Contact
There is a high level of customer contact associated with dental services.

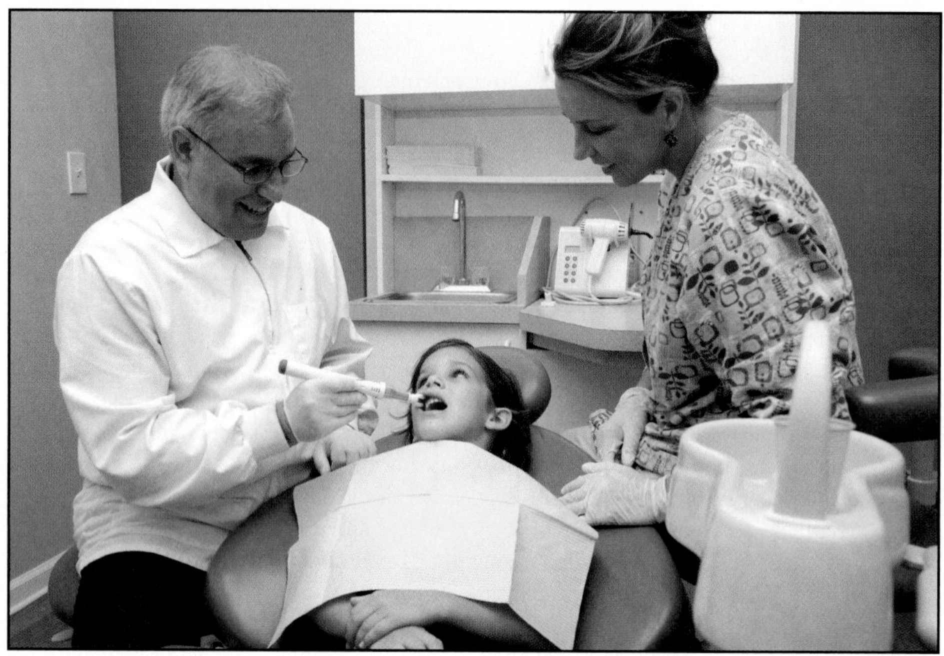

contact through technology. Note that high-contact services generally involve actions directed toward people, who must be present during production. A hairstylist's customer, for example, must be present during the styling process. Because the customer must be present, the process of production may be just as important as its final outcome. Although it is sometimes possible for the service provider to go to the customer, high-contact services typically require that the customer go to the production facility. Thus, the physical appearance of the facility may be a major component of the customer's overall evaluation of the service. Even in low-contact service situations, the appearance of the facility is important because the customer likely will need to be present to initiate and finalize the service transaction. Consider customers of auto-repair services. They bring in the vehicle and describe its symptoms but often do not remain during the repair process.

Employees of high-contact service providers are a crucial ingredient in creating satisfied customers. A fundamental relationship of customer contact is that satisfied employees lead to satisfied customers. In fact, employee satisfaction is the single most important factor in providing high service quality. Thus, to minimize the problems customer contact can create, service organizations must take steps to understand and meet the needs of employees by adequately training them, empowering them to make more decisions, and rewarding them for customer-oriented behavior.[10] The luxury hotel and five-star resort operator Ritz Carlton, which is known for providing high-quality customer service, trains all of its employees to be confident in their decisions and actively resolve customer complaints. The company gives each of its employees a personal spending budget, which can be as much as $2,000 per complaint or incident, to use at their discretion to resolve issues with customers.[11]

DEVELOPING AND MANAGING MARKETING MIXES FOR SERVICES

The characteristics of services discussed in the previous section create a number of challenges for service marketers (see Table 13.1). These challenges are especially evident in the development and management of marketing mixes for services. Although such mixes contain the four major marketing mix variables—product, distribution, promotion, and price—the characteristics of services require that marketers consider additional issues.

Table 13.1 **Service Characteristics and Marketing Challenges**

Service Characteristics	Resulting Marketing Challenges
Intangibility	Difficult for customer to evaluate. Customer does not take physical possession. Difficult to advertise and display. Difficult to set and justify prices. Service process is usually not protectable by patents.
Inseparability of production and consumption	Service provider cannot mass produce services. Customer must participate in production. Other consumers affect service outcomes. Services are difficult to distribute.
Perishability	Services cannot be stored. Balancing supply and demand is very difficult. Unused capacity is lost forever. Demand may be very time sensitive.
Heterogeneity	Service quality is difficult to control. Service delivery is difficult to standardize.
Client-based relationships	Success depends on satisfying and keeping customers over the long term. Generating repeat business is challenging. Relationship marketing becomes critical.
Customer contact	Service providers are critical to delivery. Requires high levels of service employee training and motivation. Changing a high-contact service into a low-contact service to achieve lower costs is difficult to achieve without reducing customer satisfaction.

Sources: K. Doublas Hoffman and John E. G. Bateson, *Services Marketing: Concepts, Strategies, and Cases*, 4th ed. (Mason, OH: Cengage Learning/South-Western, 2011); Valarie A. Zeithaml, A. Parasuraman, and Leonard L. Berry, *Delivering Quality Service: Balancing Customer Perceptions and Expectations* (New York: Free Press, 1990); Leonard L. Berry and A. Parasuraman, *Marketing Services: Competing Through Quality* (New York: Free Press, 1991), 5.

Development of Services

A service offered by an organization is generally a package, or bundle, of services consisting of a core service and one or more supplementary services. A core service is the basic service experience or commodity that a customer expects to receive. A supplementary service supports the core service and is used to differentiate the service bundle from those of competitors. For example, when a student attends a tutoring session for a class, the core service is the tutoring. Bundled with the core service might be access to outlines with additional information, handouts with practice questions, or online service like an e-mail address or chat room for questions outside the designated tutoring time.

As discussed earlier, heterogeneity results in variability in service quality and makes it difficult to standardize service delivery. However, heterogeneity provides one advantage to service marketers: it allows them to customize their services to match the specific needs of individual customers. Customization plays a key role in providing competitive advantage for the service provider. Being able to personalize the service to fit the exact needs of the customer accommodates individual needs, wants, or desires.[12] IBM determines a business's needs and then develops information technology services to provide a customized application. Apple's iBooks Author app allows authors to customize their books' contents, including adding interactive elements, such as diagrams, audio, and video.[13] Health care is an example of an extremely customized service. The services provided differ from one patient to the next.

Such customized services can be expensive for both provider and customer, and some service marketers therefore face a dilemma: how to provide service at an acceptable level of quality in an efficient and economic manner and still satisfy individual customer needs. To cope with this problem, some service marketers offer standardized packages. For instance, a spa may provide a number of treatments, such as hairstyling, facials, and massages for one price. When service bundles are standardized, the specific actions and activities of the service provider usually are highly specified. Automobile quick-lube providers frequently offer a service bundle for a single price. The specific work to be done on a customer's car is spelled out in detail. Various other equipment-based services are also often standardized into packages. For instance, cable television providers frequently offer several packages, such as "Basic," "Standard," and "Premier."

The characteristic of intangibility makes it difficult for customers to evaluate a service prior to purchase. A customer who is shopping for a pair of jeans can try them on before buying them, but how does this person evaluate legal advice before receiving the service? Intangibility requires service marketers like attorneys to market promises to customers. The customer is forced to place some degree of trust in the service provider to perform the service in a manner that meets or exceeds those promises. Service marketers must guard against making promises that raise customer expectations beyond what they can provide.

To cope with the problem of intangibility, marketers employ tangible cues, such as well-groomed, professional-appearing contact personnel and clean, attractive physical facilities, to help assure customers about the quality of the service. Most service providers uniform at least some of their high-contact employees. Uniforms help make the service experience more tangible and serve as physical evidence to signal quality, create consistency, and send cues to suggest a desired image.[14] Consider the professionalism, experience, and competence conveyed by an airline pilot's uniform. Life insurance companies sometimes try to make the quality of their policies more tangible by printing them on premium-quality paper and enclosing them in leather sheaths. Because customers often rely on brand names as an indicator of product quality, service marketers at organizations whose names are the same as their service brand names should strive to build a strong national image for their companies. For example, Disney, Google, and American Express try to maintain strong, positive national company images because these names are the brand names of the services they provide.

The inseparability of production and consumption and the level of customer contact also influence the development and management of services. The fact that customers take part in the production of a service means other customers can affect the outcome of the service. For instance, if a nonsmoker dines in a restaurant without a no-smoking section, the overall quality of service experienced by the nonsmoking customer declines. For this reason, many restaurants have no-smoking sections, and some prohibit smoking anywhere on their premises. Service marketers can reduce these problems by encouraging customers to share the responsibility of maintaining an environment that allows all participants to receive the intended benefits of the service.

Distribution of Services

Marketers deliver services in a variety of ways. In some instances, customers go to a service provider's facility. For instance, most health-care, dry-cleaning, and spa services are delivered at the provider's facilities. Some services are provided at the customer's home or business. Lawn care, air-conditioning and heating repair, and carpet cleaning are examples. Other services are delivered primarily at "arm's length," meaning no face-to-face contact occurs between the customer and the service provider. A number of equipment-based services are delivered at arm's length, including electric, online, cable television, and telephone services. Providing high-quality customer service at arm's length can be costly but essential in keeping customers satisfied and maintaining market share. Allstate insurance knows that customer satisfaction is important and emphasizes good public service. The company offers six months of free car insurance premiums to customers who are not satisfied with the handling of a paid auto insurance claim. The company states that it wants its customers to be satisfied with their overall experience, not just the payout of the claim.[15]

Marketing channels for services are usually short and direct, meaning the producer delivers the service directly to the end user. Some services, however, use intermediaries. For example, travel agents facilitate the delivery of airline services, independent insurance agents participate in the marketing of a variety of insurance policies, and financial planners market investment services. Service marketers are less concerned with warehousing and transportation than are goods marketers. They are, however, very concerned about inventory management, especially balancing supply and demand for services. The service characteristics of inseparability and level of customer contact contribute to the challenges of demand management. In some instances, service

© ZUMA Wire Service/Alamy

© NetPhotos/Alamy

Distribution of Services
Services can be distributed through physical facilities, such as FedEx Office, or online, through sites like Travelocity.

marketers use appointments and reservations as approaches for scheduling delivery of services. Health-care providers, attorneys, accountants, auto mechanics, restaurants, and airlines often use appointments or reservations to plan and pace delivery of their services. Southwest Airlines, for example, uses sophisticated computer systems, software, and mathematical algorithms to develop efficient routes and schedules for its more than 3,300 daily departures.[16] To increase the supply of a service, marketers use multiple service sites and also increase the number of contact service providers at each site. National and regional eye-care and hair-care services are examples.

To make delivery more accessible to customers and increase the supply of a service, as well as reduce labor costs, some service providers have replaced some contact personnel with equipment. In other words, they have changed a high-contact service into a low-contact one. For example, paying bills, renewing license plate tags or business licenses, financial services, and even computer-related services can all be done via the Internet, mail, or automated phone response systems. Changing the delivery of services from man-powered to automated has created some problems, however. Some customers complain that automated services are less personal. When designing service delivery, marketers must pay attention to the degree of personalization that customers desire.

Promotion of Services

The intangibility of services results in several promotion-related challenges to service marketers. Because it may not be possible to depict the actual performance of a service in an advertisement or display it in a store, explaining a service to customers can be a difficult task. Promotion of services typically includes tangible cues that symbolize the service. Consider Trans America, which uses its pyramid-shaped building to symbolize strength, security, and reliability. These are important features associated with insurance and other financial services. Similarly, the cupped hands Allstate uses in its ads symbolize personalized service and trustworthy, caring representatives. Although these symbols have nothing to do with the actual services, they make it much easier for customers to understand the intangible attributes associated with insurance services. To make a service more tangible, advertisements for services often show pictures of facilities, equipment, and service personnel. Marketers may also promote their services as a tangible expression of consumers' lifestyles. The California Travel & Tourism Commission, for example, runs a website called Visit California, which provides the public with information about various things to do and see throughout the state of California. Visit California's recent advertising campaign involved television advertisements that featured several famous California natives and promoted the various outdoor activities and sights that California has to offer to adventurous tourists, including its ski slopes, beaches, the Redwoods, and the Golden Gate Bridge.[17]

Compared with goods marketers, service providers are more likely to promote price, guarantees, performance documentation, availability, and training and certification of contact personnel. For example, it is common for fitness centers like Gold's Gym to promote degrees and certifications earned by trainers as a way to ensure customers that the trainers will help

Emerging Trends

Customer Service Goes Social

From Best Buy to Bank of America and beyond, a growing number of service firms are using social media to answer customers' questions, respond to complaints, and offer technical assistance. Many airlines have also jumped on the social media bandwagon. The Dutch airline KLM uses its Facebook page as a central online location to communicate service changes and help customers with everyday concerns, such as enrolling in the frequent-flyer program or rebooking a flight following a delay. More than 1 million customers have already clicked to "like" KLM on Facebook and read its updates. The airline also provides around-the-clock service support on Twitter, requesting that customers send direct messages to protect personal details.

Cable companies are going social for service as well. To address negative perceptions of its service (and to supplement traditional phone and e-mail assistance), the cable company Comcast has, since 2008, exchanged messages with customers via a Twitter account called @comcastcares. Not only do customers interact with a person instead of an automated system when they post a comment, their complaints or questions are referred to the right individual within Comcast for speedy results. Demonstrating that Comcast "cares"—in a very public forum—can change a frustrating experience into a positive experience for customers who tweet about service issues.[b]

them reach their fitness goals.[18] When preparing advertisements, service marketers are careful to use concrete, specific language to help make services more tangible in customers' minds. Service companies are also careful not to promise too much regarding their services so that customer expectations do not rise to unattainable levels.

Through their actions, service contact personnel can be directly or indirectly involved in the personal selling of services. Personal selling is often important, because personal influence can help the customer visualize the benefits of a given service. Because service contact personnel may engage in personal selling, some companies invest heavily in training. USAA, a provider of bank and insurance services for members of the U.S. military and their families, trains its employees extensively on what life is like for military families, how to provide exceptional customer service, and ways to promote the company's services. Call center employees at USAA, for example, receive up to six months of training before they are even allowed to answer customer calls.[19]

As noted earlier, intangibility makes experiencing a service prior to purchase difficult, if not impossible in some cases. A car can be test-driven, a snack food can be sampled in a supermarket, and a new brand of bar soap can be mailed to customers as a free sample. Some services can also be offered on a trial basis at little or no risk to the customer, but a number of services cannot be sampled before purchase. Promotional programs that encourage trial use of insurance, health care, or auto repair are difficult to design because, even after purchase of such services, assessing their quality may require a considerable length of time. For instance, an individual may purchase auto insurance from the same provider for 10 years before filing a claim, but the quality of the coverage is based primarily on how the customer is treated and protected when a claim is made.

Because of the heterogeneity and intangibility of services, word-of-mouth communication is particularly important in service promotion. What other people say about a service provider can have a tremendous impact on whether an individual decides to use that provider. Some service marketers attempt to stimulate positive word-of-mouth communication by asking satisfied customers to tell their friends and associates about the service and may even provide incentives to the current or new customers. Groupon, which offers discounted deals at local businesses in select cities, offers a free deal to customers who refer friends who become new customers.

Pricing of Services

Services should be priced with consumer price sensitivity, the nature of the transaction, and its costs in mind.[20] Prices for services can be established on several different bases. The prices of pest-control services, dry cleaning, carpet cleaning, and health consultations are usually based on the performance of specific tasks. Other service prices are based on time. For example, attorneys, consultants, counselors, piano teachers, and plumbers often charge by the hour or day.

Some services use demand-based pricing. When demand for a service is high, the price is also high; when demand for a service is low, so is the price. The perishability of services means that, when demand is low, the unused capacity cannot be stored and therefore is lost forever. Every empty seat on an airline flight or in a movie theater represents lost revenue. Some services are very time sensitive in that a significant number of customers desire the service at a particular time. This point in time is called *peak demand.* A provider of time-sensitive services brings in most of its revenue during peak demand. For an airline, peak demand is usually early and late in the day; for cruise lines, peak demand occurs in the winter for Caribbean cruises and in the summer for Alaskan cruises. Customers can receive better deals on services by purchasing during nonpeak times. The new travel search by Microsoft's Bing allows travelers looking to book a flight to view the cheapest dates to fly to their destination. This service allows travelers with flexibility in scheduling to save money on their flight.[21] Providers of time-sensitive services often use demand-based pricing to manage the problem of balancing supply and demand. They charge top prices during peak demand and lower prices during off-peak demand to encourage more customers to use the service. This is why the price of a matinee movie is often half the price of the same movie shown at night. Major airlines maintain sophisticated databases to help them adjust ticket prices to fill as many seats as possible on every flight. On a single day, each airline makes thousands of fare changes to maximize the use of its seating capacity and thus maximize its revenues. To accomplish this objective, many airlines have to overbook flights and discount fares. However, research suggests that overbooking as a revenue management tool can cause dissatisfied customers to take their business elsewhere in the future, and customers who are "bumped up" or upgraded as a result of the overbooking may not exhibit particularly positive responses to the upgrade.[22]

When services are offered to customers in a bundle, marketers must decide whether to offer the services at one price, price them separately, or use a combination of the two methods. For instance, some hotels offer a package of services at one price, whereas others charge separately for the room, phone service, breakfast, and even in-room safes. Some service providers offer a one-price option for a specific bundle of services and make add-on bundles available at additional charges. For example, cable television companies like Comcast and Suddenlink offer a standard package of channels for one price and offer add-on channel packages for additional charges. Telephone services, such as call waiting and caller ID, are frequently bundled and sold as a package for one price.

Going Green

"Food with Integrity" Gives Chipotle an Edge

Ringing up sales of $2 billion through more than 1,100 restaurants, Chipotle Mexican Grill is known not just for delicious burritos but also for its earth-friendly commitment to serving "food with integrity." Since Steve Ells founded Chipotle in 1993, the fast-food chain has featured top-quality, all-natural ingredients, such as beef, chicken, and pork raised in humane ways by family farmers. Most of its beans and vegetables are organically grown, following sustainable agriculture practices, and a growing percentage of its ingredients come from local producers, which saves energy and supports local businesses. Chipotle is also promoting healthy eating by adding brown rice and whole wheat tortillas to the menu.

The restaurants themselves reflect Chipotle's green marketing strategy, with furniture made from recycled materials and energy-efficient equipment. The kitchen is open and visible so customers can watch their meals cooked to order from fresh ingredients and customized by request. Although not as speedy as the typical fast-food chain's service, Chipotle restaurants can serve as many as 300 customers per hour. The company enjoys a healthy profit margin, because customers are willing to pay a premium for tasty "food with integrity," prepared just the way they like. Looking ahead, Chipotle is testing a new Asian fast-food restaurant concept, offering meat and vegetable menu items produced with the environment in mind.[c]

Because of the intangible nature of services, customers sometimes rely heavily on price as an indicator of quality. If customers perceive the available services in a service category as being similar in quality, and if the quality of such services is difficult to judge even after these services are purchased, customers may seek out the lowest-priced provider. For example, many customers seek auto insurance providers with the lowest rates. If the quality of different service providers is likely to vary, customers may rely heavily on the price-quality association. For instance, if you have to have an appendectomy, will you choose the surgeon who charges an average price of $1,500 or the surgeon who will take your appendix out for $399?

For certain types of services, market conditions may limit how much can be charged for a specific service, especially if the services in this category are perceived as generic in nature. For example, the prices charged by a self-serve Laundromat are likely to be limited by the going price for Laundromat services in a given community. Also, state and local government regulations may reduce price flexibility. Such regulations may substantially control the prices charged for auto insurance, utilities, cable television service, and even housing rentals.

SERVICE QUALITY

Delivery of high-quality services is one of the most important and difficult tasks any service organization faces. Because of their characteristics, services are very difficult to evaluate. Hence, customers must look closely at service quality when comparing services. **Service quality** is defined as customers' perceptions of how well a service meets or exceeds their expectations.[23] Research by American Express found that 70 percent of American consumers would spend an average of 13 percent more for a product from a company that provides good customer service. Consumers are two times more likely to tell other people about a bad customer service experience than a good one. More than half of the people surveyed admitted to losing their temper with a customer service representative. Finally, 81 percent of consumers believe that small businesses focus more on customer service than larger companies.[24] Note that customers, not the organization, evaluate service quality. This distinction is critical, because it forces service marketers to examine quality from the customer's viewpoint. Thus, it is important for service organizations to determine what customers expect and then develop service products that meet or exceed those expectations.

Customer Evaluation of Service Quality

The biggest obstacle for customers in evaluating service quality is the intangible nature of the service. How can customers evaluate something they cannot see, feel, taste, smell, or hear? Evaluation of a good is much easier because all goods possess **search qualities**, tangible attributes like color, style, size, feel, or fit that can be evaluated prior to purchase. Trying on a new coat and taking a car for a test-drive are examples of how customers evaluate search qualities. Services, on the other hand, have very few search qualities; instead, they abound in experience and credence qualities. **Experience qualities** are attributes, such as taste, satisfaction, or pleasure, that can be assessed only during the purchase and consumption of a service.[25] Restaurants and vacations are examples of services high in experience qualities. **Credence qualities** are attributes that customers may be unable to evaluate even after the purchase and consumption of the service. Examples of services high in credence qualities are surgical operations, automobile repairs, and legal representation. Most consumers lack the knowledge or skills to evaluate the quality of these types of services. Consequently, they must place a great deal of faith in the integrity and competence of the service provider. In hopes of having more control over their legal fate, as well as being able to better evaluate their legal services, many customers are turning to Lawyers.com. On this site, visitors can find easy-to-understand information about several areas of law, discussion forums for a variety of legal topics, videos, and more.[26]

Despite the difficulties in evaluating quality, service quality may be the only way customers can choose one service over another. For this reason, service marketers live or die by understanding how consumers judge service quality. Table 13.2 defines five dimensions consumers

service quality Customers' perceptions of how well a service meets or exceeds their expectations

search qualities Tangible attributes that can be judged before the purchase of a product

experience qualities Attributes that can be assessed only during purchase and consumption of a service

credence qualities Attributes that customers may be unable to evaluate even after purchasing and consuming a service

use when evaluating service quality: tangibles, reliability, responsiveness, assurance, and empathy. Note that all of these dimensions have links to employee performance. Of the five, reliability is the most important in determining customer evaluations of service quality.[27]

Service marketers pay a great deal of attention to the tangibles of service quality. Tangible elements, such as the appearance of facilities and employees, are often the only aspects of a service that can be viewed before purchase and consumption. Therefore, service marketers must ensure that these tangible elements are consistent with the overall image of the service. When it comes to the appearance of service personnel, one element that an organization might want to consider is if service personnel workers have visible tattoos. Research has shown that consumers draw conclusions based on visible tattoos that can affect their overall expectations of the service. Studies show that, in general, visible tattoos on white-collar workers, such as those in the medical and financial services sectors, are viewed as inappropriate because they may be viewed as unsanitary and unprofessional. However, visible tattoos on blue-collar workers, especially bartenders, auto mechanics, and hair stylists, are viewed as appropriate because they express personality.[28]

Except for the tangibles dimension, the criteria customers use to judge service quality are intangible. For instance, how does a customer judge reliability? Because dimensions like reliability cannot be examined with the senses, customers must rely on other ways of judging service. One of the most important factors in customer judgments of service quality is service expectations. Service expectations are influenced by past experiences with the service, word-of-mouth communication from other customers, and the service company's own advertising. For instance, customers are usually eager to try a new restaurant, especially when friends recommend it. These same customers may have also seen advertisements placed by the restaurant.

Service Quality
This ad communicates about the quality of service provided by Jax Desmond Worldwide, provider of protection services for executives.

Table 13.2 Dimensions of Service Quality

Dimension	Evaluation Criteria	Examples
Tangibles: Physical evidence of the service	Appearance of physical facilities Appearance of service personnel Tools or equipment used to provide the service	A clean and professional-looking doctor's office A clean and neatly attired repairperson The freshness of food in a restaurant The equipment used in a medical exam
Reliability: Consistency and dependability in performing the service	Accuracy of billing or recordkeeping Performing services when promised	An accurate bank statement A confirmed hotel reservation An airline flight departing and arriving on time
Responsiveness: Willingness or readiness of employees to provide the service	Returning customer phone calls Providing prompt service Handling urgent requests	A server refilling a customer's cup of coffee without being asked An ambulance arriving within three minutes
Assurance: Knowledge/competence of employees and ability to convey trust and confidence	Knowledge and skills of employees Company name and reputation Personal characteristics of employees	A highly trained financial adviser A known and respected service provider A doctor's bedside manner
Empathy: Caring and individual attention provided by employees	Listening to customer needs Caring about customers' interests Providing personalized attention	A store employee listening to and trying to understand a customer's complaint A nurse counseling a heart patient

Sources: Adapted from Leonard L. Berry and A. Parasuraman, *Marketing Services: Competing through Quality* (New York: Free Press, 1991); Valarie A. Zeithaml, A. Parasuraman, and Leonard L. Berry, *Delivering Quality Service: Balancing Customer Perceptions and Expectations* (New York: Free Press, 1990); A. Parasuraman, Leonard L. Berry, and Valarie A. Zeithaml, "An Empirical Examination of Relationships in an Extended Service Quality Model," *Marketing Science Institute Working Paper Series*, Report no. 90–112 (Cambridge, MA: Marketing Science Institute, 1990), 29.

As a result, they have an idea of what to expect when they visit the restaurant for the first time. When they finally dine there, the quality they experience will change the expectations they have for their next visit. That is why providing consistently high service quality is important. If the quality of a restaurant, or of any service, begins to deteriorate, customers will alter their own expectations and change their word-of-mouth communication to others accordingly.

Delivering Exceptional Service Quality

Providing high-quality service on a consistent basis is very difficult. All consumers have experienced examples of poor service: late flight departures and arrivals, inattentive restaurant servers, rude bank employees, and long lines. Obviously it is impossible for a service organization to ensure exceptional service quality 100 percent of the time. However, an organization can take many steps to increase the likelihood of providing high-quality service. First, though, the service company must consider the four factors that affect service quality: (1) analysis of customer expectations, (2) service quality specifications, (3) employee performance, and (4) management of service expectations (see Figure 13.2).[29]

Analysis of Customer Expectations

Providers need to understand customer expectations when designing a service to meet or exceed those expectations. Only then can they deliver good service. Customers usually have two levels of expectations: desired and acceptable. The desired level of expectations is what the customer really wants. If this level of expectations is provided, the customer will be very satisfied. The acceptable level of expectations is what the customer views as adequate. The difference between these two levels of expectations is called the customer's *zone of tolerance.*[30]

Service companies sometimes use marketing research, such as surveys and focus groups, to discover customer needs and expectations. For instance, American Airlines uses its online "Customer Satisfaction Survey" to measure customer satisfaction. This online survey is conducted every two weeks and generates over 200,000 responses for the airline every year. Survey results are looked at as a whole and on an individual-airport basis. Monthly survey summaries are sent out to each airport outlining their performance levels in the airline's six areas of customer service. Each location is then responsible for using this information to improve its

Figure 13.2 Service Quality Model

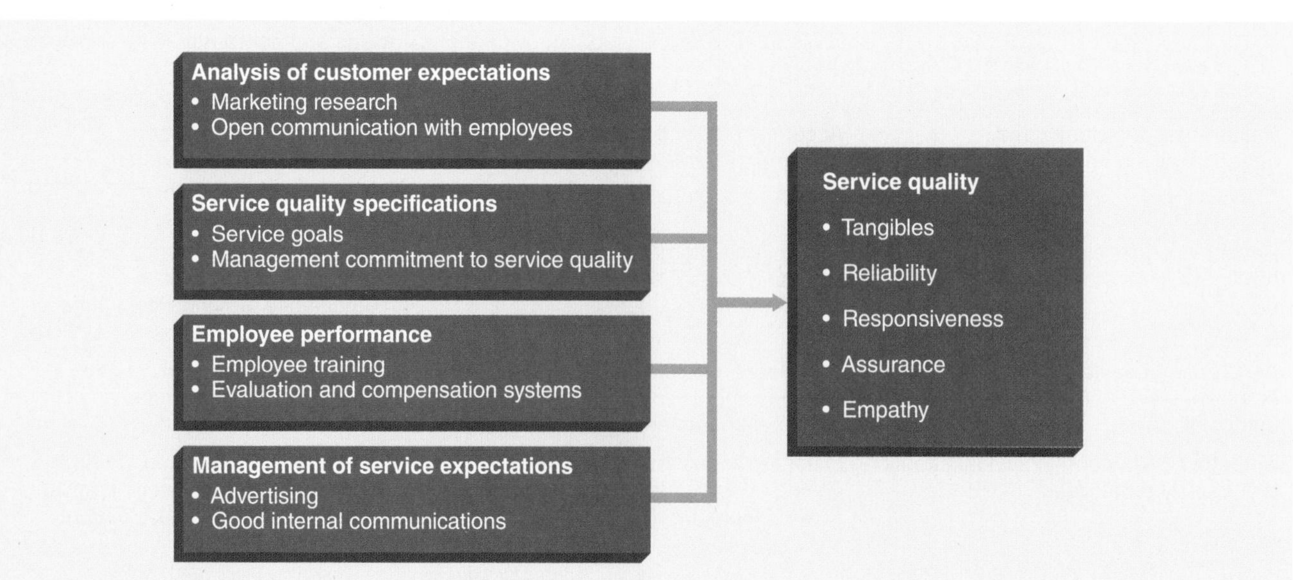

Source: Adapted from A. Parasuraman, Leonard L. Berry, and Valarie A. Zeithaml, "An Empirical Examination of Relationships in an Extended Service Quality Model," *Marketing Science Institute Working Paper Series*, Report no. 90–112, 1990. Reprinted by permission of Marketing Science Institute, and the authors.

performance.[31] Other service marketers, especially restaurants, use comment cards on which customers can complain or provide suggestions. Still another approach is to ask employees. Because customer-contact employees interact daily with customers, they are in good positions to know what customers want from the company. Service managers should regularly interact with their employees by asking their opinions on the best way to serve customers.

Service Quality Specifications

Once an organization understands its customers' needs, it must establish goals to help ensure good service delivery. These goals, or service specifications, are typically set in terms of employee or machine performance. For example, a bank may require its employees to conform to a dress code. Likewise, the bank may require that all incoming phone calls be answered by the third ring. Specifications like these can be very important in providing quality service as long as they are tied to the needs expressed by customers.

Perhaps the most critical aspect of service quality specifications is managers' commitment to service quality. Service managers who are committed to quality become role models for all employees in the organization. Such commitment motivates customer-contact employees to comply with service specifications. It is crucial that all managers within the organization embrace this commitment, especially frontline managers, who are much closer to customers than higher-level managers.

Employee Performance

Once an organization sets service quality standards and managers are committed to them, the firm must find ways to ensure that customer-contact employees perform their jobs well. Contact employees in most service industries (bank tellers, flight attendants, servers, sales clerks, etc.) are often the least-trained and lowest-paid members of the organization. Service organizations must realize that contact employees are the most important link to the customer, and thus their performance is critical to customer perceptions of service quality. Research has identified a direct relationship between the satisfaction of a company's contact employees and the satisfaction of its customers. Employee and customer satisfaction levels also have a direct relationship with customer retention and loyalty.[32] The way to ensure that employees perform well is to train them effectively so they understand how to do their jobs. Providing information about customers, service specifications, and the organization itself during the training promotes this understanding.

The evaluation and compensation system the organization uses also plays a part in employee performance. Many service employees are evaluated and rewarded on the basis of output measures, such as sales volume (automobile salespeople) or a low error rate (bank tellers). But systems using output measures overlook other major aspects of job performance, including friendliness, teamwork, effort, and customer satisfaction. These customer-oriented measures of performance may be a better basis for evaluation and reward. In fact, a number of service marketers use customer satisfaction ratings to determine a portion of service employee compensation.

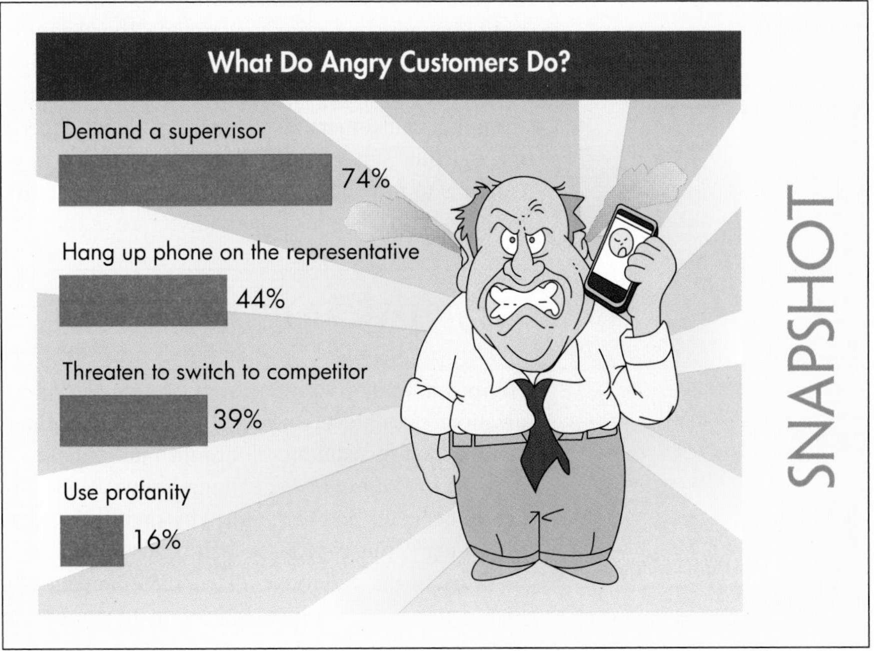

Source: American Express Global Customer Service Barometer Survey of 1,018 adults.

Marketing Debate

Is the Customer Always Right?

ISSUE: The old adage says "the customer is always right." Always?

Customers are the only reason any marketer stays in business, and that's why the customer comes first at L.L.Bean, the famous Maine retailer. If a product is defective or doesn't meet customers' expectations, L.L.Bean will provide a refund. This customer-first approach has helped the retailer thrive for more than a century.

But what about customers who hurt other customers or smash property? On Black Friday, some customers waiting to buy bargain-priced goods have started fights or broken store fixtures. What about customers who take advantage of a marketer's policies? Costco traditionally had a liberal return policy, offering a money-back guarantee on every product. A few years ago, however, the retailer noticed that some customers were returning older televisions, receiving refunds, and then buying newer models at lower prices. To prevent this abuse, Costco now offers a 90-day return policy on electronics. On the other hand, knowing that some customers returned electronics because they were unable to get them to work, the retailer created Costco Concierge Services. Now customers who buy electronics at Costco can call a free hotline for technical assistance.[d]

Management of Service Expectations

Because expectations are so significant in customer evaluations of service quality, service companies recognize they must set realistic expectations about the service they can provide. They can set these expectations through advertising and good internal communication. In their advertisements, service companies make promises about the kind of service they will deliver. As already noted, a service company is forced to make promises because the intangibility of services prevents the organization from showing the benefits in the advertisement. However, the advertiser should not promise more than it can deliver. Doing so will likely mean disappointed customers.

To deliver on promises made, a company needs to have thorough internal communication among its departments, especially management, advertising, and store operations. Assume, for example, that a restaurant's radio advertisements guarantee service within five minutes, or the meal is free. If top management or the advertising department fails to inform store operations about the five-minute guarantee, the restaurant will very likely fail to meet its customers' service expectations. Even though customers might appreciate a free meal, the restaurant will lose some credibility as well as revenue. As mentioned earlier, word-of-mouth communication from other customers also shapes customer expectations. However, service companies cannot manage this "advertising" directly. The best way to ensure positive word-of-mouth communication is to provide exceptional service quality. It has been estimated that customers tell four times as many people about bad service as they do about good service.

NONPROFIT MARKETING

Nonprofit marketing refers to marketing activities that are conducted by individuals and organizations to achieve some goal other than ordinary business goals like profit, market share, or return on investment. Nonprofit marketing is divided into two categories: nonprofit-organization marketing and social marketing. Nonprofit-organization marketing is the use of marketing concepts and techniques by organizations whose goals do not include making profits. Social marketing promotes social causes, such as AIDS research and recycling.

nonprofit marketing Marketing activities conducted to achieve some goal other than ordinary business goals such as profit, market share, or return on investment

Most of the previously discussed concepts and approaches to service products also apply to nonprofit organizations. Indeed, many nonprofit organizations mainly provide service products. In this section, we examine the concept of nonprofit marketing to determine how it differs from marketing activities in for-profit business organizations. We also explore the marketing objectives of nonprofit organizations and the development of their product strategies.

How Is Nonprofit Marketing Different?

Many nonprofit organizations strive for effective marketing activities. Charitable organizations and supporters of social causes are major nonprofit marketers in this country. Political parties, unions, religious sects, and fraternal organizations also perform marketing activities, but they are not considered businesses. Whereas the chief beneficiary of a business enterprise is whoever owns or holds stock in it, in theory, the only beneficiaries of a nonprofit organization are its clients, its members, or the public at large. The Metropolitan Opera in New York City, for example, is run by the nonprofit Metropolitan Opera Association. Many museums and performing arts institutions are run as nonprofits.

Nonprofit organizations have greater opportunities for creativity than most for-profit business organizations, but trustees or board members of nonprofit organizations are likely to have difficulty judging the performance of the trained professionals they oversee. It is harder for administrators to evaluate the performance of professors or social workers than it is for sales managers to evaluate the performance of salespeople in a for-profit organization.

Marketing in Nonprofit Organizations
Some nonprofit marketers use advertising to explain their objectives and seek support.

Another way nonprofit marketing differs from for-profit marketing is that nonprofit marketing is sometimes quite controversial. Nonprofit organizations, such as Greenpeace, the National Rifle Association, and the National Organization for Women, spend lavishly on lobbying efforts to persuade Congress, the White House, and even the courts to support their interests, in part because not all of society agrees with their aims. However, marketing as a field of study does not attempt to state what an organization's goals should be or debate the issue of nonprofit versus for-profit business goals. Marketing only tries to provide a body of knowledge and concepts to help further an organization's goals. Individuals must decide whether they approve or disapprove of a particular organization's goal orientation. Most marketers would agree that profit and consumer satisfaction are appropriate goals for business enterprises but would probably disagree considerably about the goals of a controversial nonprofit organization.

Nonprofit Marketing Objectives

The basic aim of nonprofit organizations is to obtain a desired response from a target market. The response could be a change in values, a financial contribution, the donation of services, or some other type of exchange. For example, the primary objective of the nonprofit organization Rock the Vote is "to engage and build political power for young people." The organization's website provides information on how to register to vote and cast ballots. So far, the organization has helped over 5 million young people register to vote.[33] Nonprofit marketing objectives are shaped by the nature of the exchange and the goals of the organization. These objectives should state the rationale for the organization's existence. An organization that defines its marketing objective as providing a product can be left without a purpose if the product becomes obsolete. However, servicing and adapting to the perceived needs and wants of a target public, or market, enhances an organization's chance to survive and achieve its goals.

Developing Nonprofit Marketing Strategies

Nonprofit organizations develop marketing strategies by defining and analyzing a target market and creating and maintaining a total marketing mix that appeals to that market.

Target Markets

We must revise the concept of target markets slightly to apply it to nonprofit organizations. Whereas a business seeks out target groups that are potential purchasers of its product, a nonprofit organization may attempt to serve many diverse groups. For our purposes, a **target public** is a collective of individuals who have an interest in or a concern about an organization, a product, or a social cause. The terms *target market* and *target public* are difficult to distinguish from many nonproduct or social-cause profit organizations. For example, the target public for ACCION International is anyone interested in supporting international development and relief work. However, the target market for ACCION's advertisements consists of people in developing nations who want microloans to start businesses and spur economic development.[34]

In nonprofit marketing, direct consumers of the product are called **client publics** and indirect consumers are called **general publics**.[35] For example, the client public for a university is its student body, and its general public includes parents, alumni, and trustees. The client public usually receives most of the attention when an organization develops a marketing strategy.

Developing Marketing Mixes

A marketing strategy limits alternatives and directs marketing activities toward achieving organizational goals. The strategy should include a blueprint for making decisions about product, distribution, promotion, and price. These decision variables should be blended to serve the target market.

In developing the product, nonprofit organizations usually deal with ideas and services. Problems may evolve when an organization fails to define what it is providing. What product, for example, does the Peace Corps provide? Its services include vocational training, health services, nutritional assistance, and community development. It also markets the ideas of international cooperation and the implementation of U.S. foreign policy. The product of the Peace Corps is more difficult to define than the average business product. As indicated in the first part of this chapter, services are intangible and therefore need special marketing efforts. The marketing of ideas and concepts is likewise more abstract than the marketing of tangibles, and much effort is required to present benefits.

Distribution decisions in nonprofit organizations relate to how ideas and services will be made available to clients. If the product is an idea, selecting the right media to communicate the idea will facilitate distribution. By nature, services consist of assistance, convenience, and availability. Availability is thus part of the total service. Making a product like health services available calls for knowledge of such retailing concepts as site location analysis.

Developing a channel of distribution to coordinate and facilitate the flow of nonprofit products to clients is a necessary task, but in a nonprofit setting, the traditional concept of the marketing channel may need to be revised. The independent wholesalers available to a business enterprise do not exist in most nonprofit situations. Instead, a very short channel—nonprofit organization to client—is the norm because production and consumption of ideas and services are often simultaneous.

Making promotional decisions may be the first sign that a nonprofit organization is performing marketing activities. Nonprofit organizations use advertising and publicity to communicate with clients and the public. PACER's National Center for Bullying Prevention utilizes a variety of resources and media to promote its mission. It hosts the Nation Bullying Prevention Month every October, in which thousands of schools participate. It also distributes coloring books to children, sells a CD of anti-bullying songs, and even hosts a fun run. Facebook, CNN, and Yahoo! Kids are multimedia partners of the group.[36] Direct mail remains the primary means of fundraising for social services, such as those provided by the Red Cross and Special Olympics. While direct mail remains important, some organizations have reduced their volume of direct mail in favor of e-mails or other digital communications. Environmentally focused organizations face a unique challenge in promotional materials: how to communicate using environmentally friendly products like recycled paper and environmentally sensitive inks. Red Sun Press is a nonprofit cooperative printer that provides environmentally

target public A collective of individuals who have an interest in or concern about an organization, product, or social cause

client publics Direct consumers of a product of a nonprofit organization

general publics Indirect consumers of a product of a nonprofit organization

friendly and sustainable printing services. It prints with soy ink and sources paper from businesses that are certified by the Forest Stewardship Council and the Sustainable Forestry Initiative.[37] Increasingly, nonprofits are using the Internet to reach fundraising and promotional goals through e-mail, websites, and software that permits accepting online gifts. In fact, 73 percent of nonprofits plan to increase the use of e-mail marketing and 70 percent plan to increase the use of social media. These increases come as many organizations start to limit the use of print advertisements and direct mail.[38] A new medium nonprofits are using to raise money quickly is mobile marketing. After the recent earthquake in Haiti, the Red Cross encouraged U.S. citizens to donate money to relief efforts by simply sending a text message. The Red Cross received over $43 million in text message donations alone.[39]

Many nonprofit organizations also use personal selling, although they may call it by another name. Churches and charities rely on personal selling when they send volunteers to recruit new members or request donations. The U.S. Army uses personal selling when its recruiting officers attempt to persuade men and women to enlist. Special events to obtain funds, communicate ideas, or provide services are also effective promotional activities. Amnesty International, for example, has held worldwide concert tours featuring well-known musical artists to raise funds and increase public awareness of political prisoners around the world.

Although product and promotional techniques may require only slight modification when applied to nonprofit organizations, pricing is generally quite different, and decision making is more complex. The different pricing concepts the nonprofit organization faces include pricing in user and donor markets. Two types of monetary pricing exist: *fixed* and *variable*. There may be a fixed fee for users, or the price may vary depending on the user's ability to pay. When a donation-seeking organization will accept a contribution of any size, it is using variable pricing.

The broadest definition of price (valuation) must be used to develop nonprofit marketing strategies. Financial price, an exact dollar value, may or may not be charged for a nonprofit product. Economists recognize the giving up of alternatives as a cost. **Opportunity cost** is the value of the benefit given up by selecting one alternative over another. According to this traditional economic view of price, if a nonprofit organization persuades someone to donate time to a cause or to change his or her behavior, the alternatives given up are a cost to (or a price paid by) the individual. Volunteers who answer phones for a university counseling service or a suicide hotline, for example, give up the time they could spend studying or doing other things as well as the income they might earn from working at a for-profit business organization.

For other nonprofit organizations, financial price is an important part of the marketing mix. Nonprofit organizations today are raising money by increasing the prices of their services or are starting to charge for services if they have not done so before. They are using marketing research to determine what kinds of products people will pay for. Pricing strategies of nonprofit organizations often stress public and client welfare over equalization of costs and revenues. If additional funds are needed to cover costs, the organization may solicit donations, contributions, or grants.

opportunity cost The value of the benefit given up by choosing one alternative over another

Summary

1. To understand the growth and importance of services

Services are intangible products that involve deeds, performances, or efforts that cannot be physically possessed. They are the result of applying human or mechanical efforts to people or objects. Services are a growing part of the U.S. economy. They have six fundamental characteristics: intangibility, inseparability of production and consumption, perishability, heterogeneity, client-based relationships, and customer contact.

2. To identify the characteristics of services that differentiate them from goods

Intangibility means that a service cannot be seen, touched, tasted, or smelled. Inseparability refers to the fact that the production of a service cannot be separated from its consumption by customers. Perishability means unused service capacity of one time period cannot be stored for future use. Heterogeneity is variation in service quality. Client-based relationships are interactions with customers that lead to the repeated use of a service over time. Customer contact is the interaction between providers and customers needed to deliver a service.

3. To describe how the characteristics of services influence the development of marketing mixes for services

Core services are the basic service experiences customers expect; supplementary services are those that relate to and support core services. Because of the characteristics of services, service marketers face several challenges in developing and managing marketing mixes. To address the problem of intangibility, marketers use cues that help assure customers about the quality of their services. The development and management of service products are also influenced by the service characteristics of inseparability and level of customer contact. Some services require that customers come to the service provider's facility; others are delivered with no face-to-face contact. Marketing channels for services are usually short and direct, but some services employ intermediaries. Service marketers are less concerned with warehousing and transportation than are goods marketers, but inventory management and balancing supply and demand for services are important issues. The intangibility of services poses several promotion-related challenges. Advertisements with tangible cues that symbolize the service and depict facilities, equipment, and personnel help address these challenges. Service providers are likely to promote price, guarantees, performance documentation, availability, and training and certification of contact personnel. Through their actions, service personnel can be involved directly or indirectly in the personal selling of services.

Intangibility makes it difficult to experience a service before purchasing it. Heterogeneity and intangibility make word-of-mouth communication an important means of promotion. The prices of services are based on task performance, time required, or demand. Perishability creates difficulties in balancing supply and demand because unused capacity cannot be stored. The point in time when a significant number of customers desire a service is called peak demand; demand-based pricing results in higher prices charged for services during peak demand. When services are offered in a bundle, marketers must decide whether to offer them at one price, price them separately, or use a combination of the two methods. Because services are intangible, customers may rely on price as a sign of quality. For some services, market conditions may dictate the price; for others, state and local government regulations may limit price flexibility.

4. To understand the importance of service quality and explain how to deliver exceptional service quality

Service quality is customers' perception of how well a service meets or exceeds their expectations. Although one of the most important aspects of service marketing, service quality is very difficult for customers to evaluate because the nature of services renders benefits impossible to assess before actual purchase and consumption. These benefits include experience qualities, such as taste, satisfaction, or pleasure, and credence qualities, which customers may be unable to evaluate even after consumption. When competing services are very similar, service quality may be the only way for customers to distinguish among them. Service marketers can increase the quality of their services by following the four-step process of understanding customer expectations, setting service specifications, ensuring good employee performance, and managing customers' service expectations.

5. To explore the nature of nonprofit marketing

Nonprofit marketing is marketing aimed at nonbusiness goals, including social causes. It uses most of the same concepts and approaches that apply to business situations. Whereas the chief beneficiary of a business enterprise is whoever owns or holds stock in it, the beneficiary of a nonprofit enterprise should be its clients, its members, or its public at large. The goals of a nonprofit organization reflect its unique philosophy or mission. Some nonprofit organizations have very controversial goals, but many organizations exist to further generally accepted social causes.

The marketing objective of nonprofit organizations is to obtain a desired response from a target market. Developing a nonprofit marketing strategy consists of defining and analyzing a target market and creating and maintaining a marketing mix. In nonprofit marketing, the product is usually an idea or a service. Distribution is aimed at the communication of ideas and the delivery of services. The result is a very short marketing channel. Promotion is very important to nonprofit marketing. Nonprofit organizations use advertising, publicity, and personal selling to communicate with clients and the public. Direct mail remains the primary means of fundraising for social services, but some nonprofits use the Internet for fundraising and promotional activities. Price is more difficult to define in nonprofit marketing because of opportunity costs and the difficulty of quantifying the values exchanged.

Go to www.cengagebrain.com for resources to help you master the content in this chapter as well as for materials that will expand your marketing knowledge!

Important Terms

homesourcing 419
intangibility 420
inseparability 421
perishability 421
heterogeneity 422
client-based relationships 423
customer contact 423
service quality 430
search qualities 430
experience qualities 430
credence qualities 430
nonprofit marketing 434
target public 436
client publics 436
general publics 436
opportunity cost 437

Discussion and Review Questions

1. How important are services in the U.S. economy?
2. Identify and discuss the major characteristics of services.
3. For each marketing mix element, which service characteristics are most likely to have an impact? Explain.
4. What is service quality? Why do customers find it difficult to judge service quality?
5. Identify and discuss the five components of service quality. How do customers evaluate these components?
6. What is the significance of tangibles in service marketing?
7. How do search, experience, and credence qualities affect the way customers view and evaluate services?
8. What steps should a service company take to provide exceptional service quality?
9. How does nonprofit marketing differ from marketing in for-profit organizations?
10. What are the differences among clients, publics, and customers? What is the difference between a target public and target market?
11. Discuss the development of a marketing strategy for a university. What marketing decisions must be made as the strategy is developed?

Application Questions

1. Imagine you are the owner of a new service business. What is your service? Be creative. What are some of the most important considerations in developing the service, training salespeople, and communicating about your service to potential customers?
2. As discussed in this chapter, the characteristics of services affect the development of marketing mixes for services. Choose a specific service and explain how each marketing mix element could be affected by these service characteristics.
3. In advertising services, a company must often use symbols to represent the offered product. Identify three service organizations you have seen in outdoor, television, or magazine advertising. What symbols do these organizations use to represent their services? What message do the symbols convey to potential customers?
4. Delivering consistently high-quality service is difficult for service marketers. Describe an instance when you received high-quality service and an instance when you experienced low-quality service. What contributed to your perception of high quality? Of low quality?
5. IMP A service blueprint "maps" the various processes, actions, and tangible evidence that comprise a service. It describes in detail the movement of people (customers and service providers)—for example, their interactions and the possible outcomes. A blueprint helps marketers identify operational weaknesses, critical customer-provider points of contact, and opportunities for service innovation.

   The United States Postal Service (USPS) is often the butt of jokes when it comes to service. Indeed, its design is often considered archaic, especially in comparison to its competitors. Also, its processes are clunky and time-consuming. Visit a local post office and create a blueprint of its service. Then, using this blueprint, consider how intangibility, inseparability, perishability, heterogeneity, client-based relationships, and customer contact affect the marketing of services provided by USPS.

Internet Exercise

Matchmaker.com

The Internet abounds with dating sites, but few offer as much information about their members as Matchmaker .com. Matchmaker profiles are gleaned from a survey of about 60 question and essay responses. Check out the site at **www.matchmaker.com**.

1. Classify Matchmaker.com's product in terms of its position on the service continuum.

2. How does Matchmaker.com enhance customer service and foster better client-based relationships through its Internet marketing efforts?
3. Discuss the degree to which experience and credence qualities exist in the services offered by Matchmaker.com and other dating websites.

developing your marketing plan

Products that are services rather than tangible goods present unique challenges to companies when they formulate marketing strategy. A clear comprehension of the concepts that apply specifically to service products is essential when developing the marketing plan. These concepts will form the basis for decisions in several plan areas. To assist you in relating the information in this chapter to the development of your marketing plan for a service product, focus on the following:

1. Using Figure 13.1, determine your product's degree of tangibility. If your product lies close to the tangible end of the continuum, then you may proceed to the questions in the next chapter. If your product is more intangible, then continue with this chapter's issues.
2. Discuss your product with regard to the six service characteristics. To what degree does it possess the qualities that make up each of these characteristics?
3. Using Table 13.1 as a guide, discuss the marketing challenges you are likely to experience.
4. Determine the search, experience, and credence qualities that customers are likely to use when evaluating your service product.
5. Consider how your service product relates to each of the dimensions of service quality. Using Table 13.2 as a guide, develop the evaluation criteria and examples that are appropriate for your product.

The information obtained from these questions should assist you in developing various aspects of your marketing plan found in the "Interactive Marketing Plan" exercise at **www.cengagebrain.com**.

video case 13.1

UNICEF and the Good Shirts Project

The United Nation's Children's Fund (UNICEF) was created in 1946 as a nonprofit to protect the welfare and rights of children around the world. Wherever children are threatened by natural disasters, extreme poverty, violence, disease, and other problems, UNICEF works with local and international partners to raise money and deliver services to relieve suffering and meet basic needs.

Now UNICEF has teamed up with New York–based artists Justin and Christine Gignac, plus the online T-shirt retailer Threadless, on the Good Shirts Project. This is a combination fundraiser and educational program, raising awareness of the humanitarian crisis in the Horn of Africa and raising money to provide clean water, food, health supplies, and other desperately needed items for children and adults in Somalia, Kenya, Ethiopia, Eritrea, and Djibouti. "Hundreds of thousands of children are at imminent risk of death," Gignac explains. "Obviously, we need to do something to help, and are fortunate to have been included in this effort to raise money for the U.S. Fund for UNICEF to support lifesaving relief efforts."

Good Shirts follows in the footsteps of the Gignacs' previous "Wants for Sale" art series, where they created paintings of items and experiences they wanted—and sold each painting for the amount of money they would have to pay for the item or experience. Similarly, each of the UNICEF shirts is priced at the cost of buying what the shirt shows for people in the Horn of Africa. For example, the white T-shirt featuring a big, colorful mosquito sells for $18.57, which pays for three insecticide-treated nets to protect from malaria. The white T-shirt featuring a green cargo plane sells for $300,000, the cost of chartering a flight from UNICEF's warehouse in Copenhagen to carry aid supplies to Nairobi, Kenya. In all, the artists created a dozen eye-catching T-shirts with light-hearted images "to remind people of the good they're doing by buying one," says Gignac.

Threadless produces the T-shirts and sells them online, with 100 percent of the proceeds going to UNICEF. The artists donate their time and designs, and the BBH New York ad agency provides free marketing assistance. "We're literally letting people wear their donation as a source of pride and as a means to spread the word," says a BBH executive. "If friends get a little competitive over who's being more altruistic, all the better."

To communicate with potential donors and keep the public informed about its services, UNICEF is an active user of social media. It has nearly 1 million followers on Twitter, where it uses the #goodshirts hashtag when tweeting about Good Shirts. UNICEF has nearly 2 million followers on Facebook and maintains a YouTube channel where videos are posted in multiple languages.

Good Shirts is one of a number of initiatives that UNICEF uses to call attention to world trouble-spots where children are in need of aid. When UNICEF's celebrity ambassadors, including Sarah Jessica Parker, Clay Aiken, and Laurence Fishburne, travel to these areas, they use their fame to spread UNICEF's message and attract media coverage. In a decades-old Halloween tradition, many U.S. children carry orange "Trick or Treat for UNICEF" containers and ask for donations as they go door-to-door in their costumes. No matter where in the world children are threatened, UNICEF is ready to help.[40]

Questions for Discussion

1. Identify UNICEF's target public and client publics. Who is the target market for Good Shirts' social media messages?
2. What ideas and services are involved in UNICEF's product?
3. What kinds of objectives do you think UNICEF set for the Good Shirts Project? How should UNICEF evaluate the results of this project?

case 13.2

Marketing In-Store Medical Services: Flu Shots in Aisle 6

Millions of people with minor ailments or urgent medical needs are using in-store clinics located inside drugstore chains, discount stores, and supermarkets. Across the United States, more than 1,000 stores now contain walk-in clinics, and the number is growing. Hundreds of CVS drugstores contain MinuteClinics, and hundreds of Walgreens drugstores contain Take Care clinics. Both Walmart and Target have clinics in selected stores, as do regional grocery chains such as Kroger and United Supermarkets.

In most in-store clinics, consumers meet with a nurse practitioner or a physician's assistant who is trained to treat earaches, sprained ankles, sinus infections, and similar complaints (depending on state and local regulations, doctors provide overall medical supervision but may not have to be on-site at every clinic). If needed, staff members can issue prescriptions that customers can fill immediately at the store's pharmacy. They are also ready to administer vaccinations against tetanus, influenza, and other illnesses, and provide physical checkups before youngsters go to camp or join a sports team.

© Ilene MacDonald/Alamy

The two main keys to successfully marketing in-store medical services are convenience and price. The clinics promote their convenient location inside local stores and emphasize that no appointment is necessary. Most in-store clinics offer day, evening, and weekend hours to accommodate consumers' busy schedules. Rarely do consumers have to wait more than a few minutes when they stop by to get a flu shot or have a sore throat treated. Having the pharmacy located in the next aisle is particularly convenient for consumers who walk out of the clinic with a prescription to fill.

The clinics are also handy alternatives when the family doctor's office is closed, too far away, or unable to see a patient right away. Some consumers, especially those without health insurance, may not even have family doctors. "We know that each demographic group has unique problems," observes the CEO of Take Care Health Systems, which operates clinics inside Walgreens stores. "More-affluent patients can't get in to see their doctors, while less-affluent patients often don't have doctors."

Price is another positive. The price for treatment at in-store clinics is generally far lower than at a doctor's office, let alone in the emergency room. Although most of the clinics accept popular health insurance plans as partial or full payment for services, consumers who lack insurance are price-sensitive because they must cover the costs themselves. Price is therefore an important element for marketing in-store medical services. Describing MinuteClinic's appeal, a CVS spokesperson notes: "High-quality care and lower costs combine to offer real relief to consumers struggling with the steadily increasing costs of health care."

One characteristic of services delivered in an in-store clinic is a little different from conventional medical services. Clinic staff members don't have the opportunity to develop close relationships with the people they treat, because consumers are only occasional visitors, coming in when they have an unexpected illness or know it's time for a flu shot. In contrast, family physicians can and do get to know their patients very well over the course of many visits. "When a child comes in for something minor, we use that time to talk about other things," says a pediatrician in Rochester. "All of that gets missed at the retail clinic."

For their part, the clinics aren't marketing themselves as replacements for regular medical care. Still, MinuteClinic is aware that one-third of its customers do not have a family doctor. Its chief nursing officer is ready to help with that need, too: "That's why we keep a list of local doctors who are taking new patients at each location," she says. "We want people to establish a relationship with a primary care doctor."

Recent changes to U.S. legislation affecting the healthcare industry, including provisions for expanding access to health insurance, are affecting the marketing of in-store clinics as well. Walgreens is preparing for higher demand by opening new Take Care clinics in more stores and considering whether to offer a wider range of medical services. Take Care and Walgreens jointly market the in-store clinics in Walgreens' ad campaigns and on the chain's website. In addition, Take Care uses its website plus television, radio, and direct mail to tell consumers about the features and benefits of its services. Attention, shoppers: Easy access to medical treatment is only one aisle away.[41]

Questions for Discussion

1. Which of the six basics characteristics of services are likely to have the most influence on the way in-store clinics are marketed?
2. Do you think consumers would use search qualities, experience qualities, or credence qualities to evaluate the in-store medical services? Explain your answer.
3. How do you suggest that in-store clinics like MinuteClinic and Take Care manage the service expectations of consumers seeking medical attention?

NOTES

[1]Based on information in Hayley Bosch, "Suite Life: Four Seasons New York's Ty Warner Penthouse Suite," *Forbes,* February 3, 2012, www.forbes.com; Frederic Colas and Laurel Wentz, "Four Seasons Embraces Digital Marketing, Virtual Experiences," *Advertising Age,* January 16, 2012, www.adage.com; Melanie Nayer, "Four Seasons Hotels Introduce 15-Minute Room Service Meals," *Boston Globe,* December 14, 2011, www.boston.com.

[2]Leonard L. Berry and A. Parasuraman, *Marketing Services: Competing through Quality* (New York: Free Press, 1991), 5.

[3]"About Us," Rhema Business Solutions, http://homesourcingsolutions.com/ (accessed February 24, 2012).

[4]"Top 10 Franchises for 2012," *Entrepreneur*, www.entrepreneur.com/franchise500/index.html (accessed February 24, 2012).

[5]Raymond P. Fisk, Stephen J. Grove, and Joby John, *Interactive Services Marketing* (Boston: Houghton Mifflin, 2008), 25.

[6]K. Douglass Hoffman and John E. G. Bateson, *Services Marketing: Concepts, Strategies, and Cases*, 4th ed. (Mason, OH: South-Western, 2011), 133.

[7]The information in this section is based on Hoffman and Bateson, *Services Marketing: Concepts, Strategies, and Cases*, 57; Valarie A. Zeithaml, A. Parasuraman, and Leonard L. Berry, *Delivering Quality Service: Balancing Customer Perceptions and Expectations* (New York: Free Press, 1990).

[8]J. Paul Peter and James H. Donnelly, *A Preface to Marketing Management* (Burr Ridge, IL: Irwin/McGraw-Hill, 2011).

[9]"About Pinterest," http://pinterest.com/about/help/ (accessed February 24, 2012); Lorna Smith, "How Pinterest Can Increase Your Website Traffic," Bloggertone, January 8, 2012, http://bloggertone.com/marketing/2012/01/08/how-pinterest-can-increase-your-website-traffic/.

[10]Michael D. Hartline and O. C. Ferrell, "Service Quality Implementation: The Effects of Organizational Socialization and Managerial Actions of Customer Contact Employee Behavior," *Marketing Science Institute Report*, no. 93–122 (Cambridge, MA: Marketing Science Institute, 1993).

[11]Jake Widman, "Empowered Employees Create Happy Customers," AllBusiness.com, September 23, 2011, www.allbusiness.com/create-happy-customers/16684809-1.html.

[12]Hoffman and Bateson, *Services Marketing: Concepts, Strategies, and Cases*, 69–70.

[13]Brian X. Chen and Nick Wingfield, "Apple Introduces Tools to (Someday) Supplant Print Textbooks," *The New York Times Bits Blog,* January 19, 2012, http://bits.blogs.nytimes.com/2012/01/19/apple-unveils-tools-for-digital-textbooks/?scp=2&sq=customize&st=cse.

[14]Fisk, Grove, and John, *Interactive Services Marketing*, 91.

[15]Ann Carrns, "Allstate Offers Credit to Clients Unhappy with Claims Service," *The New York Times Bucks Blog,* January 17, 2012, http://bucks.blogs.nytimes.com/2012/01/17/allstate-offers-credit-to-clients-unhappy-with-claims-service/?scp=1&sq=service%20customer%20satisfaction&st=cse.

[16]"Fact Sheet," Southwest Airlines, www.southwest.com/html/about-southwest/history/fact-sheet.html#daily_departures (accessed February 27, 2012).

[17]"Misconceptions," Visit California, www.visitcalifornia.com/Life-In-California/Behind-The-Scenes/Misconceptions/ (accessed February 27, 2012).

[18]Gold's Gym, "Meet the Trainers," www.goldsgym.com/gyms/trainers.php?gymID=0103 (accessed February 27, 2012).

[19]"USAA's Secret Sauce," *Bloomberg Businessweek*, February 18, 2010, www.businessweek.com/magazine/content/10_09/b4168040786632.htm.

[20]Hoffman and Bateson, *Services Marketing: Concepts, Strategies, and Cases*, 163.

[21]"Bing Travel," www.bing.com/travel/ (accessed November 2, 2011).

[22]*Florian v. Wangenheim*; Tomás Bayón, "Behavioral Consequences of Overbooking Service Capacity," *Journal of Marketing* 71 (October 2007): 36–47.

[23]Zeithaml, Parasuraman, and Berry, *Delivering Quality Service.*

[24]"Good Service is Good Business: American Consumers Willing to Spend More with Companies That Get Service Right, According to American Express Survey," American Express, May 3, 2011, http://about.americanexpress.com/news/pr/2011/csbar.aspx.

[25]Valarie A. Zeithaml, "How Consumer Evaluation Processes Differ between Goods and Services," in *Marketing of Services*, eds. James H. Donnelly and William R. George (Chicago: American Marketing Association, 1981), 186–190.

[26]"About Us," Laywers.com, www.lawyers.com/about-us.html (accessed February 27, 2012).

[27]A. Parasuraman, Leonard L. Berry, and Valarie A. Zeithaml, "An Empirical Examination of Relationships in an Extended Service Quality Model," *Marketing Science Institute Working Paper Services*, no. 90–112 (Cambridge, MA: Marketing Science Institute, 1990), 29.

[28]Dwane H. Dean, "Consumer Perceptions of Visible Tattoos on Service Personnel," *Managing Service Quality* 20, no. 3 (May 2010): 294–308, www.emeraldinsight.com/journals.htm?articleid=1858666&show=html.

[29]Valarie A. Zeithaml, Leonard L. Berry, and A. Parasuraman, "Communication and Control Processes in the Delivery of Service Quality," *Journal of Marketing* (April 1988): 35–48.

[30]Valarie A. Zeithaml, Leonard L. Berry, and A. Parasuraman, "The Nature and Determinants of Customer Expectations of Service," *Journal of the Academy of Marketing Science* (Winter 1993): 1–12.

[31]"Engaging Our Customers—Enhanced Customer Satisfaction," American Airlines, www.aa.com/i18n/aboutUs/corporateResponsibility/customers/engaging-our-customers.jsp (accessed February 27, 2012).

[32]"I'm Happy, You're Happy: Yet More Evidence that Satisfied Employees Make Satisfied, and Loyal, Customers," Customer Service Psychology Research, June 3, 2011, http://customerservicepsychology.wordpress.com/2011/06/03/i%e2%80%99m-happy-you%e2%80%99re-happy-yet-more-evidence-that-satisfied-employees-make-satisfied-and-loyal-customers/.

[33]"About Rock the Vote," Rock the Vote, www.rockthevote.com/about/ (accessed February 27, 2012).

[34]"Our Mission and Vision," ACCION International, www.accion.org/page.aspx?pid=501 (accessed February 27, 2012).

[35]Philip Kotler, *Marketing for Nonprofit Organizations*, 2nd ed. (Englewood Cliffs, NJ: Prentice-Hall, 1982), 37.

[36]"About Us," Pacer, www.pacer.org/bullying/about/ (accessed February 27, 2012).

[37]"Environment," Red Sun Press, http://redsunpress.com/environment.html# (accessed February 27, 2012).

[38]VerticalResponse, "VerticalResponse, Inc. Surveys the State of Non-Profits in America; Reports on Trends in Marketing Channel Use Across 2009 and 2010," press release, February 1, 2010, www.verticalresponse.com/node/1512.

[39]Amy Gahran, "Donating to Charity by Text Message: Lessons from Haiti," CNN, January 12, 2012, http://articles.cnn.com/2012-01-12/tech/tech_mobile_charity-donations-text-messages_1_text-donations-text-message-haitian-earthquake-relief?_s=PM:TECH.

[40]Based on information in David Wolinsky, "Threadless Teams with UNICEF for Charitable T-Shirts," NBC Chicago, October 13, 2011, www.nbcchicago.com; Piers Fawkes, "Justin Gignac Explains How He'll Raise Millions for UNICEF by Selling T-Shirts," *PSFK*, October 26, 2011, www.psfk.com; UNICEF, "Good Shirts Collection Launched to Help UNICEF Aid Children in the Horn of Africa," news release, October 25, 2011, www.unicefusa.org; www.unicef.org.

[41]Sandra Guy, "Walgreen Expands Hiring of Disabled, Adds More Medical Care, Fresh-Food Stores," *Chicago Sun-Times,* March 8, 2012, www.suntimes.com; Monée Fields-White, "Walgreen Stands to Reap Benefits of Health Care Reform," *Crain's Chicago Business*, March 24, 2010, www.chicagobusiness.com; Ben Sutherly, "Health Care Clinics Setting Up Shop Inside Area Kroger Stores," *Dayton Daily News* (OH), March 21, 2010, www.daytondailynews.com; "In-Store Clinics Build Niche in Changing Health Care System," *Chain Drug Review,* April 20, 2009, 71; Walecia Konrad, "A Quick Trip to the Store for Milk and a Throat Swab," *The New York Times,* October 3, 2009, B6.

Feature Notes

[a]Based on information in Maureen Morrison, "Via Agency Tapped to Handle Perdue's Marketing," *Advertising Age,* November 29, 2011, www.adage.com; Beth Snyder Bulick, "Small Agency of the Year, Gold: Via," *Advertising Age,* August 8, 2011, www.adage.com; "Via Agency, Baldwin Take Top Honors at Small Agency Awards," *Advertising Age,* July 28, 2011, www.adage.com.

[b]Based on information in Paul Demery, "For Customer Service, Shoppers Are Going Social," *Internet Retailer,* January 27, 2012, www.internetretailer.com; Rachel King, "Social Media Replacing Customer Service Channels at Banks," *ZDNet.com,* January 9, 2012, www.zdnet.com; Rohit Bhargava, "9 Ways Top Brands Use Social Media for Better Customer Service," *Mashable,* October 28, 2011, www.mashable.com.

[c]Based on information in Dan Lea, "Get Spicy with Chipotle Mexican Grill," *Idaho Press-Tribune,* January 6, 2012, www.idahopress.com; Leslie Patton, "Q&A: Chipotle Mexican Grill CEO Steve Ells," *Bloomberg Businessweek,* January 19, 2012, www.businessweek.com; David A. Kaplan, "Chipotle's Growth Machine," *Fortune,* September 12, 2011, www.fortune.com.

[d]Based on information in "L.L. Bean Celebrates 100th with a Boot on Wheels," *The Wall Street Journal,* January 16, 2012, www.wsj.com; Laarni A. Ragaza, "Costco Laptops and Desktops for the Holidays," *PC Magazine,* November 19, 2010, www.pcmag.com; Nick Carbone, "Black and Blue Friday," *Time,* November 26, 2011, www.time.com; www.costco.com.

chapter 14

Branding and Packaging

OBJECTIVES

1. To explain the value of branding
2. To understand brand loyalty
3. To analyze the major components of brand equity
4. To recognize the types of brands and their benefits
5. To understand how to select and protect brands
6. To examine three types of branding strategies
7. To understand co-branding and brand licensing
8. To describe the major packaging functions and design considerations and how packaging is used in marketing strategies
9. To examine the functions of labeling and describe some legal issues pertaining to labeling

MARKETING INSIGHTS

Who Is Joe Fresh? Will This Fresh Idea Work in the United States?

Have you met Joe Fresh? Only recently introduced to U.S. shoppers, Joe Fresh is well established in Canada, where its affordable clothing and accessories for men, women, and children are sold in hundreds of stores owned by its parent company, Loblaw. The real Joe Fresh is fashion designer Joe Mimran, who co-founded the clothing brand Club Monaco and sold it to Polo Ralph Lauren in 1999.

Now, having built Joe Fresh into a household name in Canada, Mimran and Loblaw are testing the brand's growth potential in the United States. "No matter how big you become in Canada, you're not really, truly recognized until you step outside of that market and start to expand," Mimran explains. A flagship store opened on New York's stylish Fifth Avenue in 2011, followed by other stores in the metropolitan New York area. If Joe Fresh succeeds in attracting a loyal U.S. following, the company plans as many as 800 stores within five years.

Joe Fresh's signature color is a peppy tangerine orange, reflected in the brand's logo, its store signage, and many of its products. As a fashion brand, Joe Fresh launches a new collection for each season but also stocks a selection of basic products that are always in style. Every new collection is another opportunity for Joe Fresh to differentiate itself from competing affordable fashion brands, such as the Gap, Japan's Uniqlo, and Sweden's H&M. "We compete with international brands in our own market," says Mimran. "Today, if you have a proposition that resonates, it can work across cultures and borders."[1]

Brands, components of brands, packages, and labels are all part of a product's tangible features, the verbal and physical cues that help customers identify the products they want and influence their choices when they are unsure. As such, branding and packaging play an important role in marketing strategy. A successful brand like Joe Fresh is distinct and memorable; without one, a firm could not differentiate its products, and shoppers' choices would essentially be arbitrary. A good package design is cost-effective, safe, environmentally responsible, and valuable as a promotional tool.

In this chapter, we first discuss branding, its value to customers and marketers, brand loyalty, and brand equity. Next, we examine the various types of brands. We then consider how companies choose and protect brands, the various branding strategies employed, co-branding, and brand licensing. We look at packaging's critical role as part of the product. Next, we explore the functions of packaging, issues to consider in packaging design, how the package can be a major element in marketing strategy, and packaging criticisms. Finally, we discuss the functions of labeling and relevant legal issues.

BRANDING

Marketers must make many decisions about products, including choices about brands, brand names, brand marks, trademarks, and trade names. A **brand** is a name, term, design, symbol, or any other feature that identifies one seller's product as distinct from those of other sellers. A brand may identify a single item, a family of items, or all of a seller's items.[2] Some have defined a brand as not just the physical good, name, color, logo, or ad campaign but everything associated with the product, including its symbolism and experiences. For instance, Ford Motor Company's brand represents not only the company's name, logo, and vehicles, but also the fact that it has over 100 years of experience in manufacturing motor vehicles and is the oldest car manufacturer in America that still exists today. A **brand name** is the part of a brand that can be spoken, including letters, words, and numbers (like 7Up). A brand name is often a product's only distinguishing characteristic. Without the brand name, a firm could not differentiate its products. To consumers, a brand name is as fundamental as the product itself. Indeed, many brand names have become synonymous with the product, such as Scotch Tape and Xerox copiers. Through promotional activities, the owners of these brand names try to protect them from being used as generic names for tape and photocopiers, respectively.

The element of a brand that is not made up of words—often a symbol or design—is a **brand mark**. Examples of brand marks include McDonald's golden arches, Nike's "swoosh," and the stylized silhouette of Apple's iPod. A **trademark** is a legal designation indicating that the owner has exclusive use of a brand or a part of a brand and others are prohibited by law from using it. To protect a brand name or brand mark in the United States, an organization must register it as a trademark with the U.S. Patent and Trademark Office. Recently, the Patent and Trademark Office registered almost 244,000 new trademarks in a single year.[3] Finally, a **trade name** is the full legal name of an organization, such as Ford Motor Company, rather than the name of a specific product.

brand A name, term, design, symbol, or other feature that identifies one seller's product as distinct from those of other sellers

brand name The part of a brand that can be spoken, including letters, words, and numbers

brand mark The part of a brand that is not made up of words, such as a symbol or design

trademark A legal designation of exclusive use of a brand

trade name The full legal name of an organization

Value of Branding

Both buyers and sellers benefit from branding. Brands help customers identify specific products that they do and do not like, which in turn facilitates the purchase of items that satisfy their needs and reduces the time required to purchase the product. Without brands, product selection would be quite random because buyers would have no assurance they were purchasing what they preferred. The purchase of certain brands can be a form of self-expression. For instance, clothing brand names are important to many consumers; names such as Nike, The North Face, Juicy Brand, and Levi's give manufacturers an advantage in the marketplace. A brand also helps buyers evaluate the quality of products, especially when they are unable to judge a product's characteristics; that is, a brand may symbolize a certain quality level to a

© iStockphoto.com/Nikada

Brand Mark
The apple is a familiar brand mark initiated, owned, and protected by Apple Inc.

customer, and in turn the person lets that perception of quality represent the quality of the item. A brand helps reduce a buyer's perceived risk of purchase. Customers want to purchase brands they trust, such as Amazon.com, Coca-Cola, and Walmart's Great Value brand. In addition, a psychological reward may come from owning a brand that symbolizes status. The Mercedes-Benz brand in the United States is an example.

Sellers benefit from branding because each company's brand identifies its products, which makes repeat purchasing easier for customers. Branding helps a firm introduce a new product that carries the name of one or more of its existing products, because buyers are already familiar with those brands. It also facilitates promotional efforts, because the promotion of each branded product indirectly promotes all other similarly branded products. Branding also fosters brand loyalty. To the extent that buyers become loyal to a specific brand, the company's market share for that product achieves a certain level of stability, allowing the firm to use its resources more efficiently. Once a firm develops some degree of customer loyalty for a brand, it can maintain a fairly consistent price rather than continually cutting the price to attract customers. A brand is as much of an asset as the company's building or machinery. When marketers increase their brand's value, they also raise the total asset value of the organization. Companies often spend significant resources to boost their brands' value (we discuss brand value in more detail later in this chapter). At times, marketers must decide whether to change a brand name. This is a difficult decision, because the value in the existing brand name must be given up to gain the potential to build a higher value in a new brand name.

There is a cultural dimension to branding. Most brand experiences are individual, and each consumer confers his or her own social meaning onto brands. A brand's appeal is largely at an emotional level based on its symbolic image and key associations. For some brands, such as Harley-Davidson, Google, and Apple, this can result in an almost cult-like following. These brands often develop a community of loyal customers that communicate through get-togethers, online forums, blogs, podcasts, and other means. These brands may even help consumers develop their identities and self-concepts and serve as forms of self-expression. In fact, the term *cultural branding* has been used to explain how a brand conveys a powerful myth that consumers find useful in cementing their identities.[4] It is also important to recognize that, because a brand exists independently in the consumer's mind, it is not directly controlled by the marketer. Every aspect of a brand is subject to a consumer's emotional involvement, interpretation, and memory. By understanding how branding influences purchases, marketers can facilitate customer loyalty.

Emerging Trends

Branding in China: "Defect" versus "Responds without Fail"

Can you name those sneakers with a swoosh? If you're in Boston, you'd recognize the brand as "Nike." But if you're in Beijing, you'd recognize it as "Enduring and Persevering." Nike and other Western companies have to be careful when translating or creating brands for Chinese markets. The goal is to communicate positive benefits and avoid negative associations. That's why the brand name of Tide laundry detergent is written with Chinese characters that translate as "gets rid of dirt." Similarly, Coca-Cola's Chinese brand is Kekoukele, which means "tasty fun," an appropriate benefit for a soft drink.

Knowing that horses are powerful symbols in China, many Western brands adopt a horse as part of their brand names or brand marks. For example, General Motors and its joint-venture partners in China recently introduced a sedan named the Baojun, which means "treasure horse."

Sometimes, brands intended for global markets simply don't work in China. Before Microsoft introduced its Bing search engine in China, the company learned that the character for "bing" has negative meanings, such as "disease" and "defect." As a result, Microsoft altered the brand name very slightly and launched the product as "Bi ying," which means "responds without fail."[a]

Brand Loyalty

As we just noted, creating and maintaining customer loyalty toward a brand are two of the benefits of branding. **Brand loyalty** is a customer's favorable attitude toward a specific brand. If brand loyalty is strong enough, customers may consistently purchase this brand when they need a product in that product category. Although brand loyalty may not result in a customer purchasing a specific brand all the time, the brand is at least viewed as a potentially viable choice in the variety of brands being considered for purchase. Development of brand loyalty in a customer reduces his or her risks and shortens the time spent buying the product. However, the degree of brand loyalty for products varies from one product category to another. For example, it is challenging to develop brand loyalty for most products because customers can usually judge a product's quality and do not need to refer to a brand as an indicator of quality. Brand loyalty also varies by country. Customers in France, Germany, and the United Kingdom tend to be less brand loyal than U.S. customers.

Three degrees of brand loyalty exist: recognition, preference, and insistence. **Brand recognition** occurs when a customer is aware that the brand exists and views it as an alternative purchase if the preferred brand is unavailable or if the other available brands are unfamiliar. This is the mildest form of brand loyalty. The term *loyalty* clearly is used very loosely here. One of the initial objectives when introducing a new brand is to create widespread awareness of the brand to generate brand recognition.

brand loyalty A customer's favorable attitude toward a specific brand

brand recognition The degree of brand loyalty in which a customer is aware that a brand exists and views the brand as an alternative purchase if their preferred brand is unavailable

brand preference The degree of brand loyalty in which a customer prefers one brand over competitive offerings

Brand preference is a stronger degree of brand loyalty: a customer definitely prefers one brand over competitive offerings and will purchase this brand if available. However, if the brand is not available, the customer will accept a substitute brand rather than expending additional effort finding and purchasing the preferred brand. A marketer is likely to be able to compete effectively in a market when a number of customers have developed brand preference for its specific brand. In an attempt to increase preference for its Ivory brand of soap, Procter & Gamble launched a new marketing strategy. The soap's packaging was updated to a more modern design, but the new advertisements focused on the fact that Ivory soap's formula has remained consistent throughout its over 130-year history. The taglines in the print and online ads, which include "when dirt changes its formula, so will we," appeal to consumers who value stability and simplicity, which the company hopes will encourage them to purchase Ivory brand bars of soap.[5]

When **brand insistence** occurs, a customer strongly prefers a specific brand, will accept no substitute, and is willing to spend a great deal of time and effort to acquire that brand. If a brand-insistent customer goes to a store and finds the brand unavailable, he or she will seek the brand elsewhere rather than purchase a substitute brand. Brand insistence can also apply to service products like Hilton Hotels or sports teams, such as the Chicago Bears or the Dallas Cowboys. Brand insistence is the strongest degree of brand loyalty—a brander's dream. However, it is the least-common type of brand loyalty. Customers vary considerably regarding the product categories for which they may be brand insistent. Can you think of products for which you are brand insistent? Perhaps it's a brand of deodorant, soft drink, jeans, or even pet food (if your pet is brand insistent).

Building brand loyalty is a major challenge for many marketers. Brand loyalty in general seems to be declining, partly because of marketers' increased reliance on sales, coupons, and other short-term promotions, and partly because of the sometimes overwhelming array of similar new products from which customers can choose. Thus, it is an extremely important issue. The creation of brand loyalty significantly contributes to an organization's ability to achieve a sustainable competitive advantage.

Courtesy of The Advertising Archives

Brand Insistence
Some consumers are brand insistent about their deodorant. When they find just the right brand that works with their body chemistry, they keep buying the same brand.

Brand Equity

A well-managed brand is an asset to an organization. The value of this asset is often referred to as brand equity. **Brand equity** is the marketing and financial value associated with a brand's strength in a market. Besides the actual proprietary brand assets, such as patents and trademarks, four major elements underlie brand equity: brand-name awareness, brand loyalty, perceived brand quality, and brand associations (see Figure 14.1).[6]

brand insistence The degree of brand loyalty in which a customer strongly prefers a specific brand and will accept no substitute

brand equity The marketing and financial value associated with a brand's strength in a market

Figure 14.1 Major Elements of Brand Equity

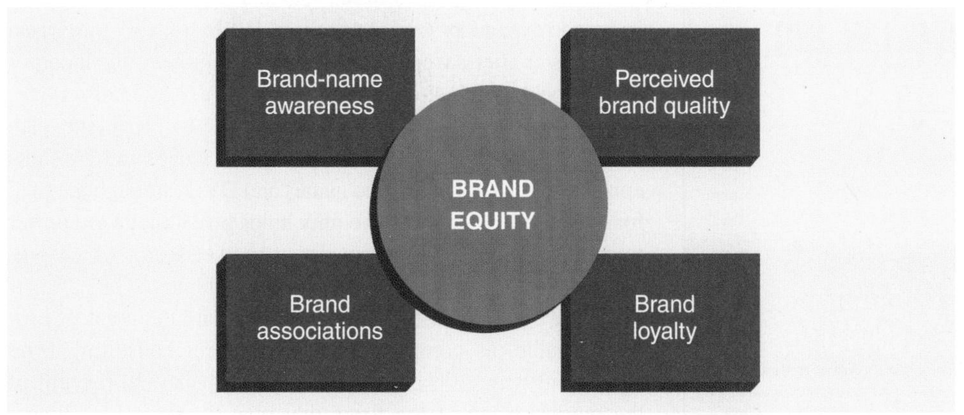

Source: Adapted with the permission of The Free Press, a division of Simon & Schuster Adult Publishing Group, from *Managing Brand Equity: Capitalizing on the Value of a Brand Name* by David A. Aaker. Copyright © 1991 by David A. Aaker. All rights reserved.

Recognition of a brand leads to brand familiarity, which in turn results in a level of comfort with the brand. A familiar brand is more likely to be selected than an unfamiliar brand, because the familiar brand is often viewed as more reliable and of more acceptable quality. The familiar brand is likely to be in a customer's consideration set, whereas the unfamiliar brand is not.

Brand loyalty is an important component of brand equity, because it reduces a brand's vulnerability to competitors' actions. Brand loyalty allows an organization to keep its existing customers and avoid spending an enormous amount of resources gaining new ones. Loyal customers provide brand visibility and reassurance to potential new customers. Because customers expect their brands to be available when and where they shop, retailers strive to carry the brands known for their strong customer following.

Customers associate a particular brand with a certain level of overall quality. A brand name may be used as a substitute for judgment of quality. In many cases, customers can't actually judge the quality of the product for themselves and instead must rely on the brand as a quality indicator. Consumers who prefer Apple products will purchase new products without conducting much research, because they know that the company delivers a consistently high level of quality. Perceived high brand quality helps support a premium price, allowing a marketer to avoid severe price competition. Also, favorable perceived brand quality can ease the introduction of brand extensions, since the high regard for the brand will likely translate into high regard for the related products.

The set of associations linked to a brand is another key component of brand equity. At times, a marketer works to connect a particular lifestyle or, in some instances, a certain personality type with a specific brand. For example, customers associate Michelin tires with protecting family members. Most consumers associate Google, on the other hand, with fun and social responsibility. This association is underscored by its informal corporate slogan: "Don't be evil." Disney's slogan, "Where dreams come true," reminds consumers that it is a brand associated with fun, fantasy, and childhood. These types of brand associations contribute significantly to the brand's equity. Brand associations are sometimes facilitated by using trade characters, such as the GEICO gecko, Snuggle the fabric softener bear, and the Pillsbury Dough Boy. Placing these trade characters in advertisements and on packages helps consumers link the ads and packages to the brands.

Stimulating Brand Associations
Geico uses the gecko as a trade character to stimulate favorable brand associations.

Although difficult to measure, brand equity represents the value of a brand to an organization. An organization may buy a brand from another company at a premium price because outright brand purchase may be less expensive and less risky than creating and developing a brand from scratch. Consider DISH Network, which decided that it would be a better business decision to buy an existing brand—Blockbuster—than to create a new brand of its own to expand its service offerings. DISH Network purchased Blockbuster after the company declared bankruptcy and incorporated Blockbuster's streaming video and DVD-by-mail services into its own service offerings, creating a $10 per-month plan where DISH Network customers can watch videos and TV show episodes online and get video games and DVDs through the mail for one monthly fee.[7] Brand equity helps give a brand the power to capture and maintain a consistent market share, which provides stability to the organization's sales volume.

Table 14.1 lists the 10 global brands with the greatest economic value, as compiled by Interbrand, a consulting firm. Interbrand's top 100 brands account for nearly 30 percent of the market value of the firms that own them. Any company that owns a brand listed in Table 14.1 would agree that the economic value of that brand is likely to be the greatest single asset the organization possesses. A brand's overall economic

Table 14.1 The World's Most Valuable Brands

Brand	Brand Value (In Millions of Dollars)
Coca-Cola	$71,861
IBM	69,905
Microsoft	59,087
Google	55,317
GE	42,808
McDonald's	35,593
Intel	35,217
Apple	33,492
Disney	29,018
Hewlett-Packard	28,479

Source: www.interbrand.com/en/best-global-brands/best-global-brands-2011.aspx (accessed February 28, 2012).

value rises and falls with the brand's profitability, brand awareness, brand loyalty, and perceived brand quality, and with the strength of positive brand associations.

Types of Brands

Brands come in three categories: manufacturer, private distributor, and generic. **Manufacturer brands** are initiated by producers and ensure that producers are identified with their products at the point of purchase—for example, Clorox, Compaq Computer, and Levi's. A manufacturer brand usually requires a producer to become involved in distribution, promotion, and, to some extent, pricing decisions. Brand loyalty is encouraged by promotion, quality control, and guarantees; it is a valuable asset to a manufacturer. The producer tries to stimulate demand for the product, which tends to encourage sellers and resellers to make the product available.

manufacturer brand A brand initiated by producers to ensure that producers are identified with their products at the point of purchase

private distributor brand A brand initiated and owned by a reseller

Private distributor brands (also called *private brands, store brands,* or *dealer brands*) are initiated and owned by resellers—that is, wholesalers or retailers. The major characteristic of private brands is that the manufacturers are not identified on the products. Retailers and wholesalers use private distributor brands to develop more efficient promotion, generate higher gross margins, and change store image. Despite the many strong national brands available to consumers, the top-selling consumer brand on this continent is Walmart's private-label brand, Great Value.[8] Private distributor brands give retailers or wholesalers freedom to purchase products of a specified quality at the lowest cost without disclosing the identities of the manufacturers. Wholesaler brands include IGA (Independent Grocers' Alliance) and Topmost (General Grocer). Familiar retailer brand names include Sears' Kenmore and JCPenney's Arizona. Many successful private brands are distributed nationally. Kenmore appliances are as well known as most manufacturer brands. Sometimes retailers with successful private distributor brands start manufacturing their own products to gain more control over

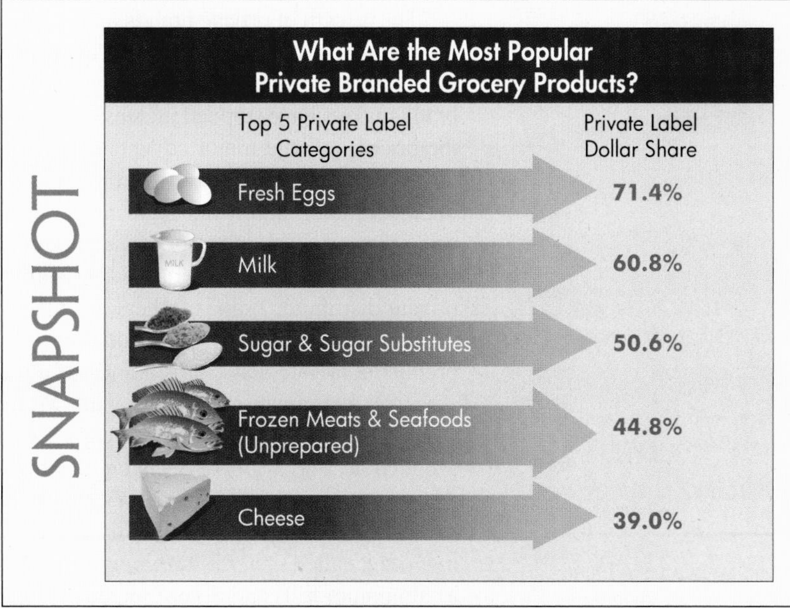

Source: PLMA's 2011 Private Label Yearbook, Private Label Manufacturer Association, 2011.

Figure 14.2 Consumers' Perceptions of Store and Manufacturers' Brands for Selected Product Groups

product costs, quality, and design in the hope of increasing profits. Sales of private labels now account for one out of every four product items sold in supermarkets, drugstores, and mass merchandisers, totaling some $93 billion of retail business.[9] Supermarket private brands are popular globally, too.

Competition between manufacturer brands and private distributor brands (sometimes called "the battle of the brands") is ongoing. To compete against manufacturer brands, retailers have tried to strengthen consumer confidence in private brands. Results of a recent study on consumer perceptions of private and manufacturer brands appear in Figure 14.2. For manufacturers, developing multiple manufacturer brands and distribution systems has been an effective means of combating the increased competition from private brands. By developing a new brand name, a producer can adjust various elements of its marketing mix to appeal to a different target market.

The growth of private brands has been steady. One reason for this is that retailers advertise the manufacturer brands, which brings customers to their stores, but sell the private brands, especially to price-sensitive customers. To compete against private brands, some manufacturer brand makers have stopped increasing prices or even have cut their prices, which has narrowed the price gap—the major advantage of buying a private brand. Traditionally, private brands have appeared in packaging that directly imitates the packaging of competing manufacturers' brands without significant legal ramifications. However, the legal risks of using look-alike packaging are increasing for private branders.

Some private distributor brands are produced by companies that specialize in making only private distributor brands; others are made by producers of manufacturer brands. At times, producers of both types of brands find it difficult to ignore the opportunities that arise from producing private distributor brands. If a producer decides not to produce a private brand for a reseller, a competitor probably will. Moreover, the production of private distributor brands allows the producer to use excess capacity during periods when its own brands are at nonpeak production. The ultimate decision of whether to produce a private or a manufacturer brand depends on a company's resources, production capabilities, and goals.

generic brand A brand indicating only the product category

Some marketers of traditionally branded products have embarked on a policy of not branding, often called *generic branding.* **Generic brands** indicate only the product category (such as aluminum foil) and do not include the company name or other identifying terms. Generic brands are usually sold at lower prices than comparable branded items. Although at one time

© Kristoffer Tripplaar/Alamy

Private Brands
Sears has initiated and developed several private brands, using Kenmore as a private brand for appliances, Craftsman for tools, and DieHard for automotive batteries.

generic brands may have represented as much as 10 percent of all retail grocery sales, today they account for less than half of 1 percent.

Selecting a Brand Name

Marketers consider a number of factors when selecting a brand name. First, the name should be easy for customers (including foreign buyers, if the firm intends to market its products in other countries) to say, spell, and recall. Short, one-syllable names, such as Cheer, often satisfy this requirement. Second, the brand name should indicate the product's major benefits and, if possible, suggest in a positive way the product's uses and special characteristics; negative or offensive references should be avoided. For example, the brand names of such household cleaning products as Ajax dishwashing liquid, Vanish toilet bowl cleaner, Formula 409 multipurpose cleaner, Cascade dishwasher detergent, and Wisk laundry detergent signify strength and effectiveness. Third, to set it apart from competing brands, the brand should be distinctive. Google, for example, renamed its online services Blogger and Picasa to Google Blogs and Google Photos, respectively, in an effort to make all of the company's products carry the same brand name.[10] If a marketer intends to use a brand for a product line, that brand must be compatible with all products in the line. Finally, a brand should be designed so that it can be used and recognized in all types of media. Finding the right brand name has become a challenging task, because many obvious product names have already been used.

How are brand names devised? Brand names can be created from single or multiple words—for example, Bic or Dodge Dart. Letters and numbers are used to create such brands as Volvo's S60 sedan or RIM's BlackBerry Bold 9900. Words, numbers, and letters are combined to yield brand names, such as Motorola's Droid X2 phone or BMW's 528i xDrive sedan. To avoid terms that have negative connotations, marketers sometimes use fabricated words that have absolutely no meaning when created—for example, Kodak and Exxon. Occasionally, a brand is simply brought out of storage and used as is or modified. Firms often maintain banks of registered brands, some of which may have been used in the past. Cadillac, for example, maintains an ever-growing bank of hundreds of trademarks. The LaSalle brand, used in the 1920s and 1930s, could be called up for a new Cadillac model in the future. Possible brand names are sometimes tested in focus groups or other settings to assess customers' reactions.

Who actually creates brand names? Brand names can be created internally by the organization. At OPI, for example, a team of six employees brainstorm possible names for the new nail lacquer colors. Some such names include "Aphrodite's Pink Nightie," "Lincoln Park After

Entrepreneurship in Marketing

EagleView's Business Brand Soars

Entrepreneurs: Chris Pershing and Dave Carlson
Business: EagleView
Founded: 2008 | Bothell, Washington
Success: The company now serves almost all of the top U.S. insurers and 20,000 contractors.

In just a few years, EagleView Technologies, a startup founded by software engineer Chris Pershing, has soared to $40 million in annual sales and made its name as a major brand in the roofing world. The company uses aerial photographs and sophisticated algorithms to provide measurements of rooftops, filling a vital need for both roofing contractors and insurance firms. The brand reflects the company's high-tech solution to what used to be a time-consuming and potentially dangerous task: climbing a ladder to painstakingly measure the size of a roof by hand.

Pershing decided to start EagleView after his brother-in-law, who sells roofing materials, complained about the difficulty of measuring a roof to accurately estimate the cost of repairing or replacing it. After investigating the market, Pershing set out to develop an automated system of calculating roof measurements based on aerial views, the "eagle view" in his brand. After months of development—and thousands of dollars in investments from family and friends—the entrepreneur perfected software to create a 3D image of any roof and accurately compute the dimensions. EagleView continues to polish its tech image as it increases market share, serving most of the top U.S. insurers and 20,000 contractors nationwide.[b]

Dark," and "Tickle My France-y."[11] Sometimes a name is suggested by individuals who are close to the product's development. Some organizations have committees that participate in brand-name creation and approval. Large companies that introduce numerous new products annually are likely to have a department that develops brand names. At times, outside consultants and companies that specialize in brand-name development are used.

Although most of the important branding considerations apply to both goods and services, branding a service has some additional dimensions. The service brand is usually the same as the company name. Financial companies, such as Fidelity Investments and Charles Schwab Discount Brokerage, have established strong brand recognition. These companies have used their names to create an image of value and friendly, timely, accurate, and knowledgeable customer assistance. Service providers (such as United Airlines) are perceived by customers as having one brand name, even though they offer multiple products (first class, business class, and coach). Because the service brand name and company name are so closely interrelated, a service brand name must be flexible enough to encompass a variety of current services, as well as new ones the company may offer in the future. Geographical references like *western* and descriptive terms like *trucking* limit the scope of possible associations with the brand name. Because Southwest Airlines now flies to many parts of the country, its name has become too limited in its scope of associations. *Humana,* with its connotations of kindness and compassion, is flexible enough to encompass all services that a hospital, insurance plan, or health-care facility offers. Frequently, a service marketer employs a symbol along with its brand name to make the brand distinctive and communicate a certain image.

Protecting a Brand

A marketer should also design a brand so that it can be protected easily through registration. A series of court decisions has created a broad hierarchy of protection based on brand type. From most protectable to least protectable, these brand types are fanciful (Exxon), arbitrary (Dr Pepper), suggestive (Spray 'n Wash), descriptive (Minute Rice), and generic (aluminum foil). Generic brands are not protectable. Surnames and descriptive, geographic, or functional names are difficult to protect.[12] Because of their designs, some brands can be legally infringed upon more easily than others. Although registration protects trademarks domestically for 10 years, and trademarks can be renewed indefinitely, a firm should develop a system for ensuring that its trademarks are renewed as needed.

To protect its exclusive rights to a brand, a company must ensure that the brand is not likely to be considered an infringement upon any brand already registered with the U.S. Patent and Trademark Office. This task may be complex because infringement is determined by the courts, which base their decisions on whether a brand causes consumers to be confused, mistaken, or deceived about the source of the product. McDonald's is one company that aggressively protects its trademarks against infringement; it has brought charges against a number of companies with *Mc* names because it fears that the use of that prefix will give consumers the impression that these companies are associated with or owned by McDonald's. Auto Shack changed its name to AutoZone when faced with legal action from Tandy Corporation, owner of Radio Shack. Tandy maintained that it owned the name *Shack*. After research showed that virtually every auto supply store in the country used *auto* in its name, *zone* was deemed the best word to pair with *auto*.

A marketer should guard against allowing a brand name to become a generic term used to refer to a general product category. Generic terms cannot be protected as exclusive brand names. For instance, *aspirin, escalator,* and *shredded wheat*—all brand names at one time—eventually were declared generic terms that refer to product classes. Thus, they could no longer be protected. To keep a brand name from becoming a generic term, the firm should spell the name with a capital letter and use it as an adjective to modify the name of the general product class, as in Kool-Aid Soft Drink Mix. Including the word *brand* just after the brand name is also helpful. An organization can deal with this problem directly by advertising that its brand is a trademark and should not be used generically. The firm can also indicate that the brand is a registered trademark by using the symbol®.

In the interest of strengthening trademark protection, Congress enacted the Trademark Law Revision Act in 1988, the only major federal trademark legislation since the Lanham Act of 1946. The purpose of this more recent legislation is to increase the value of the federal registration system for U.S. firms relative to foreign competitors and to better protect the public from counterfeiting, confusion, and deception.

A U.S. firm that tries to protect a brand in a foreign country frequently encounters problems. In many countries, brand registration is not possible; the first firm to use a brand in such a country automatically has the rights to it. In some instances, U.S. companies actually have had to buy their own brand rights from a firm in a foreign country, because the foreign firm was the first user in that country.

Marketers that are trying to protect their brands must also contend with brand counterfeiting. In the United States, for instance, one can purchase counterfeit Gucci handbags, iPod MP3 players, Baby Phat jeans, Nike sneakers, and a host of other products illegally marketed by manufacturers that do not own the brands. Annual losses caused by counterfeit products are estimated at between \$200 billion and \$250 billion for U.S. businesses, and possibly as much as \$600 billion for businesses globally.[13] Many counterfeit products are manufactured overseas—in Turkey, China, Thailand, Italy, and Colombia, for example—but some are counterfeited in the United States. Counterfeit products are often hard to distinguish from the real brands. Products most likely to be counterfeited are well-known brands that appeal to a mass market and products whose physical materials are inexpensive relative to the products' prices. Brand fraud not only results in lost revenue for the brand's owner, but it also results in a low-quality product for customers, distorts competition, affects investment levels, reduces tax revenues and legitimate employment, creates safety risks, and affects international relations. It also likely affects customers' perceptions of the brand due to the counterfeit product's inferior quality.

Protecting a Brand
Companies try to protect their brands by using certain phrases and symbols in their advertisements. Note the term "brand" after Kool-Aid, and the use of the ® symbol.

Branding Strategies

Before establishing branding strategies, a firm must decide whether to brand its products at all. If a company's product is homogeneous and similar to competitors' products, it may be difficult to brand. Raw materials like coal, sand, and farm produce are hard to brand because of the homogeneity and physical characteristics of such products.

If a firm chooses to brand its products, it may opt for one or more of the following branding strategies: individual, family, or brand extension branding. **Individual branding** is a strategy in which each product is given a different name. Nestlé S.A. is the world's largest food and nutrition company. Nestlé uses individual branding for many of its 6,000 different brands, such as NESCAFÉ coffee, PowerBar nutritional food, Maggi soups, and Häagen-Dazs ice cream. A major advantage of individual branding is that, if an organization introduces a poor product, the negative images associated with it do not contaminate the company's other products. An individual branding strategy may also facilitate market segmentation when a firm wishes to enter many segments of the same market. Separate, unrelated names can be used and each brand aimed at a specific segment.

individual branding A branding strategy in which each product is given a different name

family branding Branding all of a firm's products with the same name or part of the name

brand extension An organization uses one of its existing brands to brand a new product in a different product category

In **family branding**, all of a firm's products are branded with the same name or part of the name, such as Kellogg's Frosted Flakes, Kellogg's Rice Krispies, and Kellogg's Corn Flakes. In some cases, a company's name is combined with other words to brand items. Arm & Hammer uses its name on all its products, along with a generic description of the item, such as Arm & Hammer Heavy Duty Detergent, Arm & Hammer Pure Baking Soda, and Arm & Hammer Carpet Deodorizer. Unlike individual branding, family branding means that the promotion of one item with the family brand promotes the firm's other products. Other major companies that use family branding include Mitsubishi, Kodak, and Fisher-Price.

A **brand extension** occurs when a firm uses one of its existing brands to brand a new product in a different product category. For example, the Velveeta cheese brand recently launched a new brand extension, called Cheesy Skillets, which are one-skillet meals that compete with Hamburger Helper. This is the first major brand extension for Velveeta since it released its popular Shells and Cheese in 1984.[14] A brand extension should not be confused with a line extension, which involves using an existing brand on a new product in the same product category, such as new flavors or sizes. For instance, when the maker of Tylenol, McNeil Consumer Products, introduced Extra Strength Tylenol P.M., the new product was a line extension because it was in the same category. Researchers have found that, when a parent company with a strong brand extends its brand name into a new product category, consumers are more willing to pay a premium price for that product than comparable products with lesser-known brand names, because the consumer perceives a lower risk associated with a known brand name.[15]

Family Branding
The maker of Kellogg's cereals employs family branding on its cereals. Note that the name "Kellogg's" appears on each type of cereal.

Marketers share a common concern that, if a brand is extended too many times or extended too far outside its original product category, the brand can be significantly weakened. For example, Pillsbury tried to extend its brand into the air freshener product category. Its Pillsbury Potpourri Spritz collection, which included scents like "cinnamon roll," did not sell well and were eventually discontinued.[16] Research has found that a line extension into premium categories can be an effective strategy to revitalize a brand, but the line extension needs to be closely linked to the core brand.[17] Other research, however, suggests that diluting a brand by extending it into dissimilar product categories could have the potential to suppress consumer consideration and choice for the original brand.[18]

An organization is not limited to a single branding strategy. A company that uses primarily individual branding for many of its products may also use brand extensions. Branding strategy is influenced by the number of products and product lines the company produces, the characteristics of its target markets, the number and types of competing products available, and the size of the firm's resources.

Co-Branding

Co-branding is the use of two or more brands on one product. Marketers employ co-branding to capitalize on the brand equity of multiple brands. It is popular in a number of processed food categories and in the credit card industry. The brands used for co-branding can be owned by the same company. For example, Kraft's Lunchables product teams the Kraft cheese brand with Oscar Mayer lunchmeats, another Kraft-owned brand. The brands may also be owned by different companies. Credit card companies such as American Express, Visa, and MasterCard, for instance, team up with other brands such as General Motors, AT&T, and many airlines to co-brand and jointly promote their products.

co-branding Using two or more brands on one product

brand licensing An agreement whereby a company permits another organization to use its brand on other products for a licensing fee

Effective co-branding capitalizes on the trust and confidence customers have in the brands involved. The brands should not lose their identities, and it should be clear to customers which brand is the main brand. Nike and Apple successfully teamed up to release a co-branded running shoe, the Nike +. It syncs with an iPod to track running performance. The co-branded shoe and iPod accessories helped boost sales for both brands.[19] It is important for marketers to understand that, when a co-branded product is unsuccessful, both brands are implicated in the product failure. To gain customer acceptance, the brands involved must represent a complementary fit in the minds of buyers. Trying to link a brand like Velveeta with a brand like Nike will not achieve co-branding objectives, because customers are not likely to perceive these brands as compatible.

Co-branding can help an organization differentiate its products from those of competitors. For example, Stride gum, a brand owned by Kraft Foods, recently partnered with athlete and Olympic gold medalist Shaun White to make a new flavor of gum called Stride Whitemint.[20] By using the product development skills of a co-branding partner, an organization can create a distinctive product. Co-branding can also allow the partners to take advantage of each other's distribution capabilities.

Although co-branding has been used for a number of years, it began to grow in popularity in the 1980s when Monsanto aggressively promoted its NutraSweet product as an ingredient in such well-known brands as Diet Coke. Later, a rival sweetener, Splenda, was co-branded with Diet Coke, Starbucks, and many other brands. Intel, too, has capitalized on ingredient co-branding through its "Intel Inside" program. The effectiveness of ingredient co-branding relies heavily on continued promotional efforts by the ingredient's producer.

Co-Branding
Sandwich Combos is a co-branded product consisting of Oscar Mayer and Kraft products.

Brand Licensing

A popular branding strategy involves **brand licensing**, an agreement in which a company permits another organization to use its brand on other products for a licensing fee. Royalties may be as low as 2 percent of wholesale revenues, or higher than 10 percent. The licensee is responsible for all manufacturing, selling, and advertising functions, and bears the costs if the licensed

Marketing Debate

Brands on Campus

ISSUE: Should brands be actively marketed on college campuses?

Microsoft has student representatives demonstrating its software on more than 300 college campuses. Target sponsors freshmen events and buses incoming students to nearby stores for midnight shopping trips. Red Bull underwrites lectures, races, and other events on hundreds of colleges to boost its energy drink brand. American Eagle gives free T-shirts to student reps who help freshmen during move-in days.

Some colleges and universities have welcomed brand-supported activities and giveaways that benefit students, and most students who represent brands enjoy the experience. "We are the people who understand what kinds of things the students will be open to," explains one student rep. "It's marketing for the students, by the students."

However, students sometimes feel pressured. One told a reporter: "Although you may want to support your friends, you may not always be interested in supporting the company." An enthusiastic student rep says she posts so often to Facebook and Twitter that "my friends threaten to block me because I am constantly posting" about the brand. For their part, some school administrators are uneasy about the ongoing onslaught of on-campus marketing. Do you think brands should be doing so much marketing on campus?[c]

product fails. Not long ago, only a few firms licensed their corporate trademarks, but today licensing is a multi-billion-dollar business. The top licensing company in the world is Disney Consumer Products, with nearly $29 billion in retail sales of licensed products.[21] The NFL, the NCAA, NASCAR, and Major League Baseball are all leaders in the retail sales of licensed products.

The advantages of licensing range from extra revenues and low-cost or free publicity to new images and trademark protection. For instance, Coca-Cola has licensed its trademark for use on glassware, radios, trucks, and clothing in the hope of protecting its trademark. However, brand licensing has drawbacks. The major disadvantages are a lack of manufacturing control, which could hurt the company's name, and bombarding consumers with too many unrelated products bearing the same name. Licensing arrangements can also fail because of poor timing, inappropriate distribution channels, or mismatching of product and name.

PACKAGING

Packaging involves the development of a container and a graphic design for a product. A package can be a vital part of a product, making it more versatile, safer, and easier to use. Like a brand name, a package can influence customers' attitudes toward a product and thus affect their purchase decisions. For example, several producers of jellies, sauces, and ketchups have packaged their products in squeezable containers to make use and storage of the products more convenient, and some paint manufacturers have introduced easy-to-open and easy-to-pour paint cans. Package characteristics help shape buyers' impressions of a product at the time of purchase or during use. In this section, we examine the main functions of packaging and consider several major packaging decisions.

Packaging Functions

Effective packaging involves more than simply putting products in containers and covering them with wrappers. First, packaging materials serve the basic purpose of protecting the product and maintaining its functional form. Fluids like milk, orange juice, and hair spray need packages that preserve and protect them. The packaging should prevent damage that could affect the product's usefulness and thus lead to higher costs. Because product tampering has become a problem, several packaging techniques have been developed to counter this danger. Some packages are also designed to deter shoplifting.

Another function of packaging is to offer convenience to consumers. Consider small aseptic packages—individual-size boxes or plastic bags that contain liquids and do not require refrigeration. This packaging appeals strongly to children and young adults with active lifestyles. The size or shape of a package may relate to the product's storage, convenience of use, or replacement rate. Small, single-serving cans of vegetables, for instance, may prevent waste and make storage easier.

A third function of packaging is to promote a product by communicating its features, uses, benefits, and image. Sometimes a reusable package is developed to make the product more desirable. For example, the Cool Whip package doubles as a food storage container.

Finally, packaging can be used to communicate symbolically the quality or premium nature of a product. It can also evoke an emotional response.

Major Packaging Considerations

In developing packages, marketers must take many factors into account. Obviously one major consideration is cost. Although a variety of packaging materials, processes, and designs are available, costs vary greatly. In recent years, buyers have shown a willingness to pay more for improved packaging, but there are limits. Marketers should conduct research to determine exactly how much customers are willing to pay for effective and efficient package designs.

As already mentioned, developing tamper-resistant packaging is very important for certain products. Although no package is tamperproof, marketers can develop packages that are difficult to contaminate. At a minimum, all packaging must comply with the Food and Drug Administration's packaging regulations. However, packaging should also make any product tampering evident to resellers and consumers. Although effective tamper-resistant packaging may be expensive to develop, when balanced against the costs of lost sales, loss of consumer confidence and company reputation, and potentially expensive product liability lawsuits, the costs of ensuring consumer safety are minimal.

Marketers should also consider how much consistency is desirable among an organization's package designs. No consistency may be the best policy, especially if a firm's products are unrelated or aimed at vastly different target markets. To promote an overall company image, a firm may decide that all packages should be similar or include one major element of the design. This approach is called **family packaging**. Sometimes it is used only for lines of products, such as Campbell's soups, Weight Watchers' foods, and Planter's nuts.

A package's promotional role is an important consideration. Through verbal and nonverbal symbols, the package can inform potential buyers about the product's content, features, uses, advantages, and hazards. A firm can create desirable images and associations by its choice of color, design, shape, and texture. Many cosmetics manufacturers, for example, design their packages to create impressions of richness, luxury, and exclusivity. A package performs a promotional function when it is designed to be safer or more convenient to use if such characteristics help stimulate demand.

To develop a package that has a definite promotional value, a designer must consider size, shape, texture, color, and graphics. Beyond the obvious limitation that the package must be large enough to hold the product, a package can be designed to appear taller or shorter. Light-colored packaging may make a package appear larger, whereas darker colors may minimize the perceived size.

Colors on packages are often chosen to attract attention, and color can positively influence customers' emotions. People associate specific colors with certain feelings and experiences. Here are some examples:

- White represents sincerity, simplicity, and purity.
- Yellow is associated with cheerfulness, optimism, and friendliness.
- Red connotes excitement and stimulation.
- Pink is considered soft, nurturing, and feminine.

family packaging Using similar packaging for all of a firm's products or packaging that has one common design element

- Blue is soothing; it is also associated with intelligence, trust, and security.
- Black represents power, status, and sophistication.
- Purple is associated with dignity, quality, and luxury.
- Brown is linked to seriousness, ruggedness, and earthiness.
- Green is associated with nature and sustainability.[22]

When opting for color on packaging, marketers must judge whether a particular color will evoke positive or negative feelings when linked to a specific product. For example, rarely do processors package meat or bread in green materials because customers may associate green with mold. Marketers must also determine whether a specific target market will respond favorably or unfavorably to a particular color. Cosmetics for women are more likely to be sold in pastel packaging than are personal-care products for men. Packages designed to appeal to children often use primary colors and bold designs. A relatively recent trend in packaging is colorless packages. Clear products and packaging connote a pure, natural product.

Packaging must also meet the needs of resellers. Wholesalers and retailers consider whether a package facilitates transportation, storage, and handling. Concentrated versions of laundry detergents and fabric softeners, for example, enable retailers to offer more product diversity within the existing shelf space. Resellers may refuse to carry certain products if their packages are cumbersome.

A final consideration is whether to develop packages that are environmentally responsible. Nearly one-half of all garbage consists of discarded plastic packaging, such as polystyrene containers, plastic soft-drink bottles, and carryout bags. Plastic packaging material does not biodegrade, and paper requires the destruction of valuable forests. Consequently, many companies have changed to environmentally sensitive packaging; they are also recycling more materials. Method, the maker of eco-conscious household and personal care products, uses bottles made entirely from recycled plastic and recently started acquiring 25 percent of the plastic for the bottles from the North Pacific Gyre, a location where ocean currents have trapped floating garbage, which has accumulated over time. Method further reduces waste by offering refill packages so that users do not need to buy a new bottle every time they run out of hand soap.[23] Heinz is looking for alternatives to its plastic ketchup squeeze bottles. Other companies are also searching for alternatives to environmentally harmful packaging. In some instances, however, customers have objected to such switches, because the newer environmentally responsible packaging may be less effective or more inconvenient. Therefore, marketers must carefully balance society's desire to preserve the environment against customers' desire for convenience.

Packaging and Marketing Strategies

Packaging can be a major component of a marketing strategy. A new cap or closure, a better box or wrapper, or a more convenient container may give a product a competitive advantage. The right type of package for a new product can help it gain market recognition very quickly. Sprout Foods, for example, was started a few years ago by celebrity chef Tyler Florence. The company produces high-quality organic baby food packaged in convenient resealable pouches, which are sold individually. The package design was a first for the baby food industry, and has won several awards since it was introduced. Even though the package costs more to use than the traditional glass jar packaging, its design with the zipper closure decreases the time it takes to heat up the baby food, allows it to fit more conveniently in diaper bags, and keeps food fresh for three days after it is first opened.[24] In the case of existing brands, marketers should reevaluate packages periodically. Marketers should view packaging as a major strategic tool, especially for consumer convenience products. For instance, in the food industry, jumbo and large package sizes for such products as hot dogs, pizzas, English muffins, frozen dinners, and biscuits have been very successful. When considering the strategic uses of packaging, marketers must also analyze the cost of packaging and package changes. Table 14.2 lists the biggest packaging spenders. In this section, we examine several ways to use packaging strategically.

Table 14.2 Companies That Spend the Most on Packaging

Anheuser-Busch	Kraft Foods
Campbell Soup	Procter & Gamble
Coca-Cola	Miller Brewing
General Mills	PepsiCo

Altering the Package

At times, a marketer changes a package, because the existing design is no longer in style, especially when compared with the packaging of competitive products. Quaker Oats hired a package design company to redesign its Rice-A-Roni package to give the product the appearance of having evolved with the times while retaining its traditional taste appeal. Rice-A-Roni had been experiencing a lag in sales because of increased competition. An overhaul of the product packaging to a refreshing and more up-to-date look was credited with a 20 percent increase in sales over the previous year.

A package may be redesigned because new product features need to be highlighted or because new packaging materials have become available. An organization may decide to change a product's packaging to reposition the product or make the product safer or more convenient to use. NatureSweet, for example, altered the package for its cherry tomatoes when it introduced a clear plastic container to replace the classic red mesh bag packaging. The new plastic packaging is more sustainable than the bags, makes the product more visible to the consumer, provides more protection for the tomatoes during transport and handling, and limits ventilation, which increases the shelf life of the product.[25]

Secondary-Use Packaging

A secondary-use package can be reused for purposes other than its initial function. For example, a margarine container can be reused to store leftovers, and a jelly container can serve as a drinking glass. Customers often view secondary-use packaging as adding value to products, in which case its use should stimulate unit sales.

Category-Consistent Packaging

With category-consistent packaging, the product is packaged in line with the packaging practices associated with a particular product category. Some product categories—for example, mayonnaise, mustard, ketchup, and peanut butter—have traditional package shapes. Other product categories are characterized by recognizable color combinations, such as red and white for soup and red, white, and blue for Ritz-like crackers. When an organization introduces a brand in one of these product categories, marketers will often use traditional package shapes and color combinations to ensure that customers will recognize the new product as being in that specific product category.

Innovative Packaging

Sometimes a marketer employs a unique cap, design, applicator, or other feature to make a product distinctive. Such packaging can be effective when the innovation makes the product safer or easier to use, or provides better protection for the product. SKIN All Natural, a producer of natural skin care products, recently began using innovative airless bottles for its products after the new packaging design became available. The bottles contain a mechanism that rises to contain the remaining product after some of it is used, instead of allowing air to enter the bottle. This innovation will keep the company's skin care products from becoming contaminated from outside sources and extend shelf life without using harmful preservative chemicals.[26] In some instances, marketers use innovative or unique packages that are inconsistent with traditional packaging practices to make the brand stand out from competitors. Orville Redenbacher now offers several flavors of its microwave popcorn in packaging that converts to a convenient pop up bowl. Heinz began selling its new Dip & Squeeze Ketchup packets in stores as a result of the good consumer response to

Altering the Package
The maker of Heinz ketchup has altered the traditional narrow-mouth ketchup bottle to make its package more convenient for consumers. The package shown here is squeezable and also designed for dipping.

Going Green

In Packaging, Less Is More

A growing number of marketers are switching to smaller and simpler packaging, not just to save the planet, but also to reduce "wrap rage"—consumer frustration with difficult-to-open packages. Powerful retailers are putting their muscle behind this movement. The online retail giant Amazon.com has been pressuring manufacturers to switch to "frustration-free" packaging. Amazon defines this as packaging that is recyclable, able to be shipped without an external shipping box, and easy to open. Walmart has also been pushing manufacturers to reduce the size of packages and incorporate environmentally safe materials. In response, companies like Hewlett-Packard, Procter & Gamble, and Plantronics have been redesigning packaging for a variety of products.

Hewlett-Packard, for example, replaced the layers of cardboard that used to surround its notebook computers with a reusable messenger bag made from recycled materials. Procter & Gamble switched packaging for its Fusion ProGlide razors from a large plastic clamshell to a smaller package made from bamboo, bulrush, and other renewable sources. Plantronics completely revamped packaging for its phone headsets to make the boxes smaller, lighter, and customer-friendly. "We're trying not only to optimize our packaging to reduce waste but to fully rethink what packaging is and does," says the CEO.[d]

the products from their use in restaurants.[27] Unusual packaging sometimes requires expending considerable resources, not only on package design but also on making customers aware of the unique package and its benefit. Research suggests that uniquely shaped packages that attract attention are more likely to be perceived as containing a higher volume of product.[28]

Multiple Packaging

Rather than packaging a single unit of a product, marketers sometimes use twin packs, tripacks, six-packs, or other forms of multiple packaging. For certain types of products, multiple packaging may increase demand, because it increases the amount of the product available at the point of consumption (e.g., in one's house). It may also increase consumer acceptance of the product by encouraging the buyer to try the product several times. Multiple packaging can make products easier to handle and store, as in the case of six-packs for soft drinks; it can also facilitate special price offers, such as two-for-one sales. However, multiple packaging does not work for all types of products. One would not use additional table salt, for example, simply because an extra box is in the pantry.

Handling-Improved Packaging

A product's packaging may be changed to make it easier to handle in the distribution channel—for example, by changing the outer carton or using special bundling, shrink-wrapping, or pallets. In some cases, the shape of the package is changed. An ice cream producer, for instance, may change from a cylindrical package to a rectangular one to facilitate handling. In addition, at the retail level, the ice cream producer may be able to get more shelf facings with a rectangular package than with a round one. Outer containers for products are sometimes changed so they will proceed more easily through automated warehousing systems.

Criticisms of Packaging

The last several decades have brought a number of improvements in packaging. However, some packaging problems still need to be resolved. Some packages suffer from functional problems in that they simply do not work well. The packaging for flour and sugar is, at best, poor. Both grocers and consumers are very much aware that these packages leak and tear easily. Can anyone open and close a bag of flour without spilling at least a little bit? Certain packages, such as refrigerated biscuit cans, milk cartons with fold-out spouts, and potato chip bags, are frequently difficult to open. The traditional shapes of packages for products like ketchup and salad dressing make the product inconvenient to use. Have you ever wondered when tapping on a ketchup bottle why the producer didn't put the ketchup in a mayonnaise jar?

Although many steps have been taken to make packaging safer, critics still focus on the safety issues. Containers with sharp edges and breakable glass bottles are sometimes viewed as a threat to safety. Certain types of plastic packaging and aerosol containers represent possible health hazards.

At times, packaging is viewed as deceptive. Package shape, graphic design, and certain colors may be used to make a product appear larger than it actually is. The inconsistent use of certain size designations, such as giant, economy, family, king, and super, can lead to customer confusion.

Finally, although customers in the United States traditionally prefer attractive, effective, convenient packaging, the cost of such packaging is high.

LABELING

Labeling is very closely interrelated with packaging and is used for identification, promotional, informational, and legal purposes. Labels can be small or large relative to the size of the product and carry varying amounts of information. The sticker on a Chiquita banana, for example, is quite small and displays only the brand name of the fruit and perhaps a stock-keeping unit number. A label can be part of the package itself or a separate feature attached to the package. The label on a can of Coke is actually part of the can, whereas the label on a two-liter bottle of Coke is separate and can be removed. Information presented on a label may include the brand name and mark, the registered trademark symbol, package size and content, product features, nutritional information, potential presence of allergens, type and style of the product, number of servings, care instructions, directions for use and safety precautions, the name and address of the manufacturer, expiration dates, seals of approval, and other facts.

For many products, the label includes a **universal product code (UPC)**, a series of electronically readable lines identifying the product and providing inventory and pricing information for producers and resellers. The UPC is electronically read at the retail checkout counter.

Labels can facilitate the identification of a product by displaying the brand name in combination with a unique graphic design. For instance, Heinz ketchup is easy to identify on a supermarket shelf because the brand name is easy to read and the label has a distinctive crown-like shape. By drawing attention to products and their benefits, labels can strengthen an organization's promotional efforts. Labels may contain such promotional messages as the offer of a discount or a larger package size at the same price, or information about a new or improved product feature.

A number of federal laws and regulations specify information that must be included on the labels of certain products. Garments must be labeled with the name of the manufacturer, country of manufacture, fabric content, and cleaning instructions. Labels on nonedible items like shampoos and detergents must include both safety precautions and directions for use. Congress passed the Fair Packaging and Labeling Act, one of the most comprehensive pieces of labeling and packaging legislation. This law focuses on mandatory labeling requirements, voluntary adoption of packaging standards by firms within industries, and the provision of power to the Federal Trade Commission and the Food and Drug Administration to establish and enforce packaging regulations. A product that has come under fire recently is the printer cartridge. Consumers are pushing for more disclosure on labels about the amount of ink in each cartridge. Currently, it is difficult for consumers to compare offerings and prices without knowing the amount of ink contained in each cartridge. Companies have responded by saying ink does not fall under the Fair Packaging and Labeling Act. The National Council on Weights and Measures formed a task force to review the issue but have not yet reached a conclusion. The FDA has not weighed in on the matter.[29]

labeling Providing identifying, promotional, or other information on package labels

universal product code (UPC) A series of electronically readable lines identifying a product and containing inventory and pricing information

© Joe Marquettre/EPA/Newscom

"Made in..." Labels
The country of origin affects customers' perceptions of the product.

The Nutrition Labeling Act of 1990 requires the FDA to review food labeling and packaging, focusing on nutrition content, label format, ingredient labeling, food descriptions, and health messages. This act regulates much of the labeling on more than 250,000 products made by some 17,000 U.S. companies. Any food product for which a nutritional claim is made must have nutrition labeling that follows a standard format. Food product labels must state the number of servings per container, serving size, number of calories per serving, number of calories derived from fat, number of carbohydrates, and amounts of specific nutrients such as vitamins. In addition, new nutritional labeling requirements focus on the amounts of trans-fatty acids in food products. Although consumers have responded favorably to this type of information on labels, evidence as to whether they actually use it has been mixed. A recent study simulating a grocery store shopping experience found that, while about one-third of participants reported reading labels, only about 9 percent of participants actually looked at calorie counts and other listings on most products.[30]

Despite legislation to make labels as accurate and informative as possible, questionable labeling practices persist. The Center for Science in the Public Interest questions the practice of naming a product "Strawberry Frozen Yogurt Bars" when it contains strawberry flavoring but no strawberries, or of calling a breakfast cereal "lightly sweetened" when sugar makes up 22 percent of its ingredients. Many labels on vegetable oils say "no cholesterol," but many of these oils contain saturated fats that can raise cholesterol levels. The Food and Drug Administration amended its regulations to forbid producers of vegetable oil from making "no cholesterol" claims on their labels.

Another area of concern is "green labeling." Consumers who are committed to making environmentally responsible or natural purchasing decisions are sometimes fooled by labels that claim a product is environmentally friendly or organic. The U.S. Public Interest Research Group accused several manufacturers of "greenwashing" customers: using misleading claims to sell products by playing on customers' concern for the environment. For example, some manufacturers put a recycling symbol on labels for products made of polyvinyl chloride plastic, which cannot be recycled in the vast majority of U.S. communities.

Of concern to many manufacturers are the Federal Trade Commission's guidelines regarding "Made in U.S.A." labels, a growing problem due to the increasingly global nature of manufacturing. The FTC requires that "all or virtually all" of a product's components be made in the United States if the label says "Made in U.S.A." Although the FTC recently considered

Table 14.3 Perceived Quality and Value of Products Based on Country of Origin*

	"Made in U.S.A."		"Made in Japan"		"Made in Korea"		"Made in China"	
	Value	Quality	Value	Quality	Value	Quality	Value	Quality
U.S. adults	4.0	4.2	3.2	3.2	2.6	2.4	2.8	2.4
Western Europeans	3.3	3.4	3.5	3.5	2.8	2.4	2.9	2.4

*On a scale of 1 (low) to 5 (high).

Source: "American Demographics 2006 Consumer Perception Survey," *Advertising Age*, January 2, 2006, 9. Data by Synovate.

changing its guidelines to read "substantially all," it rejected this idea and maintains the "all or virtually all" standard. In light of this decision, the FTC ordered New Balance to stop using the "Made in U.S.A." claim on its athletic-shoe labels, because some components (rubber soles) are made in China. The "Made in U.S.A." labeling issue has not been totally resolved.[31] Table 14.3 provides insight into just how important the "Made in U.S.A." label can be for both Americans and western Europeans. It includes assessments of both quality and value for U.S.A.-, Japanese-, Korean-, and Chinese-origin labels.

Summary

1. To explain the value of branding

A brand is a name, term, design, symbol, or any other feature that identifies one seller's good or service and distinguishes it from those of other sellers. A brand name is the part of a brand that can be spoken. A brand mark is the element not made up of words. A trademark is a legal designation indicating that the owner has exclusive use of the brand or part of the brand and others are prohibited by law from using it. A trade name is the legal name of an organization. Branding helps buyers identify and evaluate products, helps sellers facilitate product introduction and repeat purchasing, and fosters brand loyalty.

2. To understand brand loyalty

Brand loyalty is a customer's favorable attitude toward a specific brand. If brand loyalty is strong enough, customers may consistently purchase a particular brand when they need a product in this product category. The three degrees of brand loyalty are brand recognition, brand preference, and brand insistence. Brand recognition occurs when a customer is aware that the brand exists and views it as an alternative purchase if the preferred brand is unavailable. With brand preference, a customer prefers one brand over competing brands and will purchase it if available. Brand insistence occurs when a customer will accept no substitute.

3. To analyze the major components of brand equity

Brand equity is the marketing and financial value associated with a brand's strength. It represents the value of a brand to an organization. The four major elements underlying brand equity include brand-name awareness, brand loyalty, perceived brand quality, and brand associations.

4. To recognize the types of brands and their benefits

A manufacturer brand, initiated by the producer, ensures that the firm is associated with its products at the point of purchase. A private distributor brand is initiated and owned by a reseller, sometimes taking on the name of the store or distributor. Manufacturers combat growing competition from private distributor brands by developing multiple brands. A generic brand indicates only the product category and does not include the company name or other identifying terms.

5. To understand how to select and protect brands

When selecting a brand name, a marketer should choose one that is easy to say, spell, and recall and that alludes to the product's uses, benefits, or special characteristics. Brand names can be devised from words, letters, numbers, nonsense words, or a combination of these. Brand names are created inside an organization by individuals, committees, or branding departments, and by outside consultants. Services as well as products are branded, often with the company name and an accompanying symbol that makes the brand distinctive or conveys a desired image.

Producers protect ownership of their brands through registration with the U.S. Patent and Trademark Office. A company must make certain the brand name it selects does not infringe on an already registered brand by confusing or deceiving consumers about the source of the product. In most foreign countries, brand registration is on a first-come, first-serve basis, making protection more difficult. Brand counterfeiting is becoming increasingly common and can undermine consumers' confidence in a brand.

6. To examine three types of branding strategies

Companies brand their products in several ways. Individual branding designates a unique name for each of a company's products, family branding identifies all of a firm's products with a single name, and brand extension branding applies an existing name to a new product in a different product category.

7. To understand co-branding and brand licensing

Co-branding is the use of two or more brands on one product. Effective co-branding profits from the trust and confidence customers have in the brands involved. Finally, through a licensing agreement and for a licensing fee, a firm may permit another organization to use its brand on other products. Brand licensing enables producers to earn extra revenue, receive low-cost or free publicity, and protect their trademarks.

8. To describe the major packaging functions and design considerations and how packaging is used in marketing strategies

Packaging involves development of a container and a graphic design for a product. Effective packaging offers protection, economy, safety, and convenience. It can influence a customer's purchase decision by promoting features, uses, benefits, and image. When developing a package, marketers must consider the value to the customer of efficient and effective packaging, offset by the price the customer is willing to pay. Other considerations include making the package tamper resistant, whether to use multiple packaging and family packaging, how to design the package as an effective promotional tool, how best to accommodate resellers, and whether to develop environmentally responsible packaging. Firms choose particular colors, designs, shapes, and textures to create desirable images and associations. Packaging can be an important part of an overall marketing strategy and can be used to target certain market segments. Modifications in packaging can revive a mature product and extend its product life cycle. Producers alter packages to convey new features or make them safer or more convenient. If a package has a secondary use, the product's value to the consumer may increase. Category-consistent packaging makes products more easily recognizable to consumers. Innovative packaging enhances a product's distinctiveness. Consumers may criticize packaging that does not work well, poses health or safety problems, is deceptive in some way, or is not biodegradable or recyclable.

9. To examine the functions of labeling and describe some legal issues pertaining to labeling

Labeling is closely interrelated with packaging and is used for identification, promotional, informational, and legal purposes. The labels of many products include a universal product code, a series of electronically readable lines identifying a product and containing inventory and pricing information. Various federal laws and regulations require that certain products be labeled or marked with warnings, instructions, nutritional information, manufacturer's identification, and the like. Despite legislation, questionable labeling practices persist, including misleading information about fat content and cholesterol, freshness, and "greenness" of packaging.

Go to www.cengagebrain.com for resources to help you master the content in this chapter as well as for materials that will expand your marketing knowledge!

Important Terms

brand 446
brand name 446
brand mark 446
trademark 446
trade name 446
brand loyalty 448
brand recognition 448
brand preference 448
brand insistence 449
brand equity 449
manufacturer brand 451
private distributor brand 451
generic brand 452
individual branding 456
family branding 456
brand extension 456
co-branding 457
brand licensing 457
family packaging 459
labeling 463
universal product code (UPC) 463

Discussion and Review Questions

1. What is the difference between a brand and a brand name? Compare and contrast a brand mark and a trademark.
2. How does branding benefit consumers and marketers?
3. What are the three major degrees of brand loyalty?
4. What is brand equity? Identify and explain the major elements of brand equity.
5. Compare and contrast manufacturer brands, private distributor brands, and generic brands.
6. Identify the factors a marketer should consider in selecting a brand name.
7. The brand name Xerox is sometimes used generically to refer to photocopiers, and Kleenex is used to refer to facial tissues. How can the manufacturers protect their brand names, and why would they want to do so?
8. What is co-branding? What major issues should be considered when using co-branding?
9. What are the major advantages and disadvantages of brand licensing?
10. Describe the functions a package can perform. Which function is most important? Why?
11. What are the main factors a marketer should consider when developing a package?
12. In what ways can packaging be used as a strategic tool?
13. What are the major criticisms of packaging?
14. What are the major functions of labeling?
15. In what ways do regulations and legislation affect labeling?

Application Questions

1. Identify two brands for which you are brand insistent. How did you begin using these brands? Why do you no longer use other brands?
2. Honda introduced an SUV called Element, a name that suggests freedom and comfort in any environment. Invent a brand name for a line of luxury sports cars that also would appeal to an international market. Suggest a name that implies quality, luxury, and value.
3. When a firm decides to brand its products, it may choose one of several strategies. Name one company that uses each of the following strategies. How does each strategy help the company?
   a. Individual branding
   b. Family branding
   c. Brand extension
4. For each of the following product categories, choose an existing brand. Then, for each selected brand, suggest a co-brand, and explain why the co-brand would be effective.
   a. Cookies
   b. Pizza
   c. Chips
   d. A sports drink
5. Packaging provides product protection; customer convenience; and promotion of image, key features, and benefits. Identify a product that uses packaging in each of these ways, and evaluate the effectiveness of the package for that function.
6. Identify a package that you believe is inferior. Explain why you think the package is inferior, and discuss your recommendations for improving it.
7. IMP As shown in Table 14.1, each of the world's most valuable brands is worth billions of dollars. These brand values change from year to year. Go to the InterBrand website, www.interbrand.com, and look at the bar chart entitled "Interact with the Best Global Brands of 2011." Of the top 10 most valuable brands in Table 14.1, which brands are at their highest values since 2000, and which brands are not at their highest values since 2000? Which brand value has increased proportionally the most since 2000, and which brand value has decreased proportionally the most since 2000? What are some of the reasons for these changes in brand value? When thinking about the reasons for changes in brand value, consider to what extent there have been changes in the major components of brand equity for these brands.

Internet Exercise

Pillsbury

Like other marketers of consumer products, Pillsbury has set up a website to inform and entertain consumers. Catering to the appeal of its most popular product spokesperson, Pillsbury has given its Dough Boy his own site. Visit him at www.doughboy.com.

1. What branding strategy does Pillsbury seem to be using with regard to the products it presents on this site?
2. How does this Pillsbury website promote brand loyalty?
3. What degree of consistency exists in Pillsbury's packaging of its products displayed on the website?

developing your marketing plan

The selection and protection of the appropriate brand name is an important part of formulating a marketing strategy. A clear understanding of how branding and packaging decisions influence a customer's choice of products is essential when developing the marketing plan. The brand name and its packaging will influence several other marketing plan decisions. Relating to the information provided in this chapter, focus on the following issues:

1. Discuss the level of brand equity your company's products currently have in the marketplace. How will brand equity affect your branding strategy?
2. Which type of branding strategy is most appropriate for your new-product idea?
3. Do any strategic opportunities exist from co-branding your new product with existing brands in your company's product mix or with other company's brands? You may want to refer to your SWOT analysis in Chapter 2.
4. Discuss the style, color, and labeling options for your product. Consider your target market's needs and your branding strategy in this discussion.

The information obtained from these questions should assist you in developing various aspects of your marketing plan found in the "Interactive Marketing Plan" exercise at **www.cengagebrain.com**.

video case 14.1

New Belgium Brews Up Strong Brand Equity

The idea for New Belgium Brewing Company began with a bicycling trip through Belgium, where some of the world's finest ales have been brewed for centuries. As Jeff Lebesch, a U.S. electrical engineer, cruised around on a fat-tired mountain bike, he wondered if he could produce such high-quality ales in his home state of Colorado. After returning home, Lebesch began to experiment in his Fort Collins basement. When his home-brewed experiments earned rave reviews from friends, Lebesch and his wife, Kim Jordan, opened New Belgium Brewing (NBB) in 1991. They named their first brew Fat Tire Amber Ale in honor of Lebesch's biking adventure.

Although the overall craft-brewing industry has done well in recent years, with sales growing steadily even during the recent economic downturn, NBB has done even better. Today, NBB is a successful $125 million company that markets 710,000 barrels of ales and pilsners every year. The entrepreneurial company has steadily expanded its distribution throughout the western United States, partnering with regional breweries to produce and sell its fresh-brewed beers in local communities farther and farther from its Colorado headquarters.

The standard product line includes Sunshine Wheat, Blue Paddle Pilsner, Abbey Ale, and 1554 Black Ale, as well as the firm's best seller, the original Fat Tire Amber Ale. NBB also markets seasonal beers, such as Frambozen, released at Thanksgiving and Christmas, and Hoptober, sold during the early fall. The firm occasionally offers one-time-only brews—such as LaFolie, a wood-aged beer—that are sold only until the batch runs out.

To reinforce the firm's commitment to old-fashioned brewing quality, NBB's packaging and labels evoke a touch of nostalgia. The Fat Tire label, for example, features an old-style cruiser bike with wide tires, a padded seat, and a basket hanging from the handlebars. All the label and packaging designs were created by the same watercolor artist, Jeff Lebesch's next-door neighbor.

NBB prices its beers to reflect high quality and set the products apart from those of more widely available brands, such as Coors and Budweiser. This pricing strategy conveys the message that the products are special but also keeps them competitive with other microbrews, such as Pete's Wicked Ale and Sierra Nevada. To demonstrate its appreciation for its retailers and business partners, NBB does not sell beer to consumers onsite at the brewery for less than the retailers charge.

Since its founding, NBB's most effective promotion has been via word-of-mouth communication by customers devoted to the brand. The company initially avoided mass advertising, relying instead on small-scale, local promotions, such as print advertisements in alternative magazines, participation in local festivals, and sponsorship of alternative sports events. Through event sponsorships, such as the Tour de Fat, NBB has raised thousands of dollars for various environmental, social, and cycling nonprofit organizations. The company is also a member of 1% for the Planet, donating 1 percent of its annual sales revenue to environmental protection groups around the world.

With expanding distribution, however, the brewery recognized a need to connect more effectively with a far-flung customer base. NBB's top management consulted with Dr. David Holt, an Oxford professor and branding expert. After studying the fast-growing company, Holt, together with NBB's marketing director, drafted a 70-page "manifesto" describing the brand's attributes, character, cultural relevancy, and promise. In particular, Holt identified an ethos of pursuing creative activities simply for the joy of doing them well and in harmony with the natural environment.

With the brand defined, NBB teamed up with Amalgamated, a New York City advertising agency, to help communicate the brand identity. The agency created a $10 million ad campaign targeting high-end beer drinkers among men ages 25 to 44, highlighting the brewery's down-to-earth, whimsical, yet thoughtful image. The grainy ads focused on a man rebuilding a cruiser bike out of used parts and then riding it along pastoral country roads. The product appeared in just five seconds of each ad between the tag lines "Follow Your Folly ... Ours Is Beer."

In addition to advertising, the company promotes its brand by engaging customers in conversations via social media, such as Twitter, Facebook, and blogs. "One of the biggest messages for craft [beer] is local and variety," says NBB's director of advertising and social media. That's why the brewer has created a series of Facebook pages, one for each of its brands and each market. It also maintains an overall Facebook company page. In all, its pages have more than 400,000 Facebook fans, who each buy an estimated $260 worth of NBB products every year. By investing time and money in social media, the company is spreading the word about its brand and reinforcing brand loyalty among current customers.

NBB's mission is: "To operate a profitable brewery which makes our love and talent manifest." From top-quality brewing to a strong belief in giving back to the local and global community, the company reinforces the positive qualities that make its brand so successful every day.[32]

Questions for Discussion

1. What has New Belgium Brewing done to increase brand recognition and brand preference?
2. How is New Belgium Brewing using packaging to support its brand image?
3. Assess New Belgium's brand equity in terms of awareness, quality, associations, and loyalty.

case 14.2

Gatorade Goes for "G" Branding

Gatorade, which single-handedly pioneered the sports drink category nearly 50 years ago, is making "G" the centerpiece of its branding efforts. Invented by researchers at the University of Florida, the original Gatorade formula was developed to help players on the college football team avoid dehydration. Other schools took notice of the Gators' performance and soon began ordering batches of Gatorade for their athletes. One by one, Gatorade attracted the interest of professional football teams, and in 1983, it was named the National Football League's official sports drink. That year, Gatorade was acquired by Quaker Oats and, in 2001, Quaker was, in turn, purchased by PepsiCo.

© Bob Levey/Getty Images

Throughout its history, Gatorade has remained the leader in sports drinks. However, in recent years, changes in customer behavior and increased competition have combined to take a toll on sales. First, increasingly health-conscious customers are seeking out low-calorie, low-sodium beverages instead of traditional sports drinks. Second, PepsiCo's main rival, Coca-Cola, has been powering up its marketing of Powerade sports drinks and winning over customers. As a result, Gatorade's market share fell to 75 percent, while Powerade's market share shot up to 24 percent.

Now, Gatorade's marketers are fighting for higher sales with new branding initiatives for specific target markets and redesigned packaging to grab customers' attention. Both the Gatorade brand name and the lightning bolt brand mark have been fine-tuned to emphasize the G and the thunderbolt while downplaying the rest of the name. The goal is to make the combination instantly recognizable as representing Gatorade, in much the same way that the Nike swoosh has become the iconic representation of that brand.

Gatorade is also introducing a series of G sports drinks targeting the specific needs of athletes. This is a change for Gatorade, which had for several years broadened its targeting and positioned the brand as a thirst-quencher for a cross-section of consumers, not just athletes. Now the brand, under its revamped G branding, is going back to its sports roots with the G Series line of drink products for casual and serious athletes at a variety of experience levels.

Gatorade Prime 01 contains vitamins and other nutrients to help athletes "start strong." Gatorade Perform 02 products include the original green Gatorade beverage for rehydration during exertion plus a low-calorie drink, branded as G2. In addition, mix-your-own powdered versions of both Perform drinks are available. Gatorade Recover 03 is a special drink developed to replenish energy and help muscles recover after any sports activity.

Thanks to a new distribution arrangement, G Series Pro—once sold to professional athletes in gyms and locker rooms—can now be purchased at 5,500 GNC stores. "This line alone, reaching a new target audience, is going to be a killer," comments GNC's CEO. "We have consumers who are extremely passionate about what they [drink]." In another new deal, Gatorade is marketing its G Natural and G2 Natural low-calorie drinks through Whole Foods Market, which specializes in natural and organic foods. Another Gatorade variation, G Series Fit, targets athletes who exercise for fitness.

Along with fine-tuning the brand and individual products, Gatorade is fine-tuning its packaging and labeling. For years, all bottles featured the full "Gatorade" brand name bisected by the brand's stylized orange lightning bolt. Today, the G has taken center stage on container labels, with a small bolt within the G and a bolder bolt as the backdrop for the product name. Overall, the G Series packaging unifies the product line while allowing each item enough distinctive touches (such as different bottle shapes) to help customers quickly find the particular product they want on crowded store shelves. The sophisticated new packaging also sets this line apart from the traditional Gatorade green-and-orange look, visually reinforcing the innovativeness of the G Series.

Gatorade's advertising and promotional efforts, including a YouTube channel and Facebook fan page, carry through the focus on athletic achievement and individual fitness. Sports stars like Serena Williams and Derek Jeter are featured, along with behind-the-scenes interviews with athletes getting ready for major sporting events. Thanks to these brand initiatives, Gatorade has increased its yearly volume sales beyond 1 billion gallons. However, it continues to lose market share, holding 70 percent of the market compared with Powerade's 28.5 percent. Looking ahead, will Gatorade's target gulp down enough G Series drinks to rebuild the brand's market share?[33]

Questions for Discussion

1. What are the marketing advantages and disadvantages of emphasizing "G" as the primary element in the Gatorade brand?
2. As Gatorade sharpens its marketing focus on athletes, should it vary its packaging for different distribution channels or different sports? Explain your answer.
3. For competitive reasons, do you think Gatorade should consider co-branding to build on the equity of another major brand name as it seeks higher sales? Why or why not?

strategic case 5

100 Years of Product Innovation at Chevrolet

General Motors' Chevrolet brand celebrated its 100th anniversary in 2011. In its 100-year history, Chevrolet embarked on many different vehicle models, some of them widely successful and others deleted from the product mix shortly after introduction. Over the years, it has transitioned from an American icon into a worldwide brand known for its quality and durability. Despite numerous ups and downs in its history, including the recent bankruptcy and bailout of parent company GM, Chevrolet is still going strong after a century of product innovation.

© Scott Olson/Getty Images

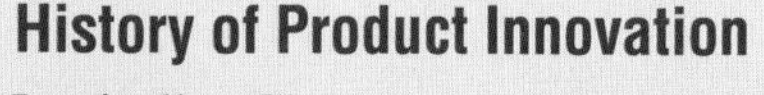

History of Product Innovation

Ironically, Chevrolet exists because of its top competitor, Ford Motor. William Durant founded Chevrolet in 1911 to compete head on with Ford's Model T. The brand was named after Louis Chevrolet, a top racer who was hired to design the first Chevrolet. Chevrolet's initial model cost $2,000. This was a high-priced vehicle at the time, which did not sit well with Durant, who wanted to compete directly against Ford on price. In 1915, Chevrolet released a less expensive model priced at $490, the same price as a Ford Model T. The company was acquired by General Motors in 1918, and Chevrolet went on to become one of GM's most popular brands.

During much of its history, Chevrolet attempted to position itself as an iconic American brand, using patriotic slogans and courting racecar drivers as endorsers to create an image of quality and sportiness. Chevrolet is also credited with being the first automobile maker to come up with the idea of planned product obsolescence. Based on this concept, Chevrolet introduces a new car model each year, a type of product modification. Like all established companies, Chevrolet vehicles underwent several successes and failures. Some vehicles that Chevy thought would succeed failed miserably, often due to safety (the Corvair) or quality (the Vega) issues. On the other hand, its sporty Corvette was immensely popular and still exists today as a sports car icon. Table 14.4 shows the entire portfolio of Chevrolet vehicle models sold in the United States.

After nearly a century in business, Chevrolet faced its greatest threat with GM's bankruptcy in 2009. The company required a massive government bailout, and although GM has begun to rebound, its reputation will take a while to recover. According to GM CEO Dan Akerson, the company "failed because we failed to innovate." However, he sees hope in Chevrolet as an innovation powerhouse and believes the brand will bring GM back from the brink of collapse.

After the Bailout

Today, Chevrolet is a worldwide brand. It achieved record global sales of 4.76 million vehicles in 2011. Although it sold the most vehicles in the United States, China saw a more than 9 percent increase in the number of Chevrolets sold at 595,068 vehicles in 2011. The company positions its vehicles along four values: durability, value, practicality, and friendliness. This lattermost value relies heavily on the customer service that Chevrolet offers among its sales staff and customer support personnel.

Chevrolet's vehicles are at all stages of the product life cycle. In the decline stage are its SUVs, as SUVs in general have become less popular due to a greater concern for the environment and rising gas prices. Rather than phasing out its SUVs, however, Chevrolet chose to revamp its SUVs to make them more eco-friendly. The company introduced SUV crossover vehicles and the Chevrolet Tahoe Hybrid in the hope of attracting those who like the style of SUVs without the gas inefficiencies. The Corvette is still going strong, although it has likely reached the maturity stage due to new product innovations and changing customer tastes. Additionally, the average Corvette owner is in his or her fifties. The Chevy Cruze is in the growth stage; in 2011, it was the best-selling compact car in the United States. Another car in the growth stage is the Chevrolet Camaro, a product that was initially deleted from the product mix in 2002. After fans demanded to have the Camaro resurrected, Chevrolet reintroduced a redesigned Camaro in 2010. The car went on to win the World Car Design of the Year. Even more popular than its cars are Chevrolet's pickup trucks. Chevrolet introduced its first truck in 1918, and sales of Chevrolet pickup trucks surpassed sales of its cars in 1989. Its Silverado pickup truck is currently in the growth stage as the second best-selling vehicle in 2011. Chevy is also seizing the opportunity to profit from a growing demand for electric vehicles with its introduction of the Chevrolet Volt. The Volt runs on electricity but will use gasoline if all of the electricity is used.

The Chevrolet brand is a model to which marketers aspire. Unlike so many other brands, it has lasted for a century due to its innovative product modifications and ability to rebound from failures. It must continue to seize market opportunities, constantly modify its products, and adapt its brand to changing customer tastes. Successfully meeting these criteria could enable the Chevrolet brand to succeed for another century.[34]

Table 14.4 Chevrolet Models Sold within the United States

Cars	SUVs/ Crossovers	Trucks/ Vans	Electric Vehicles
Sonic	Equinox	Colorado	Volt
Cruze	Traverse	Avalanche	
Malibu	Tahoe	Silverado	
Corvette	Suburban	Express	
Camaro			
Impala			
Spark			

Source: Based on data gathered from Chevrolet website, www.chevrolet .com/#happygrad (accessed January 26, 2012).

Questions

1. Evaluate the product mix brands Cruze, Camaro, and Corvette in terms of their target market.
2. How has GM managed product innovation to sustain the Chevrolet brand for over 100 years?
3. What are the challenges for the Chevrolet brand in the future?

ROLE-PLAY TEAM CASE EXERCISE 5

This role-play team exercise is designed to simulate actual marketing decision making in the real world. The entire team should read the overview and background. Each student will take on a role of a particular employee within the organization. Your instructor will provide additional information and instructions related to a team decision.

NATURE PURE*

Background

The Nature Pure product division is part of a large multinational food and beverage corporation. Based in California, the division markets juices that boast all-natural ingredients. The company began in the 1920s and has since become a staple on grocery store shelves across the country. Over the years, the brand has become associated with quality and purity. However, market share has recently been dropping, and many new competitors have been entering the marketplace. Several months ago, the company's top executives announced that overall organizational profitability should increase by an average of 5 percent over the previous year. Managers of divisions in the company unable to achieve this objective would face potential termination. The announcement placed enormous pressure on Nature Pure Product Brand Manager Peter Towne, as well as his core team of managers. Towne was determined to meet the growth target and told his team that they would do whatever it took to succeed, assuring the managers that "nobody would care how they did it" as long as they got the results.

Six months ago, Production Manager Jim Murray was approached by a supplier that the division rarely used. The supplier offered to sell the juice's main component (an apple concentrate equivalent) for 35 percent less than the company's current supplier. The new supplier explained that his firm had discovered a lower-cost component that was completely identical to the original formula, "molecule for molecule." In both taste and lab tests, no one could tell the difference. Murray immediately sent a sample of the product to the quality control supervisor for testing. After the quality control supervisor determined that the sample was not harmful, Murray and Towne decided to begin using the new concentrate as their key ingredient. On the advice of the marketing manager, they decided not to alert consumers about the change since the ingredient was deemed to be identical to the original, and because this knowledge might tarnish their brand image. Therefore, there were no modifications to the current Nature Pure labeling and packaging.

Although the quality control supervisor had numerous questions and requests for personal visits to the supplier's facilities that went unanswered, the new ingredient was used in Nature Pure juices. Ten weeks after the decision, the quality control manager did an in-house test and found something that looked like an artificial ingredient. He feared it might be a chemical additive, which would contradict the brand's claim of being "natural" and could have legal implications. Knowing that corporate had no knowledge of these activities, the quality control supervisor first approached Production Manager Jim Murray, who made light of his concerns.

*© O.C. Ferrell and Linda Ferrell, 2012. Jennifer Sawayda assisted with the development of this exercise under the direction of O.C. Ferrell and Linda Ferrell. This role-play case is not intended to represent the managerial decisions of an actual company.

However, an external "watch dog" group has now contacted the CEO and is meeting to share results of tests showing that Nature Pure contains artificial ingredients. Although the quality control supervisor has been advised not to put anything into writing yet, he is considering writing a memo to each manager expressing his concerns. He has also been keeping a journal as a record of all that has been going on, in case it is needed for future reference.

Your team consists of Product Brand Manager Peter Towne, Production Manager Jim Murray, Marketing Manager Jennifer Packard, Quality Control Supervisor George Wallis, and Supervisor of Distribution and Shipping Ralph Johnson. All of you must decide what to do in light of the fact that you have a potential product problem with the Nature Pure line. As a team, you will need to come up with an action plan to address product quality, labeling, misrepresentation of the ingredient's purity, and concerns about external watchdog groups that are claiming Nature Pure is using artificial ingredients.

Peter Towne, Product Brand Manager

You have been with the company for 15 years. After 10 years of hard work, you were appointed as product brand manager of Nature Pure juices. At first, you were excited about the prospect of taking over a well-known brand, but your enthusiasm was short-lived. Increased competition has eaten away at the brand's market share. The response from corporate headquarters was clear: meet the company's profit goals or you could lose your job, and other personnel in your division could also face termination.

Shortly afterward, Production Manager Jim Murray came to you with the news that he had been contacted by a supplier who claimed that his firm could sell Nature Pure's primary ingredient to the company for 35 percent less. Although the ingredient was not the same as the one Nature Pure was currently using, Jim claimed that the supplier guaranteed that it was identical. He had been told by the supplier that there were no tests that could determine the actual composition of the juice concentrate. You had complete faith in Jim and saw no need to meet with the supplier yourself.

You sent a sample of the ingredient to George Wallis, the quality control supervisor, for testing. The results that came back seemed to confirm the supplier's claims. The two ingredients appeared virtually indistinguishable from one another, and the new ingredient was not found to be at all harmful. Although the quality control supervisor expressed a desire to have the product tested outside the company with specialized equipment, you saw this as an unnecessary expense. The company's equipment was top-notch, and George was known for being extremely cautious.

The offer of saving so much money and keeping your division from certain doom was too good for you to pass up. You quickly agreed to ship 100,000 crates of the ingredient and begin production immediately. Since you were the product brand manager and were completely trusted to make the right decision by corporate, you didn't feel the need to let anyone outside your division know about the change in ingredients. After all, you had sampled the newly engineered product yourself and couldn't tell the difference. And despite constant badgering by George, there appeared to be nothing wrong with the product.

Two minutes ago, George appeared in your office. He stated that, after additional testing, he had found what he thinks is a chemical additive in the product. If true, this would not only contradict the supplier's assurances of a chemical-free product but would also mean that the product's labeling could be perceived as misleading. Your feelings gave way to panic when you thought of the implications this might have on both your career and the division as a whole. A product recall would certainly damage, if not destroy, the division. However, ignoring the problem would conflict with the corporation's ethics and compliance policies and, according to George, might violate consumer-protection laws. You informed the rest of the members of your team and told them you would call a meeting next week to discuss the problem. Maybe you should invite Ralph Johnson as well. Ralph is the supervisor of distribution and shipping. He might be needed to help organize a way to quickly get rid of the excess inventory should the need arise. The team agreed to put nothing in writing and referred to the situation as "our little product problem."

In previous meetings, you had reassured the group that, if there was to be a full-blown investigation, then it would just be under the guidance of the FDA. If they were found to be out of compliance, there would simply be modest fines for the company.

Jim Murray, Production Manager

You were transferred to the Nature Pure product division two years ago. Since then, you have proven to be an invaluable member of Product Brand Manager Peter Towne's team, partially because you are obsessed with making the numbers. You get along very well with Marketing Manager Jennifer Packard and Shipping and Distribution Supervisor Ralph Johnson but often butt heads with Quality Control Supervisor George Wallis, who spends an inordinate amount of time worrying about quality. Although you know George is an expert at his job, you feel George's constant concerns might be holding the division back.

When you got the news about corporate's plan to cut jobs in divisions where profit objectives were not achieved, you became concerned that a 5 percent growth goal in the current economy was too aggressive and not attainable. However, you were also inspired by Peter's challenge to meet those numbers "at any cost." When a supplier offered to sell a key component of Nature Pure beverages at 35 percent less than its normal cost, you felt your prayers had been answered. Quick calculations revealed that this decrease in the cost of supplies would save the division more than a quarter of a million dollars on its current volume. The supplier assured you that the ingredient was 100 percent identical to what you were currently using. When you asked how it was possible to sell the ingredient so cheap, the supplier claimed it was proprietary information and couldn't be disclosed. Although you felt this was strange, your elation over the possibility that many jobs could be saved trumped any initial hesitation.

After George's tests came back and found that the ingredient was not harmful, you urged Peter to go into full-scale production using the new ingredient. You thoroughly disliked George's constant reluctance concerning the product's quality and felt that the man was simply trying to make waves. Initial sales appeared excellent, and nobody could tell that Nature Pure had changed the primary ingredient.

Then George came to you with another concern. After testing the batch once again, he found what he thought was a chemical additive in its primary ingredient. Such a finding would alarm Jennifer, as it would violate the company's claims of an all-natural, pure product and might cause it to lose its market niche. But you thought it was highly unlikely that George's concerns were valid. George had conducted several tests since they first began to use the new ingredient, and nothing had shown up before. After trying unsuccessfully to calm the man down, you finally snapped, "If anything happens to get us into trouble, we'll just say that we trusted the word of our supplier and that we had no knowledge of anything questionable in our operations. Quit worrying! What we don't know…we don't know."

A few days later, you were furious to learn that George went over your head to Peter with his concerns. Although you were certain Peter wouldn't take his claims seriously, you still had some of your own doubts creep up. What if George was right? Would the authorities accept the fact that you had no knowledge about what was going on? Peter had assured George that he would follow up on his concerns, but, in the interim, they should "maintain the status quo."

Jennifer Packard, Marketing Manager

You were proud to be the only woman in your division to achieve the level of manager. From the moment Peter Towne assumed the position of product brand manager, you have been considered a valuable member of his inner circle. You too were aghast when you heard about the nearly impossible profit objectives corporate was placing upon your division. You had spent years building up the Nature Pure brand and were not about to see all your work undone. You also knew that you might not find another position that paid so well, and you needed the high income to help pay for the new house you had purchased only a few months ago, as well as your 17-year-old son's upcoming college expenses.

Although inspired by Peter's challenge to make the numbers at any cost, you didn't know how it could be accomplished. As the one responsible for advertising, promotion, and sales efforts, you were the most in tune with the market, competition, and potential for growth. So when Jim Murray, the production manager, announced that one of the suppliers could supply Nature Pure's core component at 35 percent less than what the company was currently paying, you were elated. The pressure was off your back, knowing that your division would meet the corporate profitability objectives, and you could focus on your job as usual. Your enthusiasm was soon tempered, however, by the knowledge that the core ingredient, although allegedly identical to the original, was not the same. You knew that using this substitute ingredient could contradict the brand's claims of being "all-natural" and "100% pure"—a message that you continued to promote even after the supplier of the concentrate had changed.

You felt a little better after Quality Control Supervisor George Wallis stated that his initial tests did not detect any chemical additives in the sample batch. However, you knew that the most transparent way to handle this would be to indicate the switch in ingredients on the product's packaging. Unfortunately, this could serve to undermine the brand image, which in turn could cause the division to lose its market niche as an all-natural beverage. Neither Jim nor Peter seemed very concerned. The new supplier assured them that there were no tests that could determine the actual nature of the ingredients in the product. They maintained that they wouldn't need to tell anyone since the ingredients were virtually identical. Although still a little troubled, you determined that they were right. You decided to place a very small sentence on the bottom of the package that hinted that there had been a change in one of the ingredients, but it was so mired in scientific jargon that hardly anyone would understand it. You felt that this would protect the division should problems arise in the future.

Ten weeks later, you were hit with the bad news. George had secured some new lab testing technology, and his first test on the new juices detected something that he felt was a chemical additive. The news made you feel sick. If true, then the company had misrepresented its product. Following the letter of the law would require the division to release corrective advertising and possibly institute a product recall. This could damage the brand beyond repair. You wondered if the corporation's disciplinary procedures would apply to this situation. The division acted in good faith and took the supplier's word, but you doubted the corporation would see it that way. You know there are some options to destroy inventory before an internal or external investigation might occur but are wondering how best to proceed.

George Wallis, Quality Control Supervisor

You have worked for the company for 30 years and thoroughly enjoy your job. You felt disgusted when you heard of corporate's mandate that managers in any department who did not "make the numbers" would be terminated. You are the son of one of the co-founders and admire the company's legacy and strength in the market. You love the Nature Pure brand and feel that firing employees who do not make short-term sales goals is a personal betrayal. Despite this, you feel that it is your job to work hard and with integrity to ensure to the best of your ability that these goals are met.

When Jim Murray, the production manager, informed the team that he had found a supplier willing to sell a key ingredient for Nature Pure at 35 percent less than what the company was currently paying, you knew there had to be a catch. You were quickly alarmed to find out that the ingredient being offered wasn't the same ingredient at all! You had never heard of this "new" ingredient and were fairly sure it had never been thoroughly tested. After your own tests, you could not find anything wrong with this substitute, but you strongly advised the team to allow it to be tested in an outside lab with specialized equipment. Your recommendation was rebuffed. Under continual pressure by Jim, whom you've always felt was abrasive and too focused on the bottom line, you agreed to go with the team's consensus if you could thoroughly tour the supplier's plant.

Things only got worse. When you went to visit the supplier's plant, the plant manager refused you access to the plant's production facility. Your suspicions were aroused. In the meantime, Nature Pure was using the new ingredient with virtually no indication to the public or corporate that the division had changed anything. You felt that it was wrong to market a product as being the same when a core component had been changed, even if those components were supposedly identical. And you were having severe doubts about that as well. After your clash with the supplier, you began keeping a journal of all the incidents that you felt were questionable. Your repeated attempts to batch test the supplier for quality and purity were declined.

Ten weeks after the new ingredient was used in the product, your tests confirmed your worst fears. Although you weren't 100 percent sure, you felt that you had detected an artificial ingredient in the test sample. This went against the product's claims of purity. You approached Jim with the test results but, as usual, he ignored your concerns, even when you informed him that continuing their path would violate both company policies and potentially consumer protection laws. Frustrated, you decided to go over Jim's head to Peter Towne, the product brand manager.

Peter was distressed when he heard your news. Everything was going so well and profits had never been higher. He promised to call an emergency meeting next week to discuss the problem. Then Peter told you not to put any of this down in writing. You haven't told anyone about your journal and have no intention of doing so. You feel that, if it doesn't immediately change tactics, the company is heading down a dangerous path that could lead to severe consequences.

Ralph Johnson, Supervisor of Distribution and Shipping

You have worked at the company for four years, coming from a close competitor, Mott's, a leading supplier of apple juice. Last June, you were promoted to supervisor of distribution and shipping of the Nature Pure division. You work very closely with Jim Murray, the production manager, and get along with him very well. You both have children the same age and attend many school-related functions together. You do not consider yourself to be a part of Product Brand Manager Peter Towne's inner circle of managers, which suits you just fine. You prefer to avoid the drama of directly managing a division. You also heard about the mandate from corporate that any brand not meeting next year's profit goals would result in "heads rolling." Although the news worried you, you felt it was out of your hands. Your job was to manage distribution and shipping; it was upper management's job to worry about what actions to take to increase profitability.

Six months ago, you began to hear rumors that management had decided upon a new product ingredient for the Nature Pure brand. The ingredient cost less money and would save the division enough money to allow it to meet its profit goals. The rumors seemed confirmed when you began receiving shipments from a new supplier. The choice of supplier troubled you somewhat. You knew that the reputation of this supplier was shady at best. You thought about informing management, but then remembered that Jim would know about this supplier's background. You decided that he knew what he was doing and didn't speak up.

The rumors began to worsen. You heard that George Wallis, the quality control supervisor, was denied access into the supplier's production facilities for batch testing of the product. This seemed a clear indication that the supplier was hiding something. You also knew from shipping out the product that the packaging of Nature Pure did not indicate that the product had changed in any way. To top it off, corporate had begun contacting you. They were curious about why the division was doing so well all of a sudden and requested to look at the shipping manifestos. Apparently, Nature Pure's management had failed to inform corporate about the switch in ingredients. You thought that you would be able to stall until you talked to Peter about it.

You were getting increasingly uneasy about the entire situation. But you held on to one comfort: since you didn't know what was going on, and had no intention of finding out, then you couldn't possibly be blamed if something went wrong. However, yesterday, you got an e-mail from Peter personally inviting you to a meeting next week to discuss an important issue. You think you already know the reason for this meeting. You are nervous, particularly since these meetings usually do not include you. You wonder what Peter's motivation is in inviting you.

NOTES

[1]Based on information in Sarah Nicole Pricket, "Getting Joe Fresh," *Toronto Standard,* October 15, 2011, www.torontostandard.com; Tamara Abraham, "Is Joe Fresh the New Gap?" *Daily Mail* (UK), September 17, 2011, www.dailymail.co.uk; Marina Strauss, "Joe Fresh's Global Expansion Plan," *Globe and Mail* (Canada), February 23, 2011, www.theglobeandmail.com.

[2]"Dictionary of Marketing Terms," American Marketing Association, www.marketingpower.com (accessed February 28, 2012).

[3]U.S. Bureau of the Census, *Statistical Abstract of the United States, 2012,* www.census.gov/compendia/statab/ (Table 778).

[4]Douglas Holt, "Branding as Cultural Activism," Emory Marketing Institute, www.emorymi.com/holt.shtml (accessed February 28, 2012).

[5]David Kiefaber, "Ivory Soap Gets a Bold New Look and Attitude,"*AdWeek*, October 5, 2011, www.adweek.com/adfreak/ivory-soap-gets-bold-new-look-and-attitude-135493.

[6]David A. Aaker, *Managing Brand Equity: Capitalizing on the Value of a Brand Name* (New York: Free Press, 1991), 16–17.

[7]David Daw, "DISH, Blockbuster Announce $10/Month Alternative to Netflix," *PC World*, September 23, 2011, www.pcworld.com/article/240493/dish_blockbuster_announce_10month_alternative_to_netflix.html.

[8]"Best Retail Brands 2012," Interbrand, www.interbrand.com/en/BestRetailBrands/2012.aspx (accessed February 28, 2012).

[9]"Market Profile," Private Label Manufacturer's Association, http://plma.com/storeBrands/sbt12.html (accessed March 29, 2012).

[10]Jeff Bertolucci, "Google to Rename Picasa, Blogger, Reports Say," *PC World*, July 5, 2011, www.pcworld.com/article/235067/google_to_rename_picasa_blogger_reports_say.html; Allison Fass, "Animal House," *Forbes*, February 12, 2007, 72–75.

[11]Allison Ford, "Who's Behind OPI's Punny Polish Names?" DivineCaroline, November 2011, www.divinecaroline.com/112923/119950-who-s-opi-s-punny-polish-names/2.

[12]Dorothy Cohen, "Trademark Strategy," *Journal of Marketing* (January 1986): 63.

[13]"The Truth about Counterfeiting," International Anti-Counterfeiting Coalition, www.iacc.org/about-counterfeiting/the-truth-about-counterfeiting.php (accessed November 9, 2011).

[14]Julie Jargon, "Velveeta Shows Its Sizzle Against Hamburger Helper," *The Wall Street Journal,* December 29, 2011, http://online.wsj.com/article/SB10001424052970204336104577096753420568934.html.

[15]Henrik Sattler, Franziska Völckner, Claudia Riediger, and Christian M. Ringle, "The Impact of Brand Extension Success Drivers on Brand Extension Price Premiums," *International Journal of Research in Marketing* 27, no. 4 (2010): 319–328.

[16]Garland Pollard, "Pillsbury Spritz Air Freshener, Bad Brand Extension," BrandlandUSA, January 26, 2010, www.brandlandusa.com/2010/01/26/pillsbury-spritz-air-freshener-bad-brand-extension/.

[17]Shantini Munthree, Geoff Bick, and Russell Abratt, "A Framework for Brand Revitalization," *Journal of Product & Brand Management* 15 (2006): 157–167.

[18]Chris Pullig, Carolyn J. Simmons, and Richard G. Netemeyer, "Brand Dilution: When Do New Brands Hurt Existing Brands?" *Journal of Marketing* 70 (April 2006).

[19]"Nike + iPod," Apple, www.apple.com/ipod/nike/ (accessed February 28, 2012).

[20]"Stride, The Ridiculously Long Lasting Gum, Introduces Stride Whitemint—A New Flavor Inspired By Sports Icon, Shaun White," news release, July 19, 2011, www.kraftfoodscompany.com/MediaCenter/country-press-releases/us/2011/Pages/us_pr_07192011.aspx.

[21]"License! Global Issues 2011 Top 125 Global Licensors," PR Newswire, May 18, 2011, www.prnewswire.com/news-releases/license-global-issues-2011-top-125-global-licensors-122143104.html.

[22]Lauren I. Labrecque and George R. Milne, "Exciting Red and Competent Blue: The Importance of Color in Marketing," *Journal of the Academy of Marketing Science* (January 2011), www.springerlink.com/content/u68v477973076816/.

[23]John Kalkowski, "Method Unveils Bottle Made of Ocean Plastic," *Packaging Digest*, September 16, 2011, www.packagingdigest.com/article/519357-Method_unveils_bottle_made_of_ocean_plastic.php.

[24]Lisa McTigue Pierce, "Startup Revs Up," *Packaging Digest*, November 1, 2011, www.packagingdigest.com/article/519759-Startup_revs_up.php.

[25]John Kalkowski, "NatureSweet Launches New Tomato Packaging," *Packaging Digest*, October 13, 2011, www.packagingdigest.com/article/519611-NatureSweet_launches_new_tomato_packaging.php.

[26]John Kalkowski, "Cosmetic Firm Adopts Airless Bottles for All Products," *Packaging Digest*, November 14, 2011, www.packagingdigest.com/article/520008-Cosmetic_firm_adopts_airless_bottles_for_all_products.php.

[27]Linda Casey, "Pop Up Bowls Offer Convenient Snacking with a View of Product Popping," *Packaging Digest*, April 1, 2011, www.packagingdigest.com/article/517709-Pop_Up_Bowls_offer_convenient_snacking_with_a_view_of_product_popping.php; Lisa McTigue, "Heinz Debuts Retail Version of Dip & Squeeze Ketchup Packet for At-Home Use," *Packaging Digest*, September 20, 2011, www.packagingdigest.com/article/519383-Heinz_debuts_retail_version_of_Dip_Squeeze_Ketchup_packet_for_at_home_use.php.

[28]Valerie Folkes and Shashi Matta, "The Effect of Package Shape on Consumers' Judgment of Product Volume: Attention as a Mental Contaminant," *Journal of Consumer Research* (September 2004): 390.

[29]Steve Everly, "Regulators Target Ink Cartridges," *Tennessean.com*, January 17, 2010, www.tennessean.com; "NCWM Task Group in Printer Ink and Toner Cartridges," National Conference on Weights and Measures, www.ncwm.net/content/ink (accessed February 28, 2012).

[30]Ann Lukits, "Low Readership of Nutrition Labels," *The Wall Street Journal,* December 13, 2011, http://online.wsj.com/article/SB10001424052970204319004577088763110443628.html.

[31]Federal Trade Commission, www.ftc.gov (accessed February 28, 2012).

[32]"Fat Tire, New Belgium Brewing to Break into Michigan This Summer," *Michigan Business Review,* March 12, 2012, www.mlive.com; "Fort Collins Craft Breweries Tap Success Through Social Media," *The [Fort Collins]*

Coloradoan, February 24, 2012, www.coloradoan.com; Paul Suprenard, "Climate Change in Our Own Back Yard," *St. Petersburg Times* (Florida), March 2, 2010, 7A; Jennifer Wang, "Brewing Big (With a Micro Soul)," *Entrepreneur*, November 2009, www.entrepreneur.com; Robert Baun, "What's in a Name? Ask the Makers of Fat Tire," *The [Fort Collins] Coloradoan*, October 8, 2000, E1, E3; Julie Gordon, "Lebesch Balances Interests in Business, Community," *The [Fort Collins] Coloradoan*, February 26, 2003; Del I. Hawkins, Roger J. Best, and Kenneth A. Coney, *Consumer Behavior*, 8th ed. (Burr Ridge, IL: IrwinMcGraw-Hill, 2001); David Kemp, Tour Connoisseur, New Belgium Brewing Company, personal interview by Nikole Haiar, November 21, 2000; www.newbelgium.com; Lisa Sanders, "This Beer Will Reduce Your Anxiety," *Advertising Age*, January 17, 2005, 25; Bryan Simpson, "New Belgium Brewing," http://college.hmco.com/instructorscatalog/misc/new_belgium_brewing.pdf.

[33]Shareen Pathak, "No. 2 Sports Drink Powerade Taps into Its 'Underdog' Status," *Advertising Age*, March 2, 2012, www.adage.com; Natalie Zmuda, "Gatorade Introduces G Series Fit," *Advertising Age*, May 2, 2011, www.adage.com; Jeremiah McWilliams, "PepsiCo Revamps 'Formidable' Gatorade Franchise After Rocky 2009," *The Atlanta Journal-Constitution*, March 23, 2010, www.ajc.com; Martinne Geller, "Pepsi Eyes Emerging Markets, Healthy Fare," *Reuters*, March 22, 2010, www.reuters.com; Noreen O'Leary, "Gatorade's G2 Channels All to Punch Up Its Messaging," *Brandweek*, January 4, 2010, 4; Emily Bryson and Natalie Zmuda, "What G Isn't Is a Sales Success," *Advertising Age*, August 10, 2009, 17; David Sterrett, "New Drinks in Gatorade's Playbook," *Crain's Chicago Business*, November 9, 2009, 1; Burt Helm, "Blowing Up Pepsi," *Bloomberg Businessweek*, April 27, 2009, 32; www.gatorade.com.

[34]"Chevrolet Turns 100," *Automobile*, November 2011, 53–97; James R. Healy, "100 Years of Chevy," *USA Today*, October 31, 2011, 1B, 2B; Soyoung Kim, "GM Bans Use of 'Chevy' Brand Name Internally," *Reuters*, June 10, 2010, www.reuters.com/article/2010/06/10/gm-chevy-idUSN1024152620100610 (accessed November 14, 2011); "From 0 to 100," *The Economist*, October 29, 2011, 76; "Chevrolet Camaro—World Car Design of the Year 2010," *AUSmotive.com*, April 8, 2010, www.ausmotive.com/2010/04/08/chevrolet-camaro-world-car-design-of-the-year-2010.html (accessed November 14, 2011); "Chevrolet," www.superbrands.com/za/pdfs/CHEV.pdf (accessed November 14, 2011); Joann Muller, "The Best-Selling Vehicles of 2011," *MSNBC*, November 9, 2011, www.msnbc.msn.com/id/45165770/ns/business-forbes_com/t/best-selling-vehicles/ (accessed November 21, 2011); Jason Siu, "Chevrolet Achieves Best Ever Global Sales In 2011," *AutoGuide*, January 20, 2012, www.autoguide.com/auto-news/2012/01/chevrolet-achieves-best-ever-global-sales-in-2011.html (accessed March 21, 2012).

Feature Notes

[a]Based on information in Michael Wines, "Picking Brand Names in China Is a Business Itself," *The New York Times*, November 11, 2011, www.nytimes.com; Kelvin Chan, "Global Automakers Unveil Local China Brands," *Associated Press*, April 24, 2011, www.ap.org; Kathy Chu, "Companies Launch New Brands for Asia Markets," *USA Today*, September 13, 2011, www.usatoday.com.

[b]Based on information in John Tozzi, "EagleView's Software Measures Rooftops with Photos from the Sky," *Bloomberg News*, December 8, 2011, www.bloomberg.com; Jennifer Alsever, "One Small Company Reinvents a $30 Billion Market," CNN Money, December 9, 2011, http://money.cnn.com; "EagleView Technologies Is Changing the Way Contractors Do Business," *Roofing Contractor*, July 12, 2010, www.roofingcontractor.com.

[c]Based on information in "Marketers Hitting Campus Harder than Ever," *Advertising Age*, October 16, 2011, www.adage.com; Natasha Singer, "On Campus, It's One Big Commercial," *The New York Times*, September 11, 2011, Bu 1–Bu 4; Karl Greenberg, "Chick-fil-A, MillerCoors, UPS Go to College," *MediaPost*, December 7, 2011, www.mediapost.com.

[d]Based on information in Brandi Shaffer, "P&G Reduces Plastic in Packaging Redesign," *Plastics News*, February 2, 2012, www.plasticsnews.com; Cliff Edwards, "Walmart Joining Amazon to Promote Rage-Free Packaging: Retail," *Bloomberg Businessweek*, December 2, 2011, www.businessweek.com; "Amazon to Triple 'Frustration-Free Packaging' Shipments," *Environmental Leader*, December 1, 2011, www.environmentalleader.com.

part 6

Distribution Decisions

Developing products that satisfy customers is important, but it is not enough to guarantee successful marketing strategies. Products must also be available in adequate quantities in accessible locations at the times when customers desire them. PART 6 deals with the distribution of products and the marketing channels and institutions that help to make products available. CHAPTER 15 discusses supply-chain management, marketing channels, and the decisions and activities associated with the physical distribution of products, such as order processing, materials handling, warehousing, inventory management, and transportation. CHAPTER 16 explores retailing and wholesaling, including types of retailers and wholesalers, direct marketing and selling, and strategic retailing issues.

ECONOMIC FORCES
POLITICAL FORCES
LEGAL AND REGULATORY FORCES
TECHNOLOGY FORCES
SOCIOCULTURAL FORCES
COMPETITIVE FORCES
PRODUCT
DISTRIBUTION
PROMOTION
PRICE
CUSTOMER

chapter 15

Marketing Channels and Supply-Chain Management

OBJECTIVES

1. To describe the foundations of supply-chain management
2. To explore the role and significance of marketing channels and supply chains
3. To identify types of marketing channels
4. To understand factors that influence marketing channel selection
5. To identify the intensity of market coverage
6. To examine strategic issues in marketing channels, including leadership, cooperation, and conflict
7. To examine physical distribution as a part of supply-chain management
8. To explore legal issues in channel management

MARKETING INSIGHTS

Angry Birds and Greedy Pigs Seek Expanded Distribution

Angry Birds began life as a game app in which players use digital slingshots to send digital birds hurtling toward digital pigs. Within a year, 50 million people had downloaded Angry Birds to smartphones, iPads, and other electronic gadgets, playing either the free version or paying to upgrade to premium games. Within two years, the number of players had soared to 500 million, earning parent company Rovio a healthy profit and a worldwide fan base eager for branded content and merchandise.

Rovio quickly developed a line of shirts and toys for sale through its online store. Soon it was selling 1 million stuffed pigs and birds and 1 million branded T-shirts every month through its website, along with seasonal products like Halloween costumes. To reach as many potential buyers as possible, Rovio licensed its brand so authorized products could be marketed through Amazon.com and other online and brick-and-mortar stores. In addition, Rovio opened an Angry Birds store in its home country of Finland and planned a series of company-owned stores in China, its fastest-growing market.

Looking ahead, because millions of players use Angry Birds apps every day, "our apps are becoming channels, and we can use that channel to cross-promote—to sell further content," says Rovio's CEO, Mikael Hed. The chief marketing officer envisions Angry Birds as an entertainment brand covering movies, toys, and accessories distributed globally, "just like Hello Kitty or Mickey Mouse." As long as Angry Birds games and merchandise remain popular, Rovio's revenues will be flying high.[1]

Decisions like those made by Rovio relate to the **distribution** component of the marketing mix, which focuses on the decisions and activities involved in making products available to customers when and where they want to purchase them. Choosing which channels of distribution to use is a major decision in the development of marketing strategies.

In this chapter, we focus on marketing channels and supply-chain management. First, we explore the concept of the supply chain and its various activities. Second, we elaborate on marketing channels and the need for intermediaries and then analyze the primary functions they perform. Next, we outline the types and characteristics of marketing channels, discuss how they are selected, and explore how marketers determine the appropriate intensity of market coverage for a product. We examine the strategic channel issues of leadership, cooperation, and conflict. We also look at the role of physical distribution within the supply chain, including its objectives and basic functions. Finally, we look at several legal issues that affect channel management.

distribution The decisions and activities that make products available to customers when and where they want to purchase them

supply chain All the activities associated with the flow and transformation of products from raw materials through to the end customer

operations management The total set of managerial activities used by an organization to transform resource inputs into products, services, or both

logistics management Planning, implementing, and controlling the efficient and effective flow and storage of products and information from the point of origin to consumption to meet customers' needs and wants

supply management In its broadest form, refers to the processes that enable the progress of value from raw material to final customer and back to redesign and final disposition

supply-chain management A set of approaches used to integrate the functions of operations management, logistics management, supply management, and marketing channel management so products are produced and distributed in the right quantities, to the right locations, and at the right time

FOUNDATIONS OF THE SUPPLY CHAIN

An important function of distribution is the joint effort of all involved organizations to be part of creating an effective **supply chain**, which refers to all the activities associated with the flow and transformation of products from raw materials through to the end customer. This results in a total distribution system that involves firms that are both "upstream" in the supply chain (e.g., suppliers) and "downstream" (e.g., wholesalers, retailers) to serve customers and generate competitive advantage. Historically, marketing focused on only certain downstream activities of supply chains, but today marketing professionals are recognizing that important marketplace advantages can be secured by effectively integrating important activities in the supply chain. These include operations, logistics, sourcing, and marketing channels. Integrating these activities requires marketing managers to work with their counterparts in operations management, logistics management, and supply management. **Operations management** is the total set of managerial activities used by an organization to transform resource inputs into products, services, or both.[2] **Logistics management** involves planning, implementing, and controlling the efficient and effective flow and storage of products and information from the point of origin to consumption to meet customers' needs and wants. The costs of business logistics in the United States equal around 8 percent of the nation's entire annual GDP, or over $1 trillion.[3] **Supply management** (e.g., purchasing, procurement, sourcing) in its broadest form refers to the processes that enable the progress of value from raw material to final customer and back to redesign and final disposition.

Supply-chain management is therefore a set of approaches used to integrate the functions of operations management, logistics management, supply management, and marketing channel management so products are produced and distributed in the right quantities, to the right locations, and at the right time. It includes activities like manufacturing, research, sales, advertising, shipping and, most of all, cooperating and understanding of tradeoffs throughout the whole chain to achieve optimal levels of efficiency and service. The key tasks involved in supply-chain management are outlined in Table 15.1. Supply-chain management also includes suppliers of raw materials and other components to make goods and services, logistics and transportation firms, communication firms, and other firms that indirectly take part in marketing exchanges. Thus, the supply chain includes all entities that facilitate product distribution and benefit from cooperative efforts.

Technology has improved supply-chain management capabilities on a global basis. Information technology in particular has created an almost seamless distribution process for matching inventory needs to manufacturer requirements in the upstream portion of the supply chain and to customers' requirements in the downstream portion of the chain. With integrated information sharing among chain members, costs can be reduced, service can be improved, and increased value can be provided to the end customer. Indeed, information is crucial in operating supply chains efficiently and effectively.

Table 15.1 Key Tasks in Supply-Chain Management

Marketing Activities	Sample Activities
Operations management	Organizational and system-wide coordination of operations and partnerships to meet customers' product needs.
Supply management	Sourcing of necessary resources, products, and services from suppliers to support all supply-chain members.
Logistics management	All activities designed to move the product through the marketing channel to the end user, including warehousing and inventory management.
Channel management	All activities related to selling, service, and the development of long-term customer relationships.

As demand for innovative goods and services has escalated in recent years, marketers have had to increase their flexibility and responsiveness to develop new products and modify existing ones to meet the ever-changing needs of customers. Suppliers now provide material and service inputs to meet customer needs in the upstream portion of the supply chain. Customers are increasingly a knowledge source in developing the right product in the downstream portion of the supply chain. This means that the entire supply chain is critically important in ensuring that customers get the products when, where, and how they want them. Consider Apple, the highly popular electronics brand. Apple used to be known for making many of its products in the United States. In order to keep up with demand and maintain a sufficiently large and flexible supply chain, Apple has outsourced the production of its most popular products, such as the iPod, iPad, and iPhone. Apple has a large and complicated international supply chain that is calibrated to keep up with the speed of production required to satisfy demand for Apple's highly popular products.[4] Firms must therefore be involved in the management of their own supply chains in partnership with the network of upstream and downstream organizations in the supply chain. Upstream firms provide direct or indirect input to make the product. Downstream firms are responsible for delivery of the product and after-market services to the end customers. The management of the upstream and downstream in the supply-chain activities is what is involved in managing supply chains.

Effective supply-chain management is closely linked to a market orientation. All functional areas of business (marketing, management, production, finance, and information systems) are involved in executing a customer orientation and supply-chain management. Both of these activities overlap with operations management, logistics management, and supply management. If a firm has established a marketing strategy based on continuous customer-focused leadership, then supply-chain management will be driven by cooperation and strategic coordination to ensure customer satisfaction. Managers should recognize that supply-chain management is critical to fulfilling customer requirements and requires coordination with all areas of the business. This logical association between market orientation and supply-chain management should lead to increased firm performance and competitiveness.[5]

THE ROLE OF MARKETING CHANNELS IN SUPPLY CHAINS

A **marketing channel** (also called a *channel of distribution* or *distribution channel*) is a group of individuals and organizations that direct the flow of products from producers to customers within the supply chain. The major role of marketing channels—in conjuction with operations management, logistics management, and supply management—is to make products available

marketing channel A group of individuals and organizations that direct the flow of products from producers to customers within the supply chain

Technology Facilitates Supply-Chain Management
TECSYS provides services and technology to facilitate supply-chain management for business customers.

Courtesy of TECSYS Inc.

at the right time at the right place in the right quantities. Providing customer satisfaction should be the driving force behind marketing channel decisions. Buyers' needs and behavior are therefore important concerns of channel members.

Some marketing channels are direct, meaning that the product goes directly from the producer to the customer. For instance, when a customer orders food online from Omaha Steaks, the product is sent from the manufacturer to the customer. Most channels, however, have one or more **marketing intermediaries** that link producers to other intermediaries or to ultimate consumers through contractual arrangements or through the purchase and reselling of products. Marketing intermediaries perform the activities described in Table 15.2. They also play key roles in customer relationship management, not only through their distribution activities but also by maintaining databases and information systems to help all members of the marketing channel maintain effective customer relationships. For example, eBay serves as a marketing intermediary between Internet sellers and buyers. eBay not only provides a forum for these exchanges but also helps facilitate relationships among eBay channel members and eases payment issues through its PayPal subsidiary.

marketing intermediaries Middlemen that link producers to other intermediaries or ultimate consumers through contractual arrangements or through the purchase and resale of products

Wholesalers and retailers are examples of intermediaries. Wholesalers buy and resell products to other wholesalers, retailers, and industrial customers. Retailers purchase products

Table 15.2 Marketing Channel Activities Performed by Intermediaries

Marketing Activities	Sample Activities
Marketing information	Analyze sales data and other information in databases and information systems. Perform or commission marketing research.
Marketing management	Establish strategic and tactical plans for developing customer relationships and organizational productivity.
Facilitating exchanges	Choose product assortments that match the needs of customers. Cooperate with channel members to develop partnerships.
Promotion	Set promotional objectives. Coordinate advertising, personal selling, sales promotion, publicity, and packaging.
Price	Establish pricing policies and terms of sales.
Physical distribution	Manage transportation, warehousing, materials handling, inventory control, and communication.

and resell them to the end consumers. Consider your local supermarket, which probably purchased the Tylenol or Advil on its shelves from a wholesaler. The wholesaler purchased that pain medicine, along with other over-the-counter and prescription drugs, from manufacturers like McNeil Consumer Labs and Whitehall-Robins. Chapter 16 discusses the functions of wholesalers and retailers in marketing channels in greater detail.

Supply chains start with the customer and require the cooperation of channel members to satisfy customer requirements. All members should focus on cooperation to reduce the costs of all channel members and thereby improve profits. For example, some customers prefer to purchase products from companies that have environmentally friendly products or business practices. In response to this, Dell began changing the way it packages its products. The company began using a multipack option for customers who purchase multiple systems at once. In addition, it has been working on making its packages smaller, with stronger but thinner and lighter cushioning. Dell also uses recycled boxes and bamboo packaging, and recently began trying out a new cushion made from a mushroom-based fungus material. By using sustainable packaging materials and reducing the weight and size of its products, the company has been able to reduce its footprint on the world while also saving money on its packaging, transportation, and storage costs.[6] When the buyer, the seller, marketing intermediaries, and facilitating agencies work together, the cooperative relationship results in compromise and adjustments that meet customers' needs regarding delivery, scheduling, packaging, or other requirements.

Each supply-chain member requires information from other channel members. For instance, suppliers need order and forecast information from the manufacturer; they also may need availability information from their own suppliers. Customer relationship management (CRM) systems exploit the information from supply-chain partners' information systems to help all channel members make marketing strategy decisions that develop and sustain desirable customer relationships. Thus, managing relationships with

The Role of Marketing Channels
The marketing channel for premium quality beef is different than the one for regular beef. The characteristics of a marketing channel can influence customers' perceptions of products.

supply-chain partners is crucial to satisfying customers. Companies now offer online programs that input business data into a social networking site formula. Tibbr and Yammer are two such programs. By inputting all data into a single, easy-to-use online system, businesses can achieve greater efficiencies and improve their CRM.[7]

The Significance of Marketing Channels

Although marketing channel decisions do not have to precede other marketing decisions, they are a powerful influence on the rest of the marketing mix (i.e., product, promotion, and pricing). Channel decisions are critical because they determine a product's market presence and buyers' accessibility to the product. Without effective marketing channel operations, even the best goods and services will not be successful. Consider that small businesses are more likely to purchase computers from chain specialty stores, such as Best Buy and Office Depot, putting computer companies without distribution through these outlets at a disadvantage. In fact, even Dell—which pioneered the direct-sales model in the computer industry—is now selling its computers at Best Buy. The option of buying Dell systems directly from Dell or in retail stores like Best Buy means that customers can purchase what they need when and where they want while also allowing customers to "test drive" a computer system of their choice.

Marketing channel decisions have additional strategic significance because they generally entail long-term commitments among a variety of firms (e.g., suppliers, logistics providers, and operations firms). It is usually easier to change prices or promotional strategies than to change marketing channels. Marketing channels also serve many functions, including creating utility and facilitating exchange efficiencies. Although some of these functions may be performed by a single channel member, most functions are accomplished through both independent and joint efforts of channel members.

Marketing Channels Create Utility

Marketing channels create four types of utility: time, place, possession, and form. *Time utility* is having products available when the customer wants them. Services like Movies On Demand

Entrepreneurship in Marketing

Etsy Creates a Crafty Channel

Entrepreneurs: Rob Kalin, Chris Maguire, and Haim Schoppik
Business: Etsy
Founded: 2005 | New York, New York
Success: The website has grown to $526 million in annual sales, with over 39 million unique monthly visitors from about 150 countries.

Since 2005, makers of handcrafted items have had a dedicated online channel for distributing their works: Etsy. Photographer/carpenter Rob Kalin co-founded Etsy with two friends as an Internet marketplace where he and other artisans could connect with buyers seeking creative crafts and artwork. Under Etsy's rules, all items must be handmade by the seller. The exceptions are vintage goods, which must be at least 20 years old to be offered for sale on the website.

Today, Etsy serves as a convenient yet global virtual storefront for 800,000 crafts entrepreneurs who offer a total of 13 million handmade and vintage products and ring up $526 million in annual sales. It provides apps for buyers who want to browse or search offerings via cell phone, apps for sellers who want to promote their shops, and support services like payment processing and accounting services for its craft shopkeepers.

Going beyond channel functions, Etsy encourages a sense of community among crafts lovers through social media, such as blogs, Facebook, Tumblr, Twitter, and Meetup. "It's not just handcrafted goods, but it's a handcrafted experience," explains CEO Chad Dickerson. "You can get a real message from a real seller. That's different than Walmart."[a]

allow customers to watch a movie whenever they want, unlike most video stores that are not open 24 hours a day. *Place utility* is created by making products available in locations where customers wish to purchase them. For example, shopping malls that have an ATM machine inside allow customers who need cash to withdraw money without having to go to a bank. *Possession utility* means that the customer has access to the product to use or to store for future use. Possession utility can occur through ownership or through arrangements that give the customer the right to use the product, such as a lease or rental agreement. Channel members sometimes create *form utility* by assembling, preparing, or otherwise refining the product to suit individual customer needs.

Marketing Channels Facilitate Exchange Efficiencies

Marketing intermediaries can reduce the costs of exchanges by performing certain services or functions efficiently. Even if producers and buyers are located in the same city, there are costs associated with exchanges. As Figure 15.1 shows, when four buyers seek products from four producers, 16 transactions are possible. If one intermediary serves both producers and buyers, the number of transactions can be reduced to eight. Intermediaries are specialists in facilitating exchanges. They provide valuable assistance because of their access to and control over important resources used in the proper functioning of marketing channels.

Nevertheless, the press, consumers, public officials, and even other marketers freely criticize intermediaries, especially wholesalers. Critics accuse wholesalers of being inefficient and

Figure 15.1 Efficiency in Exchanges Provided by an Intermediary

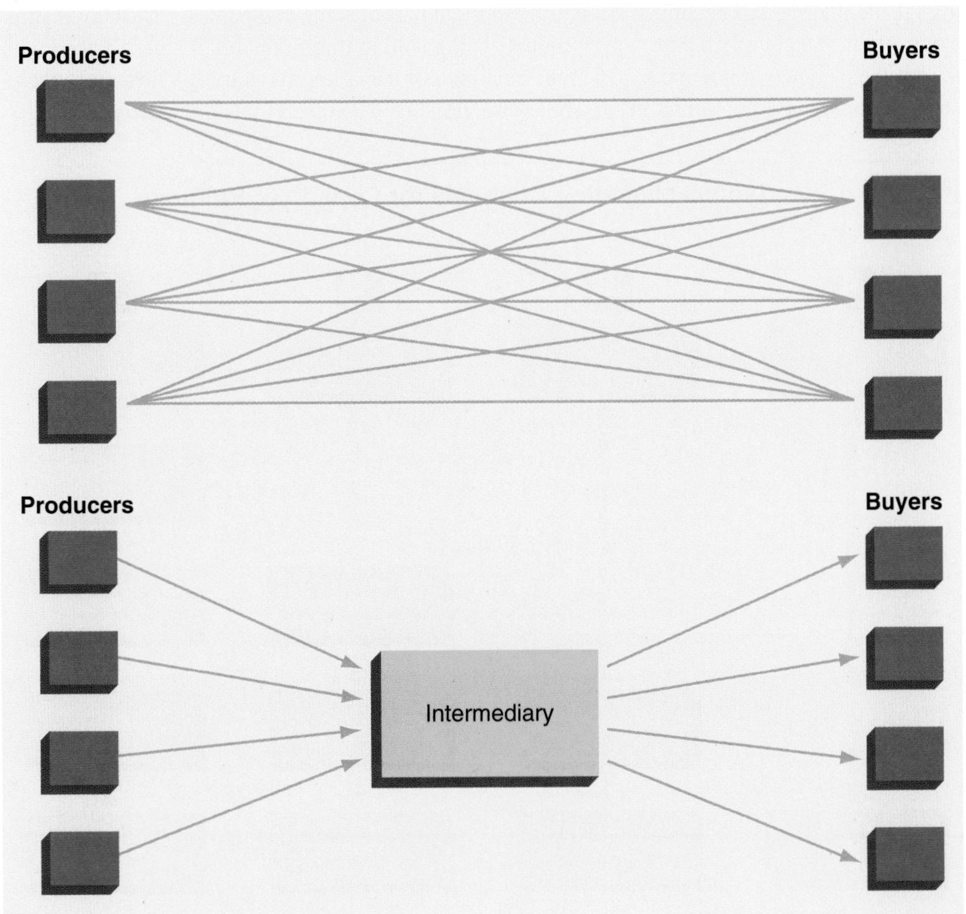

parasitic. Buyers often wish to make the distribution channel as short as possible, assuming the fewer the intermediaries, the lower the price will be.

Critics who suggest that eliminating wholesalers would lower customer prices fail to recognize that this would not eliminate the need for the services the wholesalers provide. Although wholesalers can be eliminated, their functions cannot. Other channel members would have to perform those functions, and customers still would have to pay for them. In addition, all producers would have to deal directly with retailers or customers, meaning that every producer would have to keep voluminous records and hire enough personnel to deal with a multitude of customers. Customers might end up paying a great deal more for products, because prices would reflect the costs of less-efficient channel members. Because suggestions to eliminate wholesalers come from both ends of the marketing channel, wholesalers must be careful to perform only those marketing activities that are truly desired. To survive, they must be more efficient and customer-focused than other marketing institutions.

Types of Marketing Channels

Because marketing channels that are appropriate for one product may be less suitable for others, many different distribution paths have been developed. The various marketing channels can be classified generally as channels for consumer products and channels for business products.

Channels for Consumer Products

Figure 15.2 illustrates several channels used in the distribution of consumer products. Channel A depicts the direct movement of products from producer to consumers. For instance, the legal advice given by attorneys moves through channel A. Producers, like Dell computers, that sell products directly from their factories to end users use direct marketing channels. Direct marketing via the Internet has become a critically important part of some companies' distribution strategies, often as a complement to their products being sold in traditional retail stores. Faced with the strategic choice of going directly to the customer or using intermediaries, a firm must evaluate the benefits of going direct versus the transaction costs involved in using intermediaries.

Figure 15.2 Typical Marketing Channels for Consumer Products

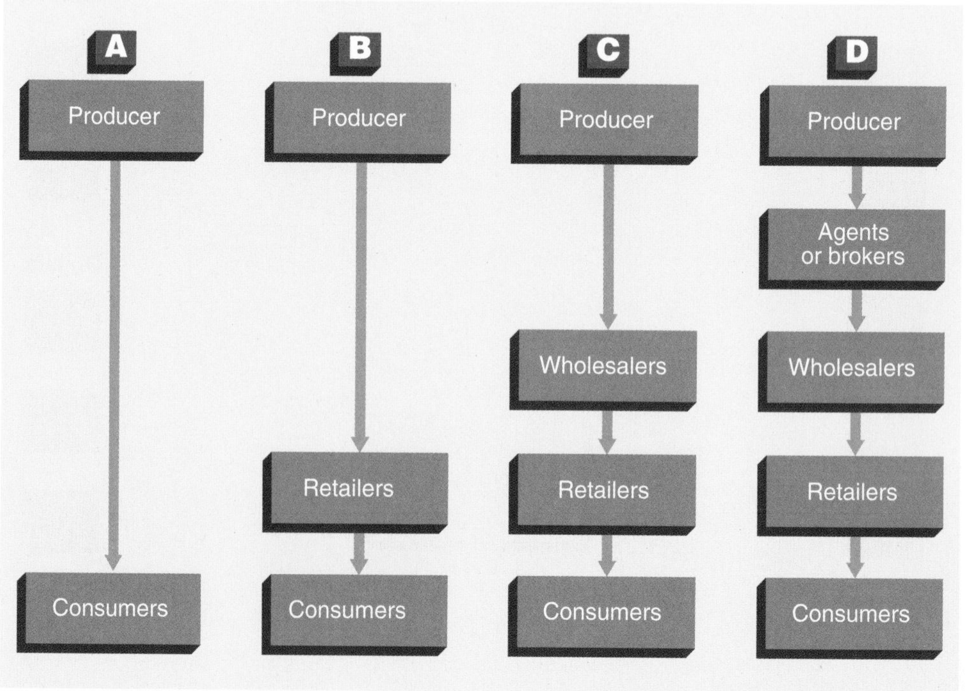

Channel B, which moves goods from the producer to a retailer and then to customers, is a frequent choice of large retailers because it allows them to buy in quantity from manufacturers. Retailers like Kmart and Walmart sell clothing, stereos, and many other items purchased directly from producers. New automobiles and new college textbooks are also sold through this type of marketing channel. Primarily nonstore retailers, such as L.L.Bean and J.Crew, also use this type of channel.

Channel C represents a long-standing distribution channel, especially for consumer products. It takes goods from the producer to a wholesaler, then to a retailer, and finally to consumers. It is a practical option for producers that sell to hundreds of thousands of customers through thousands of retailers. Consider the number of retailers marketing Wrigley's chewing gum. It would be extremely difficult, if not impossible, for Wrigley to deal directly with each retailer that sells its brand of gum. Manufacturers of tobacco products, some home appliances, hardware, and many convenience goods sell their products to wholesalers, which then sell to retailers, which in turn do business with individual consumers.

Channel D, through which goods pass from producer to agents to wholesalers to retailers and then to consumers, is used frequently for products intended for mass distribution, such as processed foods. For example, to place its cracker line in specific retail outlets, a food processor may hire an agent (or a food broker) to sell the crackers to wholesalers. Wholesalers then sell the crackers to supermarkets, vending machine operators, and other retail outlets.

Contrary to popular opinion, a long channel may be the most efficient distribution channel for some consumer goods. When several channel intermediaries perform specialized functions, costs may be lower than when one channel member tries to perform them all. In essence, this logic is similar to outsourcing part of the production to firms in low-cost countries. For the marketing channel, it means that firms that specialize in certain elements of producing a product or moving it through the channel are more effective and efficient at performing specialized tasks than the manufacturer. This results in cost efficiencies and added value to customers.

Channels for Business Products

Figure 15.3 shows four of the most common channels for business products. As with consumer products, manufacturers of business products sometimes work with more than one level of wholesalers.

Figure 15.3 Typical Marketing Channels for Business Products

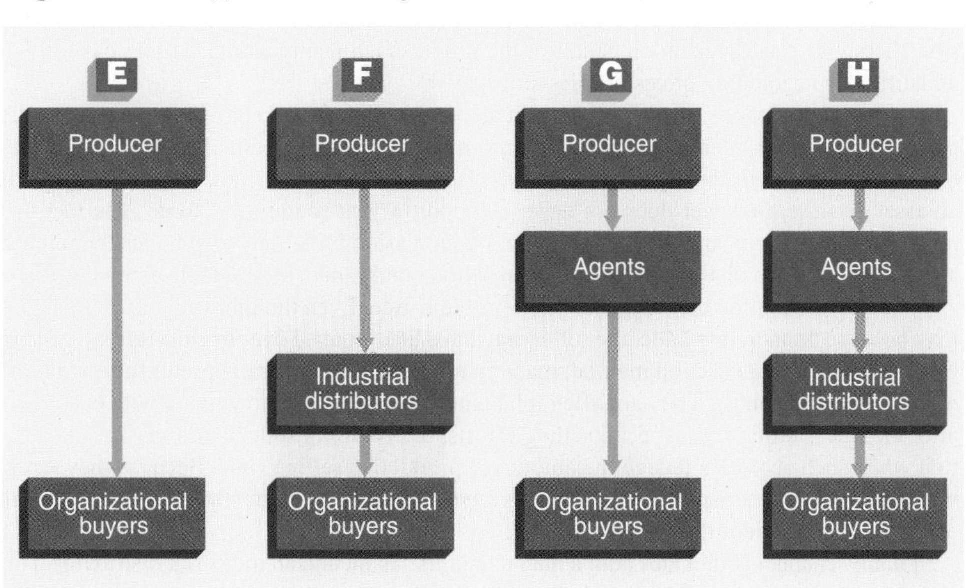

Channel E illustrates the direct channel for business products. In contrast to consumer goods, more than half of all business products, especially expensive equipment, are sold through direct channels. Business customers prefer to communicate directly with producers, especially when expensive or technically complex products are involved. For instance, buyers prefer to purchase expensive and highly complex SQL server computers directly from Dell. Similarly, Intel has established direct marketing channels for selling its microprocessor chips to computer manufacturers. In these circumstances, a customer wants the technical assistance and personal assurances that only a producer can provide.

In channel F, an industrial distributor facilitates exchanges between the producer and the customer. An **industrial distributor** is an independent business that takes title to products and carries inventories. Industrial distributors usually sell standardized items, such as maintenance supplies, production tools, and small operating equipment. Some industrial distributors carry a wide variety of product lines. Wolseley, for example, is the world's largest industrial distributor of plumbing and heating products and a leading supplier of building products. It carries a wide variety of international brands and supplies producer, government, and institutional markets worldwide.[8] Other industrial distributors specialize in one or a small number of lines. Industrial distributors are carrying an increasing percentage of business products. Overall, these distributors can be most effectively used when a product has broad market appeal, is easily stocked and serviced, is sold in small quantities, and is needed on demand to avoid high losses.

Industrial distributors offer sellers several advantages. They can perform the needed selling activities in local markets at a relatively low cost to a manufacturer and reduce a producer's financial burden by providing customers with credit services. Also, because industrial distributors usually maintain close relationships with their customers, they are aware of local needs and can pass on market information to producers. By holding adequate inventories in their local markets, industrial distributors reduce producers' capital requirements.

Using industrial distributors has several disadvantages, however. Industrial distributors may be difficult to control because they are independent firms. They often stock competing brands, so a producer cannot depend on them to sell its brand aggressively. Furthermore, because industrial distributors maintain inventories, they incur numerous expenses; consequently, they are less likely to handle bulky or slow-selling items or items that need specialized facilities or extraordinary selling efforts. In some cases, industrial distributors lack the technical knowledge necessary to sell and service certain products.

The third channel for business products, channel G, employs a *manufacturers' agent,* an independent businessperson who sells complementary products of several producers in assigned territories and is compensated through commissions. Unlike an industrial distributor, a manufacturers' agent does not acquire title to the products and usually does not take possession. Acting as a salesperson on behalf of the producers, a manufacturers' agent has little or no latitude in negotiating prices or sales terms.

Using manufacturers' agents can benefit an organizational marketer. These agents usually possess considerable technical and market information and have an established set of customers. For an organizational seller with highly seasonal demand, a manufacturers' agent can be an asset because the seller does not have to support a year-round sales force. The fact that manufacturers' agents are typically paid on a commission basis may also be an economical alternative for a firm that has highly limited resources and cannot afford a full-time sales force.

The use of manufacturers' agents is not problem-free. Even though straight commissions may be more financially viable, the seller may have little control over manufacturers' agents. Because of the compensation method, manufacturers' agents generally prefer to concentrate on their larger accounts. They are often reluctant to spend time following up with customers after the sale, putting forth special selling efforts, or providing sellers with market information when such activities reduce the amount of productive selling time. Because they rarely maintain inventories, manufacturers' agents have a limited ability to provide customers with parts or repair services quickly.

Finally, channel H includes both a manufacturers' agent and an industrial distributor. This channel may be appropriate when the producer wishes to cover a large geographic area but

industrial distributor An independent business organization that takes title to industrial products and carries inventories

maintains no sales force due to highly seasonal demand or because it cannot afford a sales force. This type of channel can also be useful for a business marketer that wants to enter a new geographic market without expanding its existing sales force.

Multiple Marketing Channels and Channel Alliances

To reach diverse target markets, manufacturers may use several marketing channels simultaneously, with each channel involving a different group of intermediaries. In particular, a manufacturer often uses multiple channels when the same product is directed to both consumers and business customers. For example, when Heinz markets ketchup for household use, the product is sold to supermarkets through grocery wholesalers or, in some cases, directly to retailers, whereas ketchup being sold to restaurants or institutions follows a different distribution channel.

In some instances, a producer may prefer **dual distribution**, the use of two or more marketing channels to distribute the same products to the same target market. For instance, Kellogg sells its cereals directly to large retail grocery chains (channel B) and food wholesalers that, in turn, sell the cereals to retailers (channel C). Another example of dual distribution is a firm that sells products through retail outlets and its own mail-order catalog or website. Procter & Gamble decided to expand its distribution strategy, which until recently included selling to wholesalers and retailers. The company recently opened an e-store, where customers can purchase all of their favorite P&G brands, including Tide, Pampers, and Pantene, directly from the company online.[9]

Dual distribution, however, can cause dissatisfaction among wholesalers and smaller retailers when they must compete with large retail grocery chains that make direct purchases from manufacturers, such as Kellogg.

A **strategic channel alliance** exists when the products of one organization are distributed through the marketing channels of another. The products of the two firms are often similar with respect to target markets or uses, but they are not direct competitors. A brand of bottled water might be distributed through a marketing channel for soft drinks, or a domestic cereal producer might form a strategic channel alliance with a European food processor. Such alliances can provide benefits for both the organization that owns the marketing channel and the company whose brand is being distributed through the channel.

dual distribution The use of two or more marketing channels to distribute the same products to the same target market

strategic channel alliance An agreement whereby the products of one organization are distributed through the marketing channels of another

Using Multiple Marketing Channels
Starbucks' Frappuccino products are available at company stores and in select grocery stores.

Selecting Marketing Channels

Selecting appropriate marketing channels is important. Although the process varies across organizations, channel selection decisions are usually significantly affected by one or more of the following factors: customer characteristics, product attributes, type of organization, competition, marketing environmental forces, and characteristics of intermediaries (see Figure 15.4).

Customer Characteristics

Marketing managers must consider the characteristics of target-market members in channel selection. As we have already seen, the channels that are appropriate for consumers are different from those for business customers. A different marketing channel will be required for business customers purchasing carpet for commercial buildings compared with consumers purchasing carpet for their homes. Business customers often prefer to deal directly with producers (or very knowledgeable channel intermediaries such as industrial distributors), especially for highly technical or expensive products, such as mainframe computers, jet airplanes, and large mining machines. Moreover, business customers are more likely to buy complex products that require strict specifications and technical assistance or to buy in considerable quantities.

Consumers, on the other hand, generally buy limited quantities of a product, purchase from retailers, and often do not mind limited customer service. Additionally, when customers are concentrated in a small geographic area, a more direct channel may be ideal, but when many customers are spread across an entire state or nation, distribution through multiple intermediaries is likely to be more efficient.

Product Attributes

The attributes of the product can have a strong influence on the choice of marketing channels. Marketers of complex and expensive products like automobiles will likely employ short

Figure 15.4 Selecting Marketing Channels

Emerging Trends

Branded Stores as Entertainment Bring in Tourists

Hershey's, Mars, and other brands are the stars of the show in showplace stores where each is the *only* brand for sale. The trend of retailing-as-entertainment has led these and other companies to tell their brand stories and put their products and memorabilia on showy display in giant stores that draw crowds of tourists day after day. Although these single-brand "worlds" bring in millions of dollars in annual sales, they're hardly competition for traditional retail channels—in fact, their role is to provide such an exciting brand experience that tourists will keep buying the brand in local stores when they get home.

For example, chocolate lovers on vacation can visit elaborate brand stores created by Hershey's and Mars. Hershey's operates Chocolate World stores in New York's Times Square; Niagara Falls, Canada; downtown Chicago; and Shanghai, China. M&M's World stores are open in busy tourist destinations like Orlando, Florida; Las Vegas, Nevada; Times Square, New York City; and Leicester Square, London. When Mars introduced Ms. Brown, one of its new brand characters for M&M's, it used the glitzy Times Square store as the backdrop.

Not long ago, Kellogg created a temporary Pop-Tarts World store in Times Square. Why? The brand's senior director explains: "Our long-term hope is to strengthen the bonding between the brand and the consumer, and that has great benefits for the brand."[b]

channels, as will marketers of perishable products, such as dairy and produce. Less-expensive, more standardized products like soft drinks and canned goods can employ longer channels with many intermediaries. In addition, channel decisions may be affected by a product's sturdiness: fragile products that require special handling are more likely to be distributed through shorter channels to minimize the risk of damage. Firms that desire to convey an exclusive image for their products may wish to limit the number of outlets available.

Type of Organization

Clearly, the characteristics of the organization will have a great impact on the distribution channels chosen. Owing to their sheer size, larger firms may be able to negotiate better deals with vendors or other channel members. Compared with small firms, they may be in a better position to have more distribution centers, which may reduce delivery times to customers. A smaller regional company that uses regional or local channel members might be in a position to better serve customers in that region compared with a larger, less-flexible organization. Compared with smaller organizations, large companies can use an extensive product mix as a competitive tool. Smaller firms may not have the resources to develop their own sales force, ship their products long distances, store or own products, or extend credit. In such cases, they may have to include other channel members that have the resources to provide these services to customers efficiently and cost effectively.

Competition

Competition is another important factor for supply-chain managers to consider. The success or failure of a competitor's marketing channel may encourage or dissuade an organization from considering a similar approach. A firm also may be forced to adopt a similar strategy to remain competitive. In a highly competitive market, it is important for a company to keep its costs low so it can offer lower prices than its competitors if necessary.

Environmental Forces

Environmental forces can also play a role in channel selection. Adverse economic conditions might force an organization to use a low-cost channel, even though customer satisfaction is reduced. In contrast, a booming economy may allow a company to choose a channel that previously had been too costly to consider. The introduction of new technology might cause an organization to add or modify its channel strategy. For instance, many marketers in a variety of industries are finding that it is valuable to maintain online social networking accounts to keep customers up-to-date on new products, offers, and events. BloomReach.com is a company offering search engine optimization services to businesses to help them compete in an increasingly digital environment. The company is staffed by former executives from Google, Cisco, and Facebook and claims to have developed technology that delivers content to consumers based on their interests and needs. This technology may help businesses more precisely target consumers who need their products.[10] Government regulations can also affect channel selection. As new labor and environmental regulations are passed, an organization may be forced to modify its existing distribution channel structure. Firms might choose to make the changes before regulations are passed to appear compliant or to avoid legal issues. Governmental regulations can also include trade agreements with other countries that complicate the supply chain.

Characteristics of Intermediaries

When an organization believes that a current intermediary is not promoting the organization's products adequately, it may reconsider its channel choices. In these instances, the company may choose another channel member to handle its products, or it might choose to eliminate intermediaries altogether and perform the eliminated intermediaries' functions itself. Alternatively, an existing intermediary may not offer an appropriate mix of services, forcing an organization to switch to another intermediary.

INTENSITY OF MARKET COVERAGE

In addition to deciding which marketing channels to use to distribute a product, marketers must determine the intensity of coverage that a product should get—that is, the number and kinds of outlets in which it will be sold. This decision depends on the characteristics of the product and the target market. To achieve the desired intensity of market coverage, distribution must correspond to behavior patterns of buyers. In Chapter 11, we divided consumer products into four categories—convenience products, shopping products, specialty products, and unsought products—according to how consumers make purchases. In considering products for purchase, consumers take into account replacement rate, product adjustment (services), duration of consumption, time required to find the product, and similar factors.[11] These variables directly affect the intensity of market coverage. As shown in Figure 15.5, the three major levels of market coverage are intensive, selective, and exclusive distribution.

Intensive Distribution

Intensive distribution uses all available outlets for distributing a product. Intensive distribution is appropriate for most convenience products like bread, chewing gum, soft drinks, and newspapers. Convenience products have a high replacement rate, require almost no service, and are often bought based on price cues. To meet these demands, intensive distribution is necessary, and multiple channels may be used to sell through all possible outlets. For example, soft drinks, snacks, laundry detergent, and pain relievers are available at convenience stores, service stations, supermarkets, discount stores, and other types of retailers. To consumers, availability means a store is located nearby, and minimum time is necessary to search for the product at the store. This ensures that consumers are provided with the greatest speed in obtaining the product, the quality they have come to expect of a certain convenience product, the flexibility to buy the product wherever it is convenient to them, and the lowest cost possible.

Sales may have a direct relationship to product availability. The successful sale of convenience products like bread and milk at service stations or gasoline at convenience grocery stores illustrates that the availability of these products is more important than the nature of the outlet. Companies like Procter & Gamble that produce consumer packaged items rely on

intensive distribution
Using all available outlets to distribute a product

Figure 15.5 Intensity of Market Coverage

intensive distribution for many of their products (e.g., soaps, detergents, food and juice products, and personal-care products) because consumers want ready availability.

Selective Distribution

Selective distribution uses only some available outlets in an area to distribute a product. Selective distribution is appropriate for shopping products; durable goods, such as televisions, stereos, and home computers, usually fall into this category. These products are more expensive than convenience goods, and consumers are willing to spend more time visiting several retail outlets to compare prices, designs, styles, and other features.

Selective distribution is desirable when a special effort, such as customer service from a channel member, is important to customers. Shopping products require differentiation at the point of purchase. Selective distribution is often used to motivate retailers to provide adequate service. Dealers can offer higher-quality customer service when products are distributed selectively, such as Apple products, which are only distributed through authorized Apple dealers and Apple stores, and high-end cosmetics, which are only available in certain department stores. Most perfumes and colognes are marketed using selective distribution in order to maintain a particular image.

Exclusive Distribution

Exclusive distribution uses only one outlet in a relatively large geographic area. Exclusive distribution is suitable for products purchased infrequently, consumed over a long period of time, or requiring service or information to fit them to buyers' needs. It is also used for expensive, high-quality products, such as Porsche, BMW, and other luxury automobiles. It is not appropriate for convenience products and many shopping products.

Exclusive distribution is often used as an incentive to sellers when only a limited market is available for products. Consider Patek Philippe watches that may sell for $10,000 or more. These watches, like luxury automobiles, are available in only a few select locations. A producer using exclusive distribution generally expects dealers to carry a complete inventory,

selective distribution Using only some available outlets in an area to distribute a product

exclusive distribution Using a single outlet in a fairly large geographic area to distribute a product

Courtesy of The Advertising Archives

Courtesy of The Advertising Archives

Comparing Intensive and Selective Distribution
Soft drinks are typically distributed through intensive distribution, whereas shoes, like Merrell, are usually distributed through selective distribution.

send personnel for sales and service training, participate in promotional programs, and provide excellent customer service. Some products are appropriate for exclusive distribution when first introduced, but as competitors enter the market and the product moves through its life cycle, other types of market coverage and distribution channels often become necessary. A problem that can arise with exclusive distribution (and selective distribution) is that unauthorized resellers acquire and sell products, violating the agreement between a manufacturer and its exclusive authorized dealers. This has been a problem for Rolex, a manufacturer of luxury watches.

STRATEGIC ISSUES IN MARKETING CHANNELS

To fulfill the potential of effective supply-chain management and ensure customer satisfaction, marketing channels require a strategic focus on certain competitive priorities and the development of channel leadership, cooperation, and the management of channel conflict. They may also require consolidation of marketing channels through channel integration.

Competitive Priorities in Marketing Channels

Much evidence exists that supply chains can provide a competitive advantage for many marketers. As mentioned earlier, effective supply-chain management has been linked to a market orientation. Because supply-chain decisions cut across all functional areas of the business, it is a competitive priority. Building the most effective and efficient supply chain can sustain a business in a variety of competitive environments.

An ongoing benchmarking study by Deloitte reveals that supply-chain problems can significantly reduce a firm's market value. The most recent report estimates that more than 80 percent of large global firms are not maximizing their returns and only about 10 percent of firms have launched campaigns to improve optimization of their supply chains. The loss to firms from not maximizing their supply chain efficiency can be up to 50 percent. Those companies that have improved their supply chains have benefited from the strongest financial returns among the firms that Deloitte studied.[12] Many well-known firms, including Amazon, Dell, FedEx, Toyota, and Walmart, owe much of their success to outmaneuvering rivals with unique supply-chain capabilities.

If supply-chain activities are not integrated, functions exist without coordination. As supply chains integrate functions, the reward is efficiency and effectiveness as well as a holistic view of the supply chain. Goal-driven supply chains, by direction of their firms, focus on the "competitive priorities" of speed, quality, cost, or flexibility as the performance objective. These priorities can generate problems for some organizations. For example, journalists revealed the appalling working conditions at Chinese factories that produce many popular electronics products, including Apple's iPad. The goal of producing the new products that customers want at a price they will pay resulted in long hours and a single-minded focus on productivity. The pressure to work excessively long hours and to be productive became so overwhelming that some workers even killed themselves. Apple, and other companies, chose to sacrifice worker safety and health in their goal of producing the number-one tablet computer.[13]

Channel Leadership, Cooperation, and Conflict

channel captain The dominant leader of a marketing channel or a supply channel

Each channel member performs a different role in the distribution system and agrees (implicitly or explicitly) to accept certain rights, responsibilities, rewards, and sanctions for nonconformity. Moreover, each channel member holds certain expectations of other channel members. Retailers, for instance, expect wholesalers to maintain adequate inventories and deliver goods on time. Wholesalers expect retailers to honor payment agreements and keep them informed of inventory needs.

Channel partnerships facilitate effective supply-chain management when partners agree on objectives, policies, and procedures for physical distribution efforts associated with the supplier's products. Such partnerships eliminate redundancies and reassign tasks for maximum system-wide efficiency.

Having an environmentally friendly supply chain is increasingly important to many organizations and their stakeholders. In order to reduce the carbon footprint of its production process, members of the U.S. auto industry partnered with suppliers and the Environmental Protection Agency. The resulting partnership, Suppliers Partnership for the Environment, is a forum for companies and their supply-chain partners to share environmental best practices and optimize supply-chain productivity. Not only do participants improve productivity, but they help reduce waste and pollution and learn from other organizations.[14] In this section, we discuss channel member behavior—including leadership, cooperation, and conflict—that marketers must understand to make effective channel decisions.

Channel Leadership

Many marketing-channel decisions are determined by give-and-take among channel partners, with the idea that the overall channel ultimately will benefit. Some marketing channels, however, are organized and controlled by a single leader, or **channel captain** (also called *channel leader*). The channel captain may be a producer, wholesaler,

Channel Leadership
Dell provides channel leadership in the distribution of its products.

or retailer. Channel captains may establish channel policies and coordinate development of the marketing mix. Walmart, for example, dominates the supply chain for its retail stores by virtue of the magnitude of its resources (especially information management) and a strong, nationwide customer base. To attain desired objectives, the captain must possess **channel power**, the ability to influence another channel member's goal achievement. The member that becomes the channel captain will accept the responsibilities and exercise the power associated with this role.

When a manufacturer's large-scale production efficiency demands that it increase sales volume, the manufacturer may exercise power by giving channel members financing, business advice, ordering assistance, advertising services, sales and service training, and support materials. For example, U.S. automakers provide these services to retail automobile dealerships. However, these manufacturers also place numerous requirements on their retail dealerships with respect to sales volume, sales and service training, and customer satisfaction.

Retailers may also function as channel captains. With the rise in power of national chain stores and private-brand merchandise, many large retailers like Walmart are taking a leadership role in the channel. Small retailers too may assume leadership roles when they gain strong customer loyalty in local or regional markets. These retailers control many brands and sometimes replace uncooperative producers. Increasingly, leading retailers are concentrating their buying power with fewer suppliers and, in the process, improving their marketing effectiveness and efficiency. Long-term commitments enable retailers to place smaller and more frequent orders as needed rather than waiting for large-volume discounts or placing huge orders and assuming the risks associated with carrying a larger inventory.

Wholesalers assume channel leadership roles as well, although they were more powerful decades ago, when many manufacturers and retailers were smaller, underfinanced, and widely scattered. Today, wholesaler leaders may form voluntary chains with several retailers, which they supply with bulk buying or management services; these chains may also market their own brands. In return, the retailers shift most of their purchasing to the wholesaler leader. The Independent Grocers' Alliance (IGA) is one of the best-known wholesaler leaders in the United States. IGA's power is based on its expertise in advertising, pricing, and purchasing knowledge that it makes available to independent business owners. Other wholesaler leaders help retailers with store layouts, accounting, and inventory control.

Channel Cooperation

Channel cooperation is vital if each member is to gain something from other members. Cooperation enables retailers, wholesalers, suppliers, and logistics providers to speed up inventory replenishment, improve customer service, and cut the costs of bringing products to the consumer.[15] Without cooperation, neither overall channel goals nor individual member goals can be realized. All channel members must recognize that the success of one firm in the channel depends in part on other member firms. Thus, marketing channel members should make a coordinated effort to satisfy market requirements. Channel cooperation leads to greater trust among channel members and improves the overall functioning of the channel. It also leads to more satisfying relationships among channel members.

There are several ways to improve channel cooperation. If a marketing channel is viewed as a unified supply chain competing with other systems, individual members will be less likely to take actions that create disadvantages for other members. Similarly, channel members should agree to direct efforts toward common objectives so channel roles can be structured for maximum marketing effectiveness, which in turn can help members achieve individual objectives. A critical component in cooperation is a precise definition of each channel member's tasks. This provides a basis for reviewing the intermediaries' performance and helps reduce conflicts, because each channel member knows exactly what is expected of it.

channel power The ability of one channel member to influence another member's goal achievement

Channel Conflict

Although all channel members work toward the same general goal—distributing products profitably and efficiently—members sometimes may disagree about the best methods for

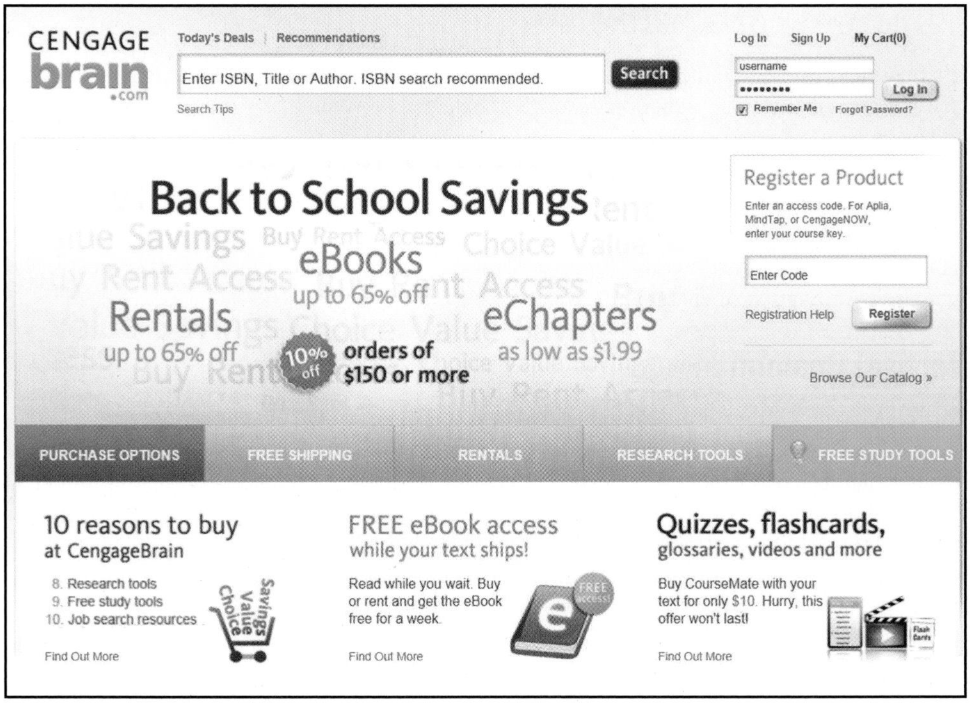

Channel Conflict
Textbook publishers, which traditionally have marketed college textbooks through campus bookstores and now sell textbooks through their own websites, may be experiencing channel conflict.

attaining this goal. However, if self-interest creates misunderstanding about role expectations, the end result is frustration and conflict for the whole channel. For individual organizations to function together, each channel member must clearly communicate and understand the role expectations. Communication difficulties are a potential form of channel conflict because ineffective communication leads to frustration, misunderstandings, and ill-coordinated strategies, jeopardizing further coordination.

The increased use of multiple channels of distribution, driven partly by new technology, has increased the potential for conflict between manufacturers and intermediaries. For instance, Hewlett-Packard makes products available directly to consumers through its website, thereby competing directly with existing distributors and retailers, such as Best Buy. Channel conflicts also arise when intermediaries overemphasize competing products or diversify into product lines traditionally handled by other intermediaries. Sometimes conflict develops because producers strive to increase efficiency by circumventing intermediaries. Such conflict is occurring in marketing channels for computer software. A number of software-only stores are establishing direct relationships with software producers, bypassing wholesale distributors altogether.

When a producer that has traditionally used franchised dealers broadens its retailer base to include other types of retail outlets, considerable conflict can arise. When Goodyear intensified its market coverage by allowing Sears and Discount Tire to market Goodyear tires, its action antagonized 2,500 independent Goodyear dealers.

Although there is no single method for resolving conflict, partnerships can be reestablished if two conditions are met. First, the role of each channel member must be specified. To minimize misunderstanding, all members must be able to expect unambiguous, agreed-upon performance levels from one another. Second, members of channel partnerships must institute certain measures of channel coordination, which requires leadership and benevolent exercise of control. To prevent channel conflict from arising, producers or other channel members may provide competing resellers with different brands, allocate markets among resellers, define policies for direct sales to avoid potential conflict over large accounts, negotiate territorial issues among regional distributors, and provide recognition to certain resellers for their importance in distributing to others.

Channel Integration

Channel members can either combine and control most activities or pass them on to another channel member. Channel functions may be transferred between intermediaries and producers and even to customers. However, a channel member cannot eliminate supply-chain functions; unless buyers themselves perform the functions, they must pay for the labor and resources needed to perform them.

Various channel stages may be combined under the management of a channel captain either horizontally or vertically. Such integration may stabilize supply, reduce costs, and increase coordination of channel members.

Vertical Channel Integration

Vertical channel integration combines two or more stages of the channel under one management. This may occur when one member of a marketing channel purchases the operations of another member or simply performs the functions of another member, eliminating the need for that intermediary. After many costly delays on the production of Boeing's 787 Dreamliner jet, the company opted to vertically integrate and buy some of its suppliers. This decision was motivated by the greater level of control a vertically integrated company has over its entire supply chain.[16]

Unlike conventional channel systems, participants in vertical channel integration coordinate efforts to reach a desired target market. In this more progressive approach to distribution, channel members regard other members as extensions of their own operations. Vertically integrated channels are often more effective against competition because of increased bargaining power and the sharing of information and responsibilities. At one end of a vertically integrated channel, a manufacturer might provide advertising and training assistance, and the retailer at the other end might buy the manufacturer's products in large quantities and actively promote them.

Integration has been successfully institutionalized in a marketing channel called the **vertical marketing system (VMS)**, in which a single channel member coordinates or manages channel activities to achieve efficient, low-cost distribution aimed at satisfying target-market customers. Vertical integration brings most or all stages of the marketing channel under common control or ownership. The Inditex Group, which owns popular clothing retailer Zara, utilizes a VMS so as to achieve channel efficiencies and maintain a maximum amount of control over the supply chain. Zara produces trendy, affordable clothing characterized by high turnover and frequently-changing options. Maintaining control over the design, manufacture, and distribution of its products allows Inditex to maintain a competitive advantage through its low prices and rapid product turnover and maximize efficiencies.[17] Because efforts of individual channel members are combined in a VMS, marketing activities can be coordinated for maximum effectiveness and economy without duplication of services. VMSs are competitive, accounting for a large share of retail sales in consumer goods.

Most vertical marketing systems take one of three forms: corporate, administered, or contractual. A *corporate VMS* combines all stages of the marketing channel, from producers to consumers, under a single owner. For example, clothing retailer The Limited established a corporate VMS that operates corporate-owned production facilities and retail stores. Supermarket chains that own food-processing plants and large retailers that purchase wholesaling and production facilities are other examples of corporate VMSs.

In an *administered VMS,* channel members are independent, but a high level of interorganizational management is achieved through informal coordination. Members of an administered VMS, for example, may adopt uniform accounting and ordering procedures and cooperate in promotional activities for the benefit of all partners. Although individual channel members maintain autonomy, as in conventional marketing channels, one channel member (such as a producer or large retailer) dominates the administered VMS so that distribution decisions take the whole system into account. Because of its size and power, Intel exercises a strong influence over distributors and manufacturers in its marketing channels, as do Kellogg (cereal) and Magnavox (televisions and other electronic products).

vertical channel integration Combining two or more stages of the marketing channel under one management

vertical marketing system (VMS) A marketing channel managed by a single channel member to achieve efficient, low-cost distribution aimed at satisfying target market customers

Under a *contractual VMS,* the most popular type of vertical marketing system, channel members are linked by legal agreements spelling out each member's rights and obligations. Franchise organizations, such as McDonald's and KFC, are contractual VMSs. Other contractual VMSs include wholesaler-sponsored groups, such as IGA (Independent Grocers' Alliance) stores, in which independent retailers band together under the contractual leadership of a wholesaler. Retailer-sponsored cooperatives, which own and operate their own wholesalers, are a third type of contractual VMS.

Horizontal Channel Integration

Combining organizations at the same level of operation under one management constitutes **horizontal channel integration**. An organization may integrate horizontally by merging with other organizations at the same level in the marketing channel. The owner of a dry-cleaning firm, for example, might buy and combine several other existing dry-cleaning establishments. Horizontal integration may enable a firm to generate sufficient sales revenue to integrate vertically as well.

Although horizontal integration permits efficiencies and economies of scale in purchasing, marketing research, advertising, and specialized personnel, it is not always the most effective method of improving distribution. Problems of size often follow, resulting in decreased flexibility, difficulties in coordination, and the need for additional marketing research and large-scale planning. Unless distribution functions for the various units can be performed more efficiently under unified management than under the previously separate managements, horizontal integration will neither reduce costs nor improve the competitive position of the integrating firm.

PHYSICAL DISTRIBUTION IN SUPPLY-CHAIN MANAGEMENT

Physical distribution, also known as *logistics,* refers to the activities used to move products from producers to consumers and other end users. Physical distribution systems must meet the needs of both the supply chain and customers. Distribution activities are thus an important part of supply-chain planning and require the cooperation of all partners.

Within the marketing channel, physical distribution activities may be performed by a producer, a wholesaler, or a retailer, or they may be outsourced. In the context of distribution, *outsourcing* is the contracting of physical distribution tasks to third parties. Most physical distribution activities can be outsourced to third-party firms that have special expertise in areas, such as warehousing, transportation, inventory management, and information technology. Ubiquiti networks, which makes wireless networking equipment, outsources its entire sales function. CEO Robert J. Perea does not believe that salespeople have an organization's best interest in mind. Instead, he relies on Ubiquiti's 50 distributors and hundreds of resellers throughout the supply chain to undertake the task of selling. Because it outsources the sales function to distributors and other channel members, Ubiquiti maintains some of the highest profit margins in the industry. Keeping prices low allows Ubiquiti to compete in developing countries, where many consumers cannot afford high prices.[18]

Cooperative relationships with third-party organizations, such as trucking companies, warehouses, and data-service providers, can help to reduce marketing channel costs and boost service and customer satisfaction for all supply-chain partners. When choosing companies through which to outsource, marketers must be cautious and use efficient firms that help the outsourcing company provide excellent customer service. They also need to recognize the importance of logistics functions like warehousing and information technology in reducing physical distribution costs associated with outsourcing.

Planning an efficient physical distribution system is crucial to developing an effective marketing strategy because it can decrease costs and increase customer satisfaction. Speed of delivery, flexibility, and quality of service are often as important to customers as costs.

horizontal channel integration Combining organizations at the same level of operation under one management

physical distribution Activities used to move products from producers to consumers and other end users

Going Green

Recyclables Travel Via Express Delivery

If you think channels work in only one direction, think again. Marketers not only have to arrange for customers to return defective or unwanted purchases, they also have to think about getting recyclable items and waste to the right places. And that's where reverse channels come in. Companies are under increased pressure from consumers, regulators, and environmental groups to make earth-friendly channel arrangements for handling recyclable and waste materials. In turn, this opens new business opportunities for marketers that can provide cost-effective reverse-channel services, especially for items that need special handling.

DHL, the delivery firm, has a division devoted to picking up recyclables and waste. The idea is to have its yellow trucks and vans carry loads in both directions (to and from businesses), while helping customers comply with strict European environmental rules. Thus, when the 800 JD Wetherspoon pubs in Great Britain receive DHL deliveries of food or beverages, they have aluminum, cardboard, and paper recyclables ready for DHL to haul away.

UPS, another package delivery service, has its own waste recycling program to ensure that electronics that should not end up in landfills are disposed of in the proper way. It has a reverse-channel deal with Toshiba in which consumers bring their broken Toshiba laptops to any U.S. UPS store. UPS sorts and tests the returns, and then transports laptops that can't be repaired to electronic-waste recycle centers for responsible disposal.[c]

Companies that have the right goods, in the right place, at the right time, in the right quantity, and with the right support services are able to sell more than competitors that do not. Even when the demand for products is unpredictable, suppliers must be able to respond quickly to inventory needs. In such cases, physical distribution costs may be a minor consideration when compared with service, dependability, and timeliness.

Customer relationship management systems exploit the information from supply-chain partners' database systems to help logistics managers identify and root out inefficiencies in the supply chain for the benefit of all marketing channel members—from the producer to the ultimate consumer. Indeed, technology is playing a larger and larger role in physical distribution within marketing channels. It has transformed physical distribution by facilitating just-in-time delivery, precise inventory visibility, and instant shipment tracking capabilities, which help companies avoid expensive mistakes, reduce costs, and even generate revenues. Information technology brings visibility to the supply chain by allowing all marketing channel members to see precisely where an item is within the supply chain at any time.[19]

Although physical distribution managers try to minimize the costs associated with order processing, inventory management, materials handling, warehousing, and transportation, decreasing the costs in one area often raises them in another. Figure 15.6 shows the percentage of total costs that physical distribution functions represent. A total-cost approach to physical distribution enables managers to view physical distribution as a system rather than a collection of unrelated activities. This approach shifts the emphasis from lowering the separate costs of individual activities to minimizing overall distribution costs.

Physical distribution managers must be sensitive to the issue of cost trade-offs. Higher costs in one functional area of a distribution system may be necessary to achieve lower costs in another. Trade-offs are strategic decisions to combine (and recombine) resources for greatest cost-effectiveness. When distribution managers regard the system as a network of integrated functions, trade-offs become useful tools in implementing a unified, cost-effective distribution strategy.

Another important goal of physical distribution involves **cycle time**, the time needed to complete a process. For instance, reducing cycle time while maintaining or reducing costs and/or maintaining or increasing customer service is a winning combination in supply chains and ultimately leads to greater end-customer satisfaction. For example, as demand for biofuels

cycle time The time needed to complete a process

Figure 15.6 Proportional Cost of Each Physical Distribution Function as a Percentage of Total Distribution Costs

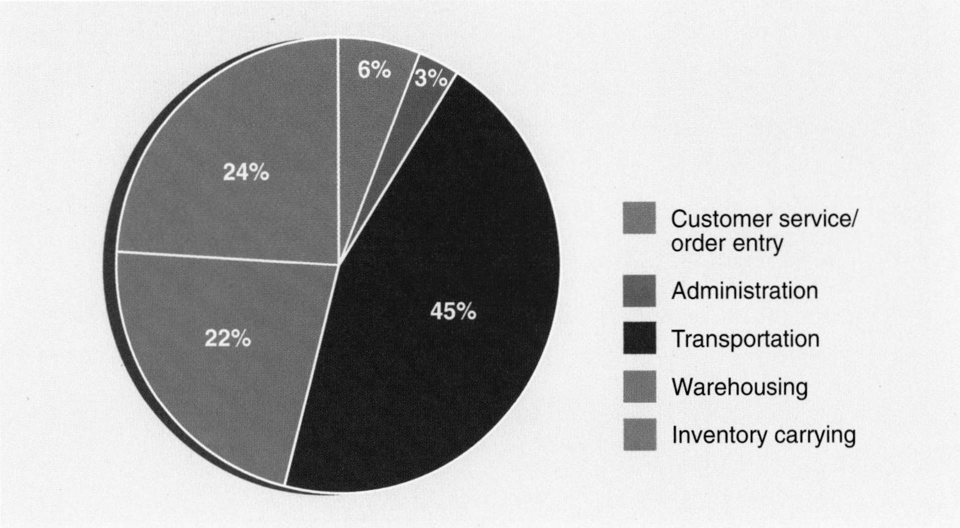

and other renewable energy sources increases, manufacturers have to develop methods for increasing production, increasing processing efficiency, and improving distribution in order to reduce cycle times. In order to meet customer demand, manufacturers have to reduce the amount of time it takes to extract the fuel, process it, and deliver it to final consumers.[20]

In the rest of this section, we take a closer look at a variety of physical distribution activities, including order processing, inventory management, materials handling, warehousing, and transportation.

Order Processing

Order processing is the receipt and transmission of sales order information. Although management sometimes overlooks the importance of these activities, efficient order processing facilitates product flow. Computerized order processing provides a database for all supply-chain members to increase their productivity. When carried out quickly and accurately, order processing contributes to customer satisfaction, decreased costs and cycle time, and increased profits.

Order processing entails three main tasks: order entry, order handling, and order delivery. Order entry begins when customers or salespeople place purchase orders via telephone, regular mail, e-mail, or website. Electronic ordering is less time consuming than a manual, paper-based ordering system and reduces costs. In some companies, sales representatives receive and enter orders personally and also handle complaints, prepare progress reports, and forward sales order information.

Order handling involves several tasks. Once an order is entered, it is transmitted to a warehouse, where product availability is verified, and to the credit department, where prices, terms, and the customer's credit rating are checked. If the credit department approves the purchase, warehouse personnel (sometimes assisted by automated equipment) pick and assemble the order. If the requested product is not in stock, a production order is sent to the factory, or the customer is offered a substitute.

When the order has been assembled and packed for shipment, the warehouse schedules delivery with an appropriate carrier. If the customer pays for rush service, overnight delivery by FedEx, UPS, DHL, or another overnight carrier is used. The customer is sent an invoice, inventory records are adjusted, and the order is delivered.

order processing The receipt and transmission of sales order information

Warehousing and Inventory Management
Warehousing and inventory management efforts are expensive but are important elements in providing customer satisfaction.

© AP Images/Ross D. Franklin

Whether a company uses a manual or an electronic order-processing system depends on which method provides the greater speed and accuracy within cost limits. Manual processing suffices for small-volume orders and is more flexible in certain situations. Most companies, however, use **electronic data interchange (EDI)**, which uses computer technology to integrate order processing with production, inventory, accounting, and transportation. Within the supply chain, EDI functions as an information system that links marketing channel members and outsourcing firms together. It reduces paperwork for all members of the supply chain and allows them to share information on invoices, orders, payments, inquiries, and scheduling. Consequently, many companies have pushed their suppliers toward EDI to reduce distribution costs and cycle times.

Inventory Management

Inventory management involves developing and maintaining adequate assortments of products to meet customers' needs. It is a key component of any effective physical distribution system. Inventory decisions have a major impact on physical distribution costs and the level of customer service provided. When too few products are carried in inventory, the result is *stockouts,* or shortages of products that, in turn, can result in brand switching, lower sales, and loss of customers. When too many products (or too many slow-moving products) are carried, costs increase, as do risks of product obsolescence, pilferage, and damage. The objective of inventory management is to minimize inventory costs while maintaining an adequate supply of goods to satisfy customers. To achieve this objective, marketers focus on two major issues: when to order and how much to order.

To determine when to order, a marketer calculates the *reorder point:* the inventory level that signals the need to place a new order. To calculate the reorder point, the marketer must know the order lead time, the usage rate, and the amount of safety stock required. The *order lead time* refers to the average time lapse between placing the order and receiving it. The *usage rate* is the rate at which a product's inventory is used or sold during a specific time period. *Safety stock* is the amount of extra inventory a firm keeps to guard against stockouts resulting from above-average usage rates and/or longer-than-expected lead times. The reorder point can be calculated using the following formula:

$$\text{reorder point} = (\text{order lead time} \times \text{usage rate}) + \text{safety stock}$$

electronic data interchange (EDI) A computerized means of integrating order processing with production, inventory, accounting, and transportation

inventory management Developing and maintaining adequate assortments of products to meet customers' needs

Thus, if order lead time is 10 days, usage rate is 3 units per day, and safety stock is 20 units, the reorder point is 50 units.

Efficient inventory management with accurate reorder points is crucial for firms that use a **just-in-time (JIT)** approach, in which supplies arrive just as they are needed for use in production or for resale. When using JIT, companies maintain low inventory levels and purchase products and materials in small quantities whenever they need them. Usually there is no safety stock, and suppliers are expected to provide consistently high-quality products. JIT inventory management requires a high level of coordination between producers and suppliers, but it eliminates waste and reduces inventory costs significantly. This approach has been used successfully by many well-known firms—including Harley-Davidson, Dell Computer, and Honda—to reduce costs and boost customer satisfaction. The efficiency gained through a JIT system has allowed Honda to branch into private jet production. The company believes that the technical know-how gained from making automobiles gives it a price and speed advantage over rival personal aircraft makers, such as Embraer and Cessna.[21] When a JIT approach is used in a supply chain, suppliers often move close to their customers.

Materials Handling

Materials handling, the physical handling of tangible goods, supplies, and resources, is an important factor in warehouse operations, as well as in transportation from points of production to points of consumption. Efficient procedures and techniques for materials handling minimize inventory management costs, reduce the number of times a good is handled, improve customer service, and increase customer satisfaction. Systems for packaging, labeling, loading, and movement must be coordinated to maximize cost reduction and customer satisfaction.

A growing number of firms are turning to radio waves to track materials tagged with radio frequency identification (RFID) through every phase of handling. RFID greatly improves the tracking of shipments and reduces cycle times. Hundreds of RFID tags can be read at a time, which represents an advantage over bar codes. RFID has many applications, from tracking inventory to paying for goods and services, and even asset management. Half of all U.S. retailers utilize RFID.[22]

just-in-time (JIT) An inventory-management approach in which supplies arrive just when needed for production or resale

materials handling Physical handling of tangible goods, supplies, and resources

Marketing Debate

Which Are More Earth-Friendly: Online or Traditional Channels?

ISSUE: Are online channels of distribution easier on the environment than traditional channels?

On two of the biggest shopping days of the year—Black Friday and Cyber Monday, the first Friday and Monday after Thanksgiving—the outdoor apparel marketer Patagonia ran online and newspaper ads headlined, "Don't Buy This Jacket." Patagonia, known for its environmental protection policies, wanted consumers to stop and think before they buy, even when choosing products made from recycled materials.

The ads rekindled debates over marketing's environmental impact, including the question of whether online channels (the focus of Cyber Monday promotions) are more earth-friendly than traditional channels (the focus of most Black Friday promotions). When customers buy online, their purchases have to be wrapped for shipment and delivered by mail or by package carrier. Shipping containers are often recyclable but still consume natural resources when manufactured. Most deliveries of online purchases rely on gasoline-powered vehicles or even jet fuel, adding to pollution. Moreover, online marketers consume considerable energy, keeping their websites and warehouses running around the clock.

Traditional channels use lots of energy in lighting, heating, and cooling local stores. Their many employees use fuel commuting to and from store locations, and their many customers use fuel when they visit different stores. Transporting merchandise to warehouses and then individual stores eats up fuel and adds to pollution—as does returning unsold inventory to the manufacturer or sending it to other outlets for sale.[d]

Product characteristics often determine handling. For example, the characteristics of bulk liquids and gases determine how they can be moved and stored. Internal packaging is also an important consideration in materials handling; goods must be packaged correctly to prevent damage or breakage during handling and transportation. Most companies employ packaging consultants during the product design process to help them decide which packaging materials and methods will result in the most efficient handling.

Unit loading and containerization are two common methods used in materials handling. With *unit loading,* one or more boxes are placed on a pallet or skid; these units can then be loaded efficiently by mechanical means, such as forklifts, trucks, or conveyer systems. *Containerization* is the consolidation of many items into a single, large container that is sealed at its point of origin and opened at its destination. Containers are usually 8 feet wide, 8 feet high, and 10 to 40 feet long. They can be conveniently stacked and shipped via train, barge, or ship. Once containers reach their destinations, wheel assemblies can be added to make them suitable for ground transportation. Because individual items are not handled in transit, containerization greatly increases efficiency and security in shipping.

Warehousing

Warehousing, the design and operation of facilities for storing and moving goods, is another important physical distribution function. Warehousing provides time utility by enabling firms to compensate for dissimilar production and consumption rates. When mass production creates a greater stock of goods than can be sold immediately, companies may warehouse the surplus until customers are ready to buy. Warehousing also helps to stabilize prices and the availability of seasonal items.

The choice of warehouse facilities is an important strategic consideration. The right type of warehouse allows a company to reduce transportation and inventory costs or improve service to customers. The wrong type of warehouse may drain company resources. Beyond deciding how many facilities to operate and where to locate them, a company must determine which type of warehouse is most appropriate. Warehouses fall into two general categories: private and public. In many cases, a combination of private and public facilities provides the most flexible warehousing approach.

Companies operate **private warehouses** for shipping and storing their own products. A firm usually leases or purchases a private warehouse when its warehousing needs in a given geographic market are substantial and stable enough to warrant a long-term commitment to a fixed facility. Private warehouses are also appropriate for firms that require special handling and storage and that want control of warehouse design and operation. Retailers like Sears and Radio Shack find it economical to integrate private warehousing with purchasing and distribution for their retail outlets. When sales volumes are fairly stable, ownership and control of a private warehouse may provide benefits, such as property appreciation. Private warehouses, however, face fixed costs, such as insurance, taxes, maintenance, and debt expense. They also limit flexibility when firms wish to move inventories to more strategic locations. Many private warehouses are being eliminated by direct links between producers and customers, reduced cycle times, and outsourcing to public warehouses.

Public warehouses lease storage space and related physical distribution facilities to other companies. They sometimes provide distribution services, such as receiving, unloading, inspecting, and reshipping products; filling orders; providing financing; displaying products; and coordinating shipments. Distribution Unlimited Inc., for example, offers a wide range of such services through its facilities in New York, which contain more than 8 million total square feet of warehouse space.[23]

Public warehouses are especially useful to firms that have seasonal production or low-volume storage needs, have inventories that must be maintained in many locations, are testing or entering new markets, or own private warehouses but occasionally require additional storage space. Public warehouses also serve as collection points during product-recall programs. Whereas private warehouses have fixed costs, public warehouses offer variable (and often lower) costs because users rent space and purchase warehousing services only as needed.

warehousing The design and operation of facilities for storing and moving goods

private warehouses Company-operated facilities for storing and shipping products

public warehouses Storage space and related physical distribution facilities that can be leased by companies

Many public warehouses furnish security for products that are used as collateral for loans, a service provided at either the warehouse or the site of the owner's inventory. *Field public warehouses* are established by public warehouses at the owner's inventory location. The warehouser becomes custodian of the products and issues a receipt that can be used as collateral for a loan. Public warehouses also provide *bonded storage,* a warehousing arrangement in which imported or taxable products are not released until the products' owners pay U.S. customs duties, taxes, or other fees. Bonded warehouses enable firms to defer tax payments on such items until they are delivered to customers.

Distribution centers are large facilities used for receiving, warehousing, and redistributing products to stores or customers. Distribution centers are specially designed for rapid flow of products. They are usually one-story buildings (to eliminate elevators) with access to transportation networks, such as major highways and/or railway lines. Many distribution centers are highly automated, with computer-directed robots, forklifts, and hoists that collect and move products to loading docks. The discount chain called Dollar Tree, for example, operates nine distribution centers around the country, which allows it to efficiently supply its more than 4,300 stores. Dollar stores generally offer a rapidly-changing assortment of merchandise and require efficient restocking capabilities. Distribution over large geographic areas can be complicated, and having strategically located distribution centers can help a company meet consumer demand.[24] Although some public warehouses offer such specialized services, most distribution centers are privately owned. They serve customers in regional markets and, in some cases, function as consolidation points for a company's branch warehouses.

Transportation

Transportation, the movement of products from where they are made to intermediaries and end users, is the most expensive physical distribution function. Today, approximately 10 percent of a company's total expenses are freight charges.[25] Because product availability and timely deliveries depend on transportation functions, transportation decisions directly affect customer service. A firm may even build its distribution and marketing strategy around a unique transportation system if that system can ensure on-time deliveries and thereby give the firm a competitive edge. Companies may build their own transportation fleets (private carriers) or outsource the transportation function to a common or contract carrier.

Transportation Modes

The basic transportation modes for moving physical goods are railroads, trucks, waterways, airways, and pipelines. Each has distinct advantages. Many companies adopt physical handling procedures that facilitate the use of two or more modes in combination. Table 15.3 shows the percentage of intercity freight carried by each transportation mode.

Railroads like Union Pacific and Canadian National carry heavy, bulky freight that must be shipped long distances over land. Railroads commonly haul minerals, sand, lumber, chemicals, and farm products, as well as low-value manufactured goods and automobiles. However, transporting chemicals via railroads can be dangerous in an accident. Currently, Clorox is changing the way it manufactures its product, eliminating chlorine gas, to make the product safer to transport via rail.[26] Railroads are especially efficient for transporting full carloads, which can be shipped at lower rates than smaller quantities, because they require less handling. Many companies locate factories or warehouses near rail lines for convenient loading and unloading.

Trucks provide the most flexible schedules and routes of all major transportation modes in the United States, because they can go almost anywhere. Because trucks have a unique ability to move goods directly from factory or warehouse to customer, they are often used in conjunction with other forms of transport that cannot provide door-to-door deliveries. Trucks are more expensive and somewhat more vulnerable to bad weather than trains. They are also subject to size and weight restrictions on the products they carry. Trucks are sometimes

distribution centers Large, centralized warehouses that focus on moving rather than storing goods

transportation The movement of products from where they are made to intermediaries and end users

Table 15.3 Characteristics and Ratings of Transportation Modes by Selection Criteria

Selection Criteria	Railroads	Trucks	Pipelines	Waterways	Airplanes
Cost	Moderate	High	Low	Very low	Very high
Speed	Average	Fast	Slow	Very slow	Very fast
Dependability	Average	High	High	Average	High
Load flexibility	High	Average	Very low	Very high	Low
Accessibility	High	Very high	Very limited	Limited	Average
Frequency	Low	High	Very high	Very low	Average
Products carried	Coal, grain, lumber, paper and pulp products, chemicals	Clothing, computers, books, groceries and produce, livestock	Oil, processed coal, natural gas	Chemicals, bauxite, grain, motor vehicles, agricultural implements	Flowers, food (highly perishable), technical instruments, emergency parts and equipment, overnight mail

criticized for high levels of loss and damage to freight and for delays caused by the rehandling of small shipments.

Waterways are the cheapest method of shipping heavy, low-value, nonperishable goods, such as ore, coal, grain, and petroleum products. Water carriers offer considerable capacity. Powered by tugboats and towboats, barges that travel along intracoastal canals, inland rivers, and navigation systems can haul at least 10 times the weight of one rail car, and oceangoing vessels can haul thousands of containers. The vast majority of international cargo is transported by water at least part of the way. However, many markets are inaccessible by water transportation unless supplemented by rail or truck. Droughts and floods also may create difficulties for users of inland waterway transportation. Nevertheless, the extreme fuel efficiency of water transportation and the continuing globalization of marketing will likely increase its use in the future.

Air transportation is the fastest but most expensive form of shipping. It is used most often for perishable goods; for high-value, low-bulk items; and for products that require quick delivery over long distances, such as emergency shipments. Some air carriers transport combinations of passengers, freight, and mail. Despite its expense, air transit can reduce warehousing and packaging costs and losses from theft and damage, thus helping to lower total costs (but truck transportation needed for pickup and final delivery adds to cost and transit time). Although air transport accounts for a small minority of total cargo carried, it is an important form of transportation in an increasingly time-sensitive business environment.[27] In fact, the success of many businesses is now based on the availability of overnight air delivery service provided by organizations, such as UPS, FedEx, DHL, RPS Air, and the U.S. Postal Service. Amazon.com, for example, ships many of the products that are ordered online via UPS within one day.

Pipelines, the most automated transportation mode, usually belong to the shipper and carry the shipper's products. Most pipelines carry petroleum products or chemicals. The Trans-Alaska Pipeline, owned and operated by a consortium of oil companies that includes ExxonMobil and BP, transports crude oil from remote oil-drilling sites in central Alaska to shipping terminals on the coast. Slurry pipelines carry pulverized coal, grain, or wood chips suspended in water. Pipelines move products slowly but continuously and at relatively low cost. They are dependable and minimize the problems of product damage and theft. However, contents are subject to as much as 1 percent shrinkage, usually from evaporation. Pipelines also have been a concern to environmentalists, who fear installation and leaks could harm plants and animals.

Choosing Transportation Modes

Logistics managers select a transportation mode based on the combination of cost, speed, dependability, load flexibility, accessibility, and frequency that is most appropriate for their products and generates the desired level of customer service. Table 15.3 shows relative ratings of each transportation mode by these selection criteria.

Marketers compare alternative transportation modes to determine whether the benefits from a more expensive mode are worth the higher costs. Companies like Port Logistics can assist marketers in analyzing various transportation options. Port Logistics is a supply chain logistics consulting firm that offers a wide range of services, such as determining the best channels and transportation options. Port Logistics even helps firms with considerations like sustainability through reducing transportation fuel outputs, increasing renewable energy usage, and reducing waste. The company demonstrated its commitment to the environment by converting its own fleet of trucks to clean power, resulting in a fleet that even meets California's stringent clean air standards.[28]

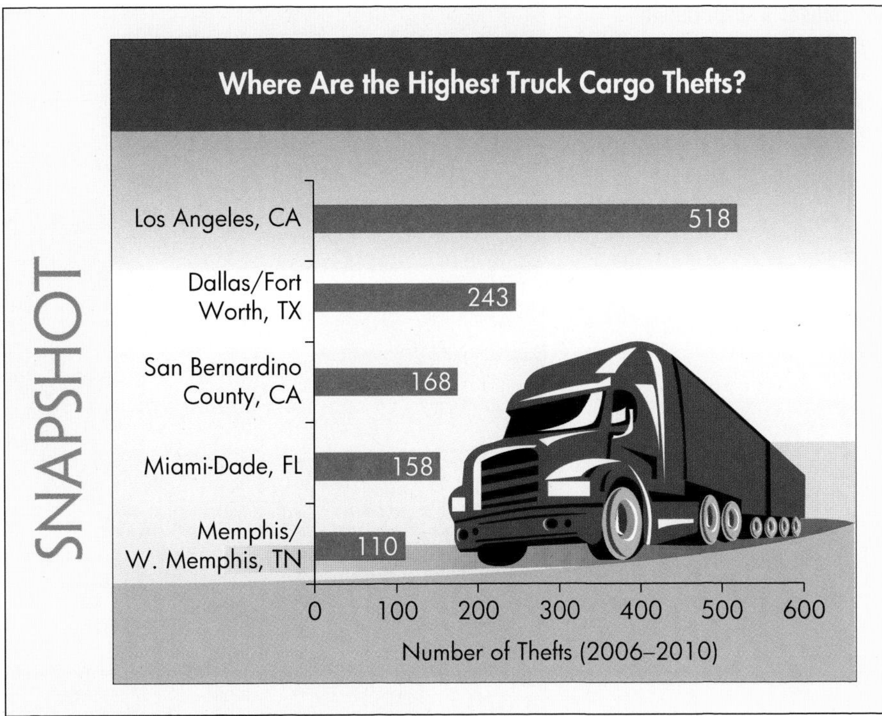

Source: "FreightWatch Special Report: US Cargo Theft: A Five-Year Review," FreightWatch, April 2, 2011, www.asisonline.org/toolkit/freightwatch.pdf.

Coordinating Transportation

To take advantage of the benefits offered by various transportation modes and compensate for deficiencies, marketers often combine and coordinate two or more modes. In recent years, **intermodal transportation**, as this integrated approach is sometimes called, has become easier because of new developments within the transportation industry. Several kinds of intermodal shipping are available. All combine the flexibility of trucking with the low cost or speed of other forms of transport. Containerization facilitates intermodal transportation by consolidating shipments into sealed containers for transport by *piggyback* (shipping that uses both truck trailers and railway flatcars), *fishyback* (shipping that uses truck trailers and water carriers), and *birdyback* (shipping that uses truck trailers and air carriers). As transportation costs have increased, intermodal shipping has gained popularity. To transport its floor cleaners to retail locations, Electrolux relies on several modes of transportation, which include water, rail, and truck carriers. The majority of products are shipped from Asia to ports in the United States, transported to the distribution center in El Paso, Texas, via rail, and finally hauled to destinations via trucks.[29]

Specialized outsource agencies provide other forms of transport coordination. Known as **freight forwarders**, these firms combine shipments from several organizations into efficient lot sizes. Small loads (less than 500 pounds) are much more expensive to ship than full carloads or truckloads, which frequently require consolidation. Freight forwarders take small loads from various marketers, buy transport space from carriers, and arrange for goods to be delivered to buyers. For instance, L'Oréal USA uses freight forwarders for shipments that are less-than-truckload, weighing less than 20,000 pounds.[30] Freight forwarders' profits come from the margin between the higher, less-than-carload rates they charge each marketer and the lower carload rates they themselves pay. Because large shipments require less handling, use of freight forwarders can speed delivery. Freight forwarders can also determine the most

intermodal transportation Two or more transportation modes used in combination

freight forwarders Organizations that consolidate shipments from several firms into efficient lot sizes

Intermodal Transportation Containers facilitate intermodal transportation, because they can be transported by ships, trains, and trucks.

efficient carriers and routes and are useful for shipping goods to foreign markets. Fracht is a major international freight forwarder, serving large and small firms all over the world through its network of international offices. The company provides services to handle major large equipment or small and delicate items.[31] Some companies prefer to outsource their shipping to freight forwarders, because the forwarders provide door-to-door service.

Another transportation innovation is the development of **megacarriers**, freight transportation companies that offer several shipment methods, including rail, truck, and air service. CSX, for example, has trains, barges, container ships, trucks, and pipelines, thus offering a multitude of transportation services. In addition, air carriers have increased their ground-transportation services. As they expand the range of transportation alternatives, carriers also put greater stress on customer service.

LEGAL ISSUES IN CHANNEL MANAGEMENT

The numerous federal, state, and local laws governing channel management are based on the general principle that the public is best served by protecting competition and free trade. Under the authority of such federal legislation as the Sherman Antitrust Act and the Federal Trade Commission Act, courts and regulatory agencies determine under what circumstances channel management practices violate this underlying principle and must be restricted. Although channel managers are not expected to be legal experts, they should be aware that attempts to control distribution functions may have legal repercussions. The following practices are among those frequently subject to legal restraint.

Dual Distribution

megacarriers Freight transportation firms that provide several modes of shipment

Earlier, we noted that some companies may use dual distribution by using two or more marketing channels to distribute the same products to the same target market. Hewlett-Packard, for example, sells computers directly to consumers through a toll-free telephone line and a website, as well as through electronics retailers like Best Buy. Courts do not consider this practice illegal when it promotes competition. A manufacturer can also legally open its own retail outlets. But the courts view as a threat to competition a manufacturer that uses company-owned outlets to dominate or drive out of business independent retailers or distributors that handle its products. In such cases, dual distribution violates the law. To avoid this interpretation, producers should use outlet prices that do not severely undercut independent retailers' prices.

Restricted Sales Territories

To tighten control over distribution of its products, a manufacturer may try to prohibit intermediaries from selling its products outside designated sales territories. Intermediaries themselves often favor this practice, because it gives them exclusive territories, allowing them to avoid competition for the producer's brands within these territories. In recent years, the courts have adopted conflicting positions in regard to restricted sales territories. Although the courts have deemed restricted sales territories a restraint of trade among intermediaries handling the same brands (except for small or newly established companies), they have also held that exclusive territories can actually promote competition among dealers handling different brands. At present, the producer's intent in establishing restricted territories and the overall effect of doing so on the market must be evaluated for each individual case.

Tying Agreements

When a supplier (usually a manufacturer or franchiser) furnishes a product to a channel member with the stipulation that the channel member must purchase other products as well, a **tying agreement** exists. Suppliers may institute tying agreements to move weaker products along with more popular items, or a franchiser may tie purchase of equipment and supplies to the sale of franchises, justifying the policy as necessary for quality control and protection of the franchiser's reputation.

A related practice is *full-line forcing,* in which a supplier requires that channel members purchase the supplier's entire line to obtain any of the supplier's products. Manufacturers sometimes use full-line forcing to ensure that intermediaries accept new products and that a suitable range of products is available to customers.

The courts accept tying agreements when the supplier alone can provide products of a certain quality, when the intermediary is free to carry competing products as well, and when a company has just entered the market. Most other tying agreements are considered illegal.

Exclusive Dealing

When a manufacturer forbids an intermediary to carry products of competing manufacturers, the arrangement is called **exclusive dealing**. Manufacturers receive considerable market protection in an exclusive-dealing arrangement and may cut off shipments to intermediaries that violate the agreement.

The legality of an exclusive-dealing contract is generally determined by applying three tests. If the exclusive dealing blocks competitors from as much as 15 percent of the market, the sales volume is large, and the producer is considerably larger than the retailer, then the arrangement is considered anticompetitive. If dealers and customers in a given market have access to similar products or if the exclusive-dealing contract strengthens an otherwise weak competitor, the arrangement is allowed.

Refusal to Deal

For more than 75 years, the courts have held that producers have the right to choose channel members with which they will do business (and the right to reject others). Within existing distribution channels, however, suppliers may not legally refuse to deal with wholesalers or dealers merely because these wholesalers or dealers resist policies that are anticompetitive or in restraint of trade. Suppliers are further prohibited from organizing some channel members in refusal-to-deal actions against other members that choose not to comply with illegal policies.

tying agreement An agreement in which a supplier furnishes a product to a channel member with the stipulation that the channel member must purchase other products as well

exclusive dealing A situation in which a manufacturer forbids an intermediary from carrying products of competing manufacturers

Summary

1. To describe the foundations of supply-chain management

The distribution component of the marketing mix focuses on the decisions and activities involved in making products available to customers when and where they want to purchase them. An important function of distribution is the joint effort of all involved organizations to be part of creating an effective supply chain, which refers to all the activities associated with the flow and transformation of products from raw materials through to the end customer. Operations management is the total set of managerial activities used by an organization to transform resource inputs into products, services, or both. Logistics management involves planning, implementation, and controlling the efficient and effective flow and storage of goods, services, and information from the point of origin to consumption in order to meet customers' needs and wants. Supply management in its broadest form refers to the processes that enable the progress of value from raw material to final customer and back to redesign and final disposition. Supply-chain management therefore refers to a set of approaches used to integrate the functions of operations management, logistics management, supply management, and marketing channel management so that products and services are produced and distributed in the right quantities, to the right locations, and at the right time. The supply chain includes all entities—shippers and other firms that facilitate distribution, as well as producers, wholesalers, and retailers—that distribute products and benefit from cooperative efforts.

2. To explore the role and significance of marketing channels and supply chains

A marketing channel, or channel of distribution, is a group of individuals and organizations that direct the flow of products from producers to customers. The major role of marketing channels is to make products available at the right time, at the right place, and in the right amounts. In most channels of distribution, producers and consumers are linked by marketing intermediaries. The two major types of intermediaries are retailers, which purchase products and resell them to ultimate consumers, and wholesalers, which buy and resell products to other wholesalers, retailers, and business customers.

Marketing channels serve many functions. They create time, place, and possession utilities by making products available when and where customers want them and providing customers with access to product use through sale or rental. Marketing intermediaries facilitate exchange efficiencies, often reducing the costs of exchanges by performing certain services and functions. Although some critics suggest eliminating wholesalers, the functions of the intermediaries in the marketing channel must be performed. As such, eliminating one or more intermediaries results in other organizations in the channel having to do more. Because intermediaries serve both producers and buyers, they reduce the total number of transactions that otherwise would be needed to move products from producer to the end customer.

3. To identify types of marketing channels

Channels of distribution are broadly classified as channels for consumer products and channels for business products. Within these two broad categories, different channels are used for different products. Although consumer goods can move directly from producer to consumers, consumer channels that include wholesalers and retailers are usually more economical and knowledge-efficient. Distribution of business products differs from that of consumer products in the types of channels used. A direct distribution channel is common in business marketing. Also used are channels containing industrial distributors, manufacturers' agents, and a combination of agents and distributors. Most producers have multiple or dual channels so the distribution system can be adjusted for various target markets.

4. To understand factors that influence marketing channel selection

Selecting an appropriate marketing channel is a crucial decision for supply-chain managers. To determine which channel is most appropriate, managers must think about customer characteristics, the type of organization, product attributes, competition, environmental forces, and the availability and characteristics of intermediaries. Careful consideration of these factors will assist a supply-chain manager in selecting the correct channel.

5. To identify the intensity of market coverage

A marketing channel is managed such that products receive appropriate market coverage. In choosing intensive distribution, producers strive to make a product available to all possible dealers. In selective distribution, only some outlets in an area are chosen to distribute a product. Exclusive distribution usually gives a single dealer rights to sell a product in a large geographic area.

6. To examine strategic issues in marketing channels, including leadership, cooperation, and conflict

Each channel member performs a different role in the system and agrees to accept certain rights, responsibilities, rewards, and sanctions for nonconformance. Although many marketing channels are determined by consensus, some are organized and controlled by a single leader, or channel captain. A channel captain may be a producer, wholesaler, or retailer.

A marketing channel functions most effectively when members cooperate; when they deviate from their roles, channel conflict can arise.

Integration of marketing channels brings various activities under one channel member's management. Vertical integration combines two or more stages of the channel under one management. The vertical marketing system (VMS) is managed centrally for the mutual benefit of all channel members. Vertical marketing systems may be corporate, administered, or contractual. Horizontal integration combines institutions at the same level of channel operation under a single management.

7. To examine physical distribution as a part of supply-chain management

Physical distribution, or logistics, refers to the activities used to move products from producers to customers and other end users. These activities include order processing, inventory management, materials handling, warehousing, and transportation. An efficient physical distribution system is an important component of an overall marketing strategy, because it can decrease costs and increase customer satisfaction. Within the marketing channel, physical distribution activities are often performed by a wholesaler, but they may also be performed by a producer or retailer or outsourced to a third party. Efficient physical distribution systems can decrease costs and transit time while increasing customer service.

Order processing is the receipt and transmission of sales order information. It consists of three main tasks—order entry, order handling, and order delivery—that may be done manually but are more often handled through electronic data interchange systems. Inventory management involves developing and maintaining adequate assortments of products to meet customers' needs. Logistics managers must strive to find the optimal level of inventory to satisfy customer needs while keeping costs down. Materials handling, the physical handling of products, is a crucial element in warehousing and transporting products. Warehousing involves the design and operation of facilities for storing and moving goods; such facilities may be privately owned or public. Transportation, the movement of products from where they are made to where they are purchased and used, is the most expensive physical distribution function. The basic modes of transporting goods include railroads, trucks, waterways, airways, and pipelines.

8. To explore legal issues in channel management

Federal, state, and local laws regulate channel management to protect competition and free trade. Courts may prohibit or permit a practice depending on whether it violates this underlying principle. Channel management practices frequently subject to legal restraint include dual distribution, restricted sales territories, tying agreements, exclusive dealing, and refusal to deal. When these practices strengthen weak competitors or increase competition among dealers, they may be permitted; in most other cases, when competition may be weakened considerably, they are deemed illegal.

Go to www.cengagebrain.com for resources to help you master the content in this chapter as well as materials that will expand your marketing knowledge!

Important Terms

distribution 482
supply chain 482
operations management 482
logistics management 482
supply management 482
supply-chain management 482
marketing channel 483
marketing intermediaries 484
industrial distributor 490
dual distribution 491
strategic channel alliance 491
intensive distribution 494
selective distribution 495
exclusive distribution 495
channel captain 497
channel power 498
vertical channel integration 500
vertical marketing system (VMS) 500
horizontal channel integration 501
physical distribution 501
cycle time 502
order processing 503
electronic data interchange (EDI) 504
inventory management 504
just-in-time (JIT) 505
materials handling 505
warehousing 506
private warehouses 506
public warehouses 506
distribution centers 507
transportation 507
intermodal transportation 509
freight forwarders 509
megacarriers 510
tying agreement 511
exclusive dealing 511

Discussion and Review Questions

1. Define supply-chain management. Why is it important?
2. Describe the major functions of marketing channels. Why are these functions better accomplished through combined efforts of channel members?
3. List several reasons consumers often blame intermediaries for distribution inefficiencies.
4. Compare and contrast the four major types of marketing channels for consumer products. Through which type of channel is each of the following products most likely to be distributed?
   a. New automobiles
   b. Saltine crackers
   c. Cut-your-own Christmas trees
   d. New textbooks
   e. Sofas
   f. Soft drinks
5. Outline the four most common channels for business products. Describe the products or situations that lead marketers to choose each channel.
6. Describe an industrial distributor. What types of products are marketed through an industrial distributor?
7. Under what conditions is a producer most likely to use more than one marketing channel?
8. Identify and describe the factors that may influence marketing channel selection decisions.
9. Explain the differences among intensive, selective, and exclusive methods of distribution.
10. "Channel cooperation requires that members support the overall channel goals to achieve individual goals." Comment on this statement.
11. Explain the major characteristics of each of the three types of vertical marketing systems (VMSs): corporate, administered, and contractual.
12. Discuss the cost and service trade-offs involved in developing a physical distribution system.
13. What are the main tasks involved in order processing?
14. Explain the trade-offs that inventory managers face when they reorder products or supplies. How is the reorder point computed?
15. Explain the major differences between private and public warehouses. How do they differ from a distribution center?
16. Compare and contrast the five major transportation modes in terms of cost, speed, and dependability.
17. Under what conditions are tying agreements, exclusive dealing, and dual distribution judged illegal?

Application Questions

1. *Supply-chain management* involves long-term partnerships among channel members that are working together to reduce inefficiencies, costs, and redundancies and develop innovative approaches to satisfy customers. Select one of the following companies and explain how supply-chain management could increase marketing productivity.
   a. Dell
   b. FedEx
   c. Nike
   d. Taco Bell
2. Marketers can select from three major levels of marketing coverage when determining the number and kinds of outlets in which to sell a product: intensive, selective, or exclusive distribution. Characteristics of the product and its target market determine the intensity of coverage a product should receive. Indicate the intensity level best suited for the following products, and explain why it is appropriate.
   a. Personal computers
   b. Deodorant
   c. Canon digital cameras
   d. Nike athletic shoes
3. Describe the decision process you might go through if you were attempting to determine the most appropriate distribution channel for one of the following:
   a. Shotguns for hunters
   b. Women's lingerie
   c. Telephone systems for small businesses
   d. Toy trucks for 2-year-olds
4. Assume that you are responsible for the physical distribution of computers at a web-based company. What would you do to ensure product availability, timely delivery, and quality service for your customers?
5. IMP Keurig is the North American leader in single-cup coffee brewing. Introduced in 1998, the Keurig system uses self-contained coffee K-Cups, which allow users to brew one cup of coffee or other hot beverage in about one minute. After the K-Cup is pierced with a nozzle, hot water is forced through its contents and filter and into a mug below. Because the K-Cup is self-contained, disposal is easy and cleanup is almost totally eliminated. Keurig was purchased by Green Mountain Coffee Roasters in 2006, and today offers more than 200 different beverages, including specialty beverages from Dunkin' Donuts, Wolfgang Puck, and Caribou Coffee.

Keurig's K-Cups are sold in many supermarkets, selected big box stores, and some specialty stores. Macy's, for example, has a small selection of popular flavors displayed next to its coffee-maker aisle. K-Cups also can be found online at specialty coffee websites as well as both the Keurig and Green Mountain Coffee Roasters e-commerce stores.

Describe the different channels used to distribute Keurig's K-Cups in terms of customer characteristics, competition, and characteristics of the intermediaries. How would you define the intensity of market coverage? Does it make sense? Are there any strategic issues in managing these marketing channels?

Internet Exercise

FedEx

Many companies lack their own distribution systems. Firms in this situation may rely on the services provided by companies like FedEx to handle their distribution. Learn more about the services provided by FedEx at www.fedex.com.

1. What tools does FedEx provide to make the shipping process easier?
2. Other than shipping products, what other services does FedEx provide?
3. Is there information on the FedEx website that would help a potential FedEx customer evaluate FedEx regarding some of the selection criteria shown in Table 15.3?

developing your marketing plan

One of the key components in a successful marketing strategy is the plan for getting the products to your customer. To make the best decisions about where, when, and how your products will be made available to the customer, you need to know more about how these distribution decisions relate to other marketing mix elements in your marketing plan. To assist you in relating the information in this chapter to your marketing plan, consider the following issues:

1. Marketing intermediaries perform many activities. Using Table 15.2 as a guide, discuss the types of activities where a channel member could provide needed assistance.
2. Using Figure 15.2 (or 15.3 if your product is a business product), determine which of the channel distribution paths is most appropriate for your product. Given the nature of your product, could it be distributed through more than one of these paths?
3. Determine the level of distribution intensity that is appropriate for your product. Consider the characteristics of your target market(s), the product attributes, and environmental factors in your deliberation.
4. Discuss the physical functions that will be required for distributing your product, focusing on materials handling, warehousing, and transportation.

The information obtained from these questions should assist you in developing various aspects of your marketing plan found in the "Interactive Marketing Plan" exercise at www.cengagebrain.com.

video case 15.1

Taza Cultivates Channel Relationships with Chocolate

Taza Chocolate is a small Massachusetts-based manufacturer of stone-ground organic chocolate made in the classic Mexican tradition. Founded in 2006, Taza markets most of its products through U.S. retailers, wholesalers, and distributors. Individual customers around the world can also buy Taza chocolate bars, baking squares, chocolate-covered nuts, and other specialty items directly from the Taza website. If they live in Somerville, Massachusetts, they might even find a Taza employee riding a "chococycle," selling products and distributing samples at an upscale food truck festival or a weekend market festival.

Taza seeks to make personal connections with all the certified organic growers who supply its ingredients. "Because our process here at the factory is so minimal," says the company's director of sales, "it's really important that we get a very high-quality ingredient. To make sure that we're getting the absolute cream of the [cocoa] crop, we have a direct face-to-face human relationship between us and the actual farmer who's producing those beans."

Dealing directly with suppliers allows Taza to meet its social responsibility goals while ensuring the kind of quality that commands a premium price. "We're a premium brand," explains the director of sales, "and because of the way we do what we do, we have to charge more than your average chocolate bar." A Taza chocolate bar that sells at a retail price of $4.50 carries a wholesale price of about $2.70. The distributor's price, however, is even lower, closer to $2.00.

Distributors buy in the largest quantities, which for Taza means a pallet load rather than a case that a wholesaler would buy. "But wholesale will always be our bread and butter, where we really move the volume and we have good margins," says Taza's director of sales. In the company's experience, distributors are very price-conscious and more interested than wholesalers in promotions and extras.

Taza offers factory tours at its Somerville site, charging a small entrance fee that includes a donation to Sustainable Harvest International. There, visitors can watch the bean-to-bar process from beginning to end, learning about the beans and the stone-ground tradition that differentiates Taza from European chocolates. Visitors enjoy product samples along the way and, at the end of the tour, they can browse through the factory store and buy freshly-made specialties like chipotle chili chocolate and ginger chocolate. On holidays like Halloween and Valentine's Day, Taza hosts special tastings and limited-edition treats to attract customers to its factory store. Its annual beer-and-chocolate pairing event, hosted with the Drink Craft Beer website, is another way to introduce Taza to consumers who appreciate quality foods and drinks.

Taza's marketing communications focus mainly on Facebook, Twitter, blogs, e-mail, and specialty food shows. Also, the company frequently offers samples in upscale and organic food stores in major metropolitan areas. As it does with its growers, Taza seeks to forge personal relationships with its channel partners. "When we send a shipment of chocolate," says the sales director, "sometimes we'll put in a little extra for the people who work there. That always helps because [it's] building that kind of human relationship."

Privately-owned Taza has begun shipping to Canada and a handful of European countries. Its channel arrangements must allow for delivering perishable products that stay fresh and firm, no matter what the weather. As a result, distributors often hold some Taza inventory in refrigerated warehouses to have ready for next-day delivery when retailers place orders.[32]

Questions for Discussion

1. Which distribution channels does Taza use, and why are they appropriate for this company?
2. In what ways does Taza benefit from selling directly to some consumers? What are some potential problems of selling directly to consumers?
3. In what ways are Taza's distribution efforts influenced by the fact that its products are organic?

case 15.2

Dell Direct and Not-So-Direct

When Michael Dell started his Texas-based computer business in 1984, he chose a distribution strategy that was radically different from that of other computer marketers. Instead of selling through wholesalers and retailers, the company dealt directly with customers. This kept costs low and allowed Dell to cater to customers' needs by building each computer to order. Using a direct channel also minimized inventory costs and reduced the risk that parts and products would become obsolete even before customers placed their orders, a constant concern in high-tech industries.

By 1997, Dell's website alone was responsible for $1 million a day in sales. Relying on the strength of its online sales, catalogs, and phone orders, Dell expanded beyond the United States and added new products for four target markets: consumers, large corporations, small businesses, and government agencies. Meanwhile, Apple, Hewlett-Packard, and other competitors were reaching out to many of the same segments with a combination of direct and indirect channels. Apple Stores, for example, proved to be major customer magnets and gave a significant boost to sales of Macintosh computers and other Apple electronics. Hewlett-Packard forged strong ties with value-added resellers (VARs), intermediaries that assemble systems of computers, servers, and other products customized to meet the special needs of business buyers.

© Eddie Seal/Bloomberg via Getty Images

Although Dell tested retail distribution on a number of occasions, it never let the experiments go on too long. In the 1990s, it tried selling PCs through a few big U.S. retail chains but soon discontinued the arrangement because the profit margins were lower than in the direct channel. Later, it opened a series of retail kiosks in major U.S. markets to display products and answer customers' questions. Unlike stores, however, the kiosks didn't actually sell anything: customers could only place orders for future delivery. Dell ultimately closed the kiosks down.

By 2007, with competitors coming on strong, Dell was ready to rethink its channel strategy. As convenient as online shopping was for many U.S. computer buyers, it was much less popular in many other countries. To gain market share domestically and internationally, Dell would have to follow consumers into stores, malls, and downtown shopping districts. The company began selling a few models through Walmart's U.S. stores, Carphone Warehouse's U.K. stores, Bic Camera's Japanese stores, and Gome's Chinese stores. In addition, it opened Dell stores in Moscow, Budapest, and other world capitals.

Soon, sales through retailers had gained enough momentum that Dell sought out other retail deals. Today, Dell sells through more than 50,000 retailers worldwide. Customers who browse the Dell website can easily find a local retail location if they want to take a product home right away. In another channel change, Dell has begun working with VAR partners that serve small- and medium-sized businesses, and it has lined up wholesalers for Europe, Latin America, and elsewhere.

As successful as Dell has been in revamping its indirect channels, selling directly to customers remains a top priority. Dell invites orders around the clock through webpages tailored to the needs of each target market. It also maintains an online outlet store to sell discontinued and refurbished products. It mails millions of catalogs and direct-mail pieces every year. And its sales force calls on government officials and big businesses that buy in volume.

Moreover, the company is a pioneer in stimulating exchanges with customers through social media, such as Facebook and Twitter. In less than three years, it generated $6.5 million in revenue from sales transactions that originated on Twitter. That may be a tiny sliver of Dell's $62 billion in annual revenue, but it demonstrates the company's flexibility in adapting to shifts in customer behavior and environmental forces, such as technological advances. The company also maintains a Social Media Listening Command Center to monitor conversations about the brand and its goods and services. With market-share and profit-margin challenges still facing the company, and global demand just picking up steam after a long, difficult recession, watch for Dell to make more channel adjustments in the coming years.[33]

Questions for Discussion

1. Is Dell using intensive, selective, or exclusive distribution for its market coverage? Why is this appropriate for Dell's products and target markets?
2. How does Dell's preference for direct channels affect its decisions about physical distribution?
3. What issues in channel conflict might arise from Dell's current distribution arrangements?

NOTES

[1]Based on information in Sherman So, "Angry Birds Head for China," *China Business,* January 18, 2012, www.atimes.com; "Angry Birds Boss: 'Piracy May Not Be a Bad Thing,'" *Guardian* (U.K.), January 30, 2012, www.guardian.co.uk; Carter Dotson, "How Mobile Games Leapt from Cult to Cultural Phenomenon," *Mashable,* January 30, 2012, www.mashable.com; Chris Reidy, "Shipments Rise for Angry Birds Merchandise," *Boston Globe,* July 19, 2011, www.boston.com; "First 'Angry Birds' Stores Will Open in China This Year," *Advertising Age,* November 2, 2011, www.adage.com.

[2]Ricky W. Griffin, *Fundamentals of Management* (Mason, OH: South-Western Cengage, 2012), 460.

[3]Lynn Adler, "U.S. Business Logistics Costs Up, Consumers May Balk," Reuters, June 15, 2011, www.reuters.com/article/2011/06/15/logistics-study-idUSN1423604020110615.

[4]Charles Duhigg and Keith Bradsher, "How the U.S. Lost Out on iPhone Work," *The New York Times,* January 21, 2012, www.nytimes.com/2012/01/22/business/apple-america-and-a-squeezed-middle-class.html.

[5]Augustine A. Lado, Antony Paulraj, and Injazz J. Chen, "Customer Focus, Supply-Chain Relational Capabilities and Performance: Evidence from U.S. Manufacturing Industries," *The International Journal of Logistics Management* 22, no. 2 (2011): 202–221.

[6]Oliver Campbell, "Dell Plans Pilot to Ship Products in Mushroom Packaging," *Direct2Dell,* April 5, 2011, http://en.community.dell.com/dell-blogs/Direct2Dell/b/direct2dell/archive/2011/04/05/dell-plans-pilot-to-ship-products-in-mushroom-packaging.aspx.

[7]Quentin Hardy, "Business Social Media: Rise of the Machines," *The New York Times,* January 20, 2012, http://bits.blogs.nytimes.com/2012/01/20/business-social-media-rise-of-the-machines/.

[8]Wolseley, www.wolseley.com (accessed March 20, 2012).

[9]"eStore," Procter & Gamble, www.pgestore.com/ (accessed March 20, 2012).

[10]Quentin Hardy, "When the Webpage Comes to You," *The New York Times,* February 22, 2012, http://bits.blogs.nytimes.com/2012/02/22/when-the-web-page-comes-to-you/.

[11]Leo Aspinwall, "The Marketing Characteristics of Goods," in *Four Marketing Theories* (Boulder, CO: University of Colorado Press, 1961), 27–32.

[12]"Unlocking the Value of Globalization," Deloitte, www.deloitte.com/assets/Dcom-Turkey/Local%20Assets/Documents/dtt_mnf_UnlockValueofGlobalizationFinal%283%29.pdf (accessed March 20, 2012), 3.

[13]Charles Duhigg and David Barboza, "Apple's iPad and the Human Costs for Workers in China," *The New York Times,* January 28, 2012, www.nytimes.com/2012/01/26/business/ieconomy-apples-ipad-and-the-human-costs-for-workers-in-china.html?_r=1&scp=1&sq=goal-driven%20supply%20chain&st=cse.

[14]Suppliers Partnership for the Environment, www.supplierspartnership.org/ (accessed March 20, 2012).

[15]Wroe Alderson, *Dynamic Marketing Behavior* (Homewood, IL: Irwin, 1965), 239.

[16]Steven Sunthang, "Boeing 787: The Dreamliner Project," Professional Management Consultancy of Australia, 2010, http://pmcaustralia.com/boeing-787.php.

[17]"Inditex Press Dossier," www.inditex.com/en/press/information/press_kit (accessed March 20, 2012), 6.

[18]Kerry A Dolan, "The Lean King: Outsourcing Helps Ex-Apple Engineer Build Wireless Powerhouse, *Forbes,* January 16, 2012, www.forbes.com/sites/kerryadolan/2011/12/28/the-lean-king-outsourcing-sales-helps-ex-apple-engineer-build-wireless-powerhouse/.

[19]Lee Pender, "The Basic Links of SCM," Supply Chain Management Research Center, www.itworld.com/CIO020501_basic_content (accessed April 18, 2012).

[20]"Improving Logistics of Raw Biofuel Materials," *Science Codex,* February 17, 2012, www.sciencecodex.com/improving_logistics_of_biofuel_raw_materials-86345.

[21]Chester Dawson, "Why Honda Says It Can Fly (and GM Won't)," *The Wall Street Journal,* January 30, 2012, http://blogs.wsj.com/japanrealtime/2012/01/30/why-honda-says-it-can-fly-and-gm-wont.

[22]Claire Swedberg, "Survey Shows Half of All U.S. Retailers Have Already Adopted Item-Level RFID," RFID Journal, January 27, 2012, www.rfidjournal.com/article/view/9168.

[23]Distribution Unlimited Inc., http://distributionunlimited.com/operations.php (accessed March 20, 2012).

[24]Jesse McKinley, "Bang for the Buck," *The New York Times*, January 11, 2012, www.nytimes.com/2012/01/12/garden/dollar-store-decor-outfitting-an-apartment.html.

[25]"Freight Payment Services: Boosting Invoice IQ," *Inbound Logistics*, September 2009.

[26]Joseph O'Reilly, "Trends: Clorox Cleans Up," *Inbound Logistics*, January 2010.

[27]David Hummels and Georg Schaur, "Time as a Trade Barrier," *National Bureau of Economic Research*, January 2012, No. 17758, http://papers.nber.org/papers/w17758#fromrss.

[28]Port Logistics, www.portlogisticsgroup.com/about-us (accessed March 20, 2012).

[29]"Intermodal Case Study: Electrolux Sweeps Up Savings," *Inbound Logistics*, October 2009.

[30]"[Case Study] Inbound Routing Compliance: L'Oreal-ity Check," *Inbound Logistics*, January 2010.

[31]Fracht, www.frachtusa.com/company/company.php (accessed March 20, 2012).

[32]"Taza Chocolate and Drink Craft Beer Prove that Beer and Chocolate Make a Perfect Pair," *Boston Globe*, February 13, 2012, www.boston.com; Rachel Leah Blumenthal, "A Tour of the Taza Chocolate Factory," CBS Local News (Boston), October 26, 2011, http://boston.cbslocal.com; Ariel Shearer, "Review: Taza Chocolate," *Boston Phoenix*, October 31, 2011, http://thephoenix.com/boston; Courtney Holland, "Sweet Batches of Local Flavor," *Boston Globe*, August 18, 2010, www.boston.com; Kerry J. Byrne, "Festival of Food Trucks," *Boston Herald*, August 6, 2010, www.bostonherald.com; Interviews with company staff and video, "Taza Cultivates Channel Relationships with Chocolate," www.tazachocolate.com.

[33]Tim Peterson, "Dell's Transformation," Direct Marketing News, February 1, 2012, www.dmnews.com; Ellen Davis, "Dell's Secret to Successful Retail Partnerships? Be N.I.C.E.," Retail's Big Blog, March 4, 2010, www.nrf.com; "Dell Bets on Social Commerce as Next Boom Area for Etail," *New Media Age*, March 25, 2010, 3; Fritz Nelson, "Who Is Dell?" *InformationWeek*, January 25, 2010, 46; Mary Ellen Slayter, "How Dell Took Social Media Mainstream," Smart Blog on Social Media, October 2, 2009, http://smartblogs.com; Jack Ewing, "Where Dell Sells with Brick and Mortar," *Bloomberg Businessweek*, October 8, 2007, www.businessweek.com; www.dell.com.

Feature Notes

[a]Based on information in Willard Spiegelman, "Etsy's Funky Brooklyn Headquarters," *Bloomberg Businessweek*, February 9, 2012, www.businessweek.com; Ryan Kim, "Etsy to Become an Indie Biz One-Stop Shop," *GigaOM*, February 2, 2012, www.gigaom.com; Nedra Rhone, "Online Crafts Site to Co-Host Atlanta Event," *Atlanta Journal-Constitution*, August 10, 2011, D1; Max Chafkin, "Rob's World," *Inc.*, April 2011, 56+.

[b]Based on information in Vidya Rao, "M&M's, NPH Unveil the New Brown in Town," MSNBC, January 31, 2012, www.msnbc.msn.com; Stephanie Clifford, "A Times Square Aura for Pop-Tarts," *The New York Times*, August 8, 2010, www.nytimes.com; www.mymms.com; www.hersheys.com.

[c]Based on information in Jonathan Bardelline, "DHL Bundles Waste, Recycling Services in Envirosolutions Arm," *GreenBiz*, June 15, 2011, www.greenbiz.com; "Logistics Companies Lend Hand to E-Waste Initiatives," *Europe Intelligence Wire*, August 23, 2011; Becky Partida, "Leaders Show Power of Reverse Logistics," *Supply Chain Management Review*, November 2011, 62.

[d]Based on information in Adelaide Lancaster, "Don't Buy This Jacket," *Forbes*, December 1, 2011, www.forbes.com; Susan Carpenter, "Online Shopping: Better for the Environment?" *Los Angeles Times*, December 16, 2011, www.latimes.com; Tim Nudd, "Ad of the Day: Patagonia," *AdWeek*, November 28, 2011, www.adweek.com.

chapter 16

Retailing, Direct Marketing, and Wholesaling

OBJECTIVES

1. To understand the purpose and function of retailers in the marketing channel
2. To identify the major types of retailers
3. To explore strategic issues in retailing
4. To recognize the various forms of direct marketing and selling
5. To examine franchising and its benefits and weaknesses
6. To understand the nature and functions of wholesaling
7. To understand how wholesalers are classified

MARKETING INSIGHTS

Bass Pro Shops Offer Outdoor Experiences Indoors

The great outdoors are inside the front doors of every Bass Pro Shops Outdoor World. The 58 cavernous stores in this North American retail chain carry tens of thousands of items for fishing, camping, hunting, and other outdoor sports. What sets Bass Pro apart from competitors is the sense of the outdoors that customers get when they step inside the stores.

For example, the walls of the store in Peoria, Illinois, feature painted murals of the neighboring countryside. A multistory waterfall spills into a 27,000-gallon aquarium stocked with native species like walleye, muskie, and bass. Customers can even try for strikes and spares in the 12-lane bowling alley. No two stores are exactly alike, because Bass Pro customizes the décor and merchandise to meet the needs and interests of local customers.

To attract both novices and long-time sports enthusiasts, Bass Pro invites customers to try many of the products on display. Interested in fly fishing? Learn from a pro who will demonstrate techniques and hand over a rod for hands-on practice. Want to test a new bow? Go to the store's archery range and notch an arrow.

The retailer educates customers with in-store seminars and online videos about everything from how to set up a tent to how to bait a hook. It also sponsors fishing tournaments, conservation fundraisers, and other events that appeal to its customers. In short, it positions itself as the place to go for outdoor products and advice in an impressive, outdoorsy atmosphere. No wonder more than 100 million shoppers visit Bass Pro Shops every year.[1]

© ZUMA Press/Newscom

Retailers like Bass Pro Shops are the most visible and accessible marketing channel members to consumers. They are an important link in the marketing channel because they are both marketers for and customers of producers and wholesalers. They perform many supply-chain functions, such as buying, selling, grading, risk taking, and developing and maintaining information databases about customers. Retailers are in a strategic position to develop relationships with consumers and partnerships with producers and intermediaries in the marketing channel.

In this chapter, we examine the nature of retailing, direct marketing, and wholesaling and their importance in supplying consumers with goods and services. First, we explore the major types of retail stores and consider strategic issues in retailing: location, retail positioning, store image, and category management. Next, we discuss direct marketing, including catalog marketing, response marketing, telemarketing, television home shopping, and online retailing. We also explore direct selling and vending. Then we look at franchising, a retailing form that continues to grow in popularity. Finally, we examine the importance of wholesalers in marketing channels, including their functions and classifications.

RETAILING

Retailing includes all transactions in which the buyer intends to consume the product through personal, family, or household use. Buyers in retail transactions are therefore the ultimate consumers. A **retailer** is an organization that purchases products for the purpose of reselling them to ultimate consumers. Although most retailers' sales are made directly to the consumer, nonretail transactions occur occasionally when retailers sell products to other businesses.

Retailing often takes place in stores or service establishments, but it also occurs through direct selling, direct marketing, and vending machines. Given the purchasing pattern trends of the past decade, there is a clear expectation that consumers will increasingly buy their goods and services online. Online shoppers prefer shopping on the Internet to avoid crowds, find lower prices, avoid the inconvenience of having to travel to stores, and have a wider selection of products. Traditionally, Black Friday, which is the Friday after Thanksgiving, has been the largest shopping day of the year. Retailers drastically mark down items to draw in customers as the Christmas holiday season kicks off. However, while still a huge shopping day for many consumers, Black Friday is not as important as it once was. More consumers are opting to skip the long lines and early wake-up times to shop online. Cyber Monday, which is the first Monday after Black Friday, is now a hugely popular shopping day as well. Traffic to retail sites rose 22 percent last year, to $1.25 billion, making it the busiest online commerce day ever. Many retailers have extended the holiday buying season by offering Cyber Monday sales for the entire week following Thanksgiving.[2]

Retailing is important to the national U.S. economy. Approximately 1.1 million retailers operate in the United States.[3] This number has remained relatively constant for the past 25 years, but sales volume has increased more than fourfold. Most personal income is spent in retail stores, and retailers in the U.S. employ more than 15.6 million people.[4]

Retailers add value for customers by providing services and assisting in making product selections. They can enhance the value of products by making buyers' shopping experiences more convenient, as in online shopping. Through their locations, retailers can facilitate comparison shopping; for example, car dealerships often cluster in the same general vicinity, as do furniture stores. Product value is also enhanced when retailers offer services, such as technical advice, delivery, credit, and repair. Finally, retail sales personnel can demonstrate to customers how products can satisfy their needs or solve problems.

The value added by retailers is significant for both producers and end consumers. Retailers are the critical link between producers and end consumers, because they provide the environment in which exchanges with ultimate consumers occur. Ultimate consumers benefit through retailers' performance of marketing functions that result in the availability of broader arrays of

retailing All transactions in which the buyer intends to consume the product through personal, family, or household use

retailer An organization that purchases products for the purpose of reselling them to ultimate consumers

Marketing Debate

Should Black Friday Start on Thanksgiving?

ISSUE: Should stores be open on major holidays like Thanksgiving?

Gap and Old Navy have been opening on Thanksgiving Day for several years, attracting shoppers eager to get an early start on Christmas and Hanukkah shopping. Walmart starts its door-buster in-store sales at 10 p.m. on Thanksgiving night, and Toys"R"Us also opens on Thanksgiving night. Target recently began a new tradition of opening at midnight on Thanksgiving, despite a petition signed by thousands of employees asking that the retailer not disrupt their family time on this family-oriented holiday.

Massachusetts is one of the few states that actually outlaws store openings on Thanksgiving and Christmas. "The spirit of the law and intent is to give people a day off," explains an official for the Massachusetts Department of Labor Standards. To comply, Macy's and other retailers wait until after midnight to open their Massachusetts stores.

Not every retailer is eager to open on Thanksgiving. JCPenney is resisting, and some others are sticking with early-morning openings on the day after Thanksgiving, one of the biggest shopping days of the year. Yet stores have also found that younger consumers, in particular—a coveted customer segment—prefer to shop on Thanksgiving night rather than early on Friday morning. Do you think stores should open on Thanksgiving and other major holidays?[a]

products that can satisfy the needs of consumers. Retailers play a major role in creating time, place, and possession utility and, in some cases, form utility.

Leading retailers like Walmart, Home Depot, Macy's, Staples, and Best Buy offer consumers a place to browse and compare merchandise to find just what they need. However, such traditional retailing is being challenged by direct marketing channels that provide home shopping through catalogs, television, and the Internet. Brick-and-mortar retailers are responding to this change in the retail environment in various ways. Many retailers utilize multiple distribution channels and complement their brick-and-mortar stores with websites where consumers can shop online. Some even offer online-only sales and merchandise in order to encourage consumers to frequent their sites as well as their stores. Major retailers like Walmart and Target have partnered with restaurant chains such as McDonald's, KFC, and Starbucks to feature in-store dining that encourages customers to stay and shop.

New store formats and advances in information technology are making the retail environment highly dynamic and competitive. As the world's largest retailer, Walmart is well positioned to offer innovative online benefits to its customers. It offers a site-to-store service, where customers can shop online and have products delivered to the store closest to them for easy in-person inspection and pickup. This service saves customers from having to pay shipping and allows them to actually see the product in person before taking it home. Walmart has established an online presence in 15 different countries, with plans to expand to others.[5] The key to success in retailing is to have a strong customer focus with a retail strategy that provides the level of service, product quality, and innovation that consumers desire. Partnerships among noncompeting retailers and other marketing channel members are providing new opportunities for retailers. For example, airports are leasing space to retailers, such as McDonald's, Sunglass Hut, and The Body Shop.

Retailers are also finding global opportunities. Many businesses see significant growth potential in international markets, especially when domestic markets become mature and saturated with limited future growth opportunities. Walmart has more stores internationally than it does in the United States. Starbucks even has stores in such tea-drinking strongholds as China, Japan, and India. While still a small portion of overall beverage consumption, the demand for coffee drinks in countries like China is growing rapidly, and Starbucks is there to meet demand.[6] On the other hand, international retailers, such as Aldi, IKEA, and Zara, have also found receptive markets in the United States.

MAJOR TYPES OF RETAIL STORES

Many types of retail stores exist. One way to classify them is by the breadth of products they offer. Two general categories include general-merchandise retailers and specialty retailers.

General-Merchandise Retailers

A retail establishment that offers a variety of product lines that are stocked in considerable depth is referred to as a **general-merchandise retailer**. The types of product offerings, mixes of customer services, and operating styles of retailers in this category vary considerably. The primary types of general-merchandise retailers are department stores, discount stores, convenience stores, supermarkets, superstores, hypermarkets, warehouse clubs, and warehouse showrooms (see Table 16.1).

Department Stores

general-merchandise retailer A retail establishment that offers a variety of product lines that are stocked in considerable depth

department stores Large retail organizations characterized by a wide product mix and organized into separate departments to facilitate marketing efforts and internal management

Department stores are large retail organizations characterized by wide product mixes and staffs of at least 25 people. To facilitate marketing efforts and internal management in these stores, related product lines are organized into separate departments—such as cosmetics, housewares, apparel, home furnishings, and appliances—to facilitate marketing and internal management. Often, each department functions as a self-contained business, and buyers for individual departments are fairly autonomous.

Department stores are distinctly service oriented. Their total product may include credit, delivery, personal assistance, merchandise returns, and a pleasant atmosphere. Although some so-called department stores are actually large, departmentalized specialty stores, most department stores are shopping stores. Consumers can compare price, quality, and service at one store with those at competing stores. Along with large discount stores, department stores are

Table 16.1 General-Merchandise Retailers

Type of Retailer	Description	Examples
Department store	Large organization offering a wide product mix and organized into separate departments	Macy's, Sears, JCPenney
Discount store	Self-service, general-merchandise store offering brand-name and private-brand products at low prices	Walmart, Target, Kmart
Convenience store	Small, self-service store offering narrow product assortment in convenient locations	7-Eleven
Supermarket	Self-service store offering complete line of food products and some nonfood products	Kroger, Safeway, Publix
Superstore	Giant outlet offering all food and nonfood products found in supermarkets, as well as most routinely purchased products	Walmart Supercenters, SuperTarget
Hypermarket	Combination supermarket and discount store; larger than a superstore	Carrefour
Warehouse club	Large-scale, members-only establishments combining cash-and-carry wholesaling with discount retailing	Sam's Club, Costco
Warehouse showroom	Facility in a large, low-cost building with large on-premises inventories and minimal service	IKEA

© Kristoffer Tripplaar/Alamy

Department Stores
Department stores like Macy's offer a wide variety of product lines.

often considered retailing leaders in a community and are found in most places with populations of more than 50,000.

Typical department stores, such as Macy's, Sears, JCPenney, Dillard's, and Neiman Marcus, obtain a large proportion of sales from apparel, accessories, and cosmetics. Other products these stores carry include gift items, luggage, electronics, home accessories, and sports equipment. Some department stores offer such services as automobile insurance, hair care, income tax preparation, and travel and optical services. In some cases, space for these specialized services is leased out, with proprietors managing their own operations and paying rent to the store. Many department stores also sell products through their websites.

Discount Stores

In recent years, department stores have been losing sales to discount stores, especially Walmart and Target. **Discount stores** are self-service, general-merchandise outlets that regularly offer brand-name and private-brand products at low prices. Discounters accept lower margins than conventional retailers in exchange for high sales volume. To keep inventory turnover high, they carry a wide but carefully selected assortment of products, from appliances to housewares to clothing. Major discount establishments also offer food products, toys, automotive services, garden supplies, and sports equipment.

In the United States, Walmart and Target are the two largest discount stores. Walmart is the largest retailer in the world, with 2 million employees. Walmart alone has more than 8,900 stores and brings in nearly $420 billion in annual revenue.[7] Not all discounters are large and international. Some, such as Meijer Inc., which has stores in the Midwest United States, are regional discounters. Most of them operate in large (50,000 to 80,000 square feet), no-frills facilities. Discount stores usually offer everyday low prices rather than relying on sales events.

Discount retailing developed on a large scale in the early 1950s, when postwar production began catching up with consumer demand for appliances, home furnishings, and other hard goods. Discount stores were often cash-only operations in warehouse districts, offering goods at savings of 20 to 30 percent over conventional retailers. Facing increased competition

discount stores Self-service, general-merchandise stores that offer brand-name and private-brand products at low prices

from department stores and other discount stores, some discounters have improved store services, atmosphere, and location, raising prices and sometimes blurring the distinction between discount store and department store. Target has grown distinctly more upscale in appearance and offerings over the years. It frequently features low-cost clothing lines by designer labels. It also has become more of a one-stop shop with food and pharmacy offerings, as well as clothing, home goods, and electronics. In a further attempt to convince customers to linger, some Target stores even feature in-store Starbucks, Jamba Juice, or Pizza Hut Express outlets.[8]

Convenience Stores

A **convenience store** is a small, self-service store that is open long hours and carries a narrow assortment of products, usually convenience items such as soft drinks and other beverages, snacks, newspapers, tobacco, and gasoline, as well as services such as automatic teller machines. The primary product offered by the "corner store" is convenience.

According to the National Association of Convenience Stores, there are more than 146,000 convenience stores in the United States alone.[9] They are typically less than 5,000 square feet; open 24 hours a day, 7 days a week; and stock about 500 items. In addition to many national chains, there are many family-owned independent convenience stores in operation. The convenience store concept was developed in 1927 when Southland Ice in Dallas began stocking milk, eggs, and other products for customers who wanted to replenish their "ice boxes."

Supermarkets

Supermarkets are large, self-service stores that carry a complete line of food products, as well as some nonfood products such as cosmetics and nonprescription drugs. Supermarkets are arranged in departments for maximum efficiency in stocking and handling products but have central checkout facilities. They offer lower prices than smaller neighborhood grocery stores, usually provide free parking, and may also cash checks.

Today, consumers make more than three-quarters of all grocery purchases in supermarkets. Even so, supermarkets' total share of the food market is declining because consumers now have widely varying food preferences and buying habits, and in many communities, shoppers can choose from several convenience stores, discount stores, and specialty food stores, as well as a wide variety of restaurants. To satisfy different market segments and different geographic locations, major retailers like Walmart and Target now have a range of store sizes offering different depth and width of grocery product offerings. To fit in an urban setting, these retailers have smaller stores with a more limited selection. Prices are generally comparable, or even lower, than other grocers and the stores feature a much wider variety of retail items.[10]

Superstores

Superstores, which originated in Europe, are giant retail outlets that carry not only food and nonfood products that are ordinarily found in supermarkets but also routinely purchased consumer products. Besides a complete food line, superstores sell housewares, hardware, small appliances, clothing, personal-care products, garden products, and tires—about four times as many items as supermarkets. Services available at superstores include dry cleaning, automotive repair, check cashing, bill paying, and snack bars. Superstores combine features of discount stores and supermarkets. Examples include Walmart Supercenters, some Kroger stores, SuperTarget stores, and Super Kmart Centers.

To cut handling and inventory costs, superstores use sophisticated operating techniques and often have tall shelving that displays entire assortments of products. Superstores can have an area of as much as 200,000 square feet (compared with 20,000 square feet in traditional supermarkets). Sales volume is two to three times that of supermarkets, partly because locations near good transportation networks help generate the in-store traffic needed for profitability.

convenience store A small self-service store that is open long hours and carries a narrow assortment of products, usually convenience items

supermarkets Large, self-service stores that carry a complete line of food products, along with some nonfood products

superstores Giant retail outlets that carry food and nonfood products found in supermarkets, as well as most routinely purchased consumer products

Hypermarkets

Hypermarkets combine supermarket and discount store shopping in one location. Larger than superstores, they range from 225,000 to 325,000 square feet and offer 45,000 to 60,000 different types of low-priced products. They commonly allocate 40 to 50 percent of their space to grocery products and the remainder to general merchandise, including athletic shoes, designer jeans, and other apparel; refrigerators, televisions, and other appliances; housewares; cameras; toys; jewelry; hardware; and automotive supplies. Many lease space to noncompeting businesses such as banks, optical shops, and fast-food restaurants. All hypermarkets focus on low prices and vast selections.

Although Kmart, Walmart, and Carrefour (a French retailer) have operated hypermarkets in the United States, most of these stores were unsuccessful and closed. Such stores may be too big for time-constrained U.S. shoppers. However, hypermarkets are more successful in Europe, South America, and Mexico and, more recently, in the Middle East and India.

Warehouse Clubs

Warehouse clubs, a rapidly growing form of mass merchandising, are large-scale, members-only selling operations that combine cash-and-carry wholesaling with discount retailing. Sometimes called *buying clubs,* warehouse clubs offer the same types of products as discount stores but in a limited range of sizes and styles. Whereas most discount stores carry around 40,000 items, a warehouse club handles only 3,500 to 5,000 products, usually acknowledged brand leaders. Sam's Club stores, for example, stock about 4,000 items. Costco leads the warehouse club industry with sales of nearly $89 billion. Sam's Club is second with almost $47 billion in store sales. A third company, BJ's Wholesale Club, which operates on the East Coast and in Ohio, has a much smaller market.[11] All these establishments offer a broad product mix, including food, beverages, books, appliances, housewares, automotive parts, hardware, and furniture.

To keep prices lower than those of supermarkets and discount stores, warehouse clubs provide few services. They generally do not advertise, except through direct mail. Their facilities, often located in industrial areas, have concrete floors and aisles wide enough for forklifts. Merchandise is stacked on pallets or displayed on pipe racks. Customers must transport

hypermarkets Stores that combine supermarket and discount store shopping in one location

warehouse clubs Large-scale, members-only establishments that combine features of cash-and-carry wholesaling with discount retailing

Warehouse Clubs
Sam's Club is a warehouse club that has a wide product mix with limited depth.

Going Green

Costco Seeks Sustainability through Improved Processes and Products

Costco is going green in a big way, putting the marketing power of its 600 warehouse stores and $87 billion in annual sales behind a multiyear sustainability strategy. First, the retailer is looking at the eco-impact of its stores. In addition to overhauling chilling units and air-conditioning systems to eliminate environmentally unfriendly refrigerants, it has installed solar panels in dozens of U.S. stores to generate clean energy. Its new stores are designed to be energy-efficient and constructed with a mix of new and recycled materials.

Just as important, the retailer is increasing its mix of sustainable private-brand products, particularly in the food department, where "everything is a limited resource commodity or relies upon a limited resource for its production," explains a Costco manager. For example, the company worked with Ugandan farmers to improve the way they grow and harvest high-quality vanilla pods. Once the vanilla is cured and processed, it is sold under Costco's Kirkland label as a baking ingredient and is mixed into other Kirkland products, such as vanilla ice cream.

Finally, Costco has teamed up with manufacturers like Seventh Generation and ConAgra to test new labels that will clearly indicate which product packages can be recycled. The goal is to educate customers about what to recycle and where, another key aspect of Costco's sustainability strategy.[b]

purchases themselves. Warehouse clubs appeal to many price-conscious consumers and small retailers unable to obtain wholesaling services from large distributors. The average warehouse club shopper has more education, a higher income, and a larger household than the average supermarket shopper.

Warehouse Showrooms

Warehouse showrooms are retail facilities with five basic characteristics: large, low-cost buildings; warehouse materials-handling technology; vertical merchandise displays; large, on-premises inventories; and minimal services. IKEA, a Swedish company, sells furniture, household goods, and kitchen accessories in warehouse showrooms and through catalogs around the world, including China and Russia. These high-volume, low-overhead operations stress fewer personnel and services. Lower costs are possible because some marketing functions have been shifted to consumers, who must transport, finance, and perhaps store larger quantities of products. Most consumers carry away purchases in the manufacturer's carton, although stores will deliver for a fee.

Specialty Retailers

In contrast to general-merchandise retailers with their broad product mixes, specialty retailers emphasize narrow and deep assortments. Despite their name, specialty retailers do not sell specialty items (except when specialty goods complement the overall product mix). Instead, they offer substantial assortments in a few product lines. We examine three types of specialty retailers: traditional specialty retailers, category killers, and off-price retailers.

warehouse showrooms Retail facilities in large, low-cost buildings with large on-premises inventories and minimal services

traditional specialty retailers Stores that carry a narrow product mix with deep product lines

Traditional Specialty Retailers

Traditional specialty retailers are stores that carry a narrow product mix with deep product lines. Sometimes called *limited-line retailers,* they may be referred to as *single-line retailers* if they carry unusual depth in one main product category. Specialty retailers commonly sell such shopping products as apparel, jewelry, sporting goods, fabrics, computers, and pet supplies. The Limited, Radio Shack, Hickory Farms, Gap, and Foot Locker are examples of retailers offering limited product lines but great depth within those lines.

Because they are usually small, specialty stores may have high costs in proportion to sales, and satisfying customers may require carrying some products with low turnover rates. However, these stores sometimes obtain lower prices from suppliers by purchasing limited lines of merchandise in large quantities. Successful specialty stores understand their customer types and know what products to carry, thus reducing the risk of unsold merchandise. Specialty stores usually offer better selections and more sales expertise than department stores, their main competitors. By capitalizing on fashion, service, personnel, atmosphere, and location, specialty retailers position themselves strategically to attract customers in specific market segments.

Category Killers

Over the past 20 years, a new breed of specialty retailer, the category killer, has evolved. A **category killer** is a very large specialty store that concentrates on a major product category and competes on the basis of low prices and enormous product availability. These stores are referred to as category killers because they expand rapidly and gain sizable market shares, taking business away from smaller, high-cost retail outlets. Examples of category killers include Home Depot and Lowe's (home improvement chains); Staples, Office Depot, and OfficeMax (office-supply chains); Barnes & Noble (bookseller); Petco and PetSmart (pet-supply chains); and Best Buy (consumer electronics).

Off-Price Retailers

Off-price retailers are stores that buy manufacturers' seconds, overruns, returns, and off-season production runs at below-wholesale prices for resale to consumers at deep discounts. Unlike true discount stores, which pay regular wholesale prices for goods and usually carry second-line brand names, off-price retailers offer limited lines of national-brand and designer merchandise, usually clothing, shoes, or housewares. The number of off-price retailers, such as T.J.Maxx, Marshalls, Stein Mart, and Burlington Coat Factory, has grown. Off-price retailers typically perform well in recessionary times, as consumers who still want to own name-brand items search for good value.

Off-price stores charge 20 to 50 percent less than department stores for comparable merchandise but offer few customer services. They often feature community dressing rooms and central checkout counters. Some of these stores do not take returns or allow exchanges. Off-price stores may or may not sell goods with the original labels intact. They turn over their inventory 9 to 12 times a year, three times as often as traditional specialty stores. They compete with department stores for the same customers: price-conscious customers who are knowledgeable about brand names.

To ensure a regular flow of merchandise into their stores, off-price retailers establish long-term relationships with suppliers that can provide large quantities of goods at reduced prices. Manufacturers may approach retailers with samples, discontinued products, or items that have not sold well. Also, off-price retailers may seek out manufacturers, offering to pay cash for goods produced during the manufacturers' off-season. Although manufacturers benefit from such arrangements, they also risk alienating their specialty and department store customers. Department stores tolerate off-price stores as long as they do not advertise brand names, limit merchandise to lower-quality items, and are located away from the department stores. When off-price retailers obtain large stocks of in-season, top-quality merchandise, tension builds between department stores and manufacturers.

category killer A very large specialty store that concentrates on a major product category and competes on the basis of low prices and product availability

off-price retailers Stores that buy manufacturers' seconds, overruns, returns, and off-season merchandise for resale to consumers at deep discounts

Traditional Specialty Stores and Off-Price Specialty Stores
Gap is a traditional specialty store, while Ross is an example of an off-price specialty retailer.

STRATEGIC ISSUES IN RETAILING

Whereas most business purchases are based on economic planning and necessity, consumer purchases may result from social and psychological influences. Because consumers shop for various reasons—to search for specific items, escape boredom, or learn about something new—retailers must do more than simply fill space with merchandise. They must make desired products available, create stimulating shopping environments, and develop marketing strategies that increase store patronage. In this section, we discuss how store location, retail positioning, store image, and category management are used strategically by retailers.

Location of Retail Stores

"Location, location, location" is a common saying among retailers (as well as realtors) because of its critical importance to success. At the same time, the retail location is the least flexible of the strategic retailing issues but is one of the most important because location dictates the limited geographic trading area from which a store draws its customers. Retailers consider various factors when evaluating potential locations, including location of the firm's target market within the trading area, kinds of products being sold, availability of public transportation, customer characteristics, and competitors' locations.

In choosing a location, a retailer evaluates the relative ease of movement to and from the site, including factors such as pedestrian and vehicular traffic, parking, and transportation. Retailers also evaluate the characteristics of the site itself. They research the types of stores in the area and the size, shape, and visibility of the lot or building under consideration. In addition, they analyze rental, leasing, or ownership terms. Retailers look for compatibility with nearby retailers because stores that complement one another draw more customers for everyone.

Many retailers choose to locate in downtown central business districts, whereas others prefer sites within various types of shopping centers. Some retailers, including Toys"R"Us, Walmart, Home Depot, and many fast-food restaurants, opt for freestanding structures that are not connected to other buildings, but many chain stores are found in planned shopping centers and malls. Sometimes, retailers choose to locate in less orthodox settings. Subway, for example, has a few outlets in nontraditional locations, including an automobile showroom in California, a ferry terminal in Seattle, a Goodwill store in South Carolina, a high school in Detroit, and a church in New York. Opening a location in unorthodox settings like these has helped Subway be more competitive and grow as a company.[12]

There are several types of shopping centers, including neighborhood, community, regional, superregional, lifestyle, power, and outlet centers. **Neighborhood shopping centers** usually consist of several small convenience and specialty stores, such as small grocery stores, gas stations, and fast-food restaurants. Many of these retailers consider their target markets to be consumers who live within 2 to 3 miles of their stores, or 10 minutes' driving time. Because most purchases are based on convenience or personal contact, there is usually little coordination of selling efforts within a neighborhood shopping center. Generally, product mixes consist of essential products, and depth of the product lines is limited. **Community shopping centers** include one or two department stores and some specialty stores, as well as convenience stores. They draw consumers looking for shopping and specialty products not available in neighborhood shopping centers. Because these centers serve larger geographic areas, consumers must drive longer distances to community shopping centers than to neighborhood centers. Community shopping centers are planned and coordinated to attract shoppers. Special events, such as art exhibits, automobile shows, and sidewalk sales, stimulate traffic. Managers of community shopping centers look for tenants that complement the centers' total assortment of products. Such centers have wide product mixes and deep product lines.

Regional shopping centers usually have the largest department stores, widest product mixes, and deepest product lines of all shopping centers. Many shopping malls are regional shopping centers, although some are community shopping centers. With 150,000 or more consumers in their target market, regional shopping centers must have well-coordinated management and marketing activities. Target markets may include consumers traveling from a distance to find products and prices not available in their hometowns. Because of the expense of leasing space in regional shopping centers, tenants are more likely to be national chains than small, independent stores. Large centers usually advertise, have special events, furnish transportation to some consumer groups, maintain their own security forces, and carefully select the mix of stores. The largest of these centers, sometimes called **superregional shopping centers**, have the widest and deepest product mixes and attract customers from many miles away. Superregional centers often have special attractions beyond stores, such as skating rinks, amusement centers, or upscale restaurants. Mall of America, in the Minneapolis area, is the largest shopping mall in the United States with 520 stores, including Nordstrom and Bloomingdale's, and 50 restaurants. The shopping center also includes a walk-through aquarium, a museum, a seven-acre Nickelodeon theme park, a 14-screen movie theater, hotels, and many special events.[13]

With traditional mall sales declining, some shopping center developers are looking to new formats that differ significantly from traditional shopping centers. A **lifestyle shopping center** is typically an open-air shopping center that features upscale specialty, dining, and entertainment stores, usually owned by national chains. They are often located near affluent neighborhoods and may have fountains, benches, and other amenities that encourage "casual browsing." Indeed, architectural design is an important aspect of these "minicities," which may include urban streets or parks, and is intended to encourage consumer loyalty by creating a sense of place. Some lifestyle centers are designed to resemble traditional "Main Street" shopping centers or may have a central theme evidenced by architecture.[14]

neighborhood shopping center A type of shopping center usually consisting of several small convenience and specialty stores

community shopping center A type of shopping center with one or two department stores, some specialty stores, and convenience stores

regional shopping center A type of shopping center with the largest department stores, widest product mixes, and deepest product lines of all shopping centers

superregional shopping center A type of shopping center with the widest and deepest product mixes that attracts customers from many miles away

lifestyle shopping center A type of shopping center that is typically open air and features upscale specialty, dining, and entertainment stores

Location
Home Depot usually locates in a free-standing building that is constructed specifically for the company, often near a shopping center.

© Erik S. Lesser/Bloomberg via Getty Images

Some shopping center developers are bypassing the traditional department store anchor and combining off-price stores and small stores with category killers in **power shopping center** formats. These centers may be anchored by stores, such as Gap, Toys"R"Us, PetSmart, and Home Depot. The number of power shopping centers is growing, resulting in a variety of formats vying for the same retail dollar.

Factory outlet malls feature discount and factory outlet stores carrying traditional manufacturer brands, such as Polo Ralph Lauren, Nike, Guess, and Sunglass Hut. Some outlet centers feature upscale products. Manufacturers own these stores and make a special effort to avoid conflict with traditional retailers of their products. Manufacturers claim their stores are in noncompetitive locations; indeed, most factory outlet centers are located outside metropolitan areas. Not all factory outlets stock closeouts and irregulars, but most avoid comparison with discount houses. Factory outlet centers attract value-conscious customers seeking quality and major brand names. They operate in much the same way as regional shopping centers, but usually draw customers, some of whom may be tourists, from a larger shopping radius. Promotional activity is at the heart of these shopping centers. Craft and antique shows, contests, and special events attract a great deal of traffic.

Retail Positioning

power shopping center A type of shopping center that combines off-price stores with category killers

retail positioning Identifying an unserved or underserved market segment and serving it through a strategy that distinguishes the retailer from others in the minds of consumers in that segment

The large variety of shopping centers and the expansion of product offerings by traditional stores have intensified retailing competition. Retail positioning is therefore an important consideration. **Retail positioning** involves identifying an unserved or underserved market segment and serving it through a strategy that distinguishes the retailer from others in the minds of those customers. Adidas, a brand mostly known for its soccer gear and footwear, is attempting to reposition some of its stores to attract the lucrative market of young fashion-conscious women. The stores dubbed NEO feature sportswear with a fashionable edge, such as shoes made of metallic leather. To promote these stores, Adidas is relying heavily on social media outlets like Twitter and Facebook. NEO already has 1,000 stores in China and has expanded around Europe. The company projects that the NEO stores will bring in an extra $1.3 billion in revenue by 2015, but only time will tell if female consumers are receptive to shopping for a

Entrepreneurship in Marketing

Personalizing Online Selling for Cyclists

Entrepreneurs: Lesley Tweedie and Alex Tweedie
Business: Roscoe Village Bike Shop
Founded: 2007 | Chicago, Illinois
Success: Starting an online marketplace where small, independent retailers can sell merchandise while running a busy neighborhood bicycle store.

Where other people saw an old tailor shop, Lesley and Alex Tweedie saw a bicycle shop for competitive cyclists, urban commuters, and families. The husband-and-wife team had already developed a business plan with the help of SCORE mentors. When they noticed a neighborhood store for rent, they became retail entrepreneurs. The owners differentiate their store with personalized service and bicycles customized for the area. For example, they sell a popular commuter bike they dubbed the "Four Star," outfitted for city streets with heavy-duty tires and full fenders. They also sell a lot of "fixie" bikes—fixed-gear, single-speed models that are low-maintenance and easy to ride on flat terrain.

Like many independent stores, Roscoe Village Bike Shop has to contend with competition from online rivals, which don't provide either in-person attention or repair services. Recently, Lesley Tweedie started a "Buy It Where You Try It" campaign, using social media to spread the message that customers will benefit by shopping locally instead of testing a product in a nearby store and then buying it online. She also launched an online marketplace to give small, Chicago-area stores like her own a virtual storefront to reach customers who prefer to buy with a click.[c]

brand largely associated with men and sports.[15] In recent years, a number of discount and specialty store chains have positioned themselves to appeal to time- and cash-strapped consumers with convenient locations and layouts as well as low prices. This strategy has helped them gain market share at the expense of large department stores.

Store Image

To attract customers, a retail store must project an image—a functional and psychological picture in the consumer's mind—that appeals to its target market. Store environment, merchandise quality, and service quality are key determinants of store image.

Atmospherics, the physical elements in a store's design that appeal to consumers' emotions and encourage buying, help to create an image and position a retailer. Barnes & Noble, for example, uses murals of authors and framed pictures of classic book covers to convey a literary image. Studies show that retailers can use different elements—music, color, and complexity of layout and merchandise presentation—to influence customer arousal based on their shopping motivation. Bars, for example, have to consider several factors when it comes to atmospherics, including music tempo and volume, lighting levels, cleanliness, and physical layout. Most bars tend to sell the same range of products, so they use atmospherics extensively to differentiate themselves and create a unique environment. In order for a bar to be successful and retain customers, it must monitor its atmospheric variables and focus on maintaining customer comfort levels, because most bar patrons are more recreationally and socially motivated, rather than task motivated. The layout, for example, should create the right flow and spread the crowd to the right places, so customers don't feel claustrophobic.[16]

Exterior atmospheric elements include the appearance of the storefront, display windows, store entrances, and degree of traffic congestion. Exterior atmospherics are particularly important to new customers, who tend to judge an unfamiliar store by its outside appearance and may not enter if they feel intimidated by the building or inconvenienced by the parking lot.

Interior atmospheric elements include aesthetic considerations, such as lighting, wall and floor coverings, dressing facilities, and store fixtures. Interior sensory elements contribute significantly to atmosphere. Caesar's Palace, the hotel and casino in Las Vegas, provides a truly memorable experience for its customers by incorporating items to reflect the hotel

atmospherics The physical elements in a store's design that appeal to consumers' emotions and encourage buying

Atmospherics
Atmospherics in a restaurant, such as McDonald's, can have very positive effects on the customer experience.

© Tim Boyle/Getty Images

theme, ancient Rome. The hotel and casino have marble floors, ancient Roman statues and fountain recreations including the Statue of David and Trevi Fountain, as well as sky-painted ceilings in the Forum Shops and white walls with plenty of columns. By providing customers with a truly authentic experience, the company hopes visitors will spend more at the casino, stores, restaurants, and bars.[17] Color can attract shoppers to a retail display. Many fast-food restaurants use bright colors, such as red and yellow, because these have been shown to make customers feel hungrier and eat faster, which increases turnover. Sound is another important sensory component of atmosphere and may range from silence to subdued background music. A low-end, family dining restaurant might play fast pop music to encourage customers to eat quickly and leave, increasing turnover and sales. A high-end restaurant, on the other hand, will opt to play soft classical music to enhance the experience and encourage diners to linger over their meals, indulging in more courses and spending more money. The owner of Grant Central Pizza in Atlanta, Georgia, was so concerned with how sound affects a diner's experience that he banned crying children from his restaurant after receiving negative customer reviews about noise levels.[18] Many retailers employ scent, especially food aromas, to attract customers. Most consumers expect the scent of a store to be congruent with the products that are sold there. For example, Starbucks should smell like its coffee, Panera like its freshly baked bread, and Yankee Candle like its scented candles.

Category Management

Category management is a retail strategy of managing groups of similar, often substitutable products produced by different manufacturers. For instance, supermarkets like Safeway use category management to determine space for products, such as cosmetics, cereals, and soups. An assortment of merchandise is both customer and strategically driven to improve performance. Category management developed in the food industry because supermarkets were concerned about highly competitive behavior among manufacturers.

category management A retail strategy of managing groups of similar, often substitutable products produced by different manufacturers

Category management is a move toward a collaborative supply-chain initiative to enhance customer value. Successful category management requires the acquisition, analysis, and sharing of sales and consumer information between the retailer and manufacturer. Walmart, for example, has developed strong supplier relationships with manufacturers like Procter & Gamble. The development of information about demand, consumer behavior, and optimal allocations of products should be available from one source. Firms like SAS provide software to manage data associated with each step of the category management decision cycle. The key is cooperative interaction between the manufacturers of category products and the retailer to create maximum success for all parties in the supply chain. Because category management can be such an important consideration for retailers, many major firms join the Category Management Association, which provides networking opportunities and information for member firms.[19]

DIRECT MARKETING AND DIRECT SELLING

Although retailers are the most visible members of the supply chain, many products are sold outside the confines of a retail store. Direct selling and direct marketing account for an increasing percentage of product sales. Products also may be sold in automatic vending machines, but these account for less than 2 percent of all retail sales.

Direct Marketing

Direct marketing is the use of the telephone, Internet, and nonpersonal media to communicate product and organizational information to customers, who can then purchase products via mail, telephone, or the Internet. Direct marketing is one type of nonstore retailing. Sales through direct marketing activities amount to $1.8 trillion per year.[20]

Nonstore retailing is the selling of products outside the confines of a retail facility. This form of retailing accounts for an increasing percentage of total sales. Direct marketing can occur through catalog marketing, direct-response marketing, telemarketing, television home shopping, and online retailing.

Catalog Marketing

In **catalog marketing**, an organization provides a catalog from which customers make selections and place orders by mail, telephone, or the Internet. Catalog marketing began in 1872, when Montgomery Ward issued its first catalog to rural families. Today, there are more than 7,000 catalog marketing companies in the United States, as well as several retail stores, such as Chico's, that engage in catalog marketing. Some organizations offer a broad array of products through a sizeable catalog. Spiegel, for example, is one of the United States' largest catalog marketing companies. Spiegel once operated department stores as well, but now exclusively sells through its print and online catalogs. Companies, such as Land's End, Pottery Barn, and Crate & Barrel, sell via catalogs and through retail stores in major metropolitan areas. These retailers generally offer considerable product depth for just a few lines of products. Still other catalog companies specialize in products from a single product line.[21]

The advantages of catalog retailing include efficiency and convenience for customers. The retailer benefits by being able to locate in remote, low-cost areas; save on expensive store fixtures; and reduce both personal selling and store operating expenses. On the other hand, catalog retailing is inflexible, provides limited service, and is most effective for a selected set of products.

Direct-Response Marketing

Direct-response marketing occurs when a retailer advertises a product and makes it available through mail or telephone orders. Generally, customers use a credit card, but other forms of payment may be permitted. Examples of direct-response marketing include a television commercial offering exercise machines, cosmetics or household cleaning products available through a toll-free number, and a newspaper or magazine advertisement for a series of

direct marketing The use of the telephone, Internet, and nonpersonal media to introduce products to customers, who can then purchase them via mail, telephone, or the Internet

nonstore retailing The selling of products outside the confines of a retail facility

catalog marketing A type of marketing in which an organization provides a catalog from which customers make selections and place orders by mail, telephone, or the Internet

direct-response marketing A type of marketing in which a retailer advertises a product and makes it available through mail or telephone orders

children's books available by filling out the form in the ad or calling a toll-free number. Direct-response marketing through TV is a $300 billion industry. The three top-selling infomercial products from last year were the Bowflex Home Gym, Carlton Sheets Real Estate Tutorial, and Proactiv Solution Acne Treatment.[22] Direct-response marketing is also conducted by sending letters, samples, brochures, or booklets to prospects on a mailing list and asking that they order the advertised products by mail or telephone. In general, products must be priced above $20 to justify the advertising and distribution costs associated with direct-response marketing.

Telemarketing

A number of organizations use the telephone to strengthen the effectiveness of traditional marketing methods. **Telemarketing** is the performance of marketing-related activities by telephone. Some organizations use a prescreened list of prospective clients. Telemarketing can help to generate sales leads, improve customer service, speed up payments on past-due accounts, raise funds for nonprofit organizations, and gather marketing data.

Currently, the laws and regulations regarding telemarketing, although in a state of flux, are becoming more restrictive. In 2003, Congress implemented a national do-not-call registry for consumers who do not wish to receive telemarketing calls. So far, more than 209 million phone numbers in the United States have been listed on the registry. The national registry is enforced by the Federal Trade Commission and the Federal Communications Commission, and companies are subject to a fine of up to $16,000 for each call made to a consumer listed on the national do-not-call registry. For instance, Rascal Scooters was forced to pay $100,000 after it was charged with using phone numbers from sweepstake forms to call consumers who were on the do-not-call registry.[23] Certain exceptions apply to do-not-call lists. A company can still use telemarketing to communicate with existing customers. In addition, charitable, political, and telephone survey organizations are not restricted by the national registry.

telemarketing The performance of marketing-related activities by telephone

television home shopping A form of selling in which products are presented to television viewers, who can buy them by calling a toll-free number and paying with a credit card

Television Home Shopping

Television home shopping presents products to television viewers, encouraging them to order through toll-free numbers and pay with credit cards. The Home Shopping Network in Florida originated and popularized this format. The most popular products sold through television home shopping are jewelry (40 percent of total sales), clothing, housewares, and electronics. Home shopping channels have grown so rapidly in recent years that more than 60 percent of U.S. households have access to home shopping programs. Home Shopping Network and QVC are two of the largest home shopping networks. Approximately 60 percent of home shopping sales revenues come from repeat purchasers.

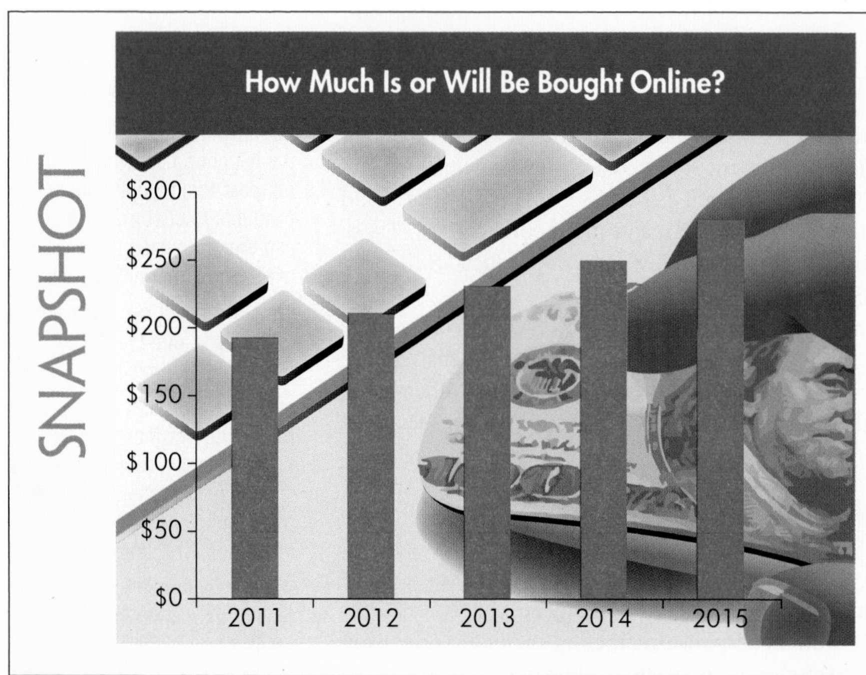

Source: Forrester.com (accessed Feb. 17, 2012).

The television home shopping format offers several benefits. Products can be demonstrated easily, and an adequate amount of time can be spent showing the product so viewers are well informed. The length of time a product is shown depends not only on the time required for doing demonstrations but also on whether the product is selling. Once the calls peak and begin to decline, a new

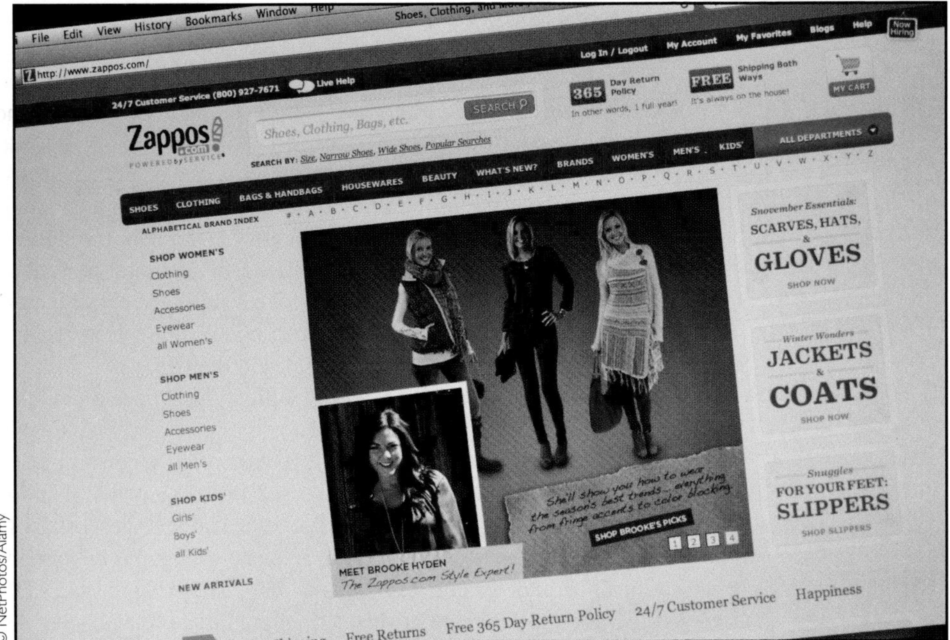

© NetPhotos/Alamy

Online Retailing
Zappo's is an online retailer of numerous products, including shoes, clothing, accessories, jewelry, eye wear, and beauty products.

product is shown. Other benefits are that customers can shop at their convenience and from the comfort of their homes.

Online Retailing

Online retailing makes products available to buyers through computer connections. The phenomenal growth of Internet use and online information services has created new retailing opportunities. Many retailers have set up websites to disseminate information about their companies and products. It is relatively rare to find a retailer who does not have a website to display its products, and many retailers also sell goods online. Increasingly, consumers expect to have multiple channels to obtain the goods and services they desire.

Consumers can perform a wide variety of shopping-related tasks online. They can purchase virtually anything via the Internet and services like eBay. They can track down rare collectibles, refill their eyeglass prescriptions, and even purchase gourmet pet products via businesses like Posh Puppy Boutique. Even banks and brokerages offer consumers access to their accounts, where they can perform a wide variety of activities, such as money transfers and stock trading. Forrester Research projects that online retail sales in the United States will climb to nearly $327 billion by 2016, up from $202 billion in 2011.[24] With advances in computer technology continuing and consumers ever more pressed for time, online retailing will continue to escalate.

More consumers than ever are shopping online now, but security remains a serious concern, with many shoppers still hesitant to use smartphones and other handheld devices to shop online. In a recent survey conducted by Wakefield Associates for Accertify Inc., 88 percent of participants said that they shop online, and two-thirds of respondents stated that they believe shopping online is more dangerous than in-store shopping in terms of identity and credit card theft. Only 7 percent of respondents trust their smartphones for shopping, and only 3 percent trust their tablet computers. The survey also found that, surprisingly, older consumers are more trusting of online shopping than younger ones.[25]

online retailing Retailing that makes products available to buyers through computer connections

direct selling Marketing products to ultimate consumers through face-to-face sales presentations at home or in the workplace

Direct Selling

Direct selling is the marketing of products to ultimate consumers through face-to-face sales presentations at home or in the workplace. The top five global direct selling companies are

© Adrian Sherratt/Alamy

Direct Selling
The Body Shop engages in direct selling by using the party plan approach through its at-home consultants. The company also markets products online as well as through catalogs and traditional brick-and-mortar retail.

Avon, Amway, Natura, Vorwerk, and Herbalife. Three of these companies, Avon, Amway, and Herbalife, are based in the United States. Direct selling is a valuable industry, with the top 10 direct sellers alone accounting for $39 billion in annual sales.[26] Direct selling was once associated with door-to-door selling but has evolved into a professional industry where most contacts with buyers are prearranged through electronic communication or personal contacts. Today, most companies identify customers through the mail, telephone, Internet, social networks, or shopping-mall intercepts and then set up appointments. Direct selling is possibly even more successful in collective societies like China, where Amway has achieved sales greater than its sales in the United States.

Although the majority of direct selling takes place on an individual, or person-to-person, basis, it sometimes also includes the use of a group, or "party," plan. With a party plan, a consumer acts as a host and invites friends and associates to view merchandise in a group setting, where a salesperson demonstrates products. The congenial party atmosphere helps to overcome customers' reluctance and encourages them to buy. Tupperware and Mary Kay were the pioneers of this selling technique, paving the way for companies like Forever Living Products International, a seller of aloe vera and honey-derived wellness products. Founded in the 1970s in Arizona, the company has grown from founder Rex Maughn's garage into the ninth-largest direct seller in the world, with annual revenues of over $1.7 billion.[27]

Direct selling has both benefits and limitations. It gives the marketer an opportunity to demonstrate the product in an environment—usually customers' homes—where it most likely would be used. The door-to-door seller can give the customer personal attention, and the product can be presented to the customer at a convenient time and location. Product categories that have been highly successful for direct selling include cosmetics and personal-care products, health products, jewelry, accessories, and household products. Personal attention to the customer is the foundation on which some direct sellers, such as Mary Kay, have built their businesses. Because commissions for salespeople are so high, ranging from 30 to 50 percent of the sales price, and great effort is required to isolate promising prospects, overall costs of direct selling make it the most expensive form of retailing. Furthermore, some customers view direct selling negatively, owing to unscrupulous and fraudulent practices used by some direct sellers in the past. Some communities even have local ordinances that control or, in some cases, prohibit direct selling. Despite these negative views held by some individuals, direct selling is still alive and well, bringing in annual revenues of $29 billion in the United States and $117 billion worldwide.[28]

Automatic Vending

automatic vending The use of machines to dispense products

Automatic vending is the use of machines to dispense products. It accounts for less than 2 percent of all retail sales. Video game machines provide an entertainment service, and most banks offer automatic teller machines (ATMs), which dispense cash and perform other services.

Automatic vending is one of the most impersonal forms of retailing. Small, standardized, routinely purchased products (e.g., chewing gum, candy, newspapers, soft drinks, or coffee) can be sold in machines because consumers usually buy them at the nearest available location. Redbox vending machines have started a new form of vending: DVD, Blu-ray disc, and video game rentals. These machines allow customers to rent movies and video games at a time that is convenient for them, without a membership and from their choice of more than

Emerging Trends

Vending Machines Go High-Tech

Coming soon to a corner or cafeteria near you: the next generation of vending machines, wired with the latest technology for a fast, convenient, and fun experience.

Want to send a friend a free cola? If you're near a PepsiCo Social Vending machine, you simply pay for a can or bottle and send a personalized text message to announce the gift, including a redeemable code for the cola. If you're at the airport and realize that you forgot your camera or cell phone charger, check out the terminal's Best Buy Express electronics vending machine. Need Wi-Fi? You can go online for free, even without buying anything, if you're standing next to an Asahi soft-drink vending machine in Tokyo.

High-tech vending machines can offer a lot of information about the products they sell. For example, buyers can swipe a finger across the touch screen of a Diji-Touch vending machine selling Kraft snacks to see nutrition facts and a 360-degree view of each item. For sheer entertainment, it's hard to beat the Lay's vending machine in Buenos Aires: drop a raw potato into the shoot, and watch as it gets washed, peeled, cut, cooked, salted, and bagged—and a finished package pops out of the machine. In reality, what customers see is a vivid one-minute video reinforcing the idea that chips are made from real potatoes.[d]

29,000 locations.[29] Machines in areas of heavy foot traffic provide efficient and continuous service to consumers. High-volume areas, such as in commercial centers of large cities or in airports, may offer a wide range of automatic vending product options. ZoomSystems, for example, operates vending machines that market products from Apple, Proactiv, Clinique, and Procter & Gamble.[30] Around the world, the trend toward increasingly novel vending options is increasing. Consumers can purchase such diverse items as freshly baked pizza and raw meat from vending machines. The Swap-O-Matic vending machine, for instance, was created by a Duke University graduate. Users can donate items to the machine in exchange for credit, which they can then use to purchase other items that have been donated. The Swap-O-Matic operates like an automated swap meet and seeks to enhance consumer awareness of the importance of recycling.[31]

Because vending machines need only a small amount of space and no sales personnel, this retailing method has some advantages over stores. The advantages are partly offset, however, by the high costs of equipment and frequent servicing and repairs.

FRANCHISING

Franchising is an arrangement in which a supplier, or franchiser, grants a dealer, or franchisee, the right to sell products in exchange for some type of consideration. The franchiser may receive some percentage of total sales in exchange for furnishing equipment, buildings, management know-how, and marketing assistance to the franchisee. The franchisee supplies labor and capital, operates the franchised business, and agrees to abide by the provisions of the franchise agreement. Table 16.2 lists the leading U.S. franchises, types of products, number of franchise outlets, and startup costs.

Because of changes in the international marketplace, shifting employment options in the United States, the expanding U.S. service economy, and corporate interest in more joint-venture activity, franchising is increasing rapidly. There are around 750,000 franchise establishments in the United States, which employ around 8 million people across a diverse variety of industries. Franchises account for more than $800 billion in annual economic output, amounting to around 3 percent of U.S. GDP.[32]

franchising An arrangement in which a supplier (franchiser) grants a dealer (franchisee) the right to sell products in exchange for some type of consideration

Franchising offers several advantages to both the franchisee and the franchiser. It enables a franchisee to start a business with limited capital and benefit from the business experience of

Table 16.2 Top U.S. Franchisers and Their Startup Costs

Rank	Franchise and Description	Number of Franchise Outlets Worldwide	Startup Costs
1	**Hampton Hotels** Mid-priced hotels	1,868	$3,745,000–$13,114,000
2	**Subway** Submarine sandwiches and salads	34,906	$84,800–$258,800
3	**7-Eleven Inc.** Convenience store	40,068	$30,800–$611,100
4	**Servpro** Insurance/disaster restoration and cleaning	1,581	$132,050–$180,450
5	**Days Inn** Hotels	1,865	$202,170–$6,764,850
6	**McDonald's** Hamburgers, chicken, salads	33,009	$1,068,850–$1,892,400
7	**Denny's Inc.** Full-service family restaurant	1,667	$1,125,505–$2,396,115
8	**H&R Block** Tax preparation and electronic filing	11,394	$35,505–$136,200
9	**Pizza Hut, Inc.** Pizza, pasta, and wings	13,432	$295,000–$2,149,000
10	**Dunkin' Donuts** Coffee, doughnuts, and baked goods	9,495	$368,900–$1,735,700

Source: "2012 Franchise 500," *Entrepreneur*, www.entrepreneur.com/franchise500/index.html (accessed April 11, 2012). © 2012 Entrepreneur Media, Inc.

Franchising
Subway is a franchise, so individual stores are owned and managed by the franchisee.

others. Moreover, nationally advertised franchises, such as Curves and Burger King, are often assured of customers as soon as they open. If business problems arise, the franchisee can obtain guidance and advice from the franchiser at little or no cost. Franchised outlets are generally more successful than independently owned businesses. Generally speaking, franchises have lower failure rates than independent retail establishments. However, franchise failure rates vary greatly depending on the particular franchise. For example, Quiznos has the highest failure rate among major franchises at 25 percent, while Pizza Hut, Burger King, and Wingstop all have failure rates below 15 percent.[33] Also, the franchisee receives materials to use in local advertising and can benefit from national promotional campaigns sponsored by the franchiser.

Through franchise arrangements, the franchiser gains fast and selective product distribution without incurring the high cost of constructing and operating its own outlets. The franchiser therefore has more capital for expanding production and advertising. It can also ensure, through the franchise agreement, that outlets are maintained and operated according to its own standards. Some franchisers, however, permit their franchisees to modify their menus, hours, or other operating elements to better match their target market's needs. The franchiser benefits from the fact that the franchisee, being a sole proprietor in most cases, is likely to be very highly motivated to succeed. Success of the franchise means more sales, which translates into higher income for the franchiser.

Franchise arrangements also have several drawbacks. The franchiser can dictate many aspects of the business: decor, menu, design of employees' uniforms, types of signs, hours of operation, and numerous details of business operations. In addition, franchisees must pay to use the franchiser's name, products, and assistance. Usually, there is a one-time franchise fee and continuing royalty and advertising fees, often collected as a percentage of sales. Franchisees often must work very hard, putting in 10- to 12-hour days six or seven days a week. In some cases, franchise agreements are not uniform; one franchisee may pay more than another for the same services. Finally, the franchiser gives up a certain amount of control when entering into a franchise agreement. Consequently, individual establishments may not be operated exactly according to the franchiser's standards.

WHOLESALING

Wholesaling refers to all transactions in which products are bought for resale, making other products, or general business operations. It does not include exchanges with ultimate consumers. A **wholesaler** is an individual or organization that sells products that are bought for resale, making other products, or general business operations. In other words, wholesalers buy products and resell them to reseller, government, and institutional users. For instance, Sysco, the nation's number-one food-service distributor, supplies restaurants, hotels, schools, industrial caterers, and hospitals with everything from frozen and fresh food and paper products to medical and cleaning supplies. Wholesaling activities are not limited to goods; service companies, such as financial institutions, also use active wholesale networks. There are approximately 435,000 wholesaling establishments in the United States, and more than half of all products sold in this country pass through these firms.[34]

Wholesalers may engage in many supply-chain management activities, including warehousing, shipping and product handling, inventory control, information system management and data processing, risk taking, financing, budgeting, and even marketing research and promotion. Regardless of whether there is a wholesaling firm involved in the supply chain, all product distribution requires the performance of these activities. In addition to bearing the primary responsibility for the physical distribution of products from manufacturers to retailers, wholesalers may establish information systems that help producers and retailers better manage the supply chain from producer to customer. Many wholesalers are using information technology and the Internet to allow their employees, customers, and suppliers to share information between intermediaries and facilitating agencies such as trucking companies and warehouse firms. Other firms are making their databases and marketing information systems available to their supply-chain partners to facilitate order processing, shipping, and product development and to share information about changing market conditions and customer desires. As a result, some wholesalers play a key role in supply-chain management decisions.

Services Provided by Wholesalers

Wholesalers provide essential services to both producers and retailers. By initiating sales contacts with a producer and selling diverse products to retailers, wholesalers serve as an extension of the producer's sales force. Wholesalers also provide financial assistance. They often pay for transporting goods; reduce a producer's warehousing expenses and inventory investment by holding goods in inventory; extend credit and assume losses from buyers who turn out to be poor credit risks; and, when they buy a producer's entire output and pay promptly or in cash, are a source of working capital. Wholesalers also serve as conduits for information within the marketing channel, keeping producers up-to-date on market developments and passing along the manufacturers' promotional plans to other intermediaries. Using wholesalers therefore gives producers a distinct advantage, because the specialized services wholesalers perform allow producers to concentrate on developing and manufacturing products that match customers' needs and wants.

wholesaling Transactions in which products are bought for resale, for making other products, or for general business operations

wholesaler An individual or organization that sells products that are bought for resale, for making other products, or for general business operations

Wholesalers support retailers by assisting with marketing strategy, especially the distribution component. Wholesalers also help retailers select inventory. They are often specialists on market conditions and experts at negotiating final purchases. In industries in which obtaining supplies is important, skilled buying is indispensable. For instance, Atlanta-based Genuine Parts Company (GPC), the nation's top automotive parts wholesaler, has more than 80 years of experience in the auto parts business, which helps it serve its customers effectively. GPC supplies more than 300,000 replacement parts (from about 150 different suppliers) to about 1,000 NAPA Auto Parts stores.[35] Effective wholesalers make an effort to understand the businesses of their customers. They can reduce a retailer's burden of looking for and coordinating supply sources. If the wholesaler purchases for several different buyers, expenses can be shared by all customers. Furthermore, whereas a manufacturer's salesperson offers retailers only a few products at a time, independent wholesalers always have a wide range of products available. Thus, through partnerships, wholesalers and retailers can forge successful relationships for the benefit of customers.

The distinction between services performed by wholesalers and those provided by other businesses has blurred in recent years. Changes in the competitive nature of business, especially the growth of strong retail chains like Walmart, Home Depot, and Best Buy, are changing supply-chain relationships. In many product categories, such as electronics, furniture, and even food products, retailers have discovered that they can deal directly with producers, performing wholesaling activities themselves at a lower cost. An increasing number of retailers are relying on computer technology to expedite ordering, delivery, and handling of goods. Thus, technology is allowing retailers to take over many wholesaling functions. However, when a wholesaler is eliminated from a marketing channel, wholesaling activities still have to be performed by a member of the supply chain, whether a producer, retailer, or facilitating agency. These wholesaling activities are critical components of supply-chain management.

Types of Wholesalers

Wholesalers are classified according to several criteria. Whether a wholesaler is independently owned or owned by a producer influences how it is classified. Wholesalers can also be grouped according to whether they take title to (own) the products they handle. The range of services provided is another criterion used for classification. Finally, wholesalers are classified according to the breadth and depth of their product lines. Using these criteria, we discuss three general types of wholesaling establishments: merchant wholesalers, agents and brokers, and manufacturers' sales branches and offices.

Merchant Wholesalers

Merchant wholesalers are independently owned businesses that take title to goods, assume risks associated with ownership, and generally buy and resell products to other wholesalers, business customers, or retailers. A producer is likely to rely on merchant wholesalers when selling directly to customers would be economically unfeasible. Merchant wholesalers are also useful for providing market coverage, making sales contacts, storing inventory, handling orders, collecting market information, and furnishing customer support. Some merchant wholesalers are even involved in packaging and developing private brands to help retail customers be competitive. Merchant wholesalers go by various names, including *wholesaler, jobber, distributor, assembler, exporter,* and *importer.* They fall into two broad categories: full service and limited service (see Figure 16.1).

merchant wholesalers Independently owned businesses that take title to goods, assume ownership risks, and buy and resell products to other wholesalers, business customers, or retailers

full-service wholesalers Merchant wholesalers that perform the widest range of wholesaling functions

Full-Service Wholesalers **Full-service wholesalers** perform the widest possible range of wholesaling functions. Customers rely on them for product availability, suitable assortments, breaking large quantities into smaller ones, financial assistance, and technical advice and service. W.L. Petrey is a full-service wholesaler of grocery and dry goods items. Petrey offers

Figure 16.1 **Types of Merchant Wholesalers**

Merchant wholesalers
Take title, assume risk, and buy and resell products to other wholesalers, to retailers, or to other business customers

Full-service wholesalers
- General merchandise
- Limited line
- Specialty line

Limited-service wholesalers
- Cash-and-carry
- Truck
- Drop shipper
- Mail order

many different services, including store design and layout, delivery, category management, and online software and communications to help customers manage orders and receive quick answers.[36] Full-service wholesalers handle either consumer or business products and provide numerous marketing services to their customers. Many large grocery wholesalers help retailers with store design, site selection, personnel training, financing, merchandising, advertising, coupon redemption, and scanning. Although full-service wholesalers often earn higher gross margins than other wholesalers, their operating expenses are also higher because they perform a wider range of functions.

Merchant Wholesaler
Grainger is a full-service, limited-line wholesaler of electrical equipment and supplies.

Full-service wholesalers are categorized as general-merchandise, limited-line, and specialty-line wholesalers. **General-merchandise wholesalers** carry a wide product mix but offer limited depth within product lines. They deal in products such as drugs, nonperishable foods, cosmetics, detergents, and tobacco. **Limited-line wholesalers** carry only a few product lines, such as groceries, lighting fixtures, or oil-well drilling equipment, but offer an extensive assortment of products within those lines. Bergen Brunswig Corporation, for example, is a limited-line wholesaler of pharmaceuticals and health and beauty aids.

general-merchandise wholesalers Full-service wholesalers with a wide product mix but limited depth within product lines

limited-line wholesalers Full-service wholesalers that carry only a few product lines but many products within those lines

specialty-line wholesalers Full-service wholesalers that carry only a single product line or a few items within a product line

rack jobbers Full-service, specialty-line wholesalers that own and maintain display racks in stores

limited-service wholesalers Merchant wholesalers that provide some services and specialize in a few functions

cash-and-carry wholesalers Limited-service wholesalers whose customers pay cash and furnish transportation

truck wholesalers Limited-service wholesalers that transport products directly to customers for inspection and selection

General-line wholesalers provide a range of services similar to those of general-merchandise wholesalers. **Specialty-line wholesalers** offer the narrowest range of products, usually a single product line or a few items within a product line. For example, Chia Seeds Direct is a specialty-line wholesaler that only sells chia seeds in large quantities.[37] **Rack jobbers** are full-service, specialty-line wholesalers that own and maintain display racks in supermarkets, drugstores, and discount and variety stores. They set up displays, mark merchandise, stock shelves, and keep billing and inventory records. Retailers need to furnish only the space. Rack jobbers specialize in nonfood items with high profit margins, such as health and beauty aids, books, magazines, hosiery, and greeting cards.

Limited-Service Wholesalers **Limited-service wholesalers** provide fewer marketing services than do full-service wholesalers and specialize in just a few functions. Producers perform the remaining functions or pass them on to customers or other intermediaries. Limited-service wholesalers take title to merchandise but often do not deliver merchandise, grant credit, provide marketing information, store inventory, or plan ahead for customers' future needs. Because they offer restricted services, limited-service wholesalers are compensated with lower rates and have smaller profit margins than full-service wholesalers. The decision about whether to use a limited-service or a full-service wholesaler depends on the structure of the marketing channel and the need to manage the supply chain to provide competitive advantage. Although certain types of limited-service wholesalers are few in number, they are important in the distribution of products like specialty foods, perishable items, construction materials, and coal.

Table 16.3 summarizes the services provided by four typical limited-service wholesalers: cash-and-carry wholesalers, truck wholesalers, drop shippers, and mail-order wholesalers. **Cash-and-carry wholesalers** are intermediaries whose customers—usually small businesses—pay cash and furnish transportation. Cash-and-carry wholesalers usually handle a limited line of products with a high turnover rate, such as groceries, building materials, and electrical or office supplies. Many small retailers whose accounts are refused by other wholesalers survive because of cash-and-carry wholesalers. **Truck wholesalers**, sometimes called *truck jobbers,* transport a limited line of products directly to customers for on-the-spot inspection and selection. They are often small operators who own and drive their own trucks. They

Table 16.3 Services That Limited-Service Wholesalers Provide

	Cash-and-Carry	Truck	Drop Shipper	Mail Order
Physical possession of merchandise	Yes	Yes	No	Yes
Personal sales calls on customers	No	Yes	No	No
Information about market conditions	No	Some	Yes	Yes
Advice to customers	No	Some	Yes	No
Stocking and maintenance of merchandise in customers' stores	No	No	No	No
Credit to customers	No	No	Yes	Some
Delivery of merchandise to customers	No	Yes	No	No

usually have regular routes, calling on retailers and other institutions to determine their needs. **Drop shippers**, also known as *desk jobbers,* take title to products and negotiate sales but never take actual possession of products. They forward orders from retailers, business buyers, or other wholesalers to manufacturers and arrange for carload shipments of items to be delivered directly from producers to these customers. They assume responsibility for products during the entire transaction, including the costs of any unsold goods. **Mail-order wholesalers** use catalogs instead of sales forces to sell products to retail and business buyers. Wholesale mail-order houses generally feature cosmetics, specialty foods, sporting goods, office supplies, and automotive parts. Mail-order wholesaling enables buyers to choose and order particular catalog items for delivery through UPS, the U.S. Postal Service, or other carriers. This is a convenient and effective method of selling small items to customers in remote areas that other wholesalers might find unprofitable to serve. The Internet has provided an opportunity for mail-order wholesalers to sell products over their own websites and have the products shipped by the manufacturers.

Agents and Brokers

Agents and brokers negotiate purchases and expedite sales but do not take title to products (see Figure 16.2). Sometimes called *functional middlemen,* they perform a limited number of services in exchange for a commission, which generally is based on the product's selling price. **Agents** represent either buyers or sellers on a permanent basis, whereas **brokers** are intermediaries that buyers or sellers employ temporarily.

Although agents and brokers perform even fewer functions than limited-service wholesalers, they are usually specialists in particular products or types of customers and can provide valuable sales expertise. They know their markets well and often form long-lasting associations with customers. Agents and brokers enable manufacturers to expand sales when resources are limited, benefit from the services of a trained sales force, and hold down personal selling costs. Table 16.4 summarizes the services provided by agents and brokers.

Manufacturers' agents, which account for more than half of all agent wholesalers, are independent intermediaries that represent two or more sellers and usually offer customers complete product lines. They sell and take orders year-round, much as a manufacturer's sales force does. Restricted to a particular territory, a manufacturer's agent handles noncompeting and complementary products. The relationship between the agent and the manufacturer is governed

drop shippers Limited-service wholesalers that take title to goods and negotiate sales but never actually take possession of products

mail-order wholesalers Limited-service wholesalers that sell products through catalogs

agents Intermediaries that represent either buyers or sellers on a permanent basis

brokers Intermediaries that bring buyers and sellers together temporarily

manufacturers' agents Independent intermediaries that represent two or more sellers and usually offer customers complete product lines

Figure 16.2 Types of Agents and Brokers

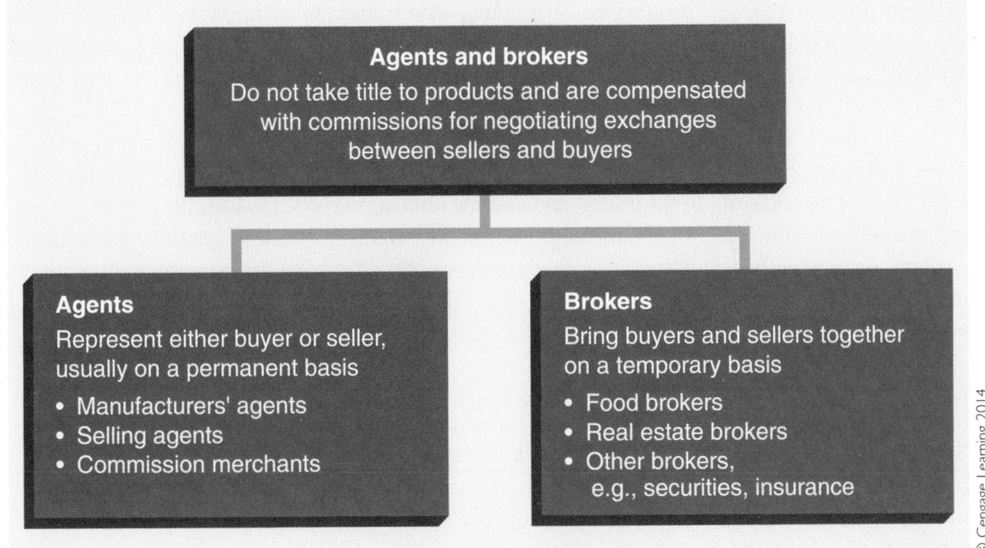

Table 16.4 Services That Agents and Brokers Provide

	Manufacturers' Agents	Selling Agents	Commission Merchants	Brokers
Physical possession of merchandise	Some	Some	Yes	No
Long-term relationship with buyers or sellers	Yes	Yes	Yes	No
Representation of competing product lines	No	No	Yes	Yes
Limited geographic territory	Yes	No	No	No
Credit to customers	No	Yes	Some	No
Delivery of merchandise to customers	Some	Yes	Yes	No

by written contracts that outline territories, selling price, order handling, and terms of sale relating to delivery, service, and warranties. Manufacturers' agents have little or no control over producers' pricing and marketing policies. They do not extend credit and may be unable to provide technical advice. Manufacturers' agents are commonly used in sales of apparel, machinery and equipment, steel, furniture, automotive products, electrical goods, and certain food items.

Selling agents market either all of a specified product line or a manufacturer's entire output. They perform every wholesaling activity except taking title to products. Selling agents usually assume the sales function for several producers simultaneously and are used often in place of marketing departments. In fact, selling agents are used most often by small producers or by manufacturers that have difficulty maintaining a marketing department because of seasonal production or other factors. In contrast to manufacturers' agents, selling agents generally have no territorial limits and have complete authority over prices, promotion, and distribution. To avoid conflicts of interest, selling agents represent noncompeting product lines. They play a key role in advertising, marketing research, and credit policies of the sellers they represent, at times even advising on product development and packaging.

Commission merchants receive goods on consignment from local sellers and negotiate sales in large, central markets. Sometimes called *factor merchants,* these agents have broad powers regarding prices and terms of sale. They specialize in obtaining the best price possible under market conditions. Most often found in agricultural marketing, commission merchants take possession of truckloads of commodities, arrange for necessary grading or storage, and transport the commodities to auction or markets where they are sold. When sales are completed, the agents deduct commission and the expense of making the sale and then turn over profits to the producer. Commission merchants also offer planning assistance and sometimes extend credit but usually do not provide promotional support.

A broker's primary purpose is to bring buyers and sellers together. Thus, brokers perform fewer functions than other intermediaries. They are not involved in financing or physical possession, have no authority to set prices, and assume almost no risks. Instead, they offer customers specialized knowledge of a particular commodity and a network of established contacts. Brokers are especially useful to sellers of certain types of products, such as supermarket products and real estate. Food brokers, for example, sell food and general merchandise to retailer-owned and merchant wholesalers, grocery chains, food processors, and business buyers.

selling agents Intermediaries that market a whole product line or a manufacturer's entire output

commission merchants Agents that receive goods on consignment from local sellers and negotiate sales in large, central markets

sales branches Manufacturer-owned intermediaries that sell products and provide support services to the manufacturer's sales force

Manufacturers' Sales Branches and Offices

Sometimes called *manufacturers' wholesalers,* manufacturers' sales branches and offices resemble merchant wholesalers' operations. **Sales branches** are manufacturer-owned intermediaries that sell products and provide support services to the manufacturer's sales force. Situated away from the manufacturing plant, they are usually located where large customers are concentrated and demand is high. They offer credit, deliver goods, give promotional assistance, and furnish other services. Customers include retailers, business buyers, and other wholesalers. Manufacturers of electrical supplies, such as Westinghouse Electric, and of plumbing supplies, such as American Standard, often have branch operations. They are also common in the lumber and automotive parts industries.

Sales offices are manufacturer-owned operations that provide services normally associated with agents. Like sales branches, they are located away from manufacturing plants, but unlike sales branches, they carry no inventory. A manufacturer's sales office (or branch) may sell products that enhance the manufacturer's own product line.

Manufacturers may set up these branches or offices to reach their customers more effectively by performing wholesaling functions themselves. A manufacturer also might set up such a facility when specialized wholesaling services are not available through existing intermediaries. A manufacturer's performance of wholesaling and physical distribution activities through its sales branch or office may strengthen supply-chain efficiency. In some situations, though, a manufacturer may bypass its sales office or branches entirely—for example, if the producer decides to serve large retailer customers directly.

sales offices Manufacturer-owned operations that provide services normally associated with agents

Summary

1. To understand the purpose and function of retailers in the marketing channel

Retailing includes all transactions in which buyers intend to consume products through personal, family, or household use. Retailers, organizations that sell products primarily to ultimate consumers, are important links in the marketing channel, because they are both marketers for and customers of wholesalers and producers. Retailers add value, provide services, and assist in making product selections.

2. To identify the major types of retailers

Retail stores can be classified according to the breadth of products offered. Two broad categories are general merchandise retailers and specialty retailers. The primary types of general merchandise retailers include department stores, which are large retail organizations organized by departments and characterized by wide product mixes in considerable depth; discount stores, which are self-service, low-price, general merchandise outlets; convenience stores, which are small self-service stores that are open long hours and carry a narrow assortment of products, usually convenience items; supermarkets, which are large self-service food stores that carry some nonfood products; superstores, which are giant retail outlets that carry all the products found in supermarkets and most consumer products purchased on a routine basis; hypermarkets, which offer supermarket and discount store shopping at one location; warehouse clubs, which are large-scale, members-only discount operations; and warehouse and catalog showrooms, which are low-cost operations characterized by warehouse methods of materials handling and display, large inventories, and minimal services.

Specialty retailers offer substantial assortments in a few product lines. They include traditional specialty retailers, which carry narrow product mixes with deep product lines; category killers, large specialty stores that concentrate on a major product category and compete on the basis of low prices and enormous product availability; and off-price retailers, which sell brand-name manufacturers' seconds and product overruns at deep discounts.

3. To explore strategic issues in retailing

To increase sales and store patronage, retailers must consider strategic issues. Location determines the trading area from which a store draws its customers and should be evaluated carefully. When evaluating potential sites, retailers take into account a variety of factors, including the location of the firm's target market within the trading area, kinds of products sold, availability of public transportation, customer characteristics, and competitors' locations. Retailers can choose among several types of locations, including freestanding structures, traditional business districts, traditional planned shopping centers (neighborhood, community, regional, and superregional), or nontraditional shopping centers (lifestyle, power, and outlet). Retail positioning involves identifying an unserved or underserved market segment and serving it through a strategy that distinguishes the retailer from others in those customers' minds. Store image, which various customers perceive differently, derives not only from atmospherics but also from location, products offered, customer services, prices, promotion, and the store's overall reputation. Atmospherics refers to the physical elements of a store's design that can be adjusted to appeal to consumers' emotions and thus induce them to buy. Category management is a retail strategy of managing groups of similar, often substitutable products produced by different manufacturers.

4. To recognize the various forms of direct marketing and selling

Direct marketing is the use of the telephone, Internet, and nonpersonal media to communicate product and organizational information to customers, who can then purchase products via mail, telephone, or the Internet. Direct marketing is a type of nonstore retailing, the selling of goods or services outside the confines of a retail facility. Direct marketing may occur through a catalog (catalog marketing), advertising (direct response marketing), telephone (telemarketing), television (television home shopping), or online (online retailing). Two other types of nonstore retailing are direct selling and automatic vending. Direct selling is the marketing of products to ultimate consumers through face-to-face sales presentations at home or in the workplace. Automatic vending is the use of machines to dispense products.

5. To examine franchising and its benefits and weaknesses

Franchising is an arrangement in which a supplier grants a dealer the right to sell products in exchange for some type of consideration. Franchise arrangements have a number of advantages and disadvantages over traditional business forms, and their use is increasing.

6. To understand the nature and functions of wholesaling

Wholesaling consists of all transactions in which products are bought for resale, making other products, or general business operations. Wholesalers are individuals or organizations that facilitate and expedite exchanges that are primarily wholesale transactions. For producers, wholesalers are a source of financial assistance and information; by performing specialized accumulation and allocation functions, they allow producers to concentrate on manufacturing products. Wholesalers provide retailers with buying expertise, wide product lines, efficient distribution, and warehousing and storage.

7. To understand how wholesalers are classified

Merchant wholesalers are independently owned businesses that take title to goods and assume ownership risks. They are either full-service wholesalers, offering the widest possible range of wholesaling functions, or limited-service wholesalers, providing only some marketing services and specializing in a few functions. Full-service merchant wholesalers include general-merchandise wholesalers, which offer a wide but relatively shallow product mix; limited-line wholesalers, which offer extensive assortments within a few product lines; specialty-line wholesalers, which carry only a single product line or a few items within a line; and rack jobbers, which own and service display racks in supermarkets and other stores. Limited-service merchant wholesalers include cash-and-carry wholesalers, which sell to small businesses, require payment in cash, and do not deliver; truck wholesalers, which sell a limited line of products from their own trucks directly to customers; drop shippers, which own goods and negotiate sales but never take possession of products; and mail-order wholesalers, which sell to retail and business buyers through direct-mail catalogs.

Agents and brokers negotiate purchases and expedite sales in exchange for a commission, but they do not take title to products. Usually specializing in certain products, they can provide valuable sales expertise. Whereas agents represent buyers or sellers on a permanent basis, brokers are intermediaries that buyers and sellers employ on a temporary basis to negotiate exchanges. Manufacturers' agents offer customers the complete product lines of two or more sellers. Selling agents market a complete product line or a producer's entire output and perform every wholesaling function except taking title to products. Commission merchants are agents that receive goods on consignment from local sellers and negotiate sales in large, central markets.

Manufacturers' sales branches and offices are owned by manufacturers. Sales branches sell products and provide support services for the manufacturer's sales force in a given location. Sales offices carry no inventory and function much as agents do.

Go to www.cengagebrain.com for resources to help you master the content in this chapter as well as for materials that will expand your marketing knowledge!

Important Terms

retailing 522
retailer 522
general-merchandise retailer 524
department stores 524
discount stores 525
convenience store 526
supermarkets 526
superstores 526
hypermarkets 527
warehouse clubs 527
warehouse showrooms 528
traditional specialty retailers 528
category killer 529
off-price retailers 529
neighborhood shopping center 531
community shopping center 531
regional shopping center 531
superregional shopping center 531

- lifestyle shopping center 531
- power shopping center 532
- retail positioning 532
- atmospherics 533
- category management 534
- direct marketing 535
- nonstore retailing 535
- catalog marketing 535
- direct-response marketing 535
- telemarketing 536
- television home shopping 536
- online retailing 537
- direct selling 537
- automatic vending 538
- franchising 539
- wholesaling 541
- wholesaler 541
- merchant wholesalers 542
- full-service wholesalers 542
- general-merchandise wholesalers 544
- limited-line wholesalers 544
- specialty-line wholesalers 544
- rack jobbers 544
- limited-service wholesalers 544
- cash-and-carry wholesalers 544
- truck wholesalers 544
- drop shippers 545
- mail-order wholesalers 545
- agents 545
- brokers 545
- manufacturers' agents 545
- selling agents 546
- commission merchants 546
- sales branches 546
- sales offices 547

Discussion and Review Questions

1. What value is added to a product by retailers? What value is added by retailers for producers and ultimate consumers?
2. What are the major differences between discount stores and department stores?
3. In what ways are traditional specialty stores and off-price retailers similar? How do they differ?
4. What major issues should be considered when determining a retail site location?
5. Describe the three major types of traditional shopping centers. Give an example of each type in your area.
6. Discuss the major factors that help to determine a retail store's image. How does atmosphere add value to products sold in a store?
7. How is door-to-door selling a form of retailing? Some consumers believe that direct-response orders bypass the retailer. Is this true?
8. If you were opening a retail business, would you prefer to open an independent store or own a store under a franchise arrangement? Explain your preference.
9. What services do wholesalers provide to producers and retailers?
10. What is the difference between a full-service merchant wholesaler and a limited-service merchant wholesaler?
11. Drop shippers take title to products but do not accept physical possession of them, whereas commission merchants take physical possession of products but do not accept title. Defend the logic of classifying drop shippers as merchant wholesalers and commission merchants as agents.
12. Why are manufacturers' sales offices and branches classified as wholesalers? Which independent wholesalers are replaced by manufacturers' sales branches? By sales offices?

Application Questions

1. Juanita wants to open a small retail store that specializes in high-quality, high-priced children's clothing. What types of competitors should she be concerned about in this competitive retail environment? Why?
2. Location of retail outlets is an issue in strategic planning. What initial steps would you recommend to Juanita (see Application Question 1) when she considers a location for her store?
3. Visit a retail store you shop in regularly or one in which you would like to shop. Identify the store, and describe its atmospherics. Be specific about both exterior and interior elements, and indicate how the store is being positioned through its use of atmospherics.
4. Contact a local retailer you patronize, and ask the store manager to describe the store's relationship with one of its wholesalers. Using your text as a guide, identify the distribution activities performed by the wholesaler. Are any of these activities shared by both the retailer and the wholesaler? How do these activities benefit the retailer? How do they benefit you as a consumer?
5. IMP Five Guys Burgers and Fries is one of the fastest growing fast food franchises in the United States. Started as a single burger joint by Jerry Murrell and his four sons—the "five guys"—in Alexandria, Virginia, the company now has more than 1,000 franchised outlets around the nation. Start-up costs for a Five Guys store range from about $150,000 to $300,000. A $25,000 franchising fee must also be paid, and ongoing royalties stand at 6 percent of sales.

Making one of these fast-food restaurants work, therefore, means acknowledging three major requirements of retailing: location, location, and location. Indeed, to recover start-up costs, and, of course, generate a profit, getting people through the door is paramount.

Franchises (like Five Guys), traditional and online retailers, and other types of channel members are all concerned with this idea of traffic. Once conducted almost exclusively by hand using "clickers," traffic is now measured using a variety of electronic and mechanical devices. One of the greatest advantages of the Internet is the ability to track online traffic behaviors. There are many consulting companies that specialize in measuring pedestrian and vehicular traffic. Most commercial real estate agents and property developers/managers use traffic data.

If you were considering becoming a Five Guys franchisee in your region, what would be the best location? What are the major factors affecting your decision?

Internet Exercise

Walmart

Walmart provides a website where customers can shop for products, search for a nearby store, and even preorder new products. The website lets browsers see what is on sale and view company information. Access Walmart's company website at www.walmart.com.

1. How does Walmart attempt to position itself on its website?
2. Compare the atmospherics of Walmart's website to the atmospherics of a traditional Walmart store. Are they consistent? If not, should they be?

developing your marketing plan

Distribution decisions in the marketing plan entail the movement of your product from the producer until it reaches the final consumer. An understanding of how and where your customer prefers to purchase products is critical to the development of the marketing plan. As you apply the information in this chapter to your plan, focus on the following issues:

1. Considering your product's attributes and your target market's (or markets') buying behavior, will your product likely be sold to the ultimate customer or to another member of the marketing channel?
2. If your product will be sold to the ultimate customer, what type of retailing establishment is most suitable to your product? Consider the product's characteristics and your target market's buying behavior. Refer to Table 16.1 for retailer types.
3. Discuss how the characteristics of the retail establishment, such as location and store image, have an impact on the consumer's perception of your product.
4. Are direct-marketing or direct-selling methods appropriate for your product and target market?
5. If your product will be sold to another member in the marketing channel, discuss whether a merchant wholesaler, agent, or broker is most suitable as your channel customer.

The information obtained from these questions should assist you in developing various aspects of your marketing plan found in the "Interactive Marketing Plan" exercise at www.cengagebrain.com.

video case 16.1

L.L.Bean: Open 24/7, Click or Brick

L.L.Bean, based in Freeport, Maine, began life as a one-product firm selling by mail in 1912. Founder Leon Leonwood Bean designed and tested every product he sold, starting with the now-iconic rubber-soled Bean Boot. Today, the catalog business that L.L.Bean began is still going strong, along with 30 U.S. stores and a thriving online retail operation. In addition, L.L.Bean is expanding its retail presence in Japan and China, where customers are particularly drawn to brand names that represent quality and a distinct personality. The company's outdoorsy image and innovative products, combined with a century-old reputation for standing behind every item, have made its stores popular shopping destinations around the world and around the Web.

Although the award-winning L.L.Bean catalog swelled in size during the 1980s and 1990s, it has slimmed down over the years as the online store has grown. Now, using sophisticated marketing database systems, L.L.Bean manages and updates the mailing lists and customer preferences for its catalogs. For targeting purposes, L.L.Bean creates 50 different catalogs that are mailed to selected customers across the United States and in 160 countries worldwide. The company's computer-modeling tools indicate which customers are interested in which products so they receive only the specialized catalogs they desire. Still, says the vice president of stores, "what we find is most customers want some sort of touch point," whether they buy online, in a store, by mail, or by phone.

© John Van Decker/Alamy

The company's flagship retail store in Freeport, Maine, like its online counterpart, is open 24 hours a day, 7 days a week, throughout the year. Even on major holidays like Thanksgiving and Christmas, when most other stores are closed, the flagship store is open for business. It stocks extra merchandise and hires additional employees for busy buying periods, as does the online store. Day or night, rain or shine, customers can walk the aisles of the gigantic Freeport store to browse an assortment of clothing and footwear for men, women, and children; try out camping gear and other sporting goods; buy home goods like blankets; and check out pet supplies. Every week, the store offers hands-on demonstrations and how-to seminars to educate customers about its products. Customers can pause for a cup of coffee or sit down to a full meal at the in-store café. Thanks to the store's enormous size and entertaining extras, it has become a tourist attraction as well as the centerpiece of L.L.Bean's retail empire.

L.L.Bean's online store continues to grow in popularity. In fact, online orders recently surpassed mail and phone orders, a first in the company's history, and the company also offers a mobile app for anytime, anywhere access via cell phone. The web-based store is busy year-round, but especially during the Christmas shopping season, when it receives a virtual blizzard of orders—as many as 120,000 orders in a day. Unlike the physical stores, which have limited space to hold and display inventory for shoppers to buy in person, the online store can offer every product in every size and color. Customers can order via the Web and have purchases sent to their home or office address or shipped to a local L.L.Bean store for pickup. This latter option is particularly convenient for customers who prefer to pay with cash rather than credit or debit cards.

At the start of L.L.Bean's second century, its dedication to customer satisfaction is as strong as when Leon Leonwood Bean began his mail-order business so many decades ago. "We want to keep . . . the customer happy and keep that customer coming back to L.L.Bean over and over," explains the vice president of e-commerce.[38]

Questions for Discussion

1. What forms of direct marketing does L.L.Bean employ? Which additional forms of direct marketing should L.L.Bean consider using?
2. Do you think L.L.Bean's website will ever entirely take the place of its mail-order catalog? Why or why not?
3. What type(s) of location do you think would be most appropriate for future L.L.Bean stores, and why?

case 16.2

Tesco Freshens Up Fresh & Easy's Retail Strategy

Tesco, the U.K. supermarket giant, is hardly a newcomer to international retailing. It's the world's third-largest retailer (behind Walmart and Carrefour) and has nearly a century of experience in its home country. Tesco embarked on a new era of global expansion in 1995 when it opened its first stores in Hungary. Within a few years, the company had stores throughout eastern Europe, as well as in Thailand and South Korea. It has added to its retail empire with new stores in China, Malaysia, India, and Japan.

By the time Tesco ventured across the Atlantic in 2007, its marketing experts had studied the U.S. retail industry for some time. They saw 4,000-square-foot convenience stores at the small end of the store spectrum. In the middle, supermarkets offered a larger assortment of foods and household items in stores of 35,000 square feet or more. At the largest stores, 200,000-square-foot superstores offered even more varieties of food and non-food products. Between these conventional store sizes, Tesco's experts identified an opportunity. "There is a gap between 4,000-square-foot stores and 35,000-square-foot-plus [stores]," explained Tesco's store design and planning director. "In Europe, that gap is filled by discount stores, but in the U.S., this segment is underserved."

Tesco set out to fill the gap with a chain of Fresh & Easy neighborhood grocery stores, each about 10,000 square feet in size. The stores would be stocked with high-quality fruits and vegetables, fresh meats, prepared meals under the store brand, and household staples carrying manufacturers' brands. Instead of fancy atmospherics, elaborate displays, and expensive shopper-reward programs, the stores would be simple, self-service, and easy to navigate for in-and-out convenience. The idea was to keep overhead costs down and pass the savings along to customers in the form of low everyday prices.

Originally, Tesco planned to open as many as 1,000 stores in the first five years. It scouted locations in California, Arizona, and Nevada and built a 1.4 million-square-foot distribution center capable of supporting an extensive store network. Even though Tesco operated everything from convenience stores to superstores in other countries, it was creating an entirely new retail brand from scratch and investing $2 billion to make it work. As part of its marketing research, the company built a prototype store inside a California warehouse to test potential shopper reaction. Only then did it finalize the retail design and begin opening stores.

However, Fresh & Easy's early results didn't live up to its parent's expectations. With rising unemployment and a deepening recession, consumers were cutting back on spending, even for food and other basics. Competition was another factor. Between supermarkets like Ralph's and Vons, natural-food grocers like Trader Joe's and Whole Foods, and convenience stores like 7-Eleven, the competitive environment was extremely challenging. Still, Tesco's management believed in Fresh & Easy's retail positioning and saw long-term profit potential in making its mark in the U.S. market.

One year into its U.S. expansion, Tesco slowed the rate of new-store openings as it fine-tuned Fresh & Easy's positioning. "After customers found the stores a little sterile, we warmed up the look, adding more graphics," says an official. "Family budgets being under pressure, we introduced more promotions and value packs." In addition, the chain installed higher shelving to increase the number of items available on the selling floor and began experimenting with smaller-size stores.

With these changes in place, Fresh & Easy launched its first-ever ad campaign to reinforce the message of fresh foods at low prices and used public relations to spotlight its support of its local communities and environmentally friendly operations. It connected with consumers through videos on YouTube, photos on Flickr, blog posts, and Twitter tweets. The retailer also made a special effort to reach out to Hispanic consumers with a Spanish-language website and Spanish-language advertising. Store by store, it adapted the merchandise mix to include more of the foods and brands favored by Hispanic shoppers in each neighborhood.

Now the U.S. venture is nearing the break-even point as Fresh & Easy stores build a loyal customer following. The economy is improving, the chain has shifted its new-store schedule into high gear, and customer feedback is positive. Looking ahead, can Fresh & Easy capture the hearts and wallets of enough U.S. shoppers to assure its long-term financial success?[39]

Questions for Discussion

1. What type of store is Fresh & Easy? Knowing that the store falls into this classification of retailers, what does that say about Fresh & Easy's marketing efforts?
2. Based on Fresh & Easy's retail positioning and marketing situation, what types of locations should it seek out as it expands its store network?
3. A few grocery retailers offer online shopping for customers' convenience. Should Fresh & Easy offer online shopping? Explain.

strategic case 6

GameStop Plays to Win

The Super Mario Bros. and Iron Man games fly off the shelves when GameStop pulls out all the stops in its video game marketing. Based in Grapevine, Texas, GameStop rings up $9 billion in annual sales as a specialty retailer of new and used video game hardware and software. Its 6,600 stores in 17 countries stock popular video game consoles and accessories from Sony, Microsoft, and Nintendo, plus thousands of games. Each 1,400-square-foot store is packed with an ever-changing merchandise assortment, some items purchased new from manufacturers or distributors and some taken as trade-ins from customers.

Founded in 1996, GameStop went through several names and mergers as it refined its retailing model and kicked off an aggressive expansion strategy that continues today, with the opening of 400 new stores every year. Its network of brick-and-mortar stores is complemented by an e-commerce site where customers can click to browse inventory, buy games and gear to be shipped to their homes, download free or paid games, and register for online game tournaments.

© Richard B. Levine/Newscom

Highly Seasonal, Highly Competitive

GameStop's business is both highly seasonal and highly competitive. Approximately 40 percent of its sales are made during the last three months of the year. In the United States, it must contend with the marketing muscle of giant discounters, such as Walmart and Target, toy stores like Toys"R"Us, and national electronics chains like Best Buy, as well as specialty stores, catalog merchants, and online retailers of all sizes. Outside the United States, GameStop also competes with multinational hypermarket retailers like Carrefour.

The company targets three customer segments: enthusiasts, casual gamers, and seasonal gift givers. In addition, some customers are value-oriented and prefer to buy used products, including older consoles and games that are no longer available as new items.

Used Games for Sale

One of GameStop's competitive advantages is its trade-in policy. Customers can bring in their games, consoles, and accessories and receive a store credit toward the purchase of other merchandise. Trade-ins must be in working condition and must include the original box and the instruction manual. GameStop's refurbishment centers in North America, Australia, and Europe test all trade-ins, fix defects when necessary, repackage the products, and ship them to stores for retail sale. Not only do trade-ins stimulate store traffic, but sales of used products result in a higher gross margin than sales of new products. Used games account for about one-fourth of GameStop's revenue and as much as 45 percent of its profits. The company recently began allowing trade-ins of non-game mobile devices, such as iPads and iPods, another way to bring customers into its stores.

The profit potential in used games has drawn competition for GameStop. The convenience store chain 7-Eleven has entered this market, selling used games through a partnership with the wholesaler Game Trading Technologies. Toys"R"Us also offers some used games and consoles and invites trade-ins, in person and by mail. Amazon.com allows game trade-ins by mail and serves as a virtual storefront for used video games sold by consumers and businesses, in addition to retailing new games and consoles.

The Right Merchandise in the Right Location

GameStop chooses store locations based on a number of factors, including demographic trends, visibility to pedestrians and vehicular traffic, and parking availability. It prefers to put stores in power shopping centers and malls that draw a high volume of customers. It also checks out the competitive situation in each area before making a final decision. Store atmospherics are designed to appeal to game players and include equipment where customers can sample games and watch videos of game clips before making a purchase.

Over the years, GameStop has developed a sophisticated information system for analyzing historic trends in store sales so it can project future demand for current and new products. This is especially important for satisfying the needs of enthusiasts, who may buy elsewhere if GameStop doesn't have the latest game or console in stock immediately after its release.

To help predict demand, GameStop invites customers to preorder new items for pick up at their local stores on or after the release date. It also tracks customer requests and monitors media coverage in advance of new-product introductions. During a busy period of new-game introductions, GameStop may have more than 1,000 new games in stock and ready for purchase. Because new games and equipment can make older products obsolete, GameStop has negotiated deals with its primary suppliers to allow returns in such instances.

Thanks to its marketing information system, GameStop knows exactly which products sell in each of its stores and what inventory is available in its distribution centers. The system automatically reorders merchandise as it sells and schedules twice-weekly shipments to replenish stock, so store shelves are never empty. On the other hand, daily analysis of inventory positions and frequent restocking allows GameStop to tailor the merchandise mix for each store while avoiding the expense of carrying too much safety stock in each store.

For high efficiency, GameStop supplies replenishment stock to U.S. stores from its 400,000-square-foot distribution center in Grapevine, Texas. Its 260,000-square-foot center in Louisville, Kentucky, is dedicated to receiving, sorting, and shipping hot new games and consoles to its stores nationwide. The company uses centrally located distribution centers to restock stores in other countries.

The Digital Dilemma

Despite GameStop's considerable investment in brick-and-mortar retailing, it sees great value in maintaining a strong online retailing presence. Game enthusiasts tend to be heavy Internet users, and GameStop wants to be where they like to be. Its website has a feature of interest to all of the targeted segments: a "wish list" where enthusiasts and casual gamers can itemize the products they would most like to receive (from gift-givers). GameStop also offers a weekly e-newsletter with exclusive discounts and advance notice of sales, tournaments, midnight openings for new releases, and other events.

Game consoles are increasingly Internet-ready and many players already play games on their personal computers, so digital game downloads are a must for GameStop. Its e-commerce site sells downloadable versions of popular games and offers hundreds of free games, some downloadable and some that play in the user's Web browser. The company tested a Facebook storefront, thinking it would appeal to its 4 million "fans," but quickly closed the "store" down because online buying is so convenient on the GameStop website.

Digital downloads pose a dilemma. GameStop's executives have been monitoring the situation in the music industry, where downloads have cut into retailers' sales of actual CDs. However, digital music files are relatively small, compared with digital game files. This means buyers would have to have a very speedy broadband Internet connection to get a game downloaded in a reasonable length of time. Still, GameStop recently began accepting in-store preorders for new digitally downloadable games, accepting trade-ins as credit toward the purchase price. "This is a great illustration of how the digital distribution model and in-store experience really complement one another," explains a GameStop official.[40]

Questions for Discussion

1. What role does physical distribution play in GameStop's retailing strategy?
2. Why would video game marketers such as Sony prefer dual distribution? What does this mean for GameStop's marketing efforts?
3. How does GameStop create time, place, possession, and form utility for customers who want to buy used video games?
4. Do you think GameStop should market used video games via vending machines placed on college campuses? Why or why not?

Role-Play Team Case Exercise 6

This role-play team exercise is designed to simulate actual marketing decision making in the real world. The entire team should read the overview and background. Each student will take on a role of a particular employee within the organization. Your instructor will provide additional information and instructions related to a team decision.

REDRIVERSHOPS.COM*

Background

RedRiverShops.com (RRS.com) is a leading online retailer. This e-commerce firm has more than 10 million customer accounts in 20 countries with sales of $900 million. The company offers products in various categories, including computers, software, music, movies, electronics, and sports equipment. RRS.com is the leading online retailer of golf and tennis equipment. The firm has 2 million feet of warehouse and distribution space to store and deliver merchandise to customers. The retailer is organized into three segments: allied electronics, integrated sports, and business-to-consumer auctions. The business-to-consumer auctions enable registered and approved businesses to offer a wide variety of products in an auction format, similar to eBay's online auctions.

RRS.com has yet to show a profit due to the high costs of building a distribution system, designing and updating a website, implementing customer transaction and service processes, and creating brand awareness through advertising. It also faces intense competition from Amazon.com and eBay. These successful firms have not merged with an outside company or developed traditional retail operations. Although RRS.com currently has $500 million in cash available for operations, it is losing about $50 million a quarter. Because acquiring additional financing has become increasingly difficult, RRS.com needs to break even in the next two-and-a-half years. As a publicly held corporation, the firm has been criticized for operating in the "red" for too long, and a number of investment firms recently downgraded RRS.com's stock from a "buy" to a "hold."

The board of directors is meeting to consider a proposal from the highly visible chief executive officer (CEO), president, and founder of RRS.com. The CEO has been able to develop an opportunity for a possible merger with a major developer of traditional shopping malls. Although not yet sure the merger is the best strategy for RRS.com, the CEO views the meeting with the board of directors as the most important aspect in the decision-making process. The CEO respects the board's ability to make the right recommendation, because the members attending the next meeting are company executives with much experience and knowledge in their respective areas of business.

A key concern is the merger of distribution functions. The supply chain for RRS.com uses large company warehouses but also uses a drop shipper approach by not taking possession of products that are shipped directly from the producer. The shopping mall sourcing of products will be very different, with retailers needing to maintain and display their inventories. On the other hand, if retailers also use the RRS.com website, they can tap into the retailer's warehouses and its drop shipper approach to fulfillment. The integration of distribution and other marketing functions is a key consideration in the merger decision. Questions relate to the advantages, disadvantages, or even the feasibility of merging these two organizations.

 Jennifer Sawayda assisted with the development of this exercise under the direction of O.C. Ferrell and Linda Ferrell. This role-play case is not intended to represent the managerial decisions of an actual company.

The proposal to be discussed at the board meeting is a merger of RRS.com with American Shopping Mall Properties (ASMP), a Houston-based real estate firm that owns 95 shopping malls in 28 states. ASMP is very profitable, with $600 million in rental income, yielding a bottom-line profit of $200 million last year. Merging a popular e-commerce portal with a successful shopping mall operator could create the ultimate "clicks-and-bricks" marriage. RRS.com could provide website exposure for shopping mall tenants who, in many cases, have well-established national brands. A joint venture with a mall tenant that markets heavy, durable products, such as washing machines and dryers, could provide an opportunity for RRS.com to market products that could be delivered and serviced by the mall store. ASMP malls could even be co-branded as RRS.com malls, creating a seamless flow between online buying and receiving and returning products in the mall.

It is time for the RRS.com board of directors to meet, discuss, and then approve or disapprove the proposed merger. You, as a member of the board of directors, have been assigned a functional role with unique information that can be used in the discussion.

Vice President of Communications

Your skills at communication have helped RRS.com become a proven technology leader. Because of your influence, the company has developed an easy-to-use search engine and the most secure payment features available in e-commerce. In addition to the U.S. website, the company operates three internationally focused websites for Japan, the European Union, and China. With the most innovative technology in the industry, RRS.com has the online platform to expand into new product lines through relationships with strategic partners. The vast computer technology and information systems developed by RRS.com have already allowed the company to sell products through co-branded (both RRS.com and a retailer or product manufacturer brand name) sections on the RRS.com website. In recent years, the company has introduced features to the e-commerce site to compete with Amazon. RRS.com has built in a recommendation engine that recommends new products to visitors based upon previous purchases. The company allows buyers to post product reviews directly onto the site. You also frequently use Facebook and Twitter to post promotional content and company updates as well as answer customer concerns.

You are concerned about the integrity of the system and the need to add additional software and hardware to upgrade the network infrastructure to accommodate increased traffic from a merger. Without these upgrades, the system could face interruptions, slower response time, and delays. Because all of the firm's equipment is at one leased facility in Houston, floods, fire, or similar events could destroy the system. Possibly of greater risk are computer viruses, electronic break-ins, and other events that could prevent servicing customers. Advancing technology and the resources needed to maintain and upgrade the websites represent a significant concern.

In addition, you are concerned about RedRiverShop's image and its possible dilution as a result of the merger with the "brick-and-mortar" shopping center. You have gone to great lengths to promote RRS.com as an online-only entity, and you continually reinforce this commitment both internally and with investors. Order processing and inventory management are also concerns if the two companies choose to merge. Your company has built an efficient order processing system for its RRS.com website. However, order processing involving retail stores would be an entirely new area requiring a complex communication system that you would have to develop. So far, your experience has dealt mainly with end consumers ordering through your site, not channel members requesting inventory shipments. If this merger occurs, it will require a great deal of thought as to the most efficient way to communicate with channel members.

Finally, you will have to work closely with the IT department to adapt RRS.com's Internet technology system to account for the new shopping malls. RRS.com will need to adapt the system to integrate its website with its retail distribution system. If the two firms merge, RRS.com will have to combine online retailing with the retailing done in its stores. Although this would take an extensive amount of time, many other companies have created successful IT systems to link their websites and their stores. Their big competitor Bass Pro Shops is one company that has had success in this area.

President, Chief Executive Officer, and Founder

Along with your role as president and CEO, you have been chairman of the board since you founded RedRiverShops in 2000. You have been successful in developing a leading e-commerce company that has the resources to pursue opportunities for forming new relationships. Through your leadership, the market value of RRS.com stock has reached $12 billion. Because the market value of American Shopping Mall Properties is $2.5 billion, RRS.com could acquire ASMP through a stock-for-stock trade. This would result in a 21 percent dilution in RRS.com's stock shares. The company would also acquire almost $3 billion in ASMP debt, because most shopping mall real estate is financed and therefore carries a heavy debt. The bottom line is that it is financially feasible for RRS.com to merge with ASMP without any cash requirements. Perhaps the greater concern is the long-run success of the merger.

You are particularly concerned with the significance and impact of the two different marketing channels. In order to be cost efficient, the channels must be able to create utility and facilitate exchange efficiencies. RRS.com has had great success in maintaining time utility, in other words, getting products to customers within a two-week time period. But will it remain as efficient after the merger? As an e-commerce firm, RRS.com did not have to worry as much about place utility, or having products available at physical locations. By adopting physical locations, RRS.com will have new inventory concerns in which it will have to maintain a sufficient amount of inventory at specific stores.

Finally, the merger will require RRS.com to make channel alliances to facilitate exchange efficiencies. If RRS.com merges, it will likely choose to adopt a dual-distribution system, or two or more marketing channels to deliver products to customers. One channel would be its e-commerce channel that it currently maintains. The other would be an expanded channel that would include retailers (through its malls), as well as the possibility of additional channel members. Because it will be expensive to adopt multiple distribution channels, RRS.com will need to work hard to make these dual-distribution channels cost efficient.

A number of advantages and disadvantages could result from the proposed merger. The new company could be profitable and some cash requirements for building warehouses and developing inventory could be reduced. RRS.com could increase traffic through websites developed for the mall stores. It could charge a fee for sales at the site, and it might have its name and logo on mall stores to increase its customer visibility. On the other hand, the CEO will lose some control over the management of the company and RRS.com will be less focused as an e-commerce company. Managers will have to spread their time over traditional as well as e-commerce operations. Taking on an additional $3 billion in debt is also a key concern. You are also concerned about investors' perceptions of this move. You see the issuance of new stock as a possible way in which to raise additional capital. But you must first convince current and potential investors of the company's commitment and faith in this extension of branding, distribution, and image. One other opportunity that you have been pondering is the possibility of opening RRS-branded stores that carry the same merchandise and use the same pricing strategy as the online operation.

Vice President of Operations and General Manager

You have been with the company for one year and were hired to streamline costs. Although RRS.com does not own any real estate, the company has been effective in leasing office facilities in Houston as well as leasing 2 million square feet of warehousing and fulfillment operations space for the company's products. In addition, infrastructure has been established to handle customer orders, supplier relationships, inventory management, and efficient shipment of products based on ordering criteria. There has been uninterrupted operation of the websites and transaction processing systems. On the other hand, continued growth will place a significant strain on management, operational, and human resource systems.

Currently, there are challenges in understanding customer demand and purchase patterns and meeting faster product life cycles. Significant risks are associated with product seasonality, accurately predicting sales, and the ability to negotiate terms with manufacturers, distributors, and other vendors. For example, some of the products sold through the site cannot be shipped overseas due to contractual limitations placed on the company by its vendors. The ability to expand leased distribution operations and maintain flexibility in the distribution of logistics systems is difficult due to the inability to predict sales increases. In fact, distribution centers are currently underutilized and operating at 60 percent of capacity.

The inventory needed to supply physical retail locations might take care of this excess capacity at your distribution centers. This merger would have the chance to create some operational efficiencies as well. American Shopping Mall Properties can make use of RRS.com warehouses and its unique drop-shipper approach. On the other hand, the merger would require RRS.com to change how it handles inventory management and materials handling. While its online store requires RRS.com to maintain enough inventory to fill orders, it does not have to worry about making sure that the right amount of product is delivered to the right stores in the right quantities. This merger would require RRS.com to take on these additional responsibilities. You realize there are many more chances for individual stores to undergo stockouts, or shortages. RRS.com will need to ship out more products to different locations, and as vice president of operations and general manager, it will be your responsibility to oversee the handling and transportation of these goods to individual stores. This increased responsibility is exciting but will also introduce a number of new challenges you must address. You are uncertain how all these functions will be managed.

Finally, competition with online and traditional stores is projected to intensify. Internet technologies foster quick comparison of prices and could reduce operating margins. Traditional retail stores may become more aggressive competitors with their own websites and strategic partnerships. However, you are skeptical that the opposite—expanding from a strictly e-commerce platform to brick-and-mortar stores—will work the same way. You feel that investing more in Internet technologies and website features could make RRS.com a more profitable enterprise and help it to compete against its rivals.

Vice President of Marketing

As vice president of marketing, you helped establish RRS.com as the number-one online store for sports and fishing equipment. *Customer Reports*, the most recognized source on rating e-commerce, has rated RRS.com as the best online store for golf and tennis equipment. Customers around the world are choosing RRS.com for online business-to-consumer auctions for a variety of products. RRS.com has maintained low competitive prices through low product gross margins. Currently, its major competitor in the sports and fishing area is Bass Pro Shops, which maintain their own stores. Bass Pro Shops have more complete product lines in sports equipment but do not offer consumer electronics. Consumer electronics is a highly competitive industry, and RRS.com faces intense competition from Best Buy and Amazon.com.

Through centralized distribution warehouses, RRS.com can physically stock all products the company needs in its inventory. Through joint agreements with UPS, FedEx, and the U.S. Postal Service, efficient delivery of products is maintained. Through advertising, RRS.com has established a brand name that has considerable value on the Internet. Overall, the company has an excellent marketing program driven by marketing research and a focus on customer value. The marketing strategy is focused on strengthening the brand name, increasing website hits, and building customer loyalty and repeat purchases. With strong competition, RRS.com has a proven track record of building customer relationships.

American Shopping Mall Properties has shopping centers across the nation ranging from regional shopping centers (large department stores and deep product mixes), to superregional shopping centers (widest and deepest product mixes), and lifestyle shopping centers (open-air shopping centers with upscale specialty, dining, and entertainment stores). These various types of shopping centers are beneficial, because they attract a diverse target market from all walks of life. However, maintaining such diverse product mixes will be challenging from both a marketing and distribution perspective.

Each type of center will require different marketing strategies. You will have to consider how to position the retailers with strategies that will serve an underserved market and distinguish them from others in the minds of consumers. You are wondering if it would be a better idea to market each variety of stores with their own brand image, or market them as RRS.com branded stores to create a cohesive brand image. Although the latter would connect the various mall stores with the RRS.com brand, you fear that the different stores and their various product mixes might confuse consumers and cause RRS.com to lose its distinctive brand identity that it has worked so hard to build.

In addition, you realize that your RRS.com credit card program has been responsible for increasing sales. The average purchase on an RRS.com credit card is 25 percent higher than the average for all other major credit cards. You are concerned about extending credit terms with the additional stores through the potential mall alliance. One other area you have been contemplating is how to relate your pricing strategy to that of the other stores you would become involved with in the malls. Do you utilize a low-margin, high-volume pricing strategy? If so, how do you improve the overall profitability of the company and generate positive cash flow?

Chief Financial Officer

RRS.com has not made a profit and has incurred significant losses since it started doing business in 2000. As of July 31, 2011, RRS.com has accumulated losses of $643 million. Losses may be significantly higher in the next year, because RRS.com must continue to invest in marketing, information technology, and operating infrastructure. Aggressive pricing, including meeting competitors' advertised online prices, has resulted in low gross margins on products. Current growth and pricing strategies will result in proportionately higher losses as sales increase. In addition, RRS.com has incurred significant debt totaling approximately $1.35 billion. If the company is unable to acquire additional funds through financial or stock markets, it could face serious liquidity problems. If cash flow is inadequate to meet service debt obligations, a major financial crisis and drop in stock value could occur. In addition, RRS.com cannot accurately forecast revenues and may experience significant fluctuations in operating costs.

Acquiring profitable ASMP shopping malls could decrease losses and help develop a more stable financial condition. However, even traditional shopping malls are subject to seasonality, business cycles, and increased competition. In addition, RRS.com would increase its debt from $1.35 billion to $4.35 billion in the merger. The newly merged organization would be under considerable financial pressure to service debt obligations. Any problems meeting these payments could result in default. Additional concerns relate to the fact that some of the malls are in less-desirable locations within their metro markets. Trends in "urban sprawl" mean that outlying malls tend to be newer and larger than those found in downtown areas.

On the other hand, your finance office has discussed a defense of the merger based on the larger distribution system. You realize that this larger distribution system would give RRS.com the ability to better negotiate deals with vendors and other channel members. The larger product mix would provide your organization with a competitive tool. These advantages could allow your company to provide products and services to your customers more efficiently and cost effectively. However, you also realize that, in order to keep costs lower than your competitors, RRS.com should carefully consider the marketing channels of its key competitors and see if this larger distribution system will enable the firm to be more efficient. You plan on bringing this fact up in the next meeting.

NOTES

[1]Based on information in Donald Heath, "Seminars Offered to Help Outdoorsmen," *Savannah Morning News*, February 8, 2012, http://savannahnow.com; Dave Haney, "Bass Pro Shops: Adding a Local Touch," *Journal Star* (Peoria, IL), September 21, 2011, www.pjstar.com; Dave Haney, "Bass Pro Visitors Amazed by New East Peoria Outdoor Center," *Journal Star* (Peoria, IL), September 20, 2011 www.pjstar.com; Danielle Altenburg, "Bass Rush: Retailer Opened First Full Day of Business," *Valley Morning Star* (Harlingen, TX), November 18, 2011, www.valleymorningstar.com.

[2]Ginger Christ, "Online Retail Sales Changing Dynamic of Holiday Shopping," *Daytona Business Journal*, January 20, 2012, www.bizjournals.com/dayton/print-edition/2012/01/20/online-retail-sales-changing-dynamic.html; Karen Talley, "Cyber Monday Sales Hit $1.25 Billion," *The Wall Street Journal*, November 29, 2011, http://online.wsj.com/article/SB10001424052970204449804577068600726857344.html?KEYWORDS=cyber+Monday.

[3]U.S. Bureau of the Census, *Statistical Abstract of the United States, 2012*, www.census.gov/compendia/statab/ (accessed April 10, 2012), Table 756.

[4]Ibid.

[5]"2011 Annual Report," Walmart, http://walmartstores.com/sites/annualreport/2011/letter.aspx (accessed April 10, 2012).

[6]Laurie Burkitt, "Starbucks Price Increase Stirs China's Netizens," *The Wall Street Journal*, February 1, 2012, http://blogs.wsj.com/chinarealtime/2012/02/01/starbucks-price-increase-stirs-chinas-netizen.

[7]"About Us," Walmart, http://walmartstores.com/AboutUs/ (accessed April 10, 2012).

[8]"Our Stores," Target, http://sites.target.com/site/en/company/page.jsp?contentId=WCMP04-031761 (accessed April 10, 2012).

[9]"About Us," National Association of Convenience Stores Online, www.nacsonline.com/NACS/About_NACS/Pages/default.aspx (accessed February 25, 2012).

[10]Alicia Ciccone, "Walmart, Target 'Small Box' Stores to Compete with Small Businesses," AOL, June 16, 2011, http://smallbusiness.aol.com/2011/06/16/walmart-target-small-box-stores-to-compete-with-small-busines/ (accessed February 25, 2012).

[11]"Sam's Club," "Costco Wholesale Corporation," "B.J.'s Wholesale Club," Hoover's Online, www.hoovers.com (accessed April 11, 2012).

[12]Julie Jargon, "Unusual Store Locations Fuel Subway's Growth," *The Wall Street Journal*, March 10, 2011, http://online.wsj.com/article/SB10001424052748704758904576188411711644134.html.

[13]Mall of America, www.mallofamerica.com (accessed April 10, 2012).

[14]"ICSC Shopping Center Definitions," International Council of Shopping Centers, http://icsc.org/srch/lib/USDefinitions.pdf (accessed April 10, 2012).

[15]Julie Cruz, "Adidas Targets Teenage Girls for $1.3 Billion in Sales," *Bloomberg*, February 13, 2012, www.bloomberg.com/news/2012-02-13/adidas-targets-teen-girl-fashion-market-for-1-3-billion-in-sales-retail.html.

[16]Rollo A. S. Grayson and Lisa S. McNeill, "Using Atmospheric Elements in Service Retailing: Understanding the Bar Environment," *Journal of Services Marketing* 23 (October 2009): 517–527.

[17]"History of Caesar's Palace," A2ZLasVegas.com, www.a2zlasvegas.com/hotels/history/h-caesars.html (accessed April 10, 2012).

[18]Scott Stump, "Restaurant Take Your Crying Kids Outside!" MSNBC, February 17, 2012, http://bites.today.msnbc.msn.com/_news/2012/02/17/10436835-restaurant-take-your-crying-kids-outside.

[19]The Category Management Association, www.cpgcatnet.org (accessed February 25, 2012).

[20]"What Is the Direct Marketing Association?" Direct Marketing Association, www.the-dma.org/aboutdma/whatisthedma.shtml (accessed April 11, 2012).

[21]"About Us," Spiegel, www.spiegel.com/about-us (accessed February 25, 2012).

[22]Davide Dukcevich, "TV's Top-Selling Infomercial Products," November 20, 2010, ABC News, http://abcnews.go.com/Business/story?id=86861&page=1.

[23]"National Do Not Call Registry Data Book for Fiscal Year 2011," Federal Trade Commission, November 2011, www.ftc.gov/os/2011/11/111130dncdatabook.pdf; "Maker of Rascal Scooters to Pay $100,000 for Violating FTC's Do Not Call Rules," Federal Trade Commission, www.ftc.gov/opa/2011/04/rascal.shtm (accessed April 10, 2012).

[24]Sucharita Mulpuru, "U.S. Online Retail Forecast, 2011 to 2016," Forrester Research, February 27, 2012, www.forrester.com/go?docid=60672.

[25]Ann Carrns, "Consumers Leery of Online Shopping with Tablets and Phones," *The New York Times*, January 27, 2012, http://bucks.blogs.nytimes.com/2012/01/27/consumers-leery-of-online-shopping-with-tablets-and-phones.

[26]J. M. Emmert, "DSN Global 100," *Direct Selling News*, June 2, 2011, http://directsellingnews.com/index.php/view/dsn_global_100_the_top_selling_companies_in_the_world.

[27]J. M. Emmert, "DSN Global 100," *Direct Selling News*, June 2, 2011, http://directsellingnews.com/index.php/view/dsn_global_100_the_top_selling_companies_in_the_world/P1.

[28]"What Is Direct Selling?" Direct Selling Association, www.directselling411.com/about-direct-selling/ (accessed April 11, 2012).

[29]"Facts about Redbox," Redbox, www.redbox.com/facts (accessed April 11, 2012).

[30]"Brands & ZoomShops," Zoom Systems, www.zoomsystems.com/our-partners/brands-zoomshop/ (accessed April 10, 2012).

[31]Tiffany Hsu, "Swap-O-Matic Vending Machine Dispenses Recycled Items from Users," *Los Angeles Times*, January 19, 2012, www.latimes.com/business/money/la-fi-mo-swap-o-matic-20120119,0,2055745.story.

[32]"Franchise Businesses Show Signs of Recovery in 2012 After Years of Restrained Growth," press release, International Franchise Association, December 19, 2011, http://franchise.org/Franchise-News-Detail.aspx?id=55623.

[33]"The Best and Worst Franchises to Own," *Inc.*, January 26, 2011, www.inc.com/articles/201101/the-best-and-worst-franchises-to-own.html.

[34]U.S. Bureau of the Census, *Statistical Abstract of the United States, 2012*, Table 1042.

[35]"Genuine Parts Company," Hoover's Online, www.hoovers.com/company/Genuine_Parts_Company/rfjcji-1.html (accessed April 11, 2012).

[36]"Our Service Solutions," W.L. Petrey, www.petrey.com/services.aspx (accessed April 11, 2012).

[37]Chia Seeds Direct, www.chiaseedsdirect.com/chse55lbwh.html (accessed April 11, 2012).

[38]"L.L. Bean Sales Grow Despite Weak Economy," Associated Press, March 9, 2012, www.suntimes.com; Kelli B. Grant, "Walmart Lets Online Shoppers Pay Cash," Smart Money, March 21, 2012, www.smartmoney.com; Michael Arndt, "Customer Service Champs: L.L. Bean Follows Its Shoppers to the Web," *Bloomberg Businessweek*, February 18, 2010, www.businessweek.com; Interviews with L.L.Bean employees and the video, "L.L. Bean Employs a Variety of Promotion Methods to Communicate with Customers"; www.llbean.com.

[39]Andrea Felsted, "Fresh & Easy Seen as Model for UK," *Financial Times*, March 6, 2012, www.ft.com; "Tesco CEO Says U.S. Business Could Break Even This Year—FT," Reuters, March 5, 2012, www.reuters.com; James Quinn, "Tesco's US Venture Sets Its Sights on Hispanic Shoppers," *The Telegraph* (U.K.), April 7, 2010, www.telegraph.co.uk; Scott Weber, "Grocery Store Shopping Is Getting Fresher, Easier," NBC News Los Angeles, April 6, 2010, www.nbclosangeles.com; Kathy Gordon, "Not So Fresh & Easy for Tesco in the U.S.," *The Wall Street Journal*, January 12, 2010, www.wsj.com; Kate Rockwood, "How Tesco Tweaked Its Fresh & Easy Concept," Fast Company, October 1, 2009, www.fastcompany.com; "Fresh & Easy Exec: Tesco Concept Fills Gap in U.S. Market," Progressive Grocer, December 13, 2009, www.progressivegrocer.com; www.freshandeasy.com.

[40]Ashley Lutz, "GameStop to J.C. Penney Shut Facebook Stores," *Bloomberg Businessweek*, February 17, 2012, www.businessweek.com; Matt Jarzemsky, "GameStop Cuts Same-Store Sales Outlook," MarketWatch, January 9, 2012, www.marketwatch.com; Emil Protalinski, "GameStop Begins Offering In-Store Digital Download Purchases," TechSpot, August 3, 2011, www.techspot.com; Brett Molina, "Want a Used Game with Your 7-11 Slurpee?" *USA Today*, April 19, 2010, www.usatoday.com; Victor Godinez, "Movie, Book, Game Companies Fight to Survive Plunge into Internet Age," *Dallas Morning News*, April 5, 2010, www.dallasnews.com; "GameStop Launches Its First Online Video Game," *Internet Retailer,* March 31, 2010, www.Internetretailer.com; Andrew Bary, "GameStop Builds a Business Selling Used Games to Teens," *Barron's Insight,* March 28, 2010, www.wsj.com; www.gamestop.com.

Feature Notes

[a]Based on information in "JCPenney Not Opening Early on Thanksgiving, CEO Says," *New York Post,* February 9, 2012, www.nypost.com; Shan Li, "Shoppers Barely Have Time for Pie," *Los Angeles Times,* November 22, 2011, www.latimes.com; Jenn Abelson, "Mass. Blue Laws Derailing Stores' Black Friday Plan," *Boston Globe,* November 15, 2011, www.boston.com; Phil Wahba and Dhanya Skariachan, "Thanksgiving Kicks Off Fight for Holiday Sales," Reuters, November 24, 2011, www.reuters.com.

[b]Based on information in Sharon Edelson, "Costco Keeps Formula as It Expands," *WWD,* January 30, 2012, 6; "Five Major Brands to Pilot New Label Designed to Promote Recycling," *Packaging Digest,* November 20, 2011; Tim Talevich, "The Chicken, the Egg, and the Future," *Costco Connection,* August 2011, 22–25; "Sustainability Initiatives Receive Recognition," *MMR,* February 8, 2010, 7.

[c]Stephanie Clifford and Claire Cain Miller, "Online Shoppers Are Rooting for the Little Guy," *The New York Times*, January 15, 2012, www.nytimes.com; Jeff Wuorio, "Business Lessons Learned in 2011," Fox Small Business Center, February 6, 2012, http://smallbusiness.foxbusiness.com; Bridget Maiellaro, "Local Boutiques Unite via New Online Shop," *Chicago Magazine*, August 2, 2011, www.chicagomag.com; Geoff Dankert, "Five Questions with Roscoe Village Bike's Lesley Tweedie," *Roscoe View Journal*, March 22, 2012, www.roscoeviewjournal.com.

[d]Based on information in Danielle Demetriou, "Japanese Vending Machines to Offer Free WiFi," *Telegraph* (U.K.), February 8, 2012, www.telegraph.co.uk; Angel Abcede, "Best Buy Uses Kiosks to Sell Upscale Devices at C-Stores, Including Murphy Express," *CSP Daily News,* January 5, 2012, www.cspnet.com; "In Argentina, Lay's Vending Machine Turns Raw Potatoes into Bags of Chips," *Advertising Age,* September 15, 2011, www.adage.com; Christina Cheddar Berk, "Vending Machines Woo Gen Y with New Technology," CNBC, October 17, 2011, www.cnbc.com.

part 7

Promotion Decisions

PART 7 focuses on communication with target market members and other relevant groups. A specific marketing mix cannot satisfy people in a particular target market unless they are aware of the product and know where to find it. Some promotion decisions relate to a specific marketing mix; others are geared toward promoting the entire organization. CHAPTER 17 discusses integrated marketing communications. It describes the communication process and the major promotional methods that can be included in promotion mixes. CHAPTER 18 analyzes the major steps in developing an advertising campaign. It also explains what public relations is and how it can be used. CHAPTER 19 deals with personal selling and sales promotion efforts, exploring the general characteristics of sales promotion and sales promotion techniques.

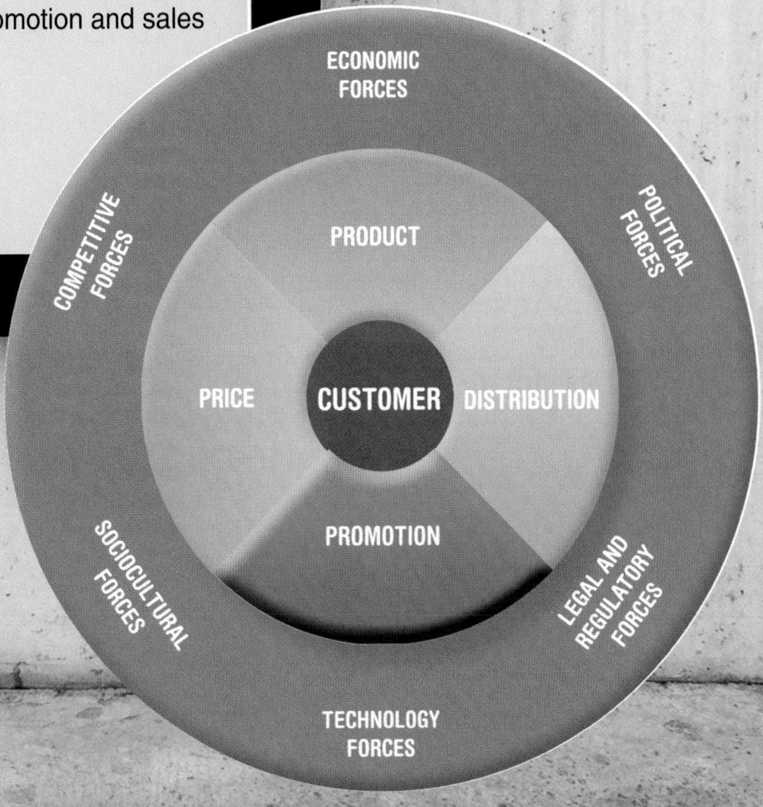

chapter 17

Integrated Marketing Communications

OBJECTIVES

1. To describe the nature of integrated marketing communications
2. To examine the process of communication
3. To understand the role and objectives of promotion
4. To explore the elements of the promotion mix
5. To examine the selection of promotion mix elements
6. To understand word-of-mouth communication and how it affects promotion
7. To understand product placement promotions
8. To examine criticisms and defenses of promotion

MARKETING INSIGHTS

Taco Bell Provides Transparent Communication in a Crisis

Does a crisis have to weaken your business? Not if you are Taco Bell. When a lawsuit accused Taco Bell's taco filling of containing less beef than required by the U.S. Department of Agriculture (USDA), the company used a carefully integrated response plan to keep sales from plummeting.

It started when consumers filed a lawsuit against Taco Bell stating that its taco filling had less than 35 percent beef, even though the USDA requires taco meat filling to have at least 40 percent beef. *USA Today* and MSNBC quickly published articles questioning the quality of Taco Bell's taco filling. Lawsuits and the resulting bad publicity can seriously jeopardize a company's revenue, regardless of whether the accusations against the company are true.

The same day that news of the lawsuit broke, Taco Bell's management team met several times to discuss the situation. To keep a crisis from overpowering a company, a business must have a crisis management team in place and a spokesperson to immediately respond to stakeholders, including the media, customers, employees, suppliers, regulators, and allies. Taco Bell responded to the media and consumers during the next few days via statements, YouTube videos, and national ads with the headline "Thank you for suing us—here's the truth about our seasoned beef." Taco Bell maintained that its taco filling contained 88 percent seasoned beef.

Thanks to its effective crisis management, sales at Taco Bell stores did not decline. Eventually, the lawsuit against Taco Bell was dropped, but the company was not quite ready to let its accusers off so easily. Instead, Taco Bell released additional advertisements reading "Would it kill you to say you're sorry?"[1]

Organizations like Taco Bell employ a variety of promotional methods to communicate with their target markets. Sometimes the messages are planned in advance, or, as was the case of Taco Bell, they may be a response to a dramatic change in the marketing environment. Providing information to customers and other stakeholders is vital to initiating and developing long-term relationships with them.

This chapter looks at the general dimensions of promotion. First, we discuss the nature of integrated marketing communications. Next, we analyze the meaning and process of communication. We then define and examine the role of promotion and explore some of the reasons promotion is used. We consider major promotional methods and the factors that influence marketers' decisions to use particular methods. Next, we explain the positive and negative effects of personal and electronic word-of-mouth communication. Finally, we examine criticisms and benefits of promotion.

THE NATURE OF INTEGRATED MARKETING COMMUNICATIONS

Integrated marketing communications refer to the coordination of promotion and other marketing efforts to ensure maximum informational and persuasive impact on customers. Coordinating multiple marketing tools to produce this synergistic effect requires a marketer to employ a broad perspective. A major goal of integrated marketing communications is to send a consistent message to customers. For instance, Tic Tac developed the integrated marketing campaign "Shake It Up" to create a more modern image for its brand. The company developed a 300-foot billboard in Times Square that viewers could scan with their mobile cameras. Those with the Tic Tac Viewr app on their phones would see a photo of themselves within the billboard that could then be uploaded to Facebook or Twitter.[2]

integrated marketing communications Coordination of promotion and other marketing efforts for maximum informational and persuasive impact

Because various units both inside and outside most companies have traditionally planned and implemented promotional efforts, customers have not always received consistent messages. Integrated marketing communications allow an organization to coordinate and manage its promotional efforts to transmit consistent messages. Integrated marketing communications also enable synchronization of promotion elements and can improve the efficiency and

Managing Promotional Efforts Pepto-Bismol is the official stomach remedy of Nathan's Famous Fourth of July International Hot Dog Eating Contest as one of its many promotional activities.

effectiveness of promotion budgets. Thus, this approach fosters not only long-term customer relationships but also the efficient use of promotional resources.

The concept of integrated marketing communications is increasingly effective for several reasons. Mass media advertising, a very popular promotional method in the past, is used less frequently today because of its high cost and lower effectiveness in reaching some target markets. Marketers can now take advantage of more precisely targeted promotional tools, such as TV, direct mail, the Internet, special-interest magazines, DVDs, cell phones, mobile applications, and outdoor boards. Database marketing is also allowing marketers to more precisely target individual customers. Until recently, suppliers of marketing communications were specialists. Advertising agencies provided advertising campaigns, sales promotion companies provided sales promotion activities and materials, and public relations organizations engaged in publicity efforts. Today, a number of promotion-related companies provide one-stop shopping for the client seeking advertising, sales promotion, and public relations, thus reducing coordination problems for the sponsoring company. Because the overall cost of marketing communications has risen significantly, marketers demand systematic evaluations of communication efforts and a reasonable return on investment.

The specific communication vehicles employed and the precision with which they are used are changing as both information technology and customer interests become increasingly dynamic. For example, companies and politicians can hold press conferences where viewers can tweet their questions and have them answered on-screen. Some companies are creating their own branded content to exploit the many vehicles through which consumers obtain information. For instance, American Express created a branded content website called OpenForum, which offers tools and advice for small businesses and entrepreneurs. OpenForum features content from business experts, articles from business publications like *Inc.*, and OpenForum's in-house team.[3]

Today, marketers and customers have almost unlimited access to data about each other. Integrating and customizing marketing communications while protecting customer privacy has become a major challenge. Through digital media, companies can provide product information and services that are coordinated with traditional promotional activities. In fact, gathering information about goods and services is one of the main reasons people go online. This has made online advertising a growing business. Marketers spent approximately $32 billion on Internet advertising in 2011.[4] College students in particular say they are influenced by Internet ads when buying online or just researching product purchases. The sharing of information and use of technology to facilitate communication between buyers and sellers are essential for successful customer relationship management.

PROMOTION AND THE COMMUNICATION PROCESS

Communication is essentially the transmission of information. For communication to take place, both the sender and receiver of information must share some common ground. They must have a common understanding of the symbols, words, and pictures used to transmit information. An individual transmitting the following message may believe he or she is communicating with you:

在工廠吾人製造化粧品，在商店吾人銷售希望。

However, communication has not taken place if you don't understand the language in which the message is written. Thus, we define **communication** as a sharing of meaning. Implicit in this definition is the notion of transmission of information because sharing necessitates transmission.

communication A sharing of meaning through the transmission of information

Figure 17.1 **The Communication Process**

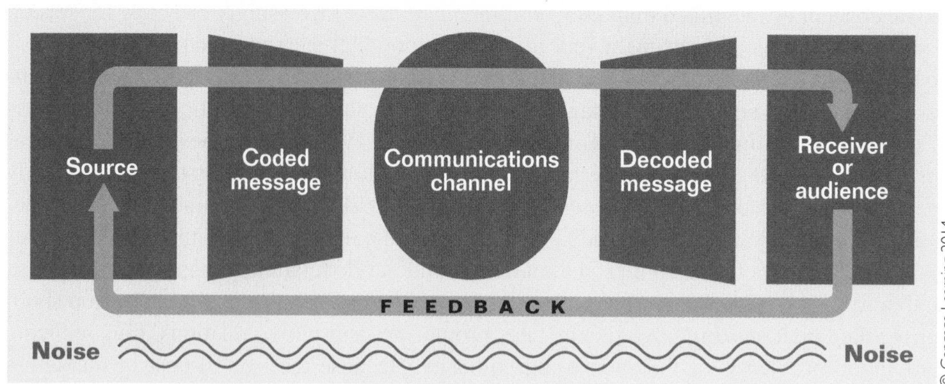

source A person, group, or organization with a meaning it tries to share with a receiver or an audience

receiver The individual, group, or organization that decodes a coded message

coding process Converting meaning into a series of signs or symbols

As Figure 17.1 shows, communication begins with a source. A **source** is a person, group, or organization with a meaning it attempts to share with an audience. A source could be an electronics salesperson wishing to communicate the attributes of 3D television to a buyer in the store or a TV manufacturer using television ads to inform thousands of consumers about its products. Developing a strategy can enhance the effectiveness of the source's communication. For example, a strategy in which a salesperson attempts to influence a customer's decision by eliminating competitive products from consideration has been found to be effective. A **receiver** is the individual, group, or organization that decodes a coded message, and an *audience* is two or more receivers.

To transmit meaning, a source must convert the meaning into a series of signs or symbols representing ideas or concepts. This is called the **coding process**, or *encoding.* When coding meaning into a message, the source must consider certain characteristics of the receiver or audience. To share meaning, the source should use signs or symbols familiar to the receiver or audience. Research has shown that persuasive messages from a source are more effective when the appeal matches an individual's personality.[5] Marketers that understand this realize the importance of knowing their target market and ensuring that an advertisement or promotion uses language the target market understands and that depicts behaviors acceptable within the culture. For instance, when Pepsodent toothpaste was sold in Southeast Asia, it promoted its teeth whitening capability. The product did not sell well because local natives chew betel nuts to blacken their teeth, which is considered more attractive than light teeth. Another example involves a U.S. telephone company whose ad campaign failed to reach Latinos with a commercial that showed a wife telling her husband to call friends and explain that they would be arriving late for dinner. First, in general, Latina women do not dictate their husband's behavior. Also, it is not customary in Latino cultures to call if you are going to be late for dinner.[6]

When coding a meaning, a source needs to use signs or symbols that the receiver or audience uses to refer to the concepts the source intends to convey. Instead of technical jargon, explanatory language that helps consumers understand the

Converting Meaning into a Concept
The MINI Countryman plays with readers' understanding of the term "biggie" in promoting its larger MINI automobile.

message is more likely to result in positive attitudes and purchase intentions. Marketers try to avoid signs or symbols that may have several meanings for an audience. For example, *soda* as a general term for soft drinks may not work well in national advertisements. Although in some parts of the United States the word means "soft drink," in other regions it may connote bicarbonate of soda, an ice cream drink, or something one mixes with alcoholic beverages.

To share a coded meaning with the receiver or audience, a source selects and uses a **communications channel**, the medium of transmission that carries the coded message from the source to the receiver or audience. Transmission media include printed words (newspapers and magazines), broadcast media (television and radio), and digital communication. Table 17.1 summarizes the leading communications channels from which people obtain information and news. Although television is still the most common source for obtaining news, the Internet is the most common source for consumers between the ages of 18 and 29 years old, at 65 percent.[7]

Table 17.1 Sources of News Information for Americans

Television	66%
Online	41%
Newspaper	31%
Radio	16%

Source: "Internet Gains on Television as Public's Main News Source," *Pew Research Center*, January 4, 2011, www.people-press.org/2011/01/04/internet-gains-on-television-as-publics-main-news-source/ (accessed February 23, 2012).

When a source chooses an inappropriate communication channel, several problems may arise. The coded message may reach some receivers, but possibly the wrong receivers. For example, dieters who adopt the Atkins low-carbohydrate diet are more likely to focus on communications that relate to their food concerns, such as "Eat Meat Not Wheat" T-shirts and fast-food chain advertisements that communicate information about the carbohydrate content of menu items. An advertiser that wants to reach this group would need to take this information into account when choosing an appropriate communications channel. At the same time, however, these messages can be easily embraced by the wrong types of receivers—those who want an excuse to eat all the meats and fatty foods they want without guilt, which is not the purpose of the Atkins diet. Thus, finding the right messages that target the right receivers can be a challenging process.

In the **decoding process**, signs or symbols are converted into concepts and ideas. Seldom does a receiver decode exactly the same meaning the source intended. When the result of decoding differs from what was coded, noise exists. **Noise** is anything that reduces the clarity and accuracy of the communication; it has many sources and may affect any or all parts of the communication process. Noise sometimes arises within the communications channel itself. Radio or television transmission difficulties, poor or slow Internet connections, and laryngitis are sources of noise. Noise also occurs when a source uses signs or symbols that are unfamiliar to the receiver or have a meaning different from the one intended. Noise may also originate in the receiver; a receiver may be unaware of a coded message when perceptual processes block it out. For example, those who do not recycle can block messages encouraging "green behaviors" such as recycling.

The receiver's response to a decoded message is **feedback** to the source. The source usually expects and normally receives feedback, although perhaps not immediately. During feedback, the receiver or audience provides the original source with a response to the message. Feedback is coded, sent through a communications channel, and decoded by the receiver, the source of the original communication. Thus, communication is a circular process, as indicated in Figure 17.1.

During face-to-face communication, such as personal selling sales promotions, verbal and nonverbal feedback can be immediate. Instant feedback lets communicators adjust messages quickly to improve the effectiveness of their communications. For example, when a salesperson realizes through feedback that a customer does not understand a sales presentation, the salesperson adapts the presentation to make it more meaningful to the customer. This is why face-to-face communication is the most adaptive and flexible, especially compared to digital, web-based, or telephone communications. In interpersonal communication, feedback occurs through talking, touching, smiling, nodding, eye movements, and other body movements and postures.

communications channel The medium of transmission that carries the coded message from the source to the receiver

decoding process Converting signs or symbols into concepts and ideas

noise Anything that reduces a communication's clarity and accuracy

feedback The receiver's response to a decoded message

When mass communication like advertising is used, feedback is often slow and difficult to recognize. Also, it may be several months or even years before the effects of this promotion will be known. Some relevant and timely feedback can occur in the form of sales increases, inquiries about products, or changes in attitude or brand awareness levels.

Each communication channel has a limit on the volume of information it can handle effectively. This limit, called **channel capacity**, is determined by the least efficient component of the communication process. Consider communications that depend on speech. An individual source can speak only so fast, and there is a limit to how much an individual receiver can take in through listening. Beyond that point, additional messages cannot be decoded; thus, meaning cannot be shared. Although a radio announcer can read several hundred words a minute, a one-minute advertising message should not exceed 150 words, because most announcers cannot articulate words into understandable messages at a rate beyond 150 words per minute.

THE ROLE AND OBJECTIVES OF PROMOTION

Promotion is communication that builds and maintains favorable relationships by informing and persuading one or more audiences to view an organization positively and accept its products. Toward this end, many organizations spend considerable resources on promotion to build and enhance relationships with current and potential customers as well as other stakeholders. For example, Procter & Gamble spends about $4.6 billion on advertising yearly.[8] Marketers also indirectly facilitate favorable relationships by focusing information about company activities and products on interest groups (such as environmental and consumer groups), current and potential investors, regulatory agencies, and society in general. For instance, some organizations promote responsible use of products criticized by society, such as tobacco, alcohol, and violent movies or video games. Companies sometimes promote programs that help selected groups. For example, Target's REDcard generates customer loyalty by allowing you to donate 1 percent of your credit card purchases to specific schools.[9]

Such cause-related marketing links the purchase of products to philanthropic efforts for one or more causes. By contributing to causes that its target markets support, cause-related marketing can help marketers boost sales, increase loyalty, and generate goodwill.

For maximum benefit from promotional efforts, marketers strive for proper planning, implementation, coordination, and control of communications. Effective management of integrated marketing communications is based on information about and feedback from customers and the marketing environment, often obtained from an organization's marketing information system (see Figure 17.2). How successfully marketers use promotion to maintain positive relationships depends to some extent on the quantity and quality of information

channel capacity The limit on the volume of information a communication channel can handle effectively

promotion Communication to build and maintain relationships by informing and persuading one or more audiences

Figure 17.2 **Information Flows Are Important in Integrated Marketing Communications**

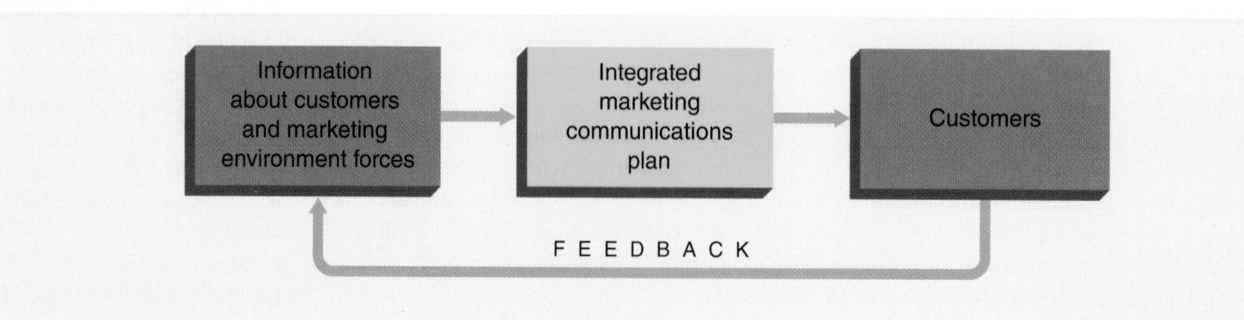

the organization receives. Because customers derive information and opinions from many different sources, integrated marketing communications planning also takes into account informal methods of communication, such as word of mouth and independent information sources on the Internet. Because promotion is communication that can be managed, we now analyze what this communication is and how it works.

Promotional objectives vary considerably from one organization to another and within organizations over time. Large firms with multiple promotional programs operating simultaneously may have quite varied promotional objectives. For the purpose of analysis, we focus on the eight promotional objectives shown in Table 17.2. Although the list is not exhaustive, one or more of these objectives underlie many promotional programs.

Creating Awareness
The producer of Ethos Water uses this advertisement to increase brand awareness and make consumers aware of its program to make clean water available in several developing countries.

Create Awareness

A considerable amount of promotion efforts focus on creating awareness. For an organization that is introducing a new product or a line extension, making customers aware of the product is crucial to initiating the product adoption process. A marketer that has invested heavily in product development strives to create product awareness quickly to generate revenues to offset the high costs of product development and introduction. Microsoft created awareness about its Windows 8 operating system months before its official launch. Microsoft allowed software developers to have an early version of Windows 8 and unveiled new features of its operating system at the Mobile World Congress before the release date. Educating consumers about its product's features is important as Windows 8 was the company's first operating system to operate on both desktop and tablet computers.[10]

Creating awareness is important for existing products, too. Promotional efforts may aim to increase awareness of brands, product features, image-related issues (such as organizational size or socially responsive behavior), or operational characteristics (such as store hours, locations, and credit availability). For instance, to inform consumers about its anti-aging products, Procter & Gamble's Olay placed advertisements in *The Huffington Post's* mobile iPhone app. The ads ran in the app's entertainment section, which targets the demographic Olay is most trying to reach—mothers.[11] Some promotional programs are unsuccessful because marketers fail to generate awareness of critical issues among a significant portion of target market members. Other times, the campaign itself is at fault. For example, a Ragu promotion featured mothers who talked about cooking but who gave a less-than-favorable view of dads in the

Table 17.2 Possible Objectives of Promotion

Create awareness	Retain loyal customers
Stimulate demand	Facilitate reseller support
Encourage product trial	Combat competitive promotional efforts
Identify prospects	Reduce sales fluctuations

kitchen. The company then made the mistake of sending the video to several Internet bloggers, including dad bloggers, resulting in backlash from these bloggers who accused Ragu of disrespecting fathers.[12]

Stimulate Demand

When an organization is the first to introduce an innovative product, it tries to stimulate **primary demand**—demand for a product category rather than for a specific brand of product—through **pioneer promotion**. Pioneer promotion informs potential customers about the product: what it is, what it does, how it can be used, and where it can be purchased. Because pioneer promotion is used in the introductory stage of the product life cycle, meaning there are no competing brands, it neither emphasizes brand names nor compares brands. When Apple introduced the new iPad (the third iteration of the iPad), it envisioned a product that would be different from desktop computers and notebooks and that would be used in and around the home for easy access of news, e-mail, entertainment, and a broad diversity of service options. The goal was to promote the iPad line as a new product category, not as a replacement for a product you might already have.[13] Therefore, the iPad line results in incremental sales and does not cannibalize existing product sales.

primary demand Demand for a product category rather than for a specific brand

pioneer promotion Promotion that informs consumers about a new product

selective demand Demand for a specific brand

To build **selective demand**, demand for a specific brand, a marketer employs promotional efforts that point out the strengths and benefits of a specific brand. Building selective demand also requires singling out attributes important to potential buyers. Selective demand can be stimulated by differentiating the product from competing brands in the minds of potential buyers. Selective demand can also be stimulated by increasing the number of product uses and promoting them through advertising campaigns, as well as through price discounts, free samples, coupons, consumer contests and games, and sweepstakes. For example, Ace Hardware offers promotions whereby consumers can receive 20 percent off everything that fits into a bag. Such a promotion supports selective demand for Ace Hardware. Promotions for large package sizes or multiple-product packages are directed at increasing consumption, which in turn can stimulate demand. In addition, selective demand can be stimulated by encouraging existing customers to use more of the product.

© AP Images/PRNewsFoto/Red Mango

Stimulate Demand
Red Mango supports sales growth with a promotional incentive for buying gift cards.

Encourage Product Trial

When attempting to move customers through the product adoption process, a marketer may successfully create awareness and interest, but customers may stall during the evaluation stage. In this case, certain types of promotion—such as free samples, coupons, test drives, or limited free-use offers, contests, and games—are employed to encourage product trial. For example, Starbucks offered free samples of its new light roast coffee, "Blonde Roast," after research showed that 54 million U.S. coffee drinkers prefer a lighter roast coffee than Starbucks house blends.[14] Whether a marketer's product is the first in a new product category, a new brand in an existing category, or simply an existing brand seeking customers, trial-inducing promotional efforts aim to make product trial convenient and low risk for potential customers.

Identify Prospects

Certain types of promotional efforts aim to identify customers who are interested in the firm's product and are likely potential buyers. A marketer may run a television advertisement encouraging the viewer to visit the company's website and share personal information in order to receive something of value from the company. Customers who respond to such a message usually have higher interest in the product, which makes them likely sales prospects. The organization can respond with phone calls, e-mail, or personal contact by salespeople.

Retain Loyal Customers

Clearly, maintaining long-term customer relationships is a major goal of most marketers. Such relationships are quite valuable. Promotional efforts directed at customer retention can help an organization control its costs, because the costs of retaining customers are usually considerably lower than those of acquiring new ones. Frequent-user programs, such as those sponsored by airlines, car rental agencies, and hotels, aim to reward loyal customers and encourage them to remain loyal. Regal Entertainment, for example, introduced the Regal Crown Club. Membership entitles consumers to earn points that can be used for free movies, popcorn, or beverages at a Regal Cinema.[15] Some organizations employ special offers that only their existing customers can use. To retain loyal customers, marketers not only advertise loyalty programs but also use reinforcement advertising, which assures current users they have made the right brand choice and tells them how to get the most satisfaction from the product.

Facilitate Reseller Support

Reseller support is a two-way street: producers generally want to provide support to resellers to assist in selling their products, and in turn they expect resellers to support their products. When a manufacturer advertises a product to consumers, resellers should view this promotion as a form of strong manufacturer support. In some instances, a producer agrees to pay a certain proportion of retailers' advertising expenses for promoting its products. For example, when a manufacturer is introducing a new consumer brand in a highly competitive product category, it may be difficult to persuade supermarket managers to carry this brand. However, if the manufacturer promotes the new brand with free samples and coupon distribution in the retailer's area, a supermarket manager views these actions as strong support and is much more likely to carry the product. To encourage wholesalers and retailers to increase their inventories of its products, a manufacturer may provide them with special offers and buying allowances. In certain industries, a producer's salesperson may provide support to a wholesaler by working with the wholesaler's customers (retailers) in the presentation and promotion of the products. Strong relationships with resellers are important to a firm's ability to maintain a sustainable competitive advantage. The use of various promotional methods can help an organization achieve this goal.

Combat Competitive Promotional Efforts

At times, a marketer's objective in using promotion is to offset or lessen the effect of a competitor's promotional or marketing programs. This type of promotional activity does not necessarily increase the organization's sales or market share, but it may prevent a sales or market share loss. A combative promotional objective is used most often by firms in extremely competitive consumer markets, such as the fast-food, convenience store, and cable/Internet/phone markets. American Airlines is following the strategies of United and Delta by offering additional leg room for passengers flying in coach. For an extra $8–$108, passengers can get an additional four to six inches of leg room. The "Main Cabin Extra" program, along with other restructuring initiatives and flight expansions, are expected to improve revenue by $1 billion.[16] It is not unusual for competitors to respond with a counter-pricing strategy or even match a competitor's pricing.

Reduce Sales Fluctuations

Demand for many products varies from one month to another because of such factors as climate, holidays, and seasons. A business, however, cannot operate at peak efficiency when sales fluctuate rapidly. Changes in sales volume translate into changes in production, inventory levels, personnel needs, and financial resources. When promotional techniques reduce fluctuations by generating sales during slow periods, a firm can use its resources more efficiently.

Promotional techniques are often designed to stimulate sales during sales slumps. For example, Snapper may offer sales prices on lawn mowers into the fall season to extend the selling season. During peak periods, a marketer may refrain from advertising to prevent stimulating sales to the point at which the firm cannot handle all of the demand. On occasion, a company advertises that customers can be better served by coming in on certain days. An Italian restaurant, for example, might distribute coupons that are valid only Monday through Wednesday because on Thursday through Sunday the restaurant is extremely busy.

To achieve the major objectives of promotion discussed here, companies must develop appropriate promotional programs. In the next section, we consider the basic components of such programs: the promotion mix elements.

THE PROMOTION MIX

Several promotional methods can be used to communicate with individuals, groups, and organizations. When an organization combines specific methods to manage the integrated marketing communications for a particular product, that combination constitutes the promotion mix for that product. The four possible elements of a **promotion mix** are advertising, personal selling, public relations, and sales promotion (see Figure 17.3). For some products, firms use all four elements; for others, they use only two or three. In this section, we provide an overview of each promotion mix element; they are covered in greater detail in the next two chapters.

Advertising

Advertising is a paid nonpersonal communication about an organization and its products transmitted to a target audience through mass media, including television, radio, the Internet, newspapers, magazines, video games, direct mail, outdoor displays, and signs on mass transit vehicles. Advertising is changing as consumers' mass media consumption habits are changing. Companies are striving to maximize their presence and impact through digital media; ads are being designed that cater to smaller, more personalized audiences; and traditional

promotion mix A combination of promotional methods used to promote a specific product

Figure 17.3 The Four Possible Elements of a Promotion Mix

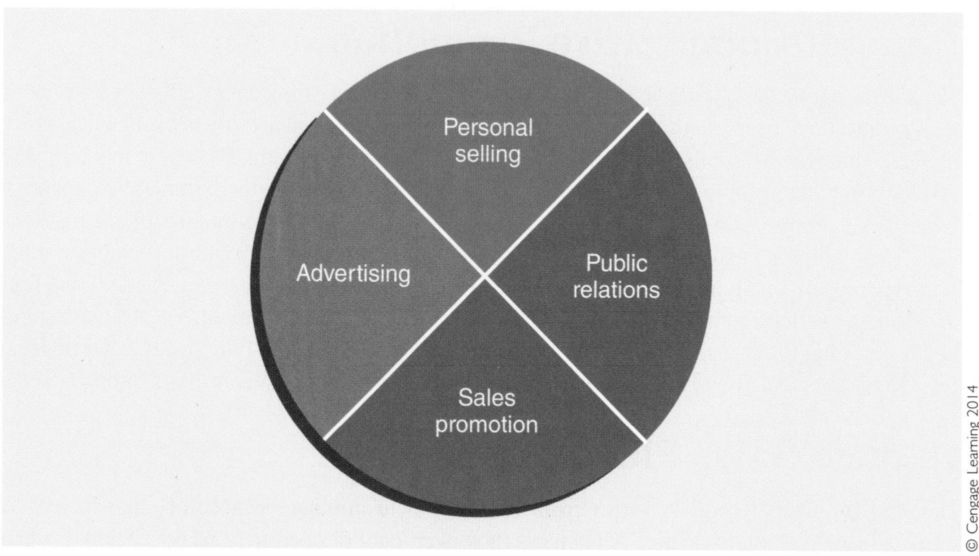

media like newspapers are in a decline due to a drop in readership. Individuals and organizations use advertising to promote goods, services, ideas, issues, and people. Being highly flexible, advertising can reach an extremely large target audience or focus on a small, precisely defined segment. For instance, Quizno's advertising focuses on a large audience of potential fast-food customers, ranging from children to adults, whereas advertising for Gulfstream jets aims at a much smaller and more specialized target market.

Advertising offers several benefits. It is extremely cost-efficient when it reaches a vast number of people at a low cost per person. For example, the cost of a four-color, full-page advertisement in the national edition of *Time* magazine costs \$320,100. With a circulation of more than 3,298,390, this makes the cost of reaching roughly a thousand subscribers \$97.00.[17] Advertising also lets the source repeat the message several times. Subway credits its promotional and advertising success to a catchy theme and heavy repetition of its "\$5.00 footlong" sub sandwich campaign. Furthermore, advertising a product a certain way can add to the product's value, and the visibility an organization gains from advertising can enhance its image. For instance, incorporating touchable elements that generate positive sensory feedback in print advertising can be a positive persuasive tool.[18] At times, a firm tries to enhance its own or its product's image by including celebrity endorsers in advertisements. For example, Louis Vuitton featured Angelina Jolie in an advertisement in its "Core Values" campaign. The campaign, set in Cambodia, shows Angelina Jolie barefoot with no makeup and wearing her own clothes with a Louis Vuitton monogrammed Alto bag slung over her shoulder.[19]

Advertising has disadvantages as well. Even though the cost per person reached may be low, the absolute dollar outlay can be extremely high, especially for commercials during

Advertising
This outdoor ad is designed to make parents aware of the implications of secondhand smoke.

Emerging Trends

The Pros and Cons to Celebrity Endorsers

Demand for celebrity endorsers is stronger than ever—and for good reason. Celebrities can create positive buzz and attract both new customers and investors. After famous chef Rachael Ray endorsed the eHow Food website, online traffic to the site jumped 56 percent. The exposure companies can get by associating with celebrities is such a lucrative opportunity that businesses often give away products in the hopes of attracting celebrity interest. For instance, at the 83rd Academy Awards, the "condolence bag" given to Academy Awards runners-up contained products worth about \$75,000.

Clearly celebrity endorsers and investors can benefit a company. However, there are many potential disadvantages as well. Sometimes the celebrity exhibits unacceptable behavior, creating bad publicity for the brand. When Tiger Woods's marital infidelity was exposed, many companies immediately dropped him as an endorser. Woods lost approximately \$20 million in endorsements in one year. In contrast, Charlie Sheen has been able to capitalize upon his "bad boy image" by appearing in a Fiat 500 Abarth ad. The ad, called "House Arrest," shows Sheen driving an Abarth at high speeds inside his home with the tagline "all bad boys are not created equal." Despite challenges, businesses feel the potential payout of being associated with a celebrity is well worth the risks.[a]

popular television shows and those associated with popular websites. High costs can limit, and sometimes preclude, use of advertising in a promotion mix. Moreover, advertising rarely provides rapid feedback. Measuring its effect on sales is often difficult, and it is ordinarily less persuasive than personal selling. In most instances, the time available to communicate a message to customers is limited to seconds, because people look at a print advertisement for only a few seconds, and most broadcast commercials are 30 seconds or less. Of course, the use of infomercials can increase exposure time for viewers; however, the format can disengage more sophisticated buyers.

Personal Selling

Personal selling is a paid personal communication that seeks to inform customers and persuade them to purchase products in an exchange situation. The phrase *purchase products* is interpreted broadly to encompass acceptance of ideas and issues. Personal selling is most extensively used in the business-to-business market and also in the business to consumer market for high-end products such as homes, cars, electronics, and furniture.

Personal selling has both advantages and limitations when compared with advertising. Advertising is general communication aimed at a relatively large target audience, whereas personal selling involves more specific communication directed at one or several individuals. Reaching one person through personal selling costs considerably more than through advertising, but personal selling efforts often have greater impact on customers. Personal selling also provides immediate feedback, allowing marketers to adjust their messages to improve communication. Such interaction helps them determine and respond to customers' information needs.

When a salesperson and a customer meet face-to-face, they use several types of interpersonal communication. The predominant communication form is language, both spoken and written. A salesperson and customer frequently use **kinesic communication**, or communication through the movement of head, eyes, arms, hands, legs, or torso. Winking, head nodding, hand gestures, and arm motions are forms of kinesic communication. A good salesperson can often evaluate a prospect's interest in a product or presentation by noting eye contact and head nodding. **Proxemic communication**, a less obvious form of communication used in personal selling situations, occurs when either person varies the physical distance separating them. When a customer backs away from a salesperson, for example, he or she may be displaying a lack of interest in the product or expressing dislike for the salesperson. Touching, or **tactile communication**, is also a form of communication, although less popular in the United States than in many other countries. Handshaking is a common form of tactile communication both in the United States and elsewhere.

Public Relations

Although many promotional activities focus on a firm's customers, other stakeholders—suppliers, employees, stockholders, the media, educators, potential investors, government officials, and society in general—are important to an organization as well. To communicate with customers and stakeholders, a company employs public relations. Public relations is a broad set of communication efforts used to create and maintain favorable relationships between an organization and its stakeholders. Maintaining a positive relationship with one or more stakeholders can affect a firm's current sales and profits, as well as its long-term survival.

Public relations uses a variety of tools, including annual reports, brochures, event sponsorship, and sponsorship of socially responsible programs aimed at protecting the environment or helping disadvantaged individuals. The goal of public relations is to create and enhance a positive image of the organization. Increasingly, marketers are going directly to consumers with their public relations efforts to bypass the traditional media intermediary (newspapers, magazines, and television). Companies like Best Buy have been creating content on YouTube with the goal of bringing viewers into the "geek world" as well as providing tutorial videos on electronics-related issues.[20]

kinesic communication Communicating through the movement of head, eyes, arms, hands, legs, or torso

proxemic communication Communicating by varying the physical distance in face-to-face interactions

tactile communication Communicating through touching

Other tools arise from the use of publicity, which is a component of public relations. Publicity is nonpersonal communication in news-story form about an organization or its products, or both, transmitted through a mass medium at no charge. A few examples of publicity-based public relations tools are news releases, press conferences, and feature articles. To generate publicity, companies sometimes give away products to celebrities in the hope that the celebrities will be seen and photographed with the product, and those photos will stimulate awareness and product trial among their fans. Companies donate large amounts of goods to "gifting suites" at major events like the Academy Awards and the Sundance Film Festival, ranging from Samsung Galaxy tabs to a $40,000 safari trip. Marketers from these companies hope the celebrity affiliation will generate publicity and create greater awareness of their brands with consumers. There is one problem, though: with the change in tax laws, if you use these gifts, you have to pay taxes on them. Therefore, many celebrities donated their "swag bags" to charity, which did not result in the celebrity end use and affiliation that marketers would ultimately like.[21] Ordinarily, public relations efforts are planned and implemented to be consistent with and support other elements of the promotion mix. Public relations efforts may be the responsibility of an individual or of a department within the organization, or the organization may hire an independent public relations agency.

Unpleasant situations and negative events, such as product tampering or an environmental disaster, may generate unfavorable public relations for an organization. For instance, Johnson & Johnson had 50 product recalls in 15 months, resulting in a feature cover story in *Bloomberg Businessweek.* After 13 million packages of Rolaid soft chews were recalled when customers found wood and metal particles in them, another 43 million bottles of Tylenol, Benadryl, Sinutab, and Rolaids were withdrawn in early 2011.[22] To minimize the damaging effects of unfavorable coverage, effective marketers have policies and procedures in place to help manage any public relations problems.

Public relations should not be viewed as a set of tools to be used only during crises. To get the most from public relations, an organization should have someone responsible for public relations either internally or externally and should have an ongoing public relations program.

Sales Promotion

Sales promotion is an activity or material that acts as a direct inducement, offering added value or incentive for the product to resellers, salespeople, or consumers. Examples include free samples, games, rebates, sweepstakes, contests, premiums, and coupons. Kraft Foods introduced a unique sampling program to award samples to specific demographics. The company released a machine that awards free samples of its Temptations desserts, but only to adults. To ensure that only adults are receiving the sample, the machine has the ability to detect facial images that can tell the difference between a child and a grown-up.[23] *Sales promotion* should not be confused with *promotion;* sales promotion is just one part of the comprehensive area of promotion. Marketers spend more on sales promotion than on advertising, and sales promotion appears to be a faster-growing area than advertising. Coupons are especially important; Table 17.3 shows the product categories with the greatest distribution of coupons.

Generally, when companies employ advertising or personal selling, they depend on these activities continuously or

Sales Promotion
McDonald's uses the Monopoly game to stimulate demand and increase sales.

Table 17.3 Top Coupon Categories

Rank	Product Category
1	Hair care
2	Eye care treatment
3	Candy and gum
4	Cosmetics
5	Butter and margarine
6	Sanitary protection products
7	First aid
8	Vitamins and supplements
9	Shaving
10	Dried fruits

Source: "Top Ten Most Popular Coupons," *Business News Daily*, February 13, 2012, www.mnn.com/money/personal-finance/stories/the-10-most-popular-coupons (accessed March 6, 2012).

cyclically. However, a marketer's use of sales promotion tends to be irregular. Many products are seasonal. Toys may be discounted in January after the holiday selling season to move excess inventory. Marketers frequently rely on sales promotion to improve the effectiveness of other promotion mix elements, especially advertising and personal selling. Americans redeemed $4.6 billion worth of coupons in 2011 out of $470 billion in savings issued by the consumer packaged goods industry.[24] Nearly two-thirds of consumers make lists before going shopping, and 51 percent indicate that coupons have a significant effect on their purchasing behavior.[25] Mobile devices are a personal technology, so they pose an unusual opportunity to reach consumers wherever they go. By 2013, mobile Internet usage will surpass desktop usage. Mobile apps can be used as tools to engage the consumer through sales promotion items such as coupons.[26]

An effective promotion mix requires the right combination of components. To see how such a mix is created, we now examine the factors and conditions affecting the selection of promotional methods that an organization uses for a particular product.

SELECTING PROMOTION MIX ELEMENTS

Marketers vary the composition of promotion mixes for many reasons. Although a promotion mix can include all four elements, frequently, a marketer selects fewer than four. Many firms that market multiple product lines use several promotion mixes simultaneously.

Promotional Resources, Objectives, and Policies

The size of an organization's promotional budget affects the number and relative intensity of promotional methods included in a promotion mix. If a company's promotional budget is extremely limited, the firm is likely to rely on personal selling because it is easier to measure a salesperson's contribution to sales than to measure the sales effectiveness of advertising. Businesses must have sizable promotional budgets to use regional or national advertising. Companies like Procter & Gamble, Unilever, General Motors, and Coca-Cola are among the leaders in worldwide media spending. Organizations with extensive promotional resources generally include more elements in their promotion mixes but having more promotional dollars to spend does not necessarily mean using more promotional methods. Researchers have found that resources spent on promotion activities have a positive influence on shareholder value.

An organization's promotional objectives and policies also influence the types of promotion selected. If a company's objective is to create mass awareness of a new convenience good, such as a breakfast cereal, its promotion mix probably leans heavily toward advertising, sales promotion, and possibly public relations. If a company hopes to educate consumers about the features of a durable good, such as a home appliance, its promotion mix may combine a moderate amount of advertising, possibly some sales promotion designed to attract customers to retail stores, and a great deal of personal selling, because this method is an efficient way to inform customers about such products. If a firm's objective is to produce immediate sales of nondurable services, the promotion mix will probably stress advertising and sales promotion. For example, dry cleaners and carpet-cleaning firms are more likely to use advertising with a coupon or discount rather than personal selling.

Characteristics of the Target Market

Size, geographic distribution, and demographic characteristics of an organization's target market help dictate the methods to include in a product's promotion mix. To some degree, market size and diversity determine composition of the mix. If the size is limited, the promotion mix will probably emphasize personal selling, which can be very effective for reaching small numbers of people. Organizations selling to industrial markets and firms marketing products through only a few wholesalers frequently make personal selling the major component of their promotion mixes. When a product's market consists of millions of customers, organizations rely on advertising and sales promotion, because these methods reach masses of people at a low cost per person. When the population density is uneven around the country, marketers may utilize regional advertising and target larger markets.

Geographic distribution of a firm's customers also affects the choice of promotional methods. Personal selling is more feasible if a company's customers are concentrated in a small area than if they are dispersed across a vast region. When the company's customers are numerous and dispersed, regional or national advertising may be more practical.

Distribution of a target market's demographic characteristics, such as age, income, or education, may affect the types of promotional techniques a marketer selects, as well as the messages and images employed. According to the U.S. Census Bureau, so-called traditional families—those composed of married couples with children—account for fewer than one-quarter of all U.S. households.[27] To reach the more than three-quarters of households consisting of single parents, unmarried couples, singles, and "empty nesters" (whose children have left home), more companies are modifying the images used in their promotions.

Characteristics of the Product

Generally, promotion mixes for business products concentrate on personal selling, whereas advertising plays a major role in promoting consumer goods. This generalization should be treated cautiously, however. Marketers of business products use some advertising to promote products. Advertisements for computers, road-building equipment, and aircrafts are fairly common, and some sales promotion is also used occasionally to promote business products. Personal selling is used extensively for consumer durables, such as home appliances, automobiles, and

Going Green

Government Cracks Down on Greenwashing

Greenwashing occurs when companies market products as being more eco-friendly than they really are. Unfortunately, greenwashing has made it difficult for consumers to pinpoint which companies' claims to trust. One study determined that as many as 95 percent of products marketed as green were guilty of at least one form of greenwashing.

In the past, the Federal Trade Commission (FTC) has cracked down on companies whose advertisements were inaccurate. For instance, when several companies advertised rayon products as being made from bamboo, the FTC sent warning letters to 78 retailers, including Walmart, Kohl's, and Gap. More recently, California sued three companies for labeling plastic bottles as biodegradable, a violation of a California labeling law.

However, not all claims of greenwashing are so easy to prove. For instance, a company might have a product that is composed of green materials but still contains one environmentally unfriendly component. Should that company be allowed to advertise itself as green? The FTC has released green guidelines to help clear up this uncertainty. These guidelines recommend actions, such as substantiating green marketing claims with evidence and avoiding ambiguous terminology. Although these guidelines do not carry the force of law, they better enable the FTC to pursue companies that violate standards with deceptive marketing practices.[b]

Characteristics of the Product
Convenience products, such as 5 Gum, are promoted mainly through advertising and sales promotion efforts.

houses, whereas consumer convenience items are promoted mainly through advertising and sales promotion. Public relations appears in promotion mixes for both business and consumer products.

Marketers of highly seasonal products often emphasize advertising—and sometimes sales promotion as well—because off-season sales generally will not support an extensive year-round sales force. Although most toy producers have sales forces to sell to resellers, many of these companies depend chiefly on advertising and strong distribution channels to promote their products.

A product's price also influences the composition of the promotion mix. High-priced products call for personal selling, because consumers associate greater risk with the purchase of such products and usually want information from a salesperson. For low-priced convenience items, marketers use advertising rather than personal selling. Research suggests that consumers visiting a store specifically to purchase a product on sale are more likely to have read flyers and purchased other sale-priced products than consumers visiting the same store for other reasons.[28]

Another consideration in creating an effective promotion mix is the stage of the product life cycle. During the introduction stage, advertising is used to create awareness for both business and consumer products. Velveeta spread awareness of its new Velveeta Cheesy Skillets product through television commercials, YouTube videos, and Facebook. Velveeta also encouraged word-of-mouth marketing by encouraging consumers to have a "Velveeta Cheesy Skillets House Party."[29] For many products, personal selling and sales promotion are also helpful in this stage. In the growth and maturity stages, consumer products require heavy emphasis on advertising, whereas business products often call for a concentration of personal selling and some sales promotion. In the decline stage, marketers usually decrease all promotional activities, especially advertising.

Intensity of market coverage is still another factor affecting the composition of the promotion mix. When products are marketed through intensive distribution, firms depend strongly on advertising and sales promotion. Many convenience products like lotions, cereals, and coffee are promoted through samples, coupons, and refunds. When marketers choose selective distribution, promotion mixes vary considerably. Items handled through exclusive distribution—such as expensive watches, furs, and high-quality furniture—typically require a significant amount of personal selling.

A product's use also affects the combination of promotional methods. Manufacturers of highly personal products, such as laxatives, nonprescription contraceptives, and feminine hygiene products, depend on advertising because many customers do not want to talk with salespeople about these products.

Costs and Availability of Promotional Methods

Costs of promotional methods are major factors to analyze when developing a promotion mix. National advertising and sales promotion require large expenditures. However, if these efforts succeed in reaching extremely large audiences, the cost per individual reached may be quite small, possibly a few pennies. Some forms of advertising are relatively inexpensive. Many small, local businesses advertise products through local newspapers, magazines, radio and television stations, outdoor displays, Internet ads, and signs on mass transit vehicles.

Another consideration that marketers explore when formulating a promotion mix is availability of promotional techniques. Despite the tremendous number of media vehicles in the United States, a firm may find that no available advertising medium effectively reaches a certain target market. The problem of media availability becomes more pronounced when marketers advertise in foreign countries. Some media, such as television, simply may not be available, or advertising on television may be illegal. For example, the advertising of cigarettes on television is banned in many countries. In addition, regulations or standards for media content may be restrictive in varying global outlets. European fashion magazines are increasingly either mandating that "real women" be used in ads (not unrealistically proportioned models) and/or that when an ad has been altered to change a person's physical appearance, this change must be noted on the ad.[30] In some countries, advertisers are forbidden to make brand comparisons on television. Other promotional methods also have limitations. For instance, a firm may wish to increase its sales force but be unable to find qualified personnel.

Push and Pull Channel Policies

Another element that marketers consider when planning a promotion mix is whether to use a push policy or a pull policy. With a **push policy**, the producer promotes the product only to the next institution down the marketing channel. In a marketing channel with wholesalers and retailers, the producer promotes to the wholesaler because, in this case, the wholesaler is the channel member just below the producer (see Figure 17.4). Each channel member in turn promotes to the next channel member. A push policy normally stresses personal selling. Sometimes sales promotion and advertising are used in conjunction with personal selling to push the products down through the channel.

As Figure 17.4 shows, a firm that uses a **pull policy** promotes directly to consumers to develop strong consumer demand for its products. It does so primarily through advertising and sales promotion. Because consumers are persuaded to seek the products in retail stores, retailers in turn go to wholesalers or the producers to buy the products. This policy is intended to pull the goods down through the channel by creating demand at the consumer level. Consumers are told that if the stores don't have it, then they should request that the stores begin carrying the product.

Push and pull policies are not mutually exclusive. At times, an organization uses both simultaneously.

push policy Promoting a product only to the next institution down the marketing channel

pull policy Promoting a product directly to consumers to develop strong consumer demand that pulls products through the marketing channel

Figure 17.4 Comparison of Push and Pull Promotional Strategies

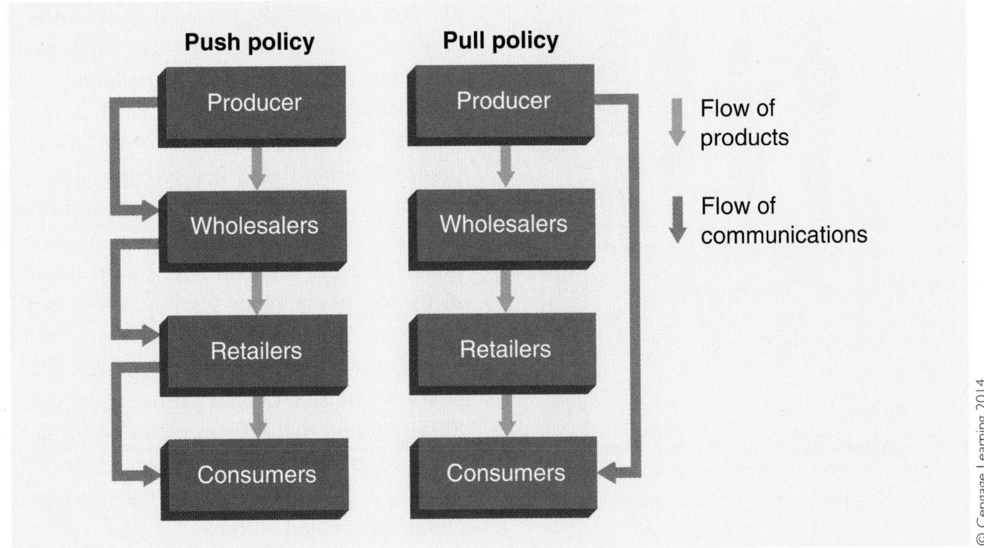

THE GROWING IMPORTANCE OF WORD-OF-MOUTH COMMUNICATIONS

When making decisions about the composition of promotion mixes, marketers should recognize that commercial messages, whether from advertising, personal selling, sales promotion, or public relations, are limited in the extent to which they can inform and persuade customers and move them closer to making purchases. Depending on the type of customers and the products involved, buyers to some extent rely on word-of-mouth communication from personal sources, such as family members and friends. **Word-of-mouth communication** is personal, informal exchanges of communication that customers share with one another about products, brands, and companies. Most customers are likely to be influenced by friends and family members when they make purchases. Word-of-mouth communication is very important when people are selecting restaurants and entertainment along with automotive, medical, legal, banking, and personal services like hair care. Vail Resorts used word-of-mouth marketing to encourage skiers to share their experiences with their friends and family right from the slopes. The company released an online and mobile app called EpicMix that allowed skiers to track where they rode, how many feet they traveled, and other useful statistics. Skiers could then use the EpicMix application to share their achievements with their friends and family without having to leave the mountain.[31] Research has identified a link between word-of-mouth communication and new-customer acquisition when there is customer involvement and satisfaction.[32] Effective marketers who understand the importance of word-of-mouth communication attempt to identify opinion leaders and encourage them to try their products in the hope that they will spread favorable publicity about them. Apple, for example, has long relied on its nearly cult consumer following to spread by word of mouth their satisfaction with Apple products, such as MacBooks, iPods, iPhones, and iPads.

word-of-mouth communication Personal informal exchanges of communication that customers share with one another about products, brands, and companies

In addition, customers are increasingly going online for information and opinions about goods and services as well as about the companies. Electronic word of mouth is communicating about products through websites, blogs, e-mail, social networks, or online forums. Users can go to a number of consumer-oriented websites, such as epinions.com and consumerreview.com. At these sites, they can learn about other consumers' feelings toward and experiences with specific products; some sites even encourage consumers to rate products they have tried. Users can also search within product categories and compare consumers' viewpoints on various brands and models. Not surprisingly, research has identified credibility as the most important attribute of a ratings website and found reducing risk and saving search effort to be the primary motives for using such sites.[33] Buyers can peruse Internet-based newsgroups, forums, and blogs to find word-of-mouth information. A consumer looking for a new cell phone service, for example, might inquire in forums about other participants' experiences and level of satisfaction to gain more information before making a purchase decision. A Nielsen Global Online Consumer Survey found that 90 percent of consumers trust recommendations they get from their friends, while 70 percent trust consumer comments posted online.[34]

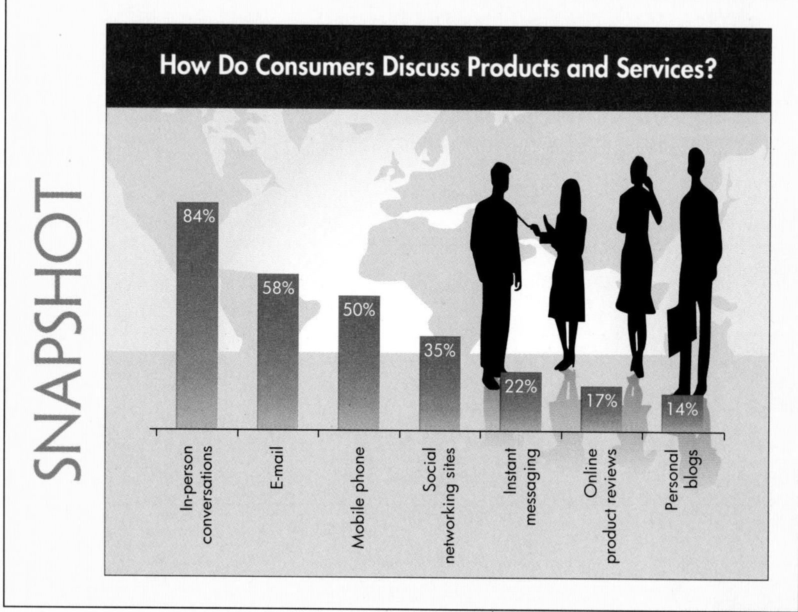

Source: E-Marketer; Word of Mouth Marketing Association. Reprinted in "Crunching the Numbers," *Inc.*, March 2012, p. 26.

The Growing Importance of Word-of-Mouth Communication Funny ads that capture consumer interest, such as this CareerBuilder.com ad, can go viral and generate a significant amount of free impact and exposure.

Electronic word of mouth is particularly important to consumers staying abreast of trends. Hundreds of blogs (such as TechCrunch, Perez Hilton, and Tree Hugger) play an essential role in propagating electronic word-of-mouth communications about everything from gossip to politics to consumer goods. They provide consumers with information on trends, reviews of products, and other information on what is new, exciting, and fashionable for consumers. These sites have become so influential in introducing consumers to new products and shaping their views about them that marketers are increasingly monitoring them to identify new trends; some firms have even attempted to influence users' votes on their favorite items. Marketers must increasingly court bloggers, who wield growing influence over consumer perception of companies, products, and services.

Buzz marketing is an attempt to incite publicity and public excitement surrounding a product through a creative event. For example, Dell used buzz marketing to spread awareness of its brand among the high school and college communities. It employed 170 brand ambassadors to visit campuses and communicate with students for an hour on the company's Facebook and Twitter pages. Dell also held a contest to award one high school with the "prom of a lifetime." Since most high school and college students purchase their first computers during these ages, Dell hopes its buzz marketing campaign will affect the students' purchasing decisions.[35]

Buzz marketing works best as a part of an integrated marketing communication program that also uses advertising, personal selling, sales promotion, and publicity. However, marketers should also take care that buzz marketing campaigns do not violate any laws or have the potential to be misconstrued and cause undue alarm. One form of buzz marketing involves stenciling or painting company logos on sidewalks. With many buildings and billboards covered with advertisements, consumers are inundated with advertisements. Companies like Microsoft and Zynga have paid for sidewalk advertisements as a unique way to catch the consumer's eye. Unfortunately, this form of marketing has also run into legal implications: namely, cities see it as "sidewalk graffiti" and have imposed fines for violators. Hence, it is important for companies to research their ideas for buzz marketing to ensure they will not conflict with existing laws.[36]

buzz marketing An attempt to incite publicity and public excitement surrounding a product through a creative event

Viral marketing is a strategy to get consumers to share a marketer's message, often through e-mail or online video, in a way that spreads dramatically and quickly. Ford, achieved success in viral marketing with its "spokespuppet," a mouthy sock puppet named Doug, who was used to promote the Ford Focus. Ford released Internet videos of Doug and had the puppet interact with users on Facebook and Twitter. The Doug videos went viral on YouTube, and his Facebook page generated more than 44,000 "Likes" (it is important to realize, however, that it is the public that determines whether something is interesting enough to "go viral").[37]

Word of mouth, no matter how it is transmitted, is not effective in all product categories. It seems to be most effective for new-to-market and more expensive products. Despite the obvious benefits of positive word of mouth, marketers must also recognize the potential dangers of negative word of mouth. This is particularly important in dealing with online platforms that can reach more people and encourage consumers to "gang up" on a company or product. As mentioned earlier, Unilever had this experience when it attempted to get a video for its Ragu sauce to go viral. Rather than positively impacting the brand, however, some notable bloggers and commentators criticized the way it portrayed dads in the kitchen.

PRODUCT PLACEMENT

A growing technique for reaching consumers is the selective placement of products within the context of television programs viewed by the target market. **Product placement** is a form of advertising that strategically locates products or product promotions within entertainment media to reach the product's target markets. Apple is considered to be an expert at product placement. It has had its iPods, iPads, and computers featured in several hit movies in recent years.[38] Such product placement has become more important due to the increasing fragmentation of television viewers who have ever-expanding viewing options and technology that can screen advertisements (e.g., digital video recorders such as TiVo). Researchers have found that 60 to 80 percent of digital video recorder users skip over the commercials when they replay programming.[39]

In-program product placements have been successful in reaching consumers as they are being entertained. Because the *X Factor* is sponsored by Pepsi, the brand is often featured

viral marketing A strategy to get consumers to share a marketer's message, often through e-mail or online videos, in a way that spreads dramatically and quickly

product placement The strategic location of products or product promotions within entertainment media content to reach the product's target market

Entrepreneurship in Marketing

The Kluger Agency Combines Music and Product Placement

Entrepreneur: Adam Kluger
The Business: The Kluger Agency (TKA)
Founded: 2008 | United States
Success: TKA represents over 75 brands and has working relationships with 17 major record labels.

One of Adam Kluger's first encounters with product placement was Abercrombie & Fitch in the 1999 song "Summer Girls." Years later, this recollection would inspire him to create The Kluger Agency, a public relations agency that successfully partners brands with music artists. Kluger's first big break was signing on to place a Vixen's Vision product into the music video of a new artist, Lady Gaga. Since then, TKA has partnered with record labels to represent brands like the soft drink Drank (in Flo Rida's "Sugar" video) and the online dating website Zoosk (in J. Randall's "Can't Sleep" and "Oo La La"). The increasing popularity of product placement into music videos or lyrics comes at an opportune time for the music industry, as product placement generates much needed revenue at a time when file-sharing and iTunes are cutting into industry profits. With an estimated $5 million in revenues, Kluger has successfully integrated his love for music and business into a profitable enterprise.[c]

in the show. Pepsi logos can be seen throughout the show, including on the cups from which the judges are drinking.[40] Reality programming in particular has been a natural fit for product placements, because of the close interchange between the participants and the product (e.g., Sears and *Extreme Makeover Home Edition;* Levi's, Burger King, Marquis Jet, and Dove and *The Apprentice;* Coca-Cola and *American Idol*). On the other hand, not all companies are happy with the way their products are placed. Abercrombie offered to pay the popular MTV show *Jersey Shore* to stop having the show's undesirable characters wear the company's apparel during the show.[41]

Product placement is not limited to U.S. television shows. The European Parliament green-lighted limited use of product placement, albeit only during certain types of programs and only if consumers were informed at the beginning of the segment that companies had paid to have their products displayed. In general, the notion of product placement has not been favorably viewed in Europe and has been particularly controversial in the United Kingdom. However, new legislation has now legalized product placement in U.K. television programs.[42]

Product Placement
Gap utilized product placement in *The Social Network.*

CRITICISMS AND DEFENSES OF PROMOTION

Even though promotional activities can help customers make informed purchasing decisions, social scientists, consumer groups, government agencies, and members of society in general have long criticized promotion. There are two main reasons for such criticism: promotion does have flaws, and it is a highly visible business activity that pervades our daily lives. Although complaints about too much promotional activity are almost universal, a number of more specific criticisms have been lodged. In this section, we discuss some of the criticisms and defenses of promotion.

Is Promotion Deceptive?

One common criticism of promotion is that it is deceptive and unethical. During the 19th and early 20th centuries, much promotion was blatantly deceptive. Although no longer widespread, some deceptive promotion still occurs. For instance, yogurt company Dannon settled with the FTC for $21 million after being sued for making deceptive claims. The FTC accused the company of advertising that its DanActive yogurt helps to prevent colds and that its Activia yogurts help to reduce irregularity, claims that the FTC determined were not backed up with sufficient evidence.[43] Many industries suffer from claims of deception from time to time. One industry that is seemingly constantly bombarded with truthfulness-related claims is the diet products and exercise equipment industry. Some promotions are unintentionally deceiving; for instance, when advertising to children, it is easy to mislead them because they are more naïve than adults and less able to separate fantasy from reality. A promotion may also mislead some receivers, because words can have diverse meanings for different people. However, not all promotion should be condemned because a small portion is flawed. Laws, government regulation, and industry self-regulation have helped decrease deceptive promotion.

Does Promotion Increase Prices?

Promotion is also criticized for raising prices, but in fact it often tends to lower them. The ultimate purpose of promotion is to stimulate demand. If it does, the business should be able to produce and market products in larger quantities and thus reduce per-unit production and marketing costs, which can result in lower prices. For example, as demand for flat-screen TVs and MP3 players has increased, their prices have dropped. When promotion fails to stimulate demand, the price of the promoted product increases because promotion costs must be added to other costs. Promotion also helps keep prices lower by facilitating price competition. When firms advertise prices, their prices tend to remain lower than when they are not promoting prices. Gasoline pricing illustrates how promotion fosters price competition. Service stations with the highest prices seldom have highly visible price signs. In addition, results of an analysis for the long-term economic growth for 64 countries indicated that there is a direct relationship between advertising and economic growth. The research found that advertising is not only related to economic growth but can also bring about economic growth. This should help clarify debates over the role of promotion in society.[44]

Does Promotion Create Needs?

Some critics of promotion claim that it manipulates consumers by persuading them to buy products they do not need, hence creating "artificial" needs. In his theory of motivation, Abraham Maslow (discussed in Chapter 7) indicates that an individual tries to satisfy five levels of needs: physiological needs, such as hunger, thirst, and sex; safety needs; needs for love and affection; needs for self-esteem and respect from others; and self-actualization needs, or the need to realize one's potential. When needs are viewed in this context, it is difficult to demonstrate that promotion creates them. If there were no promotional activities, people would still have needs for food, water, sex, safety, love, affection, self-esteem, respect from others, and self-actualization.

Although promotion may not create needs, it does capitalize on them (which may be why some critics believe promotion creates needs). Many marketers base their appeals on these needs. For instance, several mouthwash, toothpaste, and perfume advertisements associate these products with needs for love, affection, and respect. These advertisers rely on human needs in their messages, but they do not create the needs.

Does Promotion Encourage Materialism?

Another frequent criticism of promotion is that it leads to materialism. The purpose of promoting goods is to persuade people to buy them; thus, if promotion works, consumers will want to buy more and more things. Marketers assert that values are instilled in the home and that promotion does not change people into materialistic consumers. However, the behavior of today's children and teenagers contradicts this view; many insist on high-priced, brand name apparel, such as Gucci, Coach, Abercrombie & Fitch, 7 For All Mankind, Jersey Couture, and Ralph Lauren.

Does Promotion Help Customers without Costing Too Much?

Every year, firms spend billions of dollars for promotion. The question is whether promotion helps customers enough to be worth the cost. Consumers do benefit because promotion informs them about product uses, features, advantages, prices, and locations where they can buy the products. Thus, consumers gain more knowledge about available products and can make more intelligent buying decisions. Promotion also informs consumers about

Marketing Debate

Green...but Still Dangerous

ISSUE: Should cigarette manufacturers be allowed to market their products as eco-friendly?

Normally, the public doesn't mind if a company that uses organic ingredients, wind energy, and hybrid vehicles markets its brand as eco-friendly. However, when Santa Fe Natural Tobacco Company used these claims to promote its brand of cigarettes, critics were outraged. The company took out advertisements in *Esquire, Elle,* and *Mother Jones* to promote the eco-friendliness of its brand. One argument against such claims is that, because green products are thought to be healthier, consumers may be misled into believing these cigarettes are safer to smoke. The company states on the brand's website that organic cigarettes are not any safer.[d]

services—for instance, health care, educational programs, and day care—as well as about important social, political, and health-related issues. For example, several organizations, such as the California Department of Health Services, inform people about the health hazards associated with tobacco use.

Should Potentially Harmful Products Be Promoted?

Finally, some critics of promotion, including consumer groups and government officials, suggest that certain products should not be promoted at all. Primary targets are products associated with violence and other possibly unhealthy activities, such as handguns, alcohol, and tobacco. Cigarette advertisements, for example, promote smoking, a behavior proven to be harmful and even deadly. Tobacco companies, which spend billions on promotion, have countered criticism of their advertising by pointing out that advertisements for red meat and coffee are not censured, even though these products may also cause health problems. Those who defend such promotion assert that, as long as it is legal to sell a product, promoting that product should be allowed.

Summary

1. To describe the nature of integrated marketing communications

Integrated marketing communications is the coordination of promotion and other marketing efforts to ensure maximum informational and persuasive impact on customers.

2. To examine the process of communication

Communication is a sharing of meaning. The communication process involves several steps. First, the source translates meaning into code, a process known as coding or encoding. The source should employ signs or symbols familiar to the receiver or audience. The coded message is sent through a communications channel to the receiver or audience. The receiver or audience then decodes the message and usually supplies feedback to the source. When the decoded message differs from the encoded one, a condition called noise exists.

3. To understand the role and objectives of promotion

Promotion is communication to build and maintain relationships by informing and persuading one or more audiences. Although promotional objectives vary from one organization to another and within organizations over time, eight primary objectives underlie many promotional programs. Promotion aims to create awareness of a new product, a new brand, or an existing product; to stimulate primary and selective demand; to encourage product trial through the use of free samples, coupons, limited free-use offers, contests, and games; to identify prospects; to retain loyal customers; to facilitate reseller support; to combat competitive promotional efforts; and to reduce sales fluctuations.

4. To explore the elements of the promotion mix

The promotion mix for a product may include four major promotional methods: advertising, personal selling, public relations, and sales promotion. Advertising is paid nonpersonal communication about an organization and its products transmitted to a target audience through a mass medium. Personal selling is paid personal communication that attempts to inform customers and persuade them to purchase products in an exchange situation. Public relations is a broad set of communication efforts used to create and maintain favorable relationships between an organization and its stakeholders. Sales promotion is an activity or material that acts as a direct inducement, offering added value or incentive for the product, to resellers, salespeople, or consumers.

5. To examine the selection of promotion mix elements

The promotional methods used in a product's promotion mix are determined by the organization's promotional resources, objectives, and policies; characteristics of the target market; characteristics of the product; and cost and availability of promotional methods. Marketers also consider whether to use a push policy or a pull policy. With a push policy, the producer only promotes the product to the next institution down the marketing channel. Normally, a push policy stresses personal selling. Firms that use a pull policy promote directly to consumers, with the intention of developing strong consumer demand for the products. Once consumers are persuaded to seek the products in retail stores, retailers go to wholesalers or the producer to buy the products.

6. To understand word-of-mouth communication and how it affects promotion

Most customers are likely to be influenced by friends and family members when making purchases. Word-of-mouth communication is personal, informal exchanges of communication that customers share with one another about products, brands, and companies. Customers may also choose to go online to find electronic word of mouth about products or companies. Buzz marketing is an attempt to incite publicity and public excitement surrounding a product through a creative event. Viral marketing is a strategy to get consumers to share a marketer's message, often through e-mail or online videos, in a way that spreads dramatically and quickly.

7. To understand product placement promotions

Product placement is the strategic location of products or product promotions within television program content to reach the product's target market. In-program product placements have been successful in reaching consumers as they are being entertained rather than in the competitive commercial break time periods.

8. To examine criticisms and defenses of promotion

Promotional activities can help consumers make informed purchasing decisions, but they have also evoked many criticisms. Promotion has been accused of deception. Although some deceiving or misleading promotions do exist, laws, government regulation, and industry self-regulation minimize deceptive promotion. Promotion has been blamed for increasing prices, but it usually tends to lower them. When demand is high, production and marketing costs decrease, which can result in lower prices. Moreover, promotion helps keep prices lower by facilitating price competition. Other criticisms of promotional activity are that it manipulates consumers into buying products they do not need, that it leads to a more materialistic society, and that consumers do not benefit sufficiently from promotional activity to justify its high cost. Finally, some critics of promotion suggest that potentially harmful products, especially those associated with violence, sex, and unhealthy activities, should not be promoted at all.

Go to www.cengagebrain.com for resources to help you master the content in this chapter as well as for materials that will expand your marketing knowledge!

Important Terms

integrated marketing communications 566
communication 567
source 568
receiver 568
coding process 568
communications channel 569
decoding process 569
noise 569
feedback 569
channel capacity 570
promotion 570
primary demand 572
pioneer promotion 572
selective demand 572
promotion mix 574
kinesic communication 576
proxemic communication 576
tactile communication 576
push policy 581
pull policy 581
word-of-mouth communication 582
buzz marketing 583
viral marketing 584
product placement 584

Discussion and Review Questions

1. What does the term *integrated marketing communications* mean?
2. Define *communication* and describe the communication process. Is it possible to communicate without using all the elements in the communication process? If so, which elements can be omitted?
3. Identify several causes of noise. How can a source reduce noise?
4. What is the major task of promotion? Do firms ever use promotion to accomplish this task and fail? If so, give several examples.
5. Describe the possible objectives of promotion and discuss the circumstances under which each objective might be used.
6. Identify and briefly describe the four promotional methods an organization can use in its promotion mix.
7. What forms of interpersonal communication besides language can be used in personal selling?
8. How do target market characteristics determine which promotional methods to include in a promotion mix? Assume a company is planning to promote a cereal to both adults and children. Along what major dimensions would these two promotional efforts have to differ from each other?
9. How can a product's characteristics affect the composition of its promotion mix?
10. Evaluate the following statement: "Appropriate advertising media are always available if a company can afford them."
11. Explain the difference between a pull policy and a push policy. Under what conditions should each policy be used?
12. In which ways can word-of-mouth communication influence the effectiveness of a promotion mix for a product?
13. Which criticisms of promotion do you believe are the most valid? Why?
14. Should organizations be allowed to promote offensive, violent, sexual, or unhealthy products that can be legally sold and purchased? Support your answer.

Application Questions

1. The overall objective of promotion is to stimulate demand for a product. Through television advertising, the American Dairy Association promotes the benefits of drinking milk, a campaign that aims to stimulate primary demand. Advertisements for a specific brand of milk focus on stimulating selective demand. Identify two television commercials, one aimed at stimulating primary demand and one aimed at stimulating selective demand. Describe each commercial and discuss how each attempts to achieve its objective.
2. Developing a promotion mix is contingent on many factors, including the type of product and the product's attributes. Which of the four promotional methods—advertising, personal selling, public relations, or sales promotion—would you emphasize if you were developing the promotion mix for the following products? Explain your answers.
   a. Washing machine
   b. Cereal
   c. Halloween candy
   d. Compact disc
3. Suppose marketers at Falcon International Corporation have come to you for recommendations on how to promote

their products. They want to develop a comprehensive promotional campaign and have a generous budget with which to implement their plans. What questions would you ask them, and what would you suggest they consider before developing a promotional program?

4. Marketers must consider whether to use a push or a pull policy when deciding on a promotion mix (see Figure 17.4). Identify a product for which marketers should use each policy and a third product that might best be promoted using a mix of the two policies. Explain your answers.
5. IMP The SMART car was launched in the United States in 2008, thereby establishing the American "micro-car" category. Sales of SMART cars to date have not met expectations, but the introduction of the iQ from Scion and plans for small vehicles at Toyota, Hyundai, and other car manufacturers suggest that the micro-car category is not going away. An ongoing challenge for the manufacturers of micro-cars, however, is overcoming the rumors that circulate about the miniscule machines, notably the idea that micro-cars are unsafe and useless without a back seat. Develop a very simple questionnaire of four to five items and survey 10 to 15 friends or family members about their beliefs on micro-cars. Based on this information, develop a budget in terms of percentage of sales revenue to be spent for advertising, personal selling, sales promotion, and public relations.

Internet Exercise

Myspace

Myspace is not just for friends. It is also a unique promotional platform for musical artists, especially unsigned and independent artists. By creating a Myspace page, musicians can share their songs, post important dates, or even blog. Myspace music pages are different from record company websites because they feel more personal. Artists also take advantage of Myspace's viral nature by allowing other Myspace members to post their pictures, songs, and music videos on their own Myspace profile pages. Visit the website at http:// music.myspace.com, and look for your favorite artist or discover a new one.

1. Who is the target market for members?
2. What is being promoted to these individuals?
3. What are the promotional objectives of this website?
4. Is word-of-mouth communication occurring at this website? Explain.

developing your marketing plan

A vital component of a successful marketing strategy is the company's plan for communication to its stakeholders. One segment of the communication plan is included in the marketing mix as the promotional element. A clear understanding of the role that promotion plays, as well as the various methods of promotion, is important in developing the promotional plan. The following questions should assist you in relating the information in this chapter to several decisions in your marketing plan.

1. Review the communication process in Figure 17.1. Identify the various players in the communication process for promotion of your product.
2. What are your objectives for promotion? Use Table 17.2 as a guide in answering this question.
3. Which of the four elements of the promotional mix are most appropriate for accomplishing your objectives? Discuss the advantages and disadvantages of each.
4. What role should word-of-mouth communications, buzz marketing, or product placement play in your promotional plan?

The information obtained from these questions should assist you in developing various aspects of your marketing plan found in the "Interactive Marketing Plan" exercise at www.cengagebrain.com.

video case 17.1

Vans Masters Communication with the Skater-Shoe Market

For most people, surfing and skateboarding come to mind immediately when they think of southern California culture. For 40 years, Vans has embodied the California lifestyle and remains one of the preeminent skater-shoe companies. Founded in Los Angeles in 1966 by Paul Van Doren, his brother Steve, and Belgian investor Serge D'Elia, Vans quickly became a staple in southern California. Starting with a few versions of the traditional lace-up deck shoe sold out of a factory, the style of shoe became popular almost immediately. Vans rapidly increased its level of popularity by customizing shoes in all different fabrics and designs. The Van Dorens secured their local customized shoe business by selling plaid shoes to Catholic schools and sneakers with school colors to high school athletes. But when the checkered slip-on was donned by Sean Penn and his surfer buddies in the film *Fast Times at Ridgemont High,* skaters all over the country were demanding their own pairs of Vans. The shoes went from local wear to an iconic symbol in just a few years.

© iStockphoto.com/JOSE JUAN GARCIA

Contrary to many corporate success stories, the Vans company never spent much money on marketing. Paul Van Doren knew that he offered a superior product, and he relied on word of mouth to popularize the high-quality, extremely durable shoes. The most marketing Van Doren did at first was to have his children canvas their neighborhood with flyers. At all early Vans stores, signs encouraged customers to "tell a friend about Vans."

For years, Van Doren focused mostly on the manufacturing aspect of the company so that even with a minimal amount of advertising, popularity grew because Vans were, quite simply, quality shoes. It wasn't until the late 1980s and early 1990s, when manufacturing was taken overseas, that Vans turned its attention to marketing.

One of Vans' earliest forays into promotion came about by chance. As skateboarders began to discover Vans shoes, the company responded by creating styles more amenable to skating. With their skater following growing, Vans paid a few top skaters a few hundred dollars apiece to wear its shoes at skating events. In 1989, Vans produced its first signature skateboarding shoe, the Steve Caballero shoe. Since then, Vans has partnered with numerous athletes, such as Geoff Rowley, who has the best-selling signature Vans shoe to date, and Johnny Layton.

As skateboarding culture has continued to flourish over the decades, Vans' connection to the scene has remained strong. Vans' marketing and promotional team focuses on spreading interest in Vans by doing its best to remain plugged into the youth culture and fueling teenage interest in Vans products. To this end, the company advertises through print, online, TV, and sporting and music events. Currently, the key to Vans' marketing strategy is developing advertising partnerships with athletes, artists, and media outlets. People immersed in this culture want to own Vans products. Vans is not just a shoe; it is a lifestyle.

Young extreme-sports athletes, like skaters and surfers, remain Vans' most important customer base. In 1995, Vans hosted its first Triple Crown event. The Triple Crown spotlights skateboarding, surfing, snowboarding, BMX, FMX, and wakeboarding. Tony Hawk won the skateboarding competition that first year and has since become a household name. Also in 1995, Vans launched its first annual Warped Tour, blending skating with music through concerts and competitions. This use of integrated marketing allows Vans to build brand recognition, cement its integral place in the skating lifestyle, and connect with customers via giveaways and promotions, such as designing custom shoes.

In addition to events, Vans connects with its audience through magazine advertisements, television, and the Internet, especially to attract young female consumers, who represent a growing part of the Vans customer base. In the past, the company has partnered with magazines like *Teen Vogue* and *CosmoGirl* to reach the female demographic. Vans also collaborates with musicians, artists, and designers to increase brand awareness through sponsorships, music tours, and videos.

More recently, Vans has embarked upon digital marketing initiatives. For instance, Vans promotes itself through mobile apps that its fans can download in order to access Vans-related news. The company has also created a customizer on its website that allows customers to design their own pair of Vans shoes and have them delivered. Although it is more than 40 years old, Vans still connects with youth culture as well as ever—and shows no signs of slowing down.[45]

Questions for Discussion

1. Evaluate Vans' early word-of-mouth marketing strategy.
2. Why were the early Vans marketing activities related to skateboard shoes so successful?
3. How does Vans continue to capture its target market through integrated marketing?

case 17.2

Southwest Airlines Promotes Its Culture

Although Southwest Airlines started small, today, it is one of the largest airlines in the country, flying to 72 cities on more than 3,300 flights a day. The Texas-based company prides itself on its sense of humour and down-home attitude, which has been developed and advanced over the years through advertising, promotions, and public relations programs. Its national advertising campaigns ("You are now free to move about the country" and "We Love Your Bags") are success stories. This is the airline that once paid an Elvis impersonator to serenade customers at the Manchester, New Hampshire, airport to celebrate its addition of flights to Las Vegas; the airline that painted three of its aircraft with Shamu the whale in its partnership with SeaWorld. Southwest's vision is to be a low-budget airline that enables its customers to have fun flying.

The corporate culture owes a lot to the outgoing personality of the airline's co-founder, Herb Kelleher. But humor also serves as a way to make cheap travel more palatable. The Southwest Way that employees are encouraged to adopt includes displaying a Warrior Spirit, a Servant's Heart, and a Fun-LUVing attitude. It is typical for Southwest flight crews to joke with the passengers. These tactics build worldwide customer allegiance. The airline also tries to engage its customers in dialogue with its Nuts About Southwest blog and its social media presence on sites, such as Facebook, LinkedIn, and Twitter.

Southwest's "Ding" promotion is a terrific example of its use of integrated marketing communication. Customers can download software from the airline's website, and when Southwest offers a low fare, it notifies them with a "ding" sound—the same "ding" you hear when airline captains turn off the seatbelt sign; the same "ding" that precedes Southwest's well-known tagline, "You are now free to move about the country." Southwest also caters to pet-LUVing customers through its P.A.W.S. program, which allows passengers with small pets to take their pets into the airline cabin (in a carrier) for $75 each way.

One of Southwest's major campaigns is its bags-fly-free policy. Southwest Airlines allows passengers to check two bags free per customer, while most other airlines charge about $25 for checked bags (the prices go up as the number of bags increases). Baggage fees have generated much-needed revenue for many of the airlines, but Southwest recognized that it could instead profit from consumer discontent over the bag fees. In response, the company released the "Grab Your Bag. It's On!" campaign to position itself as an airline that treats its customers like people. The company released several commercials criticizing competing airlines, asking, "Why do they hate your bags?" Today, Southwest continues to heavily promote its bags-fly-free policy. Its website compares Southwest's bag charges ($0 for first two checked bags) with other airlines (up to $120) as "ridiculous" versus "ridiculously awesome." JetBlue has joined Southwest in offering two free checked bags.

More recent marketing campaigns are also stressing the positive impact that Southwest has on the communities in which it does business. Southwest stresses that its employees not only care about customer service but about serving their communities. One way in which company employees engage in community service is by the "Adopt a Pilot" program. Southwest pilots are "adopted" by classrooms across the country for four-week periods. During this time, the pilots volunteer in the classrooms and mentor the student. When traveling, the pilots will send e-mails and postcards to their students from different places. From an integrated marketing perspective, this program not only enhances Southwest's reputation as a socially responsible company, but it also spreads brand awareness among students and their parents.

Southwest spends a significant amount of money on national advertising and media, approximately $249 million in 2011. Much of this advertising discusses the benefits of Southwest as well as its caring and loving culture. However, unlike several other airlines, Southwest does not sell ad space on the exterior of its planes. Southwest maintains that it tries to keep its advertising messages related to Southwest airlines, travel-related products, and companies with which it maintains partnerships (such as SeaWorld). These limits can increase the goodwill it has with consumers who feel bombarded with marketing messages. Through effective integrated marketing, Southwest has been able to launch successful campaigns, gain market share, and thrive even during the most recent recession.[46]

Questions for Discussion

1. Describe the various promotion elements that Southwest Airlines uses in its integrated marketing communications.
2. How does the engaging and entertaining performance of Southwest flight crews contribute to promotion activities?
3. How has Southwest Airlines positioned its advertising by focusing on simple concepts like "Grab Your Bag. It's On!"?

NOTES

[1]Piet Levy, "Crisis Control," *Marketing News,* July 30, 2011, 8–9; Elizabeth Weise, "Taco Bell in a Beef over Meat Filling," *USA Today*, January 27, 2011, 3B; Sarah Skidmore and Bruce Schreiner, "'Thank You for Suing Us'—Taco Bell Fights Back on Beef Lawsuit with Ad Push," January 28, 2011, www.salon.com/news/feature/2011/01/28/taco_bell_ad_fake_meat (accessed January 28, 2011).

[2]"Tim Peterson, "Tic Tac to Erect Interactive Billboard in Times Square," *Adweek*, February 10, 2012, www.adweek.com/news/advertising-branding/tic-tac-erect-interactive-billboard-times-square-138176 (accessed March 7, 2012).

[3]Shane Snow, "How 3 Companies Took Content Marketing to the Next Level ," Mashable, May 1, 2011, http://mashable.com/2011/05/01/content-marketing-tips/ (accessed March 7, 2012); OpenForum, www.openforum.com/ (accessed March 7, 2012).

[4]Andrea Chang, "Advertising Spending Online Expected to Surpass Print This Year," *Los Angeles Times,* January 20, 2012, http://latimesblogs.latimes.com/technology/2012/01/advertising-spending-online-expected-to-surpass-print-this-year.html (accessed February 23, 2012).

[5]Salvador Ruiz and María Sicilia, "The Impact of Cognitive and/or Affective Processing Styles on Consumer Response to Advertising Appeals," *Journal of Business Research* 57 (2004): 657–664.

[6]Deborah Swallow, "Cross Cultural Marketing Blunders," August 20, 2009, www.deborahswallow.com/2009/08/20/cross-cultural-marketing-blunders (accessed April 19, 2011).

[7]"Internet Gains on Television as Public's Main News Source," *Pew Research Center,* January 4, 2011, www.people-press.org/2011/01/04/internet-gains-on-television-as-publics-main-news-source/ (accessed February 23, 2012).

[8]*Advertising Age,* June 20, 2011, copyright Crain Communications Inc., 2011; hoovers.com (accessed March 21, 2012).

[9]"REDcard: Take Charge of Education," Target, https://sites.target.com/site/en/corporate/page.jsp?contentId=PRD03-005174 (accessed March 7, 2012).

[10]Sven Grundberg and Shira Ovide, "A Test Ride for Windows 8," *The Wall Street Journal*, February 29, 2012, http://online.wsj.com/article/SB10001424052970203986604577253202516915554.html (accessed March 7, 2012).

[11]Lauren Johnson, "Olay Taps Mobile Advertising to Bolster Product Awareness," Mobile Marketer, February 14, 2012, www.mobilemarketer.com/cms/news/advertising/12116.html (accessed February 23, 2012).

[12]Aaron Perlut, "Two On Two: Does Ragu Really Hate Dads?," *Forbes,* September 30, 2011, www.forbes.com/sites/marketshare/2011/09/30/two-on-two-does-ragu-really-hate-dads/ (accessed February 23, 2012); "Marketing's Biggest Social-Media Blunders of 2011," *Advertising Age,* December 12, 2011, http://adage.com/article/special-report-book-of-tens-2011/marketing-s-biggest-social-media-blunders-2011/231503/ (accessed February 23, 2012).

[13]Nat Ives, "Publishers Gush Over iPad, but Their Publications Are More Restrained," *Advertising Age,* March 31, 2010, http://adage.com/article/media-works/publishers-gush-ipad-publications/143074/ (accessed April 19, 2011).

[14]Mike Waterhouse, "Starbucks Offering Free Samples to Introduce New Blonde Roast Coffee," News Net 5, www.newsnet5.com/dpp/news/local_news/starbucks-offering-free-samples-to-introduce-new-blonde-roast-coffee (accessed March 8, 2012).

[15]Regal Crown Club, Regal Entertainment Group, http://rcc.regalcinemas.com/CrownClub/appmanager/rcc/CrownClub?_nfpb=true&_pageLabel=CROWNCLUB (accessed March 8, 2012).

[16]Jack Nicas, "American Airlines Adds Some Leg Room in Coach," *The Wall Street Journal,* March 1, 2012, http://online.wsj.com/article/SB10001424052970203753704577255312409073878.html (accessed March 8, 2012).

[17]"2012 U.S. National Edition Rates," *Time* Media Kit, www.timemediakit.com/us/rates-specs/national.html (accessed March 8, 2012).

[18]Joann Peck and Jennifer Wiggins, "It Just Feels Good: Customers' Affective Response to Touch and Its Influence in Persuasion," *Journal of Marketing* 70 (October 2006): 56–69.

[19]Avi Dan, "Angelina Jolie in a New Louis Vuitton Ad," *Forbes,* June 14, 2011, www.forbes.com/sites/avidan/2011/06/14/angelina-jolie-in-a-new-louis-vuitton-ad/ (accessed February 23, 2012).

[20]"Geek Squad," YouTube, www.youtube.com/user/GeekSquadHQ?ob=0 (accessed February 23, 2012).

[21]Michael White, "Super Swagonomics," *Bloomberg Businessweek,* February 21–February 27, 2011, 80–81.

[22]David Voreacos, Alex Nussbaum, and Greg Farrell, "Johnson and Johnson Fights to Clear its Once-Trusted Name," *Bloomberg Businessweek*, April 4, 2011, 69.

[23]Bruce Horovitz, "New Sampling Machine Can Gauge Your Age and Sex," *USA Today,* December 14, 2011, www.usatoday.com/money/industries/food/story/2011-12-13/face-recogniton-sampling-machine/51890500/1 (accessed February 23, 2012).

[24]"Top Ten Most Popular Coupons," *Business News Daily*, February 13, 2012, www.mnn.com/money/personal-finance/stories/the-10-most-popular-coupons (accessed March 6, 2012).

[25]Doug Brooks, "How to Balance Brand Building and Price Promotion," *Ad Age,* December 29, 2009, http://adage.com/article/cmo-strategy/balance-brand-building-price-promotion/141232/ (accessed August 14, 2012).

[26]Michael Learmonth, "Marketers, It's Time to Figure Out Your Mobile-Marketing Strategy," Promotional supplement to *Advertising Age*, Spring 2011, 4.

[27]U.S. Census Bureau, American Community Survey, Fact Finder, factfinder.census.gov/servlet/ADPTable?_bm=y&-geo_id=01000US&-ds_name=ACS_2008_3YR_G00_&-_lang=en&-_caller=geoselect&-format= (accessed April 19, 2011).

[28]Rockney G. Walters and Maqbul Jamil, "Exploring the Relationships Between Shopping Trip Type, Purchases of Products on Promotion, and Shopping Basket Profit," *Journal of Business Research* 56 (2003): 17–29.

[29]Schneider Associates, "Velveeta Cheesy Skillets Forge New Ideas in Quick and Easy Dinners," Launch PR, October 13, 2011, http://launchpr.typepad.com/schneiderassociates/most_memorable_new_product/ (accessed February 23, 2012).

[30]Emma Hall, "German Magazine Ditches Models for 'Real' Women," *Advertising Age,* October 6, 2009, http://adage.com/globalnews/article?article_id=139485 (accessed April 6, 2010).

[31]"The Best of Word of Mouth," *Adweek*, November 22, 2011, www.adweek.com/sa-article/best-word-mouth-136683 (accessed March 8, 2012).

[32]Tomás Bayón, "The Chain from Customer Satisfaction via Word-of-Mouth Referrals to New Customer Acquisition," *Journal of the Academy of Marketing Science* 35 (June 2007): 233–249.

[33]Pratibha A. Dabholkar, "Factors Influencing Consumer Choice of a 'Rating Web Site': An Experimental Investigation of an Online Interactive Decision Aid," *Journal of Marketing Theory and Practice* 14 (Fall 2006): 259–273.

[34]"Global Advertising: Consumers Trust Real Friends and Virtual Strangers the Most," *NielsenWire*, July 7, 2009, http://blog.nielsen.com/nielsenwire/consumer/global-advertising-consumers-trust-real-friends-and-virtual-strangers-the-most/ (accessed April 19, 2011).

[35]"Best Buzz Marketing/Influencer Program," Event Marketer, June 14, 2011, www.eventmarketer.com/ex-awards/2011/best-buzz-marketinginfluencer-program (accessed February 21, 2012).

[36]Jim Carlton, "Logo Graffiti Gets Scrubbed," *The Wall Street Journal,* December 4–5, 2010, A3.

[37]Emily Steel and Geoffrey A. Fowler, "Big Brands Like Facebook, But They Don't Like to Pay," *The Wall Street Journal,* November 2, 2011, http://online.wsj.com/article/SB10001424052970204294504576613232804554362.html (accessed February 23, 2012);"Doug, Ford's Spokespuppet," Facebook, www.facebook.com/#!/focusdoug (accessed February 23, 2012); Josh Warner, "The 10 Most Innovative Viral Ad Videos of 2011," Mashable, December 8, 2011, http://mashable.com/2011/12/08/innovative-viral-ads-2011/#S9udCp32LdA (accessed February 23, 2012).

[38]Reuters, "Apple Deemed Top of Movie Placement Charts," February 22, 2011, www.reuters.com/article/2011/02/22/us-productplacement-idUS-TRE71L69920110222 (accessed February 23, 2012).

[39]Lynna Goch, "The Place to Be," *Best's Review,* February 2005, 64–65.

[40]Ben Sisario, "Pepsi Takes Active Role in 'X Factor,' *The New York Times,* August 5, 2011, www.nytimes.com/2011/08/05/business/media/pepsi-takes-active-role-in-x-factor.html (accessed February 23, 2012).

[41]Bruce Horovitz, "Abercrombie Reaches for PR Heaven," *USA Today*, August 18, 2011, 1B.

[42]Lilly Vitorovich, "Product Placement to Be Allowed in U.K. TV Programs," *The Wall Street Journal,* December 21, 2010, B5.

[43]"Dannon Settles FTC Deceptive Advertising Complaint," Grimes & Reese P.L.L.C., January 4, 2011, www.mlmlaw.com/blog/dannon-settles-ftc-complaint (accessed February 24, 2012).

[44]Dennis A. Kopf, Ivonne M. Torres, and Carl Enomoto, "Advertising's Unintended Consequence," *Journal of Advertising* 40, no. 4, (Winter 2011): 5–18.

[45]Jason Lee, "The History of Vans," *Sneaker Freaker,* www.sneakerfreaker.com/feature/history-of-vans/1 (accessed April 2, 2012); Vans: 40 Years of Originality, www.vans40.com (accessed April 2, 2012); Vans website, www.vans.com/ (accessed April 2, 2012).

[46]SWAMEDIA, Southwest Airlines Story Leads, www.swamedia.com/ (accessed March 15, 2011); Southwest Airlines website, www.southwest.com/ (accessed March 22, 2012); PR Newswire, "Southwest Airlines Launches New 'Grab Your Bag: It's On!' Ads," Southwest.com, March 15, 2010, www.southwest.com/about_swa/press/prindex.html?int=GFOOTER-ABOUT-PRESS (accessed May 2, 2010); "Airlines to Charge for Carry-on Bags," CBS News, April 7, 2010, www.cbsnews.com/video/watch/?id=6372838n (accessed March 22, 2012); NutsAboutSouthwest, "Southwest Airlines Bags Fly Free Commercial," September 28, 2009, www.youtube.com/ (accessed May 2, 2010); Rupal Parekh, "Southwest Airlines Looks Beyond GSD&M, Its Agency of More Than 30 Years," *Advertising Age,* February 23, 2012, http://adage.com/article/agency-news/southwest-airlines-gsd-m/232911/ (accessed March 22, 2012); Greg Stoller, "Ads Add Up for Airlines, but Some Fliers Say It's Too Much," *USA Today*, October 19, 2011, http://travel.usatoday.com/ (accessed March 22, 2012).

Feature Notes

[a]Emily Steel, "Websites Reach for the Stars," *The Wall Street Journal,* August 1, 2011, B4; Michael White, "Super Swagonomics," *Bloomberg Businessweek,* February 21–February 27, 2011, 80–81; Laura Petrecca, "The Star-Crossed Side to Celeb Investment," *USA Today,* October 10, 2011, 1B–2B; Michael McCarthy, "Gillette Ends Endorsement Deal with Tiger Woods," *USA Today,* December 24, 2010, www.usatoday.com/communities/gameon/post/2010/12/tiger-woods-dropped-as-endorser-by-gillette/1 (accessed January 6, 2011); Jonathon Welsh, "Charlie Sheen Sells Cars for Fiat in 'House Arrest' Commercial," *The Wall Street Journal,* March 2, 2012, http://blogs.wsj.com/speakeasy/2012/03/02/fiat-taps-charlie-sheen-for-house-arrest-spot/?mod=google_news_blog (accessed March 8, 2012).

[b]Federal Trade Commission, *Part 260—Guides for the Use of Environmental Marketing Claims*, http://ftc.gov/bcp/grnrule/guides980427.htm (accessed December 12, 2011); Federal Trade Commission, "FTC Warns 78 Retailers, Including Wal-Mart, Target, and Kmart, to Stop Labeling and Advertising Rayon Textile Products as 'Bamboo'," February 3, 2010, www.ftc.gov/opa/2010/02/bamboo.shtm (accessed December 12, 2011); Gwendolyn Bounds, "Misleading Claims on 'Green' Labeling," *The Wall Street Journal,* October 26, 2010, http://online.wsj.com/article/SB10001424052702303467004575574521710082414.html (accessed December 12, 2011); Cassandra Sweets, "Update: California Sues 3 Firms Over 'Greenwashing' of Bottles," *The Wall Street Journal*, October 26, 2011, http://online.wsj.com/article/BT-CO-20111026-718608.html (accessed December 12, 2011).

[c]The Kluger Agency, http://klugeragency.com/ (accessed January 11, 2011); Burt Helm, "Singing Songs of [Your Brand Here!]" *Bloomberg Businessweek,* December 6–12, 2010, 86–89.

[d]Wendy Koch, "Firm Touts Green Efforts," *USA Today*, July 27, 2011, 3A; Natural American Spirit Cigarettes, www.nascigs.com/Public/Responsible-Marketing-Policy.aspx (accessed November 2, 2011).

chapter 18

Advertising and Public Relations

OBJECTIVES

1. To describe the nature and types of advertising
2. To explore the major steps in developing an advertising campaign
3. To identify who is responsible for developing advertising campaigns
4. To examine the tools used in public relations
5. To analyze how public relations is used and evaluated

© iStockphoto.com/sorendis/iStockphoto.com/Valerie Loiseleux

MARKETING INSIGHTS

L'Oréal Slogan Celebrates 40 Years of Empowering Women

A successful company slogan may only be a few words in length, but it is a key factor in telling the story behind the brand. As brands and consumer tastes evolve, many companies change their advertising slogans over time. French cosmetics brand L'Oréal Paris is an exception. Changes to the company slogan "Because I'm Worth It" have been limited to pronouns (it recently changed its slogan to say "Because We're Worth It"). The slogan has been translated into 40 languages and continues to be a part of most L'Oréal advertising.

L'Oréal's trademark slogan was created in 1971 during a time when women were seeking to become more empowered. Created by advertising agency McCann Erickson, the slogan first appeared in a commercial with actress Joanne Dusseau speaking the words while attempting to rationalize her L'Oréal purchases. Four decades later, L'Oréal celebrated 40 years of the slogan by throwing a large party attended by the company's brand ambassadors.

Although L'Oréal is the largest cosmetics company worldwide, selling an estimated 50 products per second, sales have slipped in recent years. Experts feel that the onset of the digital age and shorter attention spans may be making the slogan less effective and more outdated. Despite these concerns, L'Oréal Paris' CEO has announced that he intends to keep the advertising slogan. Although the slogan's sense of female empowerment may not be as relevant in Europe or America, he sees opportunity in Africa and Asia where women's rights are taking hold. Combine this with L'Oréal Paris' 30 brand ambassadors, who spend a significant amount of time promoting the slogan, and L'Oréal's brand might gain the same level of prominence as it had four decades ago.[1]

Both large organizations and small companies use conventional and online promotional efforts like advertising to change their corporate images, build brand equity, launch new products, or promote current brands. In this chapter, we explore several dimensions of advertising and public relations. First, we focus on the nature and types of advertising. Next, we examine the major steps in developing an advertising campaign and describe who is responsible for developing such campaigns. We then discuss the nature of public relations and how it is used. We examine various public relations tools and ways to evaluate the effectiveness of public relations. Finally, we focus on how companies deal with unfavorable public relations.

THE NATURE AND TYPES OF ADVERTISING

advertising Paid nonpersonal communication about an organization and its products transmitted to a target audience through mass media

institutional advertising Advertising that promotes organizational images, ideas, and political issues

Advertising permeates our daily lives. At times, we view it positively; at other times, we feel bombarded and try to avoid it. Some advertising informs, persuades, or entertains us; some bores, annoys, or even offends us.

As mentioned in Chapter 17, **advertising** is a paid form of nonpersonal communication that is transmitted to a target audience through mass media, such as television, radio, the Internet, newspapers, magazines, direct mail, outdoor displays, and signs on mass transit vehicles. Advertising can have a profound impact on how consumers view certain products. In one study of children four to six years old, cereal packaged in a box with a cartoon on the cover was perceived as better tasting even when the cereal in the boxes without the cartoon on the cover was the same food. Effective advertising can influence purchase behavior throughout a lifetime.[2] Organizations use advertising to reach a variety of audiences ranging from small, specific groups, such as stamp collectors in Idaho, to extremely large groups, such as all athletic-shoe purchasers in the United States.

© AP Images/PRNewsFoto/Stonyfield Farm

Institutional Advertising
Stonyfield has created an ad to promote its efforts to help fund innovative organic farming projects, which can have a positive impact on the environment.

When asked to name major advertisers, most people immediately mention business organizations. However, many nonbusiness organizations—including governments, churches, universities, and charitable organizations—employ advertising to communicate with stakeholders. Each year, the U.S. government spends hundreds of millions of dollars in advertising to advise and influence the behavior of its citizens. Although this chapter analyzes advertising in the context of business organizations, much of the following material applies to all types of organizations. For example, the state of Wyoming increased its advertising spending on campaigns to attract tourists to the state. Tourism is the second largest industry in Wyoming. As part of its tourism initiatives, Wyoming is targeting major U.S. cities, including Chicago and Seattle. It also wants to increase its film industry incentives to attract more filmmakers to the state.[3]

Advertising is used to promote goods, services, ideas, images, issues, people, and anything else advertisers want to publicize or foster. Depending on what is being promoted, advertising can be classified as institutional or product advertising. **Institutional advertising** promotes organizational images, ideas, and political issues. It can be used to create or maintain an organizational image. Institutional advertisements may deal with broad image issues, such as organizational strengths or the friendliness of employees. They may also aim to create a more favorable view of the organization in the eyes of noncustomer groups, such as shareholders, consumer advocacy groups, potential shareholders, or the general public. When a company promotes its position on a public issue—for instance, a tax increase, sustainability, regulations, or international trade coalitions—institutional advertising is referred to as **advocacy advertising**. Such advertising may be used to promote socially approved behavior, such as recycling or moderation in consuming alcoholic beverages. Philip Morris, for example, has run television advertisements encouraging parents to talk to their children about not smoking. Research has identified a number of themes that advertisers like Philip Morris can use to increase the effectiveness of antismoking messages for adolescents.[4] This type of advertising not only has social benefits but also helps build an organization's image.

Product advertising promotes the uses, features, and benefits of products. For example, Motorola promotes features and benefits of its smartphones, such as 21 hours on a full charge for its DROID RAZR MAXX. There are two types of product advertising: pioneer and competitive. **Pioneer advertising** focuses on stimulating demand for a product category (rather than a specific brand) by informing potential customers about the product's features, uses, and benefits. Sometimes marketers will begin advertising a product before it hits the market. Apple has had great success using this type of advertising for its iPod and iPad. Product advertising that focuses on products before they are available tend to cause people to think about the product more and evaluate it more positively.[5] Pioneer advertising is also employed when the product is in the introductory stage of the product life cycle, exemplified in the launch of the Nissan Leaf in the electric car category. **Competitive advertising** attempts to stimulate demand for a specific brand by promoting the brand's features, uses, and advantages, sometimes through indirect or direct comparisons with competing brands. Cell phone service providers use competitive advertising to position their brands—for example, AT&T against Verizon. Advertising effects on sales must reflect competitors' advertising activities. The type of competitive environment will determine the most effective industry approach.

To make direct product comparisons, marketers use a form of competitive advertising called **comparative advertising**, which compares the sponsored brand with one or more identified competing brands on the basis of one or more product characteristics. Advil PM, for example, used comparative advertising to promote the effectiveness of its over-the-counter sleeping pill as compared to Tylenol PM. Often, the brands that are promoted through comparative advertisements have low market shares and are compared with competitors that have the highest market shares in the product category. Product categories that commonly use comparative advertising include soft drinks, toothpaste, pain relievers, foods, tires, automobiles, and detergents. Under the provisions of the 1988 Trademark Law Revision Act, marketers using comparative advertisements in the United States must not misrepresent the qualities or characteristics of competing products. Other countries may have laws that are stricter or less strict with regard to comparative advertising.

advocacy advertising Advertising that promotes a company's position on a public issue

product advertising Advertising that promotes the uses, features, and benefits of products

pioneer advertising Advertising that tries to stimulate demand for a product category rather than a specific brand by informing potential buyers about the product

competitive advertising Tries to stimulate demand for a specific brand by promoting its features, uses, and advantages relative to competing brands

comparative advertising Compares the sponsored brand with one or more identified brands on the basis of one or more product characteristics

Marketing Debate

Truthful but Misleading Advertisements

ISSUE: Should marketers be able to make truthful claims if those claims might mislead consumers?

Regulatory agencies and consumer groups are concerned about the possibility that an ad may be literally truthful but still misleading. Unfortunately, once consumers have an idea of what a product description means, it is difficult to change their views. For instance, many consumers believe that organic food is more nutritious because it lacks additives and pesticides. Evidence does not support this assumption. These inferences make it easier for consumers to be misled. Endorsers of products can mislead when they appear to be experts, even though their expertise might not be in that particular field. Vague definitions are also problematic. For instance, natural potato chips are perceived to be healthier, but the fats and sugars in many natural potato chip brands have not been altered significantly.[a]

Other forms of competitive advertising include reminder and reinforcement advertising. **Reminder advertising** tells customers that an established brand is still around and still offers certain characteristics, uses, and advantages. Clorox, for example, reminds customers about the many advantages of its bleach products, such as their ability to kill germs, whiten clothes, and remove stains. **Reinforcement advertising** assures current users that they have made the right brand choice and tells them how to get the most satisfaction from that brand. Insurance companies like Geico encourage potential new customers to spend 15 minutes on the phone getting an insurance quote and save 15 percent or more on their policy. Value propositions like Geico's can provide reinforcement to consumers that they are making a good decision as a new or current customer.

DEVELOPING AN ADVERTISING CAMPAIGN

reminder advertising Advertising used to remind consumers about an established brand's uses, characteristics, and benefits

reinforcement advertising Advertising that assures users they chose the right brand and tells them how to get the most satisfaction from it

advertising campaign The creation and execution of a series of advertisements to communicate with a particular target audience

target audience The group of people at whom advertisements are aimed

An **advertising campaign** involves designing a series of advertisements and placing them in various advertising media to reach a particular target audience. As Figure 18.1 shows, the major steps in creating an advertising campaign are (1) identifying and analyzing the target audience, (2) defining the advertising objectives, (3) creating the advertising platform, (4) determining the advertising appropriation, (5) developing the media plan, (6) creating the advertising message, (7) executing the campaign, and (8) evaluating advertising effectiveness. The number of steps and the exact order in which they are carried out may vary according to the organization's resources, the nature of its product, and the type of target audience to be reached. Nevertheless, these general guidelines for developing an advertising campaign are appropriate for all types of organizations.

Identifying and Analyzing the Target Audience

The **target audience** is the group of people at whom advertisements are aimed. Advertisements for the Dyson vacuum cleaner target more affluent home owners, whereas the Dirt

Figure 18.1 General Steps in Developing and Implementing an Advertising Campaign

Identifying and Analyzing the Target Audience
Banana Republic targets an older, more affluent target audience than Gap does.

Devil targets lower- to middle-income households. Identifying and analyzing the target audience are critical processes; the information yielded helps determine other steps in developing the campaign. The target audience may include everyone in the firm's target market. Marketers may, however, direct a campaign at only a portion of the target market. For instance, until recently, LEGO focused on young boys as the target market for its products. This narrower strategic focus allowed the company to tailor products to attract this demographic with much success: revenues increased 105 percent in the last six years. However, it also turned off young girls from purchasing its products, who described LEGO as a boy's company. In the past few years, the company has performed market studies on girls to reposition its brand to attract both genders.[6]

Advertisers research and analyze advertising targets to establish an information base for a campaign. Information commonly needed includes location and geographic distribution of the target group; the distribution of demographic factors, such as age, income, race, gender, and education; lifestyle information; and consumer attitudes regarding purchase and use of both the advertiser's products and competing products. The exact kinds of information an organization finds useful depend on the type of product being advertised, the characteristics of the target audience, and the type and amount of competition. Additionally, advertisers must be sure to create a campaign that will resonate with the target market. For example, privacy concerns and irritating ads lead to avoidance, but when online and direct-mail advertising personalizes the information, there is an increase in the acceptance of the ad.[7] Generally, the more an advertiser knows about the target audience, the more likely the firm is to develop an effective advertising campaign. When MIT students and their professor developed the iRobot Roomba Vacuum Cleaning Robot, they knew their target market would embrace a robot that helped in cleaning. Created in 1990, today, iRobot uses advertising to create a strong brand message and convey the benefits of the company's robotic products.[8] When the advertising target is not precisely identified and properly analyzed, the campaign may fail.

Defining the Advertising Objectives

The advertiser's next step is to determine what the firm hopes to accomplish with the campaign. Because advertising objectives guide campaign development, advertisers should define objectives carefully. Advertising objectives should be stated clearly, precisely, and in measurable terms. Precision and measurability allow advertisers to evaluate advertising success at the end of the campaign in terms of whether objectives have been met. To provide precision and measurability, advertising objectives should contain benchmarks and indicate how far the advertiser wishes to move from these standards. If the goal is to increase sales, the advertiser should state the current sales level (the benchmark) and the amount of sales increase sought through advertising. An advertising objective should also specify a time frame so that advertisers know exactly how long they have to accomplish the objective. An advertiser with average monthly sales of $450,000 (the benchmark) might set the following objective: "Our primary advertising objective is to increase average monthly sales from $450,000 to $540,000 within 12 months."

If an advertiser defines objectives on the basis of sales, the objectives focus on increasing absolute dollar sales or unit sales, increasing sales by a certain percentage, or increasing the firm's market share. Even though an advertiser's long-run goal is to increase sales, not all campaigns are designed to produce immediate sales. Some campaigns aim to increase product or brand awareness, make consumers' attitudes more favorable, heighten consumers' knowledge of product features, or create awareness of positive, healthy consumer behavior, such as nonsmoking. If the goal is to increase product awareness, the objectives are stated in terms of communication. A specific communication objective might be to increase new product feature awareness, such as increased travel point rewards on a credit card from 0 to 40 percent in the target audience by the end of six months.

Creating the Advertising Platform

Before launching a political campaign, party leaders develop a political platform stating major issues that are the basis of the campaign. Like a political platform, an **advertising platform** consists of the basic issues or selling points that an advertiser wishes to include in the advertising campaign. For instance, Best Buy advertises that, if you buy new technology now, it will buy it back when it is time to upgrade. A single advertisement in an advertising campaign may contain one or several issues from the platform. Although the platform sets forth the basic issues, it does not indicate how to present them.

An advertising platform should consist of issues important to customers. One of the best ways to determine those issues is to survey customers about what they consider most important in the selection and use of the product involved. Selling features must not only be important to customers, they should also be strongly competitive features of the advertised brand. For instance, J.Crew's Ludlow Suit collection capitalizes upon its positioning as "style with substance." The Ludlow collection is marketed as high-quality ("fine Italian fabrics"), high-value products tailored to fit the customer.[9] Although research is the most effective method for determining what issues to include in an advertising platform, customer research can be expensive.

Because the advertising platform is a base on which to build the advertising message, marketers should analyze this stage carefully. It has been found that, if the message is viewed as useful, it will create greater brand trust.[10] A campaign can be perfect in terms of selection and analysis of its target audience, statement of its objectives, media strategy, and the form of its message. For instance, when Samsung released an advertisement showing consumers waiting hours in line for a new tech product, the objective was to poke fun at the Apple lifestyle while promoting its own Galaxy S2 phones. The target audience was those who were unsure about which smartphone to purchase. Interestingly, Apple is never mentioned in the entire advertisement.[11] But the campaign will ultimately fail if the advertisements communicate information that consumers do not deem important when selecting and using the product.

Determining the Advertising Appropriation

The **advertising appropriation** is the total amount of money a marketer allocates for advertising for a specific time period. The U.K. government allocated £3 million (or $4.7 million) for advertising the London 2012 Olympics. The advertising encouraged tourists to visit the Olympics as a holiday destination. The government justified the advertisements, because the resulting revenue that would come from the Olympics would benefit local economies.[12]

advertising platform Basic issues or selling points to be included in an advertising campaign

advertising appropriation The advertising budget for a specific time period

Many factors affect a firm's decision about how much to appropriate for advertising. Geographic size of the market and the distribution of buyers within the market have a great bearing on this decision. Both the type of product advertised and the firm's sales volume relative to competitors' sales volumes also play roles in determining what proportion of revenue to spend on advertising. Advertising appropriations for business products are usually quite small relative to product sales, whereas consumer convenience items, such as the cosmetics sold by L'Oréal, generally have large advertising expenditures relative to sales. For example, Procter & Gamble spends a relatively high percentage of sales to market its product mix of cosmetics, personal care products, appliances, detergents, and pet food. Table 18.1 shows the top 10 advertisers in the United States. Retailers like Walmart usually have a much lower percent of sales spent on advertising.

Of the many techniques used to determine the advertising appropriation, one of the most logical is the **objective-and-task approach**. Using this approach, marketers determine the objectives a campaign is to achieve and then attempt to list the tasks required to accomplish them. The costs of the tasks are calculated and added to arrive at the total appropriation. This approach has one main problem: marketers sometimes have trouble accurately estimating the level of effort needed to attain certain objectives. A coffee marketer, for example, may find it extremely difficult to determine how much of an increase in national television advertising is needed to raise a brand's market share from 8 to 10 percent.

In the more widely used **percent-of-sales approach**, marketers simply multiply the firm's past sales, plus a factor for planned sales growth or decline, by a standard percentage based on both what the firm traditionally spends on advertising and the industry average. This approach, too, has a major flaw: it is based on the incorrect assumption that sales create advertising rather than the reverse. A marketer using this approach during declining sales will reduce the amount spent on advertising, but such a reduction may further diminish sales. Though illogical, this technique has been favored because it is easy to implement.

Another way to determine advertising appropriation is the **competition-matching approach**. Marketers following this approach try to match their major competitors'

objective-and-task approach Budgeting for an advertising campaign by first determining its objectives and then calculating the cost of all the tasks needed to attain them

percent-of-sales approach Budgeting for an advertising campaign by multiplying the firm's past and expected sales by a standard percentage

competition-matching approach Determining an advertising budget by trying to match competitors' advertising outlays

Table 18.1 Top 10 Advertisers

Rank	Company	Advertising Expenditures (in Millions)	Sales (in Millions)	Advertising Expenditures (as a % of Sales)
1	Procter & Gamble	$4,615	$78,938	5.8
2	AT&T	2,989	124,280	2.4
3	General Motors Co.	2,869	135,592	2.1
4	Verizon Communications	2,451	106,565	2.3
5	American Express Co.	2,223	30,242	7.4
6	Pfizer	2,124	67,809	3.1
7	Walmart Stores	2,055	408,214	0.5
8	Time Warner	2,044	18,868	10.8
9	Johnson & Johnson	2,027	61,587	3.3
10	L'Oréal	1,979	19,495	10.2

Source: Reprinted with permission from the June 20, 2011, issue of *Advertising Age*. Copyright Crain Communications Inc., 2011; hoovers.com (accessed March 21, 2012).

appropriations in absolute dollars or to allocate the same percentage of sales for advertising that their competitors do. Although a marketer should be aware of what competitors spend on advertising, this technique should not be used alone because the firm's competitors probably have different advertising objectives and different resources available for advertising. Many companies and advertising agencies review competitive spending on a quarterly basis, comparing competitors' dollar expenditures on print, radio, and television with their own spending levels. Competitive tracking of this nature occurs at both the national and regional levels. For example, AT&T spends 2.4 percent of sales on advertising, while Verizon spends 2.3 percent of sales.

At times, marketers use the **arbitrary approach**, which usually means a high-level executive in the firm states how much to spend on advertising for a certain period. The arbitrary approach often leads to underspending or overspending. Although hardly a scientific budgeting technique, it is expedient.

Deciding how large the advertising appropriation should be is critical. If the appropriation is set too low, the campaign cannot achieve its full potential. When too much money is appropriated, overspending results, and financial resources are wasted.

Developing the Media Plan

Advertisers spend tremendous amounts on advertising media. These amounts have grown rapidly during the past two decades. Figure 18.2 shows the share of advertising revenue allocated to different media categories. Although television and print still comprise a greater share of advertising revenue than digital advertising, this last category is expected to grow rapidly during the next few years. Figure 18.3 illustrates how advertising through digital media formats is estimated to increase. To derive maximum results from media expenditures, marketers must develop effective media plans. A **media plan** sets forth the exact media vehicles to be used (specific magazines, television stations, social media, newspapers, and so forth) and the dates and times the advertisements will appear. The plan determines how many people in the target audience will be exposed to the message. The method also determines, to some degree, the effects of the message on those specific target markets. Media planning is a complex task requiring thorough analysis of the target audience. Sophisticated computer models have been developed to attempt to maximize the effectiveness of media plans.

arbitrary approach Budgeting for an advertising campaign as specified by a high-level executive in the firm

media plan A plan that specifies the media vehicles to be used and the schedule for running advertisements

Developing Media Vehicles
Kia has created memorable advertising by utilizing music-loving hamsters on TV and in print promotional materials.

Figure 18.2 Proportion of Total Advertising Dollars Spent on Selected Media

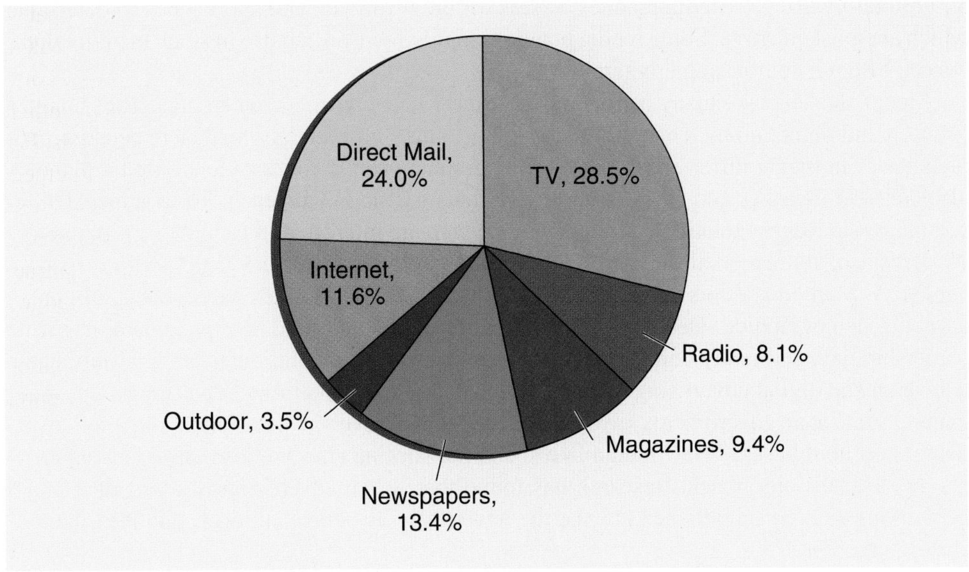

Source: "U.S. Ad Spending Totals," *Advertising Age*, June 20, 2011, pg. 18.

To formulate a media plan, the planners select the media for the campaign and prepare a time schedule for each medium. The media planner's primary goal is to reach the largest number of people in the advertising target that the budget will allow. A secondary goal is to achieve the appropriate message reach and frequency for the target audience while staying within budget. *Reach* refers to the percentage of consumers in the target audience actually exposed to a particular advertisement in a stated period. *Frequency* is the number of times these targeted consumers are exposed to the advertisement.

Media planners begin with broad decisions but eventually make very specific ones. They first decide which kinds of media to use: radio, television, newspapers, digital or online

Figure 18.3 U.S. Online Ad Spending, 2010–2015

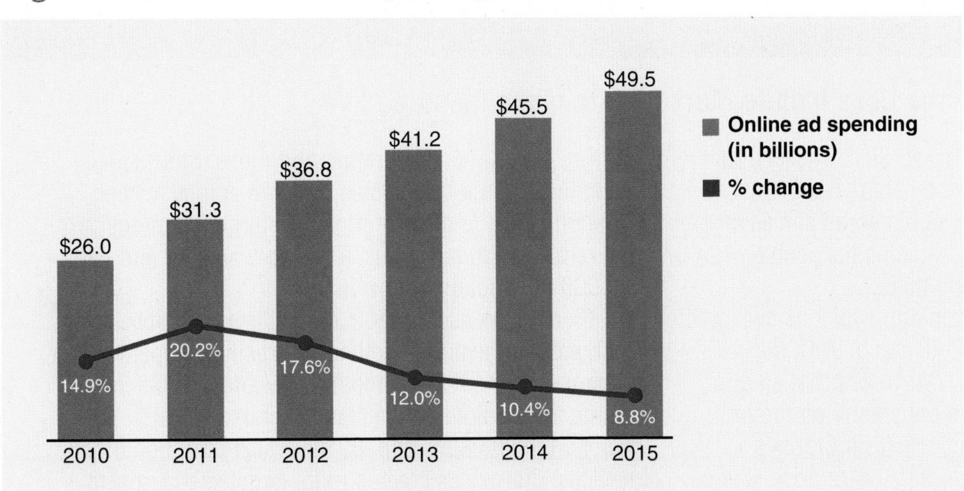

Source: "Online Advertising Market Poisted to Grow 20% in 2011," *eMarketer*, June 8, 2011, www.emarketer.com/PressRelease.aspx?R=1008432 (accessed October 17, 2012).

advertising, magazines, direct mail, outdoor displays, or signs on mass transit vehicles. Digital marketing in particular is growing, with spending on online advertising expected to exceed $49 billion by 2015.[13] Media planners assess different formats and approaches to determine which are most effective. Some media plans are highly focused and use just one medium. Others can be quite complex and dynamic.

Media planners take many factors into account when devising a media plan. They analyze location and demographic characteristics of consumers in the target audience, because people's tastes in media differ according to demographic groups and locations. Media planners also consider the sizes and types of audiences that specific media reach. For instance, *Glamour* magazine reaches relatively affluent women who are interested in fashion. Approximately 75 percent of its readership has a household income of more than $75,000 with a median age of 35. Many marketers of cosmetics, clothing, and fashion items would consider this an attractive demographic.[14] Declining broadcast television ratings and newspaper and magazine readership have led many companies to explore alternative media, including not only cable television and digital advertising but also ads on cell phones and product placements in video games. Some state governments have even made the controversial decision to allow for advertising on school buses.[15] New media like social networking sites are also attracting advertisers due to their large reach. Research has found that, when advertising is a part of a social networking site, consumers need to see the advertising as beneficial, or it may lead them to abandon the site.[16]

The rise in digital marketing is creating a dramatic shift for advertising agencies. Whereas competition came mostly from other agencies before, today, professional ad agencies face competition from amateur ad makers along with technology companies. For instance, crowdsourcing by organizations like Victor & Spoils is placing the roles of traditional advertising agencies into the hands of creative people worldwide. Digital marketing is not reduced to one medium, but can include platforms such as social networks, e-books, iPads, geotargeting, and mobile apps. Agencies that choose to embrace the new advertising media are facing challenges in adapting but are finding increased profitability along the way. One success story is the Heinz "Get Well Soon" campaign coordinated by social media marketing agency We Are Social. The campaign had two goals: generate greater awareness of Heinz's classic soups and gain more users on Heinz's U.K. Facebook fan page. During the campaign, Facebook fans could personalize their own can of "Get Well Soon" soup on the company's U.K. Facebook page and send the soup to a friend who was feeling unwell for a $3 fee. The number of fans on Heinz's U.K. Facebook page doubled as a result.[17]

Emerging Trends

Clorox Uses Mobile Marketing to Make Cleaning Fun

After nearly 100 years on the market, Clorox needed to find a way to reposition its brand and attract more customers. Its solution was to take its old brand and advertise it through a new medium while targeting the people who use Clorox products the most: mothers.

Enter the free Clorox myStain app, which is available for the iPhone, Android, and iPod Touch. With the growing use of mobile phones, Clorox felt that an app would appeal to moms who are constantly on the go. The myStain app offers instructions from Clorox's Dr. Laundry on how to deal with hard-to-remove stains, many of which go hand-in-hand with children: grass stains, pen marks, ice cream, and more. Clorox also included a game that allows users to spin a "wheel of stains" and find interesting and funny solutions for removing those stains. The app was a hit and had 75,000 downloads in one year.

Clorox also uses what it learns through mobile marketing to revamp its other advertising campaigns. For instance, many of the company's TV and print advertisements are inspired by the stains that users search for most on the myStain app. By advertising through mobile devices, Clorox has created more targeted advertising campaigns that make stain removal exciting.[b]

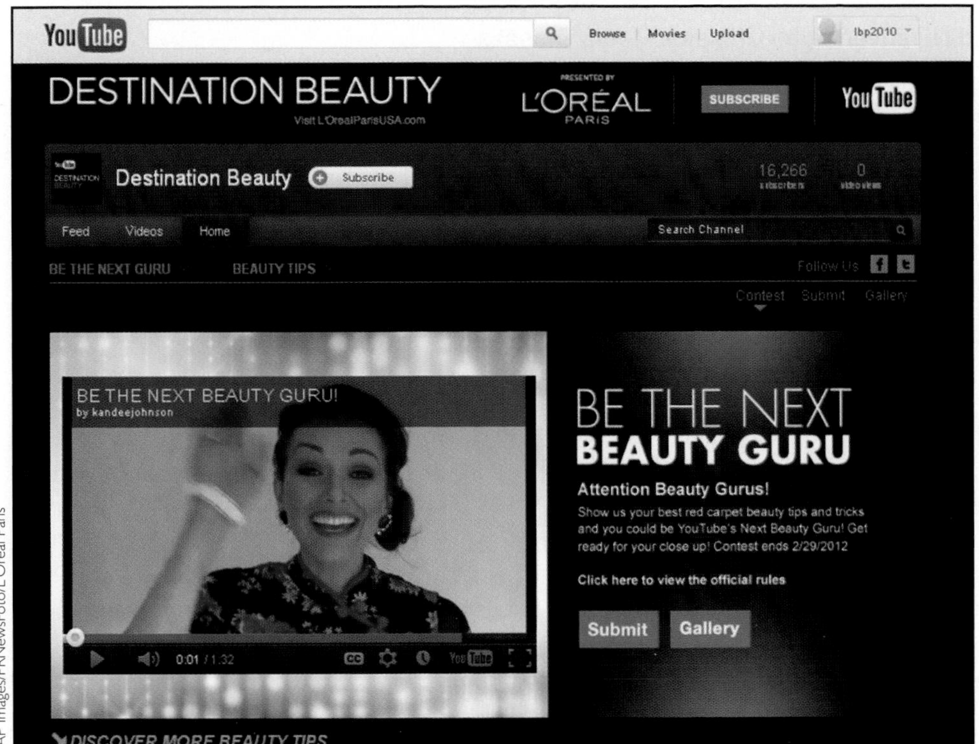

Digital Advertising
L'Oreal launched an online contest looking for their next beauty guru.

The content of the message sometimes affects media choice. Print media can be used more effectively than broadcast media to present complex issues or numerous details in single advertisements. If an advertiser wants to promote beautiful colors, patterns, or textures, media offering high-quality color reproduction, such as magazines or television, should be used instead of newspapers. For example, food can be effectively promoted in full-color magazine advertisements but far less effectively in black-and-white media.

The cost of media is an important but troublesome consideration. Planners try to obtain the best coverage possible for each dollar spent. However, there is no accurate way to compare the cost and impact of a television commercial with the cost and impact of a newspaper advertisement. A **cost comparison indicator** lets an advertiser compare the costs of several vehicles within a specific medium (such as two magazines) in relation to the number of people each vehicle reaches. The *cost per thousand impressions (CPM)* is the cost comparison indicator for magazines; it shows the cost of exposing 1,000 people to one advertisement.

Figure 18.3 shows the extent to which digital advertising is growing. Emerging media are being used more extensively in light of media fragmentation and decline in traditional media (newspapers and radio). However, although the use of newer forms of media is increasing, many companies continue to spend significant amounts of their marketing dollars advertising in more traditional forums. For instance, advertising in phone books makes up 7.6 percent of advertising dollars within the United States.[18] Media are selected by weighing the various advantages and disadvantages of each (see Table 18.2).

Like media selection decisions, media scheduling decisions are affected by numerous factors, such as target audience characteristics, product attributes, product seasonality, customer media behavior, and size of the advertising budget. There are three general types of media schedules: continuous, flighting, and pulsing. When a *continuous* schedule is used, advertising runs at a constant level with little variation throughout the campaign period. McDonald's is an example of a company that uses a continuous schedule. With a *flighting* schedule, advertisements run for set periods of time, alternating with periods in which no ads run. For example, an advertising campaign might have an ad run for two weeks, then suspend it for two weeks, and then run it again for two weeks.

cost comparison indicator A means of comparing the costs of advertising vehicles in a specific medium in relation to the number of people reached

Table 18.2 Advantages and Disadvantages of Major Media Classes

Medium	Advantages	Disadvantages
Newspapers	Reaches large audience; purchased to be read; geographic flexibility; short lead time; frequent publication; favorable for cooperative advertising; merchandising services	Not selective for socioeconomic groups or target market; short life; limited reproduction capabilities; large advertising volume limits exposure to any one advertisement
Magazines	Demographic selectivity; good reproduction; long life; prestige; geographic selectivity when regional issues are available; read in leisurely manner	High costs; 30- to 90-day average lead time; high level of competition; limited reach; communicates less frequently
Direct mail	Little wasted circulation; highly selective; circulation controlled by advertiser; few distractions; personal; stimulates actions; use of novelty; relatively easy to measure performance; hidden from competitors	Very expensive; lacks editorial content to attract readers; often thrown away unread as junk mail; criticized as invasion of privacy; consumers must choose to read the ad
Radio	Reaches 95 percent of consumers; highly mobile and flexible; very low relative costs; ad can be changed quickly; high level of geographic and demographic selectivity; encourages use of imagination	Lacks visual imagery; short life of message; listeners' attention limited because of other activities; market fragmentation; difficult buying procedures; limited media and audience research
Television	Reaches large audiences; high frequency available; dual impact of audio and video; highly visible; high prestige; geographic and demographic selectivity; difficult to ignore	Very expensive; highly perishable message; size of audience not guaranteed; amount of prime time limited; lack of selectivity in target market
Internet	Immediate response; potential to reach a precisely targeted audience; ability to track customers and build databases; highly interactive medium	Costs of precise targeting are high; inappropriate ad placement; effects difficult to measure; concerns about security and privacy
Yellow Pages	Wide availability; action and product category oriented; low relative costs; ad frequency and longevity; nonintrusive	Market fragmentation; extremely localized; slow updating; lack of creativity; long lead times; requires large space to be noticed
Outdoor	Allows for frequent repetition; low cost; message can be placed close to point of sale; geographic selectivity; operable 24 hours a day; high creativity and effectiveness	Message must be short and simple; no demographic selectivity; seldom attracts readers' full attention; criticized as traffic hazard and blight on countryside; much wasted coverage; limited capabilities

Sources: William F. Arens, *Contemporary Advertising* (Burr Ridge, IL: Irwin/McGraw-Hill, 2011); George E. Belch and Michael Belch, *Advertising and Promotion* (Burr Ridge, IL: Irwin/McGraw-Hill, 2011).

Companies like Hallmark, John Deere, and Ray-Ban use a flighting schedule. A *pulsing* schedule combines continuous and flighting schedules: during the entire campaign, a certain portion of advertising runs continuously, and during specific time periods of the campaign, additional advertising is used to intensify the level of communication with the target audience.

Creating the Advertising Message

The basic content and form of an advertising message are a function of several factors. A product's features, uses, and benefits affect the content of the message. The intensity of the advertising can also have an impact. For instance, push advertising on digital devices refers to advertising that is not requested by the user. While push advertising might alienate some consumers, younger consumers are more accepting of push advertising if the source is trusted, permission has been given, and the messages are relevant or entertaining.[19] However, research has shown that advertising that pushes too hard to the point that consumers feel uncomfortable may cause consumers to consider the product negatively. This has caused problems with green advertising.[20]

Additionally, characteristics of the people in the target audience—gender, age, education, race, income, occupation, lifestyle, life stage, and other attributes—influence both content and form. For instance, gender affects how people respond to advertising claims that use hedging words like *may* and *probably* and pledging words, such as *definitely* and *absolutely*. Researchers have found that women respond negatively to both types of claims, but pledging claims have little effect on men.[21] When Procter & Gamble promotes Crest toothpaste to children, the company emphasizes daily brushing and cavity control, focusing on fun and good flavors like bubblegum. When marketing Crest to adults, P&G focuses on functionality, stressing whitening, enamel protection, breath enhancement, and tartar and plaque control. To communicate effectively, advertisers use words, symbols, and illustrations that are meaningful, familiar, and appealing to people in the target audience.

An advertising campaign's objectives and platform also affect the content and form of its messages. If a firm's advertising objectives involve large sales increases, the message may include hard-hitting, high-impact language, symbols, and messages. Spokescharacters are visual images that can convey a brand's features, benefits, or brand personality. The spokescharacter can provide a personality and improve brand equity by directly and indirectly enhancing excitement, sincerity, and trust.[22] The Geico "gecko," Snuggle Bear, and Pillsbury Doughboy are all examples of spokescharacters or mascots. When campaign objectives aim to increase brand awareness, the message may use repetition of the brand name, words, illustrations, or characters associated with it. For example, Geico's basic message is "15 minutes could save you 15% or more on car insurance!" The Geico spokescharacter uses a nonstandard Australian accent, which has been found to positively impact evaluations of the advertising.[23] Thus, the advertising platform is the foundation on which campaign messages are built.

Choice of media obviously influences the content and form of the message. Effective outdoor displays and short broadcast spot announcements require concise, simple messages. Magazine and newspaper advertisements can include considerable detail and long explanations. Because several kinds of media offer geographic selectivity, a precise message can be tailored to a particular geographic section of the target audience. Some magazine publishers produce **regional issues**, in which advertisements and editorial content of copies appearing in one geographic area differ from those appearing in other areas. For instance, the AAA Publishing Network publishes 24 regional magazine titles, including *AAA Horizons* (Connecticut, Rhode Island, and Massachusetts), *AAA Southern Traveler* (Louisiana, Arkansas, and Mississippi), and *Western Journey* (Idaho and Washington).[24] A company advertising with the AAA Publishing Network might decide to use one message in the New England region and another in the rest of the nation. A company may also choose to advertise in only one region. Such geographic selectivity lets a firm use the same message in different regions at different times.

Copy

Copy is the verbal portion of an advertisement and may include headlines, subheadlines, body copy, and a signature. Not all advertising contains all of these copy elements. Even handwritten notes on direct-mail advertising that say, "Try this. It works!" seem to increase requests for free samples.[25] The headline is critical because often it is the only part of the copy that people read. It should attract readers' attention and create enough interest to make them want to read the body copy or visit the website. The subheadline, if there is one, links the headline to the body copy and sometimes serves to explain the headline.

Body copy for most advertisements consists of an introductory statement or paragraph, several explanatory paragraphs, and a closing paragraph. Some copywriters have adopted guidelines for developing body copy systematically: (1) identify a specific desire or problem,

regional issues Versions of a magazine that differ across geographic regions

copy The verbal portion of advertisements

(2) recommend the product as the best way to satisfy that desire or solve that problem, (3) state product benefits and indicate why the product is best for the buyer's particular situation, (4) substantiate advertising claims, and (5) ask the buyer to take action. When substantiating claims, it is important to present the substantiation in a credible manner. The proof of claims should help strengthen both the image of the product and company integrity. A shortcut explanation of what much advertising is designed to accomplish is the AIDA model. Advertising should create *awareness,* produce *interest,* create *desire,* and ultimately result in a purchase (*action*). Typeface selection can help advertisers create a desired impression using fonts that are engaging, reassuring, or very prominent.[26]

The signature identifies the advertisement's sponsor. It may contain several elements, including the firm's trademark, logo, name, and address. The signature should be attractive, legible, distinctive, and easy to identify in a variety of sizes.

Often, because radio listeners are not fully "tuned in" mentally to what they're hearing on the radio, radio copy should be informal and conversational to attract listeners' attention. Radio messages are highly perishable and should consist of short, familiar terms, which increase their impact. The length should not require a rate of speech exceeding approximately 2.5 words per second.

In television copy, the audio material must not overpower the visual material, and vice versa. However, a television message should make optimal use of its visual portion, which can be very effective for product use, applications, and demonstrations. Copy for a television commercial is sometimes initially written in parallel script form. Video is described in the left column and audio in the right. When the parallel script is approved, the copywriter and artist combine copy with visual material by using a **storyboard**, which depicts a series of miniature television screens showing the sequence of major scenes in the commercial. Beneath each screen is a description of the audio portion to be used with that video segment. Technical personnel use the storyboard as a blueprint when producing the commercial.

storyboard A blueprint that combines copy and visual material to show the sequence of major scenes in a commercial

artwork An advertisement's illustrations and layout

illustrations Photos, drawings, graphs, charts, and tables used to spark audience interest in an advertisement

Artwork

Artwork consists of an advertisement's illustrations and layout. **Illustrations** are often photographs but can also be drawings, graphs, charts, and tables. Illustrations are used to draw

Components of a Print Ad
This Jaguar ad contains most of the components of a print ad, including a headline, body copy, signature, and illustration. It does not have a subheadline.

attention, encourage audiences to read or listen to the copy, communicate an idea quickly, or convey ideas that are difficult to express. Illustrations can be more important in capturing attention than text or brand elements, independent of size.[27] They are especially important, because consumers tend to recall the visual portions of advertisements better than the verbal portions. Advertisers use a variety of illustration techniques. They may show the product alone, in a setting, or in use, or show the results of the product's use. Illustrations can also take the form of comparisons, contrasts, diagrams, and testimonials.

The **layout** of an advertisement is the physical arrangement of the illustration and the copy (headline, subheadline, body copy, and signature). These elements can be arranged in many ways. The final layout is the result of several stages of layout preparation. As it moves through these stages, the layout promotes an exchange of ideas among people developing the advertising campaign and provides instructions for production personnel.

Executing the Campaign

Execution of an advertising campaign requires extensive planning and coordination, because many tasks must be completed on time and several people and firms are involved. Production companies, research organizations, media firms, printers, and commercial artists are just a few of the people and firms contributing to a campaign.

Implementation requires detailed schedules to ensure that various phases of the work are done on time. Advertising management personnel must evaluate the quality of the work and take corrective action when necessary. After sales of Planters nut products decreased between 2005 and 2010, the company decided to revise its Mr. Peanut mascot. The silent human-sized Mr. Peanut had changed little over the years and had lost his appeal. Planters responded by making the mascot smaller and giving him a voice, provided by American actor Robert Downey Jr. Sales began to increase after the new Mr. Peanut began marketing products.[28] In some instances, changes are made during the campaign so it meets objectives more effectively. For example, an auto company focusing on gas mileage may need to add more information relative to the competition to achieve its objectives.

Evaluating Advertising Effectiveness

A variety of ways exist to test the effectiveness of advertising. They include measuring achievement of advertising objectives; assessing effectiveness of copy, illustrations, or layouts; and evaluating certain media.

Advertising can be evaluated before, during, and after the campaign. An evaluation performed before the campaign begins is called a **pretest**. A pretest usually attempts to evaluate the effectiveness of one or more elements of the message. To pretest advertisements, marketers sometimes use a **consumer jury**, a panel of existing or potential buyers of the advertised product. Jurors judge one or several dimensions of two or more advertisements. Such tests are based on the belief that consumers are more likely than advertising experts to know what influences them. Companies can also solicit the assistance of marketing research firms, such as Information Resources Inc. (IRI), to help assess ads.

To measure advertising effectiveness during a campaign, marketers usually rely on "inquiries" or responses. In a campaign's initial stages, an advertiser may use several advertisements simultaneously, each containing a coupon, form, toll-free phone number, QR code, social media, or website through which potential customers can request information. The advertiser records the number of inquiries or responses returned from each type of advertisement. If an advertiser receives 78,528 inquiries from advertisement A, 37,072 from advertisement B, and 47,932 from advertisement C, advertisement A is judged superior to advertisements B and C. Internet advertisers can also assess how many people "clicked" on an ad to obtain more product information. The outdoor advertising industry has created a system called "Eyes On" to determine the audiences likely to see an ad, with demographic and ethnographic data included. Previous measurement systems used "Daily Effective Circulation," which essentially evolved around traffic counts, not on interested audiences.[29]

layout The physical arrangement of an advertisement's illustration and copy

pretest Evaluation of advertisements performed before a campaign begins

consumer jury A panel of a product's existing or potential buyers who pretest ads

Table 18.3 Digital Advertising's Shortcomings

1.	Overly detail-focused.
2.	Too long to reach the point.
3.	Message is unclear.
4.	Boring or very unattractive design that fails to catch audience's attention.
5.	Use of "flash" technology for the sake of flash—not for effectively reaching the target audience.
6.	Often visually hard to decipher or read.
7.	Short on recognition of benefits.
8.	Focused Internet users are often angered by promotional messages that do not deliver immediate messages of interest.

Source: Adapted from Philip W. Sawyer, "Why Most Digital Ads Still Fail to Work," *Advertising Age*, January 27, 2010, http://adage.com/digitalnext/post?article_id=141751 (accessed April 9, 2010).

Evaluation of advertising effectiveness after the campaign is called a **posttest**. Advertising objectives often determine what kind of posttest is appropriate. If the objectives' focus is on communication—to increase awareness of product features or brands or to create more favorable customer attitudes—the posttest should measure changes in these dimensions. Advertisers sometimes use consumer surveys or experiments to evaluate a campaign based on communication objectives. These methods are costly, however. In posttests, generalizations can be made about why advertising is failing or why media vehicles are not delivering the desired results. Table 18.3 shows some of the beliefs about why digital advertising is failing to deliver to audiences and create the response rates that advertisers hope for.[30]

For campaign objectives stated in terms of sales, advertisers should determine the change in sales or market share attributable to the campaign. For example, the "Find Yourself" campaign launched by the Newfoundland and Labrador Island Tourism Industry led to a 7.2 percent increase in tourists during a one-year period.[31] However, changes in sales or market share brought about by advertising cannot be measured precisely; many factors independent of advertisements affect a firm's sales and market share. Competitors' actions, regulatory actions, and changes in economic conditions, consumer preferences, and weather are only a few factors that might enhance or diminish a company's sales or market share. By using data about past and current sales and advertising expenditures, advertisers can make gross estimates of the effects of a campaign on sales or market share.

Because it is difficult to determine the direct effects of advertising on sales, many advertisers evaluate print advertisements according to how well consumers can remember them. As more advertisers turn to mobile technology, measuring the recall rate of mobile advertisements is becoming increasingly important. Brands with the best mobile recall rate include Sears, Walmart, Colgate, Macy's, JCPenney, Nike, and Target.[32] Researchers have found that ads that play on the theme of social desirability are more memorable when viewed in the presence of other people.

Posttest methods based on memory include recognition and recall tests. Such tests are usually performed by research organizations through surveys. In a **recognition test**, respondents are shown the actual advertisement and asked whether they recognize it. If they do, the interviewer asks additional questions to determine how much of the advertisement each respondent read. When recall is evaluated, respondents are not shown the actual advertisement but instead are asked about what they have seen or heard recently. For Internet advertising, research suggests that the longer a person is exposed to a website containing a banner advertisement, the more likely he or she is to recall the ad.[33]

Recall can be measured through either unaided or aided recall methods. In an **unaided recall test**, respondents identify advertisements they have seen recently but are not shown any clues to help them remember. A similar procedure is used with an **aided recall test**, but respondents are shown a list of products, brands, company names, or trademarks to jog their memories. Research has shown that online advertisements have 1.8 times the aided recall rate and 1.5 times the unaided recall rate of television advertisements.[34] Several research organizations, such as Daniel Starch, provide research services that test recognition and recall of advertisements.

The major justification for using recognition and recall methods is that people are more likely to buy a product if they can remember an advertisement about it than if they cannot. However, recalling an advertisement does not necessarily lead to buying the product or brand advertised. Researchers also use a sophisticated technique called *single-source data* to help evaluate advertisements. With this technique, individuals' behaviors are tracked from television sets to checkout counters. Monitors are placed in preselected homes, and microcomputers record when the television set is on and which station is being viewed. At the

posttest Evaluation of advertising effectiveness after the campaign

recognition test A posttest in which respondents are shown the actual ad and are asked if they recognize it

unaided recall test A posttest in which respondents are asked to identify advertisements they have seen recently but are not given any recall clues

aided recall test A posttest that asks respondents to identify recent ads and provides clues to jog their memories

supermarket checkout, the individual in the sample household presents an identification card. Checkers then record the purchases by scanner, and data are sent to the research facility. Some single-source data companies provide sample households with scanning equipment for use at home to record purchases after returning from shopping trips. Single-source data supplies information that links exposure to advertisements with purchase behavior.

WHO DEVELOPS THE ADVERTISING CAMPAIGN?

An advertising campaign may be handled by an individual, a few people within a firm, a firm's own advertising department, or an advertising agency. In very small firms, one or two individuals are responsible for advertising (and for many other activities as well). Usually, these individuals depend heavily on local media (TV, radio, and newspaper) for copywriting, artwork, and advice about scheduling media.

In certain large businesses, especially large retail organizations, advertising departments create and implement advertising campaigns. Depending on the size of the advertising program, an advertising department may consist of a few multiskilled individuals or a sizable number of specialists, including copywriters, artists, social media experts, media buyers, and technical production coordinators. Advertising departments sometimes obtain the services of independent research organizations and hire freelance specialists when a particular project requires it.

Many firms employ an advertising agency to develop advertising campaigns. Barnes & Noble, for example, hired Boston advertising agency Mullen to create a marketing campaign to overhaul its Nook brand image. The campaign was estimated to cost $40 million.[35] When an organization uses an advertising agency, the firm and the agency usually develop the advertising campaign jointly. How much each participates in the campaign's total development depends on the working relationship between the firm and the agency. Ordinarily, a firm relies on the agency for copywriting, artwork, technical production, and formulation of the media plan.

Advertising agencies assist businesses in several ways. An agency, especially a large one, can supply the services of highly skilled specialists—not only copywriters, artists, and production coordinators but also media experts, researchers, and legal advisers. Agency personnel often have broad advertising experience and are usually more objective than a firm's employees about the organization's products.

Because an agency traditionally receives most of its compensation from a 15 percent commission paid by the media from which it makes purchases, firms can obtain some agency services at low or moderate costs. If an agency contracts for $400,000 of television time for a firm, it receives a commission of $60,000 from the television station. Although the traditional compensation method for agencies is changing and now includes other factors, media commissions still offset some costs of using an agency. Like advertising, public relations can be a vital element in a promotion mix. We turn to this topic next.

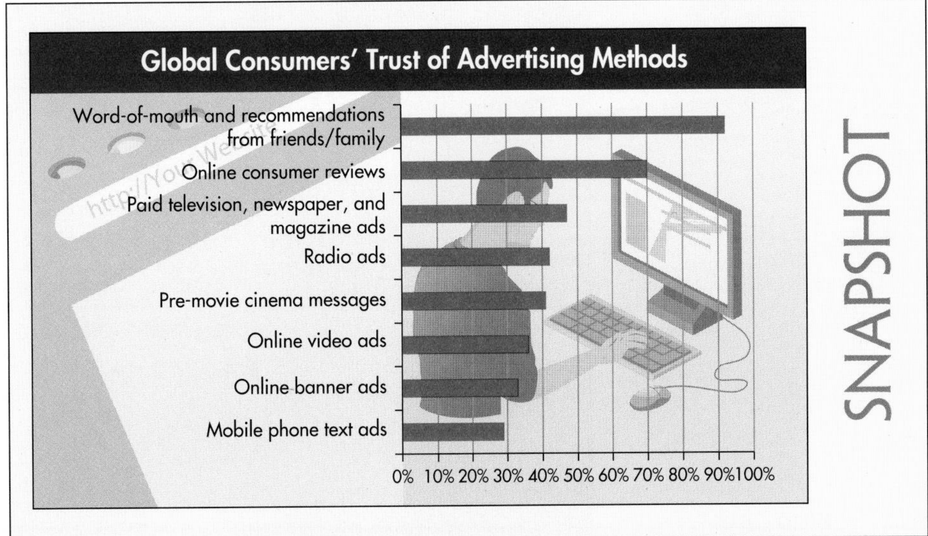

Source: Nielson, "Nielsen: Global Consumers' Trust in 'Earned' Advertising Grows in Importance," April 10, 2012, http://nielsen.com/us/en/insights/press-room/2012/nielsen-global-consumers-trust-in-earned-advertising-grows.html (accessed June 21, 2012).

PUBLIC RELATIONS

Public relations is a broad set of communication efforts used to create and maintain favorable relationships between an organization and its stakeholders. An organization communicates with various stakeholders, both internal and external, and public relations efforts can be directed toward any and all of them. A firm's stakeholders can include customers, suppliers, employees, shareholders, the media, educators, potential investors, government officials, and society in general. Research in Motion (RIM) was highly criticized for its public relations failure during a worldwide outage of the company's Blackberry devices. The company released a message to explain the problem using jargon that many consumers did not understand. As the outage continued for several days, the initial communications did little to reassure consumers that the company was working on the problem. RIM's failed response to the crisis may cause damage to consumer perceptions of the brand.[36] On the other hand, being honest with consumers and responsive to their needs develops a foundation for open communication and trust in the long run. Table 18.4 lists some of the top public relations campaigns in the past 10 years.

Public relations can be used to promote people, places, ideas, activities, and even countries. It is often used by nonprofit organizations to achieve their goals. The United Nations holds a Girl Up Pep Rally to spread awareness and raise money for girls in Africa and Latin America. Attendees write letters of advice and perform activities like carrying large jugs of water to experience the hardship that girls from these countries encounter daily.[37] Public relations focuses on enhancing the image of the total organization. Assessing public attitudes and creating a favorable image are no less important than direct promotion of the organization's products. Because the public's attitudes toward a firm are likely to affect the sales of its products, it is very important for firms to maintain positive public perceptions. In addition, employee morale is strengthened if the public perceives the firm positively.[38] Although public relations can make people aware of a company's products, brands, or activities, it can also create specific company images, such as innovativeness or dependability. Companies like Green Mountain Coffee Roasters, Patagonia, Sustainable Harvest, and Honest Tea have reputations for being socially responsible not only because they engage in socially responsible behavior but also because their actions are reported through news stories and other public relations efforts. By getting the media to report on a firm's accomplishments, public relations helps

public relations Communication efforts used to create and maintain favorable relations between an organization and its stakeholders

Public Relations
At Target, communicating with employees is part of the firm's public relations efforts.

Table 18.4 Top Five Public Relations Campaigns of the Decade

Rank	PR Agency	Client (Company or Nonprofit Organization Paying for the Campaign)	Title of PR Campaign
1	Ogilvy Public Relations	The National Heart, Lung, and Blood Institute	Red Dress Campaign
2	Patrice Tanaka and Company	Liz Claiborne	Women's Work (awareness of education of women and their families regarding domestic violence issues)
3	MGA Communications	Shell Oil Company, US Army, and the National Wildlife Agency	Rocky Mountain Arsenal clean-up and wildlife preserve campaign
4	Fleishman-Hillard	Telco Companies	Hurricane Katrina Aid for the Displaced
5	Ketchum	Frito-Lay	User-Generated Commercials—Doritos Crashes the Super Bowl

Source: "Holmes Reports Top 5 Advertising Campaigns of the Decade," January 7, 2010, www.designtaxi.com/news.php?id=30160 (accessed April 29, 2011).

the company maintain positive public visibility. Some firms use public relations for a single purpose; others use it for several purposes.

Public Relations Tools

Companies use a variety of public relations tools to convey messages and create images. Public relations professionals prepare written materials and use digital media to deliver brochures, newsletters, company magazines, news releases, blogs, managed social media sites, and annual reports that reach and influence their various stakeholders. Sometimes, organizations use less conventional tools in their public relations campaigns. Comcast, for example, holds an annual Comcast Cares Day, which brings together thousands of Comcast employees and their families to help improve their neighborhoods by cleaning schools, developing community gardens, and other acts of service. Comcast Cares Day not only enables the firm to make a positive difference but also enhances its own reputation as a socially responsible company. The campaign has been so effective that it has been inducted into the Platinum PR Awards Hall of Fame.[39]

Public relations personnel also create corporate identity materials—such as logos, business cards, stationery, signs, and promotional materials—that make firms immediately recognizable. Speeches are another public relations tool. Because what a company executive says publicly at meetings or to the media can affect the organization's image, the speech must convey the desired message clearly. Event sponsorship, in which a company pays for part or all of a special event, like a benefit concert or a tennis tournament, is another public relations tool. Examples are Coca-Cola's sponsorship of the FIFA World Cup and Special Olympics. Sponsoring special events can be an effective means of increasing company or brand recognition with relatively minimal investment. Event sponsorship can gain companies considerable amounts of free media coverage. An organization tries to ensure that its product and the sponsored event target a similar audience and that the two are easily associated in customers' minds. Many companies as well as individuals assist in their charitable giving. Bill Daniels, the founder of Cablevision who passed away in 2000, set up a fund supported with more than a billion dollars to provide financial support for many causes, including business ethics. Bill Daniels believed that ethics is integral to business success, especially in the cable industry.

Going Green

Launching a Green Public Relations Campaign

Green public relations (PR) campaigns are a tempting opportunity for businesses. Approximately 40 million U.S. consumers consider themselves environmentally friendly, prompting many organizations to jump onto the green bandwagon. However, as with every PR campaign, companies must carefully consider several different factors.

First, a PR professional must determine what claims to make about the product or business. Using ambiguous terms like "eco-friendly" does not adequately inform the consumer about how the product or business is green. Instead, PR professionals should select claims that can be substantiated. It is also important for PR professionals to use environmentally friendly marketing techniques. For instance, PR professionals could engage in digital advertising or use recycled paper to market their campaigns.

Additionally, PR professionals must choose appropriate marketing mediums. Studies have shown that consumers prefer in-store signage and online advertising; in fact, 40 percent of consumers have indicated they would like to see more green information in stores. Marketers also have a number of online outlets from which to choose. Many experts believe that the best way to connect with green-minded consumers is through social networks, online green communities, and through blogs like treehugger.com. Actively posting on these sites and referring customers to these sites to read its posts can significantly reinforce an organization's green claims.[c]

The Daniels Fund is actively supporting business ethics education in Colorado, New Mexico, Utah, and Wyoming. Public relations personnel also organize unique events to "create news" about the company. These may include grand openings with celebrities, prizes, hot-air balloon rides, and other attractions that appeal to a firm's public.

Publicity is a part of public relations. **Publicity** is communication in news-story form about the organization, its products, or both, transmitted through a mass medium at no charge. For instance, after Apple CEO Tim Cook announced that the company would introduce the new iPad, the story was covered in newspapers and television news shows throughout the world for months afterward. Although public relations has a larger, more comprehensive communication function than publicity, publicity is a very important aspect of public relations. Publicity can be used to provide information about goods or services; to announce expansions or contractions, acquisitions, research, or new-product launches; or to enhance a company's image.

The most common publicity-based public relations tool is the **news release**, sometimes called a *press release,* which is usually a single page of typewritten copy containing fewer than 300 words and describing a company event or product. A news release gives the firm's or agency's name, address, phone number, and contact person. Companies sometimes use news releases when introducing new products or making significant announcements. Dozens of organizations, including Nike, Starbucks, and clean-energy companies, are partnering to create awareness of the economic benefits of national climate and energy legislation through press releases and other media. As Table 18.5 shows, news releases tackle a multitude of specific issues. A **feature article** is a manuscript of up to 3,000 words prepared for a specific publication. A **captioned photograph** is a photograph with a brief description explaining its contents. Captioned photographs are effective for illustrating new or improved products with highly visible features.

There are several other kinds of publicity-based public relations tools. For example, a **press conference** is a meeting called to announce major news events. Media personnel are invited to a press conference and are usually supplied with various written materials and photographs. Letters to the editor and editorials are sometimes prepared and sent to newspapers and magazines. Videos may be made available to broadcasters in the hope that they will be aired.

Publicity-based public relations tools offer several advantages, including credibility, news value, significant word-of-mouth communications, and a perception of media endorsement. The public may consider news coverage more truthful and credible than an advertisement because news media are not paid to provide the information. In addition, stories regarding a new-product introduction or a new environmentally responsible company policy, for example,

publicity A news story type of communication about an organization and/or its products transmitted through a mass medium at no charge

news release A short piece of copy publicizing an event or a product

feature article A manuscript of up to 3,000 words prepared for a specific publication

captioned photograph A photograph with a brief description of its contents

press conference A meeting used to announce major news events

Table 18.5 **Possible Issues for Publicity Releases**

Support of a social cause	New products
Improved warranties	New slogan
Reports on industry conditions	Research developments
New uses for established products	Company's milestones and anniversaries
Product endorsements	Employment, production, and sales changes
Quality awards	Award of contracts
Company name changes	Opening of new markets
Interviews with company officials	Improvements in financial position
Improved distribution policies	Opening of an exhibit
International business efforts	History of a brand
Athletic event sponsorship	Winners of company contests
Visits by celebrities	Logo changes
Reports on new discoveries	Speeches of top management
Innovative business practices	Merit awards
Economic forecasts	Acquisitions and partnerships

are handled as news items and are likely to receive notice. Finally, the cost of publicity is low compared with the cost of advertising.[40]

Publicity-based public relations tools have some limitations. Media personnel must judge company messages to be newsworthy if the messages are to be published or broadcast at all. Consequently, messages must be timely, interesting, accurate, and in the public interest. It may take a great deal of time and effort to convince media personnel of the news value of publicity releases, and many communications fail to qualify. Although public relations

Entrepreneurship in Marketing

Pass Christian Soap Co. Experiences the Benefits of Publicity

Entrepreneur: Paula Lindsay
Business: Pass Christian Soap Company
Founded: 1999 | Mississippi
Success: The company sold $200,000 of products after it was discussed on a two-day *Good Morning America* special.

Pass Christian Soap Company understands the power of publicity. After *Good Morning America (GMA)* anchor Robin Roberts praised the Pass Christian Soap Company on the show, sales at the company skyrocketed. Owner Paula Lindsay claims that the company sold $200,000 in two days.

Pass Christian Soap Company advertises itself as the "makers of luxurious handmade bath and body products." Consumers also love it for its "Made in America" marketing. The idea for the company occurred when Lindsey was unable to find many domestic soap products in bath and body shops. She decided to open up Pass Christian Soap Company as a truly American business.

Since then, Pass Christian products have caught the eye of many different magazines, including *Coastal Living* and *Southern Breeze.* However, its feature on *GMA* made the difference. Sales became so intense that Lindsey hired 13 more staff workers and rented another building to complete orders. With sales remaining strong, Pass Christian Soap Company is optimistic about the future.[d]

personnel usually encourage the media to air publicity releases at certain times, they control neither the content nor the timing of the communication. Media personnel alter length and content of publicity releases to fit publishers' or broadcasters' requirements and may even delete the parts of messages that company personnel view as most important. Furthermore, media personnel use publicity releases in time slots or positions most convenient for them. Other outside public relations messages can be picked up during slow news times. Thus, messages sometimes appear in locations or at times that may not reach the firm's target audiences. Although these limitations can be frustrating, properly managed publicity-based public relations tools offer an organization substantial benefits.

Evaluating Public Relations Effectiveness

Because of the potential benefits of good public relations, it is essential that organizations evaluate the effectiveness of their public relations campaigns. Research can be conducted to determine how well a firm is communicating its messages or image to its target audiences. *Environmental monitoring* identifies changes in public opinion affecting an organization. A *public relations audit* is used to assess an organization's image among the public or to evaluate the effect of a specific public relations program. A *communications audit* may include a content analysis of messages, a readability study, or a readership survey. If an organization wants to measure the extent to which stakeholders view it as being socially responsible, it can conduct a *social audit.*

One approach to measuring the effectiveness of publicity-based public relations is to count the number of exposures in the media. To determine which releases are published in print media and how often, an organization can hire a clipping service, a firm that clips and sends news releases to client companies. To measure the effectiveness of television coverage, a firm can enclose a card with its publicity releases requesting that the television station record its name and the dates when the news item is broadcast (although station personnel do not always comply). Some multimedia tracking services exist, but they are quite costly.

Counting the number of media exposures does not reveal how many people have actually read or heard the company's message or what they thought about the message afterward. However, measuring changes in product awareness, knowledge, and attitudes resulting from the publicity campaign helps yield this information. To assess these changes, companies must measure these levels before and after public relations campaigns. Although precise measures are difficult to obtain, a firm's marketers should attempt to assess the impact of public relations efforts on the organization's sales. For example, critics' reviews of films can affect the films' box office performance. Interestingly, negative reviews (publicity) harm revenue more than positive reviews help revenue in the early weeks of a film's release.[41]

Public Relations Tools
Annual reports serve as public relations tools for a variety of stakeholders.

Dealing with Unfavorable Public Relations

Thus far, we have discussed public relations as a planned element of the promotion mix. However, companies may have to deal with unexpected and unfavorable publicity resulting from an unsafe product, an accident resulting from product use, controversial actions of employees, or some other negative event or situation. For example, the New Orleans Saints faced intense criticism after it was revealed that players were awarded bonuses for purposefully hitting opponents during games.[42] Many companies have experienced unfavorable publicity connected to contamination issues, such as salmonella in peanut butter, lead in toys, and industrial compounds in pet foods. Unfavorable coverage can have quick and dramatic effects. The global financial crisis has caused a trust breach for many companies, perhaps the greatest damage in the financial services industry. For instance, five of the nation's largest banks, including Ally Financial Inc., Bank of America Corp., Citigroup Inc., J.P. Morgan Chase & Co., and Wells Fargo & Co., were sued by New York for mortgage foreclosure abuses. The five companies agreed to pay $25 million in damages to New York. Similar lawsuits were filed by Delaware, Florida, Massachusetts, and other states.[43] The breach of trust by banks and other financial institutions has taken a toll on the industry. In one survey, less than 50 percent of global consumers indicated that they trusted banks and financial institutions, the lowest score out of all the industries listed.[44]

Negative events that generate public relations can wipe out a company's favorable image and destroy positive customer attitudes established through years of expensive advertising campaigns and other promotional efforts. For example, the public's image of BP as a socially responsible company diminished considerably after the Gulf Coast disaster. Reputation is often considered a valuable company asset. How an organization deals with unfavorable actions and outcomes can have a significant impact on firm valuation. For example, Penn State University faces a damaged reputation as the result of the negligence and wrongdoing of individuals working in the football program and the complacency of university administrators and leaders. Moreover, today's mass media, including online services and the Internet, disseminate information faster than ever before, and bad news generally receives more media attention than corporate social responsibility. Table 18.6 provides examples of public relations "gaffes" committed by major companies.

To protect its image, an organization needs to prevent unfavorable public relations or at least lessen its effect if it occurs. First and foremost, the organization should try to prevent negative incidents and events through safety programs, inspections, training, and effective quality control procedures. Experts insist that sending consistent brand messages and images throughout all communications at all times can help a brand maintain its strength even during a crisis.[45] However, because negative events can strike even the most cautious firms, an organization should have plans in place to handle them when they do occur. Firms need to establish policies and procedures for reducing the adverse impact of news coverage of a crisis

Table 18.6 Public Relations Mishaps

Organization	Mishaps
Netflix	Netflix's steep price increase and attempt to spin off its DVD business outraged consumers. CEO Reed Hastings's apology worsened matters by making consumers feel as if they had misunderstood.
Bank of America	Bank of America was planning on charging consumers $5 for using bank debit cards. It was slow to react to consumer outrage and did not drop the plan until after other banks had done so.
Penn State	Penn State appeared to turn a blind eye toward sexual abuse allegations. Not following up on reports of abuse made the college appear uncaring toward the victims.
Facebook	Facebook was highly criticized for hiring a PR firm to "smear" its competitor Google.
New Orleans Saints	It was discovered that New Orleans Saints players were awarded up to $1,500 for purposefully hitting opponents hard enough to either knock them off the field or cause them to be carried away on a cart.

Sources: Ron Torossian, "The 5 Biggest Crisis PR Blunders of 2011," *Business Insider,* December 7, 2011, http://articles.businessinsider.com/2011-12-07/strategy/30484353_1_herman-cain-joe-paterno-penn-state-for (accessed March 7, 2012); "Best and Worst PR Moves of 2011: Aflac Flies and Netflix Dives," *PR News,* December 30, 2011, www.prnewsonline.com/watercooler/Best-and-Worst-PR-Moves-of-2011-Aflac-Flies-and-Netflix-Dives_15836.html (accessed March 7, 2012); Matthew Futterman and Reed Albergotti, "NFL Flags Saints for Bounty Hunting," *The Wall Street Journal,* http://online.wsj.com/article/SB10001424052702304636404577295602826944034.html?mod=WSJ_WSJ_News_BlogsModule (accessed March 28, 2012).

or controversy. In most cases, organizations should expedite news coverage of negative events rather than try to discourage or block them. If news coverage is suppressed, rumors and other misinformation may replace facts and create public scrutiny.

An unfavorable event can easily balloon into serious problems or public issues and become very damaging. By being forthright with the press and public and taking prompt action, a firm may be able to convince the public of its honest attempts to deal with the situation, and news personnel may be more willing to help explain complex issues to the public. Dealing effectively with a negative event allows an organization to lessen, if not eliminate, the unfavorable impact on its image. For instance, after comedian Gilbert Gottfried, the voice of the Aflac duck, made what were considered to be inappropriate remarks about the earthquake and tsunami in Japan, Aflac stopped using him as a spokesman. The company immediately began holding auditions to find a new voice for the iconic duck. Despite the negative publicity that could have occurred with Gottfried's statements, Aflac was praised by public relations professionals for its quick actions and its outward sensitivity to the crisis in Japan.[46] Experts generally advise companies that are dealing with negative publicity to respond quickly and honestly to the situation and to keep the lines of communication with all stakeholders open. Digital media has enhanced the organizational ability to communicate with key stakeholders and develop dialogues on current issues.

Summary

1. To describe the nature and types of advertising

Advertising is a paid form of nonpersonal communication transmitted to consumers through mass media, such as television, radio, the Internet, newspapers, magazines, direct mail, outdoor displays, and signs on mass transit vehicles. Both business and nonbusiness organizations use advertising. Institutional advertising promotes organizational images, ideas, and political issues. When a company promotes its position on a public issue such as taxation, institutional advertising is referred to as advocacy advertising. Product advertising promotes uses, features, and benefits of products. The two types of product advertising are pioneer advertising, which focuses on stimulating demand for a product category rather than a specific brand, and competitive advertising, which attempts to stimulate demand for a specific brand by indicating the brand's features, uses, and advantages. To make direct product comparisons, marketers use comparative advertising, which compares two or more brands. Two other forms of competitive advertising are reminder advertising, which reminds customers about an established brand's uses, characteristics, and benefits, and reinforcement advertising, which assures current users they have made the right brand choice.

2. To explore the major steps in developing an advertising campaign

Although marketers may vary in how they develop advertising campaigns, they should follow a general pattern. First, they must identify and analyze the target audience, the group of people at whom advertisements are aimed. Second, they should establish what they want the campaign to accomplish by defining advertising objectives. Objectives should be clear, precise, and presented in measurable terms. Third, marketers must create the advertising platform, which contains basic issues to be presented in the campaign. Advertising platforms should consist of issues important to consumers. Fourth, advertisers must decide how much money to spend on the campaign; they arrive at this decision through the objective-and-task approach, percent-of-sales approach, competition-matching approach, or arbitrary approach.

Advertisers must then develop a media plan by selecting and scheduling media to use in the campaign. Some factors affecting the media plan are location and demographic characteristics of the target audience, content of the message, and cost of the various media. The basic content and form of the advertising message are affected by product features, uses, and benefits; characteristics of the people in the target audience; the campaign's objectives and platform; and the choice of media. Advertisers use copy and artwork to create the message. The execution of an advertising campaign requires extensive planning and coordination.

Finally, advertisers must devise one or more methods for evaluating advertisement effectiveness. Pretests are evaluations performed before the campaign begins; posttests are conducted after the campaign. Two types of posttests are a recognition test, in which respondents are shown the actual advertisement and asked whether they recognize it, and a recall test. In aided recall tests, respondents are shown a list of products, brands, company names, or trademarks to jog their memories. In unaided tests, no clues are given.

3. To identify who is responsible for developing advertising campaigns

Advertising campaigns can be developed by personnel within the firm or in conjunction with advertising agencies. A campaign created by the firm's personnel may be developed by one or more individuals or by an advertising department within the firm. Use of an advertising agency may be advantageous because an agency provides highly skilled, objective specialists with broad experience in advertising at low to moderate costs to the firm.

4. To examine the tools used in public relations

Public relations is a broad set of communication efforts used to create and maintain favorable relationships between an organization and its stakeholders. Public relations can be used to promote people, places, ideas, activities, and countries, and to create and maintain a positive company image. Some firms use public relations for a single purpose; others use it for several purposes. Public relations tools include written materials, such as brochures, newsletters, and annual reports; corporate identity materials, such as business cards and signs; speeches; event sponsorships; and special events. Publicity is communication in news story form about an organization, its products, or both, transmitted through a mass medium at no charge. Publicity-based public relations tools include news releases, feature articles, captioned photographs, and press conferences. Problems that organizations confront in using publicity-based public relations include reluctance of media personnel to print or air releases and lack of control over timing and content of messages.

5. To analyze how public relations is used and evaluated

To evaluate the effectiveness of their public relations programs, companies conduct research to determine how well their messages are reaching their audiences. Environmental monitoring, public relations audits, and counting the number of media exposures are all means of evaluating public relations effectiveness. Organizations should avoid negative public relations by taking steps to prevent negative events that result in unfavorable publicity. To diminish the impact of unfavorable public relations, organizations should institute policies and procedures for dealing with news personnel and the public when negative events occur.

Go to www.cengagebrain.com for resources to help you master the content in this chapter as well as for materials that will expand your marketing knowledge!

Important Terms

advertising 598
institutional advertising 598
advocacy advertising 599
product advertising 599
pioneer advertising 599
competitive advertising 599
comparative advertising 599
reminder advertising 600
reinforcement advertising 600
advertising campaign 600
target audience 600
advertising platform 602
advertising appropriation 602
objective-and-task approach 603
percent-of-sales approach 603
competition-matching approach 603
arbitrary approach 604
media plan 604
cost comparison indicator 607
regional issues 609
copy 609
storyboard 610
artwork 610
illustrations 610
layout 611
pretest 611
consumer jury 611
posttest 612
recognition test 612
unaided recall test 612
aided recall test 612
public relations 614
publicity 616
news release 616
feature article 616
captioned photograph 616
press conference 616

Discussion and Review Questions

1. What is the difference between institutional and product advertising?
2. What is the difference between competitive advertising and comparative advertising?
3. What are the major steps in creating an advertising campaign?
4. What is a target audience? How does a marketer analyze the target audience after identifying it?
5. Why is it necessary to define advertising objectives?
6. What is an advertising platform, and how is it used?
7. What factors affect the size of an advertising budget? What techniques are used to determine an advertising budget?
8. Describe the steps in developing a media plan.
9. What is the function of copy in an advertising message?
10. Discuss several ways to posttest the effectiveness of advertising.

11. What role does an advertising agency play in developing an advertising campaign?
12. What is public relations? Whom can an organization reach through public relations?
13. How do organizations use public relations tools? Give several examples you have observed recently.
14. Explain the problems and limitations associated with publicity-based public relations.
15. In what ways is the effectiveness of public relations evaluated?
16. What are some sources of negative public relations? How should an organization deal with unfavorable public relations?

Application Questions

1. An organization must define its objectives carefully when developing an advertising campaign. Which of the following advertising objectives would be most useful for a company, and why?
   a. The organization will spend $1 million to move from second in market share to market leader.
   b. The organization wants to increase sales from $1.2 million to $1.5 million this year to gain the lead in market share.
   c. The advertising objective is to gain as much market share as possible within the next 12 months.
   d. The advertising objective is to increase sales by 15 percent.
2. Copy, the verbal portion of advertising, is used to move readers through a persuasive sequence called AIDA: attention, interest, desire, and action. To achieve this, some copywriters have adopted guidelines for developing advertising copy. Select a print ad and identify how it (a) identifies a specific problem, (b) recommends the product as the best solution to the problem, (c) states the product's advantages and benefits, (d) substantiates the ad's claims, and (e) asks the reader to take action.
3. Advertisers use several types of publicity mechanisms. Look through some recent newspapers and magazines or use an Internet search engine and identify a news release, a feature article, or a captioned photograph used to publicize a product. Describe the type of product.
4. Negative public relations can harm an organization's marketing efforts if not dealt with properly. Identify a company that was recently the target of negative public relations. Describe the situation and discuss the company's response. What did marketers at this company do well? What, if anything, would you recommend that they change about their response?
5. IMP College can be an exciting time. New friends, sporting events, parties. But for many, it can also be a harrowing experience, with a more demanding class and homework regimen and new adult responsibilities. In order to help reduce at least one aspect of the stress for your fellow students, you have decided to launch a laundry service, which, for a set monthly fee, will pick up and deliver clothes twice per week. You have contracted with a local dry cleaner to perform the dry cleaning service. Initial reaction from friends has been very positive, but to achieve scale, you need to attract many more customers. How can you reach them most effectively and efficiently? After considerable thought, you have decided to advertise in the college newspaper and a local, free advertising paper that is distributed on campus. Create an advertising platform to communicate the basic issues or selling points that you will include in your advertising campaign.

Internet Exercise

LEGO Company

LEGO Company has been making toys since 1932 and has become one of the most recognized brand names in the toy industry. With the company motto "Only the best is good enough," it is no surprise that LEGO has developed an exciting and interactive online presence. See how the company promotes LEGO products and encourages consumer involvement with the brand by visiting LEGO's website at www.lego.com.

1. Which type of advertising is LEGO Company using on its website?
2. What target audience is LEGO attempting to reach through its website?
3. Identify the advertising objectives LEGO is attempting to achieve through its website.

developing your marketing plan

Determining the message that advertising is to communicate to the customer is an important part of developing a marketing strategy. A sound understanding of the various types of advertising and different forms of media is essential in selecting the appropriate methods for communicating the message. These decisions form a critical segment of the marketing plan. To assist you in relating the information in this chapter to the development of your marketing plan, consider the following issues:

1. What class and type of advertising would be most appropriate for your product?
2. Discuss the different methods for determining the advertising appropriation.
3. Using Table 18.2 as a guide, evaluate the different types of media and determine which would be most effective in meeting your promotional objectives (from Chapter 17).
4. What methods would you use to evaluate the effectiveness of your advertising campaign?
5. Review Table 18.5 and discuss possible uses for publicity in your promotional plan.

The information obtained from these questions should assist you in developing various aspects of your marketing plan found in the "Interactive Marketing Plan" exercise at **www.cengagebrain.com**.

video case 18.1

Pepsi Takes Different Spins on Advertising

Almost since Pepsi's creation, Pepsi and Coca-Cola have been fighting for dominance in the soft drink market. These "cola wars" have seen victories and defeats on both sides, with Pepsi gaining market share during some years and Coca-Cola gaining dominance during other years. With much of the population unable to tell the difference between the two, the question remains how to convince consumers to prefer one brand over the other. Many consumers tend to become brand loyal early on in life, requiring soft drink makers to develop creative ways to change consumer perceptions about the value of their brands. Advertising is the primary means that these businesses use to persuade consumers to favor their products.

© Stream Images/Alamy

For many years, Pepsi has been an advertising guru, spending millions on a variety of media to get its products in front of consumers. The company became skilled at using celebrity pop stars in advertisements promoting its products, such as Michael Jackson, Ray Charles, and Britney Spears. Because the Super Bowl tends to give brands some of the best exposure, Pepsi has had a constant presence at the Super Bowl for many years. In 2010, however, Pepsi deviated from its 23-year practice of Super Bowl advertisements and did something entirely different to market its brand. The company decided to engage in a type of institutional advertising in which it would promote the "social good" by agreeing to fund projects to make the world a better place. The company took the $20 million it would have spent on the Super Bowl and appropriated it to fund the Pepsi Refresh Project.

The Pepsi Refresh Project uses social media to create a platform where consumers can vote on projects to receive funding. Consumers are invited to submit ideas on the Pepsi Refresh social media site for projects that would help improve society. These project ideas are listed in four categories: (1) arts and music, (2) communities, (3) education, and (4) the Pepsi Challenge. The Pepsi Challenge asks questions about how consumers would change the world. Those with the best answers receive project funding. Consumers vote on which project ideas they like the best, and Pepsi provides money to the winners to make their project ideas a reality. Pepsi accepts 1,000 ideas each month.

The Pepsi Refresh project generated positive publicity from many major news outlets. While this publicity helped to promote the project, Pepsi had to engage in significant advertising to inform the public about the new initiative. Advertising media included TV clips, posters, buses, and even the sides of buildings. Mottos like "Vote Today, Change Tomorrow" and "Every Pepsi Refreshes the World" helped spread the image of Pepsi as a socially responsible company. While Pepsi's objectives for the project were to increase sales, it also wanted to differentiate itself from its competitors and address issues that the younger generation considered to be important. Pepsi-funded projects ranged from SOS animal shelters to eco-friendly theaters. The Pepsi Refresh social media site received 20,000 daily comments.

In 2011, Pepsi decided to resume its Super Bowl advertisements. Interestingly, Pepsi decided to use consumers once again to help it come up with a memorable Super Bowl advertisement for its Doritos brand. Similar to the Pepsi Refresh Project, consumers could submit ads and have other consumers vote on them. The winning ad was featured during the Super Bowl. This type of consumer-generated advertising encourages stakeholders to participate and interact with the brand, creating a high-involvement situation that can increase consumer loyalty.

Although Pepsi began advertising again during the Super Bowl, it also kept the Pepsi Refresh Project going. The company made the big decision to go global, extending the Pepsi Refresh Project to Europe, Asia, and Latin America. In 2012, the company announced it would also start considering projects in Canada. As the initiative continues, some of the company's objectives have evolved. The success of the initiative will largely be determined by whether the company creates consumer engagement, particularly among Millennials. In doing so, Pepsi not only spreads awareness of its brand among younger generations but is also able to discover more about this customer base, including what issues are the most important to them. By integrating consumers into its promotional activities, Pepsi has been able to extend its reach and connect to consumers in entirely new ways.[47]

Questions for Discussion

1. How did Pepsi change its advertising focus when it began the Pepsi Refresh Project?
2. Evaluate the public relations project along with why Pepsi decided to resume Super Bowl ads.
3. What does Pepsi gain in trying to encourage consumers to participate in its promotional activities?

case 18.2

Toyota Uses Advertising to Restore Trust

For decades, Toyota set the standard for quality and reliability. Known worldwide for its commitment to quality production, Toyota created the "Toyota Way," a manufacturing philosophy that emphasized continuous progress and reduced waste. Thanks to the success of the Toyota Way, Toyota became the top automobile manufacturer in the world in 2008.

However, Toyota hit a major snag that caused stakeholders to question its quality. In 2009 and 2010, the company issued a series of recalls on several of its popular models because of safety problems with accelerators, brakes, and power steering. Following the announcement of the recalls, Toyota engineers and mechanics began to search for solutions to the problems and started the process of repairing millions of cars. Many critics accused the company of acting too slowly to recall the defective cars and of trying to push the problem under the rug.

Toyota was fined $16.4 million for allegedly hiding safety defects from consumers. This came after its reputation was already tarnished by a seemingly endless number of recalls on various car models. The company became the target for late-night television jokes and seemed to constantly be in the news regarding yet another recall. This negative publicity damaged the reputation and goodwill that Toyota had developed over many years.

In the wake of massive recalls, Toyota had to adjust its advertising strategy. The world's largest carmaker pulled its national advertising campaign that promoted its cars for dependability, safety, and reliability. Toyota, which had long been the leader in automotive quality, had to scramble to figure out how to handle a growing public relations crisis resulting from recalls and a halt in sales. A series of ads were developed to deal directly with the crisis and admit that the company had strayed from keeping its eye on quality while its sales had been growing rapidly. A number of low-key ads dealt directly with the issue and promised to regain consumers' trust. Toyota also took out full-page ads in major newspapers and produced feel-good television spots featuring dealers, mechanics, and owners. The company offered no-interest loans, discount leases, and a complementary two-year maintenance program to get buyers back.

Although the situation looked dim for Toyota, a later revelation changed everything. In 2011, Toyota achieved a victory when the National Highway Traffic Safety Administration ruled that most of the accidents were caused by driver error, not mechanical problems. This cleared Toyota from several of the accusations levied against the company by media outlets and irate stakeholders. Yet the combination of the recall crisis and the natural disasters that hit Japan greatly damaged Toyota's sales, and General Motors surpassed Toyota as the world's top auto manufacturer.

However, signs now indicate that Toyota is on the rebound. The Toyota Camry and Toyota Corolla are some of the best-selling cars in the United States, and the Toyota Prius remains one of the most popular hybrids. Additionally, Toyota is still the brand of choice for many segments of the population. For instance, American minorities buy more vehicles from Toyota than any other carmaker. One reason is the fact that Toyota has become an expert at targeting advertisements to minority populations. For example, when Toyota became concerned that few African Americans were purchasing its hybrids, the company released a commercial featuring an African American couple deciding that a Toyota hybrid was the best vehicle for them. Sales of the Toyota Prius nearly doubled among African American buyers after the ad ran.

After a three-year hiatus, Toyota also began to advertise in the Super Bowl. During the 2012 Super Bowl game, Toyota released a series of ads depicting the quality and luxury of Toyota vehicles. Whereas one ad contained more of a feel-good quality and featured Toyota factory workers at different stages of the production process, another advertisement targeting first-time Millennial car buyers tried to make purchasing a Toyota vehicle into a "game" by using backdrops from Hasbro's Life board game. Although they had the same objective—promote Toyota vehicles—these different advertising messages were tailored to target specific parts of the American population.

Toyota's advertising push signals a strong message to its competitors: Toyota is fighting to regain its global dominance. Although the automaker may have more hard work ahead before it can re-obtain its high-quality status, the company appears to be well on its way to rebuilding its reputation.[48]

Questions for Discussion

1. How is Toyota using advertising to overcome negative publicity associated with a product quality issue?
2. Why did Toyota have to pull advertising for its cars' dependability, safety, and reliability during a time when it was getting so much public attention for safety recalls related to sudden acceleration?
3. What can Toyota do going forward to restore its image?

NOTES

[1]Christina Passariello and Max Colchester, "L'Oreal's Slogan Proves Timeless," *The Wall Street Journal*, November 15, 2011, B14; Amy Verner, "L'Oreal's 'Because I'm worth it' Slogan Marks a Milestone," *The Globe and Mail*, December 2, 2011, www.theglobeandmail.com/life/fashion-and-beauty/beauty/beauty-features/lorals-because-im-worth-it-slogan-marks-a-milestone/article2256825/ (accessed December 7, 2011); Kate Shapland, "It Was Worth It: L'Oreal Celebrates 40th Anniversary of Landmark Slogan," Telegraph.co.uk, November 16, 2011, http://fashion.telegraph.co.uk/beauty/news-features/TMG8894450/It-was-worth-it-LOreal-celebrates-40th-anniversary-of-landmark-slogan.html (accessed December 7, 2011); Rebecca Leffler, "L'Oreal Fetes 40th Anniversary of 'Because You're Worth It' in Paris," The Hollywood Reporter, November 14, 2011, www.hollywoodreporter.com/fash-track/l-oreal-jane-fonda-freida-pinto-261216 (accessed December 7, 2011).

[2]Nanci Hellmich, "Study: Kids Prefer Taste of Food from Cartooned Packages," *USA Today,* http://yourlife.usatoday.com/parenting-family/story/2011/03/Study-Kids-prefer-taste-of-food-from-cartooned-packages/44608794/1 (accessed March 15, 2012).

[3]Trevor Brown, "Tourism Office Seeking Millions for Advertising," Wyoming News, December 30, 2011, http://wyomingnews.com/articles/2011/12/30/news/20local_12-30-11.txt (accessed March 15, 2012); *Agency 066 Wyoming Office of Tourism Annual Report FY 2010*, www-wsl.state.wy.us/slpub/reports/2010/Tourism.pdf (accessed March 15, 2012).

[4]Marvin E. Goldberg, Cornelia Pechmann, Guangzhi Zhao, and Ellen Thomas Reibling, "What to Convey in Antismoking Advertisements for Adolescents: The Use of Protection Motivation Theory to Identify Effective Message Themes," *Journal of Marketing* (April 2003): 1–18.

[5]Micael Dahlén, Helge Thorbjørnsen, and Henrik Sjödin, "A Taste of 'Nextopia'," *Journal of Advertising* 40, no. 1 (Winter 2011): 33–44.

[6]Brad Wieners, "Lego Is for Girls," *Bloomberg Businessweek,* December 19–25, 2011, 68–73.

[7]Tae Hyun Baek and Mariko Morimoto, "Stay Away from Me," *Journal of Advertising* 41, no. 1 (Spring 2012): 59–76.

[8]"The iRobot Story," iRobot, http://store.irobot.com/shop/index.jsp?categoryId=4331595 (accessed April 29, 2011); Lisa van der Pool, "Mullen Wins iRobot Ad Biz," *Boston Business Journal,* October 21, 2011, www.bizjournals.com/boston/news/2011/10/31/mullen-wins-irobot-ad-biz.html (accessed March 7, 2012).

[9]The Ludlow Suit by J.Crew," *Fast Company,* March 2012, http://fastcompany.coverleaf.com/fastcompany/201203?pg=6#pg6 (accessed March 28, 2012).

[10]Daniel A. Sheinin, Sajeev Varki, and Christy Ashley, "The Differential Effect of Ad Novelty and Message Usefulness on Brand Judgments," *Journal of Advertising* 40, no. 3 (Fall 2011): 5–17.

[11]"THE NEXT BIG THING: Samsung Galaxy S2 Making Fun of Apple iPhone Users," www.youtube.com/watch?v=3mo5pEAHPek (accessed March 28, 2012).

[12]Jacqueline Magnay, "London 2012 Olympics: Government Expecting Games Budget Surplus," *The Telegraph,* September 13, 2011, www.telegraph.co.uk/sport/olympics/8759269/London-2012-Olympics-Government-expecting-Games-budget-surplus.html (accessed March 15, 2012).

[13]"Online Advertising Market Poised to Grow 20% in 2011," eMarketer, June 8, 2011, www.emarketer.com/PressRelease.aspx?R=1008432 (accessed March 15, 2012).

[14]Glamour Circulation/Demographics, http://condenastmediakit.com/gla/circulation.cfm (accessed April 29, 2011).

[15]Rob Jennings, "School Buses Give Ads a Ride," *USA Today,* March 17, 2011, www.usatoday.com/news/nation/2011-03-16-schoolbusads16_ST_N.htm (accessed March 15, 2012).

[16]David G. Taylor, Jeffrey E. Lewin, and David Strutton, "Friends, Fans, and Followers: Do Ads Work on Social Networks? How Gender and Age Shape Receptivity," *Journal of Advertising Research* 51, no. 1 (2011): 258–275.

[17]"Heinz Get Well Soup," *Advertising Age,* January 23, 2012, 12–13; "Like This, Follow That: It's the 10 Best Social-Media Campaigns of the Year," *Advertising Age,* December 12, 2011, http://adage.com/article/special-report-book-of-tens-2011/ad-age-s-book-tens-social-media-campaigns/231498/ (accessed March 15, 2012).

[18]Karen Weise and Cristina Alesci, "The Golden Allure of The Yellow Pages," *Bloomberg Businessweek,* March 26–April 1, 2012, 45–46.

[19]Shintaro Okazaki and Patrick Barwise, "Has the Time Finally Come for the Medium of the Future? Research on Mobile Advertising," 50th Anniversary Supplement, *Journal of Advertising Research* 51, no. 1 (2011): 59–71.

[20]Chingching Chang, "Feeling Ambivalent About Going Green," *Journal of Advertising* 40, no. 4 (Winter 2011): 19–31.

[21]Ilona A. Berney-Reddish and Charles S. Areni, "Sex Differences in Responses to Probability Markers in Advertising Claims," *Journal of Advertising* 35 (Summer 2006): 7–17.

[22]Judith Anne Garretson Folse, Richard G. Netemeyer, and Scot Burton, "Spokescharacters," *Journal of Advertising* 41, no. 1 (Spring 2012): 17–32.

[23]Andrea C. Morales, Maura L. Scott, and Eric A. Yorkston, "The Role of Accent Standardness in Message Preference and Recall," *Journal of Advertising* 41, no. 1 (Spring 2012): 33–45.

[24]AAA Publishing Network, www.aaapublishingnetwork.com/ (accessed March 28, 2012).

[25]Daniel J. Howard and Roger A. Kerin, "The Effects of Personalized Product Recommendations on Advertisement Response Rates: The 'Try This. It Works!' Technique," *Journal of Consumer Psychology* 14, no. 3 (2004): 271–279.

[26]Pamela W. Henderson, Joan L. Giese, and Joseph A. Cote, "Impression Management Using Typeface Design," *Journal of Marketing* 68 (October 2004): 60–72.

[27]Rik Pieters and Michel Wedel, "Attention Capture and Transfer in Advertising: Brand, Pictorial, and Text-Size Effects," *Journal of Marketing* 68 (April 2004): 36–50.

[28]David Welch, "Mr. Peanut Gets Smashed," *Bloomberg Businessweek,* March 12–March 18, 2012, 22–23.

[29]Andrew Hampp, "Outdoor Ad Industry Finally Gets Its Improved Metrics," *Advertising Age*, March 30, 2010, www.aef.com/industry/news/data/2010/1019 (accessed April 29, 2011).

[30]Philip W. Sawyer, "Why Most Digital Ads Still Fail to Work," *Advertising Age*, January 27, 2010, http://adage.com/digitalnext/post?article_id=141751 (accessed April 29, 2011).

[31]Kristin Laird, "Cassies Target Newfoundland Tourism Campaign," *Marketing,* January 24, 2012, www.marketingmag.ca/news/agency-news/cassies-target-newfoundland-tourism-campaign-44853 (accessed March 15, 2012).

[32]Giselle Tsirulnik, "Which Brands Have the Highest Mobile Ad Recall," *Mobile Marketer,* January 19, 2011, www.mobilemarketer.com/cms/news/research/8820.html (accessed March 21, 2012).

[33]Peter J. Danaher and Guy W. Mullarkey, "Factors Affecting Online Advertising Recall: A Study of Students," *Journal of Advertising Research* 43 (2003): 252–267.

[34]YuMe and IPG Media Lab, *YuMe and the IPG Media Lab Release Findings on the Effectiveness of Online and Televised Video Advertising*, May 24, 2011, www.vena.tv/wp-content/pdf/YuMe_IPG_Release_5.24.11.pdf (accessed March 21, 2012).

[35]Johnny Diaz, "Barnes & Noble Hires Mullen for Nook Ad Campaign," Boston.com, February 24, 2011, www.boston.com/business/articles/2011/02/24/barnes__noble_hires_mullen_for_nook_ad_campaign/ (accessed March 21, 2012).

[36]Arun Sudhaman and Paul Holmes, "The Top 10 Crises of 2011," The Holmes Report, January 25, 2012, www.holmesreport.com/featurestories-info/11377/The-Top-10-Crises-Of-2011.aspx (accessed March 21, 2012); Ron Torrosian, "BlackBerry Brand Damaged—What's Next in Crisis PR?," *Business Insider,* October 17, 2011, http://articles.businessinsider.com/2011-10-17/home/30288664_1_blackberry-service-crisis-pr-crackberry (accessed March 21, 2012).

[37]Diana Walker, "Seattle Shows Their Support for Girl Up!" Girl Up, November 14, 2011, www.girlup.org/blog/seattle-shows-their-support-for-girl-up.html (accessed March 28, 2012); "2011 PR Nonprofit Awards," *PR News*, March 18, 2011, www.prnewsonline.com/free/2011-Nonprofit-PR-Awards-Event-PR_14875.html/ (accessed March 28, 2012).

[38]George E. Belch and Michael A. Belch, *Advertising and Promotion* (Burr Ridge, IL: Irwin/McGraw-Hill, 2008), 570.

[39]"Comcast Cares Day," Comcast, www.comcast.com/corporate/about/inthecommunity/volunteer/comcastcaresday.html?SCRedirect=true (accessed March 28, 2012); "Platinum PR Awards 2011," *PR News*, www.prnewsonline.com/awards/platinumpr2011_finalists.html (accessed March 28, 2012).

[40]Belch and Belch, *Advertising and Promotion,* 580–581.

[41]Suman Basuroy, Subimal Chatterjee, and S. Abraham Ravid, "How Critical Are Critical Reviews? The Box Office Effects of Film Critics, Star Power, and Budgets," *Journal of Marketing,* October 2003: 103–117.

[42]Matthew Futterman and Reed Albergotti, "NFL Flags Saints for Bounty Hunting," *The Wall Street Journal*, http://online.wsj.com/article/SB10001424052702304636404577295602826944034.html?mod=WSJ_WSJ_News_BlogsModule (accessed March 28, 2012).

[43]Ruth Simon and Nick Timiraos, "New York to Settle Some Mortgage Claims With 5 Banks," *The Wall Street Journal,* March 13, 2012, http://online.wsj.com/article/SB10001424052702303717304577279953721486914.html (accessed March 21, 2012).

[44]Edelman, *2012 Edelman Trust Barometer,* http://trust.edelman.com/trust-download/global-results/ (accessed March 21, 2012).

[45]Deborah L. Vence, "Stand Guard: In Bad Times, An Ongoing Strategy Keeps Image Intact," *Marketing News,* November 16, 2006: 15.

[46]"Best and Worst PR Moves of 2011: Aflac Flies and Netflix Dives," *PR News,* December 30, 2011, www.prnewsonline.com/watercooler/Best-and-Worst-PR-Moves-of-2011-Aflac-Flies-and-Netflix-Dives_15836.html (accessed March 7, 2012).

[47]Pepsi Refresh, www.refresheverything.com/ (accessed March 23, 2012); Dale Buss, "Pepsi Refreshes Refresh-and Pepsi Challenge," *brandchannel,* May 11, 2011, www.brandchannel.com/home/post/2011/05/11/Pepsi-Refresh-Pepsi-Challenge.aspx (accessed March 23, 2012); "Pepsi Refresh Project Official Application Guidelines," www.refresheverything.com/official-application-guidelines (accessed March 23, 2012); Shirley Brady, "Pepsi Refresh Project Expands to Canada with $1M in Grants," *brandchannel,* January 2, 2012, www.brandchannel.com/home/post/Pepsi-Refresh-Project-Canada-010212.aspx (accessed March 23, 2012); Shelly DuBois, "How Pepsi's Crowd-Sourced Ads Beat the Super Bowl Beer Spots," *CNNMoney,* February 10, 2011, http://tech.fortune.cnn.com/2011/02/10/how-pepsis-crowd-sourced-ads-beat-the-super-bowl-beer-spots/ (accessed March 23, 2012).

[48]"What the World's Biggest Carmaker Can Learn from Other Corporate Turnarounds," *The Economist,* December 12, 2009, 11; Phil LeBeau, "Toyota Issues a 2nd Recall," *The New York Times,* January 21, 2010, www.nytimes.com/2010/01/22/business/22toyota.html (accessed March 23, 2012); "Toyota Motor Corporation," *The New York Times,* February 3, 2010, http://topics.nytimes.com/top/news/business/companies/toyota_motor_corporation/index.html (accessed March 23, 2012); Hiroko Tabuchi and Nick Bunkley, "Toyota Announces Steps to Restore Confidence on Safety," *The New York Times,* February 17, 2010, www.nytimes.com/2010/02/18/business/global/18recall.html (accessed March 23, 2012); Daisuke Wakabayashi, "Adherents Defend the Toyota 'Way,'" *The Wall Street Journal,* February 24, 2010, http://online.wsj.com/article/SB10001424052748703510204575084840073648572.html?mod=WSJ_latestheadlines (accessed March 23, 2012); Suzanne Vranica, "Toyota Pulls Ads, Hires P.R. Firm," *The Wall Street Journal,* January 27, 2010; "Analysis: Toyota's PR 'Lessons to Be Learned,'" *just-auto.com,* March 30, 2010, www.just-auto.com/article.aspx?id=103856 (accessed March 23, 2012); Rich Thomaselli, "Incentives Boost Sales but Brand Challenge Lingers on for Toyota," *AdAge,* April 12, 2010; Josh Mitchell, Mike Ramsey, and Chester Dawson, "U.S. Blames Drivers, Not Toyota," *The Wall Street Journal,* February 9, 2011, http://online.WSJ.com/article/SB10001424052748704422204576131311592922574.html (accessed March 23, 2012); Joann Muller, "The Best-Selling Cars of 2011," *Forbes,* November 2, 2011, www.forbes.com/sites/joannmuller/2011/11/02/the-best-selling-cars-of-2011/ (accessed March 23, 2012); Scott Sloan, "Georgetown Workers Featured in Toyota's Super Bowl Ad," Kentucky.com, February 3, 2012, www.kentucky.com/2012/02/03/2053529/georgetown-workers-featured-in.html (accessed March 23, 2012); Sonari Glinton, "Toyota Steers Ads to Bring in More Minority Buyers," NPR, June 30, 2011, www.npr.org/2011/06/30/137524757/toyota-steers-ads-to-bring-in-more-minority-buyers (accessed March 23, 2012); Stephen Williams, "Toyota Makes Game Out of Buying a Prius," *Advertising Age,* March 13, 2012, http://adage.com/article/news/toyota-makes-game-buying-a-prius/233294/ (accessed March 23, 2012).

Feature Notes

[a]Manoj Hastak and Michael B. Mazis (Fall 2011) "Deception by Implication: A Typology of Truthful but Misleading Advertising and Labeling Claims," *Journal of Public Policy & Marketing* 30, no. 2 (Fall 2011): 157–167; Mike Esterl, "Can This Chip Be Saved?" *The Wall Street Journal,* March 24, 2011, http://online.wsj.com/article/SB10001424052748704050204576218492608111416.html (accessed November 15, 2011); Mayo Clinic Staff, "Organic Foods: Are They Safer? More Nutritious?" June 10, 2011, www.mayoclinic.com/health/organic-food/NU00255 (accessed November 15, 2011).

[b]Christine Birkner, "Mama's Got the Magic of Mobile, Too," *Marketing News,* September 15, 2011, p. 8; "Reign of Stains on the Wane with New Clorox myStain™ Mobile App," *PRWeb,* May 19, 2010, www.prweb.com/releases/2010/05/prweb4015374.htm (accessed November 23, 2011); "Tips at Your Fingertips with the Clorox myStain App!," Clorox Mom Moments Blog, www.clorox.com/blogs/mom-moments/2010/12/22/kj-update-w-legally-approved-versiontips-at-your-fingertips-with-the-clorox-mystain-app/ (November 23, 2011); Giselle Tsirulnik, "Clorox Taps Mobile to Brand Itself an Authority in Stain Removal," *Mobile Marketer,* May 20, 2010, www.mobilemarketer.com/cms/news/database-crm/6313.html (November 23, 2011).

[c]Marcos Cordero, "Five Ways to Use Green to Grow Your Business with Marketing and PR," Intuit, September 1, 2011, http://blog.intuit.com/marketing/five-ways-to-use-green-to-grow-your-business-with-marketing-and-pr/ (accessed December 6, 2011); McMilker, "PR Tips for Green Entrepreneurs," *Ecopreneurist,* http://ecopreneurist.com/2008/01/22/pr-tips-for-green-entrepreneurs/ (accessed December 6, 2011); Associated Press, "Truth in Green Ads? Not as Much as You Think," *MSNBC,* October 6, 2010, www.msnbc.msn.com/id/39535882/ns/business-going_green/t/truth-green-ads-not-much-you-think/ (accessed December 6, 2011).

[d]Trang Pham-Bui, "Pass Soap Company's Sales Surge after GMA Exposure," *WLOX,* November 21, 2011, www.wlox.com/story/16096200/pass-soap-companys-sales-surge-after-gma-exposure?clienttype=printable (accessed December 2, 2011); "About Us," Pass Christian Soap Company, http://passsoapchristian.typepad.com/pass-christian-soap-co/about-us.html (accessed December 2, 2011); "What People Are Saying…," Pass Christian Soap Company, www.passsoap.com/press.html (accessed December 2, 2011).

chapter 19

Personal Selling and Sales Promotion

OBJECTIVES

1. To understand the major purposes of personal selling
2. To describe the basic steps in the personal selling process
3. To identify the types of sales force personnel
4. To recognize new types of personal selling
5. To understand sales management decisions and activities
6. To explain what sales promotion activities are and how they are used
7. To explore specific consumer sales promotion methods
8. To explore trade sales promotion methods

MARKETING INSIGHTS

Salesforce.com Manages Its Relationships and Reputation

Salesforce.com strives to create mutually beneficial relationships with all of its stakeholders, including customers, employees, and communities. Unlike other companies that struggled through the latest recession, Salesforce.com grew. The company earns approximately $2 billion in annual revenue and has over 100,000 customers.

Salesforce.com is a customer relationship management (CRM) vendor that provides a cloud-computing model to enable businesses to manage relationships with their customers. Because it can be difficult to manage the sales process, Salesforce.com has also begun offering a number of additional services for businesses, such as social media analytics. Users obtain the company's software through a subscription and download it directly onto their computers. The massive growth of the company in recent years indicates that customers are happy with Salesforce.com's CRM solutions.

Salesforce.com is also beloved by its employees and communities. The firm provides large bonuses and allows some of its employees to own stock in the company. The average total pay at Salesforce.com is more than $300,000. Salesforce.com's 1/1/1 Model—which stands for 1 percent time (employees are given 1 percent time to volunteer), 1 percent equity (1 percent of its capital is given to the Salesforce.com Foundation), and 1 percent product (1 percent of its products are donated or discounted to organizations such as nonprofits)—has been recognized by top ethics institutions like the Ethisphere™ Institute. Salesforce.com has donated over 240,000 employee hours to community causes, has donated or discounted licenses for its software to over 10,000 organizations, and has awarded over $21 million in grants. By selling quality CRM products and valuing its own relationships with stakeholders, Salesforce.com has achieved both high growth and a positive reputation.[1]

For many organizations, targeting customers with appropriate personal selling techniques and messages can play a major role in maintaining long-term, satisfying customer relationships, which in turn contribute to company success. Marketing strategy development should involve the sales organization during all stages of development and implementation. Top managers need extensive feedback from the sales force. Managers should strive to make information transparent and jointly analyze sales data. Sales managers should communicate marketing strategy in a language with which salespeople feel comfortable.[2] As we saw in Chapter 17, personal selling and sales promotion are two possible elements in a promotion mix. Personal selling is sometimes a company's sole promotional tool, and it is becoming increasingly professional and sophisticated, with sales personnel acting more as consultants, advisers, and sometimes as partners.

In this chapter, we focus on personal selling and sales promotion. We first consider the purposes of personal selling and then examine its basic steps. Next, we look at types of salespeople and how they are selected. After taking a look at several new types of personal selling, we discuss major sales force management decisions, including setting objectives for the sales force and determining its size; recruiting, selecting, training, compensating, and motivating salespeople; managing sales territories; and controlling and evaluating sales force performance. Then we examine several characteristics of sales promotion, reasons for using sales promotion, and sales promotion methods available for use in a promotion mix.

THE NATURE OF PERSONAL SELLING

Personal selling is paid personal communication that attempts to inform customers and persuade them to purchase products in an exchange situation. For example, a Hewlett-Packard (HP) salesperson describing the benefits of the company's servers, PCs, and printers to a small-business customer is engaging in personal selling. Likewise, a member of the American Marketing Association (AMA) manning a table at an event engages in personal selling to inform interested parties about the benefits of joining the AMA. Personal selling gives marketers the greatest freedom to adjust a message to satisfy customers' information needs. It is the most precise of all promotion methods, enabling marketers to focus on the most

personal selling Paid personal communication that attempts to inform customers and persuade them to buy products in an exchange situation

The Importance of Personal Selling
When Microsoft released the Windows Phone, representatives engaged in personal selling to inform consumers about the benefits of the new smartphone.

promising sales prospects. Personal selling is also the most effective way to form relationships with customers. Personal selling is perhaps most important with business-to-business transactions involving the purchase of expensive products. Because of the high-risk factors involved, personal selling is often necessary to assure prospective customers about the quality of the product and answer any questions.[3] Despite these benefits, personal selling is generally the most expensive element in the promotion mix. The average cost of a sales call is more than $400.[4]

Millions of people earn their living through personal selling. Sales careers can offer high income, a great deal of freedom, a high level of training, and a high degree of job satisfaction. Although the public may harbor negative perceptions of personal selling, unfavorable stereotypes of salespeople are changing thanks to the efforts of major corporations, professional sales associations, and academic institutions. Personal selling will continue to gain respect as professional sales associations develop and enforce ethical codes of conduct.[5] Developing ongoing customer relationships today requires sales personnel with high levels of professionalism as well as technical and interpersonal skills.[6]

Personal selling goals vary from one firm to another. However, they usually involve finding prospects, determining their needs, persuading prospects to buy, following up on the sale, and keeping customers satisfied. Identifying potential buyers interested in the organization's products is critical. Because most potential buyers seek information before making purchases, salespeople can ascertain prospects' informational needs and then provide relevant information. To do so, sales personnel must be well trained regarding both their products and the selling process in general.

Salespeople must be aware of their competitors. They must monitor the development of new products and keep abreast of competitors' sales efforts in their sales territories, how often and when the competition calls on their accounts, and what the competition is saying about their product in relation to its own. Salespeople must emphasize the benefits their products provide, especially when competitors' products do not offer those specific benefits. Salespeople often function as knowledge experts for the firm and provide key information for marketing decisions.[7]

Personal selling is changing today based on new technology, how customers gain information about products, and the way customers make purchase decisions. Customer information sharing through social media, mobile and Web applications, and electronic sales presentations

Entrepreneurship in Marketing

Scentsy Experiences the Sweet Smell of Success

Entrepreneurs: Orville and Heidi Thompson
Business: Scentsy
Founded: 2004 | Meridian, Idaho
Success: Over three years, Scentsy's revenue grew 2,904 percent to over $550 million.

Scentsy is a rags-to-riches story for its owners Orville and Heidi Thompson. In 2004, the couple was near bankruptcy after a failed business venture. But while Orville was manning a booth at a home show, he came across a wickless candle that used a low-watt bulb to melt scented wax candle bars. The Thompsons bought out the inventory of the product's creators and began running the business from their sheep farm. At $700,000 in debt, the couple knew they needed a strong distribution method to be successful. They chose a party plan direct-selling model, in which individuals host selling parties in their homes to create an exciting and authentic selling experience.

Although the Thompsons' first party produced sales of only $75, the second one generated $1,000. Consumers loved the idea of having the scent of a fragrant candle without worrying about the fire danger—Scentsy wax warmers can be kept on all day. Today, Scentsy has 110,000 consultants on two continents and is one of the fastest-growing direct-selling companies in the United States.[a]

are impacting the nature of personal selling. Some firms are adopting social media technology to reach business customers. "Social CRM" (customer relationship management) provides opportunities to manage data in discovering and engaging customers.[8] For instance, the cloud-computing models provided by Salesforce.com to enable firms to manage relationships with their customers can assist in personal selling sales management.

Using websites to manage orders and product information, track inventory, and train salespeople can save companies time and money. Twitter is a relatively new tool that can be used to post product information and updates, obtain prospects, recruit new salespeople, and communicate with salespeople. Facebook is another valuable tool that can supplement and support face-to-face contacts. On Facebook, salespeople can carry on conversations very similar to traditional face-to-face social networks. Mobile technology and applications provide salespeople with opportunities to offer service and connect with customers. CRM technology enables improved service, marketing and sales processes, and contact and data management and analysis. CRM can help facilitate the delivery of valuable customer experiences and provide the metrics to measure progress and sales successes.[9]

Few businesses survive solely on profits from one-time customers. For long-run survival, most marketers depend on repeat sales and thus need to keep their customers satisfied. In addition, satisfied customers provide favorable word of mouth and other communications, thereby attracting new customers. Although the whole organization is responsible for achieving customer satisfaction, much of the burden falls on salespeople, because they are almost always closer to customers than anyone else in the company and often provide buyers with information and service after the sale. Indeed, a firm's market orientation has a positive influence on salespeople's attitudes, commitment, and influence on customer purchasing intentions.[10] Additionally, studies have also shown that collaboration between sales and marketing is positively related to market orientation, which positively impacts organizational performance.[11] Such contact gives salespeople an opportunity to generate additional sales and offers them a good vantage point for evaluating the strengths and weaknesses of the company's products and other marketing mix components. Their observations help develop and maintain a marketing mix that better satisfies both the firm and its customers. Sales is no longer an isolated function in a global business world. The sales function is becoming part of a cross-functional strategic solution to customer management. This requires salespersons with both managerial and strategic skills.[12]

Prospecting
Companies often engage in prospecting at trade shows, which allow representatives to demonstrate the latest company products and collect information on consumers who might be interested in the firm's offerings. Company salespeople can later use this information in the preapproach and approach steps of the personal selling process.

ELEMENTS OF THE PERSONAL SELLING PROCESS

The specific activities involved in the selling process vary among salespeople, selling situations, and cultures. No two salespeople use exactly the same selling methods. Nonetheless, many salespeople move through a general selling process. This process consists of seven steps, outlined in Figure 19.1: prospecting, preapproach, approach, making the presentation, overcoming objections, closing the sale, and following up.

Prospecting

Developing a database of potential customers is called **prospecting**. Salespeople seek names of prospects from company sales records, trade shows, commercial databases, newspaper announcements (of marriages, births, deaths, and so on), public records, telephone directories, trade association directories, and many other sources. Sales personnel also use responses to traditional and online advertisements that encourage interested persons to send in information request forms. Seminars and meetings targeted at particular types of clients, such as attorneys or accountants, may also produce leads.

Most salespeople prefer to use referrals—recommendations from current customers—to find prospects. For example, salespeople for Cutco Cutlery, which sells high-quality knives and kitchen cutlery, first make sales calls to their friends and families and then use referrals from them to seek out new prospects. Obtaining referrals requires that the salesperson have a good relationship with the current customer and therefore must have performed well before asking the customer for help. As might be expected, a customer's trust in and satisfaction with a salesperson influences his or her willingness to provide referrals. Research shows that one

prospecting Developing a database of potential customers

Figure 19.1 General Steps in the Personal Selling Process

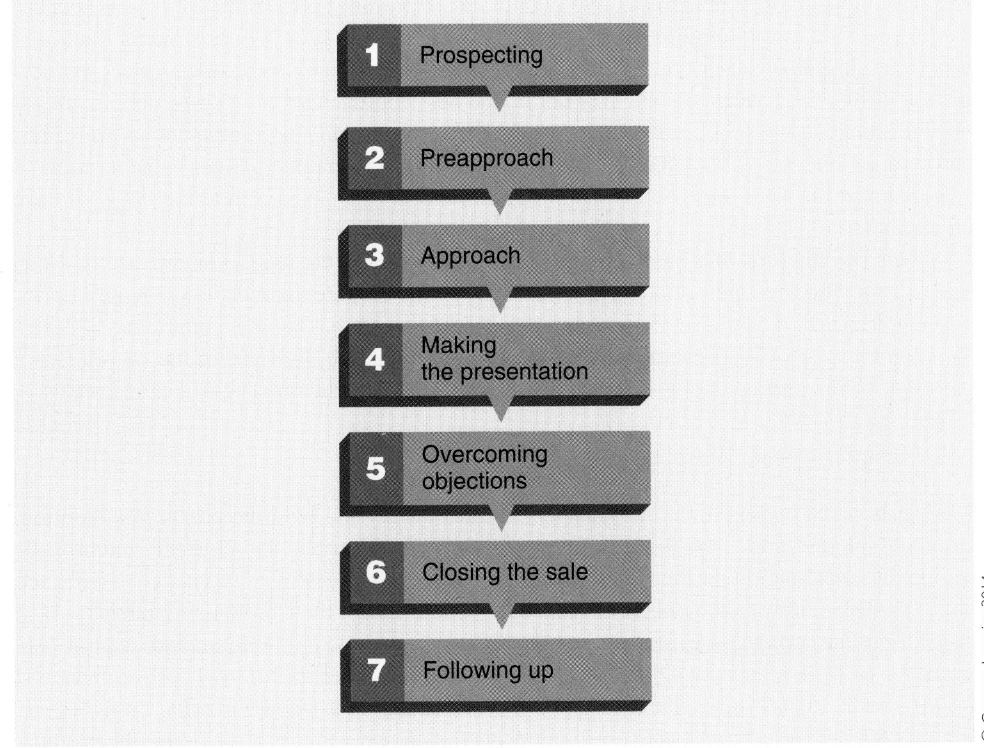

referral is as valuable as 12 cold calls.[13] Also, 80 percent of clients are willing to give referrals, but only 20 percent are ever asked. Among the advantages of using referrals are more highly qualified sales leads, greater sales rates, and larger initial transactions. Some companies even award discounts off future purchases to customers who refer new prospects to their salespeople. Consistent activity is critical to successful prospecting. Salespeople must actively search the customer base for qualified prospects that fit the target market profile. After developing the prospect list, a salesperson evaluates whether each prospect is able, willing, and authorized to buy the product. Based on this evaluation, prospects are ranked according to desirability or potential.

Preapproach

Before contacting acceptable prospects, a salesperson finds and analyzes information about each prospect's specific product needs, current use of brands, feelings about available brands, and personal characteristics. In short, salespeople need to know what potential buyers and decision makers consider most important and why they need a specific product. The most successful salespeople are thorough in their *preapproach,* which involves identifying key decision makers, reviewing account histories and problems, contacting other clients for information, assessing credit histories and problems, preparing sales presentations, identifying product needs, and obtaining relevant literature. Marketers are increasingly using information technology and customer relationship management systems to comb through databases and thus identify their most profitable products and customers. CRM systems can also help sales departments manage leads, track customers, forecast sales, and assess performance. A salesperson with a lot of information about a prospect is better equipped to develop a presentation that precisely communicates with that prospect.

Approach

The **approach**—the manner in which a salesperson contacts a potential customer—is a critical step in the sales process. In more than 80 percent of initial sales calls, the purpose is to gather information about the buyer's needs and objectives. Creating a favorable impression and building rapport with prospective clients are important tasks in the approach because the prospect's first impressions of the salesperson are usually lasting ones. During the initial visit, the salesperson strives to develop a relationship rather than just push a product. Indeed, coming across as a "salesperson" may not be the best approach because some people are put off by strong selling tactics. The salesperson may have to call on a prospect several times before the product is considered. The approach must be designed to deliver value to targeted customers. If the sales approach is inappropriate, the salesperson's efforts are likely to have poor results.

One type of approach is based on referrals, as discussed in the section on prospecting. The salesperson who uses the "cold canvass" approach calls on potential customers without prior consent. Repeat contact is another common approach: when making the contact, the salesperson mentions a previous meeting. The exact type of approach depends on the salesperson's preferences, the product being sold, the firm's resources, and the prospect's characteristics.

Making the Presentation

During the sales presentation, the salesperson must attract and hold the prospect's attention, stimulate interest, and spark a desire for the product. Salespeople who carefully monitor the selling situation and adapt their presentations to meet the needs of prospects are associated with effective sales performance.[14] Salespeople should match their influencing tactics—such as information exchange, recommendations, threats, promises, ingratiation, and inspirational appeals—to their prospects. Different types of buyers respond to different tactics, but most respond well to information exchange and recommendations, and virtually no prospects respond to threats.[15] The salesperson should have the prospect touch, hold, or use the product.

approach The manner in which a salesperson contacts a potential customer

Marketing Debate

Virtual versus Face-to-Face Sales Presentations

ISSUE: Are virtual sales presentations and meetings as effective as face-to-face?

Virtual sales presentations have been touted as a better alternative to face-to-face sales presentations due to their convenience. Yet in reality, they come with their own set of challenges. Virtual sales presentations require an adequate bandwidth, and users must be familiar with the technology to create an effective sales presentation virtually. This requires additional training for a company's sales force. The salesperson cannot always see the customer, and the customer cannot touch the product. On the other hand, virtual sales presentations can eliminate long travel times, can be sent to a large number of prospects simultaneously, and can be viewed from a location of the prospect's choosing.[b]

If possible, the salesperson should demonstrate the product or invite the prospect to use it. Automobile salespeople, for example, typically invite potential buyers to test-drive the vehicle that interests them. Audiovisual equipment and software may also enhance the presentation.

During the presentation, the salesperson must not only talk, but also listen. Nonverbal modes of communication are especially beneficial in building trust during the presentation.[16] The sales presentation gives the salesperson the greatest opportunity to determine the prospect's specific needs by listening to questions and comments and observing responses. For example, it has been found that complimenting the buyer on his or her questions adds to incremental sales.[17] Even though the salesperson plans the presentation in advance, she or he must be able to adjust the message to meet the prospect's informational needs. Adapting the message in response to the customer's needs generally enhances performance, particularly in new-task or modified rebuy purchase situations.[18]

Overcoming Objections

An effective salesperson usually seeks out a prospect's objections in order to address them. If they are not apparent, the salesperson cannot deal with them, and the prospect may not buy. One of the best ways to overcome objections is to anticipate and counter them before the prospect raises them. However, this approach can be risky, because the salesperson may mention objections that the prospect would not have raised. If possible, the salesperson should handle objections as they arise. They can also be addressed at the end of the presentation.

Closing the Sale

Closing is the stage in the personal selling process when the salesperson asks the prospect to buy the product. During the presentation, the salesperson may use a *trial close* by asking questions that assume the prospect will buy. The salesperson might ask the potential customer about financial terms, desired colors or sizes, or delivery arrangements. Reactions to such questions usually indicate how close the prospect is to buying. Properly asked questions may allow prospects to uncover their own problems and identify solutions themselves. One questioning approach uses broad questions *(what, how, why)* to probe or gather information and focused questions *(who, when, where)* to clarify and close the sale. A trial close allows prospects to indicate indirectly that they will buy the product without having to say those sometimes difficult words: "I'll take it."

A salesperson should try to close at several points during the presentation because the prospect may be ready to buy. An attempt to close the sale may result in objections. Thus, closing can uncover hidden objections, which the salesperson can then address. One closing strategy involves asking the potential customer to place a low-risk, trial order.

closing The stage in the personal selling process when the salesperson asks the prospect to buy the product

Following Up

After a successful closing, the salesperson must follow up the sale. In the follow-up stage, the salesperson determines whether the order was delivered on time and installed properly, if installation was required. He or she should contact the customer to learn if any problems or questions regarding the product have arisen. The follow-up stage is also used to determine customers' future product needs.

Following up also aids the salesperson in creating a solid relationship with the customer. New salespeople might find it difficult to understand the reasons for following up on a sale if the customer seems satisfied with the product. However, a large number of customers who stop buying products do so not out of dissatisfaction but because the company neglected to contact them.[19] Thus, the follow-up stage is vital to establishing a strong relationship and creating loyalty on the part of the buyer.

TYPES OF SALESPEOPLE

To develop a sales force, a marketing manager decides what kind of salesperson will sell the firm's products most effectively. Most business organizations use several different kinds of sales personnel. Based on the functions performed, salespeople can be classified into three groups: order getters, order takers, and support personnel. One salesperson can, and often does, perform all three functions.

Order Getters

order getters Salespeople who sell to new customers and increase sales to current customers

To obtain orders, salespeople inform prospects and persuade them to buy the product. The responsibility of **order getters** is to increase sales by selling to new customers and increasing sales to present customers. This task is sometimes called *creative selling*. It requires that salespeople recognize potential buyers' needs and give them necessary information. Order getting is frequently divided into two categories: current-customer sales and new-business sales.

Types of Salespeople
When we think of sales representatives, order getters or order takers probably come to mind. Order getters sell to new customers or increase selling to existing customers. Order takers primarily seek repeat sales. There are also support personnel who facilitate selling but are not involved in solely making sales.

Current-Customer Sales

Sales personnel who concentrate on current customers call on people and organizations that have purchased products from the firm before. These salespeople seek more sales from existing customers by following up on previous sales. Current customers can also be sources of leads for new prospects.

New-Business Sales

Business organizations depend to some degree on sales to new customers. New-business sales personnel locate prospects and convert them into buyers. Salespeople help generate new business in many organizations, but even more so in organizations that sell real estate, insurance, appliances, automobiles, and business-to-business supplies and services. These organizations depend in large part on new-customer sales.

Order Takers

Taking orders is a repetitive task salespeople perform to perpetuate long-lasting, satisfying customer relationships. **Order takers** primarily seek repeat sales, generating the bulk of many firms' total sales. One of their major objectives is to be certain that customers have sufficient product quantities where and when needed. Most order takers handle orders for standardized products that are purchased routinely and do not require extensive sales efforts. The role of order takers is changing, however, as the position moves more toward one that identifies and solves problems to better meet the needs of customers. There are two groups of order takers: inside order takers and field order takers.

Inside Order Takers

In many businesses, inside order takers, who work in sales offices, receive orders by mail, telephone, and the Internet. Certain producers, wholesalers, and retailers have sales personnel who sell from within the firm rather than in the field. Some inside order takers communicate with customers face to face; retail salespeople, for example, are classified as inside order takers. As more orders are placed electronically, the role of the inside order taker continues to change.

Field Order Takers

Salespeople who travel to customers are outside, or field, order takers. Often, customers and field order takers develop interdependent relationships. The buyer relies on the salesperson to take orders periodically (and sometimes to deliver them), and the salesperson counts on the buyer to purchase a certain quantity of products periodically. Use of small computers has improved the field order taker's inventory and order-tracking capabilities.

Support Personnel

Support personnel facilitate selling but usually are not involved solely with making sales. They engage primarily in marketing industrial products, locating prospects, educating customers, building goodwill, and providing service after the sale. There are many kinds of sales support personnel; the three most common are missionary, trade, and technical salespeople.

Missionary Salespeople

Missionary salespeople, usually employed by manufacturers, assist the producer's customers in selling to their own customers. Missionary salespeople may call on retailers to inform and persuade them to buy the manufacturer's products. When they succeed, retailers purchase

order takers Salespeople who primarily seek repeat sales

support personnel Sales staff members who facilitate selling but usually are not involved solely with making sales

missionary salespeople Support salespeople, usually employed by a manufacturer, who assist the producer's customers in selling to their own customers products from wholesalers, which are the producer's customers. Manufacturers of medical supplies and pharmaceuticals often use missionary salespeople, called *detail reps,* to promote their products to physicians, hospitals, and pharmacists.

Trade Salespeople

Trade salespeople are not strictly support personnel, because they usually take orders as well. However, they direct much effort toward helping customers—especially retail stores—promote the product. They are likely to restock shelves, obtain more shelf space, set up displays, provide in-store demonstrations, and distribute samples to store customers. Food producers and processors commonly employ trade salespeople.

Technical Salespeople

Technical salespeople give technical assistance to the organization's current customers, advising them on product characteristics and applications, system designs, and installation procedures. Because this job is often highly technical, the salesperson usually has formal training in one of the physical sciences or in engineering. Technical sales personnel often sell technical industrial products, such as computers, heavy equipment, and steel.

When hiring sales personnel, marketers seldom restrict themselves to a single category, because most firms require different types of salespeople. Several factors dictate how many of each type a particular company should have. Product use, characteristics, complexity, and price influence the kind of sales personnel used, as do the number and characteristics of customers. The types of marketing channels and the intensity and type of advertising also affect the composition of a sales force.

SELECTED TYPES OF SELLING

Personal selling has become an increasingly complex process due in large part to rapid technological innovation. Most importantly, the focus of personal selling is shifting from selling a specific product to building long-term relationships with customers by finding solutions to their needs, problems, and challenges. As a result, the roles of salespeople are changing. Among the newer philosophies for personal selling are team selling and relationship selling.

Team Selling

Many products, particularly expensive high-tech business products, have become so complex that a single salesperson can no longer be an expert in every aspect of the product and purchase process. **Team selling**, which involves the salesperson joining with people from the firm's financial, engineering, and other functional areas, is appropriate for such products. The salesperson takes the lead in the personal selling process, but other members of the team bring their unique skills, knowledge, and resources to the process to help customers find solutions to their own business challenges. Selling teams may be created to address a particular short-term situation, or they may be formal, ongoing teams. Team selling is advantageous in situations calling for detailed knowledge of new, complex, and dynamic technologies like jet aircraft and medical equipment. It can be difficult, however, for highly competitive salespersons to adapt to a team selling environment.

Relationship Selling

Relationship selling, also known as consultative selling, involves building mutually beneficial long-term associations with a customer through regular communications over prolonged periods of time. Like team selling, it is especially used in business-to-business marketing. Relationship selling involves finding solutions to customers' needs by listening to them,

trade salespeople Salespeople involved mainly in helping a producer's customers promote a product

technical salespeople Support salespeople who give technical assistance to a firm's current customers

team selling The use of a team of experts from all functional areas of a firm, led by a salesperson, to conduct the personal selling process

relationship selling The building of mutually beneficial long-term associations with a customer through regular communications over prolonged periods of time

Team Selling
Team selling is becoming more popular, especially in companies where the selling process is complex and requires a variety of specialized skills.

gaining a detailed understanding of their organizations, understanding and caring about their needs and challenges, and providing support after the sale. Sales relationships are also built on being able to recover when customers are concerned about services. Being proactive in identifying the need for recovery behaviors is a major part of relationship selling.[20] For example, contacting the customer if delivery time is longer than expected as well as explaining what happened and when the product will be delivered is important.

Relationship selling differs from traditional personal selling due to its adoption of a long-term perspective. For instance, when Sportron International Inc. began emphasizing relationship building, it saw an increase in distributor enrollment of 25 percent and a decrease in dropouts of 5 to 8 percent each month.[21] Instead of simply focusing on short-term repeat sales, relationship selling involves forming long-term connections that will result in sales throughout the relationship.[22] Relationship selling is well poised to help sellers understand their customers' individual needs. It is particularly important in business-to-business transactions as businesses often require more "individualized solutions" to meet their unique needs than the individual consumer.[23] Relationship selling has significant implications for the seller. Studies show that firms spend six times longer on finding new customers than in keeping current customers.[24] Thus, relationship selling that generates loyal long-term customers is likely to be extremely profitable for the firm both in repeat sales as well as the money saved in trying to find new customers. Finally, as the personal selling industry becomes increasingly competitive, relationship selling is one way that companies can differentiate themselves from rivals to create competitive advantages.[25]

Relationship selling efforts can be improved through sales automation technology tools that enhance interactive communication.[26] For instance, IBM's adoption of sales force automation technology allowed departments to communicate with one another more effectively and created operational efficiencies through greater collaboration and problem solving.[27] New applications for customer relationship management are also being provided through companies like Salesforce.com, whose cloud-computing model helps companies keep track of the customer life cycle without having to install any software (applications are downloaded). Social networks are being utilized in sales, adding new layers to the selling process. Salesforce CRM, for instance, now allows users to connect with their customers in real time through such networks as Twitter and Facebook. Sales force automation, which involves utilizing information technology to automatically track all stages of the sales process (a part of customer relationship management) has been found to increase salesperson professionalism and responsiveness, customer interaction frequency, and customer relationship quality.[28]

MANAGING THE SALES FORCE

The sales force is directly responsible for generating one of an organization's primary inputs: sales revenue. Without adequate sales revenue, businesses cannot survive. In addition, a firm's reputation is often determined by the ethical conduct of its sales force. Indeed, a positive ethical climate, one component of corporate culture, has been linked with decreased role stress and turnover intention and improved job attitudes and job performance in sales.[29] Research has demonstrated that a negative ethical climate will trigger higher-performing salespeople to leave a company at a higher rate than those in a company perceived to be ethical.[30] The morale and ultimately the success of a firm's sales force depend in large part on adequate compensation, room for advancement, sufficient training, and management support—all key areas of sales management. Salespeople who are not satisfied with these elements may leave. Evaluating the input of salespeople is an important part of sales force management because of its strong bearing on a firm's success. Table 19.1 provides recommendations on how to attract and retain a top-quality sales force.

We explore eight general areas of sales management: establishing sales force objectives, determining sales force size, recruiting and selecting salespeople, training sales personnel, compensating salespeople, motivating salespeople, managing sales territories, and controlling and evaluating sales force performance.

Establishing Sales Force Objectives

To manage a sales force effectively, sales managers must develop sales objectives. Sales objectives tell salespeople what they are expected to accomplish during a specified time period. They give the sales force direction and purpose and serve as standards for evaluating and controlling the performance of sales personnel. Sales objectives should be stated in precise, measurable terms; specify the time period and geographic areas involved; and be achievable.

Sales objectives are usually developed for both the total sales force and individual salespeople. Objectives for the entire force are normally stated in terms of sales volume, market

Table 19.1 Suggestions for Attracting and Retaining a Top Sales Force

Training and development	• On-the-job training • Online individual instruction • Seminars • On-site classroom instruction
Compensation	• Make sure pay mix isn't too risky (high commission, low base) for sales role • Mix base salary with commission, bonus, or both • Base bonuses/commission on reaching sales goals rather than on individual sales dollars • Maintain competitive benefits and expense reimbursement practices
Work/life autonomy	• Offer flexible hours • Consider telecommuting/work-at-home options
Product quality and service	• Ensure products and services meet customer needs • Provide the appropriate service after the sale

Source: "Attracting & Retaining a Top Sales Force," Where Great Workplaces Start, http://greatworkplace.wordpress.com/ 2010/02/10/attracting-retaining-a-top-sales-force/ (accessed September 3, 2012).

share, or profit. Volume objectives refer to dollar or unit sales. For example, the objective for an electric drill producer's sales force might be to sell $18 million worth of drills, or 600,000 drills annually. When sales goals are stated in terms of market share, they usually call for an increase in the proportion of the firm's sales relative to the total number of products sold by all businesses in that industry. When sales objectives are based on profit, they are generally stated in terms of dollar amounts or return on investment.

Sales objectives, or quotas, for individual salespeople are commonly stated in terms of dollar or unit sales volume. Other bases used for individual sales objectives include average order size, average number of calls per time period, and ratio of orders to calls.

Determining Sales Force Size

Sales force size is important, because it influences the company's ability to generate sales and profits. Moreover, size of the sales force affects the compensation methods used, salespeople's morale, and overall sales force management. Sales force size must be adjusted periodically, because a firm's marketing plans change along with markets and forces in the marketing environment. One danger in cutting back the size of the sales force to increase profits is that the sales organization may lose strength and resiliency, preventing it from rebounding when growth occurs or better market conditions prevail.

Several analytical methods can help determine optimal sales force size. One method involves determining how many sales calls per year are necessary for the organization to serve customers effectively and then dividing this total by the average number of sales calls a salesperson makes annually. A second method is based on marginal analysis, in which additional salespeople are added to the sales force until the cost of an additional salesperson equals the additional sales generated by that person. Although marketing managers may use one or several analytical methods, they normally temper decisions with subjective judgments.

Recruiting and Selecting Salespeople

To create and maintain an effective sales force, sales managers must recruit the right type of salespeople. In **recruiting**, the sales manager develops a list of qualified applicants for sales positions. Effective recruiting efforts are a vital part of implementing the strategic sales force

recruiting Developing a list of qualified applicants for sales positions

© Frances Roberts/Alamy

Recruiting and Selecting Salespeople
Career fairs are common events for recruiting salespeople. Because hiring and training costs can be so high, recruiters often have a list of qualifications they use to select the best applicants.

plan and can help assure successful organizational performance. The costs of hiring and training a salesperson are soaring, reaching more than $60,000 in some industries. Thus, recruiting errors are expensive.

To ensure that the recruiting process results in a pool of qualified applicants, a sales manager establishes a set of qualifications before beginning to recruit. Although marketers have tried for years to identify a set of traits characterizing effective salespeople, no set of generally accepted characteristics exists yet. Experts agree that good salespeople exhibit optimism, flexibility, self-motivation, good time management skills, empathy, and the ability to network and maintain long-term customer relationships. Today, companies are increasingly seeking applicants capable of employing relationship-building and consultative approaches as well as the ability to work effectively in team selling efforts.

Sales managers must determine what set of traits best fits their companies' particular sales tasks. Two activities help establish this set of required attributes. First, the sales manager should prepare a job description listing specific tasks salespeople are to perform. Second, the manager should analyze characteristics of the firm's successful salespeople, as well as those of ineffective sales personnel. From the job description and analysis of traits, the sales manager should be able to develop a set of specific requirements and be aware of potential weaknesses that could lead to failure.

A sales manager generally recruits applicants from several sources: departments within the firm, other firms, employment agencies, educational institutions, respondents to advertisements, websites (like Monster.com), and individuals recommended by current employees. The specific sources depend on the type of salesperson required and the manager's experiences and successes with particular recruiting tactics.

The process of recruiting and selecting salespeople varies considerably from one company to another. Companies intent on reducing sales force turnover are likely to have strict recruiting and selection procedures. Sales management should design a selection procedure that satisfies the company's specific needs. Some organizations use the specialized services of other companies to hire sales personnel. The process should include steps that yield the information required to make accurate selection decisions. However, because each step incurs a certain amount of expense, there should be no more steps than necessary. Stages of the selection process should be sequenced so that the more expensive steps, such as a physical examination, occur near the end. Fewer people will then move through higher-cost stages.

Recruitment should not be sporadic; it should be a continuous activity aimed at reaching the best applicants. The selection process should systematically and effectively match applicants' characteristics and needs with the requirements of specific selling tasks. Finally, the selection process should ensure that new sales personnel are available where and when needed.

Training Sales Personnel

Many organizations have formal training programs; others depend on informal, on-the-job training. Some systematic training programs are quite extensive, whereas others are rather short and rudimentary. Whether the training program is complex or simple, developers must consider what to teach, whom to train, and how to train them.

A sales training program can concentrate on the company, its products, or selling methods. Training programs often cover all three. Such programs can be aimed at newly hired salespeople, experienced salespeople, or both. Training for experienced company salespeople usually emphasizes product information or the use of new technology, although salespeople must also be informed about new selling techniques and changes in company plans, policies, and procedures. Sales managers should use ethics training to institutionalize an ethical climate, improve employee satisfaction, and help prevent misconduct. IBM's Health Care and Life Sciences Group, for example, constantly educates its sales force concerning changing trends and effective ways to reach clients. The vice president of IBM's Eastern Regional Solution Sales runs two weeks of extensive sales force training each year, part of which is used to familiarize the sales representatives with new products and services as well as current customer concerns.[31]

Emerging Trends

New Bribery Law Affects Personal Selling Industry

Bribery is a major temptation in personal selling, particularly for global businesses. Although bribery is illegal in the United States, it is sometimes an acceptable way of business in other countries. IBM was forced to pay $10 million for allegedly bribing Asian officials with cash, entertainment expenses, laptops, and cameras in exchange for sales contracts. The U.S. Foreign Corrupt Practices Act (FCPA) forbids businesses from offering such bribes to foreign officials, although facilitation payments of small monetary value are generally allowed. However, this could change as a result of the U.K. Bribery Act, passed in 2010.

The U.K. Bribery Act applies to all companies that do business in the United Kingdom, even if the bribe doesn't occur within the country. The law doesn't allow for facilitation payments, and while small gifts of hospitality are allowed, the lines between hospitality and gift-giving have changed. For instance, while it is common in personal selling to send Christmas gifts to top buyers, more "lavish" Christmas gifts like champagne and sporting events could be seen as bribes.

In response, many multinational businesses are changing their gift and entertainment policies to reflect the law. Hewlett-Packard, for instance, changed its policy so that its sales force can no longer offer anything of value to obtain business contracts. Similarly, other multinationals operating in the United Kingdom are adapting to comply with the law.[c]

PepsiCo offers 10- to 12-week sales internships to train potential sales associates and managers.[32] Ordinarily, new sales personnel require comprehensive training, whereas experienced personnel need both refresher courses on established products and training regarding new-product information and technology changes.

Sales training may be done in the field, at educational institutions, in company facilities, and/or online using web-based technology. For example, Platinum Guild International USA used web-based technologies to develop an online sales training program that retail jewelers can use to learn about the platinum industry.[33] For many companies, online training saves time and money and helps salespeople learn about new products quickly. Some firms train new employees before assigning them to a specific sales position. Others put them into the field immediately, providing formal training only after they have gained some experience. Training programs for new personnel can be as short as several days or as long as three years; some are even longer. Sales training for experienced personnel is often scheduled when sales activities are not too demanding. Because experienced salespeople usually need periodic retraining, a firm's sales management must determine the frequency, sequencing, and duration of these efforts.

Sales managers, as well as other salespeople, often engage in sales training, whether daily on the job or periodically during sales meetings. Salespeople sometimes receive training from technical specialists within their own organizations. In addition, a number of outside companies specialize in providing sales training programs. Materials for sales training programs range from videos, texts, online materials, manuals, and cases to programmed learning devices and digital media. Lectures, demonstrations, simulation exercises, role-plays, and on-the-job training can all be effective training methods. Self-directed learning to supplement traditional sales training has the potential to improve sales performance. The choice of methods and materials for a particular sales training program depends on type and number of trainees, program content and complexity, length and location, size of the training budget, number of trainers, and a trainer's expertise.

Compensating Salespeople

To develop and maintain a highly productive sales force, an organization must formulate and administer a compensation plan that attracts, motivates, and retains the most effective individuals. The plan should give sales management the desired level of control and provide sales personnel with acceptable levels of income, freedom, and incentive. It should be flexible, equitable, easy to administer, and easy to understand. Good compensation programs facilitate and encourage proper treatment of customers. Obviously, it is quite difficult to incorporate all of these requirements into a single program. Figure 19.2 shows the average salaries for sales representatives.

Developers of compensation programs must determine the general level of compensation required and the most desirable method of calculating it. In analyzing the required compensation plan, sales management must ascertain a salesperson's value to the company on the basis of the tasks and responsibilities associated with the sales position. Sales managers may consider a number of factors, including salaries of other types of personnel in the firm, competitors' compensation plans, costs of sales force turnover, and nonsalary selling expenses. The average low-level salesperson earns $50,000 to $75,000 annually (including commissions and bonuses), whereas a high-level, high-performing salesperson can make hundreds of thousands a year.

Sales compensation programs usually reimburse salespeople for selling expenses, provide some fringe benefits, and deliver the required compensation level. To achieve this, a firm may use one or more of three basic compensation methods: straight salary, straight commission, or a combination of the two. Table 19.2 lists the major characteristics, advantages, and disadvantages of each method. In a **straight salary compensation plan**, salespeople are paid a specified amount per time period, regardless of selling effort. This sum remains the same until they receive a pay increase or decrease. Although this method is easy to administer and affords salespeople financial security, it provides little incentive for them to boost selling efforts. In a **straight commission compensation plan**, salespeople's compensation is determined solely by sales for a given period. A commission may be based on a single percentage of sales or on a sliding scale involving several sales levels and percentage rates (e.g., sales under $500,000 a quarter would receive a smaller commission than sales over $500,000 each quarter). Although this method motivates sales personnel to escalate their selling efforts, it offers them little financial security, and it can be difficult for sales managers to maintain control over the sales force. Many new salespeople indicate a reluctance to

straight salary compensation plan Paying salespeople a specific amount per time period, regardless of selling effort

straight commission compensation plan Paying salespeople according to the amount of their sales in a given time period

Figure 19.2 Average Salaries for Sales Representatives

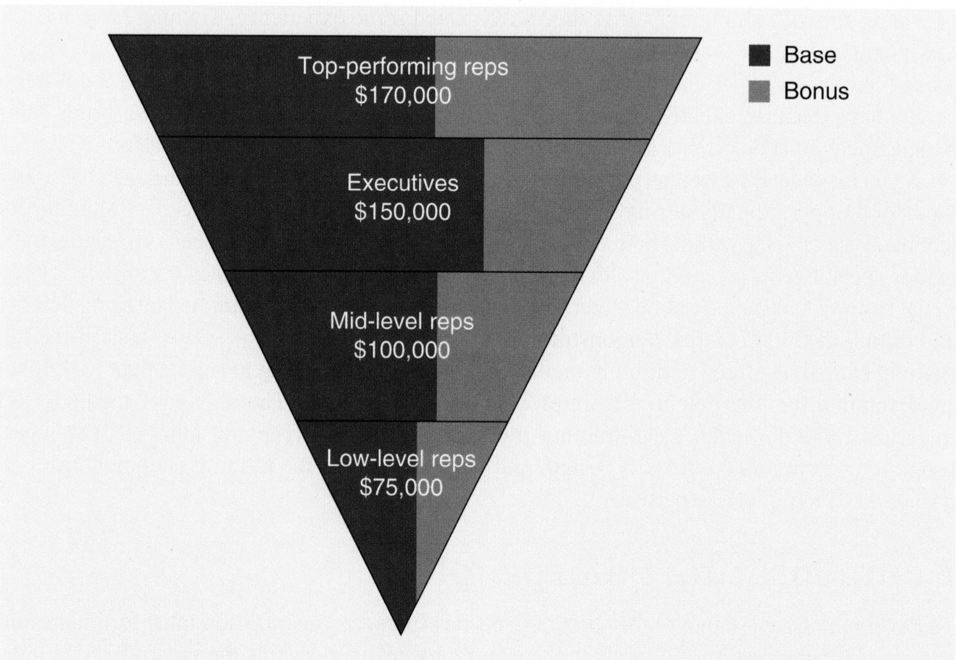

Source: Adapted from Joseph Kornik, "What's It All Worth?" *Sales and Marketing Management,* May 2007, p. 29.

Table 19.2 Characteristics of Sales Force Compensation Methods

Compensation Method	Use (%)*	When Especially Useful	Advantages	Disadvantages
Straight salary	17.5	Compensating new salespeople; firm moves into new sales territories that require developmental work; sales requiring lengthy presale and postsale services	Gives salespeople security; gives sales managers control over salespeople; easy to administer; yields more predictable selling expenses	Provides no incentive; necessitates closer supervision of salespeople; during sales declines, selling expenses remain constant
Straight commission	14	Highly aggressive selling is required; nonselling tasks are minimized; company uses contractors and part-timers	Provides maximum amount of incentive; by increasing commission rate, sales managers can encourage salespeople to sell certain items; selling expenses relate directly to sales resources	Salespeople have little financial security; sales managers have minimum control over sales force; may cause salespeople to give inadequate service to smaller accounts; selling costs less predictable
Combination	68.5	Sales territories have relatively similar sales potential; firm wishes to provide incentive but still control sales force activities	Provides certain level of financial security; provides some incentive; can move sales force efforts in profitable direction	Selling expenses less predictable; may be difficult to administer

*The figures are computed from *Dartnell's 30th Sales Force Compensation Survey,* Dartnell Corporation, Chicago, 1999.
Source: Charles Futrell, *Sales Management* (Ft. Worth: Dryden Press, 2001), 307–316.

accept the risks associated with straight commission. However, more experienced salespeople know this option can provide the greatest income potential. For these reasons, many firms offer a **combination compensation plan** in which salespeople receive a fixed salary plus a commission based on sales volume. Some combination programs require that a salesperson exceed a certain sales level before earning a commission; others offer commissions for any level of sales.

When selecting a compensation method, sales management weighs the advantages and disadvantages listed in the table. Researchers have found that higher commissions are the most preferred reward, followed by pay increases, yet preferences on pay tend to vary, depending upon the industry.[34] The Container Store, which markets do-it-yourself organizing and storage products, prefers to pay its sales staff salaries that are 50 to 100 percent higher than those offered by rivals instead of basing pay on commission plans.[35] When sales fell for the first time in 30 years, the Container Store refused to lay off staff like other companies were doing. Instead, the company froze salaries and 401(k) matches for everyone in the company and introduced sales contests as a way to motivate staff.[36]

Motivating Salespeople

Although financial compensation is an important incentive, additional programs are necessary for motivating sales personnel. The nature of the jobs, job security, and pay are considered to be the most important factors for the college student going into the sales area today.[37] A sales manager should develop a systematic approach for motivating salespeople to be productive. Effective sales force motivation is achieved through an organized set of activities performed continuously by the company's sales management.

combination compensation plan Paying salespeople a fixed salary plus a commission based on sales volume

Motivating Salespeople
Trips or vacation packages are rewards that a high-performing salesperson might receive for surpassing his or her sales goals.

Sales personnel, like other people, join organizations to satisfy personal needs and achieve personal goals. Sales managers must identify those needs and goals and strive to create an organizational climate that allows each salesperson to fulfill them. Enjoyable working conditions, power and authority, job security, and opportunity to excel are effective motivators, as are company efforts to make sales jobs more productive and efficient. At the Container Store, for example, first-year sales personnel receive 263 hours of training about the company's products.[38] A strong positive corporate culture leads to higher levels of job satisfaction and organizational commitment and lower levels of job stress.[39]

Sales contests and other incentive programs can also be effective motivators. These can motivate salespeople to increase sales or add new accounts, promote special items, achieve greater volume per sales call, and cover territories more thoroughly. However, companies need to understand salespersons' preferences when designing contests in order to make them effective in increasing sales. Some companies find such contests powerful tools for motivating sales personnel to achieve company goals. Managers should be careful to craft sales contests that support a strong customer orientation as well as motivate salespeople. In smaller firms lacking the resources for a formal incentive program, a simple but public "thank you" and the recognition from management at a sales meeting, along with a small-denomination gift card, can be very rewarding.

Salesperson turnover is one of the most critical concerns of organizations. Lower organizational commitment has been found to relate directly to job turnover. Identifying with the organization and performance are tied directly to organizational commitment that reduces turnover.[40] Properly designed incentive programs pay for themselves many times over, and sales managers are relying on incentives more than ever. Recognition programs that acknowledge outstanding performance with symbolic awards, such as plaques, can be very effective when carried out in a peer setting. The most common incentive offered by companies is cash, followed by gift cards and travel.[41] Travel reward programs can confer a high-profile honor, provide a unique experience that makes recipients feel special, and build camaraderie among award-winning salespeople. However, some recipients of travel awards may feel they already travel too much on the job. Cash rewards are easy to administer, are always appreciated by recipients, and appeal to all demographic groups. However, cash has no visible "trophy" value and provides few "bragging rights." The benefits of awarding merchandise are that the items have visible trophy value. In addition, recipients who are allowed to select the merchandise experience a sense of control, and merchandise awards can help build momentum for the sales force. The disadvantages of using merchandise are that employees may have lower perceived value of the merchandise and the company may experience greater administrative problems. Some companies outsource their incentive programs to companies that specialize in the creation and management of such programs.

Managing Sales Territories

The effectiveness of a sales force that must travel to customers is somewhat influenced by management's decisions regarding sales territories. When deciding on territories, sales managers must consider size, geographic shape, routing, and scheduling.

Creating Sales Territories

Several factors enter into the design of a sales territory's size and geographic shape. First, sales managers must construct territories that allow sales potential to be measured. Sales territories often consist of several geographic units, such as census tracts, cities, counties, or states, for which market data are obtainable. Sales managers usually try to create territories with similar sales potential, or requiring about the same amount of work. If territories have equal sales potential, they will almost always be unequal in geographic size. Salespeople with larger territories have to work longer and harder to generate a certain sales volume. Conversely, if sales territories requiring equal amounts of work are created, sales potential for those territories will often vary. Think about the effort required to sell in New York and Connecticut versus the sales effort required in a larger, less populated area like Montana and Wyoming. If sales personnel are partially or fully compensated through commissions, they will have unequal income potential. Many sales managers try to balance territorial workloads and earning potential by using differential commission rates. At times, sales managers use commercial programs to help them balance sales territories. Although a sales manager seeks equity when developing and maintaining sales territories, some inequities always prevail. A territory's size and geographical shape should also help the sales force provide the best possible customer coverage and minimize selling costs. Customer density and distribution are important factors.

Routing and Scheduling Salespeople

The geographic size and shape of a sales territory are the most important factors affecting the routing and scheduling of sales calls. Next in importance is the number and distribution of customers within the territory, followed by sales call frequency and duration. Those in charge of routing and scheduling must consider the sequence in which customers are called on, specific roads or transportation schedules to be used, number of calls to be made in a given period, and time of day the calls will occur. In some firms, salespeople plan their own routes and schedules with little or no assistance from the sales manager. In others, the sales manager maintains significant responsibility. No matter who plans the routing and scheduling, the major goals should be to minimize salespeople's nonselling time (time spent traveling and waiting) and maximize their selling time. Sales managers should try to achieve these goals so that a salesperson's travel and lodging costs are held to a minimum.

Controlling and Evaluating Sales Force Performance

To control and evaluate sales force performance properly, sales management needs information. A sales manager cannot observe the field sales force daily and, thus, relies on salespeople's call reports, customer feedback, contracts, and invoices. Call reports identify the customers called on and present detailed information about interactions with those clients. Sales personnel must often file work schedules indicating where they plan to be during specific time periods. Data about a salesperson's interactions with customers and prospects can

Evaluating Sales Performance
Sales force managers can use Xactly Incent to manage compensation plans based on sales force performance criteria. Evaluating sales force performance is crucial in determining whether sales goals are being met as well as determining areas of improvement.

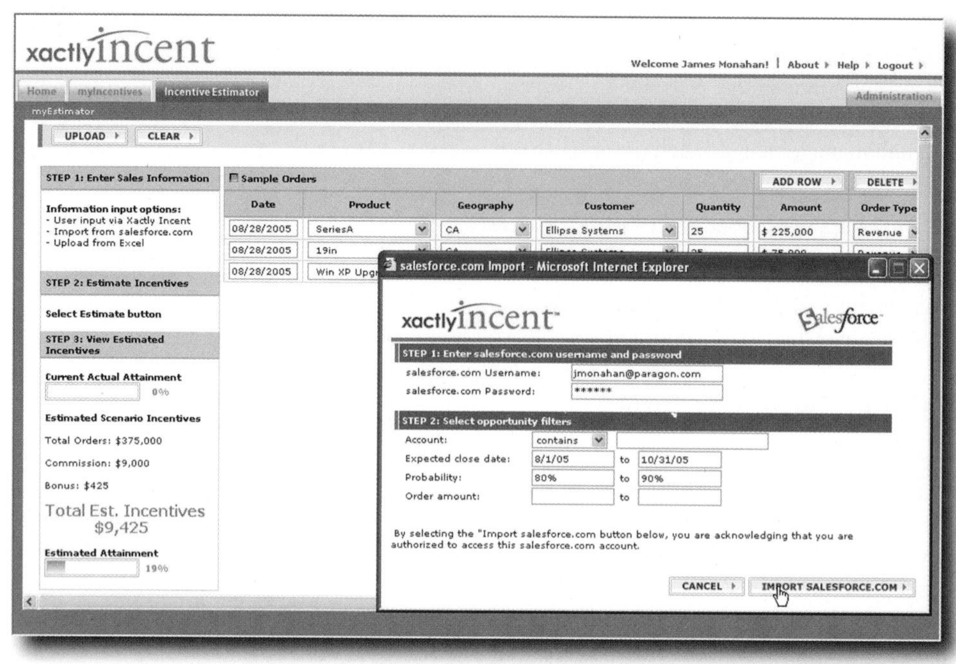

be included in the company's customer relationship management system. This information provides insights about the salesperson's performance.

Dimensions used to measure a salesperson's performance are determined largely by sales objectives, normally set by the sales manager. If an individual's sales objective is stated in terms of sales volume, that person should be evaluated on the basis of sales volume generated. Even if a salesperson is assigned a major objective, he or she is ordinarily expected to achieve several related objectives as well. Thus, salespeople are often judged along several dimensions. Sales managers evaluate many performance indicators, including average number of calls per day, average sales per customer, actual sales relative to sales potential, number of new-customer orders, average cost per call, and average gross profit per customer.

To evaluate a salesperson, a sales manager may compare one or more of these dimensions with predetermined performance standards. However, sales managers commonly compare a salesperson's performance with that of other employees operating under similar selling conditions or the salesperson's current performance with past performance. Sometimes, management judges factors that have less direct bearing on sales performance, such as personal appearance, product knowledge, and ethical standards. One concern is the tendency to reprimand top sellers less severely than poor performers for engaging in unethical selling practices.

After evaluating salespeople, sales managers take any needed corrective action to improve sales force performance. They may adjust performance standards, provide additional training, or try other motivational methods. Corrective action may demand comprehensive changes in the sales force.

THE NATURE OF SALES PROMOTION

sales promotion An activity and/or material intended to induce resellers or salespeople to sell a product or consumers to buy it

Sales promotion is an activity or material, or both, that acts as a direct inducement, offering added value or incentive for the product, to resellers, salespeople, or consumers. It encompasses all promotional activities and materials other than personal selling, advertising, and public relations. The retailer Payless, for example, often offers buy-one-get-one-free sales on its shoes, a sales promotion tactic known as a bonus or premium. In competitive markets, where products are very similar, sales promotion provides additional inducements that encourage product trial and purchase.

Marketers often use sales promotion to facilitate personal selling, advertising, or both. Companies also employ advertising and personal selling to support sales promotion activities. For example, marketers frequently use advertising to promote contests, free samples, and premiums. The most effective sales promotion efforts are highly interrelated with other promotional activities. Decisions regarding sales promotion often affect advertising and personal selling decisions, and vice versa.

Sales promotion can increase sales by providing extra purchasing incentives. Many opportunities exist to motivate consumers, resellers, and salespeople to take desired actions. Some kinds of sales promotion are designed specifically to stimulate resellers' demand and effectiveness, some are directed at increasing consumer demand, and some focus on both consumers and resellers. Regardless of the purpose, marketers must ensure that sales promotion objectives are consistent with the organization's overall objectives, as well as with its marketing and promotion objectives.

When deciding which sales promotion methods to use, marketers must consider several factors, particularly product characteristics (price, size, weight, costs, durability, uses, features, and hazards) and target market characteristics (age, gender, income, location, density, usage rate, and shopping patterns). How products are distributed and the number and types of resellers may determine the type of method used. The competitive and legal environment may also influence the choice.

The use of sales promotion has increased dramatically over the past 30 years, primarily at the expense of advertising. This shift in how promotional dollars are used has occurred for several reasons. Heightened concerns about value have made customers more responsive to promotional offers, especially price discounts and point-of-purchase displays. Thanks to their size and access to checkout scanner data, retailers have gained considerable power in the supply chain and are demanding greater promotional efforts from manufacturers to boost retail profits. Declines in brand loyalty have produced an environment in which sales promotions aimed at persuading customers to switch brands are more effective. Finally, the stronger emphasis placed on improving short-term performance results calls for greater use of sales promotion methods that yield quick (although perhaps short-lived) sales increases.[42]

In the remainder of this chapter, we examine several consumer and trade sales promotion methods, including what they entail and what goals they can help marketers achieve.

Consumer Sales Promotion Methods

Consumer sales promotion methods encourage or stimulate consumers to patronize specific retail stores or try particular products. Consumer sales promotion methods initiated by retailers often aim to attract customers to specific locations, whereas those used by manufacturers generally introduce new products or promote established brands. In this section, we discuss coupons, cents-off offers, money refunds and rebates, frequent-user incentives, point-of-purchase displays, demonstrations, free samples, premiums, consumer contests and games, and consumer sweepstakes.

Coupons

Coupons reduce a product's price and aim to prompt customers to try new or established products, increase sales volume quickly, attract repeat purchasers, or introduce new package sizes or features. Savings are deducted from the purchase price. Coupons are the most widely used consumer sales promotion technique. Although coupon usage had been spiraling downward for years, the economic downturn reversed this trend. In 2011, 3.5 billion coupons were redeemed for consumer-packaged goods alone.[43] Digital coupons via websites and mobile apps are also becoming popular. Social deal sites like Groupon, Living Social, and Crowd Cut, while not exactly in the coupon area, are encouraging consumers to look for deals or better prices. To take advantage of the new consumer interest in coupons, digital marketing—including mobile, social, and other platforms—are being used for couponing. For instance, Cold Stone Creamery is increasingly using digital coupons as incentives, allocating 20 percent of its

consumer sales promotion methods Sales promotion techniques that encourage consumers to patronize specific stores or try particular products

coupons Written price reductions used to encourage consumers to buy a specific product

Courtesy of Sara Lee Corporation

Coupons

Coupons began to make a comeback during the latest recession. While more people are getting coupons online, print materials are still a major source of coupons for many consumers.

couponing budget toward digital coupons. However, print coupons are still the most widely used and have the most redemption value.[44]

For best results, coupons should be easily recognized and state the offer clearly. The nature of the product (seasonal demand for it, life-cycle stage, and frequency of purchase) is the prime consideration in setting up a coupon promotion. Paper coupons are distributed on and inside packages, through freestanding inserts, in print advertising, on the back of cash register receipts, and through direct mail. Electronic coupons are distributed online, via in-store kiosks, through shelf dispensers in stores, and at checkout counters.[45] Figure 19.3 indicates that nearly half of the Internet users in the United States have used digital coupons, and this number is likely to grow. When deciding on the distribution method for coupons, marketers should consider strategies and objectives, redemption rates, availability, circulation, and exclusivity. The coupon distribution and redemption arena has become very competitive. To avoid losing customers, many grocery stores will redeem any coupons offered by competitors. Also, to draw customers to their stores, grocers double and sometimes even triple the value of customers' coupons.

Coupons offer several advantages. Print advertisements with coupons are often more effective at generating brand awareness than print ads without coupons. Generally, the larger the coupon's cash offer, the better the recognition generated. Coupons reward current product users, win back former users, and encourage purchases in larger quantities. Because they are returned, coupons also help a manufacturer determine whether it reached the intended target market. The advantages of using

Figure 19.3 U.S. Adult Online Coupon Users, 2009–2013

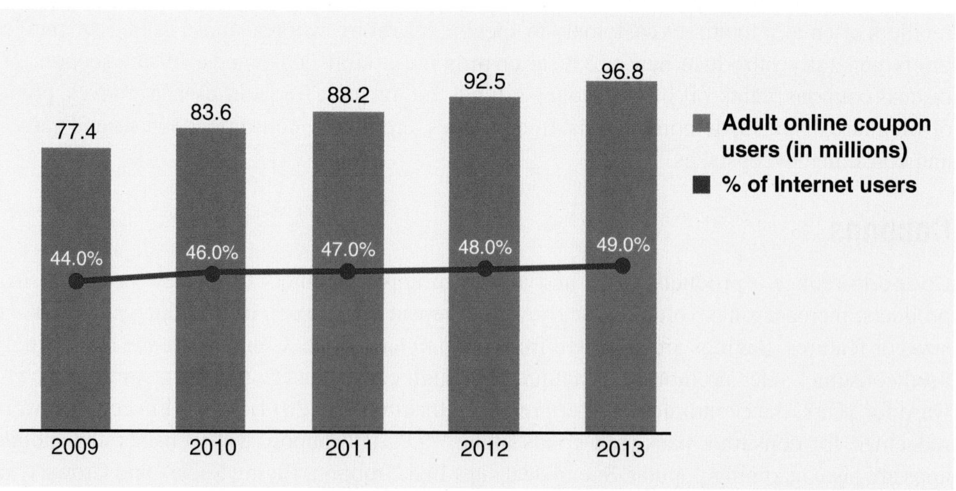

Note: Internet users ages 18+ who redeemed an online coupon/code for online or offline shopping in the past year; includes group-buying coupons and coupons/codes accessed via mobile browser or e-mail.

Source: *eMarketer*, May 2011, http://www.emarketer.com/blog/index.php/quick-stat-47-percent-online-consumers-will-redeem-digital-coupons-in-201/ (accessed April 3, 2012).

Going Green

E-Coupons Benefit a Variety of Stakeholders—Including the Environment

While coupon redemption rates have been falling in the last decade, recent years have seen an uptick in coupon usage. In fact, electronic coupon (e-coupon) redemption rates are growing rapidly. The increasing use of e-coupons benefits consumers, manufacturers, and the environment. E-coupons seem less intrusive than paper coupons, and with the growth of websites like Coupons.com, consumers can search for the digital coupons they want at their leisure. One growing trend in electronic couponing is the use of mobile devices. One study revealed that 46 percent of those owning mobile devices are willing to try mobile coupons. Manufacturers like mobile coupons as well, because they are 10 times more likely to be redeemed than paper coupons.

E-coupons also benefit the environment. They save paper because consumers can print only those coupons they want. Some stores even allow consumers to download e-coupons directly onto their rewards cards, which eliminates paper use entirely. From the manufacturer's standpoint, e-coupons reduce the costs—in paper and energy—of having to deliver coupons through direct mail. Indeed, 45 percent of people indicate that they prefer receiving mobile coupons through text messages. As more businesses and consumers realize the advantages of e-coupons, this sales promotion is likely to skyrocket.[d]

electronic coupons over paper coupons include lower cost per redemption, greater targeting ability, improved data-gathering capabilities, and greater experimentation capabilities to determine optimal face values and expiration cycles.[46]

Drawbacks of coupon use include fraud and misredemption, which can be expensive for manufacturers. Coupon fraud—including counterfeit Internet coupons as well as coupons cashed in under false retailer names—costs manufacturers hundreds of millions in losses each year.[47] Another disadvantage, according to some experts, is that coupons are losing their value; because so many manufacturers offer them, consumers have learned not to buy without some incentive, whether that pertains to a coupon, a rebate, or a refund. Furthermore, brand loyalty among heavy coupon users has diminished, and many consumers redeem coupons only for products they normally buy. It is believed that about three-fourths of coupons are redeemed by people already using the brand on the coupon. Thus, coupons have questionable success as an incentive for consumers to try a new brand or product. An additional problem with coupons is that stores often do not have enough of the coupon item in stock. This situation generates ill will toward both the store and the product.

cents-off offers Promotions that allow buyers to pay less than the regular price to encourage purchase

Source: RedPlum Survey of 23,000 adults.

Cents-Off Offers

With **cents-off offers**, buyers pay a certain amount less than the regular price shown on the label or package. Like coupons, this method can serve as a strong incentive for trying new or unfamiliar products and is commonly used in product introductions. It can stimulate product sales or multiple purchases, yield short-lived sales increases, and promote products during off-seasons. It is an easy method to control and is often used for specific purposes. If used on an ongoing basis, however, cents-off offers reduce the price for customers who would buy at the regular price and may also cheapen a product's image. In addition, the method often requires special handling by retailers who are responsible for giving the discount at the point of sale.

Money Refunds

With **money refunds**, consumers submit proof of purchase and are mailed a specific amount of money. Usually, manufacturers demand multiple product purchases before consumers qualify for money refunds. Marketers employ money refunds as an alternative to coupons to stimulate sales. Money refunds, used primarily to promote trial use of a product, are relatively low in cost. However, they sometimes generate a low response rate and, thus, have limited impact on sales.

Rebates

With **rebates**, the consumer is sent a specified amount of money for making a single product purchase. Rebates are generally given on more expensive products than money refunds and are used to encourage customers. Marketers also use rebates to reinforce brand loyalty and encourage product purchase. On larger items, such as cars, rebates are often given at the point of sale. Most rebates, however, especially on smaller items, are given after the sale, usually through a mail-in process. Research suggests that these mail-in rebates are most effective in situations where consumers require a reason to purchase an item. On the other hand, rebates for products that provide instant gratification are more effective if provided at the point of purchase.[48]

One problem with money refunds and rebates is that many people perceive the redemption process as too complicated. According to one estimate, at least 40 percent of consumers do not get their money back, because they fail to meet the requirements. Due to the high level of customer complaints, Best Buy eliminated mail-in rebates several years ago.[49] To eliminate these complications, many marketers allow customers to apply for a rebate online, which eliminates the need for forms that may confuse customers and frustrate retailers. Consumers might also have negative perceptions of manufacturers' reasons for offering rebates. They may believe the products are untested or have not sold well. If these perceptions are not changed, rebate offers may actually degrade product image and desirability.

Frequent-User Incentives

Greeting cards aren't the only products offered by Hallmark. To reward loyal customers, the company offers the Hallmark Crown Card, which allows frequent greeting card buyers to accrue points that are redeemable for merchandise and discounts.[50] Many firms develop incentive programs to reward customers who engage in repeat (frequent) purchases. For example, most major airlines offer frequent-flyer programs that reward customers who have flown a specified number of miles with free tickets for additional travel. Frequent-user incentives foster customer loyalty to a specific company or group of cooperating companies. They are favored by service businesses, such as airlines, auto rental agencies, hotels, and local coffee shops. Frequent-user programs not only reward loyal customers but also generate data that can contribute significant information about customers that helps marketers foster desirable customer relationships.

money refunds Sales promotion techniques that offer consumers a specified amount of money when they mail in a proof of purchase, usually for multiple product purchases

rebates Sales promotion techniques in which a consumer receives a specified amount of money for making a single product purchase

point-of-purchase (POP) materials Signs, window displays, display racks, and similar devices used to attract customers

Point-of-Purchase Materials and Demonstrations

Point-of-purchase (POP) materials include outdoor signs, window displays, counter pieces, display racks, and self-service cartons. Innovations in POP displays include sniff-teasers, which give off a product's aroma in the store as consumers walk within a radius of four feet,

© AP Images/PRNewsFoto/Capital One

Frequent-User Incentives
Actor Alec Baldwin, the spokesperson for Capital One, shows off the Venture Rewards credit card. Users of the credit card receive airline mileage when they make purchases. The more that customers use the card, the more airline miles they receive.

and computerized interactive displays. These items, often supplied by producers, attract attention, inform customers, and encourage retailers to carry particular products. Retailers have also begun experimenting with new forms of POP technology. For example, Macy's tested an interactive touchscreen called Beauty Spot kiosk at its stores. The kiosk allows consumers to browse through the company's cosmetics at their leisure.[51] A retailer is likely to use point-of-purchase materials if they are attractive, informative, well-constructed, and in harmony with the store's image.

Demonstrations are excellent attention-getters. Manufacturers offer them temporarily to encourage trial use and purchase of a product or to show how a product works. Because labor costs can be extremely high, demonstrations are not used widely. They can be highly effective for promoting certain types of products, such as appliances, cosmetics, and cleaning supplies. Even automobiles can be demonstrated, not only by a salesperson but also by the prospective buyer during a test drive. Cosmetics marketers, such as Estée Lauder and Clinique, sometimes offer potential customers "makeovers" to demonstrate product benefits and proper application.

Free Samples

Marketers use **free samples** to stimulate trial of a product, increase sales volume in the early stages of a product's life cycle, and obtain desirable distribution. Trader Joe's gives out free samples of its coffee hoping to entice buyers to make a purchase. Sampling is the most expensive sales promotion method because production and distribution—at local events, by mail or door-to-door delivery, online, in stores, and on packages—entail high costs. However, it can also be one of the most effective sales promotion methods: a survey by the Promotion Marketing Association's Product Sampling Council found that 92 percent of respondents said they would buy a new product that they had sampled and liked. Nonetheless, sampling's expense remains a key reason it is not used more often.[52]

Many consumers prefer to get their samples by mail. Other consumers like to sample new food products at supermarkets or try samples of new recipes featuring foods they already like. In designing a free sample, marketers should consider factors like seasonal demand for the product, market characteristics, and prior advertising. Free samples are usually inappropriate

demonstrations Sales promotion methods a manufacturer uses temporarily to encourage trial use and purchase of a product or to show how a product works

free samples Samples of a product given out to encourage trial and purchase

Free Samples
Companies, such as World's Best Cat Litter, offer free samples to encourage product trial and adoption.

for slow-turnover products. Despite high costs, use of sampling is increasing. In a given year, almost three-fourths of consumer products companies may use sampling. Distribution of free samples through websites like StartSampling.com and FreeSamples.com is growing.

Premiums

Premiums are items offered free or at a minimal cost as a bonus for purchasing a product. Like the prize in the Cracker Jack box, premiums are used to attract competitors' customers, introduce different sizes of established products, add variety to other promotional efforts, and stimulate consumer loyalty. Consumers appear to prefer premiums to discounts on products due to the perception that they are receiving something "free."[53] Creativity is essential when using premiums; to stand out and achieve a significant number of redemptions, the premium must match both the target audience and the brand's image. Premiums must also be easily recognizable and desirable. Consumers are more favorable toward a premium when the brand has high equity and there is a good fit between the product and the premium.[54] Premiums are placed on or inside packages and can also be distributed by retailers or through the mail. Examples include a service station giving a free car wash with a fill-up, a free shaving cream with the purchase of a razor, and a free plastic storage box with the purchase of Kraft Cheese Singles.

Consumer Contests

In **consumer contests**, individuals compete for prizes based on their analytical or creative skills. This method can be used to generate retail traffic and frequency of exposure to promotional messages. Contestants are usually more highly involved in consumer contests than in games or sweepstakes, even though total participation may be lower. Contests may also be used in conjunction with other sales promotional methods, such as coupons. Dunkin' Donuts holds a Create Dunkin's Next Donut Contest that gives consumers the chance to create their own donut idea and submit it to the company for the chance to win prizes. The grand prize winner wins $12,000 and might see his or her donut sold by the company as a Limited Edition donut.[55]

Consumer Games

In **consumer games**, individuals compete for prizes based primarily on chance—often by collecting game pieces like bottle caps or a sticker on a carton of French fries. Because collecting multiple pieces may be necessary to win or increase an individual's chances of winning, the game stimulates repeated business. Development and management of consumer games is often outsourced to an independent public relations firm, which can help marketers navigate federal and state laws that regulate games. Although games may stimulate sales temporarily, there is no evidence to suggest that they affect a company's long-term sales.

Marketers considering games should exercise care. Problems or errors may anger customers and could result in a lawsuit. McDonald's' wildly popular Monopoly game promotion, in which customers collect Monopoly real estate pieces on drink and French fry packages, has been tarnished by past fraud after a crime ring, including employees of the promotional firm running the game, was convicted of stealing millions of dollars in winning game pieces. McDonald's later reintroduced the Monopoly game with heightened security.[56]

premiums Items offered free or at a minimal cost as a bonus for purchasing a product

consumer contests Sales promotion methods in which individuals compete for prizes based on their analytical or creative skills

consumer games Sales promotion methods in which individuals compete for prizes based primarily on chance

Sweepstakes

Entrants in a **consumer sweepstakes** submit their names for inclusion in a drawing for prizes. The Travel Channel awarded one Grand Prize Winner a trip for two to Belize that included first-class hotel accommodations.[57] Sweepstakes are employed more often than consumer contests and tend to attract a greater number of participants. However, contestants are usually more involved in consumer contests and games than in sweepstakes, even though total participation may be lower. Contests, games, and sweepstakes may be used in conjunction with other sales promotion methods like coupons.

© AP Images/PRNewsFoto/NIVEA

Sweepstakes
NIVEA Facebook fans had the chance to enter into a consumer sweepstakes to win tickets to a live Rihanna concert.

Trade Sales Promotion Methods

To encourage resellers, especially retailers, to carry their products and promote them effectively, producers use trade sales promotion methods. **Trade sales promotion methods** attempt to persuade wholesalers and retailers to carry a producer's products and market them more aggressively. Marketers use trade sales methods for many reasons, including countering the effect of lower-priced store brands, passing along a discount to a price-sensitive market segment, boosting brand exposure among target consumers, or providing additional incentives to move excess inventory or counteract competitors. These methods include buying allowances, buy-back allowances, scan-back allowances, merchandise allowances, cooperative advertising, dealer listings, free merchandise, dealer loaders, premium or push money, and sales contests.

Trade Allowances

Many manufacturers offer trade allowances to encourage resellers to carry a product or stock more of it. One such trade allowance is a **buying allowance**, a temporary price reduction offered to resellers for purchasing specified quantities of a product. A soap producer, for example, might give retailers $1 for each case of soap purchased. Such offers provide an incentive for resellers to handle new products, achieve temporary price reductions, or stimulate purchase of items in larger-than-normal quantities. The buying allowance, which takes the form of money, yields profits to resellers and is simple and straightforward. There are no restrictions on how resellers use the money, which increases the method's effectiveness. One drawback of buying allowances is that customers may buy "forward"—that is, buy large amounts that keep them supplied for many months. Another problem is that competitors may match (or beat) the reduced price, which can lower profits for all sellers.

A **buy-back allowance** is a sum of money that a producer gives to a reseller for each unit the reseller buys after an initial promotional deal is over. This method is a secondary incentive in which the total amount of money resellers receive is proportional to their purchases during an initial consumer promotion, such as a coupon offer. Buy-back allowances foster cooperation during an initial sales promotion effort and stimulate repurchase afterward. The main disadvantage of this method is expense.

A **scan-back allowance** is a manufacturer's reward to retailers based on the number of pieces moved through the retailers' scanners during a specific time period. To participate in scan-back programs, retailers are usually expected to pass along savings to consumers through special pricing. Scan-backs are becoming widely used by manufacturers because they link trade spending directly to product movement at the retail level.

A **merchandise allowance** is a manufacturer's agreement to pay resellers certain amounts of money for providing promotional efforts like advertising or point of-purchase displays. This method is best suited to high-volume, high-profit, easily handled products. A drawback is that

consumer sweepstakes A sales promotion in which entrants submit their names for inclusion in a drawing for prizes

trade sales promotion methods Methods intended to persuade wholesalers and retailers to carry a producer's products and market them aggressively

buying allowance A temporary price reduction to resellers for purchasing specified quantities of a product

buy-back allowance A sum of money given to a reseller for each unit bought after an initial promotion deal is over

scan-back allowance A manufacturer's reward to retailers based on the number of pieces scanned

merchandise allowance A manufacturer's agreement to pay resellers certain amounts of money for providing special promotional efforts, such as setting up and maintaining a display

some retailers perform activities at a minimally acceptable level simply to obtain allowances. Before paying retailers, manufacturers usually verify their performance. Manufacturers hope that retailers' additional promotional efforts will yield substantial sales increases.

Cooperative Advertising and Dealer Listings

Cooperative advertising is an arrangement in which a manufacturer agrees to pay a certain amount of a retailer's media costs for advertising the manufacturer's products. The amount allowed is usually based on the quantities purchased. As with merchandise allowances, a retailer must show proof that advertisements did appear before the manufacturer pays the agreed-upon portion of the advertising costs. These payments give retailers additional funds for advertising. Some retailers exploit cooperative-advertising agreements by crowding too many products into one advertisement. Not all available cooperative-advertising dollars are used. Some retailers cannot afford to advertise, while others can afford it but do not want to advertise. A large proportion of all cooperative-advertising dollars is spent on newspaper advertisements.

Dealer listings are advertisements promoting a product and identifying participating retailers that sell the product. Dealer listings can influence retailers to carry the product, build traffic at the retail level, and encourage consumers to buy the product at participating dealers.

cooperative advertising An arrangement in which a manufacturer agrees to pay a certain amount of a retailer's media costs for advertising the manufacturer's products

dealer listings Advertisements that promote a product and identify the names of participating retailers that sell the product

free merchandise A manufacturer's reward given to resellers that purchase a stated quantity of products

dealer loader A gift, often part of a display, given to a retailer that purchases a specified quantity of merchandise

premium money (push money) Extra compensation to salespeople for pushing a line of goods

sales contest A sales promotion method used to motivate distributors, retailers, and sales personnel through recognition of outstanding achievements

Free Merchandise and Gifts

Manufacturers sometimes offer **free merchandise** to resellers that purchase a stated quantity of products. Occasionally, free merchandise is used as payment for allowances provided through other sales promotion methods. To avoid handling and bookkeeping problems, the "free" merchandise usually takes the form of a reduced invoice.

A **dealer loader** is a gift to a retailer that purchases a specified quantity of merchandise. Dealer loaders are often used to obtain special display efforts from retailers by offering essential display parts as premiums. For example, a manufacturer might design a display that includes a sterling silver tray as a major component and give the tray to the retailer. Marketers use dealer loaders to obtain new distributors and push larger quantities of goods.

Premium Money

Premium money (push money) is additional compensation offered by the manufacturer to salespeople as an incentive to push a line of goods. This method is appropriate when personal selling is an important part of the marketing effort; it is not effective for promoting products sold through self-service. Premium money often helps a manufacturer obtain a commitment from the sales force, but it can be very expensive. The use of this incentive must be in compliance with retailers' policies as well as state and local laws.

Sales Contest

A **sales contest** is designed to motivate distributors, retailers, and sales personnel by recognizing outstanding achievements. To be effective, this method must be equitable for all individuals involved. One advantage is that it can achieve participation at all distribution levels. Positive effects may be temporary, however, and prizes are usually expensive.

Summary

1. To understand the major purposes of personal selling

Personal selling is the process of informing customers and persuading them to purchase products through paid personal communication in an exchange situation. The three general purposes of personal selling are finding prospects, persuading them to buy, and keeping customers satisfied.

2. To describe the basic steps in the personal selling process

Many salespeople, either consciously or unconsciously, move through a general selling process as they sell products. In prospecting, the salesperson develops a database of potential customers. Before contacting prospects, the salesperson conducts a preapproach that involves finding and analyzing information about prospects and their needs. The approach is the manner in which the salesperson contacts potential customers. During the sales presentation, the salesperson must attract and hold the prospect's attention to stimulate interest and desire for the product. If possible, the salesperson should handle objections as they arise. During the closing, the salesperson asks the prospect to buy the product or products. After a successful closing, the salesperson must follow up the sale.

3. To identify the types of sales force personnel

In developing a sales force, marketing managers consider which types of salespeople will sell the firm's products most effectively. The three classifications of salespeople are order getters, order takers, and support personnel. Order getters inform both current customers and new prospects and persuade them to buy. Order takers seek repeat sales and fall into two categories: inside order takers and field order takers. Sales support personnel facilitate selling, but their duties usually extend beyond making sales.

4. To recognize new types of personal selling

The three types of support personnel are missionary, trade, and technical salespeople. The roles of salespeople are changing, resulting in an increased focus on team selling and relationship selling. Team selling involves the salesperson joining with people from the firm's financial, engineering, and other functional areas. Relationship selling involves building mutually beneficial long-term associations with a customer through regular communications over prolonged periods of time.

5. To understand sales management decisions and activities

Sales force management is an important determinant of a firm's success because the sales force is directly responsible for generating the organization's sales revenue. Major decision areas and activities are establishing sales force objectives; determining sales force size; recruiting, selecting, training, compensating, and motivating salespeople; managing sales territories; and controlling and evaluating sales force performance.

Sales objectives should be stated in precise, measurable terms and specify the time period and geographic areas involved. The size of the sales force must be adjusted occasionally because a firm's marketing plans change along with markets and forces in the marketing environment.

Recruiting and selecting salespeople involve attracting and choosing the right type of salesperson to maintain an effective sales force. When developing a training program, managers must consider a variety of dimensions, such as who should be trained, what should be taught, and how training should occur. Compensation of salespeople involves formulating and administering a compensation plan that attracts, motivates, and retains the right types of salespeople. Motivated salespeople should translate into high productivity. Managing sales territories focuses on such factors as size, shape, routing, and scheduling. To control and evaluate sales force performance, sales managers use information obtained through salespeople's call reports, customer feedback, and invoices.

6. To explain what sales promotion activities are and how they are used

Sales promotion is an activity or a material (or both) that acts as a direct inducement, offering added value or incentive for the product to resellers, salespeople, or consumers. Marketers use sales promotion to identify and attract new customers, introduce new products, and increase reseller inventories.

7. To explore specific consumer sales promotion methods

Sales promotion techniques fall into two general categories: consumer and trade. Consumer sales promotion methods encourage consumers to patronize specific stores or try a particular product. These sales promotion methods include coupons; cents-off offers; money refunds and rebates; frequent-user incentives; point-of-purchase displays; demonstrations; free samples and premiums; and consumer contests, games, and sweepstakes.

8. To explore trade sales promotion methods

Trade sales promotion techniques can motivate resellers to handle a manufacturer's products and market them aggressively. These sales promotion techniques include buying allowances, buy-back allowances, scan-back allowances, merchandise allowances, cooperative advertising, dealer listings, free merchandise, dealer loaders, premium (or push) money, and sales contests.

Go to www.cengagebrain.com for resources to help you master the content in this chapter as well as for materials that will expand your marketing knowledge!

Important Terms

personal selling 630
prospecting 633
approach 634
closing 635
order getters 636
order takers 637
support personnel 637
missionary salespeople 637
trade salespeople 638
technical salespeople 638
team selling 638
relationship selling 638
recruiting 641
straight salary compensation plan 644
straight commission compensation plan 644
combination compensation plan 645
sales promotion 648
consumer sales promotion methods 649
coupons 649
cents-off offers 651
money refunds 652
rebates 652
point-of-purchase (POP) materials 652
demonstrations 653
free samples 653
premiums 654
consumer contests 654
consumer games 654
consumer sweepstakes 655
trade sales promotion methods 655
buying allowance 655
buy-back allowance 655
scan-back allowance 655
merchandise allowance 655
cooperative advertising 656
dealer listings 656
free merchandise 656
dealer loader 656
premium money (push money) 656
sales contest 656

Discussion and Review Questions

1. What is personal selling? How does personal selling differ from other types of promotional activities?
2. What are the primary purposes of personal selling?
3. Identify the elements of the personal selling process. Must a salesperson include all these elements when selling a product to a customer? Why or why not?
4. How does a salesperson find and evaluate prospects? Do you consider any of these methods to be ethically questionable? Explain.
5. Are order getters more aggressive or creative than order takers? Why or why not?
6. Why are team selling and relationship selling becoming more prevalent?
7. Identify several characteristics of effective sales objectives.
8. How should a sales manager establish criteria for selecting sales personnel? What do you think are the general characteristics of a good salesperson?
9. What major issues or questions should management consider when developing a training program for the sales force?
10. Explain the major advantages and disadvantages of the three basic methods of compensating salespeople. In general, which method would you prefer? Why?
11. What major factors should be taken into account when designing the size and shape of a sales territory?
12. How does a sales manager, who cannot be with each salesperson in the field on a daily basis, control the performance of sales personnel?
13. What is sales promotion? Why is it used?
14. For each of the following, identify and describe three techniques and give several examples: (a) consumer sales promotion methods and (b) trade sales promotion methods.
15. What types of sales promotion methods have you observed recently? Comment on their effectiveness.

Application Questions

1. Briefly describe an experience you have had with a salesperson at a clothing store or an automobile dealership. Describe the steps the salesperson used. Did the salesperson skip any steps? What did the salesperson do well? Not so well? Would you describe the salesperson as an order getter, an order taker, or a support salesperson? Why? Did the salesperson perform more than one of these functions?
2. Leap Athletic Shoe Inc., a newly formed company, is in the process of developing a sales strategy. Market researchers have determined that sales management should segment the market into five regional territories. The sales potential

for the North region is $1.2 million; for the West region, $1 million; for the Central region, $1.3 million; for the South Central region, $1.1 million; and for the Southeast region, $1 million. The firm wishes to maintain some control over the training and sales processes because of the unique features of its new product line, but Leap marketers realize that the salespeople need to be fairly aggressive in their efforts to break into these markets. They would like to provide the incentive needed for the extra selling effort. What type of sales force compensation method would you recommend to Leap? Why?

3. Consumer sales promotions aim to increase sales of a particular retail store or product. Identify a familiar type of retail store or product. Recommend at least three sales promotion methods that could effectively promote the store or product. Explain why you would use these methods.
4. Producers use trade sales promotions to encourage resellers to promote their products more effectively. Identify which method or methods of sales promotion a producer might use in the following situations, and explain why the method would be appropriate.
   a. A golf ball manufacturer wants to encourage retailers to add a new type of golf ball to current product offerings.
   b. A life insurance company wants to increase sales of its universal life products, which have been lagging recently (the company has little control over sales activities).
   c. A light bulb manufacturer with an overproduction of light bulbs wants to encourage its grocery store chain resellers to increase their bulb inventories.
5. IMP In the cosmetics industry, sales promotions reign supreme. You manufacture and market organic skin creams, which are sold nationwide at your own "boutiques" inside various department stores. You are considering two different promotions for your newest lotion, which retails for $19.99. The first is providing free samples in select stores. Each sample will cost about 45 cents per customer. After carefully examining market research, you estimate that 15,000 customers will try the free sample, with 35 percent opting to purchase the product. The second promotion is a dollar-off coupon that provides a discount on select products. The coupons would be sent to all 100,000 current customers on your mailing list at a cost of 53 cents per customer. In the past, the coupons have had a 13 percent redemption rate. Which promotion would you adopt based upon the information provided? What is some additional information that could help you in choosing the best option?

Internet Exercise

TerrAlign

TerrAlign offers consulting services and software products designed to help a firm maximize control and deployment of its field sales representatives. See how the company provides sales territory management solutions by visiting www.terralign.com.

1. Identify three features of TerrAlign software that are likely to benefit salespeople.
2. Identify three features of TerrAlign software that are likely to benefit sales managers.
3. Why might field sales professionals object to the use of software from TerrAlign?

developing your marketing plan

When developing its marketing strategy, a company must consider the different forms of communication that are necessary to reach a variety of customers. Several types of promotion may be required. Knowledge of the advantages and disadvantages of each promotional element is necessary when developing the marketing plan. Consider the information in this chapter when evaluating your promotional mix:

1. Review the various types of salespeople described in this chapter. Given your promotional objectives (from Chapter 17), do any of these types of salespeople have a place in your promotional plan?
2. Identify the resellers in your distribution channel. Discuss the role that trade sales promotions to these resellers could play in the development of your promotional plan.
3. Evaluate each type of consumer sales promotion as it relates to accomplishing your promotional objectives.

The information obtained from these questions should assist you in developing various aspects of your marketing plan found in the "Interactive Marketing Plan" exercise at www.cengagebrain.com.

video case 19.1

Murray's Cheese Achieves Success through Personal Selling

For Murray's Cheese, personal selling is the driving force behind its success. The business has retail sales of $2,500 per square foot and a growth rate of 15 to 20 percent per year at its main store in Greenwich Village, New York. The company owns retail, wholesale, catering, and education businesses. It also has a partnership with the supermarket giant Kroger to bring Murray's customer-friendly environment to select Kroger supermarkets.

Murray's views personal selling as a core competency that sets itself apart from the competition. The key is to inform customers and persuade them to purchase products in a store environment. Murray's sales representatives understand the importance of a quick presentation, overcoming objections, and closing the sale.

Because Murray's wants its customers to be repeat buyers, there is an attempt to listen to customers, gain an understanding of their interests, and try to find the right product to satisfy their needs. Murray's Cheese began in 1940 as a wholesale butter and egg shop owned by Jewish Spanish Civil War Veteran Murray Greenberg. When the current president, Rob Kaufelt, purchased the shop in 1991, the store was little more than a local hole-in-the-wall. Kaufelt and his staff made the decision to focus on high-quality gourmet cheeses from around the world. Today, people come from all over to sample Murray's cheeses as well as take classes or attend its Cheese U boot camp to learn about cheese. Although Murray's has extended its product line to include gourmet meats, crackers, jam, chocolate, olives, pickles, and dried fruit, cheese remains its core product. In fact, Murray's Cheese has been voted by *Forbes* as "the best cheese shop." The company also received a very high rating for service in *Zagat's 2011 New York City Food Lover's Guide.*

© Yana Petruseva/Shutterstock.com

Murray's success prompted Kroger to seek it out as a partner in its supermarkets. Murray's Cheese shops can now be found in different Kroger supermarkets throughout the country. The cost that Murray's Cheese spent on advertising to become so successful: zero dollars. Instead of advertising, the company relies on in-store salespersons providing customer service and creating positive word-of-mouth communication to promote and secure its reputation.

When training its cheesemongers, the company recruits those who are passionate about both cheese and people. The company sets qualifications before beginning the recruiting process and identifies a set of traits characterizing effective salespeople who could become cheesemongers. All customers who enter Murray's Greenwich Village store get to taste free samples of cheese before they buy it. This sampling creates an image of Murray's Cheese as a customer-friendly company.

Customer relationships are so integral to Murray's that its cheesemongers taste the cheese with the customers. In this way, Murray's in-store sales force educates themselves about the cheeses they are selling and creates a valuable experience where the customer feels appreciated. "It's about sharing that knowledge and helping people have an experience that they wouldn't have been able to have on their own," said Liz Thorpe, vice president of Murray's Cheese. By establishing this unique experience, Murray's learns what customers are looking for and often succeeds in getting them to purchase more products at once and make repeat purchases.

This positive customer environment is what Murray's Cheese hopes to bring to Kroger. Those Kroger employees who sell Murray's cheeses undergo extensive training beforehand. Murray's even created a 300-page cheese service guide for these recruits. Kroger customers seem to appreciate the more attentive customer service they receive in these Murray-branded shops. In a pilot program where three Murray's Cheese shops replaced Kroger cheese departments, sales increased 50 to 100 percent. It was such a success that, under the new partnership, Murray's Cheese now has Murray's shops in Kroger supermarkets in Ohio, Georgia, Tennessee, and Texas, with plans for continued expansion.

Personal selling does not always have to be about traveling throughout sales territories, calling on prospects. Murray's in-store cheesemongers make and close sales doing what they do best: educating customers and sharing the gourmet cheese experience. With Kroger's success at promotion and Murray's strengths in personal selling, it looks to be a win-win situation for both partners. Murray's motivated cheesemongers help to satisfy the needs of their customers and achieve personal goals.[58]

Questions for Discussion

1. How would you explain the sales presentation that is most effective for selling Murray's cheese products?
2. How would you apply the concept of relationship selling to building long-term customers at Murray's Cheese?
3. Do you think that Murray's Cheese salespeople need extensive motivation and training?

case 19.2

Direct Selling in China Booms in the 21st Century

What activities come to mind when you think of the words "evil," "cultish," and "superstitious"? In China, the government has used these words to describe direct selling. Direct selling, to the benefit of consumers, involves marketing products through face-to-face sales presentations at home or in the workplace. With social media, this concept has expanded to digital person-to-person communication. In countries like China, direct selling, or as it is often called network selling, often finds prospects through relatives, friends, and neighbors. While direct selling was once criticized by the government as being a questionable activity, consumers in China respect direct selling and are aware that direct sales companies' products are often among the highest quality products available to consumers. Today, Amway's Nutrilite is the number one selling dietary supplement and the official supplement of the Chinese Olympic team.

The Chinese government's negative attitude toward direct selling was the result of prior abuses through illegal pyramid schemes, which led to riots. Pyramid schemes occur when money is exchanged for recruiting other people into the scheme. Leaders of successful schemes make the most money, while those who fail to recruit others lose out. Multilevel marketing, on the other hand, is a very legitimate activity; it is not designed to exploit others, and support is given to sell products directly to consumers.

In 2006, direct selling was allowed in China under the provision that pyramid schemes and multilevel selling were forbidden. In fact, multilevel selling and pyramid sales in China can result in serious fines and even criminal prosecution. Although some people in China still hold negative views toward direct selling, for many women, direct selling has gone from "evil" to "empowering." Today, direct selling is flourishing in China, offering women a way to earn income and maintain enough flexibility to perform domestic responsibilities.

In countries where women are not usually able to start their own businesses, direct selling offers advancement opportunities and training. Additionally, despite the worldwide economic downturn, items like cosmetics and Tupperware remain in high demand, enabling direct selling companies to flourish. Direct selling has become a multi-billion dollar industry, with Avon as a leading seller of beauty and related products. Avon sets up retail stores and provides the products to salespeople to sell directly to consumers on the streets and in their neighborhoods. Although Amway is known for being a multilevel marketer in the United States, it sells its products through the same system. The success of both of these companies has been incredible. For example, Amway's Nutrilite vitamins and Artistry cosmetics are market leaders. Direct selling cosmetics company Mary Kay also sees opportunities in China and anticipates that the country will become its largest market.

Some people do not view direct selling sales reps as authentic salespeople. But many products, even business-to-business products like telecommunications, financial services, and scientific solutions, are sold through direct selling channels. The basic approaches to personal selling are used by sales representatives from companies like Amway and Avon. The salespeople have to be involved in the personal selling process of prospecting, preapproach, approach, making the presentation, overcoming objections, and closing the sale. There are sales managers who have to recruit, train, and motivate the company's sales representatives. Many direct sales representatives develop long-term associations with the customers through regular communications over prolonged periods of time. Besides direct personal relationships and contacts, many of the sales reps are using social networking to simulate communication that would otherwise occur face-to-face. The importance of direct selling can be seen with global sales results of $10.9 billion for Amway, more than $11.3 billion for Avon, and total wholesale revenue of $66 billion for the industry. Today, there are more than 43 million sales representatives/distributors across the world.

Some Chinese officials still regard direct selling with suspicion since a common tactic of con artists is to pose as direct sellers. Therefore, China implemented laws limiting the ways direct selling companies could compensate their sales force and banned teachers, doctors, and civil servants from becoming direct sellers. Taking all of that into account, many direct sellers find the benefits outweigh the costs. Not only is direct selling flexible, it also helps women earn income in uncertain financial times when family members are out of work. Even women who do not earn much money in sales appreciate the flexibility and corporate culture. They look forward to the promise of future rewards with the company. Direct selling companies are also benefiting, with Mary Kay predicting a 30 percent sales increase in China. Although direct selling may be taken for granted in America, it is gaining an eager fan base among women in China.[59]

Questions for Discussion

1. Why are direct selling personal sales representatives legitimate or authentic salespeople?
2. Why do you think direct selling is even more successful in China than in the United States?
3. What are the social and economic benefits of the sales opportunities that are provided to women in developing countries?

strategic case 7

Indy Racing League (IRL) Focuses on Integrated Marketing Communications

For the first 17 years of its existence, the Championship Auto Racing Teams (known as CART and, later, as Champ Car) dominated auto racing in the United States. Open-wheel racing, involving cars whose wheels are located outside the body of the car rather than underneath the body or fenders as found on street cars, enjoyed greater notoriety than other forms of racing—including stock-car racing like NASCAR. However, not everyone associated with open-wheel racing in the United States welcomed the success enjoyed by CART. One person with major concerns about the direction of CART was Tony George, president of the Indianapolis Motor Speedway and founder of the Indianapolis 500.

© Mark Scheuern/Alamy

In 1994, George announced that he was creating a new open-wheel league that would compete with CART, beginning in 1996. The Indy Racing League (IRL) was divisive to open-wheel racing in the United States, as team owners were forced to decide whether to remain with CART or move to the new IRL. Only IRL members would be allowed to race in the Indianapolis 500—the world's largest spectator sport and the premiere open-wheeled racing competition. CART teams responded by planning their own event on the same day as the Indianapolis 500. The real challenge for the new IRL was developing an integrated marketing communications program to ensure maximum informational and persuasive impact on potential fans (customers). The rift between CART and the IRL resulted in both parties being unable to use the terms "IndyCar" and "Indy car." Eventually, the IRL was able to reassume the Indy Car brand name, but the temporary loss of the brand name created a challenge for promoting the new league.

A 2001 ESPN Sports Poll survey found that 56 percent of American auto racing fans said stock car racing was their favorite type of racing, with open-wheel racing third at 9 percent. The diminished appeal of open-wheel racing contributed to additional problems with sponsor relationships. Three major partners left CART, including two partners (Honda and Toyota) that provided engines and technical support to CART and its teams. During the same time, the IRL struggled to find corporate partners as a weakened economy and a fragmented market for open-wheel racing made both the IRL and CART less attractive to sponsors.

The IRL experienced ups and downs in the years following the split. Interest in IRL as measured by television ratings took a noticeable dip between 2002 and 2004, with 25 percent fewer viewers tuning in during 2004 than just two years earlier. Some sponsors pulled out, including talk-show host David Letterman. Furthermore, Tony George resigned his top positions with the IRL and the Indianapolis Motor Speedway (IMS) in July 2009. He was a proponent of using profits from IMS to support operations of the IRL, funneling an estimated hundreds of millions of dollars over the years to sustain the IRL.

In response to declining interest in IRL, marketing initiatives were taken to reverse the trend by recognizing the various promotional tools available. For instance, the league dedicated a marketing staff in 2001 to its operations. In 2005, the IRL launched a new ad campaign that targeted 18- to 34-year-old males. The campaign was part of a broader strategy to expand the association of IRL beyond a sport for middle-aged Midwestern males to a younger market. IRL has created profiles on social networking sites like Facebook and Twitter to further target this market.

In support of this effort, two developments can be noted. First, IRL has followed a trend observed in NASCAR and has involved several celebrities in the sport through team ownership. Among the celebrities involved with IRL teams are NBA star Carmelo Anthony, former NFL quarterback Jim Harbaugh, and actor Patrick Dempsey. Another celebrity involved with the IRL is rock star Gene Simmons. He is a partner in Simmons Abramson Marketing, who was hired to help the IRL devise new marketing strategies. The firm's entertainment marketing savvy is being tapped to help the IRL connect with fans on an emotional level through its drivers, whom Simmons referred to as "rock stars in rocket ships."

Second, driver personalities began to give the IRL some visibility. The emergence of Danica Patrick as a star in the IRL broadened the appeal of the league and assists in efforts to reach young males. Patrick was a 23-year-old IRL rookie in 2005, who finished fourth in the Indianapolis 500. The combination of the novelty of a female driver, her captivating looks, provocative advertising (particularly her Go Daddy ads), and personality made her the darling of American sports in 2005. Before moving on to NASCAR in 2012, Patrick's effect on the IRL was very noticeable; the IRL reported gains in event attendance, merchandise sales, website traffic, and television ratings during Patrick's rookie season. Patrick has since drawn the interest of many companies that have hired her as a product endorser, including Motorola, Boost Mobile, and XM Radio. In addition, she has appeared in photo shoots in *FHM* and the 2008 and 2009 *Sports Illustrated* swimsuit issues. Other drivers like Helio Castroneves, Scott Dixon, Ryan Hunter-Reay, and Marco Andretti, who have gained notoriety in Indy racing, also increased awareness of the IRL.

Driver personalities are critical to the promotion and communication process. Most of the drivers endorse their respective sponsors and end up in television advertising promoting the product. This is often done while showing the driver in an Indy racing car, also promoting the league. Drivers to some extent engage in personal selling by interacting with fans, signing autographs, and making personal appearances. Public relations for the drivers is important in television talk show appearances and various other word-of-mouth communication that is created when spectators start discussing the drivers. It is even possible for drivers to appear in television programs as a type of product placement, promoting themselves, the Indy League, and the IRL.

The Future

In 2008, the IRL and Champ Car decided to reunify. Although reunification was a major step toward competing against its rival NASCAR, the organization knew it needed to engage in strong integrated marketing communications if it wanted to grow its market share.

One major development for the IndyCar Series was a new television broadcast partner. ABC had televised the Indianapolis 500 for 45 years. The IRL will continue that relationship, but most of the other races on the IndyCar Series schedule (at least 13 per season) are televised by the NBC Sports Network, a cable channel that replaced ESPN as IRL's broadcast partner. While the NBC Sports Network has a smaller audience than ESPN, it covers fewer sports and plans to give the IndyCar Series more coverage than ESPN did when it owned the broadcast rights. In addition, the NBC Sports Network signed a 10-year contract with the IRL.

Perhaps the biggest development for the IRL in recent years is its acquisition of a title sponsorship. A title sponsorship is the use of a corporate brand name to be associated with all communication about the league. Due to the decline in its popularity, the IRL lacked a title sponsor for many years. In 2009, the clothing provider Izod decided to become the official title sponsor of the IRL for six years. This sponsorship is likely to be very beneficial for the IRL, particularly as it came at a time when many sponsors for NASCAR and the IRL were pulling out due to the recession.

Auto racing is the fastest-growing spectator sport in the United States. Unfortunately, the disagreement among top leadership in open-wheel racing divided the sport, leading to a period of decline in open-wheel racing, while other forms of auto racing have grown. Therefore, the new IRL must strengthen its standing in the American motorsports market. The support of major celebrities like Patrick Dempsey and the popularity of drivers like Danica Patrick have boosted the ratings of the IRL, but not enough to overtake NASCAR (and the loss of Danica Patrick as a full-time driver to NASCAR also creates a challenge). With the two major open-wheel leagues unified once more, the IRL must begin the task of reconnecting with former fans and building connections with a new audience.[60]

Questions for Discussion

1. How does the IRL utilize the various components of integrated marketing communication?
2. How do driver appearances on television and at public events contribute to promoting the IRL?
3. What is the link between sponsorships of cars and drivers by corporations and promotion of the IRL?

Role-Play Team Case Exercise 7

This role-play team exercise is designed to simulate actual marketing decision making in the real world. The entire team should read the overview and background. Each student will take on a role of a particular employee within the organization. Your instructor will provide additional information and instructions related to a team decision.

SHOCKVOLT ENERGY DRINK*

Background

Shockvolt is a popular energy drink that contains caffeine, taurine (an acid that naturally occurs in animals), glucose, sucrose, and herbal extracts. People who drink Shockvolt report feeling more energized and alert, less sleepy during the day, and more productive. Shockvolt was one of the first movers into the highly competitive energy drink market and was able to gain a 60 percent market share in just 10 years, thanks to its strategic sponsorship of college sports and flashy promotional campaigns.

Like many energy drink companies, Shockvolt targets males 18-24 years old. Shockvolt focuses its promotions on college campuses. The company sponsors nearly every major college football and basketball team in the United States, buying advertising space on billboards, banners, T-shirts, programs, and media coverage of the games. In some stadiums, the company sells Shockvolt mixed drinks or specials when purchased with a beer. In addition, the Shockvolt Girls, a team of attractive women who attend tailgating events and visit bars near campuses, hand out merchandise and free samples of Shockvolt, which are often mixed with shots of alcohol. The company also runs aggressive national advertising campaigns suggesting that drinking Shockvolt can help consumers "get more" from life, including better athletic performance thanks to increased energy.

Inspired by Shockvolt's success, many new companies have entered the energy drink market. Because there are over 1,000 energy drinks, promotions are becoming more and more extreme as competitors try to "one up" each other. Shockvolt's competitors have sponsored extreme sports, monster truck rallies, rocket launches, sky diving events, NASCAR racing, and spring break parties, and some even started their own record labels. Because of its position as the market leader, Shockvolt is starting to appear corporate and not as edgy as its competitors.

Recently, Shockvolt has faced criticism because of the risks associated with its products. A report by the Substance Abuse and Mental Health Services Administration linked the use of energy drinks to a sudden increase in emergency room visits. Consuming too much caffeine can overstimulate the nervous system and result in caffeine intoxication. Symptoms include general restlessness, anxiety, insomnia, flushing of the face, increased urination, gastrointestinal problems, irregular or rapid heartbeat, and unintentional muscle movements. In severe overdose cases, individuals may experience disorientation, hallucinations, depression, breakdown in muscle tissue, or death. In addition, many people use energy drinks like Shockvolt to fuel binge drinking because they delay blackouts, resulting in cases of alcohol poisoning on college campuses.

Although these issues are associated with all energy drinks, Shockvolt faces additional challenges because of the company's support of college athletics. Several athletic organizations

*©O.C. Ferrell and Linda Ferrell, 2012. Harper Baird assisted with the development of this exercise under the direction of O. C. Ferrell and Linda Ferrell. This role-play case is not intended to represent the managerial decisions of an actual company.

have released recommendations that Shockvolt and other energy drinks should not be used for hydration or to enhance performance due to their health risks. However, the FDA has found no conclusive evidence that Shockvolt is unsafe. Other critics are concerned about the heavy presence of Shockvolt at college campuses and sporting events, saying that they are encouraging young people to use Shockvolt and alcohol together.

In the last year, Shockvolt's market share dropped 7 percent, and executive leadership believes that the company's marketing strategies are no longer successful. Some employees believe that the marketing communications are no longer integrated, so Shockvolt is not retaining current customers, leading to a drop in sales. However, others believe that the company is not attracting new customers as it struggles to differentiate itself from its competitors. You are part of a team that is reevaluating Shockvolt's marketing strategy and deciding how to improve the company's promotions. Make sure to address all four possible elements of a promotion mix (advertising, personal selling, sales promotion, and public relations).

Public Relations Manager

As the head of public relations, it is your job to use a variety of communication tools to make sure that Shockvolt is portrayed positively in the media and work with the company's stakeholders to reduce bad publicity. As promotions in the industry have grown more extreme, controlling the coverage of Shockvolt has become more difficult.

Because stakeholder attitudes toward a firm can affect the sale of its products, it is important for Shockvolt to maintain a positive public image. You usually focus on the company's primary stakeholders, especially customers and shareholders, and you have ignored complaints from consumer organizations about the health risks associated with Shockvolt. However, you are starting to realize that assessing public opinion is just as important as direct promotion of Shockvolt.

You believe that Shockvolt needs to rebuild trust in its brand name. As a response to the allegations of health risks, you drafted a news release that states that the cardiovascular risk of drinking Shockvolt is no different than the risks associated with drinking a regular cup of coffee. The statement also argues that Shockvolt must be safe, because health authorities in several countries have approved the drink. However, you must have the approval of the marketing strategy team before you send the release or hold a press conference to make sure that it fits with the company's other marketing efforts.

The social media manager has pitched a "Get More" app for Facebook, where users can brag about how Shockvolt helped them to "get more," including better athletic performance, improved drinking performance, higher test scores, and more women. You dislike this idea because it could generate media claims that the app encourages unhealthy lifestyles and is offensive to women. You also believe that it will appear that Shockvolt is ignoring the problems associated with caffeine overdose and alcohol poisoning.

Advertising Manager

As the advertising manager, you communicate the benefits of Shockvolt through the mass media. Because the market is so competitive, it is becoming more difficult for you to combat the influence of competitors' advertising campaigns.

In your opinion, the problem with Shockvolt's marketing strategy is that it is not attracting new customers. You want to use advertising and other promotional techniques to create more of a pull policy to stimulate strong consumer demand for Shockvolt. You feel limited by Shockvolt's current advertising platform, or the company's basic selling points based on the issues that are important to customers. Shockvolt's advertising platform has always been focused on athletic performance and college sports, with commercials, billboards, and print ads that suggest that drinking Shockvolt can help consumers "get more" athletic performance.

You believe that the solution is to diversify Shockvolt's advertising platform. While this would mean moving away from Shockvolt's current niche, you think that there are other ways to reach college males, such as hosting all-night video game tournaments fueled by Shockvolt, sponsoring other events, and product placement. You think social media is a great way to learn about what is important to your target market.

The social media manager has pitched a "Get More" app for Facebook, where users can brag about how Shockvolt helped them to "get more," including better athletic performance, improved drinking performance, higher test scores, and more women. Not only will this help you gather more information about consumers, but you also think this app would help expand Shockvolt's existing national advertising campaigns to include more commercials featuring all of the ways consumers could "get more" from life.

Social Media Manager

As the social media manager, it is your responsibility to create interactive relationships between Shockvolt and consumers. You are younger than the rest of the marketing strategy team, and you think that Shockvolt needs to be more innovative in order to stay competitive. Because Shockvolt is the market leader and other companies are more extreme, you believe the company appears too corporate.

Social media is a great way to reach customers and learn more about their target market. It can be integrated with Shockvolt's other promotional techniques, but so far the company has only used social networking sites to offer online coupons and announce merchandise giveaway locations.

You would like to expand Shockvolt's social media marketing in order to attract and retain younger consumers. To increase customer loyalty, you would like to create more interactive discussions, develop online surveys, and encourage people to share pictures of themselves using Shockvolt. The company could use social media to remind customers to drink Shockvolt responsibly and prove the company is concerned about consumers.

Your department just developed a "Get More" app for Facebook, where users can brag about how Shockvolt helped them to "get more," including better athletic performance, improved drinking performance, higher test scores, and more women. While this may sound offensive, you believe that you understand young males better than the other team members and that the benefits far outweigh any bad publicity. In your opinion, not only will the app help find new customers, it will help the company gather more information about the people who drink Shockvolt.

Vice President of Marketing

As the head of the marketing department, you are concerned that the company's marketing communications aren't successfully integrated, so consumers aren't receiving a consistent message about Shockvolt. Some promotions try to make the drink seem "extreme," while others focus on product safety. While you cannot control information like press releases, you think that all communication from the company should match the company's sales, advertising, and social media goals to maximize the persuasive impact on customers.

You would like to increase the company's digital marketing efforts, especially online advertising. You think a Facebook app would be great, but you are undecided about the message conveyed by what the social media manager developed. The "Get More" app allows users to brag about how Shockvolt helped them to "get more," including better athletic performance, better drinking performance, higher test scores, and more women.

While the advertising is important, you believe that a push policy would help promote Shockvolt, because the company could use its size to its advantage and build strong relationships with retailers. Smaller companies have to fight for limited shelf space, which makes it hard for them to reach customers, no matter how much they promote their products. You would like to hire more trade salespeople who will help promote the product, restock shelves, obtain more shelf space, set up special displays, and distribute samples. You also think that offering more sales promotions to customers would encourage retailers to keep more shelf space for Shockvolt. This strategy would hinder competitors and enhance the effect of other sales promotions.

Sales Manager

You are very concerned about Shockvolt's competition in the energy drink industry. You want to increase customer loyalty so that they don't turn to a competing product, and you're willing to do whatever it takes to keep customers hooked on Shockvolt. However, you know that the most effective sales promotions are highly interrelated with other promotional activities like advertising and personal selling.

Although the current marketing methods have generated some criticism, you believe that focusing on college athletics is the best way to sell your product. You are unwilling to change the target market because marketing to college males is incredibly lucrative, and you are the only energy drink company involved in college sports. You think that Shockvolt's ad campaigns and other promotions need to be more extreme to keep customers loyal.

You would also like to increase sales promotions to encourage trials and repurchase. To go along with the increase in trade salespeople suggested by the vice president of marketing, you would like your current sales force to give retailers, distributors, and bars more point-of-purchase materials like neon signs and refrigerators featuring the Shockvolt logo. The Shockvolt Girls could also go to more stores and hand out more free samples and merchandise to shoppers. You'd also like to stimulate sales through a sweepstakes to win prizes like NCAA March Madness tickets.

The social media manager has pitched a "Get More" app for Facebook, where users can brag about how Shockvolt helped them to "get more," including better athletic performance, improved drinking performance, higher test scores, and more women. The app could be a great way to incorporate digital coupons, a customer contest, or a rewards program for loyal customers.

General Counsel

As a lawyer looking out for the best interests of Shockvolt, you are concerned about the legal and regulatory implications of some of the company's current and potential marketing campaigns.

Under pressure from several concerned consumer organizations, the Food and Drug Administration (FDA) is starting to investigate energy drinks to determine whether they are properly labeled and marketed. According to the FDA, caffeine is "generally recognized as safe" if it makes up 0.02 percent of a cola-like beverage, which is about 71 mg in a 12-ounce can. Shockvolt has 90 mg in a 9-ounce can, which means it could be classified as a liquid dietary supplement and could face stricter labeling and marketing requirements. Because energy drinks have become much more popular with adolescents over the last few years, the FDA is also scrutinizing whether or not the marketing of energy drinks could adversely impact young consumers and their behavior.

It would be very expensive for Shockvolt to have to meet the FDA regulations for dietary supplements. Because of the increased attention surrounding Shockvolt's health risks and the potential investigation by the FDA, you agree with the public relations manager that a press release highlighting the product's safety is important. Drinking a can of Shockvolt poses the same risks as drinking a cup of coffee, and you hope that this fact will reduce the amount of pressure that consumer advocate organizations are placing on the FDA and other government regulators.

The social media manager has pitched a "Get More" app for Facebook, where users can brag about how Shockvolt helped them to "get more," including better athletic performance, improved drinking performance, higher test scores, and more women. You believe that the company should tone down its messages about using Shockvolt to increase athletic performance. You don't want to give the FDA another reason to investigate whether or not Shockvolt is making unsubstantiated health claims. Furthermore, because of the increased use of Shockvolt in binge drinking, you worry that the company could be sued if it continues to appear to encourage young people to take risks. For these reasons, you do not recommend the use of the app in advertising campaigns.

NOTES

[1]"2010 World's Most Ethical Companies—Company Profile: Salesforce .com," *Ethisphere*, Q1, 32–33; Milton Moskowitz and Charles Kapelke, "25 Top-Paying Companies," CNNMoney, January 26, 2011, http://money .cnn.com/galleries/2011/pf/jobs/1101/gallery.best_companies_top_paying .fortune/index.html (accessed January 31, 2011); "Salesforce.com Named One of the 'World's Most Ethical Companies' in 2010 for the Fourth Consecutive Year," Salesforce.com, March 29, 2010, www.salesforce.com/ company/news-press/press-releases/2010/03/100329.jsp (accessed January 31, 2011); Salesforce Foundation Home Page, http://foundation.force .com/home (accessed January 31, 2011); Salesforce.com website, www .salesforce.com/company/ (accessed January 31, 2011); Chris Kanaracus, "Salesforce.com's Benioff Talks Growth, Microsoft," *CIO,* June 6, 2011, www.cio.com/article/683621/Salesforce.Com_s_Benioff_Talks_Growth_ Microsoft (accessed December 13, 2011); Steven D. Jones, "Salesforce .com Shares Weaken On Concern About Billings Growth," *The Wall Street Journal*, November 18, 2011, http://online.wsj.com/article/BT-CO-20111118-712216.html (accessed December 13, 2011).

[2]Avinash Malshe and Avipreet Sohi, "What Makes Strategy Making Across the Sales-Marketing Interface More Successful?," *Journal of the Academy of Marketing Science* 37, no. 4 (Winter 2009): 400–421.

[3]"Advantages of Personal Selling," KnowThis.com, www.knowthis.com/ principles-of-marketing-tutorials/personal-selling/advantages-of-personal-selling/ (accessed April 2, 2012).

[4]"Research and Markets: The Cost of the Average Sales Call Today Is More Than 400 Dollars," *M2 Presswire*, February 28, 2006.

[5]Jon M. Hawes, Anne K. Rich, and Scott M. Widmier, "Assessing the Development of the Sales Profession," *Journal of Personal Selling & Sales Management* 24 (Winter 2004): 27–37.

[6]Dawn R. Deeter-Schmelz and Karen Norman Kennedy, "A Global Perspective on the Current State of Sales Education in the College Curriculum, *Journal of Personal Selling & Sales Management* 31, no. 1 (Winter 2011): 55–76.

[7]Willem Verbeke, Bart Dietz, and Ernst Verwaal, "Drivers of Sales Performance: A Contemporary Meta-Analysis. Have Salespeople Become Knowledge Brokers?" *Journal of the Academy of Marketing Science* 39 (2011): 407–428.

[8]Michael Rodriguez and Robert M. Peterson, "Generating Leads via Social CRM: Early Best Practices for B2B Sales," abstract in Concha Allen (ed.), "Special Abstract Section: 2011 National Conference in Sales Management," *Journal of Personal Selling* 31, no. 4 (Fall 2011): 457–458.

[9]Ed Peelena, Kees van Montfort, Rob Beltman, and Arnoud Klerkx, "An Empirical Study into the Foundation of CRM Success," *Journal of Strategic Marketing* 17, no. 6 (December 2009): 453–471.

[10]Eli Jones, Paul Busch, and Peter Dacin, "Firm Market Orientation and Salesperson Customer Orientation: Interpersonal and Intrapersonal Influence on Customer Service and Retention in Business-to-Business Buyer–Seller Relationships," *Journal of Business Research* 56 (2003): 323–340.

[11]Kenneth Le Meunier-FitzHugh and Nigel F. Piercy, "Exploring the Relationship Between Market Orientation and Sales and Marketing Collaboration," *Journal of Personal Selling & Sales Management* 31, no. 3 (Summer 2011): 287–296.

[12]Kaj Storbacka, Pia Polsa, and Maria Sääksjärvi, "Management Practices in Solution Sales-A Multilevel and Cross-Functional Framework," *Journal of Personal Selling & Sales Management* 31, no. 1 (Winter 2011): 35–54.

[13]Julie T. Johnson, Hiram C. Barksdale Jr., and James S. Boles, "Factors Associated with Customer Willingness to Refer Leads to Salespeople," *Journal of Business Research* 56 (2003): 257–263.

[14]Ralph W. Giacobbe, Donald W. Jackson Jr., Lawrence A. Crosby, and Claudia M. Bridges, "A Contingency Approach to Adaptive Selling Behavior and Sales Performance: Selling Situations and Salesperson Characteristics," *Journal of Personal Selling & Sales Management* 26 (Spring 2006): 115–142.

[15]Richard G. McFarland, Goutam N. Challagalla, and Tasadduq A. Shervani, "Influence Tactics for Effective Adaptive Selling," *Journal of Marketing* 70 (October 2006).

[16]John Andy Wood, "NLP Revisted: Nonverbal Communications and Signals of Trustworthiness," *Journal of Personal Selling & Sales Management* 26 (Spring 2006): 198–204.

[17]John Dunyon, Valerie Gossling, Sarah Willden, and John S. Seiter, "Compliments and Purchasing Behavior in Telephone Sales Interactions," abstract in Dawn R. Deeter-Schmelz (ed.), "Personal Selling & Sales Management Abstracts," *Journal of Personal Selling & Sales Management* 31, no. 2 (Spring 2011): 186.

[18]Stephen S. Porter, Joshua L. Wiener, and Gary L. Frankwick, "The Moderating Effect of Selling Situation on the Adaptive Selling Strategy—Selling Effectiveness Relationship," *Journal of Business Research* 56 (2003): 275–281.

[19]Tammy Stanley, "Follow-Up: The Success Recipe Salespeople Don't See," *Direct Selling News*, May 2010, www.directsellingnews.com/index .php/entries_archive_display/follow_up_the_success_recipe_salespeople_ dont_see (accessed February 5, 2011).

[20]Gabriel R. Gonzalez, K. Douglas Hoffman, Thomas N. Ingram, and Raymond W. LaForge, "Sales Organization Recovery Management and Relationship Selling: A Conceptual Model and Empirical Test," *Journal of Personal Selling & Sales Management,* 30, no. 3 (Summer 2010): 223–238.

[21]Keith Harding, "Relationship Marketing," *Direct Selling News,* October 2010, www.directsellingnews.com/index.php/entries_archive_ display/relationship_marketing (accessed February 5, 2011).

[22]Barton A. Weitz and Kevin D. Bradford, "Personal Selling and Sales Management: A Relationship Marketing Perspective," *Journal of the Academy of Marketing Science* 27, no. 2 (1999): 241–254.

[23]Eli Jones, Steven P. Brown, Andris A. Zoltners, and Barton A. Weitz, "The Changing Environment of Selling and Sales Management," *Journal of Personal Selling & Sales Management* 25, no. 2 (spring 2005): 105–111.

[24]"The Right Questions and Attitudes Can Beef Up Your Sales, Improve Customer Retention," *Sell!ng* (June 2001): 3.

[25]Jones et al., 105–111.

[26]Gary K. Hunter and William D. Perreault Jr., "Making Sales Technology Effective," *Journal of Marketing* 71 (January 2007): 16–34.

[27]Robert S. Gnuse and Khalid Harris, "Conquering Acceptance Challenges of Sales Automation," *Sales & Marketing Management,* August 26, 2011, http://salesandmarketing.com/article/conquering-acceptance-challenges-sales-automation (accessed April 3, 2012).

[28]Othman Boujena, Johnston J. Wesley, and Dwight R. Merunka, "The Benefits of Sales Force Automation: A Customer's Perspective," *Journal of Personal Selling & Sales Management* 29, no. 2 (2009): 137–150.

[29]Fernando Jaramillo, Jay Prakash Mulki, and Paul Solomon, "The Role of Ethical Climate on Salesperson's Role Stress, Job Attitudes, Turnover Intention, and Job Performance," *Journal of Personal Selling & Sales Management* 26 (Summer 2006): 272–282.

[30]Christophe Fournier, John F. Tanner Jr., Lawrence B. Chonko, and Chris Manolis, "The Moderating Role of Ethical Climate on Salesperson Propensity to Leave," *Journal of Personal Selling & Sales Management* 3, no. 1 (Winter 2009–2010): 7–22.

[31]Noah Buhayar, "IBM's Secret for Making the Sale," BNET, www.bnet.com/article/ibms-secret-for-making-the-sale/313855 (accessed April 20, 2011).

[32]"Sales Internship Program at Pepsi Beverages Company," Darlene's Business Blog, March 23, 2011, http://blog.vcu.edu/dward/2011/03/sales-internship-program-at-pepsi-beverages-company.html (accessed April 3, 2012).

[33]"Online Platinum Sales Training," Platinum, www.platinumguild.com/output/page3271.asp (accessed April 3, 2012).

[34]Tara Burnthorne Lopez, Christopher D. Hopkins, and Mary Anne Raymond, "Reward Preferences of Salespeople: How Do Commissions Rate?" *Journal of Personal Selling & Sales Management* 26 (Fall 2006): pp. 381–390.

[35]Kirk Shinkle, "All of Your People Are Salesmen: Do They Know? Are They Ready?" *Investor's Business Daily,* February 6, 2002, A1.

[36]"100 Best Companies to Work For 2009," *Fortune*, February 2, 2009, money.cnn.com/magazines/fortune/bestcompanies/2009/snapshots/32.html (accessed April 20, 2011); Ellen Davis, "Container Store CEO Gives the Inside Scoop on We Love Our Employees Day," National Retail Federation Blog, February 14, 2010, http://blog.nrf.com/2010/02/14/container-store-ceo-gives-inside-scoop-on-we-love-our-employees-day/ (accessed February 5, 2011).

[37]Denny Bristow, Douglas Amyx, Stephen B. Castleberry, and James J. Cochran, "A Cross-Generational Comparison of Motivational Factors in a Sales Career Among Gen-X and Gen-Y College Students," *Journal of Personal Selling & Sales Management* 31, no. 1 (Winter 2011): 35–54.

[38]"100 Best Companies to Work For 2011," *Fortune*, February 7, 2011, http://money.cnn.com/magazines/fortune/bestcompanies/2011/snapshots/21.html (accessed February 7, 2011).

[39]John W. Barnes, Donald W. Jackson Jr., Michael D. Hutt, and Ajith Kumar, "The Role of Culture Strength in Shaping Salesforce Outcomes," *Journal of Personal Selling & Sales Management* 26 (Summer 2006): 255–270.

[40]James B. DeConinck, "The Effects of Leader-Member Exchange and Organizational Identification on Performance and Turnover Among Salespeople," *Journal of Personal Selling & Sales Management* 31, no. 1 (Winter 2011): 21–34.

[41]Patricia Odell, "Motivating the Masses," *Promo,* September 1, 2005, http://promomagazine.com/research/pitrends/marketing_motivating_masses/ (accessed April 20, 2011).

[42]George E. Belch and Michael A. Belch, *Advertising and Promotion* (Burr Ridge, IL: Irwin/McGraw-Hill, 2004), 514–522.

[43]"Press Release: Inmar Reports on 2011 Coupon Trends," inmar®, January 25, 2012, www.inmar.com/Pages/InmarArticle/Press-Release-Inmar-Releases-2011-Coupon-Trends-Report.aspx (accessed April 3, 2012).

[44]Piet Levy, "Ca$hing in on the COUPON Comeback," *Marketing News*, April 30, 2011, 14–16.

[45]Arthur L. Porter, "Direct Mail's Lessons for Electronic Couponers," *Marketing Management Journal* (Spring/Summer 2000): 107–115.

[46]Ibid.

[47]Coupon Information Corporation, www.cents-off.com/faq.php?st=1fe91 (accessed February 5, 2011).

[48]John T. Gourville and Dilip Soman, "The Consumer Psychology of Mail-in Rebates," *Journal of Product & Brand Management* 20, no. 2 (2011): 147–157.

[49]Jayne O'Donnell, "Mail-in Rebates Decline as Buyers Gripe about Hassles," *USA Today*, November 23, 2010, 1B.

[50]Crown Rewards Program," Hallmark, www.hallmark.com/online/crown-rewards/ (accessed April 3, 2012).

[51]Mark J. Miller, "Swipe This, Not That: Intel Brings Touchscreen to Retail Partners," *Brandchannel,* February 9, 2012, www.brandchannel.com/home/post/2012/02/09/Intel-Retail-Touchscreens-020912.aspx (accessed April 3, 2012).

[52]"Secret Weapon?" *Promo,* December 1, 2007, http://promomagazine.com/sampling/secret_weapon_trial_purchase_study/ (accessed April 20, 2011).

[53]Katherine Hobson, "A Sales Promotion That Works for Shoes May Not For Chocolate," *The Wall Street Journal,* February 8, 2011, http://blogs.wsj.com/health/2011/02/08/a-sales-promotion-that-works-for-shoes-may-not-for-chocolate/ (accessed April 3, 2012).

[54]Teresa Montaner, Leslie de Chernatony, and Isabel Buil, "Consumer Response to Gift Promotions," *Journal of Product & Brand Management* 20, no. 2 (2011): 101–110.

[55]"Create Dunkin's Next Donut Contest," Dunkin' Donuts, www.dunkindonuts.com/donut/ (accessed April 3, 2012).

[56]Associated Press, "Twenty-one Indicted in McDonald's Scam," *St. Petersburg Times,* September 11, 2001, www.sptimes.com/News/091101/Worldandnation/Twenty_one_indicted_i.shtml (accessed April 3, 2012).

[57]"Sweepstakes: Enter for a Chance to Win," Travel Channel, www.travelchannel.com/sweepstakes (accessed April 13, 2012).

[58]"Kroger and Murray's Cheese Launch Partnership with Opening of First of Three Murray's Cheese Departments in Cincinnati-Area Kroger Supermarkets," November 17, 2008, www.murrayscheese.com/images_global/murrays_kroger_press_release.pdf (accessed March 14, 2012); Rosalind Resnick, "Market with Meaning," *Entrepreneur*, November 6, 2009, www.entrepreneur.com/marketing/marketingideas/article203938.html# (accessed May 9, 2011); "Murray's Press," Murray's, www.murrayscheese.com/press_main.asp (accessed March 14, 2012); Kim Severson, "Murray's

Cheese Will Open 50 Locations in Kroger Markets," *The New York Times*, November 24, 2009, http://dinersjournal.blogs.nytimes.com/tag/murrays-cheese/ (accessed March 14, 2012); "Murray's Cheese Presents Cheese U Bootcamp," Murray's, www.murrayscheese.com/edu_cheeseubootcamp.asp (May 9, 2011); "The History of New York's Oldest and Best Cheese Shop," Murray's, www.murrayscheese.com/prodinfo.asp?number=ABOUT%5FMURRAYSSTORY (accessed March 14, 2012); Murray's Cheese, www.murrayscheese.com/kroger.asp (accessed March 14, 2012).

[59]David Barboza, "Direct Selling Flourishes in China," *The New York Times,* December 25, 2009, www.nytimes.com/2009/12/26/business/global/26marykay.html?_r=1&scp=1&sq=%22direct%20selling%22&st=Search (accessed March 22, 2012); Wing-Gar Cheng and Bruce Einhorn, "Amway China Sales May Rise at Least 10% as Direct Sales Rebound," *Bloomberg Businessweek*, April 9, 2010, www.businessweek.com (accessed April 12, 2010); Amway website, www.amway.com/en (accessed March 22, 2012); Avon website, www.avon.com (accessed March 22, 2012); Amway, "Direct Selling Leader Generates Double-Digit Growth in 2011," February 23, 2012, http://globalnews.amway.com/index.php?s=2933&item=122414 (accessed March 22, 2012); Bloomberg News, "Mary Kay to Invest $25 Million in China, Soon Its Largest Market," *Bloomberg,* September 19, 2011, www.bloomberg.com/news/2011-09-19/mary-kay-to-invest-25-million-in-china-soon-its-largest-market.html (accessed March 22, 2012); Reuters, "Avon Ladies See Need for Company Makeover," MSNBC, March 20, 2012, http://today.msnbc.msn.com/id/46761188/ns/today-money/t/avon-ladies-see-need-company-makeover/ (accessed March 22, 2012); "Amway Parent Surpasses USD$10.9 Billion in Sales," February 23, 2012, www.amway.com/en/ResourceCenterDocuments/Visitor/ops-amw-news-v-en--2011SalesAnnouncementNewsRelease.pdf (accessed March 26, 2012); J. M. Emmert, "The Top Direct Selling Companies in the World," *Direct Selling News*, June 2011, 18–52.

[60]Some of this material is adapted from "The Indy Racing League (IRL): Driving for First Place" by Don Roy, originally published in O. C. Ferrell and Michael D. Hartline, *Marketing Strategy*, 5th ed. (Mason, OH: South-Western Cengage Learning, 2011), 428–435. These facts are from "A Brief History of CART and Champ Car Racing," www.fsdb.net/champcar/history/index.htm; "Celebrities Who Are Revved Up Over Racing," *Street & Smith's Sports Business Journal*, May 22, 2006, 27; "Hot Wheels Announces Partnership with the IndyCar Series, Indianapolis 500," *Entertainment Newsweekly*, April 24, 2009, 140; Marty O'Brien, "Helio Castroneves Is Happier Making Headlines on the Race Tack," *Daily Press*, June 27, 2009; John Ourand, "IRL to Get at Least 7 Hours Weekly on Versus," *Street & Smith's Sports Business Journal*, February 23, 2009, 7; Jennifer Pendleton, "Danica Patrick," *Advertising Age*, November 7, 2005, S4; Anthony Schoettle, "IRL Ratings Continue Their Skid," *Indianapolis Business Journal*, November 1, 2004, 3; "Kiss Rocker Lends Voice to Indy Races," *Knight Ridder Tribune Business News*, April 1, 2006, 1; "Turnkey Sports Poll," *Street & Smith's Sports Business Journal*, May 22, 2006, 24; J. K. Wall, "Indy Racing League Sets Sights on Marketing Dollars," *Knight Ridder Tribune Business News*, May 27, 2004, 1; Scott Warfield, "IRL in Line to Court Young Males," *Street & Smith's Sports Business Journal*, November 29, 2004, 4; Jeff Wolf, "George's Ouster Clouds IRL's Future," *Las Vegas Review-Journal*, July 3, 2009; Nate Ryan, "Circuits One Again, But Gains from Split Came at Dear Cost," *USA Today*, April 17, 2008, 1C–2C; Associated Press, "Rahal-Letterman Team Out of IRL, Lacks Sponsor," *ESPN Racing*, January 29, 2009, http://sports.espn.go.com/espn/wire?section=auto&id=3868795&campaign=rsssrch=irl (accessed August 27, 2009); "Team History," *Penske Racing*, 2008, www.penskeracing.com/about/index.cfm?cid=14189 (accessed August 27, 2009); "About Andretti Green," *Andretti Green*, www.andrettigreen.com (accessed August 27, 2009); Larry Hawley, "IRL: Izod, Racing Make for Unique Match," *Indy Sports Nation,* November 4, 2009, www.fox59.com/sports/ (accessed May 4, 2010); David Newton, "Danica Adds Coke to Her Portfolio," *ESPN*, May 10, 2012, http://espn.go.com/racing/blog/_/name/newton_david/id/7916132/nascar-danica-patrick-joins-coca-cola-racing-family (accessed August 15, 2012).

Feature Notes

[a]Holly Beech, "Scentsy's Profits Continue to Rise Sharply," *Idaho Press-Tribune*, October 12, 2011, www.idahopress.com/blogs/business_to_business/scentsy-s-profits-continue-to-rise-sharply/article_d88c535e-f43f-11e0-9bf4-001cc4c002e0.html (accessed December 9, 2011); Barbara Seale, "Selling the Sweet Scent of Success," *Direct Selling News,* April 2010, www.directsellingnews.com/index.php/site/comments/selling_the_scents_of_success/ (accessed December 9, 2011); Scentsy website, http://scentsy.net/en-us/ (accessed December 9, 2011).

[b]Harvey Chipkin, "Insufficient Bandwidth Can Ruin a Meeting, Expert Says," Travel Market Report, December 5, 2011, http://travelmarketreport.com/meetings?articleID=6663&LP=1 (accessed December 9, 2011); "How to Design and Deliver Effective Sales Presentations," Slideshare, www.slideshare.net/gotomeeting/how-to-design-and-deliver-effective-virtual-sales-presentations (accessed December 9, 2011).

[c]Jessica Holzer and Shayndi Raice, "IBM Settles Bribery Charges," *The Wall Street Journal,* March 19, 2011, http://online.wsj.com/article/SB10001424052748704608504576208634150691292.html (accessed November 18, 2011); Richard Tyler, "Christmas Gifts Could Be Illegal under Bribery Act, Says PwC," *The Telegraph,* December 22, 2010, www.telegraph.co.uk/finance/yourbusiness/8217356/Christmas-gifts-could-be-illegal-under-Bribery-Act-says-PwC.html (accessed November 18, 2011); HP's Anti-Corruption Compliance Program Overview, www.hp.com/hpinfo/globalcitizenship/society/AC_Compliance_Overview.pdf (accessed November 18, 2011); O. C. Ferrell, John Fraedrich, and Linda Ferrell, *Business Ethics: Ethical Decision Making and Cases*, forthcoming 9th ed. (Mason, OH: South-Western Cengage Learning, 2013).

[d]Timothy W. Martin, "Coupons Are Hot. Clipping Is Not." *The Wall Street Journal*, February 25, 2009, http://online.wsj.com/article/SB123551425475363603.html (accessed November 30, 2011); Brandon Munson, "The Mobile Coupon: What's the Bang for the Buck?" FoodService.com, November 7, 2010, www.foodservice.com/articles/show.cfm?contentid=19550 (accessed November 30, 2011); "Go Green with Electronic Grocery Coupons," WOWPONS, June 27, 2011, www.wowponsmobilegrocerycoupons.com/Green-Shopping/go-green-with-electronic-grocery-coupons.html (accessed November 30, 2011).

Pricing Decisions

part 8

To provide a satisfying marketing mix, an organization must set a price that is acceptable to target market members. PART 8 centers on pricing decisions that can have numerous effects on other parts of the marketing mix. For example, price can influence how customers perceive the product, what types of marketing institutions are used to distribute the product, and how the product is promoted. CHAPTER 20 discusses the importance of price and looks at some characteristics of price and nonprice competition. It explores fundamental concepts, such as demand, elasticity, marginal analysis, and break-even analysis. The chapter then examines the major factors that affect marketers' pricing decisions. CHAPTER 21 discusses six major stages that marketers use to establish prices.

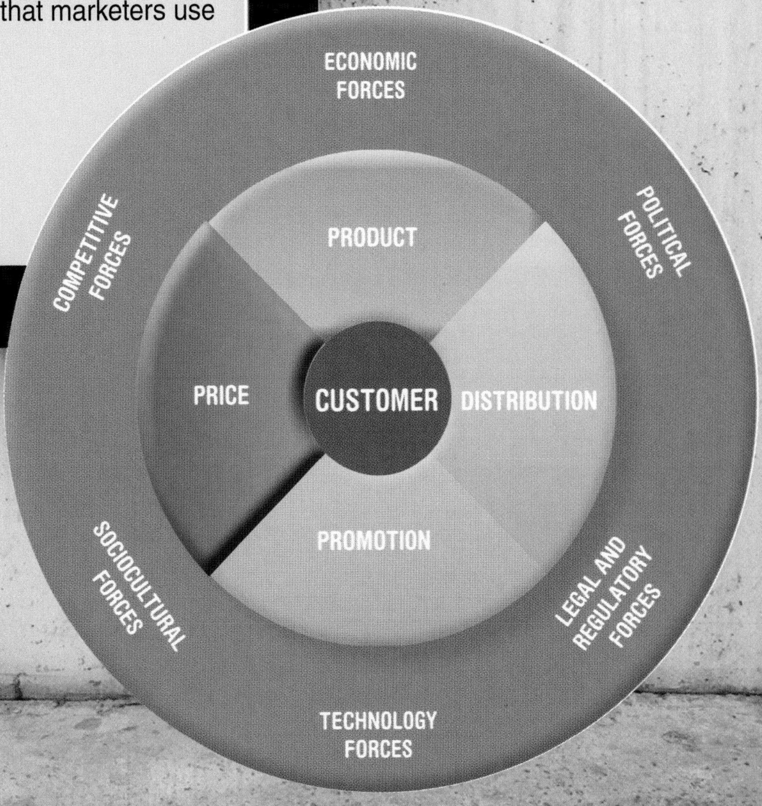

ECONOMIC FORCES
POLITICAL FORCES
LEGAL AND REGULATORY FORCES
TECHNOLOGY FORCES
SOCIOCULTURAL FORCES
COMPETITIVE FORCES
PRODUCT
DISTRIBUTION
PROMOTION
PRICE
CUSTOMER

chapter 20

Pricing Concepts

OBJECTIVES

1. To understand the role of price
2. To identify the characteristics of price and nonprice competition
3. To explore demand curves and price elasticity of demand
4. To examine the relationships among demand, costs, and profits
5. To describe key factors that may influence marketers' pricing decisions
6. To consider issues affecting the pricing of products for business markets

MARKETING INSIGHTS

Publishers and Booksellers Set E-Book Prices

More than 20 million U.S. consumers own an e-book reader—and another 20 million own an iPad or other tablet computer. No wonder sales of electronic books are going up while sales of printed books are going down. Yet the prices of e-books are bouncing up, down, and all around as publishers and retailers try to determine how different prices affect what, when, and how much customers will buy.

When Amazon.com first introduced its Kindle e-book reader, the online retailer priced electronic bestsellers (purchased wholesale from publishers) at $9.99. The idea was to encourage consumers to buy a Kindle, then click to buy bargain-priced e-book best sellers—and it worked. However, major publishers worried that low-priced e-books would change the way customers think about the prices of printed books. So when Apple's iPad became available, some publishers arranged to sell e-books through Apple's iTunes store at prices set by the publishers. They priced digital best sellers on iTunes for $12.99 and up, sometimes priced higher than printed versions, and customers continued to buy. One publishing executive explained that "there has been a change in the understanding of the value of a digital book, and that a digital book has advantages over a physical book in some cases. It's instantaneous, it's portable, it's minimal in terms of storage, and it can be retrieved from all kinds of places and devices."

Even as U.S. and European Union regulators consider the legal aspects of publishers setting e-book prices, publishers are testing whether e-books priced at 99 cents can expand the audience for the same author's full-priced e-books. "It's an experiment," says one publisher. "We're not claiming that books should cost 99 cents."[1]

Source: Bing/Impulse Research survey of 1,043 adults.

Many firms, including electronic book publishers and Amazon, use pricing as a tool to compete against major competitors. However, their rivals also may employ pricing as a major competitive tool. In some industries, firms are very successful even if they don't have the lowest prices. The best price is not always the lowest price.

In this chapter, we focus first on the nature of price and its importance to marketers. We then consider some characteristics of price and nonprice competition. Next, we discuss several pricing-related concepts, such as demand, elasticity, and break-even analysis. Then we examine in some detail the numerous factors that can influence pricing decisions. Finally, we discuss selected issues related to pricing products for business markets.

THE NATURE OF PRICE

The purpose of marketing is to facilitate satisfying exchange relationships between buyer and seller. **Price** is the value paid for a product in a marketing exchange. Many factors may influence the assessment of value, including time constraints, price levels, perceived quality, and motivations to use available information about prices.[2] In most marketing situations, the price is apparent to both buyer and seller. However, price does not always take the form of money paid. In fact, **barter**, the trading of products, is the oldest form of exchange. Money may or may not be involved. Barter among businesses, because of the relatively large values of the exchanges, usually involves trade credit. Corporate barter amounts to an estimated $12 billion in annual U.S. sales.[3] Certain websites help facilitate B2B bartering.

Buyers' interest in price stems from their expectations about the usefulness of a product or the satisfaction they may derive from it. Because consumers have limited resources, they must allocate those resources to obtain the products they most desire. They must decide whether the utility gained in an exchange is worth the buying power sacrificed. Almost anything of value—ideas, services, rights, and goods—can be assessed by a price. In our society, financial price is the measurement of value commonly used in exchanges.

As pointed out in Chapter 12, developing a product may be a lengthy process. It takes time to plan promotion and to communicate benefits. Distribution usually requires a long-term commitment to dealers that will handle the product. Often, price is the only thing a marketer can change quickly to respond to changes in demand or to actions of competitors. Under certain circumstances, however, the price variable may be relatively inflexible.

Price is a key element in the marketing mix because it relates directly to the generation of total revenue. The following equation is an important one for the entire organization:

$$\text{profit} = \text{total revenue} - \text{total costs}$$
$$\text{profit} = (\text{price} \times \text{quantity sold}) - \text{total costs}$$

Price affects an organization's profits in several ways because it is a key component of the profit equation and can be a major determinant of quantities sold. For instance, price is a top priority for Hewlett-Packard in gaining market share and improving financial performance.[4] Furthermore, total costs are influenced by quantities sold.

price The value paid for a product in a marketing exchange

barter The trading of products

Because price has a psychological impact on customers, marketers can use it symbolically. By pricing high, they can emphasize the quality of a product and try to increase the prestige associated with its ownership. By lowering a price, marketers can emphasize a bargain and attract customers who go out of their way to save a small amount of money. Thus, as this chapter details, price can have strong effects on a firm's sales and profitability.

PRICE AND NONPRICE COMPETITION

The competitive environment strongly influences the marketing mix decisions associated with a product. Pricing decisions are often made according to the price or nonprice competitive situation in a particular market. Price competition exists when consumers have difficulty distinguishing competitive offerings and marketers emphasize low prices. Nonprice competition involves a focus on marketing mix elements other than price.

Price Competition

When engaging in **price competition**, a marketer emphasizes price as an issue and matches or beats competitors' prices. To compete effectively on a price basis, a firm should be the low-cost seller of the product. If all firms producing the same product charge the same price for it, the firm with the lowest costs is the most profitable. Firms that stress low price as a key marketing mix element tend to market standardized products. A seller competing on price may change prices frequently, or at least must be willing and able to do so. For example, when AT&T and Verizon Wireless charged $50 per month for their data plans that had a limit of five gigabytes of downloads, Sprint Nextel's similar data plan was $60 per month for the same amount of data. To compete more effectively, Sprint lowered its data plan price to $50, matching the competition, and increased its download limit to six gigabytes per month. Sprint also lowered the price of its 10 gigabyte plan to $80 and increased that plan's limit to 12 gigabytes, to compete with Verizon Wireless' 10 gigabyte plan for $80.[5] Whenever competitors change their prices, the company usually responds quickly and aggressively.

Price competition gives marketers flexibility. They can alter prices to account for changes in their costs or respond to changes in demand for the product. If competitors try to gain market share by cutting prices, a company competing on a price basis can react quickly to such efforts. However, a major drawback of price competition is that competitors have the flexibility to adjust prices too. If they quickly match or beat a company's price cuts, a price war may ensue. For instance, makers of popular tablet computers have begun slashing prices

price competition Emphasizing price as an issue and matching or beating competitors' prices

Courtesy of The Advertising Archives

© Jeff Greenberg/Alamy

Price and Nonprice Competition
Generally, there is a considerable amount of price competition among brands of hair care products. However, L'Oréal products compete on the basis of nonprice competition, which emphasizes product quality.

in order to remain ahead of the competition. Asus, Nvidia, and ViewSonic all debuted tablet models retailing for less than $250. Datawind is working on the Aakash Ubislate tablet model for the Indian market, which should retail for only $35. This price would make owning a tablet computer accessible for millions of people in India. It would also put enormous price pressure on major tablet makers, such as Apple, in one of the world's largest markets.[6] Chronic price wars like this one can substantially weaken organizations.

Nonprice Competition

Nonprice competition occurs when a seller decides not to focus on price and instead emphasizes distinctive product features, service, product quality, promotion, packaging, or other factors to distinguish its product from competing brands. Thus, nonprice competition allows a company to increase its brand's unit sales through means other than changing the brand's price. Mars, for example, markets not only Snickers and M&M's but also has an upscale candy line called Ethel's Chocolate. With the tagline "eat chocolate, not preservatives," Ethel's Chocolate competes on the basis of taste, attractive appearance, and hip packaging, and, thus, has little need to engage in price competition.[7] A major advantage of nonprice competition is that a firm can build customer loyalty toward its brand. If customers prefer a brand because of nonprice factors, they may not be easily lured away by competing firms and brands. In contrast, when price is the primary reason customers buy a particular brand, a competitor is often able to attract those customers through price cuts.

Nonprice competition is effective only under certain conditions. A company must be able to distinguish its brand through unique product features, higher product quality, effective promotion, distinctive packaging, or excellent customer service. Apple is known for producing products that demand a premium price because of the capabilities and service that come with its products. One writer went as far as to say that Linux will not be able to compete with the Apple iPad, because it lacks the "magic" that Apple products have. It is difficult to define and therefore imitate Apple's magic; it is a combination of several qualities including the appearance of its products, ease of use, and product integration.[8] Buyers not only must be able to perceive these distinguishing characteristics but must also view them as important. The distinguishing features that set a particular brand apart from competitors should be difficult, if not impossible, for competitors

nonprice competition Emphasizing factors other than price to distinguish a product from competing brands

Entrepreneurship in Marketing

Buy One, Donate One Eyeglasses

Entrepreneurs: Neil Blumenthal, Andrew Hunt, Jeffrey Raider, and David Gilboa
Business: Warby Parker
Founded: 2010 | New York, New York
Success: The company donated over 100,000 pairs of eyeglasses to people in need in its second year.

Warby Parker is putting the focus on pricing and social responsibility with its new approach to eyewear marketing. The New York–based company markets affordable, retro-fashion eyeglasses directly to customers at prices that undercut competitors' prices. What's more, for every pair purchased online or in a Warby Parker showroom, the company donates one pair to someone in need.

The combination of easy-on-the-eyes styling and easy-on-the-wallet pricing has helped cofounders Neil Blumenthal and David Gilboa start to change the way customers think about eyeglasses. Instead of viewing eyewear only as vision-correction devices, Warby Parker's customers see eyeglasses through a fashion lens—as stylish accessories. Increasingly, its customers are buying different frames for different occasions, such as a pair for work and a pair for casual times with friends. If they buy online, they enjoy the convenience of free shipping and free returns, taking the risk out of ordering eyeglasses without first trying them on.

Customers feel good about buying from Warby Parker, because each purchase also covers a donation of eyeglasses. In less than two years, the company's "buy one, give one" pricing has sent more than 100,000 pairs of eyeglasses to people in need worldwide through a connection with the nonprofit organization VisionSpring.[a]

to imitate. Finally, the firm must extensively promote the brand's distinguishing characteristics to establish its superiority and set it apart from competitors in the minds of buyers.

Even a marketer that is competing on a nonprice basis cannot ignore competitors' prices. This organization must be aware of them and sometimes be prepared to price its brand near or slightly above competing brands. Therefore, price remains a crucial marketing mix component even in environments that call for nonprice competition.

ANALYSIS OF DEMAND

Determining the demand for a product is the responsibility of marketing managers, who are aided in this task by marketing researchers and forecasters. Marketing research and forecasting techniques yield estimates of sales potential, or the quantity of a product that could be sold during a specific period. These estimates are helpful in establishing the relationship between a product's price and the quantity demanded.

The Demand Curve

For most products, the quantity demanded goes up as the price goes down, and the quantity demanded goes down as the price goes up. For example, prices have fallen precipitously for LCD television sets in recent years. This change in price is largely due to high levels of competition and newer technologies, such as 3D televisions. In order to compensate, most makers of LCD TVs responded by continuing to lower prices. Thus, an inverse relationship exists between price and quantity demanded. As long as the marketing environment and buyers' needs, ability (purchasing power), willingness, and authority to buy remain stable, this fundamental inverse relationship holds.

Figure 20.1 illustrates the effect of one variable, price, on the quantity demanded. The classic **demand curve** (*D*1) is a graph of the quantity of products expected to be sold at various prices if other factors remain constant. It illustrates that, as price falls, quantity demanded usually rises. Demand depends on other factors in the marketing mix, including product quality, promotion, and distribution. An improvement in any of these factors may cause a shift to demand curve *D*2. In such a case, an increased quantity (*Q*2) will be sold at the same price (*P*).

demand curve A graph of the quantity of products expected to be sold at various prices if other factors remain constant

Many types of demand exist, and not all conform to the classic demand curve shown in Figure 20.1. Prestige products, such as selected perfumes and jewelry, tend to sell better at

Figure 20.1 Demand Curve Illustrating the Price/Quantity Relationship and Increase in Demand

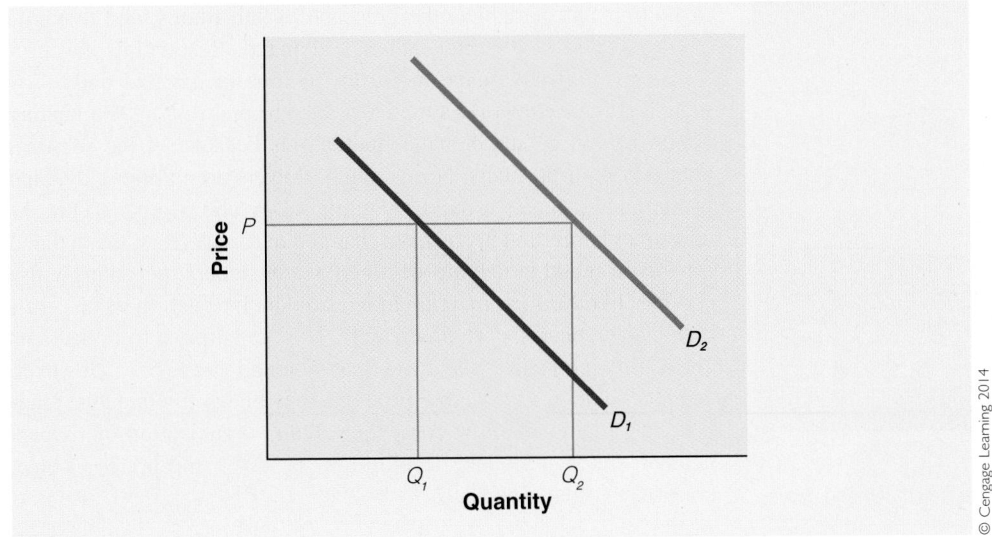

Figure 20.2 Demand Curve Illustrating the Relationship between Price and Quantity for Prestige Products

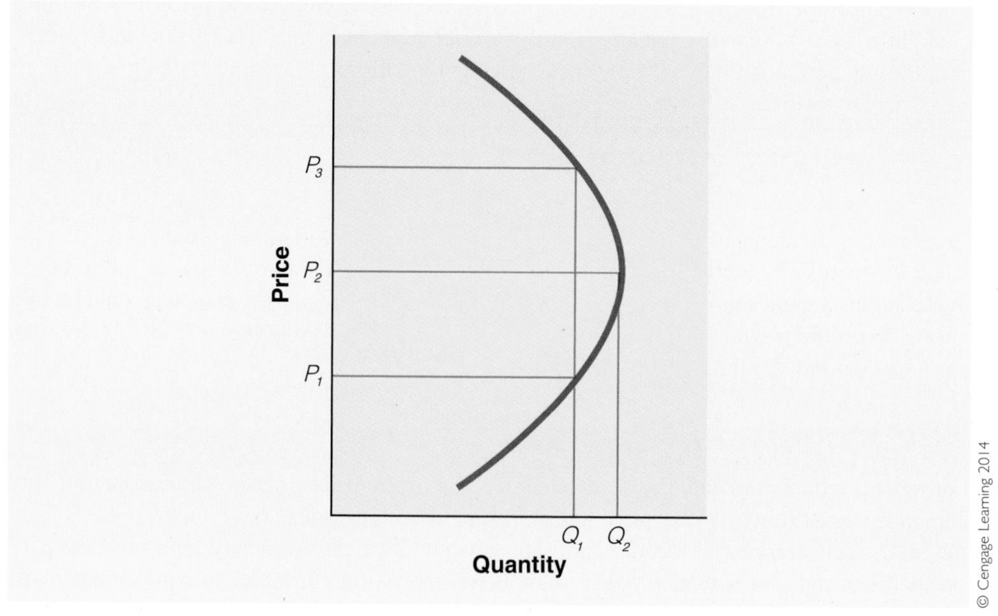

high prices than at lower ones. These products are desirable partly because their expense makes buyers feel elite. If the price fell drastically and many people owned these products, they would lose some of their appeal. The demand curve in Figure 20.2 shows the relationship between price and quantity demanded for prestige products. Quantity demanded is greater, not less, at higher prices. For a certain price range—from *P*1 to *P*2—the quantity demanded (*Q*1) goes up to *Q*2. After a certain point, however, raising the price backfires: if the price goes too high, the quantity demanded goes down. The figure shows that if price is raised from *P*2 to *P*3, quantity demanded goes back down from *Q*2 to *Q*1.

Prestige Demand
Some perfume brands have a prestige-based demand curve.

Demand Fluctuations

Changes in buyers' needs, variations in the effectiveness of other marketing mix variables, the presence of substitutes, and dynamic environmental factors can influence demand. Restaurants and utility companies experience large fluctuations in demand daily. Toy manufacturers, fireworks suppliers, and air-conditioning and heating contractors also face demand fluctuations because of the seasonal nature of their products. For example, flowers are in higher demand in the United States around Valentine's Day and Mother's Day. As consumer habits and needs have changed in recent years, the demand for movie rental stores has declined as consumers increasingly use services like Netflix or stream movies on the Internet. In some cases, demand fluctuations are predictable. It is no surprise to restaurants and utility company managers that demand fluctuates. However, changes in demand for other products may be less predictable, leading to problems for some companies. Other organizations anticipate demand fluctuations and develop new products and prices to meet consumers' changing needs.

Assessing Price Elasticity of Demand

Up to this point, we have seen how marketers identify the target market's evaluation of price and its ability to purchase and how they examine demand to learn whether price is related inversely or directly to quantity. The next step is to assess price elasticity of demand. **Price elasticity of demand** provides a measure of the sensitivity of demand to changes in price. It is formally defined as the percentage change in quantity demanded relative to a given percentage change in price (see Figure 20.3).[9] The percentage change in quantity demanded caused by a percentage change in price is much greater for elastic demand than for inelastic demand. For a product like electricity, demand is relatively inelastic: when its price increases from *P*1 to *P*2, quantity demanded goes down only a little, from *Q*1 to *Q*2. For products like recreational vehicles, demand is relatively elastic: when price rises sharply, from *P*1 to *P*2, quantity demanded goes down a great deal, from *Q*1 to *Q*2.

If marketers can determine the price elasticity of demand, setting a price is much easier. By analyzing total revenues as prices change, marketers can determine whether a product is price elastic. Total revenue is price times quantity. Thus, 10,000 cans of paint sold in one year at a price of $10 per can equals $100,000 of total revenue. If demand is *elastic,* a change in price causes an opposite change in total revenue: an increase in price will decrease total revenue, and a decrease in price will increase total revenue. *Inelastic* demand results in a change in the same direction as total revenue: an increase in price will increase total revenue, and a decrease in price will decrease total revenue. Demand for gasoline, for example, is relatively inelastic—even when prices are close to $4 per gallon—because people must still drive to work, run errands, and shop, all of which require fuel for their vehicles. Although higher gasoline prices force more consumers to change some behaviors in an effort to reduce the amount of gasoline they use, most cut spending in other areas instead because they require a certain level of fuel for weekly activities like commuting. The following formula determines the price elasticity of demand:

$$\text{price elasticity of demand} = \frac{\%\text{ change in quantity demanded}}{\%\text{ change in price}}$$

For instance, if demand falls by 8 percent when a seller raises the price by 2 percent, the price elasticity of demand is –4 (the negative sign indicating the inverse relationship between price and demand). If demand falls by 2 percent when price is increased by 4 percent, elasticity

price elasticity of demand A measure of the sensitivity of demand to changes in price

Figure 20.3 Elasticity of Demand

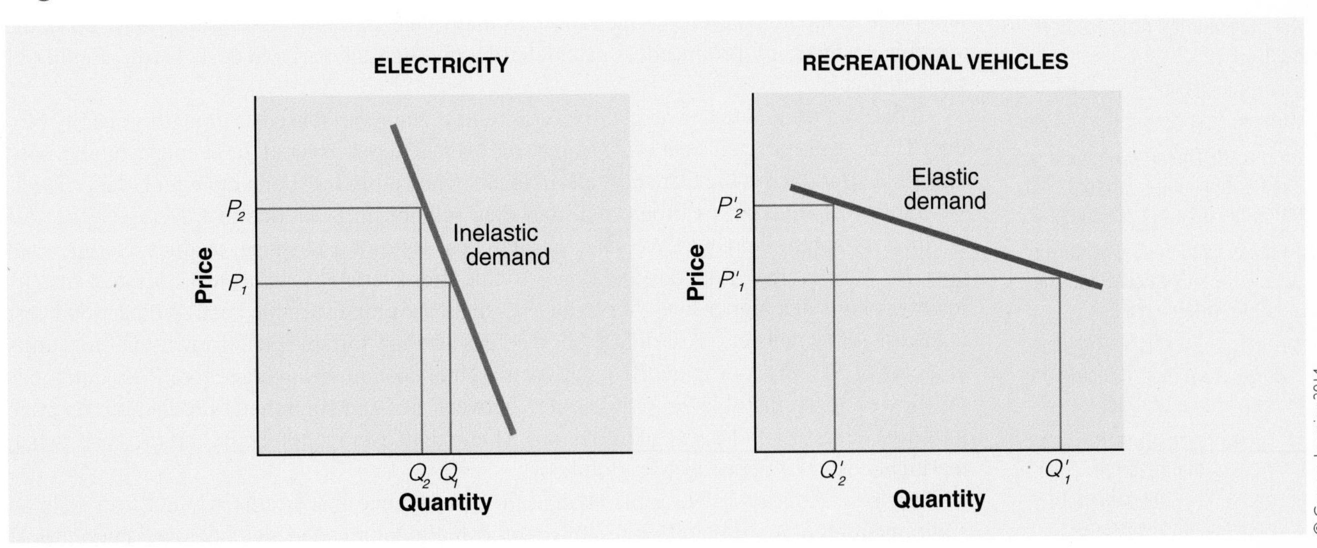

Elasticity of Demand
The demand for electricity is inelastic.

is –1/2. The less elastic the demand, the more beneficial it is for the seller to raise the price. Products without readily available substitutes and for which consumers have strong needs (e.g., electricity or appendectomies) usually have inelastic demand. Marketers cannot base prices solely on elasticity considerations. They must also examine the costs associated with different sales volumes and evaluate what happens to profits.

DEMAND, COST, AND PROFIT RELATIONSHIPS

The analysis of demand, cost, and profit is important, because customers are becoming less tolerant of price increases, forcing manufacturers to find new ways to control costs. In the past, many customers desired premium brands and were willing to pay extra for those products. Today, customers pass up certain brand names if they can pay less without sacrificing quality. To stay in business, a company must set prices that not only cover its costs but also meet customers' expectations. In this section, we explore two approaches to understanding demand, cost, and profit relationships: marginal analysis and break-even analysis.

Marginal Analysis

Marginal analysis examines what happens to a firm's costs and revenues when production (or sales volume) changes by one unit. Both production costs and revenues must be evaluated. To determine the costs of production, it is necessary to distinguish among several types of costs. **Fixed costs** do not vary with changes in the number of units produced or sold. For example, a paint manufacturer's cost of renting a factory does not change because production increases from one to two shifts a day or because twice as much paint is sold. Rent may go up, but not because the factory has doubled production or revenue. **Average fixed cost** is the fixed cost per unit produced and is calculated by dividing fixed costs by the number of units produced.

fixed costs Costs that do not vary with changes in the number of units produced or sold

average fixed cost The fixed cost per unit produced

variable costs Costs that vary directly with changes in the number of units produced or sold

average variable cost The variable cost per unit produced

total cost The sum of average fixed and average variable costs times the quantity produced

average total cost The sum of the average fixed cost and the average variable cost

marginal cost (MC) The extra cost incurred by producing one more unit of a product

marginal revenue (MR) The change in total revenue resulting from the sale of an additional unit of a product

Variable costs vary directly with changes in the number of units produced or sold. The wages for a second shift and the cost of twice as much paint are extra costs incurred when production is doubled. Variable costs are usually constant per unit; that is, twice as many workers and twice as much material produce twice as many cans of paint. **Average variable cost**, the variable cost per unit produced, is calculated by dividing the variable costs by the number of units produced.

Total cost is the sum of average fixed costs and average variable costs times the quantity produced. The **average total cost** is the sum of the average fixed cost and the average variable cost. **Marginal cost (MC)** is the extra cost a firm incurs when it produces one more unit of a product.

Table 20.1 illustrates various costs and their relationships. Notice that average fixed cost declines as output increases. Average variable cost follows a U shape, as does average total cost. Because average total cost continues to fall after average variable cost begins to rise, its lowest point is at a higher level of output than that of average variable cost. Average total cost is lowest at five units at a cost of $22.00, whereas average variable cost is lowest at three units at a cost of $10.67. As Figure 20.4 shows, marginal cost equals average total cost at the latter's lowest level. In Table 20.1, this occurs between five and six units of production. Average total cost decreases as long as marginal cost is less than average total cost and increases when marginal cost rises above average total cost.

Marginal revenue (MR) is the change in total revenue that occurs when a firm sells an additional unit of a product. Figure 20.5 depicts marginal revenue and a demand curve. Most

Table 20.1 Costs and Their Relationships

1 Quantity	2 Fixed Cost	3 Average Fixed Cost (2) ÷ (1)	4 Average Variable Cost	5 Average Total Cost (3) + (4)	6 Total Cost (5) × (1)	7 Marginal Cost
1	$40	$40.00	$20.00	$60.00	$60	
						$10
2	40	20.00	15.00	35.00	70	
						2
3	40	13.33	10.67	24.00	72	
						18
4	40	10.00	12.50	22.50	90	
						20
5	40	8.00	14.00	22.00	110	
						30
6	40	6.67	16.67	23.33	140	
						40
7	40	5.71	20.00	25.71	180	

firms in the United States face downward-sloping demand curves for their products; in other words, they must lower their prices to sell additional units. This situation means that each additional unit of product sold provides the firm with less revenue than the previous unit sold. MR then becomes less-than-average revenue, as Figure 20.5 shows. Eventually, MR reaches zero, and the sale of additional units actually hurts the firm.

However, before the firm can determine whether a unit makes a profit, it must know its cost, as well as its revenue, because profit equals revenue minus cost. If MR is a unit's addition to revenue and MC is a unit's addition to cost, MR minus MC tells us whether the unit is profitable. Table 20.2 illustrates the relationships among price, quantity sold, total revenue, marginal revenue, marginal cost, and total cost. It indicates where maximum profits are possible at various combinations of price and cost. Notice that the total cost and the marginal cost figures in Table 20.2 are calculated and appear in Table 20.1.

Figure 20.4 Typical Marginal Cost and Average Total Cost Relationship

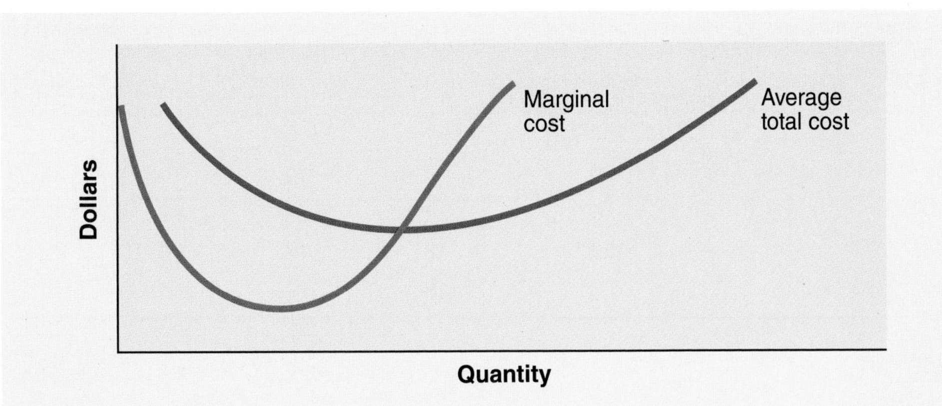

© Cengage Learning 2014

Figure 20.5 **Typical Marginal Revenue and Average Revenue Relationship**

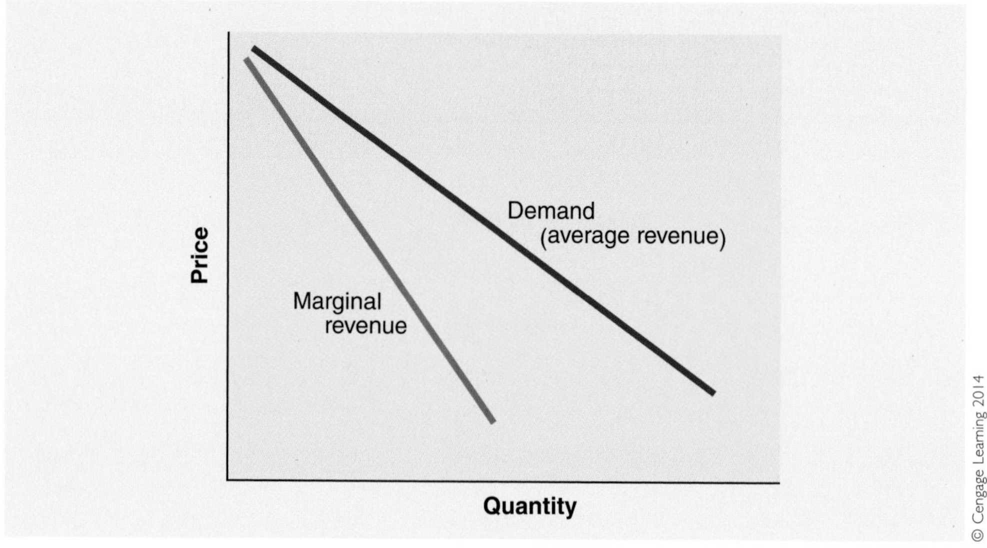

Profit is the highest where MC = MR. In Table 20.2, note that at a quantity of four units, profit is the highest and MR − MC = 0. The best price is $33, and the profit is $42. Up to this point, the additional revenue generated from an extra unit sold exceeds the additional cost of producing it. Beyond this point, the additional cost of producing another unit exceeds the additional revenue generated, and profits decrease. If the price were based on minimum average total cost—$22 (Table 20.1)—it would result in a lower profit of $40 (Table 20.2) for five units priced at $30 versus a profit of $42 for four units priced at $33.

Graphically combining Figures 20.4 and 20.5 into Figure 20.6 shows that any unit for which MR exceeds MC adds to a firm's profits, and any unit for which MC exceeds MR subtracts from profits. The firm should produce at the point where MR equals MC, because this is the most profitable level of production.

This discussion of marginal analysis may give the false impression that pricing can be highly precise. If revenue (demand) and cost (supply) remained constant, prices could be set for maximum profits. In practice, however, cost and revenue change frequently. The competitive tactics of other firms or government action can quickly undermine a company's expectations of revenue. Thus, marginal analysis is only a model from which to work. It offers little

Table 20.2 **Marginal Analysis Method for Determining the Most Profitable Price***

1 Price	2 Quantity Sold	3 Total Revenue (1) × (2)	4 Marginal Revenue	5 Marginal Cost	6 Total Cost	7 Profit (3) − (6)
$57	1	$57	$57	$60	$60	$–3
50	2	100	43	10	70	30
38	3	114	14	2	72	42
33*	**4**	**132**	**18**	**18**	**90**	**42**
30	5	150	18	20	110	40
27	6	162	12	30	140	22
25	7	175	13	40	180	–5

*Boldface indicates the best price–profit combination.

Figure 20.6 Combining the Marginal Cost and Marginal Revenue Concepts for Optimal Profit

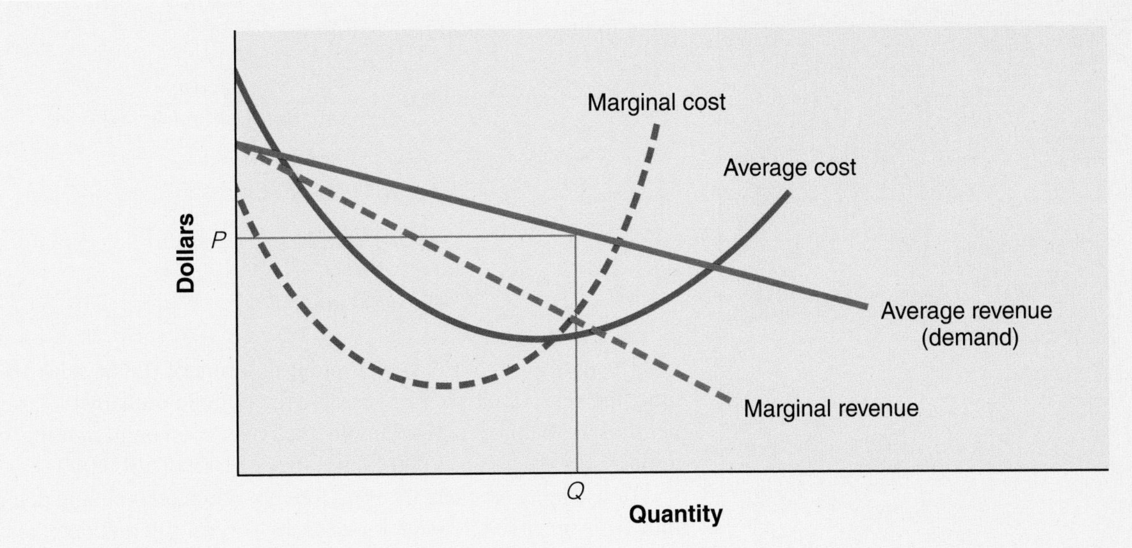

help in pricing new products before costs and revenues are established. On the other hand, in setting prices of existing products, especially in competitive situations, most marketers can benefit by understanding the relationship between marginal cost and marginal revenue.

Break-Even Analysis

The point at which the costs of producing a product equal the revenue made from selling the product is the **break-even point**. If a paint manufacturer has total annual costs of $100,000 and sells $100,000 worth of paint in the same year, the company has broken even.

break-even point The point at which the costs of producing a product equal the revenue made from selling the product

Figure 20.7 illustrates the relationships among costs, revenue, profits, and losses involved in determining the break-even point. Knowing the number of units necessary to break even is

Figure 20.7 Determining the Break-Even Point

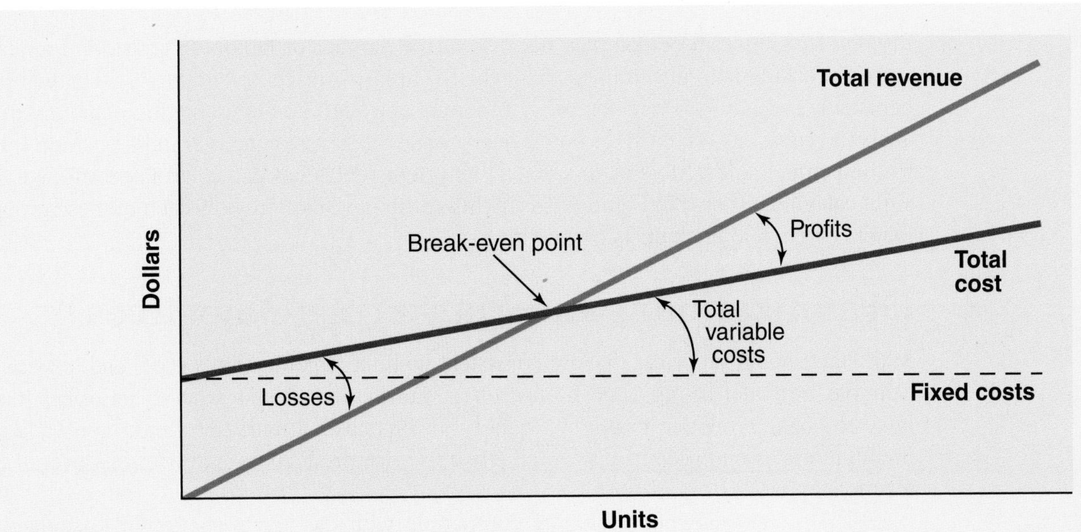

Break-Even Analysis
Many airlines do not break even.

important in setting the price. If a product priced at $100 per unit has an average variable cost of $60 per unit, the contribution to fixed costs is $40. If total fixed costs are $120,000, the break-even point in units is determined as follows:

$$\begin{aligned} \text{break-even point} &= \frac{\text{fixed costs}}{\text{per-unit contribution to fixed costs}} \\ &= \frac{\text{fixed costs}}{\text{price-variable costs}} \\ &= \frac{\$120{,}000}{\$40} \\ &= 3{,}000 \text{ units} \end{aligned}$$

To calculate the break-even point in terms of dollar sales volume, the seller multiplies the break-even point in units by the price per unit. In the preceding example, the break-even point in terms of dollar sales volume is 3,000 (units) times $100, or $300,000.

To use break-even analysis effectively, a marketer should determine the break-even point for each of several alternative prices. This determination allows the marketer to compare the effects on total revenue, total costs, and the break-even point for each price under consideration. Although this comparative analysis may not tell the marketer exactly what price to charge, it will identify highly undesirable price alternatives that should definitely be avoided.

Break-even analysis is simple and straightforward. It does assume, however, that the quantity demanded is basically fixed (inelastic) and that the major task in setting prices is to recover costs. It focuses more on how to break even than on how to achieve a pricing objective, such as percentage of market share or return on investment. Nonetheless, marketing managers can use this concept to determine whether a product will achieve at least a break-even volume.

FACTORS THAT AFFECT PRICING DECISIONS

Pricing decisions can be complex because of the number of factors to consider. Frequently, there is considerable uncertainty about the reactions to price among buyers, channel members, and competitors. Price is also an important consideration in marketing planning, market analysis, and sales forecasting. It is a major issue when assessing a brand's position relative to competing brands. Most factors that affect pricing decisions can be grouped into one of the eight categories shown in Figure 20.8. In this section, we explore how each of these groups of factors enters into price decision making.

Organizational and Marketing Objectives

Marketers should set prices that are consistent with the organization's goals and mission. For example, a retailer trying to position itself as value-oriented may wish to set prices that are quite reasonable relative to product quality. In this case, a marketer would not want to set premium prices on products but would strive to price products in line with this overall organizational goal.

Pricing decisions should also be compatible with the firm's marketing objectives. For instance, suppose one of a producer's marketing objectives is a 12 percent increase in unit

Figure 20.8 **Factors That Affect Pricing Decisions**

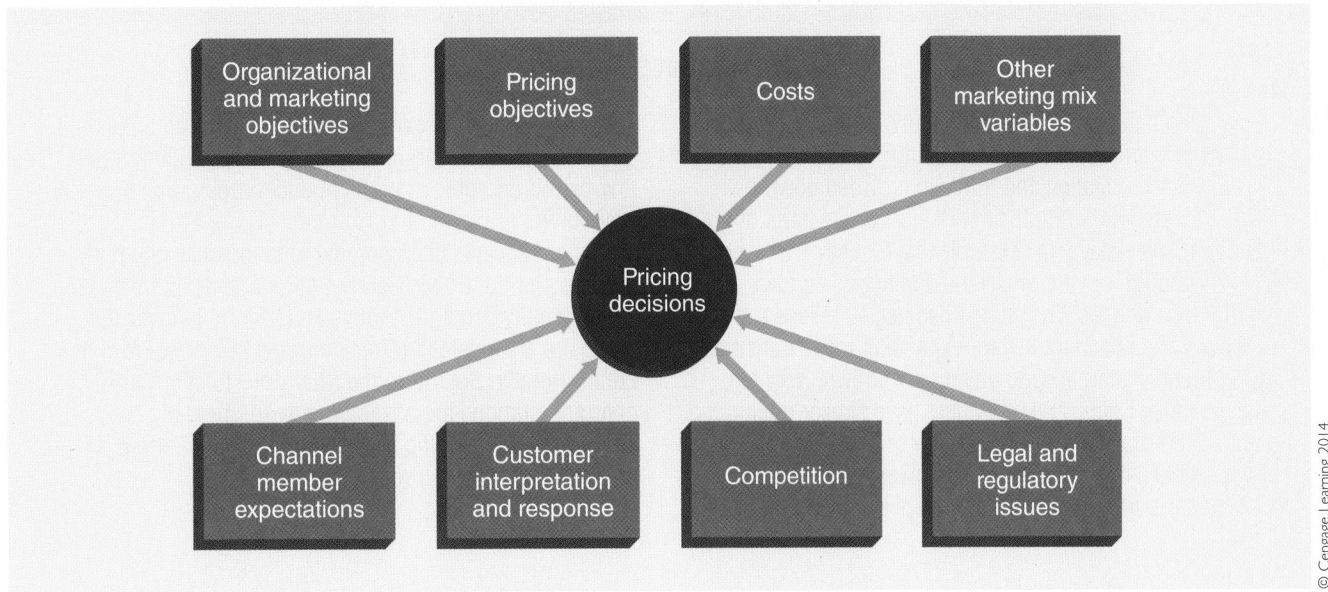

sales by the end of the following year. Assuming buyers are price-sensitive, increasing the price or setting a price above the average market price would not be in line with this objective.

Types of Pricing Objectives

The types of pricing objectives a marketer uses obviously have considerable bearing on the determination of prices. For instance, an organization that uses pricing to increase its market share would likely set the brand's price below those of competing brands of similar quality to attract competitors' customers. A marketer sometimes uses temporary price reductions in the hope of gaining market share. If a business needs to raise cash quickly, it will likely use temporary price reductions, such as sales, rebates, and special discounts. We examine pricing objectives in more detail in the next chapter.

Costs

Clearly, costs must be an issue when establishing price. A firm may temporarily sell products below cost to match competition, generate cash flow, or even increase market share, but in the long run, it cannot survive by selling its products below cost. Even a firm that has a high-volume business cannot survive if each item is sold slightly below its cost. A marketer should be careful to analyze all costs so they can be included in the total cost associated with a product.

To maintain market share and revenue in an increasingly price-sensitive market, many marketers have concentrated on reducing costs. Sony, for example, was able to remain in business during the recession by eliminating more than 20,000 jobs, closing 20 percent of its plants, and redesigning its supply chain to cut costs by more than $3 billion. The company also reduced the production costs of its televisions, digital cameras, and video game consoles.[10]

Labor-saving technologies, a focus on quality, and efficient manufacturing processes have brought productivity gains that translate into reduced costs and lower prices for customers. After years of being hampered by production delays, Boeing turned to its own workers to clear up production bottlenecks. Demand for 737 jets has soared recently, and Boeing designated innovation teams to define and solve the many problems that have slowed down production. Through the changes implemented by innovation teams, Boeing hopes to keep costs down and boost production from 31.5 jets per month to 41 by 2014.[11]

Going Green

Driven to Save the Planet

Can pricing be used to save the planet? A small but growing number of international cities are using "congestion pricing" to reduce pollution and traffic in crowded downtown areas. Drivers who bring their cars into certain parts of London on weekdays, for example, have to pay £10 (about $15)—although drivers of electric and hybrid cars are exempt from the fee. The charge has helped relieve traffic problems and raised money for expanding mass transit as an ecofriendly alternative to driving downtown. Now big cities in India, China, and elsewhere have similar pricing plans. Cities are also pricing highway tolls to manage the environmental impact of traffic, by lowering or eliminating fees for car-pool vehicles and for off-peak driving.

Because electric cars are greener than traditional gasoline-powered cars, many cities are providing free or low-priced charging stations to encourage greener driving downtown. In Florida, for example, Winter Park's charging stations are available in popular locations like city parking lots and the Public Safety Building, part of the city's sustainability program. Hotels and resorts all over the globe are also installing free charging stations. From the Lenox Hotel in Boston to the Sheraton Hotel in Waikiki, charging stations are attracting environmentally conscious customers and helping to save the planet by letting drivers of electric cars recharge without charge.[b]

Besides considering the costs associated with a particular product, marketers must take into account the costs the product shares with others in the product line. Products often share some costs, particularly the costs of research and development, production, and distribution. Most marketers view a product's cost as a minimum, or floor, below which the product cannot be priced.

Other Marketing Mix Variables

All marketing mix variables are highly interrelated. Pricing decisions can influence evaluations and activities associated with product, distribution, and promotion variables. A product's price frequently affects the demand for that item. A high price, for instance, may result in low unit sales, which in turn may lead to higher production costs per unit. Conversely, lower per-unit production costs may result from a low price. For many products, buyers associate better product quality with a high price and poorer product quality with a low price. This perceived price–quality relationship influences customers' overall image of products or brands. For example, some individuals view Mercedes Benz vehicles as higher quality than other brands and are willing to pay a higher price. Individuals who associate quality with a high price are likely to purchase products with well-established and recognizable brand names.

The price of a product is linked to several dimensions of its distribution. Premium-priced products are often marketed through selective or exclusive distribution. Lower-priced products in the same product category may be sold through intensive distribution. For instance, high-end Cross pens are distributed through selective distribution and disposable Bic pens through intensive distribution. Moreover, an increase in physical distribution costs, such as shipping, may have to be passed on to customers. When fuel prices increase significantly, some distribution companies pass on these additional costs through surcharges or higher prices. When setting a price, the profit margins of marketing channel members, such as wholesalers and retailers, must also be considered. Channel members must be adequately compensated for the functions they perform.

Price may determine how a product is promoted. Bargain prices are often included in advertisements. Premium prices are less likely to be advertised, though they are sometimes included in advertisements for upscale items like luxury cars or fine jewelry. Higher-priced products are more likely than lower-priced ones to require personal selling. Furthermore, the price structure can affect a salesperson's relationship with customers. A complex pricing structure takes longer to explain to customers, is more likely to confuse potential buyers, and may cause misunderstandings that result in long-term customer dissatisfaction. Anyone who has tried to decipher his or her cell phone bill will empathize with the frustration that complex pricing structures can bring about. Trying to decipher charges for anytime, weekend, daytime, and roaming minutes, not to mention charges for smartphone data usage, can be confusing.

Channel Member Expectations

When making price decisions, a producer must consider what members of the distribution channel expect. A channel member certainly expects to receive a profit for the functions it performs. The amount of profit expected depends on what the intermediary could make if it were handling a competing product instead. Also, the amount of time and the resources required to carry the product influence intermediaries' expectations.

Channel members often expect producers to give discounts for large orders and prompt payment. At times, resellers expect producers to provide several support activities, such as sales training, service training, repair advisory service, cooperative advertising, sales promotions, and perhaps a program for returning unsold merchandise to the producer. These support activities clearly have associated costs that a producer must consider when determining prices.

Customers' Interpretation and Response

When making pricing decisions, marketers should address a vital question: How will our customers interpret our prices and respond to them? *Interpretation* in this context refers to what the price means or what it communicates to customers. Does the price mean "high quality" or "low quality," or "great deal," "fair price," or "rip-off"? Customer *response* refers to whether the price will move customers closer to purchase of the product and the degree to which the price enhances their satisfaction with the purchase experience and with the product after purchase.

Customers' interpretation of and response to a price are to some degree determined by their assessment of value, or what they receive compared with what they give up to make the purchase. In evaluating what they receive, customers consider product attributes, benefits, advantages, disadvantages, the probability of using the product, and possibly the status associated with the product. In assessing the cost of the product, customers will likely consider its price, the amount of time and effort required to obtain it, and perhaps the resources required to maintain it after purchase.

At times, customers interpret a higher price as higher product quality. They are especially likely to make this price–quality association when they cannot judge the quality of the product themselves. This is not always the case, however. Whether price is equated with quality depends on the types of customers and products involved. Obviously marketers that rely on customers making a price–quality association and that provide moderate- or low-quality products at high prices will be unable to build long-term customer relationships.

When interpreting and responding to prices, how do customers determine if the price is too high, too low, or about right? In general, they compare prices with internal or external reference prices. An **internal reference price** is a price developed in the buyer's mind through experience with the product. It reflects a belief that a product should cost approximately a certain amount. To arrive at an internal reference price, consumers may consider one or more values, including what they think the product "ought" to cost, the price usually charged for it, the last price they paid, the highest and lowest amounts they would be willing to pay, the price of the brand they usually buy, the average price of similar products, the expected future price, and the typical discounted price.[12] Research has found that less-confident consumers tend to have higher internal reference prices than consumers with greater confidence, and frequent buyers—perhaps because of their experience and confidence—are more likely to judge high prices unfairly.[13] As consumers, our experiences have given each of us internal reference prices for a number of products. For instance, most of us have a reasonable idea of how much to pay for a six-pack of soft drinks, a loaf of bread, or a cup of coffee.

internal reference price A price developed in the buyer's mind through experience with the product

© AP Images/PRNewsFoto/Pizza Hut

External Reference Price
Advertisements, like this one, provide information that customers use to establish or change their reference prices.

For the product categories with which we have less experience, we rely more heavily on external reference prices. An **external reference price** is a comparison price provided by others, such as retailers or manufacturers. Some grocery and electronics stores, for example, will show other stores' prices next to their price of a particular good if their price is lower than the competitor's. This provides a reference point for consumers unfamiliar with the product category. Customers' perceptions of prices are also influenced by their expectations about future price increases, what they paid for the product recently, and what they would like to pay for the product. Other factors affecting customers' perceptions of whether the price is right include time or financial constraints, the costs associated with searching for lower-priced products, and expectations that products will go on sale.

Buyers' perceptions of a product relative to competing products may allow the firm to set a price that differs significantly from rivals' prices. If the product is deemed superior to most of the competition, a premium price may be feasible. However, even products with superior quality can be overpriced. Strong brand loyalty sometimes provides the opportunity to charge a premium price. On the other hand, if buyers view a product less than favorably (though not extremely negatively), a lower price may generate sales.

In the context of price, buyers can be characterized according to their degree of value consciousness, price consciousness, and prestige sensitivity. Marketers that understand these characteristics are better able to set pricing objectives and policies. **Value-conscious** consumers are concerned about both price and quality of a product.[14] During recessions, customers become more value and price conscious and tend to limit discretionary spending. In an effort to regain market share after a period of declining sales, The International House of Pancakes (IHOP) launched a new menu appealing to value-conscious consumers. The 7 for $7 menu features a wide range of offerings, including steak, crepes, and a vegetable omelet. Denny's has a similar menu for value-conscious diners, with options priced at $2, $4, $6, and $8. These value-conscious consumers may perceive value as quality per unit of price or as not only economic savings but also the additional gains expected from one product over a competitor's brand. The first view is appropriate for commodities like bottled water, bananas, and gasoline. If a value-conscious consumer perceives the quality of gasoline to be the same for Exxon and Shell, he or she will go to the station with the lower price. For consumers looking not just for economic value but additional gains they expect from one brand over another, a product differentiation value could be associated with benefits and features that are believed to be unique.[15] For example, a BMW may be considered to be better than a Cadillac.

Price-conscious individuals strive to pay low prices. They want the lowest prices, even if the products are not of the highest quality. Amazon.com has long been known for a willingness to sacrifice profit margins in favor of offering the lowest prices. Although not popular with competing retailers, Amazon's Price Check feature encourages customers to compare prices and shop at Amazon for the best deals.[16] Price-conscious consumers might also shop at Walmart due to its "Everyday Low Price" guarantee.

Prestige-sensitive buyers focus on purchasing products that signify prominence and status. For instance, Tiffany & Co. is known for its stunning jewelry designs and has been a premier jeweler worldwide for over 175 years. Its Soleste diamond ring, with a 1.35 carat yellow diamond and several smaller white diamonds, is priced at $30,000.[17]

Some consumers vary in their degree of value, price, and prestige consciousness. In some market segments, consumers "trade up" to higher-status products in categories, such as automobiles, home appliances, restaurants, and even pet food, yet remain price conscious regarding cleaning and grocery products. This trend has benefited marketers like Starbucks, BMW, Whole Foods, and PETCO, which can charge premium prices for high-quality, prestige products.

external reference price A comparison price provided by others

value conscious Concerned about price and quality of a product

price conscious Striving to pay low prices

prestige sensitive Drawn to products that signify prominence and status

Emerging Trends

The Great Pretenders: Renting Upscale Art, Fashion, and Jewelry

One of the latest high-tech twists in rentals is click to rent high-end products like couture fashion or original art for a few days or a few months. Rentals are nothing new—tuxedo rentals have been around for many years. What's new is the ability to browse thousands of available items on the Web, get one-on-one expert assistance, and reserve a rental for the next day, the next month, or the next year, all without leaving your keyboard. Thanks to rentals, you can make a big impression without a big investment or try before you buy expensive items.

Interested in art but not sure what to buy? Artsicle rents paintings and other original artworks for a month (or longer), starting at $25 per month. Going to a wedding or a dressy event? Rent high fashion apparel and accessories, at a fraction of what you'd pay to buy. For example, RenttheRunway.com carries dozens of designer names, with rentals priced at about 10 percent of the retail price, plus shipping and insurance fees. Adorn.com rents diamond necklaces, bracelets, and earrings for very special occasions. New for the Night, a Houston-area fashion rental business, invites local customers to check styles online and then visit the showroom to try on clothing before renting. And in the long run, designer brands benefit from high-end rentals, because these increase brand awareness and preference, says New for the Night's owner.[c]

Competition

A marketer needs to know competitors' prices so it can adjust its own prices accordingly. This does not mean a company will necessarily match competitors' prices; it may set its price above or below theirs. However, for some organizations, matching competitors' prices is an important strategy for survival.

When adjusting prices, a marketer must assess how competitors will respond. Will competitors change their prices and, if so, will they raise or lower them? In Chapter 3, we described several types of competitive market structures. The structure that characterizes the industry to which a firm belongs affects the flexibility of price setting. For example, because of reduced pricing regulation, firms in the telecommunications industry have moved from a monopolistic market structure to an oligopolistic one, which has resulted in significant price competition.

When an organization operates as a monopoly and is unregulated, it can set whatever prices the market will bear. However, the company may not price the product at the highest-possible level to avoid government regulation or penetrate a market by using a lower price. If the monopoly is regulated, it normally has less pricing flexibility; the regulatory body lets it set prices that generate a reasonable but not excessive return. A government-owned monopoly may price products below cost to make them accessible to people who otherwise could not afford them. Transit systems, for example, sometimes operate this way. However, government-owned monopolies sometimes charge higher prices to control demand. In some states with state-owned liquor stores, the price of liquor is higher than in states where liquor stores are not owned by a government body.

The automotive and airline industries exemplify oligopolies, in which only a few sellers operate and barriers to competitive entry are high. Companies in such industries can raise their prices in the hope that competitors will do the same. When an organization cuts its price to gain a competitive edge, other companies are likely to follow suit. Thus, very little advantage is gained through price cuts in an oligopolistic market structure.

A market structure characterized by monopolistic competition has numerous sellers with product offerings that are differentiated by physical characteristics, features, quality, and brand images. The distinguishing characteristics of its product may allow a company to set a different price than its competitors. However, firms in a monopolistic competitive market structure are likely to practice nonprice competition, discussed earlier in this chapter.

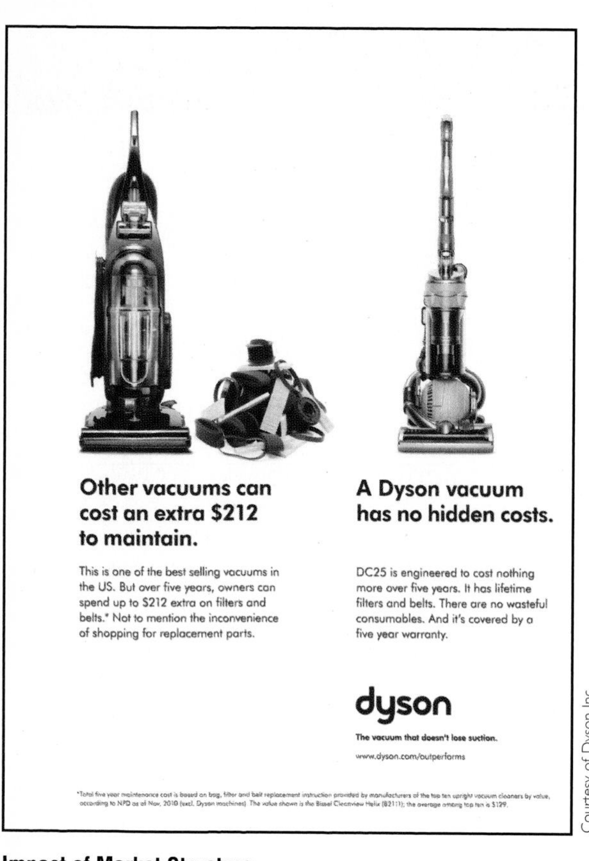

Courtesy of Dyson Inc.

Impact of Market Structure
The vacuum cleaner industry is an example of an oligopoly, because there are relatively few vacuum cleaner manufacturers.

Under conditions of perfect competition, many sellers exist. Buyers view all sellers' products as the same. All firms sell their products at the going market price, and buyers will not pay more than that. This type of market structure, then, gives a marketer no flexibility in setting prices. Farming, as an industry, has some characteristics of perfect competition. Farmers sell their products at the going market price. At times, for example, corn, soybean, and wheat growers have had bumper crops and been forced to sell them at depressed market prices. In countries in which farm subsidies are provided, the effects of perfect competition are reduced.

Legal and Regulatory Issues

Legal and regulatory issues influence pricing decisions. To curb inflation, the federal government can invoke price controls, freeze prices at certain levels, or determine the rates at which firms may increase prices. In some states and many other countries, regulatory agencies set prices on such products as insurance, dairy products, and liquor.

Many regulations and laws affect pricing decisions and activities in the United States. The Sherman Antitrust Act prohibits conspiracies to control prices, and in interpreting the act, courts have ruled that price-fixing among firms in an industry is illegal. Marketers must refrain from fixing prices by developing independent pricing policies and setting prices in ways that do not even hint at collusion. The U.S. Justice Department recently found Japanese auto supplier Yazaki, which supplies products to companies like Honda and Toyota, guilty of price-fixing. The Justice Department levied the largest-ever single fine, $470 million, for the offense. Additionally, four of Yazaki's executives were sentenced to two years in jail for the price-fixing arrangements that occurred over the course of a decade. Another Japanese auto supplier, Denso, was also found guilty of price-fixing and fined $78 million.[18] Both the Federal Trade Commission Act and the Wheeler-Lea Act prohibit deceptive pricing. Some other nations and trade agreements have similar prohibitions. Determining what is anticompetitive in different countries can be complicated. For example, a French judge recently determined that the free Google Maps service is anticompetitive and illegal. The court ruled that Google must pay a French mapmaker, Bottin Cartogrophes, $660,000 in damages.[19] In establishing prices, marketers must guard against deceiving customers.

The Robinson-Patman Act has had a particularly strong impact on pricing decisions. For various reasons, marketers may wish to sell the same type of product at different prices. Provisions in the Robinson-Patman Act, as well as those in the Clayton Act, limit the use of such price differentials. **Price discrimination**, the practice of employing price differentials that tend to injure competition by giving one or more buyers a competitive advantage over other buyers, is prohibited by law. Currently, the biggest U.S. oil company, ExxonMobil Corp., is facing a lawsuit from some of its operators in New Jersey. Exxon apparently divides stations into zones and charges different rates to each zone for gasoline, and it also delivers gasoline on a schedule that saves Exxon money while costing the operator more. Operators cite the Robinson-Patman Act as one of the laws violated by their supplier.[20] However, not all price differentials are discriminatory. A marketer can use price differentials if they do not hinder competition, result from differences in the costs of selling or transportation to various customers, or arise because the firm has had to cut its price to a particular buyer to meet competitors' prices. Airlines, for example, may charge different customers different prices for the same flights based on the availability of seats at the time of purchase. As a result, flyers sitting in adjacent seats may have paid vastly different fares because one passenger booked weeks

price discrimination
Employing price differentials that injure competition by giving one or more buyers a competitive advantage

Marketing Debate

Should Cash and Credit Prices Differ?

ISSUE: Should marketers be allowed to charge one price for credit purchases and another for cash purchases?

Many gas stations (and some other marketers) set one price for credit purchases and a lower price for cash purchases. No, credit customers aren't being charged more—in fact, adding a surcharge to a credit-card purchase is illegal in 10 states, and the credit-card companies don't allow extra fees, either. However, marketers can offer a discount for paying with cash, as long as the two prices are clearly disclosed. But should cash and credit prices differ?

Marketers that accept Visa, MasterCard, American Express, and other credit cards have to pay fees to have credit transactions processed, usually about 2 to 3 percent of the amount charged. Their prices reflect these fees, passing them along to customers who use credit. Because cash transactions aren't subject to these processing fees, marketers can set lower prices for cash-paying customers, as many (but not all) gas stations do.

Yet customers who are attracted by the low cash-discount price may not even notice that there are two prices until they hand over a credit card. Also, some say that cash discounts should be offered only on sizable or luxury purchases, not on smaller, everyday purchases of necessities. Finally, some critics argue that marketers should absorb the credit-card fees as a cost of doing business and set one price regardless of how the buyer pays. What do you think?[d]

ahead, whereas the other booked on the spur of the moment a few days before when only a few seats were still available.

PRICING FOR BUSINESS MARKETS

Business markets consist of individuals and organizations that purchase products for resale, use those products in their own operations, or produce other products. Establishing prices for this category of buyers sometimes differs from setting prices for consumers. Differences in the size of purchases, geographic factors, and transportation considerations require sellers to adjust prices. In this section, we discuss several issues unique to the pricing of business products, including discounts, geographic pricing, and transfer pricing.

Price Discounting

Producers commonly provide intermediaries with discounts, or reductions, from list prices. Although many types of discounts exist, they usually fall into one of five categories: trade, quantity, cash, seasonal, and allowance. Table 20.3 summarizes some reasons to use each type of discount and provides examples. Such discounts can be a significant factor in a marketing strategy.

Trade Discounts

A reduction off the list price given by a producer to an intermediary for performing certain functions is called a **trade (functional) discount**. A trade discount is usually stated in terms of a percentage or series of percentages off the list price. Intermediaries are given trade discounts as compensation for performing various functions, such as selling, transporting, storing, final processing, and perhaps providing credit services. Although certain trade discounts are often a standard practice within an industry, discounts vary considerably among industries. It is important that a manufacturer provide a trade discount large enough to offset the intermediary's costs, plus a reasonable profit, to entice the reseller to carry the product.

trade (functional) discount A reduction off the list price a producer gives to an intermediary for performing certain functions

Table 20.3 Discounts Used for Business Markets

Type	Reasons for Use	Examples
Trade	To attract and keep effective resellers by compensating them for performing certain functions, such as transportation, warehousing, selling, and providing credit	A college bookstore pays about (functional) one-third less for a new textbook than the retail price a student pays.
Quantity	To encourage customers to buy large quantities when making purchases and, in the case of cumulative discounts, to encourage customer loyalty	Large department store chains purchase some women's apparel at lower prices than do individually owned specialty stores.
Cash	To reduce expenses associated with accounts receivable and collection by encouraging prompt payment of accounts	Numerous companies serving business markets allow a 2 percent discount if an account is paid within 10 days.
Seasonal	To allow a marketer to use resources more efficiently by stimulating sales during off-peak periods	Florida hotels provide companies holding national and regional sales meetings with deeply discounted accommodations during the summer months.
Allowance	In the case of a trade-in allowance, to assist the buyer in making the purchase and potentially earning a profit on the resale of used equipment; in the case of a promotional allowance, to ensure that dealers participate in advertising and sales support programs	A farm equipment dealer takes a farmer's used tractor as a trade-in on a new one. Nabisco pays a promotional allowance to a supermarket for setting up and maintaining a large, end-of-aisle display for a two-week period.

Quantity Discounts

Deductions from list price that reflect the economies of purchasing in large quantities are called **quantity discounts**. Quantity discounts are used in many industries and pass on to the buyer cost savings gained through economies of scale.

Quantity discounts can be either cumulative or noncumulative. **Cumulative discounts** are quantity discounts aggregated over a stated time period. Purchases totaling $10,000 in a three-month period, for example, might entitle the buyer to a five percent, or $500, rebate. Such discounts are intended to reflect economies in selling and encourage the buyer to purchase from one seller. **Noncumulative discounts** are one-time reductions in prices based on the number of units purchased, the dollar value of the order, or the product mix purchased. Like cumulative discounts, these discounts should reflect some economies in selling or trade functions.

quantity discounts Deductions from the list price for purchasing in large quantities

cumulative discounts Quantity discounts aggregated over a stated time period

noncumulative discounts One-time price reductions based on the number of units purchased, the dollar value of the order, or the product mix purchased

cash discount A price reduction given to buyers for prompt payment or cash payment

seasonal discount A price reduction given to buyers for purchasing goods or services out of season

Cash Discounts

A **cash discount**, or price reduction, is given to a buyer for prompt payment or cash payment. Accounts receivable are an expense and a collection problem for many organizations. A policy to encourage prompt payment is a popular practice and sometimes a major concern in setting prices.

Discounts are based on cash payments or cash paid within a stated time. For instance, "2/10 net 30" means that a 2 percent discount will be allowed if the account is paid within 10 days. If the buyer does not make payment within the 10-day period, the entire balance is due within 30 days without a discount. If the account is not paid within 30 days, interest may be charged.

Seasonal Discounts

A price reduction to buyers that purchase goods or services out of season is a **seasonal discount**. These discounts let the seller maintain steadier production during the year. For example, it is usually much cheaper to purchase and install an air-conditioning unit in the winter than it is in the summer. This is because demand for air conditioners is very low during the winter in most parts of the country, and price therefore is also lower than in peak-demand season.

Allowances

Another type of reduction from the list price is an **allowance**, a concession in price to achieve a desired goal. Trade-in allowances, for example, are price reductions granted for turning in a used item when purchasing a new one. Allowances help make the buyer better able to make the new purchase. Another example is a promotional allowance, a price reduction granted to dealers for participating in advertising and sales support programs intended to increase sales of a particular item.

Geographic Pricing

Geographic pricing involves reductions for transportation costs or other costs associated with the physical distance between buyer and seller. Prices may be quoted as F.O.B. (free-on-board) factory or destination. An **F.O.B. factory** price indicates the price of the merchandise at the factory, before it is loaded onto the carrier, and thus excludes transportation costs. The buyer must pay for shipping. An **F.O.B. destination** price means the producer absorbs the costs of shipping the merchandise to the customer. This policy may be used to attract distant customers. Although F.O.B. pricing is an easy way to price products, it is sometimes difficult to administer, especially when a firm has a wide product mix or when customers are widely dispersed. Because customers will want to know about the most economical method of shipping, the seller must be informed about shipping rates.

To avoid the problems involved in charging different prices to each customer, **uniform geographic pricing**, sometimes called *postage-stamp pricing,* may be used. The same price is charged to all customers regardless of geographic location, and the price is based on average shipping costs for all customers. Paper products and office equipment are often priced on a uniform basis.

Zone pricing sets uniform prices for each of several major geographic zones; as the transportation costs across zones increase, so do the prices. For instance, a Florida manufacturer's prices may be higher for buyers on the Pacific coast and in Canada than for buyers in Georgia.

Base-point pricing is a geographic pricing policy that includes the price at the factory, plus freight charges from the base point nearest the buyer. This approach to pricing has virtually been abandoned because of its questionable legal status. The policy resulted in all buyers paying freight charges from one location, such as Detroit or Pittsburgh, regardless of where the product was manufactured.

When the seller absorbs all or part of the actual freight costs, **freight absorption pricing** is being used. The seller might choose this method because it wishes to do business with a particular customer or to get more business; more business will cause the average cost to fall and counterbalance the extra freight cost. This strategy is used to improve market penetration and retain a hold in an increasingly competitive market.

Transfer Pricing

Transfer pricing occurs when one unit in an organization sells a product to another unit. The price is determined by one of the following methods:

- *Actual full cost:* calculated by dividing all fixed and variable expenses for a period into the number of units produced.
- *Standard full cost:* calculated based on what it would cost to produce the goods at full plant capacity.
- *Cost plus investment:* calculated as full cost plus the cost of a portion of the selling unit's assets used for internal needs.
- *Market-based cost:* calculated at the market price less a small discount to reflect the lack of sales effort and other expenses.

The choice of transfer pricing method depends on the company's management strategy and the nature of the units' interaction. An organization must also ensure that transfer pricing is fair to all units involved in the transactions.

allowance A concession in price to achieve a desired goal

geographic pricing Reductions for transportation and other costs related to the physical distance between buyer and seller

F.O.B. factory The price of merchandise at the factory before shipment

F.O.B. destination A price indicating the producer is absorbing shipping costs

uniform geographic pricing Charging all customers the same price, regardless of geographic location

zone pricing Pricing based on transportation costs within major geographic zones

base-point pricing Geographic pricing that combines factory price and freight charges from the base point nearest the buyer

freight absorption pricing Absorption of all or part of actual freight costs by the seller

transfer pricing Prices charged in sales between an organization's units

Summary

1. To understand the role of price

Price is the value paid for a product in a marketing exchange. Barter, the trading of products, is the oldest form of exchange. Price is a key element in the marketing mix, because it relates directly to generation of total revenue. The profit factor can be determined mathematically by multiplying price by quantity sold to get total revenue and then subtracting total costs. Price is the only variable in the marketing mix that can be adjusted quickly and easily to respond to changes in the external environment.

2. To identify the characteristics of price and nonprice competition

A product offering can compete on either a price or a nonprice basis. Price competition emphasizes price as the product differential. Prices fluctuate frequently, and price competition among sellers is aggressive. Nonprice competition emphasizes product differentiation through distinctive features, service, product quality, or other factors. Establishing brand loyalty by using nonprice competition works best when the product can be physically differentiated and the customer can recognize these differences.

3. To explore demand curves and price elasticity of demand

An organization must determine the demand for its product. The classic demand curve is a graph of the quantity of products expected to be sold at various prices if other factors hold constant. It illustrates that, as price falls, the quantity demanded usually increases. However, for prestige products, there is a direct positive relationship between price and quantity demanded: demand increases as price increases. Next, price elasticity of demand, the percentage change in quantity demanded relative to a given percentage change in price, must be determined. If demand is elastic, a change in price causes an opposite change in total revenue. Inelastic demand results in a parallel change in total revenue when a product's price is changed.

4. To examine the relationships among demand, costs, and profits

Analysis of demand, cost, and profit relationships can be accomplished through marginal analysis or break-even analysis. Marginal analysis examines what happens to a firm's costs and revenues when production (or sales volume) is changed by one unit. Marginal analysis combines the demand curve with the firm's costs to develop a price that yields maximum profit. Fixed costs do not vary with changes in the number of units produced or sold; average fixed cost is the fixed cost per unit produced. Variable costs vary directly with changes in the number of units produced or sold. Average variable cost is the variable cost per unit produced. Total cost is the sum of average fixed cost and average variable cost times the quantity produced. The optimal price is the point at which marginal cost (the cost associated with producing one more unit of the product) equals marginal revenue (the change in total revenue that occurs when one additional unit of the product is sold). Marginal analysis is only a model; it offers little help in pricing new products before costs and revenues are established.

Break-even analysis, determining the number of units that must be sold to break even, is important in setting price. The point at which the costs of production equal the revenue from selling the product is the break-even point. To use break-even analysis effectively, a marketer should determine the break-even point for each of several alternative prices. This makes it possible to compare the effects on total revenue, total costs, and the break-even point for each price under consideration. However, this approach assumes the quantity demanded is basically fixed and the major task is to set prices to recover costs.

5. To describe key factors that may influence marketers' pricing decisions

Eight factors enter into price decision making: organizational and marketing objectives, pricing objectives, costs, other marketing mix variables, channel member expectations, customer interpretation and response, competition, and legal and regulatory issues. When setting prices, marketers should make decisions consistent with the organization's goals and mission. Pricing objectives heavily influence price-setting decisions. Most marketers view a product's cost as the floor below which a product cannot be priced. Because of the interrelationship among the marketing mix variables, price can affect product, promotion, and distribution decisions. The revenue channel members expect for their functions must also be considered when making price decisions.

Buyers' perceptions of price vary. Some consumer segments are sensitive to price, but others may not be. Thus, before determining price, a marketer needs to be aware of its importance to the target market. Knowledge of the prices charged for competing brands is essential to allow the firm to adjust its prices relative to competitors'. Government regulations and legislation also influence pricing decisions.

6. To consider issues affecting the pricing of products for business markets

The categories of discounts include trade, quantity, cash, seasonal, and allowance. A trade discount is a price reduction for performing such functions as storing, transporting, final processing, or providing credit services. If an intermediary purchases in large enough quantities, the producer gives a quantity discount, which can be either cumulative or noncumulative.

A cash discount is a price reduction for prompt payment or payment in cash. Buyers who purchase goods or services out of season may be granted a seasonal discount. An allowance, such as a trade-in allowance, is a concession in price to achieve a desired goal.

Geographic pricing involves reductions for transportation costs or other costs associated with the physical distance between buyer and seller. With an F.O.B. factory price, the buyer pays for shipping from the factory. An F.O.B. destination price means the producer pays for shipping; this is the easiest way to price products, but it is difficult to administer. When the seller charges a fixed average cost for transportation, it is using uniform geographic pricing. Zone prices are uniform within major geographic zones; they increase by zone as transportation costs increase. With base-point pricing, prices are adjusted for shipping expenses incurred by the seller from the base point nearest the buyer. Freight absorption pricing occurs when a seller absorbs all or part of the freight costs.

Transfer pricing occurs when a unit in an organization sells products to another unit in the organization. Methods used for transfer pricing include actual full cost, standard full cost, cost plus investment, and market-based cost.

Go to www.cengagebrain.com for resources to help you master the content in this chapter as well as for materials that will expand your marketing knowledge!

Important Terms

price 674
barter 674
price competition 675
nonprice competition 676
demand curve 677
price elasticity of demand 679
fixed costs 680
average fixed cost 680
variable costs 680
average variable cost 680
total cost 680
average total cost 680
marginal cost (MC) 680
marginal revenue (MR) 680
break-even point 683
internal reference price 687
external reference price 688
value conscious 688
price conscious 688
prestige sensitive 688
price discrimination 690
trade (functional) discount 691
quantity discounts 692
cumulative discounts 692
noncumulative discounts 692
cash discount 692
seasonal discount 692
allowance 693
geographic pricing 693
F.O.B. factory 693
F.O.B. destination 693
uniform geographic pricing 693
zone pricing 693
base-point pricing 693
freight absorption pricing 693
transfer pricing 693

Discussion and Review Questions

1. Why are pricing decisions important to an organization?
2. Compare and contrast price and nonprice competition. Describe the conditions under which each form works best.
3. Why do most demand curves demonstrate an inverse relationship between price and quantity?
4. List the characteristics of products that have inelastic demand, and give several examples of such products.
5. Explain why optimal profits should occur when marginal cost equals marginal revenue.
6. Chambers Company has just gathered estimates for conducting a break-even analysis for a new product. Variable costs are $7 a unit. The additional plant will cost $48,000. The new product will be charged $18,000 a year for its share of general overhead. Advertising expenditures will be $80,000, and $55,000 will be spent on distribution. If the product sells for $12, what is the break-even point in units? What is the break-even point in dollar sales volume?
7. In what ways do other marketing mix variables affect pricing decisions?
8. What types of expectations may channel members have about producers' prices? How might these expectations affect pricing decisions?
9. How do legal and regulatory forces influence pricing decisions?
10. Compare and contrast a trade discount and a quantity discount.
11. What is the reason for using the term *F.O.B.?*
12. What are the major methods used for transfer pricing?

Application Questions

1. Price competition is intense in the fast-food, air travel, and personal computer industries. Discuss a recent situation in which companies had to meet or beat a rival's price in a price-competitive industry. Did you benefit from this situation? Did it change your perception of the companies and/or their products?
2. Customers' interpretations and responses regarding a product and its price are an important influence on marketers' pricing decisions. Perceptions of price are affected by the degree to which a customer is value conscious, price conscious, or prestige sensitive. Discuss how value consciousness, price consciousness, and prestige sensitivity influence the buying decision process for the following products:
   a. A new house.
   b. Weekly groceries for a family of five.
   c. An airline ticket.
   d. A soft drink from a vending machine.
3. IMP As discussed in this chapter, customers interpret and respond to prices in different ways, depending on the type of product, perceptions of product quality, and the customer's ability to judge product quality independent of the price. Because customers lack the ability to judge product quality, they sometimes use the price of the product as an indicator of product quality. Thus, the price–quality relationship can influence the purchase of some products. For each one of the following, indicate whether customers rely heavily, moderately, or hardly at all on the price to judge the quality of a product.

   Airfare in coach ______________________

   Appendectomy ______________________

   Baby food ______________________

   Cell phone service ______________________

   Cosmetics ______________________

   Dog food ______________________

   Electricity ______________________

   Furniture ______________________

   Gasoline ______________________

   Haircut ______________________

   Hotel room ______________________

   Jewelry ______________________

   Tanning salon ______________________

   Used car ______________________

Internet Exercise

Autobytel

Autobytel offers car buyers a free, comprehensive website to find the invoice prices for almost all car models. The browser can also access a listing of all the latest new-car rebates and incentives. Visit this company's site at **www.autobytel.com**.

1. Find the lowest-priced Lexus available today, and examine its features. Which Lexus dealer is closest to you?
2. If you wanted to purchase this Lexus, what are the lowest monthly payments you could make over the longest time period?
3. Is this free site more credible than a "pay" site? Why or why not?

developing your marketing plan

The appropriate pricing of a product is an important factor in developing a successful marketing strategy. The price contributes to the profitability of the product and can deter competition from entering the market. A clear understanding of pricing concepts is essential in developing a strategy and marketing plan. Consider the information in this chapter when focusing on the following issues:

1. Does your company currently compete based on price or nonprice factors? Should your new product continue with this approach?
2. Discuss the level of elasticity of demand for your product. Is additional information needed for you to determine its elasticity?
3. At various price points, calculate the break-even point for sales of your product.
4. Using Figure 20.8 as a guide, discuss the various factors that affect the pricing of your product.

The information obtained from these questions should assist you in developing various aspects of your marketing plan found in the "Interactive Marketing Plan" exercise at **www.cengagebrain.com**.

video case 20.1

Pricing Renewable Energy Projects: Think Long-Term

John Miggins, a sales representative for Standard Renewable Energy in Oklahoma, tells customers to think long-term when they're thinking about buying renewable energy equipment for residential or commercial use. Although solar panels or a wind turbine will allow customers to generate enough power to replace much or all of the electricity they currently buy from a utility company, the out-of-pocket cost is hardly a quick fix for kilowatt sticker shock. Installing a wind turbine can cost $17,500, and a solar power set-up for an average home can cost up to $40,000.

Still, demand for renewable energy equipment has been steadily rising for more than a decade as consumers and businesses have become interested in environmentally friendly power sources. Manufacturers around the world are constantly introducing new, high-efficiency offerings for homes, factories, and other buildings. At the same time, the combination of technological advances, higher supply, and increased global competition has put downward pressure on prices. At one point, so many manufacturers were making so many silicon solar panels that the glut and the competition pushed panel prices down by 50 percent in one year.

© iStockphoto.com/gmalandra

These dramatic price drops, and a variety of governmental tax incentives for buying energy-efficient products for homes and businesses, are bringing the cost of renewable energy much closer to the cost of energy from conventional sources, such as coal and nuclear power. As prices move ever lower, the market expands, because more consumers and business buyers see solar and wind generation as viable alternatives to their current power sources. These days, small and mid-size solar panel installations and wind turbines are popping up in many places, like homes and individual businesses. In addition, power companies are installing renewable energy equipment to generate electricity on a large scale.

John Miggins warns his customers against expecting a quick return on their investment in renewable energy equipment. He says businesses that install solar panels usually get 60 percent of their investment back within six years and 100 percent back within 10 years. Consumer installations don't earn back their cost as quickly as commercial installations, simply because homes don't use as much electricity as businesses. Miggins also recognizes that customers care about things other than price—they also want a feeling of security and a sense of confidence in the seller who provides their new energy equipment.

Because Miggins works for Standard Renewable Energy, his prices take into account the company's buying power and sales volume. The pieces of equipment he orders for customers are bundled with larger deliveries to the company's facilities, which reduces the shipping costs paid by individual buyers. And toward the end of a month, when Miggins wants to close deals and make his sales quota, customers are likely to get an even better price when they place an order.[21]

Questions for Discussion

1. When pricing its products, what external factors should Standard Renewable Energy pay particular attention to, and why?
2. How are value-conscious, price-conscious, and prestige-conscious customers likely to react to the price of a wind turbine?
3. Does geographic pricing affect what business customers pay for a wind turbine they buy from Standard Renewable Energy compared to prices paid by nonbusiness customers? Explain your answer.

case 20.2

Take You Out to the Ball Game? Let Me Check the Price First

When the Chicago White Sox play the Chicago Cubs, the Sox raise single-game ticket prices, because the cross-town rivalry attracts so many local fans. The Atlanta Braves raise ticket prices when the Yankees come to town, knowing that fans will flock to the stadium for this matchup. The San Francisco Giants, Minnesota Twins, Oakland Athletics, and other baseball teams also change single-game ticket prices depending on demand. This trend toward dynamic pricing is now spreading to other sports. The Washington Capitals hockey team and the Washington Wizards basketball team are two of a growing list of teams that use this pricing approach for single-game tickets (not for season tickets).

Before baseball's Giants instituted dynamic pricing, team marketers wondered how fans would react. "They are familiar with this type of pricing in the airline and hotel industry," says the head of ticket sales, "but this was a big leap for a sports team to implement the idea into the box office." Although the Giants had been varying prices depending on which team was visiting, its marketers knew that demand was higher at certain points in the season and on different days of the week. Switching to dynamic pricing enables the Giants to stimulate demand during slower periods and increase revenue during periods of peak demand.

The Chicago White Sox team uses dynamic pricing because "we want to get as many bodies in the park as possible," explains the head of marketing. The team has a committee that meets weekly to review sales data for individual games and for the season, and decide on price changes for the coming week. Except for seats that have been sold to season ticket holders, single-game tickets may be priced up or down at any time. Buyers who get their tickets well in advance usually get the best prices, especially for games scheduled early in the season and games against teams that aren't high in the standings. Filling seats also means higher revenues from team merchandise, parking fees, and food sales.

Marketers for the Minnesota Twins like the flexibility of dynamic pricing. In the past, they had to set prices months before the season started, to have time to print brochures and tickets. Now they can make last-minute price adjustments after checking weather forecasts, team rankings, player trades, pitching lineups, and other factors. If they've priced tickets for a particular game too low—meaning sales are much better than expected—or too high, they can boost ticket sales by making price changes as game day approaches. The Twins also use dynamic pricing to get fans excited about specially priced "Steal of the Week" single-game tickets that are offered online only.

Will all major league sports teams eventually adopt dynamic pricing? The answer depends on whether fans raise a fuss over price changes, and whether the teams currently using it are successful in filling seats and raising revenue. Some teams are testing such pricing on a small scale, applying it only to designated seating sections or specific games to determine public reaction. But if a baseball team hits a home run in pricing, chances are good that it will expand this dynamic approach to the rest of its stadium and the rest of its schedule.[22]

Questions for Discussion

1. How does dynamic pricing allow a team to judge the price elasticity of demand for a particular game and then use this information in future pricing decisions?
2. What other marketing mix variables must teams consider when using dynamic pricing to set ticket prices? Why?
3. Do you think price competition plays a role in the way baseball teams price their single-game tickets? Explain your answer.

NOTES

[1]Based on information in Charles Cooper, "So How Much Is a Fair Price to Pay for an E-book?" CBS News, February 24, 2012, www.cbsnews.com; Alexandra Alter, "A Sneak Preview—For Books," *The Wall Street Journal,* February 17, 2012, www.wsj.com; Jeffrey A. Trachtenberg, "E-book Readers Face Sticker Shock," *The Wall Street Journal,* December 15, 2011, www.wsj.com.

[2]Rajneesh Suri and Kent B. Monroe, "The Effects of Time Constraints on Consumers' Judgements of Prices and Products," *Journal of Consumer Research* (June 2003): 92.

[3]"Modern Trade & Barter," International Reciprocal Trade Association, www.irta.com/modern-trade-a-barter.html (accessed April 12, 2012).

[4]"Hewlett-Packard," Case Study, Professional Pricing Society, www.pricingsociety.com/Page5024.aspx (accessed April 18, 2012).

[5]"Sprint Data Plan Price Drops After Just 2 Weeks," *Huffington Post,* November 14, 2011, www.huffingtonpost.com/2011/11/14/sprint-data-plan-price_n_1093654.html.

[6]David Pogue, "Sampling the Future of Gadgetry," *The New York Times,* January 11, 2012, www.nytimes.com/2012/01/12/technology/personaltech/in-las-vegas-its-the-future-of-high-tech-state-of-the-art.html?; Michael Casey, "India's $35 iPad Competitor Captures Interest," *The Wall Street Journal,* January 26, 2012, http://blogs.wsj.com/davos/2012/01/26/indias-35-ipad-competitor-captures-hope-challenges-of-globalization/.

[7]"About Us," Ethel M. Chocolates, www.ethelm.com/about_us/default.aspx (accessed April 18, 2012).

[8]Jim Zemlin, "Linux Can Compete with the iPad on Price, But Where's the Magic?" *The Linux Foundation,* January 28, 2010, www.linux-foundation.org/weblogs/jzemlin/2010/01/.

[9]*Dictionary of Marketing Terms,* American Marketing Association, www.marketingpower.com/_layouts/Dictionary.aspx (accessed April 18, 2012).

[10]Daisuke Wakabayashi, "Cost Cutting Pays Off at Sony," *The Wall Street Journal,* February 5, 2010, http://online.wsj.com.

[11]David Kesmodel, "Boeing Teams Speed Up 737 Output," *The Wall Street Journal,* February 7, 2012, http://online.wsj.com/article/SB10001424052970203436904577155204034907744.html.

[12]Russell S. Winer, *Pricing* (Cambridge, MA: Marketing Science Institute, 2005), 20.

[13]Manoj Thomas and Geeta Menon, "When Internal Reference Prices and Price Expectations Diverge: The Role of Confidence," *Journal of Marketing Research* XLIV (August 2007): 401–409.

[14]Lichtenstein, Ridgway, and Netemeyer, "Price Perceptions and Consumer Shopping Behavior."

[15]Gerald E. Smith and Thomas T. Nagle, "A Question of Value," *Marketing Management* (July/August 2005): 39–40.

[16]David Streitfeld, "Amazon's Revenues Disappoint," *The New York Times,* February 1, 2012, www.nytimes.com/2012/02/01/technology/amazon-shares-drop-as-revenues-fall-short.html.

[17]Tiffany & Co., www.tiffany.com (accessed April 12, 2012).

[18]Nick Bunkley, "Japanese Auto Makers are Fined, and Executives Agree to Prison, in a Price-Fixing Case," *The New York Times,* January 31, 2012, www.nytimes.com/2012/01/31/business/japanese-auto-suppliers-fined-in-us-price-fixing-case.html.

[19]Don Reisinger, "Google Must Pay $660,000 for Offering Google Maps for Free," *CNET,* February 2, 2012, http://news.cnet.com/8301-13506_3-57370274-17/google-must-pay-$660000-for-offering-google-maps-for-free/.

[20]David Voreacos, "Exxon's New Jersey Franchisees Sue over Fuel Prices, Rent," *Bloomberg News,* December 10, 2009, www.bloomberg.com/apps/news?pid=20670001&sid=acvF_jEdjKME.

[21]Based on information in Diane Cardwell, "Renewable Sources of Power Survive, But in a Patchwork," *The New York Times,* April 10, 2012, www.nytimes.com; James Murray, "McKinsey: Solar Will Be Cost Competitive Within a Decade," *Business Green,* April 18, 2012, www.businessgreen.com; Ucilia Wang, "First Solar Struggles Amid Decline of Thin-Film Solar Market," *Forbes,* April 18, 2012, www.forbes.com.

[22]Based on information in Doug Williams, "Dynamic Pricing Is New Trend in Ticket Sales," ESPN, April 23, 2012, http://espn.go.com; Patrick Rishe, "Dynamic Pricing: The Future of Ticket Pricing in Sports," *Forbes,* January 6, 2012, www.forbes.com; Tim Tucker, "Braves Join New Trend in Ticketing: Dynamic Pricing," *Atlanta Journal-Constitution,* February 15, 2012, www.ajc.com; Ed Sherman, "White Sox Get Dynamic about Ticket Pricing," Crain's Chicago Business, February 2, 2012, www.chicagobusiness.com.

Feature Notes

[a]Based on information in Alex Williams, "On Spec: Vintage-Style Glasses Online," *The New York Times,* January 18, 2012, www.nytimes.com; "Warby Parker Revolutionizes Eyewear Market by Borrowing from Apple, Zappos," *Advertising Age,* November 27, 2011, www.adage.com; Andrew Maclean, "Warby Parker," *Inc.,* November 24, 2011, www.inc.com.

[b]Based on information in Michele Hanson, "Congestion Charge—Fined for Paying the Wrong Way," *Guardian* (U.K.), January 23, 2012, www.guardian.co.uk; Chanchal Pal Chauhan, "Delhi May Soon Levy Congestion Fee on Vehicles," *Economic Times,* April 8, 2011, www.economictimes.indiatimes.com; "Are Electric Car-Charging Stations the New Must-Have Hotel Amenity?" *Budget Travel,* January 31, 2012, www.foxnews.com; Isaac Babcock, "Electric Cars Charge for Free in Winter Park," *Winter Park Observer* (FL), February 22, 2012, www.wpmobserver.com.

[c]Based on information in Christina Uticone, "New for the Night," *Houston Pres,* February 13, 2012, www.houstonpress.com; Christina Binkley, "Fashion 101: Rent the Runway Targets Students," *The Wall Street Journal,* April 7, 2011, www.wsj.com; Graeme McMillan, "Artsicle Wants to Decorate Your Home with Fine Art," *Time,* March 1, 2011, www.time.com; Anne D'Innocenzio, "Rental Sites Make It Easy and Inexpensive to Look Red Carpet Ready," Associated Press, March 6, 2011, www.boston.com.

[d]Based on information in Christina Couch, "Bonus or Bogus: Who Pays for Rewards Credit Cards?" *Fox Business,* February 20, 2012, www.oxbusiness.com; Rafi Mohammed, "Should You Offer Different Prices for Cash and Credit?" *Harvard Business Review,* July 27, 2011, www.hbr.org; Halah Touryalai, "Cash or Credit at the Pump? The Choice Is Costing You," *Forbes,* October 21, 2011, www.forbes.com.

chapter 21

Setting Prices

OBJECTIVES

1. To describe the six major stages of the process used to establish prices
2. To explore issues related to developing pricing objectives
3. To understand the importance of identifying the target market's evaluation of price
4. To examine how marketers analyze competitors' prices
5. To describe the bases used for setting prices
6. To explain the different types of pricing strategies

MARKETING INSIGHTS

Good, Better, Best Western

In a world filled with hotel choices, from high-priced luxury suites to low-priced basic rooms, what does the Best Western brand stand for? With a chain-wide range of rates stretching from $60 to $500 per night, consumers and business travelers didn't always know what amenities to expect when they checked into a Best Western hotel or resort. So Best Western decided to add descriptive brand names to differentiate three tiers of quality, service, and pricing among its thousands of hotels worldwide.

Under the new pricing strategy, hotels that carry the Best Western brand charge mid-priced room rates with standard amenities, such as free high-speed Internet access and free local phone calls. One tier up is the Best Western Plus brand, hotels with upper-mid-priced rooms, better-quality furnishings, and additional free amenities. The top tier is the Best Western Premier brand. These are the most expensive hotels with larger rooms, premium furnishings, top-quality linens, and luxury extras like turndown service.

Corporations have responded particularly well to this three-tier strategy. The head of marketing for Best Western International says that corporations "could see some of their more senior executives adopting the Best Western Premier, they clearly saw where their mid-level executives would fit with Best Western Plus, and a lot of the commercial business really lines up strategically with Best Western." The strategy is also helping the company attract the growing segment of businesspeople in India and other nations who are willing to pay for better- and best-quality accommodations when they travel beyond the big cities.[1]

© AP Images/PRNewsFoto/Best Western International

Because price has such a profound impact on a firm's success, finding the right pricing strategy is crucial. Marketers at Best Western successfully implemented a three-tier pricing strategy. Selecting a pricing strategy is one of the fundamental components of the process of setting prices.

In this chapter, we examine six stages of a process that marketers can use when setting prices. Figure 21.1 illustrates these stages. Stage 1 is the development of a pricing objective that is compatible with the organization's overall marketing objectives. Stage 2 entails assessing the target market's evaluation of price. Stage 3 involves evaluating competitors' prices, which helps determine the role of price in the marketing strategy. Stage 4 requires choosing a basis for setting prices. Stage 5 is the selection of a pricing strategy, or the guidelines for using price in the marketing mix. Stage 6, determining the final price, depends on environmental forces and marketers' understanding and use of a systematic approach to establishing prices. These stages are not rigid steps that all marketers must follow. Rather, they are guidelines that provide a logical sequence for establishing prices.

DEVELOPMENT OF PRICING OBJECTIVES

The first step in setting prices is developing **pricing objectives**—goals that describe what a firm wants to achieve through pricing. Developing pricing objectives is an important task, because pricing objectives form the basis for decisions for other stages of the pricing process. Thus, pricing objectives must be stated explicitly, and the statement should include the time frame for accomplishing them.

Marketers must ensure that pricing objectives are consistent with the firm's marketing and overall objectives, because pricing objectives influence decisions in many functional areas, including finance, accounting, and production. A marketer can use both short- and long-term pricing objectives and can employ one or multiple pricing objectives. For instance, a firm may wish to increase market share by 18 percent over the next three years, achieve a 15 percent return on investment, and promote an image of quality in the marketplace.

pricing objectives Goals that describe what a firm wants to achieve through pricing

Figure 21.1 Stages for Establishing Prices

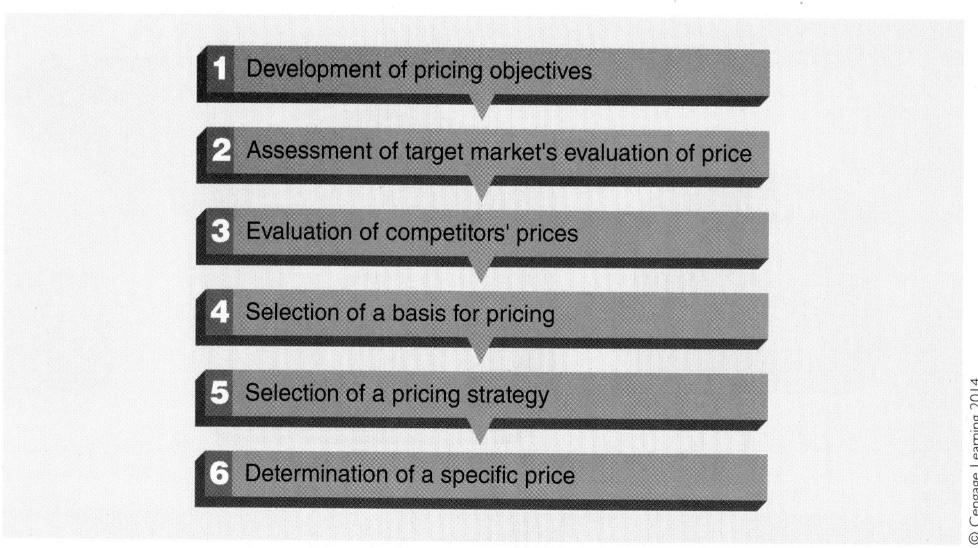

Table 21.1 Pricing Objectives and Typical Actions Taken to Achieve Them

Objective	Possible Action
Survival	Adjust price levels so the firm can increase sales volume to match organizational expenses
Profit	Identify price and cost levels that allow the firm to maximize profit
Return on investment	Identify price levels that enable the firm to yield targeted ROI
Market share	Adjust price levels so the firm can maintain or increase sales relative to competitors' sales
Cash flow	Set price levels to encourage rapid sales
Status quo	Identify price levels that help stabilize demand and sales
Product quality	Set prices to recover research and development expenditures and establish a high-quality image

In this section, we examine some of the pricing objectives companies might set for themselves. Table 21.1 shows the major pricing objectives and typical actions associated with them.

Survival

Survival is one of the most fundamental pricing objectives. Most organizations will tolerate setbacks, such as short-run losses and internal upheaval, if necessary for survival. For instance, during the recent economic downturn, some businesses were forced to reduce their prices in order to survive. Because price is a flexible variable, it is sometimes used to keep a company afloat by increasing sales volume to levels that match expenses.

Profit

Although a business may claim that its objective is to maximize profits for its owners, the objective of profit maximization is rarely operational, because its achievement is difficult to measure. Because of this difficulty, profit objectives tend to be set at levels that the owners and top-level decision makers view as satisfactory. Specific profit objectives may be stated in terms of either actual dollar amounts or a percentage of sales revenues.

Return on Investment

Pricing to attain a specified rate of return on the company's investment is a profit-related pricing objective. Most pricing objectives based on return on investment (ROI) are achieved by trial and error, because not all cost and revenue data needed to project the return on investment are available when setting prices. General Motors, for example, uses ROI pricing objectives. Many pharmaceutical companies also use ROI pricing objectives because of their great investment in research and development.

Market Share

Many firms establish pricing objectives to maintain or increase market share, a product's sales in relation to total industry sales. Kimberly-Clark Corporation recently tried to raise the price of its Huggies diapers, only to meet with strong consumer pushback and a 7 percent loss of market share. To counter the negative reactions to the price increase and regain market share, the company issued diaper coupons to consumers.[2] Many firms recognize that high relative market shares often translate into higher profits. The Profit Impact of Market Strategies (PIMS) studies, conducted over the past 50 years, have shown that both market share and product quality influence profitability.[3] Thus, marketers often use an increase in market share as a primary pricing objective.

Maintaining or increasing market share need not depend on growth in industry sales. Remember that an organization can increase its market share even if sales for the total industry are flat or decreasing. On the other hand, a firm's sales volume may increase while its market share decreases if the overall market is growing.

Cash Flow

Some companies set prices so they can recover cash as quickly as possible. Financial managers understandably seek to quickly recover capital spent to develop products. This objective may have the support of a marketing manager who anticipates a short product life cycle. Although it may be acceptable in some situations, the use of cash flow and recovery as an objective oversimplifies the contribution of price to profits. If this pricing objective results in high prices, competitors with lower prices may gain a large share of the market.

Status Quo

In some cases, an organization is in a favorable position and, thus, may set an objective of status quo. Status quo objectives can focus on several dimensions, such as maintaining a certain market share, meeting competitors' prices, achieving price stability, and maintaining a favorable public image. A status quo pricing objective can reduce a firm's risks by helping to stabilize demand for its products. The use of status quo pricing objectives sometimes

Cash Flow Pricing Objective
The pricing objective for this retailer is cash flow.

Emerging Trends

Panera Cares: Pay What You Want

"Take what you need, leave your fair share." That's what signs tell customers who eat at the Panera Cares Community Cafés in Missouri, Michigan, and Oregon. In these pay-what-you-want restaurants, people with little money can still enjoy a full meal without paying the full price. The menu boards in Panera Cares cafés look just like those in the 1,500 other Panera cafés throughout the United States and Canada, with one exception: instead of prices, they show "suggested funding levels."

Why not give the restaurant food away? Panera's Operation DoughNation already donates up to $150 million worth of unsold bakery items every year to groups that feed the hungry. But Panera's CEO also envisioned a small chain of "shared responsibility" cafés, where customers who can afford to pay add a little extra to cover meals for customers who can't afford to pay. "This is not about a handout," he explains. "This is about a hand up, and every one of us has a need for that at some point in our lives."

Although Panera Cares restaurants don't aim for profits, they do aim to cover costs, reaching the break-even point when revenues reach 80 percent of suggested funding levels. So far, the company finds that 60 percent of customers pay the suggested amount, 20 percent pay more, and 20 percent pay nothing or much less than the suggested amount.[a]

minimizes pricing as a competitive tool, leading to a climate of nonprice competition in an industry. Professionals like accountants and attorneys often operate in such an environment.

Product Quality

A company may have the objective of leading its industry in product quality. This goal normally dictates a high price to cover the costs of achieving high product quality and, in some instances, the costs of research and development. For example, Starbucks recently acquired the premium juice company Evolution Fresh with the aim to give the juice market the premium treatment the company has given coffee. The company plans to sell bottled juices as well as open a series of juice bars offering high-end, premium juices. Starbucks hopes to take advantage of the healthful image of juice and draw in customers looking to detox, lose weight, or introduce more fruit into their diets.[4] As previously mentioned, the PIMS studies have shown that both product quality and market share are good indicators of profitability. The products and brands that customers perceive to be of high quality are more likely to survive in a competitive marketplace. High quality usually enables a marketer to charge higher prices for the product.

Product Quality
This ad for the Apple iPhone focuses on the high quality of Apple's premium products.

ASSESSMENT OF THE TARGET MARKET'S EVALUATION OF PRICE

After developing pricing objectives, marketers must assess the target market's evaluation of price next. Despite the general assumption that price is a major issue for buyers, the importance of price

Table 21.2 Examples of Perceptions of Product Value

Basic, Cost-Effective Product	Expensive, Time-Saving Product
Whole loose bagels, $0.59 each	Sliced packaged bagels, $0.65 each
Whole broccoli, $1.49/lb	Florets broccoli, $3.99/lb
Whole carrots, $1.49/lb	Baby carrots, $3.99/lb
Whole chicken, $1.49/lb	Cut-up chicken, $1.99/lb
Whole feta cheese, $3.23/8 oz	Crumbled feta cheese, $8.65/8 oz
Whole Granny Smith apples, $1.99/lb	Sliced Granny Smith apples, $3.97/lb
Lean ground chuck (ground), $3.99/lb	Lean ground chuck (patties), $5.99/lb

Source: "Supermarket Smarts," *Consumer Reports ShopSmart*, www.shopsmartmag.org/files/Supermarket_smarts.pdf (accessed April 13, 2012).

depends on the type of product, the type of target market, and the purchase situation. For instance, buyers are probably more sensitive to gasoline prices than luggage prices. With respect to the type of target market, adults may have to pay more than children for certain products. The purchase situation also affects the buyer's view of price. Most moviegoers would never pay in other situations the prices charged for soft drinks, popcorn, and candy at movie concession stands. By assessing the target market's evaluation of price, a marketer is in a better position to know how much emphasis to put on price in the overall marketing strategy. Information about the target market's price evaluation may also help a marketer determine how far above the competition the firm can set its prices.

Today, because some consumers are seeking less-expensive products and shopping more selectively, some manufacturers and retailers are focusing on the value of their products. Value combines a product's price and quality attributes, which customers use to differentiate among competing brands. Consumers are looking for good deals on products that provide better value for their money. They may also view products that have highly desirable attributes, such as organic content or time-saving features, as having great value. Consumers are also increasingly willing to pay a higher price for food that is convenient and time saving, as illustrated in Table 21.2. Companies that offer both low prices and high quality, like Target and Amazon, have altered consumers' expectations about how much quality they must sacrifice for low prices. Understanding the importance of a product to customers, as well as their expectations about quality and value, helps marketers correctly assess the target market's evaluation of price.

EVALUATION OF COMPETITORS' PRICES

In most cases, marketers are in a better position to establish prices when they know the prices charged for competing brands, the third step in establishing prices. Discovering competitors' prices may be a regular function of marketing research. Some grocery and department stores, for example, have full-time comparative shoppers who systematically collect data on prices. Companies may also purchase price lists, sometimes weekly, from syndicated marketing research services.

Uncovering competitors' prices is not always easy, especially in producer and reseller markets. Competitors' price lists are often closely guarded. Even if a marketer has access to competitors' price lists, those lists may not reflect the actual prices at which competitive products are sold, because those prices may be established through negotiation.

Knowing the prices of competing brands can be very important for a marketer. Competitors' prices and the marketing mix variables that they emphasize partly determine how important price will be to customers. A marketer in an industry in which price competition prevails needs competitive price information to ensure its prices are the same as, or lower than, competitors' prices. In some instances, an organization's prices are designed to be slightly above competitors' prices to give its products an exclusive image. In contrast, another company may use price as a competitive tool and price its products below those of competitors. The Kindle Fire tablet computer from Amazon, for example, is priced at less than half what Apple's cheapest iPad 2 costs. Although the Kindle Fire does not have a camera, microphone, or 3G connection like the iPad, it still offers Wi-Fi connectivity with access to games, movies, books, magazines, music, and other applications. The Kindle Fire also uses Amazon's cloud computing technology, runs on Google's Android operating system, and includes access to the Android application store.[5]

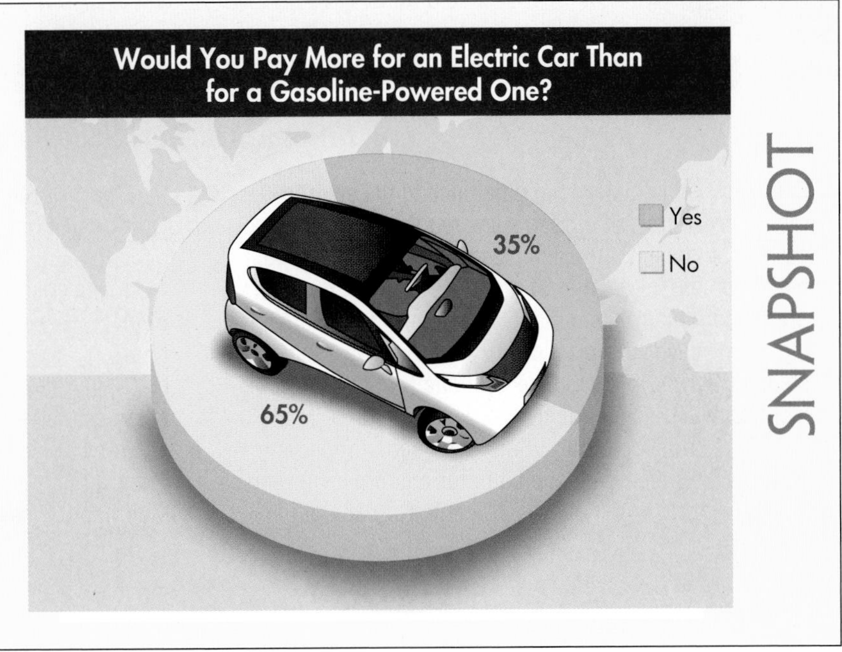

Source: Deloitte survey of 13,000 consumers.

SELECTION OF A BASIS FOR PRICING

The fourth step involves selecting a basis for pricing: cost, demand, or competition. The selection of the basis to use is affected by the type of product, the market structure of the industry, the brand's market share position relative to competing brands, and customer characteristics. Although we discuss each basis separately in this section, an organization generally considers two or all three of these dimensions, even if one is the primary basis on which it determines prices. For example, if a company is using cost as a basis for setting prices, marketers in that firm are also aware of and concerned about competitors' prices. If a company is using demand as a basis for pricing, those making pricing decisions still must consider costs and competitors' prices. Indeed, cost is a factor in every pricing decision, because it establishes a price minimum below which the firm will not be able to recoup its production and other costs; demand likewise sets an effective price maximum above which customers are unlikely to buy the product. Setting appropriate prices can be difficult for firms. A high price may reduce demand for the product, but a low price will hurt profit margins. Firms must weigh many different factors when setting prices, including costs, competition, customer buying behavior and price sensitivity, manufacturing capacity, and product life cycles.

Cost-Based Pricing

With **cost-based pricing**, a dollar amount or percentage is added to the cost of the product. Thus, this approach involves calculations of desired profit margins. Cost-based pricing does not necessarily take into account the economic aspects of supply and demand, nor must it relate to just one pricing strategy or pricing objective. Cost-based pricing is straightforward and easy to implement. Two common forms of cost-based pricing are cost-plus and markup pricing.

cost-based pricing Adding a dollar amount or percentage to the cost of the product

Going Green

Can a Nickel Change Behavior?

Can a few cents make a big difference to the environment? When Ireland passed a law requiring shoppers to pay about 20 cents for each plastic bag, usage plummeted by 94 percent in a matter of months. Similarly, demand dropped dramatically in India when retailers began charging a few rupees per plastic bag. Now some U.S. cities are stepping up efforts to reduce litter and keep bags out of landfills, with retailers doing their part as well.

For example, although San Francisco stopped supermarkets from using plastic bags for customer purchases in 2007, stores must charge 10 cents for each paper bag, part of the city's push for zero waste by 2020. Other cities have also imposed bans or bag charges or both.

Meanwhile, retailers are taking the initiative to get rid of plastic bags or discourage use by charging customers. Metro, a Canadian supermarket chain, began charging a nickel per bag in 2009. Within a month, bag usage had fallen by half—and within 18 months, bag usage was down by 80 percent. "Five cents might not be a lot of money, but it seems to be enough to make people change their habits," says a Metro manager.[b]

Cost-Plus Pricing

With **cost-plus pricing**, the seller's costs are determined (usually during a project or after a project is completed), and then a specified dollar amount or percentage of the cost is added to the seller's cost to establish the price. When production costs are difficult to predict, cost-plus pricing is appropriate. Projects involving custom-made equipment and commercial construction are often priced using this technique. The government frequently uses such cost-based pricing in granting defense contracts. One pitfall for the buyer is that the seller may increase costs to establish a larger profit base. Furthermore, some costs, such as overhead, may be difficult to determine. In periods of rapid inflation, cost-plus pricing is popular, especially when the producer must use raw materials that are fluctuating in price. In industries in which cost-plus pricing is common and sellers have similar costs, price competition may not be especially intense.

Markup Pricing

With **markup pricing**, commonly used by retailers, a product's price is derived by adding a predetermined percentage of the cost, called *markup,* to the cost of the product. For instance, most supermarkets mark up prices by at least 25 percent, whereas warehouse clubs like Costco and Sam's Club have a very low average markup of 14 percent.[6] One markup that might shock you is the average markup for popcorn in movie theaters, which is about 900 percent. Popcorn is not expensive, but consumers are willing to pay the markup to enhance their movie experience by enjoying warm, buttery popcorn at the theater.[7] Although the percentage markup in a retail store varies from one category of goods to another—35 percent of cost for hardware items and 100 percent of cost for greeting cards, for example—the same percentage is often used to determine the prices on items within a single product category, and the percentage markup may be largely standardized across an industry at the retail level. Using a rigid percentage markup for a specific product category reduces pricing to a routine task that can be performed quickly.

Markup can be stated as a percentage of the cost or as a percentage of the selling price. The following example illustrates how percentage markups are determined and points out the differences in the two methods. Assume a retailer purchases a can of tuna at 45 cents, adds 15 cents to the cost, and then prices the tuna at 60 cents. Here are the figures:

$$\text{markup as percentage of cost} = \frac{\text{markup}}{\text{cost}}$$

$$= \frac{15}{45}$$

$$= 33.3\%$$

cost-plus pricing Adding a specified dollar amount or percentage to the seller's cost

markup pricing Adding to the cost of the product a predetermined percentage of that cost

$$\text{markup as percentage of selling price} = \frac{\text{markup}}{\text{selling price}}$$
$$= \frac{15}{60}$$
$$= 25.0\%$$

Obviously, when discussing a percentage markup, it is important to know whether the markup is based on cost or selling price.

Markups normally reflect expectations about operating costs, risks, and stock turnovers. Wholesalers and manufacturers often suggest standard retail markups that are considered profitable. To the extent that retailers use similar markups for the same product category, price competition is reduced. In addition, using rigid markups is convenient and is the major reason retailers, which face numerous pricing decisions, favor this method.

Demand-Based Pricing

Marketers sometimes base prices on the level of demand for the product. When **demand-based pricing** is used, customers pay a higher price when demand for the product is strong and a lower price when demand is weak. For example, hotels that otherwise attract numerous travelers often offer reduced rates during lower-demand periods. Some telephone companies, such as Sprint and AT&T, also use demand-based pricing by charging peak and off-peak rates or offering free cell phone minutes during off-peak times. While demand-based pricing is a common practice with cell phone minutes, airplane seats, and hotel rooms, some concerts and sporting events have also implemented demand-based pricing for ticket sales. Ticketmaster recently partnered with a company called MarketShare to start using demand-based pricing on tickets for concerts, and baseball, basketball, and hockey games sold on its website. Now, if a concert or game is selling out quickly, Ticketmaster will be aware of this, and can increase ticket prices and improve profits for those more popular events.[8]

To use this pricing basis, a marketer must be able to estimate the amounts of a product consumers will demand at different prices. The marketer then chooses the price that generates the highest total revenue. Obviously, the effectiveness of demand-based pricing depends on the marketer's ability to estimate demand accurately. Compared with cost-based pricing, demand-based pricing places a firm in a better position to reach higher profit levels, assuming buyers value the product at levels sufficiently above the product's cost.

demand-based pricing Pricing based on the level of demand for the product

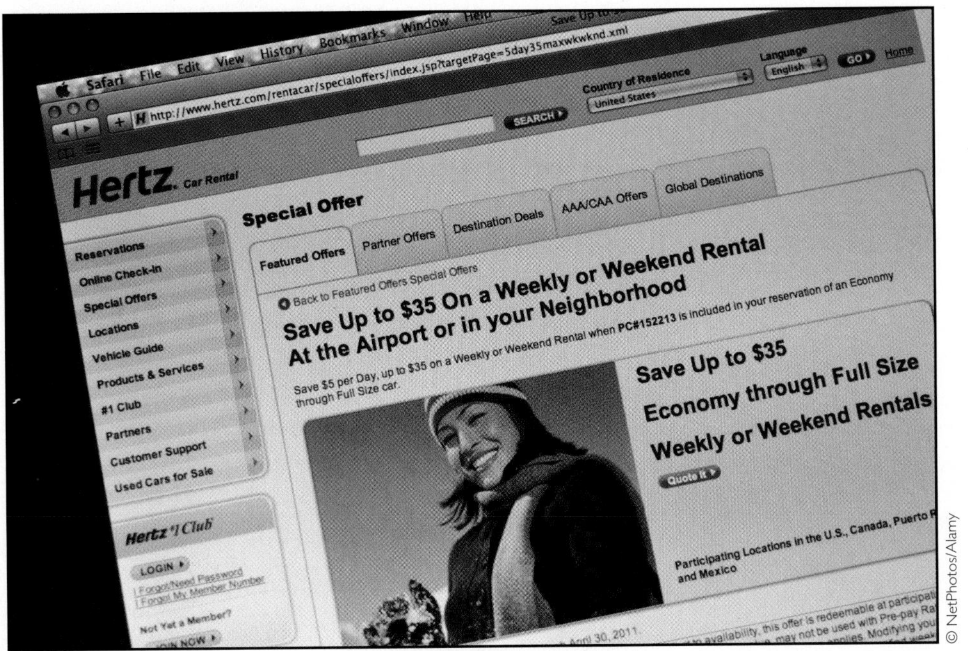

Demand-Based Pricing
Car rental companies often engage in demand-based pricing. When demand for rental cars is high, then the rental rates will be higher. Conversely, when the demand for rental cars is low, then the rental rates will be lower.

Competition-Based Pricing

With **competition-based pricing**, an organization considers costs to be secondary to competitors' prices. The importance of this method increases when competing products are relatively homogeneous and the organization is serving markets in which price is a key purchase consideration. A firm that uses competition-based pricing may choose to price below competitors' prices or at the same level. The movie delivery business is becoming more competitive, with firms like Netflix and Blockbuster offering consumers the option to have DVDs and video games delivered to their homes or streamed online. Verizon recently partnered with Redbox after seeing a window of opportunity in this growing industry. Verizon jumped into the industry shortly after Netflix released its hugely unpopular plan to nearly double rates for consumers who both stream movies and have DVD delivery. Redbox and Verizon offer a movie plan for around $6, which is considerably less than Netflix's rate, wherein consumers can select DVDs from Red Box movie locations and stream movies online.[9]

Although not all introductory marketing texts have exactly the same price, they do have similar prices. The price the bookstore paid to the publishing company for this textbook was determined on the basis of competitors' prices. Competition-based pricing can help a firm achieve the pricing objective of increasing sales or market share. Competition-based pricing may necessitate frequent price adjustments. For instance, for many competitive airline routes, fares are adjusted often.

SELECTION OF A PRICING STRATEGY

competition-based pricing Pricing influenced primarily by competitors' prices

After choosing a basis for pricing, the next step is to select a pricing strategy, an approach or a course of action designed to achieve pricing and marketing objectives. Generally, pricing strategies help marketers solve the practical problems of establishing prices. Table 21.3 lists the most common pricing strategies, which we discuss in this section.

Table 21.3 Common Pricing Strategies

Differential Pricing	**Psychological Pricing**
Negotiated pricing	Reference pricing
Secondary-market pricing	Bundle pricing
Periodic discounting	Multiple-unit pricing
Random discounting	Everyday low prices
	Odd-even pricing
New-Product Pricing	Customary pricing
Price skimming	Prestige pricing
Penetration pricing	
	Professional Pricing
Product-Line Pricing	
Captive pricing	**Promotional Pricing**
Premium pricing	Price leaders
Bait pricing	Special-event pricing
Price lining	Comparison discounting

Differential Pricing

An important issue in pricing decisions is whether to use a single price or different prices for the same product. Using a single price has several benefits. A primary advantage is simplicity. A single price is easily understood by both employees and customers, and because many salespeople and customers dislike having to negotiate a price, it reduces the chance of an adversarial relationship developing between marketer and customer. The use of a single price does create some challenges, however. If the single price is too high, some potential customers may be unable to afford the product. If it is too low, the organization loses revenue from those customers who would have paid more had the price been higher.

Differential pricing means charging different prices to different buyers for the same quality and quantity of product. As a student, you might be familiar with differential pricing for your tuition. Some colleges charge a higher tuition for certain majors, such as business, engineering, and medicine. These higher fees are called differential tuition.[10] For differential pricing to be effective, the market must consist of multiple segments with different price sensitivities, and the method should be used in a way that avoids confusing or antagonizing customers. Customers who are paying the lower prices should not be able to resell the product to the individuals and organizations that are paying the higher prices, unless that is the seller's intention. Differential pricing can occur in several ways, including negotiated pricing, secondary-market discounting, periodic discounting, and random discounting.

Negotiated Pricing

Negotiated pricing occurs when the final price is established through bargaining between seller and customer. If you buy a house, for example, you are likely to negotiate the final price with the seller. Negotiated pricing occurs in a number of industries and at all levels of distribution. Even when there is a predetermined stated price or a price list, manufacturers, wholesalers, and retailers may negotiate to establish the final sales price. Consumers commonly negotiate prices for houses, cars, and used equipment. Negotiation can be very important in setting a good price and all negotiators should enter into a discussion with a good strategy. This involves preparing negotiation tactics and understanding all the variables and risks at play. Managing personal chemistry between the negotiators is just as important as settling on prices. The negotiation process can help build relationships and increase understanding between different parties in a supply chain relationship.[11]

Secondary-Market Pricing

Secondary-market pricing means setting one price for the primary target market and a different price for another market. Often the price charged in the secondary market is lower. However, when the costs of serving a secondary market are higher than normal, secondary-market customers may have to pay a higher price. Examples of secondary markets include a geographically isolated domestic market, a market in a foreign country, and a segment willing to purchase a product during off-peak times. For example, some restaurants offer special "early-bird" prices during the early evening hours, movie theaters offer senior citizen and afternoon matinee discounts, and some textbooks and pharmaceutical products are sold for considerably less in certain foreign countries than in the United States. Secondary markets give an organization an opportunity to use excess capacity and stabilize the allocation of resources.

Periodic Discounting

Periodic discounting is the temporary reduction of prices on a patterned or systematic basis. Most retailers, for example, have annual holiday sales. Some women's apparel stores have two seasonal sales each year: a winter sale in the last two weeks of January and a summer sale in the first two weeks of July. Automobile dealers regularly discount prices on current models in the fall, when the next year's models are introduced. From the marketer's point of view, a

differential pricing Charging different prices to different buyers for the same quality and quantity of product

negotiated pricing Establishing a final price through bargaining between seller and customer

secondary-market pricing Setting one price for the primary target market and a different price for another market

periodic discounting Temporary reduction of prices on a patterned or systematic basis

major problem with periodic discounting is that, because the discounts follow a pattern, customers can predict when the reductions will occur and may delay their purchases until they can take advantage of the lower prices.

Random Discounting

To alleviate the problem of customers knowing when discounting will occur, some organizations employ **random discounting**. That is, they temporarily reduce their prices on an unsystematic basis. When price reductions of a product occur randomly, current users of that brand are likely unable to predict when the reductions will occur and, thus, will not delay their purchases. Random discounting can be useful to attract new customers or draw attention to a relatively new product. Many grocery store items, such as a new kind of yogurt or cereal, will use frequent random discounting. Marketers must be careful not to use random discounting too often, however. If customers always suspect another sale will be around the corner, they may delay purchase of the item until it goes back on sale. For instance, Dove may temporarily reduce the price of one of its bar soaps in the hope of attracting new customers.

Whether they use periodic discounting or random discounting, retailers often employ tensile pricing when putting products on sale. *Tensile pricing* refers to a broad statement about price reductions as opposed to detailing specific price discounts. Examples of tensile pricing would be statements like "20 to 50 percent off," "up to 75 percent off," and "save 10 percent or more." Generally, using and advertising the tensile price that mentions only the maximum reduction (such as "up to 50 percent off") generates the highest customer response.[12]

New-Product Pricing

random discounting Temporary reduction of prices on an unsystematic basis

Setting the base price for a new product is a necessary part of formulating a marketing strategy. The base price is easily adjusted (in the absence of government price controls), and its establishment is one of the most fundamental decisions in the marketing mix. The base price can be set high to recover development costs quickly or provide a reference point for developing discount prices for different market segments. When a marketer sets base prices, it also considers how quickly competitors will enter the market, whether they will mount a strong campaign

Random Discounting
This advertisement promotes an in-store sale based upon random pricing.

on entry, and what effect their entry will have on the development of primary demand. Two strategies used in new-product pricing are price skimming and penetration pricing.

Price Skimming

Price skimming means charging the highest possible price that buyers who most desire the product will pay. This approach provides the most flexible introductory base price. Demand tends to be inelastic in the introductory stage of the product life cycle.

Price skimming can provide several benefits, especially when a product is in the introductory stage of its life cycle. A skimming policy can generate much-needed initial cash flows to help offset sizable development costs. Price skimming protects the marketer from problems that arise when the price is set too low to cover costs. When a firm introduces a product, its production capacity may be limited. A skimming price can help keep demand consistent with the firm's production capabilities. The use of a skimming price may attract competition into an industry, because the high price makes that type of business appear quite lucrative. New-product prices should be based on both the value to the customer and competitive products.

Penetration Pricing

With **penetration pricing**, prices are set below those of competing brands to penetrate a market and gain a large market share quickly. This approach is less flexible for a marketer than price skimming, because it is more difficult to raise a penetration price than to lower or discount a skimming price. It is not unusual for a firm to use a penetration price after having skimmed the market with a higher price.

Penetration pricing can be especially beneficial when a marketer suspects that competitors could enter the market easily. If penetration pricing allows the marketer to gain a large market share quickly, competitors may be discouraged from entering the market. In addition, because the lower per-unit penetration price results in lower per-unit profit, the market may not appear to be especially lucrative to potential new entrants.

Product-Line Pricing

Rather than considering products on an item-by-item basis when determining pricing strategies, some marketers employ product-line pricing. **Product-line pricing** means establishing and adjusting the prices of multiple products within a product line. When marketers use product-line pricing, their goal is to maximize profits for an entire product line rather than focusing on the profitability of an individual product. Product-line pricing can lend marketers flexibility in price setting. For example, marketers can set prices so that one product is quite profitable while another increases market share due to having a lower price than competing products.

Before setting prices for a product line, marketers evaluate the relationship among the products in the line. When products in a line are complementary, sales increases in one item raise demand for other items. For instance, desktop printers and toner cartridges are complementary products. When products in a line function as substitutes for one another, buyers of one product in the line are unlikely to purchase one of the other products in the same line. In this case, marketers must be sensitive to how a price change for one of the brands may affect the demand not only for that brand but also for the substitute brands. For instance, if decision makers at Procter & Gamble were considering a price change for Tide detergent, they would be concerned about how the price change might influence sales of Cheer, Bold, and Gain.

When marketers employ product-line pricing, they have several strategies from which to choose. These include captive pricing, premium pricing, bait pricing, and price lining.

Captive Pricing

With **captive pricing**, the basic product in a product line is priced low, whereas items required to operate or enhance it are priced higher. Printer companies have used this pricing

price skimming Charging the highest possible price that buyers who most desire the product will pay

penetration pricing Setting prices below those of competing brands to penetrate a market and gain a significant market share quickly

product-line pricing Establishing and adjusting prices of multiple products within a product line

captive pricing Pricing the basic product in a product line low, while pricing related items higher

Captive Pricing
Products that require component replacement on a regular basis, such as printers, may be relatively inexpensive, but the replacement components are premium priced. This type of pricing is referred to as captive pricing.

strategy: providing relatively low-cost, low-margin printers and selling ink cartridges to generate significant profits.

Premium Pricing

Premium pricing is often used when a product line contains several versions of the same product; the highest-quality products or those with the most versatility are given the highest prices. Apple has historically utilized premium pricing on its products, which, combined with sleek styling and unique features, has lent an aura of desirability to its goods. The premium sticker price correlates to a better product in the minds of consumers, and competitors have struggled to keep up. Other products in the line are priced to appeal to price-sensitive shoppers or to buyers who seek product-specific features.

Marketers that use a premium strategy often realize a significant portion of their profits from premium-priced products. Examples of product categories that commonly use premium pricing are small kitchen appliances, beer, ice cream, and cable television service.

Bait Pricing

To attract customers, marketers may put a low price on one item in the product line with the intention of selling a higher-priced item in the line; this strategy is known as **bait pricing**. For example, a computer retailer might advertise its lowest-priced computer model, hoping that when customers come to the store, they will purchase a higher-priced one. This strategy can facilitate sales of a line's higher-priced products. As long as a retailer has sufficient quantities of the advertised low-priced model available for sale, this strategy is considered acceptable. In contrast, *bait and switch* is an activity in which retailers have no intention of selling the bait product; they use the low price merely to entice customers into the store to sell them higher-priced products. Bait and switch is considered unethical, and in some states it is illegal.

premium pricing Pricing the highest-quality or most versatile products higher than other models in the product line

bait pricing Pricing an item in a product line low with the intention of selling a higher-priced item in the line

price lining Setting a limited number of prices for selected groups or lines of merchandise

Price Lining

When an organization sets a limited number of prices for selected groups or lines of merchandise, it is using **price lining**. A retailer may have various styles and brands of similar-quality men's shirts that sell for $15 and another line of higher-quality shirts that sell for $22. Price

Figure 21.2 **Price Lining**

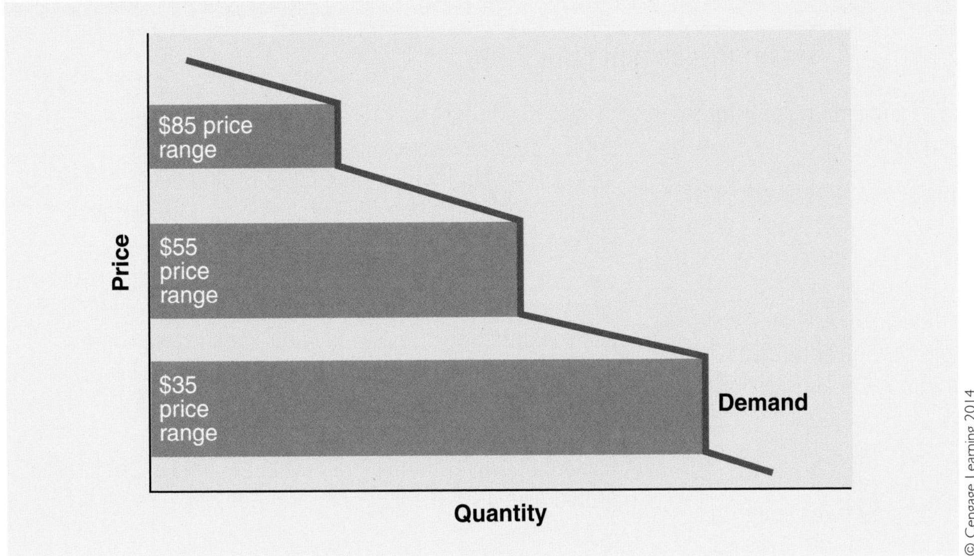

lining simplifies customers' decision making by holding constant one key variable in the final selection of style and brand within a line.

The basic assumption in price lining is that the demand for various groups or sets of products is inelastic. If the prices are attractive, customers will concentrate their purchases without responding to slight changes in price. Thus, a women's dress shop that carries dresses priced at $85, $55, and $35 may not attract many more sales with a drop to $83, $53, and $33. The "space" between the price of $85 and $55, however, can stir changes in consumer response. With price lining, the demand curve looks like a series of steps, as shown in Figure 21.2.

Psychological Pricing

Learning the price of a product is not always a pleasant experience for customers. It is sometimes surprising (as at a movie concession stand) and sometimes downright horrifying; most of us have experienced some sort of "sticker shock." Consumers are likely to have negative reactions to incomplete or unclear pricing information, especially when it is conveyed through misleading communications. **Psychological pricing** attempts to influence a customer's perception of price to make a product's price more attractive. In this section, we consider several forms of psychological pricing: reference pricing, bundle pricing, multiple-unit pricing, everyday low prices (EDLP), odd-even pricing, customary pricing, and prestige pricing.

Reference Pricing

Reference pricing means pricing a product at a moderate level and displaying it next to a more expensive model or brand in the hope that the customer will use the higher price as an external reference price (i.e., a comparison price). Because of the comparison, the customer is expected to view the moderate price favorably. Reference pricing is based on the "isolation effect," meaning an alternative is less attractive when viewed by itself than when compared with other alternatives. When you go to CVS to buy aspirin, CVS' private-label aspirin may appear especially attractive, because it offers most of the important attributes of the more expensive alternatives on display and at a lower price.

psychological pricing Pricing that attempts to influence a customer's perception of price to make a product's price more attractive

reference pricing Pricing a product at a moderate level and displaying it next to a more expensive model or brand

Marketing Debate

Travel Prices and Fine Print

ISSUE: Should customers have to check the fine print to know how much travel services cost?

What is the real price of a room at a resort hotel or a seat on an airplane? In many cases, customers don't know until they follow the asterisk in an ad or read the fine print at the bottom of the screen or page. Because many travel services are subject to taxes and fees that are not always prominently disclosed, customers may be surprised when a bargain turns out to not be as good as it appeared at first glance.

Airlines and travel websites often promote low fares to grab attention and boost sales in a hurry. After customers complained about "hidden" fees and taxes added at the end of a purchase, U.S. regulators began requiring airlines to disclose the full price at the start. Some airlines objected, saying that fees and taxes should be disclosed separately, because they're imposed by the government and not under the airline's pricing control.

A growing number of resort hotels are adding mandatory all-in-one fees to cover parking, fitness center facilities, Internet access, and other services, saying that bundled pricing is more convenient for guests. However, guests who don't take advantage of these services sometimes grumble about the higher price, especially when they aren't aware of the extra fees at the time of booking. Should fees be in the fine print or in the price?[c]

Bundle Pricing

Bundle pricing is packaging two or more products together, usually complementary ones, to be sold at a single price. Many fast-food restaurants, for example, offer combination meals at a price that is lower than the combined prices of each item priced separately. Most telephone and cable television providers bundle local telephone service, broadband Internet access, and digital cable or satellite television for one monthly fee. To attract customers, the single bundled price is usually considerably less than the sum of the prices of the individual products. The opportunity to buy the bundled combination of products in a single transaction may be of value to the customer as well. Telecommunications companies frequently bundle their services. Along with cable, Internet, and telephone services, Comcast, for example, even offers movie and TV show streaming as part of some of its service bundles. Consumers may find it easier and more affordable to receive all of their telecommunications services bundled by one provider.[13] Bundle pricing can allow companies to develop multiple bundles, each containing a different combination of its available goods or services, which then appeal to consumers in different target markets. Bundle pricing facilitates customer satisfaction and, when slow-moving products are bundled with those with a higher turnover, can help stimulate sales and increase revenues. It may also help foster customer loyalty and improve customer retention. Selling products as a package rather than individually may also result in cost savings. Bundle pricing is commonly used for banking and travel services, computers, and automobiles with option packages.

Multiple-Unit Pricing

Multiple-unit pricing occurs when two or more identical products are packaged together and sold at a single price. This normally results in a lower per-unit price than the price regularly charged. Multiple-unit pricing is commonly used for twin-packs of potato chips, four-packs of light bulbs, and six- and 12-packs of soft drinks. Customers benefit from the cost savings and convenience this pricing strategy affords. A company may use multiple-unit pricing to attract new customers to its brands and, in some instances, to increase consumption of them. When customers buy in larger quantities, their consumption of the product may increase. For instance, multiple-unit pricing may encourage a customer to buy larger quantities of snacks,

bundle pricing Packaging together two or more complementary products and selling them at a single price

multiple-unit pricing Packaging together two or more identical products and selling them at a single price

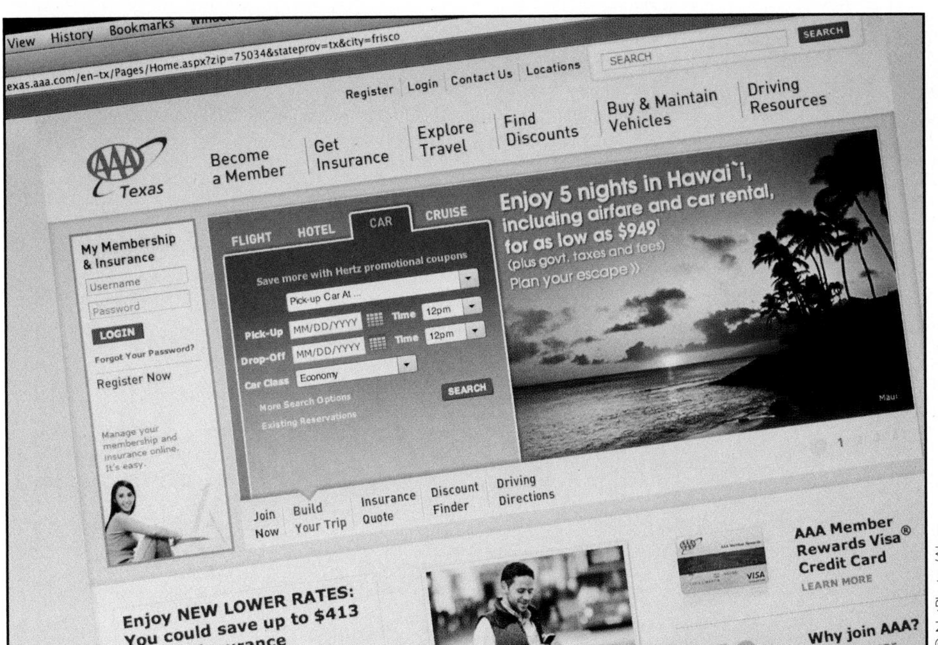

© NetPhotos/Alamy

Bundle Pricing
This Hawaiian vacation offer for airfare, a five-night hotel stay, and a five-day car rental, all for $949, is an example of bundle pricing.

which are likely to be consumed in higher volume at the point of consumption simply because they are available. However, this is not true for all products. For instance, greater availability at the point of consumption of light bulbs, bar soap, and table salt is not likely to increase usage.

Discount stores and especially warehouse clubs, like Sam's Club and Costco, are major users of multiple-unit pricing. For certain products in these stores, customers receive significant per-unit price reductions when they buy packages containing multiple units of the same product, such as an eight-pack of canned tuna fish.

Everyday Low Prices (EDLP)

To reduce or eliminate the use of frequent short-term price reductions, some organizations use an approach referred to as **everyday low prices (EDLP)**. With EDLP, a marketer sets a low price for its products on a consistent basis rather than setting higher prices and frequently discounting them. Everyday low prices, though not deeply discounted, are set far enough below competitors' prices to make customers feel confident they are receiving a fair price. EDLP is employed by retailers like Walmart and manufacturers like Procter & Gamble. Indeed, Walmart has already trademarked the phrase "Always Low Prices. Always." A company that uses EDLP benefits from reduced losses from frequent markdowns, greater stability in sales, and decreased promotional costs.

One of the major problems with EDLP is that customers can respond to it in several different ways. Over the last few years, many marketers have inadvertently "trained" customers to expect and seek out deeply discounted prices. In some product categories, such as apparel, finding the deepest discount has become almost a national consumer sport. Thus, failure to provide deep discounts can be a problem for certain marketers. In some instances, customers do not believe everyday low prices are simply what marketers claim they are but are instead a marketing gimmick.

everyday low prices (EDLP) Pricing products low on a consistent basis

odd-even pricing Ending the price with certain numbers to influence buyers' perceptions of the price or product

Odd-Even Pricing

Through **odd-even pricing**—ending the price with certain numbers—marketers try to influence buyers' perceptions of the price or the product. Odd pricing assumes more of a product will be sold at $99.95 than at $100. Theoretically, customers will think, or at least tell friends, that the product is a bargain—not $100, but $99 and change. Also, customers will supposedly

Everyday Low Prices
Walmart is a major user of everyday low prices.

think the store could have charged $100 but instead cut the price to the last cent, to $99.95. Some claim, too, that certain types of customers are more attracted by odd prices than by even ones. Researchers have found that women are more likely to respond to odd-ending prices than men are.[14] However, research on the effect of odd-even prices has demonstrated conflicting results; one recent study found that odd prices that end in 5 or 9 failed to trigger the threshold of consumer response.[15] Nonetheless, odd prices are far more common today than even prices.

Even prices are often used to give a product an exclusive or upscale image. An even price will supposedly influence a customer to view the product as being a high-quality, premium brand. A shirt maker, for example, may print on a premium shirt package a suggested retail price of $42.00 instead of $41.95; the even price of the shirt is used to enhance its upscale image.

Customary Pricing

With **customary pricing**, certain goods are priced primarily on the basis of tradition. Recent economic uncertainties have made most prices fluctuate fairly widely, but the classic example of the customary, or traditional, price is the price of a candy bar. For years, a candy bar cost 5 cents. A new candy bar would have had to be something very special to sell for more than a nickel. This price was so sacred that, rather than change it, manufacturers increased or decreased the size of the candy bar itself as chocolate prices fluctuated. Today, of course, the nickel candy bar has disappeared. However, most candy bars still sell at a consistent, but obviously higher, price. Thus, customary pricing remains the standard for this market.

Prestige Pricing

customary pricing Pricing on the basis of tradition

prestige pricing Setting prices at an artificially high level to convey prestige or a quality image

With **prestige pricing**, prices are set at an artificially high level to convey prestige or a quality image. Prestige pricing is used especially when buyers associate a higher price with higher quality. Garmin, for example, offers a wide range of GPS systems for navigation and sports activities. Although many of its products offer similar benefits, consumers associate its higher priced products with higher quality and performance. For example, its 910XT GPS running

Table 21.4 Sample Prestige Product Prices

Prestige Product	Brand	Price
Women's Cashmere Sweater	Brunello Cucinelli Scoop Neck	$1,200
Men's Dress Watch	Girard-Perregaux Rose Gold 1966 Full Calendar	$22,680
Crystal Stemware	Baccarat Harcourt	$195/piece
Sheets	Frette Chelonia Pizzo Queen Set	$2,745

Source: "Gift Guide: Shop Global for the Best Luxury Buys," *Smart Money*, November 29, 2011, www.smartmoney.com.

watch has most of the same features as the older Forerunner 205 but costs nearly $400 more and has sleeker styling.[16]

Typical product categories in which selected products are prestige priced include perfumes, liquor, jewelry, and cars. Although appliances have not traditionally been prestige priced, upscale appliances have appeared in recent years to capitalize on the willingness of some consumer segments to "trade up" for high-quality products. These consumers do not mind paying extra for a Sub-Zero refrigerator, a Viking commercial range, or a Whirlpool Duet washer and dryer, because these products offer high quality as well as a level of prestige. If these producers lowered their prices dramatically, the new prices would be inconsistent with the perceived high-quality images of their products. From golf clubs to handbags, prestige products are selling at record levels. Consider some of the prestige products shown in Table 21.4 that were selected as the best by *Smart Money* magazine.

Professional Pricing

Professional pricing is used by people who have great skill or experience in a particular field. Professionals often believe their fees (prices) should not relate directly to the time and effort spent in specific cases. Rather, a standard fee is charged regardless of the problems involved in performing the job. Some doctors' and lawyers' fees are prime examples, such as $75 for an office visit, $2,000 for an appendectomy, and $995 for a divorce. Other professionals set prices in other ways. Like other marketers, professionals have costs associated with facilities, labor, insurance, equipment, and supplies. Certainly, costs are considered when setting professional prices.

The concept of professional pricing carries the idea that professionals have an ethical responsibility not to overcharge customers. In some situations, a seller can charge customers a high price and continue to sell many units of the product. Medicine offers several examples. If a person with diabetes requires one insulin treatment per day to survive, she or he will probably buy that treatment whether its price is $1 or $10. In fact, the patient will probably purchase the treatment even if the price rose. In these situations, sellers could charge exorbitant fees. Drug companies claim that, despite their positions of strength in this regard, they charge ethical prices rather than what the market will bear.

Promotional Pricing

As an ingredient in the marketing mix, price is often coordinated with promotion. The two variables are sometimes so closely interrelated that the pricing policy is promotion-oriented. Types of promotional pricing include price leaders, special-event pricing, and comparison discounting.

professional pricing Fees set by people with great skill or experience in a particular field

© Karen Bleier/AFP/Getty Images/Newscom

Price Leaders
The retail grocery industry commonly uses price leaders.

Price Leaders

Sometimes, a firm prices a few products below the usual markup, near cost, or below cost, which results in prices known as **price leaders**. This type of pricing is used most often in supermarkets and restaurants to attract customers by giving them especially low prices on a few items. Management hopes that sales of regularly priced products will more than offset the reduced revenues from the price leaders.

Special-Event Pricing

To increase sales volume, many organizations coordinate price with advertising or sales promotions for seasonal or special situations. **Special-event pricing** involves advertised sales or price cutting linked to a holiday, a season, or an event. If the pricing objective is survival, special sales events may be designed to generate the necessary operating capital. Special-event pricing entails coordination of production, scheduling, storage, and physical distribution. Whenever a sales lag occurs, special-event pricing is an alternative that marketers should consider.

Comparison Discounting

Comparison discounting sets the price of a product at a specific level and simultaneously compares it with a higher price. The higher price may be the product's previous price, the price of a competing brand, the product's price at another retail outlet, or a manufacturer's suggested retail price. Customers may find comparative discounting informative, and it can have a significant impact on their purchases. However, overuse of comparison pricing may reduce customers' internal reference prices, meaning they no longer believe the higher price is the regular or normal price.[17]

Because this pricing strategy has occasionally led to deceptive pricing practices, the Federal Trade Commission has established guidelines for comparison discounting. If the

price leaders Products priced near or even below cost.

special-event pricing Advertised sales or price cutting linked to a holiday, a season, or an event

comparison discounting Setting a price at a specific level and comparing it with a higher price

Entrepreneurship in Marketing

Zafirro's $100,000 Razor

Entrepreneur: Hayden Hamilton
Business: Zafirro
Founded: 2011 | Portland, Oregon
Success: The Zafirro Iridium razor was named one of "The 50 Best Inventions" by *Time* magazine in 2011.

If you buy the Zafirro Iridium razor, you'll never need to buy another razor again—not ever. The sleek handle is made from a high-tech combination of stainless steel and iridium, a rare but ultra-strong metal, and secured by platinum screws. The whisper-thin blades are made from sapphire and are so durable that they carry a 20-year guarantee. Zafirro's CEO says the target market is collectors and wealthy consumers worldwide who "appreciate extremely well-made products, regardless of their cost." The firm is making only 99 of these limited-edition razors and setting a prestige price of $100,000 to reinforce the luxury image.

Months after announcing the iridium razor, start-up Zafirro added two new products to its product line. The Zafirro Gold razor, made with 18-karat gold, in addition to incorporating a sapphire blade, is priced at $18,000 and offers four years of free service and resharpening. The Zafirro Titanium, which also comes with a sapphire blade, is priced at $2,000, including two years of free service and resharpening. Zafirro's CEO says these new models are "mainstream luxury" products that incorporate the best engineering and design features of the original iridium model. Can Oregon-based Zafirro build on its prestige-pricing strategy as it expands into new product categories?[d]

higher price against which the comparison is made is the price formerly charged for the product, the seller must have made the previous price available to customers for a reasonable period of time. If the seller presents the higher price as the one charged by other retailers in the same trade area, it must be able to demonstrate that this claim is true. When the seller presents the higher price as the manufacturer's suggested retail price, the higher price must be similar to the price at which a reasonable proportion of the product was sold. Some companies' suggested retail prices are so high that very few products are actually sold at those prices. In such cases, comparison discounting would be deceptive. Carrefour and Walmart stores in China were subjected to an investigation and fines after they were charged with deceptive pricing. The retailers were accused of stating that the original prices on items were higher than they were, making discounts look deceptively large. The retailers were also accused of charging more than the marked price at check out. Walmart's CEO of its Chinese operations resigned after a barrage of negative publicity following this incident.[18]

DETERMINATION OF A SPECIFIC PRICE

A pricing strategy will yield a certain price, the final step in the process. However, this price may need refinement to make it consistent with circumstances as well as pricing practices in a particular market or industry. Pricing strategies should help in setting a final price. If they are to do so, marketers must establish pricing objectives; have considerable knowledge about target market customers; and determine demand, price elasticity, costs, and competitive factors. Also, the way pricing is used in the marketing mix will affect the final price.

In the absence of government price controls, pricing remains a flexible and convenient way to adjust the marketing mix. In many situations, prices can be adjusted quickly—over a few days or even in minutes. Such flexibility is unique to this component of the marketing mix.

Summary

1. To describe the six major stages of the process used to establish prices

The six stages in the process of setting prices are (1) developing pricing objectives, (2) assessing the target market's evaluation of price, (3) evaluating competitors' prices, (4) choosing a basis for pricing, (5) selecting a pricing strategy, and (6) determining a specific price.

2. To explore issues related to developing pricing objectives

Setting pricing objectives is critical, because pricing objectives form a foundation on which the decisions of subsequent stages are based. Organizations may use numerous pricing objectives, including short-term and long-term ones, and different objectives for different products and market segments. Pricing objectives are overall goals that describe the role of price in a firm's long-range plans. There are several major types of pricing objectives. The most fundamental pricing objective is the organization's survival. Price can usually be easily adjusted to increase sales volume or combat competition to help the organization stay alive. Profit objectives, which are usually stated in terms of sales dollar volume or percentage change, are normally set at a satisfactory level rather than at a level designed to maximize profits. A sales growth objective focuses on increasing the profit base by raising sales volume. Pricing for return on investment (ROI) has a specified profit as its objective. A pricing objective to maintain or increase market share links market position to success. Other types of pricing objectives include cash flow, status quo, and product quality.

3. To understand the importance of identifying the target market's evaluation of price

Assessing the target market's evaluation of price tells the marketer how much emphasis to place on price and may help determine how far above the competition the firm can set its prices. Understanding how important a product is to customers relative to other products, as well as customers' expectations of quality, helps marketers correctly assess the target market's evaluation of price.

4. To examine how marketers analyze competitors' prices

A marketer needs to be aware of the prices charged for competing brands. This allows the firm to keep its prices in line with competitors' prices when nonprice competition is used. If a company uses price as a competitive tool, it can price its brand below competing brands.

5. To describe the bases used for setting prices

The three major dimensions on which prices can be based are cost, demand, and competition. When using cost-based pricing, the firm determines price by adding a dollar amount or percentage to the cost of the product. Two common cost-based pricing methods are cost-plus and markup pricing. Demand-based pricing is based on the level of demand for the product. To use this method, a marketer must be able to estimate the amounts of a product buyers will demand at different prices. Demand-based pricing results in a high price when demand for a product is strong and a low price when demand is weak. In the case of competition-based pricing, costs and revenues are secondary to competitors' prices.

6. To explain the different types of pricing strategies

A pricing strategy is an approach or a course of action designed to achieve pricing and marketing objectives. Pricing strategies help marketers solve the practical problems of establishing prices. The most common pricing strategies are differential pricing, new-product pricing, product-line pricing, psychological pricing, professional pricing, and promotional pricing.

When marketers employ differential pricing, they charge different buyers different prices for the same quality and quantity of products. For example, with negotiated pricing, the final price is established through bargaining between seller and customer. Secondary-market pricing involves setting one price for the primary target market and a different price for another market; often, the price charged in the secondary market is lower. Marketers employ periodic discounting when they temporarily lower their prices on a patterned or systematic basis; the reason for the reduction may be a seasonal change, a model-year change, or a holiday. Random discounting occurs on an unsystematic basis.

Two strategies used in new-product pricing are price skimming and penetration pricing. With price skimming, the organization charges the highest price that buyers who most desire the product will pay. A penetration price is a low price designed to penetrate a market and gain a significant market share quickly.

Product-line pricing establishes and adjusts the prices of multiple products within a product line. This strategy includes captive pricing, in which the marketer prices the basic product in a product line low and prices related items higher; premium pricing, in which prices on higher-quality or more versatile products are set higher than those on other models in the product line; bait pricing, in which the marketer tries to attract customers by pricing an item in the product line low with the intention of selling a higher-priced item in the line; and price lining, in which the organization sets a limited number of prices for selected groups or lines of merchandise.

Psychological pricing attempts to influence customers' perceptions of price to make a product's price more attractive. With reference pricing, marketers price a product at a moderate level and position it next to a more expensive model or brand. Bundle pricing is packaging together two or more complementary products and selling them at a single price. With multiple-unit pricing, two or more identical products are packaged together and sold at a single price. To reduce or eliminate use of frequent short-term price reductions, some organizations employ everyday low pricing (EDLP), setting a low price for products on a consistent basis. When employing odd-even pricing, marketers try to influence buyers' perceptions of the price or the product by ending the price with certain numbers. Customary pricing is based on traditional prices. With prestige pricing, prices are set at an artificially high level to convey prestige or a quality image.

Professional pricing is used by people who have great skill or experience in a particular field, therefore allowing them to set the price. This concept carries the idea that professionals have an ethical responsibility not to overcharge customers. As an ingredient in the marketing mix, price is often coordinated with promotion. The two variables are sometimes so closely interrelated that the pricing policy is promotion-oriented. Promotional pricing includes price leaders, special-event pricing, and comparison discounting.

Price leaders are products priced below the usual markup, near cost, or below cost. Special-event pricing involves advertised sales or price cutting linked to a holiday, season, or event. Marketers that use a comparison discounting strategy price a product at a specific level and compare it with a higher price.

Once a price is determined by using one or more pricing strategies, it needs to be refined to a final price consistent with the pricing practices in a particular market or industry.

Go to www.cengagebrain.com for resources to help you master the content in this chapter as well as materials that will expand your marketing knowledge!

Important Terms

Discussion and Review Questions

1. Identify the six stages in the process of establishing prices.
2. How does a return on an investment pricing objective differ from an objective of increasing market share?
3. Why must marketing objectives and pricing objectives be considered when making pricing decisions?
4. Why should a marketer be aware of competitors' prices?
5. What are the benefits of cost-based pricing?
6. Under what conditions is cost-plus pricing most appropriate?
7. A retailer purchases a can of soup for 24 cents and sells it for 36 cents. Calculate the markup as a percentage of cost and as a percentage of selling price.
8. What is differential pricing? In what ways can it be achieved?
9. For what types of products would price skimming be most appropriate? For what types of products would penetration pricing be more effective?
10. Describe bundle pricing, and give three examples using different industries.
11. What are the advantages and disadvantages of using everyday low prices?
12. Why do customers associate price with quality? When should prestige pricing be used?
13. Are price leaders a realistic approach to pricing? Explain your answer.

Application Questions

1. Price skimming and penetration pricing are strategies that are commonly used to set the base price of a new product. Which strategy is more appropriate for the following products? Explain.
   a. Short airline flights between cities in Florida
   b. A Blu-ray player
   c. A backpack or book bag with a lifetime warranty
   d. Season tickets for a newly franchised NBA basketball team
2. Price lining is used to set a limited number of prices for selected lines of merchandise. Visit a few local retail stores to find examples of price lining. For what types of products and stores is this practice most common? For what types of products and stores is price lining not typical or feasible?
3. Professional pricing is used by people who have great skill in a particular field, such as doctors, lawyers, and business consultants. Find examples (advertisements, personal contacts) that reflect a professional pricing policy. How is the price established? Are there any restrictions on the services performed at that price?
4. Organizations often use multiple pricing objectives. Locate an organization that uses several pricing objectives, and discuss how this approach influences the company's marketing mix decisions. Are some objectives oriented toward the short term and others toward the long term? How does the marketing environment influence these objectives?
5. IMP Diamond marketers sometimes employ prestige pricing. This is especially true at high-end jewelers like Tiffany's, whose signature blue box conveys exclusivity and status. A pair of their diamond earrings, for example, may be priced considerably higher than "generic" diamond earrings. Identify three prestige brands in different product categories. Compare each prestige-priced brand to regularly priced brands in each product category, and calculate the price differentials. In each product category, is the price difference justifiable? Explain.

Internet Exercise

T-Mobile

T-Mobile has attempted to position itself as a low-cost cellular phone service provider. A person can purchase a calling plan, a cellular phone, and phone accessories at its website. Visit the company's website at www.t-mobile.com.

1. Determine the various nationwide calling rates available in your city.
2. How many different calling plans are available in your area?
3. What type of pricing strategy is T-Mobile using on its rate plans in your area?

developing your marketing plan

Setting the right price for a product is a crucial part of a marketing strategy. Price helps to establish a product's position in the mind of the consumer and can differentiate a product from its competition. Several decisions in the marketing plan will be affected by the pricing strategy that is selected. To assist you in relating the information in this chapter to the development of your marketing plan, focus on the following:

1. Using Table 21.1 as a guide, discuss each of the seven pricing objectives. Which pricing objectives will you use for your product? Consider the product life cycle, competition, and product positioning for your target market during your discussion.
2. Review the various types of pricing strategies in Table 21.3. Which of these is the most appropriate for your product?
3. Select a basis for pricing your product (cost, demand, and/or competition). How will you know when it is time to revise your pricing strategy?

The information obtained from these questions should assist you in developing various aspects of your marketing plan found in the "Interactive Marketing Plan" exercise at www.cengagebrain.com.

video case 21.1

Pricing at the Farmers' Market

Whether they're outside the barn or inside the city limits, farmers' markets are becoming more popular as consumers increasingly seek out fresh and local foods. Today, more than 7,000 farmers' markets are open in the United States, selling farm products year-round or only in season. Although some are located within a short drive of the farms where the fruits and vegetables are grown, many operate only on weekends, setting up stands in town squares and city parks to offer a combination of shopping and entertainment. "These markets are establishing themselves as part of our culture in ways that they didn't used to be, and that bodes well for their continued growth," says the director of LocalHarvest.org, which produces a national directory of farmers' markets.

© iStockphoto.com/Dan Moore

Selling directly to the public enables farmers to build relationships with local shoppers and encourage repeat buying week after week as different items are harvested. It also allows farmers to realize a larger profit margin than if they sold to wholesalers and retailers. This is because the price at which intermediaries buy must have enough room for them to earn a profit when they resell to a store or to consumers. Farmers who market to consumers without intermediaries can charge almost as much—or sometimes even more than—consumers would pay in a supermarket. In many cases, consumers are willing to pay a higher price for top-quality local products, and even more for products that have been certified organic by a recognized authority. Competition is a factor, however. Consumers who browse the farmer's market will quickly see the range of prices that farmers are charging that day for peppers, peaches, or pumpkins. Competition between farmer's markets is another issue, as a new crop of markets appears every season.

Urban Farmz, like other vendors, is adding unique and complementary merchandise to its traditional lineup of agricultural items. Diversifying by selling certified organic soap at its stand, online, and to wholesale accounts will "juice up the brand," as Caleb says. The producers of the organic soap sell it for $14 per bar on their own website, and they ask Urban Farmz to avoid any conflict by selling at a higher price. Thinking fast, Caleb suggests a retail price of $15.95 per bar, saying that this will give Urban Farmz a reasonable profit margin.

Will buyers accept this price? It's time for some competitive homework. The lavender-lemon verbena scent is very popular, and certified-organic products have cachet. Caleb thinks that visitors to the Urban Farmz website will probably not click away to save a dollar or two by buying elsewhere, because then they'll have to pay the other site's shipping fee, as well as the Urban Farmz site's shipping fee. Urban Farmz will also have to set a separate wholesale price when it sells the soap to local restaurants. Will this new soap be the product that boosts Urban Farmz's profits and turns the name into a lifestyle brand?[19]

Questions for Discussion

1. In the pursuit of profits, how might Urban Farmz use a combination of cost-based, demand-based, and competition-based pricing for the products it sells? Explain your answer.
2. Urban Farmz wants to price the organic soap at $15.95 per bar, while the soap maker prices the same soap at $14 per bar. What perceptions do you think consumers will have of each price? What recommendations do you have regarding this price difference?
3. Would you recommend that Urban Farmz use promotional pricing at the farmers' markets where it regularly sells its products? If so, which techniques would you suggest, and why?

case 21.2

JCP Switches to EDLP

When Ron Johnson left Apple to become CEO of JCPenney in late 2011, he discovered that the department store had been running 590 different promotions every year, counting sales, discounts, coupons, clearance events, and other price reductions. But years of competing on price—like so many of its competitors—hadn't done very much to boost JCPenney's revenue or profits. Worse, research showed that customers were shopping at its stores only four times a year. "We haven't given the customer enough reasons to love us," he remembers thinking.

Digging deeper into the company's history, Johnson learned that the founder, James Cash Penney, was well known for his "fair and square" dealings with customers. That became the starting point for the company's switch to everyday low pricing. "People are disgusted with the lack of integrity on pricing," Johnson explained, referring to the retailing industry's reliance on price promotions to attract customers, especially during holiday shopping periods.

Starting in 2012, JCPenney set the price of all merchandise about 40 percent lower than the regular price charged in 2011, a "fair and square" everyday price. This new price policy didn't entirely eliminate price reductions. For example, the retailer planned 12 "month-long values" sales to bring customers into its 1,100 stores every month. It also publicized its first and third Fridays as the days when slow-moving products would be marked down for clearance at the "best" prices. JCPenney began using its Facebook page to prove how "fair and square" its everyday low prices really are by contrasting the "before" and "after" prices of specific items.

Price isn't the only part of JCPenney's marketing mix that's being overhauled. The company now has a new logo, a red-outlined square with the initials "jcp" in one corner, updating the image and echoing the "fair and square" pricing approach. The retailer is also renovating its stores to reflect a "town square" layout of 80 to 100 boutiques and adding new designer product lines to call attention to the company's transformation. For customers who want to shop or browse without going to a store, JCPenney continues to promote its extensive online offerings as well as its apps for cell-phone users. Instead of weekly sales fliers, it mails monthly catalogs featuring merchandise for men, women, children, and the home. The products, not the prices, are the stars of these magazine-like catalogs.

"We want to be the favorite store for everyone, for all Americans, rich and poor, young and old," the CEO says. To do that, JCPenney will have to convince customers that its everyday low prices are fair, compared with the bewildering barrage of coupons and sales that other department stores offer to bargain-hunters. It will also have to make its department stores as appealing as possible, with brand-name products that customers recognize and want to buy—from JCPenney.[20]

Questions for Discussion

1. What is JCPenney doing to influence the target market's evaluation of the value of its merchandise?
2. How do you think competitors should respond to JCPenney's everyday low prices? Explain your answer.
3. Would you suggest that JCPenney reveal the markup it uses to arrive at its prices as a way to convince customers that its everyday prices really are low?

strategic case 8

Newspapers Test Pricing for Digital Editions

Pricing is one of the most difficult challenges facing U.S. newspapers in the 21st century. The entire industry is feeling a tremendous financial squeeze. Revenues from display advertising have plummeted as many marketers engage customers via social media, Internet ads, special events, daily deal sites, and other promotional methods that sidestep newspapers. Just as important, revenues from paid classified ads have also slumped. Instead of buying classified ads to fill job openings, sell new or used cars, and sell or trade household items, large numbers of consumers and businesses are turning to auction websites, online employment sites, and social media sites.

Looking at trends in paid newspaper subscriptions, the news isn't much better. During the first decade of this century, weekday newspaper circulation fell by 17 percent, and the outlook for a turnaround in print subscriptions is not positive. One reason is that some people—younger consumers, in particular—prefer to get their news online or from television. With the rise of mobile devices like smartphones, tablet computers, and e-book readers, on-the-go consumers have a quick and easy way to click for news, at any time and from any place. The printed newspaper doesn't have the very latest news—but online sources do. Another reason is that many cash-strapped subscribers have cut back on buying newspapers, either because they're worried about their jobs or because they're saving money for other purchases.

© Lourens Smak/Alamy

In short, newspapers simply can't continue to do business as they did in the last century and expect to prosper in this century. Once-strong newspapers like the *Rocky Mountain News* have been forced to shut down, while others (like the *Christian Science Monitor*) have abandoned print in favor of online-only editions. Now, with fewer paying customers and fewer advertisers, newspapers are taking a long, hard look at their pricing strategies to find new ways of improving circulation revenues and profits in the digital age. Some newspapers continue to offer news for free, on the basis that this builds their brands online and offers extra value to readers who want to see updated news whenever it breaks. Other newspapers are trying a *paywall,* allowing only paid subscribers to see online content that's "walled off" to prevent free access.

Pricing the Digital *Wall Street Journal*

How do you price the online version of a print newspaper for readers? Should the Internet or mobile edition be entirely free because there are no print costs? Should it be free to customers who subscribe to the print edition? Should some content be free and some fee-only? Or should you set a price for reading almost anything other than today's headlines?

The Wall Street Journal was one of the first newspapers to confront these questions and try to find pricing approaches that made sense for its situation. A national newspaper that's heavy on U.S. and international business news, the *Journal* also covers general news and politics, economics, investment issues, the arts, and lifestyle trends. Many of its subscribers are professionals, investors, or businesspeople who need to follow the latest happenings in their field and stay updated on world events.

During the mid-1990s, the *Journal* recognized that it had an unusual opportunity to pioneer a new pricing strategy for online news content. It started with a free website, quickly attracted 600,000 registered users, and within a few months, it announced a change to subscriber pricing. Once the site set its prices at $49 per year for online-only access and $29 for print subscribers who wanted to view online material, only 5 percent of the registered users chose to pay for access.

The *Journal* was prepared for this kind of response. Whereas other newspapers were testing prices for individual articles or for weekly access, the *Journal* believed it offered subscribers long-term value that they wouldn't appreciate if they could pay for content by the article or by the week. "It's easier for people to see the total value of a package if you have to pay for it all," said the online editor. Giving business readers a comprehensive overview of global markets day after day means "we're not a news site, we're a competitive advantage tool," said another *Journal* executive.

Despite the steep drop in visitors after the *Journal* began selling subscriptions, the site had 100,000 paid subscribers within a year. Within two years, it had 200,000 paid subscribers and was nearly at the break-even point. Since then, the *Journal* has increased its online subscription prices and instituted subscription pricing for access via apps on mobile devices. Today, the newspaper has more than 500,000 digital subscribers, including 80,000 who access the online edition by phone, tablet, or e-book reader. Non-subscribers have access to a limited amount of the *Journal*'s online content, and new-subscriber deals encourage people to sign up rather than be casual visitors. Thanks to the *Journal* site's loyal and lucrative subscriber base, a growing number of major advertisers are willing to pay to reach this audience online, which contributes millions more to the newspaper's bottom line.

Pricing Digital Versions of Gannett Newspapers

Unlike *The Wall Street Journal,* which attracts many business readers, Gannett newspapers are for the general public. In addition to *USA Today,* its national newspaper, Gannett also owns 80 other papers in 30 states. No two of these local papers are exactly alike: some (like the *Indianapolis Star* in Indianapolis, Indiana) serve big cities, while others (like the *Times Recorder* in Zanesville, Ohio) serve smaller communities. In recent years, Gannett's circulation revenue has been dropping, and the company has decided to increase revenue by instituting monthly subscription pricing for the digital versions of its local newspapers. *USA Today* was not included in this new pricing strategy, because of its national distribution.

To start, Gannett tested pricing for online access to three of its local newspaper sites to learn about "consumer engagement and willingness to pay for unique local content," says a spokesperson. Based on the results of those tests, which included full access via computer and mobile devices, Gannett then announced that 80 of its local papers would limit non-subscriber access to digital content. Each local paper was responsible for setting the price, following the general principle that non-subscribers could view no more than 15 articles per month (or as few as five if the paper wants to be more restrictive). To view more content, consumers could choose a monthly subscription for digital-only access using a wide range of devices or a monthly subscription combining print and digital access. Even subscribing to Sunday-only editions will be sufficient to qualify for digital access, if a local paper chooses to price content in that way.

Will consumers pay for digital versions of local newspapers? Some experts believe that local residents will pay for in-depth local coverage and the very latest news, which they can't easily get for free from other sources. If consumers like to read a particular columnist or a regular feature that only appears in the local paper, they will have to pay to see that content online or in print. With the rapid penetration of tablet computers and smartphones, the ability to access local content digitally is increasingly more appealing than reading a once-a-day newspaper in print. Other experts say that consumers have grown accustomed to unlimited online access over the years, and they won't be receptive to paying for what was previously free. However, if consumers find themselves reaching the preset limit of how many articles they can read online, they may find that it's easier to pay than to have to click around and find the content elsewhere for free.

Gannett expects its new digital pricing strategy to increase revenues by as much as $100 million per year, once the pricing is implemented by all 80 papers. "This is a turning point for us," says an executive. Meanwhile, other local newspapers are testing different ways to price online content, also hoping that subscribers will sign up and then remain loyal. Will paywalls pay off?[21]

Questions for Discussion

1. When *The Wall Street Journal* began charging for online access, the number of visitors to its site dropped dramatically and slowly began rising again. What does this suggest about the price elasticity of demand for its products?
2. Would consumers have an internal reference price for digital newspaper content? Explain your answer.
3. What type of psychological pricing are Gannett and *The Wall Street Journal* using when they offer print and digital subscriptions together for one price? What do you think of this approach to pricing?
4. Should Gannett and *The Wall Street Journal* be looking at competitors' prices when setting their own prices? Why or why not?

ROLE-PLAY TEAM CASE EXERCISE 8

This role-play team exercise is designed to simulate actual marketing decision making in the real world. The entire team should read the overview and background. Each student will take on a role of a particular employee within the organization. Your instructor will provide additional information and instructions related to a team decision.

CLEAN TECHNOLOGIES INC.*

Background

Two former employees of a large chemical manufacturer founded Clean Technologies Inc. (CTI) in 1995. One of the company's product lines consists of three soy-based powders with additives to enhance their moisture-absorbing properties. The products are used to absorb and eliminate excess moisture in a variety of consumer and organizational settings. In their powdered form, CTI products can absorb as much as 10 times their weight in moisture. The products are environmentally friendly, a critical value of CTI. The company has been acknowledged for accomplishments in the area of environmental sensitivity, and the products have undergone numerous tests for safety and high quality.

Initially, CTI targeted the industrial market with the Slab Clean brand. Slab Clean is marketed primarily to commercial establishments for the purpose of eliminating moisture and oil from paved surfaces. The product soaks up spills and can then be swept dry. The product is colored white to enhance its visibility and ease of removal. Slab Clean is distributed in 64-ounce tin containers with adjustable lids for application. The retail price of Slab Clean is $8.50 per 64-ounce container, with a manufacturing cost of $2.50. The product is available to industrial buyers through catalogs and, more recently, through AutoZone, Discount Auto Parts, and other consumer automotive outlets. It has been so successful that it is now being distributed in the same stores as CTI's other soy-based powders. CTI positions its Slab Clean product as a better deal than its closest competitor, which prices its 32-ounce absorbent product at $8.99. Slab Clean generates the company's second-highest sales levels.

In 2000, CTI expanded its product line to try and include other goods targeted at distinctly different end users. One of these new products, Pet Fresh, is used in pet litter boxes to facilitate moisture and odor absorption. Pet Fresh has the same formulation as Slab Clean, but the product is beige so that it blends with other pet litter products. The product is available in a 32-ounce plastic container with an adjustable lid for application. Pet Fresh is distributed through major discount stores, such as Walmart, Target, Kmart, and supermarkets. The suggested retail price is $8.00 per 32-ounce container, with a manufacturing cost of $1.75. Pet Fresh has become CTI's best-selling product. Currently, CTI has no major competitors in this category.

The final derivative product is Baby Fresh, which is used in place of traditional baby powder. Developed in 2010 as a relatively new addition to CTI's product line, Baby Fresh has the lowest sales. Because tests of CTI's first two products indicated that their high moisture absorption properties caused rashes and irritated babies' skin with prolonged use, Baby Fresh's moisture-absorbing properties were modified to make it absorb five times its weight in

*© O.C. Ferrell and Linda Ferrell, 2012. Jennifer Sawayda assisted with the development of this exercise under the direction of O.C. Ferrell and Linda Ferrell. This role-play case is not intended to represent the managerial decisions of an actual company.

moisture. Baby Fresh is also purified to meet federal regulations for consumers' personal use. The product is white in color, the same as Slab Clean. Baby Fresh is sold in 8-ounce plastic containers for a suggested retail price of $6.00, with a product cost of $1.50. This is a higher price than competing product Johnson & Johnson's Baby Powder, which retails from between $3.84 to $5.29 for a 22-ounce container. Despite the fact that CTI is charging a higher price for a smaller size, the company feels its higher price point creates a premium image for the brand. Baby Fresh is distributed through major discount chains like Target, Walmart, Kmart, Toys"R"Us, supermarkets, and baby supply stores throughout the country.

While there is a slight difference in manufacturing costs, differences in packaging and quantity result in about the same cost per product. Pricing objectives are based on a return on investment pricing strategy, in which the company hopes to maintain a specified amount of return on each product. CTI also evaluates its competitors' prices when making pricing decisions. For Slab Fresh, CTI wants consumers to realize that they are receiving twice the content at a lower price than competing products. Consumers thereby feel that they are receiving a good deal. On the other hand, the company is using a premium pricing strategy for its Pet Fresh and Baby Fresh brands to signify their quality and superior performance.

Thus, it came as a real surprise that several consumer advocate groups are now reporting that some consumers are buying Slab Clean and Pet Fresh as a replacement for Baby Fresh. While the products are clearly labeled for their intended purpose, the fact that their ingredients are almost identical has led some consumers to believe that the same benefits can be derived from Slab Clean and Pet Fresh. An investigative news program, *1-Hour,* is going to do a story on this issue in the next several weeks. A meeting has been called to discuss product misuse and pricing. Dana Lewis, marketing manager, Marty Byrne, director of research and development, Kay Oliver, general council, Randy McAdams, chief financial officer and pricing administrator, and Kyle Sanders, vice president of sales, will attend the meeting. Of key concern are any relationships among pricing, size of containers, and consumer perceptions leading to product misuse.

Dana Lewis, Marketing Manager

You are the marketing manager in charge of overseeing the design and implementation of marketing strategies for Slab Clean, Pet Fresh, and Baby Fresh. You have been with the company since graduating from a prestigious business school and aspire to move into executive management one day. Additionally, your grandfather is one of the founders of CTI.

You have three product managers who report to you, one for each of the different products within the product line. Traditionally, you have favored a rather "hands off" approach when working with your product managers, in order to grant them greater flexibility, autonomy, and creativity. The product manager for Pet Fresh, for example, recently implemented price discounts for wholesalers to better support the product line. The product manager for Slab Clean has created an innovative online coupon for distributors to relay to customers through their corporate websites. Although you have a good working relationship with most employees at CTI, you believe the chief financial officer/pricing administrator and the vice president of sales do not really understand the long-term priorities of "new marketing" approaches.

You prefer a relationship-building approach with customers, rather than an insistence on immediate sales, and you believe that the best way to build relationships with large retailers and wholesalers is by developing new products and applications on a regular basis. You enjoy working closely with the director of research and development on new product development. The director of research and development actually came up with the idea that led to the start-up of CTI.

You and the pricing administrator are particularly interested in how consumers are interpreting the prices of the three brands. The intention of the company is to portray Slab Clean as a good deal compared to rival products, Pet Fresh as a one-of-a-kind product, and Baby Fresh as a superior product offering. Your department has created advertising to market these characteristics. However, you also know that the majority of consumers attracted to these types of products are value-conscious. Although they desire a high-quality product, they are also extremely concerned with price. You wonder if your company has priced Baby Fresh too high for its package size.

Last month, at a trade meeting, a few of your distributors indicated that some customers are using company products in ways in which they were not intended to be used. Because you were aware of only a few incidents, you did not report the misuse or document it in any manner.

Late yesterday, you received a communication from the general counsel indicating there may be a potential problem with customers' misusing Slab Clean and Pet Fresh. The CEO has requested that you meet to come up with a comprehensive action plan to resolve this matter.

Marty Byrne, Director of Research and Development

You are the director of research and development at CTI. Your mission is twofold: (1) to locate and identify the best environmentally sensitive resources and processes for all of the products CTI manufactures, distributes, and sells, and (2) to come up with at least one new product (or derivative/alternative use for an existing product) every two years.

You have been with CTI almost since its inception, when you were a struggling graduate student. The company funded your biohazard research and your still-unfinished doctorate. You have been a pacesetter with the organization but are looked upon with some disfavor. You are often criticized for your overzealous push for innovation in product development. Some think you are too big a risk-taker for the well-being of the organization, and many in the organization complain bitterly about the elitist compensation and benefits you have at your disposal for yourself and your department. You take it all in stride, knowing that CTI's market expansion is due in large part to your creativity and that of your staff.

CTI went public three years ago and has performed well since, a fact that should sit very well at next month's shareholders' meeting. One of the issues on the agenda is the adoption of tighter corporate governance mechanisms, including methods for incorporating stakeholders' concerns into CTI's strategic planning efforts and how the product fits into the overall organization.

Pricing decisions are also an issue, because they influence evaluations and activities associated with the product. CTI is using an EDLP (everyday low prices) strategy for its Slab Clean brand to position it as a better deal than its competitors. It is using a premium pricing strategy for its Pet Fresh and Baby Fresh brands. These different strategies may make it harder for the company to achieve a solid brand identity. You believe that the firm is unsure about whether it wants to be perceived as a company that gives consumers good deals or as a company offering premium products. You have also heard rumors that channel members are charging more for carrying Slab Clean products than for Pet Fresh or Baby Fresh because its bulkier 64-ounce packages take up more room. There has been talk about redesigning the product, or at least its packaging, to reduce the amount of shelf space it requires.

Late yesterday, you received a communication from the general counsel indicating there may be a potential problem with customers misusing Slab Clean and Pet Fresh. The CEO has requested that you meet to come up with a comprehensive action plan to resolve this matter. A meeting has been scheduled.

Kay Oliver, General Council

You are the general counsel for CTI. You report directly to the CEO, who has just informed you that consumers are buying Pet Fresh and, in some instances, Slab Clean for use as a baby powder on their children. Everyone in the company is well aware that Slab Clean and Pet Fresh are not intended for the same use as Baby Fresh, which is why Baby Fresh is a reformulated product. The CEO wants an action plan from several key executives and managers within the organization to address this issue.

You are deeply concerned about this revelation, because the moisture-absorbing properties of CTI's three products differ, even though the ingredients listed on each product's label make them appear identical. You believe that the current pricing differentials are encouraging consumers to purchase the larger quantities of Slab Clean and Pet Fresh to substitute for Baby Fresh in order to save money. You realize that, although Pet Fresh and Slab Clean are technically more expensive than Baby Fresh, customers perceive they can save money, because they receive significantly more product for only a few dollars more.

You are concerned not only about consumers misusing the product and the long-term implications of such use but also about the potential for civil litigation. The company never placed any kind of disclaimer on the packaging stating that Slab Clean and Pet Fresh were not intended for use on people. You are currently conducting an investigation into the alleged incidents of product misuse.

Right now, you are checking to see what the company has done to prevent any product misunderstanding by reviewing the following:

1. Different labeling
2. Different packaging
3. Different pricing
4. Varying channels of distribution
5. Derivative names

Your greatest concern lies in the fact that the company was aware that Slab Clean and Pet Fresh are too harsh for use on babies, but the products are not specifically labeled to discourage customers from using them on their children. Looking at the list of ingredients on the packaging, the products appear basically the same in composition and formulation.

The CEO has also informed you that the news program *1-Hour* is preparing a story on the product misuse, which will air in the next several weeks. As the company's legal counsel, you are mindful of the company's need to act quickly and responsibly to protect consumers, distributors, and the owners. You have called an emergency meeting to discuss the issue.

Randy McAdams, Chief Financial Officer and Pricing Administrator

You are the chief financial officer for CTI. You have traditionally managed the company's financial, accounting, and pricing decisions with a firm hand. You were hired right after the company introduced Slab Clean and deftly guided the company through its initial public offering three years ago. You look forward to presenting information on CTI's continued financial success with shareholders at the annual meeting next month. In addition to the re-election of two officers (including yourself), one of the issues on the agenda is the issuance of stock to support future research and development efforts and expansion of the CTI product lines and applications.

Your previous position was with a major producer of soy, the primary ingredient in all of the CTI brand products. You were hired for your reputation as a cost-cutter. Because you have so much responsibility for the financial success of CTI, you are insistent that the sales force and sales management meet their sales and market share goals. Fortunately, you have a great relationship with the vice president of sales.

When pricing the three different product lines, you were more concerned about competitor prices than costs. You want to blow the competition out of the water. To do so requires you to carefully consider competitive offerings. For Slab Clean, the competition for environmentally friendly oil absorbents was high, so you decided to keep prices low and offer larger package sizes to undercut the competition. Because Pet Fresh does not have comparable competitors, you felt your company could charge a higher price. Baby Fresh is not only environmentally friendly but has passed numerous safety tests. You feel that a higher price point is needed to signal to consumers the quality of the product.

Although you priced the three types of products differently according to their objectives, the prices are within a few dollars of one another despite the difference in package size and function. This did not bother you until yesterday, when you received a communication from the general counsel indicating there may be a potential problem with customers misusing Slab Clean and Pet Fresh. From the general counsel and CEO, you have learned that some lower-income families and cost-conscious adults are using the less expensive Pet Fresh and Slab Clean in lieu of Baby Fresh. The CEO wants you to remind the meeting attendees that product liability juries generally find in favor of the possessive where babies and toddlers are concerned, even in the face of evidence of the possessive's own culpability. You also need to make sure the attendees remember the shareholders' meeting coming up next month and the CEO's strong position that good ethical practices are good business.

You wonder if perhaps the closeness in price has confused customers into purchasing a product for which it was not intended. The CEO has requested that you meet to come up with a comprehensive action plan to resolve this matter.

Kyle Sanders, Vice President of Sales

As vice president of sales and marketing, you are responsible for, essentially, the economic viability of CTI. With more than 14 years of sales and sales management experience, you have been with the company for more than six years. Since joining CTI, you have risen from regional sales manager to vice president.

You were heavily involved with every aspect of developing and testing the Baby Fresh product. You recognized the potential for the consumer application for such a product and helped foster buy-in for the product idea from many departments throughout the organization. In fact, you were instrumental in rushing the product tests to get the introduction off on schedule.

You have a tenuous relationship with the marketing and research and development departments, mainly because you feel they do not always understand the realities of selling products in intensely competitive consumer markets and retailers (e.g., national discount chains), which put enormous pressure on you to trim your margins.

When you heard about the prices that CTI was charging for its products, you were initially concerned. Although you feel that the everyday low prices strategy will certainly attract consumers, you have spent enough time in the industry to know that competitors will quickly retaliate. Either they will try to portray the brand as being inferior to theirs, or they could lower their own prices to match those of Slab Clean, setting off a price war. CTI is using a price skimming approach for Pet Fresh. Although it is a unique product, you feel it might backfire. Since cat litter costs pet owners anywhere from $7 to $16 on average (depending on the type and package size), at the time, you were unsure whether consumers would go for something meant to supplement—not replace—cat litter. So far, your fears have proved unfounded, as Pet Fresh has become your company's best-selling product. However, you recently heard rumors that a competitor was working on a similar product, which would increase competition and might force CTI to lower the price of Pet Fresh. You are also concerned about the lower sales of Baby Fresh and feel its high price is to blame.

Another concern is the fact that the products are so close in price, despite their vastly different functions. You have already fielded questions from channel members who are confused as to why your company was selling the same product to entirely different industries. Your company recognizes that these products are vastly different, but if channels members are having trouble differentiating the products, what about customers? You would like your company to adopt a pricing strategy that would better separate these products.

Late yesterday, you received a communication from the general counsel indicating there may be a potential problem with customers misusing Slab Clean and Pet Fresh. The CEO has requested that you meet to come up with a comprehensive action plan to resolve this matter.

NOTES

[1]Based on information in Megha Paul, "India Is a Growth Driver," *Travel Talk-India,* February 15, 2012, www.travtalkindia.com; Michael B. Baker, "Best Western Launches Segmented Brands in Three Tiers, *Business Travel News,* March 21, 2011, 22; Tanya Mohn, "Best Western Gives Names to Higher Levels," *The New York Times,* February 6, 2011, TR-2.

[2]John Detrixhe and Cordell Eddings, "Huggies Price Cut Shows Why Bond Market Backs Bernanke QE3," *Bloomberg News*, February 6, 2012, www.bloomberg.com/news/2012-02-06/huggies-price-cut-shows-why-bond-market-backing-bernanke-considering-qe3.html.

[3]"The Profit Impact of Market Strategies (PIMS) Overview," The Strategic Planning Institute, http://pimsonline.com/about_pims_db.htm (accessed April 18, 2012).

[4]Lisa Jennings, "Dripping with Potential," *National Restaurant News*, February 6, 2012, http://nrn.com/article/dripping-potential.

[5]Brad Stone, "Amazon, the Company That Ate the World," *Bloomberg Businessweek*, September 28, 2011, www.businessweek.com/magazine/the-omnivore-09282011.html.

[6]John Miley, "Warehouse Stores: Deal or No Deal?" Kiplinger, June 9, 2011, www.kiplinger.com/quiz/warehouse-store-deals/.

[7]"America's Biggest Rip-Offs," CNN, February 2, 2010, http://money.cnn.com/galleries/2010/news/1001/gallery.americas_biggest_ripoffs/2.html.

[8]Dan Frommer, "Get Ready to Pay More for Popular Concerts and Sporting Events," Business Insider, April 18, 2011, http://articles.businessinsider.com/2011-04-18/tech/30039355_1_ticket-pricing-live-nation-entertainment-ticket-inventory.

[9]Amy Chozick, "Verizon Teaming with Redbox for DVD and Streaming Service," *The New York Times,* February 6, 2012, http://mediadecoder.blogs.nytimes.com/2012/02/06/verizon-teaming-with-redbox-for-dvd-and-streaming-service/.

[10]"Differential Tuition at Mays Business School," Mays Business School, http://mays.tamu.edu/tuition/ (accessed April 18, 2012).

[11]Keld Jensen, "What's Your Negotiation Strategy?," *Forbes*, February 23, 2012, www.forbes.com/sites/keldjensen/2012/02/23/whats-your-negotiation-strategy/.

[12]Marla Royne Stafford and Thomas F. Stafford, "The Effectiveness of Tensile Pricing Tactics in the Advertising of Services," *Journal of Advertising* (Summer 2000): 45–56.

[13]Ricky Aristotle Muniarriz, "This is No Netflix Killer," MSNBC, February 22, 2012, www.msnbc.msn.com/id/46485559/ns/business-motley_fool/.

[14]Christine Harris and Jeffrey Bray, "Price Endings and Consumer Segmentation," *Journal of Product & Brand Management* 16 (March 2007): 200–205.

[15]Ralk Wagner and Kai-Stefan Beinke, "Identifying Patterns of Customer Response to Price Endings," *Journal of Product & Brand Management*, 15 (May 2006): 341–351.

[16]Sayantani Ghosh and Sruthi Ramakrishnan, "Garmin Finds New Direction with Fitness Gadgets," Reuters, February 22, 2012, www.reuters.com/article/2012/02/22/us-garmin-idUSTRE81L0SG20120222.

[17]Bruce L. Alford and Brian T. Engelland, "Advertised Reference Price Effects on Consumer Price Estimates, Value Perception, and Search Intention," *Journal of Business Research* (May 2000): 93–100.

[18]Laurie Burkitt, "Walmart Names New Chief Executive for China," *The Wall Street Journal,* February 7, 2012, http://online.wsj.com/article/SB10001424052970204136404577207723629587432.html; Owen Fletcher, "China Charges Carrefour, Walmart with Deceptive Pricing," *The Wall Street Journal,* January 26, 2011, http://online.wsj.com/article/SB10001424052748704062604576105672306973968.html.

[19]Based on information in "Urban Farmz" video, Southwestern Cengage, 2011; Jennifer Shutt, "Market Benefits Farmers, Residents," *Delmarva Now* (Salisbury, MD), April 18, 2012, www.delmarvanow.com; Jenna Telesca, "Farmers' Markets Grow 17%, Continuing Trend," *Supermarket News,* August 22, 2011, www.supermarketnews.com; Katie Zezima, "In Parts of the U.S., Farmers' Markets Are Testing the Limits of Productivity," *The New York Times,* August 20, 2011, www.nytimes.com; Elizabeth Weise, "Fresh Crop of Farmers Markets Is Spring Up," *USA Today,* August 8, 2011, 5B.

[20]Based on information in Laura Gunderson, "J.C. Penney Perks Up Its Image and Slashes Its Prices," *Oregonian,* April 7, 2012, www.oregonlive.com; Susanna Kim, "What to Expect: J.C. Penney's New Pricing Strategy," ABC News, January 31, 2012, http://abcnews.go.com; Jennifer Reingold, "Ron Johnson's Rx for JC Penney," *Fortune,* January 25, 2012, www.fortune.com; www.jcpenney.com; Stephanie Clifford, "J.C. Penney to Revise Pricing Methods and Limit Promotions," *The New York Times,* January 25, 2012, www.nytimes.com.

[21]Based on information in "Newspapers Erect Pay Walls in Hunt for New Revenue," *The Wall Street Journal,* April 3, 2012, www.wsj.com; Tom Rosenstiel, Mark Jurkowitz, and Hong Ji, "The Search for a New Business Model," *Pew Research Center's Journalism.org,* March 5, 2012, www.journalism.org; Russell Adams, "Papers Put Faith in Paywalls," *The Wall Street Journal,* March 4, 2012, www.wsj.com; Jeff Bercovici, "Gannett Building Paywalls Around All Its Papers Except *USA Today,*" *Forbes,* February 22, 2012, www.forbes.com; Justin Ellis, "From Salinas to Burlington: Can an Army of Paywalls Big and Small Buoy Gannett?" *Nieman Journalism Lab,* February 28, 2012, www.niemanlab.org; Elizabeth Gardner, "200,000 Paying for Wall St. Journal Interactive," *InternetWorld,* April 20, 1998, 10.

Feature Notes

[a]Based on information in Sylvia Rector, "Panera, Others Are Planning More Pay-What-You-Can Cafes," *Detroit Free Press,* February 22, 2012, www.freep.com; Peter Korn, "A Gentle Nudge Helps Panera Cares Fulfill Mission, Get Paid," *Portland Tribune* (OR), December 29, 2011, www.portlandtribune.com; Sarah Skidmore, "Panera Opens Pay-What-You-Wish Location in Oregon," Associated Press, January 12, 2011, http://abcnews.go.com; "Year Later, Pay-What-You-Want Panera a Success," *Cleveland Plain Dealer,* May 16, 2011, www.cleveland.com.

[b]Based on information in "Fewer Plastic Shopping Bags Handed Out," *Canadian Press*, January 3, 2011, www.cbc.ca/news; Kate Galbraith, "Should Plastic Bags Be Banned?" *The New York Times*, February 8, 2012, www.nytimes.com; William Yardley, "Seattle Bans Plastic Bags, and Sets a

Charge for Paper," *The New York Times*, December 20, 2011, www.nytimes.com; "Demand for Carry Bags Dips After Extra Charges," *The Times of India*, July 20, 2011, http://articles.timesofindia.indiatimes.com.

[c]Based on information in Christopher Elliott, "Bill Aims to Scuttle New Airfare Pricing Rule," *Chicago Tribune*, February 7, 2012, www.chicagotribune.com; "Rule Takes Surprises Out of Airfares," *San Francisco Chronicle*, February 14, 2012, www.sfgate.com; Rob Lovitt, "Mandatory Resort Fees Frustrate Hotel Guests," MSNBC, January 10, 2011, www.msnbc.com; David Segal, "Name Your Price, Then Get Ready for the Fees," *The New York Times*, September 10, 2011, www.nytimes.com.

[d]Based on information in "Angel Oregon Names This Year's Semifinalist Startups," *Oregonian*, January 25, 2012, www.oregonlive.com; Amanda Kooser, "$2,000 Zafirro Titanium Razor Has Sapphire Blades," *CNet News*, September 12, 2011, www.cnet.com; Kristiano Ang, "Is This Razor Worth $100,000?" *The Wall Street Journal*, August 19, 2011, www.wsj.com.

© Mike Stratton / © iStockphoto.com/hh5800 / © iStockphoto.com/sorendis

appendix A

Financial Analysis in Marketing*

Our discussion in this book focuses more on fundamental concepts and decisions in marketing than on financial details. However, marketers must understand the basic components of financial analyses to be able to explain and defend their decisions. In fact, they must be familiar with certain financial analyses to reach good decisions in the first place. To control and evaluate marketing activities, they must understand the income statement and what it says about their organization's operations. They also need to be familiar with performance ratios, which compare current operating results with past results and with results in the industry at large. We examine the income statement and some performance ratios in the first part of this appendix. In the second part, we discuss price calculations as the basis for price adjustments. Marketers are likely to use all these areas of financial analysis at various times to support their decisions and make necessary adjustments in their operations.

THE INCOME STATEMENT

The income, or operating, statement presents the financial results of an organization's operations over a certain period. The statement summarizes revenues earned and expenses incurred by a profit center, whether a department, a brand, a product line, a division, or the entire firm. The income statement presents the firm's net profit or net loss for a month, quarter, or year.

Table A.1 (on page A-2) is a simplified income statement for Stoneham Auto Supplies, a fictitious retail store. The owners, Rose Costa and Nick Schultz, see that net sales of $250,000 are decreased by the cost of goods sold and by other business expenses to yield a net income of $83,000. Of course, these figures are only highlights of the complete income statement, which appears in Table A.2 (on page A-3).

The income statement can be used in several ways to improve the management of a business. First, it enables an owner or a manager to compare actual results with budgets for various parts of the statement. For example, Rose and Nick see that the total amount of merchandise sold (gross sales) is $260,000. Customers returned merchandise or received allowances (price reductions) totaling $10,000. Suppose the budgeted amount was only $9,000. By checking the tickets for sales returns and allowances, the owners can determine why these events occurred and whether the $10,000 figure could be lowered by adjusting the marketing mix.

After subtracting returns and allowances from gross sales, Rose and Nick can determine net sales, the amount the firm has available to pay its expenses. They are pleased with this figure because it is higher than their sales target of $240,000.

A major expense for most companies that sell goods (as opposed to services) is the cost of goods sold. For Stoneham Auto Supplies, it amounts to 18 percent of net sales. Other expenses are treated in various ways by different companies. In our example, they are broken down into standard categories of selling expenses, administrative expenses, and general expenses.

The income statement shows that, for Stoneham Auto Supplies, the cost of goods sold was $45,000. This figure was derived in the following way. First, the statement shows that merchandise in the amount of $51,000 was purchased during the year. In paying the invoices

*We gratefully acknowledge the assistance of Jim L. Grimm, Professor Emeritus, Illinois State University, in writing this appendix.

Table A.1 Simplified Income Statement for a Retailer

Stoneham Auto Supplies Income Statement for the Year Ended December 31, 2012	
Net sales	$250,000
Cost of goods sold	– 45,000
Gross margin	$205,000
Expenses	– 122,000
Net income	$83,000

associated with these inventory additions, purchase (cash) discounts of $4,000 were earned, resulting in net purchases of $47,000. Special requests for selected merchandise throughout the year resulted in $2,000 in freight charges, which increased the net cost of delivered purchases to $49,000. When this amount is added to the beginning inventory of $48,000, the cost of goods available for sale during 2012 totals $97,000. However, the records indicate that the value of inventory at the end of the year was $52,000. Because this amount was not sold, the cost of goods that were sold during the year was $45,000.

Rose and Nick observe that the total value of their inventory increased by 8.3 percent during the year:

$$\frac{\$52{,}000 - \$48{,}000}{\$48{,}000} = \frac{\$4{,}000}{\$48{,}000} = \frac{1}{12} = 0.08333, \text{ or } 8.33\%$$

Further analysis is needed to determine whether this increase is desirable or undesirable (note that the income statement provides no details concerning the composition of the inventory held on December 31; other records supply this information). If Nick and Rose determine that inventory on December 31 is excessive, they can implement appropriate marketing action.

Gross margin is the difference between net sales and cost of goods sold. Gross margin reflects the markup on products and is the amount available to pay all other expenses and provide a return to the owners. Stoneham Auto Supplies had a gross margin of $205,000:

Net Sales	$250,000
Cost of Goods Sold	– 45,000
Gross Margin	205,000

Stoneham's expenses (other than cost of goods sold) during 2012 totaled $122,000. Observe that $53,000, or slightly more than 43 percent of the total, constituted direct selling expenses:

$$\frac{\$53{,}000 \text{ selling expenses}}{\$122{,}000 \text{ total expenses}} = 0.434, \text{ or } 43\%$$

The business employs three salespeople (one full time) and pays competitive wages. The selling expenses are similar to those in the previous year, but Nick and Rose wonder whether more advertising is necessary because the value of inventory increased by more than 8 percent during the year.

The administrative and general expenses are essential for operating the business. A comparison of these expenses with trade statistics for similar businesses indicates that the figures are in line with industry amounts.

Net income, or net profit, is the amount of gross margin remaining after deducting expenses. Stoneham Auto Supplies earned a net profit of $83,000 for the fiscal year ending

Table A.2 Income Statement for a Retailer

Stoneham Auto Supplies Income Statement for the Year Ended December 31, 2012			
Gross Sales			**$260,000**
Less: Sales returns and allowances			10,000
Net Sales			**$250,000**
Cost of Goods Sold			
Inventory, January 1, 2012 (at cost)		$48,000	
Purchases	$51,000		
Less: Purchase discounts	4,000		
Net purchases	$47,000		
Plus: Freight-in	2,000		
Net cost of delivered purchases		$49,000	
Cost of goods available for sale		$97,000	
Less: Inventory, December 31, 2012		$52,000	
Cost of goods sold			$45,000
Gross Margin			**$205,000**
Expenses			
Selling expenses			
Sales salaries and commissions	$32,000		
Advertising	16,000		
Sales promotions	3,000		
Delivery	2,000		
Total selling expenses		$53,000	
Administrative expenses			
Administrative salaries	$20,000		
Office salaries	20,000		
Office supplies	2,000		
Miscellaneous	1,000		
Total administrative expenses		$43,000	
General expenses			
Rent	$14,000		
Utilities	7,000		
Bad debts	1,000		
Miscellaneous	4,000		
(local taxes, insurance, interest, depreciation)			
Total general expenses		$26,000	
Total expenses			$122,000
Net Income			**$83,000**

Table A.3 **Cost of Goods Sold for a Manufacturer**

ABC Manufacturing Income Statement for the Year Ended December 31, 2012				
Cost of Goods Sold				
Finished Goods Inventory January 1, 2012				**$50,000**
Cost of Goods Manufactured				
Work-in-process inventory, January 1, 2012			$20,000	
Raw materials inventory, January 1, 2012	$40,000			
Net cost of delivered purchases	$240,000			
Cost of goods available for use	$280,000			
Less: Raw materials inventory, December 31, 2012	$42,000			
Cost of goods placed in production		$238,000		
Direct labor		32,000		
Manufacturing overhead				
Indirect labor	$12,000			
Supervisory salaries	10,000			
Operating supplies	6,000			
Depreciation	12,000			
Utilities	$10,000			
Total manufacturing overhead		$50,000		
Total manufacturing costs			$320,000	
Total work-in-process			$340,000	
Less: Work-in-process inventory, December 31, 2012			$22,000	
Cost of goods manufactured				$318,000
Cost of Goods Available for Sale				**$368,000**
Less: Finished goods inventory, December 31, 2012				48,000
Cost of Goods Sold				**$320,000**

December 31, 2012. Note that net income on this statement is figured before payment of state and federal income taxes.

Income statements for intermediaries and for businesses that provide services follow the same general format as that shown for Stoneham Auto Supplies in Table A.2. The income statement for a manufacturer, however, differs somewhat in that the "purchases" portion is replaced by "cost of goods manufactured." Table A.3 shows the entire Cost of Goods Sold section for a manufacturer, including cost of goods manufactured. In other respects, income statements for retailers and manufacturers are similar.

Performance Ratios

Rose and Nick's assessment of how well their business did during fiscal year 2012 can be improved through the use of analytical ratios. Such ratios enable a manager to compare the results for the current year with data from previous years and industry statistics. However, comparisons of the current income statement with income statements and industry statistics from other years are not very meaningful, because factors like inflation are not accounted for when comparing dollar amounts. More useful comparisons can be made by converting these figures to a percentage of net sales, as this section shows.

The first analytical ratios we discuss, the operating ratios, are based on the net sales figure from the income statement.

Operating Ratios

Operating ratios express items on the income, or operating, statement as percentages of net sales. The first step is to convert the income statement into percentages of net sales, as illustrated in Table A.4. After making this conversion, the manager looks at several key operating ratios: two profitability ratios (the gross margin ratio and the net income ratio) and the operating expense ratio.

For Stoneham Auto Supplies, these ratios are determined as follows (see Tables A.2 and A.4 for supporting data):

$$\text{gross margin ratio} = \frac{\textit{gross margin}}{\textit{net sales}} = \frac{\$205{,}000}{\$250{,}000} = 82\%$$

$$\text{net income ratio} = \frac{\textit{net income}}{\textit{net sales}} = \frac{\$83{,}000}{\$250{,}000} = 33.2\%$$

$$\text{operating expense ratio} = \frac{\textit{total expenses}}{\textit{net sales}} = \frac{\$122{,}000}{\$250{,}000} = 48.8\%$$

The gross margin ratio indicates the percentage of each sales dollar available to cover operating expenses and achieve profit objectives. The net income ratio indicates the percentage of each sales dollar that is classified as earnings (profit) before payment of income taxes. The operating expense ratio calculates the percentage of each dollar needed to cover operating expenses.

If Nick and Rose believe the operating expense ratio is higher than historical data and industry standards, they can analyze each operating expense ratio in Table A.4 to determine which expenses are too high and then take corrective action. After reviewing several key operating ratios, Nick and Rose, like many managers, will probably want to analyze all the items on the income statement. By doing so, they can determine whether the 8 percent increase in the value of their inventory was necessary.

Inventory Turnover Rate

The inventory turnover rate, or stock-turn rate, is an analytical ratio that can be used to answer the question "Is the inventory level appropriate for this business?" The inventory turnover rate indicates the number of times an inventory is sold (turns over) during one year. To be useful, this figure must be compared with historical turnover rates and industry rates.

The inventory turnover rate is computed (based on cost) as follows:

$$\text{inventory turnover} = \frac{\textit{cost of goods sold}}{\textit{average inventory at cost}}$$

Table A.4 Income Statement Components as Percentage of Net Sales

Stoneham Auto Supplies Income Statement as a Percentage of Net Sales for the Year Ended December 31, 2012			
		Percentage of Net Sales	
Gross Sales			**103.8%**
Less: Sales returns and allowances			3.8
Net Sales			**100.0%**
Cost of Goods Sold			
Inventory, January 1, 2012 (at cost)		19.2%	
Purchases	20.4%		
Less: Purchase discounts	1.6		
Net purchases	18.8%		
Plus: Freight-in	0.8		
Net cost of delivered purchases		19.6	
Cost of goods available for sale		38.8%	
Less: Inventory, December 31, 2012 (at cost)		20.8	
Cost of goods sold			18.0
Gross Margin			**82.0%**
Expenses			
Selling expenses			
Sales salaries and commissions	12.8%		
Advertising	6.4		
Sales promotions	1.2		
Delivery	0.8		
Total selling expenses		21.2%	
Administrative expenses			
Administrative salaries	8.0%		
Office salaries	8.0		
Office supplies	0.8		
Miscellaneous	0.4		
Total administrative expenses		17.2%	
General expenses			
Rent	5.6%		
Utilities	2.8		
Bad debts	0.4		
Miscellaneous	1.6		
Total general expenses		10.4%	
Total expenses			48.8
Net Income			33.2%

Rose and Nick would calculate the turnover rate from Table A.2 as follows:

$$\frac{\textit{cost of goods sold}}{\textit{average inventory at cost}} = \frac{\$45{,}000}{\$50{,}000} = 0.9$$

Their inventory turnover is less than once per year (0.9 times). The industry average is 2.8 times. This figure convinces Rose and Nick that their investment in inventory is too large and they need to reduce their inventory.

Return on Investment

Return on investment (ROI) is a ratio that indicates management's efficiency in generating sales and profits from the total amount invested in the firm. For Stoneham Auto Supplies, the ROI is 41.5 percent, which compares well with competing businesses.

We use figures from two different financial statements to arrive at ROI. The income statement, already discussed, gives us net income. The balance sheet, which states the firm's assets and liabilities at a given point in time, provides the figure for total assets (or investment) in the firm.

The basic formula for ROI is

$$\text{ROI} = \frac{\textit{net income}}{\textit{total investment}}$$

For Stoneham Auto Supplies, net income is $83,000 (see Table A.2). If total investment (taken from the balance sheet for December 31, 2012) is $200,000, then

$$\text{ROI} = \frac{\$83{,}000}{\$200{,}000} = 0.415, \text{ or } 41.5\%$$

The ROI formula can be expanded to isolate the impact of capital turnover and the operating income ratio separately. Capital turnover is a measure of net sales per dollar of investment; the ratio is figured by dividing net sales by total investment. For Stoneham Auto Supplies,

$$\text{capital turnover} = \frac{\textit{net sales}}{\textit{total investment}} = \frac{\$250{,}000}{\$200{,}000} = 1.25$$

ROI is equal to capital turnover times the net income ratio. The expanded formula for Stoneham Auto Supplies is

$$\begin{aligned}\text{ROI} &= \frac{\textit{net sales}}{\textit{total investment}} \times \frac{\textit{net income}}{\textit{net sales}}\\ &= \frac{\$250{,}000}{\$200{,}000} \times \frac{\$83{,}000}{\$250{,}000}\\ &= (1.25)\,(33.2\%) = 41.5\%\end{aligned}$$

PRICE CALCULATIONS

An important step in setting prices is selecting a basis for pricing, as discussed in Chapter 21. The systematic use of markups, markdowns, and various conversion formulas helps in calculating the selling price and evaluating the effects of various prices.

Markups

As discussed in the text, markup is the difference between the selling price and the cost of the item; that is, selling price equals cost plus markup. The markup must cover cost and contribute to profit; thus, markup is similar to gross margin on the income statement.

Markup can be calculated on either cost or selling price as follows:

$$\text{markup as percentage of cost} = \frac{\textit{amount added to cost}}{\textit{cost}} = \frac{\textit{dollar markup}}{\textit{cost}}$$

$$\text{markup as percentage of selling price} = \frac{\textit{amount added to cost}}{\textit{selling price}} = \frac{\textit{dollar markup}}{\textit{selling price}}$$

Retailers tend to calculate the markup percentage on selling price.

To review the use of these markup formulas, assume an item costs \$10 and the markup is \$5:

$$\text{selling price} = \text{cost} + \text{markup}$$

$$\$15 = \$10 + \$5$$

Thus,

$$\text{markup percentage on cost} = \frac{\$5}{\$10} = 50\%$$

$$\text{markup percentage on selling price} = \frac{\$5}{\$15} = 33\tfrac{1}{3}\%$$

It is necessary to know the base (cost or selling price) to use markup pricing effectively. Markup percentage on cost will always exceed markup percentage on price, given the same dollar markup, as long as selling price exceeds cost.

On occasion, we may need to convert markup on cost to markup on selling price, or vice versa. The conversion formulas are as follows:

$$\text{markup percentage on selling price} = \frac{\textit{markup percentage on cost}}{\textit{100\%} + \textit{markup percentage on cost}}$$

$$\text{markup percentage on cost} = \frac{\textit{markup percentage on selling price}}{\textit{100\%} - \textit{markup percentage on selling price}}$$

For instance, if the markup percentage on cost is $33\tfrac{1}{3}$ percent, the markup percentage on selling price is

$$\frac{33\tfrac{1}{3}\%}{100\% + 33\tfrac{1}{3}\%} = \frac{33\tfrac{1}{3}\%}{1.33\tfrac{1}{3}\%} = 25\%$$

If the markup percentage on selling price is 40 percent, the corresponding percentage on cost is as follows:

$$\frac{40\%}{100\% - 40\%} = \frac{40\%}{60\%} = 66\tfrac{2}{3}\%$$

Finally, we can show how to determine selling price if we know the cost of the item and the markup percentage on selling price. Assume an item costs \$36 and the usual markup percentage on selling price is 40 percent. Remember that selling price equals markup plus cost. Thus, if

$$100\% = 40\% \text{ of selling price} + \text{cost}$$

then,

$$60\% \text{ of selling price} = \text{cost}$$

In our example, cost equals \$36. Therefore,

$$0.6X = \$36$$

$$X = \frac{\$36}{0.6}$$

$$\text{selling price} = \$60$$

Alternatively, the markup percentage could be converted to a cost basis as follows:

$$\frac{40\%}{100\% - 40\%} = \frac{40\%}{60\%} = 66\tfrac{2}{3}\%$$

The selling price would then be computed as follows:

$$\begin{aligned}\text{selling price} &= 66\tfrac{2}{3}\%\ (\text{cost}) + \text{cost}\\ &= 66\tfrac{2}{3}\%\ (\$36) + \$36\\ &= \$24 + \$36 = \$60\end{aligned}$$

If you keep in mind the basic formula—selling price equals cost plus markup—you will find these calculations straightforward.

Markdowns

Markdowns are price reductions a retailer makes on merchandise. Markdowns may be useful on items that are damaged, priced too high, or selected for a special sales event. The income statement does not express markdowns directly because the change in price is made before the sale takes place. Therefore, separate records of markdowns would be needed to evaluate the performance of various buyers and departments.

The markdown ratio (percentage) is calculated as follows:

$$\text{markdown percentage} = \frac{\textit{dollar markdowns}}{\textit{net sales in dollars}}$$

In analyzing their inventory, Nick and Rose discover three special automobile jacks that have gone unsold for several months. They decide to reduce the price of each item from \$25 to \$20. Subsequently, these items are sold. The markdown percentage for these three items is

$$\text{markdown percentage} = \frac{3(\$5)}{3(\$20)} = \frac{\$15}{\$60} = 25\%$$

Net sales, however, include all units of this product sold during the period, not just those marked down. If 10 of these items were already sold at \$25 each, in addition to the three items sold at \$20, the overall markdown percentage would be

$$\begin{aligned}\text{markdown percentage} &= \frac{3(\$5)}{10(\$25) + 3(\$20)}\\ &= \frac{\$15}{\$250 + \$60} = \frac{\$15}{\$310} = 4.8\%\end{aligned}$$

Discussion and Review Questions

1. How does a manufacturer's income statement differ from a retailer's income statement?
2. Use the following information to answer parts a, b, and c:

Tea Company

Fiscal Year Ended June 30, 2013	
Net sales	$500,000
Cost of goods sold	300,000
Net income	50,000
Average inventory at cost	100,000
Total assets (total investment)	200,000

   a. What is the inventory turnover rate for Tea Company? From what sources will the marketing manager determine the significance of the inventory turnover rate?
   b. What is the capital turnover ratio? What is the net income ratio? What is the return on investment (ROI)?
   c. How many dollars of sales did each dollar of investment produce for Tea Company?
3. Product A has a markup percentage on cost of 40 percent. What is the markup percentage on selling price?
4. Product B has a markup percentage on selling price of 30 percent. What is the markup percentage on cost?
5. Product C has a cost of $60 and a usual markup percentage of 25 percent on selling price. What price should be placed on this item?
6. Apex Appliance Company sells 20 units of product Q for $100 each and 10 units for $80 each. What is the markdown percentage for product Q?

appendix B

Sample Marketing Plan

This sample marketing plan for a hypothetical company illustrates how the marketing planning process described in Chapter 2 might be implemented. If you are asked to create a marketing plan, this model may be a helpful guide, along with the concepts in Chapter 2.

Star Software Inc. Marketing Plan

I. EXECUTIVE SUMMARY

Star Software Inc. is a small, family-owned corporation in the first year of a transition from first-generation to second-generation leadership. Star Software sells custom-made calendar programs and related items to about 400 businesses, which use the software mainly for promotion. As Star's business is highly seasonal, its 18 employees face scheduling challenges, with greatest demand during October, November, and December. In other months, the equipment and staff are sometimes idle. A major challenge facing Star Software is how to increase profits and make better use of its resources during the off-season.

An evaluation of the company's internal strengths and weaknesses and external opportunities and threats served as the foundation for this strategic analysis and marketing plan. The plan focuses on the company's growth strategy, suggesting ways it can build on existing customer relationships, and on the development of new products and/or services targeted to specific customer niches. Since Star Software markets a product used primarily as a promotional tool by its clients, it is currently considered a business-to-business marketer.

1 **The Executive Summary,** one of the most frequently read components of a marketing plan, is a synopsis of the marketing plan. Although it does not provide detailed information, it does present an overview of the plan so readers can identify key issues pertaining to their roles in the planning and implementation processes. Although this is the first section in a marketing plan, it is usually written last.

II. ENVIRONMENTAL ANALYSIS

2 **The Environmental Analysis** presents information regarding the organization's current situation with respect to the marketing environment, the current target market(s), and the firm's current marketing objectives and performance.

Founded as a commercial printing company, Star Software Inc. has evolved into a marketer of high-quality, custom-made calendar software and related business-to-business specialty items. In the mid-1960s, Bob McLemore purchased the company and, through his full-time commitment, turned it into a very successful family-run operation. In the near future, McLemore's 37-year-old son, Jonathan, will take over as Star Software's president and allow the elder McLemore to scale back his involvement.

A. The Marketing Environment

3 This section of the environmental analysis considers relevant **external environmental** forces, such as competitive, economic, political, legal and regulatory, technological, and sociocultural forces.

1. *Competitive forces.* The competition in the specialty advertising industry is very strong on a local and regional basis but somewhat weak nationally. Sales figures for the industry as a whole are difficult to obtain since very little business is conducted on a national scale.

   The competition within the calendar industry is strong in the paper segment and weak in the software-based segment. Currently, paper calendars hold a dominant market share of approximately 65 percent; however, the software-based segment is growing rapidly. The 35 percent market share held by software-based calendars is divided among many different firms. Star Software, which holds 30 percent of the software-based calendar market, is the only company that markets a software-based calendar on a national basis. As software-based calendars become more popular, additional competition is expected to enter the market.

2. *Economic forces.* Nationwide, many companies have reduced their overall promotion budgets as they face the need to cut expenses. However, most of these reductions have occurred in the budgets for mass media advertising (television, magazines, and newspapers). While overall promotion budgets are shrinking, many companies are diverting a larger percentage of their budgets to sales promotion and specialty advertising. This trend is expected to continue as a weak, slow-growth economy forces most companies to focus more on the "value" they receive from their promotion dollars. Specialty advertising, such as can be done with a software-based calendar, provides this value.
3. *Political forces.* There are no expected political influences or events that could affect the operations of Star Software.
4. *Legal and regulatory forces.* In recent years, more attention has been paid to "junk mail." A large percentage of specialty advertising products are distributed by mail, and some of these products are considered "junk." Although this label is attached to the type of products Star Software makes, the problem of junk mail falls on Star's clients and not on the company itself. While legislation may be introduced to curb the tide of advertising delivered through the mail, the fact that more companies are diverting their promotion dollars to specialty advertising indicates that most do not fear the potential for increased legislation.
5. *Technological forces.* A major technological trend involves the growing popularity of tablet computers. Tablet computers, such as the Apple iPad and Samsung Galaxy Tab, provide consumers with increased mobility and application services. Tablet computers have begun taking market share away from desktop, laptop, and netbook computers. As this trend continues, current software-based calendar products will have to be adapted to match the new technology.
6. *Sociocultural forces.* In today's society, consumers have less time for work or leisure. The hallmarks of today's successful products are convenience and ease of use. In short, if the product does not save time and is not easy to use, consumers will simply ignore it. Software-based calendars fit this consumer need quite well. A software-based calendar also fits in with other societal trends: a move away from paper and hard copies, the need to automate repetitive tasks, and the growing dependence on information technology, for example.

4 The analysis of current target markets assesses demographic, geographic, psychographic, and product usage characteristics of the target markets. It also assesses the current needs of each of the firm's target markets, anticipated changes in those needs, and determines how well the organization's current products are meeting those needs.

4 B. Target Market(s)

By focusing on a commitment to service and quality, Star Software has effectively implemented a niche differentiation strategy in a somewhat diverse marketplace. Its ability to differentiate its product has contributed to superior annual returns. Its target market consists of manufacturers or manufacturing divisions of large corporations that move their products through dealers, distributors, or brokers. Its most profitable product is a software program for a PC-based calendar, which can be tailored to meet client needs by means of artwork, logos, and text. Clients use this calendar software as a promotional tool, providing a disk to their customers as an advertising premium. The calendar software is not produced for resale.

The calendar software began as an ancillary product to Star's commercial printing business. However, due to the proliferation of new computer technology, the computer calendar soon became more profitable for Star than its wall and desktop paper calendars. This led to the sale of the commercial printing plant and equipment to employees. Star Software has maintained a long-term relationship with these former employees, who have added capabilities to reproduce computer disks and whose company serves as Star's primary supplier of finished goods. Star's staff focuses on further development and marketing of the software.

C. Current Marketing Objectives and Performance

Star Software's sales representatives call on potential clients and, using a template demonstration disk, help them create a calendar concept. Once the sale has been finalized, Star completes the concept, including design, copywriting, and customization of the demonstration disk. Specifications are then sent to the supplier, located about 1,000 miles away, where the disks are produced. Perhaps what most differentiates Star from its competitors is its high level of service. Disks can be shipped to any location the buyer specifies. Since product development and customization of this type can require significant amounts of time and effort, particularly during the product's first year, Star deliberately pursues a strategy of steady, managed growth. Star Software markets its products on a company-specific basis. It has an annual reorder rate of approximately 90 percent and an average customer-reorder relationship of about eight years. The first year in dealing with a new customer is the most stressful and time-consuming for Star's salespeople and product developers. Subsequent years are faster and significantly more profitable. A company must set marketing objectives, measure performance against those objectives, and then take corrective action if needed.

The company is currently debt free except for the mortgage on its facility. However, about 80 percent of its accounts receivable are billed during the last three months of the calendar year. Seasonal account billings, along with the added travel of Star's sales staff during the peak season, pose a special challenge to the company. The need for cash to fund operations in the meantime requires the company to borrow significant amounts of money to cover the period until customer billing occurs. Star Software's marketing objectives include increases in both revenues and profits of approximately 10 percent over the previous year. Revenues should exceed $4 million, and profits are expected to reach $1.3 million.

III. SWOT ANALYSIS

A. Strengths

5 **Strengths** are competitive advantages or core competencies that give the organization an advantage in meeting the needs of its customers.

1. Star Software's product differentiation strategy is the result of a strong market orientation, commitment to high quality, and customization of products and support services.
2. There is little turnover among employees, who are well compensated and liked by customers. The relatively small staff size promotes camaraderie with coworkers and clients, and fosters communication and quick response to clients' needs.
3. A long-term relationship with the primary supplier has resulted in shared knowledge of the product's requirements, adherence to quality standards, and a common vision throughout the development and production process.
4. The high percentage of reorder business suggests a satisfied customer base, as well as positive word-of-mouth communication, which generates some 30 percent of new business each year.

B. Weaknesses

6 **Weaknesses** are limitations a firm has in developing or implementing a marketing strategy.

1. The highly centralized management hierarchy (the McLemores) and the lack of managerial backup may impede creativity and growth. Too few people hold too much knowledge.
2. Despite the successful, long-term relationship with the supplier, single sourcing could make Star Software vulnerable in the event of a natural disaster, strike, or dissolution of the current supplier. Contingency plans for suppliers should be considered.
3. The seasonal nature of the product line creates bottlenecks in productivity and cash flow, places excessive stress on personnel, and strains the facilities.

4. Both the product line and the client base lack diversification. Dependence on current reorder rates could breed complacency, invite competition, or create a false sense of customer satisfaction. The development of a product that would make the software calendar obsolete would probably put Star out of business.
5. While the small size of the staff fosters camaraderie, it also impedes growth and new-business development.
6. Star Software is reactive rather than assertive in its marketing efforts because of its heavy reliance on positive word-of-mouth communication for obtaining new business.
7. Star's current facilities are crowded. There is little room for additional employees or new equipment.

7 **Opportunities** are favorable conditions in the environment that could yield rewards for an organization if acted on properly.

7 C. Opportunities

1. Advertising expenditures in the United States exceed $132 billion annually. More than $25 billion of this is spent on direct-mail advertising and another $20 billion on specialty advertising. Star Software's potential for growth is significant in this market.
2. Technological advances have not only freed up time for Americans and brought greater efficiency but have also increased the amount of stress in their fast-paced lives. Laptops, tablet computers, and mobile technology have become commonplace, and personal information managers have gained popularity.
3. As U.S. companies look for ways to develop customer relationships rather than just close sales, reminders of this relationship could come in the form of acceptable premiums or gifts that are useful to the customer.
4. Computer-based calendars are easily distributed nationally and globally. The globalization of business creates an opportunity to establish new client relationships in foreign markets.

8 **Threats** are conditions or barriers that may prevent the organization from reaching its objectives.

8 D. Threats

1. Reengineering, right-sizing, and outsourcing trends in management may alter traditional channel relationships with brokers, dealers, and distributors, or eliminate them altogether.
2. Calendars are basically a generic product. The technology, knowledge, and equipment required to produce such an item, even a computer-based one, are minimal. The possible entry of new competitors is a significant threat.
3. Theft of trade secrets and software piracy through unauthorized copying are difficult to control.
4. Specialty advertising through promotional items relies on gadgetry and ideas that are new and different. As a result, product life cycles may be quite short.
5. Single-sourcing can be detrimental or even fatal to a company if the buyer–supplier relationship is damaged or if the supplying company has financial difficulty.
6. Competition from traditional paper calendars and other promotional items is strong.

9 During the development of a marketing plan, marketers attempt to match internal strengths to external opportunities. In addition, they try to convert internal weaknesses into strengths and external threats into opportunities.

9 E. Matching Strengths to Opportunities/ Converting Weaknesses and Threats

1. The acceptance of technological advances and the desire to control time create a potential need for a computer-based calendar.
2. Star Software has more opportunity for business growth during its peak season than it can presently handle because of resource (human and capital) constraints.
3. Star Software must modify its management hierarchy, empowering its employees through a more decentralized marketing organization.
4. Star Software should discuss future growth strategies with its supplier and develop contingency plans to deal with unforeseen events. Possible satellite facilities in other geographic locations should be explored.

5. Star Software should consider diversifying its product line to satisfy new market niches and develop nonseasonal products.
6. Star Software should consider surveying its current customers and its customers' clients to gain a better understanding of their changing needs and desires.

IV. MARKETING OBJECTIVES

10 The development of marketing objectives is based on environmental analysis, SWOT analysis, the firm's overall corporate objectives, and the organization's resources. For each objective, this section should answer the question, "What is the specific and measurable outcome and time frame for completing this objective?"

Star Software Inc. is in the business of helping other companies market their products and/or services. Besides formulating a market-oriented and customer-focused mission statement, Star Software should establish an objective to achieve cumulative growth in net profit of at least 50 percent over the next five years. At least half of this 50 percent growth should come from new, nonmanufacturing customers and from products that are nonseasonal or that are generally delivered in the off-peak period of the calendar cycle.

To accomplish its marketing objectives, Star Software should develop benchmarks to measure progress. Regular reviews of these objectives will provide feedback and possible corrective actions on a timely basis. The major marketing objective is to gain a better understanding of the needs and satisfaction of current customers. Because Star Software is benefiting from a 90 percent reorder rate, it must be satisfying its current customers. Star could use the knowledge of its successes with current clients to market to new customers. To capitalize on its success with current clients, the company should establish benchmarks to learn how it can improve the products it now offers through knowledge of clients' needs and specific opportunities for new-product offerings. These benchmarks should be determined through marketing research and Star's marketing information system.

Another objective should be to analyze the billing cycle Star now uses to determine if there are ways to bill accounts receivable in a more evenly distributed manner throughout the year. Alternatively, repeat customers might be willing to place orders at off-peak cycles in return for discounts or added customer services.

Star Software should also create new products that can use its current equipment, technology, and knowledge base. It should conduct simple research and analyses of similar products or product lines with an eye toward developing specialty advertising products that are software based but not necessarily calendar related.

V. MARKETING STRATEGIES

11 The marketing plan clearly specifies and describes the target market(s) toward which the organization will aim its marketing efforts. The difference between this section and the earlier section covering target markets is that the earlier section deals with present target markets, whereas this section looks at future target markets.

A. Target Market(s)

Target Market 1: Large manufacturers or stand-alone manufacturing divisions of large corporations with extensive broker, dealer, or distributor networks

Example: An agricultural chemical producer, like Dow Chemical, distributes its products to numerous rural "feed and seed" dealers. Customizing calendars with Chicago Board of Trade futures or USDA agricultural report dates would be beneficial to these potential clients.

Target Market 2: Nonmanufacturing, nonindustrial segments of the business-to-business market with extensive customer networks, such as banks, medical services, or financial planners

Example: Various sporting goods manufacturers distribute to specialty shop dealers. Calendars could be customized to the particular sport, such as golf (with PGA, Virginia Slims, or other tour dates), running (with various national marathon dates), or bowling (with national tour dates).

Target Market 3: Direct consumer markets for brands with successful licensing arrangements for consumer products, like Coca-Cola

Example: Products with major brand recognition and fan club membership, such as Harley-Davidson motorcycles or the Bloomington Gold Corvette Association, could provide additional markets for customized computer calendars. Environmental or political groups represent a nonprofit market. Brands with licensing agreements for consumer products could provide a market for consumer computer calendars in addition to the specialty advertising product, which would be marketed to manufacturers/dealers.

Target Market 4: Industry associations that regularly hold or sponsor trade shows, meetings, conferences, or conventions

Example: National associations, such as the National Dairy Association or the American Marketing Association, frequently host meetings or annual conventions. Customized calendars could be developed for any of these groups.

12 Though the marketing mix section in this plan is abbreviated, this component should provide considerable details regarding each element of the marketing mix: product, price, distribution, and promotion.

12 B. Marketing Mix

1. *Products.* Star Software markets not only calendar software but also the service of specialty advertising to its clients. Star's intangible attributes are its ability to meet or exceed customer expectations consistently, its speed in responding to customers' demands, and its anticipation of new-customer needs. Intangible attributes are difficult for competitors to copy, thereby giving Star Software a competitive advantage.
2. *Price.* Star Software provides a high-quality specialty advertising product customized to its clients' needs. The value of this product and service is reflected in its premium price. Star should be sensitive to the price elasticity of its product and overall consumer demand.
3. *Distribution.* Star Software uses direct marketing. Since its product is compact, lightweight, and nonperishable, it can be shipped from a central location direct to the client via UPS, FedEx, or the U.S. Postal Service. The fact that Star can ship to multiple locations for each customer is an asset in selling its products.
4. *Promotion.* Because 90 percent of Star's customers reorder each year, the bulk of promotional expenditures should focus on new-product offerings through direct-mail advertising and trade journals or specialty publications. Any remaining promotional dollars could be directed to personal selling (in the form of sales performance bonuses) of current and new products.

13 This section of the marketing plan details how the firm will be organized—by functions, products, regions, or types of customers—to implement its marketing strategies. It also indicates where decision-making authority will rest within the marketing unit.

13 VI. MARKETING IMPLEMENTATION

A. Marketing Organization

Because Star's current and future products require extensive customization to match clients' needs, it is necessary to organize the marketing function by customer groups. This will allow Star to focus its marketing efforts exclusively on the needs and specifications of each target customer segment. Star's marketing efforts will be organized around the following customer groups: (1) manufacturing group; (2) nonmanufacturing, business-to-business group; (3) consumer product licensing group; and (4) industry associations group. Each group will be headed by a sales manager who will report to the marketing director (these positions must be created). Each group will be responsible for marketing Star's products within that customer segment. In addition, each group will have full decision-making authority. This represents a shift from the current, highly centralized management hierarchy. Frontline salespeople will be empowered to make decisions that will better satisfy Star's clients.

These changes in marketing organization will enable Star Software to be more creative and flexible in meeting customers' needs. Likewise, these changes will overcome the current lack of diversification in Star's product lines and client base. Finally, this new marketing organization will give Star a better opportunity to monitor the activities of competitors.

B. Activities, Responsibilities, and Timetables for Completion

14 This component of the marketing plan outlines the specific activities required to implement a marketing strategy, determines who is responsible for performing these activities, and outlines when these activities should be accomplished, based on a specified schedule.

All implementation activities are to begin at the start of the next fiscal year on April 1. Unless specified, all activities are the responsibility of Star Software's next president, Jonathan McLemore.

- On April 1, create four sales manager positions and the position of marketing director. The marketing director will serve as project leader of a new business analysis team, to be composed of nine employees from a variety of positions within the company.
- By April 15, assign three members of the analysis team to each of the following projects: (1) research potential new-product offerings and clients, (2) analyze the current billing cycle and billing practices, and (3) design a customer survey project. The marketing director is responsible.
- By June 30, the three project groups will report the results of their analyses. The full business analysis team will review all recommendations.
- By July 31, develop a marketing information system to monitor client reorder patterns and customer satisfaction.
- By July 31, implement any changes in billing practices as recommended by the business analysis team.
- By July 31, make initial contact with new potential clients for the current product line. Each sales manager is responsible.
- By August 31, develop a plan for one new-product offering, along with an analysis of its potential customers. The business analysis team is responsible.
- By August 31, finalize a customer satisfaction survey for current clients. In addition, the company will contact those customers who did not reorder this year's product line to discuss their concerns. The marketing director is responsible.
- By December, implement the customer satisfaction survey with a random sample of 20 percent of current clients who reordered this year's product line. The marketing director is responsible.
- By February, implement a new-product offering, advertising to current customers and to a sample of potential clients. The business analysis team is responsible.
- By March, analyze and report the results of all customer satisfaction surveys and evaluate the new-product offering. The marketing director is responsible.
- Reestablish the objectives of the business analysis team for the next fiscal year. The marketing director is responsible.

VII. PERFORMANCE EVALUATION

15 This section details how the performance of the marketing strategy will be evaluated. Performance standards will be established against which to compare actual performance.

A. Performance Standards and Financial Controls

A comparison of the financial expenditures with the plan goals will be included in the project report. The following performance standards and financial controls are suggested:

- The total budget for the billing analysis, new-product research, and the customer survey will be equal to 60 percent of the annual promotional budget for the coming year.
- The breakdown of the budget within the project will be a 20 percent allocation to the billing cycle study, a 30 percent allocation to the customer survey and marketing information system development, and a 50 percent allocation to new-business development and new-product implementation.
- Each project team is responsible for reporting all financial expenditures, including personnel salaries and direct expenses, for its segment of the project. A standardized reporting form will be developed and provided by the marketing director.

- The marketing director is responsible for adherence to the project budget and will report overages to the company president on a weekly basis. The marketing director is also responsible for any redirection of budget dollars as required for each project of the business analysis team.
- Any new-product offering will be evaluated on a quarterly basis to determine its profitability. Product development expenses will be distributed over a two-year period, by calendar quarters, and will be compared with gross income generated during the same period.

B. Measuring Actual Performance

To analyze the effectiveness of Star Software's marketing strategy, it is necessary to compare its actual performance with plan objectives. To facilitate this analysis, monitoring procedures should be developed for the various activities required to bring the marketing strategy to fruition. These procedures include, but are not limited to, the following:

- A project management concept will be used to evaluate the implementation of the marketing strategy by establishing time requirements, human resource needs, and financial or budgetary expenditures.
- A perpetual comparison of actual and planned activities will be conducted on a monthly basis for the first year and on a quarterly basis after the initial implementation phase. The business analysis team, including the marketing director, will report its comparison of actual and planned outcomes directly to the company president.
- Each project team is responsible for determining what changes must be made in procedures, product focus, or operations as a result of the studies conducted in its area.

glossary

© Mike Stratton / © iStockphoto.com/hh5800 / © iStockphoto.com/sorendis

accessory equipment Equipment that does not become part of the final physical product but is used in production or office activities

advertising Paid nonpersonal communication about an organization and its products transmitted to a target audience through mass media

advertising appropriation The advertising budget for a specific time period

advertising campaign The creation and execution of a series of advertisements to communicate with a particular target audience

advertising platform Basic issues or selling points to be included in an advertising campaign

advocacy advertising Advertising that promotes a company's position on a public issue

aesthetic modifications Changes relating to the sensory appeal of a product

agents Intermediaries that represent either buyers or sellers on a permanent basis

aided recall test A posttest that asks respondents to identify recent ads and provides clues to jog their memories

allowance A concession in price to achieve a desired goal

approach The manner in which a salesperson contacts a potential customer

arbitrary approach Budgeting for an advertising campaign as specified by a high-level executive in the firm

artwork An advertisement's illustrations and layout

Asia-Pacific Economic Cooperation (APEC) An alliance that promotes open trade and economic and technical cooperation among member nations throughout the world

Association of Southeast Asian Nations (ASEAN) An alliance that promotes trade and economic integration among member nations in Southeast Asia

atmospherics The physical elements in a store's design that appeal to consumers' emotions and encourage buying

attitude An individual's enduring evaluation of feelings about and behavioral tendencies toward an object or idea

attitude scale A means of measuring consumer attitudes by gauging the intensity of individuals' reactions to adjectives, phrases, or sentences about an object

automatic vending The use of machines to dispense products

average fixed cost The fixed cost per unit produced

average total cost The sum of the average fixed cost and the average variable cost

average variable cost The variable cost per unit produced

bait pricing Pricing an item in a product line low with the intention of selling a higher-priced item in the line

balance of trade The difference in value between a nation's exports and its imports

barter The trading of products

base-point pricing Geographic pricing that combines factory price and freight charges from the base point nearest the buyer

benefit segmentation The division of a market according to benefits that consumers want from the product

Better Business Bureau (BBB) A system of nongovernmental, independent, local regulatory agencies supported by local businesses that helps settle problems between customers and specific business firms

blogs Web-based journals (short for "weblogs") in which writers editorialize and interact with other Internet users

brand A name, term, design, symbol, or other feature that identifies one seller's product as distinct from those of other sellers

brand competitors Firms that market products with similar features and benefits to the same customers at similar prices

brand equity The marketing and financial value associated with a brand's strength in a market

brand extension An organization uses one of its existing brands to brand a new product in a different product category

brand insistence The degree of brand loyalty in which a customer strongly prefers a specific brand and will accept no substitute

brand licensing An agreement whereby a company permits another organization to use its brand on other products for a licensing fee

brand loyalty A customer's favorable attitude toward a specific brand

brand manager The person responsible for a single brand

brand mark The part of a brand that is not made up of words, such as a symbol or design

brand name The part of a brand that can be spoken, including letters, words, and numbers

brand preference The degree of brand loyalty in which a customer prefers one brand over competitive offerings

brand recognition The degree of brand loyalty in which a customer is aware that a brand exists and views the brand as an alternative purchase if their preferred brand is unavailable

breakdown approach Measuring company sales potential based on a general economic forecast for a specific period and the market potential derived from it

break-even point The point at which the costs of producing a product equal the revenue made from selling the product

brokers Intermediaries that bring buyers and sellers together temporarily

buildup approach Measuring company sales potential by estimating how much of a product a potential buyer in a specific geographic area will purchase in a given period, multiplying the estimate by the number of potential buyers, and adding the totals of all the geographic areas considered

bundle pricing Packaging together two or more complementary products and selling them at a single price

business analysis Evaluating the potential impact of a product idea on the firm's sales, costs, and profits

business (organizational) buying behavior The purchase behavior of producers, government units, institutions, and resellers

business cycle A pattern of economic fluctuations that has four stages: prosperity, recession, depression, and recovery

business market Individuals, organizations, or groups that purchase a specific kind of product for resale, direct use in producing other products, or use in general daily operations

business products Products bought to use in a firm's operations, to resell, or to make other products

business services Intangible products that many organizations use in their operations

buy-back allowance A sum of money given to a reseller for each unit bought after an initial promotion deal is over

buying allowance A temporary price reduction to resellers for purchasing specified quantities of a product

buying behavior The decision processes and actions of people involved in buying and using products

buying center The people within an organization who make business purchase decisions

buying power Resources, such as money, goods, and services, that can be traded in an exchange

buzz marketing An attempt to incite publicity and public excitement surrounding a product through a creative event

captioned photograph A photograph with a brief description of its contents

captive pricing Pricing the basic product in a product line low, while pricing related items higher

cash-and-carry wholesalers Limited-service wholesalers whose customers pay cash and furnish transportation

cash discount A price reduction given to buyers for prompt payment or cash payment

catalog marketing A type of marketing in which an organization provides a catalog from which customers make selections and place orders by mail, telephone, or the Internet

category killer A very large specialty store that concentrates on a major product category and competes on the basis of low prices and product availability

category management A retail strategy of managing groups of similar, often substitutable products produced by different manufacturers

cause-related marketing The practice of linking products to a particular social cause on an ongoing or short-term basis

centralized organization A structure in which top-level managers delegate little authority to lower levels

cents-off offers Promotions that allow buyers to pay less than the regular price to encourage purchase

channel capacity The limit on the volume of information a communication channel can handle effectively

channel captain The dominant leader of a marketing channel or a supply channel

channel power The ability of one channel member to influence another member's goal achievement

client-based relationships Interactions that result in satisfied customers who use a service repeatedly over time

client publics Direct consumers of a product of a nonprofit organization

closing The stage in the personal selling process when the salesperson asks the prospect to buy the product

co-branding Using two or more brands on one product

codes of conduct Formalized rules and standards that describe what the company expects of its employees

coding process Converting meaning into a series of signs or symbols

cognitive dissonance A buyer's doubts shortly after a purchase about whether the decision was the right one

combination compensation plan Paying salespeople a fixed salary plus a commission based on sales volume

commercialization Refining and finalizing plans and budgets for full-scale manufacturing and marketing of a product

commission merchants Agents that receive goods on consignment from local sellers and negotiate sales in large, central markets

communication A sharing of meaning through the transmission of information

communications channel The medium of transmission that carries the coded message from the source to the receiver

community shopping center A type of shopping center with one or two department stores, some specialty stores, and convenience stores

company sales potential The maximum percentage of market potential that an individual firm within an industry can expect to obtain for a specific product

comparative advertising Compares the sponsored brand with one or more identified brands on the basis of one or more product characteristics

comparison discounting Setting a price at a specific level and comparing it with a higher price

competition Other organizations that market products that are similar to or can be substituted for a marketer's products in the same geographic area

competition-based pricing Pricing influenced primarily by competitors' prices

competition-matching approach Determining an advertising budget by trying to match competitors' advertising outlays

competitive advantage The result of a company matching a core competency to opportunities it has discovered in the marketplace

competitive advertising Tries to stimulate demand for a specific brand by promoting its features, uses, and advantages relative to competing brands

component parts Items that become part of the physical product and are either finished items ready for assembly or items that need little processing before assembly

concentrated targeting strategy A market segmentation strategy in which an organization targets a single market segment using one marketing mix

concept testing Seeking a sample of potential buyers' responses to a product idea

conclusive research Research designed to verify insights through objective procedures and to help marketers in making decisions

consideration set A group of brands within a product category that a buyer views as alternatives for possible purchase

consistency of quality The degree to which a product has the same level of quality over time

consumer buying behavior The decision processes and purchasing activities of people who purchase products for personal or household use and not for business purposes

consumer buying decision process A five-stage purchase decision process that includes problem recognition, information search, evaluation of alternatives, purchase, and postpurchase evaluation

consumer contests Sales promotion methods in which individuals compete for prizes based on their analytical or creative skills

consumer games Sales promotion methods in which individuals compete for prizes based primarily on chance

consumer jury A panel of a product's existing or potential buyers who pretest ads

consumer market Purchasers and household members who intend to consume or benefit from the purchased products and do not buy products to make profits

consumer misbehavior Behavior that violates generally accepted norms of a particular society

consumer products Products purchased to satisfy personal and family needs

consumer sales promotion methods Sales promotion techniques that encourage consumers to patronize specific stores or try particular products

consumer socialization The process through which a person acquires the knowledge and skills to function as a consumer

consumer sweepstakes A sales promotion in which entrants submit their names for inclusion in a drawing for prizes

consumerism Organized efforts by individuals, groups, and organizations to protect consumers' rights

contract manufacturing The practice of hiring a foreign firm to produce a designated volume of the domestic firm's product or a component of it to specification; the final product carries the domestic firm's name

convenience products Relatively inexpensive, frequently purchased items for which buyers exert minimal purchasing effort

convenience store A small self-service store that is open long hours and carries a narrow assortment of products, usually convenience items

cooperative advertising An arrangement in which a manufacturer agrees to pay a certain amount of a retailer's media costs for advertising the manufacturer's products

copy The verbal portion of advertisements

core competencies Things a company does extremely well, which sometimes give it an advantage over its competition

corporate strategy A strategy that determines the means for utilizing resources in the various functional areas to reach the organization's goals

cost-based pricing Adding a dollar amount or percentage to the cost of the product

cost comparison indicator A means of comparing the costs of advertising vehicles in a specific medium in relation to the number of people reached

cost-plus pricing Adding a specified dollar amount or percentage to the seller's cost

coupons Written price reductions used to encourage consumers to buy a specific product

credence qualities Attributes that customers may be unable to evaluate even after purchasing and consuming a service

crowdsourcing Combines the words *crowd* and *outsourcing* and calls for taking tasks usually performed by a marketer or researcher and outsourcing them to a crowd, or potential market, through an open call

cultural relativism The concept that morality varies from one culture to another and that business practices are therefore differentially defined as right or wrong by particular cultures

culture The accumulation of values, knowledge, beliefs, customs, objects, and concepts that a society uses to cope with its environment and passes on to future generations

cumulative discounts Quantity discounts aggregated over a stated time period

customary pricing Pricing on the basis of tradition

customer advisory boards Small groups of actual customers who serve as sounding boards for new-product ideas and offer insights into their feelings and attitudes toward a firm's products and other elements of its marketing strategy

customer contact The level of interaction between provider and customer needed to deliver the service

customer forecasting survey A survey of customers regarding the types and quantities of products they intend to buy during a specific period

customer relationship management (CRM) Using information about customers to create marketing strategies that develop and sustain desirable customer relationships

customer services Human or mechanical efforts or activities that add value to a product

customers The purchasers of organizations' products; the focal point of all marketing activities

cycle analysis An analysis of sales figures for a three- to five-year period to ascertain whether sales fluctuate in a consistent, periodic manner

cycle time The time needed to complete a process

database A collection of information arranged for easy access and retrieval

dealer listings Advertisements that promote a product and identify the names of participating retailers that sell the product

dealer loader A gift, often part of a display, given to a retailer that purchases a specified quantity of merchandise

decentralized organization A structure in which decision-making authority is delegated as far down the chain of command as possible

decline stage The stage of a product's life cycle when sales fall rapidly

decoding process Converting signs or symbols into concepts and ideas

Delphi technique A procedure in which experts create initial forecasts, submit them to the company for averaging, and then refine the forecasts

demand-based pricing Pricing based on the level of demand for the product

demand curve A graph of the quantity of products expected to be sold at various prices if other factors remain constant

demonstrations Sales promotion methods a manufacturer uses temporarily to encourage trial use and purchase of a product or to show how a product works

department stores Large retail organizations characterized by a wide product mix and organized into separate departments to facilitate marketing efforts and internal management

depression A stage of the business cycle when unemployment is extremely high, wages are very low, total disposable income is at a minimum, and consumers lack confidence in the economy

depth of product mix The average number of different products offered in each product line

derived demand Demand for business products that stems from demand for consumer products

descriptive research Research conducted to clarify the characteristics of certain phenomena to solve a particular problem

differential pricing Charging different prices to different buyers for the same quality and quantity of product

differentiated targeting strategy A strategy in which an organization targets two or more segments by developing a marketing mix for each segment

digital marketing Uses all digital media, including the Internet and mobile and interactive channels, to develop communication and exchanges with customers

digital media Electronic media that function using digital codes; when we refer to digital media, we are referring to media available via computers, cellular phones, smartphones, and other digital devices that have been released in recent years

direct marketing The use of the telephone, Internet, and nonpersonal media to introduce products to customers, who can then purchase them via mail, telephone, or the Internet

direct ownership A situation in which a company owns subsidiaries or other facilities overseas

direct-response marketing A type of marketing in which a retailer advertises a product and makes it available through mail or telephone orders

direct selling Marketing products to ultimate consumers through face-to-face sales presentations at home or in the workplace

discount stores Self-service, general-merchandise stores that offer brand-name and private-brand products at low prices

discretionary income Disposable income available for spending and saving after an individual has purchased the basic necessities of food, clothing, and shelter

disposable income After-tax income

distribution The decisions and activities that make products available to customers when and where they want to purchase them

distribution centers Large, centralized warehouses that focus on moving rather than storing goods

drop shippers Limited-service wholesalers that take title to goods and negotiate sales but never actually take possession of products

dual distribution The use of two or more marketing channels to distribute the same products to the same target market

dumping Selling products at unfairly low prices

early adopters People who adopt new products early, choose new products carefully, and are viewed as "the people to check with" by later adopters

early majority Individuals who adopt a new product just prior to the average person

electronic data interchange (EDI) A computerized means of integrating order processing with production, inventory, accounting, and transportation

electronic marketing (e-marketing) The strategic process of distributing, promoting, and pricing products, and discovering the desires of customers using digital media and digital marketing

embargo A government's suspension of trade in a particular product or with a given country

environmental analysis The process of assessing and interpreting the information gathered through environmental scanning

environmental scanning The process of collecting information about forces in the marketing environment

ethical issue An identifiable problem, situation, or opportunity requiring a choice among several actions that must be evaluated as right or wrong, ethical or unethical

European Union (EU) An alliance that promotes trade among its member countries in Europe

evaluative criteria Objective and subjective product characteristics that are important to a buyer

everyday low prices (EDLP) Pricing products low on a consistent basis

exchange controls Government restrictions on the amount of a particular currency that can be bought or sold

exchanges The provision or transfer of goods, services, or ideas in return for something of value

exclusive dealing A situation in which a manufacturer forbids an intermediary from carrying products of competing manufacturers

exclusive distribution Using a single outlet in a fairly large geographic area to distribute a product

executive judgment A sales forecasting method based on the intuition of one or more executives

experience qualities Attributes that can be assessed only during purchase and consumption of a service

experimental research Research that allows marketers to make causal inferences about relationships

expert forecasting survey Sales forecasts prepared by experts outside the firm, such as economists, management consultants, advertising executives, or college professors

exploratory research Research conducted to gather more information about a problem or to make a tentative hypothesis more specific

exporting The sale of products to foreign markets

extended decision making A consumer decision-making process employed when purchasing unfamiliar, expensive, or infrequently bought products

external reference price A comparison price provided by others

external search An information search in which buyers seek information from sources other than their memories

family branding Branding all of a firm's products with the same name or part of the name

family packaging Using similar packaging for all of a firm's products or packaging that has one common design element

feature article A manuscript of up to 3,000 words prepared for a specific publication

Federal Trade Commission (FTC) An agency that regulates a variety of business practices and curbs false advertising, misleading pricing, and deceptive packaging and labeling

feedback The receiver's response to a decoded message

first-mover advantage The ability of an innovative company to achieve long-term competitive advantages by being the first to offer a certain product in the marketplace

fixed costs Costs that do not vary with changes in the number of units produced or sold

F.O.B. destination A price indicating the producer is absorbing shipping costs

F.O.B. factory The price of merchandise at the factory before shipment

focus-group interview An interview that is often conducted informally, without a structured questionnaire, in small groups of 8 to 12 people, to observe interaction when members are exposed to an idea or a concept

franchising An arrangement in which a supplier (franchiser) grants a dealer (franchisee) the right to sell products in exchange for some type of consideration

free merchandise A manufacturer's reward given to resellers that purchase a stated quantity of products

free samples Samples of a product given out to encourage trial and purchase

freight absorption pricing Absorption of all or part of actual freight costs by the seller

freight forwarders Organizations that consolidate shipments from several firms into efficient lot sizes

full-service wholesalers Merchant wholesalers that perform the widest range of wholesaling functions

functional modifications Changes affecting a product's versatility, effectiveness, convenience, or safety

General Agreement on Tariffs and Trade (GATT) An agreement among nations to reduce worldwide tariffs and increase international trade

general-merchandise retailer A retail establishment that offers a variety of product lines that are stocked in considerable depth

general-merchandise wholesalers Full-service wholesalers with a wide product mix but limited depth within product lines

general publics Indirect consumers of a product of a nonprofit organization

generic brand A brand indicating only the product category

generic competitors Firms that provide very different products that solve the same problem or satisfy the same basic customer need

geodemographic segmentation A method of market segmentation that clusters people in zip code areas and smaller neighborhood units based on lifestyle and demographic information

geographic pricing Reductions for transportation and other costs related to the physical distance between buyer and seller

globalization The development of marketing strategies that treat the entire world (or its major regions) as a single entity

good A tangible physical entity

government markets Federal, state, county, or local governments that buy goods and services to support their internal operations and provide products to their constituencies

green marketing A strategic process involving stakeholder assessment to create meaningful long-term relationships with customers while maintaining, supporting, and enhancing the natural environment

gross domestic product (GDP) The market value of a nation's total output of goods and services for a given period; an overall measure of economic standing

growth stage The product life-cycle stage when sales rise rapidly, profits reach a peak, and then they start to decline

heterogeneity Variation in quality

heterogeneous market A market made up of individuals or organizations with diverse needs for products in a specific product class

homesourcing A practice whereby customer contact jobs are outsourced into workers' homes

homogeneous market A market in which a large proportion of customers have similar needs for a product

horizontal channel integration Combining organizations at the same level of operation under one management

hypermarkets Stores that combine supermarket and discount store shopping in one location

hypothesis An informed guess or assumption about a certain problem or set of circumstances

idea A concept, philosophy, image, or issue

idea generation Seeking product ideas to achieve organizational objectives

illustrations Photos, drawings, graphs, charts, and tables used to spark audience interest in an advertisement

import tariff A duty levied by a nation on goods bought outside its borders and brought into the country

importing The purchase of products from a foreign source

impulse buying An unplanned buying behavior resulting from a powerful urge to buy something immediately

income For an individual, the amount of money received through wages, rents, investments, pensions, and subsidy payments for a given period

individual branding A branding strategy in which each product is given a different name

industrial distributor An independent business organization that takes title to industrial products and carries inventories

inelastic demand Demand that is not significantly altered by a price increase or decrease

information inputs Sensations received through sight, taste, hearing, smell, and touch

in-home (door-to-door) interview A personal interview that takes place in the respondent's home

innovators First adopters of new products

inseparability The quality of being produced and consumed at the same time

installations Facilities and nonportable major equipment

institutional advertising Advertising that promotes organizational images, ideas, and political issues

institutional markets Organizations with charitable, educational, community, or other nonbusiness goals

intangibility The characteristic that a service is not physical and cannot be perceived by the senses

integrated marketing communications Coordination of promotion and other marketing efforts for maximum informational and persuasive impact

intensive distribution Using all available outlets to distribute a product

intermodal transportation Two or more transportation modes used in combination

internal reference price A price developed in the buyer's mind through experience with the product

internal search An information search in which buyers search their memories for information about products that might solve their problem

international marketing Developing and performing marketing activities across national boundaries

introduction stage The initial stage of a product's life cycle; its first appearance in the marketplace, when sales start at zero and profits are negative

inventory management Developing and maintaining adequate assortments of products to meet customers' needs

joint demand Demand involving the use of two or more items in combination to produce a product

joint venture A partnership between a domestic firm and a foreign firm or government

just-in-time (JIT) An inventory-management approach in which supplies arrive just when needed for production or resale

kinesic communication Communicating through the movement of head, eyes, arms, hands, legs, or torso

labeling Providing identifying, promotional, or other information on package labels

laggards The last adopters, who distrust new products

late majority Skeptics who adopt new products when they feel it is necessary

late-mover advantage The ability of later market entrants to achieve long-term competitive advantages by not being the first to offer a certain product in a marketplace

layout The physical arrangement of an advertisement's illustration and copy

learning Changes in an individual's thought processes and behavior caused by information and experience

level of involvement An individual's degree of interest in a product and the importance of the product for that person

level of quality The amount of quality a product possesses

licensing An alternative to direct investment that requires a licensee to pay commissions or royalties on sales or supplies used in manufacturing

lifestyle An individual's pattern of living expressed through activities, interests, and opinions

lifestyle shopping center A type of shopping center that is typically open air and features upscale specialty, dining, and entertainment stores

limited decision making A consumer decision-making process used when purchasing products occasionally or needing information about an unfamiliar brand in a familiar product category

limited-line wholesalers Full-service wholesalers that carry only a few product lines but many products within those lines

limited-service wholesalers Merchant wholesalers that provide some services and specialize in a few functions

line extension Development of a product that is closely related to existing products in the line but is designed specifically to meet different customer needs

logistics management Planning, implementing, and controlling the efficient and effective flow and storage of products and information from the point of origin to consumption to meet customers' needs and wants

mail-order wholesalers Limited-service wholesalers that sell products through catalogs

mail survey A research method in which respondents answer a questionnaire sent through the mail

manufacturer brand A brand initiated by producers to ensure that producers are identified with their products at the point of purchase

manufacturers' agents Independent intermediaries that represent two or more sellers and usually offer customers complete product lines

marginal cost (MC) The extra cost incurred by producing one more unit of a product

marginal revenue (MR) The change in total revenue resulting from the sale of an additional unit of a product

market A group of individuals and/or organizations that have needs for products in a product class and have the ability, willingness, and authority to purchase those products

market density The number of potential customers within a unit of land area

market growth/market share matrix A helpful business tool, based on the philosophy that a product's market growth rate and its market share are important considerations in determining its marketing strategy

market manager The person responsible for managing the marketing activities that serve a particular group of customers

market opportunity A combination of circumstances and timing that permits an organization to take action to reach a particular target market

market orientation An organizationwide commitment to researching and responding to customer needs

market potential The total amount of a product that customers will purchase within a specified period at a specific level of industry-wide marketing activity

market segment Individuals, groups, or organizations sharing one or more similar characteristics that cause them to have similar product needs

market segmentation The process of dividing a total market into groups with relatively similar product needs to design a marketing mix that matches those needs

market share The percentage of a market that actually buys a specific product from a particular company

market test Making a product available to buyers in one or more test areas and measuring purchases and consumer responses to marketing efforts

marketing The process of creating, distributing, promoting, and pricing goods, services, and ideas to facilitate satisfying exchange relationships with customers and to develop and maintain favorable relationships with stakeholders in a dynamic environment

marketing channel A group of individuals and organizations that direct the flow of products from producers to customers within the supply chain

marketing citizenship The adoption of a strategic focus for fulfilling the economic, legal, ethical, and philanthropic social responsibilities expected by stakeholders

marketing concept A managerial philosophy that an organization should try to satisfy customers' needs through a coordinated set of activities that also allows the organization to achieve its goals

marketing cost analysis Analysis of costs to determine which are associated with specific marketing efforts

marketing decision support system (MDSS) Customized computer software that aids marketing managers in decision making

marketing environment The competitive, economic, political, legal and regulatory, technological, and sociocultural forces that surround the customer and affect the marketing mix

marketing ethics Principles and standards that define acceptable marketing conduct as determined by various stakeholders

marketing implementation The process of putting marketing strategies into action

marketing information system (MIS) A framework for managing and structuring information gathered regularly from sources inside and outside the organization

marketing intermediaries Middlemen that link producers to other intermediaries or ultimate consumers through contractual arrangements or through the purchase and resale of products

marketing management The process of planning, organizing, implementing, and controlling marketing activities to facilitate exchanges effectively and efficiently

marketing mix Four marketing activities—product, pricing, distribution, and promotion—that a firm can control to meet the needs of customers within its target market

marketing objective A statement of what is to be accomplished through marketing activities

marketing plan A written document that specifies the activities to be performed to implement and control the organization's marketing strategies

marketing research The systematic design, collection, interpretation, and reporting of information to help marketers solve specific marketing problems or take advantage of marketing opportunities

marketing strategy A plan of action for identifying and analyzing a target market and developing a marketing mix to meet the needs of that market

markup pricing Adding to the cost of the product a predetermined percentage of that cost

Maslow's hierarchy of needs The five levels of needs that humans seek to satisfy, from most to least important

materials handling Physical handling of tangible goods, supplies, and resources

maturity stage The stage of a product's life cycle when the sales curve peaks and starts to decline, and profits continue to fall

media plan A plan that specifies the media vehicles to be used and the schedule for running advertisements

megacarriers Freight transportation firms that provide several modes of shipment

merchandise allowance A manufacturer's agreement to pay resellers certain amounts of money for providing special promotional efforts, such as setting up and maintaining a display

merchant wholesalers Independently owned businesses that take title to goods, assume ownership risks, and buy and resell products to other wholesalers, business customers, or retailers

micromarketing An approach to market segmentation in which organizations focus precise marketing efforts on very small geographic markets

mission statement A long-term view, or vision, of what the organization wants to become

missionary salespeople Support salespeople, usually employed by a manufacturer, who assist the producer's customers in selling to their own customers

modified rebuy purchase A new-task purchase that is changed on subsequent orders or when the requirements of a straight rebuy purchase are modified

money refunds Sales promotion techniques that offer consumers a specified amount of money when they mail in a proof of purchase, usually for multiple product purchases

monopolistic competition A competitive structure in which a firm has many potential competitors and tries to develop a marketing strategy to differentiate its product

monopoly A competitive structure in which an organization offers a product that has no close substitutes, making that organization the sole source of supply

motive An internal energizing force that directs a person's behavior toward satisfying needs or achieving goals

MRO supplies Maintenance, repair, and operating items that facilitate production and operations but do not become part of the finished product

multinational enterprise A firm that has operations or subsidiaries in many countries

multiple sourcing An organization's decision to use several suppliers

multiple-unit pricing Packaging together two or more identical products and selling them at a single price

National Advertising Review Board (NARB) A self-regulatory unit that considers challenges to issues raised by the National Advertising Division (an arm of the Council of Better Business Bureaus) about an advertisement

negotiated pricing Establishing a final price through bargaining between seller and customer

neighborhood shopping center A type of shopping center usually consisting of several small convenience and specialty stores

new-product development process A seven-phase process for introducing products: idea generation, screening, concept testing, business analysis, product development, test-marketing, and commercialization

new-task purchase An organization's initial purchase of an item to be used to perform a new job or solve a new problem

news release A short piece of copy publicizing an event or a product

noise Anything that reduces a communication's clarity and accuracy

noncumulative discounts One-time price reductions based on the number of units purchased, the dollar value of the order, or the product mix purchased

nonprice competition Emphasizing factors other than price to distinguish a product from competing brands

nonprobability sampling A sampling technique in which there is no way to calculate the likelihood that a specific element of the population being studied will be chosen

nonprofit marketing Marketing activities conducted to achieve some goal other than ordinary business goals such as profit, market share, or return on investment

nonstore retailing The selling of products outside the confines of a retail facility

North American Free Trade Agreement (NAFTA) An alliance that merges Canada, Mexico, and the United States into a single market

North American Industry Classification System (NAICS) An industry classification system that generates comparable statistics among the United States, Canada, and Mexico

objective-and-task approach Budgeting for an advertising campaign by first determining its objectives and then calculating the cost of all the tasks needed to attain them

odd-even pricing Ending the price with certain numbers to influence buyers' perceptions of the price or product

off-price retailers Stores that buy manufacturers' seconds, overruns, returns, and off-season merchandise for resale to consumers at deep discounts

offshore outsourcing The practice of contracting with an organization to perform some or all business functions in a country other than the country in which the product or service will be sold

offshoring The practice of moving a business process that was done domestically at the local factory to a foreign country, regardless of whether the production accomplished in the foreign country is performed by the local company (e.g., in a wholly owned subsidiary) or a third party (e.g., subcontractor)

oligopoly A competitive structure in which a few sellers control the supply of a large proportion of a product

online fraud Any attempt to conduct fraudulent activities online, including deceiving consumers into releasing personal information

online retailing Retailing that makes products available to buyers through computer connections

online survey A research method in which respondents answer a questionnaire via e-mail or on a website

on-site computer interview A variation of the shopping mall intercept interview in which respondents complete a self-administered questionnaire displayed on a computer monitor

operations management The total set of managerial activities used by an organization to transform resource inputs into products, services, or both

opinion leader A member of an informal group who provides information about a specific topic to other group members

opportunity cost The value of the benefit given up by choosing one alternative over another

order getters Salespeople who sell to new customers and increase sales to current customers

order processing The receipt and transmission of sales order information

order takers Salespeople who primarily seek repeat sales

organizational (corporate) culture A set of values, beliefs, goals, norms, and rituals that members of an organization share

outsourcing The practice of contracting noncore operations with an organization that specializes in that operation

patronage motives Motives that influence where a person purchases products on a regular basis

penetration pricing Setting prices below those of competing brands to penetrate a market and gain a significant market share quickly

percent-of-sales approach Budgeting for an advertising campaign by multiplying the firm's past and expected sales by a standard percentage

perception The process of selecting, organizing, and interpreting information inputs to produce meaning

performance standard An expected level of performance against which actual performance can be compared

periodic discounting Temporary reduction of prices on a patterned or systematic basis

perishability The inability of unused service capacity to be stored for future use

personal interview survey A research method in which participants respond to survey questions face-to-face

personal selling Paid personal communication that attempts to inform customers and persuade them to buy products in an exchange situation

personality A set of internal traits and distinct behavioral tendencies that result in consistent patterns of behavior in certain situations

physical distribution Activities used to move products from producers to consumers and other end users

pioneer advertising Advertising that tries to stimulate demand for a product category rather than a specific brand by informing potential buyers about the product

pioneer promotion Promotion that informs consumers about a new product

podcast Audio or video file that can be downloaded from the Internet with a subscription that automatically delivers new content to listening devices or personal computers; podcasts offer the benefit of convenience, giving users the ability to listen to or view content when and where they choose

point-of-purchase (POP) materials Signs, window displays, display racks, and similar devices used to attract customers

population All the elements, units, or individuals of interest to researchers for a specific study

posttest Evaluation of advertising effectiveness after the campaign

power shopping center A type of shopping center that combines off-price stores with category killers

premium money (push money) Extra compensation to salespeople for pushing a line of goods

premium pricing Pricing the highest-quality or most versatile products higher than other models in the product line

premiums Items offered free or at a minimal cost as a bonus for purchasing a product

press conference A meeting used to announce major news events

prestige pricing Setting prices at an artificially high level to convey prestige or a quality image

prestige sensitive Drawn to products that signify prominence and status

pretest Evaluation of advertisements performed before a campaign begins

price The value paid for a product in a marketing exchange

price competition Emphasizing price as an issue and matching or beating competitors' prices

price conscious Striving to pay low prices

price discrimination Employing price differentials that injure competition by giving one or more buyers a competitive advantage

price elasticity of demand A measure of the sensitivity of demand to changes in price

price leaders Products priced near or even below cost

price lining Setting a limited number of prices for selected groups or lines of merchandise

price skimming Charging the highest possible price that buyers who most desire the product will pay

pricing objectives Goals that describe what a firm wants to achieve through pricing

primary data Data observed and recorded or collected directly from respondents

primary demand Demand for a product category rather than for a specific brand
private distributor brand A brand initiated and owned by a reseller
private warehouses Company-operated facilities for storing and shipping products
probability sampling A type of sampling in which every element in the population being studied has a known chance of being selected for study
process materials Materials that are used directly in the production of other products but are not readily identifiable
producer markets Individuals and business organizations that purchase products to make profits by using them to produce other products or using them in their operations
product A good, a service, or an idea
product adoption process The five-stage process of buyer acceptance of a product: awareness, interest, evaluation, trial, and adoption
product advertising Advertising that promotes the uses, features, and benefits of products
product competitors Firms that compete in the same product class but market products with different features, benefits, and prices
product deletion Eliminating a product from the product mix when it no longer satisfies a sufficient number of customers
product design How a product is conceived, planned, and produced
product development Determining if producing a product is technically feasible and cost effective
product differentiation Creating and designing products so that customers perceive them as different from competing products
product features Specific design characteristics that allow a product to perform certain tasks
product item A specific version of a product that can be designated as a distinct offering among a firm's products
product life cycle The progression of a product through four stages: introduction, growth, maturity, and decline
product line A group of closely related product items viewed as a unit because of marketing, technical, or end-use considerations
product-line pricing Establishing and adjusting prices of multiple products within a product line
product manager The person within an organization who is responsible for a product, a product line, or several distinct products that make up a group
product mix The composite, or total, group of products that an organization makes available to customers
product modifications Changes in one or more characteristics of a product
product placement The strategic location of products or product promotions within entertainment media content to reach the product's target market
professional pricing Fees set by people with great skill or experience in a particular field
promotion Communication to build and maintain relationships by informing and persuading one or more audiences
promotion mix A combination of promotional methods used to promote a specific product
prospecting Developing a database of potential customers
prosperity A stage of the business cycle characterized by low unemployment and relatively high total income, which together ensure high buying power (provided the inflation rate stays low)
proxemic communication Communicating by varying the physical distance in face-to-face interactions
psychological influences Factors that in part determine people's general behavior, thus influencing their behavior as consumers
psychological pricing Pricing that attempts to influence a customer's perception of price to make a product's price more attractive
public relations Communication efforts used to create and maintain favorable relations between an organization and its stakeholders
public warehouses Storage space and related physical distribution facilities that can be leased by companies
publicity A news story type of communication about an organization and/or its products transmitted through a mass medium at no charge
pull policy Promoting a product directly to consumers to develop strong consumer demand that pulls products through the marketing channel
pure competition A market structure characterized by an extremely large number of sellers, none strong enough to significantly influence price or supply
push policy Promoting a product only to the next institution down the marketing channel
quality The overall characteristics of a product that allow it to perform as expected in satisfying customer needs
quality modifications Changes relating to a product's dependability and durability
quantity discounts Deductions from the list price for purchasing in large quantities
quota A limit on the amount of goods an importing country will accept for certain product categories in a specific period of time
quota sampling A nonprobability sampling technique in which researchers divide the population into groups and then arbitrarily choose participants from each group
rack jobbers Full-service, specialty-line wholesalers that own and maintain display racks in stores
random discounting Temporary reduction of prices on an unsystematic basis
random factor analysis An analysis attempting to attribute erratic sales variations to random, nonrecurrent events
random sampling A form of probability sampling in which all units in a population have an equal chance of appearing in the sample, and the various events that can occur have an equal or known chance of taking place
raw materials Basic natural materials that become part of a physical product
rebates Sales promotion techniques in which a consumer receives a specified amount of money for making a single product purchase
receiver The individual, group, or organization that decodes a coded message
recession A stage of the business cycle during which unemployment rises and total buying power declines, stifling both consumer and business spending

reciprocity An arrangement unique to business marketing in which two organizations agree to buy from each other

recognition test A posttest in which respondents are shown the actual ad and are asked if they recognize it

recovery A stage of the business cycle in which the economy moves from recession or depression toward prosperity

recruiting Developing a list of qualified applicants for sales positions

reference group A group that a person identifies with so strongly that he or she adopts the values, attitudes, and behavior of group members

reference pricing Pricing a product at a moderate level and displaying it next to a more expensive model or brand

regional issues Versions of a magazine that differ across geographic regions

regional shopping center A type of shopping center with the largest department stores, widest product mixes, and deepest product lines of all shopping centers

regression analysis A method of predicting sales based on finding a relationship between past sales and one or more independent variables, such as population or income

reinforcement advertising Advertising that assures users they chose the right brand and tells them how to get the most satisfaction from it

relationship marketing Establishing long-term, mutually satisfying buyer–seller relationships

relationship selling The building of mutually beneficial long-term associations with a customer through regular communications over prolonged periods of time

reliability A condition that exists when a research technique produces almost identical results in repeated trials

reminder advertising Advertising used to remind consumers about an established brand's uses, characteristics, and benefits

research design An overall plan for obtaining the information needed to address a research problem or issue

reseller markets Intermediaries that buy finished goods and resell them for a profit

retail positioning Identifying an unserved or underserved market segment and serving it through a strategy that distinguishes the retailer from others in the minds of consumers in that segment

retailer An organization that purchases products for the purpose of reselling them to ultimate consumers

retailing All transactions in which the buyer intends to consume the product through personal, family, or household use

roles Actions and activities that a person in a particular position is supposed to perform based on expectations of the individual and surrounding persons

routinized response behavior A consumer decision-making process used when buying frequently purchased, low-cost items that require very little search-and-decision effort

sales analysis Analysis of sales figures to evaluate a firm's performance

sales branches Manufacturer-owned intermediaries that sell products and provide support services to the manufacturer's sales force

sales contest A sales promotion method used to motivate distributors, retailers, and sales personnel through recognition of outstanding achievements

sales force forecasting survey A survey of a firm's sales force regarding anticipated sales in their territories for a specified period

sales forecast The amount of a product a company expects to sell during a specific period at a specified level of marketing activities

sales offices Manufacturer-owned operations that provide services normally associated with agents

sales promotion An activity and/or material intended to induce resellers or salespeople to sell a product or consumers to buy it

sample A limited number of units chosen to represent the characteristics of a total population

sampling The process of selecting representative units from a total population

scan-back allowance A manufacturer's reward to retailers based on the number of pieces scanned

screening Selecting the ideas with the greatest potential for further review

search qualities Tangible attributes that can be judged before the purchase of a product

seasonal analysis An analysis of daily, weekly, or monthly sales figures to evaluate the degree to which seasonal factors influence sales

seasonal discount A price reduction given to buyers for purchasing goods or services out of season

secondary data Data compiled both inside and outside the organization for some purpose other than the current investigation

secondary-market pricing Setting one price for the primary target market and a different price for another market

segmentation variables Characteristics of individuals, groups, or organizations used to divide a market into segments

selective demand Demand for a specific brand

selective distortion An individual's changing or twisting of information that is inconsistent with personal feelings or beliefs

selective distribution Using only some available outlets in an area to distribute a product

selective exposure The process by which some inputs are selected to reach awareness and others are not

selective retention Remembering information inputs that support personal feelings and beliefs and forgetting inputs that do not

self-concept A perception or view of oneself

selling agents Intermediaries that market a whole product line or a manufacturer's entire output

service An intangible result of the application of human and mechanical efforts to people or objects

service quality Customers' perceptions of how well a service meets or exceeds their expectations

shopping mall intercept interview A research method that involves interviewing a percentage of individuals passing by "intercept" points in a mall

shopping products Items for which buyers are willing to expend considerable effort in planning and making purchases

single-source data Information provided by a single marketing research firm

situational influences Influences that result from circumstances, time, and location that affect the consumer buying decision process

social class An open group of individuals with similar social rank

social influences The forces other people exert on one's buying behavior

social network Web-based meeting place for friends, family, coworkers, and peers that allow users to create a profile and connect with other users for purposes such as getting acquainted, keeping in touch, and building a work-related network

social responsibility An organization's obligation to maximize its positive impact and minimize its negative impact on society

sociocultural forces The influences in a society and its culture(s) that change people's attitudes, beliefs, norms, customs, and lifestyles

sole sourcing An organization's decision to use only one supplier

source A person, group, or organization with a meaning it tries to share with a receiver or an audience

Southern Common Market (Mercosur) An alliance that promotes the free circulation of goods, services, and production factors, and has a common external tariff and commercial policy among member nations in South America

special-event pricing Advertised sales or price cutting linked to a holiday, a season, or an event

specialty products Items with unique characteristics that buyers are willing to expend considerable effort to obtain

specialty-line wholesalers Full-service wholesalers that carry only a single product line or a few items within a product line

stakeholders Constituents who have a "stake," or claim, in some aspect of a company's products, operations, markets, industry, and outcomes

statistical interpretation Analysis of what is typical and what deviates from the average

storyboard A blueprint that combines copy and visual material to show the sequence of major scenes in a commercial

straight commission compensation plan Paying salespeople according to the amount of their sales in a given time period

straight rebuy purchase A routine purchase of the same products under approximately the same terms of sale by a business buyer

straight salary compensation plan Paying salespeople a specific amount per time period, regardless of selling effort

strategic alliance A partnership that is formed to create a competitive advantage on a worldwide basis

strategic business unit (SBU) A division, product line, or other profit center within the parent company

strategic channel alliance An agreement whereby the products of one organization are distributed through the marketing channels of another

strategic marketing management The process of planning, implementing, and evaluating the performance of marketing activities and strategies, both effectively and efficiently

strategic performance evaluation Establishing performance standards, measuring actual performance, comparing actual performance with established standards, and modifying the marketing strategy, if needed

strategic philanthropy The synergistic use of organizational core competencies and resources to address key stakeholders' interests and achieve both organizational and social benefits

strategic planning The process of establishing an organizational mission and formulating goals, corporate strategy, marketing objectives, and marketing strategy

strategic windows Temporary periods of optimal fit between the key requirements of a market and the particular capabilities of a company competing in that market

stratified sampling A type of probability sampling in which the population is divided into groups with a common attribute and a random sample is chosen within each group

styling The physical appearance of a product

subculture A group of individuals whose characteristics, values, and behavioral patterns are similar within the group and different from those of people in the surrounding culture

supermarkets Large, self-service stores that carry a complete line of food products, along with some nonfood products

superregional shopping center A type of shopping center with the widest and deepest product mixes that attracts customers from many miles away

superstores Giant retail outlets that carry food and nonfood products found in supermarkets, as well as most routinely purchased consumer products

supply chain All the activities associated with the flow and transformation of products from raw materials through to the end customer

supply-chain management A set of approaches used to integrate the functions of operations management, logistics management, supply management, and marketing channel management so products are produced and distributed in the right quantities, to the right locations, and at the right time

supply management In its broadest form, refers to the processes that enable the progress of value from raw material to final customer and back to redesign and final disposition

support personnel Sales staff members who facilitate selling but usually are not involved solely with making sales

sustainability The potential for the long-term well-being of the natural environment, including all biological entities, as well as the interaction among nature and individuals, organizations, and business strategies

sustainable competitive advantage An advantage that the competition cannot copy

SWOT analysis Assessment of an organization's strengths, weaknesses, opportunities, and threats

tactile communication Communicating through touching

target audience The group of people at whom advertisements are aimed

target market A specific group of customers on whom an organization focuses its marketing efforts

target public A collective of individuals who have an interest in or concern about an organization, product, or social cause

team selling The use of a team of experts from all functional areas of a firm, led by a salesperson, to conduct the personal selling process

technical salespeople Support salespeople who give technical assistance to a firm's current customers

technology The application of knowledge and tools to solve problems and perform tasks more efficiently

telemarketing The performance of marketing-related activities by telephone

telephone depth interview An interview that combines the traditional focus group's ability to probe with the confidentiality provided by telephone surveys

telephone survey A research method in which respondents' answers to a questionnaire are recorded by an interviewer on the phone

television home shopping A form of selling in which products are presented to television viewers, who can buy them by calling a toll-free number and paying with a credit card

test marketing A limited introduction of a product in geographic areas chosen to represent the intended market

time series analysis A forecasting method that uses historical sales data to discover patterns in the firm's sales over time and generally involves trend, cycle, seasonal, and random factor analyses

total budget competitors Firms that compete for the limited financial resources of the same customers

total cost The sum of average fixed and average variable costs times the quantity produced

trade (functional) discount A reduction off the list price a producer gives to an intermediary for performing certain functions

trade name The full legal name of an organization

trade sales promotion methods Methods intended to persuade wholesalers and retailers to carry a producer's products and market them aggressively

trade salespeople Salespeople involved mainly in helping a producer's customers promote a product

trademark A legal designation of exclusive use of a brand

trading company A company that links buyers and sellers in different countries

traditional specialty retailers Stores that carry a narrow product mix with deep product lines

transfer pricing Prices charged in sales between an organization's units

transportation The movement of products from where they are made to intermediaries and end users

trend analysis An analysis that focuses on aggregate sales data over a period of many years to determine general trends in annual sales

truck wholesalers Limited-service wholesalers that transport products directly to customers for inspection and selection

tying agreement An agreement in which a supplier furnishes a product to a channel member with the stipulation that the channel member must purchase other products as well

unaided recall test A posttest in which respondents are asked to identify advertisements they have seen recently but are not given any recall clues

undifferentiated targeting strategy A strategy in which an organization designs a single marketing mix and directs it at the entire market for a particular product

uniform geographic pricing Charging all customers the same price, regardless of geographic location

universal product code (UPC) A series of electronically readable lines identifying a product and containing inventory and pricing information

unsought products Products purchased to solve a sudden problem, products of which customers are unaware, and products that people do not necessarily think of buying

validity A condition that exists when a research method measures what it is supposed to measure

value A customer's subjective assessment of benefits relative to costs in determining the worth of a product

value analysis An evaluation of each component of a potential purchase

value conscious Concerned about price and quality of a product

variable costs Costs that vary directly with changes in the number of units produced or sold

vendor analysis A formal, systematic evaluation of current and potential vendors

venture team A cross-functional group that creates entirely new products that may be aimed at new markets

vertical channel integration Combining two or more stages of the marketing channel under one management

vertical marketing system (VMS) A marketing channel managed by a single channel member to achieve efficient, low-cost distribution aimed at satisfying target market customers

viral marketing A strategy to get consumers to share a marketer's message, often through e-mail or online videos, in a way that spreads dramatically and quickly

warehouse clubs Large-scale, members-only establishments that combine features of cash-and-carry wholesaling with discount retailing

warehouse showrooms Retail facilities in large, low-cost buildings with large on-premises inventories and minimal services

warehousing The design and operation of facilities for storing and moving goods

wealth The accumulation of past income, natural resources, and financial resources

wholesaler An individual or organization that sells products that are bought for resale, for making other products, or for general business operations

wholesaling Transactions in which products are bought for resale, for making other products, or for general business operations

width of product mix The number of product lines a company offers

wiki Type of software that creates an interface that enables users to add or edit the content of some types of websites

willingness to spend An inclination to buy because of expected satisfaction from a product, influenced by the ability to buy and numerous psychological and social forces

word-of-mouth communication Personal informal exchanges of communication that customers share with one another about products, brands, and companies

World Trade Organization (WTO) An entity that promotes free trade among member nations by eliminating trade barriers and educating individuals, companies, and governments about trade rules around the world

zone pricing Pricing based on transportation costs within major geographic zones

name index

© Mike Stratton / © iStockphoto.com/hh5800 / © iStockphoto.com/sorendis

organization index

A

B

C

D

E

F

G

H

I

J

K

L

O

P

Q

R

S

T

U

V

W

X

Y

Z

subject index

© Mike Stratton / © iStockphoto.com/hh5800 / © iStockphoto.com/sorendis

C

D

E

F

G

H

I

J

K

L

M

N

O

Q

R

S

T

U

V

W

Y

Z

Global Economic Watch

Your source for turning today's challenges into tomorrow's solutions.

Impact on Society

To get started:

1. Go to: **academic.cengage.com/login**
2. Click on "Create My Account."
3. Select user type "Student."
4. Enter account information and the access code below.

ACCESS CODE
See Inside Front Cover
www.cengage.com/login

5. Record your e-mail address and password for future visits.

Tips and Troubleshooting

Keep a record of your e-mail address and password.

You will need them every time you sign in.

Your access code is NOT your password!

You will use this access code only once when you first access your eResources. Once your access code is successfully authenticated, you will not be asked for it again.

Problems with your access code?
For tech support, visit our website at **www.cengage.com/support**

For tech support, visit our website at **www.cengage.com/support**

Note: All media assets accessible through this program are available to college and university students in the United States and Canada. Some restrictions may apply in other markets or countries. Please contact Cengage Learning for details.

Global Economic Watch

Impact on Social Media and Marketing

SOUTH-WESTREN
CENGAGE Learning™

Australia • Brazil • Japan • Korea • Mexico • Singapore • Spain • United Kingdom • United States

Global Economic Watch: Impact on Social Media and Marketing

Sr. Art Director: Michelle Kunkler

Cover Design: Rose Alcorn

Cover Images: © Alan Gallyer / iStockphoto

For product information and technology assistance, contact us at
Cengage Learning Customer & Sales Support, 1-800-354-9706

For permission to use material from this text or product,
submit all requests online at **www.cengage.com/permissions**
Further permissions questions can be emailed to
permissionrequest@cengage.com

ISBN-13: 978-1-111-06734-2
ISBN-10: 1-111-06734-1

South-Western Cengage Learning
5191 Natorp Boulevard
Mason, OH 45040
USA

Cengage Learning products are represented in Canada by
Nelson Education, Ltd.

For your course and learning solutions, visit **www.cengage.com**
Purchase any of our products at your local college store or at our
preferred online store **www.ichapters.com**

Printed in the United States of America
1 2 3 4 5 6 7 13 12 11 10 09

Global Economic Watch: Impact on Social Media and Marketing

SOCIAL MEDIA/WEB 2.0—INTRODUCTION

The philosophy of social media marketing is as different from traditional marketing as Miley Cyrus is from Ella Fitzgerald.

Traditional marketing is based on broadcasting a very carefully designed and tightly controlled message to a well-targeted audience in order to generate the desired action. Social media marketing is based on communication to develop a "relationship" with an interested audience in order to engage and build a loyal community that will spread messages and generate positive word of mouth buzz.

Gary Vaynerchuk transformed his family's traditional (or as *traditional* as a Vaynerchuk can be) $4 million/year New Jersey liquor store business, "Shoppers Discount Liquors," into a $60+ million/year global wine and information business, "Wine Library," in less than six years via social media. How?

First, Gary realized that people had a passion for and collected wine much like he and his friends were passionate about and collected baseball cards when he was a youngster. In 2006 Gary launched the Wine Library TV (WLTV) show (http://tv.winelibrary.com), a video blog or video podcast—Vlog or Vcast (blog or podcast with video)—where he tastes and reviews wine in his own unique style. It's the unique style that has taken WLTV viral, with just the right combination of expert information and total, unfiltered, in-your-face "Crush It" honesty. The Vcast is distributed on iTunes, and Gary promotes the show via Twitter, Facebook, his website, and speaking engagements. Today over 90,000 people ("Vayniacs," as his fans have self-named themselves) view the show *every* day. Gary says, "An investment of just a few thousand dollars in social media returned more to me than millions of dollars in conventional advertising." I tend to agree.

That being said, we all aren't cut out to be a Gary Vaynerchuk. We all do, however, have access to the tools and formula Gary used to take his business global. The tools are what we call, collectively, "social media."

Social (Latin: socius, meaning companion, ally, associate)—the interaction of organisms with other organisms and to their collective betterment and co-existence

Media (singular medium)—storage and transmission tools used to store and deliver information or data

Social Media—tools that enable the interaction of people with other people to their collective health, wealth, and happiness

The development of new technology has enabled people to gather in online communities; in effect, technology has changed the way people interact with one another. These people are your clients—your market. If your clients and prospects are there, doesn't it make sense for you to be there, too? And *that* is why it's important for businesses to know about social media. It's where the people are.

It's a new world.

SOCIAL MEDIA/WEB 2.0—HISTORY

Before "social media" there was Web. 2.0, which is a buzzword meaning the "new and improved" Internet.

Information Age listed three qualities that Web 2.0 has in common with the dawn of Web 1.0:

1. It is overhyped;
2. It is poorly understood; and
3. It is, without doubt, revolutionizing business.

Depending on whom you listen to, "Web 2.0" was coined in 2004 or 2005 by Tim O'Reilly and/or Dale Dougherty, co-founders of O'Reilly Media, a company that distributes, publishes and promotes the work of knowledge leaders and innovators. (Read "What Is Web 2.0" on the O'Reilly site at http://www.oreillynet.com/pub/a/oreilly/tim/news/2005/09/30/what-is-web-20.html.)

After the 2000–2001 Internet bubble-bust, many were pooh-poohing the web as being overhyped and overrated. In 2004, O'Reilly and Dougherty were participating in a brainstorming session and noted that "far from having 'crashed,'" the web was more important than ever, with "exciting new appli-

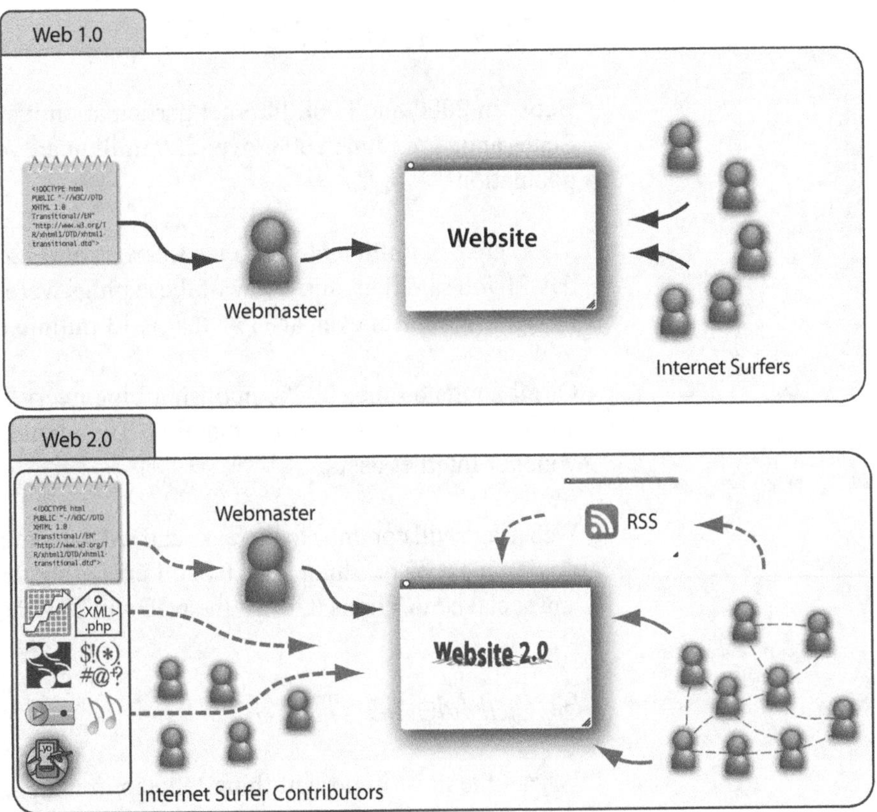

cations and sites popping up with surprising regularity." The Web 2.0 Conference (and buzzword) was born.

One perspective is that Web 2.0 is the evolved web, from a document delivery system to a communication platform. It's not just about interaction between people, but the way people interact with the web that enables that interaction between people. Internet interaction.

Another way to look at Web 2.0 is that it describes website functionality that has moved beyond the "publication-only" type to a platform for interaction between people. "Social media" is another, less technical term often used to mean the same thing. With regard to marketing, other terms you'll likely hear include "new media," "inbound marketing," "social marketing," to name a few. It all basically means the same thing—using online facilities to build relationships with people online, form communities of fans to generate word of mouth, buzz, and forward messages.

A Few Facts to Consider

Between 2000 and 2008 Internet participation increased 131% in the United States and, as of June 2008, over 220 million are online. That is 72.5% of our population.

There are 112 million blogs on the Internet, and 120,000 new blogs start every day. If you said that only a few of these blogs were actually active, you would be right: 11%. But even at 11%, that is 13 million blogs.

Of all adults online, 11.2% publish a blog every month and even more read and comment on other blogs monthly. The numbers are much higher for the younger Internet users.

Web usage will continue to increase and will become a part of everyday life, like driving a car or brushing your teeth. Leveraging the power of communication and social connections through the web will become not only useful but vital.

Social Media, The Tool

What's the most important thing to keep in mind about social media marketing? Remember that it's still **marketing**. Social media is another tool to help you reach marketing objectives.

Well, actually, social media is a set of tools. Among them are blogs, micro-blogs (Twitter, Plurk, etc.), social networks (Facebook, LinkedIn, MySpace, etc.), forum and review sites, wikis, podcasts, Vcasts, and YouTube, to name a few.

There are two important questions to which you should answer "yes" before you throw yourself and your business into social media in a big way.

#1 Do you have a website, and is it ready for social media success? By "ready" I mean are the content and technology up to date, is the design user- and search-engine friendly, does it positively reflect your brand/image, does it clearly explain your value proposition, and are there clear calls to action?

#2 Do you have a concise marketing plan? I don't mean a marketing thesis; I mean a clear outline of your business objective(s), marketing strategy, primary target market, product/service benefits, etc.

Getting involved in social media means you will "get to know" literally hundreds, if not thousands, of people. These people will be getting to know you and your business as well.

You want to make sure:

- You are investing your limited resources (time and money) getting to know the right people for your business objective, and
- Those "right people" get to "know" you and your business as you would like them to.

It isn't rocket science. It's not very sexy, and many won't think it's fun. Heck, when you get down to it, it's not even social media, per se. It's marketing; and, if you want to grow your business in the most effective and efficient way possible, build the toolbox first, *then* begin adding the tools.

SOCIAL MEDIA AND YOUR BUSINESS

Your business's web presence isn't limited to your website, and social media isn't exclusively a marketing tool. Your market is online on blogs, social networks, music sites, review forums, etc. They are on these sites talking, sharing, and giving their opinions about a multitude of things, including your products and services as well as their opinions about your competitor's products and services. How could that knowledge help your business?

Business Cases for Social Media

- Early warning on problems; market shifts
- Product development; speed "design-to-market" timeline
- Customer service; customer support
- Marketing: publicity-promotion-brand/reputation management
- SEO; drive web traffic
- Collaboration and internal communication
- Education; training
- Productivity and efficient office administration

Most small businesses use social media primarily as a marketing tool and to drive web traffic. Social media is relatively inexpensive and easy to launch, both important characteristics to small businesses, guerrilla marketers. The major expense of participation for the small business owner is time; time to plan, time to participate, and time to evaluate.

Why haven't more businesses joined the "conversation"? A couple of reasons:

1. It's new. It's a change. It's the unknown.
2. People are afraid of giving up control of the message.

This document will hopefully help with reason 1. Reason 2, however, will require changing your outlook on how you conduct business.

"What if someone leaves a negative comment about my service?" you ask. My response is, "They're saying it anyway, whether you see it or not." If not on your blog or to you on Twitter, then to their friends, colleagues, and associates. Hearing it directly and quickly is an advantage that gives you an opportunity to interact and respond. For example, say you get a complaint about the design of a product. You can respond with something like, "Here's why the designers created it that way. I understand this was a problem for you. How would you recommend we improve it?" You are now a person, not a company. You are speaking to another person, your client. The client feels validated. Others reading the exchange will see this. You are engaging and establishing a relationship with your market.

Do you wonder what is being said about you? Progressive companies are online where their market is, monitoring, participating, and creating online communities of their own.

MARKETING WITH SOCIAL MEDIA

Think about your own marketing efforts. Is your marketing one-way or two-way? Do you broadcast, or do you converse? Consider your website, for example; does it engage your site visitors? Does it invite participation?

Traditional Marketing	Social Media Marketing
• One-way	• Two-way
• Top-down	• Grassroots; bottom-up
• Return on investment	• Return on influence
• Building a pipeline	• Building a community of fans
• It's business	• It's personal

Many businesses approach social media as a list of technologies to be set up—a blog here, a podcast there. Before investing your limited resources remember:

First, it is important to think of social media as a marketing tactic used to achieve a business objective, not social media as a technology goal. Like traditional advertising or PR, social media is another powerful tool in the marketing toolbox.

Second, remember that social media marketing is still **marketing**: the process you use to *identify, anticipate, and satisfy your clients' needs, profitably.*

Marketing with social media adds a different dimension to the traditional customer profile. In addition to defining your target market's demographics and psychographics, you must now understand your market's *technographics*.

Where your market demographics are statistical characteristics like age, income, and marital status and psychographics describe your market's attitudes, values, and opinions, technographics describe your market based on their ownership, use patterns, and feelings toward different types of technologies. ("Technographics" is a term coined in 1985 by Dr. Edward Forrester (Forrester Research [www.forrester.com]) in a study of VCR users.)

Forrester's Technographic Ladder

Forrester has six different technographic group categories that are segmented based on participation with technology—and participation at one level may or may not overlap with participation at other levels.

Creators: Publish a blog; publish original content on a web page; upload user created video/audio/music;

Critics: Rate or review products or services; comment on blogs; contribute to online forums; contribute or edit wikis

Collectors: Use RSS feeds; vote for websites; add tags for web pages or photos

Joiners: Maintain a profile on a social networking site; visit social networking sites

Spectators: Read blogs; listen to podcasts; watch online video; read online forums

Inactives: None of the above

Groups include consumers participating in at least one activity a month.

Before embarking on a social media, or any marketing program for that matter, make sure you have clearly defined:

1. Your marketing objective,
2. Your market, and
3. Your message.

You've heard this before. It is still marketing. Know your objective, know your market, and then pick the tools to deliver the message.

Since social media—Web 2.0—is an important marketing tool, you now need to look at your market and answer these questions:

1. What kind of relationship do you want to build with them?
2. What are they ready for?

Now the question is, "How do you know what your market is ready for?" Fortunately, there is a lot of information out there. That doesn't mean it's not cumbersome to do the research, but you can find what you need. Forrester is a great source of information. They are in the information business and, therefore, much of the "good stuff" is for sale in reports and webcasts. They do have a vast amount available for free on their site as well as in blog entries of Forrester employees, such as Josh Bernoff's (http://bernoff.com/).

In the meantime, the chart on page 9 will give you a starting point.

To get more specific technographic information about your market, use Forrester's online tool: http://www.forrester.com/Groundswell/profile_tool.html. This can help you determine "what they're ready for."

Social Media—Align Tactics with Objectives

Objective: Deepen community and loyalty to brand around your brand, product, or service.

Social Media Tactic: Social networks, online groups and forums

Objective: Establish your personal brand as expert in your field.

Social Media Tactic: Blogs, podcasts, videos, micro-blogging

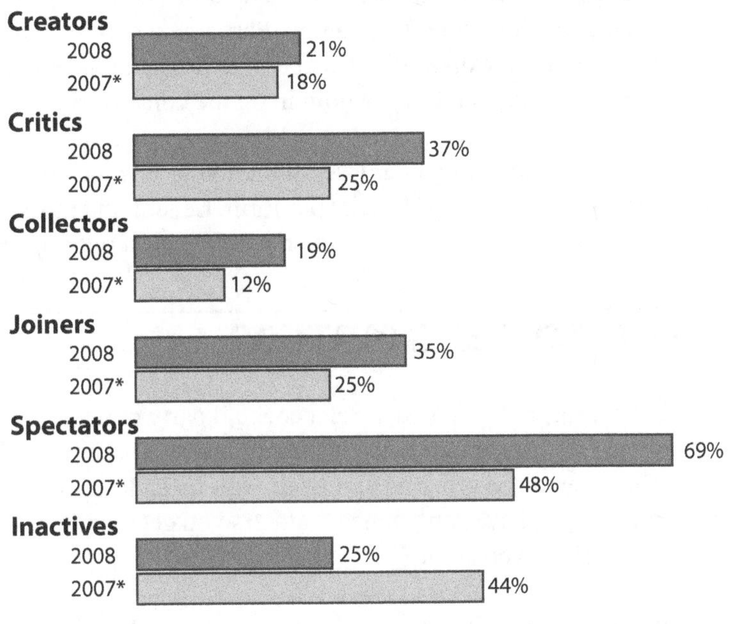

Objective: Give quick status or product updates, real-time event notice, brief comment; viral word-of-mouth marketing launch pad.

Social Media Tactic: Micro-blogging, micro-messaging

Objective: Provide forum for clients to ask questions; discuss product and services; give opinions, definitions, and/or reviews.

Social Media Tactic: User forums and wiki sites

Objective: Provide platform for satisfied clients and fans to promote you and generate referrals.

Social Media Tactic: Widgets and video and/or photosharing

Objective: Network with peers and others of similar interest

Social Media Tactic: Social networks

We're in the early stages of the new world of social media. Small businesses should be involved *now*. Understand the landscape; stay informed of the changes and evolving technology. Participate and be represented on some of the leading networks, like Facebook and LinkedIn. Publish a blog, create a Twitter account, and follow/join in on the conversations.

It's not a zero-sum game. Use all the tools. The web will continue to evolve into more and more of a social platform. Leveraging the power and social connections of the web will become not only useful but imperative.

WHAT CAN YOU DO TO GET STARTED?

Listen. Just as when you are at a cocktail party or networking event, you don't barge into a room and start blabbing away. You look and listen and decide which person or group to approach. You listen to the conversation and chime in when you have something to add. As you get more comfortable, you initiate topics of conversation.

It's the same online. Set up a Twitter account. Follow me (www.twitter.com/lynnelle); see who I follow and look at their stream of comments. Do any "conversations" look interesting or pertinent to what you do? Follow them. Look at who they're following . . . and so on. Watch the conversation. Listen first; then engage.

Do the same with blogs. Search for blogs you find interesting and/or pertinent to you and your business. You can use Google's blog search (www.blogsearch.google.com) or Technorati (www.technorati.com), two of the most popular. There are also others out there. Find a few that you like and follow them. Read an interesting entry? You agree, disagree, have something to add? Leave a comment.

Join LinkedIn (www.linkedin.com), Facebook (www.facebook.com), and/or another social network. Set up your profile, look for those you know who are also there, and connect. As with blogging, look at what others are doing and begin to participate.

As you get more comfortable, you will begin to move up the "ladder."

SOCIAL NETWORKS

Professional Networking Sites

Social networks can attract large numbers of people who are eager to engage with their favorite brands and personalities. To succeed in marketing with social networks it is important to engage in a personal relationship with those "following" you by providing something of value. Promotions are good, and even better would be information or *content* (pictures, videos, etc.) that your "fans" can pass on to their friends.

LinkedIn: LinkedIn is a popular networking site where alumni, business associates, recent graduates, and other professionals connect online.

Facebook: Now no longer just for college kids who want to post party pics, businesses vie for advertising opportunities, event promotion, and more on this social networking site.

Ecademy: "Connecting business people" through an online network, blog, and message board chats. BlackStar is Ecademy's pay-membership program, which has exclusive member benefits.

Plaxo: Organize your contacts and stay updated with feeds from Digg, Amazon.com, del.icio.us, and more. You can create your own "dashboard"/ home page site with Plaxo.

Tribe: Cities like Philadelphia, Boston, San Francisco, New York, and Chicago have unique online communities on tribe. Doing business here? You can search for favorite restaurants, events, clubs, and more.

Networking for Professionals: This online community combines the Internet with special events in the real world. Post photos, videos, résumés, and clips on your individual profile.

Blogs

The word "blog" is a contraction of "web log." The basic definition of blog is a *log of thoughts, ideas, useful links, photos, videos, or the latest news.*

A blog is a website in which the content is a series of frequent entries—or posts, normally arranged in reverse chronological order so that the most recent entry is always on top of the site. The objective of marketing your blog is to develop a loyal readership of your posts—a community of like-minded people who care what you have to say and engage in conversation with you by way of comments to your posts.

From a business perspective there are several potential reasons to blog. But, as always, it depends on what you want. Blogs are no different from channels like video, print, audio, presentations, and so on. They all deliver results—but of varying kind. The kind you can expect from blogs is mainly about stronger relationships with important target groups. There are a number of business reasons to blog, among them:

- Become recognized as the expert in your area of focus
- Build/monitor customer relationships
- Manage media relations
- Test ideas or products
- Improve search engine optimization

The most popular choices for free blogging software and hosting are:

- Blogger (blogger.com)—This site is owned by Google.
- WordPress (wordpress.com)—Professional web developers are building entire websites on the WordPress platform. There is also a paid subscription-based WordPress service.

Others include:

- B2evolution (b2evolution.net)
- Nucleus (nucleuscms.org)
- CreateBlog (createblog.com)
- Movable Type (movabletype.org)
- TypePad (not free, but well known and well respected)

There are others but these are the most reliable, state-of-the art, open-source, and free.

Micro-Blogs

Micro-blogging is a form of blogging where entries are limited to brief updates (usually 140 characters or fewer). Entries can be text-only or micromedia, such as photos or audio clips, and can either be viewed by any of the bloggers subscribers *(followers)* or can be directed to a single person. Your entries can be uploaded from a computer, mobile phone, or other IM-enabled device.

Twitter is the most popular and best recognized micro-blogging interactive site—period. It has an estimated active account base of well over 1.5 million. Think of Twitter (and any micro-blog) as a cross between instant messaging (IM) and a chat room, because it is an open forum, but "open" only to those you follow and/or who follow you.

The ways to use Twitter for marketing are very similar to how you'd use blogging, just shorter and include more real-time messages.

There are a number of business reasons to blog, among them:

- Become recognized as the expert in your area of focus
- Build/monitor customer relationships
- Manage media relations
- Test ideas or products
- Improve search engine optimization

You're hearing a theme now—to be successful you have to engage your followers and provide relevant value. Pass on helpful links, comments, and resources and ask insightful questions.

Good resource on how to get started on Twitter are available from www.hubspot.com and marketingprofs.com

Twitter.com (www.twitter.com)—Other micro-blogs include Jaiku (owned by Google), Pownce, and Plurk.

Podcasts

At its most basic, podcasting is a method for delivering audio (and now video) over the Internet. An MP3 file is placed on the web for listeners to download and listen to on their computer or a portable M3P player such as an iPod, thus the term "podcasting."

What's the difference between an MP3 and a podcast? At the audio level, there is no difference. The delivery of the audio file is what separates the two. You can place an MP3 on your site, and say that you have a "podcast"—and many people are doing just that. Creating the audio file itself is easy. Most computers have a basic audio recording and editing program pre-loaded, such as Windows Media. Plug in a microphone and you're set to go.

But a podcast is an audio file that is set up so that it can be accessed/delivered via an RSS feed, whether from your website, the iTunes site, or some other RSS host/directory server.

Podcast Resources

How-to-Podcast information can be found at http://www.sweetwater.com/feature/podcasting/index.php.

Audacity 1.2.3 is another free voice recorder/editing program. It is simple enough for first-time users, compatible with both Mac and Windows, and available via a free download at http://audacity.sourceforge.net.

Forums

The discussion and Q/A forums on social and professional networking sites offer great opportunities to introduce your brand and expertise into a targeted group. Again, consistency and offering value—in the form of information, links, and thoughtful and relevant questions—are the keys to success here.

LinkedIn group discussion forums and Q/A section

Facebook group & fan page discussion forums

Professional association forums

Yelp.com; AngiesList.com, and other company/customer review forums eBay, Amazon.com, Travelocity.com, and other product/service specific review forums

Medical, hobby, religious, political forums

Additional Web 2.0 Reading

February 2008—*BusinessWeek:* "Social Media Will Change Your Business," http://tinyurl.com/2gj3yz

July 2008—*Forbes Magazine*: "The Business Value of Social Networking," http://tinyurl.com/5tt4sj

Videos

We don't all learn the same way; some learn and engage through reading, and some of us like the movie version. It's one thing to read about something, someone, or a company, but it's a completely different thing to watch and hear an interesting and relevant message. However, if you think it's as simple as uploading a video from your Flip and waiting for the e-mails to pour in demanding your products or services, you're going to be really disappointed. Again, it's important to understand and gear your efforts to the community aspect of video viewers and to what attracts them. What does video do for your marketing?

- **Video Gives Your Brand a Literal Voice:** The tone, emotion, and personality can come through in video as well as the message.

- **Videos Are Marketing's Annuity:** Once the video is published, it is online in perpetuity and will continue to get traffic even after the initial launch buzz.

- **Video Is Another Distribution Channel for Your Content:** Successful social media efforts are based on providing valuable and relevant content to interested audiences. Your content needs to have multiple distribution channels (blog post, Tweet, video, e-mail message, etc.). You should be experimenting with several in a coordinated way.

- **Videos Are Easier to Produce Than You Think:** You don't have to be a Martin Scorsese to produce a video for your business. Depending on your objective, a handheld Flip video, or even something taken with your mobile phone, can be good for impromptu customer testimonials, a quick "fyi," or other casual messages. It doesn't need to be perfect.

If you want a more professional and formal corporate message, it still doesn't have to cost a fortune. Online video is low resolution so no fancy camera is necessary. The most important things to remember are the sound quality and lighting (don't shoot the video in front of a bright window). Other than that, keep in mind that a successful marketing video:

- Focuses on something interesting that people will want to forward and share with friends.
- Is real and authentic. Like in all of your social media efforts, there are no tricks—just the message.
- Is "tagged," which means "keywords" are assigned to the video when uploaded to help in search results. What are the words that your ideal viewer will use in the search box to find your video if he or she doesn't know you or the video exist?

YouTube is by far the most popular video-sharing site. Other popular video sites include Vimeo, Blip.tv, and Viddler.

Case Study

Here's a small-business case study from Jason Falls at www.socialmediaexplorer.com. This is a solid illustration of how a sound strategy, an understanding of social media, and a small investment can make measurable differences for regular, everyday, brick-and-mortar businesses.

Martell Home Builders in Moncton, New Brunswick, Canada

The first thing that hits you about Martell is their URL—http://www.themartellexperience.com. And, that, in essence, captures what Martell is about. Hiring them to build your house gives you an experience. Watch this video: http://www.youtube.com/watch?v=T_L4Pq0u9QQ

I've never had a house built but have heard horror stories of the project being thousands of dollars over budget, months behind schedule, and problem after problem with the contractor, permits, and more. What defines Martell's unique selling proposition is what Pierre Martell alluded to in the video: transparency. You're going to know where he is at all times. You're going to know what's going on with your house at all times. And because Martell is seen and wants to see you as a person, going the extra mile to build and nurture the relationship beyond the project is important.

So far, none of this has to do with social media. The strategy that dictates Martell's business plan is not focused on social media; it's holistic. Advertising, customer relations, vendor relations, public relations, website execution, social media, and more, are all tactics of communicating the message: **Martell will give the customer a home building and buying experience like no other.** Whether intentional or not, Martell went through the strategic process and:

1. Established their objectives,

2. Defined their audience,

3. Developed strategies to achieve those objectives, and only THEN

4. Decided on the tools (online and offline) to use to execute that strategy.

So, how does social media play into Martell's strategy? First, the customer-accessible project management tool, which appears to be Basecamp-based (www.basecamphq.com), is a powerful internal communications platform with all sorts of Web 2.0 bells and whistles. If it is, in fact, Basecamp/GroupHub software, the communication in the project can be managed via e-mail (easy for the client) and all the activity streams can be subscribed to via RSS. Pierre Martell understands the most important audience he has is the current customer base and makes sure they have access to their project status at all times.

The on-site website experience uses a number of social media tools and strategies that help make Martell Home Builders stand out among their competitors. The main content on the front page is dated, blog-type entries, giving them the opportunity to increase their relevance to search engines with fresh content. They admit not using it optimally to date, but the RSS feed is clearly offered and the opportunity to use a blog mechanism to drive website content is there. Their YouTube videos are positioned as website content, as is their latest entries on Twitter. They've even developed a posting and RSS feed of interesting articles from around the web as recommended reading, providing added value to site visitors. And they have images displayed of their homes in a SmugMug badge.

(They were kicked off Flickr for violating the terms of service. Not to get off on a tangent, but Flickr refuses to grow a spine when it comes to their non-commercial policy. They ban people who are reported by the community for being in violation of terms, but not everyone is in violation of the terms. When I asked them recently how a business could use Flickr, they said they couldn't, but then the community decides so they won't prevent you. This is a cop-out, spineless and unfair to all users. Large corporations have their entire photo catalog on Flickr and Martell's pictures of homes in progress—not homes they are selling—gets banned? Give me a break. Grow a set Flickr. Either get rid of the term or enforce it across the board.)

The off-site social media elements stick to the strategy of communicating the Martell experience. Their Twitter stream is all about updating their customers and followers as to what is going on with current projects, company efforts, land purchases, and more. Their Facebook page gives a little different and more in-depth version of what's happening with the company, including a recent wall post indicating a website refresh is coming and the content/blog will kick into a higher gear soon. The YouTube channel is peppered with trade show booth interviews done with many different personalities and experts on home building, decorating, and design, which also stirs up quite a bit of differentiation attention at the trade show. What other home builder is going to invite folks by to be interviewed for their YouTube channel?

And did you catch the subtlety of the SmugMug images? They're not pictures of homes they're trying to sell. They're picture of in-progress builds. It may seem innocuous, but in the social space it's the difference in knowing what consumers will find acceptable and what they'll find interesting. Martell is providing value beyond that of competitors by not being about sales first, at least in this regard.

But What Is the ROI?

First, understand examining the ROI on Martell Homes' efforts in social media has very little to do with their social media efforts. Martell gives us a perfect example of a business whose success stems from the uniqueness in their business model. The Martell Experience is what can be credited with the ROI. The social media tools only help create it. Are they getting business because of their participation in social media? Maybe. Are they creating an experience with social media tools as contributing components that bring in customers? Damn right.

Martell Homes sold 16 units in 2007. They are on schedule to sell 40 in 2008 and hope for 100 in 2009—and in a tough economy. But here's where some social media payoff may come to play—80% of their homes are sold direct to consumer, with no real estate agents adding more to the bottom line for Martell. Would that be possible without an "experience" online? Bet not.

What Pierre Martell has done is embraced the notion that to have **meaningful connection and relationships** with consumers in today's world, you have to operate your business in a very human way. With a focus on transparency, openness, and the establishment of a real and powerful relationship with his